Ilya Kabakov
Artist Books / Künstlerbücher
1958 – 2009
Catalogue Raisonné

Ilya Kabakov
Artist Books / Künstlerbücher
1958 – 2009
Catalogue Raisonné

Editor / Herausgeber
Matthias Haldemann

Editing / Bearbeitet
Nicole Seeberger, Marco Obrist, Matthias Haldemann

Introduction / Einleitung
Matthias Haldemann

A Dialogue with Ilya Kabakov / Dialog mit Ilya Kabakov
by / von Matthias Haldemann

Kunsthaus Zug

KERBER ART

Contents / Inhalt

Introduction

Matthias Haldemann

Books have played an important role in the work of Ilya Kabakov from the very beginning. From 1956 through 1989 he enjoyed considerable success as an official state-trained illustrator of children's books in the Soviet Union. He can thus be said to have developed his artistic work from books, even if, at the time, these censured works served primarily as a means of earning money and can only be regarded with certain reservations as part of his oeuvre. Indeed, this already published segment of his work is not included in the present catalogue of his artist's books.

Yet it was not only this official work that was consistently so closely linked to books; the same applies to his unofficial artwork dating back to the 1960s. In fact, one could go so far as to assert that Kabakov's work can only truly be understood in relation to the book.

The unofficial Moscow artists were, in general, greatly influenced by literature above all, reflecting the fact that, from the eighteenth century onward and well into the Soviet era, Russian culture had essentially been a book culture. The group of Moscow conceptualists, of which Kabakov was a key member and which included artists, intellectuals, and litterateurs, met regularly for long and open discussions "around the kitchen table." Publications known as "samizdat," which they had themselves produced and "published" in very small numbers, were passed around for discussion. These handwritten or typed notebooks and portfolios were officially prohibited, which is why they were often either copied or committed to memory. In these works the connection between word and image is paramount.

Kabakov also began producing samizdat publications in the 1970s. Within this framework he composed seminal texts dealing with various subjects, formulated his own artistic concepts, and developed ideas for installations. Both conceptually and in terms of content, many of his books – though created under completely different conditions since he emigrated to the West – have continued to reveal the influence of those early writings. The simple volumes served as the intellectual seeds from which his enormous output of drawings, albums, paintings, installations, sculptures, and architectural inventions gradually emerged as fully fledged works.

Books have remained an indispensible part of Kabakov's life. On the one hand, he uses them to present new projects; on the other, these projects – once they have been successfully realized – are documented in this medium. His numerous artist's books represent the intellectual brackets enclosing the material works, placed before and after the execution of every project. The simple "autodidactic" layout of Kabakov's books provides a stark contrast to the experimental, avant-garde approach adopted in East and West alike, the reason being that his "books without aesthetic" (Kabakov) are not so much concerned with material form as with intellectual content.

The present catalogue raisonné not only reveals Ilya Kabakov both as an author of texts and as the person responsible for the layout, but also in many instances as a book author. There are extensive tracts devoted to art in Moscow in the 1960s and 1970s, to the subject of the fly, the concept of the "total" installation, the relationship between text and visuality, or to projects executed in the public realm. The Russian samizdat books were in many cases the precursors of the texts the artist has written in the West.

In this context, it is interesting to point out that Kabakov's extensive oeuvre is characterized by certain recurring motifs and themes that have adopted ever new "aggregate states" and have served to configure striking series of works over the decades, as well as to forge links between the various genres he has used. The fly, for instance, having first emerged in an early samizdat book, went on to become the theme of various publications. Then Kabakov devoted a large installation work to the fly, which in turn was enhanced by a number of books. Most recently, the fly installation has figured in multipartite "super" installations already presented in book form but not yet executed.

The fly motif is, however, not Kabakov's own discovery but figures as a free "quotation" from Gogol and Dostoyevsky, for example. It is as if the fly has traversed the different eras and worlds of other authors, figuratively speaking, while at the same time buzzing around in Kabakov's creative cosmos. Its free flight – flitting between nature and civilization, between "heaven and garbage" – establishes a meta-level transcending all boundaries of space and time, art and literature, word and image.

The way in which the book has accompanied Kabakov's artistic work, however, is different from what is generally the case with other artists. From a very early stage it also played a central role in his art. This is especially true of his idiosyncratic "album" genre, a book-like, word-image-narration concept dating from the 1970s. Indeed, many of his drawings appear like independent "illustrations" whose texts seem to have been lost. The paintings also frequently resemble opened books, statistics, tables, et cetera. He even conceives of many of his installations figuratively as "books with room chapters"; some installations have even been expressly dedicated to the concept of the book or the library.

The color white forms one point of convergence for Kabakov's illustrations, drawings, paintings, albums, and books. Kabakov has derived many qualities from white over the course of his artistic life, using it as a motif or symbol in a number of ways. In his work, it can ultimately be traced back to the paper-white of books. Large areas of white were already a conspicuous feature of his children's book illustrations. White provides a free space for the imagination amidst the ideologically and aesthetically controlled world of motifs.

Dialogue forms a second point of intersection in Kabakov's labyrinthine oeuvre. While modernist art was endeavoring to assert its autonomy in opposition to the word and all things literary, the Moscow conceptualists were primarily and explicitly concerned with the spoken word. The latter has a significant background in the Russian literature of the eighteenth and nineteenth centuries. Indeed, novels by Dostoyevsky and Chekov were already being termed "vocal spaces." Such vocal spaces are something we are familiar with from Kabakov's installations. He is also the undisputed master of epic narratives and reflective commentaries. Endless dialogues with friends, as well as between fictive characters or "personages" (Kabakov), pervade his oeuvre. Visual art originates in speech and ultimately ends in dialogue. For Kabakov himself, art is thus above all founded upon dialogue, since thought is itself an inner dialogue. Ultimately his work emerges in response to the idea of a meta-text, since the individual object is to be incorporated into the general horizon of a possible cultural tradition, into a "sea of voices."

We have prefixed this catalogue raisonné with three parts of a dialogue with the artist on the idea of the book. As always with Kabakov, artistic practice and discourse cannot be separated from one another. The same applies to this oeuvre catalogue, which in Kabakov's case takes on the form of a paradoxical construction: it is simultaneously an academic catalogue and an artist's book, and thus in turn an integral part of the very oeuvre it summarizes. It is a constituent of the whole and, at the same time, the whole itself – a world created from numerous worlds composed of the most varied contexts.

For Kabakov, speech means analysis, interpretation, commentary, but ultimately also imagination and discovery. In a manner that is imaginative, critical, educated, humorous, objective, emotional, eloquent, and creative, this endless, hovering voice always also describes a possible absence, a mysterious nothingness. In speaking, the voice remains silent. This recalls the white to be found in the artist's books, drawings, and paintings. Kabakov accordingly also refers to "white writing," which creates meaning just as it continuously dissolves this meaning.

Kabakov's art harks back to the premodernism of the nineteenth century in East and West, and in view of its stark opposition to modernism may strike some in the West as strange. The divergences and similarities between Kabakov's work and modernism create new perspectives on the various paths art has pursued throughout the twentieth century right up to the present. At the same time, it also permits a critical analysis of the often unchallenged premises of modern art, for example the way it defines the relationship between abstraction and realism.

In response to his own negative experiences of reality in the Soviet Union, Kabakov had to come up with alternatives to the utopian avant-garde. If his work was to be able to achieve any intellectual freedom under the most difficult imaginable conditions of a dictatorship, then this could only be done with a deep faith in a universal culture of humanity founded upon the classical model. Kabakov registers, as it were, the individual history of Soviet barbarity in the annals of the great humanist tradition. And as far as his "normal" books are concerned, his belief is that they will one day find their place in the universal library of collective memory to serve as a reminder for later generations. They are intended to be read and viewed as sober documents rather than as artistic experiments that are only to be understood with difficulty.

Thanks to his fantasized art chronicle, the Soviet Union – the first lost civilization of the modern era – can be experienced by outsiders as more than just a closed chapter of history. It can become a highly unsettling means of experiencing the still-potent dialectic of the Enlightenment as felt in the East and the West. In the work of Kabakov, culture succeeds in integrating the foreign and alien, even into its own self.

If the ideologized total reality of the Soviet Union could only be experienced as something unreal and fictive, there being no real alternative, then artistic fiction presented a possible means of escape for the consciousness. Reading in particular offered an imaginary free space: a book can explore a better, humane, and cultured world.

Whatever the average person in the Soviet Union set out to personally plan, it inevitably remained an idea that could never be pursued to fruition. As such, the normal Soviet citizen was predestined, as "personage," to assume the role of the literary antihero in the works of Kabakov, to take one's place in the universal "vocal space" – standing, in a manner of speaking, alongside the underground man and the idiot (Fyodor Dostoyevsky), the doctor confined to a sickroom (Anton Chekhov), Captain Nemo (Jules Verne), the writer Marcel whom life defeats (Marcel Proust), Joseph K., a man paralyzed by the anonymous might of the authorities (Franz Kafka), the imaginary invalid on the Magic Mountain (Thomas Mann), or the idle man without qualities (Robert Musil), to name but a few.

Kabakov's artistic imagination, however, is not quixotic, but rather formulates a painful metaphor for reality: the articulated longing for "normality" ultimately remains unfulfilled. As an artist-Sisyphus, Kabakov is himself an antihero. Whatever he produces dissolves again into nothingness, or rather into books. Like a double-sided Matryoshka, the development goes from the small to the large and back to the small again – from the book of ideas to the materialized reality of the artwork and then back into a book of recollection. All the works hover in the betwixt and between, and are at once realized and unrealized, visible and invisible, realistic and utopian, material and spiritual. This dualism is in keeping with the character of the book, which is at all times – distinguishably – both material object and intellectual content.

I am indebted to Ilya and Emilia Kabakov for the confidence they have placed in me and would like to offer my deepest gratitude to them for their willingness to engage in conversations and for their commitment to the preparation and realization of this book.

I would also like to thank Nicole Seeberger and Dr. Marco Obrist of the Kunsthaus Zug for the compilation of this catalogue raisonné and for the many valuable discussions on the subject. My thanks go to Hubert Beck, Judith Rosenthal, and Andrew Ennis of Frankfurt am Main, Maria Porudominskaja of Cologne, and Ann Marie Bohan of Dublin for the translations, as well as to Dawn Michelle d'Atri and Katrin Günther for editing the English and German texts. Nord Stream AG of Zug has generously provided the financial basis for this academic undertaking, and I hereby extend my heartfelt thanks to this company for their contribution. I would also like to express my appreciation to the Kerber Verlag publishing house for the production and distribution of the book and for what has been a very fruitful collaborative process. We moreover gratefully acknowledge the valuable information and support we have received from Prof. Dr. Luzius Keller, Zug; Walther König, Cologne; Prof. Dr. Verena Lenzen, Lucerne; Gabriele Leupold, Berlin; and Monika Sommerhalder, Lucerne.

In an age of new communication technologies, this book of books may perhaps seem something of an anachronism to many. If, however, life means narrated life, as is especially the case in the Jewish intellectual tradition, then we as readers take part in Kabakov's "life novel." In the case of Kabakov, that which is being narrated can as little be separated from the narrator as from the reader. The self formulates itself by means of a dialogue in the act of narration. In the spirit of this observation, I wish us all an inspiring perusal.

Zug, October 2009

Einleitung

Matthias Haldemann

Das Buch spielt im Werk von Ilya Kabakov von Beginn an eine zentrale Rolle. Von 1956 bis 1989 war er als offizieller, staatlich ausgebildeter Kinderbuchillustrator in der Sowjetunion erfolgreich tätig. Er entwickelte seine bildkünstlerische Tätigkeit folglich vom Buch aus, wenngleich diese zensurierte Arbeit seinerzeit in erster Linie dem Gelderwerb diente und nur unter Vorbehalt dem eigenen Œuvre zugerechnet werden darf. Im vorliegenden Verzeichnis seiner eigenen Künstlerbücher ist dieser bereits publizierte Teil seines Werks nicht enthalten.

Doch nicht nur die offizielle, sondern auch Kabakovs inoffizielle bildkünstlerische Arbeit seit den 1960er-Jahren erfolgte stets in enger Anbindung an das Buch, mehr noch: Sie lässt sich vom Buch her eigentlich erst richtig verstehen.

Ganz allgemein waren die inoffiziellen Moskauer Künstler vor allem von der Literatur geprägt, da die russische Kultur seit dem 18. Jahrhundert und bis in die Sowjetzeit immer primär eine Buchkultur gewesen war. Der Kreis der Moskauer Konzeptualisten um Kabakov, dem Künstler, Intellektuelle und Literaten angehörten, traf sich regelmäßig zu langen, freien Gesprächen „am Küchentisch“. Dort reichte man selber angefertigte und in kleiner Auflage „verlegte“ Publikationen – Samisdat genannt – als Diskussionsbeiträge herum. Die hand- oder maschinenschriftlichen Hefte und Mappen waren offiziell verboten, weshalb man sie oft abschrieb oder memorierte. Die Verbindung von Wort und Bild ist für sie kennzeichnend.

Kabakov hat seit den 1970er-Jahren auch selbst Samisdat-Publikationen gemacht und darin grundlegende Texte über verschiedene Themen verfasst, eigene künstlerische Konzepte formuliert und Installationen vorbereitet. Bis heute lassen viele seiner Bücher, die seit der Emigration in den Westen unter völlig veränderten Voraussetzungen entstehen, eine konzeptionelle und inhaltliche Prägung durch diese frühen Schriften erkennen. Überhaupt scheint sich sein enormes Gesamtwerk mit Zeichnungen, Alben, Bildern, Installationen, Skulpturen und Architekturinterventionen aus den einfachen Heften als geistigen Keimzellen schrittweise ins Großräumliche entfaltet zu haben.

Bücher sind für Kabakov stets unverzichtbare Begleiter geblieben. Zum einen werden in ihnen neue Projekte präsentiert und zum andern werden diese nach erfolgter Realisation in diesem Medium dokumentiert. Die zahlreichen Künstlerbücher sind gleichsam die geistigen Klammern der materiellen Werke, stehen vor und nach jeder Ausführung. Mit ihrem einfachen, „autodidaktischen“ Layout unterscheiden sie sich stark vom experimentellen Ansatz der Avantgarde in West und Ost. Denn nicht die materielle Form soll bei den „Ohne-Ästhetik-Büchern“ (Kabakov) im Vordergrund stehen, sondern der geistige Inhalt.

Im vorliegenden Catalogue Raisonné tritt Ilya Kabakov nicht nur als Layout-Verantwortlicher und Textautor auf, sondern mehrmals auch als Buchautor. Umfangreiche Abhandlungen hat er der Kunst in Moskau der 1960er- und 1970er-Jahre, der Fliege, der „totalen“ Installation, dem Verhältnis von Text und

Visualität, oder den Projekten im öffentlichen Raum gewidmet. Diesen im Westen entstandenen Schriften gehen oft russische Samisdat-Hefte voraus.

Kabakovs umfangreiches Œuvre kennzeichnen dabei wiederkehrend bestimmte Motive und Themen, die in immer neuen „Aggregatszuständen" über Jahrzehnte markante Werkreihen konfigurieren und die verschiedenartigen Gattungen verbinden. So taucht zum Beispiel die Fliege erstmals bereits in einem frühen Samisdat-Heft auf, wird zum Thema mehrerer Publikationen, dann widmet ihr der Künstler eine große Installation, die wiederum diverse Bücher ergänzen. Zuletzt figuriert die Fliegen-Installation in mehrteiligen „Super"-Installationen, die Kabakov in Büchern bereits vorgestellt, bisher aber noch nicht realisiert hat.

Dabei ist das Fliegenmotiv selbst nicht seine Erfindung, figuriert eher als freies „Zitat" von Gogol und Dostojewski beispielsweise. Als bewege sich die Fliege im übertragenen Sinn durch die Epochen und Welten anderer Autoren, so schwirrt sie zugleich im Kabakov'schen Werkkosmos herum. Ihr freier Flug zwischen Natur und menschlicher Zivilisation, „Himmel und Müll" etabliert eine Metaebene jenseits aller Grenzen von Raum und Zeit, Kunst und Literatur, Wort und Bild.

Das Buch begleitet Kabakovs bildnerisches Werk aber nicht nur, wie das bei anderen Künstlern meist der Fall ist. Auch bildkünstlerisch spielt es für ihn schon früh eine zentrale Rolle. Dies trifft besonders für die eigenwillige Gattung „Album", eine buchartige Wort-Bild-Narration aus den 1970er-Jahren, zu. Überhaupt muten viele seiner Zeichnungen wie verselbstständigte „Illustrationen" an, deren Text verloren gegangen zu sein scheint. Und die Bilder gleichen häufig aufgeschlagenen Büchern, Statistiken, Tabellen etc. Selbst die Installationen versteht Kabakov im übertragenen Sinn als „Bücher mit Raumkapiteln"; einzelne hat er konkret dem Buch und der Bibliothek gewidmet.

Ein Konvergenzpunkt von Kabakovs Illustration, Zeichnung, Malerei, „Album" und Buch bildet das Weiß. Ihm hat er im Laufe seines Schaffens viele Qualitäten abgewonnen, hat es als Motiv und Symbol unterschiedlich eingesetzt. Dessen Ursprung geht bei ihm letztlich auf das Papierweiß der Bücher zurück. Bereits die Kinderbuchillustrationen zeichnen sich durch auffallend viel Weiß aus, das inmitten von ideologisch und ästhetisch kontrollierten Motivwelten einen Freiraum für die Fantasie offen hält.

Ein zweiter Konvergenzpunkt des labyrinthischen Gesamtwerks von Kabakov ist der Dialog. Während die Kunst der Moderne ihre Autonomie gerade gegen das Wort und alles Literarische zu behaupten sucht, beziehen die Moskauer Konzeptualisten sich explizit und primär auf das gesprochene Wort. Dies hat eine wichtige Vorgeschichte in der russischen Literatur des 18. und 19. Jahrhunderts. Schon Romane von Dostojewski und Tschechow wurden als „Raum von Stimmen" bezeichnet. Räume mit Stimmen kennen wir auch von Kabakovs Installationen. Das epische Erzählen und reflektierende Kommentieren beherrscht ihr Autor wie kaum ein zweiter. Endlose Dialoge mit Freunden, aber auch zwischen fiktiven Figuren, „Personagen" (Kabakov), durchziehen sein Schaffen. Bildnerische Kunst entspringt dem Sprechen und mündet schließlich wieder ins Gespräch. Für Kabakov selbst ist die Kunst deshalb vor allem dialogisch angelegt, da bereits das Denken ein innerer Dialog ist. Letztlich entwirft sein Werk sich auf einen Metatext, denn das Einzelne soll in den allgemeinen Horizont einer möglichen kulturellen Tradition eingerückt werden, in ein „Meer von Stimmen".

Dem vorliegenden Gesamtverzeichnis haben wir drei Teile eines Dialoges mit dem Künstler über das Buch vorangestellt. Wie immer bei Kabakov lassen sich

Kunstpraxis und Diskurs darin nicht trennen. Das gilt ebenso für diesen Œuvrekatalog, der sich bei ihm als paradoxe Konstruktion erweist: Er ist wissenschaftliches Verzeichnis und Künstlerbuch zugleich, und damit wiederum ein Bestandteil jenes Œuvres, das er zusammenfasst. In einem ist er Teil und Ganzes. Eine Welt aus lauter Welten, die sich ihrerseits in verschiedenste Kontexte einreiht.

Sprechen bedeutet für Kabakov analysieren, interpretieren, kommentieren, letztlich aber auch imaginieren und erfinden. Fantasievoll, kritisch, gebildet, humorvoll, sachlich, emotional, eloquent und kreativ umschreibt diese endlose und zugleich schwebende Stimme aber immer auch ein mögliches Abwesendes, ein geheimnisvolles Nichts. Sprechend schweigt sie. Das erinnert an das Weiß der Bücher, Zeichnungen und Bilder. Kabakov spricht denn auch vom „weißen Schreiben", das Sinn ebenso produziert, wie es ihn fortlaufend auflöst.

Kabakovs für manche im Westen vielleicht fremde, weil in scharfer Opposition zum Modernismus formulierte Kunst führt zurück auf die Vormoderne des 19. Jahrhunderts in Ost und West. Von dort her lassen sich mit ihr die verschiedenen Wege der Kunst durchs 20. Jahrhundert bis in die Gegenwart auf Divergenzen und Gemeinsamkeiten hin neu bedenken, aber auch bezüglich ihrer oft unhinterfragten Prämissen kritisch analysieren. Exemplarisch gilt das für das Verhältnis von Abstraktion und Realismus.

Aus seinen eigenen, negativen Realitätserfahrungen in der Sowjetunion musste Kabakov zur utopischen Avantgarde alternative Schlüsse ziehen. Wenn sich sein Werk unter den denkbar schwierigsten Bedingungen einer Diktatur geistig überhaupt frei auszubilden vermochte, dann nur im tiefen Vertrauen auf eine universelle Menschheitskultur nach klassischem Vorbild. In die große humanistische Tradition schreibt Kabakov die partikulare Geschichte der barbarischen Sowjetunion ein. Und von seinen „normalen" Büchern erhofft er sich, dass sie sein Werk dereinst in das kollektive Gedächtnis der universellen Bibliothek einreihen werden, um Erinnerung zu stiften für die künftige Nachwelt. Als nüchterne „Dokumente" sollen sie gelesen und betrachtet werden, kein schwer verständliches Kunstexperiment sein.

Dank seiner fantasierten Kunstchronik kann die Sowjetunion als erste untergegangene Zivilisation der Moderne auch für Außenstehende mehr sein als ein abgeschlossenes Vergangenheitskapitel. Sie kann zum erschreckenden Erfahrungsgegenstand werden für die in Ost und West erlittene und bis heute immer wieder wirksame Dialektik der Aufklärung. Beispielhaft integriert die Kultur damit das Fremde bei Kabakov, auch im eigenen Selbst.

Wenn die ideologisierte Totalrealität der Sowjetunion als unwirklich und fiktiv erlebt werden musste und es keine reale Alternative dazu gab, dann konnte die künstlerische Fiktion dem Bewusstsein einen möglichen Ausweg eröffnen. Einen imaginären Freiraum bot namentlich das Lesen: Im Buch ließ sich eine bessere, humane und kulturelle Welt erkunden.

Was immer der einfache Sowjetmensch auch plante, es musste als Idee meist unrealisiert bleiben. Damit war er prädestiniert, um bei Kabakov als „Personage" die Rolle literarischer Antihelden zu übernehmen und sich einzufinden im universellen Raum der Stimmen: sozusagen neben dem Mann im Kellerloch und dem Idioten (Fjodor Dostojewski), dem im Krankenzimmer eingesperrten Arzt (Anton Tschechow), neben Kapitän Nemo (Jules Verne), dem am Leben scheiternden Autor Marcel (Marcel Proust), dem von der anonymen Behördenmacht paralysierten Josef K. (Franz Kafka), dem eingebildeten Kranken auf dem Zauberberg (Thomas

Mann), oder neben dem untätigen Mann ohne Eigenschaften (Robert Musil), um nur einige Beispiele anzuführen.

Kabakovs künstlerische Imagination ist aber nicht weltfremd, sondern formuliert eine schmerzliche Realitätsmetapher: Die artikulierte Sehnsucht nach „Normalität" bleibt als Utopie letztlich unerfüllt. Als Künstler-Sisyphos ist er selber ein Antiheld. Was immer er produziert, es löst sich wieder in Nichts auf, besser: in Bücher. Wie bei einer „zweiseitigen" Matrjoschka führt die Entwicklung vom Kleinen zum Großen und vom Großen wieder zum Kleinen – vom Ideenbuch zur materialisierten Kunstrealität und zurück ins Buch der Erinnerung. Schwebend bleiben alle Werke im Dazwischen, sind realisiert und unrealisiert, sichtbar und unsichtbar, real und utopisch, materiell und geistig. Diesem Dualismus entspricht die Eigenart des Buches, das immer klar unterscheidbar beides zugleich ist: materielles Objekt und geistiger Inhalt.

Ilya und Emilia Kabakov schulde ich für ihr Vertrauen, die Gesprächsbereitschaft und das Engagement bei der Vorbereitung und Realisation dieses Buchs einen großen Dank!

Weiter danke ich Dr. Marco Obrist und Nicole Seeberger vom Kunsthaus Zug für die Redaktion und Bearbeitung des Verzeichnisses sowie für die vielen wertvollen Gespräche über das Thema. Hubert Beck, Judith Rosenthal und Andrew Ennis, Frankfurt am Main, sowie Maria Porudominskaja, Köln, und Ann Marie Bohan, Dublin, ist für die Übersetzungsarbeit sehr zu danken, daneben Dawn Michelle d'Atri für das englische und Katrin Günther für das deutsche Lektorat. Die Firma Nord Stream AG, Zug, hat großzügig die finanziellen Voraussetzungen für dieses wissenschaftliche Unternehmen geschaffen – herzlichen Dank! Und dem Kerber Verlag danke ich für die sorgfältige Produktion und den Vertrieb des Buches sowie für die sehr gute Zusammenarbeit. Wichtige Informationen und Unterstützung erhielten wir dankenswerterweise von Prof. Dr. Luzius Keller, Zug; Walther König, Köln; Prof. Dr. Verena Lenzen, Luzern; Gabriele Leupold, Berlin; Monika Sommerhalder, Luzern.

In einer Zeit neuer Kommunikationstechniken mag dieses Buch der Bücher manchem vielleicht schon anachronistisch anmuten. Wenn Leben aber erzähltes Leben bedeutet, wie besonders in der jüdischen Geistestradition, dann nehmen wir als betrachtende Leser Teil am „Lebensroman" Kabakov. Das Erzählte ist hier vom Erzähler so wenig abzutrennen wie vom Leser. Im Erzählten formuliert sich das eigene Selbst dialogisch mit. In diesem Sinn wünsche ich uns allen eine inspirierende Lektüre.

Zug, Oktober 2009

A Dialogue with Ilya Kabakov by Matthias Haldemann

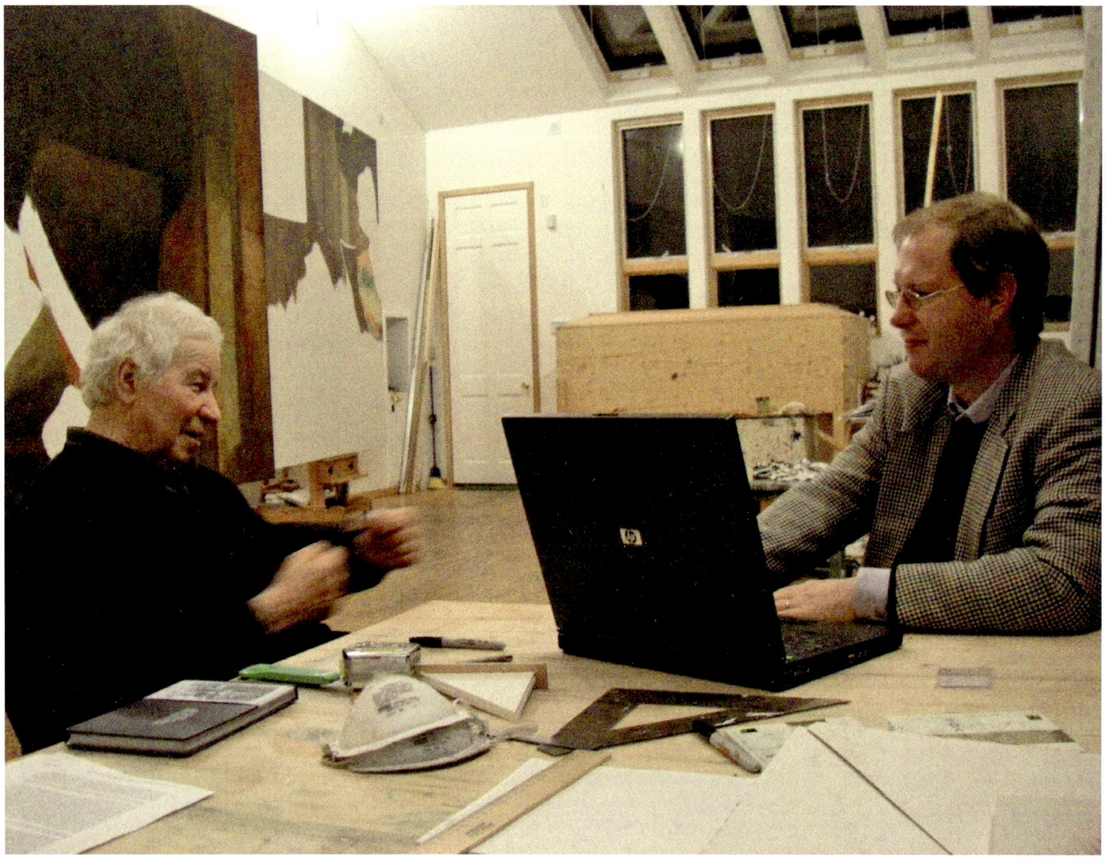

A Dialogue with Ilya Kabakov by Matthias Haldemann[1]

It is thanks only to books that consciousness exists.

MH: You are a trained children's book illustrator and therefore have had a professional relationship to the theme of the book from the very beginning. Can you say something about your initial relationship to the book?

IK: Naturally. At the art institute I learned the profession of children's book illustrator. Nevertheless, I have to say that those works were not associated with affinity or great interest, but merely served the purpose of survival in the Soviet context. Why? Of course the book illustration, especially for children's books, is in principle an interesting artistic challenge. But in the Soviet situation there were so many censored elements and restrictions that you couldn't feel free. It was as if someone were saying: "Please, dear bird, go on flying, but without wings." That was a paradoxical, regressive, or even to an extent sadistic situation. You had to produce imagery, but within a framework and under censorship.

The censorship of Soviet art had begun in the mid-1930s. Before that, Russian children's book illustration had naturally been very interesting and avant-garde; members of a movement that was strong and free had produced wonderful works. But from the 1930s onward, everything was very closely controlled. When I started working for the Moscow Children's Book Publishing Company in 1956, this was the only means of earning money. The government had book illustration completely under its control, almost to the same extent as the literary texts. You had a choice: either you followed the rules or you didn't get the job. There was no way out. You couldn't change the system.

For my first book I submitted a drawing I thought was good. I took it to the editor (there was a certain art editor for each book). But he said, "No, this face isn't good." Or: "The rabbit's physiognomy isn't perfect." I didn't understand why, because I had practically drawn from nature. I wasn't told in any detail what was wrong with the drawings. It was an education system like in Tibet: "The teachers beat you on the head with a stick, but don't explain what mistake you're making." And after the tenth lash, you suddenly understand of your own accord: "Ah, THAT'S what it is!" I had this "satori" after the editor had rejected my drawing, which I had reworked every time, for the twelfth time. Then I had the revelation: "You can't look at your drawing with your own eyes; you have to put yourself in the editor's position and look at your own drawing with the anonymous eyes of this art editor whose job it is to carry out censorship." Once I had assumed his psychological position and submitted the new drawings with the rabbit or the child's face, he said: "This is perfect!"

Such psychological pressure and psychological perversion are interesting: for ultimately, these were no longer my own drawings, even though I had naturally

[1] Editor's note: The ensuing dialogues with Ilya Kabakov were held in German on January 12, 14, and 16, 2009 in Mattituck, Long Island, USA. The phrasing and the tone have been retained in the English translation.

made them with my own hand. From that point on, all of my drawings were therefore approved immediately, without objections. Now suddenly things became totally easy for me. Why? The editor in the children's book publishing company was like a ticket inspector on the bus. Usually the artist thinks of himself as an individual personality and makes a drawing which expresses his individuality and assumes that this aspect will be heeded. But the work of the editor turned out to be precisely the opposite. He was as strict as an inspector. You took a portfolio of drawings to him, and while he was paging through them he sat there and chatted with a colleague: "Yesterday I was in the cinema and it was very interesting."– He inspected the drawings like tickets. When he found something individual, it was like a "mistake." If there was even just one single individual effect in your standardized drawing, you had to do the whole thing over again. The editor looked through anonymous eyes. Like a censor. On a personal level they were very nice, but in art they didn't want any personal originality.

Just the schema, the standardized idea.

Yes, just the schema.
All I wanted was the money, and I calculated how many books I would have to do every year to earn enough. Not to get rich, just to survive. In the first year of my career as a children's book illustrator, it took me maybe four to five months for one children's book. But in order to earn enough money, you had to do four books a year. So I soon started working faster and producing the books very pragmatically. Then, during my last year in Moscow, it took me only a month and a half to earn my wages. That was optimal.

Okay, that's a summarized version of what I wrote in the foreword to my book about my children's books entitled »Children's Book Illustrator as a Social Character«.

But when I started working with installations – in the West I was much more concerned with installations than with pictures – the important question arose: "What remains after the exhibition is over?" A picture keeps existing even without an exhibition, but an installation is very ephemeral and is almost never preserved after an exhibition. All that remains are the memories of it, but nothing is left for "history." But I'm more interested in the perspective of future generations than in that of my contemporaries. What remains of art for a long time afterward, goes down in history? The best means of remembering is books. But then the question arises: "How do you represent the lost art?"

Bygone or lost art?

Yes, lost art. Essentially, the installation is a lost art. How do you represent this art for the next generation? The answer that came to my mind was the idea of various "narrative" means of preservation.

The first such means would be the detailed description of the installation concept. What shape should it take? What impression should it make on the viewer? Naturally, there are lots of artists who don't concern themselves with the viewer. That's the old topic: "Artists work for themselves or for God." The "normal" artist is not interested in the viewer. "God and you, those are the best criteria for your work."

I myself, however, have never been the essential criterion for my art and its quality. As criteria go, other people are more important to me than I myself. Why? I proceed on the assumption that the viewer is not an idiot. There are well-informed people with scholarly knowledge of art, people who have "seen a lot." I'm not talking here about some unique "maternal" position that works like the relationship between mother and child. Naturally, for the child, the mother is the only person, but the viewer is not a mother. He is a very cold, well-informed flaneur. He has an entire pantheon of wonderful works in his head. He's got Michelangelo, Raphael, and great contemporary artists sitting there. And with this precarious "golden yardstick" he is now measuring your work. Yes, he has brought along this terrible instrument: the golden yardstick! With this yardstick, his eyes, and his mind he passes judgment on every work. But such passing of judgment can prove fatal for your work. The viewer will simply remain silent and pass by your work, and this silence sounds out like the final shot!

Now a brief comment on the subject: "How would you like to tell the man with the golden yardstick about your work?"

There is, for example, a very strange situation which I myself have experienced frequently. Usually an artist who has been invited to the art academy for a lecture has visited the students beforehand in their studios to say a few words to them about their works. And there are almost always lots of sketches and pictures hanging on the walls of such studios, or a number of objects standing around. But often you find yourself in a place where there is nothing at all to see – no artworks, just empty walls. You're surprised, but the student remains perfectly calm and says, "Okay, have a seat and I'll tell you about my new idea." Then he goes on and on, nonstop, and very aggressively. What I find interesting about his remarks: he doesn't describe a plastic form, but rather what he intends to do. He talks about his negative reactions to war, for example the war in South Africa. He talks about the program, but not about artistic matters. You notice that he doesn't have the slightest idea about the formal realization.

And this example takes us back to what we were talking about a minute ago: "How do I explain the no-longer-existing object-installation to the unknown viewer?"

Now, my catalogue raisonné of the installations seems to represent an example of such possibilities. The first part of the text consists of a presentation of the concept. It explains the intention that lies behind the respective work, the "concept" upon which the work was originally founded. To understand an artwork, it seems to me that an explanation of how it emerged and evolved is very important. A clear and well-wrought narrative physiognomy is the basis of the visual depiction, and verbal explanation is its chief principle. That is totally contrary to the modernist tradition, which says: "Art begins where words end. Language falls silent; henceforth art speaks." It's the absolute opposite. For me, visual art is solely like a realization of words, of an idea.

So that's the first part, the concept. The second, simpler part deals with the technical description. The proportions, distances, dimensions, color, light, and the various elements of an artwork are described in a visually clear manner. This is of course a very prosaic, bureaucratic part. But if a person has the patience to read everything, then he begins to understand the material aspect of the installation, step by step so to speak.

The third linguistic level is a brief narrative on the music, sound, or voices in the installation. And the last part consists of commentary on an installation which has already been realized.

So whereas the first three parts precede the realization of the work, this last part comes about afterward, so to speak. Of concern here is the discussion with an imaginary critic about what has succeeded and what has failed. In the catalogue raisonné there is a dialogue between Kabakov and Bakstein. Here Bakstein is a "sparring partner," like in tennis or boxing. He is a "false" partner, but nevertheless important for the readers as regards the explanation of the work. They receive answers to his questions: "Why did you do this this way, and that that way?"

Naturally there's also a visual part, likewise addressing various aspects of development: initial sketches, various ground plans, then detail studies, overall views, and finally photos as documentation of the realization, with overall and detail views.

It's like the story of a destroyed building, for example a ruin. Maybe my art school played an important role here, because there were wonderful books there about the Roman catacombs, about ruins or drawings by Piranesi. I wasn't only interested in the finished work, but also in the process of analysis, particularly in learning to understand the plan. I was especially interested in plans, because they show the main idea of a building; then came photos, et cetera. That activated my fantasy for possible reconstructions. In my youth, this was very important to me, and I think this slow process of structuring a book with the various detailed views can also be helpful to the viewer of a no-longer-existing installation and stimulate his interest. You learn something about the context and become acquainted with various technical aspects, so that gradually an image of the installation's original appearance begins to form in your mind.

Something I find very interesting is the fact that your books on individual installations are not merely documentations of works which have been realized. Rather, this deconstruction into various areas of reality – language, image, photography, sketch, and documentation – leads the reader/viewer to put together his or her own image from these elements. And all of the elements are given equal emphasis, with the initial design often being placed even more prominently than the reproduction of the work. There is no hierarchy between the initial idea, the final work, and the reproduction.

Absolutely.

And the result is not exactly the same for every reader/viewer, is it?

No, no.

Which means that in the book, the artwork once again becomes an element of the imagination – even if it was built as an installation?

Absolutely, exactly. It's like the investigation of a detective, a Sherlock Holmes. There are various elements which come together like a puzzle. But you never succeed in putting the puzzle together, because then another piece turns up and then another one.

Actually, that's very interesting. For example, I look at a book with Rembrandt sketches and drawings and think: "Ah!" And automatically a puzzle starts going in my mind, bringing forth a painting. Naturally you need to know certain things about the culture and the various contexts that led to the installation in order to put the puzzle together. In the case of my work, you need to know something about Russian culture, conceptual art, about the situation in the Soviet Union. You need this knowledge of the various contextual levels in order to understand the concept: the pyramid needs another huge pyramid. But for normal cultural people, that's par for the course and totally normal.

But exactly – you said it yourself at the beginning – it's a narrative. For me, this act of assembling the parts is also a form of narrative and becomes a story. And I can design this story to be bigger, more colorful, and more complex, depending on how much I know about these contexts, or it will just remain a simpler story. Nevertheless, it is still alive and stimulates fantasy. And I can also relate it to my own story. Not only do I need to be familiar with the right historical contexts, but I can also incorporate my own?

Yes, absolutely.

Also in the sense of a dialogue?

Absolutely, yes. It's a special book genre for the subject »Gesamtkunstwerk«, or "synthesis of the arts." In its sequence, a book about an installation is a whole, like a sphere. That's why there's a part with photos and, like equally important sections, there are also dialogues with Boris Groys. A book of this kind is like a fantasy cloud. Just like the fantastic stories by Jules Verne. Like a children's book, the book not only contains information. In every book is the whole world. My pompous book about installations possesses the naïve claim of functioning like a model of the universe. It's an attempt to create an illusory – but in any case a universal – "model."

There's something I notice when I look at the development of your oeuvre. I have the impression that, initially, the individual work – a drawing, an album, an installation – was like a model of the world. But over the decades, all of these works – which gradually and successively emerged from one another – have become a world in and of themselves, a cosmos in its own right, with a wide range of different areas, with large parts and smaller parts, with centers and peripheries. Your books actually tell the story of how this world of Kabakov emerges, transforms, grows, et cetera. A river of ideas with ever new branches, merging in a sea from which new rivers spring. This is a very fascinating notion. So is it once again about a story?

Yes. The small model of the world becomes a big model of the world, like in the Matryoshka system. But the principle is different from that of a novel. There is no succession. Every minute and every object functions as a self-contained unit.

But then the question arises as to what, actually, is the book? Books always contain an autobiographical element: "the fear of death." They embody the idea of eternity which they touch on. It's something that remains from your short stay in the world. And nearly every book has a dramaturgical principle with two simultaneous levels.

Can you give an example of this?

There's a level for what we can perhaps call simple people and another level that is directed toward "intelligent" consciousness. For example, one book is called »My Mother's Album«. It was a long-cherished wish of mine to make it in great honor of my mother, who had an unhappy life. In the late years of her life – she was already eighty-two – I asked her to write her memoirs, spanning from her childhood to the present moment. She did, and then she gave me her extensive notebook, which made me very happy. When I came to the West, my first wish was to print this biography of my mother. Naturally this book comprised a gigantic amount of informational material. But it nevertheless needed a certain concept, because – it seemed to me – it was supposed to become a special artwork. That's why I hit on the idea of presentation on two levels. The first level addresses the theme of "my mother's suffering," because her whole life was filled with suffering; she was so unhappy. In other words, this book was not to be read without tears, because the situation of this helpless person – which my mother was – reflected a complete disaster. And this life took place against the background of the Socialist "paradise" allegedly taking place throughout the land. We were supposedly living in the real paradise, with happiness prevailing in every area of life. Accordingly, the upper part of each page of this invented book/album contains photos with captions from magazines: "How much sausage there is in this shop," "What percentage of happy people are now living in a sanatorium," et cetera. And in the lower section is my mother's text, an entirely different "voice." Utopia and reality are directly related to one another.

That's a simple example of a construction with two levels. Important is which level you're on, but the best thing is to contemplate both simultaneously.

In my other books, there is material about the installations and, at the same time, also a dialogue with Boris Groys, who carries out an inner analysis of certain motifs or contexts – especially of contexts. The author conducts a discussion with the analyst, philosopher, and critic. It's like between doctor and patient, like when the patient tells the doctor what has happened to him and the doctor explains why. It's a bit like a Freudian psychotherapy session.

A theatrical play with two roles?

Absolutely. In principle it's possible to exchange them, although with Boris it looks unrealistic. Of course it's theater for two actors.

This brings us to another topic related to your books. With Western artists, publications usually accompany their work in a kind of subordinate function, conveying information about it. In other words, there's the artistic oeuvre on the one hand and, at a certain distance to it, the discourse on the other. There exists a clear hierarchy between the primary art and the secondary discourse.

With you it's different. Already starting with the dialogue with Boris Groys. The discourse becomes an integral element of the work and the two can no longer be distinguished. And the books on your work – the great majority of them were conceived by you, and you also do the layout – are also part of the work. The discourse is an integral part of the artistic work, which is itself also always a discourse. A reciprocal relationship connects the two. This culminates in the scholarly catalogues raisonnés of the installations, the paintings, and now the books as well, which in turn – as publications conceived and designed by Kabakov – are parts of the overall oeuvre, which they at the same time document objectively.

You're absolutely right. For me there would be something false about a "serious and profound discourse" about my art! Self-irony and humor play a major role. And there is no so-called résumé, no last word about a work. There are just various jumps, smaller ones, bigger ones, with any and all opinions remaining fragmentary. A serious explanation is impossible. Only various attempts from various angles are possible. When it comes down to it, there is no hitting the target dead center!

No direct hit.

So that the bird is dead. (laughter)

So in your work the visual is related to language. You wrote an extensive book about that, entitled »The Text as the Basis of Visual Expression«. Except your understanding of "text" is a very special one. It is strongly related to the conception of the spoken language, the "voice." The text is accordingly not a law, not a norm, not a rule or truth, but – as a voice – comes from life?

That's very perceptive. When I'm asked "What does this picture mean?," I always think about what role I should answer in. I have ten roles: the serious, the idiotic, et cetera, but all of them are authentic. All of them!

The concern is not with the written, literary, scholarly text. Only spoken language plays a role. It is completely free and not tied to any style. One interesting theme is the "long and free dialogue."

I lived in the Soviet Union for thirty years during the relatively stable Brezhnev period, a time of stagnation. Life was like grey weather. A permanent state. No sun, but also no disaster. And the people had lots of free time. They could drink, dance, do sports. The artists, too, had lots of free time and got together in the evenings. Just talking was a completely normal activity. In the kitchen there was a bottle, and you talked. You talked with huge enthusiasm – because speech, "the dialogue," was the only thing that was "us." There were no exhibitions, no means of selling anything, no criticism, no viewers. There was nothing, just talking in the cellar or the attic, for quite a long period. Like in a prison cell or a hospital room.

That was the reason for this conversational practice and the major text production which emerged from it. The free artists' dialogue was also a special genre and has fortunately been preserved in archives in the form of audio cassettes, texts, and already published books.

But works also emerged from that as well. Which takes us back to our starting point. You talked about your official work as a children's book illustrator, and about adapting to censorship. So with you, there was this difficulty in dealing with books. But at the same time there was also this unofficial circle of artists, writers, and critics who spent a great deal of time talking, and producing texts on that basis, which resulted in very simple, unofficial publications referred to as "samizdats." I'm thinking of the so-called "barrack poetry" by the Lianosovo Group, for example, by Rabin, Kholin, Rubinstein, Prigov; incidentally, for a number of them you also illustrated children's books. That was how your free work with the book began, wasn't it?

Absolutely. There's one positive aspect of Soviet life that shouldn't be forgotten, despite the generally gloomy memories of the past. Today everything is viewed completely negatively, the constant fear, et cetera. That's correct. But the positive aspects were education and the health care system.

The main principle of Soviet education was universalism. Lenin had this idea of the new human being as the culmination of cultural history. He – this new human being, a kind of peculiar superman – was the quintessence, the final stage of human evolution. Now the tradition of universal education had already existed in the nineteenth century, especially in the German »Gymnasium«: the Goethe principle. Youth were educated in widely differing disciplines, whether they needed that knowledge later on in life or not. But an entire universe was supposed to be created in their heads.

This tradition was adopted by the Soviet school. A diversified education was programmed, and essentially you could "know everything." But there an "independent education" also existed. Spontaneously organized groups of pupils would study certain subjects outside of school, purely because they were interested. In our group, for example, which consisted of five children, each one of us pursued a different "discipline." Each one of us was a "specialist" – either on theater, on classical music or philosophy – and supplied the others with books or "lectures" which we composed ourselves.

Our Soviet "school culture" existed exclusively within the book culture. We knew the major figures in the history of painting, Russian literature, world philosophy, the music of the world, and so forth. In our group, each of us gave lectures on his or her particular subject. The music person, for example, also took care of getting tickets for the conservatory concerts for the rest of the group. That's a paradox: life was very dark, conservative, depressing, but our imaginations led us to entirely different worlds; we lived on different "islands." We escaped from the terrible life surrounding us to the few remaining "oases" – the museum, the philharmonic orchestra, the reading room. It's also interesting to note that the Soviet authorities created wonderful reading rooms. You could get any work of classical literature you wanted there. But nothing contemporary, and no information about the outside world, no. But as much as you wanted about classical literature. Why? There was this prevalent idea that we were the abstract children of classical culture. It was not an active contemporary situation.

Like living in the past.

That's why the classical image continued to exist or, more specifically, it glowed in your mind. With Beuys, for example, an interest in classical art is not apparent at first glance. The classical development is like a corridor buried in the nineteenth century. For us, however, this corridor was always present. All we remembered was Rembrandt, or classical Russian art, et cetera.

No modern art.

No modern art. The Russian avant-garde did not play the slightest role for me. It didn't interest me. All we saw was the painting of the nineteenth century, up to Vrubel; and Vrubel was already banned. And we only had knowledge of Western art up to the Barbizon School, because the Impressionists had already been banned. There was everyday life in the Soviet Union and, at the back, like a tail, classicism.

The classical tail in Russia was first and foremost wonderful literature. So, again, the book?

Of course. The main theme of our discussions was the meaning of culture in the Soviet Union. We were completely aware that Soviet culture was not culture. Not a good culture, not a bad culture, but essentially no culture at all! So you had to look to an earlier cultural tradition for your ideal, a tradition preceding the Soviet period. This was the Russian culture of the nineteenth century, and the non-Soviet contemporary culture of the time.

Another good thing was that there were lots of translations of contemporary Western literature, primarily English and German, for example by Fitzgerald, Remarque, Grass, among others. But Russian culture formed the basis or the cornerstone of our cultural horizon. For us, culture was classical Russian culture. Naturally we were also familiar with the unofficial literature of the Soviet Union – Akhmatova, Pasternak, and the poets of the "Silver Age" – and we had ways of obtaining it. But our background reflected the earlier authors of the nineteenth century – Chekhov, Dostoyevsky.

Why literature and not painting? For us, the Moscow conceptualists, there was no good-quality painting, and it didn't provide us with a practicable artistic model. The ideals were music and, above all, literature. As a result, we had no contact to the Soviet realist tradition. We viewed the stars of the nineteenth century, like Surikov and Repin, negatively and mockingly. But we didn't mock Tolstoy, Dostoyevsky, and Chekhov, for they formed our foundation. When you worked, you constantly heard a voice in your inner ear: "What would Chekhov say about your works?" But never: "What would Repin say?"

In Chekhov there are heroes who in a certain sense reemerge in your works as characters, whether in the albums, the installations, then also in the books, for example with Bakstein's commentaries. I mean the literary concept of figures who function above all by way of their voices. Is that something that became relevant and productive again for your generation in a new way and in a different context, also under the influence of contemporary Western impulses?

That's a good point. Just a minute ago I was talking about the great influence of Russian literature. But the concern wasn't solely with literature or with art, but with the more fundamental ethical questions: "What is a good human being?" and "What would be the ideal mentality for you?"

Naturally the Russian intellectual is the ideal figure for your viewer or critic. Who is he, and when was he born? The Russian intellectual was born in the age of Enlightenment and comes from the West. During the era of Catherine II, the books of Voltaire, Montesquieu, and especially Rousseau made their way to Russia, all of which had a major impact. This "inundation" took place in Russia by way of two "channels." The first area to be affected was science – chemistry, geology, history, et cetera – laying the groundwork for the fantastic Russian universities with their famous professors. The second current was in the area of ethics. There was this idea that the enlightened intellectuals were to bring light to the darkness of the masses, to educate them as new human beings. In Russian the word "Enlightenment" is derived from the word "light," like in English. The enthusiasm associated with the Enlightenment was very important for the Russian intellectuals and continued to prevail throughout the nineteenth century.

The democratic Russian writers were also this type of classical Russian intellectual. Chekhov is the best example: he unites the enlightened intellectual with his educational slant and ingenious talents as a writer. The combination of artist and intellectual is the best quality of the Russian writer. The same applies to Mandelstam, Akhmatova, and especially to Pasternak.

In other words, it was also to continue into the twentieth century: a new dark age came about, which once again required enlightenment?

Yes, but unfortunately this was already a different age; the continuity of the ages had been interrupted.

But this generation also adhered to the "educated artist type"?

Absolutely. And that explains the position of the last generation – our generation – better. There's a long span from the age of Catherine the Great in the eighteenth century to our generation at the end of the twentieth. The intelligentsia had developed for two hundred years before its "obliteration" and destruction. Everyone says there's no intelligentsia in Russia anymore. Yet the memory of the intelligentsia still remains. It was the hope of Russian history. Without this intelligentsia, in my opinion, there is no longer any hope for this country.

So that makes clearer what I mean. Especially for the conceptual artist in Russia, the question as to the meaning of art, its significance, is an important subject. Because he's also a human being, not just an artist. Accordingly, he differs somewhat from the Western artist type, as I see him. Naturally, I don't want to generalize. Although there are lots of "intelligent" artists in the West, for example Boltanski. But for me the "normal" Western artist is different. For example Warhol, who was always very active, aggressive, enterprising. He was more of a spontaneous, sensitive, deceptive "character," who skillfully manipulated the contemporary public and the commercial structures, the way Jeff Koons and Damien Hirst do today, for example – peculiar artist/businessman centaurs. Of course, apart from him, there are also artists characterized by profound historical backgrounds and intellectual reflection, like Donald Judd or Mark Rothko.

But with an entirely different way of reflecting.

The Russian intellectual tradition was for the most part a utopian one. Like with Chekhov, who remained a doctor all his life out of a sense of moral obligation, in order to help. The element of distance and the reciprocal relationship between the person and the artist is the main underlying principle of the Russian intellectual: "I'm a writer, but nevertheless I'm also an intellectual." That's why art of that kind also needs intelligent viewers.

Who are willing and able to read the works.

Right. Not a spontaneous viewer, not a collector or gallery owner. Just a normal, intelligent person.

I'd like to talk about another context that also takes us back to the book. At the end of the eighteenth century and beginning of the nineteenth, there was yet another root for the art of the late nineteenth and of the twentieth centuries; I am referring to Romanticism, particularly in philosophy. According to statements you yourself have made, you were already preoccupied with Romanticism at an early stage. Its philosophy differentiates between sensual reality and consciousness. The concept of a unified whole no longer exists; instead, thought and the outer world are considered two separate things.

You have said repeatedly that the figures in your albums, installations, and texts emerge from consciousness as voices, embodying certain aspects of consciousness and at the same time addressing the consciousnesses of the reader/viewer. So you're strongly concerned with the conceptual, the psychological, the emotional?

And the book really does mirror that: on the one hand there's its outward, physical form, the object-like quality, and on the other hand the aspect of content, the language, which itself cannot be illustrated – it has to be read, that is, deciphered. So the book represents two contrary facets, the material and the conceptual.

Yes, exactly. That's what I mean.

Therefore: "the world as a book"?

Yes, exactly. The book culture is an long-standing tradition. For me, since Gutenberg the printed book has been like a deep well which people go to for knowledge like they go to a well for water. It is thanks only to books that consciousness exists. There's no other system that encompasses philosophy and the various aspects of life in so concentrated a manner. Books contain everything.

I'm aware that these days everyone uses the computer and the book is something very conservative. I have no idea what role it's going to play in the future. A new epoch is developing with new means of communication and new communication needs.

I, by contrast, was born in the Soviet Union, where there was no such thing as contemporary life. Naturally, back then there was also no future, because we believed that the Soviet Union would remain the way it was forever, for five thousand years. History had come to a halt. All we had was the past. Naturally, the past contained a huge reservoir of knowledge. It was as if everything had come to a standstill, like in an amphitheater, on whose stage the same play was performed again and again.

From childhood onward, my thoughts did not concentrate on change, but on watching this "play." I was willing to remain seated in this "amphitheater" forever, so to speak. All artists existed in it together. Raphael alongside Eduard Manet. It was the same with music. Despite the development of music, Bach was there right next to Mozart and Shostakovich. There were also second- and third-rate figures in this amphitheater. A kind of pyramid system prevailed. This was already in my head during my school days, despite the fact that I tried to look at things thoroughly and from a perspective distinguished by a certain distance. Yet for some reason I was already convinced of the existence of this pyramid, and of the fact that you couldn't change this system.

Earlier I talked about the man with the golden yardstick. For me this yardstick is not horizontally aligned but vertically. I know that this principle is not perfect, because every artist is a cosmos unto himself who needs his own evaluation criteria, not criteria from the outside. But I can't change that anymore.

Let's go back to the question of the distinction between sensual reality and consciousness, a distinction the book is capable of bringing about, as you said. That presumably explains why literature or also music – ultimately immaterial art forms – were better suited for a conceptual approach than painting, which is perhaps too physical, or too external? Just a hypothesis.

Well . . . that's the paradox.
I'm very pessimistic as far as my profession – painting and the craft of painting – is concerned. But it's too late to change. I hit upon this profession entirely by chance, when I started going to art school. I was never particularly enthusiastic about handling complicated painting techniques.

Out of skepticism?

Great skepticism, yes. Also with regard to my works. That's why I see them as projects. But we also shouldn't lose sight of the fact that Rothko also referred to his works as "experiments."

Would it be correct to say that in the early phase of samizdat, when you produced the albums, you applied techniques of contemporary literature to the visual sphere, while also of course combining the latter with literature? I'm thinking about the connection between word and image, about the hybrid genre of the album, which is both at the same time – book and drawing – but also neither one, and about the boundary crossings between the two mediums: independent texts can become elements of installations; paintings look like designs for book pages. Later, in the West, the book, the reading room, and the dialogue also became themes of exhibition installations, which in turn were accompanied by books, and so on.

Yes. What can I say about this communication between visual and narrative material on the same page, as is the case in the albums?

What interests me is the connection and the conflict between the image and the text, the relativity and the contingency for the one or the other. Not the absurd qualities, like in Surrealism. Relationships exist and they are very rich, complicated, and difficult to depict. But without congruency. There is air – there is distance – between text and image. The image explains something about the text, and the text explains something about the image, but in some other, special sense. There's something the two have in common, but on a different level, in a different space. But in which space? –

That's the conceptual space, where the two come together, a space of consciousness.

At the same time, there's a difference for simple people and intelligent people. Simple people perceive only a picture and a poorly written text. They say: "I didn't understand what he was talking about." In the case of intelligent people, a direct connection of this kind provokes a new allusion to an unidentified space, toward which both the image and the text are directed, and in which they're both floating together, arm in arm.

Blinking

MH: In our first dialogue we talked about the content and language of your books. But for me there's a second important aspect of your books that has to do with the viewer/reader: the aspect of "time." In general, of course, it takes time to read or look at a book. If the book is a major work of literature, it even lays claim to a little chunk of your "lifetime." You have written in detail about the significance of time for your albums. But what does time mean for your books? Is there a correlation to the albums? You later also made books about the albums.

IK: Yes, the subject of time. How much time does it take to read my "books"? They are not literature or poetry, but more like information books. The appearance and design of these books – who is interested? Normal people read texts as literature or poetry – there's a long praxis and tradition of this. But my information books can be a bit problematic for the reader; I'm aware of that.
In the case of an artist's manifesto by Kandinsky or Malevich, it is clear to me as a reader that I have to read the text in order to understand what the artist wants to say. With my books, however, there is no ambition of being a manifesto, a program, or a textbook. So what can the viewer expect of them? What genre do they belong to?

The simple reader essentially uses these catalogues or books only because he is looking for certain information about an installation. Or he is interested in the content of my theoretical books, for example »On the "Total" Installation« or »Public Projects or the Spirit of a Place«. But there aren't very many of these, only about four or five. All of the other books serve as an orientation for works already executed.

One problem for the reader consists in the fact that it takes him some time to distinguish between documentary and informative elements, on the one hand, and the various commentaries, on the other. The commentaries do not merely come at the end, after the extensive informational part, but are interspersed, mixed in like a soup ingredient. It's a mixture of very cold information and very emotional commentaries. A mixed salad with cold and hot ingredients.

There's even a problem in reading the text. The informational text has a very cold and stringent rhythm, like a set of drums. The commentaries, on the other hand, have an emotional, beautiful melody. But there's no program for it. The texts are strongly improvised. For the artist/author, however, the bureaucratic text is also emotional. The numbers and depictions all reflect various different meanings for him. He is perfectly aware of that and arranges the information accordingly. For the outsider, however, it all remains very relative. These cold, geometric depictions are not capable of arousing his fantasy or imagination. So in most cases, he presumably can't understand how these emotional, or even philosophical, commentaries could come about by way of such bureaucratic things. I well understand this problem. There is no continuity between the two parts – information and commentary – for they are separated by a step.

This I noticed after I wrote the book »Die 60er und 70er Jahre: Aufzeichnungen über das inoffizielle Leben in Moskau (The 1960s and 1970s: Notes on Unofficial Life in Moscow)«. Usually memoirs have a rhythm. They revolve around time, the context, one's circle of friends, personal matters – a normal narrative rhythm. There's a long tradition of that. Normal breathing. The reader is calm and understands this melody so carefully created by the voice. Yet in my memories of the 1960s, there are these two different parts again. Right in the middle of the text part, I put a list of works with the names, titles, dimensions, and owners of the paintings, along with information about where they have been discussed in literature; then I continue the story. It's a bad situation for the flow of reading. When the reader arrives at the information section, he thinks: "OK, I'm not interested in this; this is for other people. I'm interested in the artist descriptions and everything having to do with them."

But this mixture of two genres – documentation and description of projects, on the one hand, and storytelling, on the other – this arrhythmic quality of the texts is something I can't change, because for me it's organic, essential, and I like it very much. But I do understand the difficulties the readers have with it.

When I endeavor to control the viewer's reactions to my artworks, I have to pay very careful attention to form and design, and this applies particularly to the installations. These "books," however, are intended for more difficult reading. They're not easy to read: documentation, narrative, commentary, et cetera.

That's the puzzle.

Yes, that's the subject of "time." How much time does it take for the reader to understand what it's all about? It is my hope that the reader is not just a normal reader of literature, because my texts are made for very slow, arrhythmic reading. In other words, the text doesn't flow through the reader but functions more like a fragment of something.

The idea of the fragment as opposed to the whole is related to memories of my childhood, but it also has to do with the present. I never take the time to start a book at the beginning, to continue reading it the next day, et cetera. It's strange. I usually open a book in the middle and read just two or three sentences. I'm not interested in what is going to happen in a novel, or how. I'm not interested in intrigues or crimes. I'm not a detective-like reader. Of interest to me is the author's style, the flow of his text, the way he handles language, various aspects of the hidden content, his main idea. Not what he says, but what he wants to say. For me, a brief excerpt suffices. That's all I need time for.

I take one of my catalogues but don't look at everything, just at three, four pages and the commentaries. The fragment provokes and stimulates the imagination. My analysis intersects the text vertically. When I read, all I need time for is this analysis. I only require little time, but enough to concentrate.

What you're saying makes me think of something having to do with dialogue. Dialogue – of the manner in which you are having with me at the moment, for example – is, on the contrary, not fragmented but more like a calm, slow current, with a certain distance, with irony and humor. An epic narrative, which takes quite some time, sometimes even goes on for several days.

For me, however, one aspect of this current is a kind of circling. The dialogue doesn't just proceed linearly from one point to the next but in a sense revolves, taking on a "spatial" quality as a result. The departures from and returns to the subject are related to this process.

It reminds me of Russian literature. For example, it has been said of Dostoyevsky that his characters don't undergo any real development, but are virtually imprisoned in a room they can't escape. His lengthy books are almost totally devoid of external action. Over more than two hundred pages, the first chapter of the novel »The Idiot«, for example, describes a single day, the return of the Russian hero to St. Petersburg from Switzerland. The narrative has its own "closed" space, even if it continues over hundreds of pages. Almost nothing happens, like standstill in motion, ceaseless reflection, an unending conversation, a circling and revolving of various often contradictory thoughts and voices. For me, there is also something physical about that.

Yes, of course; that is very perceptive. The text creates a form. For me, a round of dialogue is always devoted to a certain subject and the related problems. When it is finished, a circle has been formed. By way of a line or spiral, you then proceed to the next ring. It's a bit like a dance. Yes, a dance. There are also certain similarities with the idea of the series, with a subject and variations of views on it. It's like a rabbit hopping to one point, then jumping to the next, and hopping on again from there. The series first came about in the albums, but then the principle remained the same with all of the books. Dancing at a certain spot, and then going on dancing at somewhere else. That's how my memoirs of the 1960s and 1970s came about. And it also applies to the books »The Text as the Basis of Visual Expression«, »On the "Total" Installation«, and »Public Projects or the Spirit of a Place«. There's always a subject and the dancing around this center, the core.
This style is comparable to a didactic lesson for students. Once Kaspar König gave me a teaching appointment at the art school in Frankfurt am Main, Germany. At the beginning of the first lesson, I said to the students: "I'll talk, and you just listen. If you have a question, ask it at the end." This style is absolutely undemocratic and would be completely crazy for a present-day art school. Because normally the professor sits down with the students and discusses various topics with them. But above all the students discuss issues with other students. For example, Joseph Kosuth once said to me: "I just sit there, and the others talk."

I, on the contrary, was employing the old German style: "The professor comes and says what he wants to say and what he knows. The students open their mouths like little children and take what the professor puts in them." My students stayed to the very end, altogether sixteen lessons. Then one of the participants said to me: "I'm not sure if those were serious lessons; that was a performance, wasn't it? And as a performance we found it very interesting."

Later I made a book about it: »On the "Total" Installation«. Every lesson, every chapter, is devoted to a single topic. I dance on the same spot and invent various positions, like a machine, an air hammer (knocks on the table and laughs). That's the principle with a theme and variations, like in music, very organic. The subject: "dancing in my rooms."

From one room to the next. And that, in turn, is related to the installations, which you once compared to books. Just as you proceed from chapter to chapter, in an installation you proceed from room to room, following a dramaturgy.

Yes, exactly, But there is no development. A room is a room. Every single room is like a monad or a sphere. A monad is like a room without windows.

That reminds me of your book about the 1960s and 1970s. When I first read it, I was very surprised. Why?

Here an artist is writing almost exclusively about others, about his friends and colleagues, especially in parts two and three. This continues for a very long time, altogether over more than two hundred pages. As I was reading, I kept asking myself: "Where, in fact, is Kabakov? Who is Kabakov? Why does he write about everyone else but not about himself?" Only when you get to the end do you understand how the book works: the fact that essentially everyone, as described by you, also has something of Kabakov; that the figure Kabakov is not presented as a positive form – "I'm this and that, and I can do this and that, and I want this and that" – but rather in a certain sense as a negative form. In the figure's interior a void and openness exist. But it nevertheless has a clear outline; it is a figure defined by its surroundings, by the context, or from the outside in. I would say: Kabakov appears as a "Luftmensch" – empty inside but still having consistency. Perhaps this form can ultimately also be compared to a sphere, which is defined from the outside, from every direction, but not from the inside?

Yes, that's an interesting topic: "Where is the author?" For the reader, for normal people, it's clear that when talking to somebody, they're either talking about themselves or about other people. Those are two different vantage points. With the first, you observe yourself, and with the second, you observe your surroundings, the overall situation. But nevertheless, tradition determines the spot at which a person is standing when observing others. This person has a traditional role: he is a historian, curator, psychologist, sociologist, or, for example, a biographer. In this situation the author is like a compact and self-contained figure. What is that? When he writes about a country or a situation and knows exactly what he's talking about. He is certain that that's the way it is. He writes either in an authoritarian style or a soft style, et cetera.

Things get very difficult, however, when he starts talking about the others while at the same time talking about himself and saying: "I'm not sure what I'm talking about; my figures are driving me to despair. This text is not completely serious." "Oh, it's not serious, is it? You're crazy!" No, on the one hand it is serious, but on the other hand it isn't serious. When you write about other people and it is at one point a sound text, and then a despairing text – the result is a restless and unclear position. For example: You go to the doctor and the doctor tells you about his biography. That's paradoxical. I'm sick and you're my doctor, but here I'm in a perverted position: I'm the doctor and you're sick. It's a totally schizophrenic situation.
(laughter)
There's a resemblance to Dostoyevsky. On the one hand the personage Dostoyevsky talks about other people, and on the other hand, he is simultaneously talking about himself. He says: "What I say about the others is totally wrong

because I'm not sure what I mean. At this moment this is what I think, but a few minutes later I say: 'No, that's a false story'." Then he starts telling the story over again, with new variations.

It's a situation in limbo. In our conceptual circle, there's a term for it: "blinking." This blinking is a quick change of position, so fast that the reader/listener doesn't understand where the other person's position is. In the first position he's like an object, but a second later he's like a subject. In the case of the first character he's the narrator, but in the case of the second figure he despairs about the story. It's like stepping on the gas and braking. There's no movement for the author.

But this style is very good – like a salad style. Like when you mash a potato with a fork and eat spinach and a pickle or an onion, and everything simultaneously. (gesticulates)

The text about the 1960s and 1970s is totally subjective. But gradually, as you read, you understand the author's tendencies. What does he want to say? He wants to say that there is a common context and common figures. The artist is not a separate artist, regardless of how he might see himself, and he has tendencies toward various figures: a metaphysical one, a religious one, a social one, and so forth. And the idea is to discover this bouquet or this bush, with a root from which this bush will grow. And even though every part of this bush grows separately, all of these growths as well as the roots go back to one and the same stock.

On the one hand this is very subjective, and on the other hand it corresponds in part to a theory or a utopian construction. What the author wants to say is: "There is an overall sphere." It's like a family with various brothers and sisters, who are nevertheless a family. And the concept of this book is to tell about this family. There are different generations, different places of birth, but nevertheless a family exists to which all of these figures belong. That's a Russian tradition: "When they are dead, they will rise again together." Not only the one or the other, but all of them together, everything, like with Nikolay Fyodorov.

Like a body?

Yes, a body. It's an old Russian tradition. That's where the main idea for this book came from: "to tell about this group as a whole, an entirety, so that we rise up together from the grave of history, embracing life."

Later you also did the installation on Noma, in which you chose the form of the circle with an open, empty center to represent the inner family circle of Moscow conceptualism. Everyone had his or her own room around the edge, but together everyone formed a whole.

The unofficial artists, that's a family. But the conceptualist circle, that's something completely different. It's more like a chapter of the Rosicrucian Order. It has secret terminology and a covenant of secrecy. The meanings are placed as if on a ring around an empty center.

But from what you say, can we draw the conclusion that the artist figure Kabakov is not an autonomous person who emerged from within himself – fell from the sky, so to speak – but is shaped and influenced by all these relatives?

Yes, to an extent. Sure.

And of course vice versa as well – a reciprocal effect?

I didn't see myself as an isolated figure, but as partially responsible for a group mentality. It's a bit like with Vadim Zakharov, who also has this tendency toward family responsibility.

Let's turn to another (related) aspect, namely, that you are not only Kabakov the artist and the person, but also the figure or "personage" Kabakov, which plays a role of its own in your work. There's this duplication. And that clearly begins in the albums; you have said that their figures embodied various states of consciousness which are connected with you. And it continues in the book »The Text as the Basis of Visual Expression« in which you write about the installations under the heading: »Wie ich zu meiner eigenen Figur wurde and Wo ich zu meiner eigenen Figur wurde (How I Became My Own Figure and Where I Became My Own Figure)«. Or, to take this even further: most recently in Moscow, in 2008, with the project »An Alternative History of Art«, where three artists exhibited – Rosenthal, Kabakov, and Spivak – all three of whom you invented as fictional figures. They exhibited together in a museum that you had invented. You produced the catalogue and wrote the biographies. You were everything at once: the artists (several simultaneously), the curator, the author, the book designer, the museum architect. All of these roles from the art world you assumed yourself, and on that basis made an installation as an artistic work.

Yes, that's a very interesting topic: "Where do the figures come from?" Why does he need these fictional figures or fictional faces? What is the underlying reason? Naturally, the reason has to do with my youth, which I spent living with other people, and which had a special psychological effect on me.

At my art school, and later at the art institute as well, I observed myself and my fellow pupils and students while learning. Back then, the important questions for me were: "Who am I? Where am I? What do I mean?" I didn't have the normal subject feeling: "I exist." But: "Everyone exists except me." I didn't feel like a subject or body, but like something unreal, like a cloud or some immaterial substance. Without a sense of myself, without self-reflection, without a name. When I heard the name "Kabakov," my first reaction was: "Who's that?" There was absolutely no subjective basis within myself, no tripod, no central axis. Absolutely nothing. There's this permanent feeling, a huge complex: "What do I mean?"

I read a lot of books and immediately absorbed everything – various stories, various situations. And I understood that there are people who "have the right" to be in this world. They are alive and function as students, professors, or artists who painted the pictures in the Tretyakov Gallery. In contrast, I myself felt like an eye or a fly, like someone who just observes. But not like someone who takes everything to a conclusion, to an outcome. And that's why there was this constantly recurring question: "What should I do in this world?"

Naturally I learned a profession, we talked about that, but that, too, was fictive. I did what the professors wanted, but not what I myself wanted. I had no subjective interest in the activities of illustration or painting, et cetera. That is the underlying reason for the emergence of figures, the awareness of "figures." And the other reason is: I wasn't interested in life itself. Neither food, nor dancing, nor going for a walk, nor just sitting interested me – in my case, all functions were like those of a golem. For example, I had to wash myself, dress myself. But I wasn't interested in clothing. There were no reactions to reality, so to speak. Imitation, yes. I was good at football, I played volleyball, but that was like a wild reaction. I understood "the wild." But what I didn't know was what I wanted to do as a person. I didn't have any desires. I sat there, and every action was difficult and meaningless for me. It was a very frustrating situation – a long period without the slightest interruption.

For example: an artist like Repin painted a picture – I also painted a picture. And then I looked at it and compared it to the Repin picture and said: "Isn't it good? How can I improve it so that I might get closer to the painting by Repin?" That was an imitation.

It's like you are repeating the process of developing a photograph: first you put the negative in a chemical bath, and then, very slowly, a picture appears. That's how art works for me. I'm the person who makes this picture. But where's the guy who decided to carry out these actions? I'm some unknown person who realizes a work with the help of paper or a canvas.

And then that's how it gradually developed, became a permanent preoccupation. In other words: "I became an artist." I myself didn't exist, but slowly, very slowly, the artist became bigger, like a cake rising in the oven. What ultimately came about was a monster. (laughter)

I realized that a new monster had come into the world. I didn't know what contact existed between me and this monster. But the monster grew like a golem. The artist is a construction like a golem. And to this day, when somebody talks about the artist Kabakov and somebody says: "Kabakov!," I ask: "Who's that? – Oh, it's the monster! It makes a lot of installations and books." Like a rabbit in the circus. (bangs on the table) He has to "work." When he stops hopping, a huge void emerges, a nothingness. That's reality. And this golem keeps on incessantly hopping like a rabbit, and keeps producing something or other.

For example, today I painted. The golem feels very good because today he's functioning like an artist; he has a brush and he paints. He's a serious figure. That's why for me the term "personage" is the best and the correct designation for this golem. I myself am the golem from the parable of my biography. For no biography of my life exists. There is no life as such, and also no biography.

In the Soviet Union I preoccupied myself with painting every day. But a big problem was where I could get something to eat. Back then there were lots of problems. You had to stand in line in order to buy food. But I was too lazy to stand in line and often went hungry. For the golem, that was the problem of the stomach.

But fortunately, when I had completely "gone under," Emilia came. She took this golem and said: "Golem come here!", "Come and eat!," "Come and sleep!," "Today we're off to New York!" – "OK." (laughter)
To this day, life has remained a void; I have developed absolutely no interest in life. I have neither a negative nor a positive relationship to it.

Neutral.

Neutral, yes. It's like with Pavel Pepperstein. He also doesn't care what he eats. He's also a monster, a golem. (laughter) But he's a very good observer. He's like a fly, like an anonymous eye. He understands and observes everything.
For example, in the early phase, when I was working for the children's book publisher, a friend asked me: "Ilya. What did a musketeer in France look like? What did he wear on his head?" "No problem," I replied. I didn't know the answer from books. But my fantasy extended way back into the past. Like an airplane or a fly, I covered a great distance and landed in France, in eighteenth-century Paris, wandered through the streets, looked around, and came to a tavern. There sat a musketeer. I walked around him and took a very close look at him, from the back, his head, the shoes, et cetera. And then I quickly sketched him, to help me remember. That's this very free and mobile way of seeing. For example today people talk about the Chinese. OK, so I go to China and see everything in front of me – it's like a moving picture.

That was a commentary. But to return to the personages. For me the personages are the same as real people. They're like figures of life. That's why Rosenthal and Spivak are also personages, without bodies and without historical reality. For me the question "Does Rosenthal exist or not?" is absurd. Maybe he exists, maybe he doesn't. "Do you exist, or do you not exist?" That is very problematic.

This subject has to do with the relationship between mind/soul and body. Every person feels like an emigrant in his body. It is the temporary room or house; someone is in there – coincidentally and temporarily. That's why there's this distance between me and my "social" figure. And the social figures are like monsters, too. When we look at politicians or philosophers – they're also various figures, "representatives" of a certain theory or construct. But the normal person and the monster, those are two entirely different things.

My pessimistic view of this problem is very simple: if you're a normal person with a body and a soul and don't concern yourself with the world, just working until retirement, as did my parents, then there's no program. It's very simple: "I live because I was born." Like a bird. The bird was born; that's why it sings. That's the fundamental idea: "Being born and living until the end."

But parallel to that there's another situation, with a program. I don't know who gives each person his program. Showing the way he's supposed to do things. In the eighteenth century, for example, there was this romantic theory: "The human being was born to carry out a mission." Just being born is not enough for life; it also needs a human mission. You have to look for it, as a violinist, a politician, or someone who spreads a message. But when you start carrying out this mission you're a monster.

Here, a big question arises: "Does the monster bear responsibility for itself or are you responsible for this monster?" That is a very problematic aspect. I ask myself when this monster in me starting working and why it came about. Why is it always there, and where does it get its energy? For example we talk to our grandmother and ask her: "Now that you're retired you have a lot of free time. Why don't you pick up a pencil and write your memoirs? Because your biography is very interesting." Her answer is simple: "I don't even have enough energy for my own life, so I certainly don't have any extra energy for other things."

What that means is that the monster requires extra energy. It doesn't get its energy from its body, but from a different source or a different reservoir. That, in turn, is a special topic. I will limit myself now to the aspect of the "artist figure."

There is great resemblance here to Dostoyevsky's personages. Dostoyevsky was very sick, psychopathic. His brain was unstable, and as a result he had problems with time, and with answers, for example. Once he was sitting and talking to the writers Turgenev and Belinsky and they asked him: "What do you think, Fyodor Mikhailovich?" Dostoyevsky went blank and couldn't answer, because his brain wasn't flexible enough. This frightened him and he became very nervous. Suddenly he jumped up from his chair and dashed out. After about ten minutes or so, outside somewhere along the street, the answer occurred to him. Half an hour later he returned and wanted to answer the question, but the idiots had already forgotten what it had been all about. (laughter)

That's typical. His novels are answers to questions posed in other places, in other times, by other people. He conducts dialogues with these people, but they are not present.

The word "dialogue" takes us back to the topic of conversation. The term "dialogicity" was used for Dostoyevsky's concept of the novel. The dialogic principle also applies to the individual. For Dostoyevsky, it is not just the ego that is of central importance, but also the dialogue with himself and others. He spread himself out like a kaleidoscope in various different, contradictory characters as alter egos. The ego accordingly no longer has a fixed position, but is constantly in motion. And this manifests itself in the dialogue. A little while ago you used the word "blinking" for this.

Yes, exactly. That's Bakhtin's theory. Dostoyevsky's personages were part of himself and not part of himself.

To return to the monsters, the personages, and the inner void: in your case the void is also openness, isn't it? – A space where you can do what you like? It offers opportunities for very different figures. This reminds me of an author and a novel that was very important for you in the 1970s, as you once told me: Robert Musil's »The Man Without Qualities«. This figure not only distinguishes itself by a sense of reality, but also – and above all – by its sense of possibility. For this figure, reality, as it exists, is of equal value to various possible ways it could be instead.

Yes, but then he does nothing. Nothing happens.

According to Musil, the concern is with conveying the sense of possibility and the sense of reality as a human goal. Taking a refuse heap of things and facts, as it were, and using them again and again to synthesize a possible utopian world.

Yes, Musil is very close to my consciousness, like part of my own experience. The division into two persons was very widespread in the Soviet society. In my case, the best example is the rift – the life of the official artist and that of the unofficial artist. Nevertheless, it was easier for me than for others. At the children's book publisher's we always had a lot of fun, laughed a lot, told each other anecdotes; I was a one-hundred-percent "pleasant" person. But for my unofficial friends I was very acrimonious, sad, and pessimistic. Like a bad man during the day and a good man at night. In English literature these two figures are well known: »Dr. Jekyll and Mr. Hyde« by Robert Louis Stevenson.

Speaking of these two sides, I'd like to finish by returning to the topic of the dialogue. Can we say that the same applies to dialogue as to your paintings and books? You once said to me that the paintings are paintings and yet not paintings. They were just pretending to be paintings, but were only actually paintings to a limited extent. This also applies to the personages and the books. They are partially real, partially fiction, like Gogol's hero who has lost his nose. And the dialogue really does show similarities. While the dialogue, the way you conduct it, is always related to a theme, it explains, it contemplates, but it doesn't pin the subject down for good. It's more like circling around the topic, ultimately like a commentary, an interpretation based on one's own imagination, with no unequivocal answers to certain questions. More like a process which goes on and on and never comes to an end.

For me there's something very fundamental behind that, which – as you have claimed – also applies to the installations, namely the paradox of free confinement or confined freedom.

The dialogue is bound to something, a theme, a question, and in that sense it is not free as an answer. At the same time, it also has these possibilities of constant reinterpretation – opening it up, making it independent, liberating it. It is thus essentially endless.

It seems to me that this freedom gives the listener/reader of the dialogue the opportunity to connect with it himself, to link his own thoughts with it. Then the dialogue leaves the people, so to speak, creating a general human context and existing on a meta-level?

That's a very good topic: "the dramaturgy." In every one of my artworks, particularly in the installations, there's this paradox, this dramatic moment.

I'm not only interested in the usual installations made of objects for the free viewer. What I'm interested in is the closed room. Why? Because the closed room is like a theater or a film – or like a dream, which grabs you and starts "gobbling you up." You're either a victim or a prisoner. You feel like a dog locked up in a kennel. The room functions like claustrophobia. When you enter it, you normally lose no time in looking for a way out of this world. You can either use the same door you entered through, or you look for another "door" or a window to exit, to disappear.

In the Soviet Union there were lots of situations in which it wasn't so easy to find this door. That's why normal people were very frustrated and depressed. The dramaturgy is therefore a kind of challenge to the viewer: "Please look for freedom in a different way. Do not only use the normal, physical doors as exits. There is also an exit as a mental act. There is freedom on a different level, in different spaces."

In every installation there's this stairway, this ladder, where the person/viewer searches for the exit, or can find it. Or it's a poetic, metaphysical, paradoxical, or irony-laden ladder, but there's an exit all the same. "This depression is not permanent; it's not stable, and not hopeless" – that's the dramaturgy. You always have to overcome some difficulty or other so that, later, something will happen . . .

You offer various means for this liberation?

It's like an exit from the labyrinth.

But you have already been laying out clues leading to this exit?

Like various labyrinths: a mental labyrinth, a constructive labyrinth. The installations are essentially a model of life or of this world: a metaphor for the "universal." And naturally there is an exit from this world.

If I may close by coming back to the topic of the book – can the book also be understood as a metaphor for this world?

Yes. Yes, exactly.

Both closed and open?

Yes, yes, of course. The book is the labyrinth. If it's a good book, then it's a never-ending labyrinth.

White Writing

MH: I don't know whether the reader will really follow our long dialogue this far once it's in print. I assume he or she will have left it earlier, having paged through the illustrations for a while and then put the book back on the shelf. We should nevertheless carry on and conduct a "dialogue after the dialogue," as it were, a dialogue without listeners/readers. A fitting topic here is "absence."

You once said that your paintings aren't entirely paintings, and your books only partially appear as books, and that the artist himself is a monster. And for me, your most confined and darkest installations, which seem to have no exit, have the quality of stage sets the visitor can enter, that is, they also show that they are "false." They may be physically present but, at the same time, they're also absent at a higher level due to their shoddiness and makeshift character: deliberately made illusions, phantoms, or, indeed, monsters. In the end, they no longer have the threatening quality one senses at first.

Absence plays a major role particularly in your drawings, albums and paintings, in which context the topic of "white" is very important. We haven't talked about this aspect yet.

There has been the tradition of the white ground in modern painting since Cézanne, and naturally also in the Russian avant-garde. For me, the white in your work is a counter element to the illustrative, pictorial aspect. It could even be said that by showing something in white, it is at the same time veiled or concealed. In other words, that which we see may well have emerged from white and may just as well vanish again into white, so that everything is present-absent. The dramaturgy of the albums demonstrates this idea very clearly.
There is also a relationship here to an emptiness or a void. In our last dialogue you talked about the labyrinth. Being lost, without orientation, is something that plays a role in your installations and in your books.

Now it seems to me that, when you talk, you also remain silent and absent in a certain sense. Pavel Pepperstein proposed the term "transnarrativity" for the special narrative form of Moscow conceptualism. What he means is a form of narrative that simultaneously goes through or beyond itself, not depending solely on words and their meaning but also introducing another element. Paper-white also figures as a theme in literature, not only in painting. I'm thinking here of Mallarmé, who talks about paper-white in poems. In your books, white plays an important role as well, both in your children's books and in your artist's books.

So I would like to pose the following question. For me, there is, in your work, not only the cold white of emptiness or the warm white of light, but also the white of nothingness – which plays an important role in Eastern culture, particularly in East Asian painting. It signifies openness. An absence that is openness – something afloat, free, perhaps even something meditative. With reference to Pepperstein we could use the term "transvisuality." Do you see it this way as well – the nothingness of absence as a potential and a possibility for meaning?

IK: Of course white is a theme. In my work, white has many different meanings, levels, and qualities. There is, however, a central meaning: "white as space."

When I start a painting or drawing, I see the white surface as a three-dimensional space with great depth and great potential. This potential not only relates to me as the productive artist who paints or draws something on "the white," but it also lurks, so to speak, in every viewer as his special "ability" to comprehend.

Initially, a painting consists of realistic elements and depicts the "simple view of reality." How do my works differ from the realistic depiction of still lifes, landscapes, or portraits executed from the Renaissance to the nineteenth century? Renaissance techniques also dealt with space, but a space generated entirely by the figures and the landscapes. Nature is space. And the master putting this world on the canvas was naturally making a copy of the big world. He looked at the world through an open window and considered what he could paint. It was with diligence and great respect that he copied the space on the other side of the window. Therein lies the holiness of such a painting, when it becomes a mirror and reproduces the qualities of the world.

I've often worked with such depictions of nature. With views, lighting, highlights, colors, reality, et cetera. But I have treated the motifs in a special way. This is because my white picture already has three-dimensional space, so for realistic spatiality there is actually no space left. I have lost faith in three-dimensional, representational reality for my painting. Reality, in and of itself, has three dimensions, but when it encounters the depth of white space in my painting, it loses its spatiality. I treat it like a surface, essentially like a reproduction. As if one had affixed a piece of cloth or paper to the surface, like a curtain shrouding my white three-dimensionality. That's the best explanation for my painterly intention: a painted curtain covering up "the white."

This pasting-over principle of reality has many consequences and can cause considerable problems. It doesn't leave any means of creating a work with two spaces: real space and white space. There is no relationship between the two in my painting. Real space is two-dimensional. There are, however, various ways in which this flat space of depicted reality might encounter the three-dimensional white.

This two-dimensional, realistic depiction, for example, covers the entire picture. Then various measures are required in order to make it clear that the work is not about three-dimensionality. The white forces its way through in the form of a "hole," or in some way or other, and destroys this wonderful, so-called realistic painting. It says: "There's nothing there, just a foil."

In the second variation I don't paint so illusionistically. Prior to Impressionism and Expressionism, three-dimensional space required illusionistic painting. Expressionism says: "This isn't reality, it's my reaction to reality." But I'm not interested in that kind of manipulation of color and form. What I'm interested in is the process by which "reality" behaves on the white. This gives my paintings an anonymous, mediocre quality: it's not "good" painting, but it also isn't "very bad" painting. It's like the painting of an autodidact. Without personal style. No, it's spaceless painting with an anonymous technique. It's not important what the painting looks like; the most important thing is its communication with the white.

This concept is very difficult to understand if you haven't had much experience handling white. For example, the reactions of a number of Russian painters to my last show in Moscow were surprisingly negative. For them it was just painting. They didn't understand the aspect of the communication between the painting and the empty white elements. On the one hand, from their perspective there are already enough empty elements in the serious and exceptional works by Malevich and Mondrian. On the other hand, to them realism represents poor-quality Socialist Realism, which is very unpleasant to view. They did not realize that my work is a combination of the two.

White has also come to take on other meanings for me. It works like a light. In other words, in my paintings – and especially in my drawings – it creates not only space, but illuminated space. Like a screen on which the light comes to us from the depths. Like cosmic energy or another "thin" form of matter. When you stand in front of this white image, you are permeated by this energy or this light – at least that's how I experience it.

Yet another variation of white is the impression of a void or a nothingness. Here the white is not spatial, but flat. It has a double meaning: whereas an artist or someone with an imagination can recognize a deep space in it, for simple people it is merely a normal empty surface, filled with nothingness. You have to work with this nothingness. How many elements and how much mass of reality do you need when you encounter the white "nothingness"? How can communication be facilitated on this surface? What figures function within it?

And the last meaning of white is the natural white material – in other words, logically: snow. I would like to repeat what Boris Groys said in »Under the Snow«. Snow is a symbol of white and radiates a sense of calm, evoking Russian memories, nostalgia, longing. White snow is an element which covers everything on the surface of the earth – snow is like a lost memory and stands for forgetting, oblivion. Boris also says that, with my last works, for example the great white paintings for a chapel, the artist was directing his attention more and more to the subject of oblivion. Only a few realistic elements remain behind as fragments of the past. Oblivion increases, and emptiness spreads, like in a computer which no longer works properly and loses data.

To return from painting and drawing to language and Pepperstein's concept of "transnarrativity" – to the white in language, so to speak. On listening more closely, one notices that, in your speech, the informational content of what you say continually dissolves into nothingness again, so that a "white or empty space" is created?

Yes, yes, exactly. It's called "white writing." It means writing so much that people fall asleep. That so many words generate speechlessness. That's also very important for me.

That brings me to my next question. This mass of speech production – including our long dialogue over the course of days, which perhaps nobody at all will even read because it's too long and the end seems out of sight, as were there no end – it evokes a movement that goes on and on . . .

And it's like with an old LP that has a scratch and gets stuck.

In the overabundance, what we ultimately find is an absence, nothingness?

Yes, exactly.

And, as you said, absence comes about due to the fact that one can hardly remember this overabundance and one forgets what one has read and what one has seen. There we have the labyrinthine element again: you keep getting lost all over again.

That applies particularly to scholarly interpreters of your work. At the beginning there are usually a lot of questions, but normally in the course of an extended preoccupation with an artistic oeuvre many things become resolved of their own accord. One receives important information, knows more and more, and becomes ever better acquainted with the work. In your case, it's completely different. The more information obtained – the longer one preoccupies oneself with you and your oeuvre – the larger the labyrinth. It's essentially a standstill.

Yes, exactly. Essentially it's a negative reaction to scholarship and knowledge: consciousness as a machine fostering not communication but oblivion. In our culture there are very old roots for this in religious texts. It's called "apophatism." It expresses everything in negative terms: "This doesn't exist, and that doesn't exist, and neither does the other thing. What does exist? I don't know. All I know is: everything around me doesn't exist."

It's not like when someone paints just one single picture; then he knows what he's doing. But when you paint five hundred pictures, you know absolutely nothing. (laughter)

Exactly. There are even art historians who have experienced "despair" while preoccupying themselves with your oeuvre, because they have never been able to arrive at a conclusion or a result – they have become lost in the labyrinth or have just managed to get away from the monster threatening to imprison and devour them.

That's an interesting idea: that the artist is a monster and works without there being a reason for his production.

Like Sisyphus?

Absolutely. His production lacked identity but it nevertheless continued. That's a good question: "Why does this tragic automatism work? What is the purpose of this nonstop production?"

This also reflects a profound question about emptiness. The respective topic is called: "the empty center."

There is only one possible principle. If you look directly at your goal and ask yourself: "What do I see?," you'll recognize nothing. If you expect openness and clarity, you'll get nothing. The result remains elusive. But while you are looking straight ahead, something happens in your peripheral vision. Something important turns up, something emotional, some information; there are answers, communication. Not on your direct viewing axis, but somewhere in your angle of vision, at the edge of your field of vision.

And this also has something to do with the topic of white or emptiness. The focus of our interest is always wrong. In other words, we don't know what we are seeing. And we can't know what will reveal itself to us outside our direct focus. Our interest behaves in a very paradoxical manner: you need a point of interest, which you direct straight toward an empty center; then around the edge you receive various information as a gift. But if you show no interest, nothing will reveal itself to you on the ring outside the center. This double view, or double effect, presupposes your interest and an empty center. It requires a central interest, which remains, however, without an immediate result. Nevertheless, at the edge, something turns up which has something to do with your search. The significant aspect, the truth, always lies on the edge, not in the middle. It's a paradox, but life is a paradox. Life has no simple logic, but it has paradoxical logic.

Take, for example, portrait art. You can compare portraits by Franz Hals and Rembrandt. In the case of Franz Hals you see a simple face with a nose, lips, eyes, ears, et cetera. All of the elements are in place – good portrait painting, showing people talking, laughing, et cetera. Then, when you look at a portrait by Rembrandt, a strange movement of the subject's eyes comes about. The strange effect of "aliveness" is directly related to the very evident way in which the artist had calculated the "peripheral view." For when you look at one of the portrait subject's eyes, you suddenly see that his mouth moves a bit, but if you look at his mouth, suddenly his eye moves a little, and so forth. That is the theme of focusing and defocusing: "the central view and the second view." Every element functions with this additional movement. This leads to a very lively effect, because you can't stabilize your view; the painting has no primary focal point.

The result is communication. The animated person in the portrait – having been aroused to life – observes with his lively gaze. But it is a mirror-image effect, because you're not really only just seeing this man, but also yourself in the presence of the painted, yet real, person. This is particularly true of the painting »The Sampling Officials« at the Rijksmuseum in Amsterdam. When you stand in front of it, you see six different forms of communication with the viewer: one figure is sinister, another is smiling, a third is thinking "he's a good man," while the fourth is saying, "no, he's not a good man." Those are various aspects of your fate. You look at it and don't know which one is right.

The entire range of possibilities is spread out, and you don't know how it's going to end. Or what opinion of you will ultimately prevail at the guild.

And the "double view" also occurs again: when you look at this face, you also see the one next to it; you see both at the same time. Rembrandt was a master at painting a good overall scene.

And if the focus is so animated, you always see two together, not just the one or the other. That's another dialogue?

They revolve together. When the one stands still, the other turns; it's like a film, a kinetic effect.

Like flipping something over – fascinating. Perhaps that concept can be applied to our dialogue. You said the consequence of talking for a long time is forgetting. Forgetting is the one thing. But by way of forgetting, memory also returns. That's also a kind of movement, an interdependent oscillation between forgetting and remembering. But the memory is not simply that which factually once happened or existed, because it had been forgotten, but it comes back as something new, something all its own, doesn't it? Memory as a creative act?

Absolutely. This topic is very interesting, and that's a very good comment. The topic of "extra information." The message to the viewer requires a second element. The one element is simple: a good, clear answer. But in parallel there's an alternative, which cancels out this good answer. You work with both. It's like with money. The right hand gives you the money, the left hand takes it away again. A double movement – the one gives you the truth, the other says: "No, that's a false truth." A paradoxical effect of defocusing comes about in the viewer's consciousness, which is very interesting. The viewer says: "Actually I understood everything, but 10 percent, or one single element, is something different." And he looks for what accounts for this differentness, but there is always one last remaining bit, a reserve he can't grasp.

A white spot.

A white surface that I haven't been able to grasp, can't comprehend. And later this effect works well in memory. You say: "In that moment I didn't understand absolutely everything." There has to be this remainder, this reserve. Naturally there are artists who work without reserves. (laughter)

That can also have something to do with the different phases of life. In one's youth or one's mature period, there's usually a clear impression, and as one becomes advanced in age a certain reserve accumulates. For example Claude Monet. As a painter he was very clear throughout his life, but in his late work – in the water lily and Japanese bridge paintings – he was clearly working with a reserve.

Forgetting plays a role here as well. In front of these indistinct, blurry paintings, you see, in a sense, how you had forgotten what you know. The motifs dissolve in color.

And you no longer understand what you see in front of your eyes.

It's in limbo.

And even so, many artists work quite "clearly." The Symbolist program or that of Viennese Art Nouveau is particularly strange. They used religious or irrational motifs, but their works still have a very aesthetic feel today. Everything is clear, there are no reserves, no secret elements in these paintings. Everything is over and done with. Good, but already over and done with. Edvard Munch, on the other hand, is an artist with huge reserves. Of course there's also a lot of clarity in his work: the expressive qualities, the emotionality, the sexuality. But still there's a reserve – and you can look at his works again and again.

Every time you look at them, you see them differently, because you yourself have changed and are able to discover something new?

Yes, exactly. In addition to the main idea there's a large reserve.

That brings me back to the subject of forgetting again. With reference to our dialogue, the following could be said: when one has forgotten something and remembers its meaning as a new creation, as it were, then the conversation's past is not just simply past, but also lies ahead of one like the future. One enters the future by reinterpreting the bygone in the act of remembering.

And that brings me full circle back to what we were saying about history at the beginning. That history doesn't just represent what is past; what lies behind us is over and uninteresting. Precisely the opposite is the case: by remembering what is past, I paradoxically arrive at something new. With creative memory, history is reinvented and becomes part of personal history and a possible future?

Yes, that's what I mean. We see that in the work of many old artists, artists of the Renaissance, the Baroque, especially the Baroque. Baroque artists frequently worked with memories. Whereby there are problematic elements here as well, for the past should be alive and not be aestheticized.

Or historicized.

Or historicized. The past is a secret.

The Russian group »Mir Iskusstva« (World of Art), for example, worked with the past, with the Rococo for instance. But that's not particularly interesting, because what they produced were contrived reconstructions, aestheticizations of various museum objects.

But the past is like a large, mysterious room. In the Baroque, for example, artists like Rembrandt or particularly Caravaggio show us this. The latter works with two "times." On the one hand, he uses a great, dark black which is essentially completely asensual, since you can't discern anything in it at all. Of course you suspect that something lies concealed behind this darkness. Many scientific analyses have been carried out, but nothing has been found beneath the black. On the other hand, his vibrant figures have a strong physical presence and create temporal presence. They are naturalistically painted, without fantasy, like a photograph.

The combination of this naturalistic depiction with the absolutely black space of the surroundings results in a connection between the present and the past, as it were. The tension is particularly strong between the figures at the bottom and the upper three quarters of the painting, where it is absolutely dark. A kind of pressure builds up. It's incredible. There's a similar, intuitively created effect in Velázquez's »Las Meninas« in the Prado in Madrid. In a large proportion of the painting there is absolutely nothing, empty space. But that's the strongest element of this painting. Yes, it's a very important topic: "How does the past function when the artist intuitively leaves space free – that is, without any subject – for this past?"

A gap.

Yes, an empty space.

Also for the imagination, so that you sense that there's something there, a secret, another space?

A reserve. In the music of the great composers there are also many empty elements which function as reserves.

And isn't it the emptiness then that is quasi the means of redefining that which borders on the emptiness, but redefining it in an equivocal manner? In other words, the emptiness is not simply void of meaning but indirectly generates meaning again.

Yes, absolutely. Today, the meaning of Caravaggio's subjects has long disappeared, and his technique is not particularly interesting. But this reserve – the emptiness or the dark nothingness – still works today.

This is also very striking in the late works of Cézanne, I mean his white surface areas on the canvas. The individual dab of color doesn't mean anything in and of itself, but in conjunction with the white it becomes a house, a tree, anything. That's particularly true of the watercolors.

Yes, the unfinished state.

It can become anything and at the same time remains a fragment.

The principle of "the unfinished" is also very interesting. It also works with Toulouse-Lautrec.

With Toulouse-Lautrec there's also a connection to East Asian painting, in which white played a major role.

But let's return to your manner of speaking, which never reaches its goal but is a kind of circling, a going-back-and-forth, always leaving something unresolved in the process. You explained that. The concern here, as in the paintings with the double view, is with movement, here as a process of speaking and reading. And while the process itself is meaningless, it makes sense as a means of experiencing something. But an experience of this kind should never actually come to completion. When talking and reading, I thus get an inkling of a reserve, an open space. But once the thought has been expressed, the idea drawn or built, or published in a book, then it is fixed and materialized. Then it's like a hull, a shell, or a piece of refuse which remains behind. Your work stimulates me to carry on this movement further and further, like a ritual, so as not to get stuck at a standstill with mere empty hulls.

The unrealized projects are also part of this principle. There's the idea that a human being has talent and strengths and comes into the world with a mission to realize something valuable. This result then represents the climax of long and hard activity. A good result is like a good building. There's a principle that we are born into this world to build an important building. The ideal example is Leonardo da Vinci, who produced the »Mona Lisa«.

There is also an alternative principle: "unrealized projects." The second figure of the Renaissance is Michelangelo. He is the best example of a loser. Michelangelo started a large number of gigantic projects which were never realized, for example the tomb of Pope Julius. But he wasn't particularly sad about that fact. For me this is a good metaphor for explaining the system: we come into this world, but we don't understand what we're doing here. We start living and realizing our works, but at the end we still haven't understood the role played by this little fragment, our activity.

It's like with a train. We arrive at a station and get off the train, but the train continues on, and we don't know its schedule or the connections. It's an interesting principle: there's a huge circle, and we're just a fragment, a tiny part of it. We don't understand where the beginning of this circle is, or what happens with us and our works. Our fate is just a segment of the curve, but not the entire circle. So there is the unknown in the past and in the future. The fate of the human being and his works is essentially very fragmentary. That's why there's a reserve for the memory of the past and the vision of the future. Every human being and every artist has the same fate. Michelangelo is a good example of that.

Eternal failure?

Undertaking a new attempt, over and over again.

In the area of linguistic thought, which functions very logically, one is also trapped to a certain extent. One can't experience the fragmentary, because one is trapped in the space of linguistic logic. Kleist proposed an alternative model for escaping the linguistic system of human finitude: the constant advance from one paradox to the next in an inconclusible process of consciousness. And I've noticed that, in this dialogue, you have often formulated paradoxical images and have even talked about a paradoxical logic of life. Do you also see the production of paradoxes as a means of opening up finite language to infiniteness?

Only that – only that.
But what I find interesting about the Baroque is the great experience with the cosmos. Michelangelo and Caravaggio worked with cosmic constructions. They understood that – at the end of this world – a secret, other cosmic dimension exists. In the Sistine Chapel you see figures which come flying at you like cosmonauts – the effect of flying.

This brings me, in conclusion, to just such a paradox. The way you have constructed your entire oeuvre, the way you talk and write, it's all a narrative, in a special way of course. We have talked about that. A kind of novel which – and this is my paradox – was written by "a luftmensch in the underground."[1] On the one hand, you're captive in a space, in a situation, in a body, or in a way of thinking, while at the same time having the perspective from above – from the air.

You need an ascent. It works like a vertical movement, like a balloon. Because life is a deep well. There's a way out at the top, in vertical movement. Every good work functions like an elevator. Everything good, in art or in literature, functions like a draught of air. You read, and then an unknown vertical force pulls you up, as if through an air tunnel. And naturally, there are many works which push you down. In the classical works it's under control – there's a great vertical pull in them, a lot of air.

[1] The reference here is to Dostoyevsky's Notes from the Underground, in German *Aufzeichnungen aus dem Kellerloch*.

Every evening before I go to sleep I read Pasternak – not much, three or four poems. It's so healthy, a kind of therapy. He talks about nothing; life is very trivial. He was naïve and lived as a simple man. But the effect of his poetry is like a huge vertical air pump that rises up. Always, in every work. No pressure. When he talks about tragedy or longing, the result of this poetry is always a lot of air. It's good therapy.

Breathing, oxygen.

It has a balancing effect, makes for good breathing. Pasternak essentially had a very pessimistic view of life. But he nevertheless sensed a great "air world" in life and – as a further quality – possessed huge wings. He flew. That's the idea of a reserve, of a reservoir of air, or of the sky. In metaphorical terms, the sky is energy, there for the taking, a reserve you can fly to for a free float. But that's a huge topic: "flying, cosmonauts, the cosmic." Boris Groys handled that in his book »The Man Who Flew into Space from His Apartment«. Collective dreams: "Leave our earth; there's not enough space for life here."

It's too confined.

It's interesting, because there we can note a strong contrast to the American mentality. Why? Because here people live very comfortably. The people here think: "This is our earth, and we're the people on the earth." They don't come into the world for tragedy, but to live. The earth is here to be lived on, very simple. No stoicism like in England, for example, and also not like German Romanticism, which considered the earth not as a means of life but as a means of suffering. That's particularly true of the Russians – that's where the center of suffering is. (laughter)

For the Americans it's no problem: "I was born and I'm happy." The earth is the place for human beings. It's unique. No ideology and no religion pointing to a different world. The other world is this world. Very simple.

A real utopia.

A real utopia. I really like that. But still, I don't have any contacts. (laughter) I'm a cosmonaut, but on a good planet.

Dialog mit Ilya Kabakov von Matthias Haldemann

Dialog mit Ilya Kabakov von Matthias Haldemann[1]

Das Bewusstsein ist nur dank Büchern entstanden.

MH: Du bist ausgebildeter Kinderbuchillustrator und hast deshalb von Anfang an ein professionelles Verhältnis zum Thema Buch gehabt. Kannst du etwas über deine anfängliche Beziehung zum Buch sagen?

IK: Natürlich habe ich am Kunstinstitut den Beruf des Kinderbuchillustrators gelernt. Trotzdem muss ich sagen, dass diese Tätigkeit für mich nicht mit Liebe und einem großen Interesse verbunden war, sondern nur dem Überleben in der sowjetischen Situation diente. Warum? Natürlich ist die Buchillustration, besonders für Kinderbücher, im Prinzip eine interessante künstlerische Aufgabe. Aber in der sowjetischen Situation gab es so viele zensurierte Elemente und Grenzen, dass man sich nicht frei fühlen konnte. Man sagte: „Bitte, lieber Vogel, flieg weiter, aber ohne Flügel." Das war eine paradoxe, regressive oder zum Teil sogar sadistische Situation. Du musstest zeichnen, aber innerhalb eines Rahmens und unter Zensur.

Die Zensur war in der sowjetischen Kunst Mitte der 1930er-Jahre entstanden. Vorher war die russische Kinderbuchillustration natürlich sehr interessant und avantgardistisch gewesen; Mitglieder einer starken und freien Bewegung hatten wunderbare Arbeiten gemacht. Aber ab den 1930er-Jahre wurde dann sehr stark kontrolliert. Als ich im Jahre 1956 zum Moskauer Kinderbuchverlag kam, gab es für mich nur diese Möglichkeit Geld zu verdienen. Der Staat hatte die Buchillustration total unter Kontrolle, fast genauso wie die literarischen Texte. Du hattest die Wahl: Entweder du folgtest diesen Regeln oder du bekamst den Auftrag nicht. Es gab keinen Ausweg. Dieses System konntest du nicht ändern.

Für mein erstes Buch schlug ich eine Zeichnung vor, von der ich dachte, sie sei gut. Ich brachte sie zum Redakteur (für jedes Buch gab es bestimmte Kunstredakteure). Der sagte aber: „Nein, dieses Gesicht ist nicht gut.", oder: „Diese Physiognomie des Hasen ist nicht perfekt gemacht." Ich verstand nicht warum, denn ich zeichnete praktisch nach der Natur. Mir wurde nicht ausführlich erklärt, was schlecht war. Das war ein Erziehungssystem wie im Tibet: „Die Lehrer schlagen dir mit dem Stock auf den Kopf, aber erklären nicht, was dein Fehler ist." Und nach dem zehnten Schlag verstehst du dann plötzlich selber: „Aha, das ist es also!" Dieser „Satori" kam mir, nachdem der Redakteur meine vielmals überarbeitete Zeichnung zwölf Mal abgelehnt hatte. Dann kam mir die Erleuchtung: „Du darfst deine Zeichnung nicht mit deinen Augen sehen; du musst dich in die Position des Redakteurs versetzen und deine eigenen Zeichnungen mit den anonymen Augen dieses zensierenden Kunstredakteurs betrachten." Hatte ich seine psychologische Position einmal eingenommen und legte ihm die neuen Zeichnungen mit einem Hasen oder einem Kindergesicht vor, meinte er sogleich: „Das ist perfekt!"

Dieser psychologische Druck und diese psychologische Perversion sind interessant: Denn es waren letztendlich nicht mehr meine Zeichnungen, obwohl ich sie natürlich mit meiner Hand gemacht hatte. Fortan wurden alle meine Zeichnungen

[1] *Anm. des Herausgebers: Die folgenden Dialoge mit Ilya Kabakov wurden am 12., 14. und 16. Januar 2009 in Mattituck, Long Island, USA, auf Deutsch geführt. Ausdrucksweise und Ton wurden in der englischen Übersetzung beibehalten.*

ganz normal und ohne Beanstandung abgesegnet. Auf einmal wurde jetzt alles einfach für mich. Warum? Der Redakteur im Kinderbuchverlag funktionierte wie ein Buskontrolleur. Der Künstler nimmt normalerweise an, er sei eine individuelle Persönlichkeit, macht eine Zeichnung, die seine Individualität ausdrückt, und denkt, dass man dies beachten würde. Aber die Arbeit des Redakteurs funktionierte gerade umgekehrt. Er war streng wie ein Kontrolleur. Du brachtest eine Mappe mit Zeichnungen und beim Durchblättern saß er da und plauderte gleichzeitig mit einem Kollegen: „Gestern war ich im Kino und es war sehr interessant." – Er kontrollierte die Zeichnungen wie Tickets. Wenn er etwas Individuelles entdeckte, war das wie ein „Fehler". Wenn es in deiner Standardzeichnung nur einen einzigen individuellen Effekt gab, musstest du sie gleich wiederholen. Der Redakteur schaute mit anonymen Augen. Wie ein Zensor. Als Menschen waren es sehr sympathische Leute, doch in der Kunst wollten sie keine persönliche Eigenständigkeit.

Nur das Schema.

Ja, nur das Schema.
Ich wollte nur das Geld und rechnete, wie viele Bücher im Jahr ich machen musste, um genug zu bekommen. Nicht um reich zu werden, zum Überleben. Im ersten Jahr meiner Kinderbuchillustratorenkarriere brauchte ich jährlich vielleicht zwischen vier und fünf Monate für ein Kinderbuch. Um genug Geld zu bekommen, musste man aber vier Bücher im Jahr machen. Also arbeitete ich bald schnell und produzierte diese Bücher sehr pragmatisch. Dann, im letzten Jahr meines Lebens in Moskau, benötigte ich für meinen Lohn nur noch eineinhalb Monate. Das war optimal.

Okay, das ist kurz erzählt, was ich im Vorwort des Buches über meine Kinderbücher erzählt habe unter dem Titel »Children's Book Illustrator as a Social Character«.

Als ich jedoch an den Installationen zu arbeiten begann, im Westen, beschäftigte ich mich mehr mit den Installationen als mit den Bildern, kam die wichtige Frage auf: „Was bleibt nach der Ausstellung zurück?" Ein Bild existiert auch ohne Ausstellung, aber eine Installation ist sehr vergänglich und wird nach dem Ende der Ausstellung fast nie erhalten. Nur die Erinnerungen daran bleiben, aber für „die Geschichte" bleibt nichts. Aber mich interessiert der Blick künftiger Generationen mehr als derjenige der Zeitgenossen. Was kann von der Kunst lange Zeit danach in der Geschichte bestehen bleiben? Das beste Mittel der Erinnerung sind die Bücher. Doch da stellt sich die Frage: „Wie repräsentiert man die verlorene Kunst?"

Vergangene oder verlorene Kunst?

Ja, verlorene. Die Installation ist im Prinzip eine verlorene Kunst. Wie repräsentiert man diese Kunst für die nächste Generation? Als Antwort kam mir die Idee verschiedener „narrativer" Erhaltungsmöglichkeiten.

Als erstes wäre da eine detaillierte Beschreibung des Konzeptes einer Installation. Welche Gestalt soll sie haben? Welchen Eindruck soll sie auf den Betrachter machen? Natürlich gibt es viele Künstler, die sich nicht um den Betrachter kümmern. Das ist das alte Thema: „Künstler arbeiten für sich selbst oder für Gott." Die Betrachter interessieren den „normalen" Künstler nicht: „Gott und du, das sind die besten Kriterien deiner Arbeit."

Ich selbst war aber niemals das Kriterium für meine Kunst und ihre Qualität. Andere Personen sind als Kriterium für mich wichtiger als ich selbst. Warum? Ich gehe davon aus, dass der Betrachter kein Idiot ist. Es gibt gut informierte Personen mit kunstwissenschaftlichen Kenntnissen, die „vieles gesehen" haben. Und hier geht es nicht um irgendeine einzigartige „mütterliche" Position, die wie das Verhältnis von Mutter und Kind funktioniert. Natürlich ist ihr Kind für die Mutter der einzige Mensch, aber der Betrachter ist keine Mutter. Er ist ein sehr kalter und informierter Flaneur. In seinem Kopf existiert ein Pantheon wunderbarer Arbeiten. Dort sind sowohl Michelangelo als auch Raffael und auch große zeitgenössische Künstler. Und mit diesem gefährlichen „goldenen Meter" misst er nun deine Arbeit. Ja, er hat dieses schreckliche Instrument mitgebracht: Den goldenen Meter! Mit diesem Maß, dem Auge und dem Kopf urteilt er über jede Arbeit. Aber solch ein Urteilen kann sich als tödlich für deine Arbeit erweisen. Der Betrachter wird einfach schweigen und vorbeigehen, und dieses Schweigen tönt wie der letzte Schuss!

Nun ein kleiner Kommentar zum Thema: „Wie möchtest du dem Mann mit dem goldenen Meter von deiner Arbeit erzählen?"

Es gibt zum Beispiel eine sehr merkwürdige Situation, die ich mehrmals selber erlebt habe. Normalerweise besucht ein Künstler, den man in eine Kunstakademie für eine Vorlesung einlädt, vorher die Studenten in ihren Werkräumen, um einige Worte über ihre Arbeiten zu sagen. Fast immer hängen in solchen kleinen Räumen viele Skizzen und Bilder an den Wänden, oder es stehen einige Objekte herum. Doch häufig kommst du an Orte, wo überhaupt nichts zu sehen ist, keine Kunstwerke, nur leere Wände. Du bist überrascht, aber der Student bleibt ganz ruhig und sagt: „Okay, setz dich bitte, und ich erzähle dir von meiner neuen Idee." Dann erzählt er im Nonstopstil und sehr aggressiv. Was mich an seinen Erklärungen interessiert: Er beschreibt keine plastische Form, sondern schildert, was er tun will, spricht zum Beispiel von seinen negativen Reaktionen auf den Krieg, etwa in Südafrika usw. Er redet über das Programm, aber nicht über künstlerische Dinge. Man merkt, dass er keine Vorstellung von einer formalen Umsetzung im Kopf hat.

Und dieses Beispiel führt uns wieder zum vorhin besprochenem Thema: „Wie erkläre ich dem unbekannten Betrachter die verschwundene Objekt-Installation?"

Nun, mein Catalogue Raisonné der Installationen erscheint als ein Beispiel für solche Möglichkeiten. Der erste Teil des Textes besteht aus der Darlegung des Konzeptes. Das erklärt, welche Absicht hinter der einen oder anderen Arbeit steht, welches „Konzept" ihr ursprünglich zugrunde liegt. Für das Verständnis eines Kunstwerkes scheint mir die Begründung seiner Entstehung sehr wichtig zu sein. Eine gut und deutlich dargelegte narrative Physiognomie ist die Grundlage der visuellen Darstellung und das Erklären mit Worten ist ihr Hauptprinzip. Das steht im absoluten Gegensatz zur modernistischen Tradition, die sagt: „Die Kunst beginnt, wo die Wörter enden. Die Sprache verstummt, fortan spricht die Kunst." Es ist absolut das Gegenteil. Für mich ist die visuelle Kunst allein wie eine Realisation von Wörtern, einer Idee.

Das ist also der erste Teil, das Konzept. Der zweite, einfachere Teil behandelt die technische Beschreibung. Visuell klar beschreibt man die Proportionen, Distanzen, Maße, die Farbe, das Licht, die verschiedenen Elemente eines Kunstwerkes. Das ist ein durchaus trockener, bürokratischer Teil. Aber wenn jemand die Geduld hat, um alles zu lesen, dann fängt er sozusagen Schritt für Schritt an die materielle Seite der Installation zu verstehen.

Die dritte Sprachebene ist eine kleine Erzählung über die Musik, den Ton oder die Stimmen in einer Installation. Und der letzte Teil sind Kommentare über eine bereits realisierte Installation.

Während die ersten drei Teile also vor einer Realisation stehen, entsteht dieser letzte, vierte Teil sozusagen danach. Hier geht es um die Diskussion mit einem imaginären Kritiker über das Gelungene oder Misslungene. Im Catalogue Raisonné ist es ein Dialog zwischen Kabakov und Backstein. Backstein ist hier ein „Sparringspartner" wie beim Tennis oder Boxen. Er ist falsch, aber für die Leser zur Erklärung des Werkes trotzdem wichtig. Auf seine Frage: „Warum ist das so gemacht und das so?", erhalten sie Antworten.

Dieser beschriebene narrative Teil erinnert an die Erschaffung einer „Installationspuppe". Natürlich gibt es daneben auch den visuellen Teil, ebenfalls mit verschiedenen Entstehungsaspekten: ersten Skizzen, verschiedenen Grundrissen, dann Detailentwürfen, Gesamtansichten und schließlich Fotos als Dokumentation der Realisation mit Gesamt- und Einzelansichten.

Das ist wie die Geschichte eines zerstörten Baus, zum Beispiel einer Ruine. Hierbei spielt meine Kunstschule vielleicht eine wichtige Rolle, wo es wunderbare Bücher über die römischen Katakomben, über Ruinen oder Piranesi-Zeichnungen gab. Mich interessierte nicht nur das fertige Werk, sondern der Prozess der Analyse, insbesondere das Verstehenlernen des Plans. Pläne interessierten mich besonders, denn sie zeigen die Hauptidee eines Baus; danach kamen die Fotos etc. Das aktivierte meine Fantasie für mögliche Rekonstruktionen. Das war in der Jugend sehr wichtig für mich, und ich glaube, dass dieser langsame Buchaufbau mit den verschieden detaillierten Ansichten auch für den Betrachter einer verschwundenen Installation hilfreich sein kann und sein Interesse stimulieren wird. Man erfährt etwas vom Kontext und lernt verschiedene technische Aspekte kennen, sodass im Kopf allmählich eine Vorstellung von dem ursprünglichen Aussehen der Installation entsteht.

Was mich dabei sehr interessiert, ist, dass deine Bücher über einzelne Installationen nicht nur Dokumentationen von realisierten Werken sind. Sondern dass dieses Zerlegen in verschiedene Realitätsbereiche, in Sprache, Bild, Fotografie, Skizze und Dokumentation dazu führt, dass der Leser/Betrachter sich aus diesen Elementen eine eigene Vorstellung zusammenbaut. Alle Elemente treten ja gleichwertig auf, der Entwurf ist oft sogar prominenter platziert als die Werkreproduktion. Es gibt keine Hierarchie zwischen Entwurf, finalem Werk und Reproduktion.

Absolut.

Und das Ergebnis ist nicht für jeden Leser/Betrachter genau gleich, oder?

Nein, nein.

Das bedeutet, dass das Kunstwerk, selbst wenn es als Installation gebaut wurde, im Buch nachträglich wieder zu einem Element der Imagination wird?

Absolut, genau. Das ist wie die Untersuchung eines Detektivs, eines Sherlock Holmes. Es gibt verschiedene Elemente, die wie bei einem Puzzle zusammenkommen.

Das Puzzle gelingt aber nicht, denn es kommt immer noch ein weiteres Teil dazu und noch eines.

Denn in Wirklichkeit ist das sehr interessant. Ich betrachte zum Beispiel ein Rembrandtbuch mit Skizzen und Zeichnungen und denke: „Aha!" Und wie eine Maschine kommt in mir ein Puzzle in Gang, das ein Gemälde hervorbringt. Natürlich brauchst du für diese Puzzlearbeit bestimmte Kenntnisse über die Kultur und die verschiedenen Kontexte, die zur Installation führten. In meinem Fall über die russische Kultur, die Konzeptkunst, über die Situation in der Sowjetunion. Man benötigt diese Kenntnisse der verschiedenen kontextuellen Ebenen, um das Konzept zu verstehen: Die Pyramide braucht noch eine weitere riesige Pyramide. Aber für normale kulturelle Leute ist das selbstverständlich und ganz normal.

Aber eben – du hast es am Anfang gesagt – es ist narrativ. Dieses Zusammenbauen ist für mich auch eine Erzählform und wird zu einer Geschichte. Und diese Geschichte kann ich größer, farbiger und komplexer ausgestalten, je nachdem wie viel ich von diesen Kontexten weiß, oder sie bleibt eben eine einfachere Geschichte. Trotzdem ist sie lebendig und stimuliert die Fantasie. Ich kann damit auch meine eigene Geschichte verbinden. Ich brauche nicht nur die historisch richtigen Kontexte zu kennen, sondern kann auch meine eigenen einbringen?

Ja, absolut.

Im Sinne eines Dialoges auch?

Absolut, ja. Das ist ein spezielles Buchgenre für das Thema „Gesamtkunstwerk". Ein Buch über eine Installation ist in seiner Reihenfolge ein Ganzes, eine Art Kugel. Deshalb gibt es auch einen Bereich mit Fotos und wie gleichberechtigte Teile hat es dort auch Dialoge mit Boris Groys. So ein Buch ist wie eine Fantasiewolke. Genauso wie die fantastischen Geschichten von Jules Verne. Wie ein Kinderbuch beinhaltet das Buch nicht nur Informationen. In jedem Buch ist die ganze Welt. Mein pompöses Buch über Installationen besitzt den naiven Anspruch, wie ein Modell des Universums zu funktionieren. Es ist der Versuch ein illusorisches, aber auf jeden Fall universelles „Modell" zu erschaffen.

Da fällt mir etwas auf, wenn ich die Entwicklung deines Werkes betrachte. Ich habe den Eindruck, dass am Anfang zuerst das Einzelwerk, eine Zeichnung, ein Album, eine Installation, als Modell für die Welt stand. Aber im Laufe der Jahrzehnte sind alle diese Arbeiten, die langsam und sukzessiv auseinander hervorgingen, selber zu einer Welt geworden, zu einem eigenen Kosmos mit ganz verschiedenen Bereichen, mit großen Teilen und kleineren, mit Zentren und Rändern. Deine Bücher erzählen eigentlich die Geschichte, wie diese Welt von Kabakov entsteht, sich transformiert und weiter wächst usw. Ein Strom der Ideen mit immer neuen Ablegern, die sich in einem Meer sammeln, wovon dann wieder neue Flüsse abzweigen. Das ist etwas sehr Faszinierendes. Es handelt sich also wieder um eine Geschichte?

Ja. Das kleine Weltmodell wird zum großen Weltmodell, wie beim Matrjoschka-System. Das Prinzip ist aber anders als bei einem Roman. Es gibt kein Nacheinander. Jede Minute und jedes Objekt funktionieren als geschlossene Einheiten.

Aber was ist das dann überhaupt – das Buch? Bücher enthalten immer ein autobiografisches Moment: „Die Furcht vor dem Tod". Sie verkörpern die Idee der Ewigkeit, die sie berühren. Da ist etwas, das von deinem kurzen Besuch auf der Welt bleibt. Und fast jedes Buch hat ein dramaturgisches Prinzip mit zwei Ebenen gleichzeitig.

Kannst du dafür ein Beispiel geben?

Es gibt eine Ebene, sagen wir für einfache Leute, und eine andere, die an das „intelligente" Bewusstsein gerichtet ist. Ich bringe ein Beispiel aus einem meiner Bücher. Das Buch heißt »Das Album meiner Mutter«. Es war ein alter Wunsch, es zur großen Ehre meiner Mutter, die ein unglückliches Leben hatte, zu machen. Ich bat sie in ihren letzten Lebensjahren, sie war bereits 82 Jahre alt, ihre Memoiren zu schreiben von der Kindheit bis zu jenem Moment. Sie tat es und übergab mir ihr umfangreiches Heft, was mich sehr glücklich machte. Als ich in den Westen kam, war mein erster Wunsch, diese Biografie meiner Mutter zu drucken. Natürlich umfasst sie ein gigantisches Informationsmaterial. Aber es brauchte dennoch zusätzlich ein bestimmtes Konzept, denn es sollte, wie mir schien, ein besonderes Kunstwerk werden. Darum kam mir die Idee der Präsentation mit zwei Ebenen. Die erste Ebene hat als Thema das „Leiden meiner Mutter", weil ihr ganzes Leben nur ein Leiden war; sie war so unglücklich. Man sollte dieses Buch also nicht ohne Tränen lesen, weil die Situation dieser hilflosen Menschen, wie meine Mutter einer war, eine totale Katastrophe war. Und dieses Leben fand vor dem Hintergrund eines im ganzen Land verkündeten sozialistischen „Paradieses" statt. Wir lebten im realen Paradies. In jedem Lebensbereich herrschte dieses Glück. So enthält jeder obere Seitenteil des ausgedachten Buch-Albums Fotos mit Legenden aus Magazinen: „Wie viel Wurst gibt es in diesem Geschäft", „Wie viel Prozent glückliche Leute leben heute in einem Sanatorium" usw. Und im unteren Teil steht der Text meiner Mutter, eine ganz andere „Stimme". Utopie und Realität sind direkt miteinander verbunden.

Das ist ein einfaches Beispiel für die Konstruktion mit zwei Ebenen. Es kommt darauf an, auf welcher du stehst, aber am besten ist es, wenn du beide zusammen betrachtest.

In meinen anderen Büchern gibt es Material über die Installationen und gleichzeitig auch einen Dialog mit Boris Groys, der eine Innenanalyse bestimmter Motive oder Kontexte gibt, besonders der Kontexte. Der Autor führt eine Diskussion mit dem Analytiker, Philosophen und Kritiker. Das ist wie zwischen Doktor und Patient. Wenn der Patient erzählt, was mit ihm passiert ist, und der Doktor ihm erklärt warum. Das ist ein bisschen wie ein freudianisches, psychotherapeutisches Gespräch.

Ein Theaterspiel mit zwei Rollen?

Absolut. Im Prinzip kann man sie auch tauschen, obwohl es mit Boris unrealistisch aussieht. Natürlich ist das ein Theater für zwei Akteure.

Das bringt uns auf ein anderes Thema im Zusammenhang der Bücher. Bei westlichen Künstlern begleiten die Publikationen ihr Werk meistens in einer eher dienenden Funktion und verbreiten Informationen darüber. Das bedeutet, es gibt einerseits das künstlerische Werk und in der Distanz dazu andererseits auch den Diskurs. Es besteht eine klare Hierarchie zwischen der primären Kunst und dem sekundären Diskurs.

Bei dir ist das anders. Es beginnt ja schon beim Dialog mit Boris Groys. Der Diskurs wird zu einem Bestandteil des Werks und beide kann man nicht mehr genau auseinanderhalten. Auch die Bücher über dein Werk – die allermeisten sind ja von dir konzipiert und du machst auch ihr Layout – sind ein Teil des Werks. Der Diskurs ist Bestandteil der künstlerischen Arbeit, die selbst immer auch ein Diskurs ist. Beide verbindet ein Wechselverhältnis. Das kulminiert im wissenschaftlichen Œuvrekatalog der Installationen, der Bilder und hier nun auch der Bücher, die als von Kabakov konzipierte und gestaltete Publikationen wiederum Teile seines Gesamtwerkes sind, das sie zugleich objektiv dokumentieren.

Absolut richtig. Für mich würde ein „seriöser und tiefer Diskurs" über meine Arbeiten ein bisschen falsch aussehen! Selbstironie und Humor spielen darin eine große Rolle. Und es gibt kein sogenanntes „Resümee", ein letztes Wort über eine Arbeit. Es gibt nur verschiedene Sprünge, nähere und weitere, jegliche Meinungen bleiben immer fragmentarisch. Eine seriöse Erklärung ist unmöglich. Nur verschiedene Versuche von verschiedenen Seiten sind möglich. Im Prinzip kann es keinen Schuss in die Mitte der Zielscheibe geben!

Keinen Treffer.

Dass der Vogel getötet wird. (Lachen)

Das Visuelle ist bei dir also auf die Sprache bezogen. Du hast darüber ein umfangreiches Buch geschrieben mit dem Titel „Der Text als Grundlage des Visuellen". Nur ist dein Textverständnis eben ein besonderes. Es hängt stark mit der Auffassung von der gesprochenen Sprache, der „Stimme" zusammen. Der Text ist folglich kein Gesetz, keine Norm, keine Regel oder Wahrheit, sondern er kommt als Stimme aus dem Leben?

Das ist sehr gut bemerkt. Auf die Frage: „Was bedeutet dieses Bild?", überlege ich mir jeweils, in welcher Rolle ich darauf am besten antworten soll. Ich habe zehn Rollen: die seriöse, die idiotische usw., doch alle sind richtig. Alle!

Es geht nicht um den schriftlichen, literarischen, wissenschaftlichen Text. Nur die Rede spielt eine Rolle. Sie ist ganz frei und an keinen Stil gebunden. Ein interessantes Thema ist das „lange und freie Gespräch".

Ich lebte während der relativ stabilen Periode der Breschnjewzeit, einer Stagnation, dreißig Jahre lang in der Sowjetunion. Das Leben war wie graues Wetter. Ein Dauerzustand. Keine Sonne, aber auch keine Katastrophe. Und die Leute hatten viel freie Zeit. Sie konnten trinken, tanzen oder Sport treiben. Auch die Künstler hatten viel freie Zeit und saßen am Abend zusammen. Einfach nur zu reden war eine ganz normale Beschäftigung. In der Küche war eine Flasche und man redete. Man sprach mit riesigem Enthusiasmus – denn die Sprache, „das Gespräch", war das einzige, was „uns" war. Es gab keine Ausstellungen, keine Verkaufsmöglichkeit, keine Kritik, keine Betrachter. Es gab nichts, nur das Gespräch im Keller oder auf dem Dachboden während einer langen Zeit. Wie in der Zelle eines Gefängnisses oder einer Klinik.

Das war der Grund für die Gesprächspraktik und die hieraus gewonnene, große Textproduktion. Das freie Künstlergespräch war auch ein besonderes Genre und ist heute zum Glück in Archiven in Form von Audiokassetten, Texten und bereits erschienenen Büchern erhalten geblieben.

Aber daraus sind ja auch wieder Werke entstanden. Das bringt uns an den Anfang des Gesprächs zurück. Du hast von deiner offiziellen Tätigkeit als Kinderbuchillustrator gesprochen und vom Ausrichten auf die Zensur. Es gab bei dir also diesen schwierigen Umgang mit dem Buch. Aber daneben existierte der inoffizielle Kreis von Künstlern, Schriftstellern und Kritikern, die viel gesprochen und daraus Texte produziert haben, was zu ganz einfachen, „Samisdat" genannten, inoffiziellen Publikationen führte. Ich denke da zum Beispiel an die sogenannte „Barackenpoesie" der Lianosowo-Gruppe, an Rabin, Cholin, Rubinstein, Prigow; für einige hast du übrigens auch Kinderbücher illustriert. Das war der Anfang deines freien Umgangs mit dem Buch, oder?

Absolut. Heute, bei der allgemein düsteren Erinnerung an die Vergangenheit, darf man eine positive Seite des sowjetischen Lebens nicht vergessen. Heute sieht man alles total negativ, die permanente Angst usw. Das ist schon richtig. Aber die positive Seite, das waren die Bildung und das Gesundheitswesen.

Das Hauptprinzip der sowjetischen Erziehung war der Universalismus. Lenin hatte die Idee vom neuen Menschen als Höhepunkt der Kulturgeschichte. Er – dieser neue Mensch, ein eigenartiger Superman – erreicht das Entwicklungsziel der gesamten Menschheit. Die Tradition der universellen Bildung hatte es zuvor aber bereits im 19. Jahrhundert gegeben, besonders beim deutschen Gymnasium: Das Goethe-Prinzip. Dem Studenten wurden ganz verschiedene Disziplinen beigebracht, unabhängig davon, ob er diese Kenntnisse im späteren Leben brauchen würde oder nicht. Doch in seinem Kopf sollte ein ganzes Universum entstehen.

Diese Tradition wurde von der sowjetischen Schule übernommen. Eine vielseitige Bildung wurde programmiert, im Prinzip konnte man „alles wissen". Außerdem existierte aber auch eine „selbstständige Bildung". Spontan organisierte Gruppen von Schülern beschäftigten sich außerhalb der Schule auf eigenen Wunsch mit speziellen Fächern. Bei unserer Gruppe zum Beispiel, die aus fünf Freunden bestand, ging jedes Kind einer anderen „Disziplin" nach. Jeder war ein „Spezialist", entweder für das Theater, für die klassische Musik oder die Philosophie und versorgte die anderen mit Büchern oder eigenen „Vorträgen".

Unsere sowjetische „Schulkultur" bestand ausschliesslich in der Buchkultur. Wir kannten die großen Figuren der Malereigeschichte, der russischen Literatur, der Weltphilosophie, der Weltmusik usw. und hielten in der Gruppe Vorträge über das eigene Gebiet. Wer sich zum Beispiel mit Musik beschäftigte, kümmerte sich auch um die Konzerttickets für das Konservatorium. Das ist ein Paradox: Das Leben war sehr dunkel, konservativ und deprimierend, aber unsere Fantasie führte uns in ganz andere Welten, wir lebten auf anderen „Inseln". Wir flohen von dem uns umgebenden schlimmen Leben in einige wenige erhaltene „Oasen" – das Museum, die Philharmonie, den Lesesaal. Es ist auch interessant, dass die sowjetische Macht wunderbare Lesesäle schuf. Was du an klassischer Literatur wolltest, bekamst du dort. Aber nichts Zeitgenössisches und keine Information über die andere Welt , nein. Doch über die klassische Literatur, so viel du wolltest. Warum? Es herrschte die Vorstellung, wir wären die abstrakten Kinder der klassischen Kultur. Das war keine lebendige zeitgenössische Situation.

Wie ein Leben in der Vergangenheit.

Deshalb blieb das klassische Bild bestehen, besser gesagt, es leuchtete in deinem Kopf. Bei Beuys, zum Beispiel, gibt es auf den ersten Blick kein Interesse für die klassische Kunst. Die klassische Entwicklung ist wie ein im 19. Jahrhundert vergrabener Korridor. Für uns war dieser Korridor jedoch immer präsent. Wir erinnerten uns nur an Rembrandt oder an die russische Klassik usw.

Keine Moderne?

Keine Moderne. Die russische Avantgarde spielte für mich keine Rolle. Das interessierte mich nicht. Wir sahen nur das Bild des 19. Jahrhunderts bis Wrubel; Wrubel war bereits verboten. Und die westliche Kunst kannten wir nur bis zur Schule von Barbizon, weil schon die Impressionisten verboten waren. Es gab den sowjetischen Alltag und auf der Hinterseite, als Schwanz, die Klassik.

Der klassische Schwanz in Russland war vor allem eine großartige Literatur. Also wieder das Buch?

Natürlich. Das Hauptthema unserer Diskussionen war die Bedeutung der Kultur in der Sowjetunion. Wir wussten hundertprozentig, dass die sowjetische Kultur keine war. Keine gute oder schlechte Kultur, sondern im Prinzip gar keine! Du musstest deshalb nach einer früheren kulturellen Tradition als Ideal suchen, die vor der Sowjetzeit lag. Das waren die russische Kultur des 19. Jahrhunderts und die nichtsowjetische Kultur der damaligen Gegenwart.

Gut war auch, dass es viele Übersetzungen westlicher zeitgenössischer Literatur gab, in erster Linie englische und deutsche, zum Beispiel von Fitzgerald, Remarque, Grass etc. Aber die russische Kultur bildete die Basis oder den Eckstein unseres kulturellen Horizonts. Kultur war für uns die klassische russische Kultur. Natürlich kannten wir und besorgten uns die inoffizielle Literatur der Sowjetunion, wie Achmatova, Pasternak und die Dichter des „silbernen" Jahrhunderts. Aber unser Background waren frühere Autoren des 19. Jahrhunderts, Tschechow, Dostojewski.

Warum Literatur und keine Malerei? Die Malerei hatte für uns Moskauer Konzeptualisten aus vielen Gründen keine gute Qualität und stellte kein brauchbares künstlerisches Modell dar. Die Ideale waren die Musik und vor allem die Literatur. Deshalb bestand kein Kontakt zur sowjetischen realistischen Tradition. Wir schauten negativ und ironisch auf die Stars des 19. Jahrhunderts wie Surikow und Repin. Aber zu Tolstoi, Dostojewski und Tschechow hatten wir kein ironisches Verhältnis, denn sie bildeten unser Fundament. Wenn du gearbeitet hast, dann hast du stets ihre Stimmen im inneren Ohr gehört: „Was sagt wohl Tschechow über deine Arbeiten?", aber nie: „Was sagt Repin?"

Bei Tschechow gibt es Helden, die sozusagen als Personagen in deinen Arbeiten wiederkehren, sei es in den Alben, Installationen, dann auch in den Büchern, mit Backsteins Kommentaren beispielsweise. Ich meine das literarische Konzept mit

Figuren, die vor allem über ihre Stimmen funktionieren. Das ist etwas, das bei eurer Generation auf neue Weise und in einem anderen Kontext, auch unter dem Einfluss zeitgenössischer westlicher Impulse, wieder aktuell und produktiv wurde?

Das ist ein gutes Thema. Ich sprach eben vom großen Einfluss der russischen Literatur. Doch es ging nicht nur um die Literatur oder um die Kunst, sondern um die grundsätzliche ethische Frage: „Was ist ein guter Mensch?" und „Was wäre die ideale Mentalität für dich?"

Natürlich ist der intelligente russische Mensch die ideale Figur für deinen Betrachter oder Kritiker. Wer ist er, wann wurde er geboren? Der russische Intellektuelle wurde im Zeitalter der Aufklärung geboren und stammt aus dem Westen. Während der Zeit von Katharina der Zweiten gelangten Bücher von Voltaire, Montesquieu und besonders von Rousseau nach Russland, die allesamt einen großen Einfluss hatten. Diese „Überflutung" geschah in Russland durch zwei „Kanäle". Als erstes betraf das die Wissenschaft, die Chemie, Geologie, Geschichte usw., was die Basis schuf für die fantastischen russischen Universitäten mit ihren berühmten Professoren. Die zweite Strömung betraf die Moral. Die Idee entstand, dass die aufgeklärten Intellektuellen Licht in die Dunkelheit der Massen bringen sollten, um sie zu neuen Menschen zu erziehen. Im Russischen stammt das Wort „Aufklärung" vom Wort „Licht" ab. Dieser Enthusiasmus der Aufklärung war für den intelligenten russischen Menschen sehr wichtig und herrschte im ganzen 19. Jahrhundert vor.

Die russischen Schriftsteller-Demokraten waren auch solche klassische russische intelligente Menschen. Tschechow ist das beste Beispiel dafür: Er vereint den aufgeklärten Intellektuellen mit seinem erzieherischen Aspekt und den genialen Schriftsteller. Die Kombination von Künstler und intelligentem Mensch ist die beste Eigenschaft der russischen Schriftsteller. Das gilt auch noch für Mandelstam, Achmatova, aber in erster Linie für Pasternak.

Das heißt, es ging auch im 20. Jahrhundert weiter: Es kam eine neue dunkle Zeit, die erneut der Aufklärung bedurfte?

Ja, aber leider war dies schon eine andere Zeit, die Verbundenheit der Zeiten ist abgerissen.

Aber auch diese Generation folgte dem Typus des gebildeten Künstlers?

Absolut. Das erklärt nun besser die Position der letzten, unserer Generation. Es gibt eine lange Brücke von der Zeit Katharina der Großen im 18. Jahrhundert bis zu unserer Generation am Ende des 20. Jahrhunderts. Zweihundert Jahre Entwicklung der Intelligenz bis zu ihrer „Auslöschung" und Zerstörung. Alle sagen, dass es heute in Russland keine Intelligenz mehr gibt. Trotzdem bleibt die Erinnerung an die Intelligenz. Sie war die Hoffnung der russischen Geschichte. Ohne diese Intelligenz gibt es, nach meiner Meinung, nun keine Hoffnung mehr für diesen Staat.

Damit wird nun deutlicher, was ich meine. Besonders für den konzeptualistischen Künstler in Russland ist die Frage nach der Bedeutung der Kunst, ihres Sinns, ein wichtiges Thema. Er ist eben auch ein Mensch, nicht nur Künstler. Damit unterscheidet er sich etwas vom Typ des westlichen Künstlers, so wie ich ihn sehe. Ich will natürlich nicht pauschalisieren. Obwohl es viele „intelligente" Künstler im Westen gibt, zum Beispiel Boltanski. Der „normale" westliche Künstler ist für mich jedoch anders. Zum Beispiel Warhol – immer sehr aktiv, aggressiv, geschäftstüchtig. Das ist eher ein spontaner, sensibler, täuschender „Charakter", der das zeitgenössische Publikum und die kommerziellen Strukturen gekonnt manipulierte, so wie es heute beispielsweise Jeff Koons und Damien Hirst machen – eigenartige Kentauren von Künstler und Geschäftsmann. Natürlich existieren daneben auch immer Künstler mit einem tiefen historischen Hintergrund und einer intellektuellen Reflexion wie Donald Judd oder Mark Rothko.

Aber mit einer völlig anderen Art der Reflexion.

Die russische intellektuelle Tradition war zum großen Teil eine utopische. Wie bei Tschechow, der zeitlebens aus moralischer Verpflichtung Arzt war, um zu helfen. Die Distanz und Wechselbeziehung zwischen Mensch und Künstler ist das Hauptprinzip des intelligenten russischen Menschen: „Ich bin ein Dichter, aber trotzdem bin ich auch noch ein intelligenter Mensch." Und deshalb braucht eine solche Kunst auch einen intelligenten Betrachter.

Der lesen kann und will.

Ja. Kein spontaner Betrachter, kein Sammler oder Galerist. Sondern eine normale, intelligente Person.

Ich komme auf einen weiteren Zusammenhang, der uns wieder zum Buch zurückführt. Am Ende des 18. und am Anfang des 19. Jahrhunderts gibt es noch eine andere Wurzel für die Kunst des späten 19. und des 20. Jahrhunderts, ich meine die Romantik, besonders in der Philosophie. Die Romantik hat dich nach eigenen Aussagen schon früh beschäftigt. Ihre Philosophie unterscheidet zwischen sinnlicher Realität und Bewusstsein. Da existiert nicht mehr die Vorstellung einer Einheit, sondern von der Trennung des Denkens und der äußeren Welt.

Du hast mehrfach gesagt, dass die Personagen in deinen Alben, Installationen und Texten als Stimmen dem Bewusstsein entspringen, bestimmte Seiten des Bewussteins verkörpern und sich auch wieder an das Bewusstsein der Leser/Betrachter wenden würden. Es geht dir dabei also sehr stark um das Geistige, Psychologische und Emotionale?

Und beim Buch ist es ja tatsächlich so: Es hat zum einen die äußere physische Seite, das Objekthafte, und zum anderen die inhaltliche Seite, die Sprache, welche selbst unanschaulich ist; sie muss man lesen, das heißt dechiffrieren. Das Buch repräsentiert also zwei konträre Seiten, die materielle und die geistige.

Ja, genau so. Das meine ich.

Deshalb auch: „Die Welt als Buch"?

Ja, genau. Die Buchkultur ist eine alte Tradition. Für mich ist das gedruckte Buch seit Gutenberg wie ein tiefer Brunnen, worin die Leute nach Wasser wie nach Wissen suchen. Das Bewusstsein ist nur dank Büchern entstanden. Es existiert kein anders System, das die Philosophie und die verschiedenen Lebensas-

pekte so konzentriert umfasst. Im Buch gibt es alles. Ich weiß, dass heute alle den Computer benutzen und das Buch etwas sehr Konservatives ist. Welche Rolle es in Zukunft spielen wird, weiß ich nicht. Eine neue Epoche entsteht mit neuen Kommunikationsmitteln und neuen Kommunikationsbedürfnissen.

Ich wurde dagegen in der Sowjetunion geboren, in der kein zeitgenössisches Leben existierte. Natürlich gab es damals auch keine Zukunft, weil man glaubte, die Sowjetunion würde für alle Ewigkeit, während fünftausend Jahren, so bleiben wie sie war. Die Geschichte stoppte. Wir hatten nur Vergangenheit. Sie enthielt freilich ein riesiges Reservoir an Wissen. Alles blieb stehen wie in einem Amphitheater, auf dessen Bühne immer wieder dasselbe Stück gespielt wurde.

Mein Denken konzentrierte sich seit der Kindheit nicht auf die Veränderung, sondern auf das Betrachten dieses „Stücks". Ich war sozusagen damit einverstanden, ewig in einem solchen „Amphitheater" zu sitzen. Alle Künstler existierten darin gemeinsam. Raffael gleichzeitig wie Eduard Manet. Dasselbe in der Musik. Trotz der Musikentwicklung „saß" dort Bach direkt neben Mozart und Schostakowitsch. Auch Figuren der zweiten und dritten Klasse gab es in diesem Amphitheater. Alles existierte nach dem Pyramidensystem. Das war schon während der Schulzeit in meinem Kopf, und das, obwohl ich versucht habe, gründlich und mit einer gewissen Distanz zu schauen. Doch aus irgendwelchen Gründen war ich bereits von der Existenz einer solchen Pyramide überzeugt und auch davon, dass man dieses System nicht ändern konnte.

Ich habe vorher über den Mann mit dem goldenen Meter gesprochen. Dieser Meter ist für mich nicht horizontal, sondern vertikal ausgerichtet. Ich weiß, dass dieses Prinzip nicht perfekt ist, weil jeder Künstler ein eigener Kosmos ist, der seine eigenen, keine fremden Beurteilungskriterien braucht. Aber ich kann es nicht mehr ändern.

Kehren wir noch einmal zurück zur Unterscheidung von sinnlicher Realität und Bewusstsein, die gerade durch das Buch entsteht, wie du gesagt hast. Das erklärt womöglich, warum für eine solche geistige Ausrichtung die Literatur oder auch die Musik als etwas letztlich Immaterielles besser geeignet waren als die dafür vielleicht zu physische oder äußerliche Malerei? Eine Hypothese.

Ah ja. Das ist das Paradox.

Ich bin sehr pessimistisch, was meinen Beruf, die Malerei und ihr Handwerk betrifft. Aber es ist zu spät, um zu wechseln. Ich bin ganz zufällig auf diesen Beruf gekommen, als ich zur Kunstschule kam. Ich hatte nie einen großen Enthusiasmus für den Umgang mit den komplizierten Maltechniken.

Eine Skepsis?

Große Skepsis, ja. Skepsis auch hinsichtlich meiner Arbeiten. Darum verstehe ich sie als Projekte. Aber es ist nicht zu vergessen, dass auch Rothko für seine Werke von „Experiment" gesprochen hat.

Kann man sagen, dass du in der Frühzeit des Samisdat, als die Alben entstanden, Verfahren der zeitgenössischen Literatur in den bildnerischen Bereich übertragen hast, und diesen natürlich auch mit der Literatur kombiniert hast? Ich denke an die Verbindung von Wort und Bild, an die Zwischengattung Album, die beides zugleich ist, Buch und Zeichnung, und doch keines von beidem, und an die intermediären Grenzgänge: Selbstständige Texte können zu Bestandteilen von

Installationen werden, Bilder sehen wie gestaltete Buchseiten aus. Das Buch, der Lesesaal und das Gespräch sind später im Westen auch Themen von Ausstellungsinstallationen geworden, die wiederum von Büchern begleitet wurden usw.

Ja. Was kann ich über diese Kommunikation von visuellem und narrativem Material auf demselben Blatt sagen, wie es etwa bei den Alben der Fall ist?

Mich interessieren die Verbindung und der Konflikt zwischen dem Visuellen und dem Text, die Relativität und die Bedingung für das eine oder das andere. Nicht das Absurde wie beim Surrealismus. Beziehungen gibt es und sie sind sehr reich, kompliziert und schwer darstellbar. Aber keine Deckungsgleichheit. Es gibt Luft, Distanz zwischen Text und Bild. Das Bild erklärt etwas vom Text, und der Text erklärt etwas vom Bild, aber in irgendeinem anderen, besonderen Sinn. Es existiert das Gemeinsame, aber auf einer anderen Ebene, in einem anderen Raum. Aber in welchem Raum? –

Das ist eben der Denkraum, wo beides zusammenkommt, ein Bewusstseinsraum.

Dabei gibt es einen Unterschied für einfache und intelligente Leute. Für einfache Leute handelt es sich bloß um ein Bild und einen schlechten Text. Sie sagen: „Ich habe nicht verstanden, wovon er spricht." Bei intelligenten Leuten provoziert eine solch direkte Verbindung einen neuen Hinweis auf einen nicht identifizierten Raum, auf den sowohl das Bild als auch der Text gerichtet sind und in dem sie zusammen, Arm in Arm, gleiten.

Blinzeln

MH: Wir haben uns beim ersten Gespräch über den Inhalt und die Sprache deiner Bücher unterhalten. Es gibt für mich aber noch einen zweiten wichtigen Aspekt bei deinen Büchern, der mit dem Betrachter/Leser zu tun hat: die „Zeit". Ganz allgemein braucht man ja Zeit, um ein Buch zu lesen oder anzusehen. Wenn es sich um ein größeres literarisches Werk handelt, benötigt man sogar ein Stück „Lebenszeit", um es zu bewältigen. Du hast ausführlich über die Bedeutung der Zeit für deine Alben geschrieben. Welche Bedeutung hat die Zeit aber für deine Bücher? Gibt es einen Zusammenhang zu den Alben? Du hast über die Alben später auch Bücher gemacht.

IK: Ja das Thema Zeit. Wie viel Zeit braucht man, um meine „Bücher" zu lesen? Sie sind keine Literatur oder Poesie, sondern gleichen Informationsbüchern. Das Aussehen und die Gestalt dieser Bücher, wen interessiert das? Die normalen Leute lesen Texte wie Literatur oder Poesie – da gibt es eine lange Praxis und Tradition. Aber meine Informationsbücher sind für den Leser ein bisschen problematisch, das habe ich verstanden.

Bei einem Künstlermanifest von Kandinsky oder Malewitsch ist mir als Leser klar, dass ich den Text lesen muss, um zu verstehen, was der Künstler sagen will. Aber bei meinen Büchern gibt es keine Ambition ein Manifest zu sein, ein Programm oder ein Lehrbuch. Was kann der Betrachter also von ihnen erwarten? Welchem Genre gehören sie an?

Im Prinzip benutzt der einfache Leser diese Kataloge oder Bücher nur, weil er nach einer bestimmten Information über eine Installation sucht. Oder er hat ein inhaltliches Interesse für meine wenigen theoretischen Bücher, zum Beispiel »Über die „totale" Installation« oder »Public Projects or the Spirit of a Place«. Solche gibt es aber nicht viele, nur vier oder fünf. Alle anderen Bücher dienen der Orientierung über bereits gemachte Arbeiten.

Ein Problem für den Leser besteht darin, dass er Zeit braucht, um zu unterscheiden einerseits zwischen den dokumentarischen und informativen Elementen und andererseits den verschiedenen Kommentaren. Die Kommentare stehen nicht einfach am Ende des umfangreichen Informationsteils, sondern befinden sich wie in einer Suppe mittendrin. Es ist eine Mischung von sehr kalten Informationen und sehr emotionalen Kommentaren. Ein gemischter Salat mit Kaltem und Warmem.

Selbst beim Lesen des Textes gibt es ein Problem. Der Informationstext hat einen sehr kalten und strengen Rhythmus, wie bei einem Schlagzeug. Die Kommentare dagegen haben eine emotionale, schöne Melodie. Es gibt dafür aber kein Programm. Die Texte sind sehr improvisiert. Für den Künstler/Autor hingegen ist auch dieser bürokratische Text emotional. Alle Zahlen und Darstellungen haben für ihn viele Bedeutungen. Er weiß das genau und arrangiert die Informationen entsprechend. Für den Aussenstehenden bleibt das alles jedoch sehr relativ. Diese kalten, geometrischen Darstellungen können seine Fantasie oder Vorstellungskraft nicht wecken. Darum kann er meist wohl nicht verstehen, wie es zu diesen emo-

tionalen oder sogar philosophischen Kommentaren über derartig bürokratische Dinge kommen konnte. Dieses Problem verstehe ich gut. Es gibt keine Kontinuität zwischen beiden Textteilen Information und Kommentar; beide trennt eine Stufe.

Das habe ich bemerkt, nachdem ich das Buch »Die 60er und 70er Jahre. Aufzeichnungen über das inoffizielle Leben in Moskau« geschrieben hatte. Normalerweise haben Memoiren einen Rhythmus. Es ist die Rede von der Zeit, vom Kontext, vom Freundeskreis, von Persönlichem; ein normaler Erzählrhythmus. Dafür gibt es eine lange Tradition. Ein normales Atmen. Der Leser ist ruhig und versteht diese sorgfältig von der Stimme hervorgebrachte Melodie. Doch bei den Erinnerungen an die 1960er-Jahre sind wieder diese zwei verschiedenen Teile vorhanden. Mitten im Textteil bringe ich eine Werkliste mit den Namen, Titeln, Maßen und Besitzern der Bilder sowie mit den Angaben über ihre Publikation, dann setze ich die Erzählung fort. Zum Lesen ist das eine schlechte Situation. Wenn der Leser zum Informationsteil kommt, denkt er: „Okay, das interessiert mich nicht, das ist für andere Leute. Mich interessieren die Beschreibungen der Künstler und alles was damit zu tun hat."

Aber diese Mischung von zwei Genres – Dokumentation und Beschreibung von Projekten einerseits und Erzählung andererseits – diese Arhythmik der Texte kann ich nicht ändern, denn sie ist für mich organisch und gefällt mir sehr. Dennoch verstehe ich die Schwierigkeiten der Leser damit.

Wenn ich mich bei meinen Kunstwerken darum bemühe, die Reaktionen der Betrachter zu kontrollieren, muss ich mich sehr genau um Form und Gestalt kümmern, das gilt besonders für die Installationen. Aber diese „Bücher" sind für ein erschwertes Lesen gedacht. Sie sind nicht leicht zu lesen: Dokumentation, Erzählung, Kommentare usw.

Das ist das Puzzle.

Ja. Das ist das Thema „Zeit". Wie viel Zeit braucht der Leser, um zu verstehen, worum es geht? Ich habe die Hoffnung, dass der Leser nicht nur ein normaler Literaturleser ist, denn meine Texte sind für das sehr langsame und arhythmische Lesen gemacht. Das heißt, der Text geht nicht durch den Leser hindurch, sondern funktioniert eher wie ein Fragment von irgendetwas.

Die Idee des Fragments statt eines Ganzen hängt mit der Erinnerung an meine Kindheit zusammen; sie hat aber auch mit heute zu tun. Ich nehme mir nie die Zeit, um ein Buch am Anfang zu beginnen, morgen weiterzulesen usw. Das ist seltsam. Ich öffne ein Buch normalerweise in der Mitte und lese nur zwei, drei Sätze. Mich interessiert nicht, was wie in einem Roman passieren wird, eine Intrige oder ein Verbrechen. Ich bin kein detektivartiger Leser. Mich interessieren der Stil des Autors, die Bewegungen seines Textes, der Umgang mit der Sprache, verschiedene Aspekte des verborgenen Inhalts, seine Hauptidee. Nicht was er sagt, sondern was er sagen will. Mir genügt ein kurzer Textausschnitt. Zeit brauche ich nur dafür.

Ich nehme einen meiner Kataloge, sehe mir aber nicht alles an, sondern nur drei, vier Seiten und die Kommentare. Das Fragment provoziert und stimuliert die Fantasie. Meine Analyse geht vertikal durch den Text hindurch. Zeit benötige ich beim Lesen nur für dieses Analysieren. Ich brauche dafür nur wenig Zeit, aber ausreichend Zeit zur Konzentration.

Das bringt mich auf einen Gedanken, der mit dem Gespräch zu tun hat. Das Gespräch, wie du es zum Beispiel jetzt gerade mit mir führst, ist dagegen nicht fragmentiert, sondern eher ein ruhiges, langsames Fließen, mit einer gewissen Distanz, mit Ironie und Humor. Ein episches Erzählen, das längere Zeit dauert, sich manchmal sogar über mehrere Tage hinzieht.

Zu diesem Fließen gehört für mich aber auch eine Art von Kreisen. Das Gespräch schreitet nicht einfach linear von einem Punkt zum nächsten voran, sondern dreht sich gewissermaßen und bekommt damit eine „räumliche" Qualität. Das Entfernen und wieder Annähern des Themas hängen damit zusammen.

Das erinnert mich an die russische Literatur. Zum Beispiel wurde von Dostojewski gesagt, seine Romanfiguren würden eigentlich gar keine Entwicklung durchmachen, sondern seien wie in einem Raum gefangen, aus dem sie nicht entweichen könnten. Seine dicken Bücher kennen fast keine äußere Handlung. So beschreibt das erste Kapitel des Romans „Der Idiot" auf über 200 Seiten nur einen einzigen Tag, die Rückkehr des russischen Helden aus der Schweiz nach St. Petersburg. Die Erzählung hat einen eigenen, „geschlossenen" Raum, wenn sie auch über Hunderte von Seiten geht. Es passiert fast nichts, wie ein bewegter Stillstand, eine ewige Reflexion, ein endloses Gespräch, ein Kreisen und Drehen von verschiedenen, oft gegensätzlichen Gedanken und Stimmen. Das hat für mich auch wieder etwas Körperliches.

Ja, sicher. Das ist gut bemerkt. Der Text bildet eine Form. Eine Gesprächsrunde ist bei mir jeweils einem Thema und seinen Problemen gewidmet. Ist sie fertig, ist ein Kreis entstanden. Uber eine Linie oder Spirale kommt man dann zum nächsten Ring. Das ist ein bisschen wie ein Tanz. Ja, ein Tanz. Es besteht auch eine Nähe zur Idee der Serie, mit einem Thema und Variationen von Ansichten darüber. Das ist wie ein Hase, der an einem Punkt hüpft, dann zum nächsten springt und von dort aus weiter hüpft. Die Serie trat erstmals in den Alben auf, doch dann blieb das Prinzip bei allen Büchern dasselbe. Ein Tanzen an einer bestimmten Position und dann ein Weitertanzen an einer anderen. So sind die Erinnerungen an die 1960er- und 1970er-Jahre entstanden. Das gilt auch für die Bücher »Der Text als Grundlage des Visuellen«, »Über die „totale" Installation« und »Public Projects or the Spirit of a Place«. Immer gibt es ein Sujet und das Tanzen um dieses Zentrum.

Dieser Stil ist mit einer didaktischen Lektion für Studenten vergleichbar. Einmal bekam ich von Kaspar König einen Lehrauftrag an der Kunstschule in Frankfurt am Main, Deutschland. Am Anfang der ersten Lektion sagte ich zu den Studenten: „Ich spreche, und sie hören nur zu. Wenn Sie eine Frage haben, stellen Sie sie erst am Ende." Dieser Stil ist absolut undemokratisch und für eine heutige Kunstschule völlig verrückt. Denn normalerweise sitzt der Professor mit den Studenten zusammen und diskutiert über verschiedene Themen. Besonders diskutieren die Studenten aber mit anderen Studenten. Zum Beispiel sagte mir Joseph Kosuth einmal: „Ich sitze nur da und die anderen sprechen."

Ich dagegen wandte den alten deutschen Stil an: „Der Professor kommt und sagt was er will und was er weiß. Die Studenten öffnen wie Kinder den Mund und bekommen, was man in sie hinein legt." Meine Studenten blieben bis zur letzten Lektion, es waren insgesamt 16. Danach sagte mir eine Teilnehmerin: „Ich bin nicht sicher, ob das seriöse Lektionen waren, das war doch eine Performance, oder? Und als Performance war es für uns sehr interessant."

Ich habe später ein Buch daraus gemacht: »Über die „totale" Installation«. Jede Lektion, jedes Kapitel ist nur einem Thema gewidmet. Ich tanze am gleichen Platz und erfinde verschiedene Positionen, wie eine Maschine, ein Presslufthammer (klopft auf den Tisch und lacht). Das ist das Prinzip mit Thema und Variationen, wie in der Musik, sehr organisch. Das Sujet: „Tanzen in meinen Räumen".

Von einem Raum zum anderen. Das hat wieder mit den Installationen zu tun, die du einmal mit einem Buch verglichen hast. Wie man von Kapitel zu Kapitel fortschreitet, so auch von Raum zu Raum, entlang einer Dramaturgie.

Ja genau. Aber es gibt keine Entwicklung. Raum ist Raum. Jeder einzelne ist wie eine Monade oder eine Kugel. Eine Monade ist wie ein Raum ohne Fenster.

Das erinnert mich an dein Buch über die 1960er- und 1970er-Jahre. Es hat mich beim Lesen zuerst sehr überrascht. Warum?

Hier schreibt ein Künstler eigentlich fast nur über die anderen, über seine Freunde und Kollegen, besonders im zweiten und dritten Teil. Das geht sehr lange so, insgesamt über mehr als zweihundert Seiten. Beim Lesen habe ich mich immer wieder gefragt: „Wo ist eigentlich Kabakov? Wer ist Kabakov? Warum schreibt er über alle anderen, aber nicht über sich selbst?" Und erst ganz am Schluss versteht man dann, wie das Buch funktioniert: Dass nämlich im Grunde alle, so wie sie von dir beschrieben werden, auch etwas von Kabakov haben. Dass die Figur Kabakov nicht als Positiv-Form dargestellt wird – „ich bin das und das, und ich kann das und das, und ich will das und das" –, sondern gewissermaßen als eine Negativ-Form. In Innern der Figur existiert eine Leere und Offenheit. Dennoch hat sie einen klaren Umriss, eine Gestalt, die von der Umgebung, vom Kontext oder vom Rand her definiert ist.

Ich würde sagen: Kabakov erscheint als ein „Luftmensch". Innen leer, aber doch mit einer Konsistenz. Vielleicht kann man diese Form letztlich auch mit einer Kugel vergleichen, die von außen aus allen Richtungen definiert wird, aber nicht von innen?

Ja, das ist ein interessantes Thema: „Wo ist der Autor?" Für den Leser, für normale Leute ist klar, dass wenn sie mit jemandem sprechen, sie entweder über sich oder über andere reden. Das sind zwei verschiedene Blickrichtungen. Bei der ersten beobachtet man sich selbst und bei der zweiten beobachtet man die Umgebung, die Gesamtsituation. Aber trotzdem bestimmt die Tradition, in welcher Position der Mensch steht, wenn er die anderen beobachtet. Er hat eine traditionelle Rolle: Er ist Historiker, Kurator, Psychologe, Soziologe oder er ist zum Beispiel ein Biograf. In dieser Situation ist der Autor wie eine kompakte und geschlossene Figur. Was ist das? Wenn er über ein Land oder eine Situation schreibt, und er genau weiß, was er sagt. Er ist sicher, dass es so ist. Er schreibt entweder autoritär oder weich usw.

Es wird aber sehr schwierig, wenn er über die anderen zu reden beginnt und dabei gleichzeitig über sich selbst spricht und sagt: „Ich bin nicht sicher, was ich sage, ich verzweifle an meinen Figuren. Dieser Text ist nicht ganz seriös." „Ach, der ist nicht seriös? Du bist verrückt!" Nein, auf der einen Seite ist er seriös, aber auf der anderen Seite ist er nicht seriös. Wenn du über andere schreibst und es einmal ein sicherer Text, dann wieder ein verzweifelnder Text wird – das ergibt eine unruhige und unklare Position. Zum Beispiel: Du kommst zum Doktor, und der Doktor

erzählt dir von seiner Biografie. Das ist paradox. Ich bin krank und du bist mein Arzt, aber hier befinde ich mich in einer pervertierten Position: Ich bin der Arzt und du bist krank. Das ist eine absolut schizophrene Situation.
(Lachen)

Da ist eine Nähe zu Dostojewski. Die Personage Dostojewski spricht zum einen über andere und zum anderen gleichzeitig über sich selbst. Er sagt: „Was ich über die anderen sage, ist total falsch, weil ich nicht sicher bin, was ich meine. In diesem Moment bin ich dieser Meinung, aber nach einigen Minuten sage ich: ‚Nein, das ist eine falsche Erzählung'". Dann beginnt er wieder von Neuem zu erzählen, mit neuen Varianten.

Das ist eine schwebende Situation. In unserem konzeptualistischen Kreis gibt es dafür den Begriff „Blinzeln". Dieses Blinzeln ist ein schneller Positionswechsel; so schnell, dass der Leser/Hörer nicht versteht, wo die Position des anderen ist. Bei der ersten Position ist dieser wie ein Objekt, aber in der nächsten Sekunde ist er wie ein Subjekt. Bei der ersten Figur ist er der Erzähler und bei der zweiten Figur verzweifelt er über die Erzählung. Das ist wie Gas geben und Bremsen. Für den Autor gibt es keine Bewegung.

Aber dieser Stil ist sehr gut – wie ein Salatstil. Wie als wenn du mit der Gabel eine Kartoffel zerdrückst, Spinat und eine Gurke oder eine Zwiebel isst und das alles gleichzeitig. (Gestikuliert)

Der Text über die 1960er- und 1970er-Jahre ist total subjektiv. Aber langsam versteht man beim Lesen die Tendenzen des Autors. Was will er sagen? Er will sagen, dass es einen gemeinsamen Kontext und gemeinsame Figuren gibt. Der Künstler ist kein separater Künstler, egal was er über sich selbst denken mag, er hat Tendenzen zu verschiedenen Figuren: einer metaphysischen, religiösen, einer sozialen etc. Und die Idee liegt darin, dieses Bukett oder diesen Busch zu entdecken, mit einer Wurzel, aus der dieser Busch wachsen wird. Und obwohl jeder Teil dieses Busches separat wächst, haben all diese Auswüchse und die Wurzel ein und denselben Stammbaum.

Das ist auf der einen Seite sehr subjektiv und auf der anderen Seite entspricht es zum Teil auch einer Theorie oder einer utopischen Konstruktion. Der Autor will damit sagen: „Es gibt eine Gesamtkugel." Das ist wie eine Familie mit verschiedenen Brüdern oder Schwestern, die trotzdem eine Familie sind. Und die Idee dieses Buches ist, von dieser Familie zu erzählen. Es gibt verschiedene Generationen, verschiedene Geburtsorte, aber trotzdem existiert eine Familie, zu der all diesen Figuren gehören. Das ist eine russische Tradition: „Wenn sie gestorben sind, auferstehen sie zusammen." Nicht nur der eine oder der andere, sondern alle gemeinsam, alles, wie bei Nikolai Fjodorow.

Wie ein Körper?

Ein Körper, ja. Das ist eine alte russische Tradition. Von dort stammt die Hauptidee dieses Buches: „Über die Gesamtheit dieser Gruppe zu erzählen, damit wir zusammen aus dem Grab der Geschichte wieder zum Leben kommen."

Du hast ja später auch die Installation über Noma gemacht, wo du für den engeren Familienkreis des Moskauer Konzeptualismus die Form des Kreises gewählt hast mit einer offenen, leeren Mitte. Um sie herum hatte jeder sein Zimmer, doch alle bildeten zusammen ein Ganzes.

Die inoffiziellen Künstler, das ist eine Familie. Aber der konzeptualistische Kreis, das ist etwas ganz anderes. Das ist eher ein „Rosenkreuzer-Zirkel". Er hat geheime Begriffe und eine geheime Basis. Die Bedeutungen sind wie auf einem Ring um ein leeres Zentrum platziert.

Aber man kann aus dem Gesagten auch ableiten, dass die Künstlerfigur Kabakov keine autonome Person ist, die aus sich selbst heraus entstanden ist, quasi vom Himmel gefallen ist, sondern geprägt ist von all diesen Verwandten?

Ein bisschen, ja. Ja sicher.

Und umgekehrt natürlich auch – eine Wechselwirkung?

Ich fühlte mich nicht als Einzelfigur, sondern zum Teil verantwortlich für eine Gruppenmentalität. Das ist ein bisschen wie Vadim Zakharov, der auch diese Tendenz zu einer Familienverantwortung hat.

Kommen wir noch auf ein weiteres Thema, das damit zusammenhängt, nämlich, dass du nicht nur der Künstler und die Person Kabakov bist, sondern auch die Figur oder „Personage" Kabakov, die in deinem Werk eine eigene Rolle spielt. Es gibt diese Doppelung. Und das beginnt ganz deutlich bei den Alben, über deren Figuren du gesagt hast, sie verkörperten verschiedene Bewusstseinszustände, die mit dir zusammenhingen. Und das geht dann weiter im Buch »Der Text als Grundlage des Visuellen«, worin du über die Installationen unter dem Titel schreibst: »Wie ich zu meiner eigenen Figur wurde« und »Wo ich zu meiner eigenen Figur wurde«. Oder, um das noch etwas weiter zu treiben, zuletzt in Moskau 2008 mit dem Projekt »Alternative Geschichte der Kunst«, wo drei Künstler ausgestellt haben: Rosenthal, Kabakov und Spivak, die du alle drei als fiktive Figuren erfunden hast. Sie haben in einem Museum gemeinsam ausgestellt, das du erfunden hast. Du hast den Katalog gemacht und die Biografien geschrieben. Du warst alles in einem: die Künstler, mehrere gleichzeitig, der Kurator, der Autor, der Buchgestalter, der Museumsarchitekt. Du hast alle diese Rollen, die mit dem Kunstbetrieb zusammenhängen, selbst übernommen und daraus eine Installation als künstlerisches Werk gemacht.

Ja. Das ist ein sehr interessantes Thema: „Woher stammen die Figuren?" Warum braucht es diese fiktiven Figuren oder fiktiven Gesichter? Was ist der Grund dafür? Der Grund hat natürlich mit meiner Jugend zu tun, die ich in einer Wohngemeinschaft verbracht habe, und mit einem besonderen psychologischen Effekt.

In meiner Kunstschule und später auch im Kunstinstitut habe ich mich und meine Mitschüler und Studentennachbarn beim Lernen beobachtet. Die wichtigen Fragen für mich waren damals: „Wer bin ich? Wo bin ich? Was bedeute ich?" Ich hatte nicht das normale, subjektive Gefühl: „Ich bin da." Sondern: „Alle sind da, alle bis auf mich." Ich fühlte mich selbst nicht als Subjekt oder als Körper, sondern als etwas Irreales, wie eine Wolke oder eine immaterielle Substanz. Ohne Selbstgefühl oder Selbstreflexion, ohne Namen. Wenn ich „Kabakov" gehört habe, war meine erste Reaktion: „Wer ist das denn?" In mir war absolut keine subjektive Basis, kein Stativ, keine Mittelachse vorhanden. Absolut nichts. Da ist das permanente Gefühl, ein riesiger Komplex: „Was bedeute ich?"

Ich las viele Bücher und griff alles auf Anhieb auf – verschiedene Geschichten, verschiedene Situationen. Und ich verstand, dass es Leute gibt, die „das Recht haben" in dieser Welt zu sein. Sie sind lebendig und funktionieren als Studenten, Professoren oder als Künstler, die die Gemälde in der Tretjakow-Galerie gemacht haben. Dagegen fühlte ich mich aber wie ein Auge oder eine Fliege, als jemand, der nur beobachtet. Aber nicht wie jemand, der alles zu einem Resultat führt. Und darum war die immer wieder aufkommende Frage: „Was soll ich in dieser Welt machen?"

Natürlich erlernte ich einen Beruf, wir haben darüber gesprochen, aber das war ja auch fiktiv. Ich machte, was die Professoren wollten, aber nicht, was ich selber wollte. Es gab kein subjektives Interesse für diese Tätigkeit der Illustration oder der Malerei usw. Das ist der tiefe Grund für das Auftauchen von Figuren, das Bewusstsein von „Figuren".

Und der zweite Grund ist: Ich hatte kein Interesse am Leben selbst. Mich interessierten weder Essen noch Tanzen, Spazieren oder einfach nur Sitzen – alle Funktionen waren für mich wie bei einem Golem. Ich musste mich zum Beispiel waschen oder kleiden. Aber ich hatte kein Interesse an Kleidern. Es gab keine Reaktionen auf die Realität sozusagen. Imitation, ja. Ich war ein guter Fußballer, ich spielte Volleyball, aber das war wie eine wilde Reaktion. „Das Wilde" verstand ich. Aber was ich selbst als Mensch machen wollte, das wusste ich nicht. Ich hatte keinen Wunsch nach irgendetwas. Ich saß da und jede Handlung war für mich sehr schwer und sinnlos. Es war eine sehr frustrierende Situation – eine lange Zeit ohne jegliche Unterbrechung.

Zum Beispiel: Ein Künstler wie Repin malte ein Bild. – Ich malte auch ein Bild. Und dann guckte ich es an und verglich es mit dem Repin-Bild und sagte: „Ist das nicht gut? Wie kann ich es verbessern, damit ich mich dem Bild von Repin annähere?" Das war eine Imitation.

Du wiederholst quasi den Entwicklungsprozess einer Fotografie: Zuerst legst du das Negativ in ein Wasserbecken mit Chemie, und dann kommt langsam ein Bild zum Vorschein. Die Kunst funktionierte für mich in diesem Sinne. Ich bin die Person, die dieses Bild macht. Aber wer ist derjenige, der sich entschieden hat so zu handeln? Ich bin jemand Unbekannter, der mithilfe von Papier oder einer Leinwand ein Werk realisiert.

Und dann, so entwickelte es sich nach und nach, wurde das zu einer permanenten Beschäftigung. Das heißt: „Ich wurde Künstler." Ich selbst existierte nicht, aber der Künstler wurde langsam, langsam immer größer, wie ein Kuchen, der aufgeht. Im Endeffekt entstand ein Monster. (Lachen)

Mir wurde klar, dass ein neues Monster auf diese Welt gekommen war. Welcher Kontakt zwischen mir und diesem Monster bestand, das wusste ich nicht. Aber das Monster wuchs wie ein Golem. Der Künstler ist eine Konstruktion wie ein Golem. Und bis heute, wenn man über den Künstler Kabakov spricht und jemand sagt: „Kabakov!", frage ich: „Wer ist da? – Aha, das ist das Monster! Es macht viele Installationen und Bücher." Wie ein Hase im Zirkus. (Schlägt auf den Tisch) Er muss „arbeiten". Wenn er aufhört zu hüpfen, entsteht eine riesige Leere, ein Nichts. Das ist die Realität. Und dieser Golem hüpft permanent wie ein Hase und stellt immer wieder irgendwas her.

Zum Beispiel habe ich heute gemalt. Der Golem fühlt sich ganz gut, denn er funktioniert wie ein Künstler; er hat seine Pinsel und malt. Er ist eine seriöse Figur. Darum ist der Begriff „Personage" für mich die beste und richtige Bezeich-

nung für diesen Golem. Ich bin selbst der Golem aus der Parabel meiner Biografie. Denn eine Biografie meines Lebens existiert nicht. Es gibt kein Leben an sich und auch keine Biografie.

In der Sowjetunion beschäftigte ich mich jeden Tag mit der Malerei. Aber ein großes Problem war, woher ich Nahrung bekommen konnte. Damals gab es viele Probleme. Man stand Schlange, um Nahrung zu kaufen. Ich war aber zu faul zum Anstehen und blieb oftmals hungrig. Das war für den Golem das Problem des Magens.

Aber zu meinem Glück kam, als ich komplett „untergegangen war", Emilia. Sie nahm diesen Golem und sagte: „Golem komm hierher!", „Komm zum Essen!", „Komm zum Schlafen!", „Heute fahren wir nach New York!" – „Okay". (Lachen)

Das Leben ist bis zum heutigen Tag ein Nichts geblieben, es ist absolut kein Interesse für das Leben entstanden. Ich habe dazu weder ein negatives noch ein positives Verhältnis.

Neutral.

Neutral, ja. Das ist wie bei Pavel Pepperstein. Ihm ist es auch egal, was er isst. Er ist auch ein Monster, ein Golem. (Lachen) Aber er ist ein sehr guter Beobachter. Er ist wie eine Fliege, wie ein anonymes Auge. Er versteht und beobachtet alles.

Zum Beispiel fragte mich einmal ein Freund in der Anfangszeit beim Kinderbuchverlag: „Ilya. Wie sah ein Musketier in Frankreich aus? Was hatte er für eine Kopfbedeckung?" „Kein Problem." Ich wusste das nicht von den Büchern. Aber meine Fantasie ging ganz weit in die Vergangenheit zurück. Wie ein Flugzeug oder eine Fliege legte ich eine große Distanz zurück und landete in Frankreich, im Paris des XVIII. Jahrhunderts, bewegte mich durch die Straßen, sah mich um und gelangte zu einer Taverne. Dort saß ein Musketier. Ich ging um ihn herum und sah ihn mir genau an, von hinten, den Kopf, die Schuhe usw. Und dann habe ich ihn ganz schnell gezeichnet, um ihn mir zu merken. Das ist diese ganz freie und bewegliche Sichtweise. Heute spricht man zum Beispiel von den Chinesen. Okay, dann bewege ich mich zu den Chinesen und sehe alles vor mir – das ist wie ein bewegter Film.

Das war ein Kommentar. Aber zurück zu den Personagen. Die Personagen sind für mich dasselbe wie reale Leute. Sie sind wie Figuren des Lebens. Darum sind auch Rosenthal und Spivak Personagen, ohne Körper und ohne historische Realität. Die Frage: „Gibt's Rosenthal oder nicht?", ist für mich absurd. Vielleicht gibt's ihn, vielleicht nicht. „Bist du, oder bist du nicht?" Das ist sehr problematisch.

Dieses Sujet betrifft das Verhältnis von Geist/Seele und Körper. Jeder Mensch fühlt sich wie ein Emigrant im Körper. Dieser ist der provisorische Raum oder ein Haus; dort befindet sich jemand – zufällig und vorübergehend. Darum besteht zwischen mir und meiner „sozialen" Figur eine Distanz. Und die sozialen Figuren sind ja auch wie Monster. Wenn wir uns Politiker oder Philosophen ansehen – das sind auch verschiedene Gestalten, „Repräsentanten" einer Theorie oder einer Konstruktion. Aber der normale Mensch und das Monster, das ist etwas ganz Unterschiedliches.

Mein pessimistischer Blick auf dieses Problem ist ganz einfach: Wenn du ein normaler Mensch bist mit einem Körper und einer Seele und dich nicht mit die-

ser Welt beschäftigst, nur arbeitest bis zur Pension, wie meine Eltern, dann gibt es kein Programm. Es ist ganz einfach: „Ich lebe, weil ich geboren bin." Wie ein Vogel. Der Vogel wurde geboren, darum singt er. Das ist die fundamentale Idee: „Geboren werden und leben bis zum Ende."

Aber daneben gibt es eine andere Situation mit einem Programm. Ich weiß nicht, wer jedem Menschen sein eigenes Programm gibt. Dass er es so machen muss oder soll. Zum Beispiel gab es im 18. Jahrhundert die romantische Theorie: „Der Mensch ist für eine Mission geboren." Geboren zu sein ist nicht genug für das Leben, es braucht eine menschliche Mission. Du musst sie suchen, als Geiger, Politiker oder als jemand der eine Botschaft verbreitet. Aber wenn du diese Mission zu realisieren beginnst, bist du ein Monster.

Da kommt eine große Frage auf: „Hat das Monster eine Verantwortung oder bist du selber für dieses Monster verantwortlich?" Das ist ein sehr problematischer Aspekt. Ich frage mich selbst, wann dieses Monster bei mir zu funktionieren begann und warum es entstand. Warum ist es permanent da, und woher bekommt es die Energie? Zum Beispiel sprechen wir mit unserer Großmutter und fragen sie: „Jetzt, als Pensionärin, hast du viel Freizeit. Warum nimmst du nicht den Bleistift und schreibst deine Memoiren, weil deine Biografie sehr interessant ist?" Ihre Antwort ist einfach: „Meine Energie reicht nicht einmal für mein Leben aus, ich habe keine Extraenergie für andere Sachen."

Das heißt, dass das Monster Extraenergie braucht. Es bekommt seine Energie nicht von seinem Körper, sondern aus einem anderen Bassin oder einer anderen Zisterne. Das wiederum ist ein besonderes Thema. Ich beschränke mich jetzt nur auf den Aspekt der „Künstler-Figur".

Da besteht eine große Nähe zu den Personagen von Dostojewski. Dostojewski war sehr krank, psychopathisch. Sein Gehirn war instabil, sodass er Probleme hatte mit der Zeit und mit Antworten beispielsweise. Er saß einmal mit den Schriftstellern Turgenjew und Belinski bei einem Gespräch zusammen und wurde gefragt: „Was meinst du dazu, Fjodor Michailowitsch?" Dostojewski war blockiert und konnte nicht antworten, da sein Gehirn dafür nicht flexibel genug war. Er erschrak und wurde sehr nervös. Plötzlich sprang er vom Stuhl auf und stürzte hinaus. Als er irgendwo auf der Straße war, so nach zehn Minuten, kamen ihm die Antworten in den Sinn. Er kehrte nach einer halben Stunde zurück und wollte jetzt antworten, doch die Idioten hatten schon vergessen, worum es gegangen war. (Lachen)

Das ist typisch. Seine Romane sind die Antworten auf solche Fragen, die sich in anderen Räumen, in einer anderen Zeit, bei anderen Leuten stellen. Er führt Dialoge mit diesen Leuten, doch sie sind nicht anwesend.

Das Stichwort „Dialog" führt uns wieder zum Gespräch zurück. Man hat für Dostojewskis Romankonzept den Begriff der „Dialogizität" verwendet. Das dialogische Prinzip gilt auch für die Einzelperson. Nicht das Ich allein ist bei Dostojewski primär, sondern immer schon ein Dialog mit sich selbst und mit anderen. So hat er sich kaleidoskopartig in verschiedene, gegensätzliche Romanfiguren als Alter egos aufgefächert. Das Ich hat folglich keine feste Position mehr, sondern ist in Bewegung. Und diese manifestiert sich im Dialog. Du hast in unserem Gespräch dafür von „Blinzeln" gesprochen.

Ja, genau. Das ist die Theorie von Bachtin. Dostojewskis Personagen waren Teil von ihm selbst, und auch nicht.

Zurück zu den Monstern, den Personagen und zur inneren Leere. Die Leere ist bei dir doch auch eine Offenheit, ein Freiraum? Sie bietet die Möglichkeit für ganz verschiedenartige Figuren. Das erinnert mich an einen Autor und einen Roman, der für dich in den 1970er-Jahren sehr wichtig war, wie du mir einmal gesagt hast: Robert Musils »Der Mann ohne Eigenschaften«. Diese Figur zeichnet sich nicht nur durch Wirklichkeitssinn aus, sondern vor allem auch durch ihren Möglichkeitssinn. Für sie ist die Realität, so wie sie besteht, gleichwertig mit den verschiedenen Möglichkeiten, wie sie auch noch sein könnte.

Ja, aber dann macht er nichts. Es geschieht nichts.

Nach Musil geht es um die Vermittlung von Möglichkeitssinn und Wirklichkeitssinn als menschliches Ziel. Quasi darum, aus einem Müllhaufen von Dingen und Fakten immer wieder eine mögliche utopische Welt zu synthetisieren.

Ja, Musil ist meinem Bewusstsein sehr nahe, wie ein Teil meiner eigenen Erfahrungen. Die Trennung in zwei Menschen war in der sowjetischen Gesellschaft sehr verbreitet. Bei mir ist das beste Beispiel dafür der Riss – das Leben der offiziellen und der inoffiziellen Künstler. Und doch war es für mich leichter als für andere. Im Kinderbuchverlag war es immer sehr lustig, es wurde gelacht, und man erzählte sich Anekdoten; ich war eine zu einhundert Prozent „angenehme“ Person. Aber für meine inoffiziellen Freunde war ich sehr böse, traurig und pessimistisch. Wie ein schlechter Mann am Tag und ein guter Mann in der Nacht. In der englischen Literatur sind diese zwei Figuren bekannt: »Dr. Jekyll and Mr. Hyde« von Robert Louis Stevenson.

Wenn wir diese zwei Seiten so erörtern, möchte ich zum Schluss noch einmal auf das Gespräch zurückkommen. Kann man sagen, dass für das Gespräch das Gleiche gilt wie für deine Bilder und Bücher? Du hast mir einmal gesagt, dass die Bilder Bilder seien und doch auch keine Bilder. Sie täten nur so, als ob sie Bilder wären, aber seien es nur zum Teil. So ist es auch mit den Personagen und den Büchern. Die sind zum Teil etwas Reales und zum Teil Fiktion, wie der Held mit der verlorenen Nase bei Gogol. Und ähnlich ist es doch auch beim Gespräch. Das Gespräch, so wie du es führst, ist zwar immer auf ein Thema bezogen, es erklärt, es reflektiert, doch es fasst den Gegenstand nicht, fixiert ihn nicht endgültig. Es ist eher ein Umkreisen, ein Kommentieren letztlich, ein Interpretieren mit der eigenen Fantasie, kein eindeutiges Antworten auf bestimmte Fragen. Eher ein Prozess, der immer weitergeht und zu keinem Ende kommt.

Für mich steht da etwas ganz Grundsätzliches dahinter, was nach deiner Aussage auch für die Installationen zutrifft, nämlich das Paradox freier Unfreiheit bzw. unfreier Freiheit.

Das Gespräch ist an etwas gebunden, ein Thema, eine Frage, insofern ist es als Antwort unfrei. Und es hat gleichzeitig aber auch diese Möglichkeiten immer neuer Deutungen, die es öffnen, verselbstständigen und befreien. Im Prinzip ist es damit endlos.

Ich denke, dass diese Freiheit dem Zuhörer/Leser des Gesprächs die Chance gibt, sich damit selber zu verbinden, eigene Gedanken damit zu verknüpfen. Dann tritt das Gespräch quasi aus den Personen heraus, schafft einen allgemeinen menschlichen Zusammenhang und bewegt sich auf einer Metaebene?

Das ist ein sehr gutes Thema: „Die Dramaturgie". Bei jedem meiner Kunstwerke, besonders bei den Installationen, gibt es dieses Paradox, dieses dramatische Moment.

Mich interessieren nicht nur die üblichen Installationen aus Objekten für freie Betrachter. Mich interessiert der geschlossene Raum. Warum? Weil der geschlossene Raum wie ein Theater oder wie ein Film ist – oder wie ein Traum, der dich packt und zu „fressen" beginnt. Du bist ein Opfer oder ein Gefangener. Du fühlst dich wie ein eingesperrter Hund. Der Raum funktioniert wie eine Klaustrophobie. Wenn du ihn betrittst, suchst du normalerweise gleich in der nächsten Minute nach dem Ausgang aus dieser Welt. Du kannst entweder dieselbe Tür benützen, durch die du eingetreten bist, oder du suchst nach einer anderen „Tür" oder einem Fenster, um rauszugehen, um zu verschwinden.

Es gab in der Sowjetunion viele Situationen, in denen es nicht so leicht war, diese Türe zu finden. Darum waren die normalen Leute sehr frustriert und depressiv. Die Dramaturgie ist also eine Aufforderung an die Betrachter: „Suchen Sie die Freiheit bitte auf andere Weise. Benutzen Sie als Ausgang nicht nur die normalen physischen Türen. Es gibt auch einen Ausgang als mentale Aktion. Es gibt eine Freiheit auf einer anderen Ebene, in anderen Räumen."

In jeder Installation gibt es diese Treppe, diese Leiter, wo der Mensch/Betrachter diesen Ausgang suchen und finden kann. Oder es ist eine poetische, metaphysische, paradoxe oder eine ironische Leiter, aber trotzdem gibt es einen Ausgang. „Diese Depression ist nicht permanent, sie ist nicht stabil und nicht aussichtslos" – das ist die Dramaturgie. Du musst immer irgendeine Schwierigkeit überwinden, damit dann später irgendetwas passiert ...

Du bietest Möglichkeiten zu dieser Befreiung?

Es ist wie ein Ausgang aus dem Labyrinth.

Aber du legst schon Fäden, die zu diesem Ausgang führen?

Wie verschiedene Labyrinthe: mentales Labyrinth, konstruktives Labyrinth. Die Installationen sind im Prinzip ein Modell des Lebens oder dieser Welt: eine Metapher des „Universellen". Und natürlich gibt es einen Ausgang aus dieser Welt.

Und wenn ich zum Schluss noch einmal auf das Buch zurückkomme, dann kann man es eben auch als eine Metapher für diese Welt verstehen?

Ja, ja – genau.

Gleichzeitig geschlossen und offen?

Ja, ja – sicher. Das Buch ist das Labyrinth. Wenn es ein gutes Buch ist, dann ist es ein unendliches Labyrinth.

Das weiße Schreiben

MH: Ich weiß nicht, ob der Leser unserem langen Gespräch bis hierher gefolgt sein wird, wenn es einmal gedruckt sein wird. Ich vermute, dass er es früher verlassen hat, vielleicht noch etwas im Abbildungsteil des Buches geblättert und es dann wieder ins Regal gestellt hat. Dennoch sollten wir weitersprechen und quasi ein „Gespräch nach dem Gespräch" führen, ein Gespräch ohne Zuhörer/Leser. Dazu passt das Thema „Abwesenheit".

Du hast einmal gesagt, dass deine Bilder nicht ganz Bilder seien und deine Bücher zum Teil wie Bücher schienen, der Künstler selbst ein Monstrum sei. Und für mich sind deine engsten und dunkelsten Installationen, die scheinbar gar keinen Ausgang haben, so etwas wie begehbare Bühnenbilder; sie zeigen also auch, dass sie „falsch" sind. Sie sind zwar physisch anwesend, zugleich aber auf einer höheren Ebene wegen ihrer Schäbigkeit und provisorischen Machart auch abwesend: bewusst gemachte Illusionen, Phantome oder eben Monster. Dadurch verlieren sie ihre Bedrohlichkeit.

Die Abwesenheit spielt aber besonders für deine Zeichnungen, Alben und Bilder eine große Rolle, wobei das Thema „Weiß" wichtig ist; darüber haben wir noch nicht gesprochen.

Es gibt die Tradition des weißen Grundes in der Malerei der Moderne seit Cézanne, natürlich auch in der russischen Avantgarde. Bei dir ist das Weiß für mich eine Gegenelement zum Illustrativ-Bildhaften. Man könnte sagen, dass im Zeigen von Etwas durch das Weiß zugleich etwas verhüllt oder verschwiegen wird. Oder anders formuliert, dass das, was man sieht, womöglich aus dem Weiß aufgetaucht ist oder darin wieder verschwinden wird, dass somit alles anwesend-abwesend ist. Die Dramaturgie der Alben veranschaulicht dies ganz deutlich.

Damit hängt auch die Leere zusammen. Du hast das letzte Mal vom Labyrinth gesprochen. Das Verlorensein, die Frage der Orientierungslosigkeit, das spielt bei den Installationen und bei den Büchern eine Rolle.

Mir scheint es nun, dass du auch beim Erzählen in einer gewissen Weise schweigst und abwesend bist. Pavel Pepperstein hat für die besondere Erzählform des Moskauer Konzeptualismus den Begriff „Transnarrativität" vorgeschlagen. Er meint damit ein Erzählen, das gleichzeitig durch sich hindurch- oder über sich hinausgeht. Das nicht bei den Worten und ihrer Bedeutung bleibt, sondern etwas Zusätzliches ins Spiel bringt. Das Papierweiß kommt ja auch in der Literatur als Thema vor, nicht nur in der Malerei. Ich denke an Mallarmé, der in Gedichten über das Papierweiß spricht. Auch in deinen Büchern spielt das Weiß eine wichtige Rolle, in den Kinderbüchern genauso wie in den Künstlerbüchern.

Ich komme zu meiner Frage. Für mich gibt es bei dir nicht nur das kalte Weiß der Leere oder das warme Weiß des Lichts, sondern auch das weiße Nichts – das in der östlichen Kultur und besonders in der ostasiatischen Malerei eine wichtige Rolle spielt. Es markiert eine Offenheit. Eine Abwesenheit, die eine Offenheit ist, etwas Schwebendes, Freies, vielleicht sogar etwas Meditatives. In Bezug auf Pepperstein könnte man von „Transvisualität" sprechen. Siehst du das auch so – das Nichts der Abwesenheit als Potenzial und als Möglichkeit von Sinn?

IK: Natürlich ist das Weiß ein Thema. Das Weiß hat in meinen Werken viele verschiedene Bedeutungen, Ebenen und Qualitäten. Doch es gibt eine Hauptbedeutung: „das Weiß als Raum".

Wenn ich mit einem Bild oder einer Zeichnung beginne, sehe ich die weiße Leinwand wie einen dreidimensionalen Raum, mit einer großen Tiefe und einem großen Potenzial. Dieses Potenzial bezieht sich nicht nur auf mich als produzierenden Künstler, der etwas auf „das Weiß" malt oder zeichnet, sondern es verbirgt sich sozusagen in jedem Betrachter als seine besondere „Fähigkeit" des Verstehens.

Zuerst besteht ein Bild aus realistischen Elementen und stellt das „einfache Bild der Wirklichkeit" dar. Wo ist bei mir der Unterschied zur realistischen Darstellung von Stillleben, Landschaften oder Porträts von der Renaissance bis ins 19. Jahrhundert? Die Technik der Renaissance arbeitete auch mit dem Raum, der aber ganz von den Figuren und den Landschaften erzeugt wird. Die Natur ist der Raum. Und natürlich machte der Meister, wenn er diese Welt aufs Bild brachte, eine Kopie der großen Welt. Er schaute durch das offene Fenster in die Welt und überlegte, was er malen konnte. Mit Fleiß und großem Respekt kopierte er den Raum dahinter. Darin liegt das Heilige eines solchen Bildes, wenn es zu einem Spiegel wird und die Qualität der Welt wiedergibt.

Ich habe oft mit dieser Naturdarstellung gearbeitet. Mit den Ansichten, der Beleuchtung, den Reflexen, den Farben, der Realität usw. Aber ich habe die Motive auf besondere Art behandelt. Denn mein weißes Bild hat schon einen dreidimensionalen Raum, und es gibt deshalb für die realistische Räumlichkeit eigentlich gar keinen Platz. Ich habe den Glauben an die dreidimensionale, gegenständliche Realität für meine Malerei verloren. Die Realität an sich hat drei Dimensionen, aber wenn sie in meinem Bild mit der Tiefe des weißen Raumes zusammentrifft, verliert sie ihre Räumlichkeit. Ich behandle sie als Fläche, im Grunde als eine Reproduktion. Als ob man ein Tuch oder ein Papier aufkleben würde – wie ein Vorhang vor meiner weißen Dreidimensionalität. Das ist die beste Erklärung für meine malerische Absicht: ein Malerei-Vorhang, der „das Weiß" abdeckt.

Dieses Klebeprinzip der Realität hat viele Konsequenzen und Probleme. Es lässt keine Möglichkeit für eine Arbeit mit zwei Räumen, dem realen Raum und dem weißen Raum. Zwischen beiden existiert keine Beziehung in meiner Malerei. Der reale Raum ist flach. Doch es gibt verschiedene Varianten der Begegnung dieses flächigen Raumes der dargestellten Realität mit dem dreidimensionalen Weiß.

Diese flächige realistische Darstellung bedeckt zum Beispiel das ganze Bild. Dann braucht es einige Maßnahmen, um zu verdeutlichen, dass es sich um keine Dreidimensionalität handelt. Das Weiß dringt in Form eines „Loches" hindurch, oder auf irgendeine andere Art, und zerstört diese wunderbare, sogenannte realistische Malerei. Es sagt: „Da ist nichts, nur eine Folie."

Die zweite Variante besteht darin, dass ich nicht so illusionistisch male. Bis zum Impressionismus und zum Expressionismus brauchte der dreidimensionale Raum eine illusionistische Malerei. Der Expressionismus sagt: „Das ist keine Realität, das ist meine Reaktion darauf." Doch diese Manipulation mit Farbe und Form interessiert mich nicht. Mich interessiert der Vorgang, wie sich die „Realität" auf dem Weiß verhält. Dadurch erhält meine Malerei eine anonyme, durchschnittliche Qualität: Sie ist keine „gute" Malerei, aber sie ist auch keine „sehr schlechte". Sie ist wie von einem Autodidakten gemacht. Kein persönlicher Stil. Nein, das ist eine raumlose Malerei mit einer anonymen Technik. Wichtig ist nicht, wie die Malerei aussieht, das Wichtigste ist ihre Kommunikation mit dem Weiß. Dieses Konzept ist sehr schwer zu verstehen, wenn man wenig Erfahrung im Umgang mit dem Weiß hat. Zum Beispiel kamen bei meiner letzten Ausstellung in Moskau von russischen Malern überraschend negative Reaktionen. Für sie war das nur Malerei. Sie haben nicht verstanden, worum es bei der Kommunikation zwischen der Malerei und den weißen leeren Elementen geht. Einerseits gibt es für sie bereits genügend leere Elemente in den seriösen und außergewöhnlichen Kunstwerken von Malewitsch und Mondrian. Und zum anderen ist Realismus für sie der schlechte sozialistische Realismus, der sehr unangenehm anzusehen ist. Die Kombination von beidem haben sie nicht wahrgenommen.

Inzwischen hat das Weiß bei mir auch andere Bedeutungen bekommen. Es funktioniert auch wie ein Licht. Das heißt, dass es in meiner Malerei und besonders in meiner Zeichnung nicht nur einen Raum, sondern einen beleuchteten Raum schafft. Wie ein Bildschirm, bei dem das Licht aus der Tiefe zu uns kommt. Wie eine kosmische Energie oder eine andere „dünne" Materie. Wenn Du vor dem weißen Bild stehst, durchdringt dich diese Energie oder dieses Licht – in jedem Fall erlebe ich es so.

Noch eine Variante des Weiß ist der Eindruck einer Leere oder eines Nichts. Dann ist das Weiß nicht räumlich, sondern flach. Es hat eine Doppelbedeutung: Während ein Künstler oder jemand mit Fantasie darin einen tiefen Raum erkennen kann, handelt es sich für einfache Leute nur um eine normale, mit Nichts gefüllte, leere Oberfläche. Man muss mit diesem Nichts arbeiten: Wie viele Elemente und wie viel Masse der Realität braucht man, wenn man auf das weiße „Nichts" trifft? Wie kann eine Kommunikation auf dieser Fläche entstehen? Welche Figuren funktionieren darin?

Und der letzte Sinn des Weiß ist das weiße Naturmaterial; logischerweise ist das der Schnee. Ich wiederhole jetzt, was Boris Groys im Buch »Under the Snow« gesagt hat. Der Schnee ist ein Symbol für das Weiß und strahlt eine Ruhe aus, weckt russische Erinnerungen, Nostalgie und Sehnsucht. Der weiße Schnee ist ein Element, das alles, was es auf der Erdoberfläche gibt, zudeckt – der Schnee ist wie ein verlorenes Gedächtnis und steht für das Vergessen. Boris sagt auch, dass der Künstler mit meinen letzten Arbeiten, zum Beispiel den großen weißen Bildern für eine Kapelle, mehr und mehr das Vergessen thematisiere. Nur einige realistische Elemente blieben als Fragmente der Vergangenheit übrig. Das Vergessen nehme zu und eine Leere breite sich wie bei einem Computer aus, der nicht mehr richtig funktioniert und Daten verliert.

Von der Malerei und der Zeichnung wieder zurück zur Sprache und zu Peppersteins Begriff der „Transnarrativität". Sozusagen zum Weiß in der Sprache. Man kann feststellen, dass sich bei deinem Sprechen der Informationsgehalt dessen, was erzählt wird, fortwährend auch wieder auflöst, sodass ein „weißer oder leerer Raum" entsteht?

Ja, ja, genau. Das heißt „Das weiße Schreiben". Es bedeutet, so viel zu schreiben, dass die Leute einschlafen. So viele Wörter erzeugen eine Sprachlosigkeit. Das ist für mich auch sehr wichtig.

Das bringt mich zur nächsten Frage. Diese Masse der Sprachproduktion – auch unser langes Gespräch über Tage, vielleicht liest gar niemand mehr mit, weil es zu lang ist und man an kein Ende kommt, es gar kein Ende gibt –, sie evoziert eine Bewegung, die immer weitergeht ...

Und das ist wie bei einer alten Langspielplatte, die einen Kratzer hat und stehen bleibt.

In der Fülle liegt dann eben auch wieder eine Abwesenheit, das Nichts?

Ja genau.

Und wie du sagtest: Weil man sich an diese Fülle kaum erinnern kann und vergisst, was man gelesen und was man gesehen hat. Das hat wieder etwas Labyrinthisches: Man verliert sich dabei immer wieder von Neuem.

Das gilt besonders für die wissenschaftlichen Interpreten deiner Arbeit. Am Anfang hat man gewöhnlich immer viele Fragen, doch normalerweise klären sich etliche Dinge während der längeren Beschäftigung mit einem künstlerischen Werk. Man erhält wichtige Informationen, weiß immer mehr und wird immer vertrauter mit dem Werk. Bei dir ist das ganz anders. Je mehr Informationen man bekommt, je länger man sich mit dir und deinem Werk beschäftigt, desto größer wird das Labyrinth, es ist eigentlich ein Stillstand.

Ja – genau. Das ist im Prinzip eine negative Reaktion auf die Wissenschaft und das Wissen: Das Bewusstsein nicht als Maschine der Verständigung, sondern für das Vergessen. Dafür gibt es bei uns alte Wurzeln in religiösen Texten. Der Name ist „Apophatismus". Er spricht über das Negative: „Das gibt es nicht, dieses auch nicht, und das gibt es auch nicht. Was gibt es überhaupt? Das weiß ich nicht. Ich weiß nur eines: Alles was mich umgibt gibt es nicht."

Das ist nicht so, wie wenn einer nur ein einziges Bild macht; dann weiß er, was er macht. Wenn du aber fünfhundert Bilder machst, dann weißt du absolut nichts. (Lachen)

Genau. Es gibt ja auch Kunsthistoriker, die „verzweifelten", als sie sich mit deinem Werk befassten, weil sie nie zu einem Ergebnis kamen, sich im Labyrinth verloren oder noch rechtzeitig vor diesem Monstrum flüchteten, das einen da gefangen zu nehmen und zu verschlingen droht.

Das ist eine interessante Idee: Dass der Künstler ein Monster ist und arbeitet, ohne dass es einen Grund für seine Produktion gibt.

Wie Sisyphus?

Absolut. Seine Produktion hat keine Identität, aber trotzdem geht sie weiter. Das ist eine gute Frage: „Weshalb funktioniert dieser tragische Automatismus? Was ist der Zweck dieser Nonstop-Produktion?" Das ist auch eine tiefe Frage nach der Leere. Das Thema dazu heißt „Das leere Zentrum".

Es gibt nur ein mögliches Prinzip: Wenn du direkt auf dein Ziel blickst und dich fragst: „Was sehe ich?", dann erkennst du nichts. Wenn du Offenheit und Klarheit erwartest, wirst du nichts bekommen. Das Resultat bleibt dir verborgen. Doch während du geradeaus blickst, passiert irgendetwas in deinem weiteren

Gesichtsfeld. Etwas Wichtiges taucht auf, etwas Emotionales, eine Information; es gibt Antworten, eine Kommunikation. Aber nicht auf der direkten Blickachse, sondern irgendwo im Blickwinkel, am Rand des Gesichtsfeldes.

Und das hat auch mit dem Thema des Weiß oder der Leere zu tun. Das Zentrum unseres Interesses ist immer falsch. Das heißt, wir wissen nicht, was wir sehen. Und wir können nicht wissen, was sich uns außerhalb des zentrierten Blickes zeigen wird. Mit unserem Interesse verhält es sich paradox: Du brauchst ein Interesse, das du direkt auf ein leeres Zentrum richtest, dann erhältst du am Rande verschiedene Informationen zum Geschenk. Wenn du aber kein Interesse hast, dann wird sich auch nichts auf dem Ring außerhalb des Zentrums zeigen. Dieser Doppelblick oder Doppeleffekt setzt dein Interesse und ein leeres Zentrum voraus. Es braucht ein zentrales Interesse, das aber ohne unmittelbares Resultat bleibt. Trotzdem entsteht am Rand etwas, das mit deiner Suche zu tun hat. Das Bedeutende, die Wahrheit liegt immer am Rand, nicht in der Mitte. Das ist paradox, aber das Leben ist paradox. Das Leben hat keine einfache Logik, aber es hat eine paradoxale Logik.

Zum Beispiel die Porträtkunst. Man kann die Porträts von Franz Hals und Rembrandt vergleichen. Bei Franz Hals siehst du ein einfaches Gesicht mit Nase, Lippen, Augen, Ohren usw. Alle Elemente sind an ihrem Platz. Eine gute Porträtmalerei, die Menschen zeigt, die sprechen, lachen usw. Wenn du dagegen ein Porträt von Rembrandt betrachtest, entsteht beim Dargestellten eine seltsame Augenbewegung. Der seltsame Effekt des „Lebendigen" hängt mit dem gut erkennbaren, vom Künstler berechneten Seitenblick zusammen. Wenn du nämlich ein Auge des Dargestellten betrachtest, dann siehst du plötzlich, dass sich sein Mund etwas bewegt; siehst du aber auf den Mund, bewegt sich plötzlich das Auge ein bisschen usw. Das ist das Thema von Fokussieren und Entfokussieren: „der zentrale Blick und der zweite Blick". Jedes Element funktioniert mit dieser zusätzlichen Bewegung. Das ergibt einen sehr lebendigen Effekt, denn du kannst den Blick nicht stabilisieren; das Bild hat keinen primären Blickpunkt.

So entsteht eine Kommunikation. Der lebendige, zum Leben erweckte Mensch auf dem Porträt schaut mit seinem lebendigen Blick. Aber es ist ein Spiegeleffekt, weil du eigentlich nicht nur diesen Mann siehst, sondern dich selbst in der Anwesenheit des gemalten, aber realen Menschen. Das gilt besonders für das Gemälde »Die Meister der Sankt-Lukas-Gilde in Haarlem« im Rijksmuseum, Amsterdam. Wenn du davor stehst, siehst du sechs verschiedene Kommunikationsvarianten mit dir. Eine Figur ist böse, eine lächelt, die dritte denkt: „Das ist ein guter Mann", die vierte sagt: „Nein, du bist kein guter Mann." Das sind verschiedene Aspekte deines Schicksals. Du siehst hin und weißt nicht, welcher der richtige ist.

Alle Möglichkeiten sind gleichzeitig aufgefächert, und man weiß nicht, wie es ausgehen wird. Welche Meinung über dich sich bei der Gilde durchsetzen wird.

Und auch der Doppelblick entsteht wieder: Wenn Du dieses Gesicht betrachtest, siehst du auch das andere daneben, du siehst beide zusammen. Rembrandt versteht es, ein gutes Gesamtbild zu machen.

Und wenn der Fokus so beweglich ist, sieht man immer zwei zusammen, nicht das eine oder das andere. Das ist wieder ein Dialog?

Die drehen zusammen. Wenn das eine steht, dreht sich das andere, das ist wie ein Film, ein kinetischer Effekt.

Wie ein Umklappen – spannend. Vielleicht kann man das auf unser Gespräch übertragen. Du hast gesagt, die Folge des langen Sprechens sei das Vergessen. Das Vergessen ist das eine. Doch über das Vergessen kehrt auch das Erinnern zurück. Das ist doch auch eine Art von Bewegung, ein Oszillieren von vergessen und erinnern, die einander bedingen. Aber die Erinnerung ist nicht einfach das, was faktisch einmal gewesen ist, denn man hat es ja vergessen, sondern sie kommt als etwas Neues und Eigenes zurück, oder? Das Erinnern als etwas Kreatives?

Absolut. Das Thema ist sehr interessant, und das ist eine sehr gute Anmerkung dazu. Das Thema der „Extrainformationen". Die Mitteilung an den Betrachter braucht ein zweites Element. Das eine Element ist einfach, eine gute und klare Antwort. Aber parallel gibt es eine Alternative, die diese gute Antwort annulliert. Du arbeitest mit beiden. Das ist wie mit dem Geld. Die rechte Hand gibt dir das Geld, die linke nimmt es dir wieder weg. Eine Doppelbewegung – die eine gibt dir die Wahrheit und die zweite sagt: „Nein, das ist eine falsche Wahrheit." Es entsteht ein paradoxer Effekt des Entfokussierens im Bewusstsein des Betrachters, was sehr interessant ist. Dieser meint: „Ich habe eigentlich alles verstanden, doch zehn Prozent oder ein einzelnes Element sind etwas Anderes." Und er sucht immer, worin dieses Andere besteht, aber es bleibt da stets eine Reserve.

Ein weißer Fleck.

Eine weiße Fläche, die ich nicht gepackt habe, nicht fassen kann. Und später funktioniert dieser Effekt in der Erinnerung gut, man sagt: „In jenem Moment habe ich nicht ganz alles verstanden." Es braucht diese Reserve. Natürlich gibt es Künstler, die ohne Reserven arbeiten. (Lachen)

Das kann auch mit den verschiedenen Lebensabschnitten zusammenhängen. In der Jugend oder in der Zeit der Reife gibt es normalerweise einen klaren Eindruck, und mit dem Alter entsteht eine gewisse Reserve. Zum Beispiel Claude Monet. Er war als Maler während seines ganzen Lebens sehr klar, doch im Spätwerk, bei den Seerosen- und bei den japanischen Brückenbildern, da arbeitete er eindeutig mit einer Reserve.

Da spielt das Vergessen auch eine Rolle. Man sieht quasi vor diesen undeutlichen und unscharfen Gemälden, wie man vergisst, was man kennt. Die Motive lösen sich in der Farbe auf.

Und du verstehst nicht mehr, was vor deinen Augen steht.

Es ist in der Schwebe.

Aber trotzdem arbeiten viele Künstler ziemlich „klar". Besonders komisch ist das Programm des Symbolismus oder des Wiener Jugendstils. Dort wurden sakrale oder irrationale Motive verwendet, aber trotzdem wirkt das heute sehr ästhetisch. Alles ist klar, es gibt keine Reserven, keine geheimen Elemente in diesen Bildern. Alles ist gegessen. Gut, aber schon gegessen. Dagegen ist zum Beispiel Edvard Munch ein

Künstler mit riesigen Reserven. Bei ihm ist zwar auch viel Klarheit vorhanden: das Expressive, die Emotionalität, die Sexualität. Aber trotzdem gibt es eine Reserve, denn man kann seine Werke immer und immer wieder betrachten.

Man sieht sie wieder anders, weil man sich auch selber verändert hat und Neues entdecken kann?

Ja, genau. Neben der Hauptidee existiert eine große Reserve.

Das bringt mich nochmals auf das Vergessen zurück. Bezogen auf unser Gespräch kann man Folgendes sagen: Wenn man etwas vergessen hat und sich dessen Sinn quasi als Neuschöpfung erinnert, dann ist die Vergangenheit des Gesprächs nicht einfach bloß Vergangenheit, sondern liegt wie die Zukunft vor einem. Man geht in die Zukunft, indem man das Vergangene erinnernd uminterpretiert.

Ich komme damit auf das zurück, was wir am Anfang über die Geschichte gesagt haben. Dass die Geschichte nicht einfach das Vergangene repräsentiert; was hinter einem liegt, ist vorbei und uninteressant. Sondern es ist gerade umgekehrt: Indem ich mich des Vergangenen erinnere, komme ich paradoxerweise auf etwas Neues. Mit der schöpferischen Erinnerung wird die Geschichte neu erfunden und wird zum Bestandteil der eigenen Geschichte und zu einer möglichen Zukunft?

Ja, das meine ich. Das sehen wir bei vielen alten Künstlern, in der Renaissance, im Barock, besonders im Barock. Die Barockkünstler arbeiteten oft mit Erinnerungen. Wobei es hier auch problematische Elemente gibt, denn die Vergangenheit muss lebendig sein und darf nicht ästhetisiert werden.

Oder historisiert.

Und nicht historisiert. Die Vergangenheit ist ein Geheimnis. Zum Beispiel hat die russische Gruppe »Mir Iskusstva«, Welt der Kunst, mit der Vergangenheit gearbeitet, etwa mit dem Rokoko. Doch das ist nicht so interessant, weil es ausgedachte Rekonstruktionen sind, Ästhetisierungen einiger musealer Objekte.

Aber die Vergangenheit ist wie ein großer geheimnisvoller Raum. Im Barock beispielsweise zeigen dies Künstler wie Rembrandt oder besonders Caravaggio. Letzterer arbeitet mit zwei Zeiten. Er verwendet zum einen ein großes, dunkles Schwarz, das im Prinzip völlig unsinnlich ist, da man darin gar nichts erkennen kann. Natürlich vermutet man, dass sich hinter diesem Dunkel etwas verbirgt. Es wurden viele wissenschaftliche Farbanalysen gemacht, doch man konnte unter dem Schwarz nichts entdecken. Zum andern haben seine lebendigen Figuren eine starke Präsenz und schaffen eine Gegenwart. Sie sind naturalistisch gemalt, ohne Fantasie, wie ein Foto.

Die Kombination dieser naturalistischen Darstellung mit dem absolut schwarzen Raum der Umgebung ergibt quasi eine Verbindung von Gegenwart und Vergangenheit. Besonders stark ist die Spannung zwischen den Figuren unten und den oberen Dreivierteln des Bildes, wo es absolut dunkel ist. Ein Druck baut sich auf. Das ist unglaublich. Einen ähnlichen, intuitiv entstandenen Effekt gibt es auch bei »Las Meninas« von Velázquez im Prado in Madrid. Auf dem größten Teil des Bildes ist absolut nichts, ein leerer Raum. Doch das ist das stärkste Moment dieser Malerei. Ja, das ist ein wichtiges Thema: „Wie funktioniert die Vergangenheit, wenn der

Künstler intuitiv einen Platz ohne Sujet für diese Vergangenheit frei lässt?"

Eine Leerstelle.

Eine leere Stelle, ja.

Auch für die Imagination, damit man spürt, das da etwas ist, ein Geheimnis, ein anderer Raum?

Eine Reserve. Auch in der Musik gibt es bei großen Komponisten viele leere Elemente als Reserven.

Und die Leere ist dann quasi auch das Mittel, um das, was an die Leere grenzt, wieder zu definieren, aber vieldeutig zu definieren, oder? Die Leere ist also nicht einfach ohne Sinn, sondern sie generiert indirekt auch wieder Sinn.

Ja absolut. Die Bedeutung von Caravaggios Sujets ist heute verschwunden; auch seine Technik ist nicht so interessant. Aber diese Reserve – die Leere oder das dunkle Nichts – das funktioniert auch heute noch.

Das ist auch beim späten Cézanne sehr eindrücklich, ich meine seine weißen Leinwandflecke. Der einzelne Farbfleck bedeutet für sich nichts, aber mit dem Weiß zusammen wird er zum Haus, zum Baum, kann alles werden. Das gilt besonders für die Aquarelle.

Ja, das Unfertige.

Er kann alles werden und ist gleichzeitig Fragment.

Das Prinzip des Unvollendeten ist auch sehr interessant. Das funktioniert auch bei Toulouse-Lautrec.

Bei Toulouse-Lautrec besteht auch eine Verbindung zur ostasiatischen Malerei, für die das Weiß eine große Rolle spielte.

Aber kommen wir noch einmal auf dein Sprechen zurück, das nie zu seinem Ziel kommt, sondern ein Kreisen ist, ein Vorwärts- und Zurückgehen, das dabei immer etwas offen lässt. Du hast das ausgeführt. Es geht dabei wie bei den Bildern mit dem Doppelblick auch um Bewegung, hier als Prozess des Sprechens und Lesens. Und der Prozess hat selber zwar keine Bedeutung, aber als Erfahrungsweise macht er Sinn. Eine solche Erfahrung darf aber eigentlich nie abgeschlossen sein. Beim Sprechen und Lesen bekomme ich so die Ahnung einer Reserve, eines offenen Raumes. Aber wenn der Gedanke einmal ausgesprochen ist, die Idee gezeichnet oder gebaut ist, in einem Buch publiziert ist, dann ist sie fixiert und materialisiert. Dann ist sie wie eine Hülse, eine Schale oder wie ein Stück Müll, das zurückbleibt. Dein Werk stimuliert mich, diese Bewegung wie in einem Ritual immer weiterzuführen, um nicht bei den bloßen Hülsen stehen zu bleiben.

Zu diesem Prinzip gehören die unrealisierten Projekte. Es gibt die Idee, dass ein Mensch Talent und Kraft hat und mit einer Mission auf die Welt kommt, um etwas Wertvolles zu realisieren. Dieses Resultat stellt dann den Höhepunkt seiner langen und schweren Beschäftigung dar. Ein gutes Resultat ist wie ein guter Bau. Es gibt das Prinzip, dass man in diese Welt geboren wird, um einen wichtigen Bau zu machen. Das ideale Beispiel dafür ist Leonardo da Vinci, der die »Mona Lisa« schuf.

Dazu gibt es ein Alternativprinzip: „Unrealisierte Projekte". Die zweite Figur der Renaissance ist Michelangelo. Er ist das beste Beispiel des Verlierers. Michelangelo machte viele gigantische Projekte, die nie realisiert wurden; zum Beispiel das Grabmal für Papst Julius. Aber er war deswegen nicht so traurig. Das ist für mich eine gute Metapher, um das System zu erklären: Wir kommen auf diese Welt; doch was wir hier machen, verstehen wir nicht. Wir beginnen zu leben und unsere Arbeiten zu realisieren, aber am Ende haben wir noch immer nicht verstanden, welche Rolle dieses kleine Fragment, unsere Tätigkeit, spielt.

Das ist wie bei einem Zug. Wir erreichen mit dem Zug eine Station und steigen aus, aber der Zug geht weiter und wir kennen weder den Fahrplan noch die Anschlüsse. Das ist ein interessantes Prinzip: Es gibt einen riesigen Zirkel, und wir sind nur ein Fragment, ein kleiner Teil davon. Wir verstehen nicht, wo der Anfang dieses Zirkels ist, was mit uns und mit unseren Werken geschieht. Unser Schicksal ist nur ein Segment des Bogens, aber nicht der ganze Zirkel. Darum gibt es Unbekanntes in der Vergangenheit und in der Zukunft. Das Schicksal des Menschen und seiner Werke ist im Prinzip sehr fragmentarisch. Deshalb besteht eine Reserve für das Gedächtnis der Vergangenheit und für die Vorstellung von der Zukunft. Jeder Mensch und jeder Künstler hat dasselbe Schicksal. Michelangelo ist dafür ein gutes Beispiel.

Ein ewiges Scheitern?

Immer wieder neu probieren.

Im Bereich des sprachlichen Denkens, das sehr logisch funktioniert, ist man doch auch ein Stück weit gefangen. Man kommt nicht zu dieser Erfahrung des Fragmentarischen, weil man im Raum der Sprachlogik gefangen ist. Kleist hat ein alternatives Modell vorgeschlagen, um aus dem Sprachsystem menschlicher Endlichkeit herauszukommen: dass man in einem unabschließbaren Bewusstseinsprozess stets von einem Paradox zum nächsten fortschreiten solle. Und mir ist aufgefallen, dass du in diesem Gespräch sehr oft paradoxe Bilder formuliert hast und sogar von einer paradoxalen Logik des Lebens gesprochen hast. Siehst du die Produktion von Paradoxen auch als eine Möglichkeit, die endliche Sprache auf eine Unendlichkeit hin zu öffnen?

Nur diese – nur diese. Aber was mich am Barock interessiert, das ist die große Erfahrung mit dem Kosmos. Michelangelo und Caravaggio arbeiteten mit kosmischen Konstruktionen. Sie verstanden, dass es am Ende dieser Welt eine geheime andere, kosmische Dimension gibt. In der Sixtinischen Kapelle sieht man Figuren, die wie Kosmonauten zu dir geflogen kommen – der Effekt des Fliegens.

Das bringt mich zum Schluss auf ein solches Paradox. So wie du dein gesamtes Werk aufbaust, so wie du sprichst und schreibst, das ist alles eine Erzählung, narrativ, freilich auf eine besondere Weise. Wir haben davon gesprochen. Eine Art Roman, der – so mein Paradox – von einem „Luftmenschen im Kellerloch" geschrieben wurde. Man ist einerseits in einem Raum gefangen, in einer Situation, in einem Körper oder in einem Denken und gleichzeitig hat man die Perspektive von oben – eben aus der Luft.

Man braucht einen Aufstieg. Er funktioniert wie eine vertikale Bewegung, wie ein Luftballon. Denn das Leben ist ein tiefer Brunnen. Oben hat er einen Ausgang, in der vertikalen Bewegung. Jedes gute Werk funktioniert wie ein Aufzug. Alle guten Sachen, in der Kunst oder in der Literatur, funktionieren wie ein Luftzug. Du liest, und dann zieht dich eine unbekannte vertikale Kraft hinauf wie durch einen Lufttunnel. Und natürlich gibt es viele Werke, die dich hinunter drücken. In den klassischen Werken ist das unter Kontrolle, in ihnen ist ein großer vertikaler Zug, viel Luft.

Ich lese jeden Abend vor dem Schlafen Pasternak, nicht viel, drei, vier verschiedene Gedichte. Das ist so gesund, eine Therapie. Er spricht über nichts, das Leben ist sehr trivial. Er war naiv und lebte als einfacher Mann. Aber die Wirkung seiner Poesie ist wie eine große vertikale Luftpumpe, die nach oben geht. Immer, in jedem Werk. Kein Druck. Wenn er über Tragik spricht oder über Sehnsüchte, ist das Resultat dieser Poesie immer viel Luft. Das ist eine gute Therapie.

Atmen, Sauerstoff.

Das gleicht aus, gibt einen guten Atem. Pasternak hatte im Prinzip eine sehr pessimistische Sicht des Lebens. Trotzdem fühlte er eine große „Luftwelt" im Leben und besaß – als weitere Qualität – große Flügel. Er flog. Das ist die Idee einer Reserve, eines Luftreservoirs oder des Himmels. Der Himmel ist, metaphorisch gesprochen, geschenkte Energie, eine Reserve, wohin man für ein freies Schweben fliegen kann. Aber das ist ein großes Thema: „Das Fliegen, die Kosmonauten, das Kosmische". Boris Groys hat das in seinem Buch »Der Mensch, der aus seinem Zimmer in den Kosmos flog« behandelt. Kollektive Träume: „Verlasst unsere Erde, dort ist nicht genug Platz zum Leben."

Sie ist zu eng.

Das ist interessant, denn darin besteht ein großer Kontrast zur Mentalität der Amerikaner. Warum? Weil man hier sehr komfortabel lebt. Die Leute von hier meinen: „Das ist unsere Erde, und wir sind die Menschen auf der Erde." Sie kommen nicht für eine Tragik auf die Welt, sondern um zu leben. Die Erde ist zum Leben da, ganz einfach. Kein Stoizismus wie in England zum Beispiel, auch nicht wie die Romantik in Deutschland, die meinte, die Erde sei nicht zum Leben, sondern für das Leiden da. Das gilt besonders auch für die Russen – dort ist das Zentrum des Leidens. (Lachen)

Für die Amerikaner ist das kein Problem: „Ich wurde geboren und ich bin glücklich." Die Erde ist ein Platz für die Menschen. Das ist unikal. Keine Ideologie und keine Religion von einer anderen Welt. Die andere Welt ist diese Welt. Sehr einfach.

Eine reale Utopie.

Eine reale Utopie. Das gefällt mir sehr. Aber trotzdem habe ich keine Kontakte. (Lachen) Ich bin ein Kosmonaut, aber auf einem guten Planeten.

Annotations to the Catalogue Raisonné
Erläuterungen zum Werkverzeichnis

Explanatory Notes on the Catalogue Raisonné of Artist's Books

Numbering and Sequence

This oeuvre catalogue of Ilya Kabakov's artist's books encompasses 137 works dating from between 1958 and 2008, catalogued in chronological order according to publication date. There was no artist's book published in 2009.

Criteria for Inclusion

All publications in whose design the artist was directly involved have been included in this catalogue. Distinctions must be made here between idea, concept, and layout. Also included in the catalogue are books to which Ilya Kabakov contributed as text author, even where he was not involved in the design. A further criterion is a minimum edition of two.

Technical Data

The technical data refer to the title, year of publication, editor, place of publication, publishing company, dimensions (of cover), number of pages, number of illustrations (black-and-white and color illustrations separately), and type of binding.

Edition

The number of editions and the number of copies per edition are included in cases where these figures are given in the publication's edition notice. Special editions containing signed and dated freehand drawings by the artist are listed separately. The editions of the early samizdat publications generally consisted of ten copies.

Genres

Distinctions are made between the following genres: samizdat (books published by the author himself in small editions during the Soviet period), exhibition catalogue, thematic publication, oeuvre catalogue, libretto.

Information on Content

In the case of exhibition catalogues, the exhibition title, place, and date are mentioned. Exhibition catalogues on installations generally consist of texts, studies, and plans; thematic publications serving as documentations of installations bearing the same title moreover include photos of the works executed and commentaries. This standard information has been omitted in the oeuvre catalogue for reasons of space. The names of the text authors and the languages are also given. In the case of Kabakov texts used repeatedly, the titles and places are noted.
Brief information is provided on the contents of the theoretical and literary books. The information on the contents of the Russian samizdat publications is based on information provided orally by the artist.

References

With regard to references, the catalogue numbers of those artist's books are given in which the same texts, or parts thereof, were reused. Where the same text also appears in an installation, reference is made to the catalogue raisonné of the installations. In publications about installations or paintings, reference is likewise made to the respective catalogues raisonnés.

Abbreviations

b/w = black and white / *schwarz-weiss*
cm = centimeter / *Zentimeter*
col. = color / *Farbe*
CRI = Ilya Kabakov: Installations 1983–2000, Catalogue Raisonné, 2 vols., ed. Toni Stooss (Düsseldorf: Richter Verlag, 2003).
CRP = Ilya Kabakov: Paintings / *Gemälde* 1957–2008, Catalogue Raisonné, 2 vols., ed. Renate Petzinger and/ *und* Emilia Kabakov, Museum Wiesbaden (Bielefeld: Kerber Verlag, 2008).
ed. = editor / *Herausgeber*
ill./ills. = illustrations / *Abbildung(en)*
cat. = catalogue / *Katalog*
no./nos. = number(s) / *Nummer*
p./pp. = page(s) / *Seite(n)*
vol./vols. = volume(s) / *Band (Bände)*

Bibliography

The bibliography at the end of the catalogue raisonné encompasses publications to which Ilya Kabakov contributed neither in the role of author nor in the role of conceiver and/or designer.

Matthias Haldemann and
Nicole Seeberger

Erläuterungen zum Werkverzeichnis der Künstlerbücher

Nummerierung und Reihenfolge

Das vorliegende Werkverzeichnis von Ilya Kabakovs Künstlerbüchern umfasst 137 Nummern von 1958 bis 2008. Die chronologische Reihenfolge richtet sich nach dem Erscheinungsdatum. 2009 erschien kein Künstlerbuch.

Aufnahmekriterien

Es sind alle die Publikationen aufgenommen, bei denen der Künstler direkt an der Gestaltung beteiligt war; dabei ist zu unterscheiden zwischen Idee, Konzept und Layout. Verzeichnet sind auch jene Bücher, deren Textautor Ilya Kabakov ist, selbst wenn er bei der Gestaltung nicht mitwirkte. Ein weiteres Kriterium ist eine Mindestauflage von zwei Exemplaren.

Technische Angaben

Die technischen Angaben beziehen sich auf Titel, Erscheinungsjahr, Herausgeber, Erscheinungsort, Verlag, Maße (Umschlaggröße), Anzahl der Seiten und der Abbildungen (schwarz-weiße und farbige getrennt), Bindungsart.

Edition / Auflage

Die Auflagenzahl und Auflagenhöhe werden aufgeführt, wenn sie im Impressum der Publikation genannt sind. Vorzugsausgaben mit einer signierten und datierten Orignialzeichnung des Künstlers sind gesondert erfasst. Die Auflage der frühen Samisdat-Publikationen beträgt in der Regel zehn Exemplare.

Gattungen

Als Gattungen werden unterschieden: Samisdat (im Selbstverlag während der Sowjetzeit erschienene Publikationen in kleiner Auflage), Ausstellungskatalog, thematische Publikation, Werkverzeichnis, Libretto.

Inhaltsangaben

Bei Ausstellungskatalogen sind Ausstellungstitel, -ort und Datum erwähnt. Ausstellungskataloge über Installationen bestehen in der Regel aus Texten, Entwürfen und Plänen; thematische Publikationen als Dokumentationen gleichnamiger Installationen beinhalten zudem auch Fotos der ausgeführten Werke und Kommentare. Auf diese Standardangaben wurde im Werkkatalog aus Platzgründen verzichtet. Des Weiteren sind die Namen der Textautoren und die Sprachen aufgeführt. Bei Kabakov-Texten, die mehrfach verwendet wurden, sind jeweils die Titel und Orte aufgeführt.

Kurze Inhaltsangaben werden zu theoretischen oder literarischen Büchern gemacht. Die Inhaltsangaben zu russischen Samisdat-Publikationen beruhen auf mündlichen Mitteilungen des Künstlers.

Verweise

Bei den Verweisen sind die Katalognummern jener Künstlerbücher aufgeführt, in denen dieselben Texte, oder Teile davon, wiederverwendet wurden. Tritt derselbe Text auch in einer Installation auf, erfolgt ein Verweis auf das Werkverzeichnis der Installationen. Bei Publikationen über Installationen oder Gemälde wird ebenfalls auf die entsprechenden Werkverzeichnisse verwiesen.

Abkürzungen

b/w = black and white / *schwarz-weiß*
cm = centimeter / *Zentimeter*
col. = color / *Farbe*
CRI = Ilya Kabakov, Installations 1983–2000, Catalogue Raisonné, 2 Vols., Ed. Toni Stooss, Richter Verlag, Düsseldorf 2003.
CRP = Ilya Kabakov, Paintings / *Gemälde* 1957–2008, Catalogue Raisonné, 2 Vols., Ed. Renate Petzinger and / *und* Emilia Kabakov, Museum Wiesbaden, Kerber Verlag, Bielefeld 2008.
Ed. = Editor / *Herausgeber*
Ill./ills. = illustrations / *Abbildung(en)*
Kat. = Catalog / *Katalog*
No./Nos. = number(s) / *Nummer*
p./pp. = page(s) / *Seite(n)*
Vol./Vols. = Volume(s) / *Band (Bände)*

Literaturverzeichnis

Das Literaturverzeichnis im Anschluss an den Werkkatalog umfasst Publikationen, die von Ilya Kabakov weder als Autor verfasst noch von ihm konzipiert und/oder gestaltet wurden.

Matthias Haldemann und
Nicole Seeberger

1 A Sea of Thoughts | *Ein Meer von Gedanken*

1958

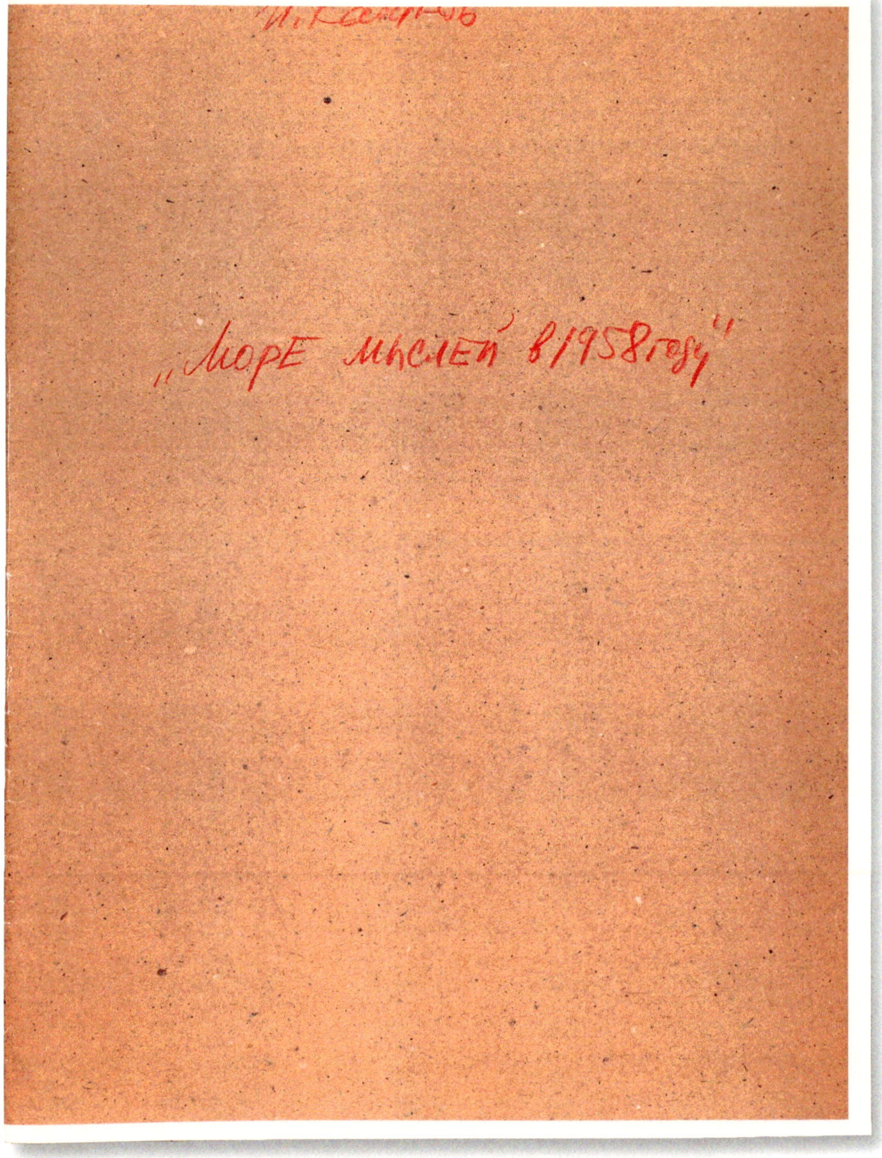

Ilya Kabakov
Moscow: published by the author
28 x 21.8 cm
27 pp.
loose sheets, cardboard cover
lose Blätter, Kartonumschlag
edition: 10 copies

thematic publication | *thematische Publikation*

layout by Ilya Kabakov | *Layout von Ilya Kabakov*

Kabakov's notes, numbered in the margin and cataloged; Russian.

Notizen Kabakovs, am Rand mit einer Nummer gekennzeichnet und katalogisiert; russisch.

see also | *siehe auch*

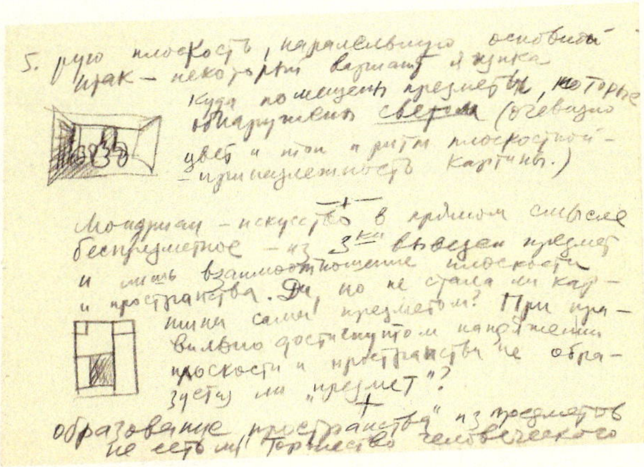

5. [illegible] плоскость, параллельную основной [illegible] – некоторый вариант [illegible]
куда помещены предметы, которые обнаружены сверху (очевидно цвет и [illegible] и ритм плоскостей – принадлежность картины.)

Мондриан – искусство в прямом смысле беспредметное – из 3-ки выведен предмет и лишь взаимоотношение плоскости и пространства. Да, но не стала ли картина сама предметом? При правильно достигнутом напряжении плоскости и пространства не образуется ли „предмет"?

образование „пространства" из предметов не есть ли торжество человеческого

14. Особенностью Рембрандтовских картин является присутствие тела, которого сейчас нет в картине. Он вне картины или [illegible]? (Близость к Сикстинской мадонне.)
анатомия.
смотрит
Д-р
„полость для „X".

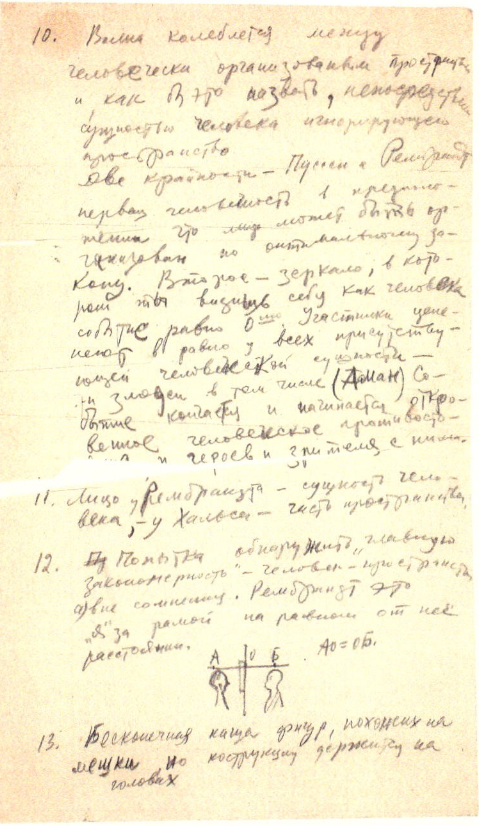

10. [illegible] колеблется между человечески организованным пространством и как бы это назвать, непосредственным существом человека игнорирующего пространство
Две крайности – Пуссен и Рембрандт
первая человечность [illegible] может быть [illegible] организован по оптимальному [illegible]. Второе – зеркало, в котором ты видишь себя как человека [illegible] Участника [illegible] у всех присутствующих человеческой сущности – и злодеи в том числе (Аман) [illegible] контакту и начинается [illegible] человеческое противостояние [illegible] героев и зрителя с [illegible]

11. Лицо у Рембрандта – сущность человека, – у Хальса – часть пространства.

12. Попытка обнаружить „главную закономерность" – человек – пространство [illegible]. Рембрандт это „Я" за рамой на равном от нее расстоянии.
А О Б
АО = ОБ.

13. Бесконечная каша фигур, похожих на мешки, но конструкцию держит на головах

2 Today is July 4, 1977... | *Heute ist der 4. Juli 1977...*

1977

Ilya Kabakov
Moscow: published by the author
30 x 21.9 cm
9 pp.
staplebound, cardboard cover
Drahtheftung, Kartonumschlag
edition: 10 copies

thematic publication | *thematische Publikation*

layout by Ilya Kabakov | *Layout von Ilya Kabakov*

Reflecting and drawing some conclusions on July 4, 1977, Kabakov sees himself at the high point of his life to date; Russian.

Kabakov zieht am 4. Juli 1977 ein Fazit und sieht sich auf dem Höhepunkt seines bisherigen Lebens; russisch.

see also | *siehe auch*

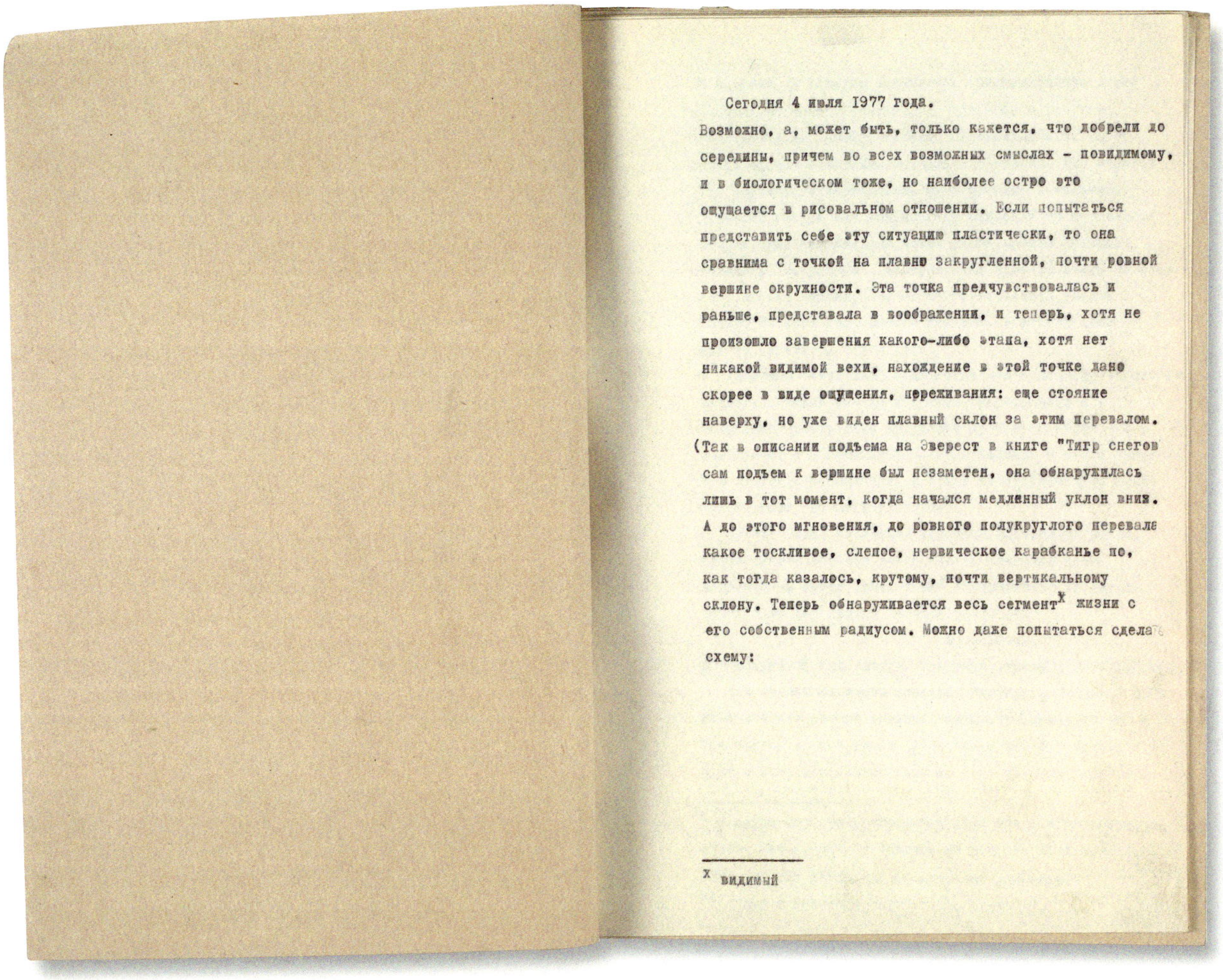

Сегодня 4 июля 1977 года.

Возможно, а, может быть, только кажется, что добрели до середины, причем во всех возможных смыслах - повидимому, и в биологическом тоже, но наиболее остро это ощущается в рисовальном отношении. Если попытаться представить себе эту ситуацию пластически, то она сравнима с точкой на плавно закругленной, почти ровной вершине окружности. Эта точка предчувствовалась и раньше, представала в воображении, и теперь, хотя не произошло завершения какого-либо этапа, хотя нет никакой видимой вехи, нахождение в этой точке дано скорее в виде ощущения, переживания: еще стояние наверху, но уже виден плавный склон за этим перевалом. (Так в описании подъема на Эверест в книге "Тигр снегов сам подъем к вершине был незаметен, она обнаружилась лишь в тот момент, когда начался медленный уклон вниз. А до этого мгновения, до ровного полукруглого перевала какое тоскливое, слепое, нервическое карабканье по, как тогда казалось, крутому, почти вертикальному склону. Теперь обнаруживается весь сегмент[x] жизни с его собственным радиусом. Можно даже попытаться сделать схему:

---

[x] видимый

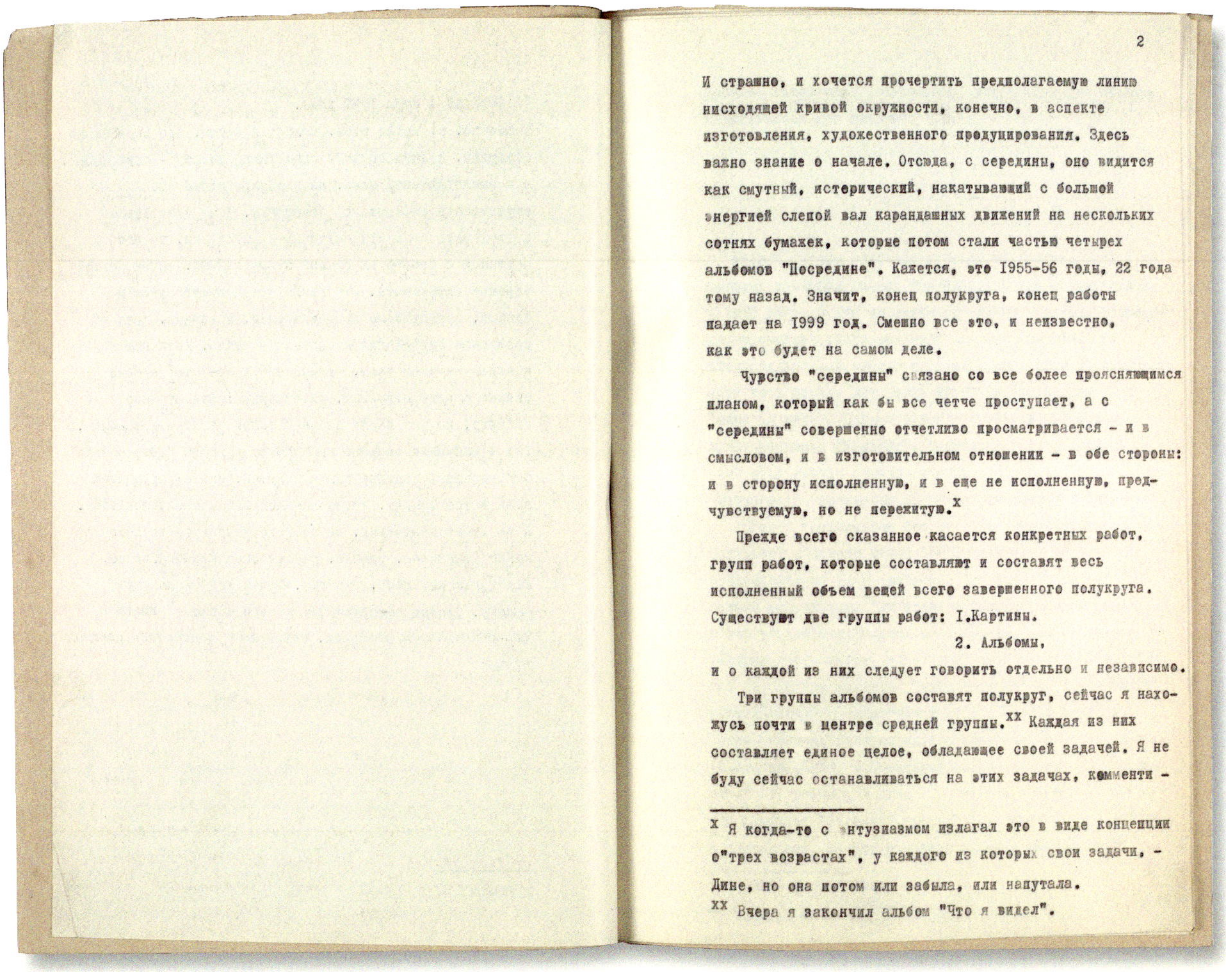

2

И страшно, и хочется прочертить предполагаемую линию нисходящей кривой окружности, конечно, в аспекте изготовления, художественного продуцирования. Здесь важно знание о начале. Отсюда, с середины, оно видится как смутный, истерический, накатывавший с большой энергией слепой вал карандашных движений на нескольких сотнях бумажек, которые потом стали частью четырех альбомов "Посредине". Кажется, это 1955-56 годы, 22 года тому назад. Значит, конец полукруга, конец работы падает на 1999 год. Смешно все это, и неизвестно, как это будет на самом деле.

Чувство "середины" связано со все более проясняющимся планом, который как бы все четче проступает, а с "середины" совершенно отчетливо просматривается - и в смысловом, и в изготовительном отношении - в обе стороны: и в сторону исполненную, и в еще не исполненную, предчувствуемую, но не пережитую.[x]

Прежде всего сказанное касается конкретных работ, групп работ, которые составляют и составят весь исполненный объем вещей всего завершенного полукруга. Существуют две группы работ: I.Картины.

2. Альбомы,

и о каждой из них следует говорить отдельно и независимо.

Три группы альбомов составят полукруг, сейчас я нахожусь почти в центре средней группы.[xx] Каждая из них составляет единое целое, обладающее своей задачей. Я не буду сейчас останавливаться на этих задачах, комменти -

---

[x] Я когда-то с энтузиазмом излагал это в виде концепции о"трех возрастах", у каждого из которых свои задачи, - Дине, но она потом или забыла, или напутала.

[xx] Вчера я закончил альбом "Что я видел".

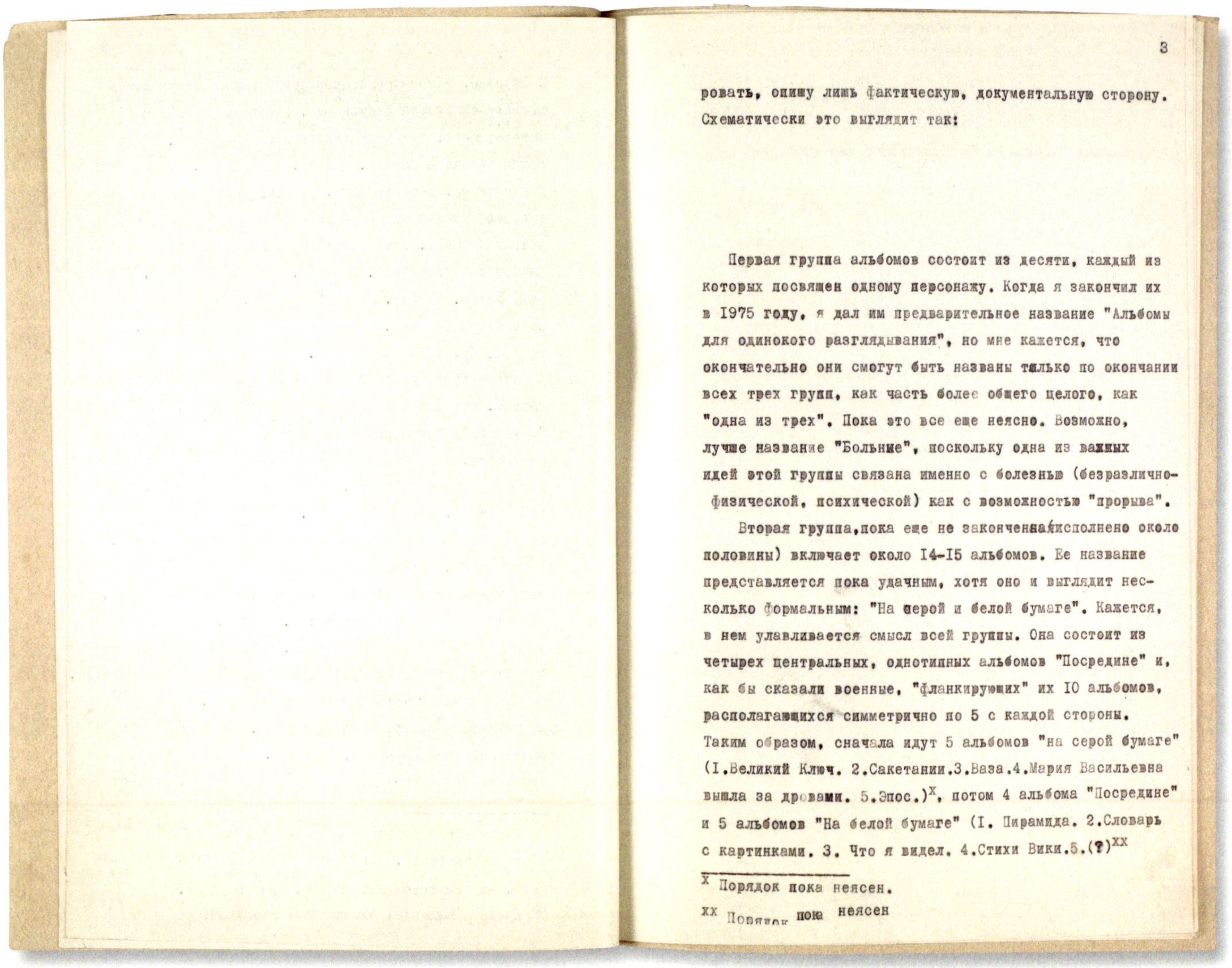

3

ровать, опишу лишь фактическую, документальную сторону. Схематически это выглядит так:

Первая группа альбомов состоит из десяти, каждый из которых посвящен одному персонажу. Когда я закончил их в 1975 году, я дал им предварительное название "Альбомы для одинокого разглядывания", но мне кажется, что окончательно они смогут быть названы тлько по окончании всех трех групп, как часть более общего целого, как "одна из трех". Пока это все еще неясно. Возможно, лучше название "Больные", поскольку одна из важных идей этой группы связана именно с болезнью (безразлично-физической, психической) как с возможностью "прорыва".

Вторая группа, пока еще не закончена (исполнено около половины) включает около 14–15 альбомов. Ее название представляется пока удачным, хотя оно и выглядит несколько формальным: "На серой и белой бумаге". Кажется, в нем улавливается смысл всей группы. Она состоит из четырех центральных, однотипных альбомов "Посредине" и, как бы сказали военные, "фланкирующих" их 10 альбомов, располагающихся симметрично по 5 с каждой стороны. Таким образом, сначала идут 5 альбомов "на серой бумаге" (1. Великий Ключ. 2. Сакетании. 3. Ваза. 4. Мария Васильевна вышла за дровами. 5. Эпос.)[x], потом 4 альбома "Посредине" и 5 альбомов "На белой бумаге" (1. Пирамида. 2. Словарь с картинками. 3. Что я видел. 4. Стихи Вики. 5. (?)[xx]

---

x Порядок пока неясен.

xx Порядок пока неясен

3 TEN Characters (Text of the Albums) | *ZEHN Charaktere (Text der Alben)*

1978

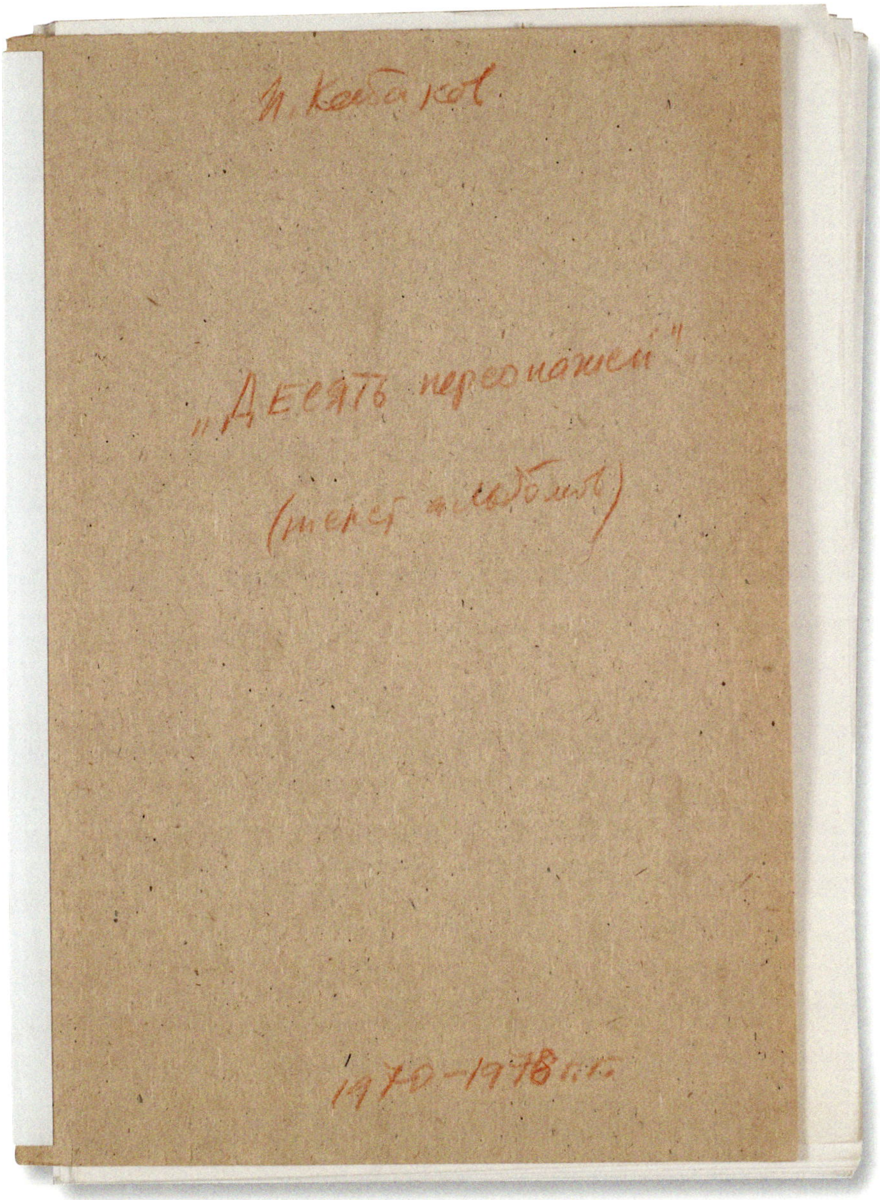

Ilya Kabakov
Moscow: published by the author
29.8 x 21.2 cm
63 pp.
quick bind, cardboard cover
Schnellhefter, Kartonumschlag
edition: 10 copies

thematic publication | *thematische Publikation*

layout by Ilya Kabakov | *Layout von Ilya Kabakov*

Texts for the series of albums entitled »10 Characters«; Russian.

Texte der Albumserie »10 Charaktere«; russisch.

see also | *siehe auch* no. 16; no. 21; no. 68; no. 100; CRI, vol. 1, no. 6, pp. 76–81

" ДЕСЯТЬ ПЕРСОНАЖЕЙ "

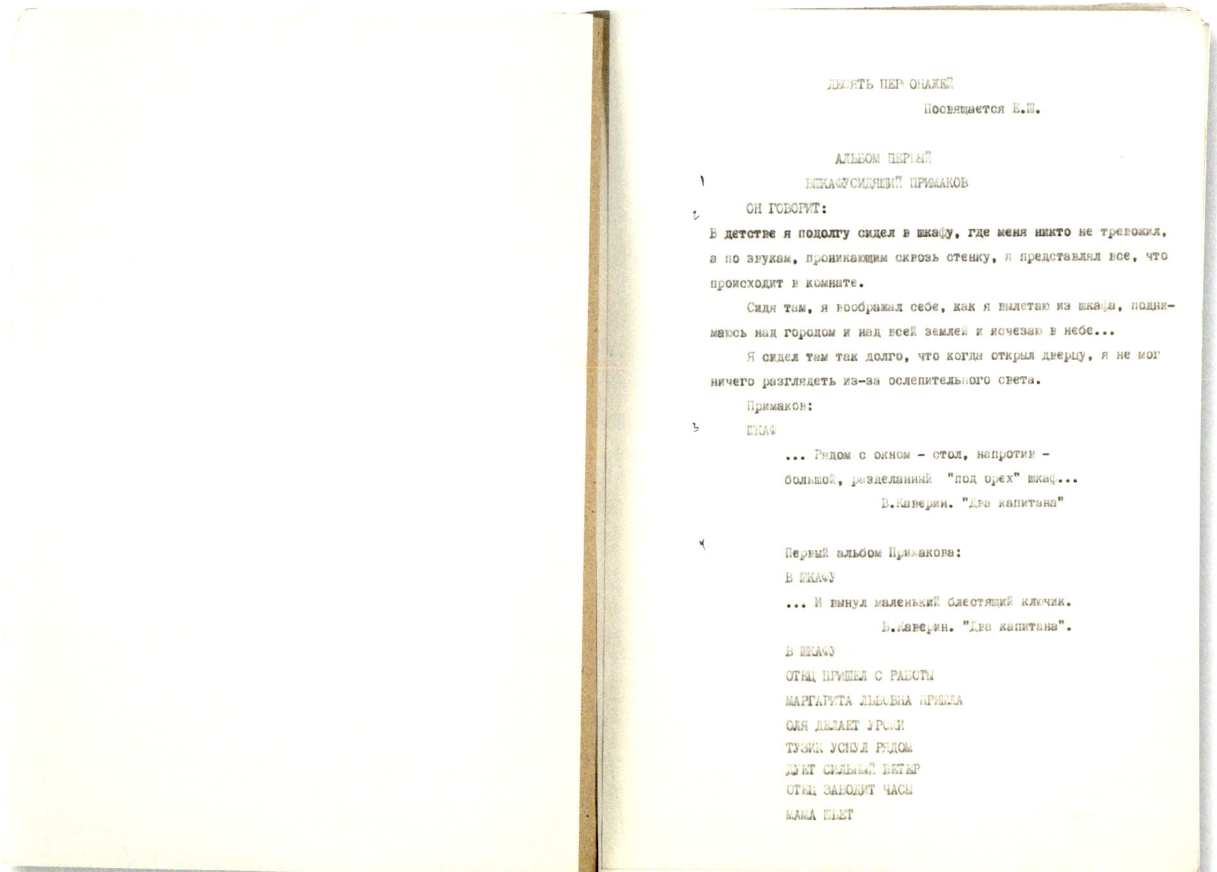

ДЕСЯТЬ ПЕРСОНАЖЕЙ

Посвящается Е.Ш.

АЛЬБОМ ПЕРВЫЙ

1 ШКАФУСИДЯЩИЙ ПРИМАКОВ

2 ОН ГОВОРИТ:

В детстве я подолгу сидел в шкафу, где меня никто не тревожил, а по звукам, проникающим сквозь стенку, я представлял все, что происходит в комнате.

Сидя там, я воображал себе, как я вылетаю из шкафа, поднимаюсь над городом и над всей землей и исчезаю в небе...

Я сидел там так долго, что когда открыл дверцу, я не мог ничего разглядеть из-за ослепительного света.

Примаков:

3 ШКАФ

... Рядом с окном - стол, напротив - большой, разделанный "под орех" шкаф...

В.Каверин. "Два капитана"

4 Первый альбом Примакова:

В ШКАФУ

... И вынул маленький блестящий ключик.

В.Каверин. "Два капитана".

В ШКАФУ

ОТЕЦ ПРИШЕЛ С РАБОТЫ

МАРГАРИТА ЛЬВОВНА ПРИШЛА

ОЛЯ ДЕЛАЕТ УРОКИ

ТУЗИК УСНУЛ РЯДОМ

ДУЕТ СИЛЬНЫЙ ВЕТЕР

ОТЕЦ ЗАВОДИТ ЧАСЫ

МАМА ШЬЕТ

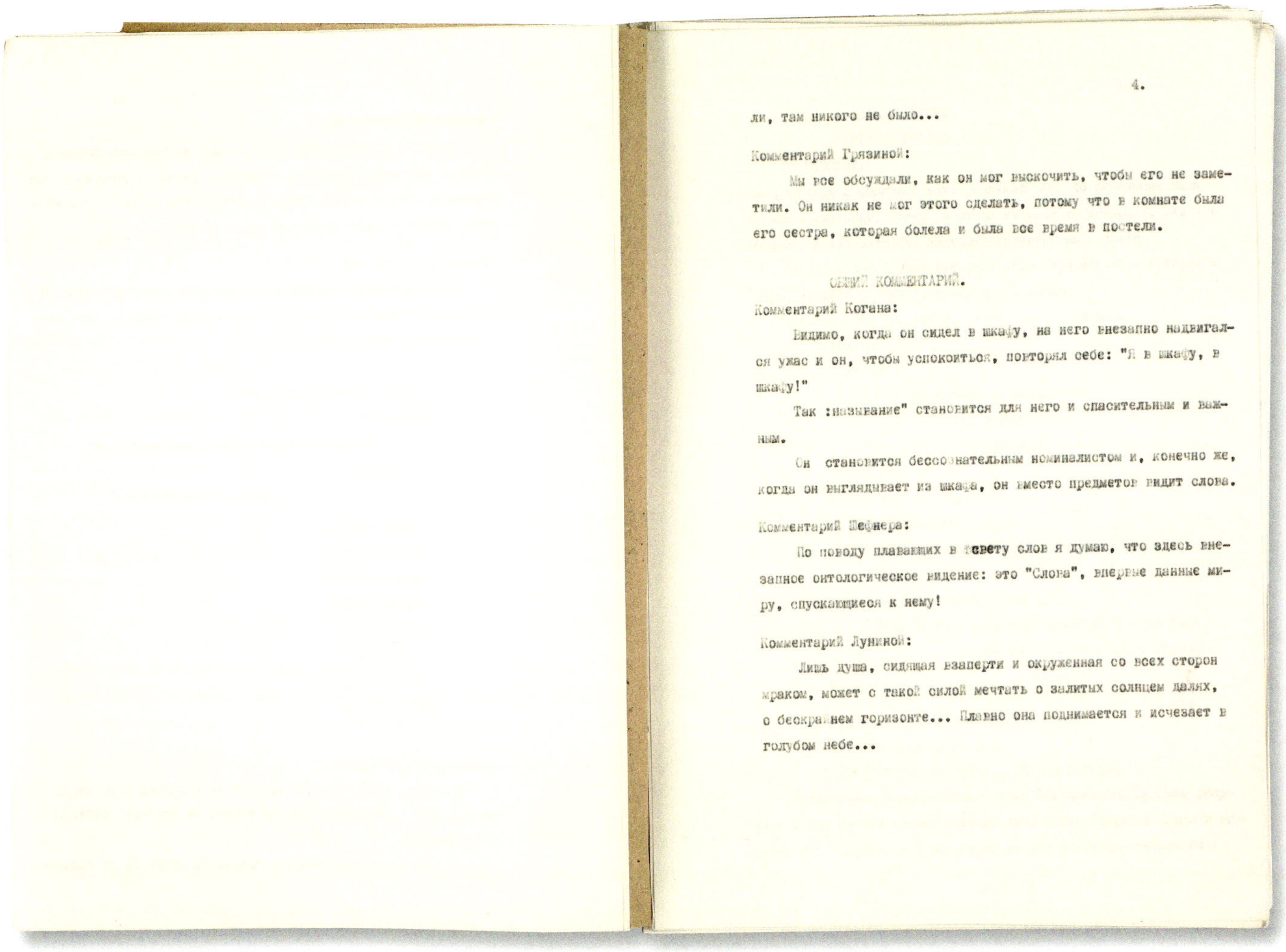

4.

ли, там никого не было...

Комментарий Грязиной:

Мы все обсуждали, как он мог выскочить, чтобы его не заметили. Он никак не мог этого сделать, потому что в комнате была его сестра, которая болела и была все время в постели.

ОБЩИЙ КОММЕНТАРИЙ.

Комментарий Когана:

Видимо, когда он сидел в шкафу, на него внезапно надвигался ужас и он, чтобы успокоиться, повторял себе: "Я в шкафу, в шкафу!"

Так :называние" становится для него и спасительным и важным.

Он становится бессознательным номиналистом и, конечно же, когда он выглядывает из шкафа, он вместо предметов видит слова.

Комментарий Шефнера:

По поводу плавающих в свету слов я думаю, что здесь внезапное онтологическое видение: это "Слова", впервые данные миру, спускающиеся к нему!

Комментарий Луниной:

Лишь душа, сидящая взаперти и окруженная со всех сторон мраком, может с такой силой мечтать о залитых солнцем далях, о бескрайнем горизонте... Плавно она поднимается и исчезает в голубом небе...

4 Rhombus | *Rhombus*

1980

Ilya Kabakov
Moscow: published by the author
30.2 x 21.3 cm
23 pp.
stapled, cardboard cover
Drahtheftung, Kartonumschlag
edition: 10 copies

thematic publication | *thematische Publikation*

layout by Ilya Kabakov | *Layout von Ilya Kabakov*

The positions held by the four artists Vladimir Yankilevsky, Erik Bulatov, Eduard Steinberg, and Ilya Kabakov represent for Kabakov the four principal trends that were prevalent in the Soviet art scene of the time; Russian.

Die Positionen der vier Künstler Wladimir Jankilewski, Erik Bulatov, Eduard Shteinberg und Ilya Kabakov repräsentieren für Kabakov die vier aktuellen Haupttendenzen der damaligen sowjetischen Kunstszene; russisch.

see also | *siehe auch*

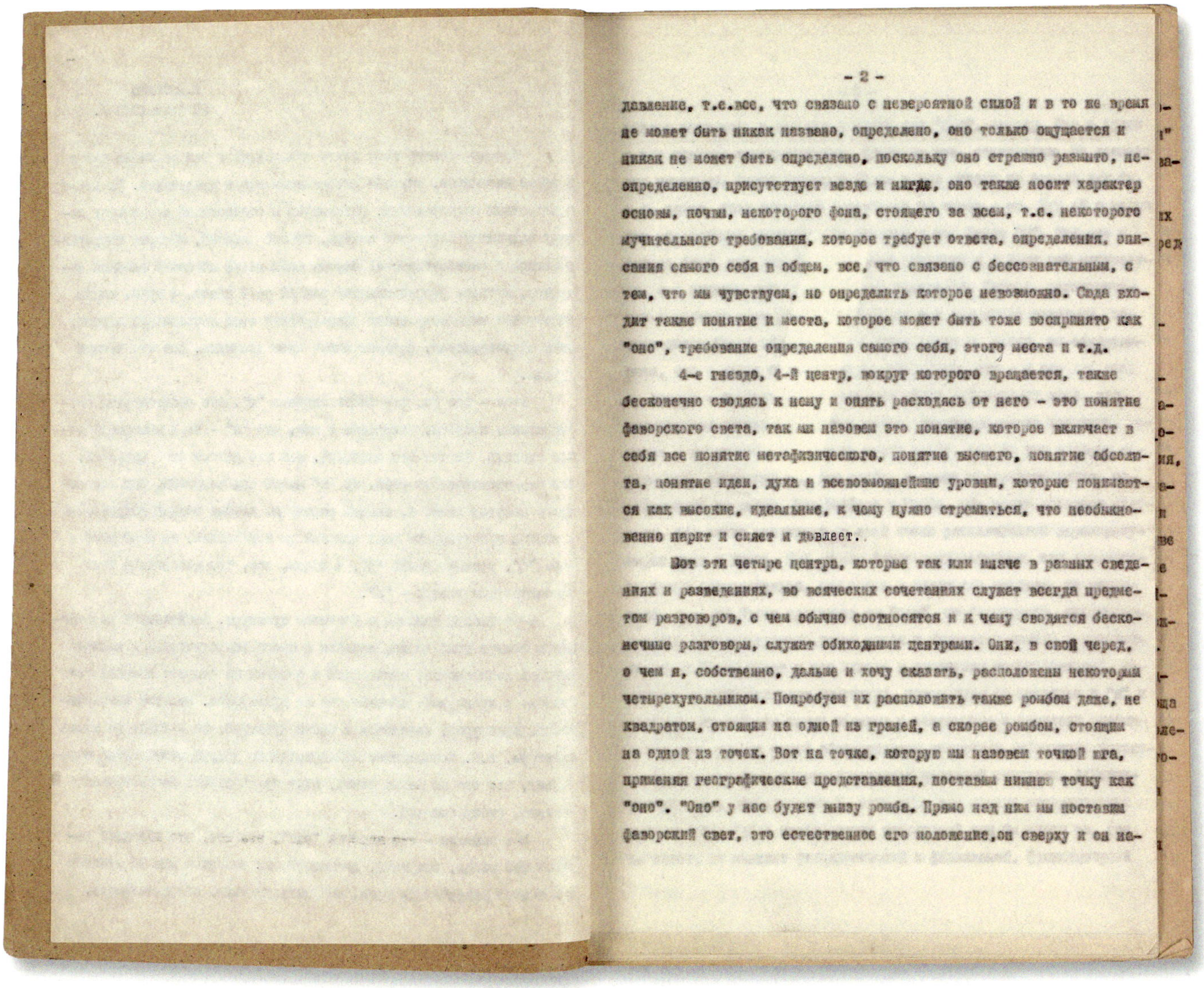

- 2 -

давление, т.е.все, что связано с невероятной силой и в то же время не может быть никак названо, определено, оно только ощущается и никак не может быть определено, поскольку оно страшно размыто, неопределенно, присутствует везде и нигде, оно также носит характер основы, почвы, некоторого фона, стоящего за всем, т.е. некоторого мучительного требования, которое требует ответа, определения, описания самого себя в общем, все, что связано с бессознательным, с тем, что мы чувствуем, но определить которое невозможно. Сюда входит также понятие и места, которое может быть тоже воспринято как "оно", требование определения самого себя, этого места и т.д.

4-е гнездо, 4-й центр, вокруг которого вращается, также бесконечно сводясь к нему и опять расходясь от него - это понятие фаворского света, так мы назовем это понятие, которое включает в себя все понятие метафизического, понятие высшего, понятие абсолюта, понятие идеи, духа и всевозможнейшие уровни, которые понимаются как высокие, идеальные, к чему нужно стремиться, что необыкновенно парит и сияет и довлеет.

Вот эти четыре центра, которые так или иначе в разных сведениях и разведениях, во всяческих сочетаниях служат всегда предметом разговоров, с чем обычно соотносятся и к чему сводятся бесконечные разговоры, служат обиходными центрами. Они, в свой черед, о чем я, собственно, дальше и хочу сказать, расположены некоторым четырехугольником. Попробуем их расположить также ромбом даже, не квадратом, стоящим на одной из граней, а скорее ромбом, стоящим на одной из точек. Вот на точке, которую мы назовем точкой юга, применяя географические представления, поставим нижнюю точку как "оно". "Оно" у нас будет внизу ромба. Прямо над ним мы поставим фаворский свет, это естественное его положение, он сверху и он на-

5 In our Shek | *In unserer Wohnungsverwaltung*

1981

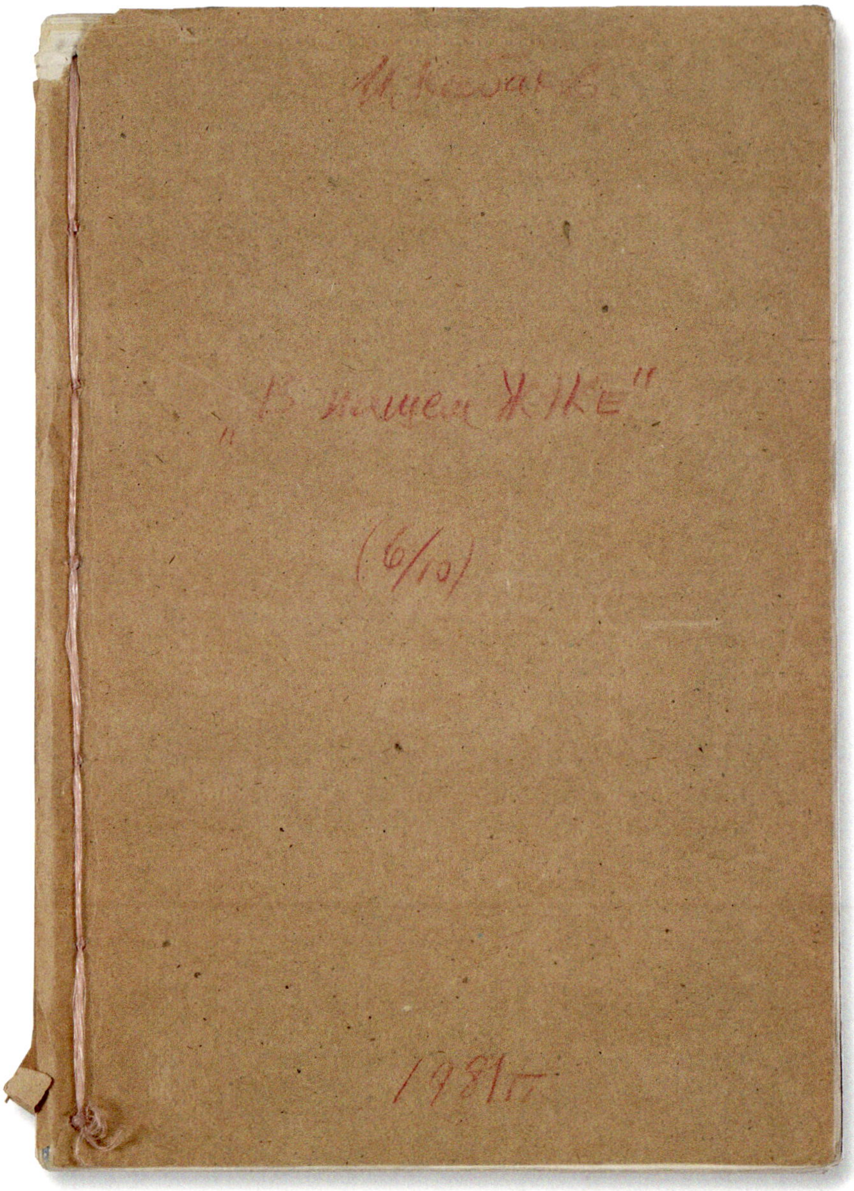

Ilya Kabakov
Moscow: published by the author
30.3 x 21.6 cm
184 pp. with 51 (5 color) ills.
seven punched holes, held together with a string, cardboard cover
sieben ausgestanzte Löcher, zusammengehalten mit einer Schnur, Kartonumschlag
edition: 10 copies

thematic publication | *thematische Publikation*

layout by Ilya Kabakov | *Layout von Ilya Kabakov*

A book portraying proponents of Moscow conceptualism and fictitious artists in the form of a fictitious propaganda pamphlet from the "SHEK," the residential management authority in a small urban residential area. Texts by Erik Bulatov, Ilya Kabakov, Oleg Vassilyev, and a dialogue between Erik Bulatov and Boris Groys on »The Existential Space in the Picture«; Russian.

Ein Buch mit Vertretern des Moskauer Konzeptualismus und fiktiven Künstlern in Form einer fiktiven Propagandabroschüre des „SHEK", der Wohnungsverwaltung eines kleinen städtischen Wohnbereichs. Texte von Erik Bulatov, Ilya Kabakov, Oleg Wassiljew und ein Dialog von Erik Bulatov und Boris Groys über »Der existentielle Raum des Bildes«; russisch.

see also | *siehe auch* no. 74

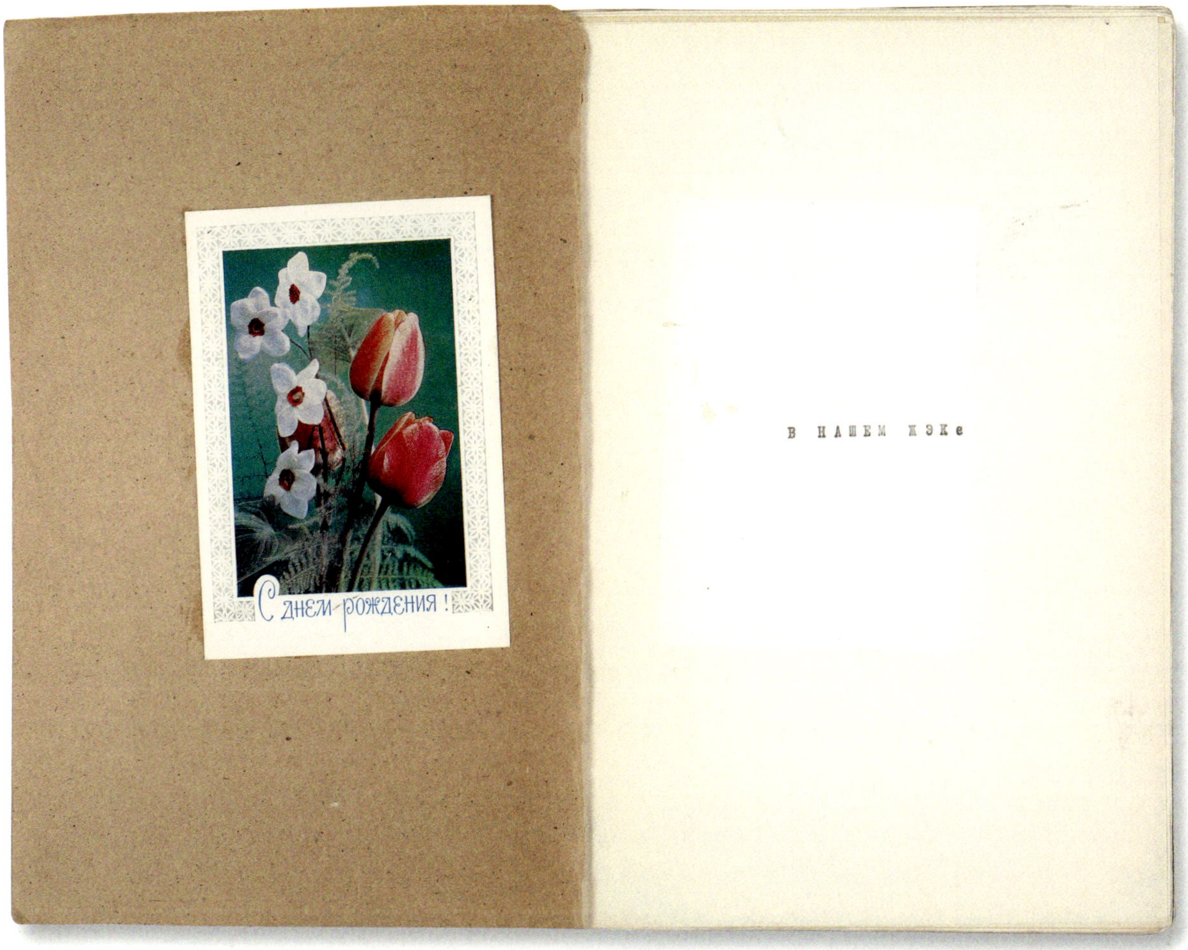
С днем рождения !
В НАШЕМ ЖЭКе

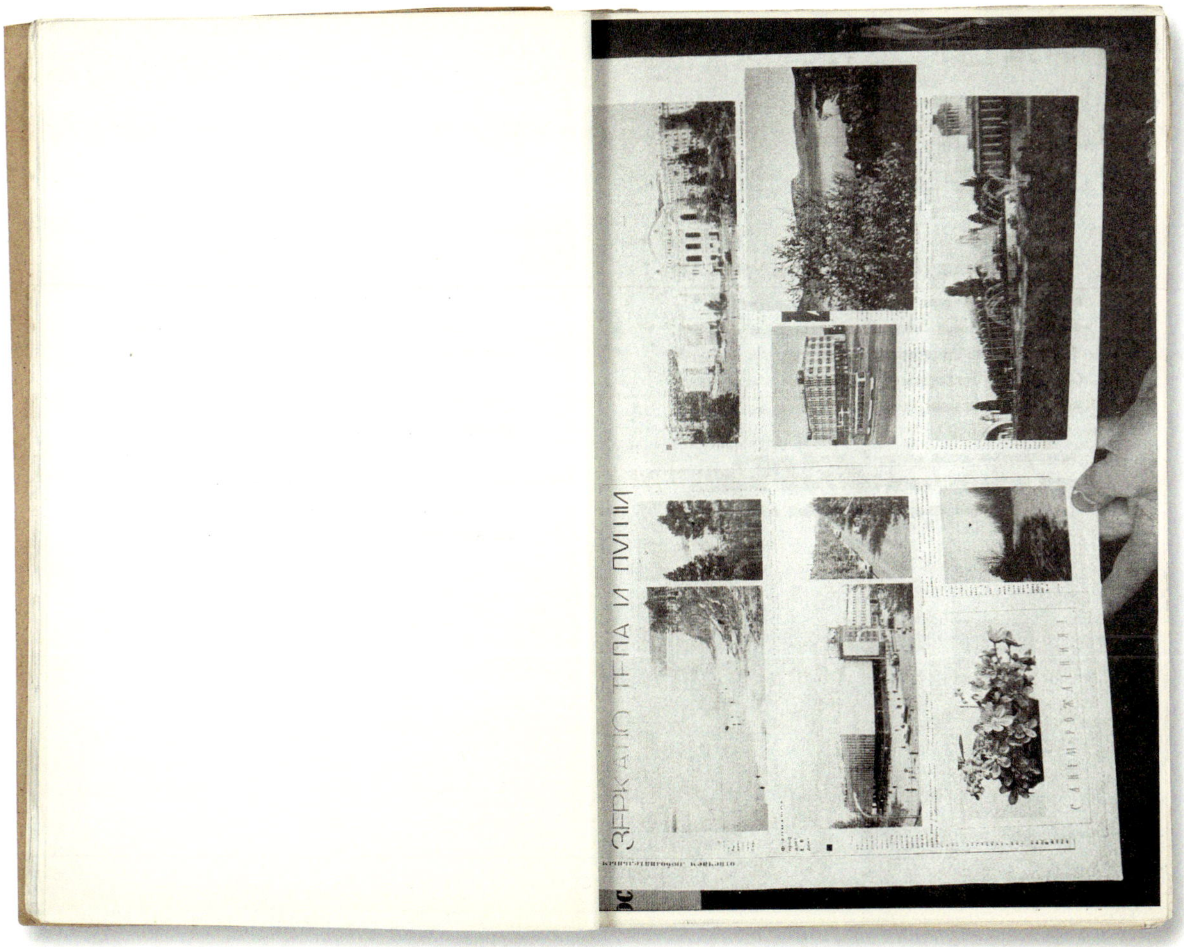

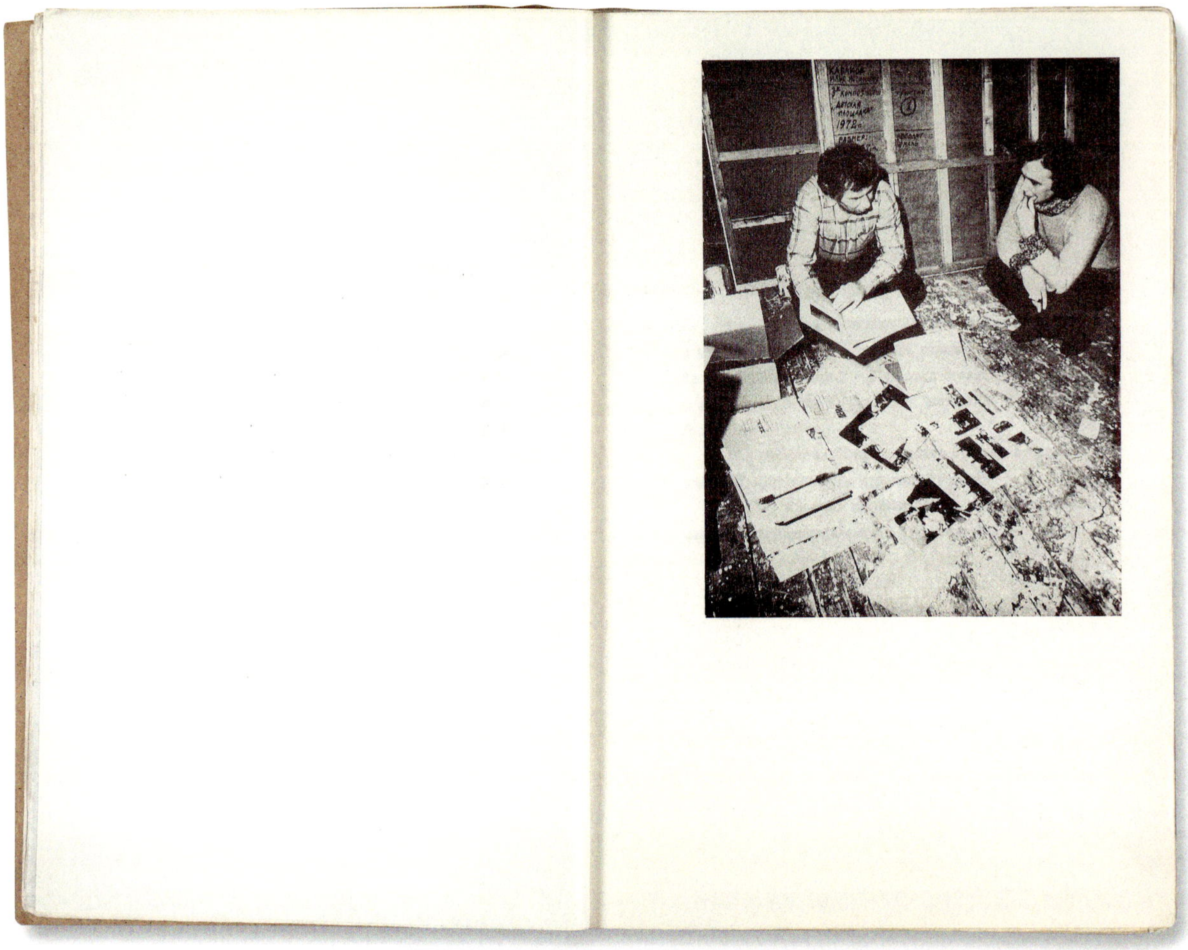

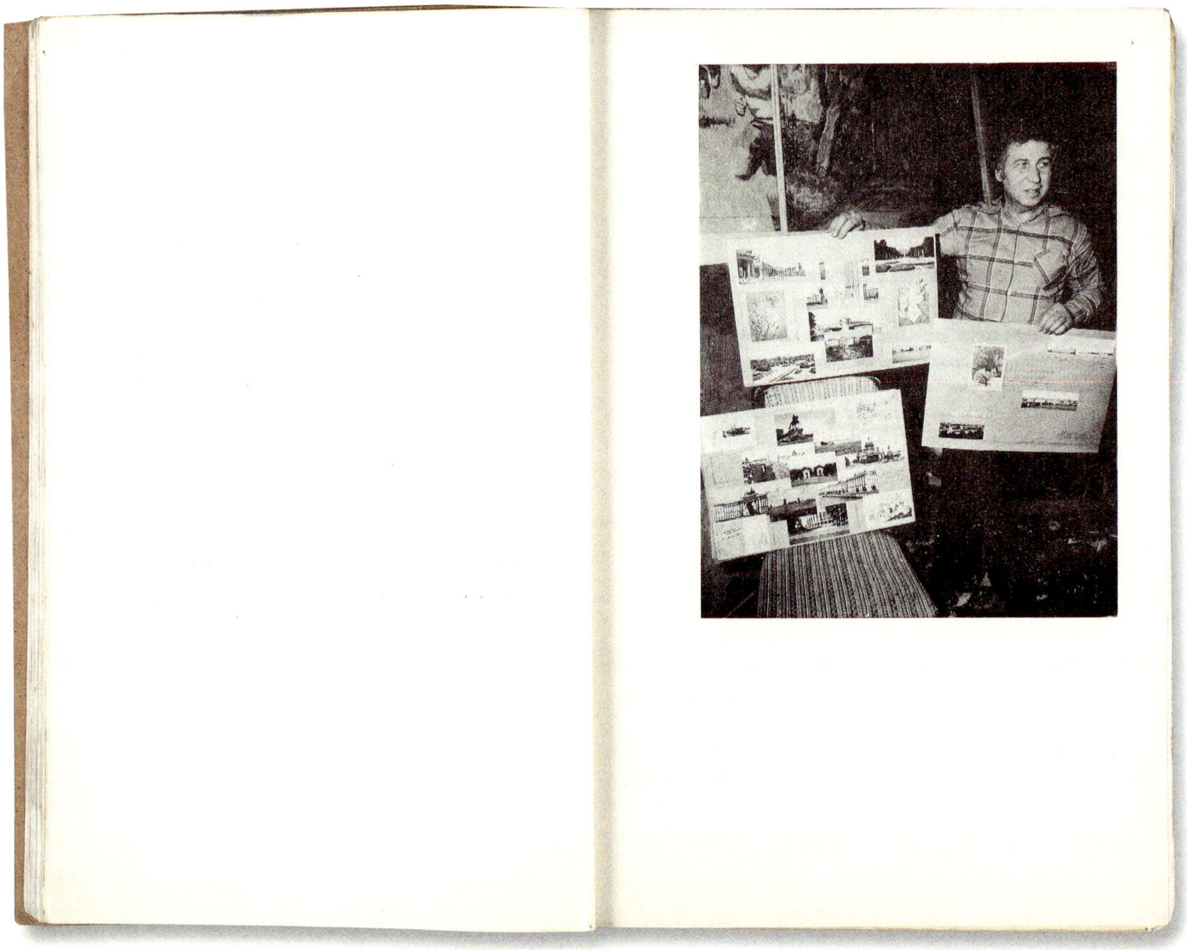

6 … It's All About Leafing Through the Pages | *… Es geht nur ums Blättern*

1981

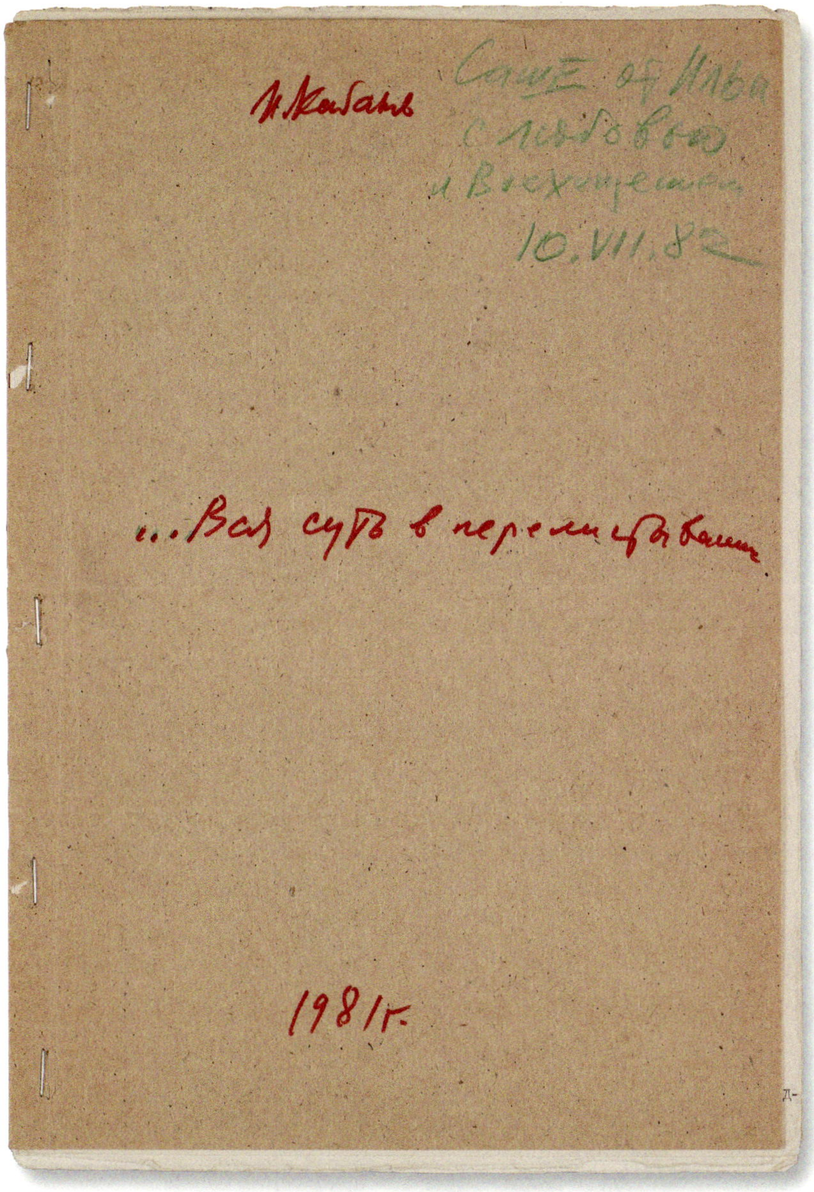

Ilya Kabakov
Moscow: published by the author
30.3 x 21.3 cm
5 pp.
stapled, cardboard cover
Drahtheftung, Kartonumschlag
edition: 10 copies

thematic publication | *thematische Publikation*

layout by Ilya Kabakov | *Layout von Ilya Kabakov*

Kabakov considers the leafing through of album pages a temporal and rhythmic motif. Inscription on the title page: "For Sascha from Ilya with love and admiration, 10. VII. 82"; Russian.

Kabakov versteht das Blättern von Albumseiten als ein zeitliches und rhythmisches Motiv. Widmung auf der Titelseite: „Für Sascha von Ilya in Liebe und Bewunderung, 10. VII. 82"; russisch.

see also | *siehe auch*

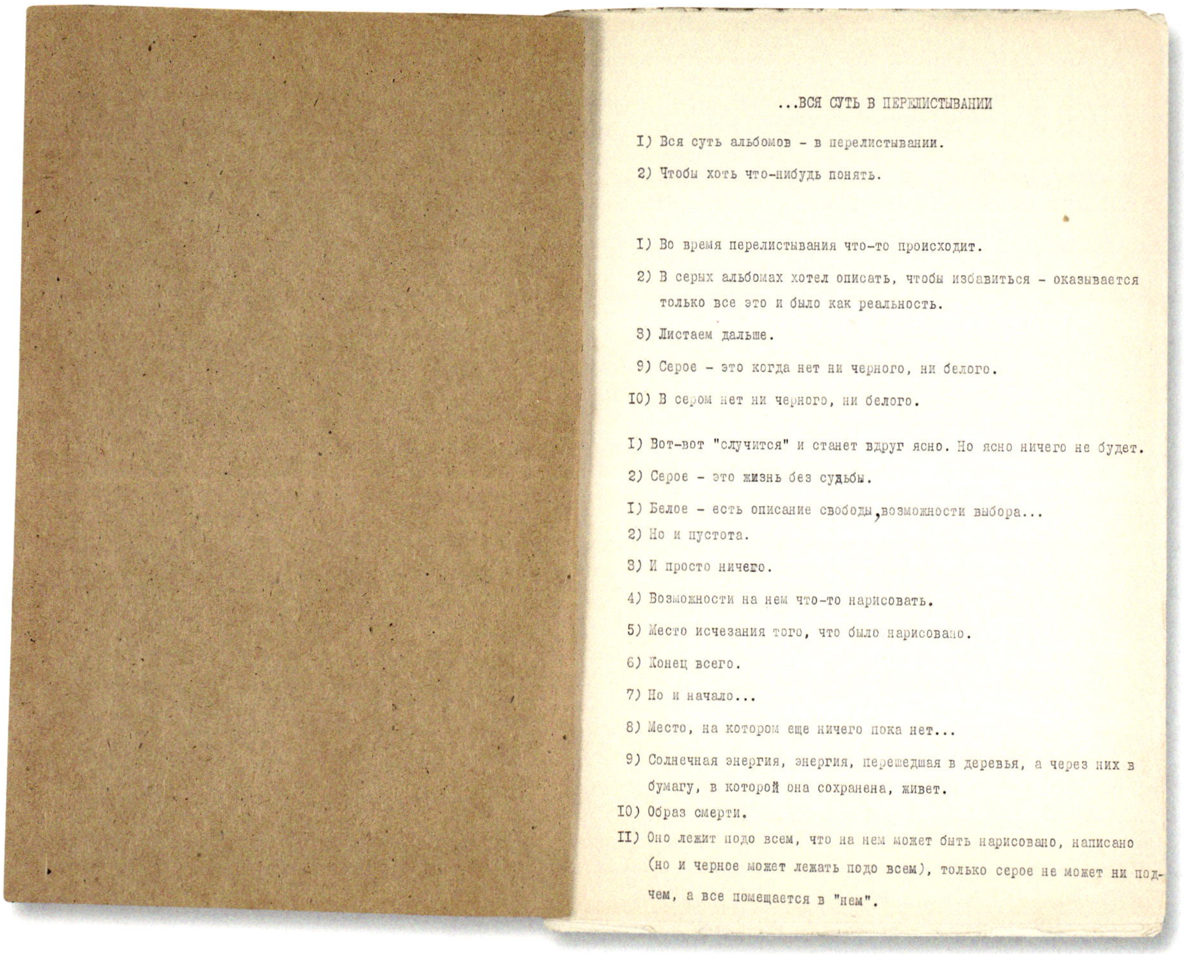

...ВСЯ СУТЬ В ПЕРЕЛИСТЫВАНИИ

I) Вся суть альбомов - в перелистывании.

2) Чтобы хоть что-нибудь понять.

I) Во время перелистывания что-то происходит.

2) В серых альбомах хотел описать, чтобы избавиться - оказывается только все это и было как реальность.

3) Листаем дальше.

9) Серое - это когда нет ни черного, ни белого.

I0) В сером нет ни черного, ни белого.

I) Вот-вот "случится" и станет вдруг ясно. Но ясно ничего не будет.

2) Серое - это жизнь без судьбы.

I) Белое - есть описание свободы, возможности выбора...

2) Но и пустота.

3) И просто ничего.

4) Возможности на нем что-то нарисовать.

5) Место исчезания того, что было нарисовано.

6) Конец всего.

7) Но и начало...

8) Место, на котором еще ничего пока нет...

9) Солнечная энергия, энергия, перешедшая в деревья, а через них в бумагу, в которой она сохранена, живет.

I0) Образ смерти.

II) Оно лежит подо всем, что на нем может быть нарисовано, написано (но и черное может лежать подо всем), только серое не может ни под-чем, а все помещается в "нем".

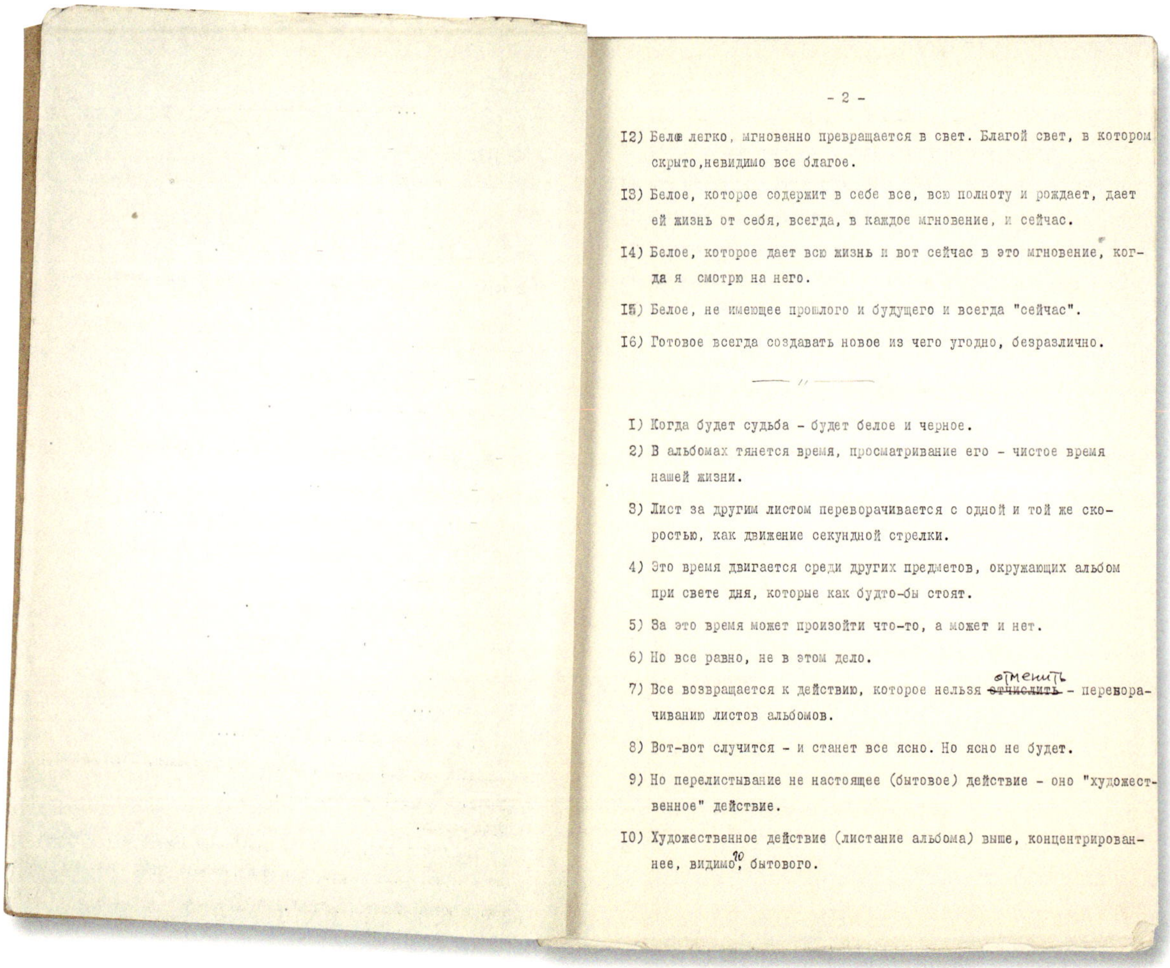

\- 2 -

I2) Белое легко, мгновенно превращается в свет. Благой свет, в котором скрыто, невидимо все благое.

I3) Белое, которое содержит в себе все, всю полноту и рождает, дает ей жизнь от себя, всегда, в каждое мгновение, и сейчас.

I4) Белое, которое дает всю жизнь и вот сейчас в это мгновение, когда я смотрю на него.

I5) Белое, не имеющее прошлого и будущего и всегда "сейчас".

I6) Готовое всегда создавать новое из чего угодно, безразлично.

—— // ——

I) Когда будет судьба - будет белое и черное.

2) В альбомах тянется время, просматривание его - чистое время нашей жизни.

3) Лист за другим листом переворачивается с одной и той же скоростью, как движение секундной стрелки.

4) Это время двигается среди других предметов, окружающих альбом при свете дня, которые как будто-бы стоят.

5) За это время может произойти что-то, а может и нет.

6) Но все равно, не в этом дело.

7) Все возвращается к действию, которое нельзя ~~отчислить~~ отменить - переворачиванию листов альбомов.

8) Вот-вот случится - и станет все ясно. Но ясно не будет.

9) Но перелистывание не настоящее (бытовое) действие - оно "художественное" действие.

I0) Художественное действие (листание альбома) выше, концентрированнее, видимо то, бытового.

7 Tested! | *Geprüft!*

1981

Ilya Kabakov
Moscow: published by the author
21.2 x 29.6 cm
10 pp. with 1 b/w ills.
formerly stapled, loose sheets, cardboard cover
vormals Drahtheftung, lose Blätter, Kartonumschlag
edition: 10 copies

thematic publication | *thematische Publikation*

layout by Ilya Kabakov | *Layout von Ilya Kabakov*

Kabakov's text »Tested!« accompanying the painting of the same name was also published in the book »The Text as the Basis of Visual Expression«; Russian.

Kabakovs Text »Geprüft!« zum gleichnamigen Gemälde erschien auch im Buch »Der Text als Grundlage des Visuellen«; russisch.

see also | *siehe auch* no. 111; CRP, vol. 1, no. 62, pp. 124–125, 406–408

„Проверена!"
260х380см Орг. Эм.
1981г.

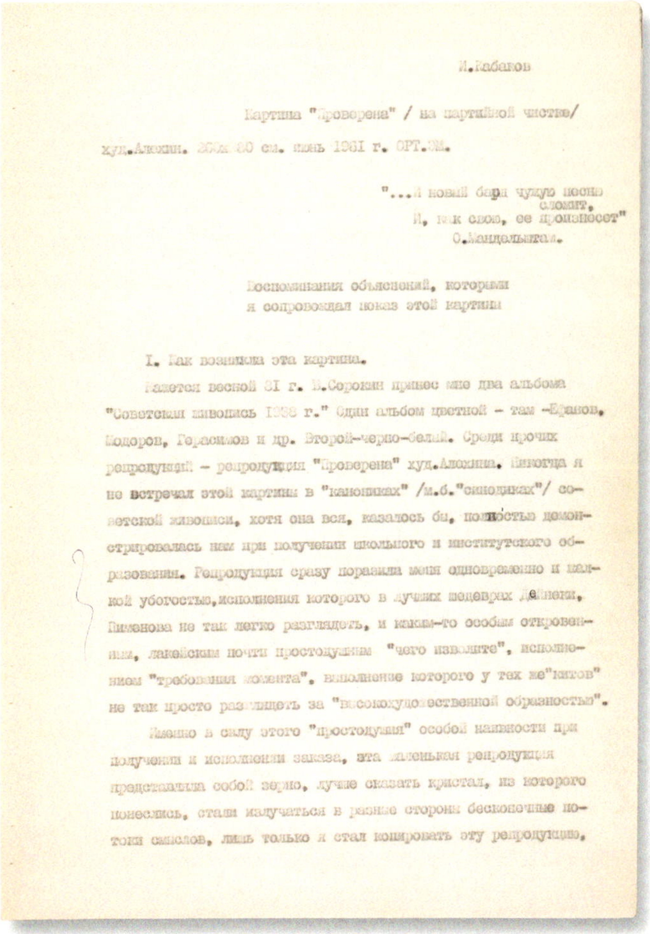

И.Кабаков

Картина "Проверена" / на партийной чистке/

худ.Алохин. 260х380 см. июнь 1981 г. ОРГ.ЭМ.

"...И новый бард чужую песню
сложит,
И, как свою, ее произносет"
О.Мандельштам.

Воспоминания объяснений, которыми
я сопровождал показ этой картины

I. Как возникла эта картина.

Кажется весной 81 г. В.Сорокин принес мне два альбома "Советская живопись 1938 г." Один альбом цветной – там –Ефанов, Модоров, Герасимов и др. Второй–черно–белый. Среди прочих репродукций – репродукция "Проверена" худ.Алохина. Никогда я не встречал этой картины в "каноних" /м.б."синодиках"/ советской живописи, хотя она вся, казалось бы, полностью демонстрировалась нам при получении школьного и институтского образования. Репродукция сразу поразила меня одновременно и жалкой убогостью,исполнения которого в лучших шедеврах Дейнеки, Пименова не так легко разглядеть, и каким–то особым откровенным, лакейским почти простодушием "чего изволите", исполнением "требования момента", выполнение которого у тех же"китов" не так просто разглядеть за "высокохудожественной образностью".

Именно в силу этого "простодушия" особой наивности при получении и исполнении заказа, эта маленькая репродукция представляла собой зерно, лучше сказать кристал, из которого понеслись, стали излучаться в разные стороны бесконечные потоки смыслов, лишь только я стал копировать эту репродукцию,

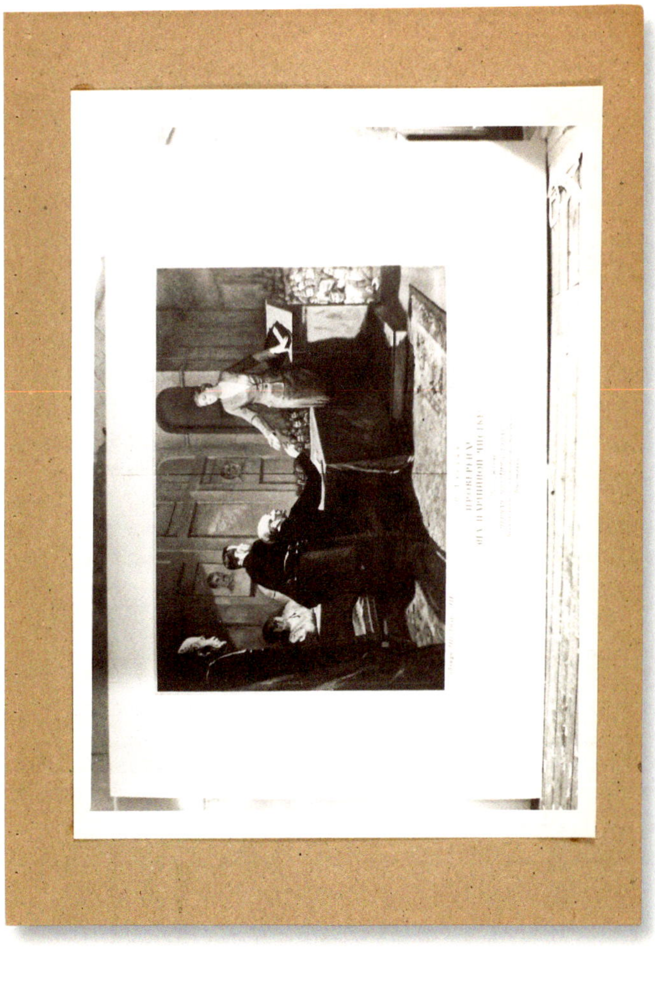

8 On the Subject of the Local Language | *Über die lokale Sprache*

1982

Ilya Kabakov
Moscow: published by the author
29.6 x 21.2 cm
11 pp.
formerly stapled, loose sheets, cardboard cover
vormals Drahtheftung, lose Blätter, Kartonumschlag
edition: 10 copies

thematic publication | *thematische Publikation*

layout by Ilya Kabakov | *Layout von Ilya Kabakov*

Kabakov likens the Soviet Union to a huge garbage pit. The text was published in 1992 in the book »Life of Flies« as the chapter »The Fly as a Subject and Basis for Philosophical Discourse« and forms part of the installation »The Fly with the Wings«; Russian.

Kabakov spricht von der Sowjetunion als einer riesigen Abfallgrube. Der Text wurde 1992 im Buch »Das Leben der Fliegen« als Kapitel »Die Fliege als Ursache und Grundlage des philosophischen Diskurses« publiziert und gehört zur Installation »Fliege mit Flügeln«; russisch.

see also | *siehe auch* no. 9; no. 33; no. 37; no. 38; no. 50; no. 56; no. 134

О МЕСТНОМ ЯЗЫКЕ

Глядя на эту выставку "Муха с крыльями" я одновременно и удивлен и не удивлен таким количеством текста, которое присутствует на этой, так сказать, выставке „изобразительного искусства". Удивлен тем, что, казалось бы, что общего между словом и изображением – ведь, если ты хорошо нарисовал, то зачем тебе текст, ведь все, что ты хотел, можешь включить в свое изображение?

А не удивлен потому, что мне кажется очевидным, и эта выставка лишний раз подтверждает, что все изобразительное искусство имеет у нас опору и поддержку в слове, в рассказе, короче в литературе. У нас всякое изобразительное восприятие связано со словом, любое изображение как бы приглашает "составить рассказ по увиденной картинке". И вот что бы мне хотелось сказать в связи с этим.

В этом центральном месте словесной культуры мы видим прежде всего мощную традицию русской литературы XIX века, в которой были сосредоточены и находили свое отражение все проблемы, тревожащие современное ей общество, и то, что многие окололитературные и внелитературные проблемы находили себе прежде всего словесное выражение и то, что иные искусства опирались на литературу и были объяснены и сами себя понимали через нее.

Возможно, что здесь сказалась и традиция христианских текстов и, тексты уже светские, взяли на себя все морализирующие, философские, педагогические и просветительские функции, сосредоточив их как раз в литературе, а не в пластике, напри-

\- 2 -

мер одновременно, как на Западе.

Как бы там ни было, язык, текст у нас и по сей день несет главную содержательную и художественную нагрузку, стягивая и сосредотачивая в себе все проблемы современной местной культуры.

Но за это время, а точнее с начала 20-х годов нашего века, сам этот язык внутри себя претерпел значительные изменения. Это уже не совсем тот язык как прежде, какие-то глубокие внутренние изменения произошли в нем на глубинном уровне, хотя внешне он напоминает русский язык классической литературы прошлого века. Что-то произошло не только с лексической, но, прежде всего, с семантической стороной его, а в отношении между словом и его значением. И это явление коснулось не только обыденного языка, но и, прежде всего, языка художественного, который не может не отразить происшедшую перемену.

x x x

Если воспользоваться этническими представлениями о разделенности Севера и Юга России и Запада и Востока Украины, то можно дать ту же характеристику этой проблемы в плоскости отношений "культуры – некультуры".

Можно представить [illegible] России, начиная от границы Вологды, как стабильный, [illegible] этно-культурный массив, наподобие скального [illegible] массива в геологии, со своими традициями, представлениями, языком, обрядами, короче тем, о чем мы можем говорить как о "культуре".

Приблизительно то же самое можно говорить и о культуре Украины к западу от Киева, также с ее достаточно устойчи-

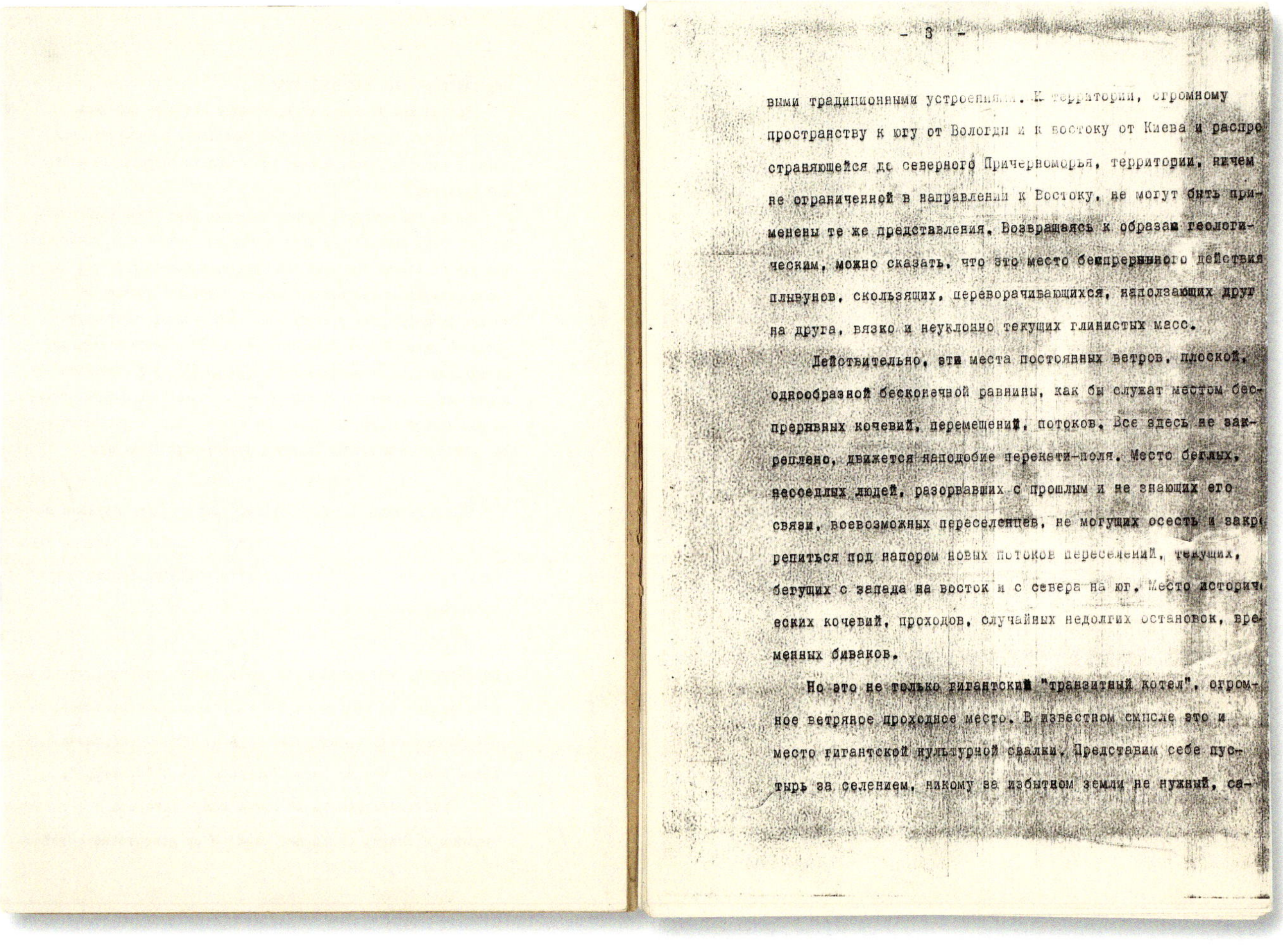

\- 3 -

вими традиционными устроениями. К территории, огромному
пространству к югу от Вологды и к востоку от Киева и распро
страняющейся до северного Причерноморья, территории, ничем
не ограниченной в направлении к Востоку, не могут быть при-
менены те же представления. Возвращаясь к образам геологи-
ческим, можно сказать, что это место беспрерывного действия
плывунов, скользящих, переворачивающихся, наползающих друг
на друга, вязко и неуклонно текущих глинистых масс.

Действительно, эти места постоянных ветров, плоской,
однообразной бесконечной равнины, как бы служат местом бес-
прерывных кочевий, перемещений, потоков. Все здесь не зак-
реплено, движется наподобие перекати-поля. Место беглых,
несоседлых людей, разорвавших с прошлым и не знающих его
связи, всевозможных переселенцев, не могущих осесть и закр
репиться под напором новых потоков переселений, текущих,
бегущих с запада на восток и с севера на юг. Место историч
еских кочевий, проходов, случайных недолгих остановок, вре-
менных биваков.

Но это не только гигантский "транзитный котел", огром-
ное ветряное проходное место. В известном смысле это и
место гигантской культурной свалки. Представим себе пус-
тырь за селением, никому за избытком земли не нужный, са-

9 The Fly with the Wings | *Fliege mit Flügeln*

1982

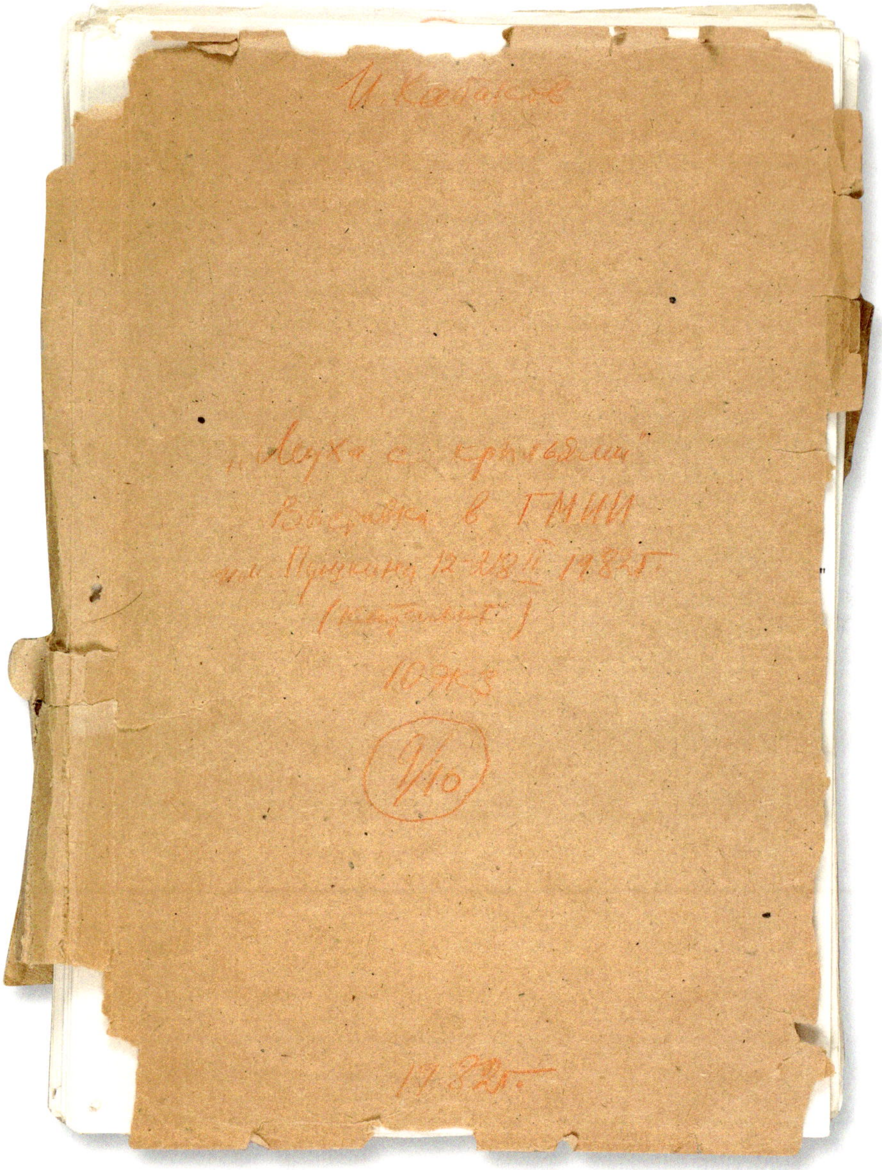

Ilya Kabakov
Moscow: published by the author
33.3 x 22.6 cm
169 pp. (partly doubled sided)
with 20 b/w ills.
loose sheets, cardboard cover
lose Blätter, Kartonumschlag
edition: 10 copies

exhibition catalogue | *Ausstellungskatalog*

layout by Ilya Kabakov | *Layout von Ilya Kabakov*

For the fictional installation that allegedly took place in the White Hall of the Pushkin State Museum of Fine Arts, Moscow, from February 12 to 28, 1982. The book contains all of Kabakov's texts that were published in 1992 as the chapter »The Fly as a Subject and Basis for Philosophical Discourse« in the book »Life of Flies«, including »The Ant« and »On the Subject of the Local Language«; Russian.

Zur fiktiven Installation die angeblich im Weissen Saal, Staatliches Puschkin-Museum, Moskau, vom 12. – 28. Februar 1982 stattfand. Das Heft umfasst sämtliche Texte Kabakovs, die 1992 unter dem Kapitel »Die Fliege als Ursache und Grundlage des philosophischen Diskurses« im Buch »Das Leben der Fliegen« publiziert wurden, darunter »Die Ameise« und »Über die lokale Sprache«; russisch.

see also | *siehe auch* no. 8; no. 33; no. 43; no. 44; no. 37; no. 38; no. 50; no. 56; no. 134; CRI, vol. 1, no. 3, pp. 60–65

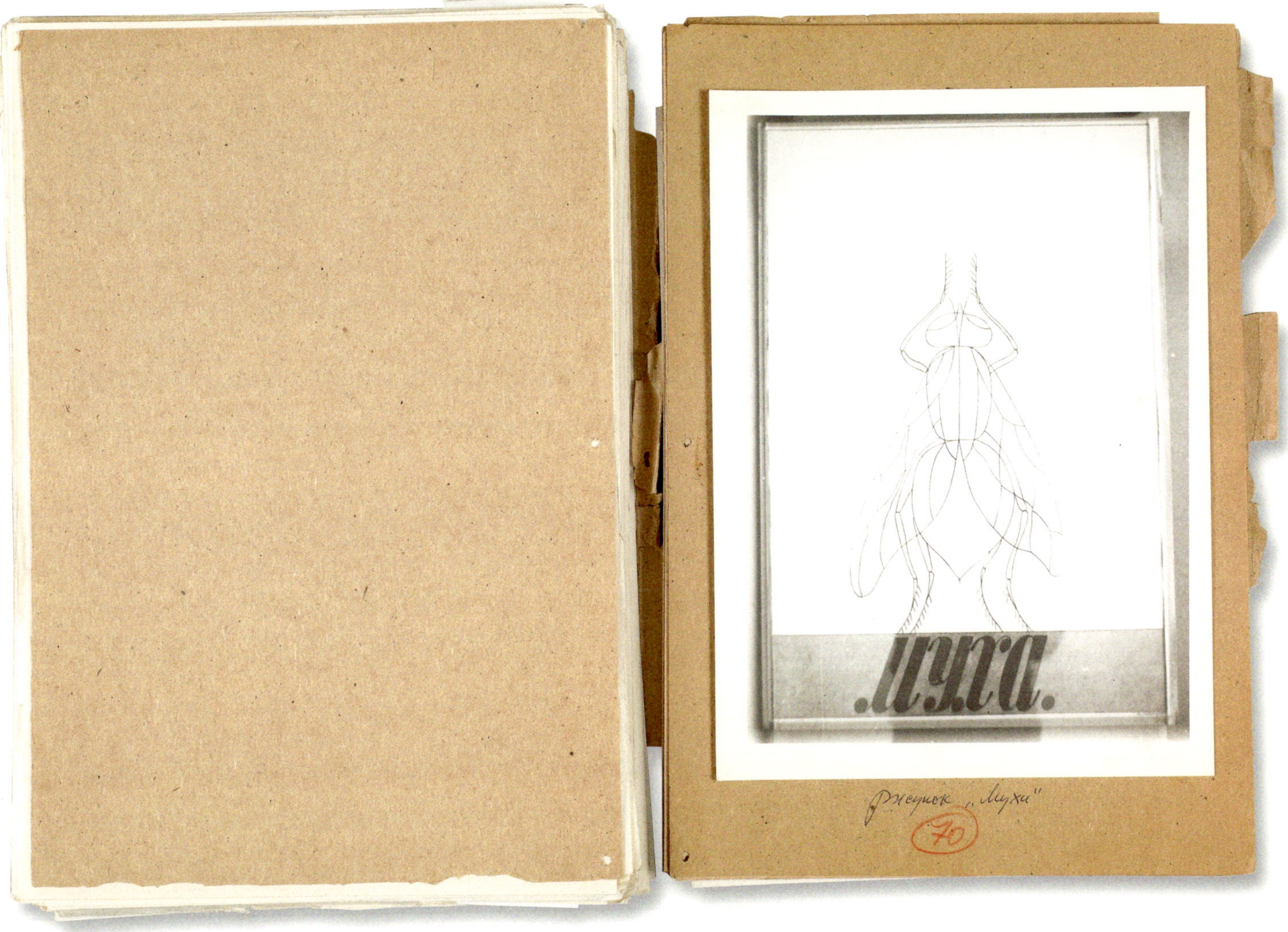
Рисунок „Мухи"
70

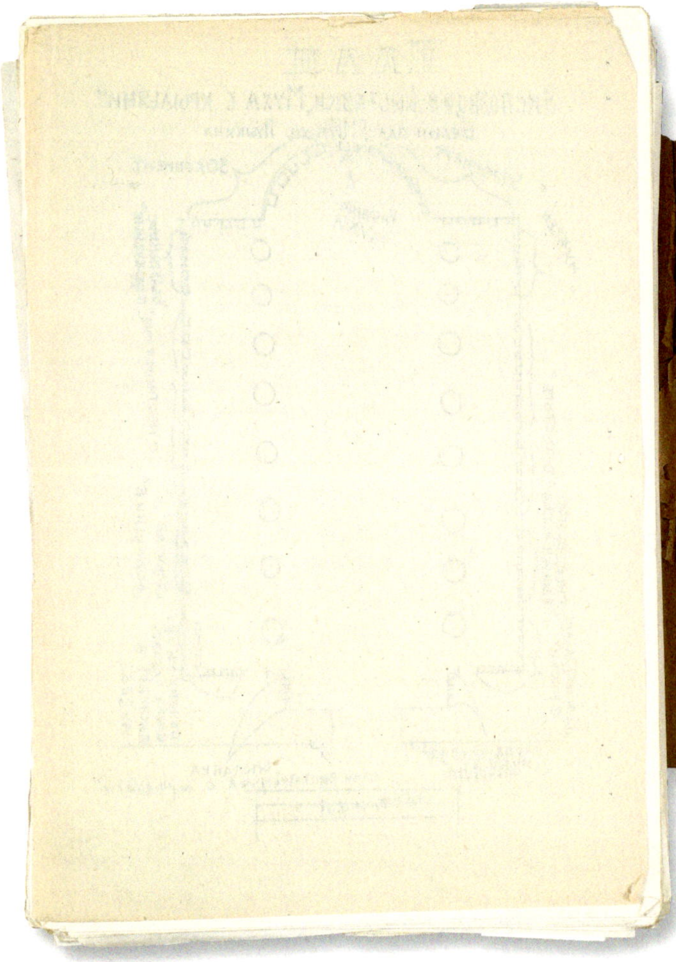

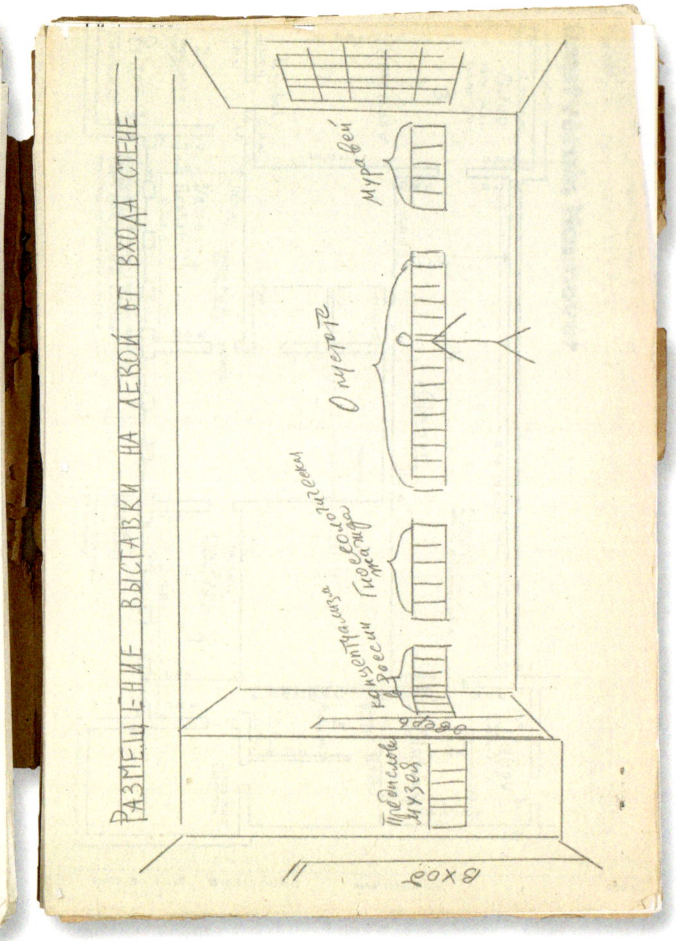

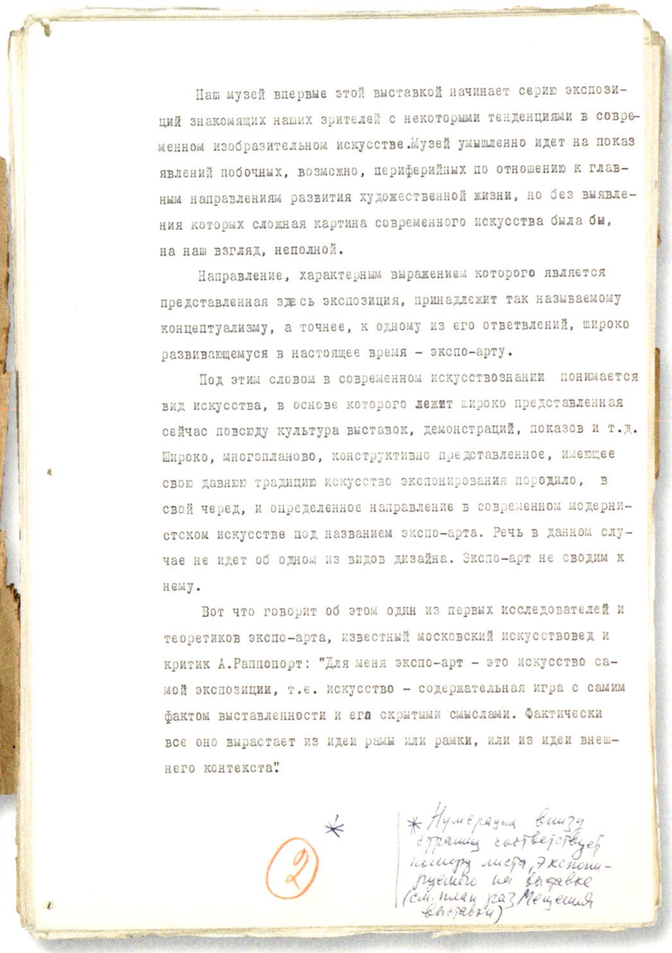

Наш музей впервые этой выставкой начинает серию экспозиций знакомящих наших зрителей с некоторыми тенденциями в современном изобразительном искусстве. Музей умышленно идет на показ явлений побочных, возможно, периферийных по отношению к главным направлениям развития художественной жизни, но без выявления которых сложная картина современного искусства была бы, на наш взгляд, неполной.

Направление, характерным выражением которого является представленная здесь экспозиция, принадлежит так называемому концептуализму, а точнее, к одному из его ответвлений, широко развивающемуся в настоящее время – экспо-арту.

Под этим словом в современном искусствознании понимается вид искусства, в основе которого лежит широко представленная сейчас повсюду культура выставок, демонстраций, показов и т.д. Широко, многопланово, конструктивно представленное, имеющее свою давнюю традицию искусство экспонирования породило, в свой черед, и определенное направление в современном модернистском искусстве под названием экспо-арта. Речь в данном случае не идет об одном из видов дизайна. Экспо-арт не сводим к нему.

Вот что говорит об этом один из первых исследователей и теоретиков экспо-арта, известный московский искусствовед и критик А.Раппопорт: "Для меня экспо-арт – это искусство самой экспозиции, т.е. искусство – содержательная игра с самим фактом выставленности и его скрытыми смыслами. Фактически все оно вырастает из идеи рамы или рамки, или из идеи внешнего контекста".

(2) *

* Нумерация внизу страницы соответствует номеру листа, экспонируемого на выставке (см. план размещения выставки)

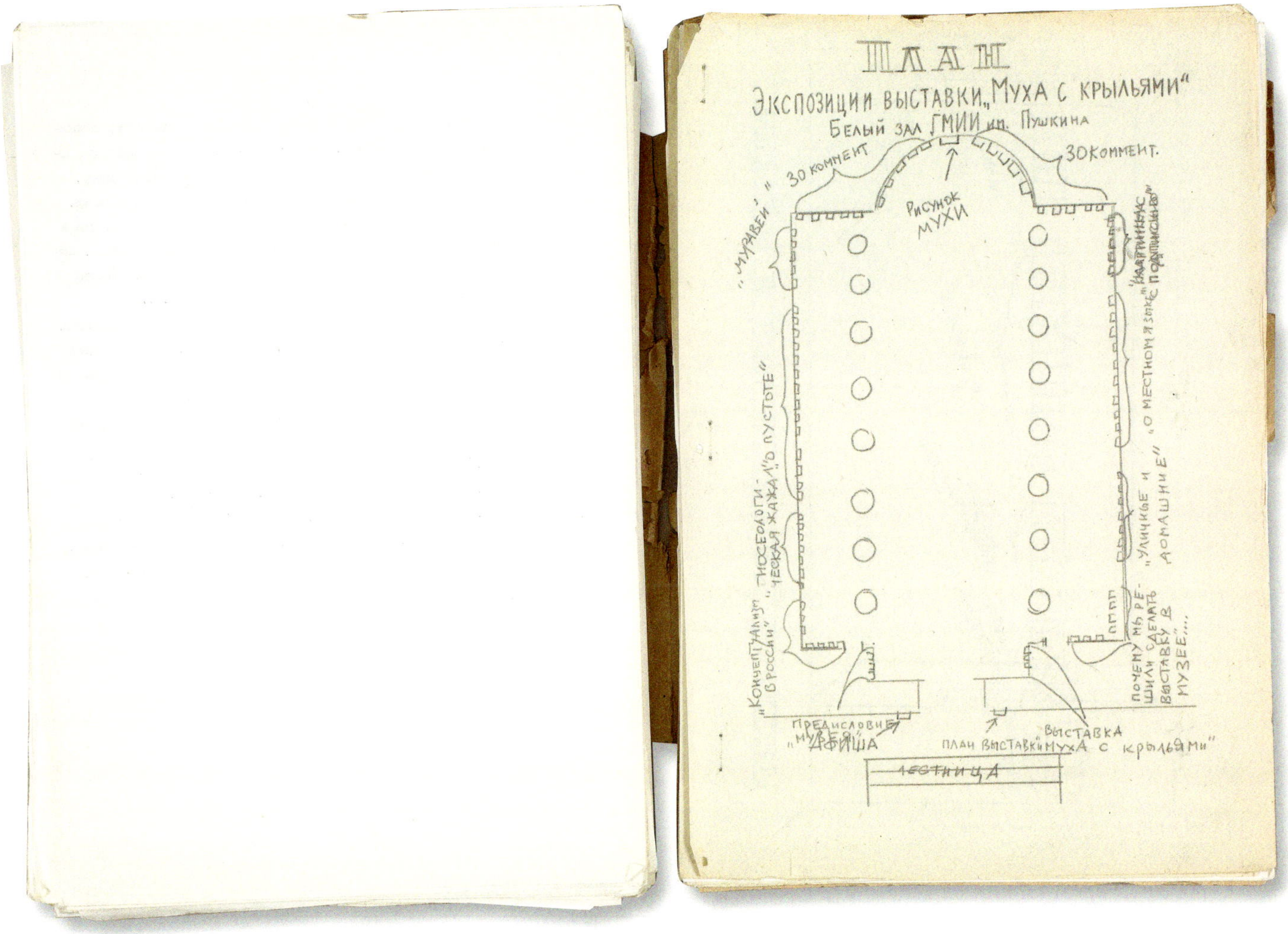
ПЛАН
Экспозиции выставки „Муха с крыльями“
Белый зал ГМИИ им. Пушкина
30 коммент
30 коммент.
Рисунок мухи
„Муравей“
„о местном языке“
„Уличные и домашние“
Почему мы решили сделать выставку в музее...
Предисловие „музея“
Афиша
Выставка
План выставки „Муха с крыльями“

10 New Rhombus | *Neuer Rhombus*

1983

Ilya Kabakov
Moscow: published by the author
29.7 x 21 cm
3 pp. with 1 b/w ill.
stapled, cardboard cover
Drahtheftung, Kartonumschlag
edition: 10 copies

thematic publication | *thematische Publikation*

layout by Ilya Kabakov | *Layout von Ilya Kabakov*

Kabakov uses a rhombus to explain everyday life in the Soviet Union. The vertical line stretches from the "Soviet garbage" and "dirt on the ground" to the "sky," while a horizontal line represents the movement from East to West; Russian.

Kabakov erklärt den sowjetischen Alltag mit einem Rhombus. Die vertikale Linie reicht vom „sowjetischen Müll" und „Schmutz am Boden" in den „Himmel", während eine horizontale Linie die Bewegung von Ost nach West repräsentiert; russisch.

see also | *siehe auch*

НОВЫЙ РОМБ.
7 мая 1983 г.

Молодое, совсем молодое русско изобразительное искусство имеет своим началом петровские "парсуны" и среднеевропейскую парадную живопись в ХУШ веке и один из вариантов типовой "академии" вплоть до конца XIX в. Проблема "Запада и Востока", их противостояние и сходство, отталкиваня и притяжения начались в самом конце XIX в. с мирискусников и ее напряжение существует до сих пор. (передвижники полностью находятся в сфере действия "жанра" по традиционной академической шкале, лишь поменяв сюжеты с сентиментальных на обличительные).

Эта неразрешенность "сюда-туда", "отсюда-оттуда" связана,вне сомнения, с отсутствием "языка" живописи специально местного - ка это счастливо случилось в русской литературе со времен Пушкина.

Но мало этого. Нерешенность в изобразительном языке ситуации "оттуда-отсюда" усугубляется нерешенностью, вернее неопределенностью в решении ситуации "священное-профаническое" - в ситуации, касающейся, повторяю, нашего изоискусства. По-прежнему идея о священной, духовной эманации, которая должна содержаться в художественном произведении, ее необычайный сакральный смысл - все это идущее от традиции иконописи в сегодняшний день также затрудняет получение вменяемых результатов.

Итак в сфере культуры решение затруднено ситуацией "как у них, так и у нас", идущей от петровских времен. В сфере "духа" решение затруднено мечтой о "иконной" духовности и ее влиянии, и уже не каноническим предметом, который изготавливает художник, ушедший из мастерских по изготовлению икон, да и за неимением таковых. (Гибриды, желающие соединить и то и другое, возникают постоянно - достаточно указать на Петрова-Водкина).

- 2 -

Тем не менее за это время, т.е. начало XIX - конец XX вв, как кажется проявляется в первой тенденции - назовем их "культурой" а с точки зрения второй тенденции - "профанической" - особые две линии, две струи, что ли, которые можно было бы вычленить и назвать, как специфически местные:

1) Линия, идущая через Зорянко-Федотова к Лактионову.

2) Линия В.Васнецова - Кустодиева.

Первая линия - особого непредвзятого, беззаветного рассказа, лишенного спекуляции и всевозможных сверхобобщений.

Вторая линия - откровенный лубок, где автор изготавливает лубковую доску, близкую к базарному ковру, опять-таки лишенную всякого "художественного" эстетического изыска.

* *
*

Тенденция "духовка" тоже в истории новой живописи не дремлет и проявляется во все новых и новых вспышках визионерства, пророчества и водительства (Чекрыгин, Малевич, Штейнберг).

Таким образом мы можем изобразить ~~ромб~~ фигуры нерешенной ситуации в русском "изо" к сегодняшнему дню в виде ромба

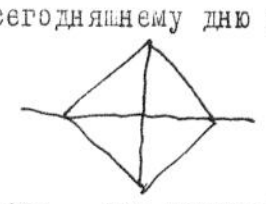

где горизонтальная ось - ось местной культуры колышется на "Запад-Восток" и обратно, а вертикальная - вверх, к небу и вниз - к дну, грязи и пыли.

11 Without Culture | *Ohne Kultur*

1983

Ilya Kabakov
Moscow: published by the author
29.5 x 21 cm
4 pp.
stapled, cardboard cover
Drahtheftung, Kartonumschlag
edition: 10 copies

thematic publication | *thematische Publikation*

layout by Ilya Kabakov | *Layout von Ilya Kabakov*

Kabakov's analysis of the situation of unofficial artists in Moscow at the time; Russian.

Kabakovs Analyse der damaligen Situation inoffizieller Künstler in Moskau; russisch.

see also | *siehe auch*

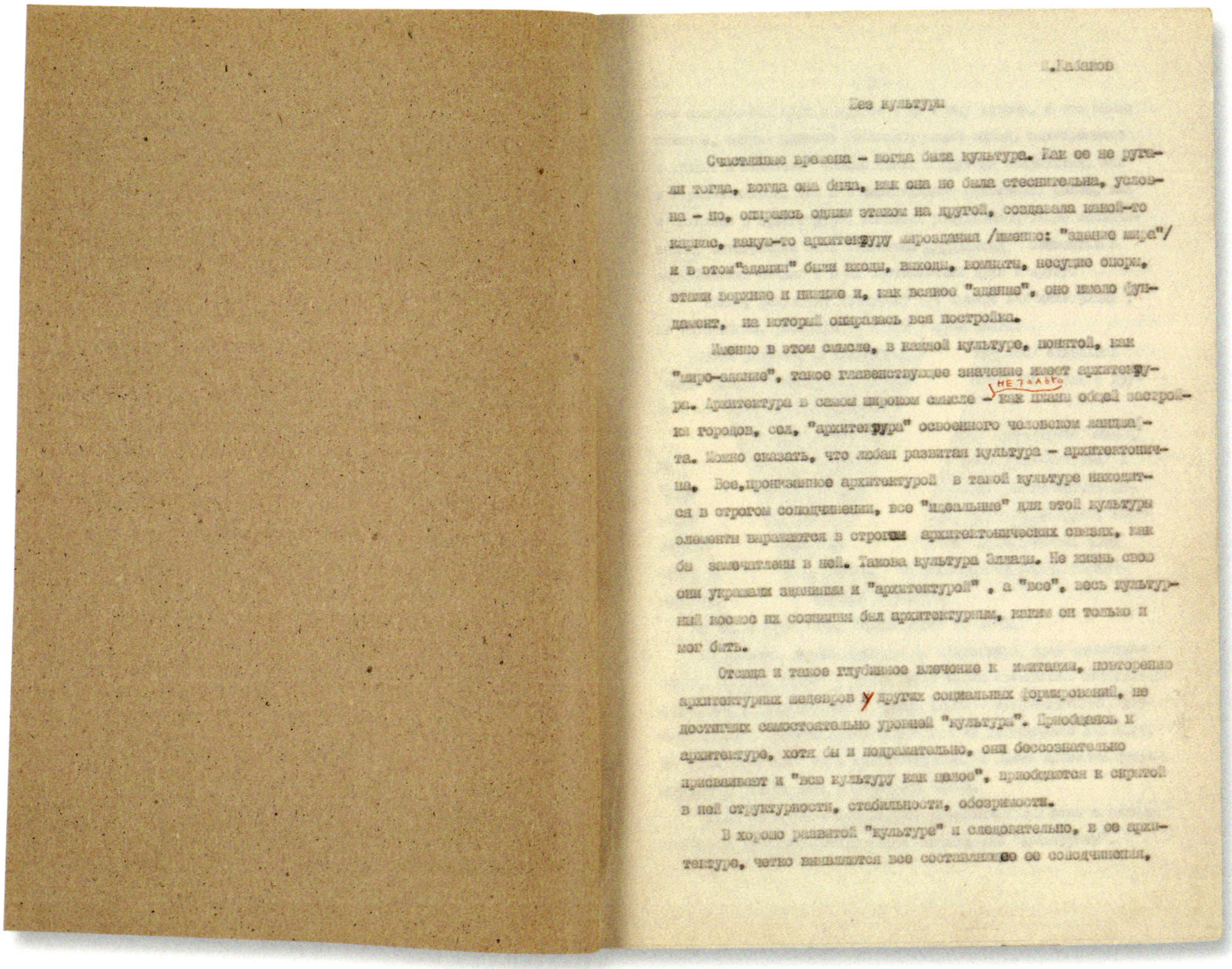

И.Кабаков

Без культуры

Счастливые времена – когда была культура. Как ее не ругали тогда, когда она была, как она не была стеснительна, условна – но, опираясь одним этажом на другой, создавала какой-то каркас, какую-то архитектуру мироздания /именно: "здание мира"/ и в этом "здании" были входы, выходы, комнаты, несущие опоры, этажи верхние и нижние и, как всякое "здание", оно имело фундамент, на который опиралась вся постройка.

Именно в этом смысле, в каждой культуре, понятой, как "миро-здание", такое главенствующее значение имеет архитектура. Архитектура в самом широком смысле – не только как планы общей застройки городов, сел, "архитектура" освоенного человеком ландшафта. Можно сказать, что любая развитая культура – архитектонична. Все, пронизанное архитектурой в такой культуре находится в строгом соподчинении, все "идеальные" для этой культуры элементы выражаются в строгих архитектонических связях, как бы запечатлены в ней. Такова культура Эллады. Не жизнь свою они украшали зданиями и "архитектурой", а "все", весь культурный космос их сознания был архитектурным, каким он только и мог быть.

Отсюда и такое глубинное влечение к имитации, повторению архитектурных шедевров у других социальных формирований, не достигших самостоятельно уровней "культура". Приобщаясь к архитектуре, хотя бы и подражательно, они бессознательно присваивают и "всю культуру как целое", приобщаются к скрытой в ней структурности, стабильности, обозримости.

В хорошо развитой "культуре" и следовательно, в ее архитектуре, четко выявляются все составляющие ее соподчинения,

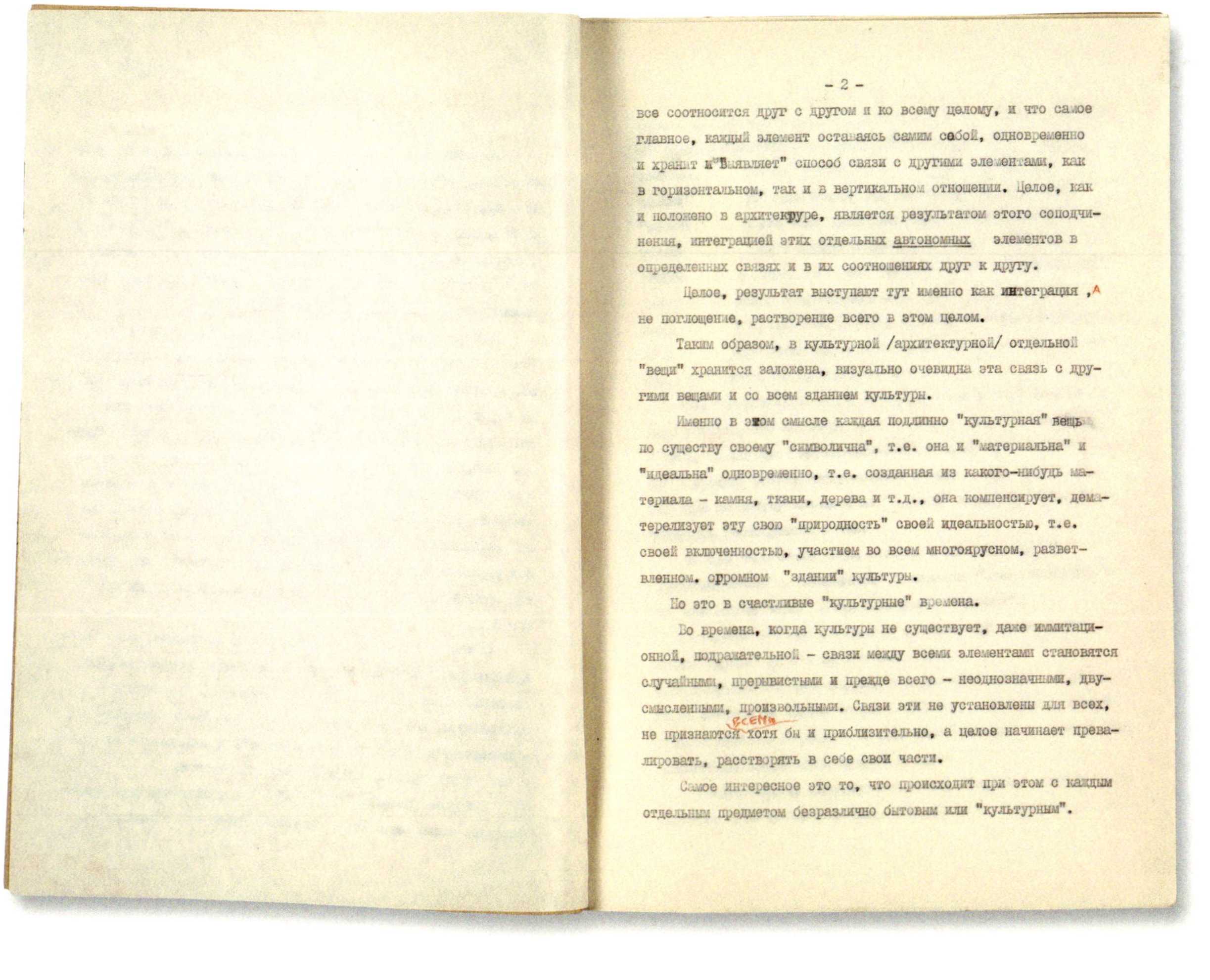

\- 2 -

все соотносится друг с другом и ко всему целому, и что самое главное, каждый элемент оставаясь самим собой, одновременно и хранит и "выявляет" способ связи с другими элементами, как в горизонтальном, так и в вертикальном отношении. Целое, как и положено в архитектуре, является результатом этого соподчинения, интеграцией этих отдельных автономных элементов в определенных связях и в их соотношениях друг к другу.

Целое, результат выступают тут именно как интеграция, а не поглощение, растворение всего в этом целом.

Таким образом, в культурной /архитектурной/ отдельной "вещи" хранится заложена, визуально очевидна эта связь с другими вещами и со всем зданием культуры.

Именно в этом смысле каждая подлинно "культурная" вещь по существу своему "символична", т.е. она и "материальна" и "идеальна" одновременно, т.е. созданная из какого-нибудь материала – камня, ткани, дерева и т.д., она компенсирует, дематерелизует эту свою "природность" своей идеальностью, т.е. своей включенностью, участием во всем многоярусном, разветвленном. огромном "здании" культуры.

Но это в счастливые "культурные" времена.

Во времена, когда культуры не существует, даже иммитационной, подражательной – связи между всеми элементами становятся случайными, прерывистыми и прежде всего – неоднозначными, двусмысленными, произвольными. Связи эти не установлены для всех, не признаются всеми хотя бы и приблизительно, а целое начинает превалировать, расстворять в себе свои части.

Самое интересное это то, что происходит при этом с каждым отдельным предметом безразлично бытовым или "культурным".

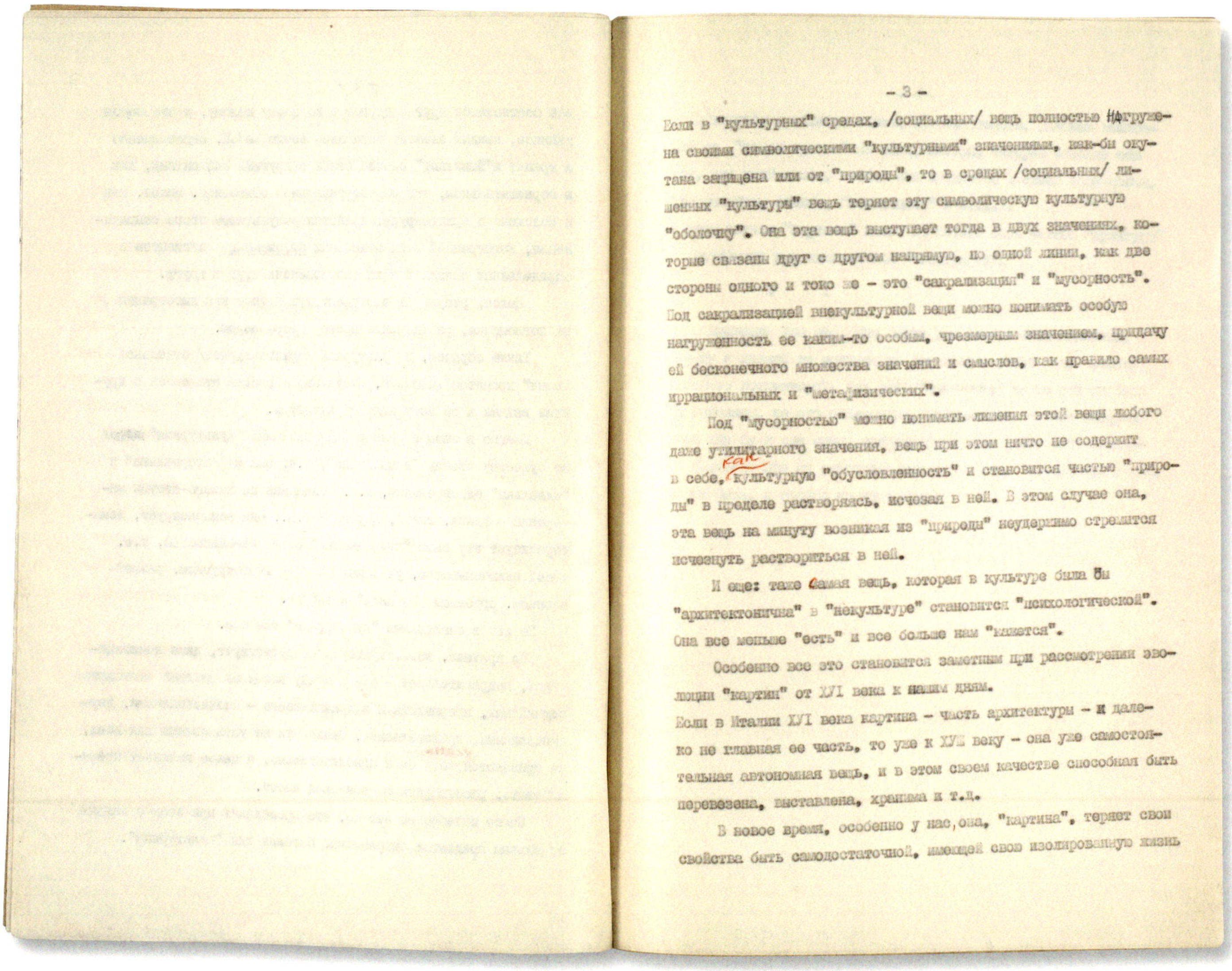

- 3 -

Если в "культурных" средах, /социальных/ вещь полностью нагружена своими символическими "культурными" значениями, как-бы окутана защищена или от "природы", то в средах /социальных/ лишенных "культуры" вещь теряет эту символическую культурную "оболочку". Она эта вещь выступает тогда в двух значениях, которые связаны друг с другом напрямую, по одной линии, как две стороны одного и того же - это "сакрализация" и "мусорность". Под сакрализацией внекультурной вещи можно понимать особую нагруженность ее каким-то особым, чрезмерным значением, придачу ей бесконечного множества значений и смыслов, как правило самых иррациональных и "метафизических".

Под "мусорностью" можно понимать лишения этой вещи любого даже утилитарного значения, вещь при этом ничто не содержит в себе, как культурную "обусловленность" и становится частью "природы" в пределе растворяясь, исчезая в ней. В этом случае она, эта вещь на минуту возникая из "природы" неудержимо стремится исчезнуть раствориться в ней.

И еще: таже самая вещь, которая в культуре была бы "архитектонична" в "некультуре" становится "психологической". Она все меньше "есть" и все больше нам "кажется".

Особенно все это становится заметным при рассмотрении эволюции "картин" от XVI века к нашим дням.
Если в Италии XVI века картина - часть архитектуры - и далеко не главная ее часть, то уже к XVII веку - она уже самостоятельная автономная вещь, и в этом своем качестве способная быть перевезена, выставлена, хранима и т.д.

В новое время, особенно у нас, она, "картина", теряет свои свойства быть самодостаточной, имеющей свою изолированную жизнь

12 Complete Overview of the Work | *Gesamtübersicht über die Arbeit*

1984

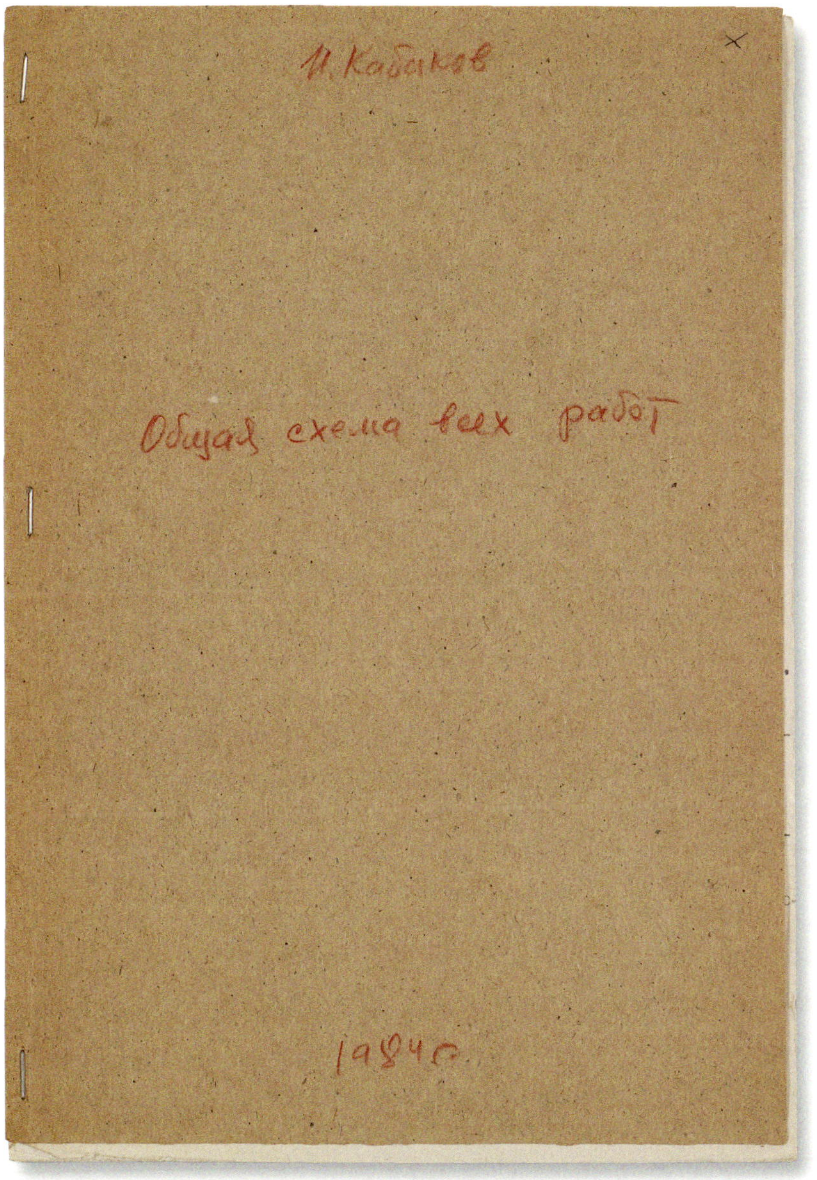

Ilya Kabakov
Moscow: published by the author
29.9 x 21 cm
3 pp. with 8 b/w ills.
stapled, cardboard cover
Drahtheftung, Kartonumschlag
edition: 10 copies

thematic publication | *thematische Publikation*

layout by Ilya Kabakov | *Layout von Ilya Kabakov*

Portrayal of all of Kabakov's work in the form of a diagram with a horizontal and vertical axis. The horizontal axis extends from left to right: »Pictures without Text, Pictures with Text, Screen Walls, Exhibitions, Portfolios, Boxes, Novel with Images, and Text without Pictures«. The following are located in an upward direction on the vertical axis: »Dirt, Garbage, Garbage Pit, Garbage Can, Album, Screen Walls, Exhibitions, Almost Empty Pictures, Empty Drawings«, and »Emptiness«; it leads from the »Soiled Ground« to the »Metaphysical Emptiness«; Russian.

Darstellung von Kabakovs Gesamtwerk in Diagrammform mit einer horizontalen und einer vertikalen Achse. Die horizontale Achse umfasst von links nach rechts: »Bilder ohne Text, Bilder mit Text, Schirmwände, Ausstellungen, Mappen, Schachteln, Roman mit Bildern und Text ohne Bilder«. Auf der vertikalen Achse stehen von unten nach oben: »Schmutz, Müll, Müllgrube, Mülleimer, Album, Schirmwände, Ausstellungen, Fast leere Bilder, leere Zeichnungen« und »Leere«; sie führt vom »Verschmutzen Boden« in die Metaphysische »Leere«; russisch.

see also | *siehe auch*

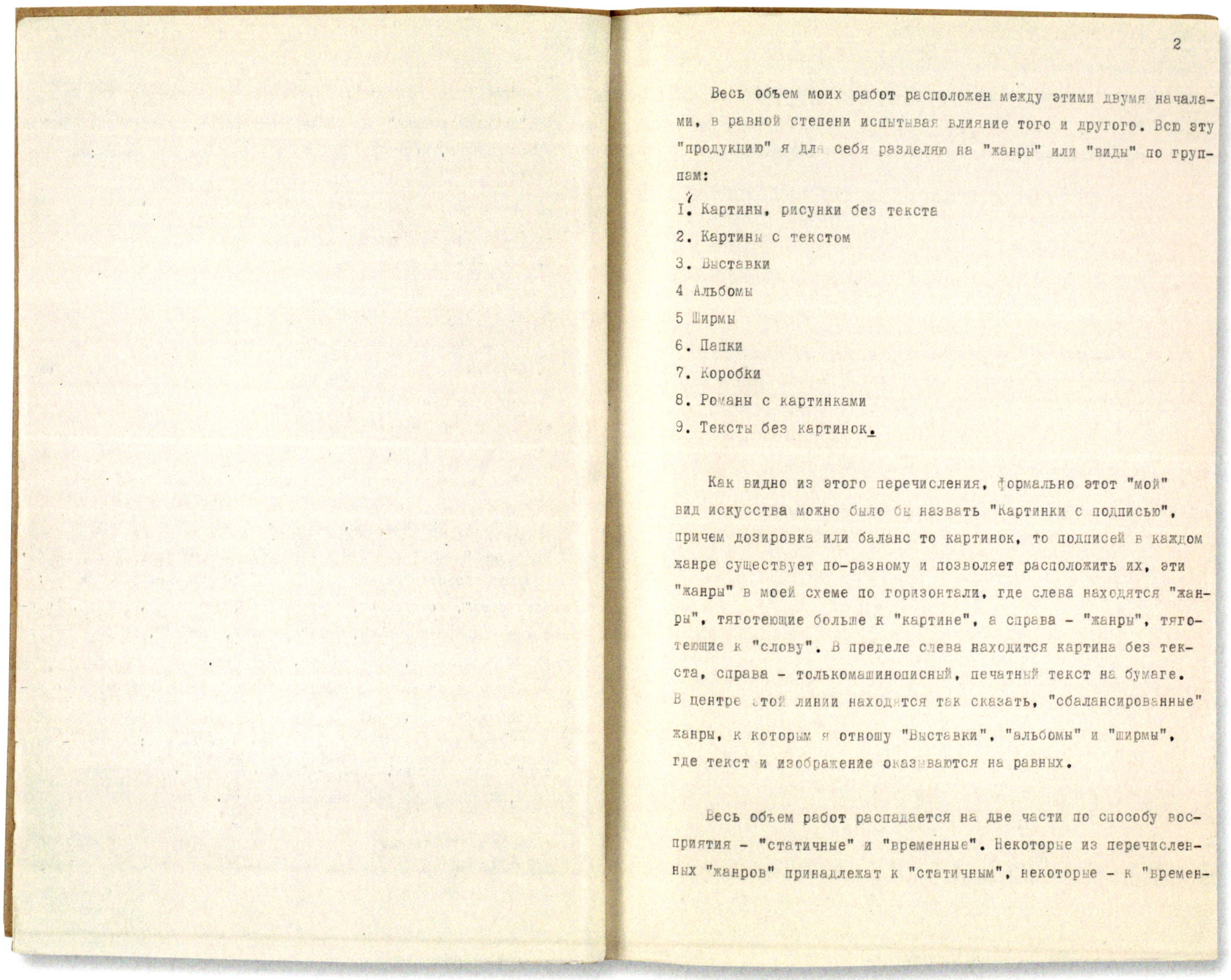

2

Весь объем моих работ расположен между этими двумя началами, в равной степени испытывая влияние того и другого. Всю эту "продукцию" я для себя разделяю на "жанры" или "виды" по группам:

1. Картины, рисунки без текста
2. Картины с текстом
3. Выставки
4 Альбомы
5 Ширмы
6. Папки
7. Коробки
8. Романы с картинками
9. Тексты без картинок.

Как видно из этого перечисления, формально этот "мой" вид искусства можно было бы назвать "Картинки с подписью", причем дозировка или баланс то картинок, то подписей в каждом жанре существует по-разному и позволяет расположить их, эти "жанры" в моей схеме по горизонтали, где слева находятся "жанры", тяготеющие больше к "картине", а справа - "жанры", тяготеющие к "слову". В пределе слева находится картина без текста, справа - толькомашинописный, печатный текст на бумаге. В центре этой линии находятся так сказать, "сбалансированные" жанры, к которым я отношу "Выставки", "альбомы" и "ширмы", где текст и изображение оказываются на равных.

Весь объем работ распадается на две части по способу восприятия - "статичные" и "временные". Некоторые из перечисленных "жанров" принадлежат к "статичным", некоторые - к "времен-

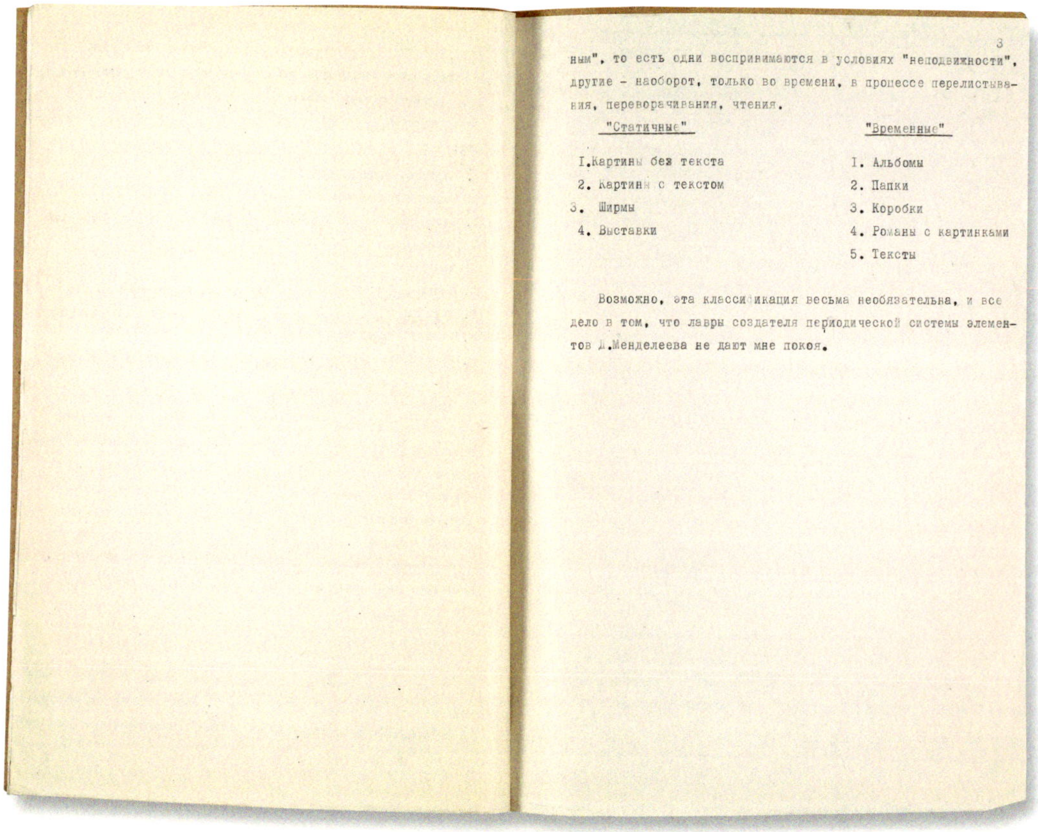

3

ным", то есть одни воспринимаются в условиях "неподвижности", другие - наоборот, только во времени, в процессе перелистывания, переворачивания, чтения.

"Статичные"	"Временные"
I.Картины без текста	I. Альбомы
2. Картины с текстом	2. Папки
3. Ширмы	3. Коробки
4. Выставки	4. Романы с картинками
	5. Тексты

Возможно, эта классификация весьма необязательна, и все дело в том, что лавры создателя периодической системы элементов Д.Менделеева не дают мне покоя.

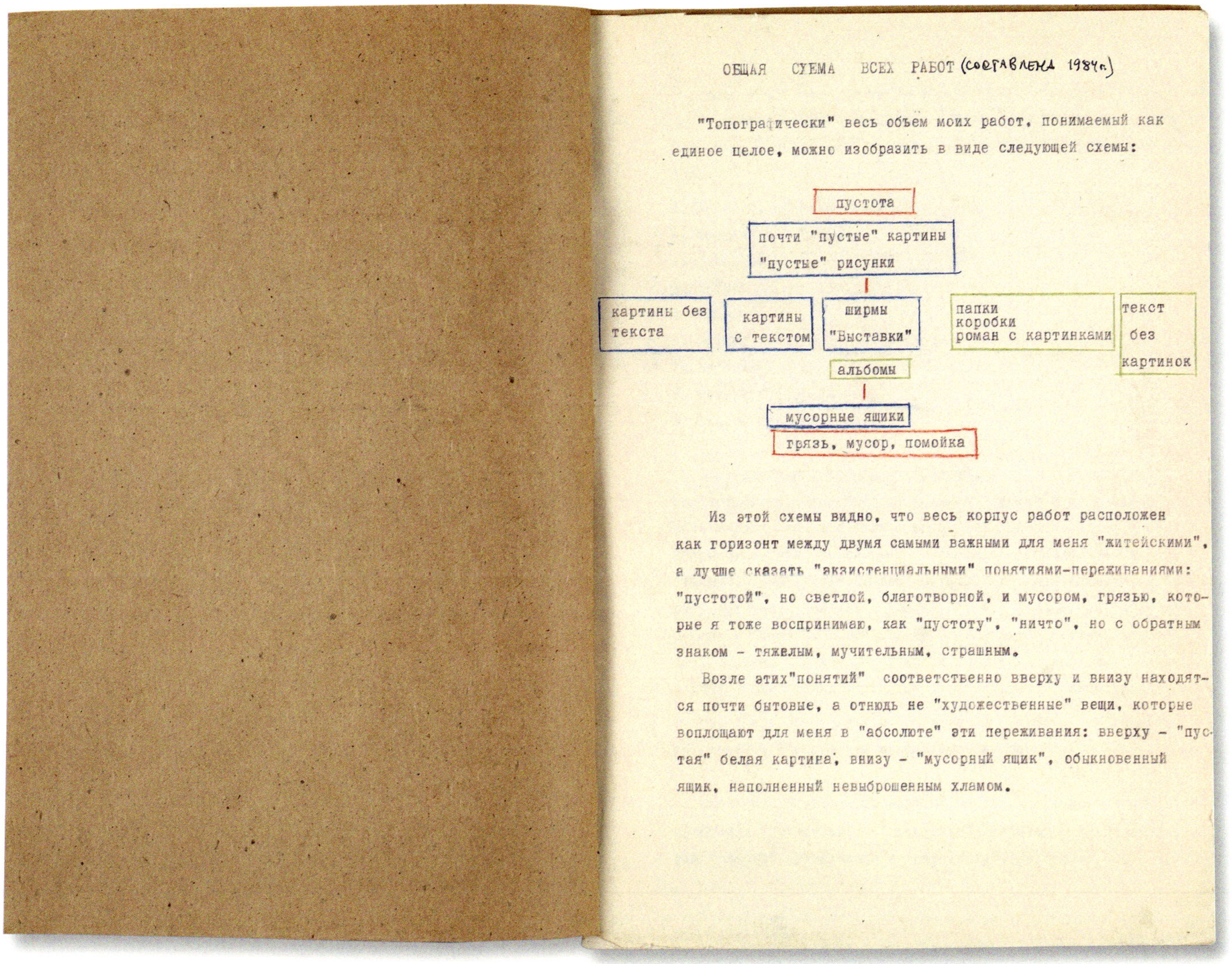

ОБЩАЯ СУЕМА ВСЕХ РАБОТ (составлена 1984г.)

"Топографически" весь объем моих работ, понимаемый как единое целое, можно изобразить в виде следующей схемы:

Из этой схемы видно, что весь корпус работ расположен как горизонт между двумя самыми важными для меня "житейскими", а лучше сказать "акзистенциальными" понятиями-переживаниями: "пустотой", но светлой, благотворной, и мусором, грязью, которые я тоже воспринимаю, как "пустоту", "ничто", но с обратным знаком – тяжелым, мучительным, страшным.

Возле этих"понятий" соответственно вверху и внизу находятся почти бытовые, а отнюдь не "художественные" вещи, которые воплощают для меня в "абсолюте" эти переживания: вверху – "пустая" белая картина, внизу – "мусорный ящик", обыкновенный ящик, наполненный невыброшенным хламом.

13 Shovel | *Schaufel*

1984

Ilya Kabakov
Moscow: published by the author
30 x 21.4 cm
11 pp. with 2 b/w ills.
stapled, cardboard cover
Drahtheftung, Kartonumschlag
edition: 10 copies

thematic publication | *thematische Publikation*

layout by Ilya Kabakov | *Layout von Ilya Kabakov*

Texts by Ilya Kabakov accompanying the painting of the same name; Russian.

Texte von Ilya Kabakov zum gleichnamigen Gemälde; russisch.

see also | *siehe auch* CRP, vol. 1, no. 110, pp. 190–192, 409–410

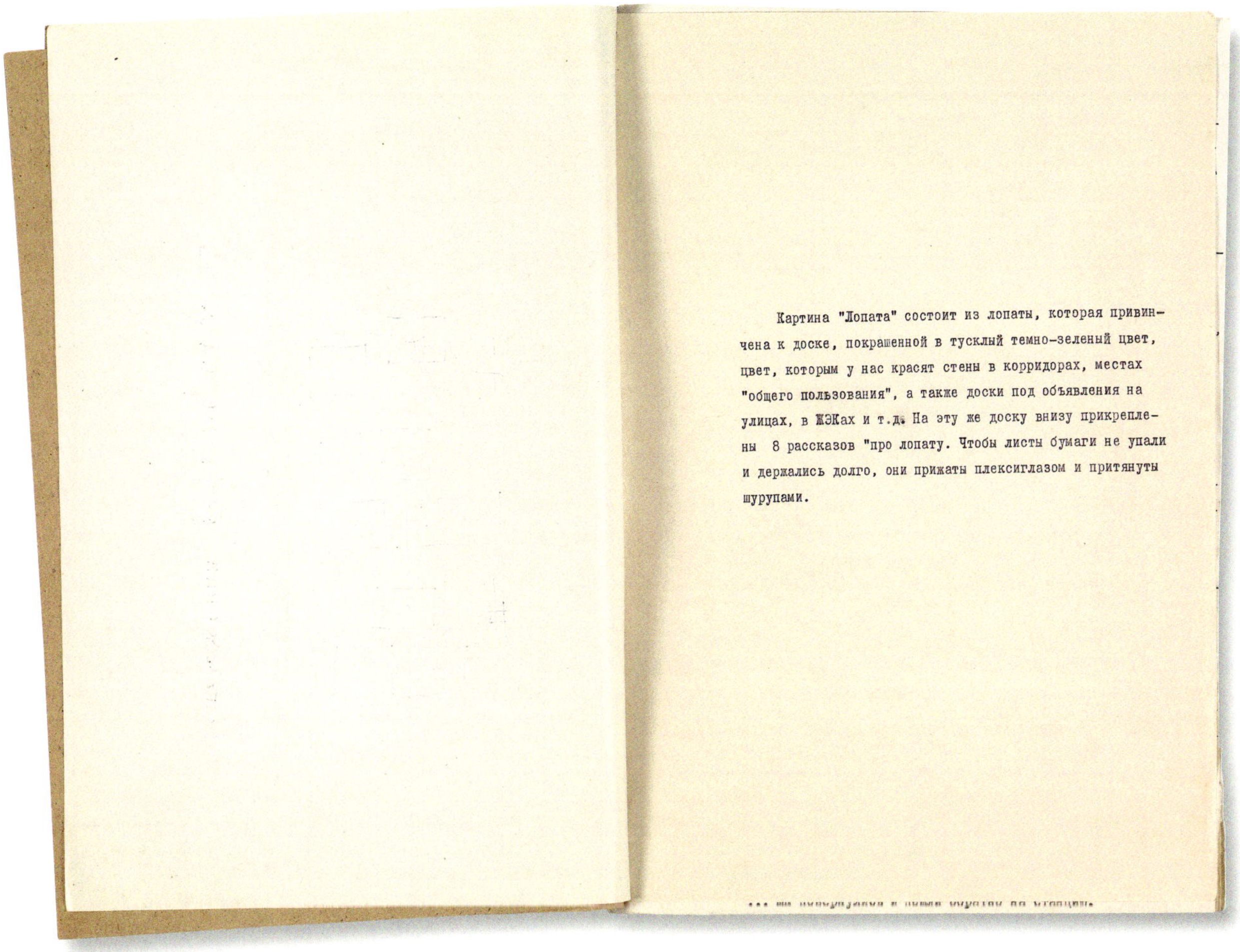

Картина "Лопата" состоит из лопаты, которая привинчена к доске, покрашенной в тусклый темно-зеленый цвет, цвет, которым у нас красят стены в корридорах, местах "общего пользования", а также доски под объявления на улицах, в ЖЭКах и т.д. На эту же доску внизу прикреплены 8 рассказов "про лопату. Чтобы листы бумаги не упали и держались долго, они прижаты плексиглазом и притянуты шурупами.

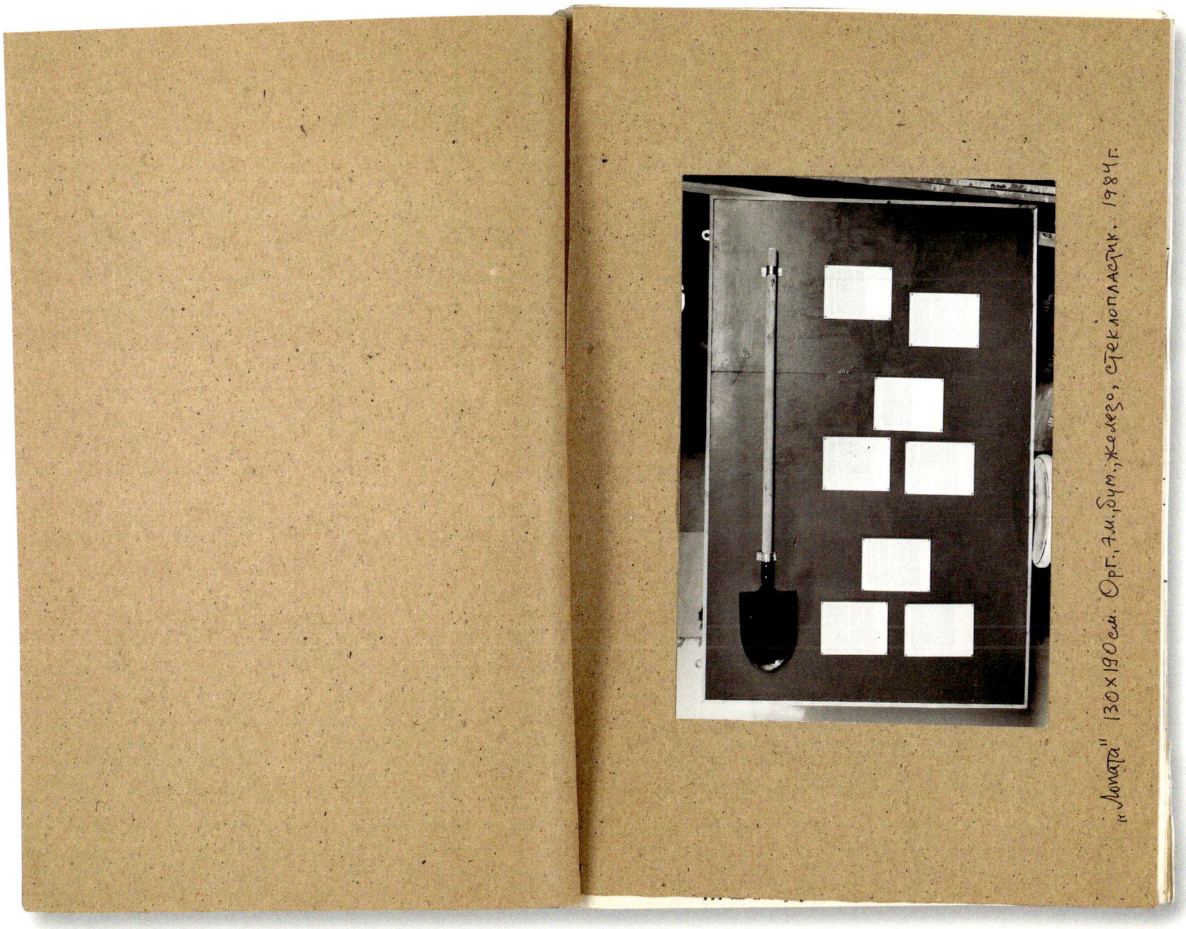

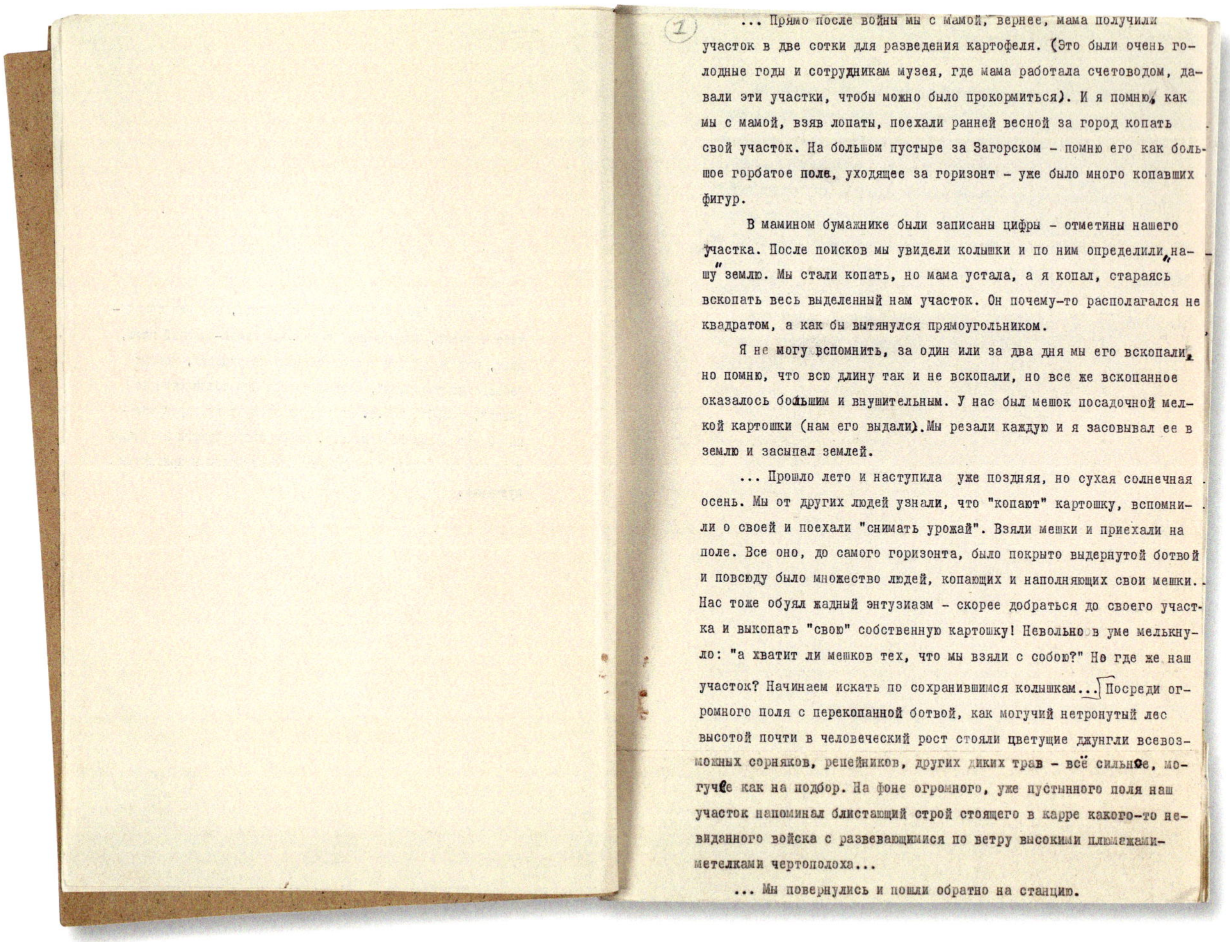

... Прямо после войны мы с мамой, вернее, мама получили участок в две сотки для разведения картофеля. (Это были очень голодные годы и сотрудникам музея, где мама работала счетоводом, давали эти участки, чтобы можно было прокормиться). И я помню, как мы с мамой, взяв лопаты, поехали ранней весной за город копать свой участок. На большом пустыре за Загорском – помню его как большое горбатое поле, уходящее за горизонт – уже было много копавших фигур.

В мамином бумажнике были записаны цифры – отметины нашего участка. После поисков мы увидели колышки и по ним определили „нашу" землю. Мы стали копать, но мама устала, а я копал, стараясь вскопать весь выделенный нам участок. Он почему-то располагался не квадратом, а как бы вытянулся прямоугольником.

Я не могу вспомнить, за один или за два дня мы его вскопали, но помню, что всю длину так и не вскопали, но все же вскопанное оказалось большим и внушительным. У нас был мешок посадочной мелкой картошки (нам его выдали). Мы резали каждую и я засовывал ее в землю и засыпал землей.

... Прошло лето и наступила уже поздняя, но сухая солнечная осень. Мы от других людей узнали, что "копают" картошку, вспомнили о своей и поехали "снимать урожай". Взяли мешки и приехали на поле. Все оно, до самого горизонта, было покрыто выдернутой ботвой и повсюду было множество людей, копающих и наполняющих свои мешки. Нас тоже обуял жадный энтузиазм – скорее добраться до своего участка и выкопать "свою" собственную картошку! Невольно в уме мелькнуло: "а хватит ли мешков тех, что мы взяли с собою?" Но где же наш участок? Начинаем искать по сохранившимся колышкам... Посреди огромного поля с перекопанной ботвой, как могучий нетронутый лес высотой почти в человеческий рост стояли цветущие джунгли всевозможных сорняков, репейников, других диких трав – всё сильные, могучие как на подбор. На фоне огромного, уже пустынного поля наш участок напоминал блистающий строй стоящего в карре какого-то невиданного войска с развевающимися по ветру высокими плюмажами-метелками чертополоха...

... Мы повернулись и пошли обратно на станцию.

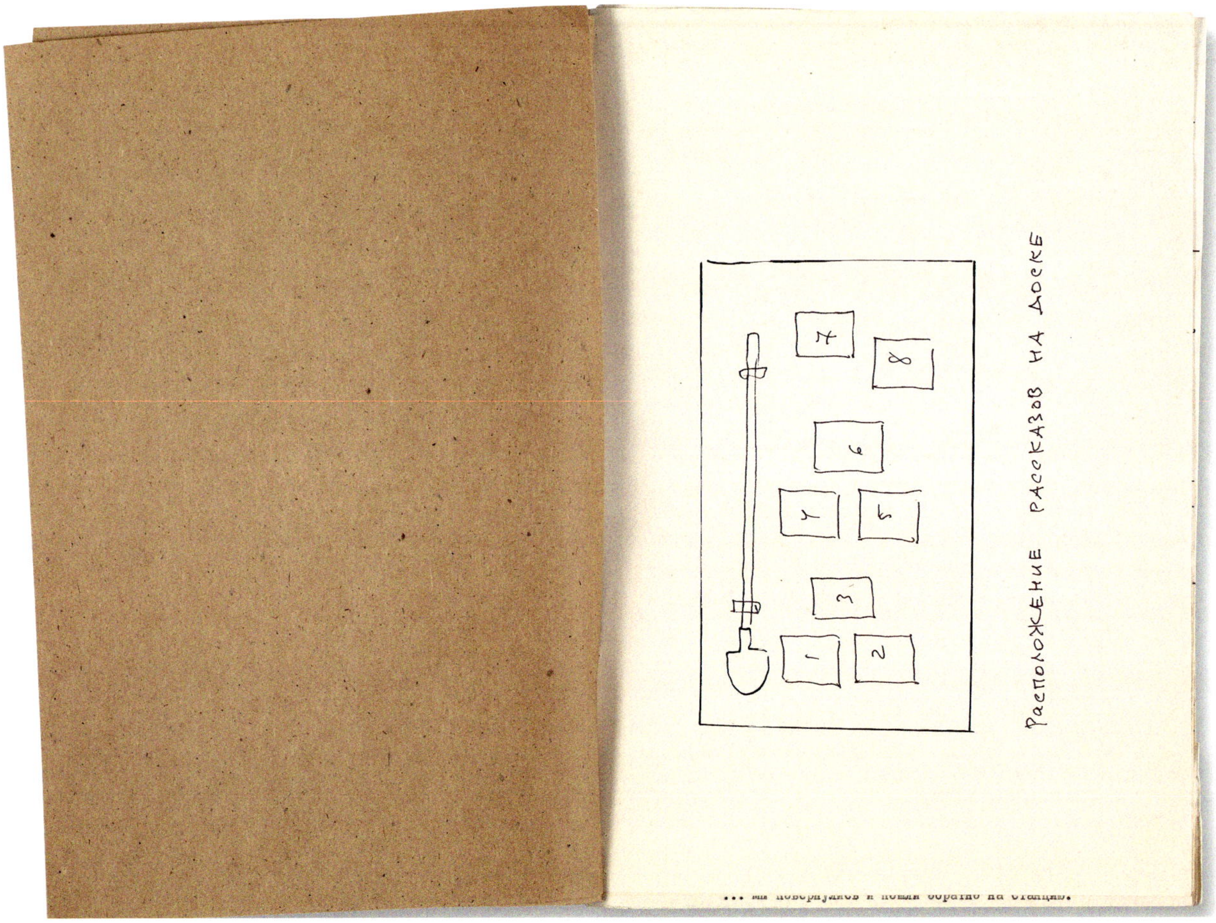

14 The Seventies | *Die 70er Jahre*

1984

Ilya Kabakov
Moscow: published by the author
31.8 x 23 cm
139 pp. with 1 b/w ill.
quick bind, two screws, cardboard cover
Schnellhefter, zwei Schrauben, Kartonumschlag
edition: 10 copies

thematic publication | *thematische Publikation*

layout by Ilya Kabakov | *Layout von Ilya Kabakov*

Ilya Kabakov depicts his own artistic development within the context of the unofficial art scene in Moscow in the 1970s. The text was published in 1999 and 2008 as Part 2 in the book »The Sixties and the Seventies: Notes About Unofficial Life in Moscow«; published in German in 2001 and in Japanese in 2007; Russian.

Ilya Kabakov schildert den eigenen künstlerischen Werdegang im Kontext der inoffiziellen Kunst in Moskau in den 1970er Jahren. Der Text wurde 1999 und 2008 als Teil 2 im Buch »Die 60er und 70er Jahre. Aufzeichnungen über das inoffizielle Leben in Moskau« publiziert; 2001 deutsche Ausgabe und 2007 japanische Ausgabe; russisch.

see also | *siehe auch* no. 107; no. 116; no. 131; no. 136

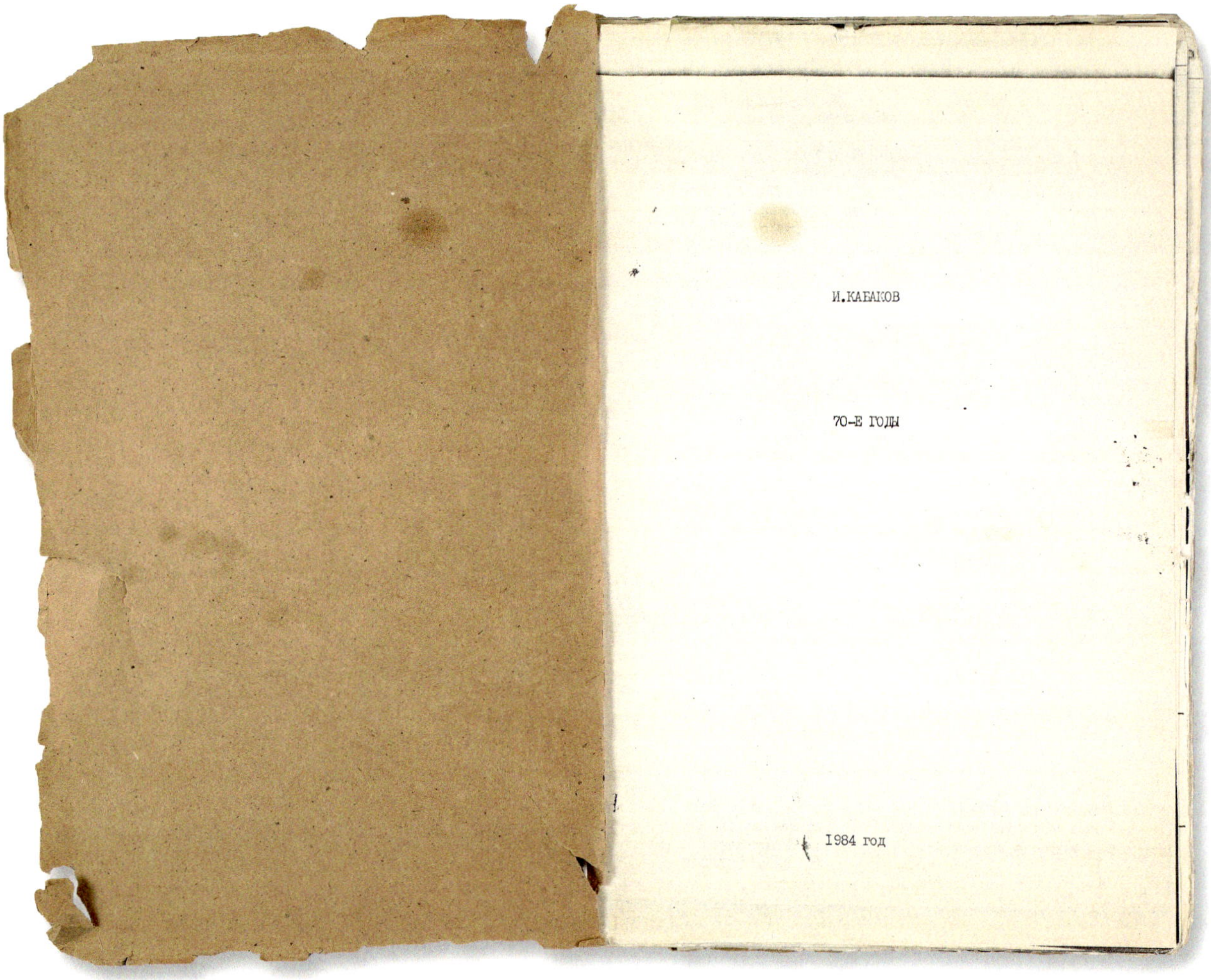

И.КАБАКОВ

70-Е ГОДЫ

1984 год

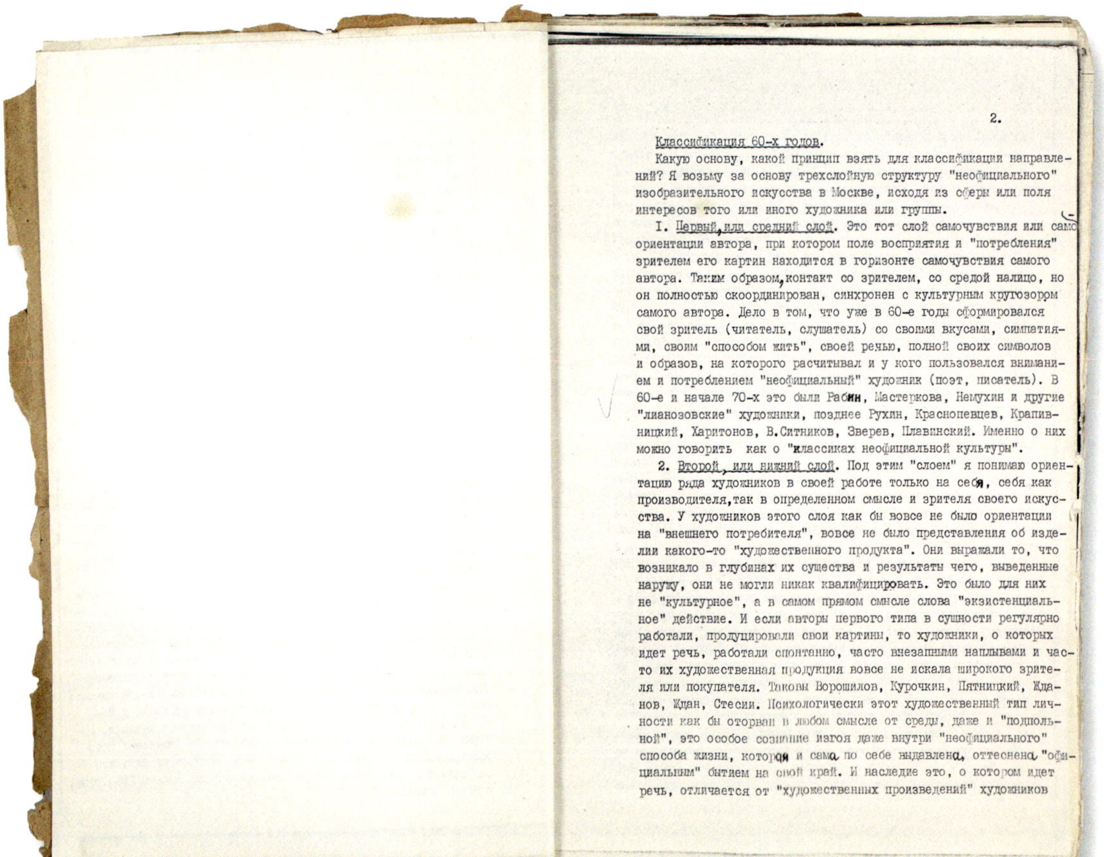

2.

Классификация 60-х годов.

Какую основу, какой принцип взять для классификации направлений? Я возьму за основу трехслойную структуру "неофициального" изобразительного искусства в Москве, исходя из сферы или поля интересов того или иного художника или группы.

I. Первый, или средний слой. Это тот слой самочувствия или само ориентации автора, при котором поле восприятия и "потребления" зрителем его картин находится в горизонте самочувствия самого автора. Таким образом, контакт со зрителем, со средой налицо, но он полностью скоординирован, синхронен с культурным кругозором самого автора. Дело в том, что уже в 60-е годы сформировался свой зритель (читатель, слушатель) со своими вкусами, симпатиями, своим "способом жить", своей речью, полной своих символов и образов, на которого расчитывал и у кого пользовался вниманием и потреблением "неофициальный" художник (поэт, писатель). В 60-е и начале 70-х это были Рабин, Мастеркова, Немухин и другие "лианозовские" художники, позднее Рухин, Краснопевцев, Крапивницкий, Харитонов, В.Ситников, Зверев, Плавинский. Именно о них можно говорить как о "классиках неофициальной культуры".

2. Второй, или нижний слой. Под этим "слоем" я понимаю ориентацию ряда художников в своей работе только на себя, себя как производителя, так в определенном смысле и зрителя своего искусства. У художников этого слоя как бы вовсе не было ориентации на "внешнего потребителя", вовсе не было представления об изделии какого-то "художественного продукта". Они выражали то, что возникало в глубинах их существа и результаты чего, выведенные наружу, они не могли никак квалифицировать. Это было для них не "культурное", а в самом прямом смысле слова "экзистенциальное" действие. И если авторы первого типа в сущности регулярно работали, продуцировали свои картины, то художники, о которых идет речь, работали спонтанно, часто внезапными наплывами и часто их художественная продукция вовсе не искала широкого зрителя или покупателя. Таковы Ворошилов, Курочкин, Пятницкий, Жданов, Ждан, Стесин. Психологически этот художественный тип личности как бы оторван в любом смысле от среды, даже и "подпольной", это особое сознание изгоя даже внутри "неофициального" способа жизни, которая и сама по себе выдавлена, оттеснена "официальным" бытием на свой край. И наследие это, о котором идет речь, отличается от "художественных произведений" художников

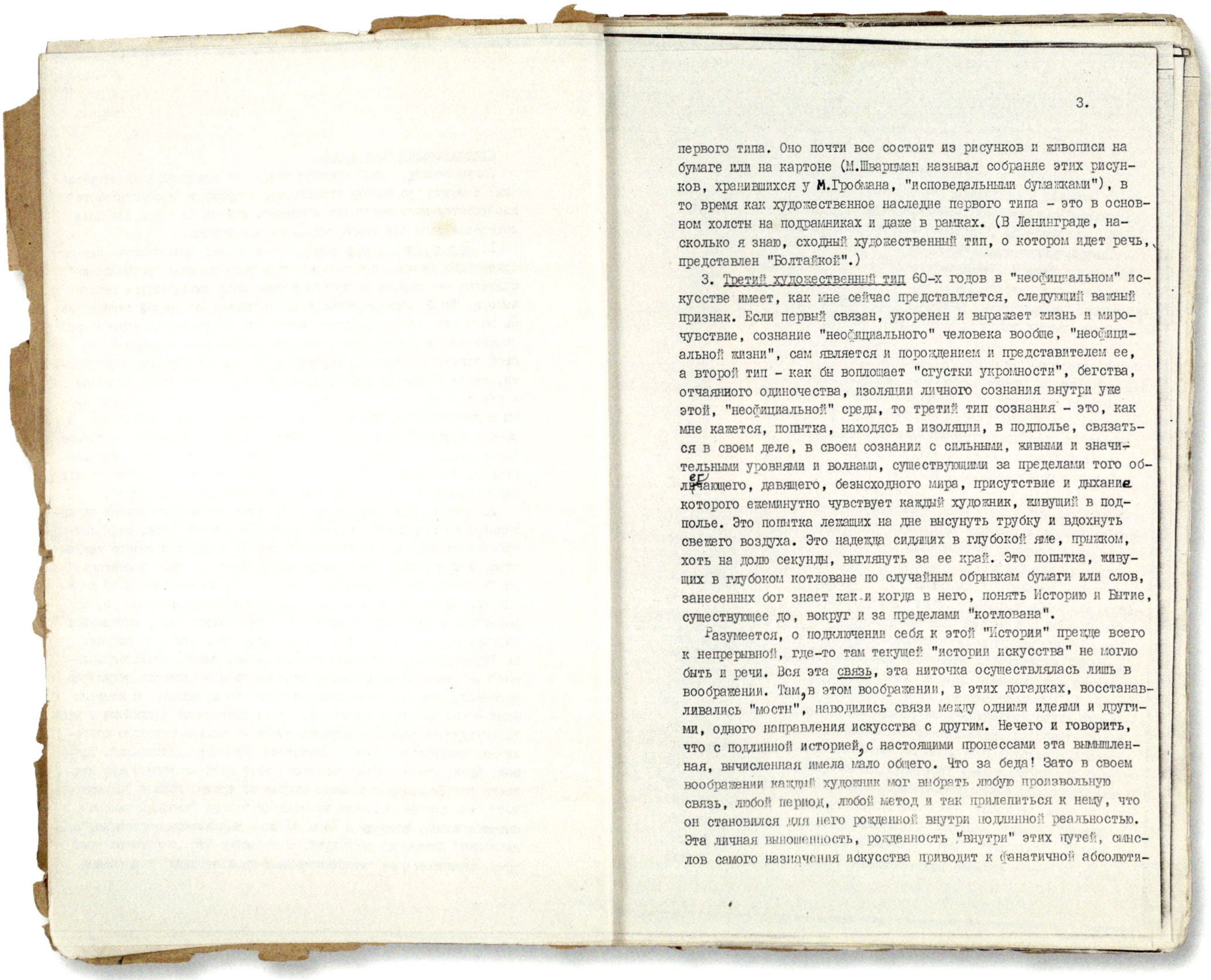

3.

первого типа. Оно почти все состоит из рисунков и живописи на бумаге или на картоне (М.Шварцман называл собрание этих рисунков, хранившихся у М.Гробмана, "исповедальными бумажками"), в то время как художественное наследие первого типа - это в основном холсты на подрамниках и даже в рамках. (В Ленинграде, насколько я знаю, сходный художественный тип, о котором идет речь, представлен "Болтайкой".)

3. Третий художественный тип 60-х годов в "неофициальном" искусстве имеет, как мне сейчас представляется, следующий важный признак. Если первый связан, укоренен и выражает жизнь и мирочувствие, сознание "неофициального" человека вообще, "неофициальной жизни", сам является и порождением и представителем ее, а второй тип - как бы воплощает "сгустки укромности", бегства, отчаянного одиночества, изоляции личного сознания внутри уже этой, "неофициальной" среды, то третий тип сознания - это, как мне кажется, попытка, находясь в изоляции, в подполье, связаться в своем деле, в своем сознании с сильными, живыми и значительными уровнями и волнами, существующими за пределами того облегающего, давящего, безысходного мира, присутствие и дыхание которого ежеминутно чувствует каждый художник, живущий в подполье. Это попытка лежащих на дне высунуть трубку и вдохнуть свежего воздуха. Это надежда сидящих в глубокой яме, прыжком, хоть на долю секунды, выглянуть за ее край. Это попытка, живущих в глубоком котловане по случайным обрывкам бумаги или слов, занесенных бог знает как и когда в него, понять Историю и Бытие, существующее до, вокруг и за пределами "котлована".

Разумеется, о подключении себя к этой "Истории" прежде всего к непрерывной, где-то там текущей "истории искусства" не могло быть и речи. Вся эта связь, эта ниточка осуществлялась лишь в воображении. Там, в этом воображении, в этих догадках, восстанавливались "мосты", наводились связи между одними идеями и другими, одного направления искусства с другим. Нечего и говорить, что с подлинной историей, с настоящими процессами эта вымышленная, вычисленная имела мало общего. Что за беда! Зато в своем воображении каждый художник мог выбрать любую произвольную связь, любой период, любой метод и так прилепиться к нему, что он становился для него рожденной внутри подлинной реальностью. Эта личная выношенность, рожденность "внутри" этих путей, смыслов самого назначения искусства приводит к фанатичной абсолюти-

15 Three 'Russian' Paintings | *Drei ,russische' Bilder*

1984

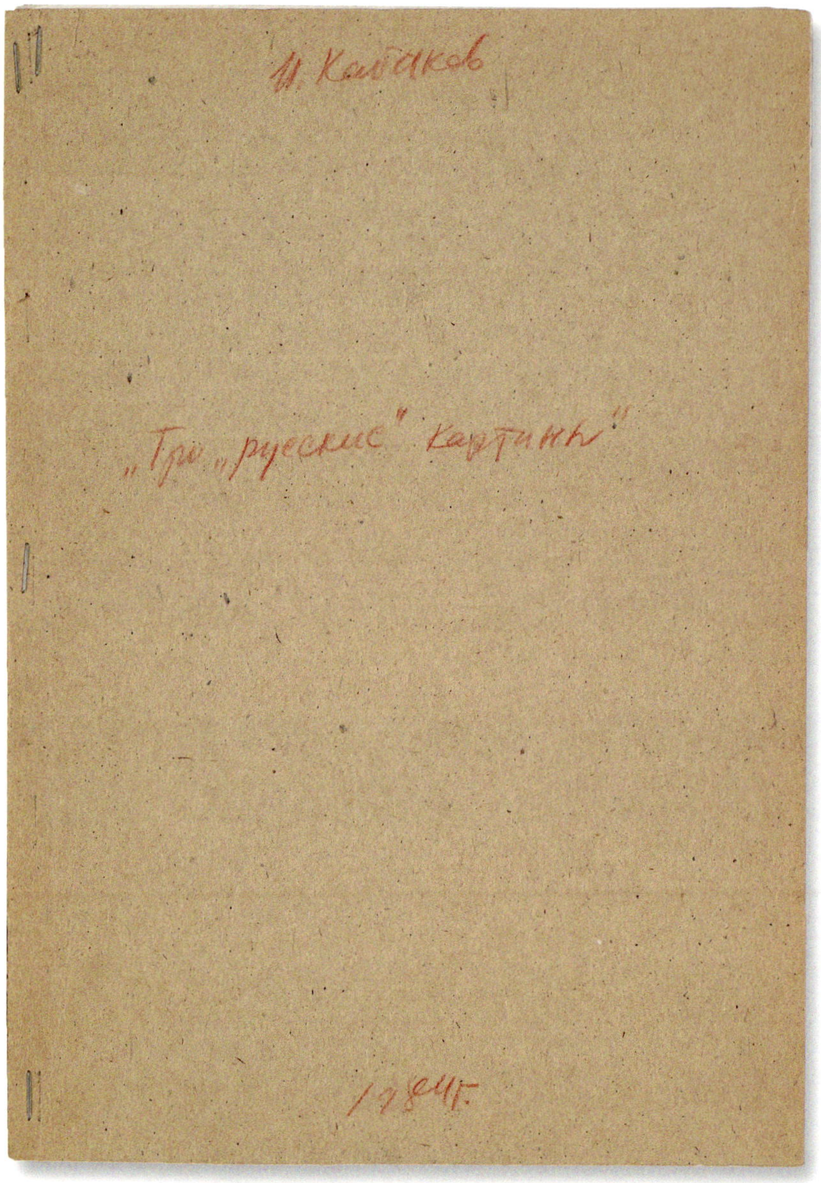

Ilya Kabakov
Moscow: published by the author
29.5 x 21 cm
8 pp. with 4 b/w ills.
stapled, cardboard cover
Drahtheftung, Kartonumschlag
edition: 10 copies

thematic publication | *thematische Publikation*

layout by Ilya Kabakov | *Layout von Ilya Kabakov*

Documentation of the installation of the same name featuring the paintings »Ivan Trofimovich Goes to Collect Wood, In the Corner, They Lie Below« from 1969 and with an »Explanation Table« from 1980 containing Kabakov's explanations of the paintings; Russian.

Dokumentation der gleichnamigen Installation mit den Gemälden »Iwan Trofimowitsch fährt Holz holen, In der Ecke, Sie liegen unten« von 1969 sowie mit einer »Erklärungstafel« von 1980 mit Kabakovs Bilderläuterungen; russisch.

see also | *siehe auch* CRI, vol. 1, no. 57, pp. 374–379; CRP, vol. 1, nos. 30–32, pp. 73–75, no. 54, p. 110

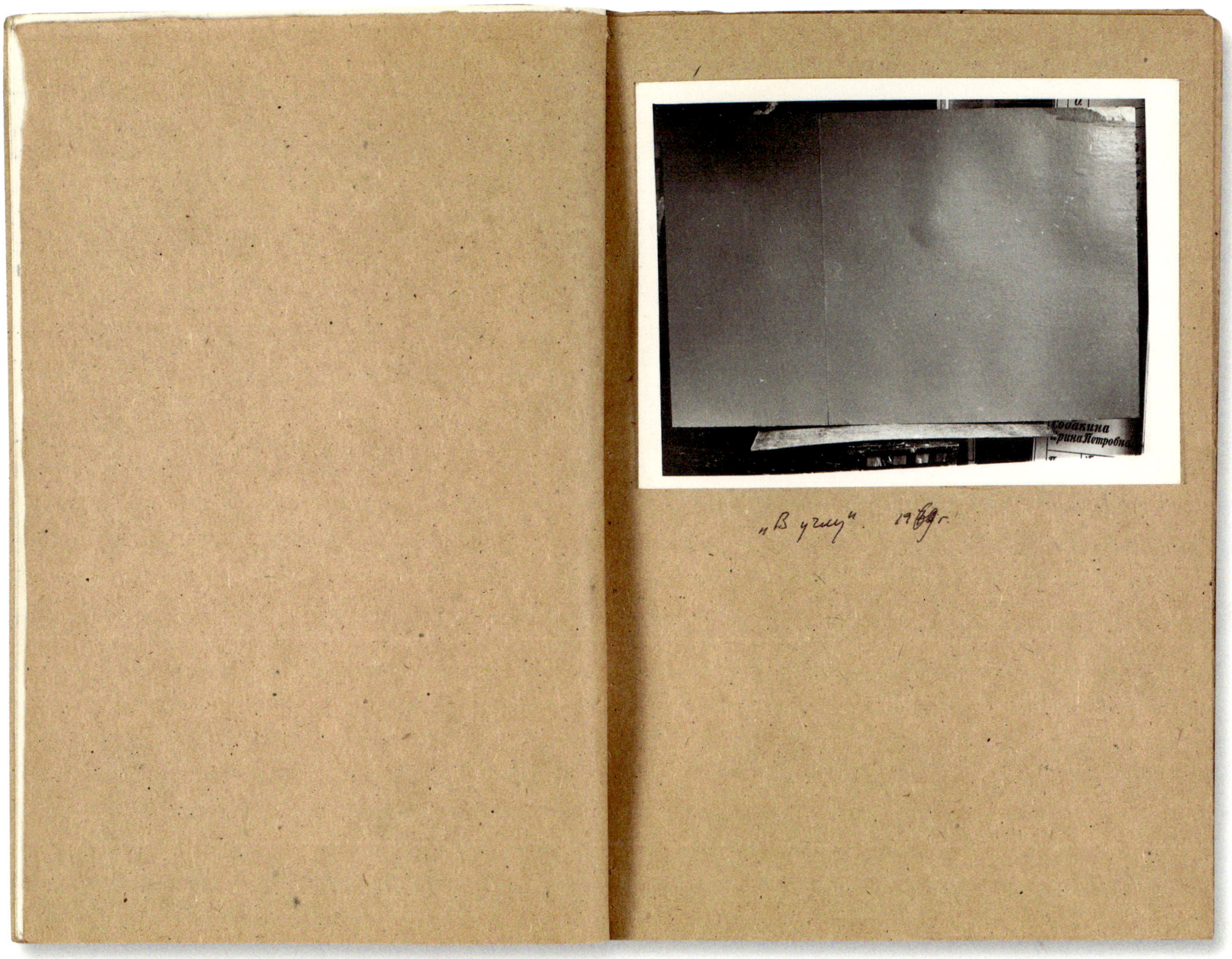

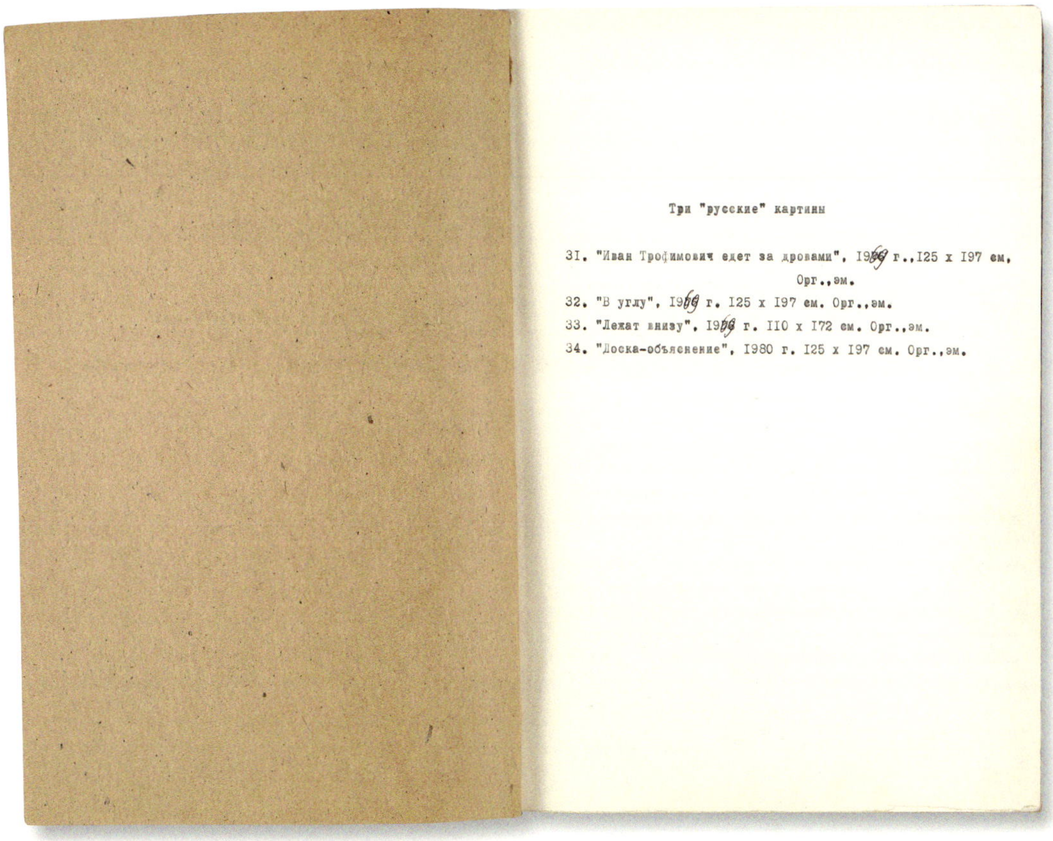

Три "русские" картины

31. "Иван Трофимович едет за дровами", 1969 г., I25 x I97 см, Орг., эм.
32. "В углу", 1969 г. I25 x I97 см. Орг., эм.
33. "Лежат внизу", 1969 г. II0 x I72 см. Орг., эм.
34. "Доска-объяснение", I980 г. I25 x I97 см. Орг., эм.

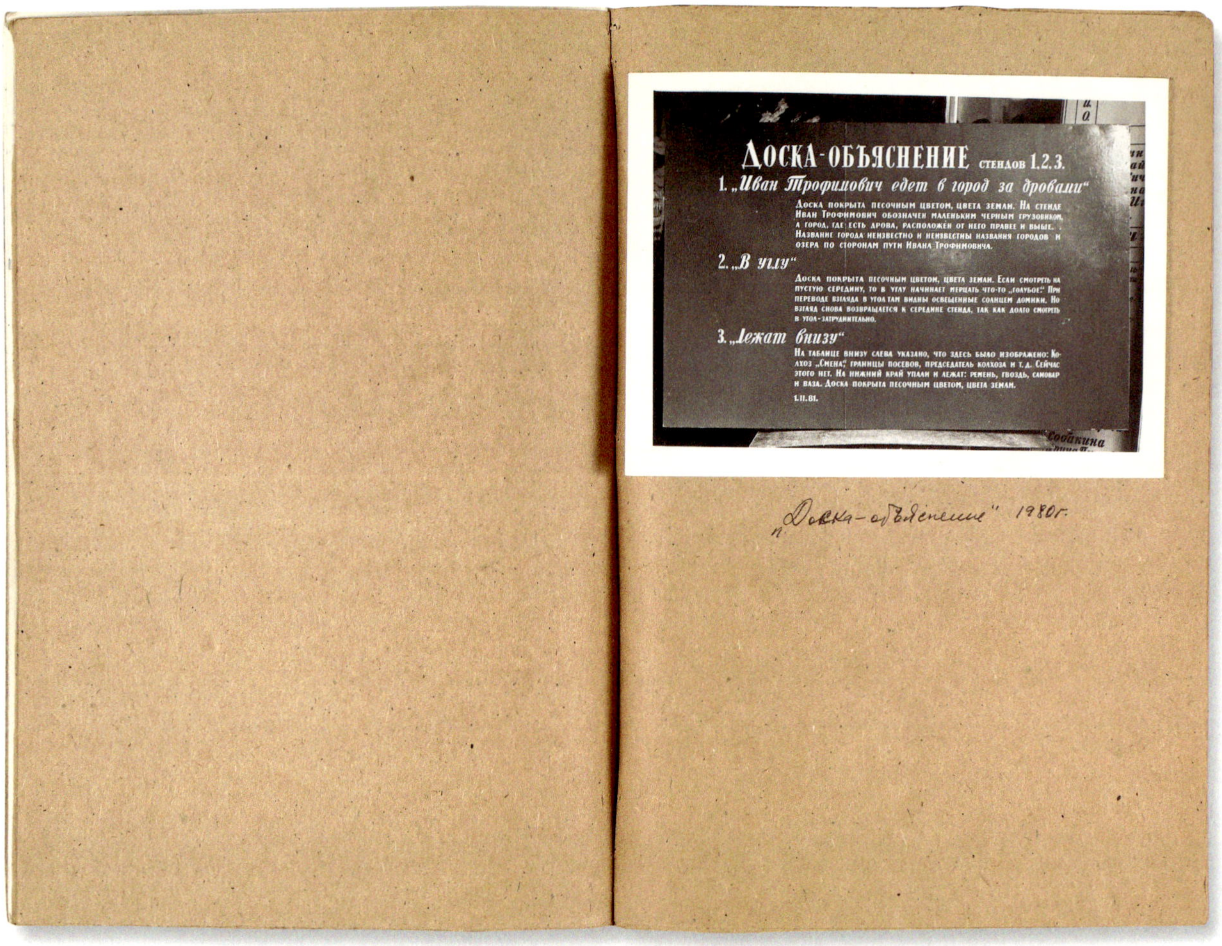
Доска-объяснение стендов 1.2.3.
1. „Иван Трофимович едет в город за дровами“
Доска покрыта песочным цветом, цвета земли. На стенде Иван Трофимович обозначен маленьким черным грузовиком, а город, где есть дрова, расположен от него правее и выше. Название города неизвестно и неизвестны названия городов и озера по сторонам пути Ивана Трофимовича.
2. „В углу“
Доска покрыта песочным цветом, цвета земли. Если смотреть на пустую середину, то в углу начинает мерцать что-то „голубое“. При переводе взгляда в угол там видны освещенные солнцем домики. Но взгляд снова возвращается к середине стенда, так как долго смотреть в угол - затруднительно.
3. „Лежат внизу“
На табличке внизу слева указано, что здесь было изображено: Колхоз „Смена“, границы посевов, председатель колхоза и т. д. Сейчас этого нет. На нижний край упали и лежат: ремень, гвоздь, самовар и ваза. Доска покрыта песочным цветом, цвета земли.
1.II.81.
Собакина
„Доска-объяснение“ 1980 г.

Собакина
Ирина Петровна
„Иван Трофимович едет за дровами“
1969 г.

16 The Window. Arkhipov Looking Through the Window

Das Fenster. Der aus dem Fenster schauende Archipow

1985

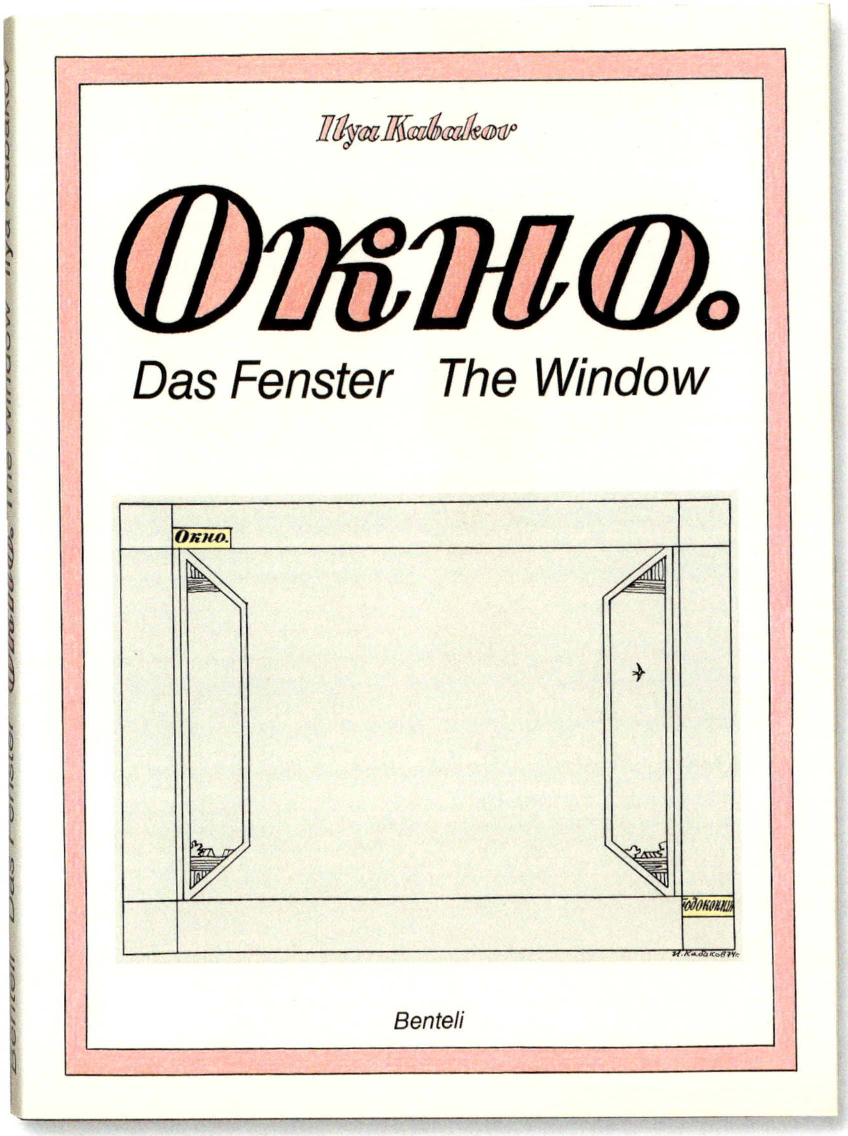

Ilya Kabakov
Bern: Benteli Verlag
32.6 x 24.7 cm
142 pp. with 52 (50 color) ills.
stitchbound, clothbound with blind blocking, dustjacket
Fadenheftung, Leinen mit Blindprägung, Schutzumschlag
edition: a limited edition of the book includes an original drawing by Ilya Kabakov, numbered A1-20, B1-20, C1-20

thematic publication | *thematische Publikation*

layout by Ilya Kabakov | *Layout von Ilya Kabakov*

For the exhibition »Am Rande« by Ilya Kabakov, Kunsthalle Bern, Bern, August 31 to November 18, 1985. Texts by Jean-Hubert Martin, Claudia Jolles, and Ilya Kabakov. The book illustrates Ilya Kabakov's tenth album »Arkhipov Looking Through the Window« from the »10 Characters« album series (1972–1975) and exists in a reciprocal relationship with the »On the Margins« paintings; German, English, Russian.

Zur Ausstellung »Am Rande« von Ilya Kabakov, Kunsthalle Bern, Bern, 31. August – 18. November 1985. Texte von Jean-Hubert Martin, Claudia Jolles und Ilya Kabakov.

Das Buch illustriert Ilya Kabakovs 10. Album »Der aus dem Fenster schauende Archipow« aus der Albumserie »10 Personen« (1972–1975) und steht in wechselseitiger Beziehung mit den Gemälden »Am Rande«; deutsch, englisch, russisch.

see also | *siehe auch* no. 3; no. 21; no. 68; no. 100

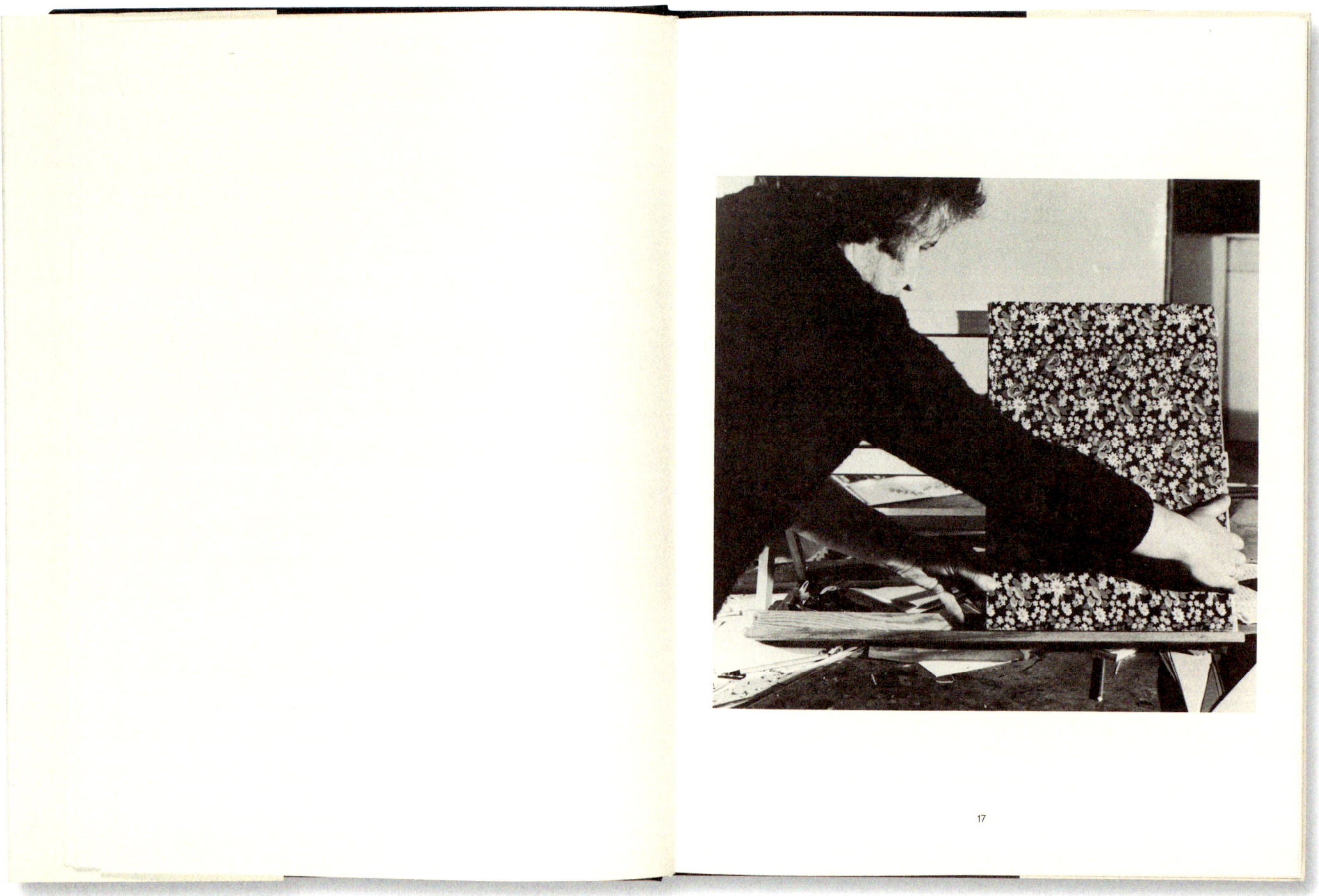
17

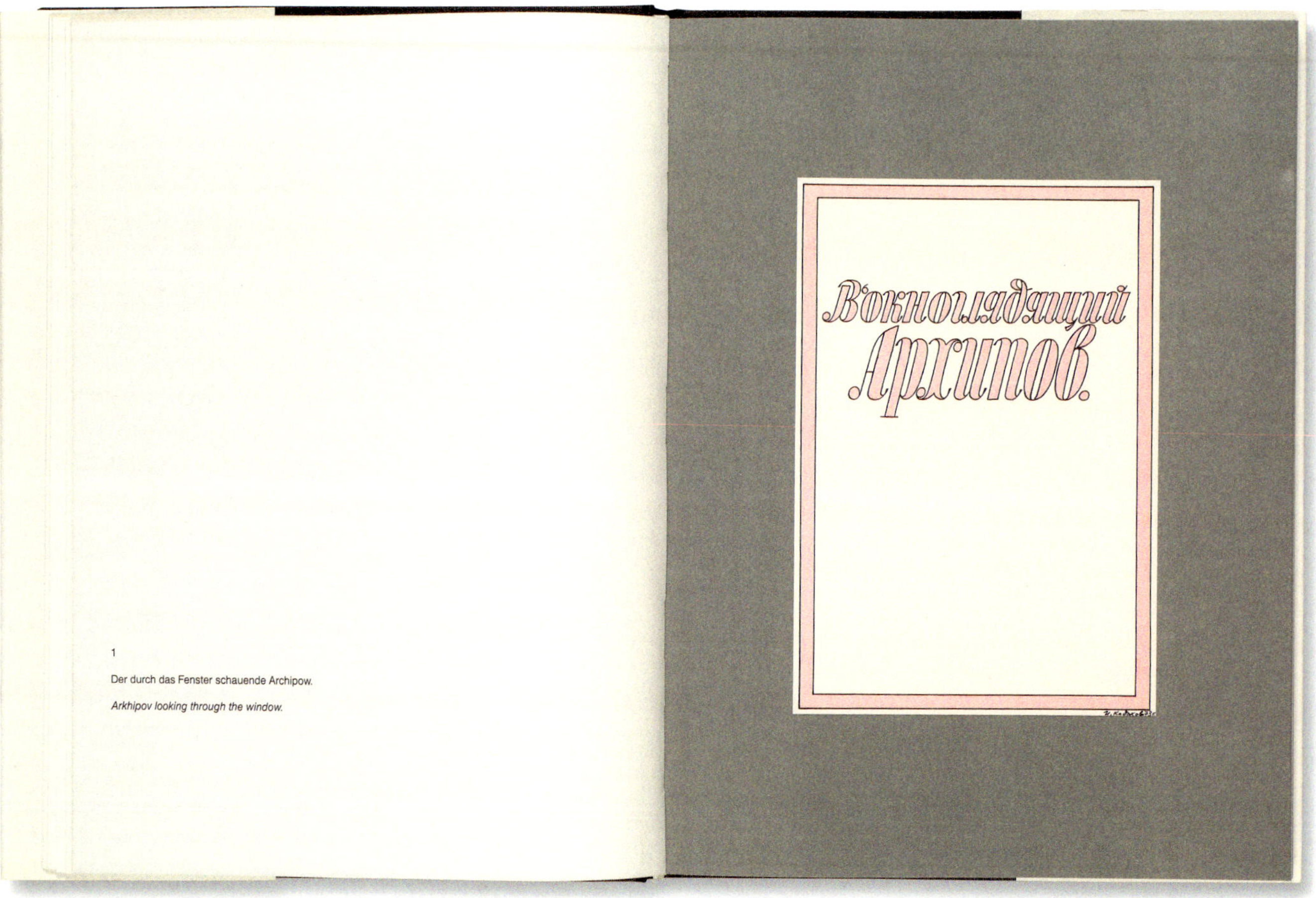
1
Der durch das Fenster schauende Archipow.
Arkhipov looking through the window.
Вокноглядящий
Архипов.

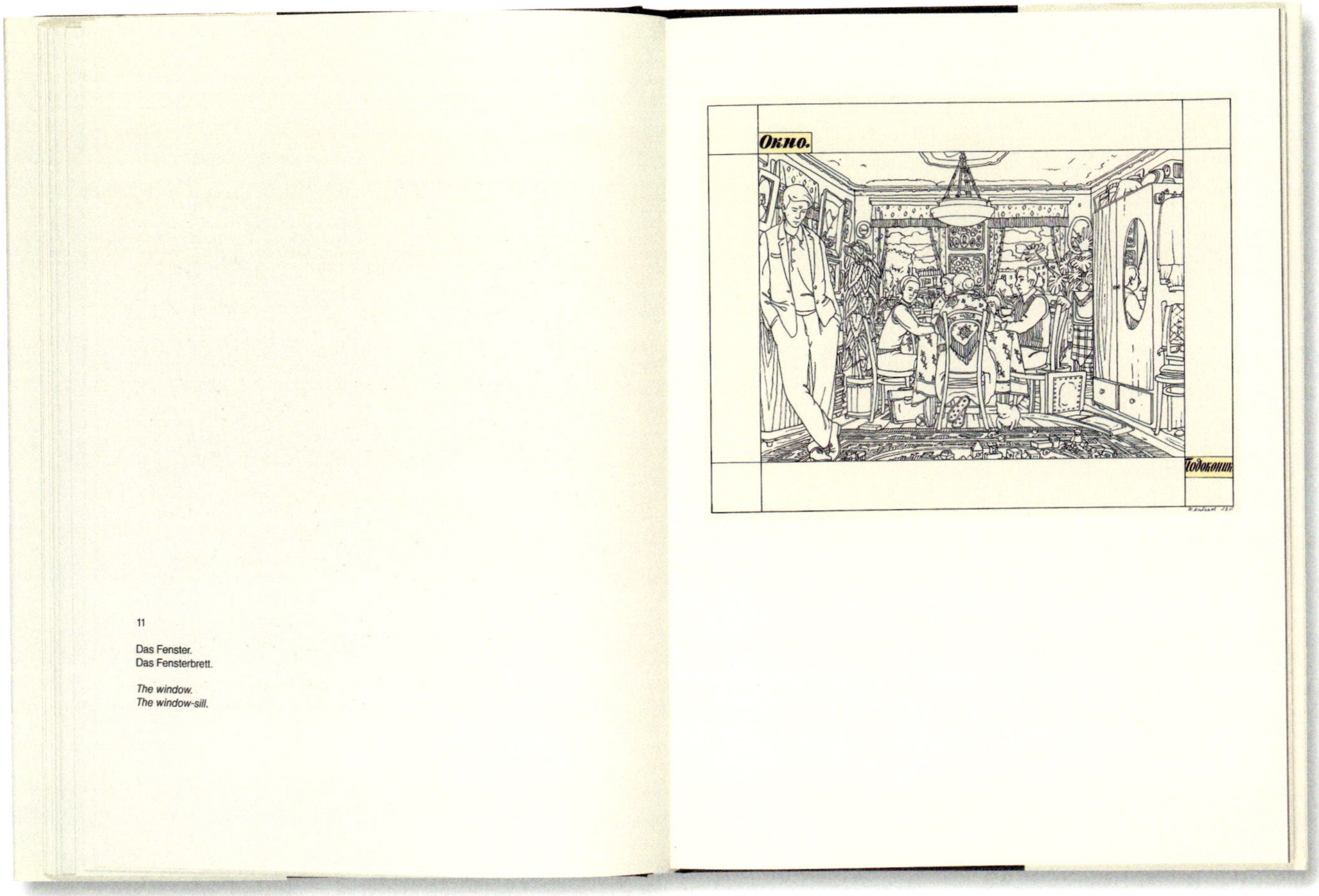
Окно.
Подоконник
11
Das Fenster.
Das Fensterbrett.
The window.
The window-sill.

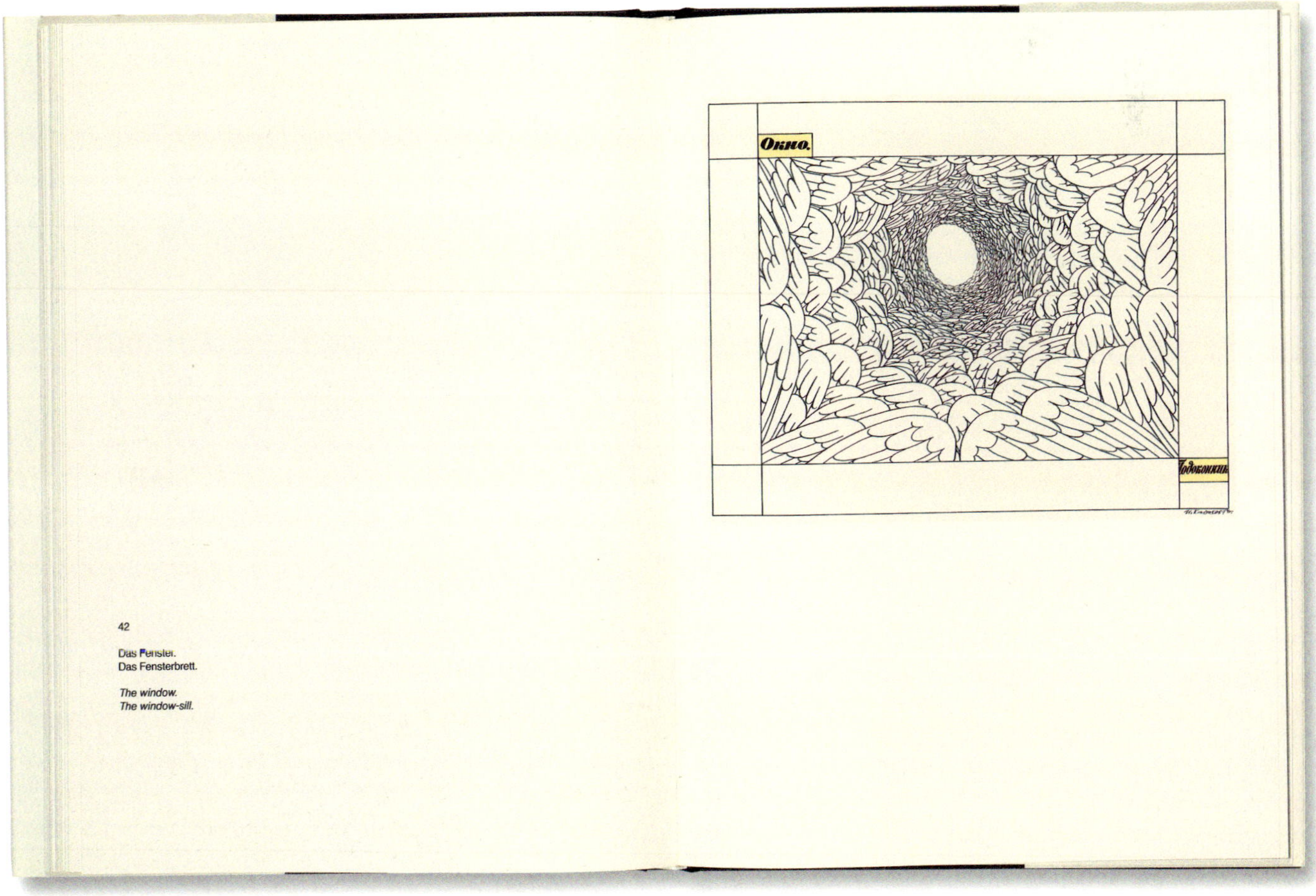
Окно.
Подоконник
42
Das Fenster.
Das Fensterbrett.
The window.
The window-sill.

17 Dust, Dirt, Garbage | *Staub, Schmutz, Müll*

1985

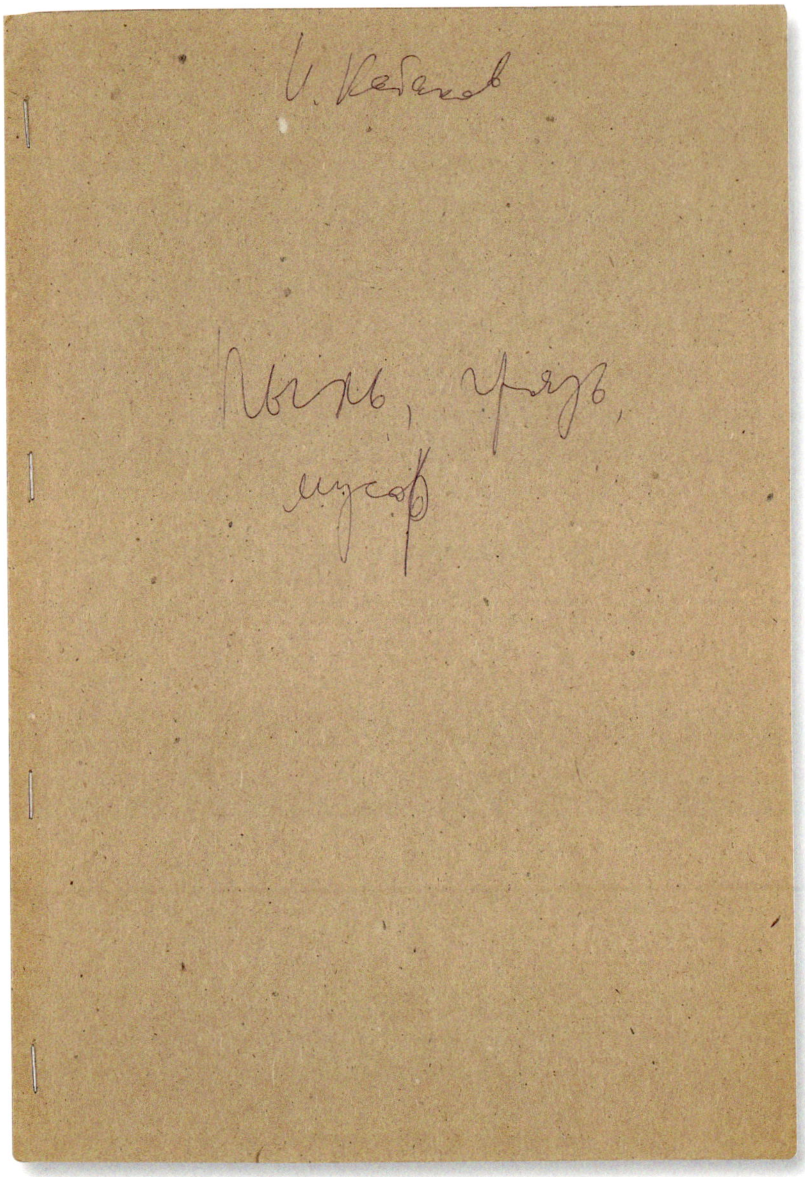

Ilya Kabakov
Moscow: published by the author
29.5 x 20.9 cm
7 pp.
stapled, cardboard cover
Drahtheftung, Kartonumschlag
edition: 10 copies

thematic publication | *thematische Publikation*

layout by Ilya Kabakov | *Layout von Ilya Kabakov*

Kabakov characterizes the work of the three artists Michail Schwarzman, Eduard Steinberg and Vladimir Yankilevsky with dust, dirt, and garbage; Russian.

Kabakov charakterisiert die Arbeit der drei Künstler Michail Schwarzman, Eduard Steinberg und Wladimir Jankilewski mit Staub, Schmutz und Müll; russisch.

see also | *siehe auch*

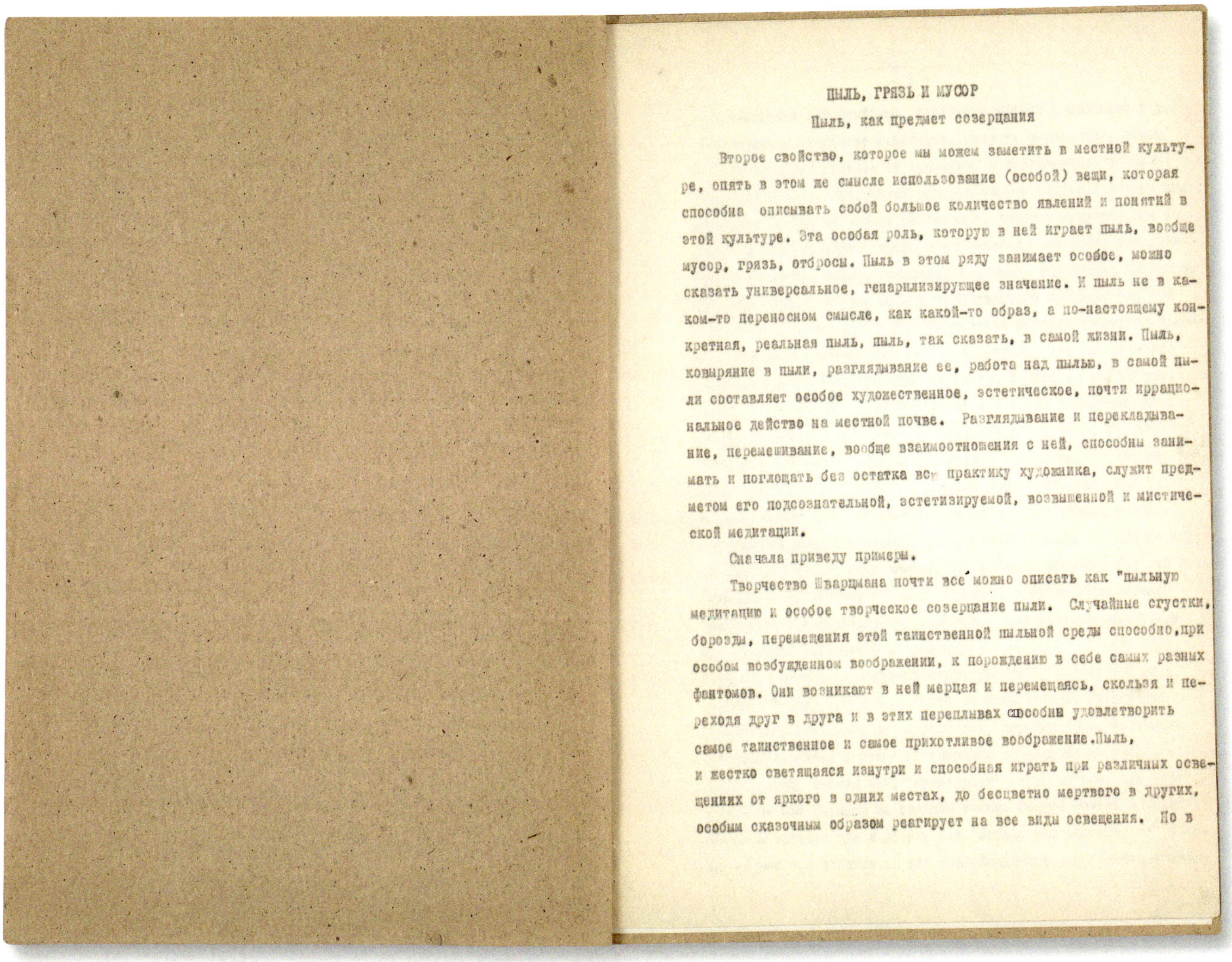

ПЫЛЬ, ГРЯЗЬ И МУСОР

Пыль, как предмет созерцания

Второе свойство, которое мы можем заметить в местной культуре, опять в этом же смысле использование (особой) вещи, которая способна описывать собой большое количество явлений и понятий в этой культуре. Эта особая роль, которую в ней играет пыль, вообще мусор, грязь, отбросы. Пыль в этом ряду занимает особое, можно сказать универсальное, генарилизирующее значение. И пыль не в каком-то переносном смысле, как какой-то образ, а по-настоящему конкретная, реальная пыль, пыль, так сказать, в самой жизни. Пыль, ковыряние в пыли, разглядывание ее, работа над пылью, в самой пыли составляет особое художественное, эстетическое, почти иррациональное действо на местной почве. Разглядывание и перекладывание, перемешивание, вообще взаимоотношения с ней, способны занимать и поглощать без остатка всю практику художника, служит предметом его подсознательной, эстетизируемой, возвышенной и мистической медитации.

Сначала приведу примеры.

Творчество Шварцмана почти всё можно описать как "пыльную медитацию и особое творческое созерцание пыли. Случайные сгустки, борозды, перемещения этой таинственной пыльной среды способно, при особом возбужденном воображении, к порождению в себе самых разных фантомов. Они возникают в ней мерцая и перемещаясь, скользя и переходя друг в друга и в этих переплывах способны удовлетворить самое таинственное и самое прихотливое воображение. Пыль,
и жестко светящаяся изнутри и способная играть при различных освещениях от яркого в одних местах, до бесцветно мертвого в других, особым сказочным образом реагирует на все виды освещения. Но в

18 Nikolai Petrovich | *Nikolai Petrowitsch*

1985

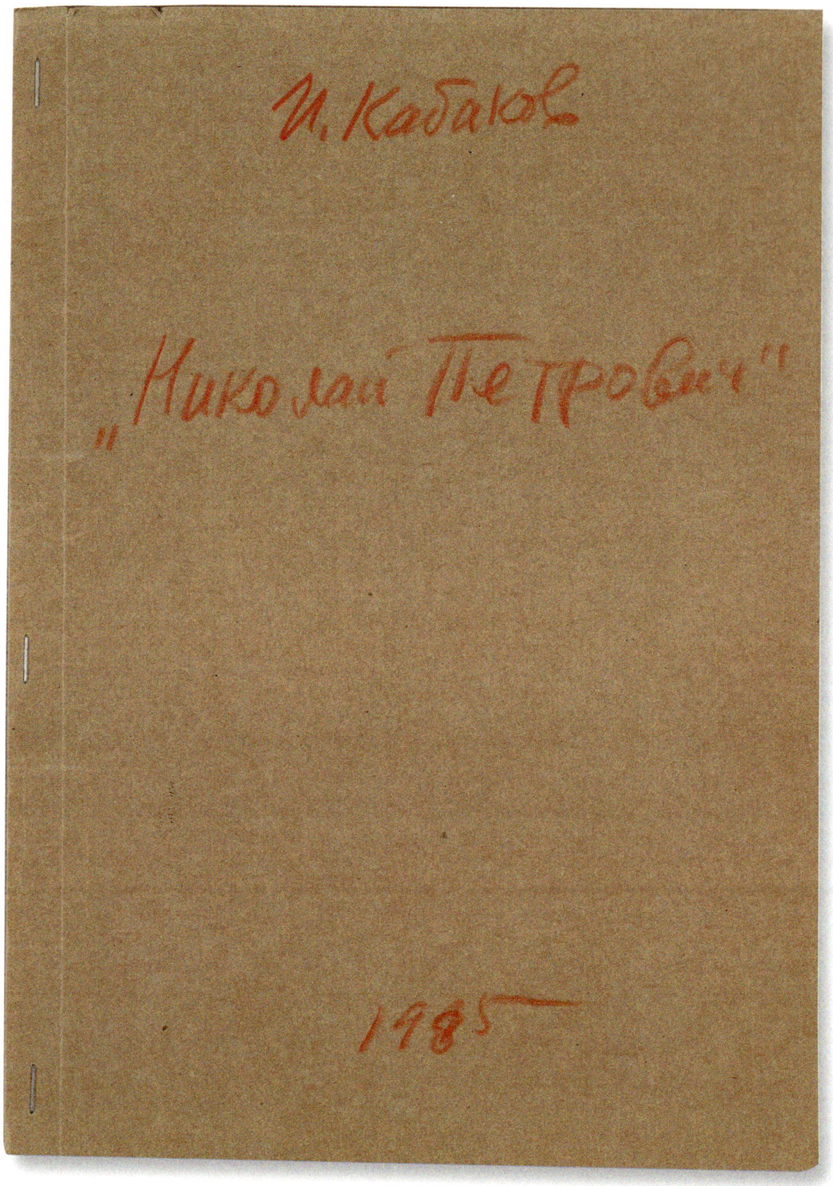

Ilya Kabakov
Moscow: published by the author
29.3 x 21.3 cm
17 pp.
stapled, cardboard cover
Drahtheftung, Kartonumschlag
edition: 10 copies

thematic publication | *thematische Publikation*

layout by Ilya Kabakov | *Layout von Ilya Kabakov*

Text by Ilya Kabakov; Russian. The text was published in 1987 in »A-Ya«, no. 7, a magazine founded by the sculptor Igor Shelkovski and published in Paris; reprinted in »The Text as the Basis of Visual Expression« and in the catalogue raisonné of the paintings«.

Text von Ilya Kabakov; russisch. Er erschien 1987 in der vom Bildhauer Igor Schelkowski gegründeten und in Paris publizierten Zeitschrift »A-Ya«, Nr. 7; Wiederabdruck im Buch »Der Text als Grundlage des Visuellen« und im Werkverzeichnis der Gemälde.

see also | *siehe auch* no. 111; CRP, vol. 1, no. 59, pp. 118–119, 406

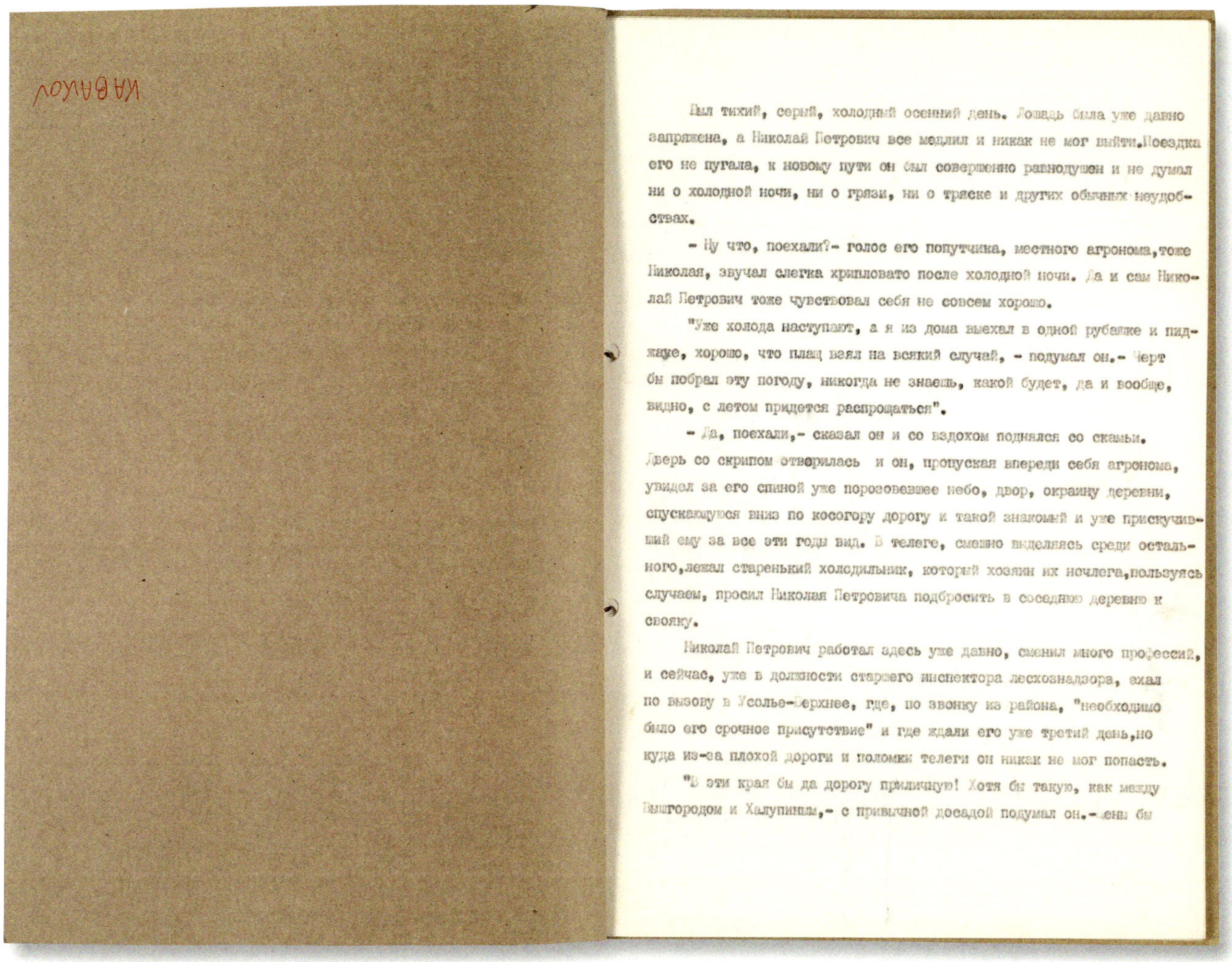

Был тихий, серый, холодный осенний день. Лошадь была уже давно запряжена, а Николай Петрович все медлил и никак не мог выйти. Поездка его не пугала, к новому пути он был совершенно равнодушен и не думал ни о холодной ночи, ни о грязи, ни о тряске и других обычных неудобствах.

– Ну что, поехали?– голос его попутчика, местного агронома, тоже Николая, звучал слегка хрипловато после холодной ночи. Да и сам Николай Петрович тоже чувствовал себя не совсем хорошо.

"Уже холода наступают, а я из дома выехал в одной рубашке и пиджаке, хорошо, что плащ взял на всякий случай, – подумал он.– Черт бы побрал эту погоду, никогда не знаешь, какой будет, да и вообще, видно, с летом придется распрощаться".

– Да, поехали,– сказал он и со вздохом поднялся со скамьи. Дверь со скрипом отворилась и он, пропуская впереди себя агронома, увидел за его спиной уже порозовевшее небо, двор, окраину деревни, спускающуюся вниз по косогору дорогу и такой знакомый и уже прискучивший ему за все эти годы вид. В телеге, смешно выделяясь среди остального, лежал старенький холодильник, который хозяин их ночлега, пользуясь случаем, просил Николая Петровича подбросить в соседнюю деревню к свояку.

Николай Петрович работал здесь уже давно, сменил много профессий, и сейчас, уже в должности старшего инспектора лесхознадзора, ехал по вызову в Усолье-Верхнее, где, по звонку из района, "необходимо было его срочное присутствие" и где ждали его уже третий день, но куда из-за плохой дороги и поломки телеги он никак не мог попасть.

"В эти края бы да дорогу приличную! Хотя бы такую, как между Вышгородом и Халупиным,– с привычной досадой подумал он.– Лены бы

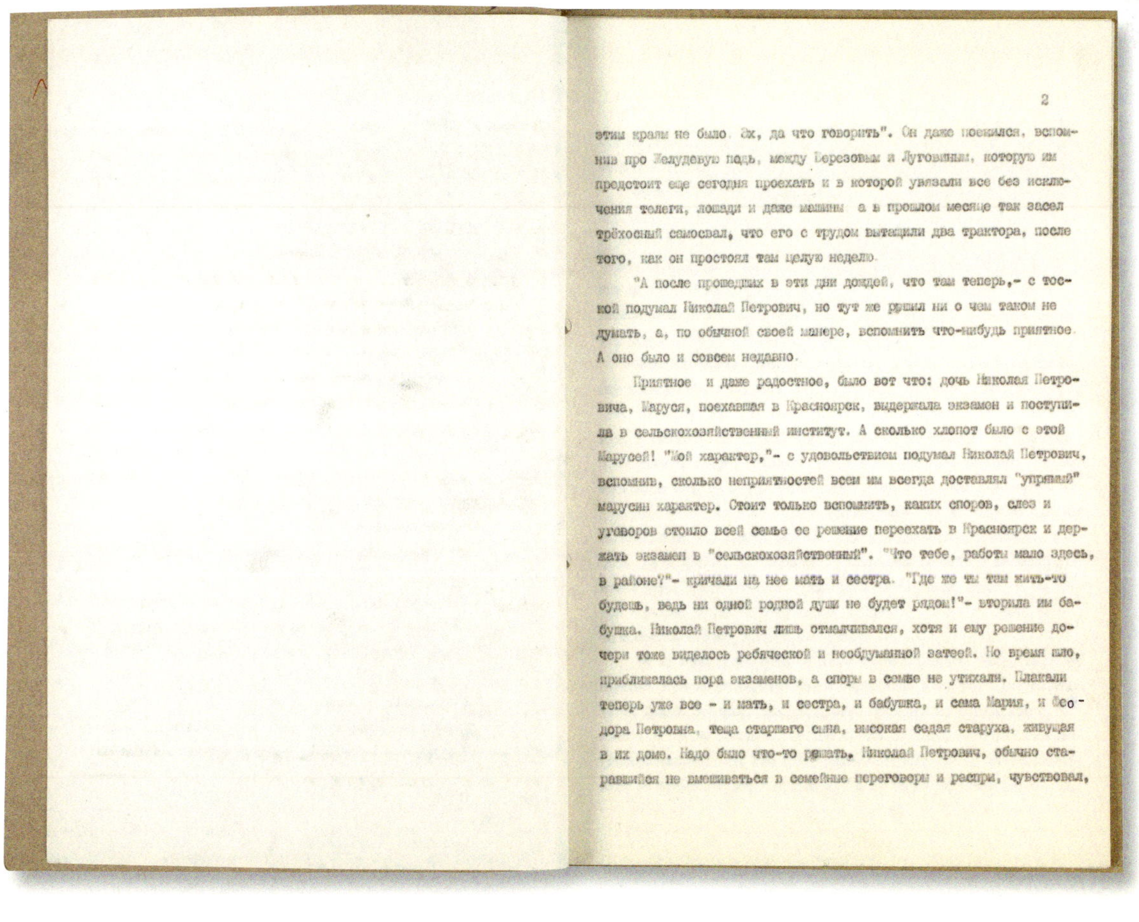

2

этим краям не было. Эх, да что говорить". Он даже поежился, вспомнив про Желудевую падь, между Березовым и Луговиным, которую им предстоит еще сегодня проехать и в которой увязали все без исключения телеги, лошади и даже машины, а в прошлом месяце так засел трёхосный самосвал, что его с трудом вытащили два трактора, после того, как он простоял там целую неделю.

"А после прошедших в эти дни дождей, что там теперь,– с тоской подумал Николай Петрович, но тут же решил ни о чем таком не думать, а, по обычной своей манере, вспомнить что-нибудь приятное. А оно было и совсем недавно.

Приятное и даже радостное, было вот что: дочь Николая Петровича, Маруся, поехавшая в Красноярск, выдержала экзамен и поступила в сельскохозяйственный институт. А сколько хлопот было с этой Марусей! "Мой характер,"– с удовольствием подумал Николай Петрович, вспомнив, сколько неприятностей всем им всегда доставлял "упрямый" марусин характер. Стоит только вспомнить, каких споров, слез и уговоров стоило всей семье ее решение переехать в Красноярск и держать экзамен в "сельскохозяйственный". "Что тебе, работы мало здесь, в районе?"– кричали на нее мать и сестра. "Где же ты там жить-то будешь, ведь ни одной родной души не будет рядом!"– вторила им бабушка. Николай Петрович лишь отмалчивался, хотя и ему решение дочери тоже виделось ребяческой и необдуманной затеей. Но время шло, приближалась пора экзаменов, а споры в семье не утихали. Плакали теперь уже все – и мать, и сестра, и бабушка, и сама Мария, и Федора Петровна, теща старшего сына, высокая седая старуха, живущая в их доме. Надо было что-то решать. Николай Петрович, обычно старавшийся не вмешиваться в семейные переговоры и распри, чувствовал,

19 Ropes | *Leinen*

1985

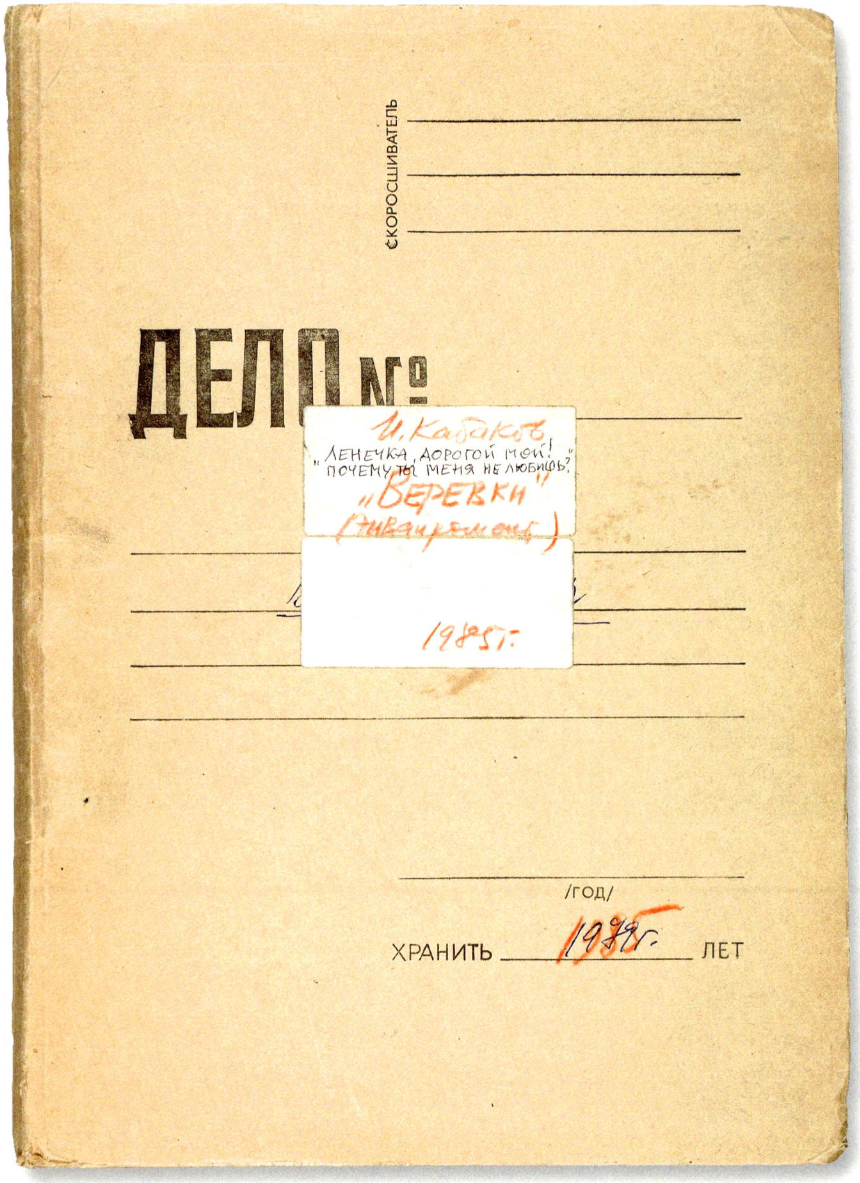

Ilya Kabakov
Moscow: published by the author
31.1 x 23 cm
124 pp. with 12 b/w ills.
quick bind, two punched holes, cardboard cover, label on the cover
Schnellhefter, zwei ausgestanzte Löcher, Kartonumschlag, Etikette auf dem Umschlag
edition: 10 copies

thematic publication | *thematische Publikation*

layout by Ilya Kabakov | *Layout von Ilya Kabakov*

Documentation of the 1985 installation of the same name in Kabakov's studio on Sretenski Boulevard, later entitled »16 Ropes«. Inscription on the title page: "Lyoneshka, my friend! Why do you not love me?"; Russian.

Dokumentation zur gleichnamigen Installation in Kabakovs Atelier am Sretenski-Boulevard von 1985, die später mit »16 Leinen« betitelt wurde. Widmung auf der Titelseite: „Ljonetschka, mein Freund! Warum liebst du mich nicht?"; russisch.

see also | *siehe auch* no. 34; CRI, vol. 1, no. 4, pp. 66–71

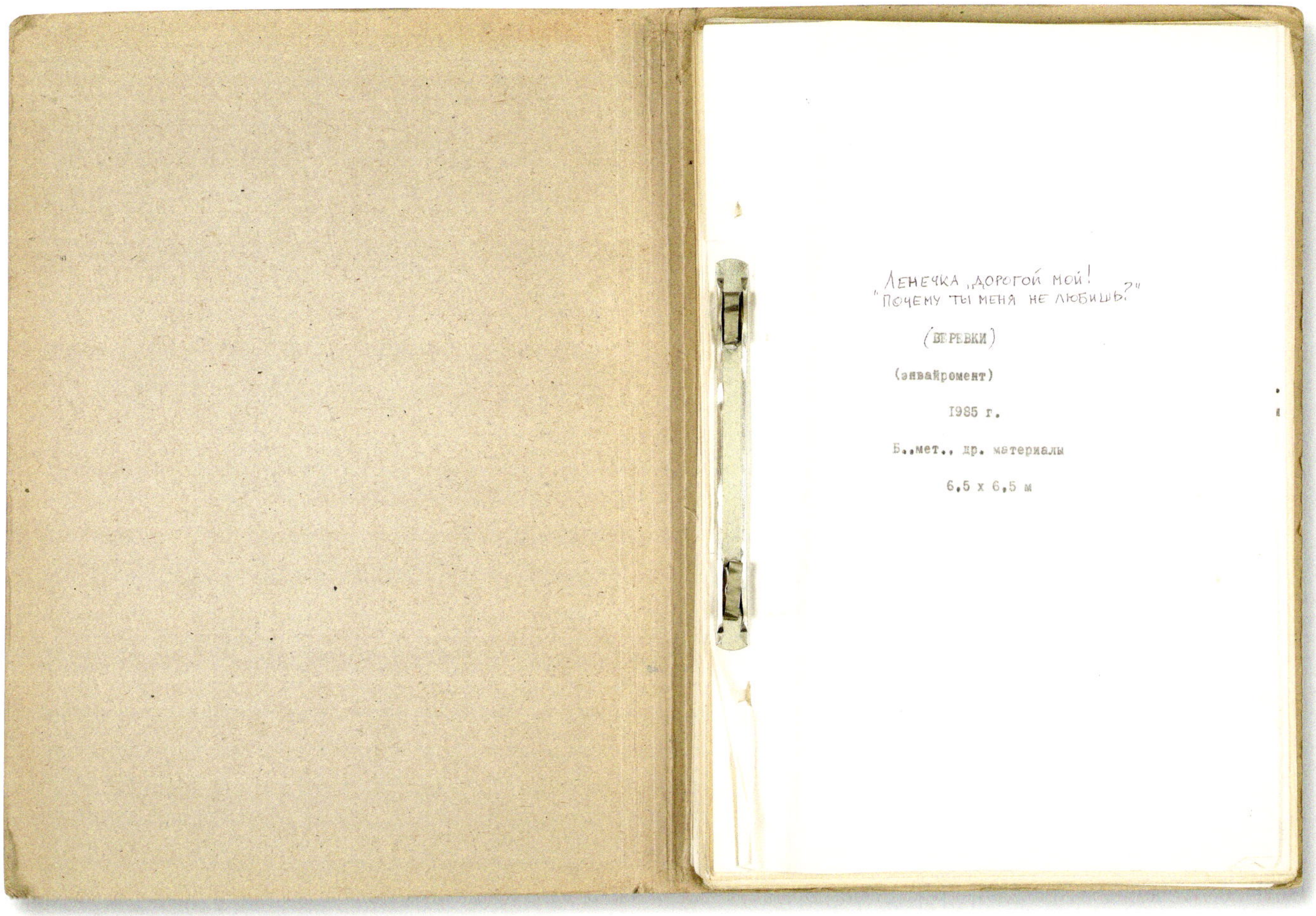
"Ленечка, дорогой мой!
"Почему ты меня не любишь?"
(Веревки)
(энвайромент)
1985 г.
Б., мет., др. материалы
6,5 х 6,5 м

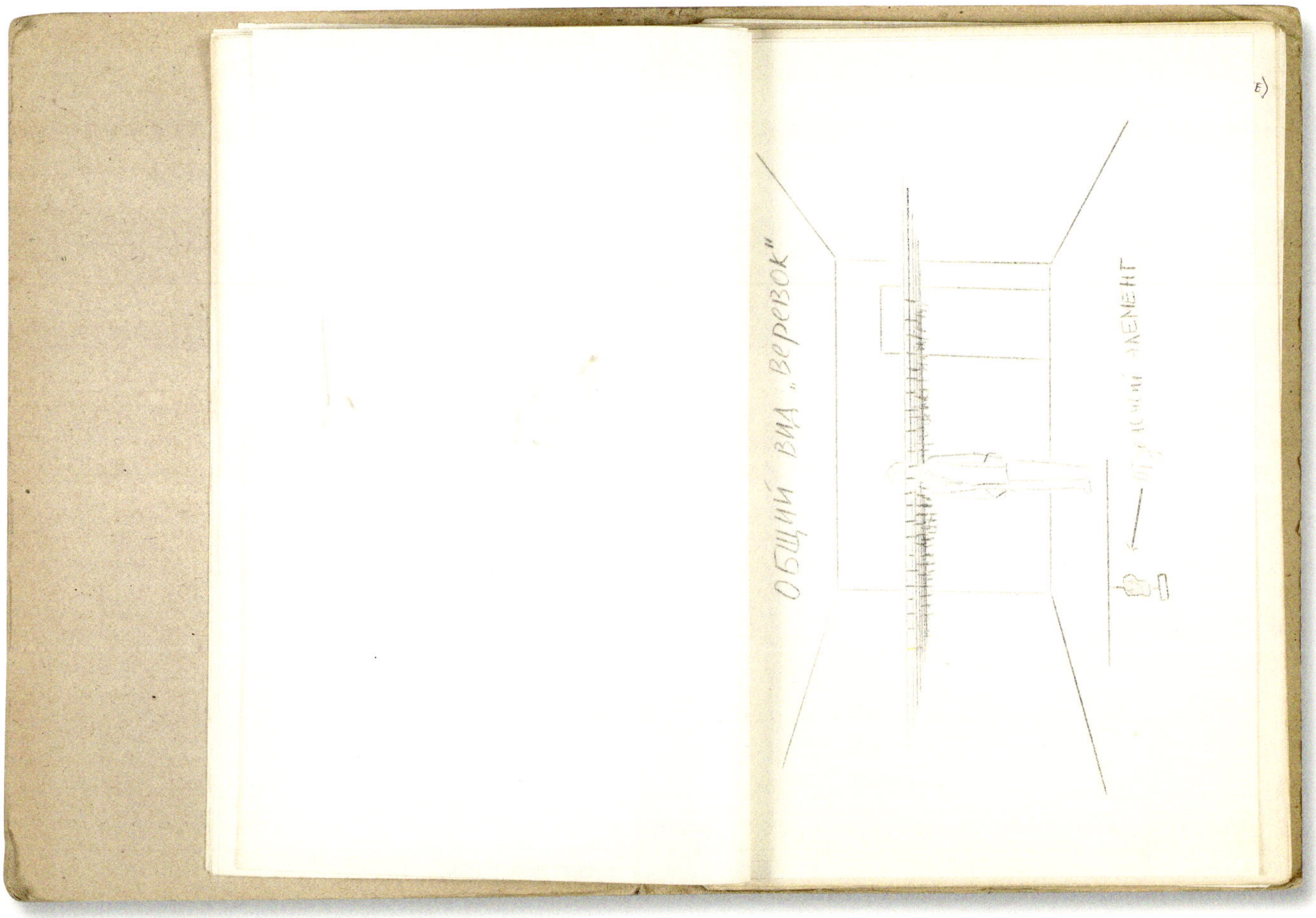
е)
Общий вид „Веревок"

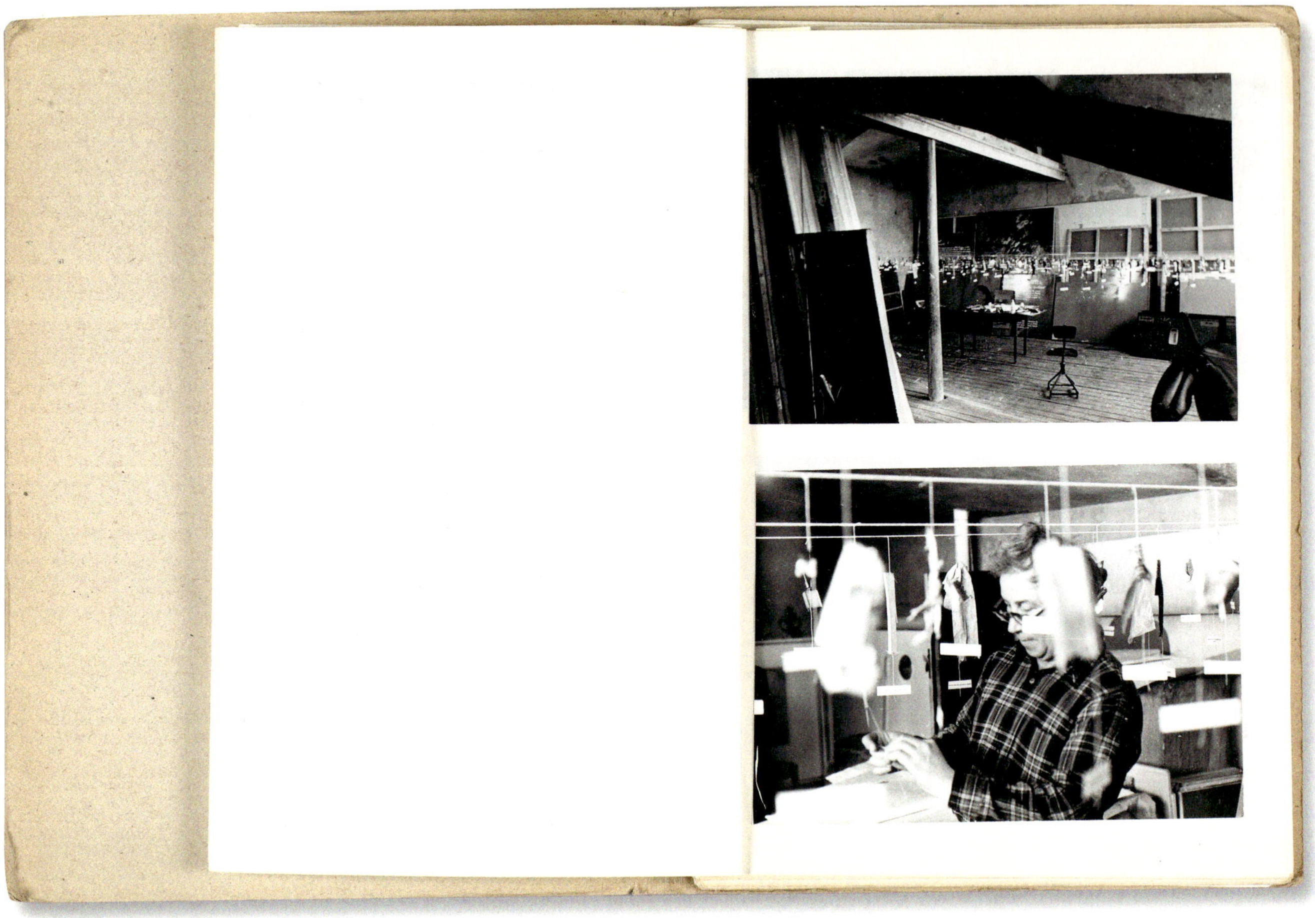

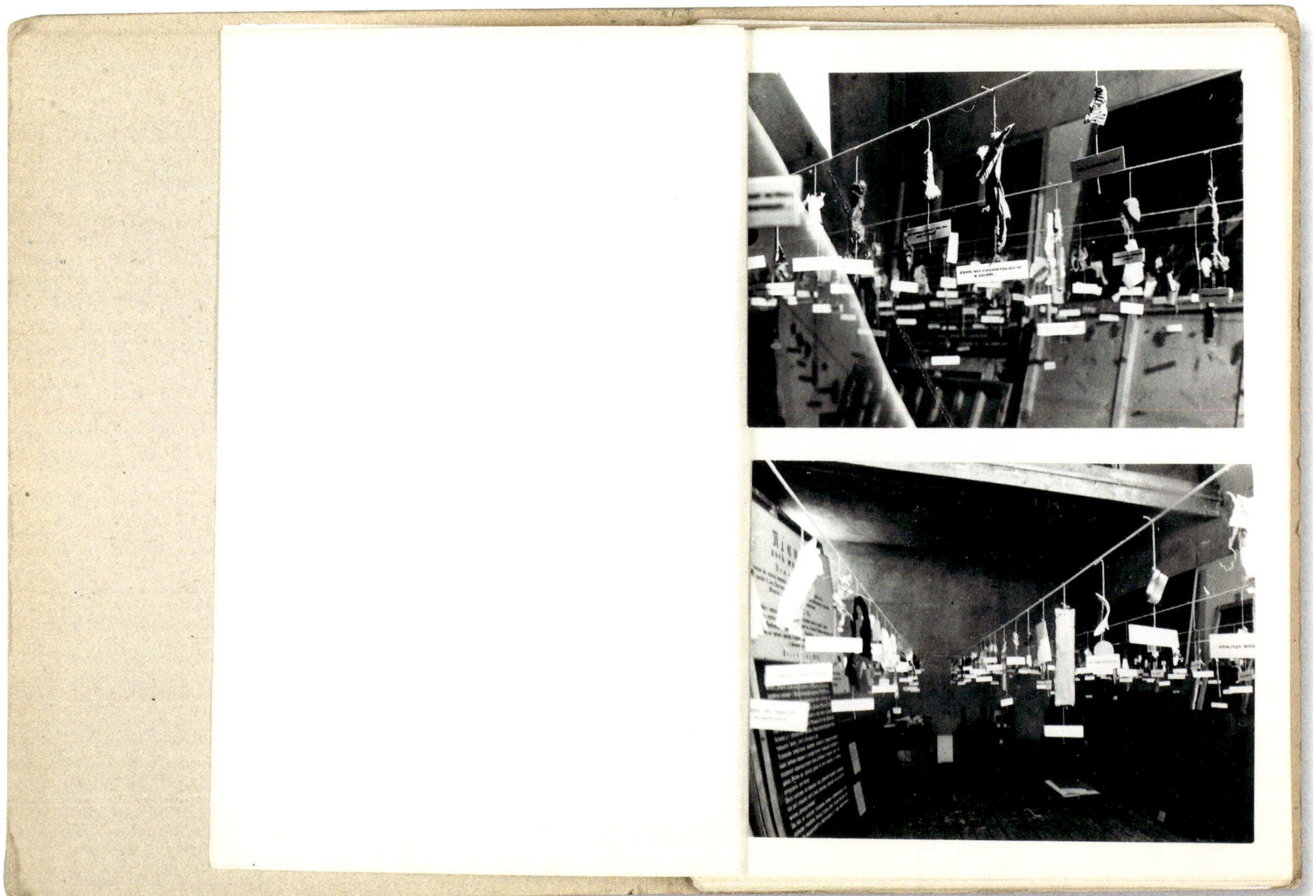

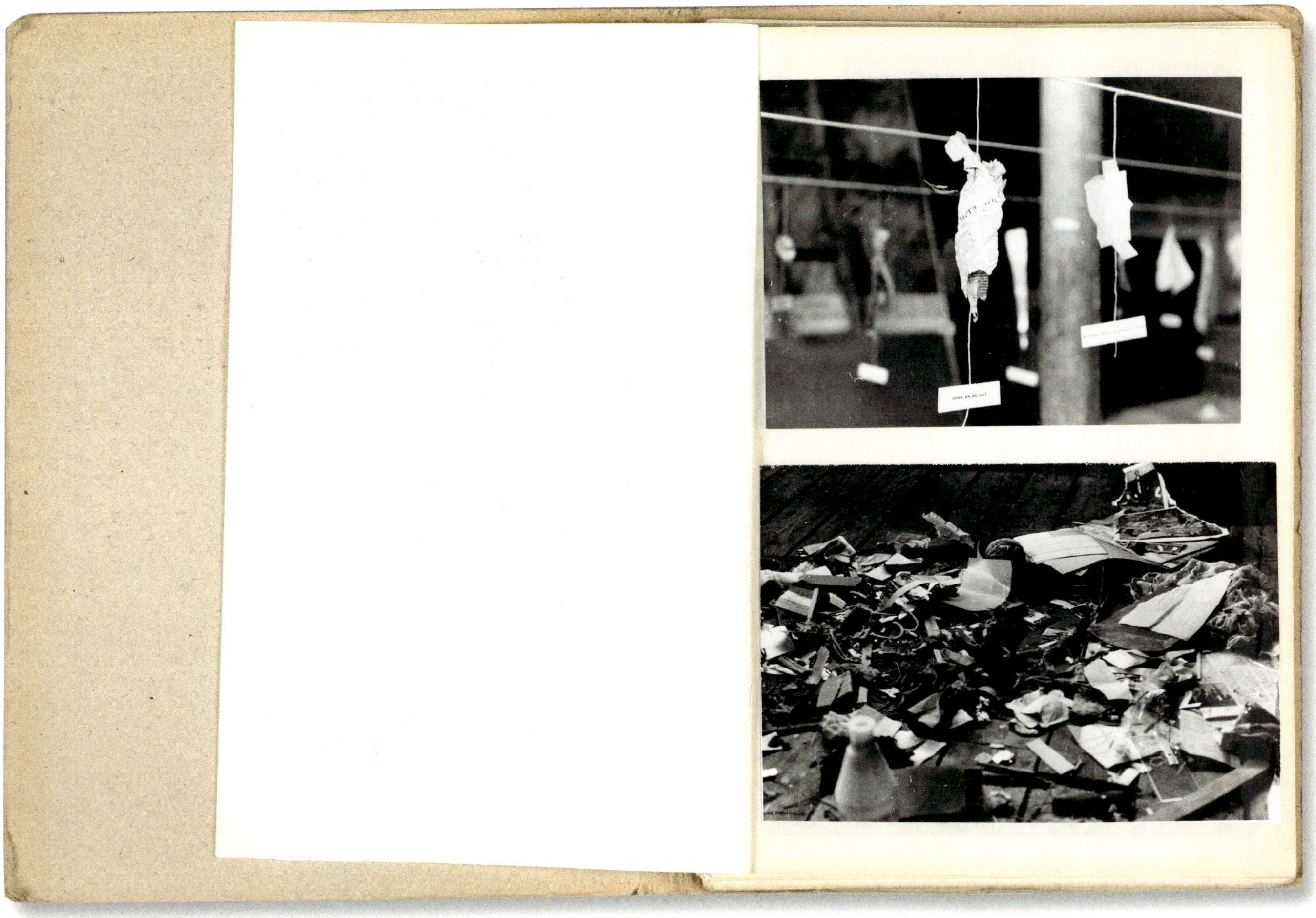

20 The Artist as an Acting Figure | *Der Künstler als handelnde Figur*

1985

Ilya Kabakov
Moscow: published by the author
28 x 22.2 cm
43 pp. with 31 b/w ills.
stapled, cardboard cover
Drahtheftung, Kartonumschlag
edition: 10 copies

thematic publication | *thematische Publikation*

layout by Ilya Kabakov | *Layout von Ilya Kabakov*

Text about the artist; the pictures are supposedly by the fictitious artist figure; Russian.

Text über den Künstler; die Abbildungen stammen angeblich von der fiktiven Künstlerfigur; russisch.

see also | *siehe auch*

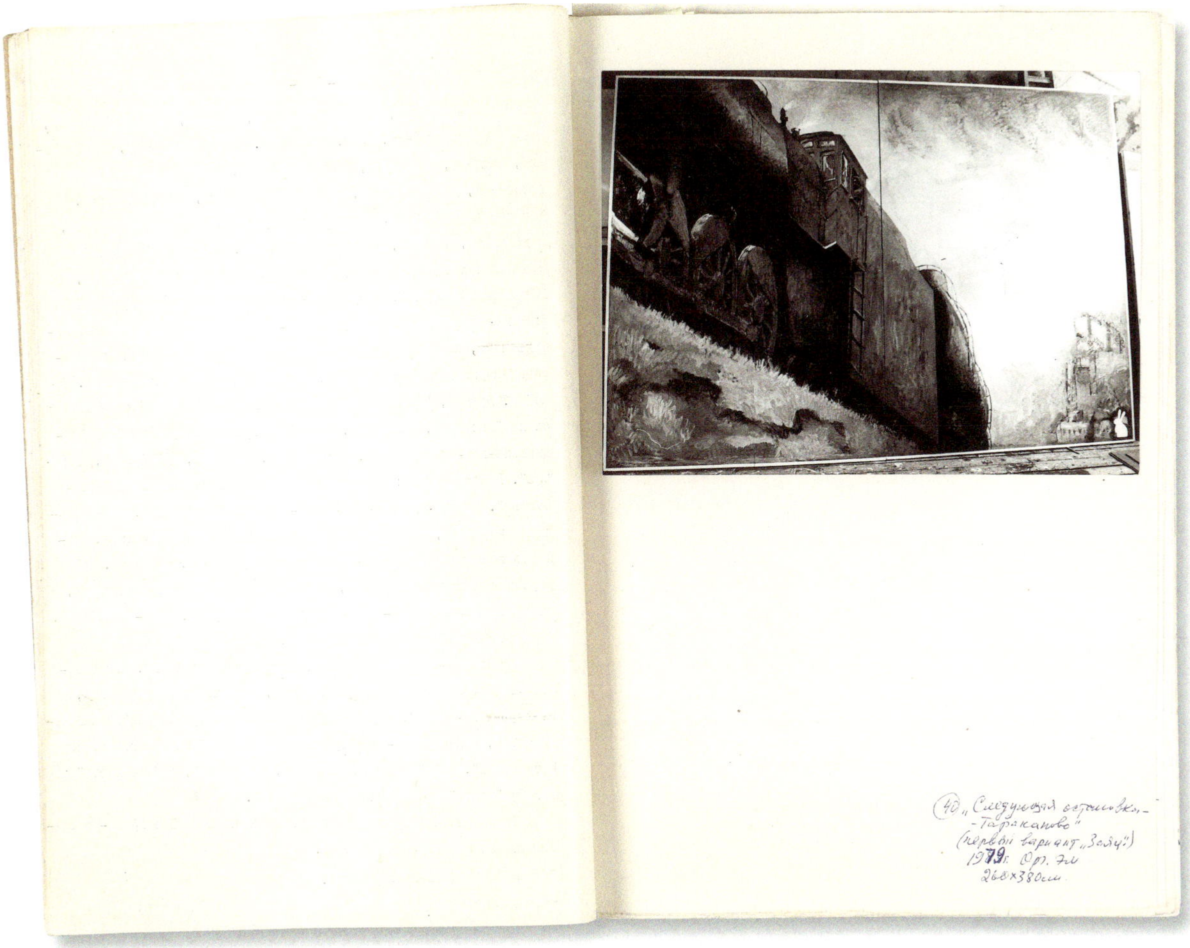
(40) „Следующая остановка-
-Тараканово"
(первый вариант „Заяц")
1979г. Орг. Эм
260x380см

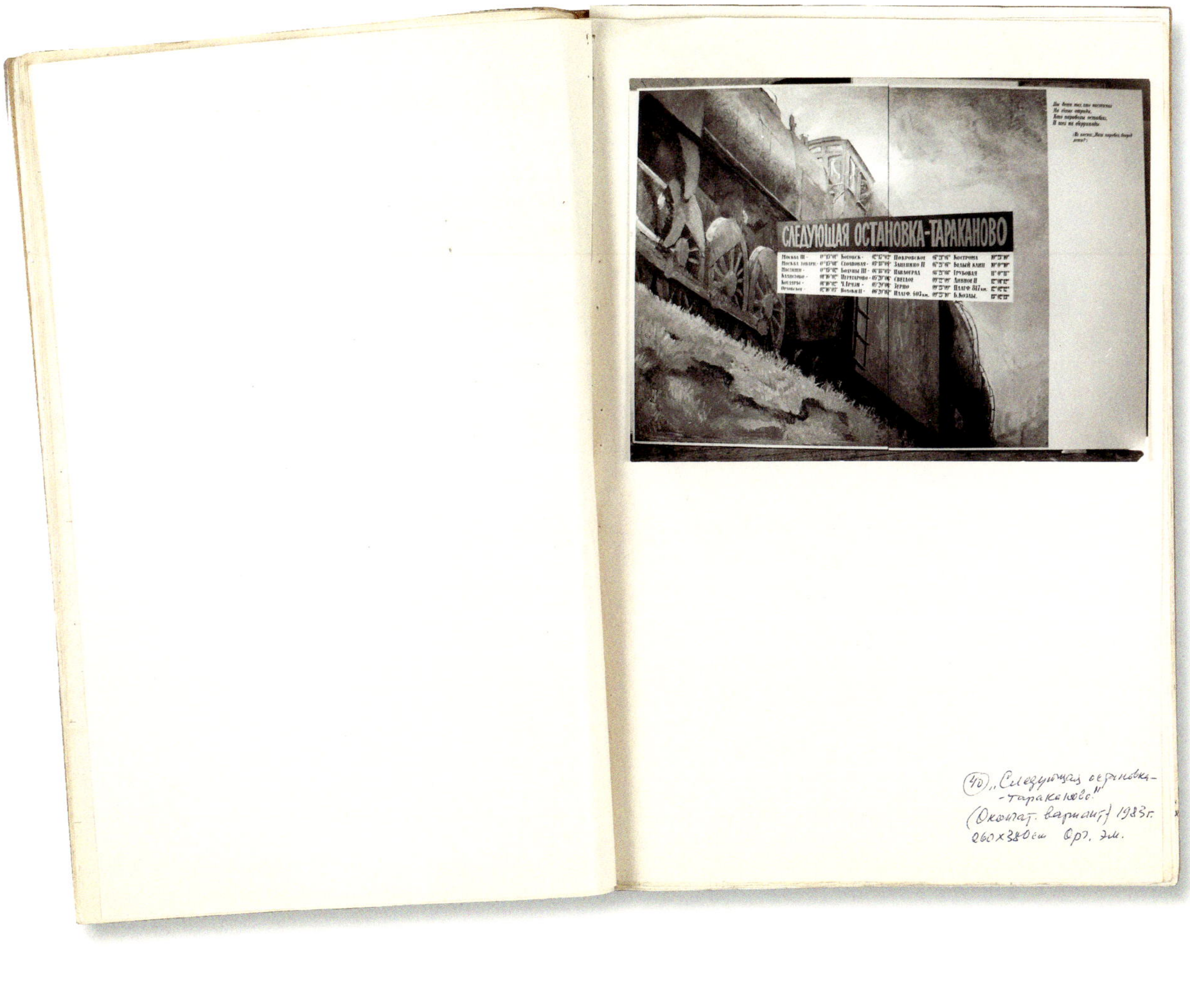
СЛЕДУЮЩАЯ ОСТАНОВКА-ТАРАКАНОВО
(40) „Следующая остановка-
-тараканово"
(Оконч. вариант) 1983г.
260x380см Орг. Эм.

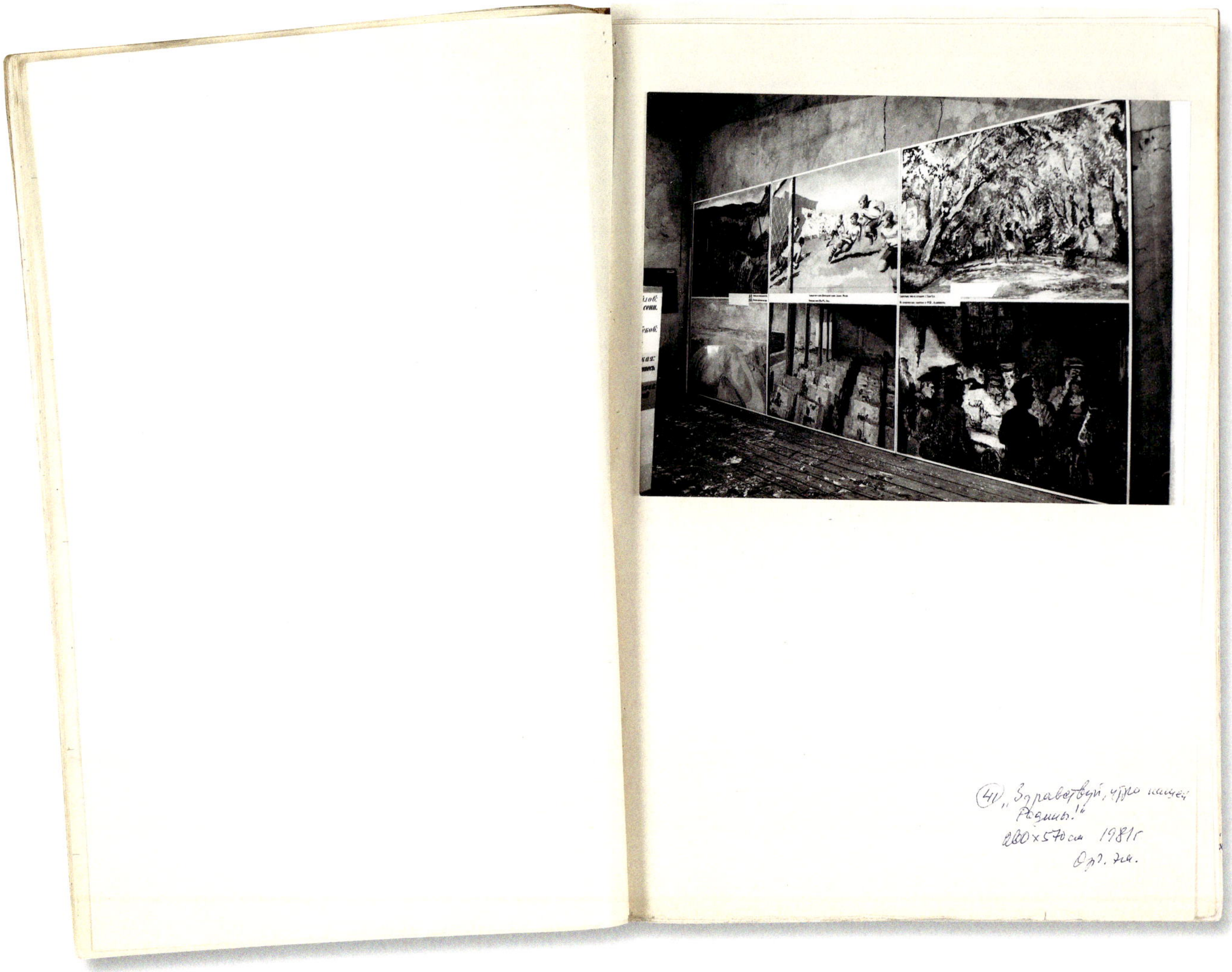
(41) „Здравствуй, утро нашей Родины!"
260×570 см 1981 г
Орг. эм.

21 10 Albums | *10 Alben*

1988

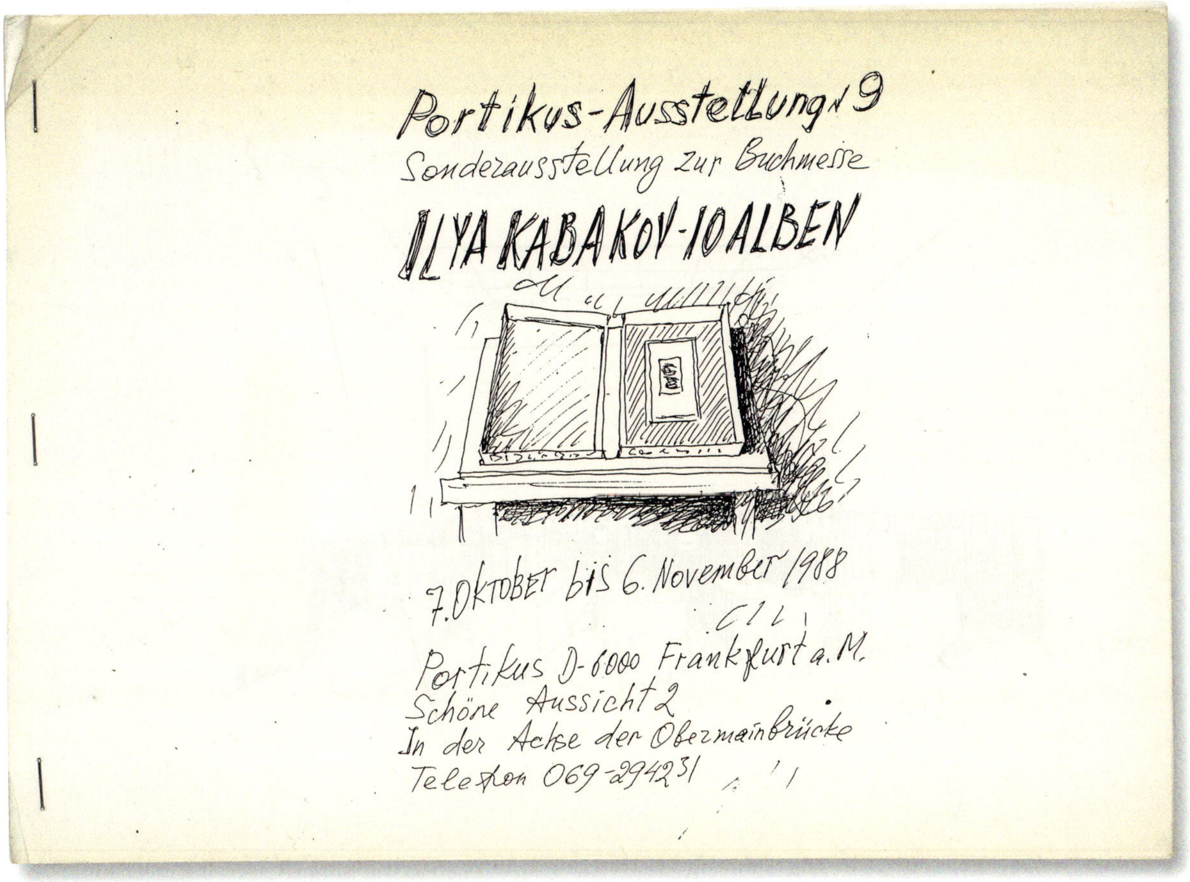

Portikus
Frankfurt a. M.: Portikus
21 x 29.7 cm
30 (partly double-sided) photocopied pp. with 6 b/w ills.
stapled, plastic cover
Drahtheftung, Plastikumschlag

exhibition catalogue | *Ausstellungskatalog*

layout by Ilya Kabakov | *Layout von Ilya Kabakov*

For the installation of the same name for the »Portikus Exhibition 9« at the Frankfurt Book Fair at Portikus, Frankfurt am Main, October 8 to November 6, 1988. Texts by Ilya Kabakov; German.

Zur gleichnamigen Installation für die »Portikus-Ausstellung 9« anlässlich der Frankfurter Buchmesse 1988 im Portikus, Frankfurt am Main, 8. Oktober – 6. November 1988. Texte von Ilya Kabakov; deutsch.

see also | *siehe auch* no. 3; no. 16; no. 68; no. 100; CRI, vol. 1, no. 6, pp. 76–81

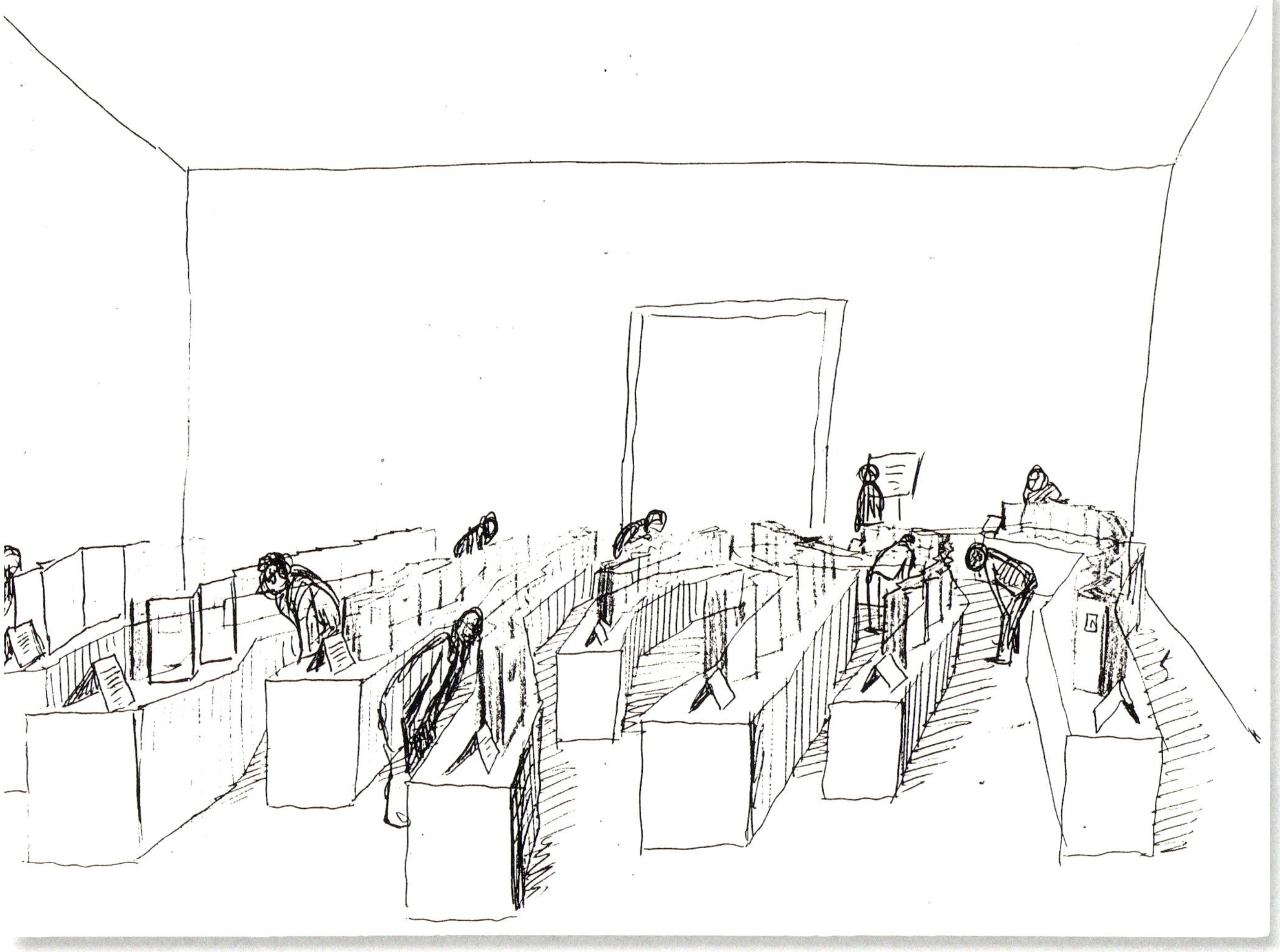

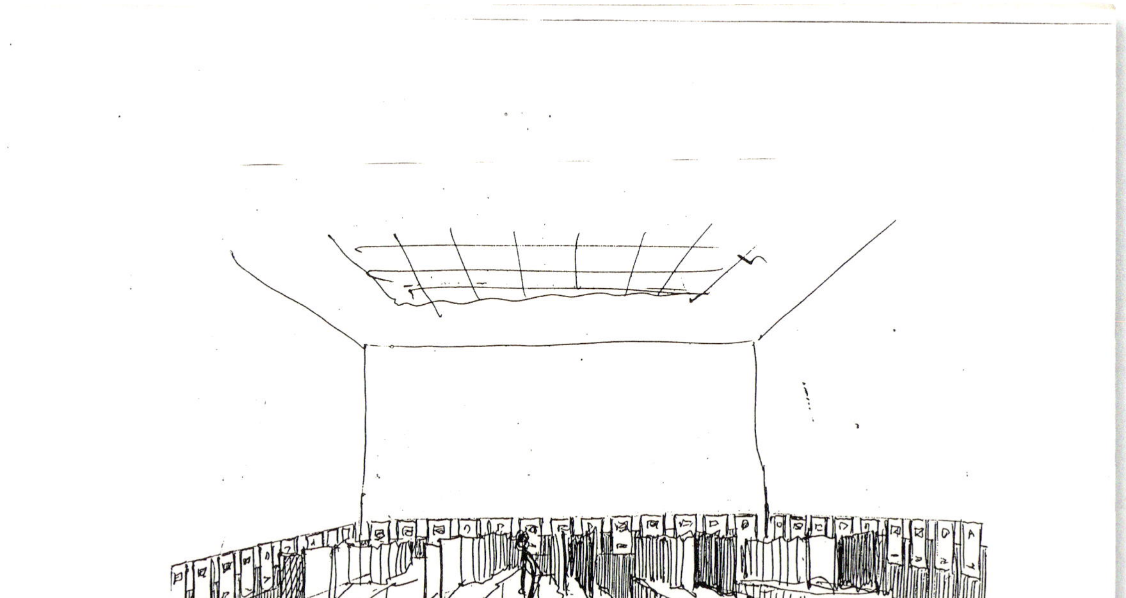

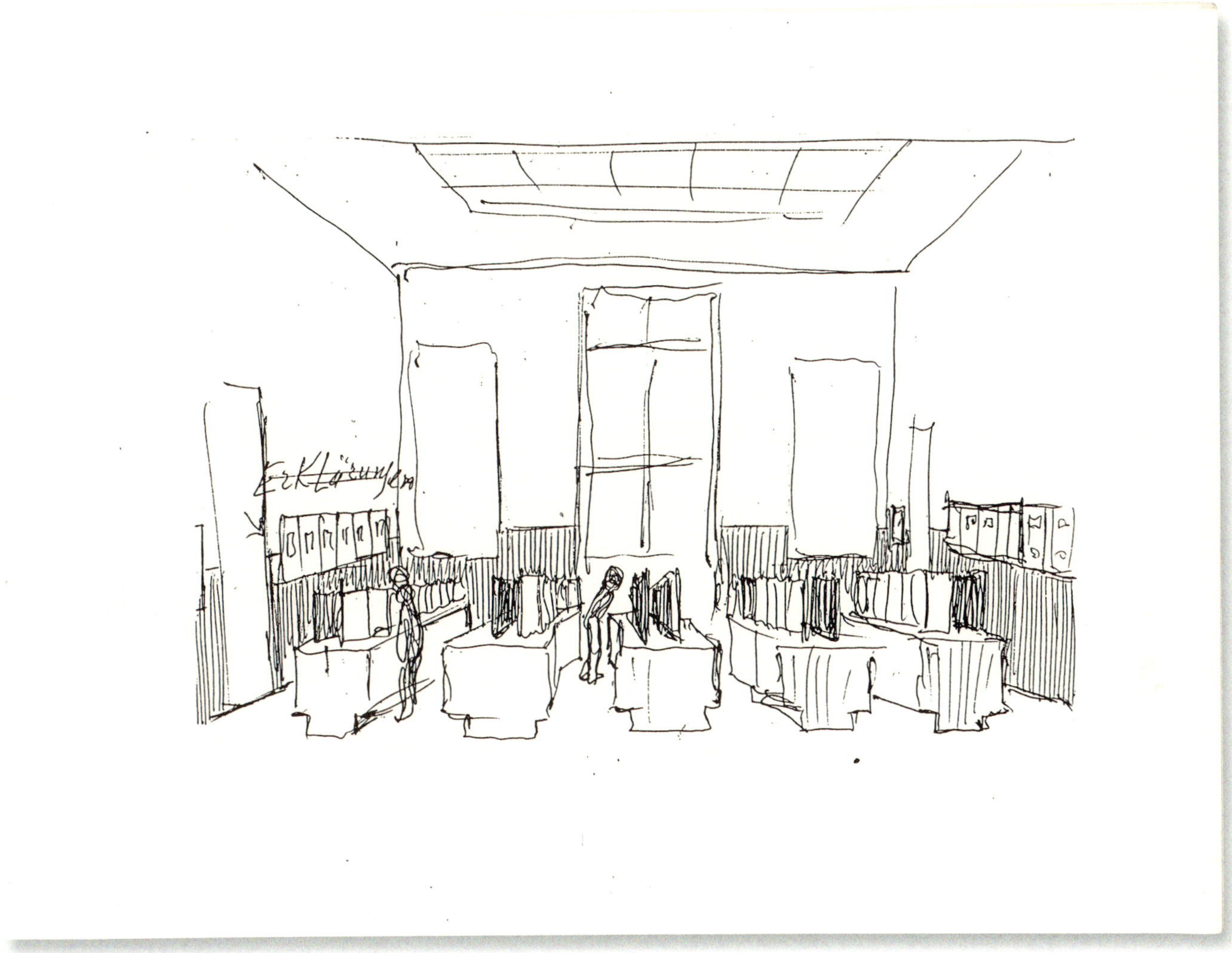
Erklärungen

22 10 Characters | *10 Charaktere*

1988

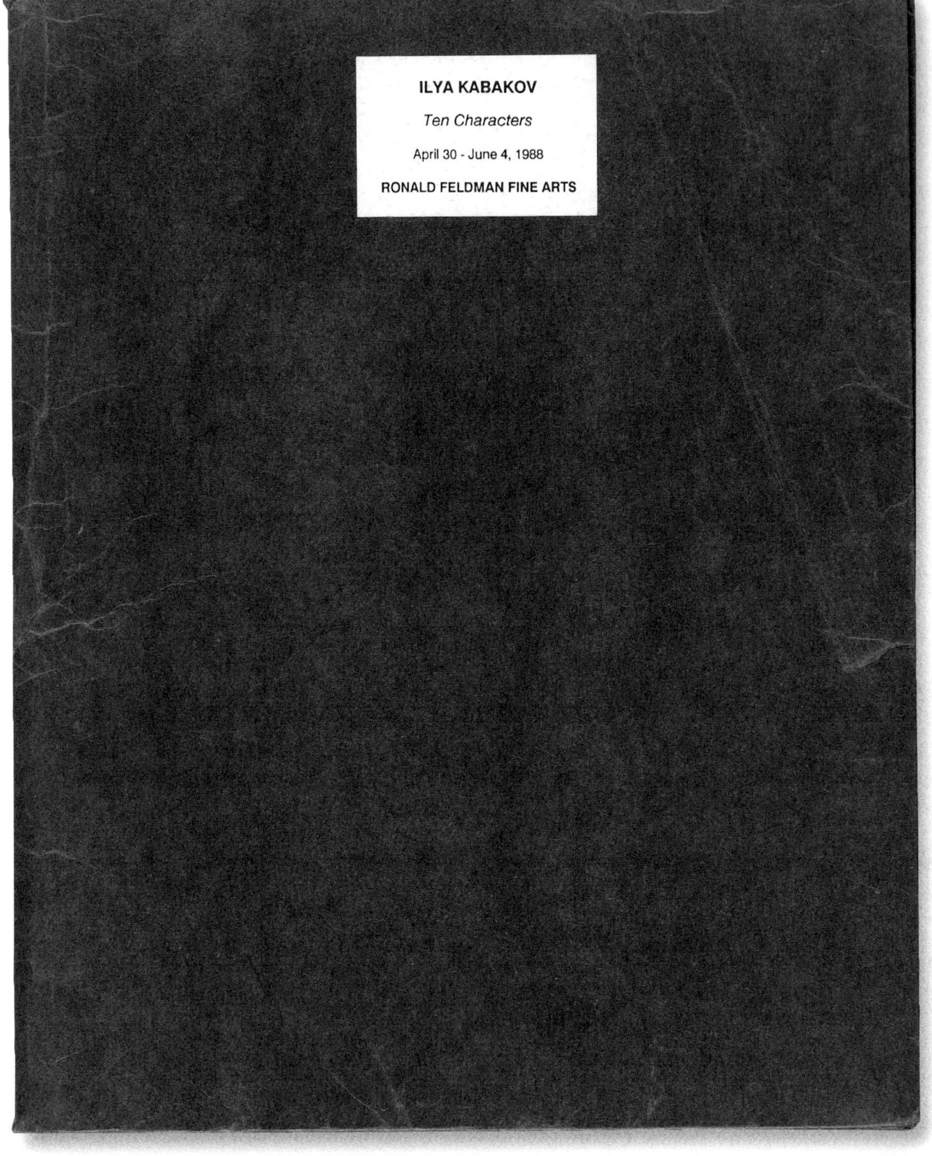

Ilya Kabakov
New York: published by the author
29.7 x 24 cm
84 photocopied pp. with 15 b/w ills.
loose sheets, cardboard cover, label on the cover
lose Blätter, Kartonumschlag, Etikette auf dem Umschlag

exhibition catalogue | *Ausstellungskatalog*

layout by Ilya Kabakov | *Layout von Ilya Kabakov*

For the installation of the same name at the Ronald Feldman Fine Arts Gallery, New York, April 30 to June 4, 1988. Text by Ilya Kabakov; English.

Zur gleichnamigen Installation, Galerie Ronald Feldman Fine Arts, New York, 30. April – 4. Juni 1988. Text von Ilya Kabakov; englisch.

see also | *siehe auch* no. 48; no. 53; no. 54; no. 63; no. 76; no. 89; CRI, vol. 1, no. 15, pp. 132–145; CRP, vol. 1, no. 49, pp. 101–102, no. 57, pp. 114–115, no. 67, p. 132, no. 73, pp. 141–142, no. 114, pp. 196–197, no. 128, p. 213, no. 129, p. 214

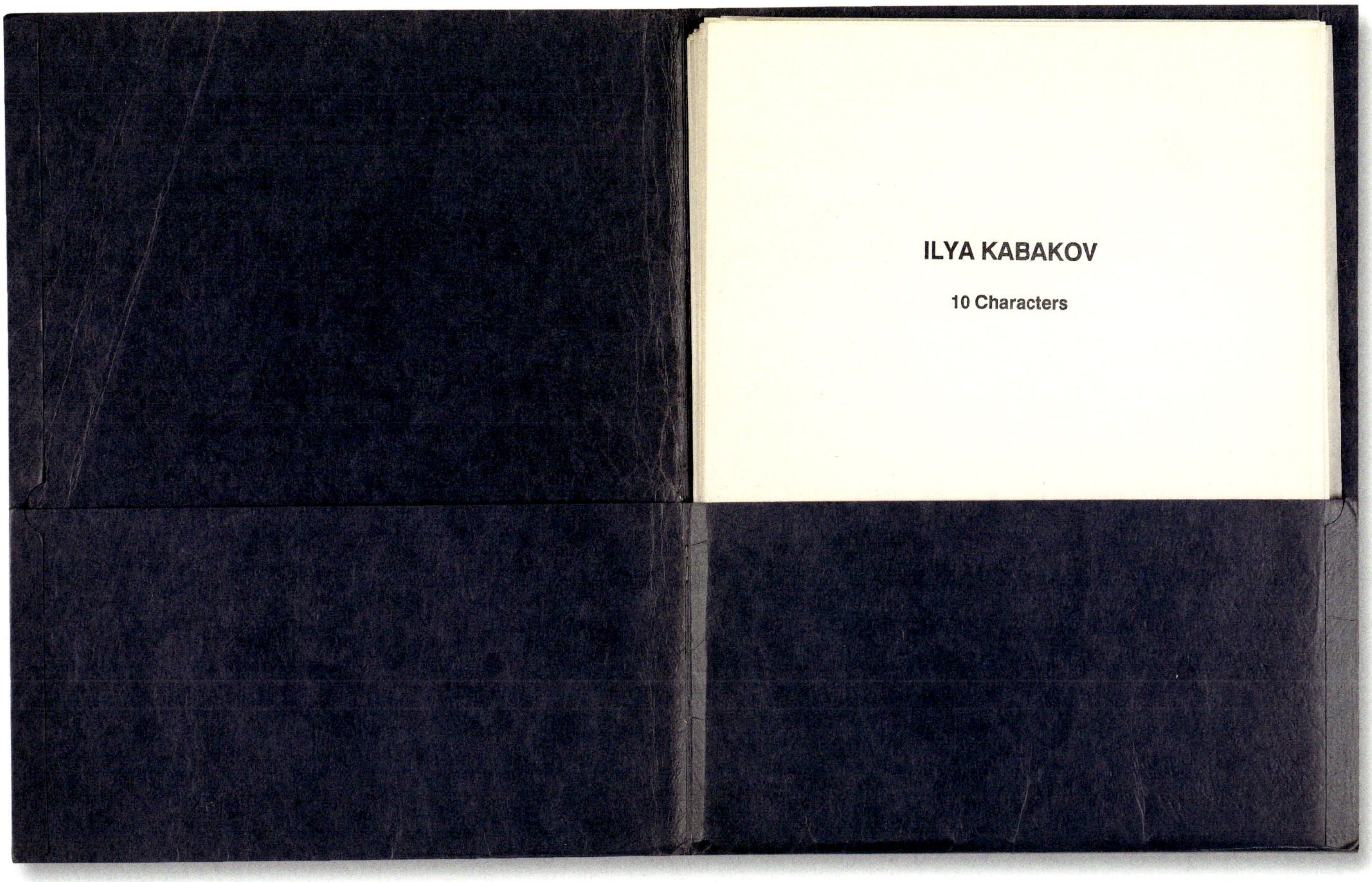
ILYA KABAKOV
10 Characters

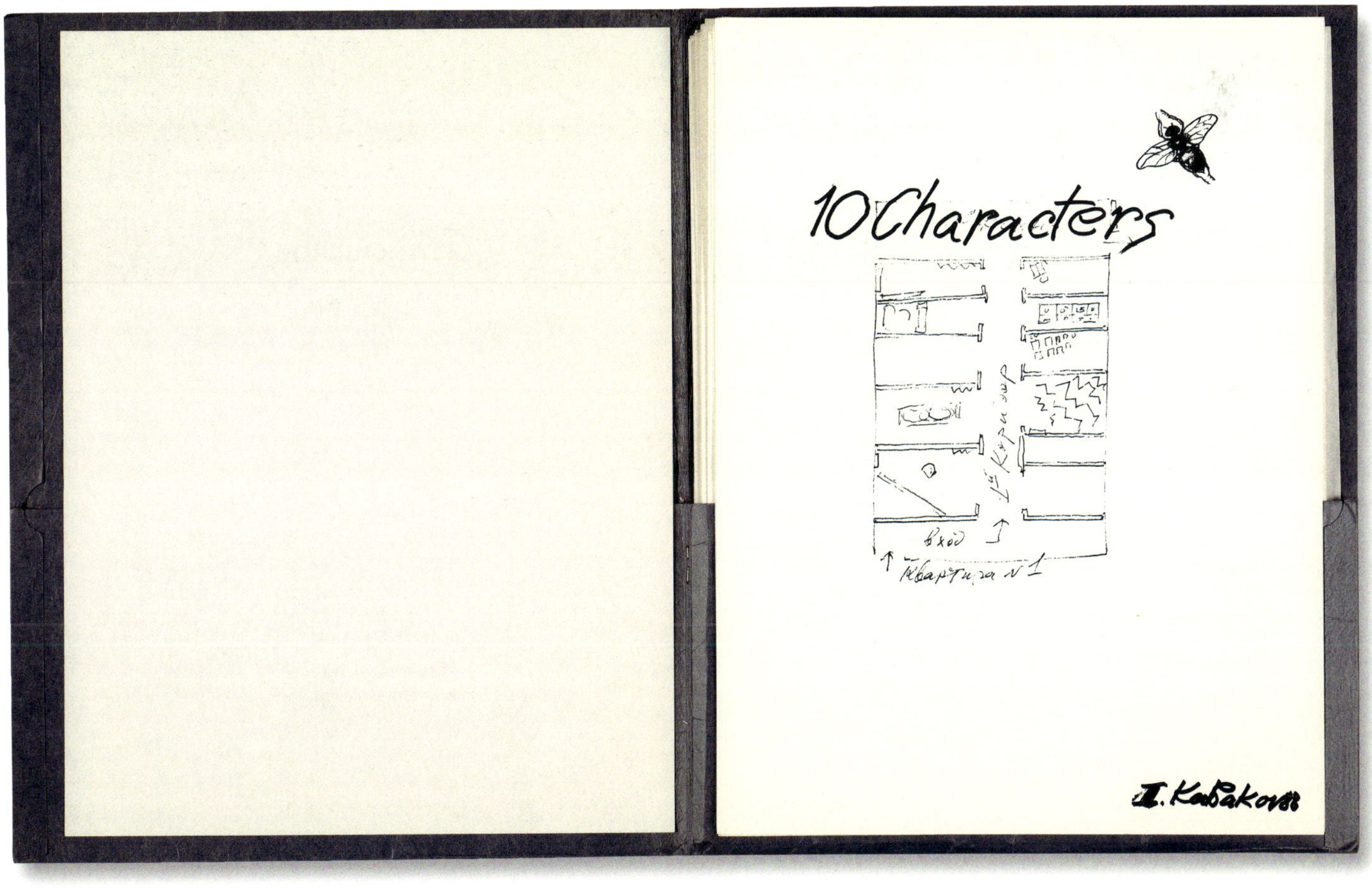
10Characters

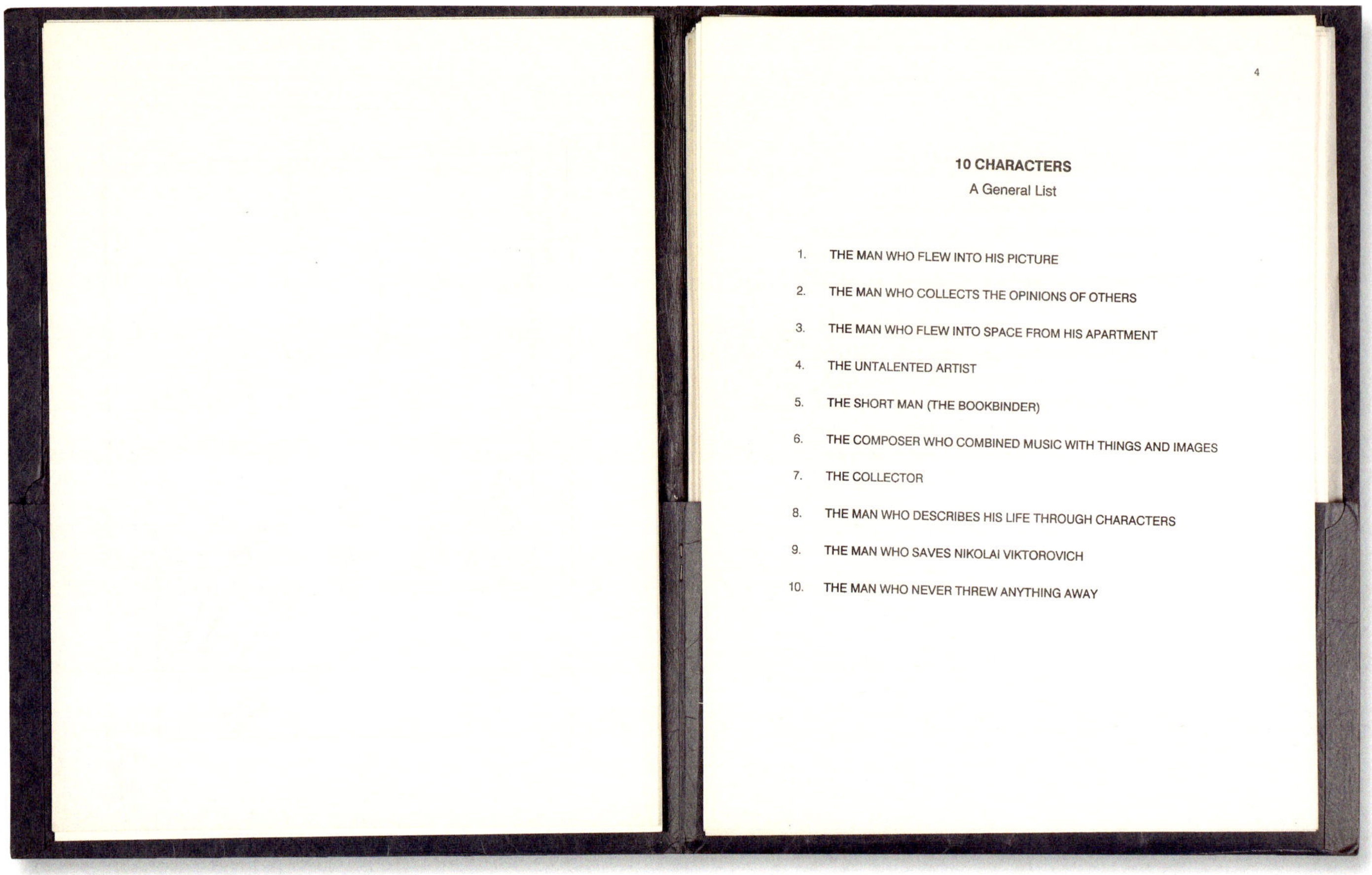

4

10 CHARACTERS
A General List

1. THE MAN WHO FLEW INTO HIS PICTURE
2. THE MAN WHO COLLECTS THE OPINIONS OF OTHERS
3. THE MAN WHO FLEW INTO SPACE FROM HIS APARTMENT
4. THE UNTALENTED ARTIST
5. THE SHORT MAN (THE BOOKBINDER)
6. THE COMPOSER WHO COMBINED MUSIC WITH THINGS AND IMAGES
7. THE COLLECTOR
8. THE MAN WHO DESCRIBES HIS LIFE THROUGH CHARACTERS
9. THE MAN WHO SAVES NIKOLAI VIKTOROVICH
10. THE MAN WHO NEVER THREW ANYTHING AWAY

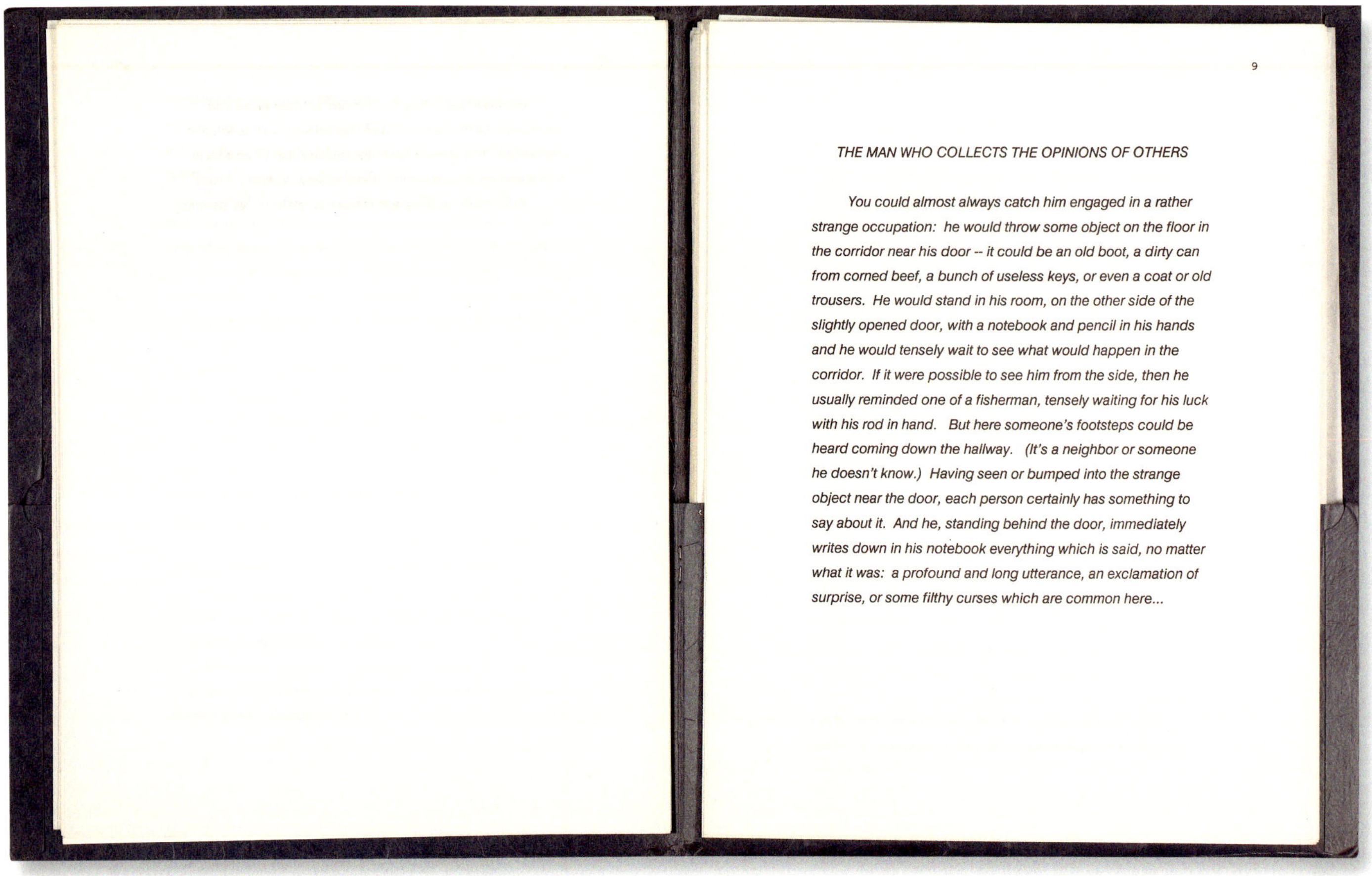

9

THE MAN WHO COLLECTS THE OPINIONS OF OTHERS

You could almost always catch him engaged in a rather strange occupation: he would throw some object on the floor in the corridor near his door -- it could be an old boot, a dirty can from corned beef, a bunch of useless keys, or even a coat or old trousers. He would stand in his room, on the other side of the slightly opened door, with a notebook and pencil in his hands and he would tensely wait to see what would happen in the corridor. If it were possible to see him from the side, then he usually reminded one of a fisherman, tensely waiting for his luck with his rod in hand. But here someone's footsteps could be heard coming down the hallway. (It's a neighbor or someone he doesn't know.) Having seen or bumped into the strange object near the door, each person certainly has something to say about it. And he, standing behind the door, immediately writes down in his notebook everything which is said, no matter what it was: a profound and long utterance, an exclamation of surprise, or some filthy curses which are common here...

23 Before Supper | *Vor dem Abendessen*

1988

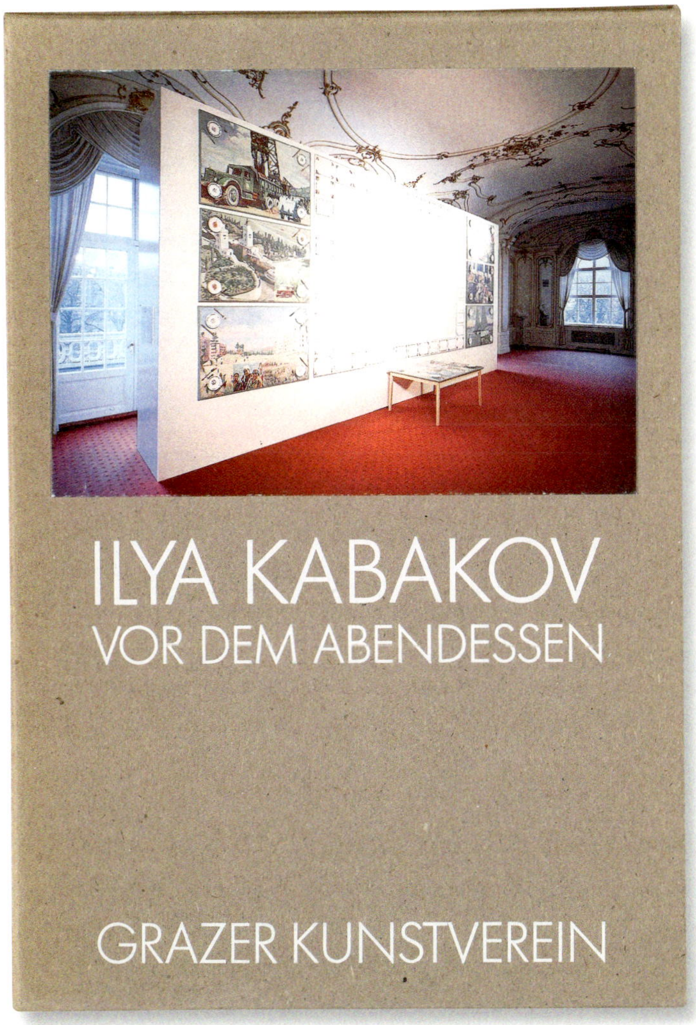

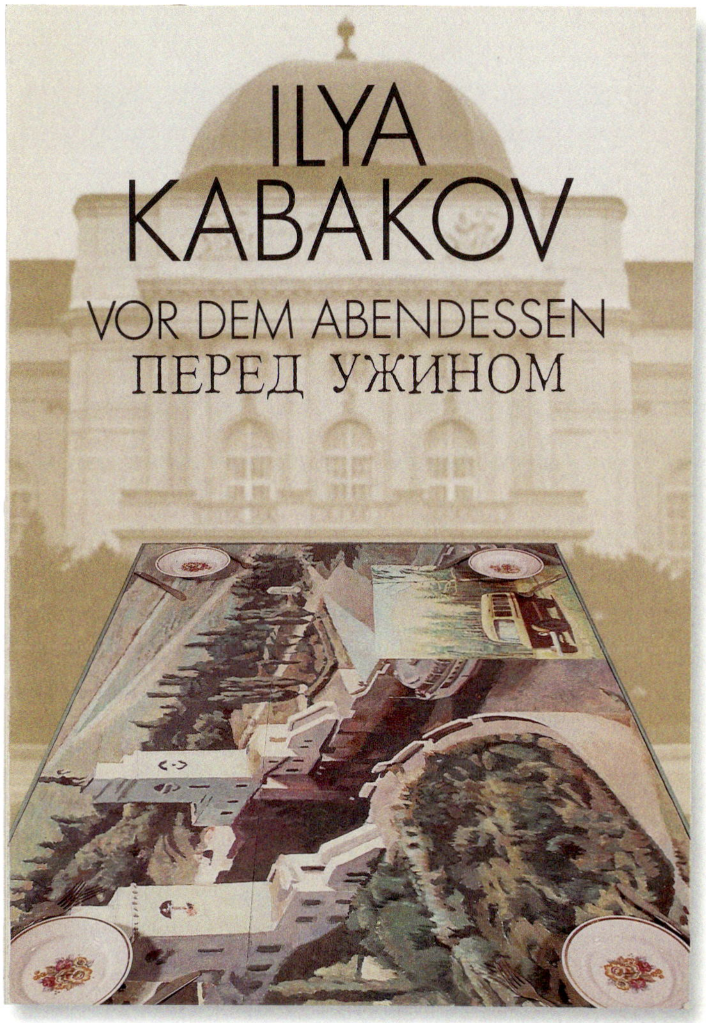

Grazer Kunstverein
Graz: Grazer Kunstverein
24 x 17 cm
[32] pp. with 21 (9 color) ills.
concertina-folded brochure, cardboard slipcase
Leporello, Kartonschuber

exhibition catalogue | *Ausstellungskatalog*

layout by Ilya Kabakov | *Layout von Ilya Kabakov*

For the installation of the same name in the foyer of the Graz Opera House, Graz, March 20 to April 8, 1988. Text by Ilya Kabakov; German, Russian.

Zur gleichnamigen Installation, Foyer der Grazer Oper, Graz, 20. März – 8. April 1988. Text von Ilya Kabakov; deutsch, russisch.

see also | *siehe auch* CRI, vol. 1, no. 14, pp. 126–131; CRP, vol. 1, nos. 131–137, pp. 217–223

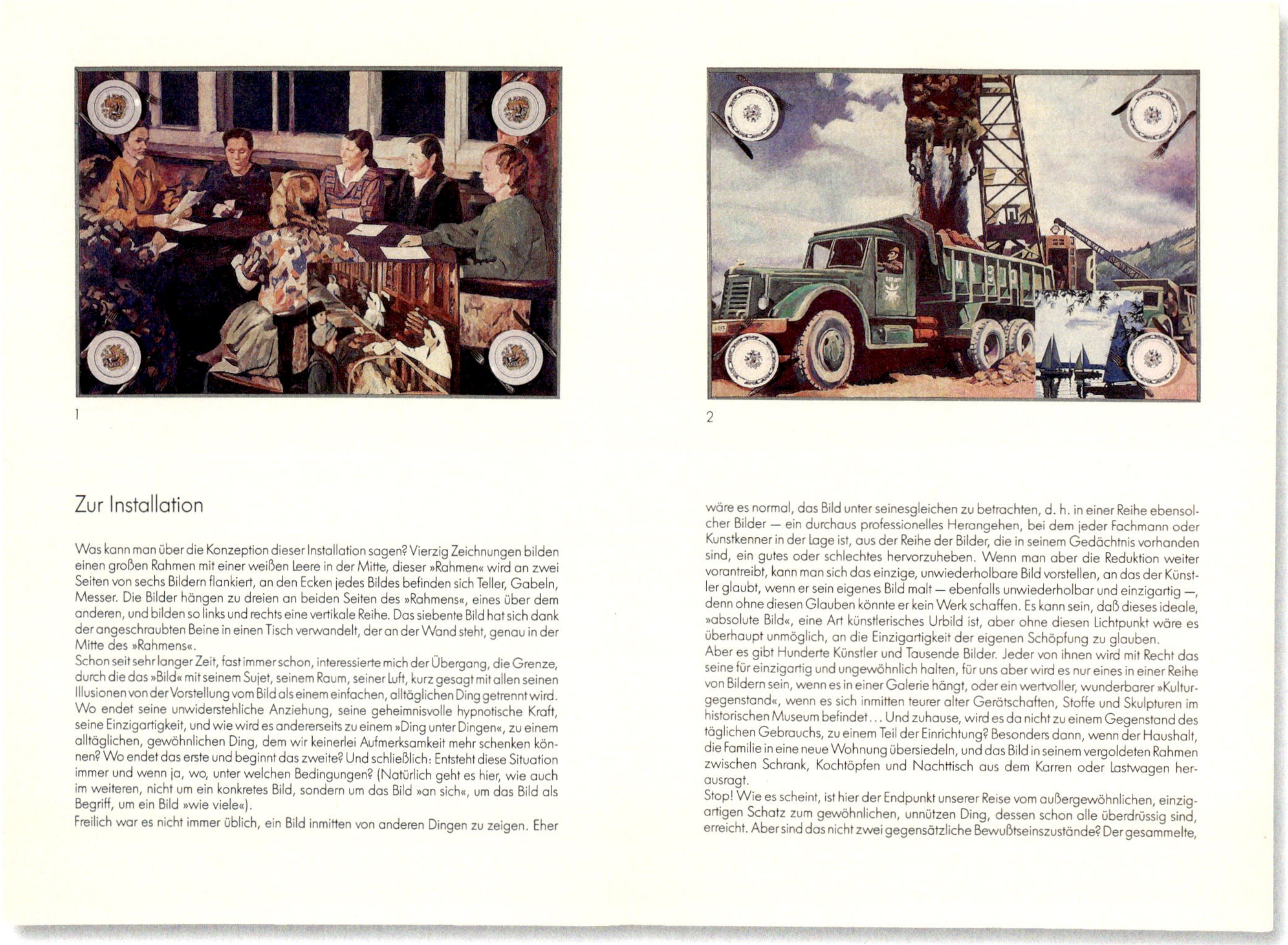

1

2

Zur Installation

Was kann man über die Konzeption dieser Installation sagen? Vierzig Zeichnungen bilden einen großen Rahmen mit einer weißen Leere in der Mitte, dieser »Rahmen« wird an zwei Seiten von sechs Bildern flankiert, an den Ecken jedes Bildes befinden sich Teller, Gabeln, Messer. Die Bilder hängen zu dreien an beiden Seiten des »Rahmens«, eines über dem anderen, und bilden so links und rechts eine vertikale Reihe. Das siebente Bild hat sich dank der angeschraubten Beine in einen Tisch verwandelt, der an der Wand steht, genau in der Mitte des »Rahmens«.
Schon seit sehr langer Zeit, fast immer schon, interessierte mich der Übergang, die Grenze, durch die das »Bild« mit seinem Sujet, seinem Raum, seiner Luft, kurz gesagt mit allen seinen Illusionen von der Vorstellung vom Bild als einem einfachen, alltäglichen Ding getrennt wird. Wo endet seine unwiderstehliche Anziehung, seine geheimnisvolle hypnotische Kraft, seine Einzigartigkeit, und wie wird es andererseits zu einem »Ding unter Dingen«, zu einem alltäglichen, gewöhnlichen Ding, dem wir keinerlei Aufmerksamkeit mehr schenken können? Wo endet das erste und beginnt das zweite? Und schließlich: Entsteht diese Situation immer und wenn ja, wo, unter welchen Bedingungen? (Natürlich geht es hier, wie auch im weiteren, nicht um ein konkretes Bild, sondern um das Bild »an sich«, um das Bild als Begriff, um ein Bild »wie viele«).
Freilich war es nicht immer üblich, ein Bild inmitten von anderen Dingen zu zeigen. Eher wäre es normal, das Bild unter seinesgleichen zu betrachten, d. h. in einer Reihe ebensolcher Bilder — ein durchaus professionelles Herangehen, bei dem jeder Fachmann oder Kunstkenner in der Lage ist, aus der Reihe der Bilder, die in seinem Gedächtnis vorhanden sind, ein gutes oder schlechtes hervorzuheben. Wenn man aber die Reduktion weiter vorantreibt, kann man sich das einzige, unwiederholbare Bild vorstellen, an das der Künstler glaubt, wenn er sein eigenes Bild malt — ebenfalls unwiederholbar und einzigartig —, denn ohne diesen Glauben könnte er kein Werk schaffen. Es kann sein, daß dieses ideale, »absolute Bild«, eine Art künstlerisches Urbild ist, aber ohne diesen Lichtpunkt wäre es überhaupt unmöglich, an die Einzigartigkeit der eigenen Schöpfung zu glauben.
Aber es gibt Hunderte Künstler und Tausende Bilder. Jeder von ihnen wird mit Recht das seine für einzigartig und ungewöhnlich halten, für uns aber wird es nur eines in einer Reihe von Bildern sein, wenn es in einer Galerie hängt, oder ein wertvoller, wunderbarer »Kulturgegenstand«, wenn es sich inmitten teurer alter Gerätschaften, Stoffe und Skulpturen im historischen Museum befindet... Und zuhause, wird es da nicht zu einem Gegenstand des täglichen Gebrauchs, zu einem Teil der Einrichtung? Besonders dann, wenn der Haushalt, die Familie in eine neue Wohnung übersiedeln, und das Bild in seinem vergoldeten Rahmen zwischen Schrank, Kochtöpfen und Nachttisch aus dem Karren oder Lastwagen herausragt.
Stop! Wie es scheint, ist hier der Endpunkt unserer Reise vom außergewöhnlichen, einzigartigen Schatz zum gewöhnlichen, unnützen Ding, dessen schon alle überdrüssig sind, erreicht. Aber sind das nicht zwei gegensätzliche Bewußtseinszustände? Der gesammelte,

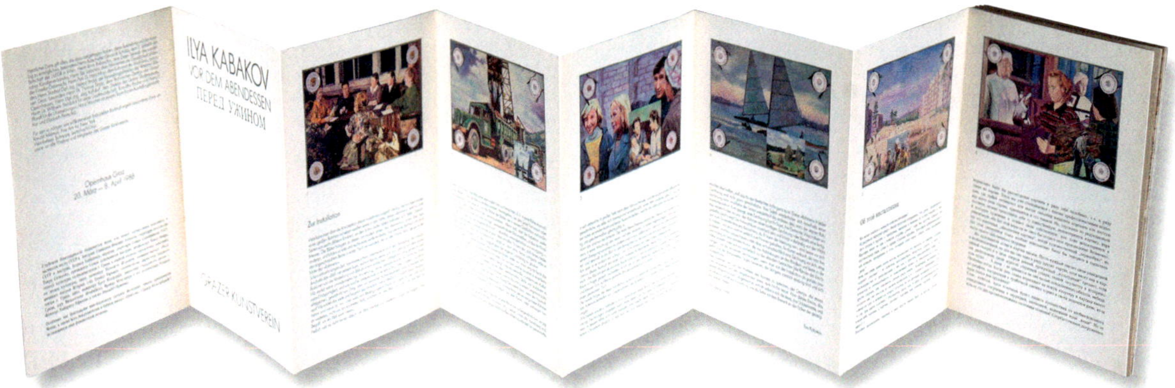

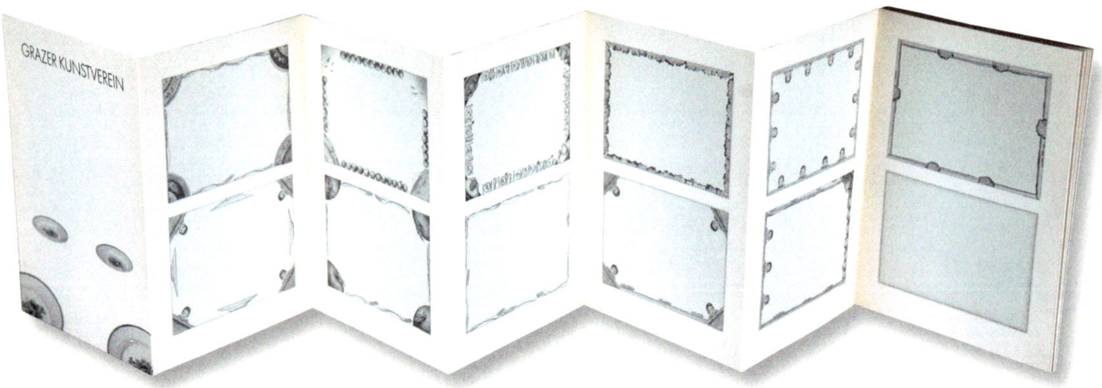

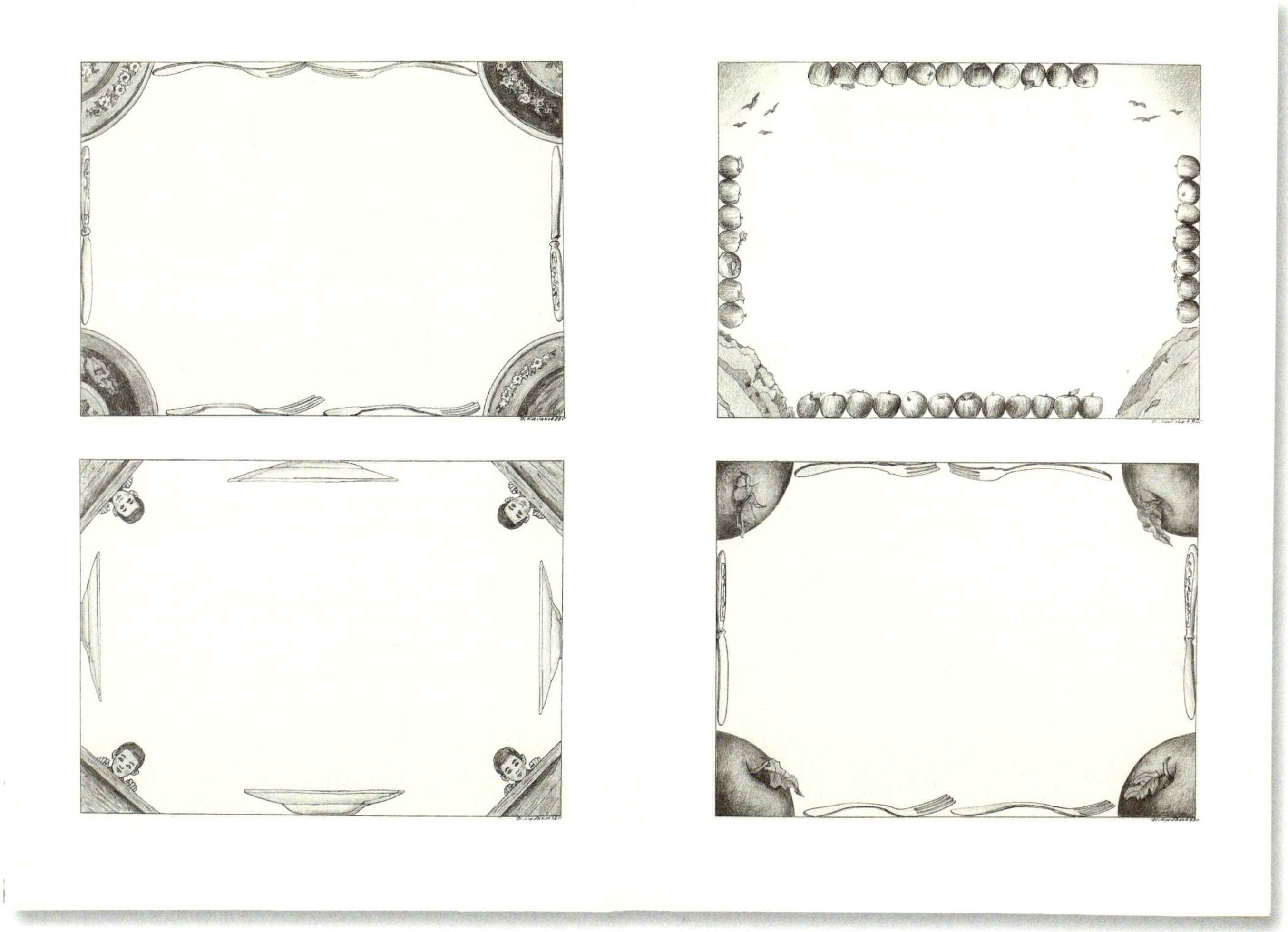

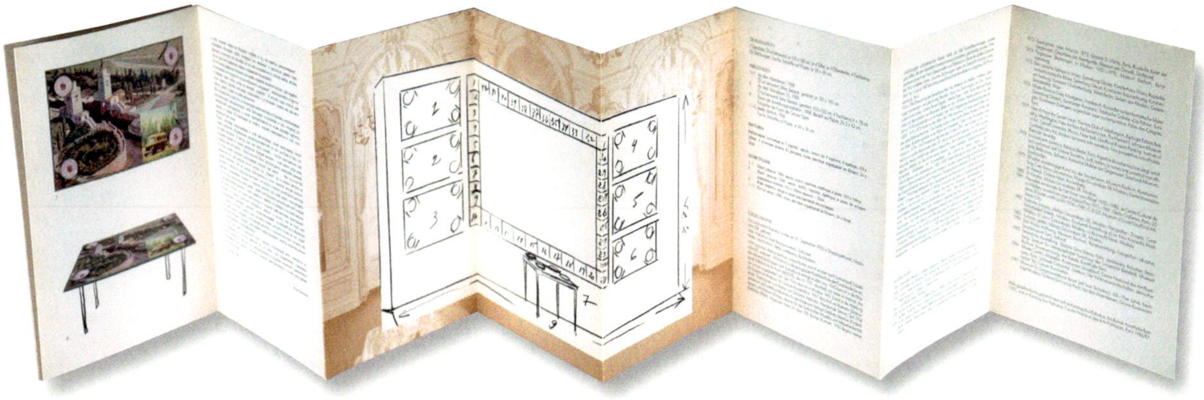

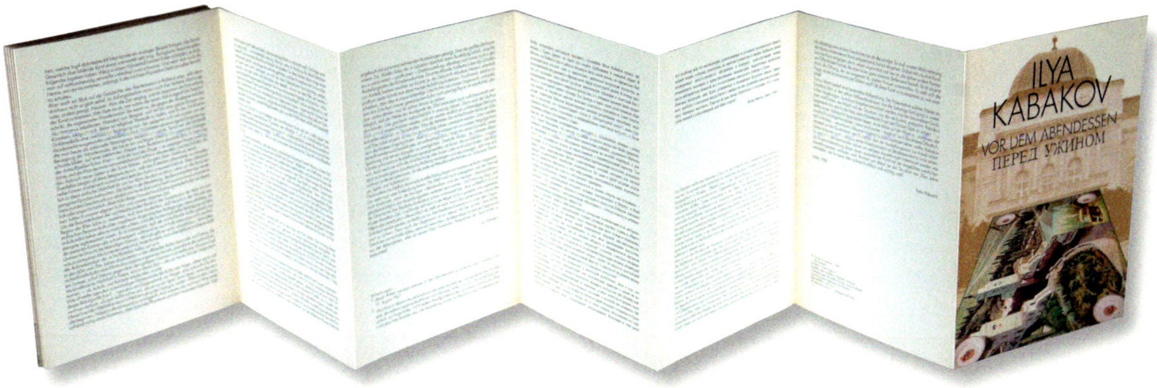
ILYA
KABAKOV
VOR DEM ABENDESSEN
ПЕРЕД УЖИНОМ

24 Who Are These Little Men? | *Wer sind die kleinen Männchen?*

1989

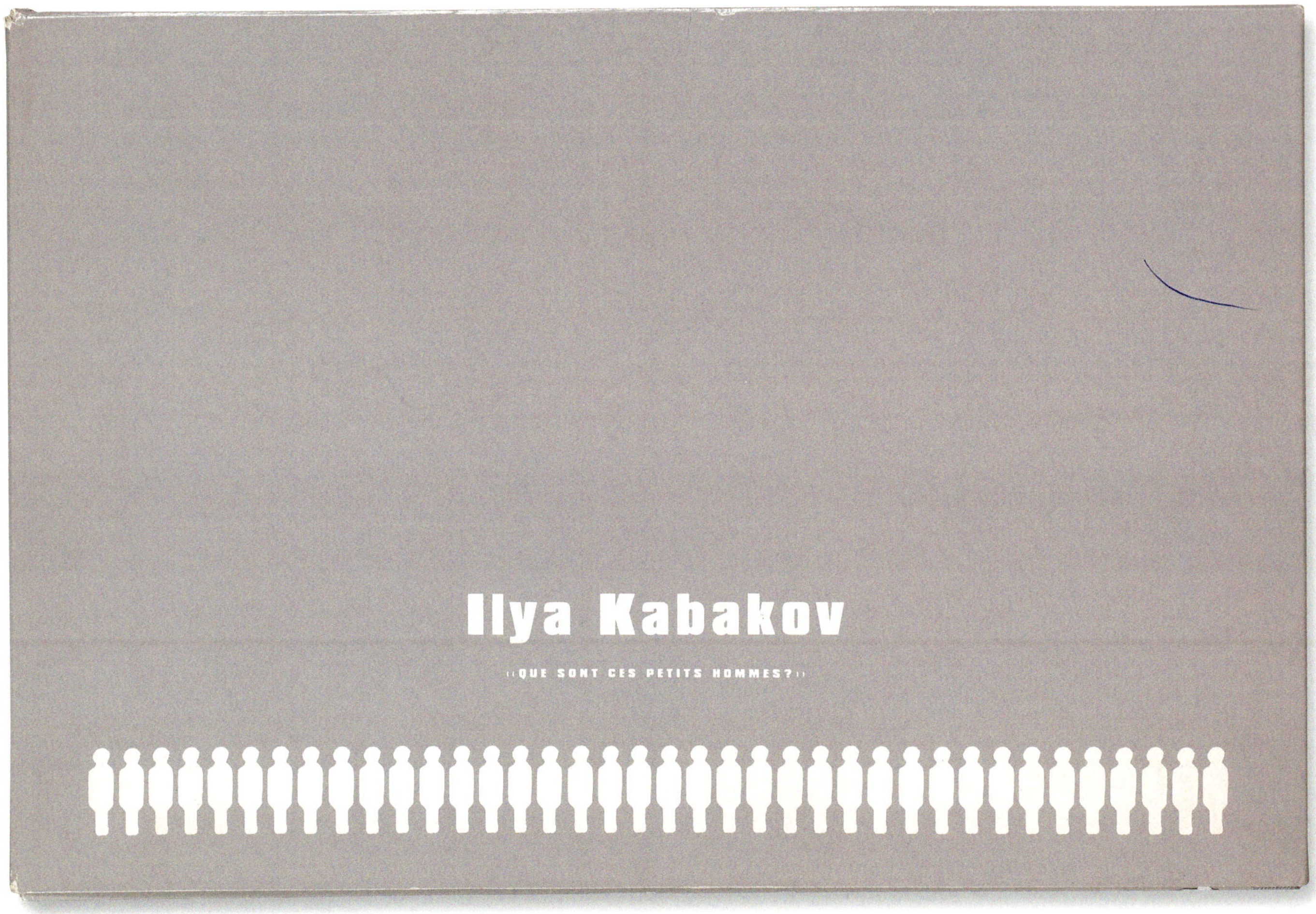

Galerie de France
Paris: Galerie de France
22.6 x 34.1 cm
[22] pp. with 33 (25 color) ills.
concertina-folded brochure,
cardboard slipcase
Leporello, Kartonschuber

exhibition catalogue | *Ausstellungskatalog*

layout by Ilya Kabakov | *Layout von Ilya Kabakov*

For the exhibition of the same name at the Galerie de France, Paris, January 19 to March 4, 1989. Texts, drawings, and reproductions of the paintings in the five installations: »Old Furniture and Little White Men, Three Nights, The Garden in the Corner, Trousers in the Corner«, and »Incident in the Corridor near the Kitchen«; Russian, French, English.

Zur gleichnamigen Ausstellung, Galerie de France, Paris, 19. Januar – 4. März 1989. Texte, Zeichnungen und Abbildungen der Gemälde in den fünf Installationen »Alte Möbel und weisse Männchen, Drei Nächte, Der Garten in der Ecke, Die Hose in der Ecke« und »Zwischenfall im Korridor neben der Küche«; russisch, französisch, englisch.

see also | *siehe auch* CRI, vol. 1, nos. 23–27, pp. 186–209; CRP, vol. 1, nos. 138–142, pp. 224–231

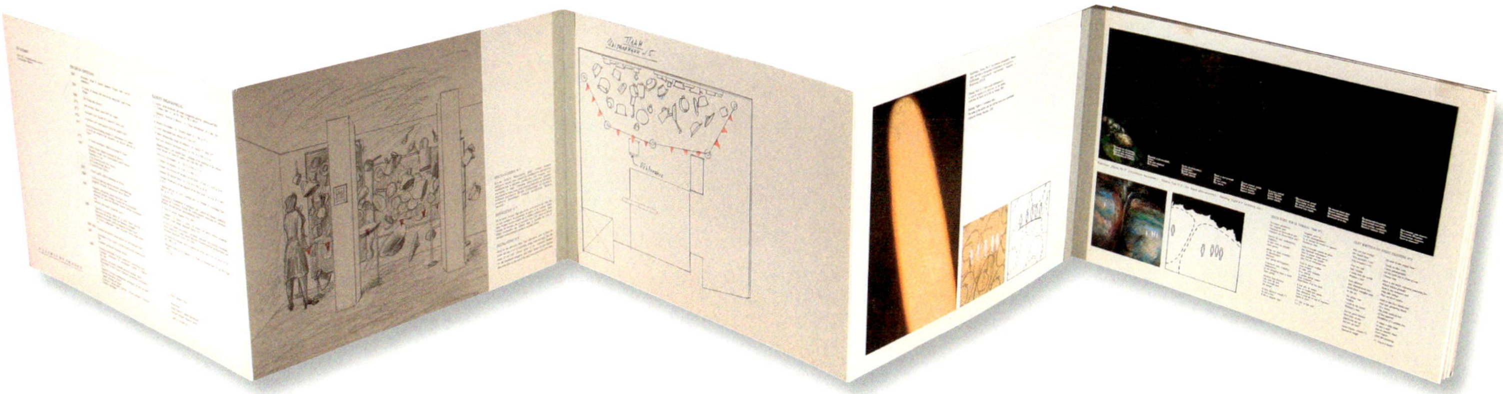

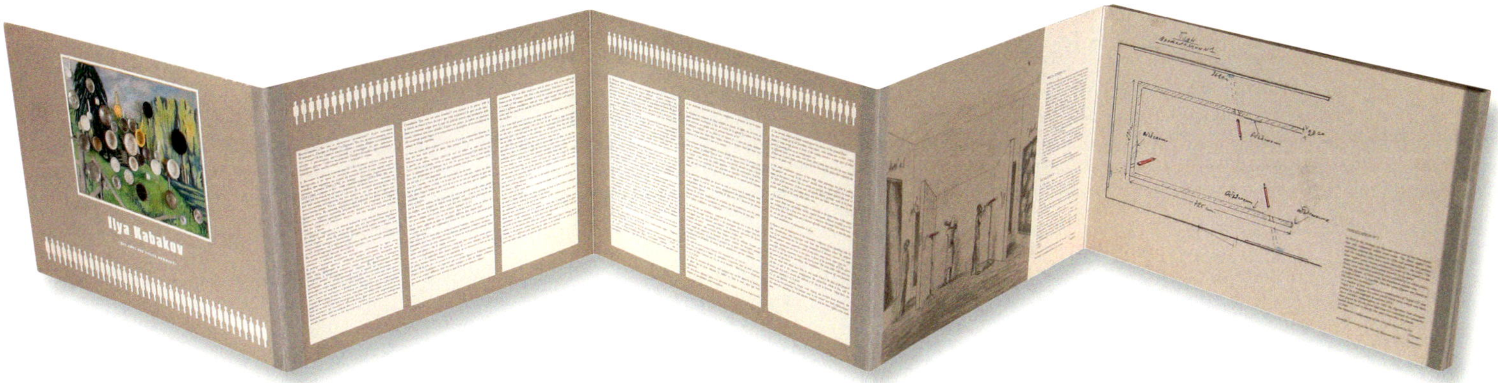
Ilya Kabakov

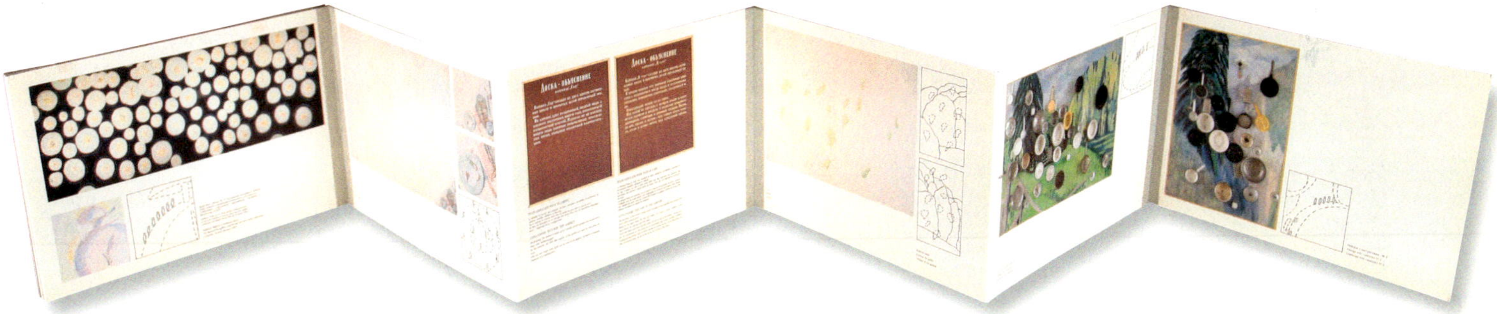

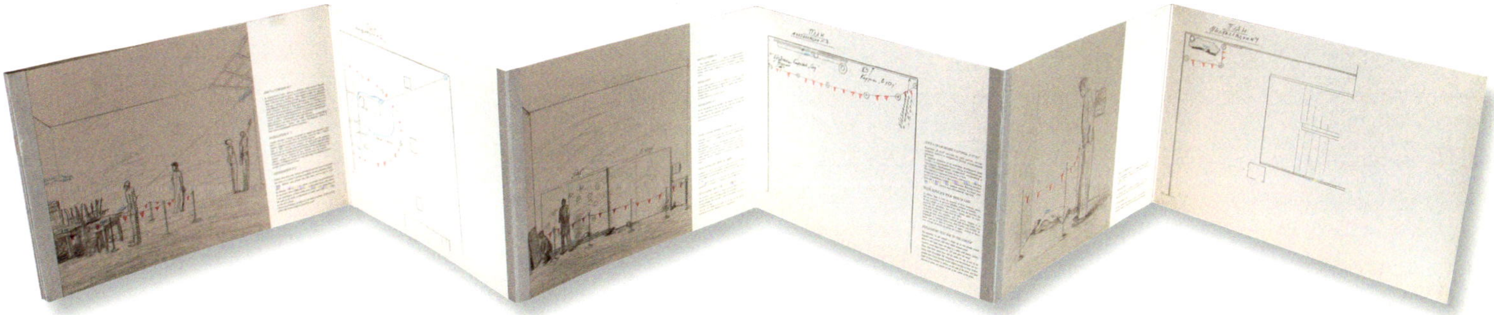

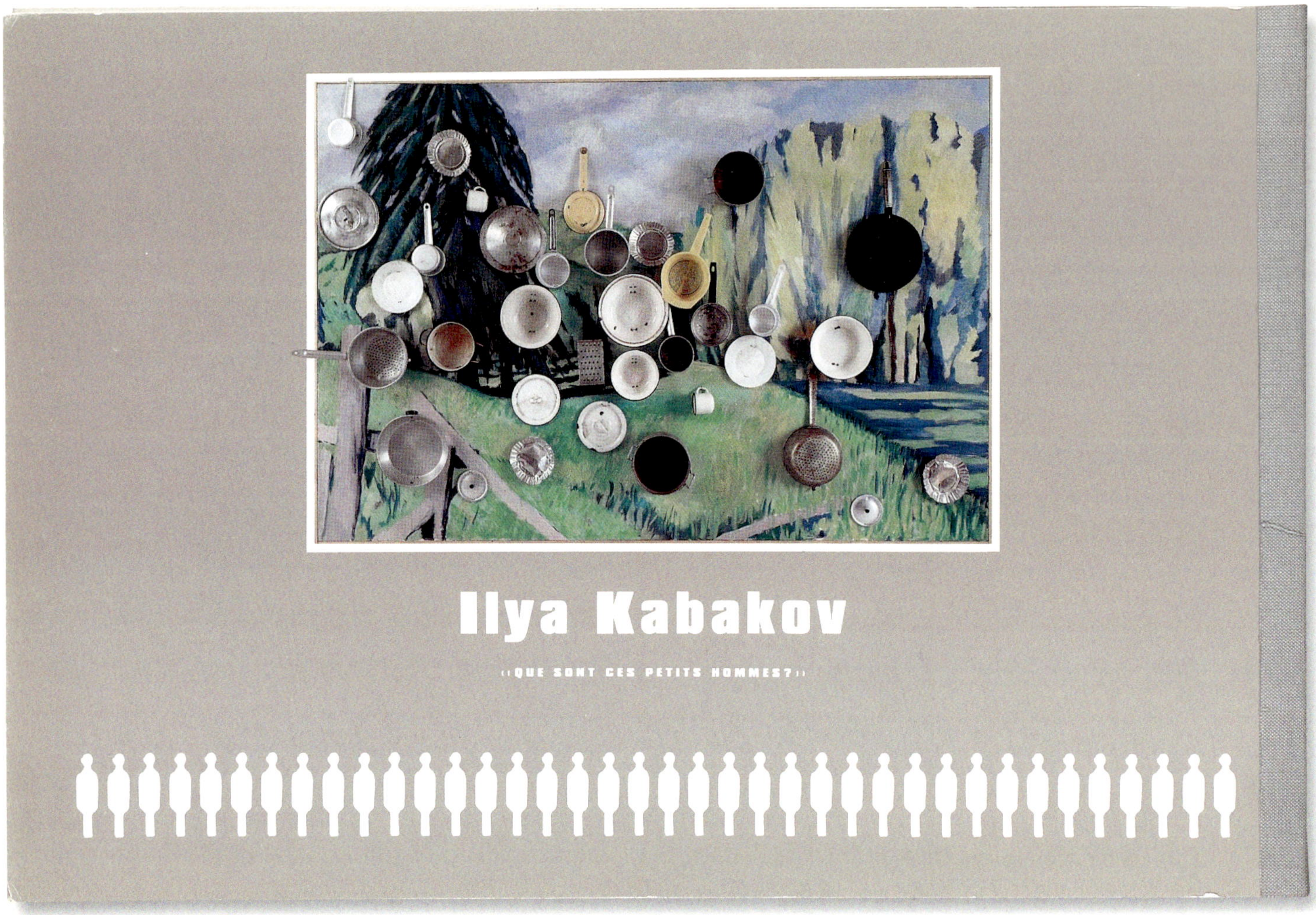
Ilya Kabakov
«QUE SONT CES PETITS HOMMES?»

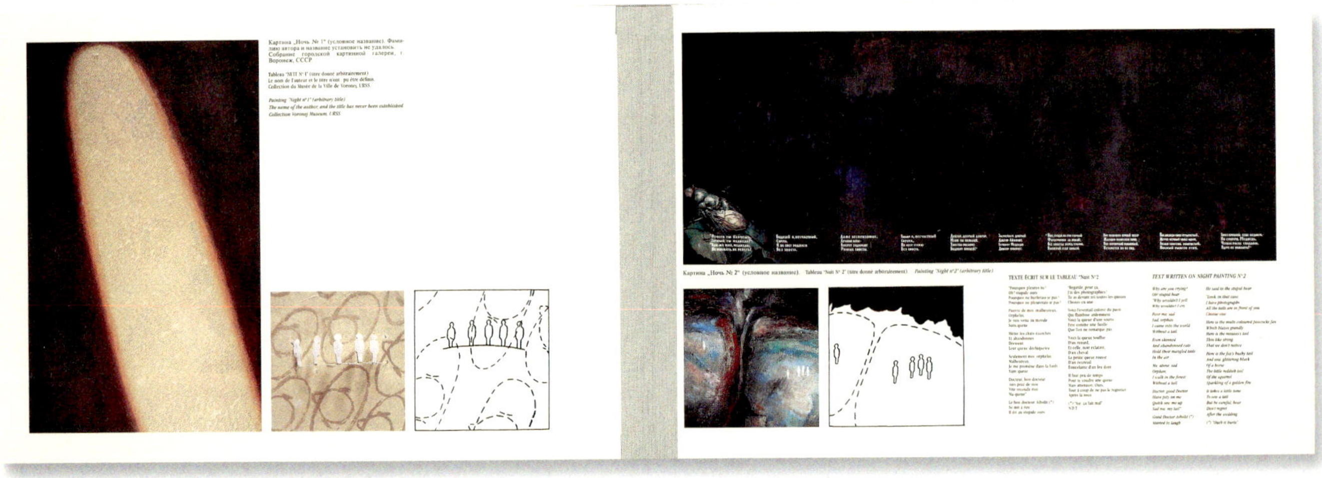

25 The Communal Apartment | *Die Kommunalwohnung*

1989

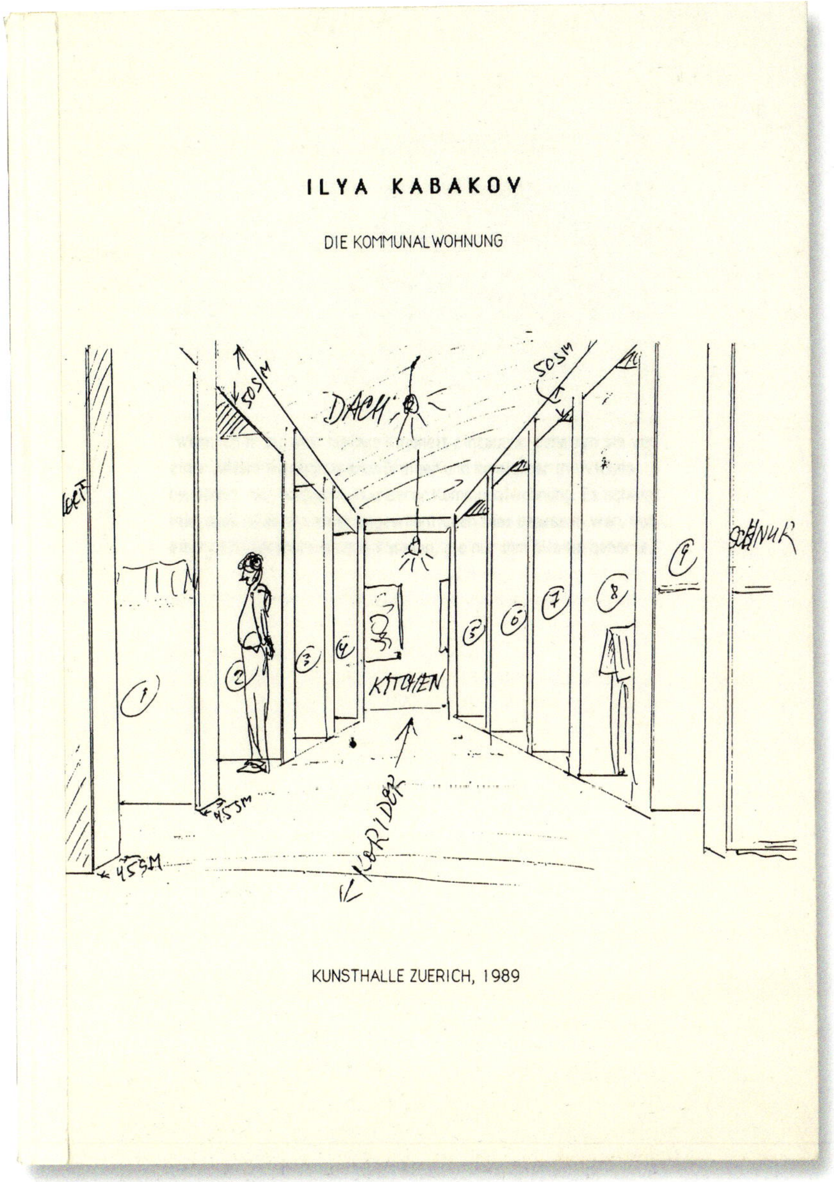

Kunsthalle Zürich
Zürich: Kunsthalle Zürich
29.7 x 21.1 cm
26 photocopied pp. with 3 b/w ills.
adhesive binding, plastic cover
Klebebindung, Plastikumschlag

exhibition catalogue | *Ausstellungskatalog*

layout by Ilya Kabakov | *Layout von Ilya Kabakov*

For the exhibition »The Ship – The Communal Apartment: Two Installations by Ilya Kabakov«, Kunsthalle Zürich, Zurich, June 2 to July 30, 1989. Texts by Ilya Kabakov; German.

Zur Ausstellung »Das Schiff – Die Kommunalwohnung, zwei Installationen von Ilya Kabakov«, Kunsthalle Zürich, Zürich, 2. Juni – 30. Juli 1989. Texte von Ilya Kabakov; deutsch.

see also | *siehe auch* no. 22; no. 48; no. 53; no. 54; no. 63; no. 89; CRI, vol. 1, no. 15, pp. 132–145; CRP, vol. 1, no. 49, pp.101–102, no. 57, pp. 114–115, no. 67, p. 132, no. 73, pp. 141–142, no. 114, pp. 196–197, no. 128, p. 213, no. 129, p. 214

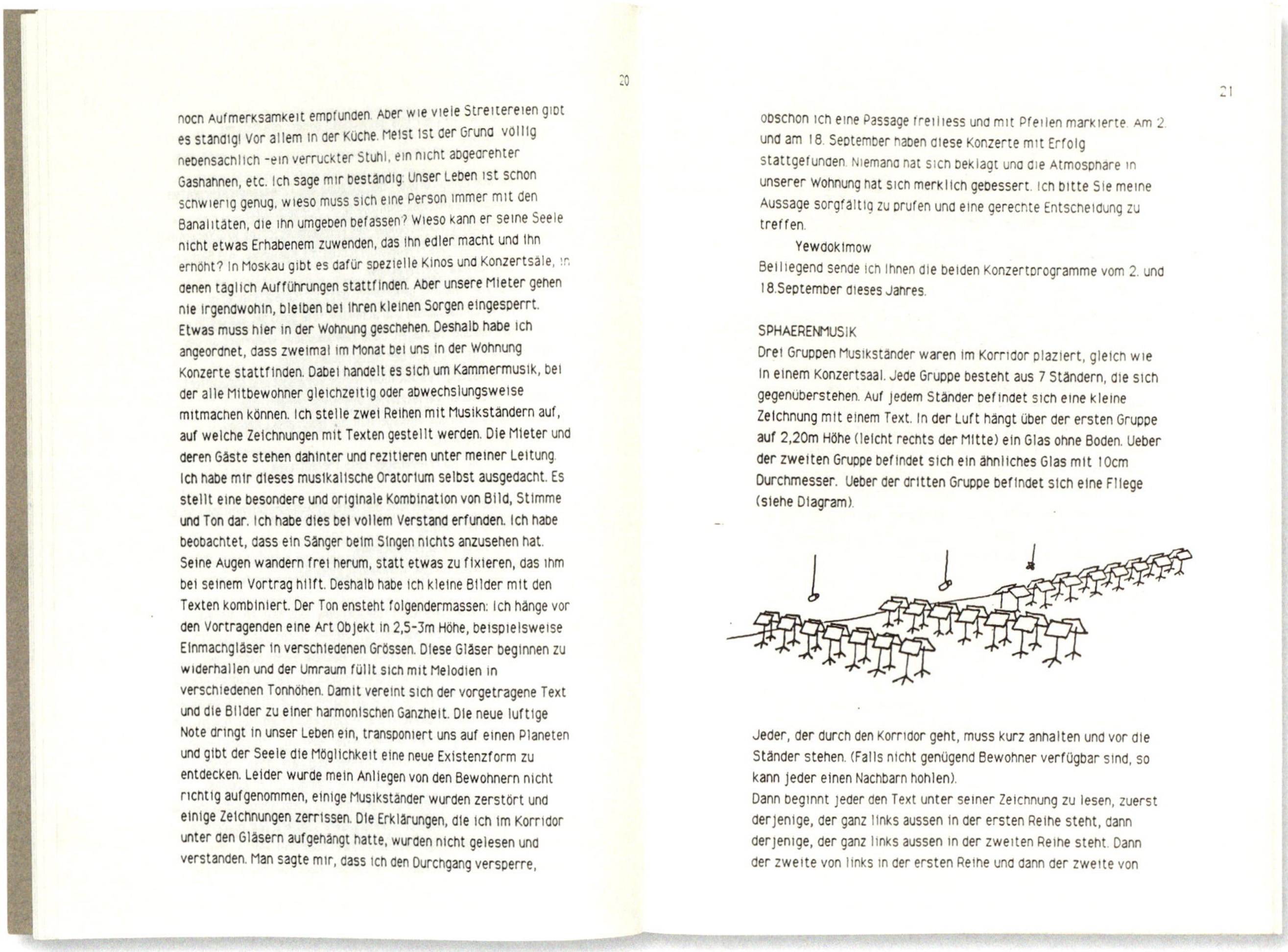

20

noch Aufmerksamkeit empfunden. Aber wie viele Streitereien gibt es ständig! Vor allem in der Küche. Meist ist der Grund völlig nebensächlich -ein verrückter Stuhl, ein nicht abgedrehter Gashahnen, etc. Ich sage mir beständig: Unser Leben ist schon schwierig genug, wieso muss sich eine Person immer mit den Banalitäten, die ihn umgeben befassen? Wieso kann er seine Seele nicht etwas Erhabenem zuwenden, das ihn edler macht und ihn erhöht? In Moskau gibt es dafür spezielle Kinos und Konzertsäle, in denen täglich Aufführungen stattfinden. Aber unsere Mieter gehen nie irgendwohin, bleiben bei ihren kleinen Sorgen eingesperrt. Etwas muss hier in der Wohnung geschehen. Deshalb habe ich angeordnet, dass zweimal im Monat bei uns in der Wohnung Konzerte stattfinden. Dabei handelt es sich um Kammermusik, bei der alle Mitbewohner gleichzeitig oder abwechslungsweise mitmachen können. Ich stelle zwei Reihen mit Musikständern auf, auf welche Zeichnungen mit Texten gestellt werden. Die Mieter und deren Gäste stehen dahinter und rezitieren unter meiner Leitung. Ich habe mir dieses musikalische Oratorium selbst ausgedacht. Es stellt eine besondere und originale Kombination von Bild, Stimme und Ton dar. Ich habe dies bei vollem Verstand erfunden. Ich habe beobachtet, dass ein Sänger beim Singen nichts anzusehen hat. Seine Augen wandern frei herum, statt etwas zu fixieren, das ihm bei seinem Vortrag hilft. Deshalb habe ich kleine Bilder mit den Texten kombiniert. Der Ton ensteht folgendermassen: Ich hänge vor den Vortragenden eine Art Objekt in 2,5-3m Höhe, beispielsweise Einmachgläser in verschiedenen Grössen. Diese Gläser beginnen zu widerhallen und der Umraum füllt sich mit Melodien in verschiedenen Tonhöhen. Damit vereint sich der vorgetragene Text und die Bilder zu einer harmonischen Ganzheit. Die neue luftige Note dringt in unser Leben ein, transponiert uns auf einen Planeten und gibt der Seele die Möglichkeit eine neue Existenzform zu entdecken. Leider wurde mein Anliegen von den Bewohnern nicht richtig aufgenommen, einige Musikständer wurden zerstört und einige Zeichnungen zerrissen. Die Erklärungen, die ich im Korridor unter den Gläsern aufgehängt hatte, wurden nicht gelesen und verstanden. Man sagte mir, dass ich den Durchgang versperre,

21

obschon ich eine Passage freiliess und mit Pfeilen markierte. Am 2. und am 18. September haben diese Konzerte mit Erfolg stattgefunden. Niemand hat sich beklagt und die Atmosphäre in unserer Wohnung hat sich merklich gebessert. Ich bitte Sie meine Aussage sorgfältig zu prüfen und eine gerechte Entscheidung zu treffen.

Yewdokimow

Beiliegend sende ich Ihnen die beiden Konzertprogramme vom 2. und 18.September dieses Jahres.

SPHAERENMUSIK

Drei Gruppen Musikständer waren im Korridor plaziert, gleich wie in einem Konzertsaal. Jede Gruppe besteht aus 7 Ständern, die sich gegenüberstehen. Auf jedem Ständer befindet sich eine kleine Zeichnung mit einem Text. In der Luft hängt über der ersten Gruppe auf 2,20m Höhe (leicht rechts der Mitte) ein Glas ohne Boden. Ueber der zweiten Gruppe befindet sich ein ähnliches Glas mit 10cm Durchmesser. Ueber der dritten Gruppe befindet sich eine Fliege (siehe Diagram).

Jeder, der durch den Korridor geht, muss kurz anhalten und vor die Ständer stehen. (Falls nicht genügend Bewohner verfügbar sind, so kann jeder einen Nachbarn hohlen).

Dann beginnt jeder den Text unter seiner Zeichnung zu lesen, zuerst derjenige, der ganz links aussen in der ersten Reihe steht, dann derjenige, der ganz links aussen in der zweiten Reihe steht. Dann der zweite von links in der ersten Reihe und dann der zweite von

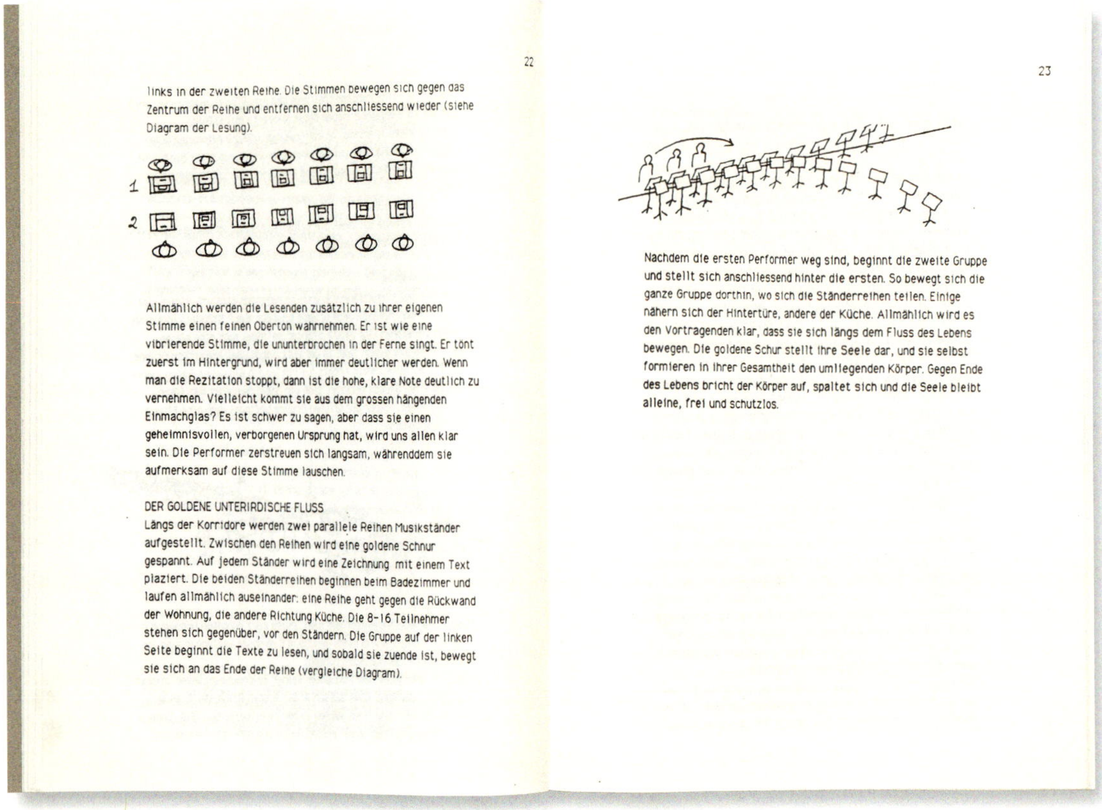

22

links in der zweiten Reihe. Die Stimmen bewegen sich gegen das Zentrum der Reihe und entfernen sich anschliessend wieder (siehe Diagram der Lesung).

Allmählich werden die Lesenden zusätzlich zu ihrer eigenen Stimme einen feinen Oberton wahrnehmen. Er ist wie eine vibrierende Stimme, die ununterbrochen in der Ferne singt. Er tönt zuerst im Hintergrund, wird aber immer deutlicher werden. Wenn man die Rezitation stoppt, dann ist die hohe, klare Note deutlich zu vernehmen. Vielleicht kommt sie aus dem grossen hängenden Einmachglas? Es ist schwer zu sagen, aber dass sie einen geheimnisvollen, verborgenen Ursprung hat, wird uns allen klar sein. Die Performer zerstreuen sich langsam, währenddem sie aufmerksam auf diese Stimme lauschen.

DER GOLDENE UNTERIRDISCHE FLUSS

Längs der Korridore werden zwei parallele Reihen Musikständer aufgestellt. Zwischen den Reihen wird eine goldene Schnur gespannt. Auf jedem Ständer wird eine Zeichnung mit einem Text plaziert. Die beiden Ständerreihen beginnen beim Badezimmer und laufen allmählich auseinander: eine Reihe geht gegen die Rückwand der Wohnung, die andere Richtung Küche. Die 8-16 Teilnehmer stehen sich gegenüber, vor den Ständern. Die Gruppe auf der linken Seite beginnt die Texte zu lesen, und sobald sie zuende ist, bewegt sie sich an das Ende der Reihe (vergleiche Diagram).

23

Nachdem die ersten Performer weg sind, beginnt die zweite Gruppe und stellt sich anschliessend hinter die ersten. So bewegt sich die ganze Gruppe dorthin, wo sich die Ständerreihen teilen. Einige nähern sich der Hintertüre, andere der Küche. Allmählich wird es den Vortragenden klar, dass sie sich längs dem Fluss des Lebens bewegen. Die goldene Schur stellt ihre Seele dar, und sie selbst formieren in ihrer Gesamtheit den umliegenden Körper. Gegen Ende des Lebens bricht der Körper auf, spaltet sich und die Seele bleibt alleine, frei und schutzlos.

26 The Ship | *Das Schiff*

1989

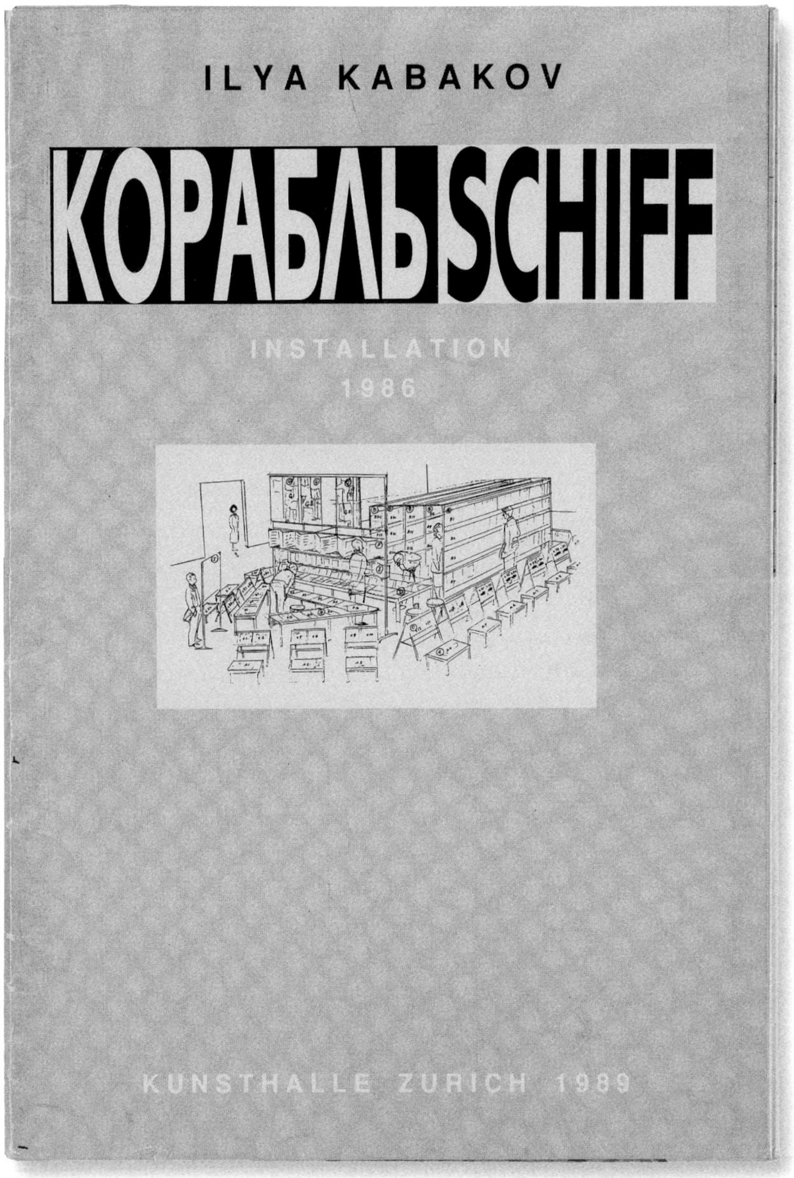

Kunsthalle Zürich
Zürich: Kunsthalle Zürich
23,9 x 16,6 cm
[32] pp. with 27 (12 color) ills.
concertina-folded brochure
Leporello

exhibition catalogue | *Ausstellungskatalog*

layout by Ilya Kabakov | *Layout von Ilya Kabakov*

For the exhibition »The Ship – The Communal Apartment: Two Installations by Ilya Kabakov«, Kunsthalle Zürich, Zurich, June 2 to July 30, 1989. Texts by Claudia Jolles and Ilya Kabakov; German.

Zur Ausstellung »Das Schiff – Die Kommunalwohnung, zwei Installationen von Ilya Kabakov« in der Kunsthalle Zürich, Zürich, 2. Juni – 30. Juli 1989. Texte von Claudia Jolles und Ilya Kabakov; deutsch.

see also | *siehe auch* CRI, vol.1, no. 10, pp. 102–107

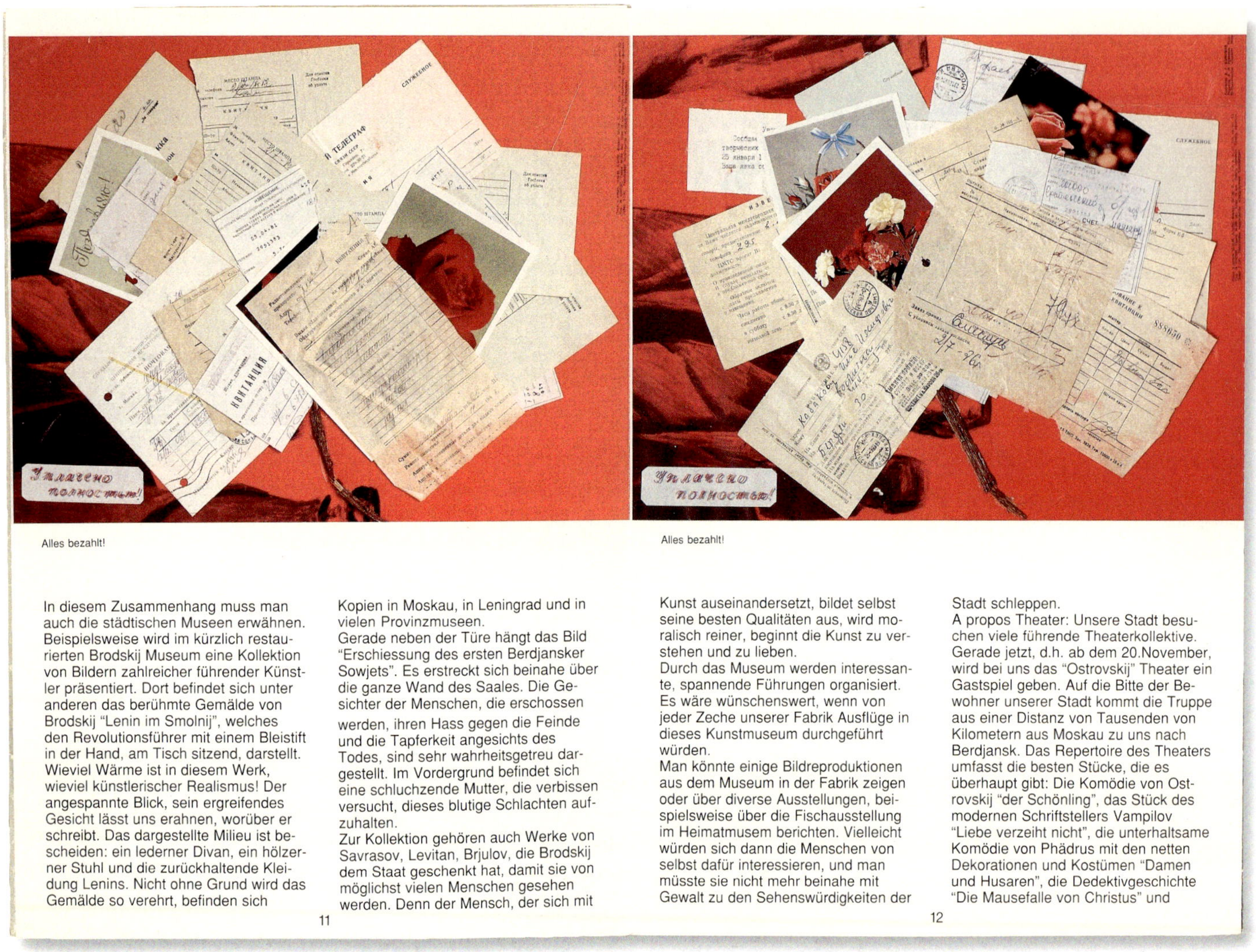

Alles bezahlt!

Alles bezahlt!

In diesem Zusammenhang muss man auch die städtischen Museen erwähnen. Beispielsweise wird im kürzlich restaurierten Brodskij Museum eine Kollektion von Bildern zahlreicher führender Künstler präsentiert. Dort befindet sich unter anderen das berühmte Gemälde von Brodskij "Lenin im Smolnij", welches den Revolutionsführer mit einem Bleistift in der Hand, am Tisch sitzend, darstellt. Wieviel Wärme ist in diesem Werk, wieviel künstlerischer Realismus! Der angespannte Blick, sein ergreifendes Gesicht lässt uns erahnen, worüber er schreibt. Das dargestellte Milieu ist bescheiden: ein lederner Divan, ein hölzerner Stuhl und die zurückhaltende Kleidung Lenins. Nicht ohne Grund wird das Gemälde so verehrt, befinden sich Kopien in Moskau, in Leningrad und in vielen Provinzmuseen.

Gerade neben der Türe hängt das Bild "Erschiessung des ersten Berdjansker Sowjets". Es erstreckt sich beinahe über die ganze Wand des Saales. Die Gesichter der Menschen, die erschossen werden, ihren Hass gegen die Feinde und die Tapferkeit angesichts des Todes, sind sehr wahrheitsgetreu dargestellt. Im Vordergrund befindet sich eine schluchzende Mutter, die verbissen versucht, dieses blutige Schlachten aufzuhalten.

Zur Kollektion gehören auch Werke von Savrasov, Levitan, Brjulov, die Brodskij dem Staat geschenkt hat, damit sie von möglichst vielen Menschen gesehen werden. Denn der Mensch, der sich mit

11

Kunst auseinandersetzt, bildet selbst seine besten Qualitäten aus, wird moralisch reiner, beginnt die Kunst zu verstehen und zu lieben.

Durch das Museum werden interessante, spannende Führungen organisiert. Es wäre wünschenswert, wenn von jeder Zeche unserer Fabrik Ausflüge in dieses Kunstmuseum durchgeführt würden.

Man könnte einige Bildreproduktionen aus dem Museum in der Fabrik zeigen oder über diverse Ausstellungen, beispielsweise über die Fischausstellung im Heimatmusem berichten. Vielleicht würden sich dann die Menschen von selbst dafür interessieren, und man müsste sie nicht mehr beinahe mit Gewalt zu den Sehenswürdigkeiten der Stadt schleppen.

A propos Theater: Unsere Stadt besuchen viele führende Theaterkollektive. Gerade jetzt, d.h. ab dem 20.November, wird bei uns das "Ostrovskij" Theater ein Gastspiel geben. Auf die Bitte der Bewohner unserer Stadt kommt die Truppe aus einer Distanz von Tausenden von Kilometern aus Moskau zu uns nach Berdjansk. Das Repertoire des Theaters umfasst die besten Stücke, die es überhaupt gibt: Die Komödie von Ostrovskij "der Schönling", das Stück des modernen Schriftstellers Vampilov "Liebe verzeiht nicht", die unterhaltsame Komödie von Phädrus mit den netten Dekorationen und Kostümen "Damen und Husaren", die Dedektivgeschichte "Die Mausefalle von Christus" und

12

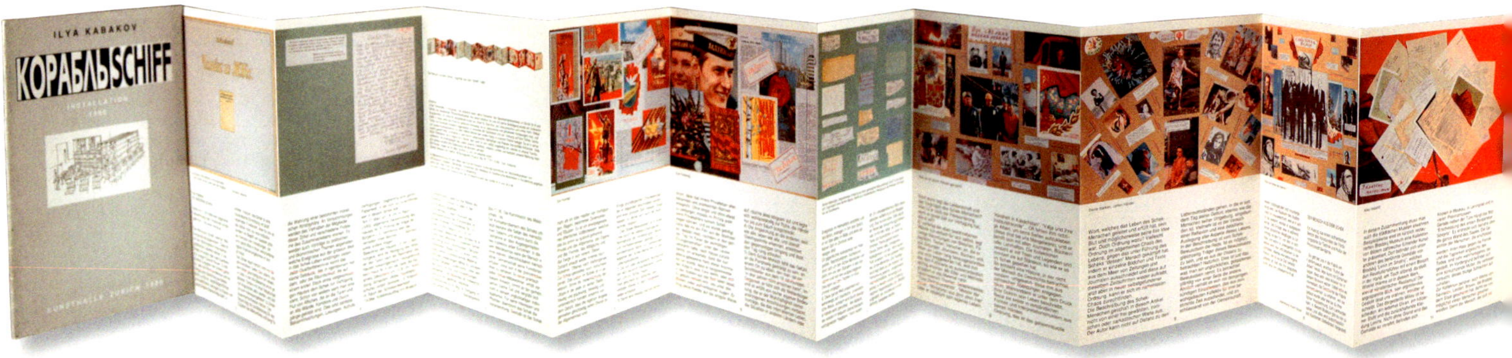

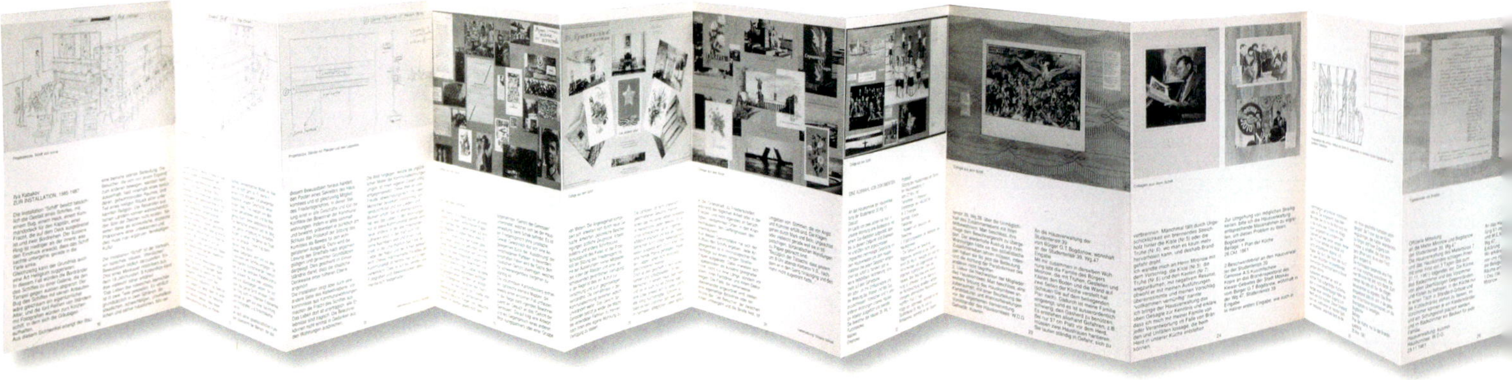

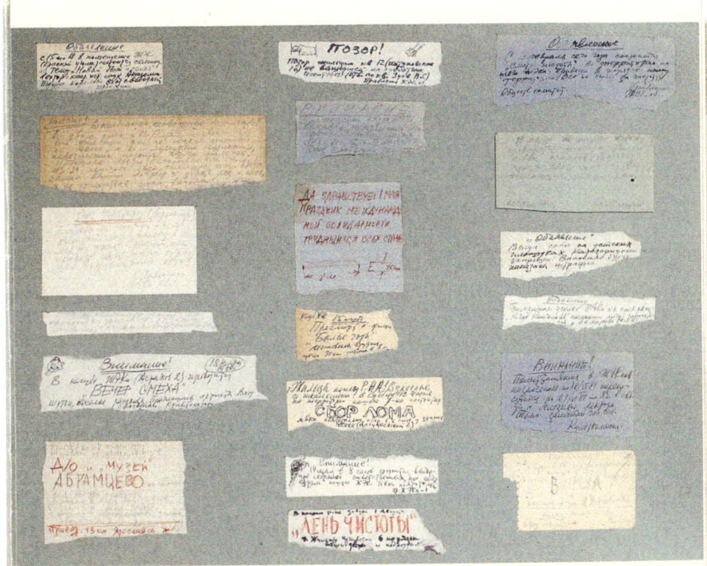

Diverse Mitteilungen, beispielsweise: Einladung zu einem gemeinsamen Museumsbesuch, Aufruf "für die Sauberkeit", Organisation eines Bunten Abends, Beitritt zum Handarbeitszirkel, Beteiligung an der freiwilligen Sonntagsarbeit, der Kartoffelernte.

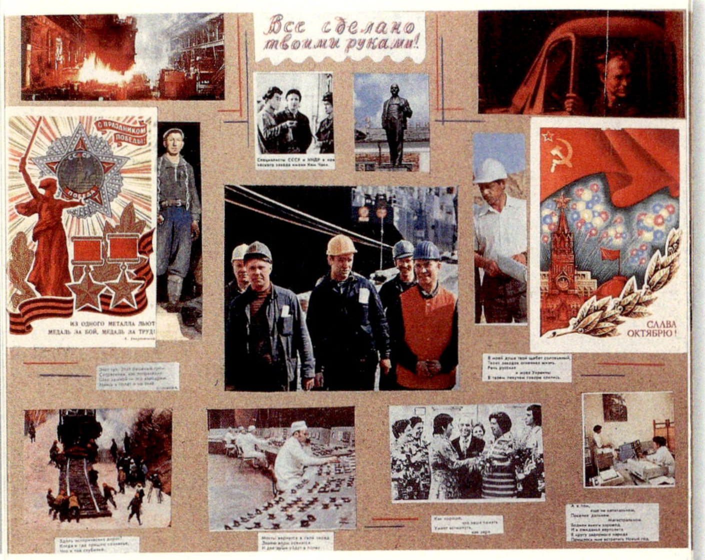

Alles ist mit deinen Händen gemacht!

Ereignisse im Heimatland vorstellen und beurteilen, erzeugen in ihm das Gefühl, er sei über alles im Bilde und stehe als kleiner Gott im Zentrum einer riesigen Welt.
Ein gigantisches Kaleidoskop von Fotografien, Reproduktionen, Karikaturen, dreht sich um den Schek-Menschen und blickt ihm von den Ständern in den Korridoren und von den aufgeschlagenen Zeitungen auf den Tischen im Klubzimmer entgegen.
6) Diese ganze Welt präsentiert sich keineswegs auf chaotische, unverständliche Weise, sondern wird durch besorgte Hände wohl geordnet. Alle Materialien werden in bequem überschaubarer, vorzugsweise "tragbarer" Form vermittelt. Ein charakteristisches Mittel dieser optischen Aufklärung ist die Wandzeitung. Dies ist eine kleine Tafel, die an der Wand des Versammlungszimmers oder im Korridor hängt, auf welche Texte und Illustrationen zu einem bestimmten Thema geklebt werden.
Dieses Ordnen alles Umliegenden, Katalogisieren und das "Allem-seinen-Platz-zuweisen" ist die süsseste Pflicht des Schek-Menschen. Das Hauptgewicht liegt dabei auf der Auswahl und Formulierung positiver, inhaltschwerer Informationsblöcke, die würdig sind, gezeigt zu werden und der Schaffung negativer Gegenbeispiele, die, öffentlich aufgestellt, der Verurteilung und der Ächtung übergeben werden.

7

Doch worin liegt die Leidenschaft und das Vergnügen des Schek-Menschen? Was tut er nach der Pensionierung, wenn er soviel Zeit zur Verfügung hat, wie er will?
Er verfertigt die oben beschriebenen Wände nun einfach für sich selbst, legt riesige Sammlungen von Bildchen, Fotografien, Texten, Verschen an, die er aus Zeitungen, Journalen, Büchern und Alben ein Leben lang herausgeschnitten und nicht weggeworfen hat, weil ihm das dort Publizierte so ausserordentlich wichtig erschien. Mit Eifer und Methode gruppiert er das Material nach verschiedenen Themen, beispielsweise: "Tiere Zentralrusslands", "Meister der Kunst", "Miniaturen aus dem alten Iran". Oder er reflektiert sein eigenes Leben: "Kindheit in Kasachstan", "Valja und ihre Institutsfreunde"... Oft fehlen ihm richtige Alben, um seine Serien aufzukleben (diese sind bei uns Mangelware), und er behilft sich mit alten Journalen, Büchern oder Lehrheften. Die Kollektionen versieht er mit Titeln und Legenden und montiert sie auf Ständern, so wie er es im Schek gesehen hat.
So entsteht eine Historie, in der nicht der Mensch die Geschichte betrachtet, sondern -umgekehrt- diese ihm aus zahlreichen Abbildungen entgegenblickt. Währenddem er unter dem Druck ihrer Doktrin sein Leben beschreibt, fliesst sie selber in verständlichen Formen und Interpretationsmustern aus seinen Händen.
Ordnung, das ist das geheimnisvolle

8

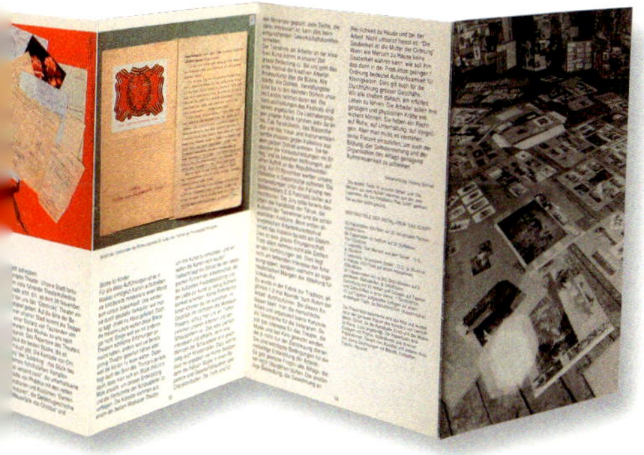

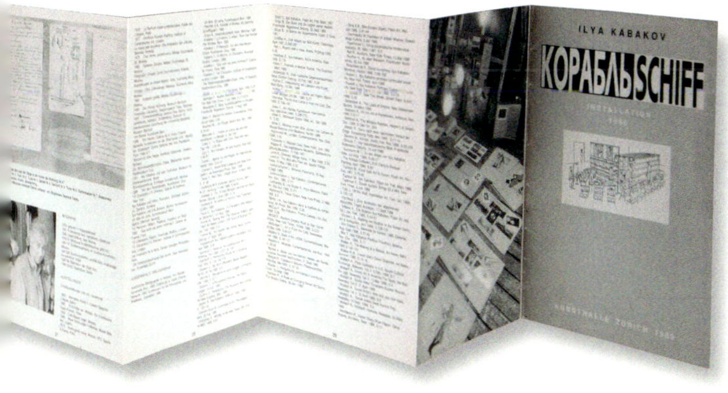

27 Exhibition of a Book | *Ausstellung eines Buches*

1989

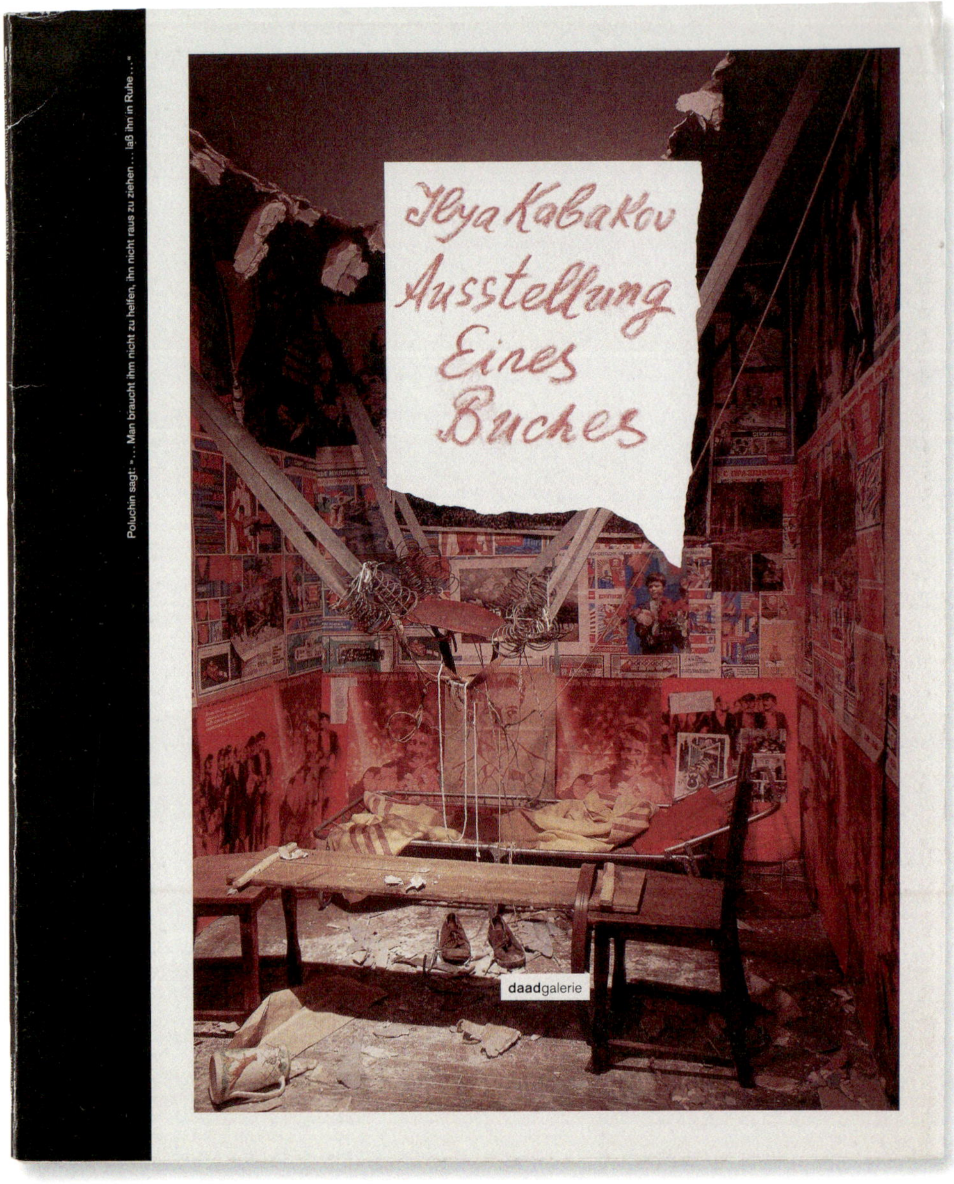

Berliner Künstlerprogramm des DAAD
Berlin: DAAD
26.2 x 21.8 cm
[32] pp. with 15 (11 color) ills.
concertina-folded brochure,
cardboard slipcase
Leporello, Kartonschuber

exhibition catalogue | *Ausstellungskatalog*

layout by Ilya Kabakov | *Layout von Ilya Kabakov*

For the installation of the same name at the DAAD Galerie, Berlin Artists-in-Residence Program of the German Academic Exchange Service (DAAD), Berlin, December 9, 1989 to January 28, 1990. The texts are based on the dialogues conducted by Joseph Backstein, Boris Groys, and Ilya Kabakov in 1989: »Fear, Voices, Being Means Speaking, Characters, Zek, The West, Communal Apartment, Emptiness, Garbage«, and »Flight«; they are components of »The Art of Flight«, which was published at a later date.

Zur gleichnamigen Installation, DAAD-Galerie, Berliner Künstlerprogramm des Deutschen Akademischen Austausch Dienstes, Berlin, 9. Dezember 1989 – 28. Januar 1990. Die Texte basieren auf den 1989 geführten Dialogen von Josef Bakstein, Boris Groys und Ilya Kabakov: »Angst, Stimmen, Sein heisst sprechen, Personen, Zek, Der Westen, Kommunalwohnung, Leere, Müll« und »Flucht«; sie sind Bestandteile der späteren Publikation »Die Kunst des Fliehens«.

see also | *siehe auch* no. 47; CRI, vol. 1, no. 29, pp. 216–221

SEIN HEISST SPRECHEN

Forts. von S. 5A

der Drang zu sprechen war entschieden stärker als das, was mich zurückhielt. Die Grundsituation kann man ›Sprechen vor der Entscheidung zu sprechen‹ nennen. Dadurch trat die Situation ein, daß ich mir als ein ER, das spricht, gegenüberstand. Ich sagte mir: Warum redet DER eigentlich dauernd und sagt trotzdem nicht das, was er sagen will? Das Auseinandertreten von Sprecher und dem, der diesen Sprecher hört, geschah in meiner frühen Kindheit und führte später dazu, daß ich das ›sprechende Ich‹ einholen mußte. Wie ein Läufer auf dem Feld mußte ich den, der dauernd sprach, einholen, um ihn zu fragen: bist du dir denn sicher, daß das, was du sagst, überhaupt mit dem, was du sagen willst, übereinstimmt?

Das ist meine erste Erinnerung. Meine zweite Erinnerung hängt mit dem Zeichnen zusammen. Das war schon in der Kunstschule und wiederholte sich später im Institut. Während ich malte, spürte ich plötzlich ganz intensiv, daß ich nicht weiß, was und warum ich das zeichnen soll, was ich zeichne. Im Gegensatz zu anderen Malern hatte ich weder eigene künstlerische Ambitionen noch Talent, weder die Aggressivität noch auch nur den Wunsch, jemanden zu erstaunen. Das Zeichnen war für mich da, bevor ich beschlossen hatte, Maler zu werden und zu zeichnen! Alles war verkehrt herum. Der Karren lief, das Pferd zockelte hinterher. Das Zeichnen war zuerst da, der Wunsch dazu kam später. Das hatte zur Folge, daß ich so zeichnete, wie es mir vor den Lehrern im Moment am wenigsten riskant erschien. Ich konnte kaum zeichnen, nicht daß ich einfach mittelmäßig zeichnete, sondern ich war schlicht unbegabt, so daß ich jeden Augenblick in der Gefahr schwebte, von der Schule zu fliegen. Ich mußte so zeichnen, daß sie mich zähneknirrschend behielten! Daraus folgte, daß ich so zeichnen mußte, daß sie keine Handhabe hatten, mich aus dem Institut zu schmeißen. Meine ganze Aufmerksamkeit konzentrierte sich darauf, diejenigen Pinselbewegungen, Linien, Flecken, Farben und Stellen auf der Leinwand bzw. dem Papier zu treffen, die dem Schuldurchschnitt entsprachen und verhinderten, daß ich flog. Es ging nie darum, sich hervorzutun; ich mußte mich abstrampeln, um nicht der Schlechteste zu sein – denn der fliegt. Deshalb imitierte ich ständig a) die Situation von jemand, der zeichnet, b) das, was dieser Maler zeichnet. Wenn der Lehrer hinter mir stand, ahmte ich mit einer Bleistiftbewegung und der Kopfhaltung einen Schüler nach, der mit großem Eifer das vor ihm stehende Modell betrachtet, das heißt, ich inszenierte die durchaus theatralische Situation: ein Maler steht vor seiner Staffelei und zeichnet. Die Hand darf nicht zu schnell über das Papier gleiten, damit der Lehrer hinter deinem Rücken nicht dahinterkommt, daß ich gar nichts sehe; andererseits darf die Hand sich auch nicht so langsam bewegen, daß der Lehrer denkt, ich schliefe.«

B. Groys – I. Kabakov: »Dialoge«, 1989

Aus dem Album: »Fliegender Komarov«, 1972–75, Feder, schwarze Tusche, aquarelliert, 1 von 32 Blättern, je 25 x 35 cm, Centre Georges Pompidou, Paris

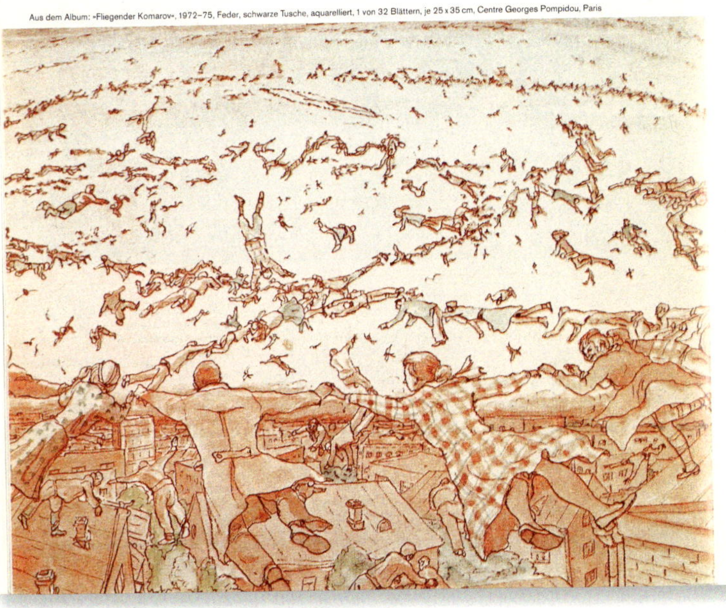

Der Plan für die meisten Themen entstand im Frühling 1971 in Chost. Diese Themen nahmen sofort die Form von Personen an; es bildeten sich sogleich die fiktiven Personen Komarow, Barmin u. a. heraus. Das heißt, ich war mir schon damals darüber im klaren, daß die »Personen« keine natürlichen Menschen sind, sondern literarische Gestalten, die von diesem Thema bzw. Zustand durchdrungen sind und dieses Thema bzw. diesen Zustand als einzigen Lebensinhalt von A bis Z durchleben.

Hier ein kurzer Überblick über diese Themen:

1. »Der im Schrank sitzende Komarov«
Thema ist die Finsternis des Bewußtseins, das nichts sieht, Blindheit. Dieses Nichts-sehen-Können gilt sowohl für die Situation des völlig »Eingeschlossenen« als auch für den Flug in die absolute »Leere«.

2. »Der Witzbold«
Die Dummheit, Oberflächlichkeit des Witzes; Ironie, die mit all ihren Anspielungen nur scheinbar vielsagend ist. Die typische, ephemere »Seichtheit« jeglichen »geistreichen« Getues.

3. »Der großzügige Barmin«
Der Alptraum des »Namens« als soziales Etikett, die Rolle des Namens als Stempel des Kollektivs. Das manische Aufzählen, Durchgehen von Namen bei totalem Unverständnis für den Sinn der »Benennung«. Die nicht-sakrale »Namengebung«. Selbstherrliche, willkürliche »Initiation«.

4. »Der Selbstquälerische«
Das Bewußtsein, das hinter den »Schleier« dringt. Alles Echte liegt »hinter einem Vorhang« verborgen. Zerreißen dieser »Schleier«, Erweiterung der »Öffnung«, hinter dem alten taucht ein neuer Schleier auf, hinter einem jeden findet sich der nächste …

»Die 70er Jahre«, MS, 1984

Als er eines Tages an seiner Biographie saß, merkte er plötzlich, daß sie ihm, obwohl doch nur von ihm selbst die Rede war, als Biographie eines einzelnen nicht gelingen wollte. Sie ging ihm aber leicht als Biographie mehrerer Personen von der Hand. Er wunderte sich unheimlich und erschrak sogar darüber – denn er wußte ja sehr wohl, daß es einzig und allein um ihn ging. Und trotzdem standen diese verschiedenen Personen so klar vor seinen Augen, ihre Charaktere zeichneten sich so deutlich ab, daß er sogar die Stimmen hörte, mit denen jede sprach.

Um von dieser seltsamen Vorstellung loszukommen, stellte er eine Reihe Alben her, Sammlungen von Zuständen, Zeichnungen und Erläuterungen. Jedes Album verkörperte eine bestimmte Person, einen Teil seiner selbst. So entstanden große Gruppen von zehn und mehr »Personen«.

»Der Mann, der sich über andere beschreibt«, Installation »10 Personen«, Galerie R. Feldman, New York 1987

Zweimal im Monat nahm er seine Notenständer und stellte sie im Flur der Kommunalwohnung auf, so daß sie sich in zwei Reihen gegenüberstanden; er legte auf jeden eine kleine Zeichnung mit einem Text darunter und hängte an einer dünnen Schnur zwei Konservengläser ohne Boden sowie eine kleine Fliege aus Papier auf …

Er wollte von allen Bewohnern der Kommunalwohnung, daß sie für einen Moment ihr Zimmer verlassen, sich vor die Notenständer stellen, die Zeichnungen betrachten und die Texte zu zweit laut vorlesen. Diese merkwürdigen Programme hielt er nicht für eine persönliche Laune, er tat das nicht für sich. Er sah in diesen Konzerten die Möglichkeit, die Nachbarn in einem gemeinsamen künstlerischen Akt zu vereinen, sie an höheren geistigen Zuständen teilhaben zu lassen. Aufgrund der Beschwerden der Nachbarn wurde er etliche Male vom Ehrengericht zur Ordnung gerufen.

»Der Komponist«,
Installation »10 Personen«,
Galerie R. Feldman, New York 1987

Er sammelte immer Unmengen von Postkarten. Sie wurden im Nachbarhaus angeboten, er kaufte sie und sammelte alle ohne Ausnahme: Postkarten mit Blumen, historischen Denkmälern, Porträts von Berühmtheiten, Stadtansichten, Meerestiere … Er klebte sie alle sorgfältig in Alben, und wenn es mal wieder keine gab, klebte er sie einzeln auf ein Blatt Papier, das er ordentlich zurechtgeschnitten hatte. Jedes dieser immer nach einem festen System geordneten Blätter mit den fein säuberlich aufgeklebten Postkarten und Ausschnitten versah er mit einer prächtigen Überschrift und verzierte es mit Ornamenten, bunten Winkeln und Streifen …

»Der Sammler«, Installation »10 Personen«,
Galerie R. Feldman, New York 1987

6B

Ilya Kabakov
Ausstellung eines Buches

Herausgeber
Berliner Künstlerprogramm des DAAD
Direktor: Joachim Sartorius
Katalog: Ingrid Mössinger und Ilya Kabakov
Texte aus dem Russischen: Birgit Veit
Fotos: G. Kisewalter, I. Makarevich
Ausstellungsorganisation: Ingrid Mössinger
Druckhaus Hentrich, Berlin

ISBN 3-89357-017-9

Wir danken der Stiftung Deutsche Klassenlotterie für die Unterstützung von Ausstellung und Katalog.

Biographie

Ilya Kabakov wurde am 30. 9. 1933 in Dnepropetrovsk, Ukraine, geboren. Die Mutter, Bejla Judelevna Soloduchina, war Buchhalterin und der Vater, Josif Benzionovitch Kabakov, Schlosser. Während des Krieges evakuierte man die Familie nach Samarkand. Ilya Kabakov besuchte die ebenfalls nach dorthin ausgelagerte Kunstschule der Kunstakademie Leningrad. Bis 1951 studierte er dann an der Kunstschule von Moskau und trat anschließend in das Moskauer Kunstinstitut Surikov ein. 1957 beendete er sein Studium als Buchillustrator und arbeitete für verschiedene Kinderbuchverlage und Zeitschriften.

Einzelausstellungen (Auswahl)

1985 Galerie Dina Vierni, Paris
1985/86 »Am Rande«, Kunsthalle Bern; Galerie de la Veille Charité, Marseille; Kunstverein der Rheinlande und Westfalen, Düsseldorf; Centre National des Arts Plastiques, Paris
1987 Museum für Gegenwartskunst, Basel (mit Ivan Tschuikov)
1988 »Vor dem Abendessen«, Kunstverein Graz; »10 Personen« (Zimmer), Galerie R. Feldman, New York; Bonner Kunstverein (mit E. Bulatov) »10 Personen« (Alben), Portikus, Frankfurt a. M.
1989 »Que sont ces petits hommes?«, Galerie de France, Paris; De Appel, Amsterdam; ICA, Philadelphia »10 Personen« (Zimmer), ICA, London »Die Kommunalwohnung – Das Schiff«, Kunsthalle Zürich.

VORWORT

Grundlage der Installation ist der Text der zwischen Boris Groys und Ilya Kabakov im Jahre 1989 geführten »Dialoge«.

Die Themenvorschläge für die »Dialoge« stammen von Kabakov.

1. Angst
2. Stimmen
3. Sein heißt sprechen. Personen
4. ŽEK · ЖЭК
5. Der Westen
6. Kommunalwohnung
7. Leere
8. Müll
9. Flucht

Die Seiten mit dem Text der Dialoge ziehen sich wie eine Eisenbahnlinie sukzessive durch den Ausstellungsraum, wobei jedes »Thema«, zusätzlich illustriert durch Fotos, Zeichnungen und weitere Texte, gleichsam eine »Station« dieser Eisenbahnlinie darstellt.

Als Ergänzung zu den »Dialogen« sind im Katalog Ausschnitte aus verschiedenen – teils veröffentlichten, teils unveröffentlichten – Aufsätzen abgedruckt.

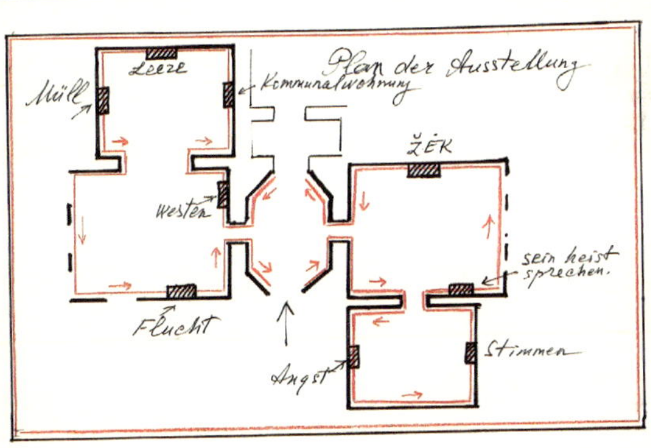

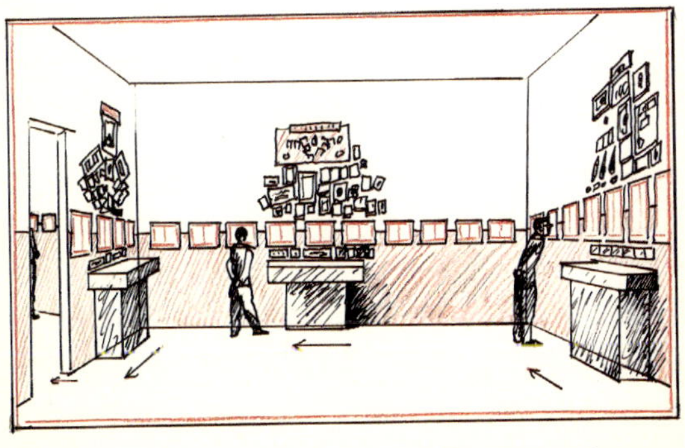

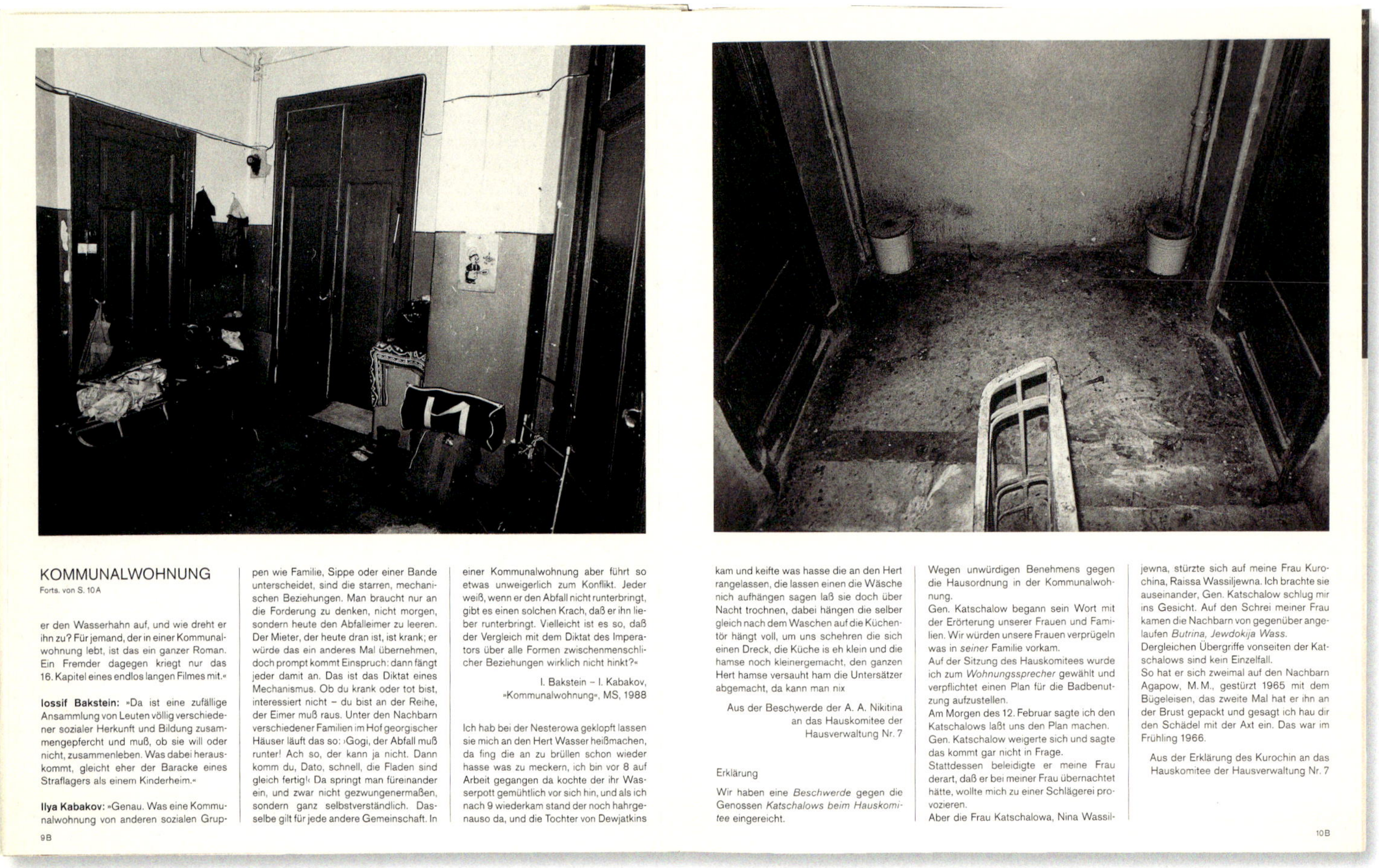

KOMMUNALWOHNUNG

Forts. von S. 10A

er den Wasserhahn auf, und wie dreht er ihn zu? Für jemand, der in einer Kommunalwohnung lebt, ist das ein ganzer Roman. Ein Fremder dagegen kriegt nur das 16. Kapitel eines endlos langen Filmes mit.«

Iossif Bakstein: »Da ist eine zufällige Ansammlung von Leuten völlig verschiedener sozialer Herkunft und Bildung zusammengepfercht und muß, ob sie will oder nicht, zusammenleben. Was dabei herauskommt, gleicht eher der Baracke eines Straflagers als einem Kinderheim.«

Ilya Kabakov: »Genau. Was eine Kommunalwohnung von anderen sozialen Gruppen wie Familie, Sippe oder einer Bande unterscheidet, sind die starren, mechanischen Beziehungen. Man braucht nur an die Forderung zu denken, nicht morgen, sondern heute den Abfalleimer zu leeren. Der Mieter, der heute dran ist, ist krank; er würde das ein anderes Mal übernehmen, doch prompt kommt Einspruch: dann fängt jeder damit an. Das ist das Diktat eines Mechanismus. Ob du krank oder tot bist, interessiert nicht – du bist an der Reihe, der Eimer muß raus. Unter den Nachbarn verschiedener Familien im Hof georgischer Häuser läuft das so: ›Gogi, der Abfall muß runter! Ach so, der kann ja nicht. Dann komm du, Dato, schnell, die Fladen sind gleich fertig!‹ Da springt man füreinander ein, und zwar nicht gezwungenermaßen, sondern ganz selbstverständlich. Dasselbe gilt für jede andere Gemeinschaft. In einer Kommunalwohnung aber führt so etwas unweigerlich zum Konflikt. Jeder weiß, wenn er den Abfall nicht runterbringt, gibt es einen solchen Krach, daß er ihn lieber runterbringt. Vielleicht ist es so, daß der Vergleich mit dem Diktat des Imperators über alle Formen zwischenmenschlicher Beziehungen wirklich nicht hinkt?«

I. Bakstein – I. Kabakov, »Kommunalwohnung«, MS, 1988

Ich hab bei der Nesterowa geklopft lassen sie mich an den Hert Wasser heißmachen, da fing die an zu brüllen schon wieder hasse was zu meckern, ich bin vor 8 auf Arbeit gegangen da kochte der ihr Wasserpott gemühtlich vor sich hin, und als ich nach 9 wiederkam stand der noch hahrgenauso da, und die Tochter von Dewjatkins kam und keifte was hasse die an den Hert rangelassen, die lassen einen die Wäsche nich aufhängen sagen laß sie doch über Nacht trochnen, dabei hängen die selber gleich nach dem Waschen auf die Küchentör hängt voll, um uns schehren die sich einen Dreck, die Küche is eh klein und die hamse noch kleinergemacht, den ganzen Hert hamse versauht ham die Untersätzer abgemacht, da kann man nix

Aus der Beschwerde der A. A. Nikitina an das Hauskomitee der Hausverwaltung Nr. 7

Erklärung

Wir haben eine *Beschwerde* gegen die Genossen *Katschalows beim Hauskomitee* eingereicht.

Wegen unwürdigen Benehmens gegen die Hausordnung in der Kommunalwohnung.

Gen. Katschalow begann sein Wort mit der Erörterung unserer Frauen und Familien. Wir würden unsere Frauen verprügeln was in *seiner* Familie vorkam.

Auf der Sitzung des Hauskomitees wurde ich zum *Wohnungssprecher* gewählt und verpflichtet einen Plan für die Badbenutzung aufzustellen.

Am Morgen des 12. Februar sagte ich den Katschalows laßt uns den Plan machen.

Gen. Katschalow weigerte sich und sagte das kommt gar nicht in Frage.

Stattdessen beleidigte er meine Frau derart, daß er bei meiner Frau übernachtet hätte, wollte mich zu einer Schlägerei provozieren.

Aber die Frau Katschalowa, Nina Wassiljewna, stürzte sich auf meine Frau Kurochina, Raissa Wassiljewna. Ich brachte sie auseinander, Gen. Katschalow schlug mir ins Gesicht. Auf den Schrei meiner Frau kamen die Nachbarn von gegenüber angelaufen *Butrina, Jewdokija Wass.*

Dergleichen Übergriffe vonseiten der Katschalows sind kein Einzelfall.

So hat er sich zweimal auf den Nachbarn Agapow, M. M., gestürzt 1965 mit dem Bügeleisen, das zweite Mal hat er ihn an der Brust gepackt und gesagt ich hau dir den Schädel mit der Axt ein. Das war im Frühling 1966.

Aus der Erklärung des Kurochin an das Hauskomitee der Hausverwaltung Nr. 7

9B

10B

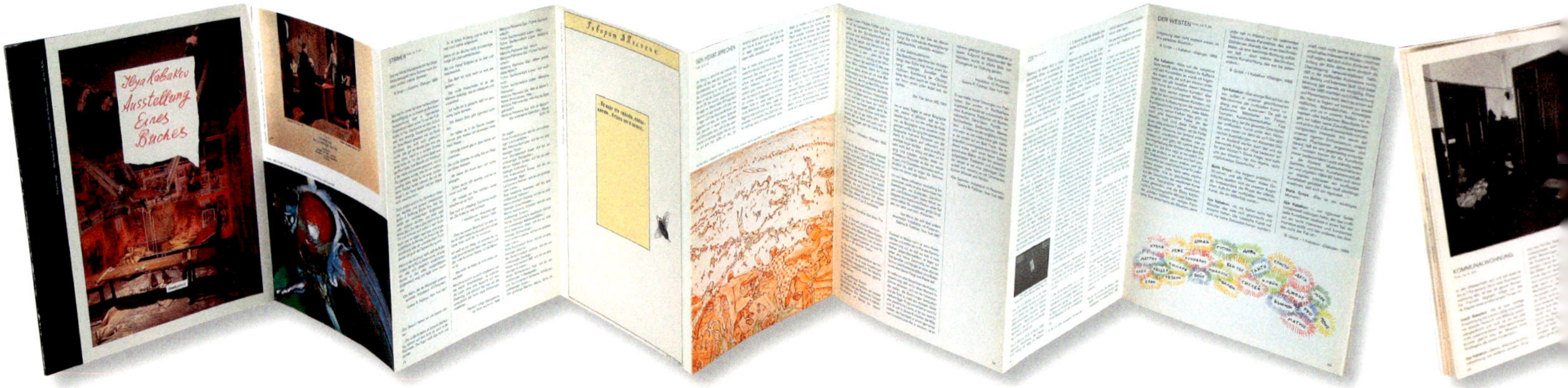

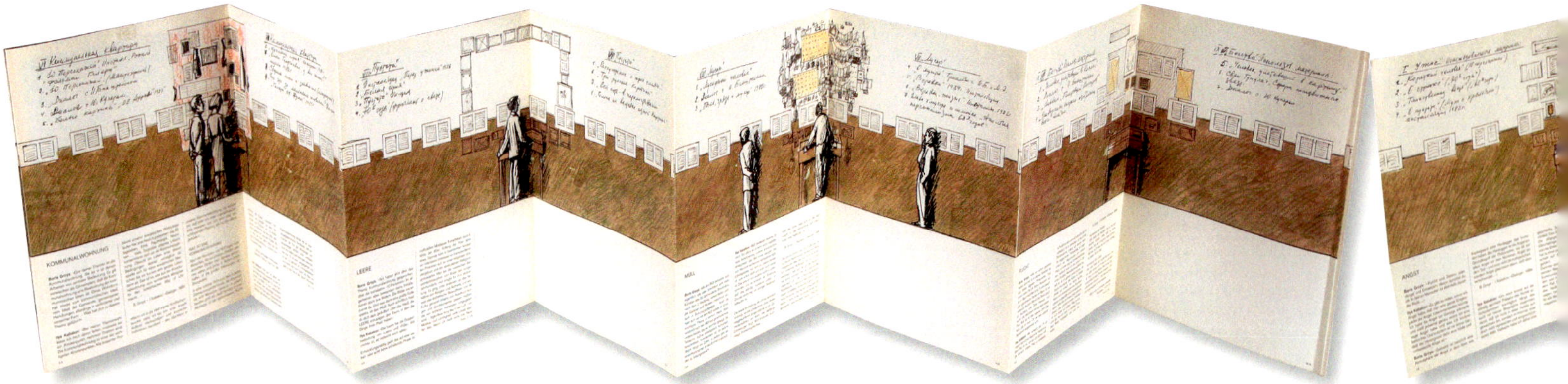

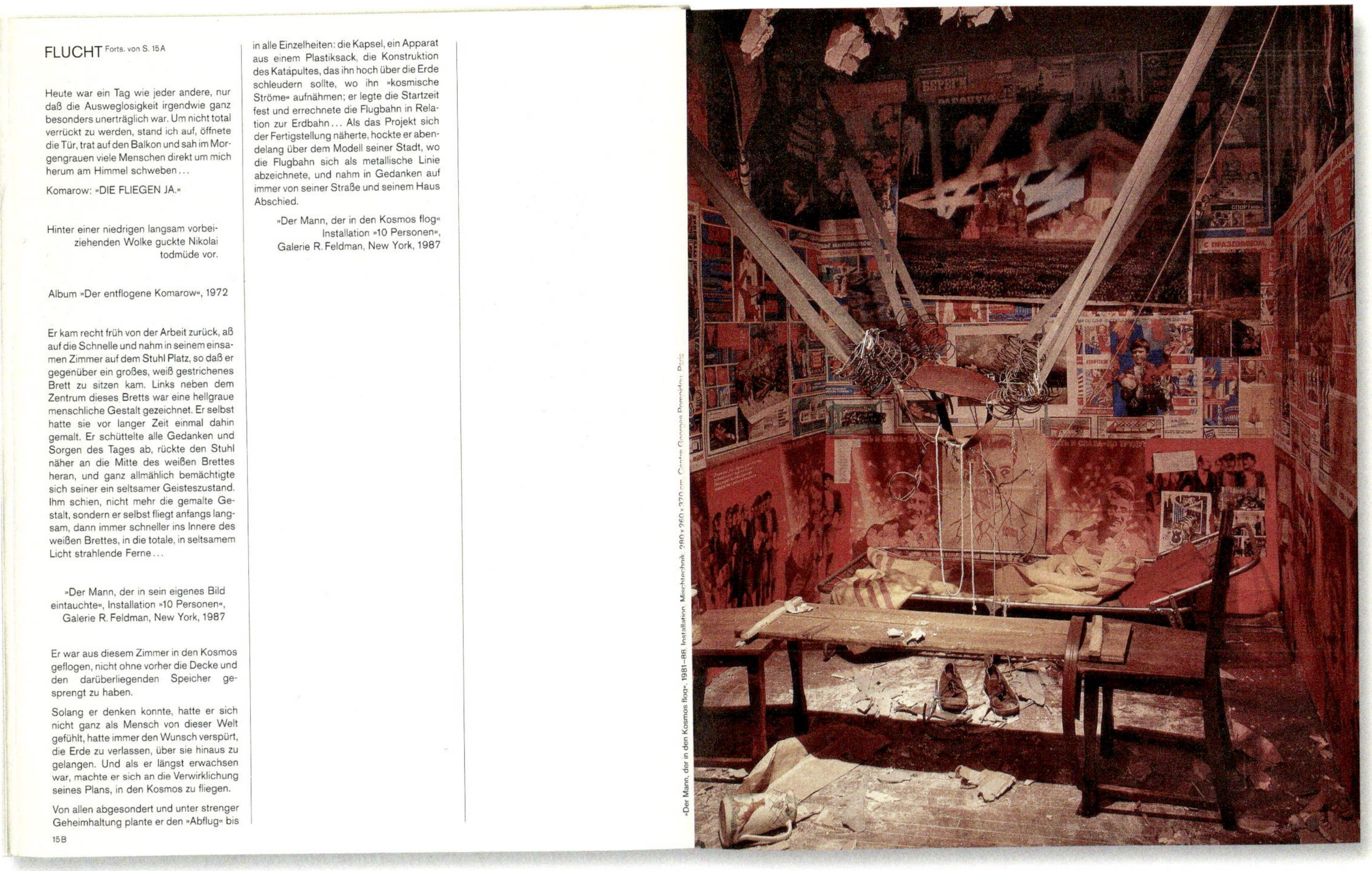

FLUCHT Forts. von S. 15A

Heute war ein Tag wie jeder andere, nur daß die Ausweglosigkeit irgendwie ganz besonders unerträglich war. Um nicht total verrückt zu werden, stand ich auf, öffnete die Tür, trat auf den Balkon und sah im Morgengrauen viele Menschen direkt um mich herum am Himmel schweben ...

Komarow: »DIE FLIEGEN JA.«

Hinter einer niedrigen langsam vorbeiziehenden Wolke guckte Nikolai todmüde vor.

Album »Der entflogene Komarow«, 1972

Er kam recht früh von der Arbeit zurück, aß auf die Schnelle und nahm in seinem einsamen Zimmer auf dem Stuhl Platz, so daß er gegenüber ein großes, weiß gestrichenes Brett zu sitzen kam. Links neben dem Zentrum dieses Bretts war eine hellgraue menschliche Gestalt gezeichnet. Er selbst hatte sie vor langer Zeit einmal dahin gemalt. Er schüttelte alle Gedanken und Sorgen des Tages ab, rückte den Stuhl näher an die Mitte des weißen Brettes heran, und ganz allmählich bemächtigte sich seiner ein seltsamer Geisteszustand. Ihm schien, nicht mehr die gemalte Gestalt, sondern er selbst fliegt anfangs langsam, dann immer schneller ins Innere des weißen Brettes, in die totale, in seltsamem Licht strahlende Ferne ...

»Der Mann, der in sein eigenes Bild eintauchte«, Installation »10 Personen«, Galerie R. Feldman, New York, 1987

Er war aus diesem Zimmer in den Kosmos geflogen, nicht ohne vorher die Decke und den darüberliegenden Speicher gesprengt zu haben.

Solang er denken konnte, hatte er sich nicht ganz als Mensch von dieser Welt gefühlt, hatte immer den Wunsch verspürt, die Erde zu verlassen, über sie hinaus zu gelangen. Und als er längst erwachsen war, machte er sich an die Verwirklichung seines Plans, in den Kosmos zu fliegen.

Von allen abgesondert und unter strenger Geheimhaltung plante er den »Abflug« bis in alle Einzelheiten: die Kapsel, ein Apparat aus einem Plastiksack, die Konstruktion des Katapultes, das ihn hoch über die Erde schleudern sollte, wo ihn »kosmische Ströme« aufnähmen; er legte die Startzeit fest und errechnete die Flugbahn in Relation zur Erdbahn ... Als das Projekt sich der Fertigstellung näherte, hockte er abendelang über dem Modell seiner Stadt, wo die Flugbahn sich als metallische Linie abzeichnete, und nahm in Gedanken auf immer von seiner Straße und seinem Haus Abschied.

»Der Mann, der in den Kosmos flog« Installation »10 Personen«, Galerie R. Feldman, New York, 1987

15B

»Der Mann, der in den Kosmos flog«, 1981–88, Installation, Mischtechnik, 280 x 260 x 370 cm, Centre Georges Pompidou, Paris

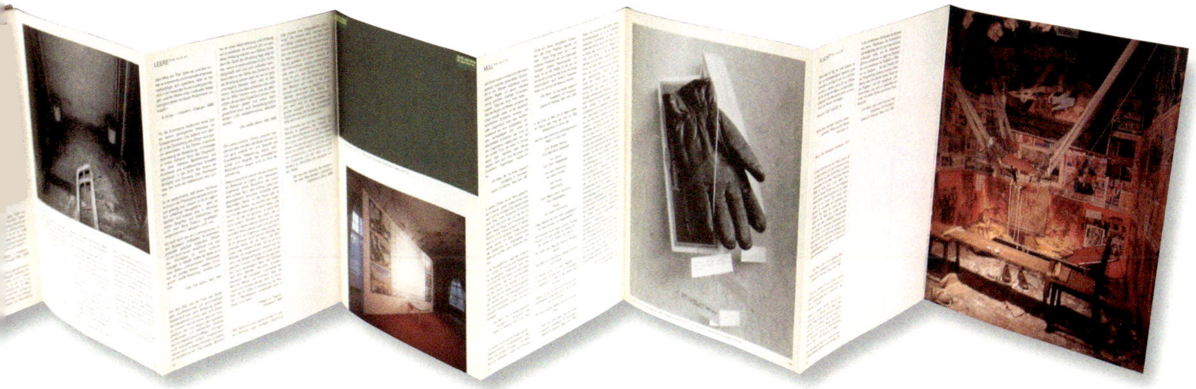

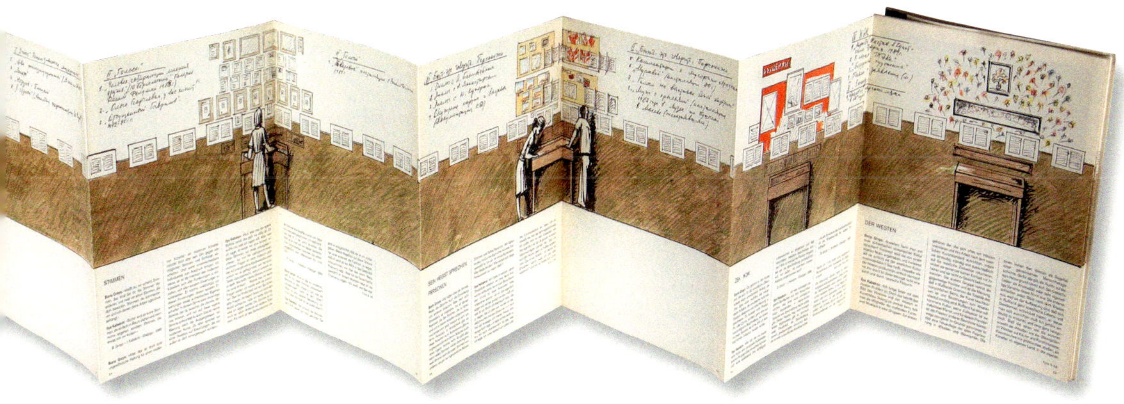

28 He Lost His Mind, Undressed, and Ran Away Naked

Er wurde verrückt, zog sich aus und rannte nackt davon

1990

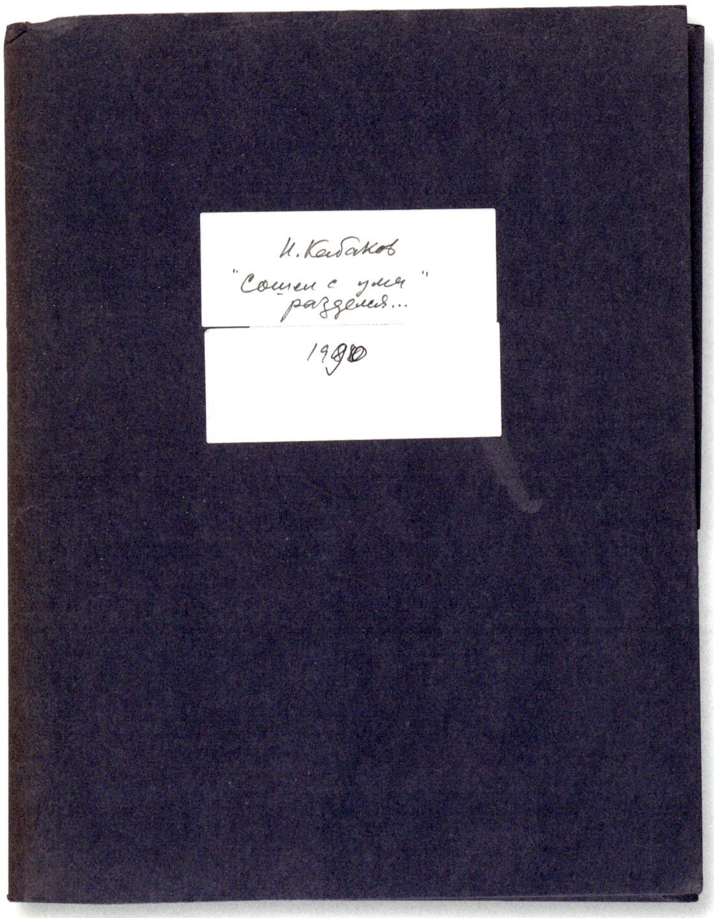

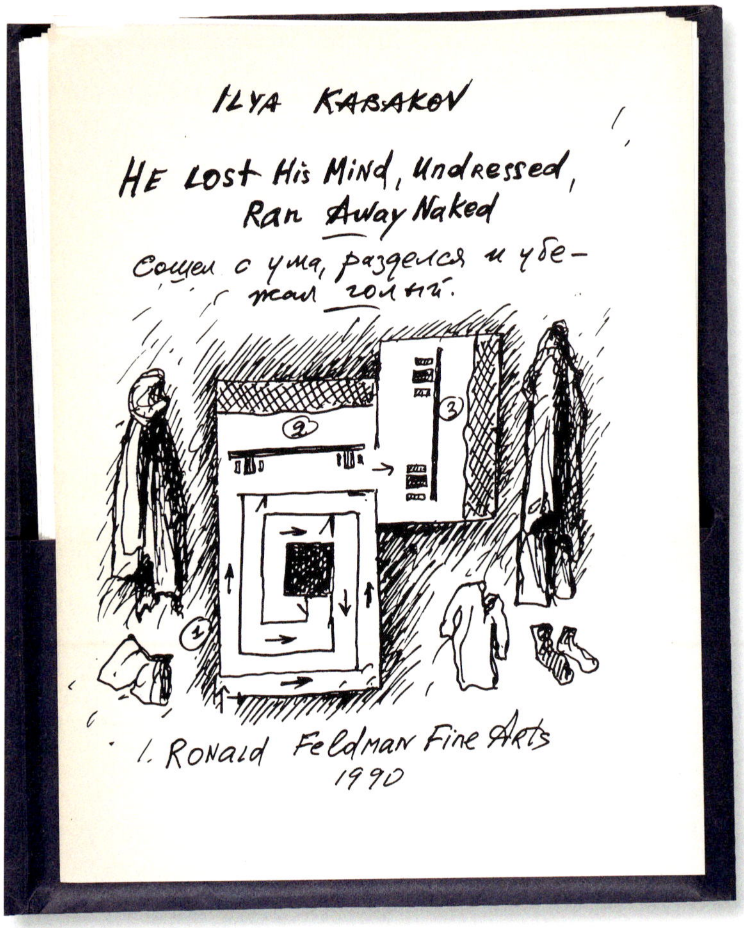

Ilya Kabakov
New York: published by the author
29.7 x 24 cm
96 (partly double-sided) photocopied pp. (2 foldouts) with 12 b/w ills.
loose sheets, cardboard cover, label on the cover
lose Blätter, Kartonumschlag, Etikette auf dem Umschlag
edition: 100 copies

exhibition catalogue | *Ausstellungskatalog*

layout by Ilya Kabakov | *Layout von Ilya Kabakov*

For the installation of the same name at the Ronald Feldman Fine Arts Gallery, New York, January 6 to February 3, 1990. Texts by Joseph Backstein, Sven Gundlakh, Ilya Kabakov, and two dialogues between Joseph Backstein and Ilya Kabakov on »The Man Who Flew Into His Picture« and »What is a Communal Apartment?«; Russian, English.

Zur gleichnamigen Installation, Ronald Feldman Fine Arts Gallery, New York, 6. Januar – 3. Februar 1990. Texte von Josef Bakstein, Sven Gundlakh, Ilya Kabakov sowie zwei Dialoge von Josef Bakstein und Ilya Kabakov über »Der Mann, der in sein Bild eintritt« und »Was ist eine Kommunalwohnung?«; russisch, englisch.

see also | *siehe auch* no. 29; CRI, vol. 1, no. 30, pp. 222–227; CRP, vol. 1, no. 56, pp. 112–113, 405–406, no. 65, p. 129, no. 85, pp. 155–156, no. 97, pp. 171–173, no. 102, pp. 178–179, 409, nos. 149–159, pp. 239–249

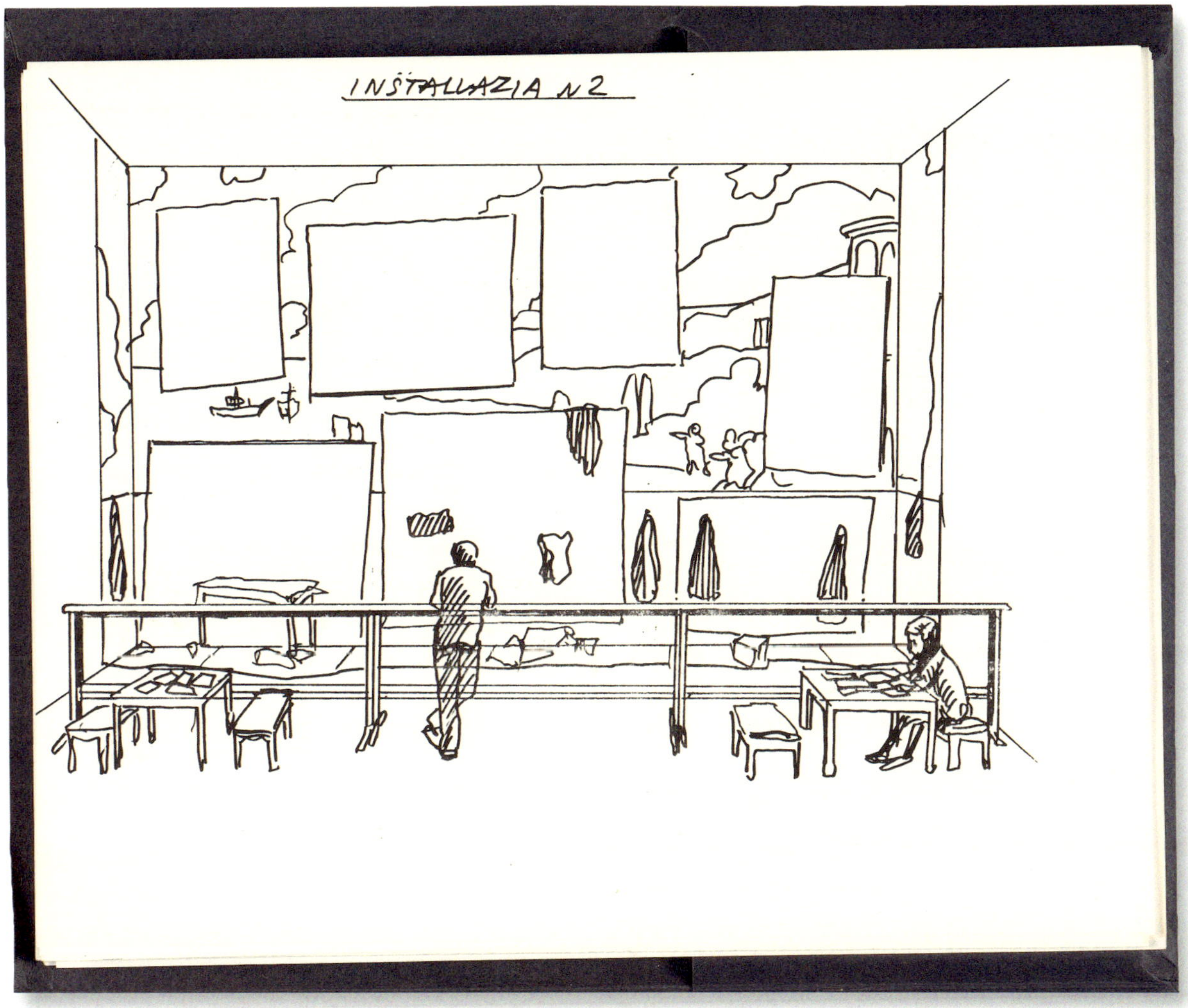
INSTALLAZIA N2

29 He Lost His Mind, Undressed, and Ran Away Naked

Er wurde verrückt, zog sich aus und rannte nackt davon

1990

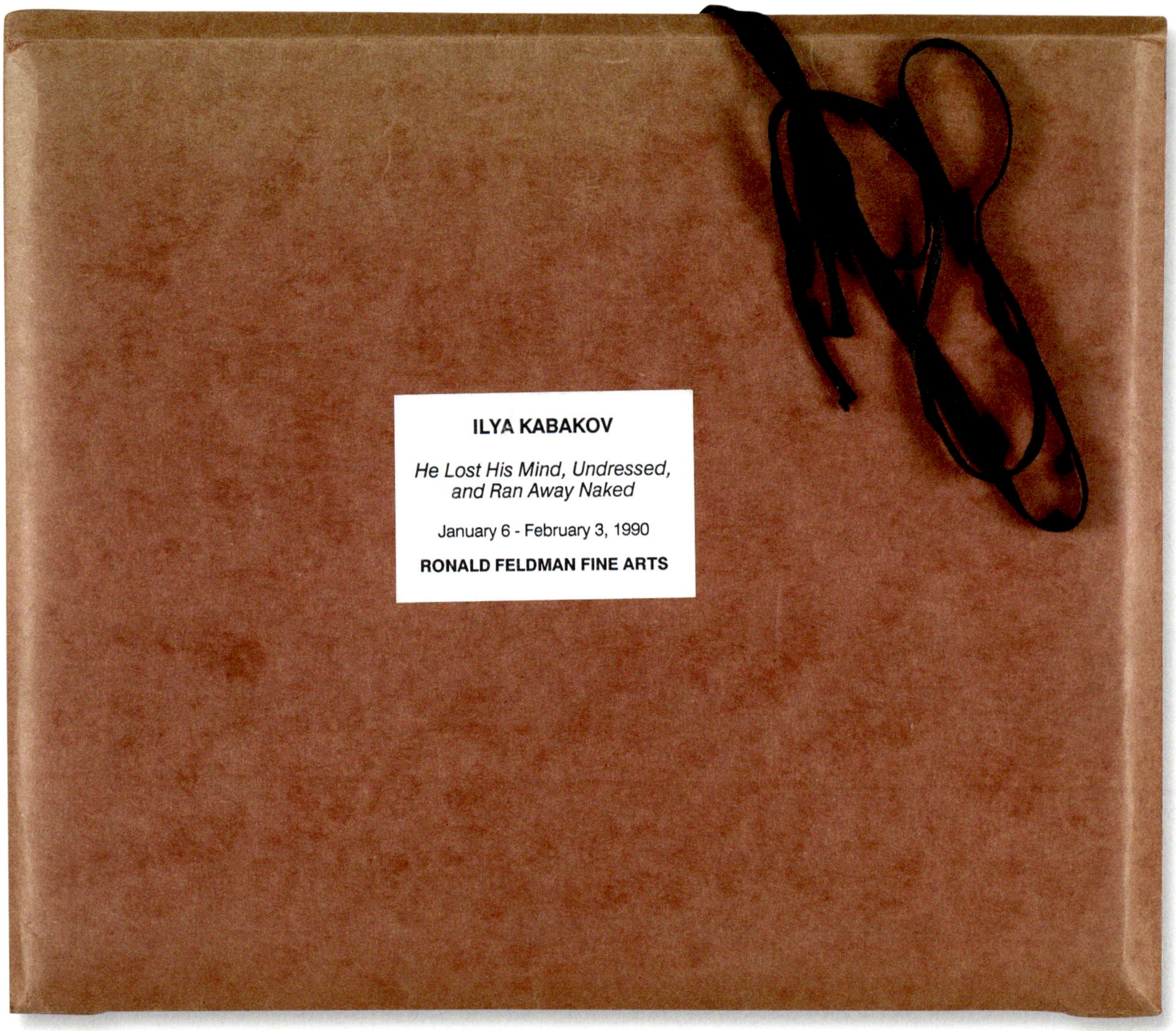

Ilya Kabakov
New York: published by the author
24 x 29.5 cm
96 (partly double-sided) photocopied pp. (2 foldouts) with 12 b/w ills.
loose sheets, cardboard cover, bound together with a ribbon, label on the cover
lose Blätter, Kartonumschlag, zusammengehalten mit einem Band, Etikette auf dem Umschlag
edition: 100 copies

exhibition catalogue | *Ausstellungskatalog*

layout by Ilya Kabakov | *Layout von Ilya Kabakov*

For the installation of the same name at the Ronald Feldman Fine Arts Gallery, New York, January 6 to February 3, 1990. Texts by Joseph Backstein, Sven Gundlakh, Ilya Kabakov, and two dialogues between Ilya Kabakov and Joseph Backstein on »The Man Who Flew Into His Picture and What is a Communal Apartment?«; English.

Zur gleichnamigen Installation, Ronald Feldman Fine Arts Gallery, New York, 6. Januar – 3. Februar 1990. Texte von Josef Bakstein, Sven Gundlakh, Ilya Kabakov sowie zwei Dialoge von Ilya Kabakov und Josef Bakstein über »Der Mann, der in sein Bild eintritt« und »Was ist eine Kommunalwohnung?«; englisch.

see also | *siehe auch* no. 28; CRI, vol. 1, no. 30, pp. 222–227; CRP, vol. 1, no. 56, pp. 112–113, 405–406, no. 65, p. 129, no. 85, pp. 155–156, no. 97, pp. 171–173, no. 102, pp. 178–179, 409, nos. 149–159, pp. 239–249

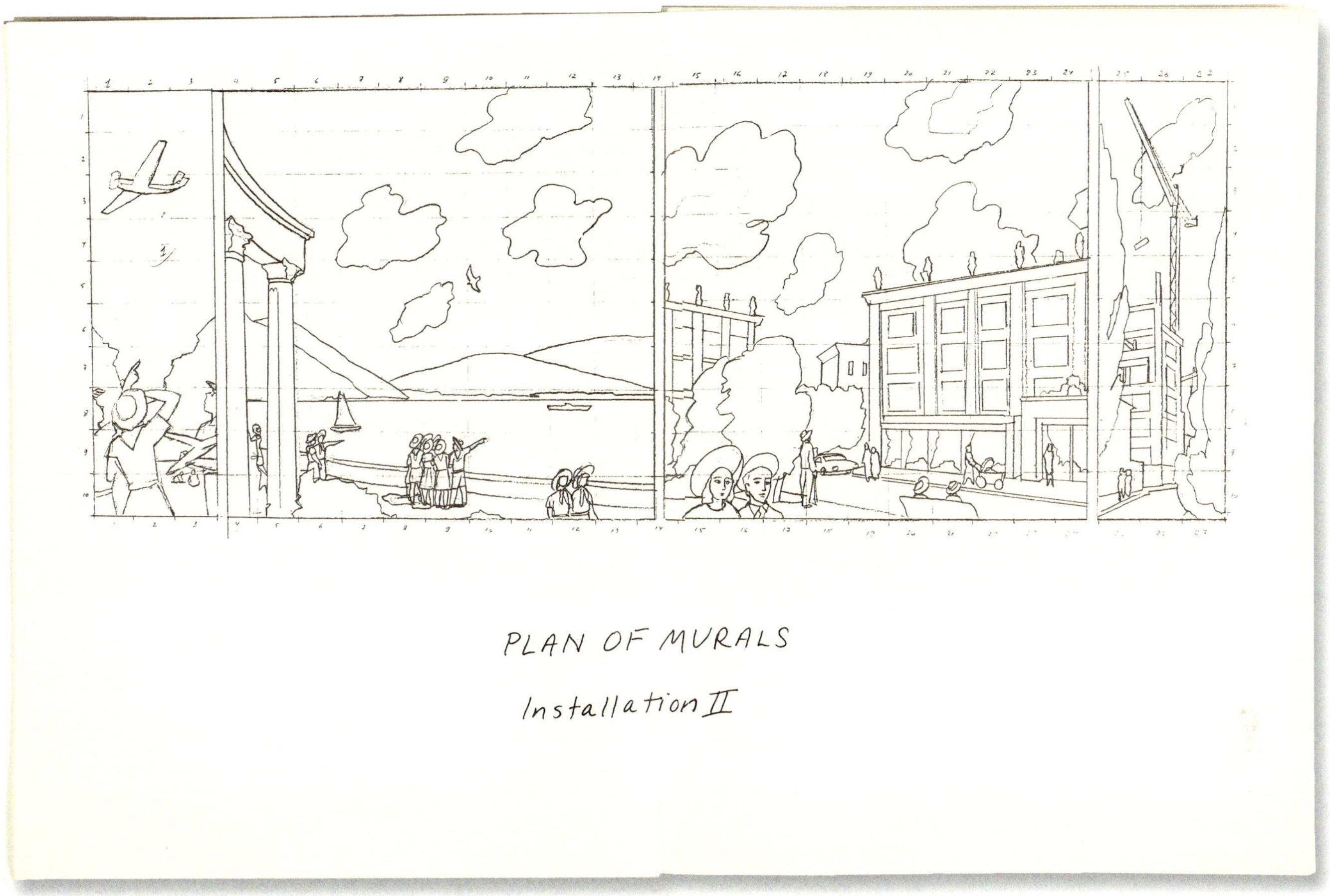
PLAN OF MURALS
Installation II

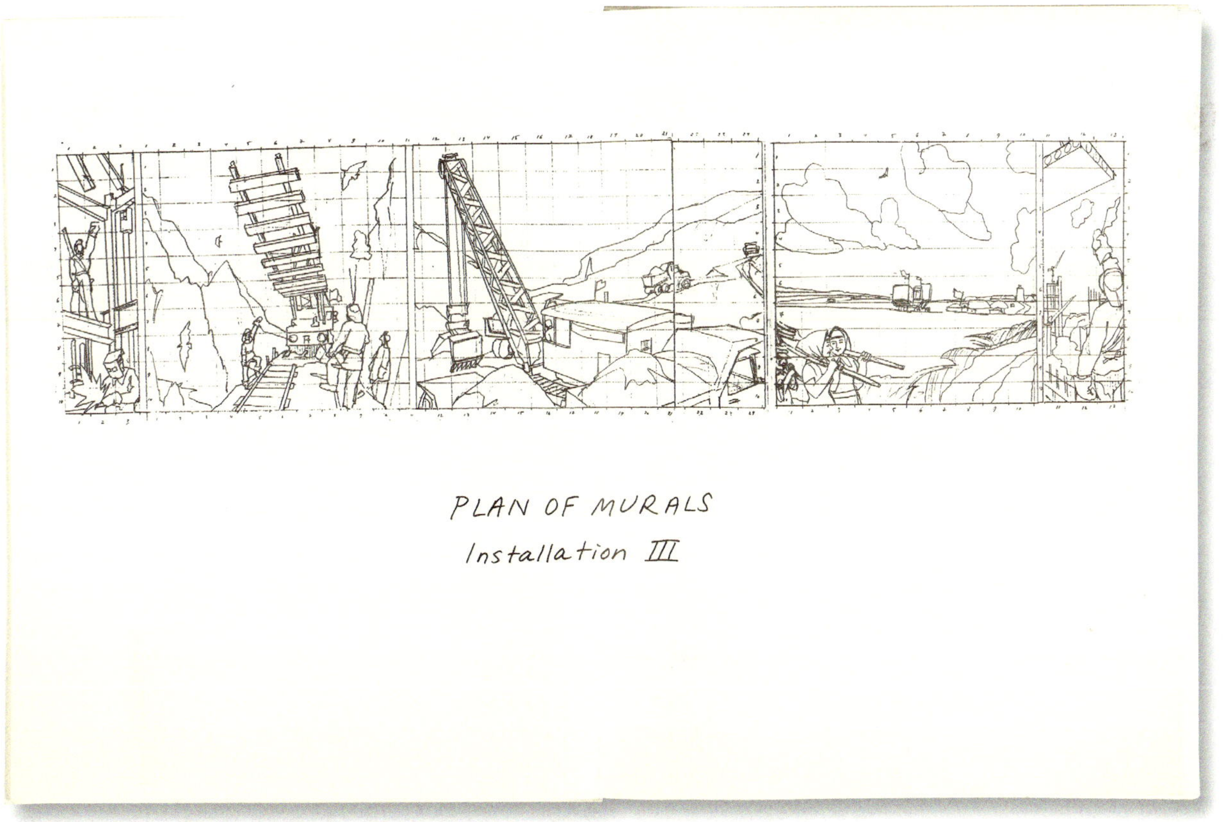
PLAN OF MURALS
Installation III

30 The Rope of Life and Other Installations

Das Seil des Lebens und andere Installationen

1990

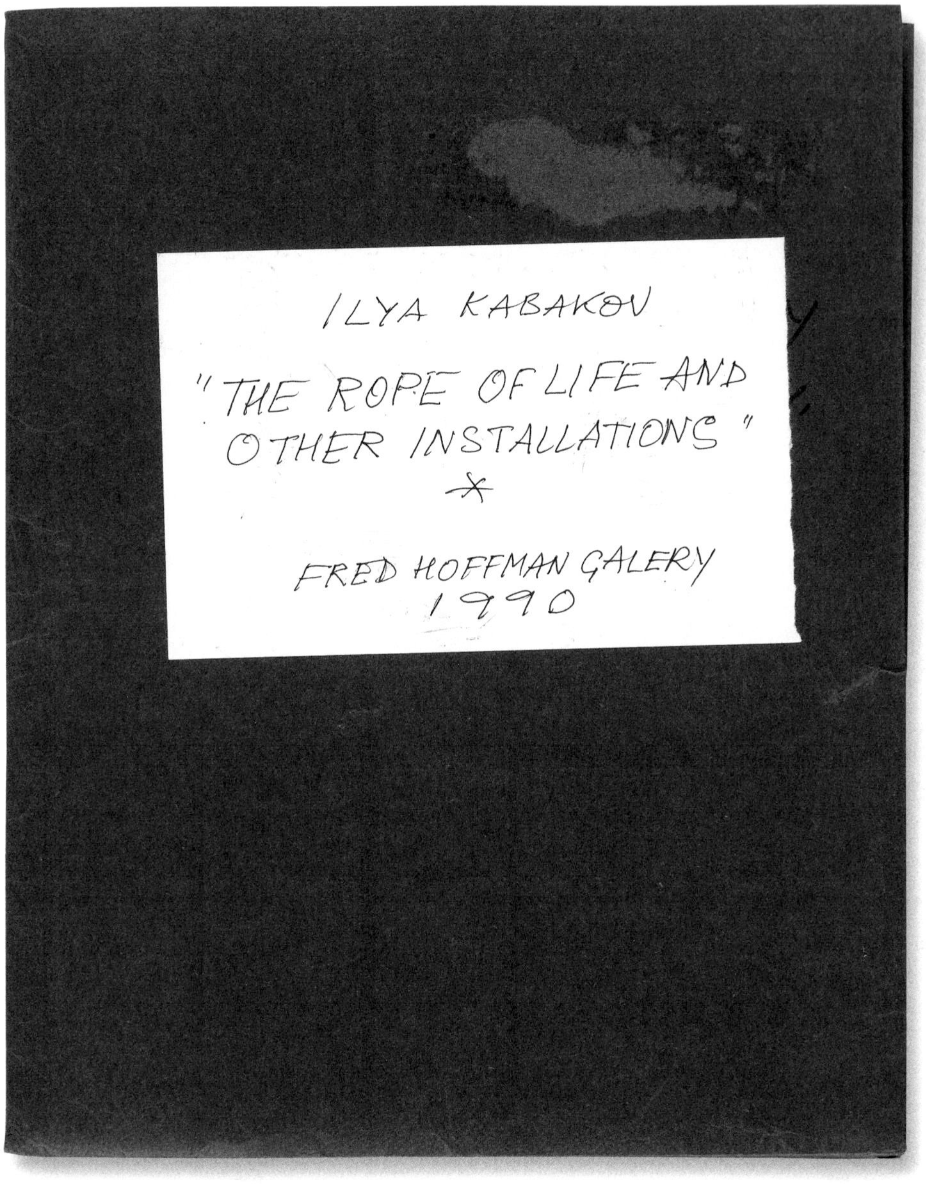

Ilya Kabakov
New York: published by the author
28 x 21.7 cm
47 photocopied pp. with 13 b/w ills.
loose sheets, cardboard cover,
label on the cover
lose Blätter, Kartonumschlag, Etikette auf dem Umschlag

exhibition catalogue | *Ausstellungskatalog*

layout by Ilya Kabakov | *Layout von Ilya Kabakov*

For the installation of the same name at the Fred Hoffman Gallery, Santa Monica, CA, January 13 to February 10, 1990. Texts by Ilya Kabakov; English.

Zur gleichnamigen Installation, Fred Hoffman Gallery, Santa Monica, CA, 13. Januar – 10. Februar 1990. Texte von Ilya Kabakov; englisch.

see also | *siehe auch* no. 31; no. 81; CRI, vol. 1, no. 7, pp. 82–87

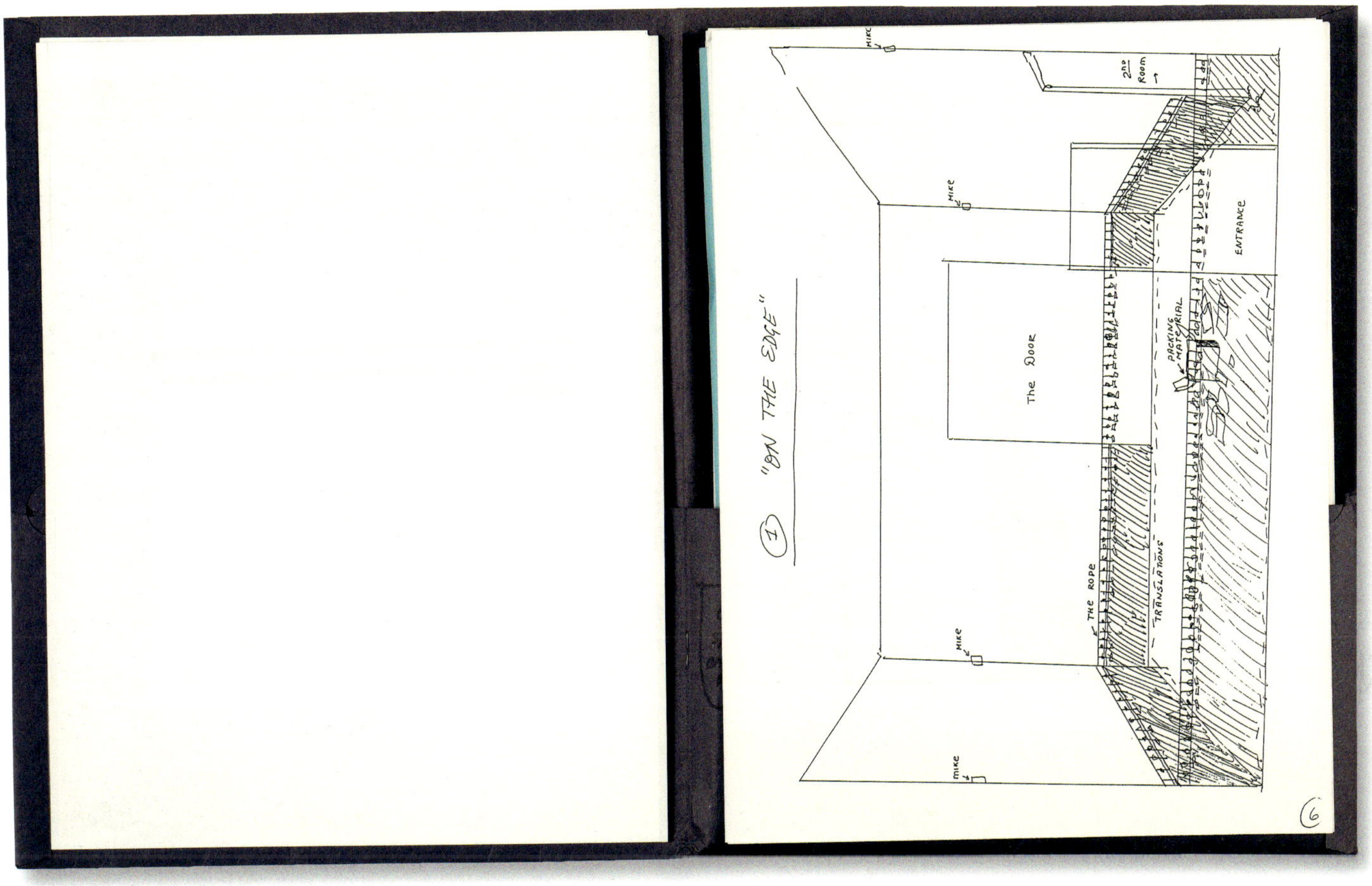

1 "ON THE EDGE"
MIKE
The Door
THE ROPE
"TRANSLATIONS"
PACKING MATERIAL
2ND Room
ENTRANCE
6

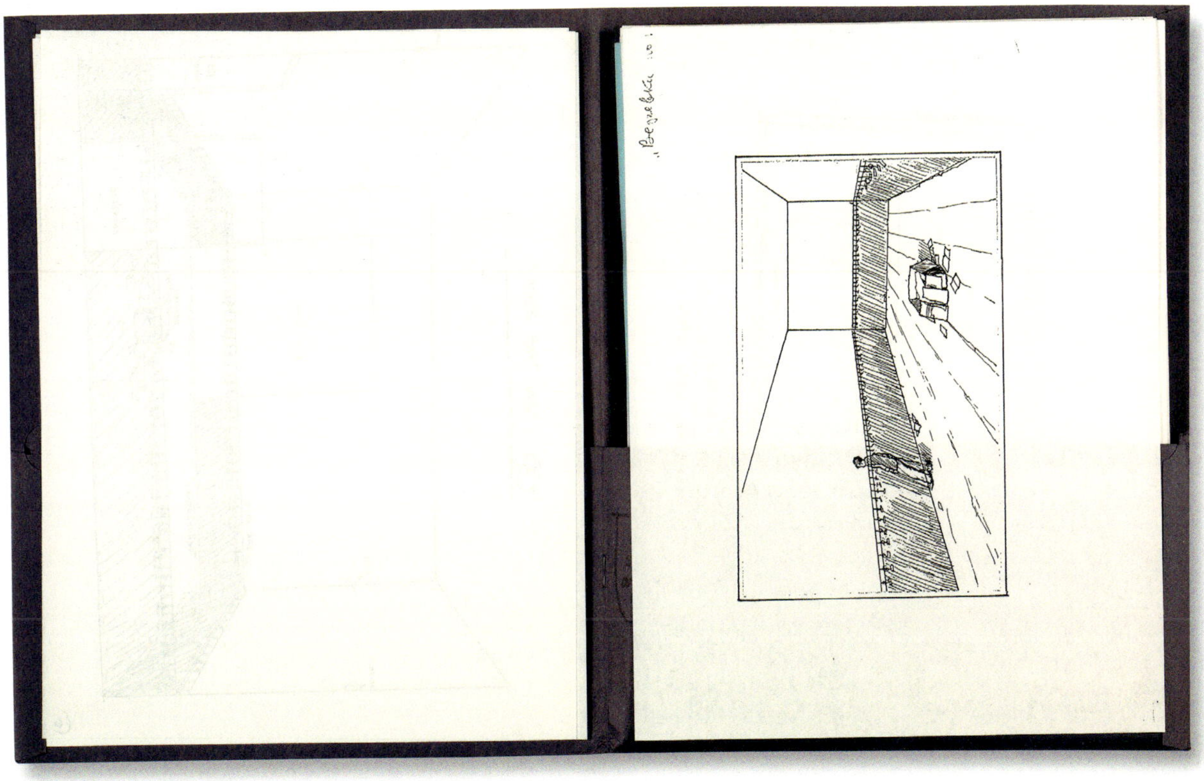

31 The Rope of Life and Other Installations

Das Seil des Lebens und andere Installationen

1990

Fred Hoffmann Gallery
Santa Monica: Fred Hoffmann Gallery
28 x 21.7 cm
47 photocopied pp. with 16 b/w ills.
loose sheets, cardboard cover,
label on the cover
lose Blätter, Kartonumschlag, Etikette auf dem Umschlag

exhibition catalogue | *Ausstellungskatalog*

layout by Ilya Kabakov | *Layout von Ilya Kabakov*

For the installation of the same name at the Fred Hoffman Gallery, Santa Monica, CA, January 13 to February 10, 1990. Texts by Ilya Kabakov; English.

Zur gleichnamigen Installation, Fred Hoffman Gallery, Santa Monica, CA, 13. Januar – 10. Februar 1990. Texte von Ilya Kabakov; englisch.

see also | *siehe auch* no. 30; no. 81; CRI, vol. 1, no. 7, pp. 82–87

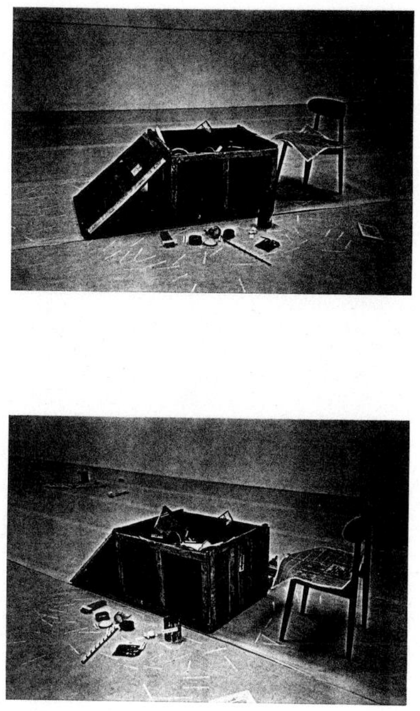

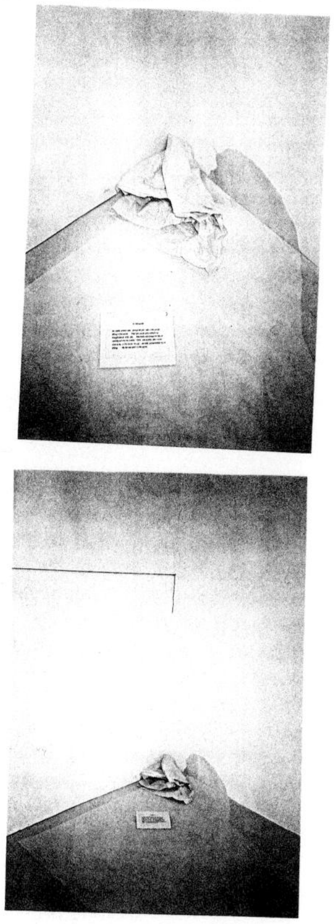

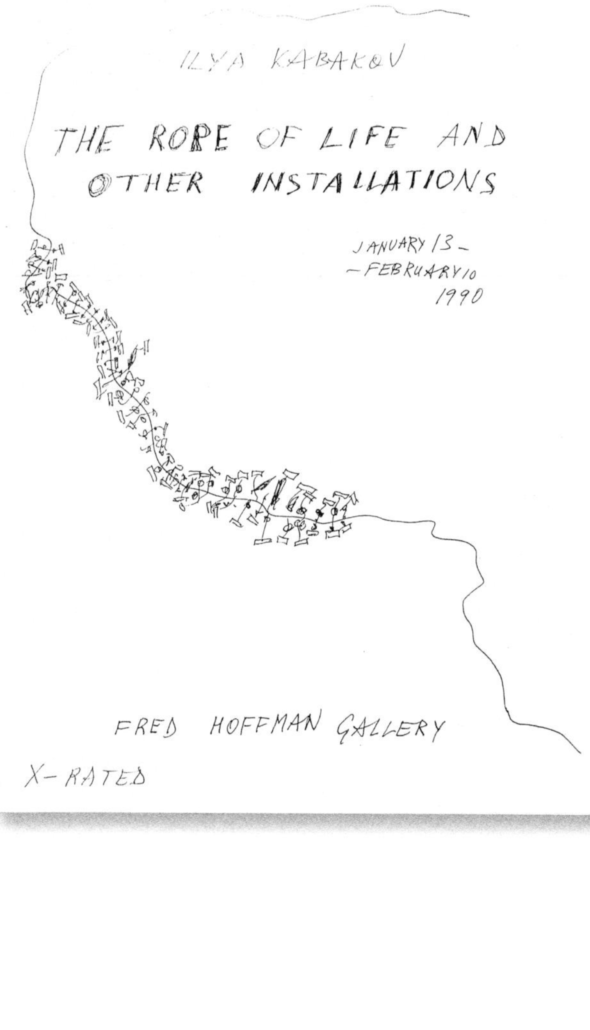
ILYA KABAKOV
THE ROPE OF LIFE AND
OTHER INSTALLATIONS
JANUARY 13 –
– FEBRUARY 10
1990
FRED HOFFMAN GALLERY
X-RATED

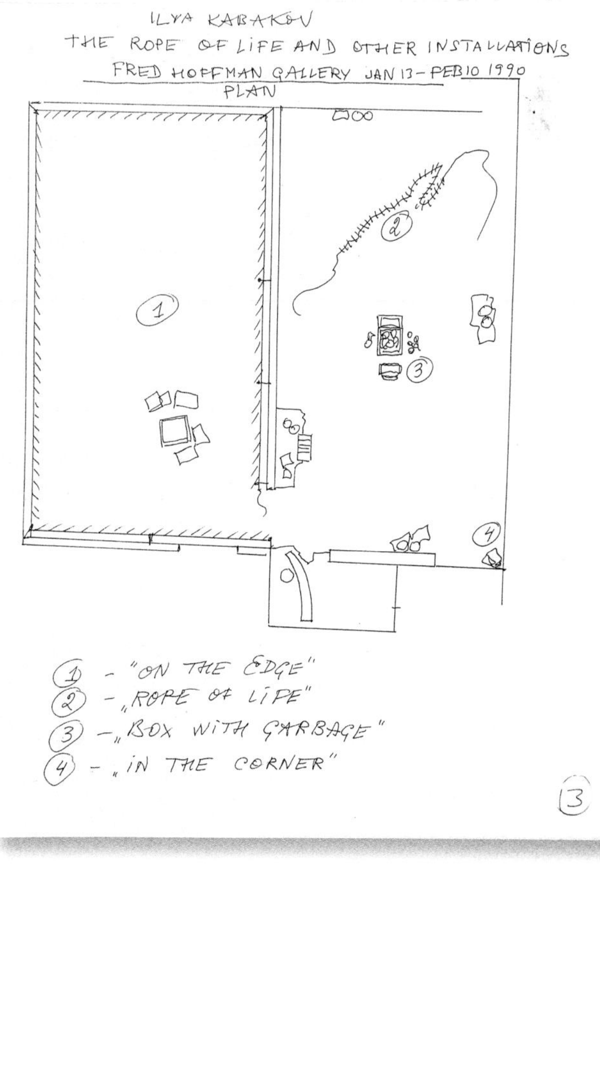
ILYA KABAKOV
THE ROPE OF LIFE AND OTHER INSTALLATIONS
FRED HOFFMAN GALLERY JAN 13 – FEB 10 1990
PLAN
1
2
3
4
1 – "ON THE EDGE"
2 – „ROPE OF LIFE"
3 – „BOX WITH GARBAGE"
4 – „IN THE CORNER"
3

32 Seven Exhibitions of a Painting | *Sieben Ausstellungen eines Bildes*

1990

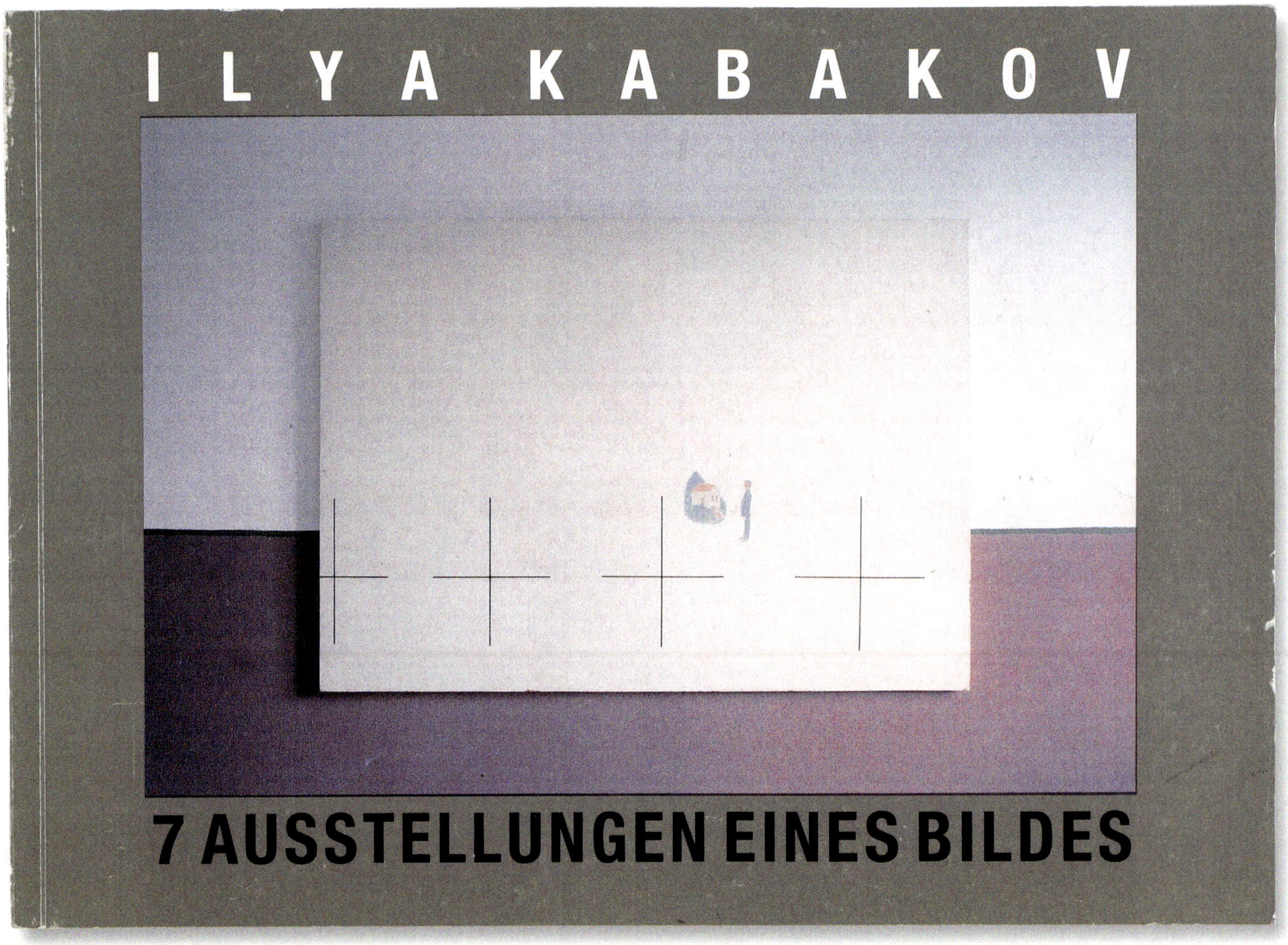

Kasseler Kunstverein
Kassel: Kasseler Kunstverein
21 x 29.7 cm
[52] pp. with 31 b/w ills.
adhesive binding, softback
Klebebindung, broschiert

exhibition catalogue | *Ausstellungskatalog*

layout by Ilya Kabakov | *Layout von Ilya Kabakov*

For the installation of the same name at the Kasseler Kunstverein, Kassel, May 13 to June 24, 1990. Texts by Boris Groys and Ilya Kabakov. The painting »The Ripped Off Landscape« is part of the installation; German.

Zur gleichnamigen Installation im Kasseler Kunstverein, Kassel, 13. Mai – 24. Juni 1990. Texte von Boris Groys und Ilya Kabakov. Das Gemälde »Die heruntergerissene Landschaft« ist Teil der Installation; deutsch.

see also | *siehe auch* CRI, vol. 1, no. 34, pp. 244–249; CRP, vol. 1, no. 37, pp. 82–83, no. 45, p. 96, no. 47–48, pp. 98–100, no. 93, p. 167

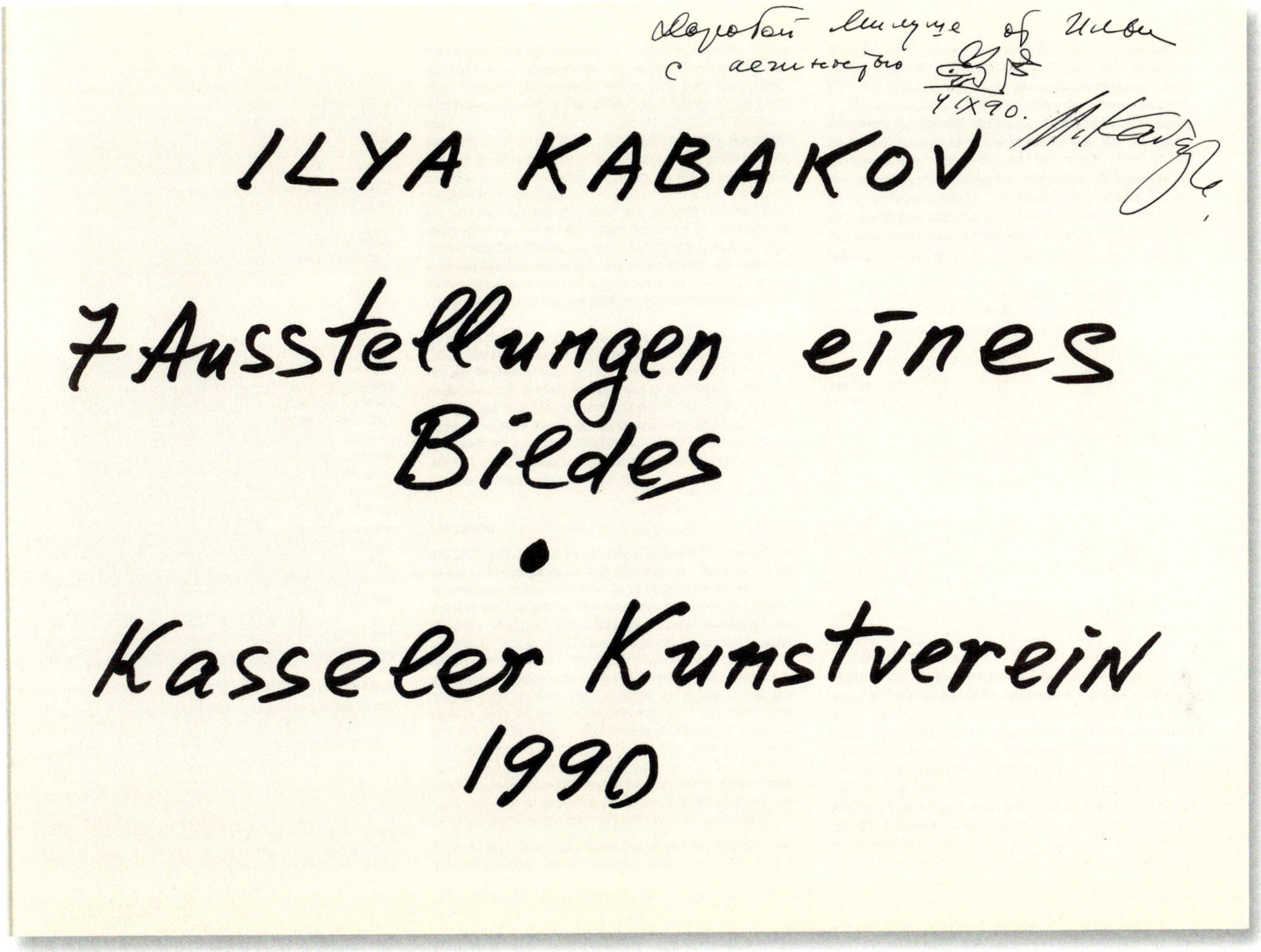
ILYA KABAKOV
7 Ausstellungen eines Bildes
Kasseler Kunstverein
1990
4.IX.90.

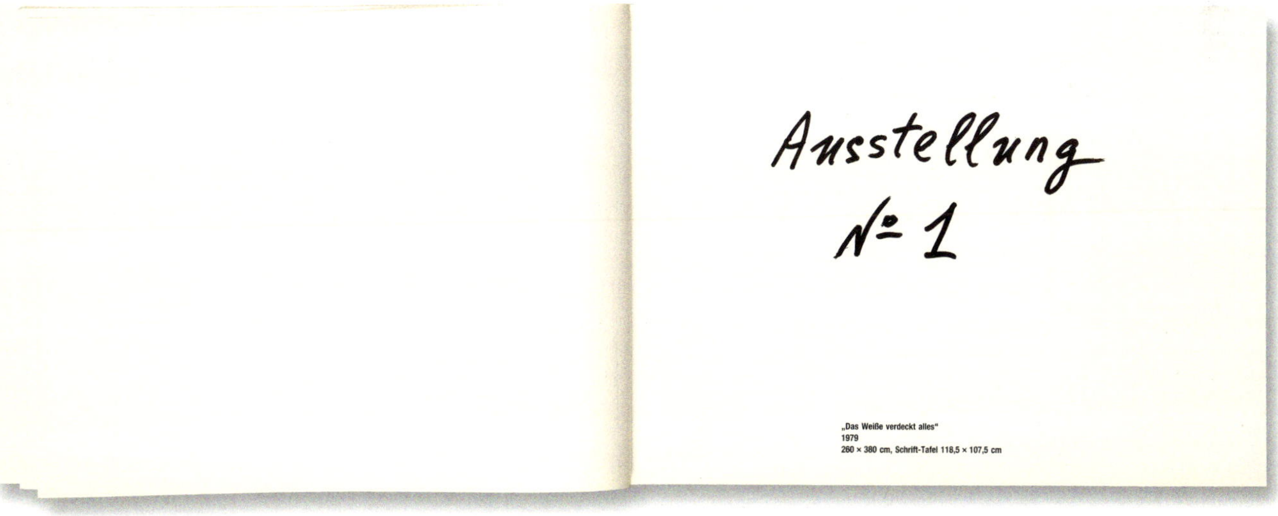
Ausstellung
№ 1
„Das Weiße verdeckt alles"
1979
260 × 380 cm, Schrift-Tafel 118,5 × 107,5 cm

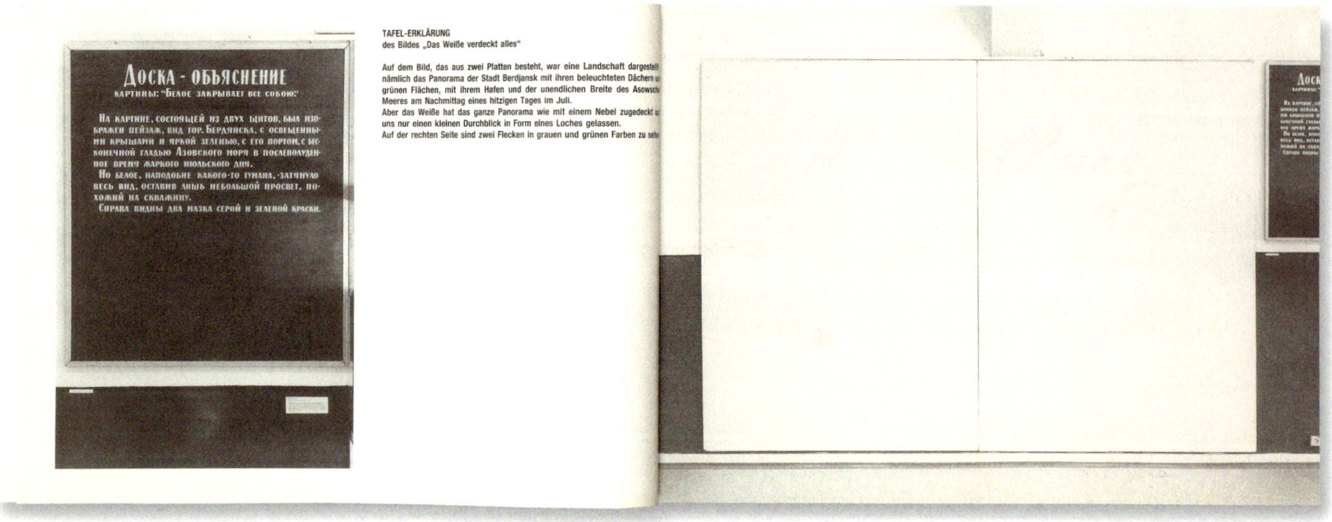
Доска - объяснение
картины: "Белое закрывает все собою:"
На картине, состоящей из двух щитов, был изображен пейзаж, вид гор. Бердянска, с освещенными крышами и яркой зеленью, с его портом, с бесконечной гладью Азовского моря в послеполуденное время жаркого июльского дня.
Но белое, наподобие какого-то тумана, затянуло весь вид, оставив лишь небольшой просвет, похожий на скважину.
Справа видны два мазка серой и зеленой краски.
TAFEL-ERKLÄRUNG
des Bildes „Das Weiße verdeckt alles"
Auf dem Bild, das aus zwei Platten besteht, war eine Landschaft dargestel
nämlich das Panorama der Stadt Berdjansk mit ihren beleuchteten Dächern
grünen Flächen, mit ihrem Hafen und der unendlichen Breite des Asowsch
Meeres am Nachmittag eines hitzigen Tages im Juli.
Aber das Weiße hat das ganze Panorama wie mit einem Nebel zugedeckt
uns nur einen kleinen Durchblick in Form eines Loches gelassen.
Auf der rechten Seite sind zwei Flecken in grauen und grünen Farben zu se

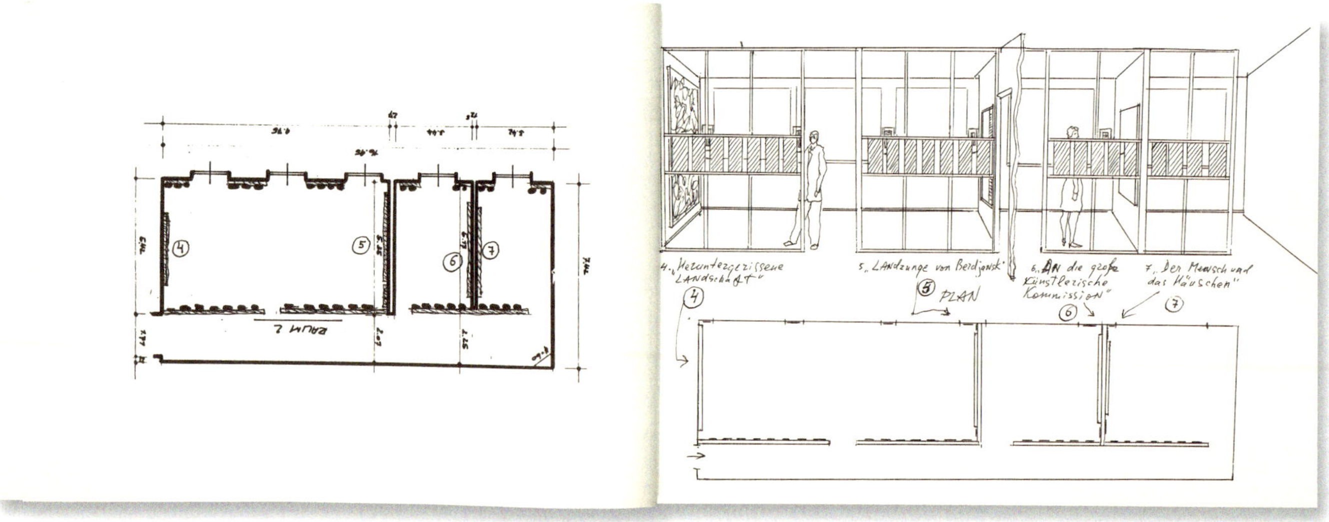
RAUM 2
4. „Heruntergerissene Landschaft"
5. „Landzunge von Berdjansk"
6. „Die große künstlerische Kommission"
7. „Der Mensch und das Häuschen"
PLAN

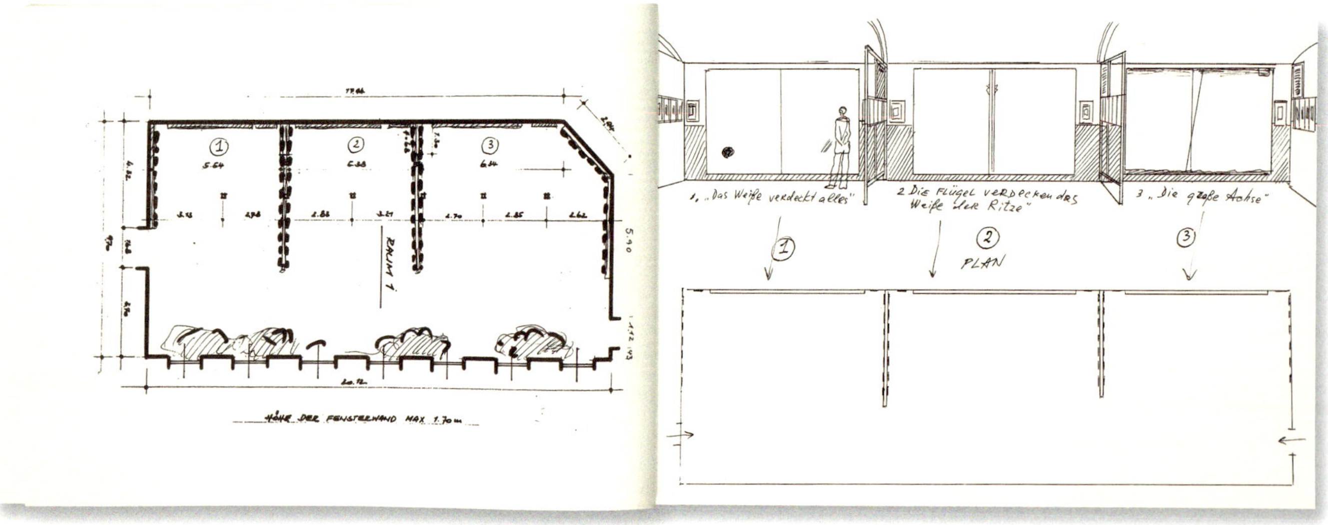
RAUM 1
HÖHE DER FENSTERWAND MAX. 1.70 m
1. „Das Weiße verdeckt alles"
2 Die Flügel verdecken das Weiße der Ritze
3. „Die große Achse"
PLAN

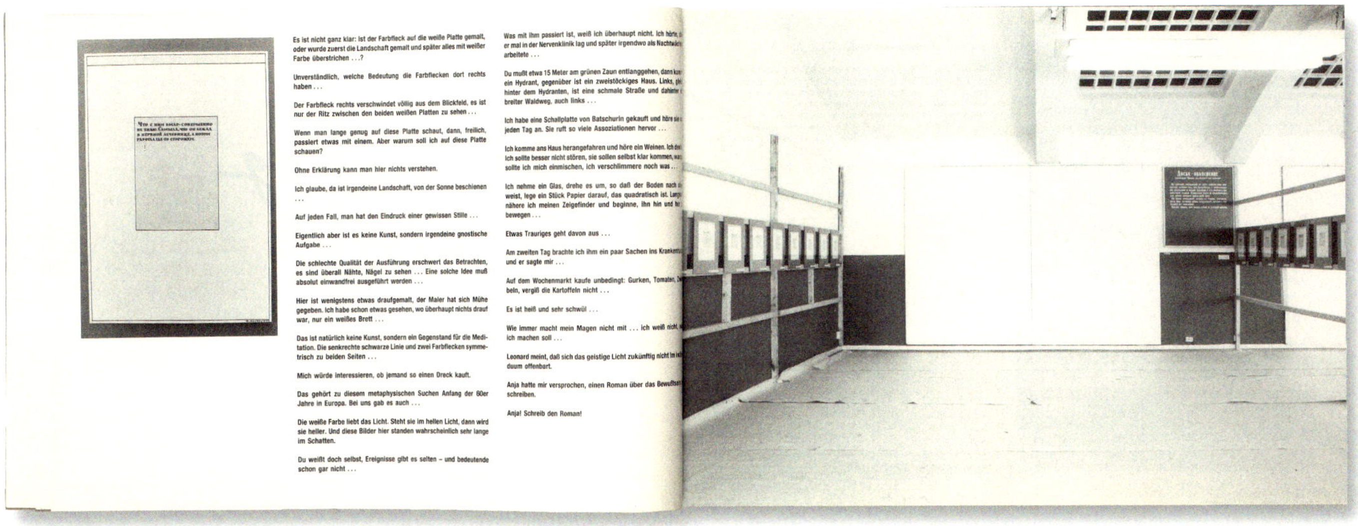

Es ist nicht ganz klar: Ist der Farbfleck auf die weiße Platte gemalt, oder wurde zuerst die Landschaft gemalt und später alles mit weißer Farbe überstrichen ...?

Unverständlich, welche Bedeutung die Farbflecken dort rechts haben ...

Der Farbfleck rechts verschwindet völlig aus dem Blickfeld, es ist nur der Ritz zwischen den beiden weißen Platten zu sehen ...

Wenn man lange genug auf diese Platte schaut, dann, freilich, passiert etwas mit einem. Aber warum soll ich auf diese Platte schauen?

Ohne Erklärung kann man hier nichts verstehen.

Ich glaube, da ist irgendeine Landschaft, von der Sonne beschienen ...

Auf jeden Fall, man hat den Eindruck einer gewissen Stille ...

Eigentlich aber ist es keine Kunst, sondern irgendeine gnostische Aufgabe ...

Die schlechte Qualität der Ausführung erschwert das Betrachten, es sind überall Nähte, Nägel zu sehen ... Eine solche Idee muß absolut einwandfrei ausgeführt werden ...

Hier ist wenigstens etwas draufgemalt, der Maler hat sich Mühe gegeben. Ich habe schon etwas gesehen, wo überhaupt nichts drauf war, nur ein weißes Brett ...

Das ist natürlich keine Kunst, sondern ein Gegenstand für die Meditation. Die senkrechte schwarze Linie und zwei Farbflecken symmetrisch zu beiden Seiten ...

Mich würde interessieren, ob jemand so einen Dreck kauft.

Das gehört zu diesem metaphysischen Suchen Anfang der 60er Jahre in Europa. Bei uns gab es auch ...

Die weiße Farbe liebt das Licht. Steht sie im hellen Licht, dann wird sie heller. Und diese Bilder hier standen wahrscheinlich sehr lange im Schatten.

Du weißt doch selbst, Ereignisse gibt es selten – und bedeutende schon gar nicht ...

Was mit ihm passiert ist, weiß ich überhaupt nicht. Ich hörte, er mal in der Nervenklinik lag und später irgendwo als arbeitete ...

Du mußt etwa 15 Meter am grünen Zaun entlanggehen, dann ein Hydrant, gegenüber ist ein zweistöckiges Haus. Links, hinter dem Hydranten, ist eine schmale Straße und breiter Waldweg, auch links ...

Ich habe eine Schallplatte von Batschurin gekauft und höre jeden Tag an. Sie ruft so viele Assoziationen hervor ...

Ich komme ans Haus herangefahren und höre ein Weinen. Ich sollte besser nicht stören, sie sollen selbst klar kommen, sollte ich mich einmischen, ich verschlimmere noch was ...

Ich nehme ein Glas, drehe es um, so daß der Boden weist, lege ein Stück Papier darauf, das quadratisch ist. nähere ich meinen Zeigefinder und beginne, ihn hin und bewegen ...

Etwas Trauriges geht davon aus ...

Am zweiten Tag brachte ich ihm ein paar Sachen ins und er sagte mir ...

Auf dem Wochenmarkt kaufe unbedingt: Gurken, Tomaten, beln, vergiß die Kartoffeln nicht ...

Es ist heiß und sehr schwül ...

Wie immer macht mein Magen nicht mit ... ich weiß nicht, ich machen soll ...

Leonard meint, daß sich das geistige Licht zukünftig nicht im duum offenbart.

Anja hatte mir versprochen, einen Roman über das schreiben.

Anja! Schreib den Roman!

33 The Fly with the Wings | *Fliege mit Flügeln*

1990

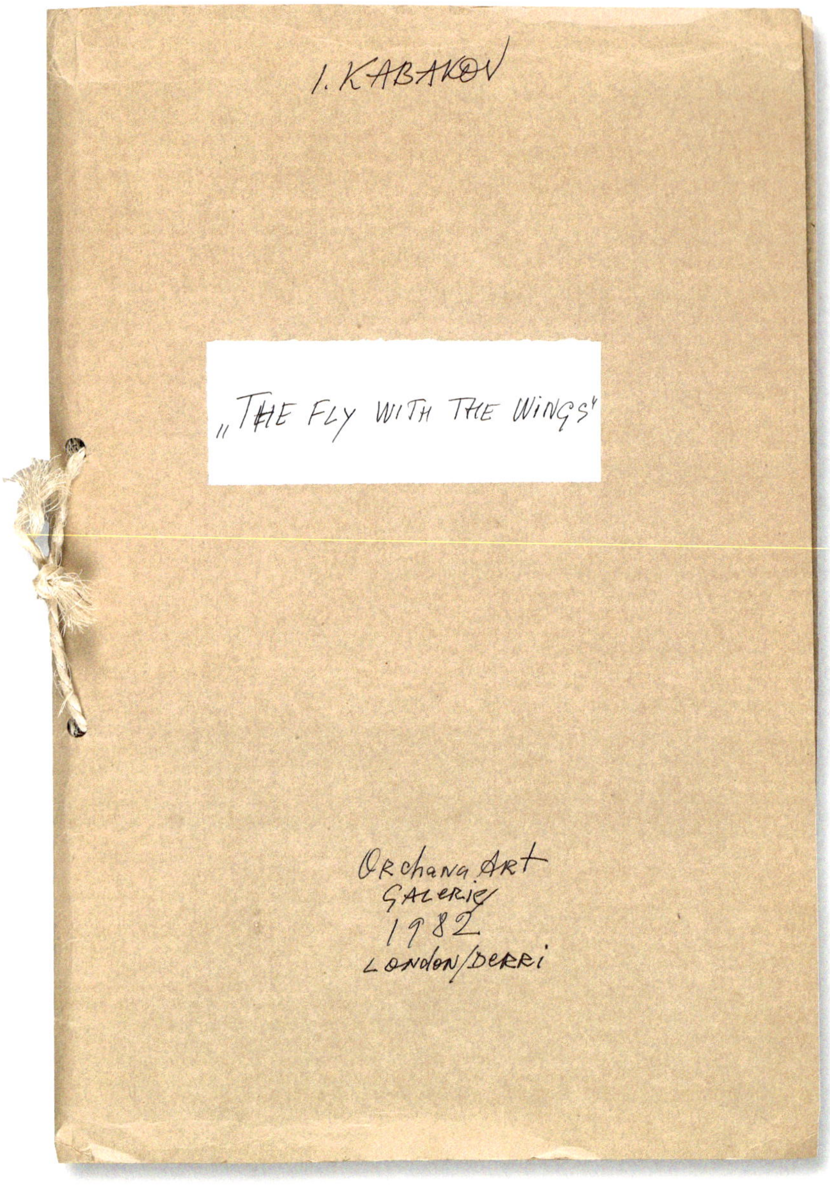

Ilya Kabakov
Londonderry: Orchard Gallery
33.3 x 22.6 cm
66 photocopied pp. with 7 b/w ills.
two punched holes, held together with a string, cardboard cover, label on the cover
zwei ausgestanzte Löcher, zusammengehalten mit einer Schnur, Kartonumschlag, Etikette auf dem Umschlag

exhibition catalogue | *Ausstellungskatalog*

layout by Ilya Kabakov | *Layout von Ilya Kabakov*

For the installation of the same name for the exhibition »New Works for Different Places: TSWA Four Cities Project« at the Orchard Gallery, Londonderry, Northern Ireland, September 1 to 29, 1990. Ilya Kabakov's texts were published in 1992 in the chapter entitled »The Fly as a Subject and Basis for Philosophical Discourse« in the book »Life of Flies«; Russian, English.

Zur gleichnamigen Installation für die Ausstellung »New Works for Different Places: TSWA Four Cities Project«, Orchard Gallery, Londonderry, Nordirland, 1. – 29. September 1990. Die Texte von Ilya Kabakov erschienen 1992 unter dem Titel »Die Fliege als Ursache und Grundlage des philosophischen Diskurses« im Buch »Das Leben der Fliegen«; russisch, englisch.

see also | *siehe auch* no. 8; no. 9; no. 43; no. 44; no. 37; no. 38; no. 50; no. 56; no. 134; CRI, vol. 1, no. 3, pp. 60–65

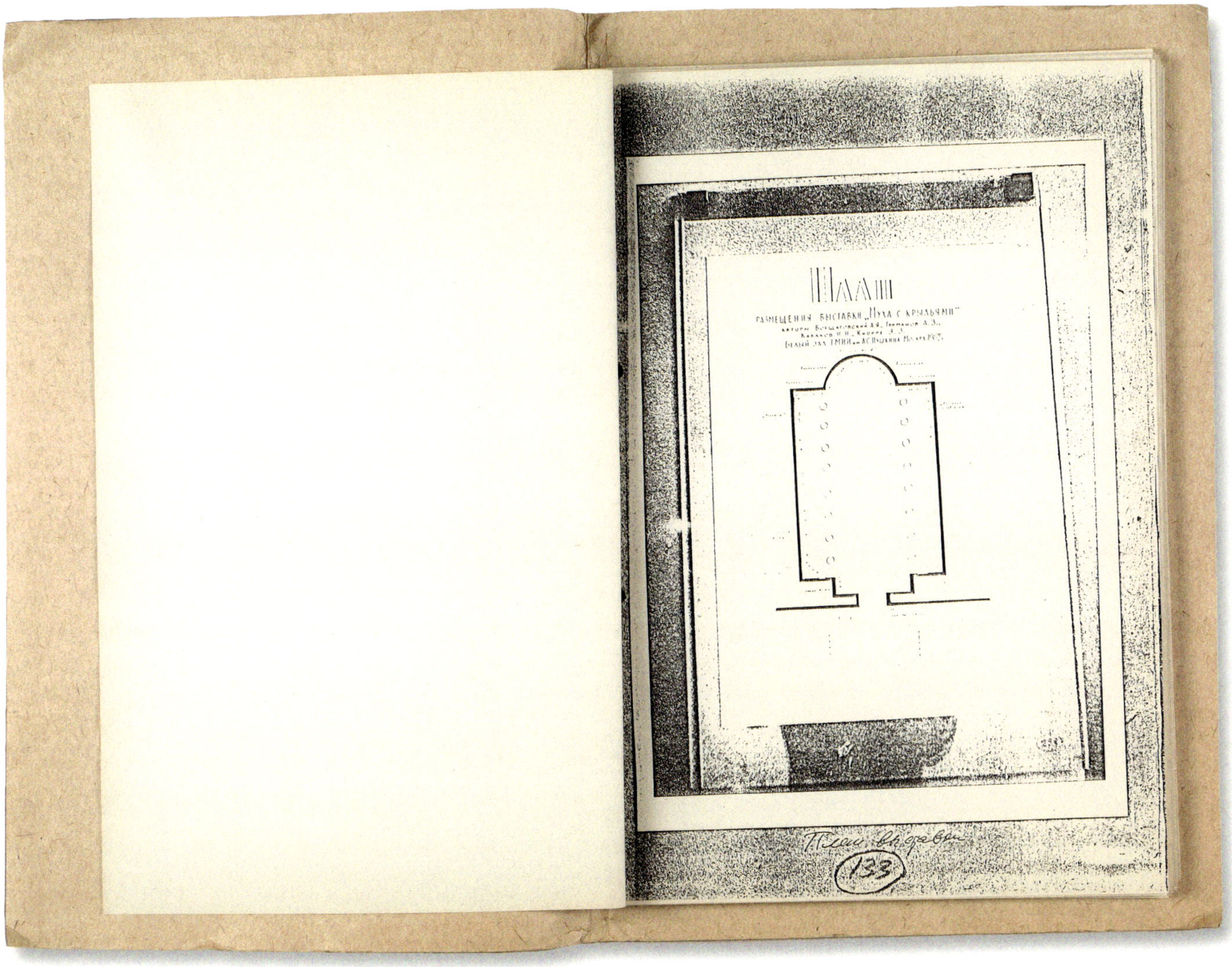
План
размещения выставки „Муха с крыльями"
133

34 16 Ropes | *16 Seile*

1991

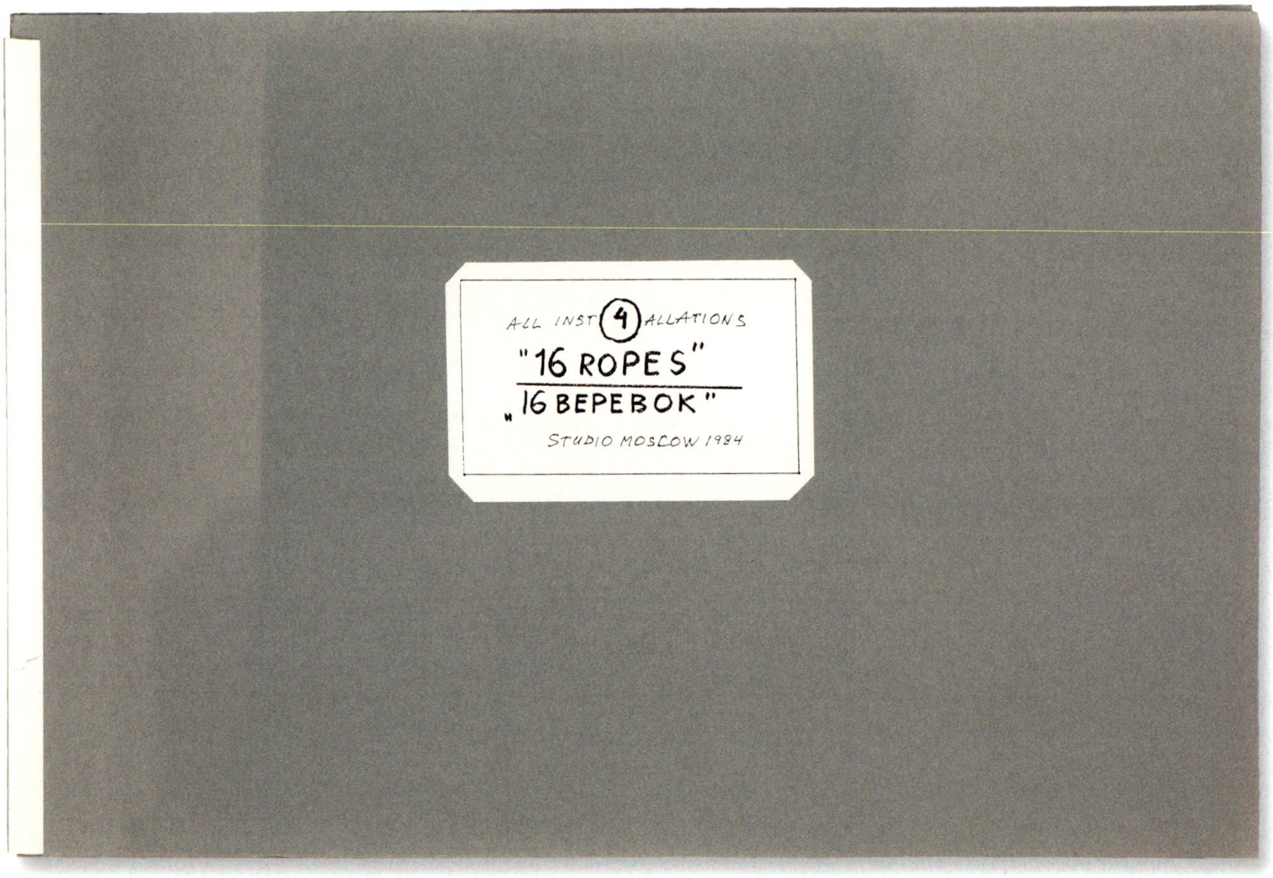

Ilya Kabakov
New York: published by the author
27.9 x 43.3 cm
19 photocopied pp. with 16 (5 color) ills.
quick bind, cardboard cover, label on the cover
Schnellhefter, Kartonumschlag, Etikette auf dem Umschlag
edition: 16 copies

thematic publication | *thematische Publikation*

layout by Ilya Kabakov | *Layout von Ilya Kabakov*

Documentation of the installation of the same name, which was created for the first time in 1984 in Kabakov's Moscow studio. Text by Ilya Kabakov and a dialogue between Joseph Backstein and Ilya Kabakov; English, Russian.

Dokumentation der gleichnamigen Installation, die 1984 in Kabakovs Moskauer Atelier erstmals realisiert wurde. Text von Ilya Kabakov und ein Dialog von Josef Bakstein und Ilya Kabakov; englisch, russisch.

see also | *siehe auch* no. 19; CRI, vol. 1, no. 4, pp. 66–71

④
„16 ROPES"
„16 ВЕРЕВОК"
1984
Мастерская. Москва
STUDIO MOSKOW.

1984

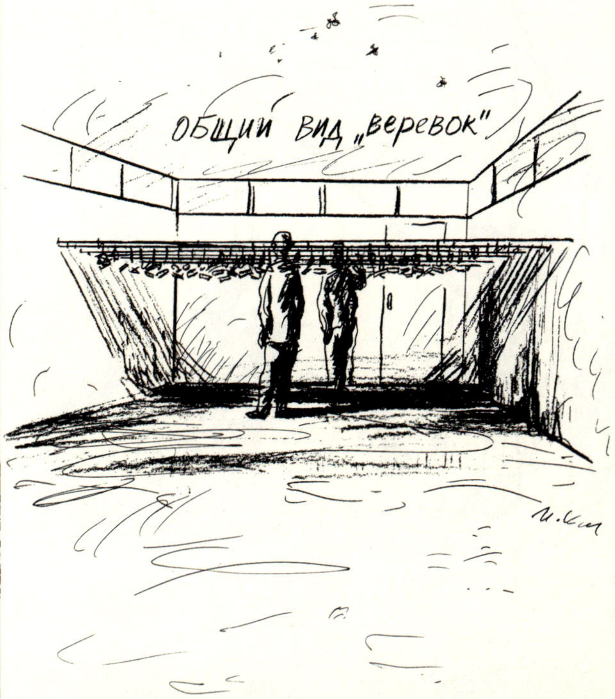

when I say what they say, and where I will tell them only what they expect.

. . . And now we are "interacting", everyone at the same time, everything as one. It is not important that when I am speaking, no one listens to me and everyone just waits for me to stop -- to say a phrase in their own turn, which I too will not particularly care about. What is important is that contact has emerged, exists, we are standing next to each other, we are not afraid of one another, everything is going on "normally" between us. We attain a unity, my neighbor and I find a commonality, and we, which is especially important, enter into a similar commonality will everyone else, too, through this speech we are connected to "our entire world" -- for we know, we HEAR: EVERYONE speaks like this.

I am delivered from my loneliness, no one is whining in me anymore, no one is moaning, contorting, suffering. What happiness it is to calm down, to become quiet, to be together with others, to become "like everyone" and to muffle the voice resounding inside you so that it cannot be heard at all.

Description of the Installation

The hall is a closed dwelling, square in layout, with windows located high above. Or there are none at all. The length and width of the walls of the hall is 10 meters. 16 ropes are stretched between the walls of the hall horizontally and parallel to one another at eye level, ie. approximately 168 cm., so that together they form a single horizontal surface. The distance between the stretched ropes is 42

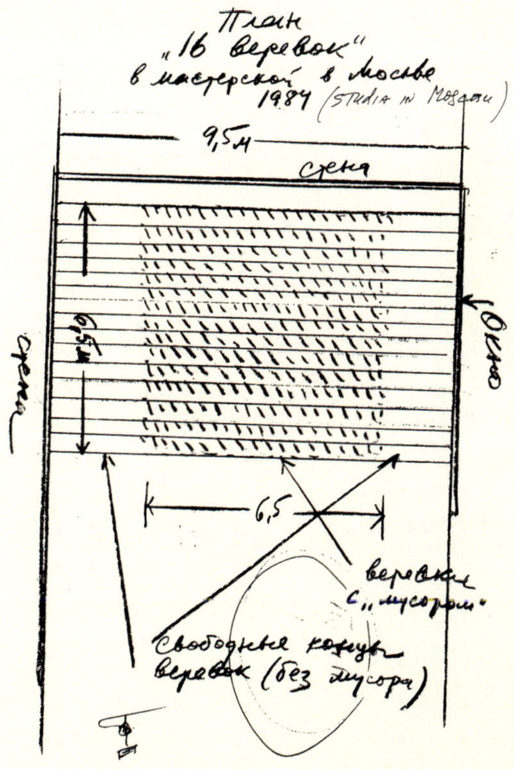

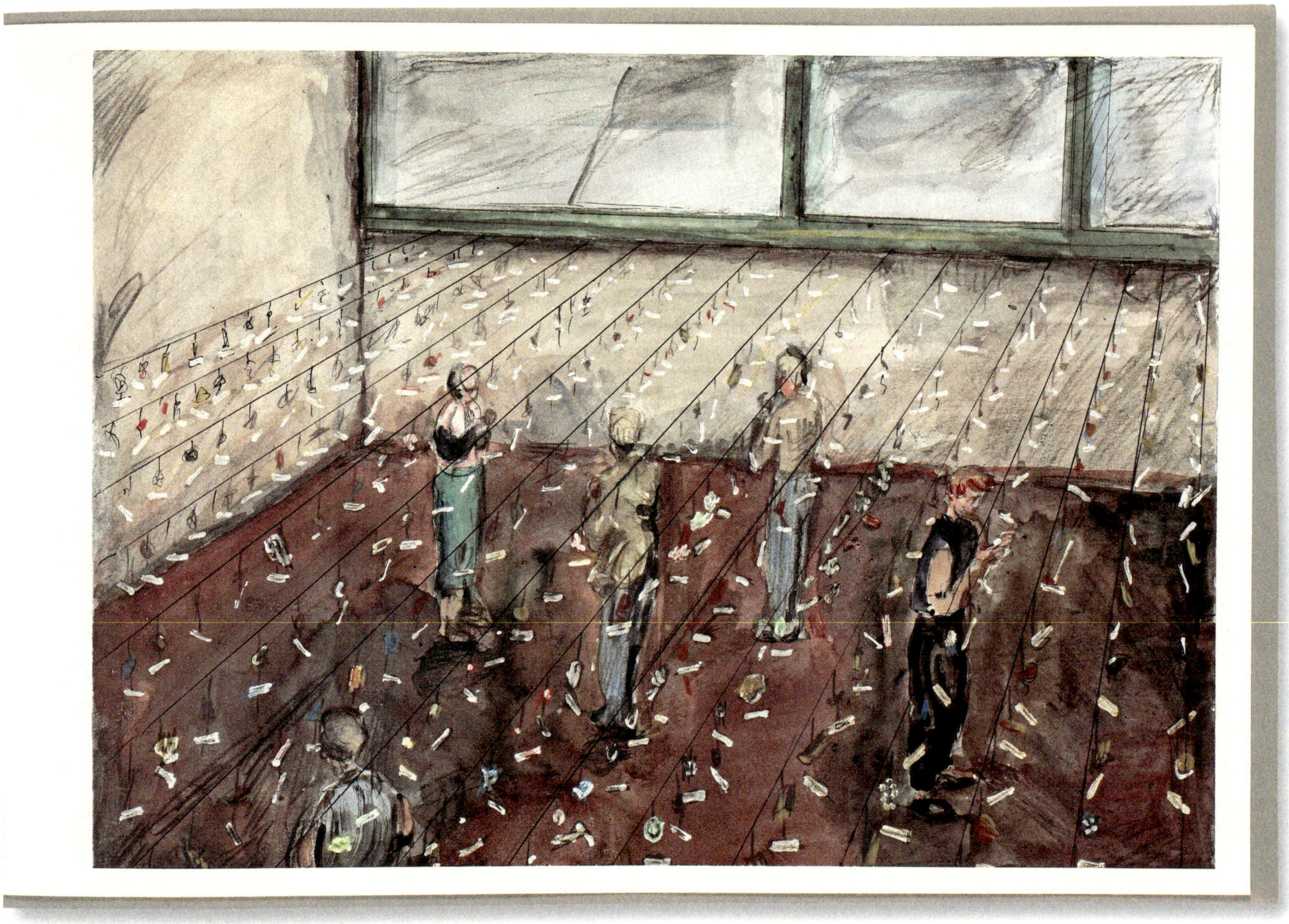

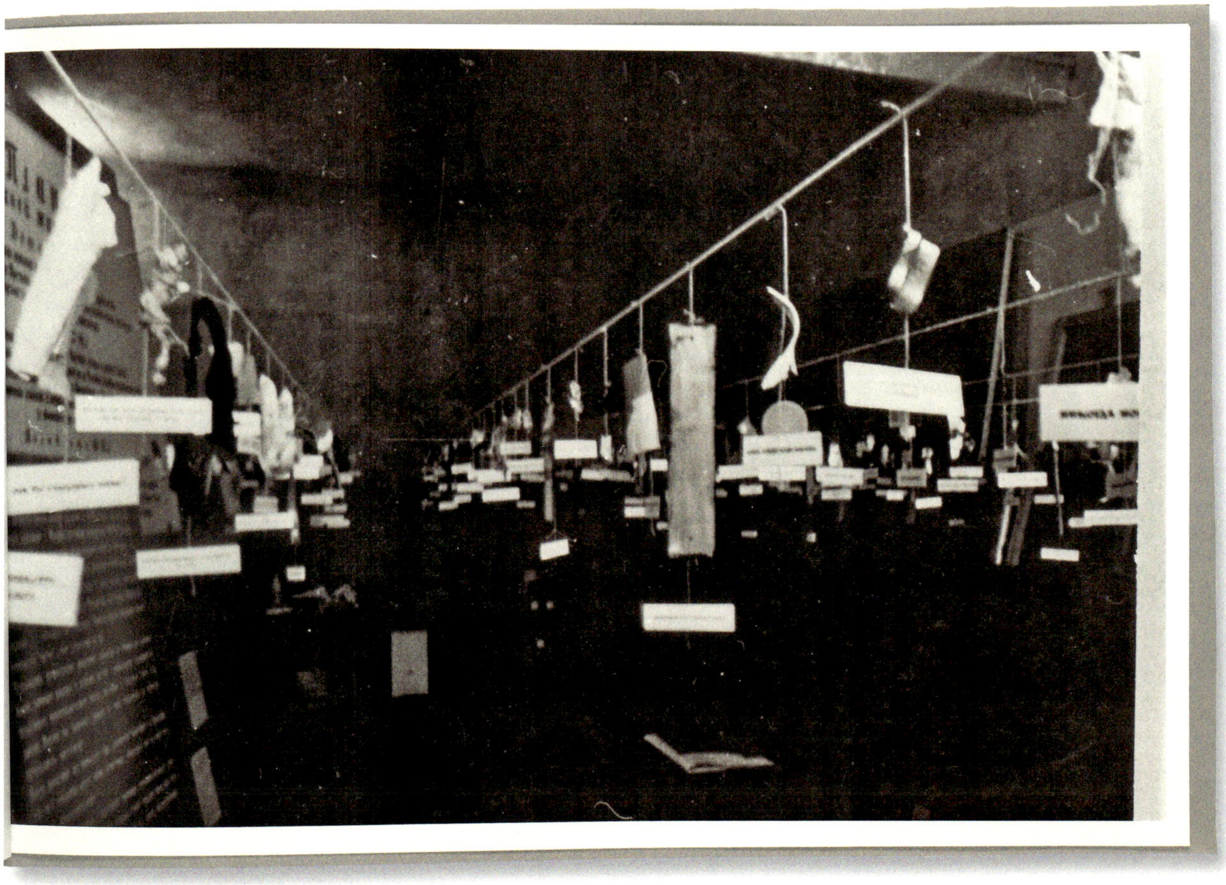

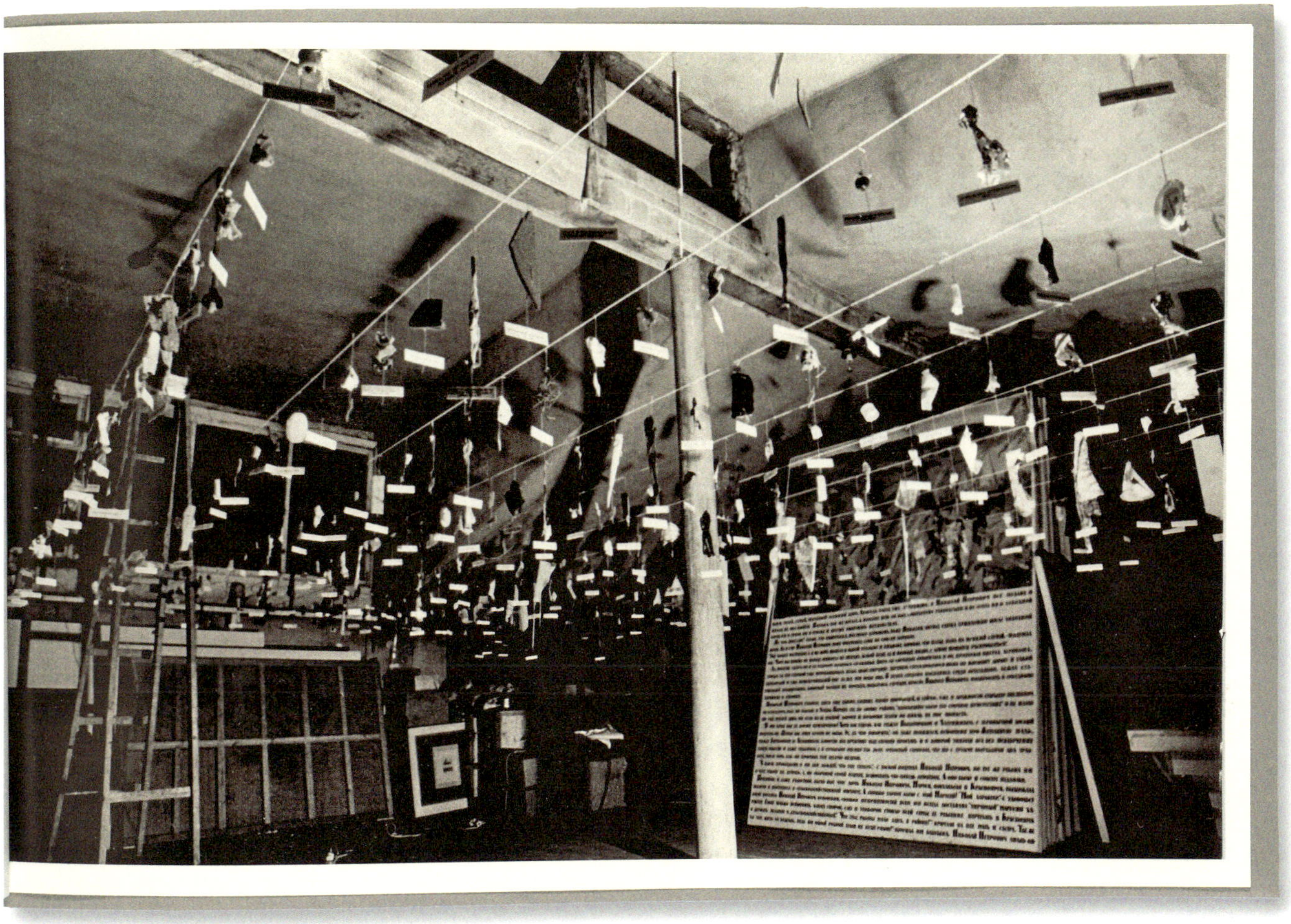

35 My Homeland (The Flies) | *Meine Heimat (Die Fliegen)*

1991

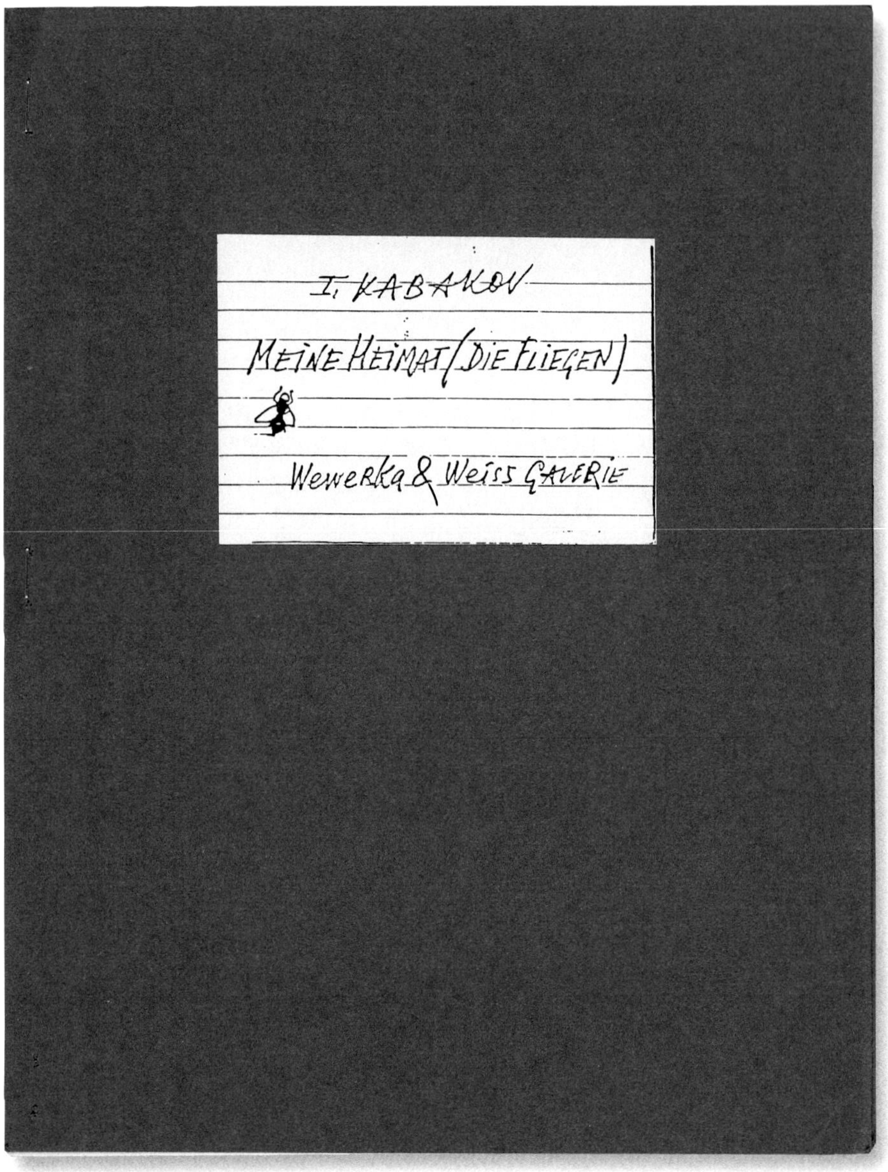

Ilya Kabakov
Berlin: Wewerka & Weiss Galerie
29.7 x 21 cm
12 photocopied pp. with 6 b/w ills.
stapled, cardboard cover, label on the cover
Drahtheftung, Kartonumschlag, Etikette auf dem Umschlag

exhibition catalogue | *Ausstellungskatalog*

layout by Ilya Kabakov | *Layout von Ilya Kabakov*

For the installation of the same name at the Wewerka & Weiss Galerie, Berlin, February 4 to March 23, 1991. Text by Ilya Kabakov on »New Findings on the 'Dancing' Civilization of Flies (F)« which also appeared in 1992 in the book »Life of Flies«; German.

Zur gleichnamigen Installation, Wewerka & Weiss Galerie, Berlin, 4. Februar – 23. März 1991. Text von Ilya Kabakov über »Neue Erkenntnisse über die ‚tanzende' Zivilisation der Fliegen (F)«, der auch 1992 im Buch »Das Leben der Fliegen« erschien; deutsch.

see also | *siehe auch* no. 36; no. 50; no. 134; CRI, vol. 1, no. 40, pp. 278–283

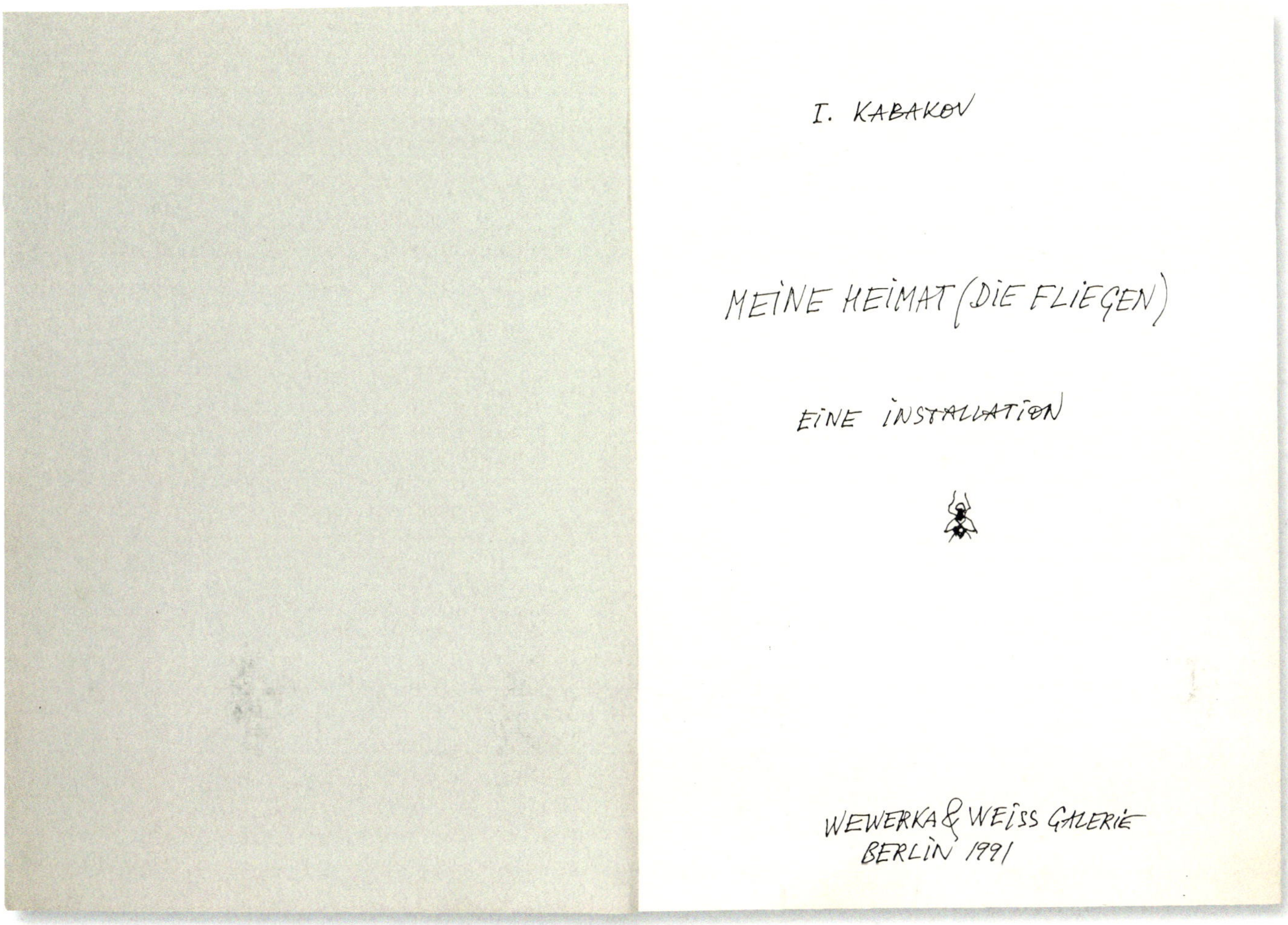
I. KABAKOV
MEINE HEIMAT (DIE FLIEGEN)
EINE INSTALLATION
WEWERKA & WEISS GALERIE
BERLIN 1991

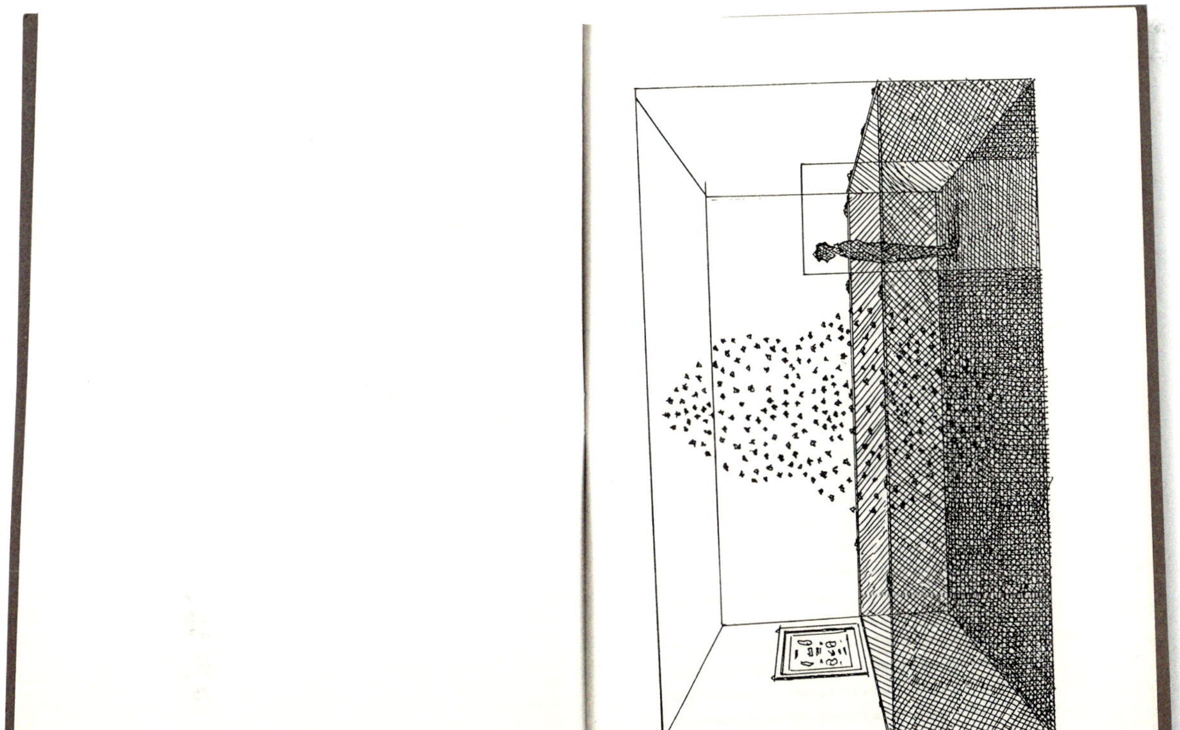

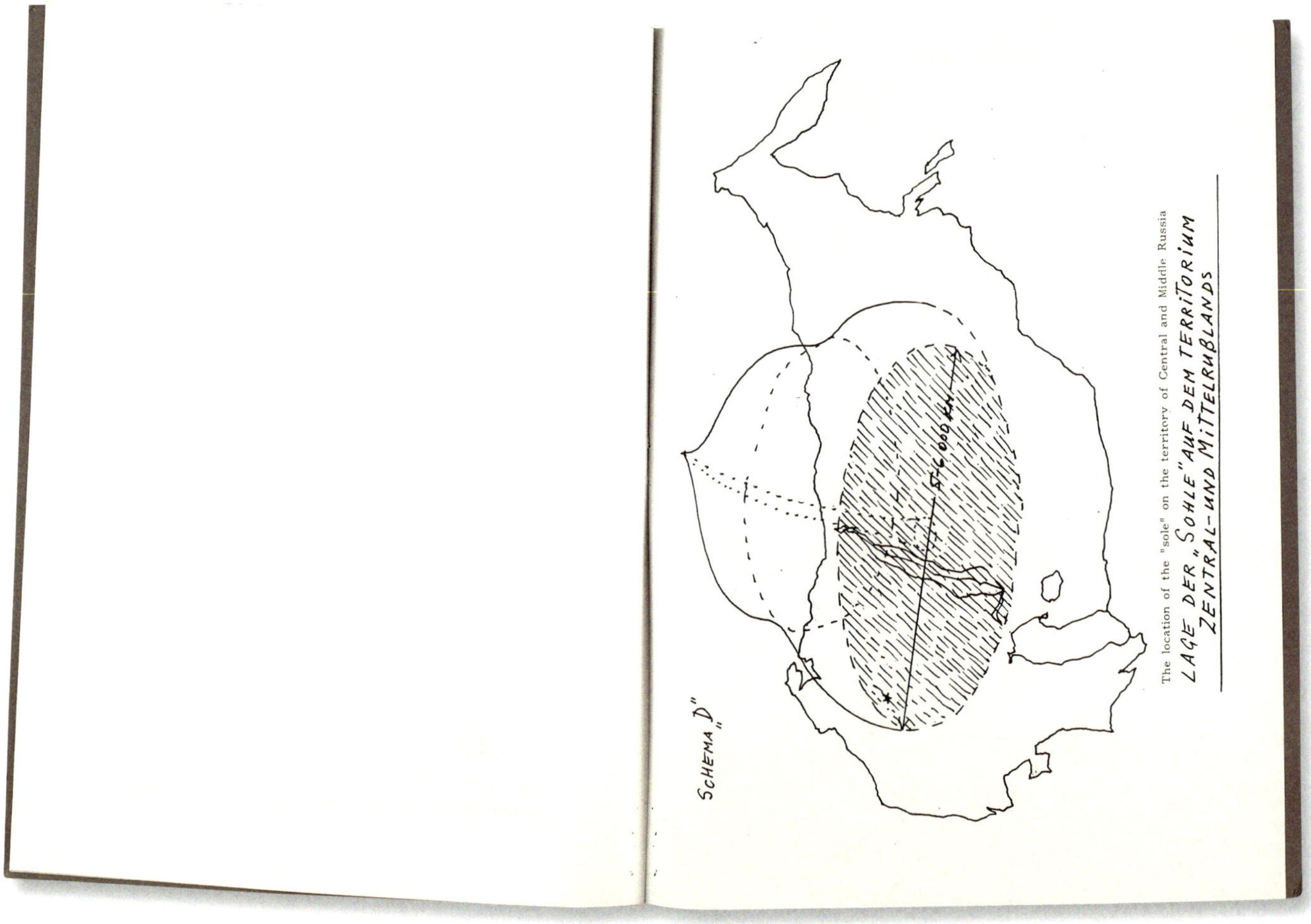
SCHEMA „D"
The location of the "sole" on the territory of Central and Middle Russia
LAGE DER „SOHLE" AUF DEM TERRITORIUM
ZENTRAL- UND MITTELRUßLANDS

36 My Homeland (The Flies) | *Meine Heimat (Die Fliegen)*

1991

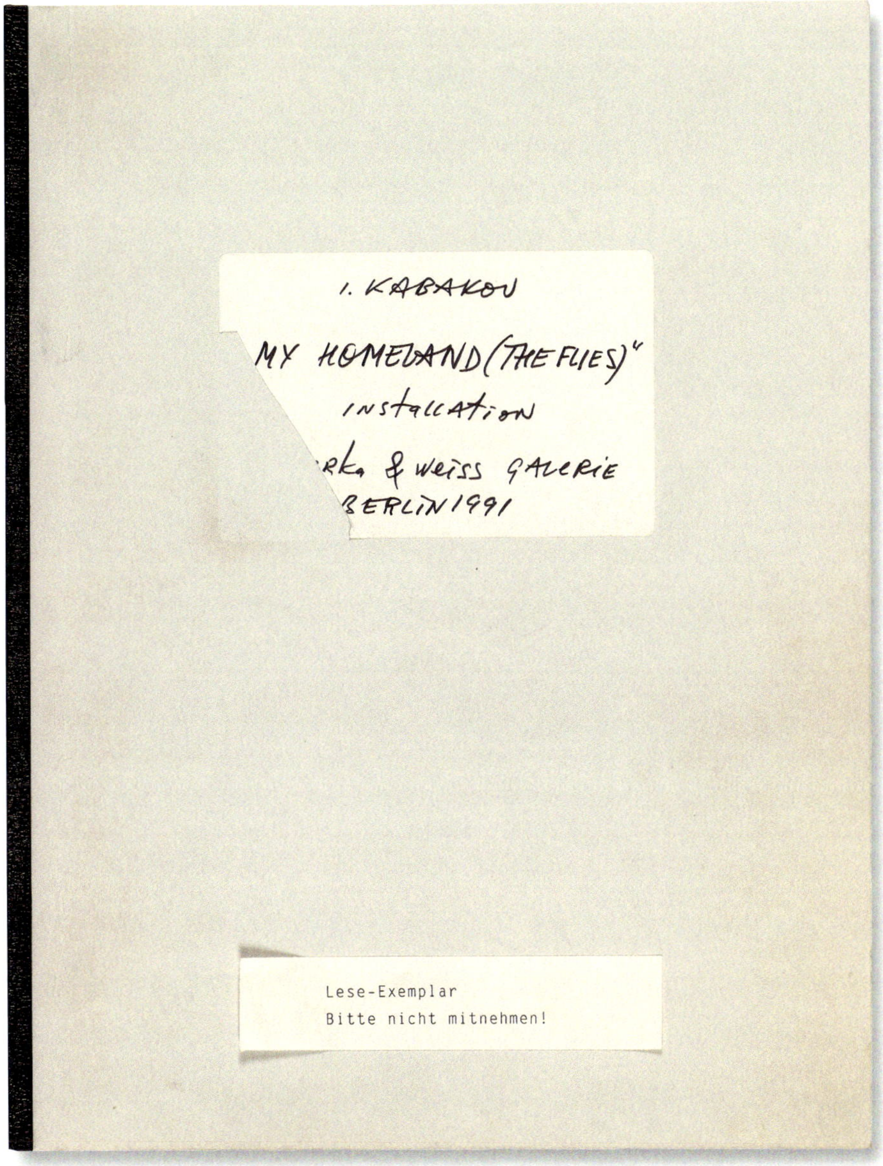

Ilya and Emilia Kabakov
New York: published by Ilya and Emilia Kabakov
29.7 x 21 cm
39 photocopied pp. with 20 (6 color) ills.
quick bind, paper cover, label on the cover
Schnellhefter, Papierumschlag, Etikette auf dem Umschlag
edition: 500 copies

thematic publication | *thematische Publikation*

layout by Ilya Kabakov | *Layout von Ilya Kabakov*

Documentation of the installation of the same name at the Wewerka & Weiss Galerie, Berlin, February 4 to March 23, 1991. Texts by Ilya Kabakov. Ilya Kabakov's text on »New Findings on the 'Dancing' Civilization of Flies (F)« also appeared in 1992 in the book »Life of Flies«; German, English, Russian.

Dokumentation der gleichnamigen Installation, Wewerka & Weiss Galerie, Berlin, 4. Februar – 23. März 1991. Texte von Ilya Kabakov. Der Text über »Neue Erkenntnisse über die ‚tanzende' Zivilisation der Fliegen (F)« von Ilya Kabakov erschien 1992 auch im Buch »Das Leben der Fliegen«; deutsch, englisch, russisch.

see also | *siehe auch* no. 35; no. 50; no. 134; CRI, vol. 1, no. 40, pp. 278–283

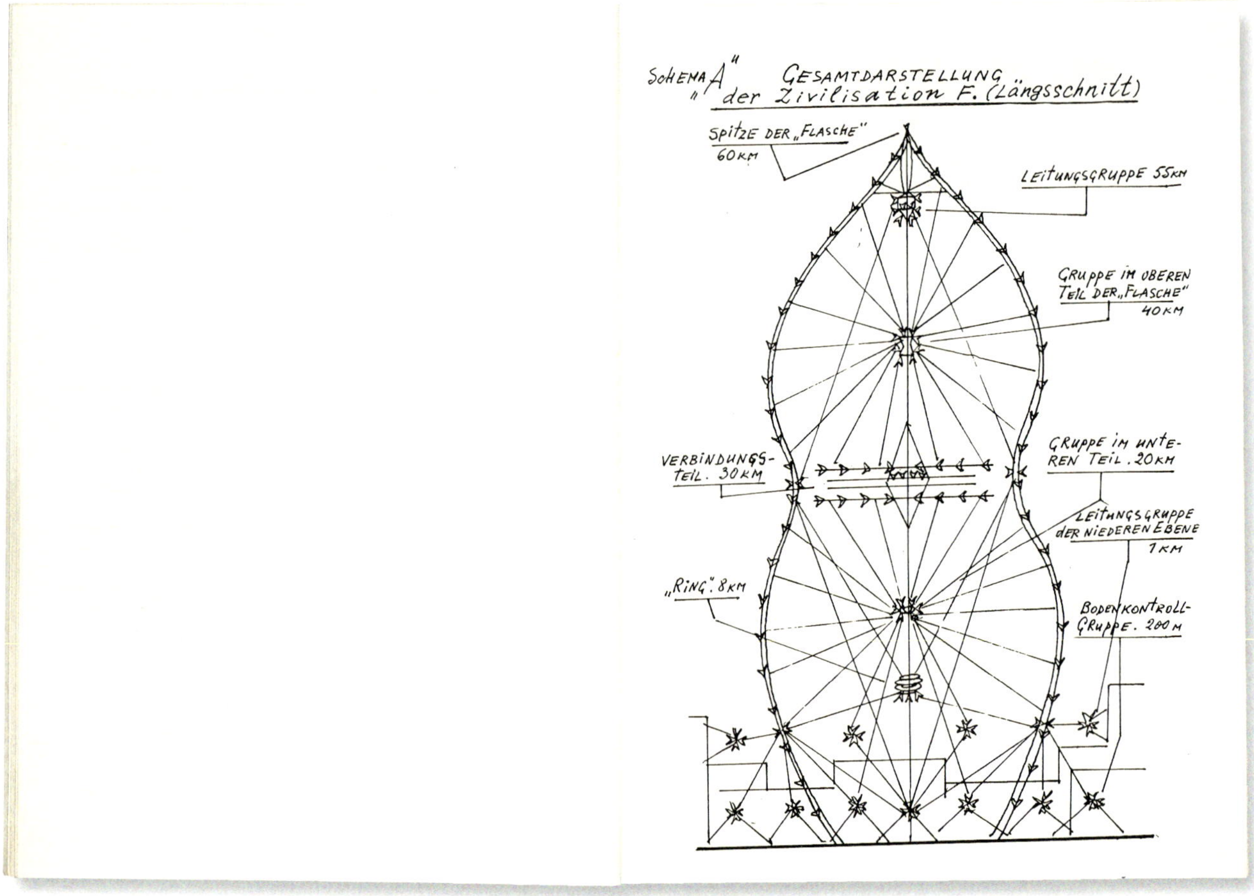
SCHEMA „A" GESAMTDARSTELLUNG der Zivilisation F. (Längsschnitt)
SPITZE DER „FLASCHE" 60KM
LEITUNGSGRUPPE 55KM
GRUPPE IM OBEREN TEIL DER „FLASCHE" 40KM
VERBINDUNGS-TEIL. 30KM
GRUPPE IM UNTE-REN TEIL. 20KM
LEITUNGSGRUPPE DER NIEDEREN EBENE 1KM
„RING". 8KM
BODENKONTROLL-GRUPPE. 200 M

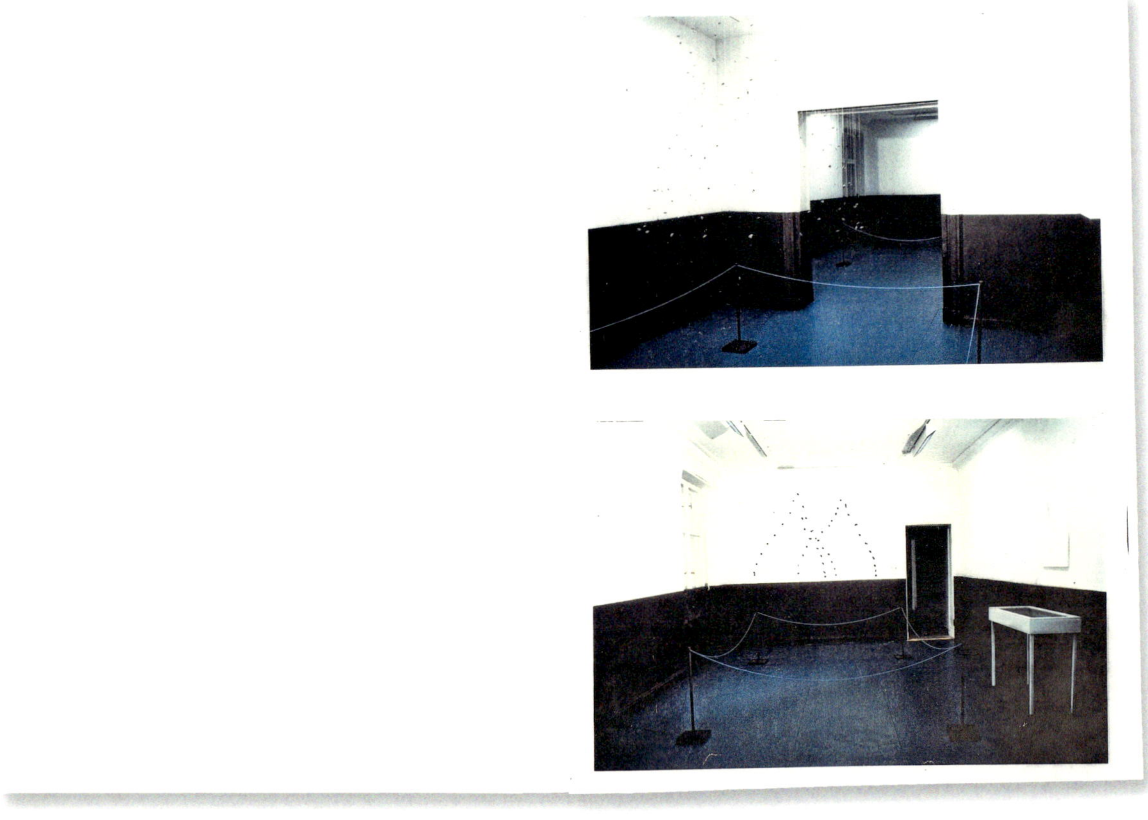

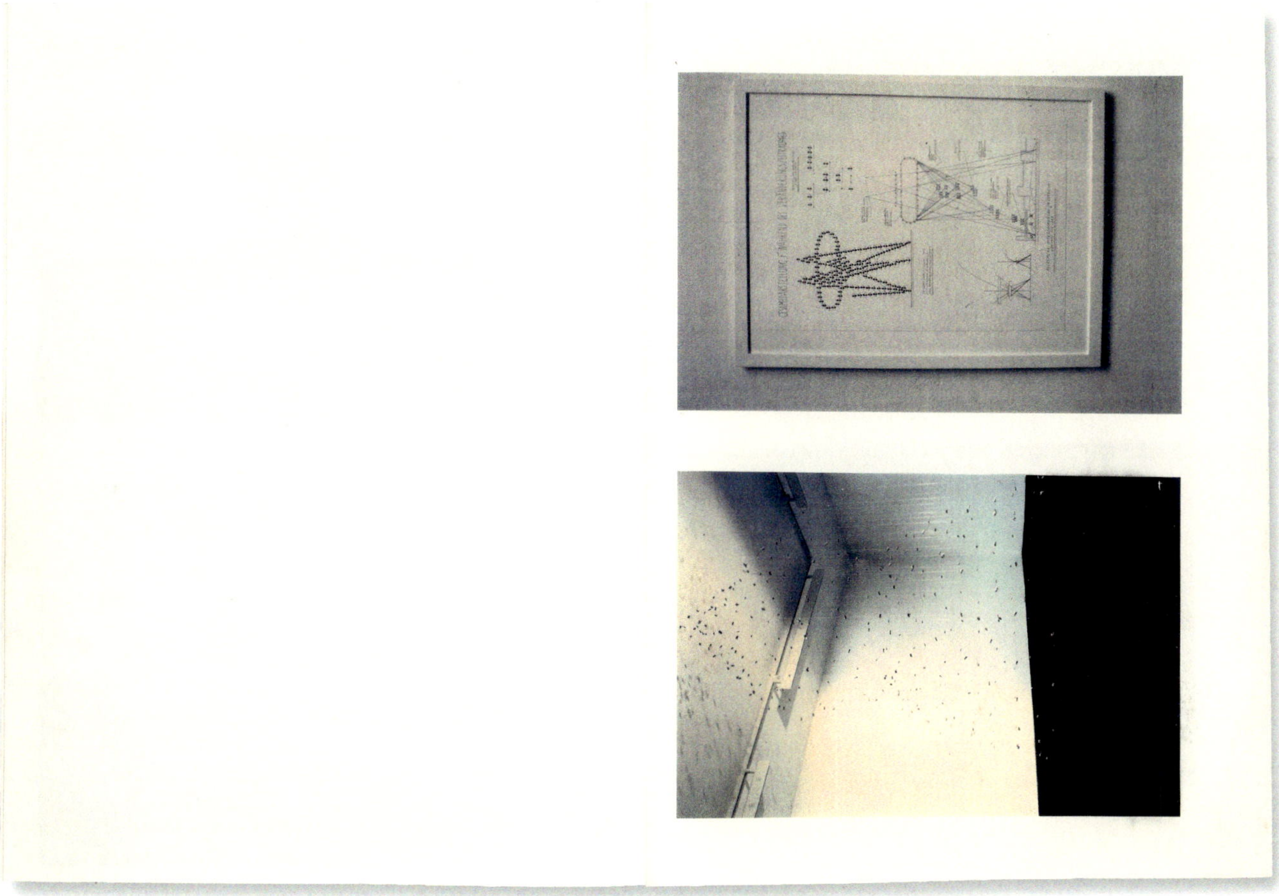

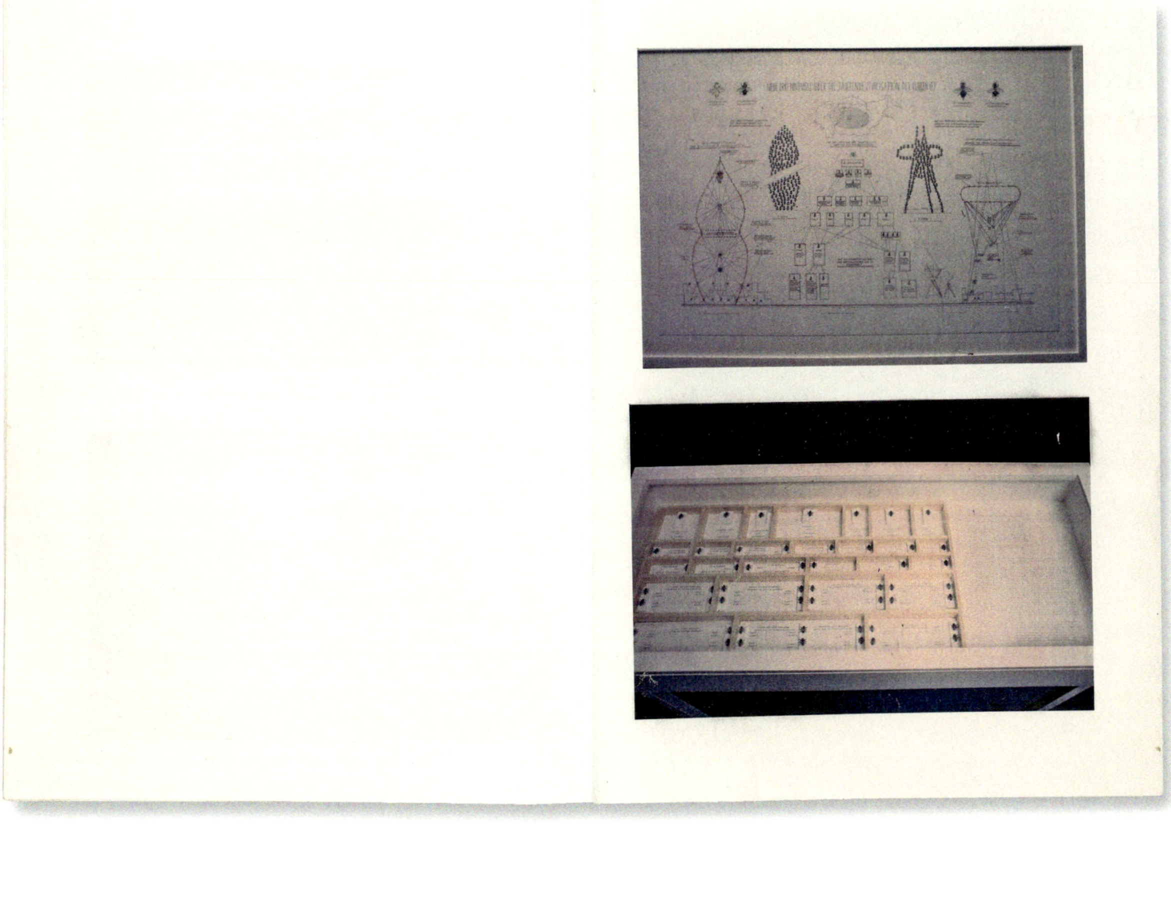

37 The Fly with the Wings | *Fliege mit Flügeln*

1991

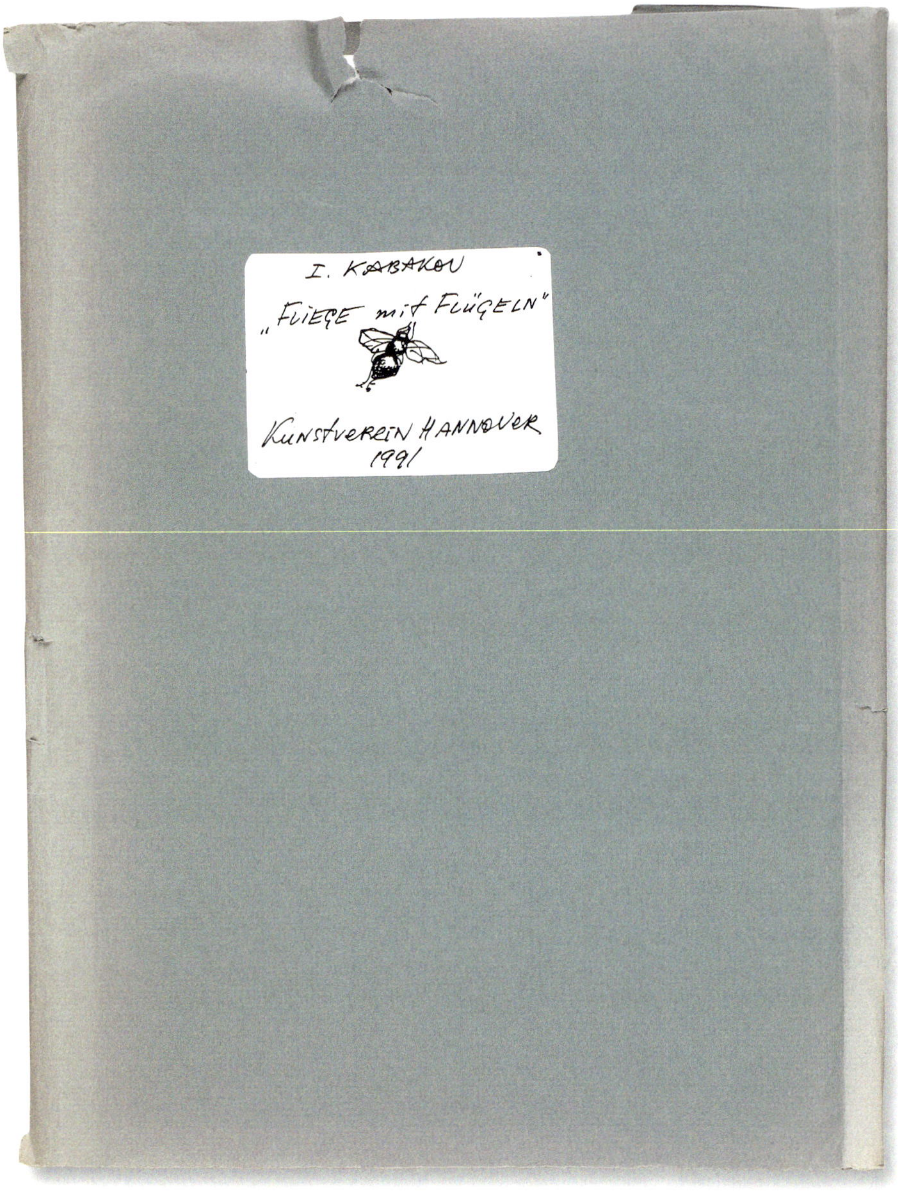

Ilya Kabakov
New York: published by the author
30.3 x 22.8 cm
90 photocopied pp. with 10 b/w (incl. 2 foldouts) ills.
adhesive binding, plastic cover, paper cover, label on the cover
Klebebindung, Plastikumschlag, Papierumschlag, Etikette auf dem Umschlag
edition: 100 copies

exhibition catalogue | *Ausstellungskatalog*

layout by Ilya Kabakov | *Layout von Ilya Kabakov*

For the installation of the same name for the exhibition »Art, Europe: Soviet Union« at the Kunstverein Hannover, Hanover, June 22 to August 25, 1991. Texts by Ilya Kabakov, which were published in 1992 as the chapter entitled »The Fly as a Subject and Basis for Philosophical Discourse« in the book »Life of Flies«; Russian, German.

Zur gleichnamigen Installation für die Ausstellung »Kunst, Europa: Sowjetunion«, Kunstverein Hannover, Hannover, 22. Juni – 25. August 1991. Texte von Ilya Kabakov, die 1992 unter dem Kapitel »Die Fliege als Ursache und Grundlage des philosophischen Diskurses« im Buch »Das Leben der Fliegen« publiziert wurden; russisch, deutsch.

see also | *siehe auch* no. 8; no. 9; no. 33; no. 43; no. 44; no. 38; no. 50; no. 56; no. 134; CRI, vol. 1, no. 3, pp. 60–65

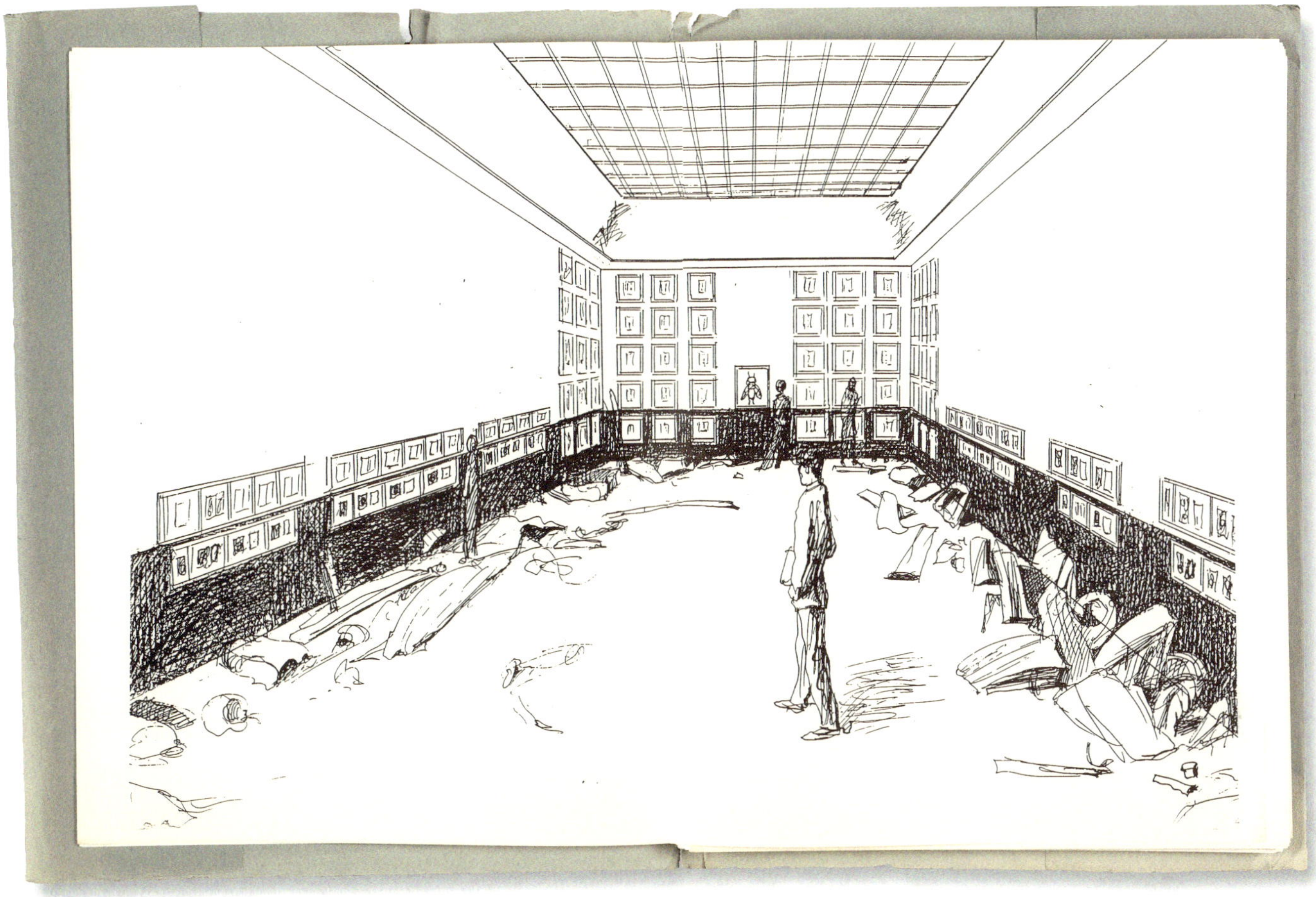

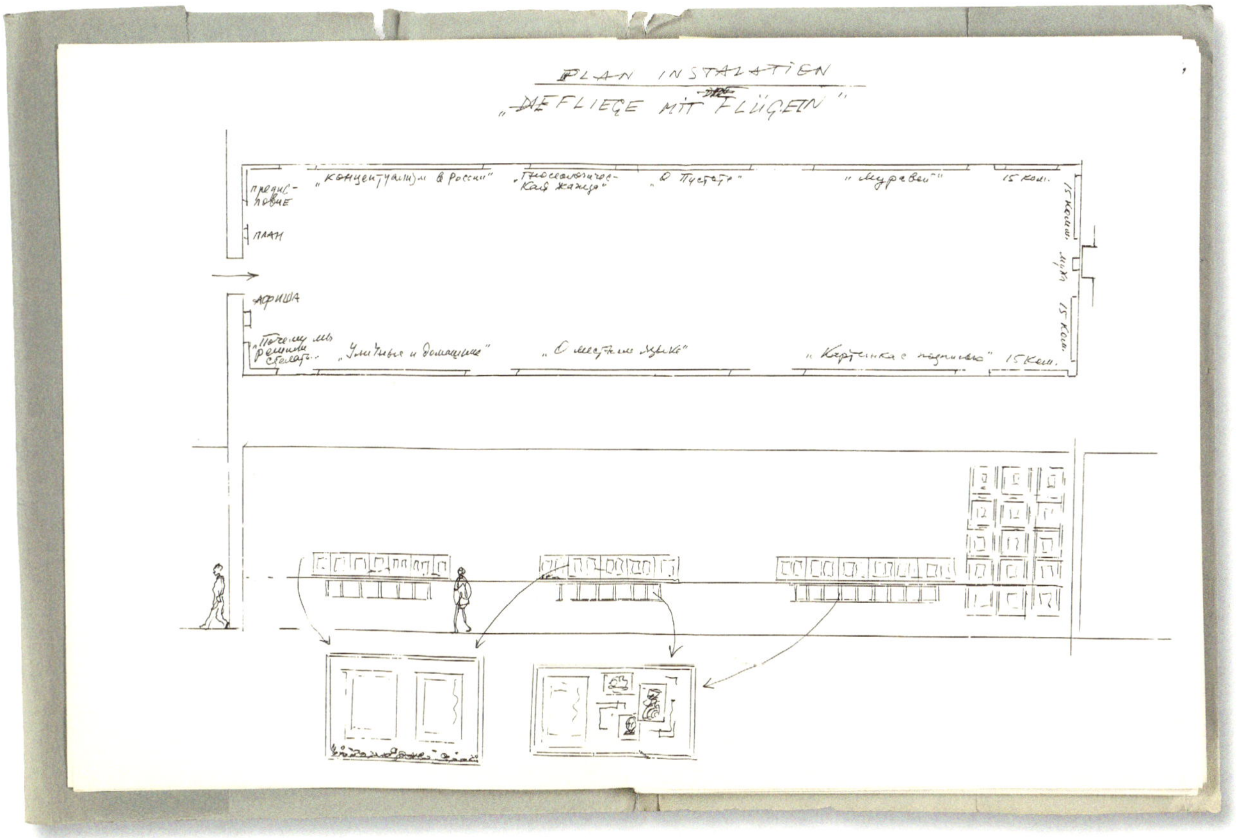
PLAN INSTALATIEN
„FLIEGE MIT FLÜGELN"
„Концептуализм в России"
„О пустоте"
„Муравей"
15 Ком.
План
Афиша
„Картинка с надписью"

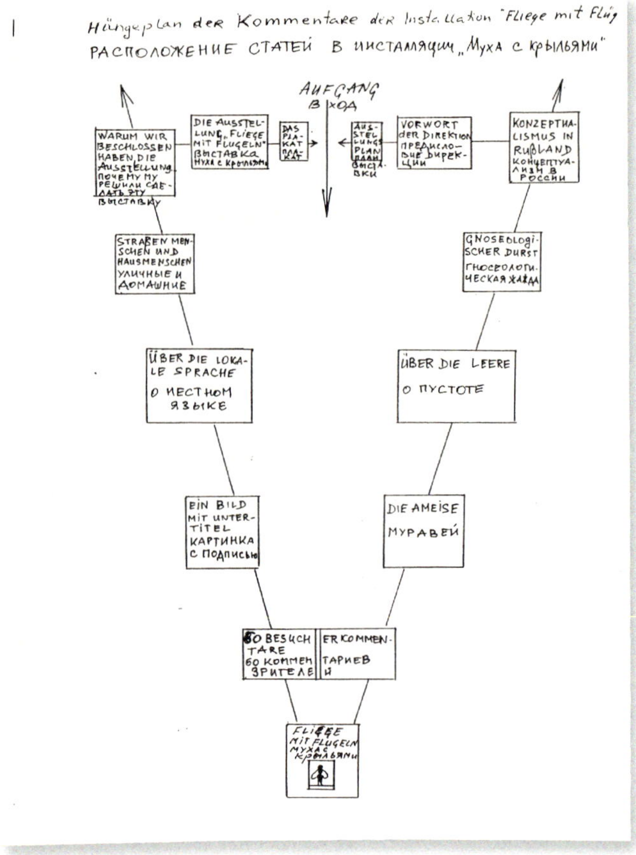
Hängeplan der Kommentare der Installation "Fliege mit Flüg
РАСПОЛОЖЕНИЕ СТАТЕЙ В ИНСТАЛЛЯЦИИ „Муха с крыльями"
AUFGANG
ВХОДА
WARUM WIR BESCHLOSSEN HABEN, DIE AUSSTELLUNG. ПОЧЕМУ МЫ РЕШИЛИ СДЕЛАТЬ ЭТУ ВЫСТАВКУ
DIE AUSSTELLUNG „FLIEGE MIT FLÜGELN" ВЫСТАВКА МУХА С КРЫЛЬЯМИ
DAS PLAKAT ПЛАКАТ
AUSSTELLUNGSPLAN ПЛАН ВЫСТАВКИ
VORWORT DER DIREKTION ПРЕДИСЛОВИЕ ДИРЕКЦИИ
KONZEPTUALISMUS IN RUßLAND КОНЦЕПТУАЛИЗМ В РОССИИ
STRAßENMENSCHEN UND HAUSMENSCHEN УЛИЧНЫЕ И ДОМАШНИЕ
GNOSEOLOGISCHER DURST ГНОСЕОЛОГИЧЕСКАЯ ЖАЖДА
ÜBER DIE LOKALE SPRACHE О МЕСТНОМ ЯЗЫКЕ
ÜBER DIE LEERE О ПУСТОТЕ
EIN BILD MIT UNTERTITEL КАРТИНКА С ПОДПИСЬЮ
DIE AMEISE МУРАВЕЙ
60 BESUCHER KOMMENTARE 60 КОММЕНТАРИЕВ ЗРИТЕЛЕЙ
FLIEGE MIT FLÜGELN МУХА С КРЫЛЬЯМИ

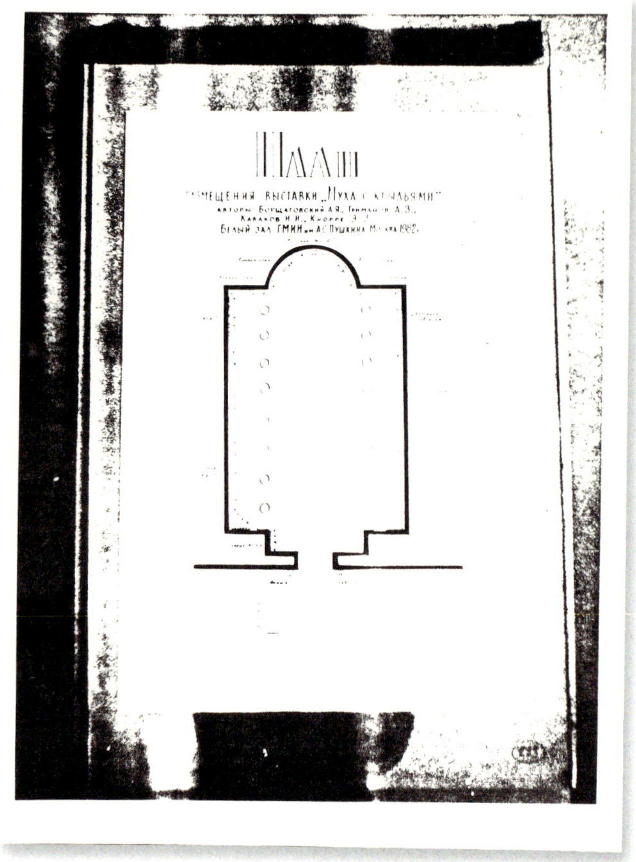
План
выставки „Муха
Кабаков И. И.

38 The Fly with the Wings | *Fliege mit Flügeln*

1991

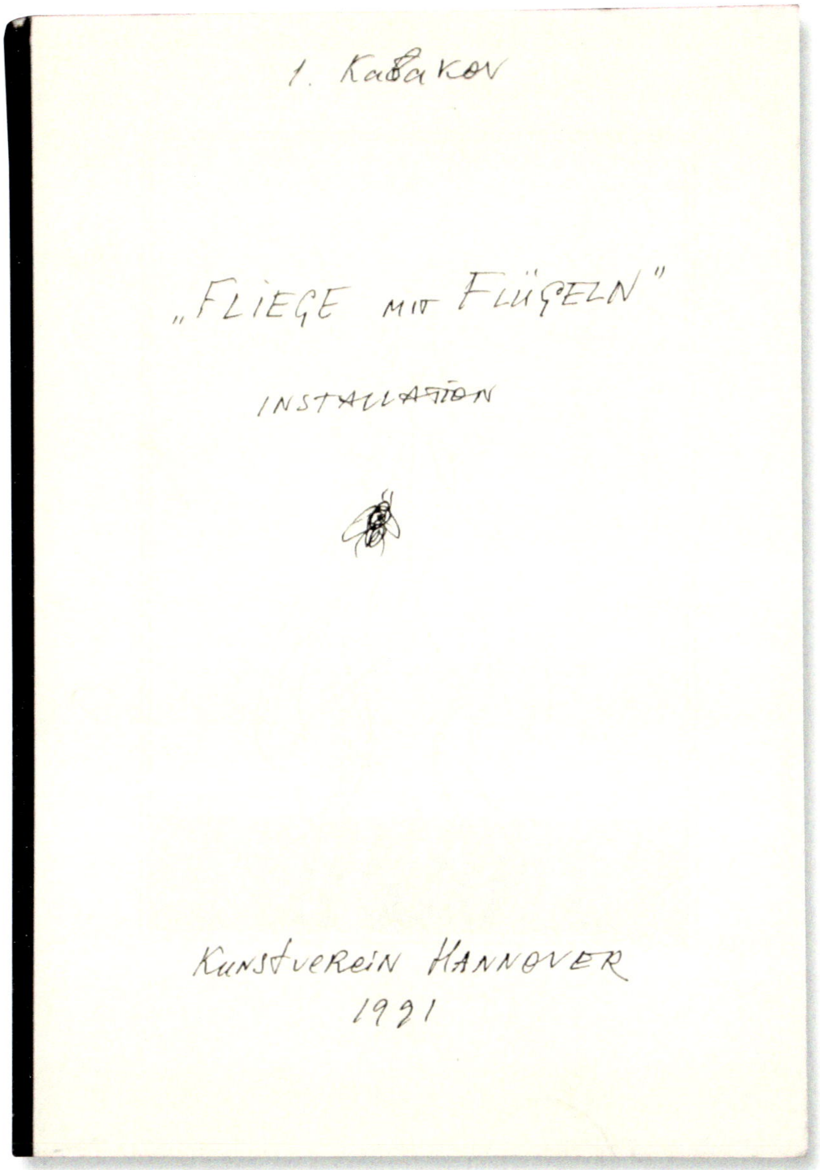

Ilya Kabakov
New York: published by the author
30 x 21.3 cm
166 photocopied pp. with 8 b/w ills.
adhesive binding
Klebebindung
edition: 100 copies

exhibition catalogue | *Ausstellungskatalog*

layout by Ilya Kabakov | *Layout von Ilya Kabakov*

For the installation of the same name for the exhibition »Art, Europe: Soviet Union« at the Kunstverein Hannover, Hanover, June 22 to August 25, 1991. Texts by Ilya Kabakov, which were published in 1992 as the chapter entitled »The Fly as a Subject and Basis for Philosophical Discourse« in the book »Life of Flies«; Russian, German.

Zur gleichnamigen Installation für die Ausstellung »Kunst, Europa: Sowjetunion«, Kunstverein Hannover, Hannover, 22. Juni – 25. August 1991. Texte von Ilya Kabakov, die 1992 unter dem Kapitel »Die Fliege als Ursache und Grundlage des philosophischen Diskurses« im Buch »Das Leben der Fliegen« publiziert wurden; russisch, deutsch.

see also | *siehe auch* no. 8; no. 9; no. 33; no. 43; no. 44; no. 37; no. 50; no. 56; no. 134; CRI, vol. 1, no. 3, pp. 60–65

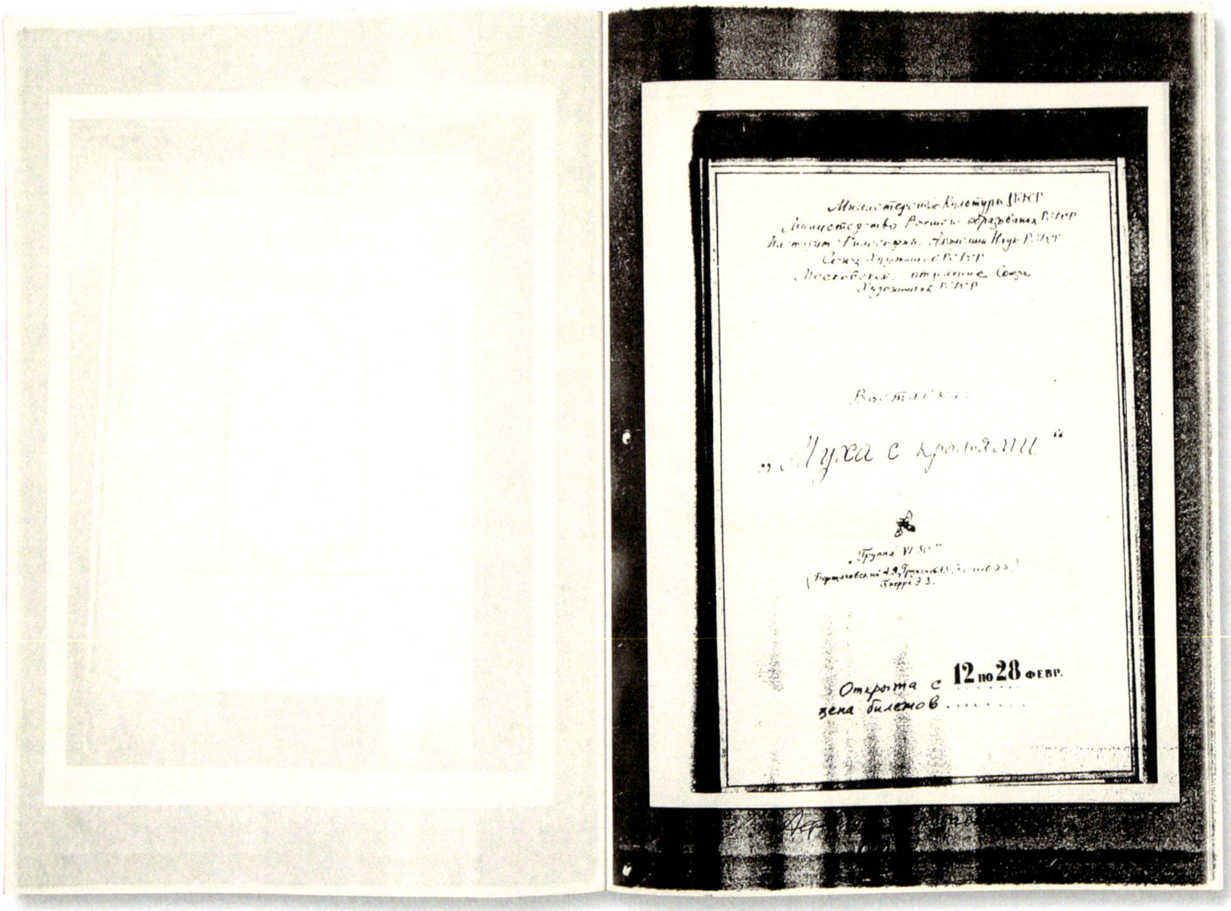
„Муха с крыльями“
Открыта с 12 по 28 февр.
цена билетов ....

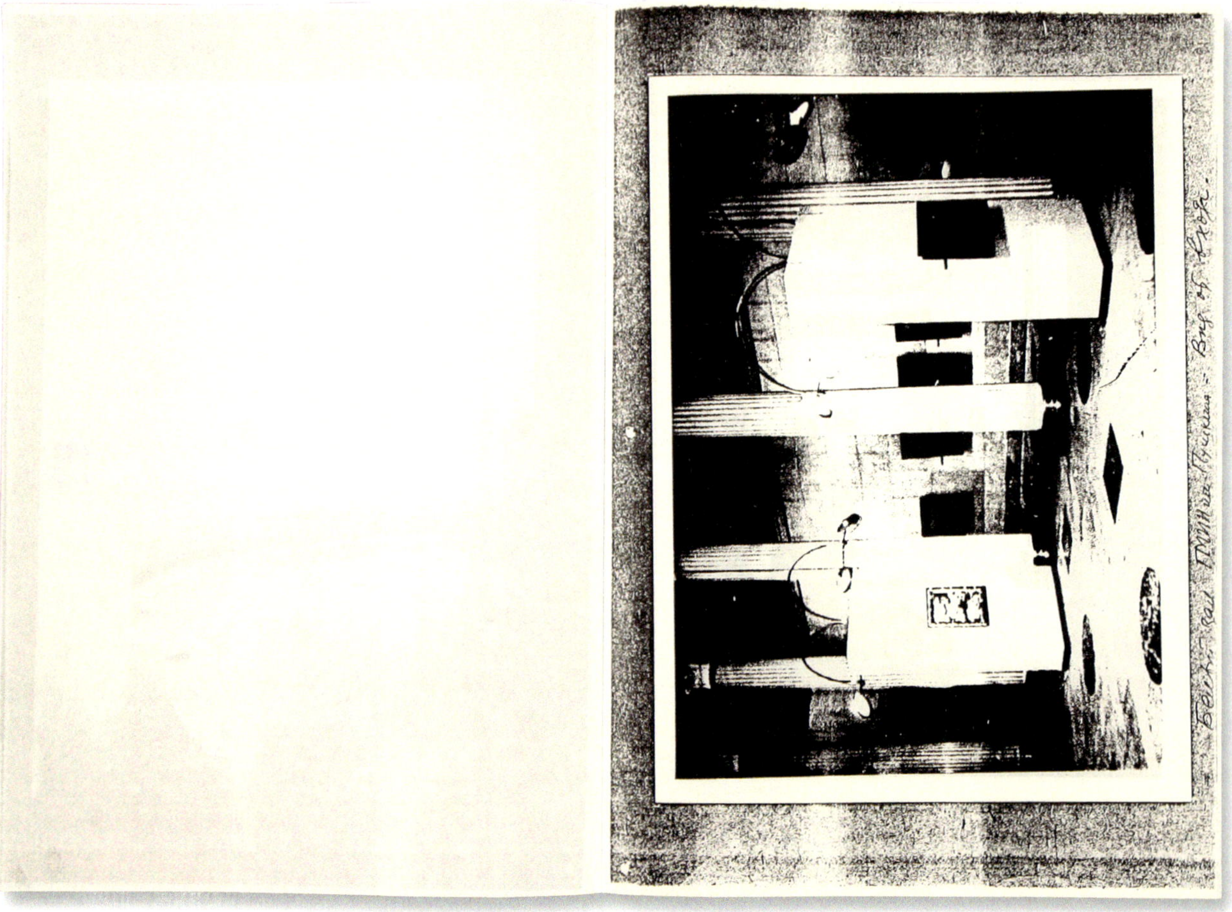

39 In the Communal Kitchen | *In der Gemeinschaftsküche*

1991

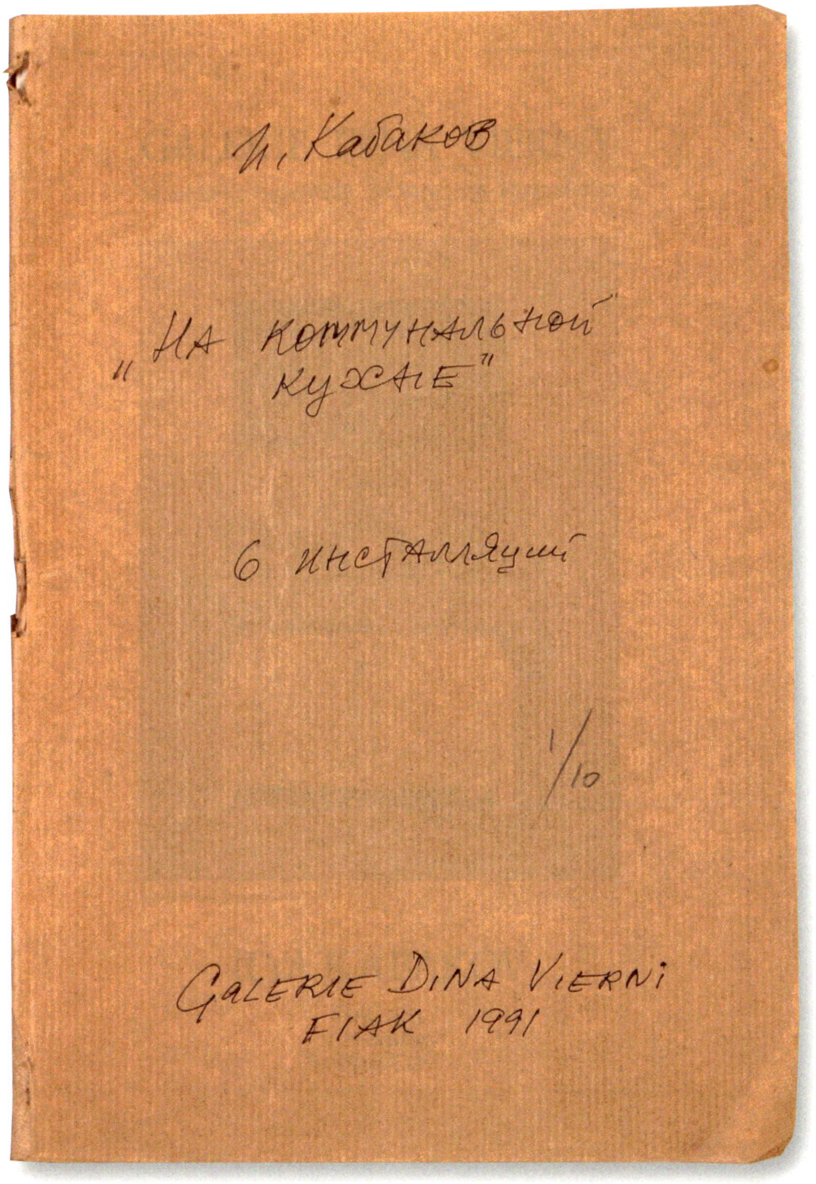

Ilya Kabakov
Paris: Dina Vierny
30 x 22 cm
39 pp. with 19 b/w and 1 color ill.
loose sheets, paper cover
lose Blätter, Papierumschlag
edition: 10 copies

thematic publication | *thematische Publikation*

layout by Ilya Kabakov | *Layout von Ilya Kabakov*

Published for the FIAC art fair, Paris, October 4 to 13, 1991. Texts by Ilya and Emilia Kabakov; Russian, English.

Erschien zur Kunstmesse FIAC, Paris, 4. – 13. Oktober 1991. Texte von Ilya und Emilia Kabakov; russisch, englisch.

see also | *siehe auch*

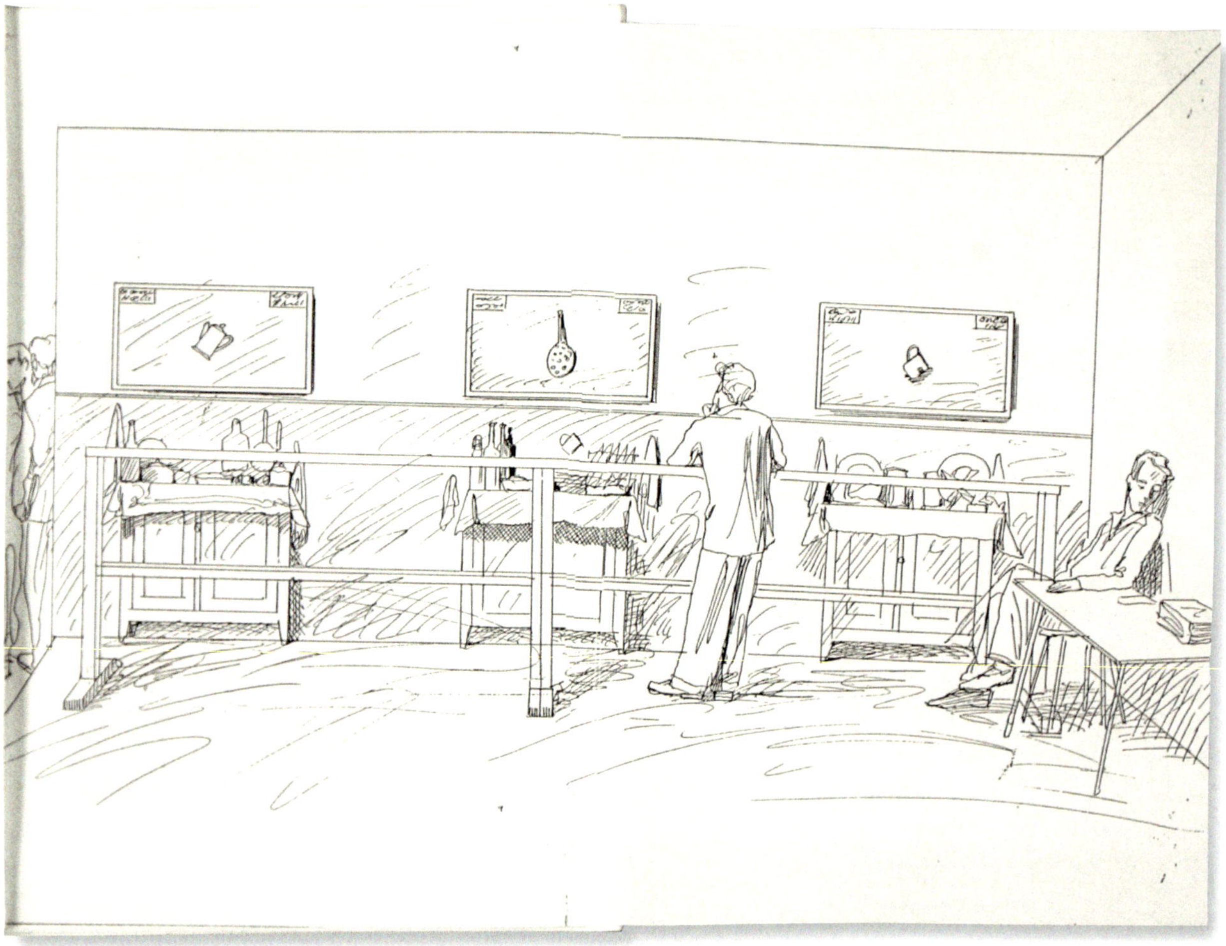

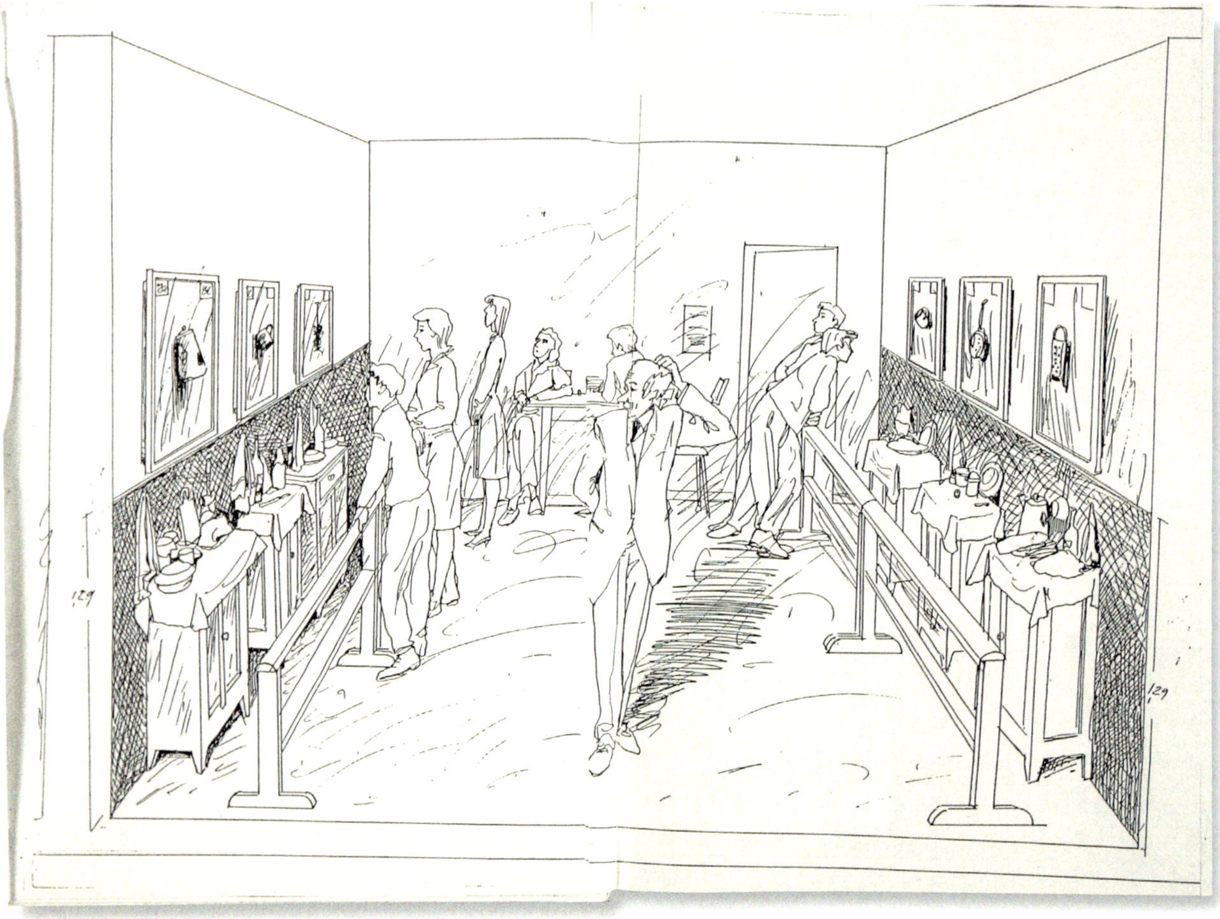

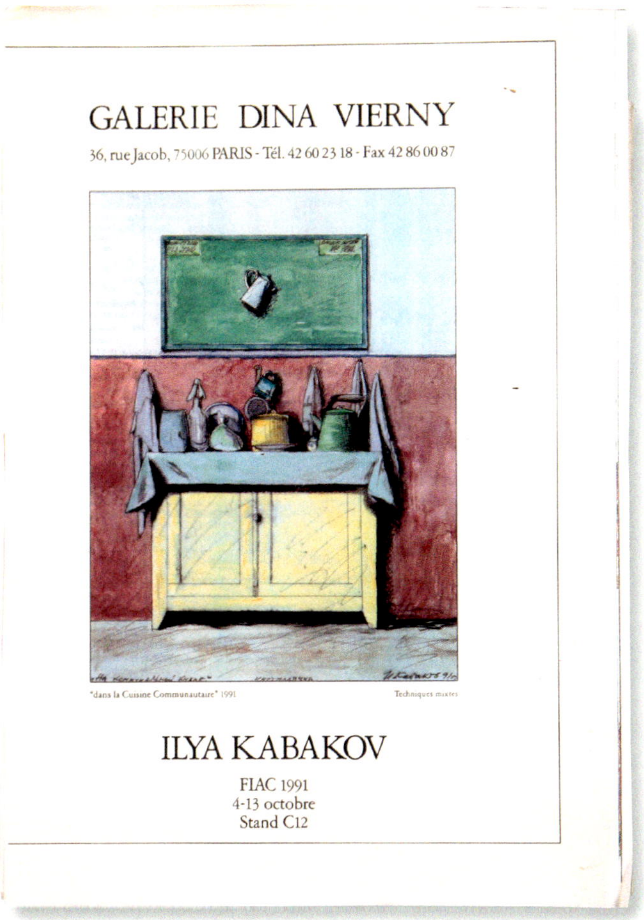
GALERIE DINA VIERNY

36, rue Jacob, 75006 PARIS - Tél. 42 60 23 18 - Fax 42 86 00 87

"dans la Cuisine Communautaire" 1991 — Techniques mixtes

ILYA KABAKOV

FIAC 1991
4-13 octobre
Stand C12

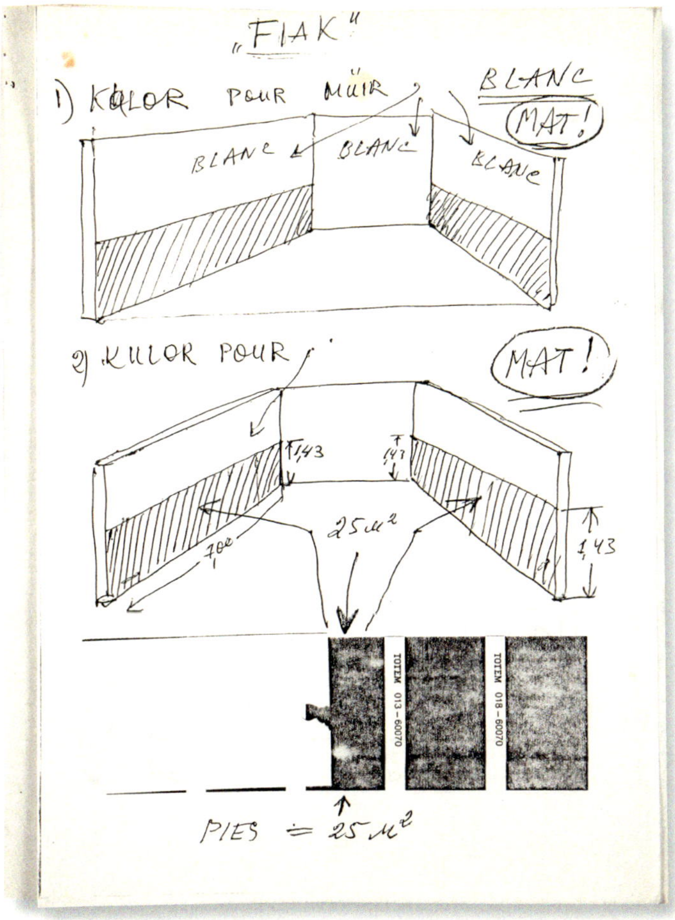

40 Community Kitchen and Labyrinth (My Mother's Album)

Die Gemeinschaftsküche und Labyrinth (Album meiner Mutter)

1991

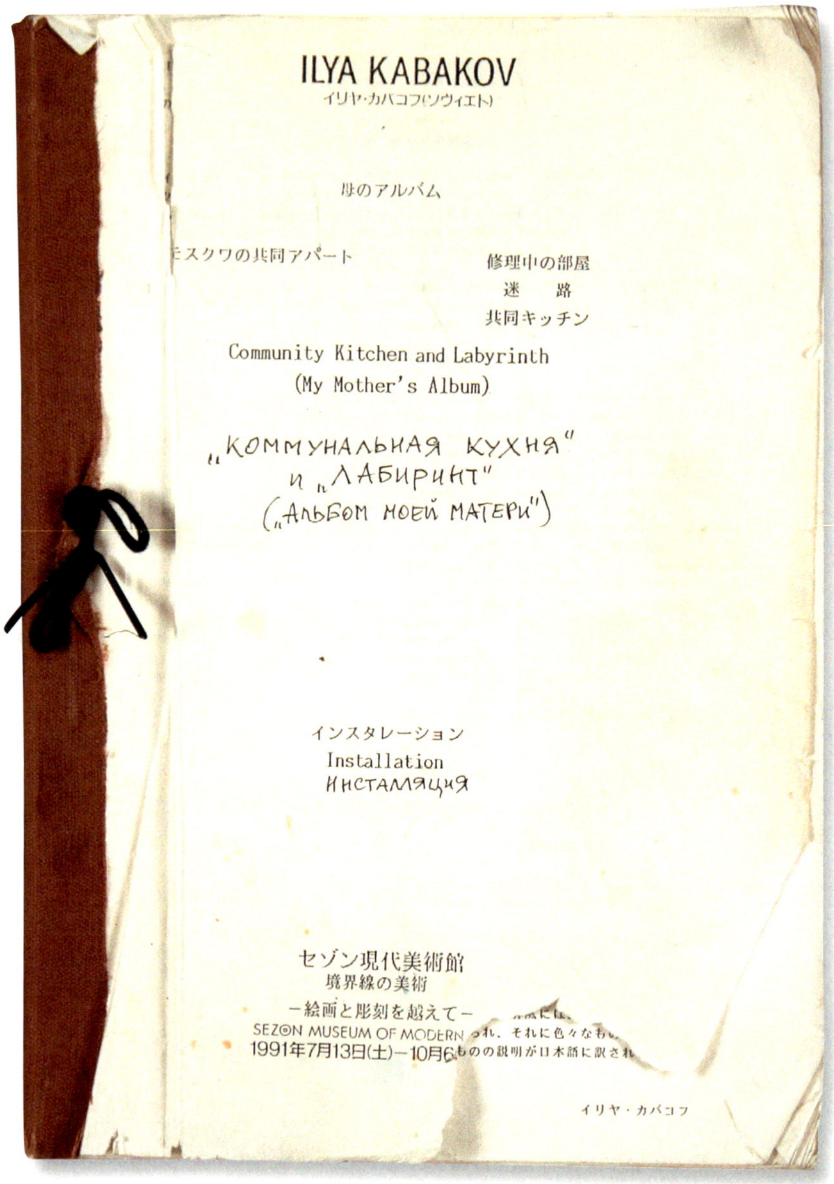

Sezon Museum of Modern Art
Karuizawa: Sezon Museum of Modern Art
29.8 x 21.2 cm
237 (partly double-sided) photocopied pp. (12 foldouts) with 47 b/w ills. two punched holes, held together with a string
zwei ausgestanzte Löcher, zusammengehalten mit einer Schnur

exhibition catalogue | *Ausstellungskatalog*

layout by Ilya Kabakov | *Layout von Ilya Kabakov*

For the installations of the same name at the Sezon Museum of Modern Art, Karuizawa, Nagano, Japan, July 13 to October 6, 1991. Text by Ilya Kabakov; Japanese, English, Russian.

Zu den gleichnamigen Installationen, Sezon Museum of Modern Art, Karuizawa, Nagano, Japan, 13. Juli – 6. Oktober 1991. Text von Ilya Kabakov; japanisch, englisch, russisch.

see also | *siehe auch* no. 75; CRI, vol. 1, no. 48, pp. 318–323; CRP, vol. 1, nos. 185–216, pp. 270–286

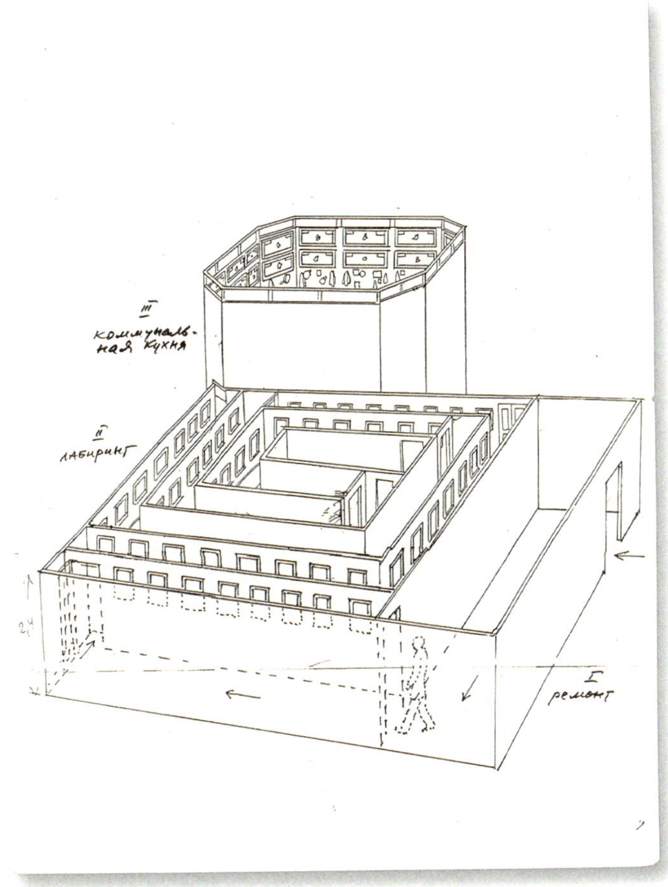
III коммунальная кухня
II лабиринт
I ремонт

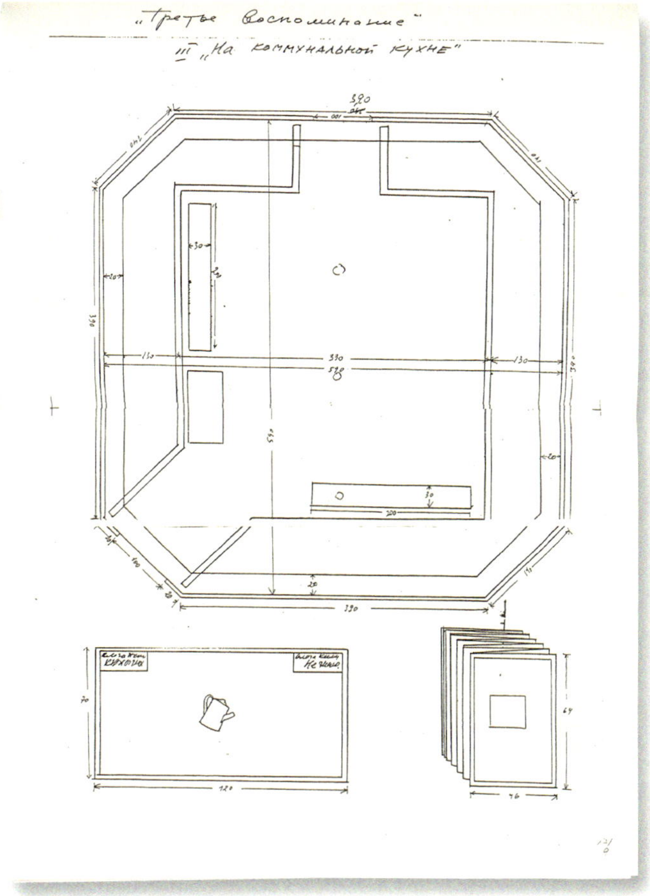
„Третье воспоминание"
III „На коммунальной кухне"

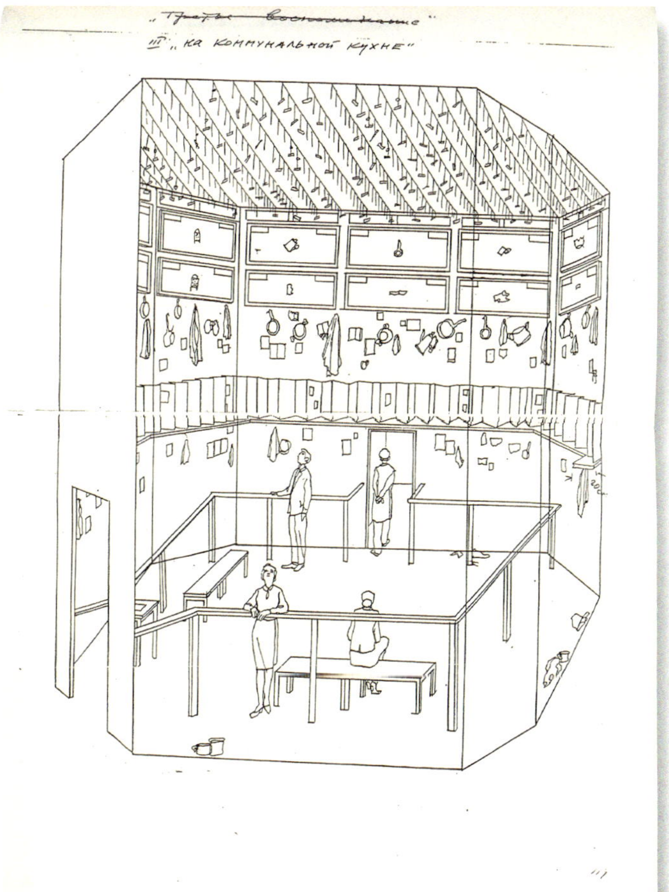
„Третье воспоминание"
III „На коммунальной кухне"

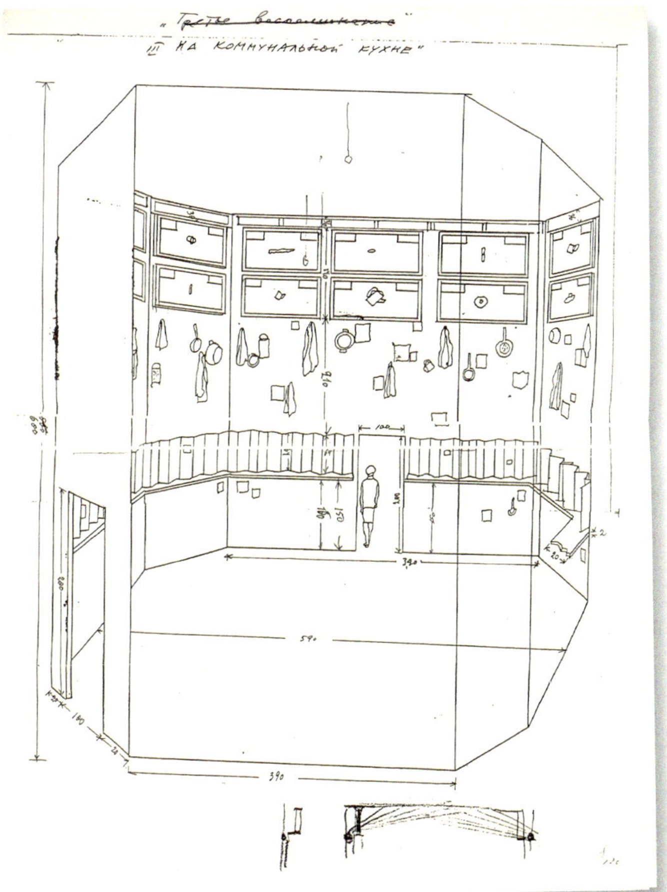
„Третье воспоминание"
III „На коммунальной кухне"

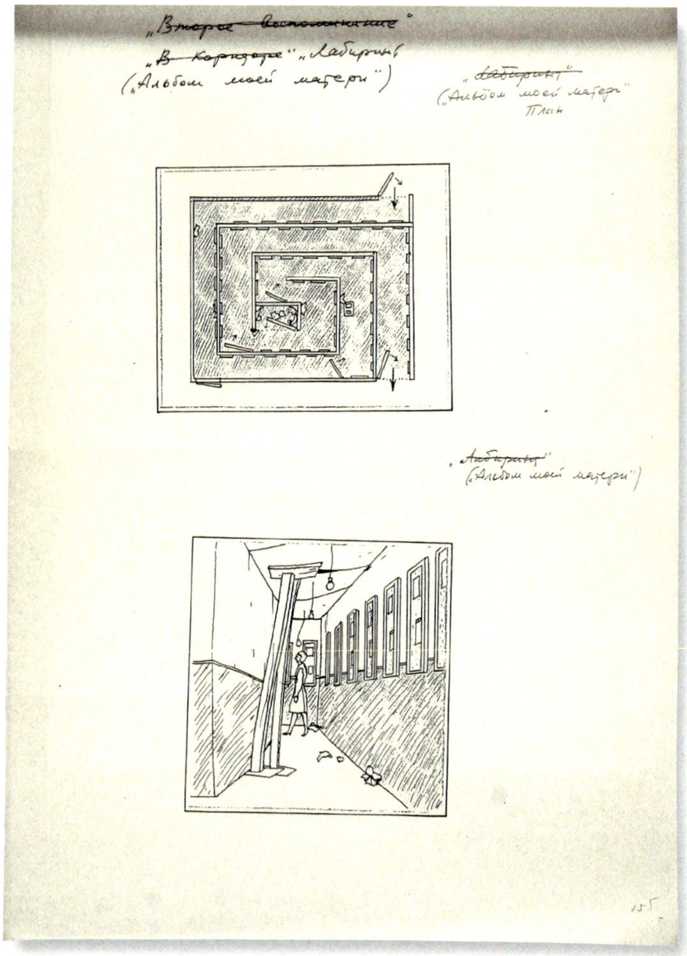
„Второе воспоминание"
„В коридоре" „Лабиринт"
(„Альбом моей матери")
„Лабиринт"
(„Альбом моей матери"
План
„Лабиринт"
(„Альбом моей матери")

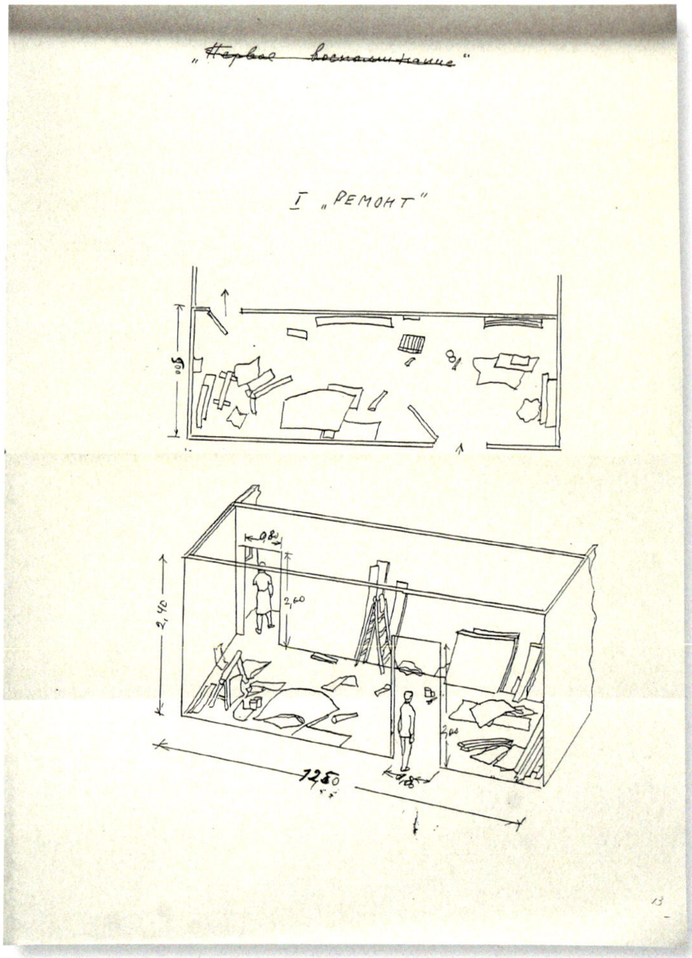
„Первое воспоминание"
I „РЕМОНТ"
2,40

41 Mental Institution or Institute of Creative Research

Das Irrenhaus oder Institut für kreative Forschung

1991

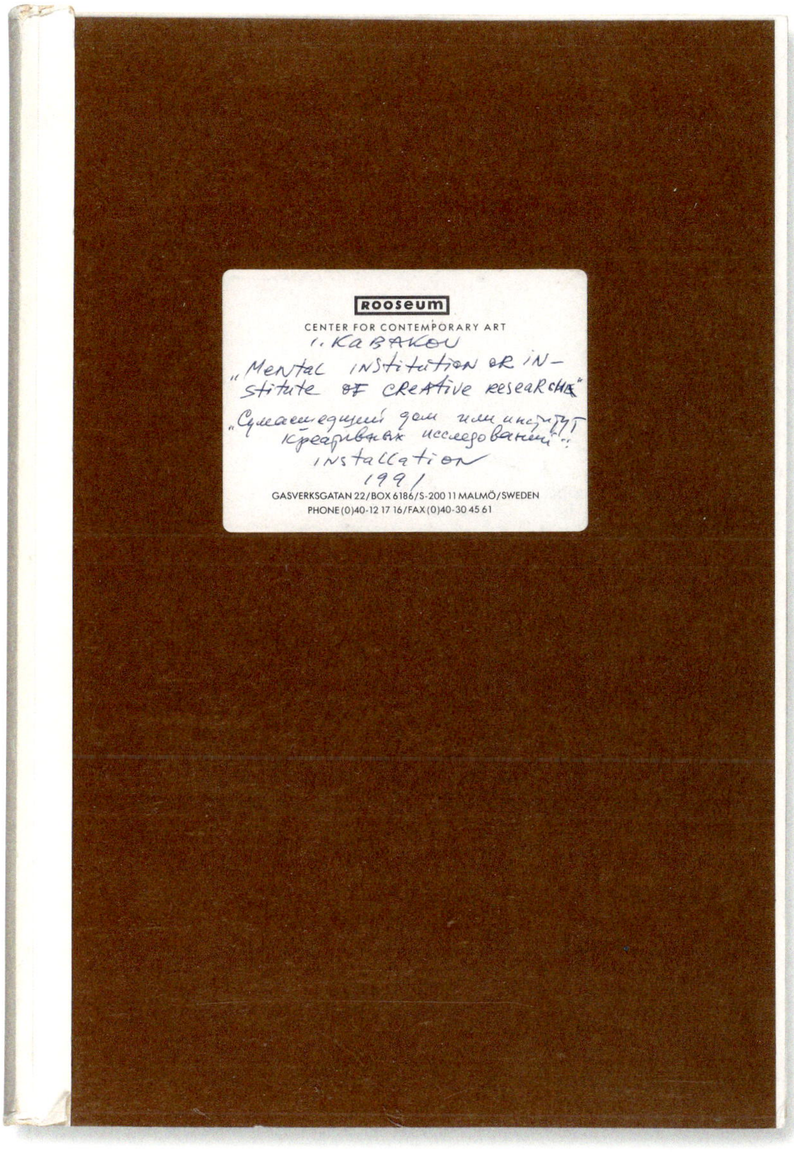

Rooseum, Center for Contemporary Art
Malmö: Rooseum, Center for Contemporary Art
29.8 x 21.2 cm
167 (partly double-sided) photocopied pp. with 68 b/w ills.
adhesive binding, plastic cover
Klebebindung, Plastikumschlag

exhibition catalogue | *Ausstellungskatalog*

layout by Ilya Kabakov | *Layout von Ilya Kabakov*

Documentation of the installation of the same name for the exhibition »Trans/Mission – Konst i interkulturell limbo«, Rooseum, Center for Contemporary Art, Malmö, August 27 to October 27, 1991. Texts by Ilya Kabakov; Russian, English, Swedish.

Dokumentation der gleichnamigen Installation für die Ausstellung »Trans/Mission – Konst i interkulturell limbo«, Rooseum, Center for Contemporary Art, Malmö, 27. August – 27. Oktober 1991. Texte von Ilya Kabakov; russisch, englisch, schwedisch.

see also | *siehe auch* no. 57; CRI, vol. 1, no. 50, pp. 330–335; CRP, vol. 1, no. 220, p. 290, nos. 222–224, pp. 292–294

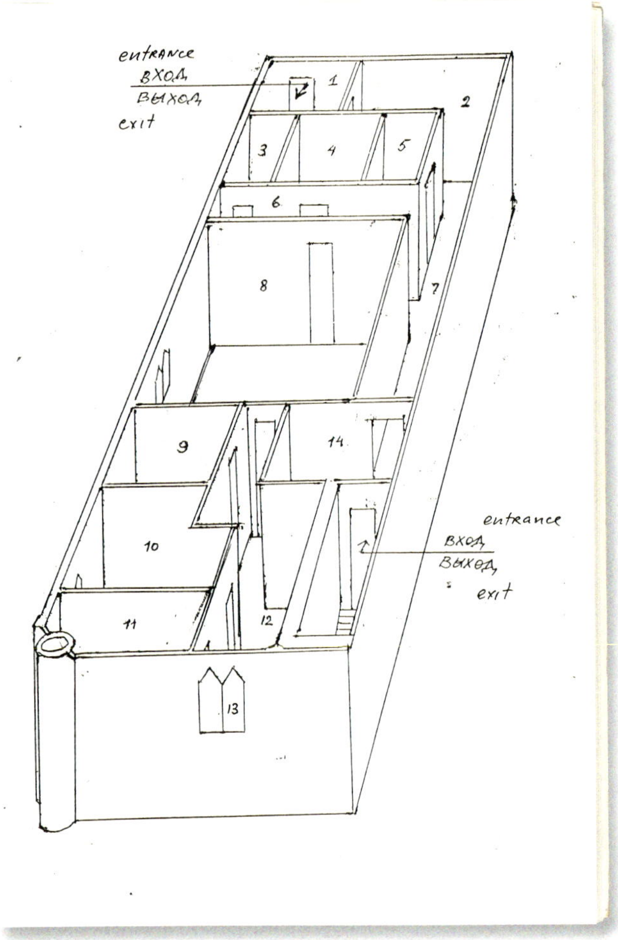
entrance
вход
выход
exit
entrance
вход
выход
exit

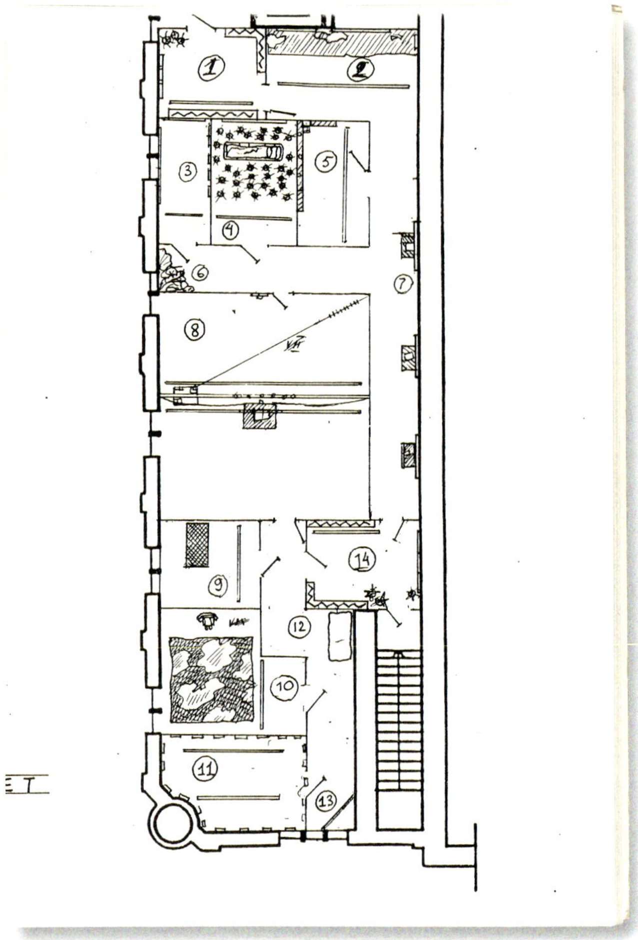

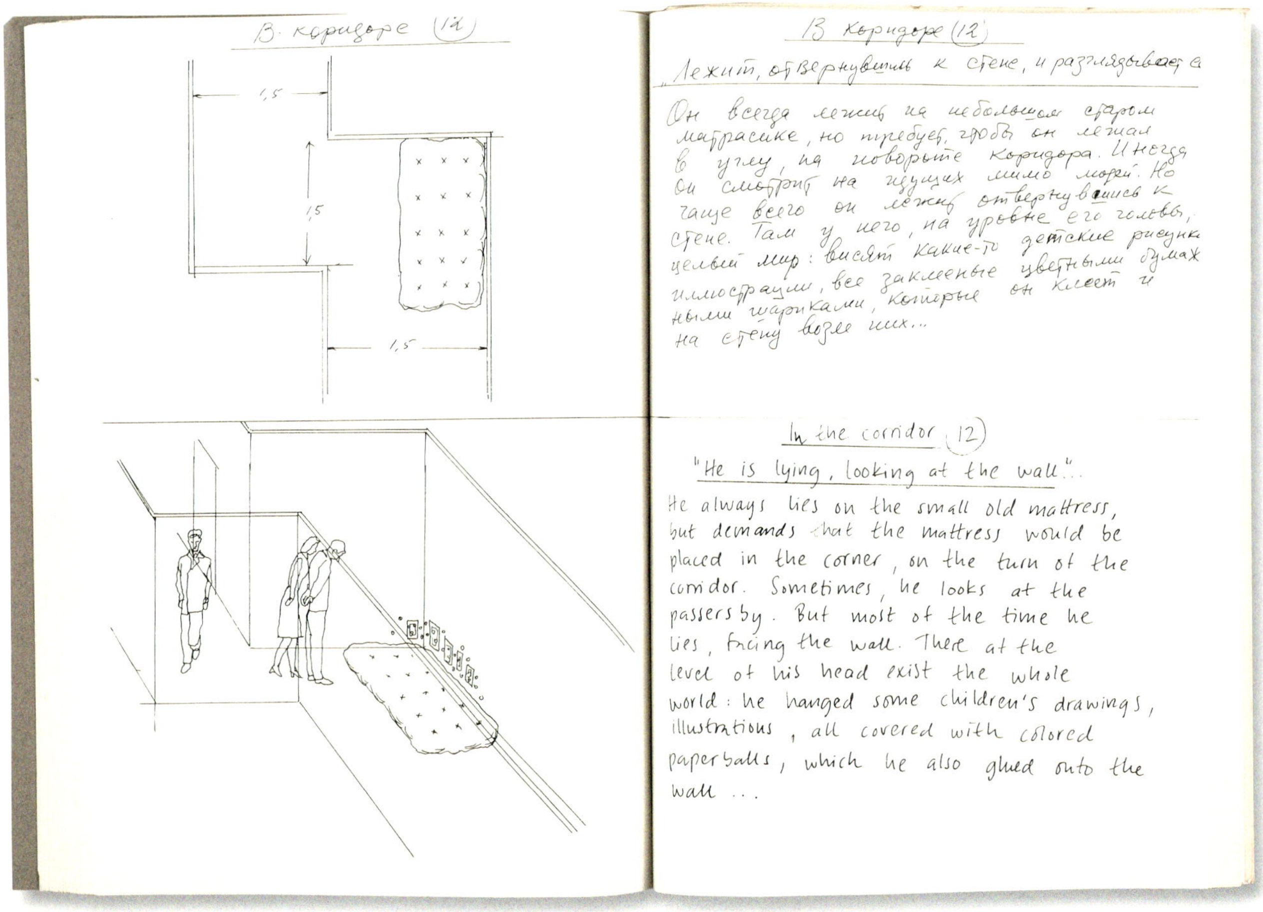
В коридоре (12)
В коридоре (12)
1,5
1,5
1,5
In the corridor (12)
"He is lying, looking at the wall"...
He always lies on the small old mattress, but demands that the mattress would be placed in the corner, on the turn of the corridor. Sometimes, he looks at the passers by. But most of the time he lies, facing the wall. There at the level of his head exist the whole world: he hanged some children's drawings, illustrations, all covered with colored paperballs, which he also glued onto the wall ...

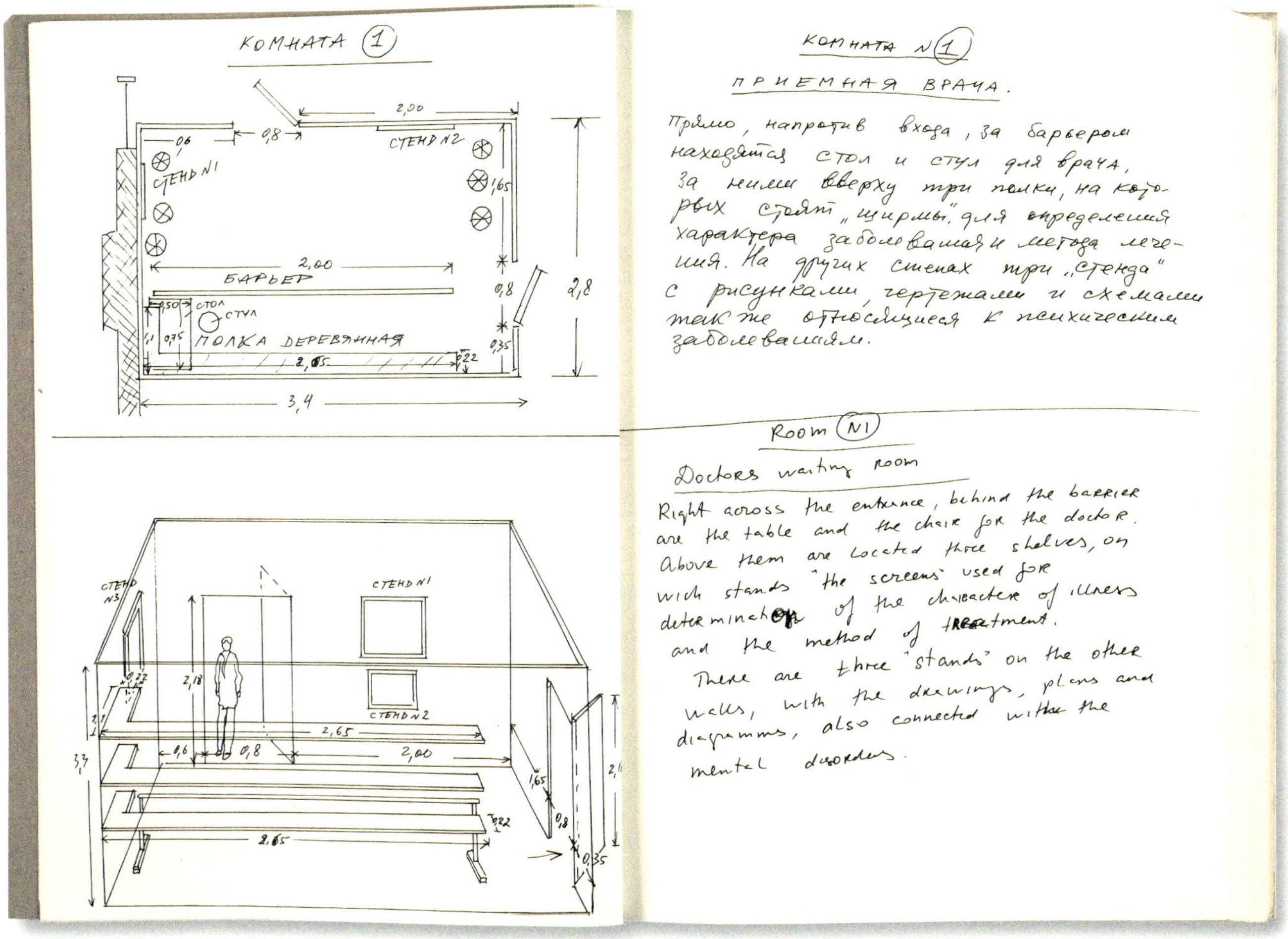

КОМНАТА N(1)

ПРИЕМНАЯ ВРАЧА.

Прямо, напротив входа, за барьером находятся стол и стул для врача, За ними вверху три полки, на которых стоят „ширмы" для определения характера заболевания и метода лечения. На других стенах три „стенда" с рисунками, чертежами и схемами так же относящиеся к психическим заболеваниям.

Room (N1)

Doctors waiting room

Right across the entrance, behind the barrier are the table and the chair for the doctor. Above them are located three shelves, on wich stands "the screens" used for determination of the character of illness and the method of treatment.

There are three "stands" on the other walls, with the drawings, plans and diagramms, also connected with the mental disorders.

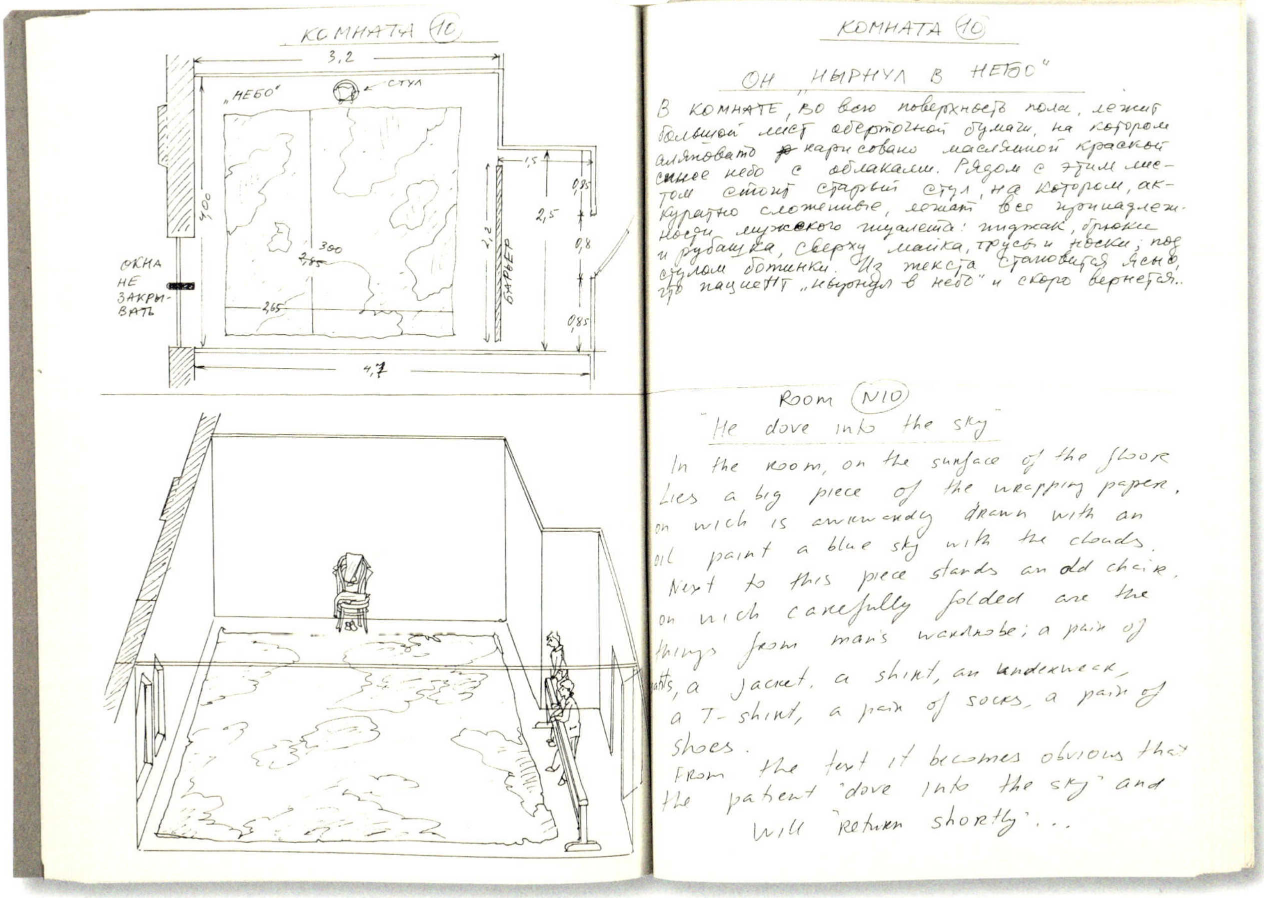

КОМНАТА (10)

ОН „НЫРНУЛ В НЕБО"

В КОМНАТЕ, во всю поверхность пола, лежит большой лист обёрточной бумаги, на котором аляповато нарисовано масляной краской синее небо с облаками. Рядом с этим листом стоит старый стул, на котором, аккуратно сложенные, лежат все принадлежности мужского туалета: пиджак, брюки и рубашка, сверху майка, трусы и носки; под стулом ботинки. Из текста становится ясно, что пациент „нырнул в небо" и скоро вернется..

Room (N10)

"He dove into the sky"

In the room, on the surface of the floor lies a big piece of the wrapping paper, on wich is awkwardy drawn with an oil paint a blue sky with the clouds. Next to this piece stands an old chair, on wich carefully folded are the things from man's wardrobe; a pair of pants, a jacket, a shirt, an underwear, a T-shirt, a pair of socks, a pair of shoes.

From the text it becomes obvious that the patient "dove into the sky" and will "return shortly"...

42 52 Dialogues in the Communal Kitchen | *52 Dialoge in der Gemeinschaftsküche*

1991

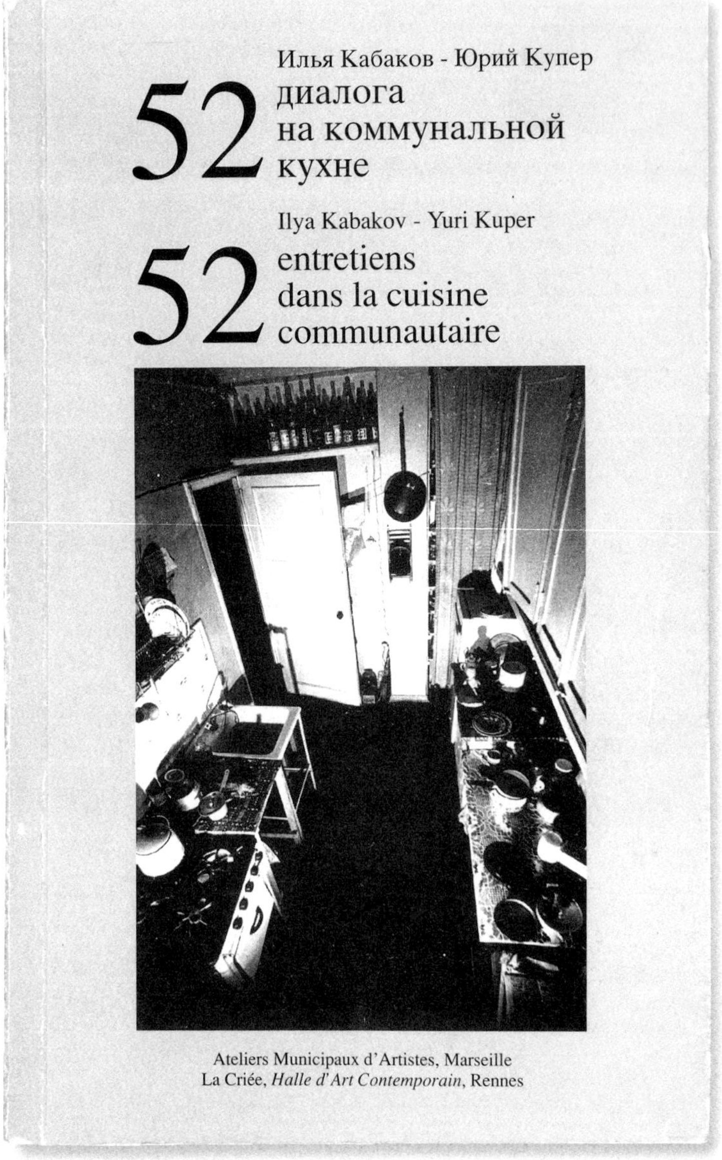

Ateliers Municipaux d'Artistes, Marseille; La Criée, Halle d'Art Contemporain, Rennes Marseille/Rennes: Ateliers Municipaux d'Artistes, La Criée, Halle d'Art Contemporain
20 x 12.5 cm
405 pp. with 53 b/w ills.
adhesive binding, softback with flaps
Klebebindung, broschiert mit Umschlagsklappe

exhibition catalogue | *Ausstellungskatalog*

layout by Ilya Kabakov | *Layout von Ilya Kabakov*

For the installation of the same name at the Ateliers Municipaux d'Artistes, Marseille, December 20, 1991 to January 25, 1992 and at La Criée, Halle d'Art Contemporain, Rennes, July 4 to September 26, 1992. Dialogues between Ilya Kabakov and Yuri Kuper; Russian, French.

Zur gleichnamigen Installation, Ateliers Municipaux d'Artistes, Marseille, 20. Dezember 1991 – 25. Januar 1992 und La Criée, Halle d'Art Contemporain, Rennes, 4. Juli – 26. September 1992. Dialoge von Ilya Kabakov und Yuri Kuper; russisch, französisch.

see also | *siehe auch* CRI, vol. 1, no. 55, pp. 360–365

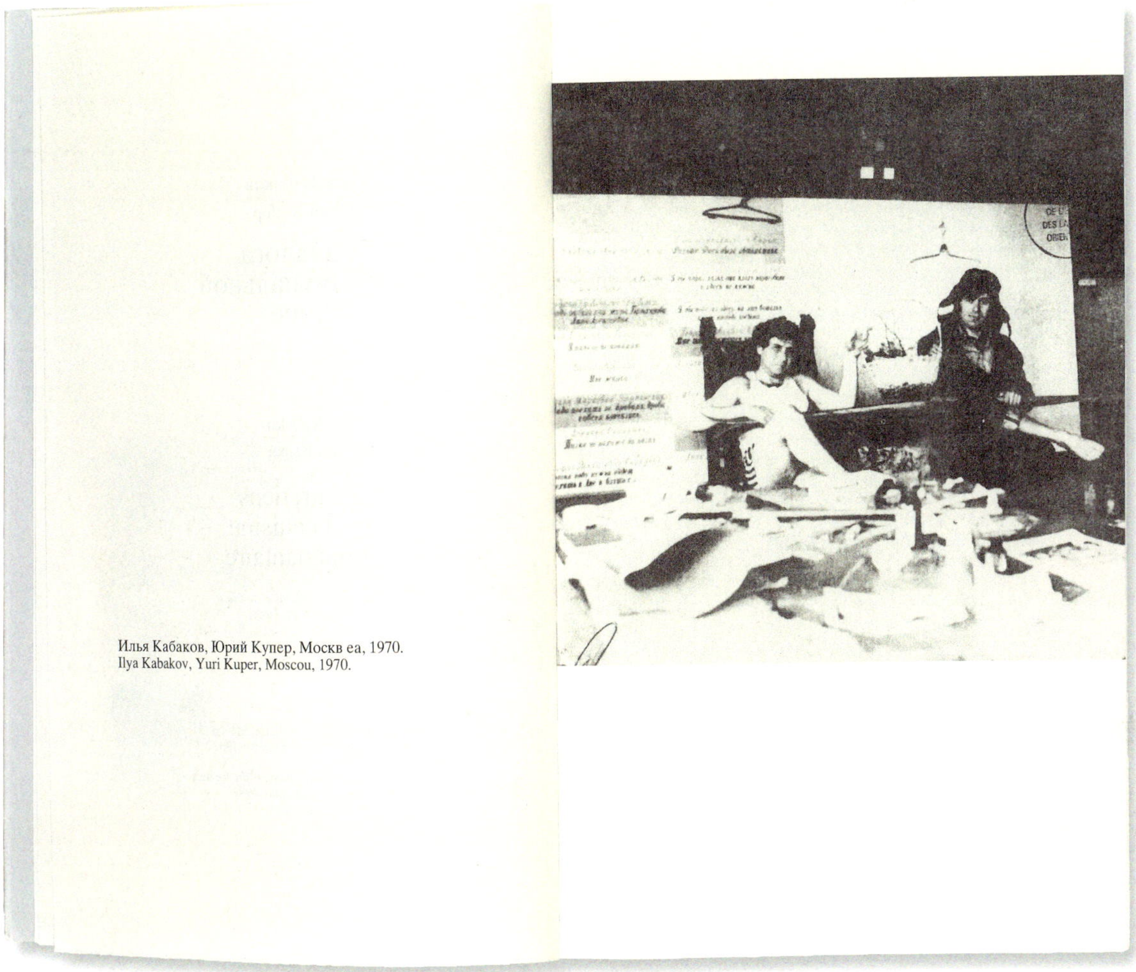
Илья Кабаков, Юрий Купер, Москв еа, 1970.
Ilya Kabakov, Yuri Kuper, Moscou, 1970.

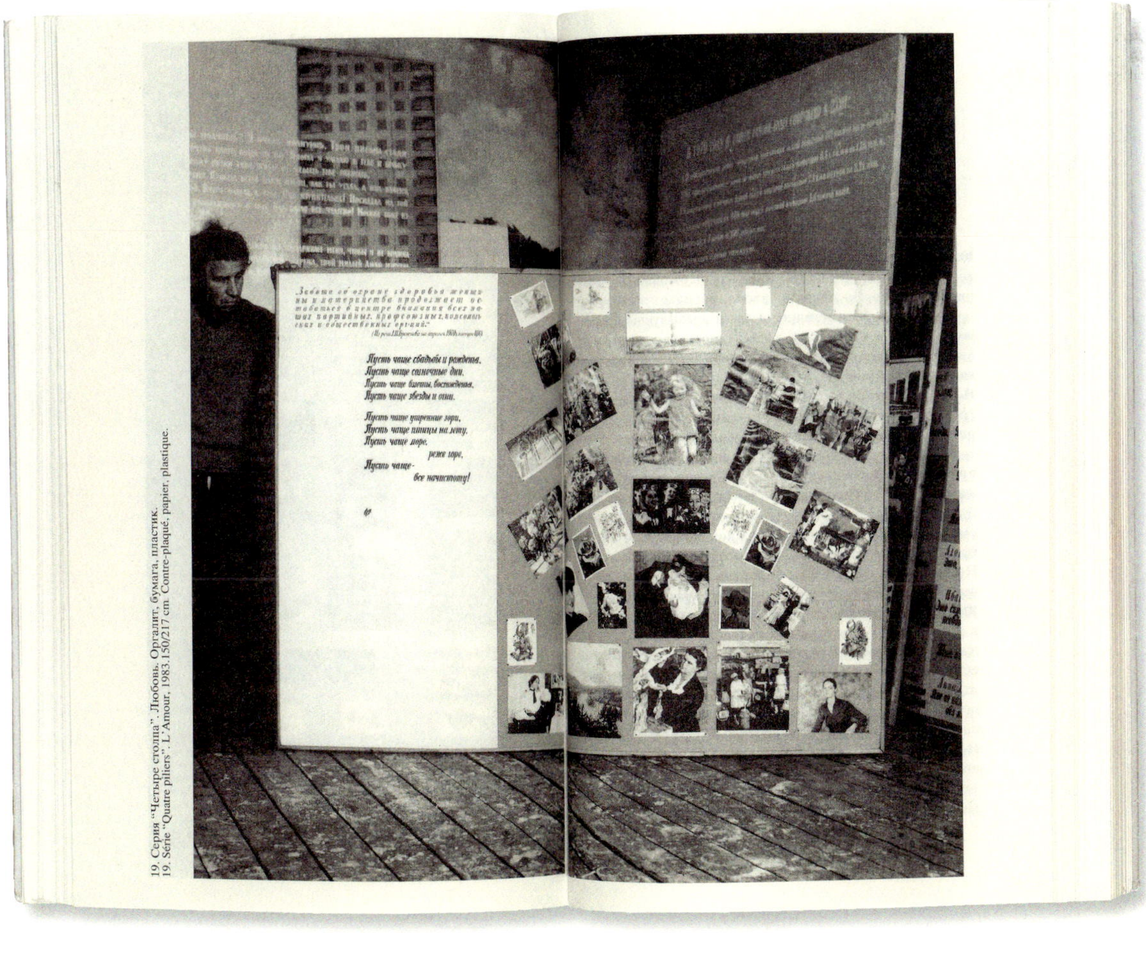
19. Серия "Четыре столпа". Любовь. Оргалит, бумага, пластик.
19. Série "Quatre piliers". L'Amour, 1983.150/217 cm Contre-plaqué, papier, plastique.

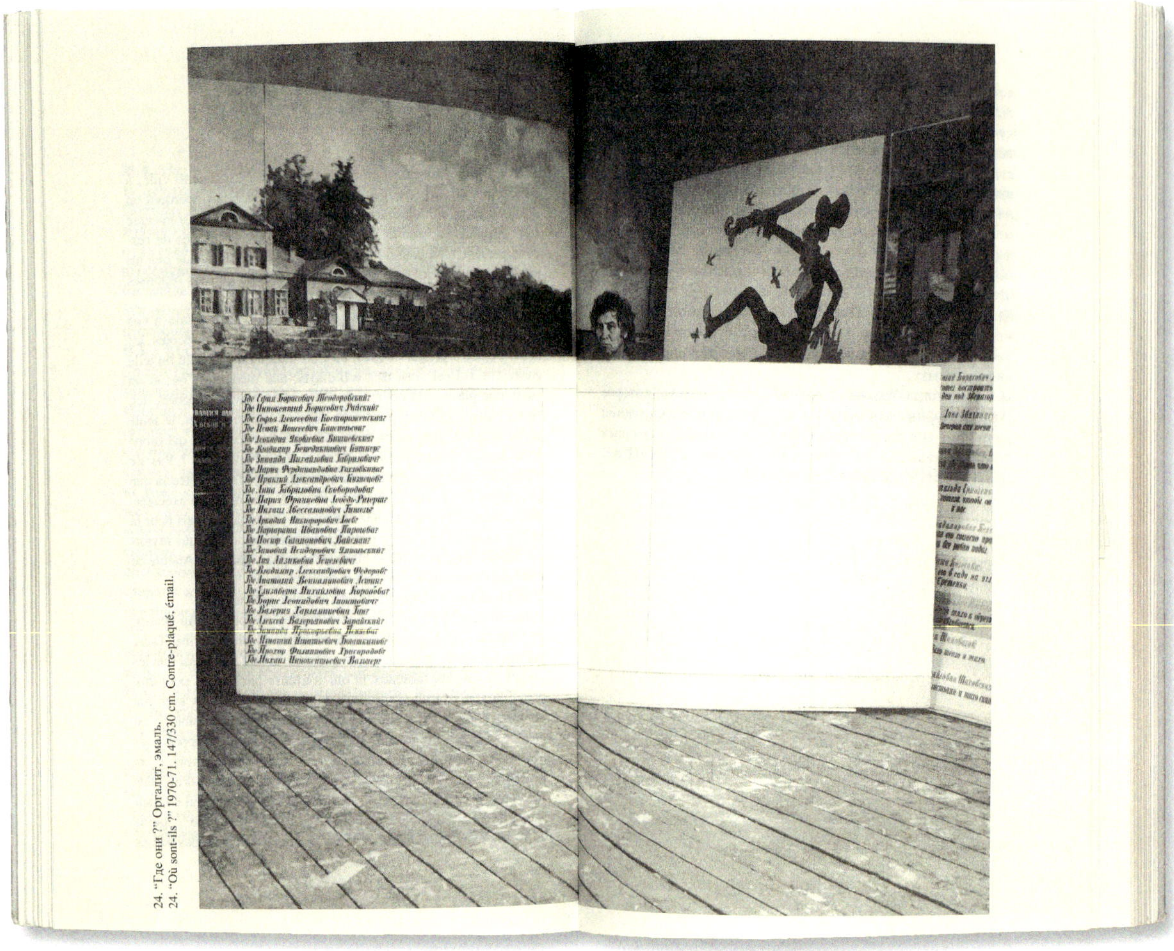
24. "Где они ?" Оргалит, эмаль.
24. "Où sont-ils ?" 1970-71. 147/330 cm. Contre-plaqué, émail.

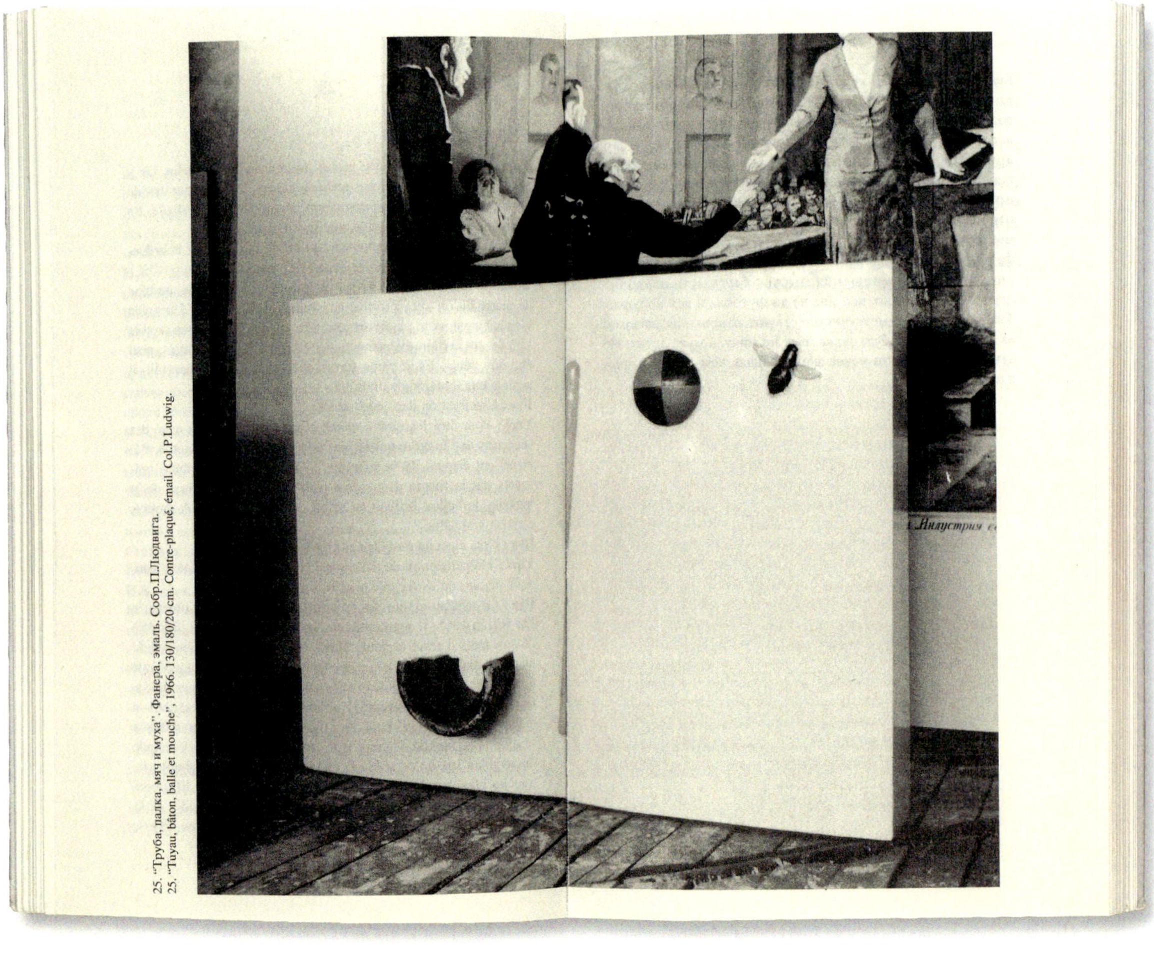
25. "Труба, палка, мяч и муха". Фанера, эмаль. Собр.П.Людвига.
25. "Tuyau, bâton, balle et mouche", 1966. 130/180/20 cm. Contre-plaqué, émail. Col.P.Ludwig.

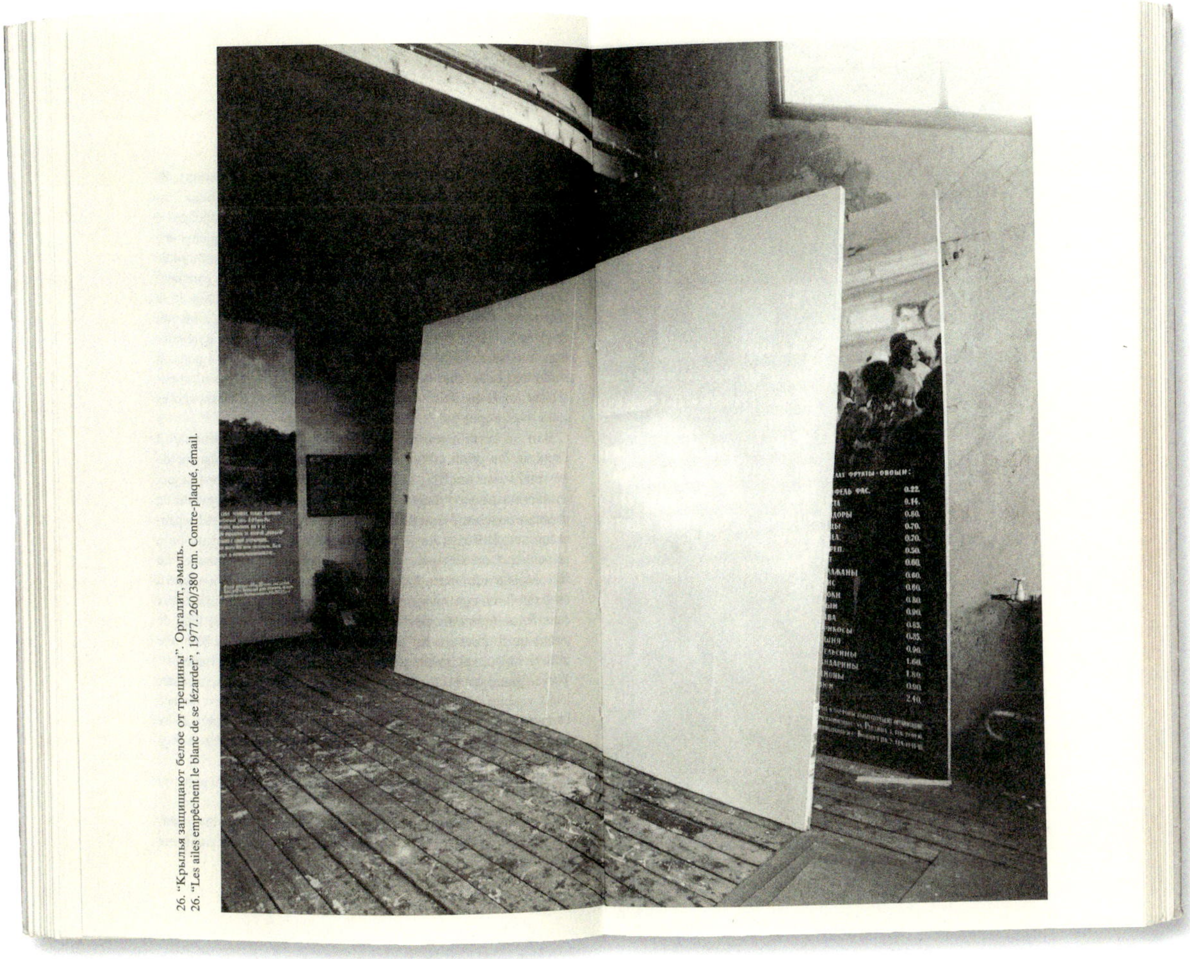
26. "Крылья защищают белое от трещины". Оргалит, эмаль.
26. "Les ailes empêchent le blanc de se lézarder", 1977. 260/380 cm. Contre-plaqué, émail.

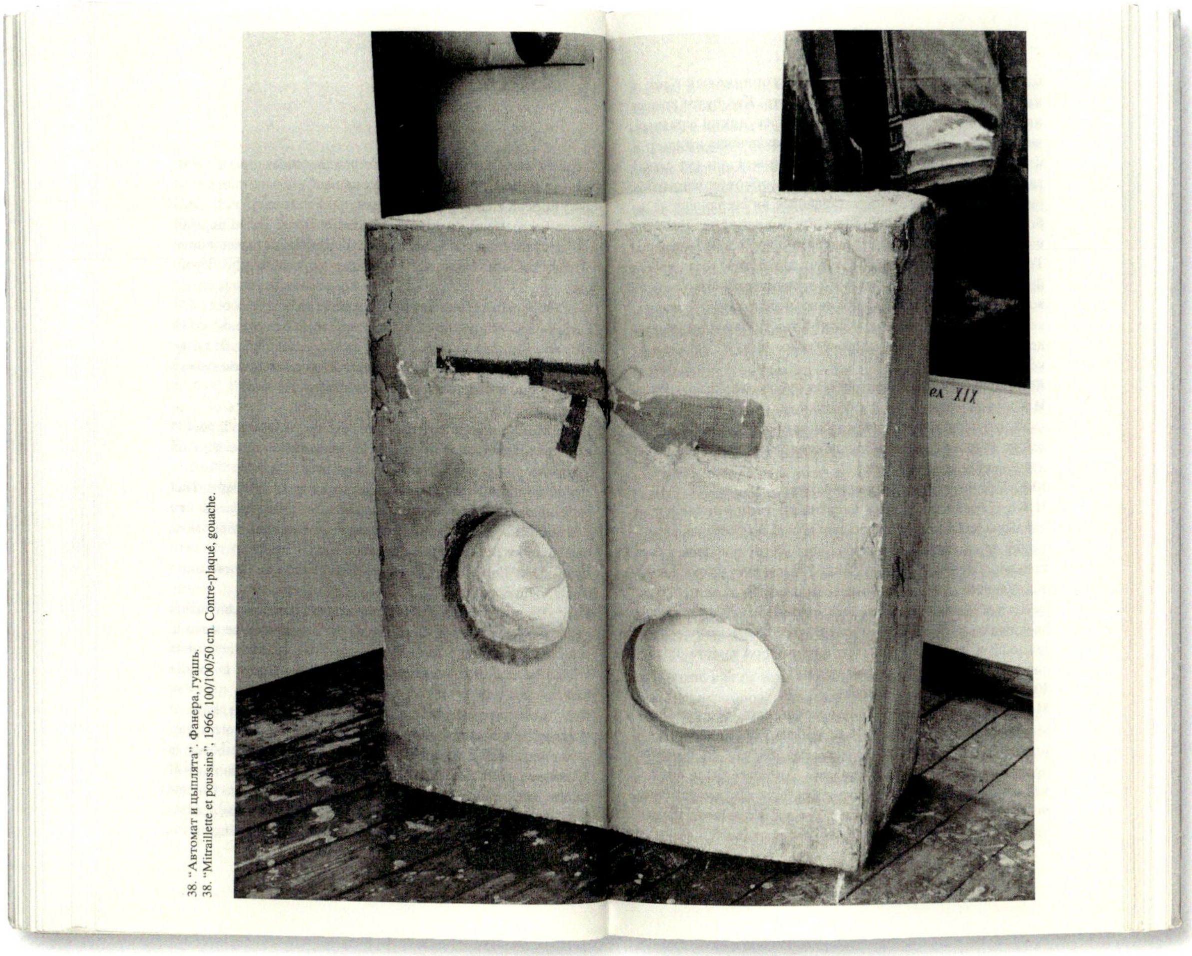
38. "Автомат и цыплята". Фанера, гуашь.
38. "Mitraillette et poussins", 1966. 100/100/50 cm. Contre-plaqué, gouache.

43 The Ant | *Die Ameise*

1991

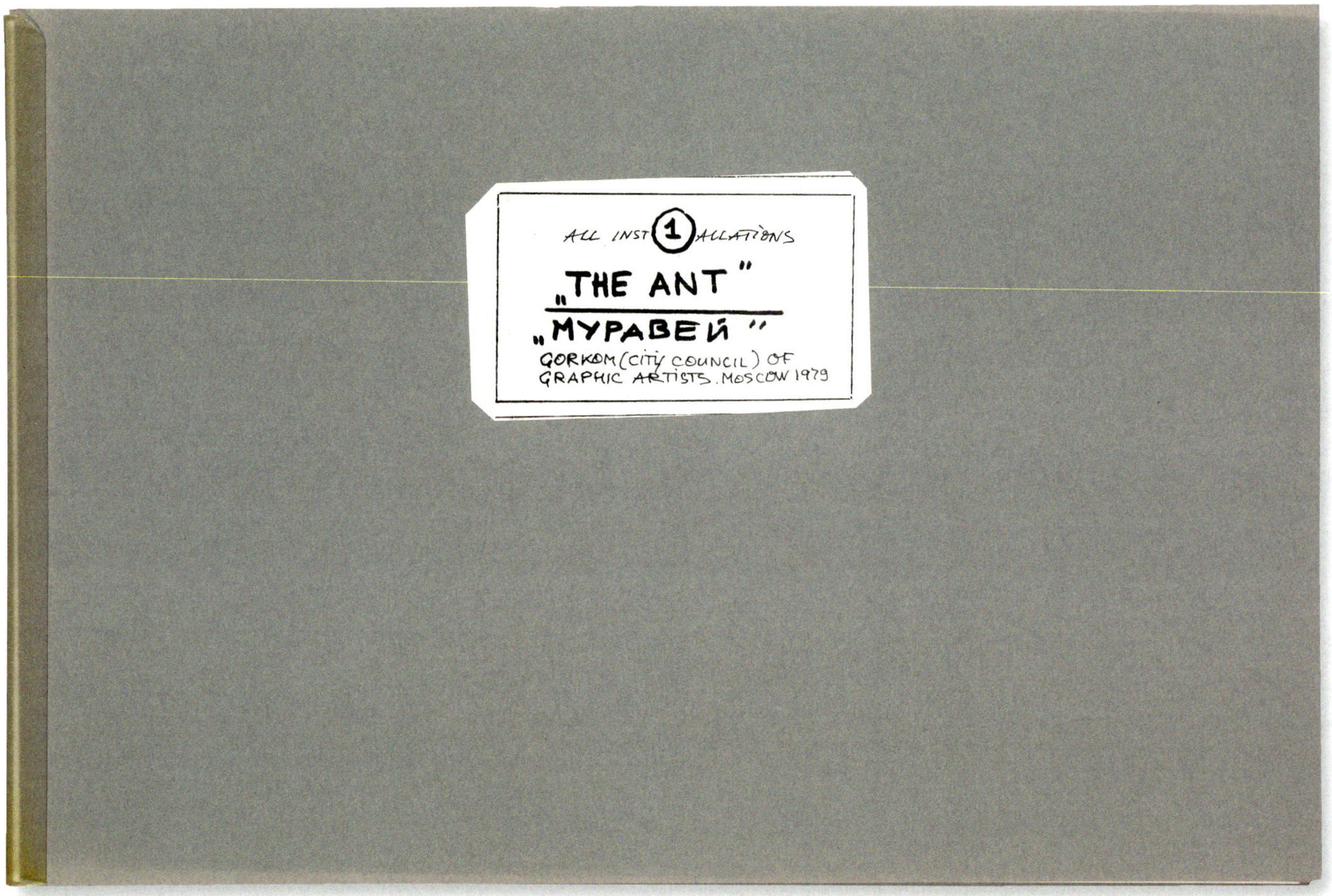

Ilya Kabakov
New York: published by the author
27.9 x 43.3 cm
14 photocopied pp. with 8 (3 color) ills. quick bind, cardboard cover, label on the cover
Schnellhefter, Kartonumschlag, Etikette auf dem Umschlag
edition: 7 copies

thematic publication | *thematische Publikation*

layout by Ilya Kabakov | *Layout von Ilya Kabakov*

For the installation of the same name for the exhibition »Vystavka grafiki« at Obédinjennyj Komitet Hudojnikov – Grafikov, GORKOM, City Council of Graphic Artists, Moscow, May 5 to 25, 1983. The text by Ilya Kabakov on »The Ant« was also published in the book »Life of Flies«, 1992; Russian, English.

Zur gleichnamigen Installation für die Ausstellung »Vystavka grafiki«, Obédinjennyj Komitet Hudojnikov – Grafikov, GORKOM, City Council of Graphic Artists, Moskau, 5. – 25. Mai 1983. Der Text von Ilya Kabakov über »Die Ameise« erschien auch im Buch »Das Leben der Fliegen«, 1992; russisch, englisch.

see also | *siehe auch* no. 44; no. 50; CRI, vol. 1, no. 1, pp. 50–53

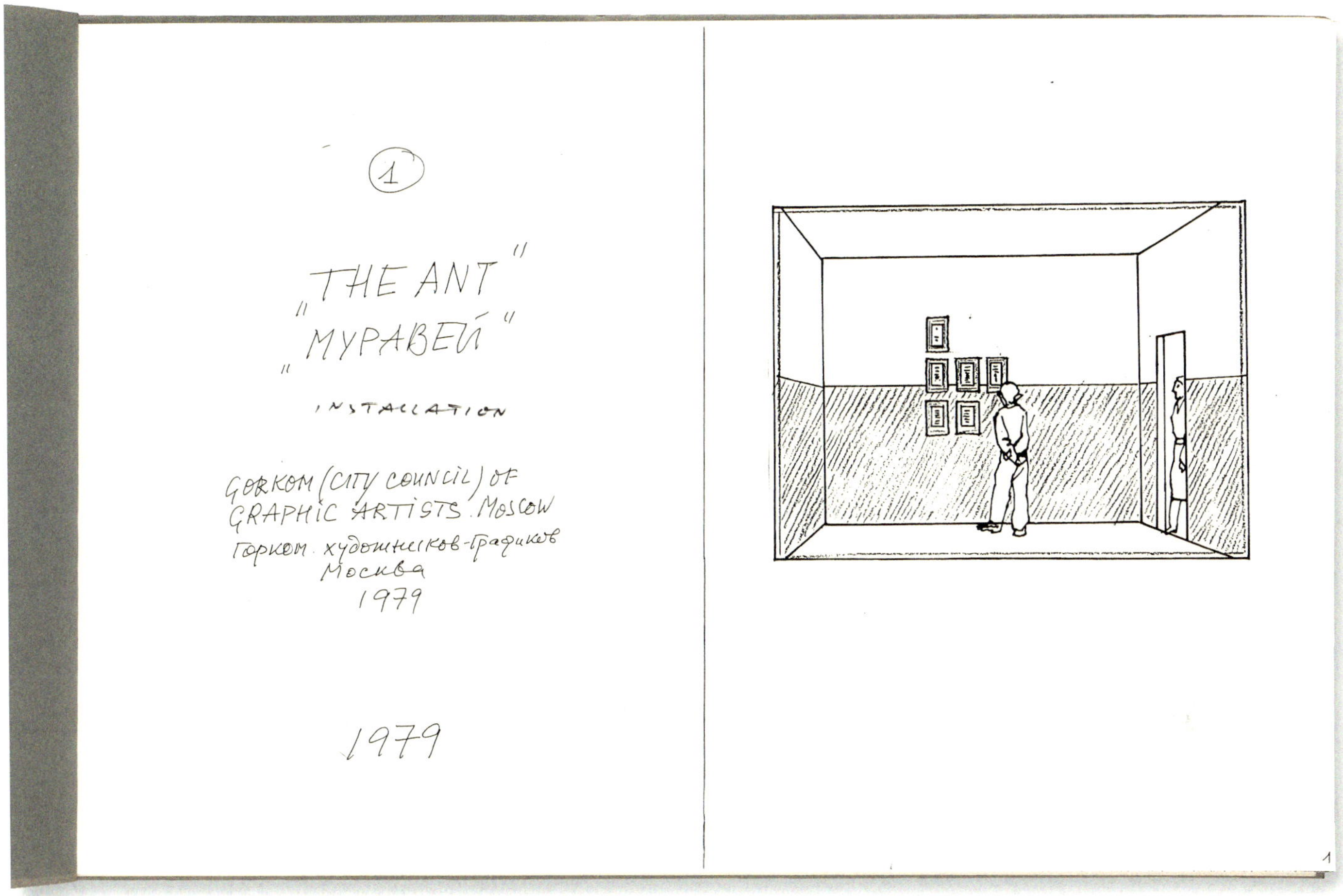
1
„THE ANT"
„МУРАВЕЙ"
INSTALLATION
GORKOM (CITY COUNCIL) OF
GRAPHIC ARTISTS. MOSCOW
Горком художников-графиков
Москва
1979
1979
1

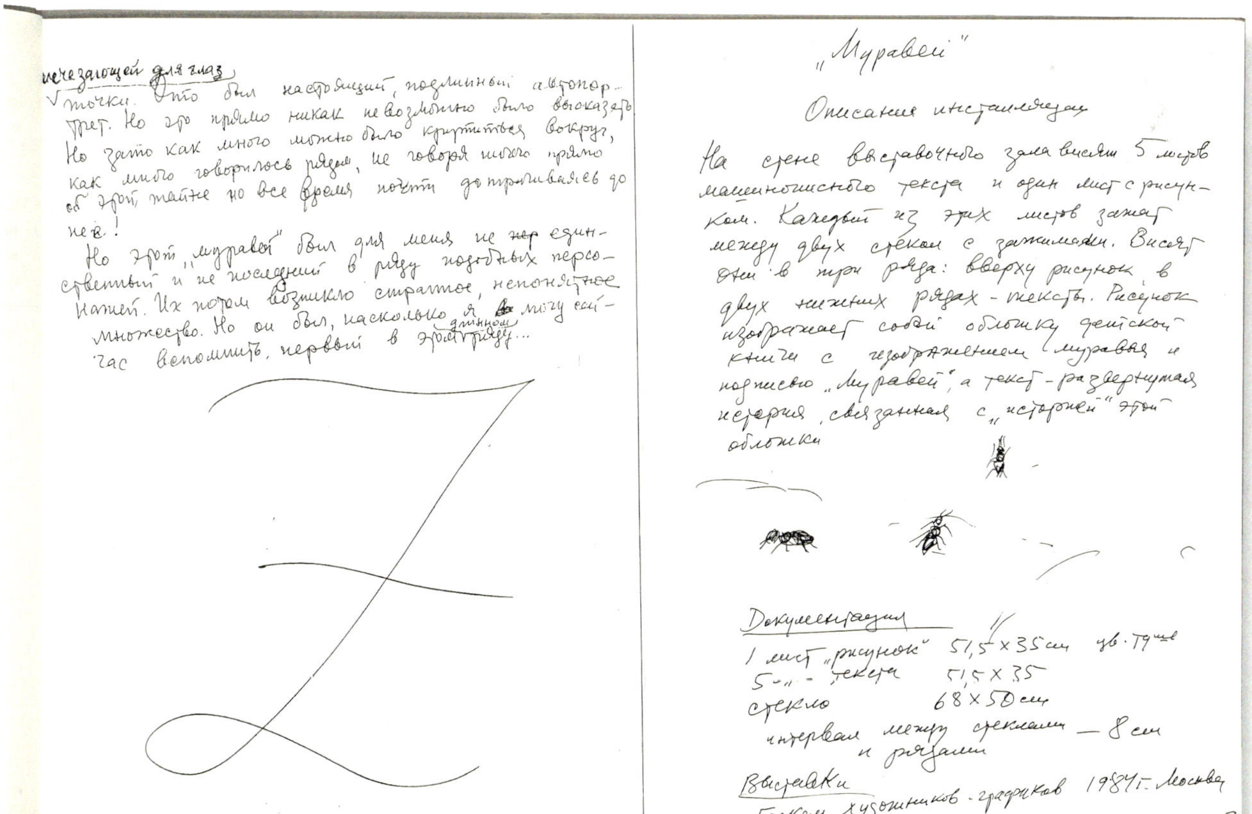
исчезающей для глаз точки. Это был настоящий, подлинный автопортрет. Но его прямо никак невозможно было высказать. Но зато как много можно было крутиться вокруг, как много говорилось рядом, не говоря ничего прямо об этой тайне но все время почти дотрагиваясь до нее!
Но этот „муравей" был для меня не единственный и не последний в ряду подобных персонажей. Их потом возникло странное, непонятное множество. Но он был, насколько я могу сейчас вспомнить, первый в этом длинном ряду...
„Муравей"
Описание инсталляции
На стене выставочного зала висят 5 листов машинописного текста и один лист с рисунком. Каждый из этих листов зажат между двух стекол с зажимами. Висят они в три ряда: вверху рисунок, в двух нижних рядах – тексты. Рисунок изображает собой обложку детской книги с изображением муравья и подписью „Муравей", а текст – развернутая история, связанная с „историей" этой обложки
Документация
1 лист „рисунок" 51,5 × 35 см цв. туш
5 –„– „текста" 51,5 × 35
стекло 68 × 50 см
интервал между стеклами и рядами — 8 см
Выставки
Горком художников-графиков 1984 г. Москва
7

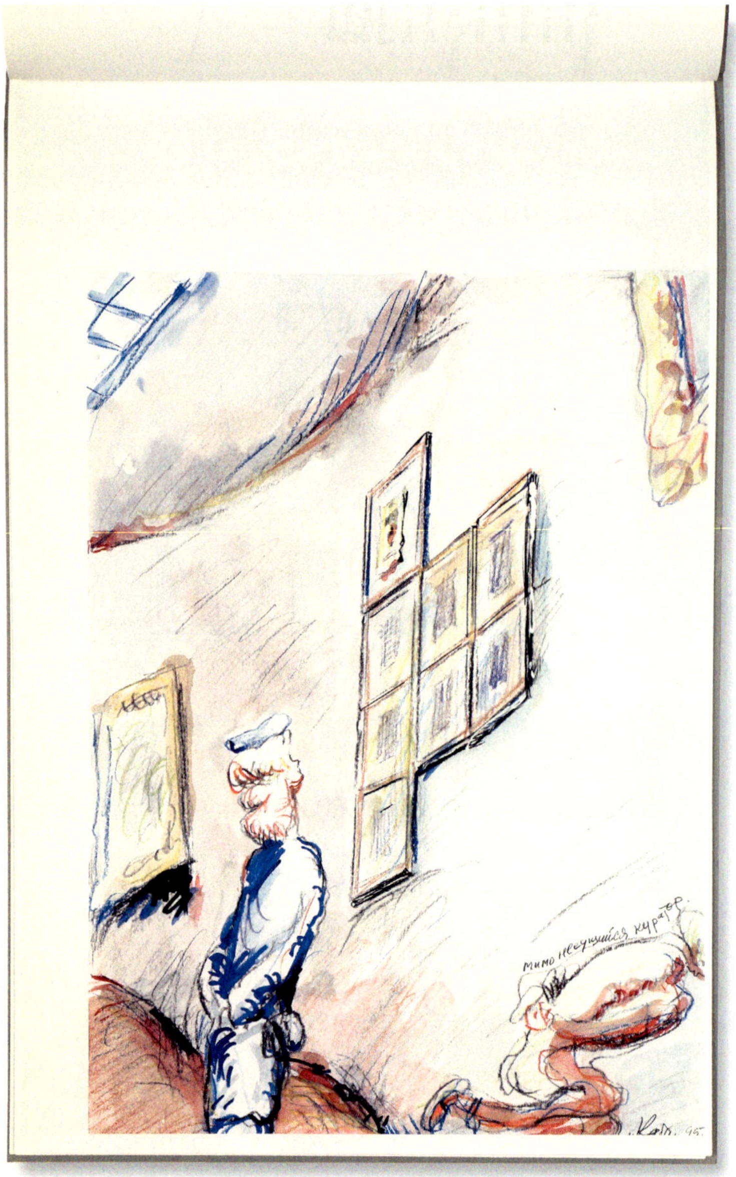
мимо несущийся куратор.
Кол. 95

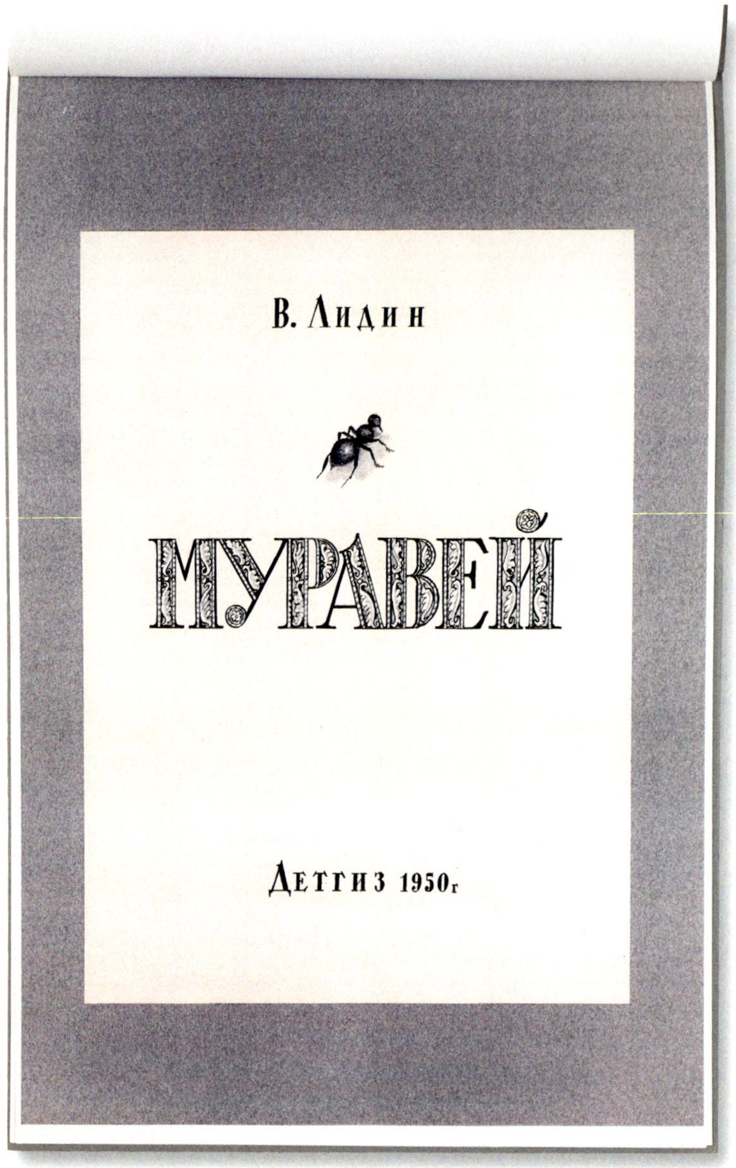
В. Лидин
МУРАВЕЙ
Детгиз 1950г

44 The Ant | *Die Ameise*

1991

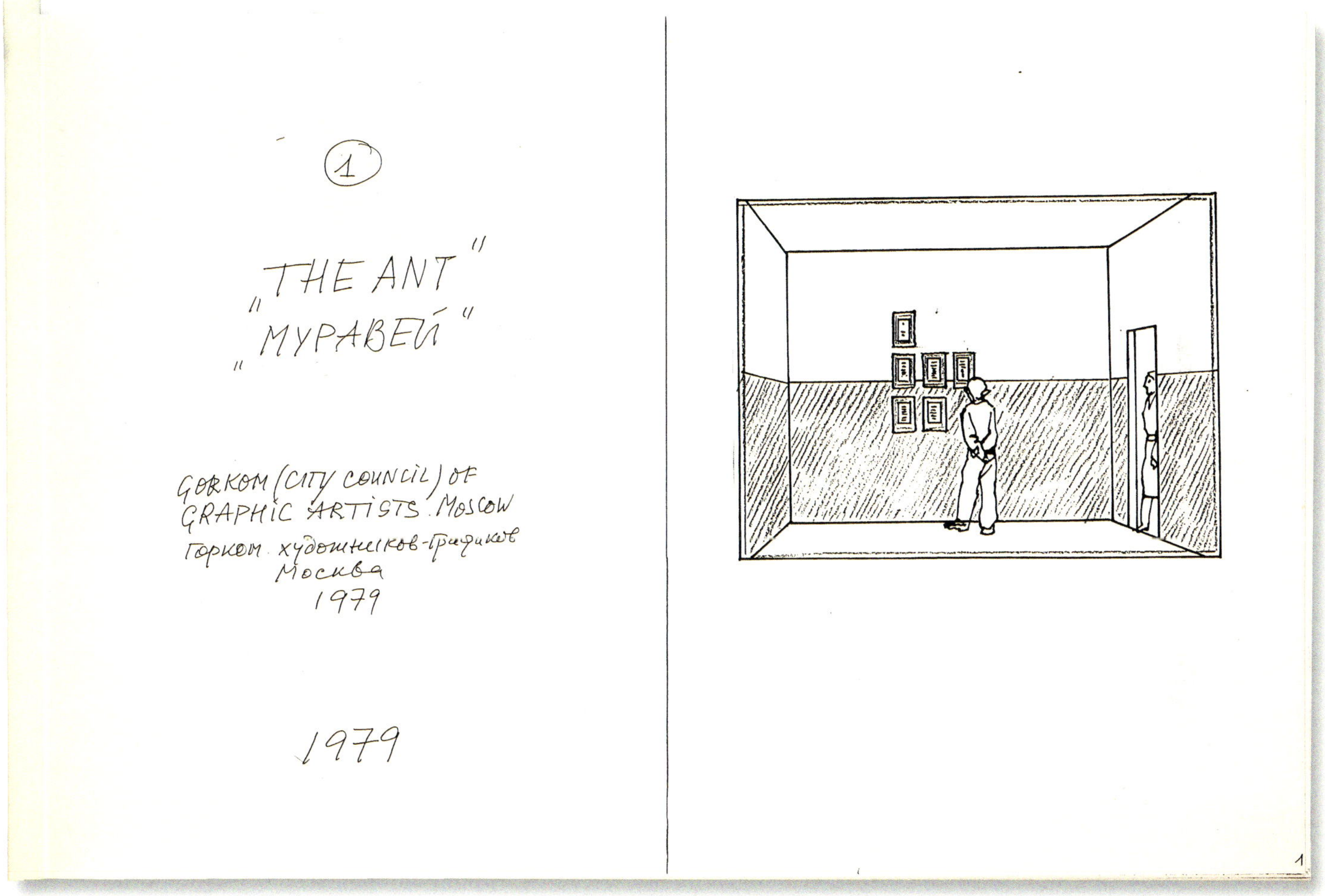

Ilya Kabakov
New York: published by the author
27.9 x 43.3 cm
11 photocopied pp. with 5 b/w ills.
quick bind
Schnellhefter
edition: 2 copies

thematic publication | *thematische Publikation*

layout by Ilya Kabakov | *Layout von Ilya Kabakov*

For the installation of the same name for the exhibition »Vystavka grafiki« at Obédinjennyj Komitet Hudojnikov – Grafikov, GORKOM, City Council of Graphic Artists, Moscow, May 5 to 25, 1983. The text by Ilya Kabakov on »The Ant« was also published in the book »Life of Flies«, 1992; Russian, English.

Zur gleichnamigen Installation für die Ausstellung »Vystavka grafiki«, Obédinjennyj Komitet Hudojnikov – Grafikov, GORKOM, City Council of Graphic Artists, Moskau, 5. – 25. Mai 1983. Der Text von Ilya Kabakov über »Die Ameise« erschien auch im Buch »Das Leben der Fliegen«, 1992; russisch, englisch.

see also | *siehe auch* no. 43; no. 50; CRI, vol. 1, no. 1, pp. 50–53

этого муравья. Возможно, он был тем для нас, чем была китайская картина, развернутая и повешенная по случаю прихода гостей. Но там был один лишь вечер, а здесь? Муравей был отправной точкой для наших бесконечных импровизаций на протяжении целого лета и многих таких лет подряд...

Может быть, причиной была лишь наша молодость и тот избыток сил, которому был достаточен лишь повод, чтобы?...

Возможно. Но дело было, конечно, и в самом МУРАВЬЕ. Много раз я спрашивал потом себя, возможен был бы "эффект муравья" (так мы его называли), если бы висела перед нами репродукция Венеры Джорджоне, или, в нижнем ярусе шкалы - фотографии какого-нибудь стакана или блюдца?

Никогда.

"Эффект муравья" был возможен потому, что само графические это изделие находилось, по-моему, в середине, если можно так сказать, шкалы от стакана внизу до Джорджоне на самом верху ее. Но можно еще точнее. Наш МУРАВЕЙ находился у той самой черты, у той грани, где нехудожественный продукт может, способен перейти в художественный, но... никогда перейти не может.

И нам наглядно было это усилие при взгляде на муравья, котором мы как бы помогали своим воображением это сделать, подобно тому, как мы наблюдаем взлет прыгуна, который собирается перелететь через планку и который каждый раз задевает ее, и она летит вниз. И вот это-то внутреннее "подсаживание", которое невольно делает зритель на стадионе, и держало нас постоянно в нервном напряжении

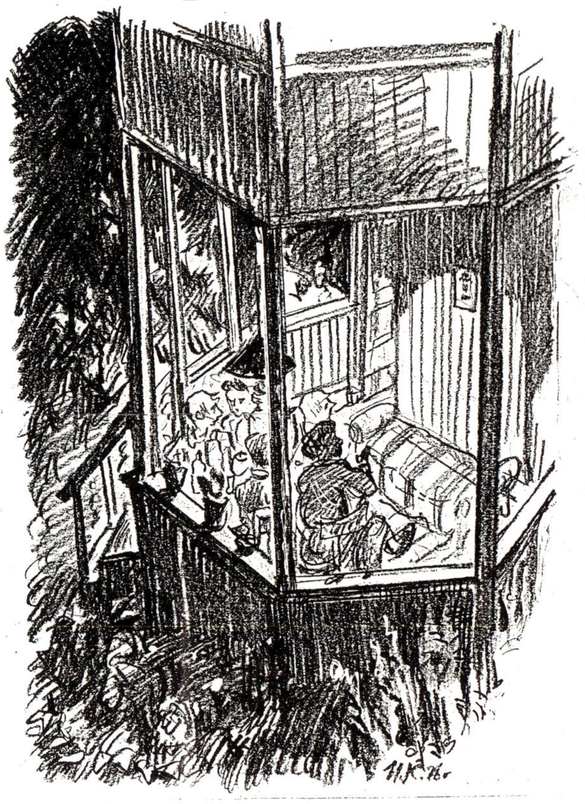

9

45 A Rope – A Life | *Das Seil – Das Leben*

1991

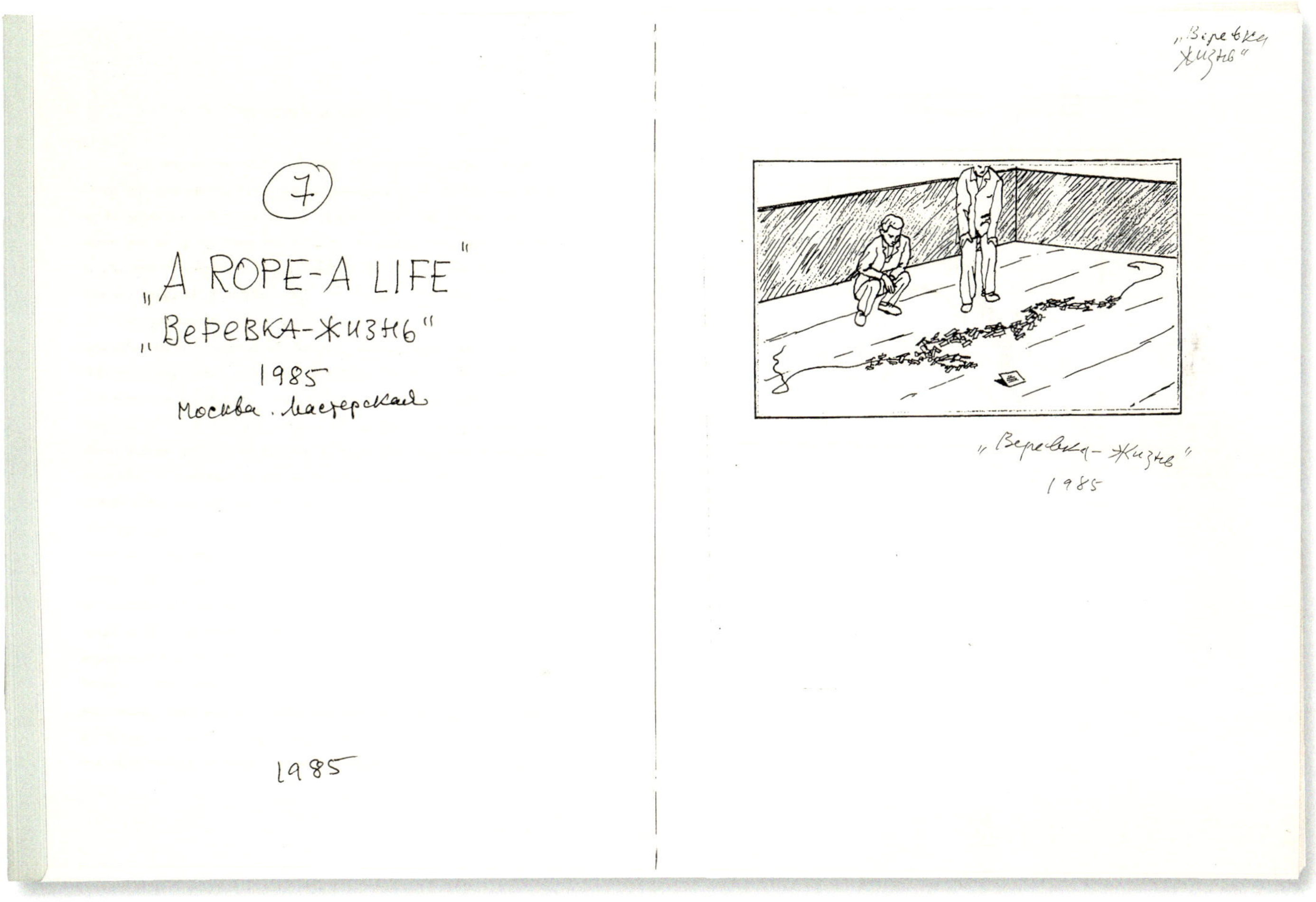

Ilya Kabakov
New York: published by the author
27.9 x 43.3 cm
12 photocopied pp. with 7 b/w ills.
quick bind
Schnellhefter
edition: 19 copies

thematic publication | *thematische Publikation*

layout by Ilya Kabakov | *Layout von Ilya Kabakov*

Documentation of the installation of the same name, which was created for the first time in 1985 in Kabakov's studio in Moscow and has been exhibited since 1995 in the collection of the Museum für Moderne Kunst, Frankfurt am Main under the name »The Rope of Life«. Text by Ilya Kabakov; Russian, English.

Dokumentation der gleichnamigen Installation, die 1985 erstmals in Kabakovs Atelier in Moskau realisiert wurde und sich als »Das Seil des Lebens« seit 1995 in der Sammlung des Museum für Moderne Kunst, Frankfurt am Main befindet. Text von Ilya Kabakov; russisch, englisch.

see also | *siehe auch* no. 30; no. 31; no. 81; CRI, vol. 1, no. 7, pp. 82–87

Autumn 1957

Painting in the room. The masterpiece. White walls. Six square meters.

Winter 1957

The boredom of the Moscow visits.

Summer 1958

The voyage on the South river. Erik, Oleg, Michael. The wood jam on the river. The complete happiness.

Summer 1958

Decided to get married. Mother leaves for Berdiansk alone.

Autumn 1958

We live on Mlikova street. Three in one room with my mother-in-law. Painting there my masterpiece.

Winter 1958

Renting a room for work (as a studio) in Sviblovo with M. Ignatiev. Painting my masterpiece.

Spring 1959

The journey to Svanetia. Erik, Oleg, Michael. Erik saved all of us from falling to the abyss.

Summer 1959

The slavery for mother-in-law. The summer house in Valentinovka. The shopping bags with food. 8 books a year.

Spring 1960

The room with a heavy desk on Novoslobodskaya. The series "The Shower". Leonard didn't see it.

Spring 1960

In Detgiz meet Ulo. We decide to rent a studio.

August 7, 1960

Galia is born.

Autumn 1960

Bought a house in Berdiansk for mother for 2.800 rubles. By the sea in Liskach.

Autumn 1960

Together with Ulo and Oleg, we rent a basement - dark and damp- on Taganka. Grnia sleeps over on his books.

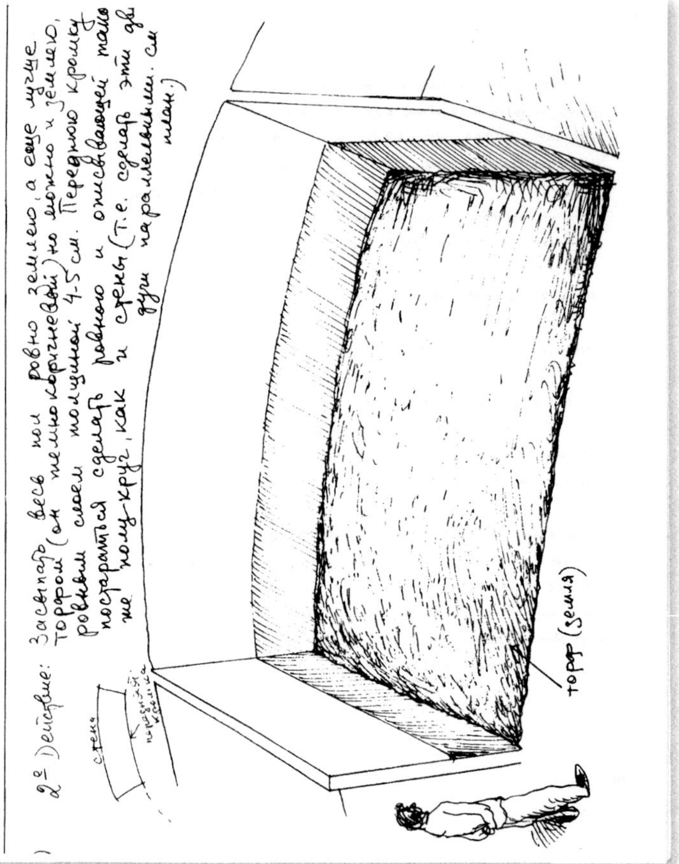

"ВЕРЕВКА-ЖИЗНЬ"

Одно из самых увлекательных занятий и состояний: еще жить, но как бы и не жить, не участвовать во всей этой жизни, во всех ее перипетиях, а жить уже как бы "потом" и видеть всю эту свою жизнь как бы со стороны, с какой-то высоты даже и, если возможно, уже как бы и прожитую. Жить как бы уже будучи мертвым. Быть мертвым (странное и желанное сочетание). И возможно, это одно из самых легких, чудных состояний: безо всяких чувств, без боли, усталости и неизвестности впереди - все видеть, парить надо всем и, самое важное, - быть избавленным от неизвестной и длительной своей жизни, в которой ты ни в чем не уверен, где ты не знаешь: действуешь ли ты по своей воле или что-то само с тобой происходит по чьей-то указке. А уже мертвый, ты видишь свою жизнь целиком, можешь свободно перелетать от начала к концу и обратно, подобно какому-то легкому беззвучному летающему аппарату, устремляющемуся то к истоку реки, то к ее устью; могущему зависнуть над любой точкой этой реки, спуститься - ниже, ниже, совсем низко к окну какого-нибудь дома на берегу этой реки и заглянуть в окно... Вдруг вновь подняться вверх и быстро помчаться вдоль изгибов ее берегов... Вдоль реки, по которой плыву я реальный, не зная и страшась того, что окажется за следующим поворотом, испытывая постоянный страх перевернуться на скользком бревне, на котором я сижу всю свою жизнь; ничего не понимая ни в себе, ни вокруг себя, ни в проплывающем мимо ландшафте, задыхаясь от ужаса и боясь опрокинуться с головой в холодную воду...

И все же, как это "путешествие" вдоль жизни выглядит сверху, из легкого воздушного пространства? Не похожа ли она хотя бы отчасти на длинный шнур, лежащий на полу, со многими изгибами, петлями и поворотами? А составившие ее события? Не кажутся ли они грязными мусорными остатками, привязанными к ней, одинаковыми в своей неразличимости?

И, быть может, этот наблюдатель еще и потому плывет и движется вдоль этой жизни вперед и назад, что самому эту веревку-жизнь кто-то специально разложил на полу перед ним для его обозрения, но пройдет срок, и, собрав веревку и мусор в единый ком, в спутанный узел, засунут в небольшой мешок и отнесут, положат куда-то... А что же наблюдатель? Куда отправится он? Что станет с ним? Невозможно ничего об этом сказать - ведь, сказать по правде, и сам он был только потому, что была эта веревка, с ней он только и был связан и как же он без нее, когда ее возьмут, положат в пакет и унесут неизвестно куда?..

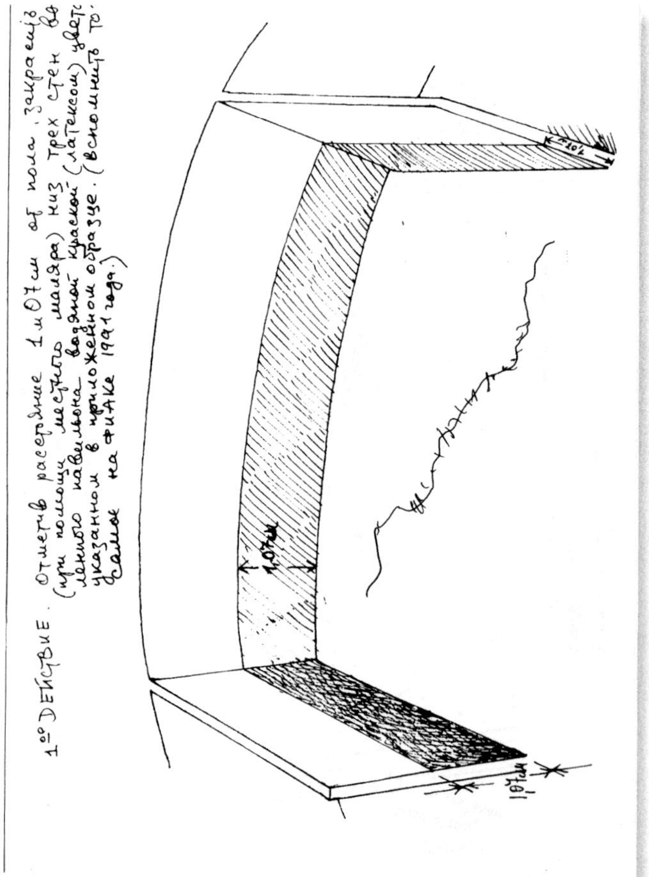

utumn 1960

m renting a room from "general's widow". Drawing some images on aper.

inter 1960

aking money for "living" and for "co-op". Books in Detgiz and Malish.

inter 1960

he baby. The carriage. The boredom of going out for a walk with the aby. In the evening I am making books. Two, three without stopping.

inter 1961

m making drawings in the basement. Ulo across from me is making aintings. At the chair's leg the white mushroom is growing.

pring 1961

omething gets out of me to the paper.

utumn 1961

he journey to mother's house.

ummer 1961

e rent a house in Valentinovka. The heat and the shopping bags with ood.

ummer 1963

t Erik's summer house. The oil landshaft from the upper terrace.

inter 1963

oving to a different basement, across from Majakovsky museum. x-apartment.

utumn 1963

he Manyesz exposition.

inter 1964

ross country skiing around Moscow. Spending night in the snow around he camp fire.

ummer 1963

he journey to Germany, to Saxony. The forest, the castles.

utumn 1966

oving to the third basement on Taganka, deep and small.

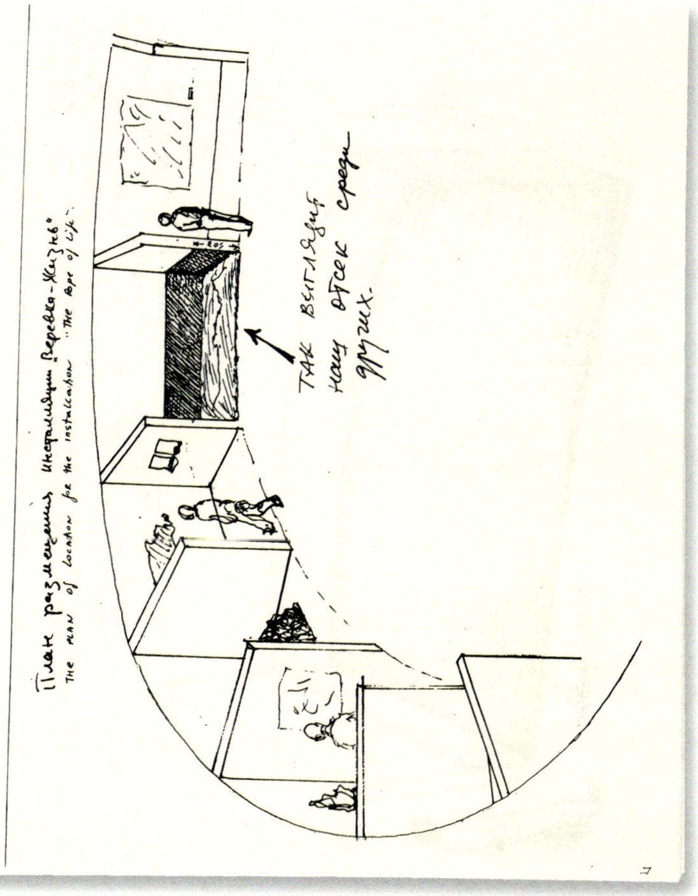

46 Rope Along the Edge | *Das Seil am Rand entlang*

1991

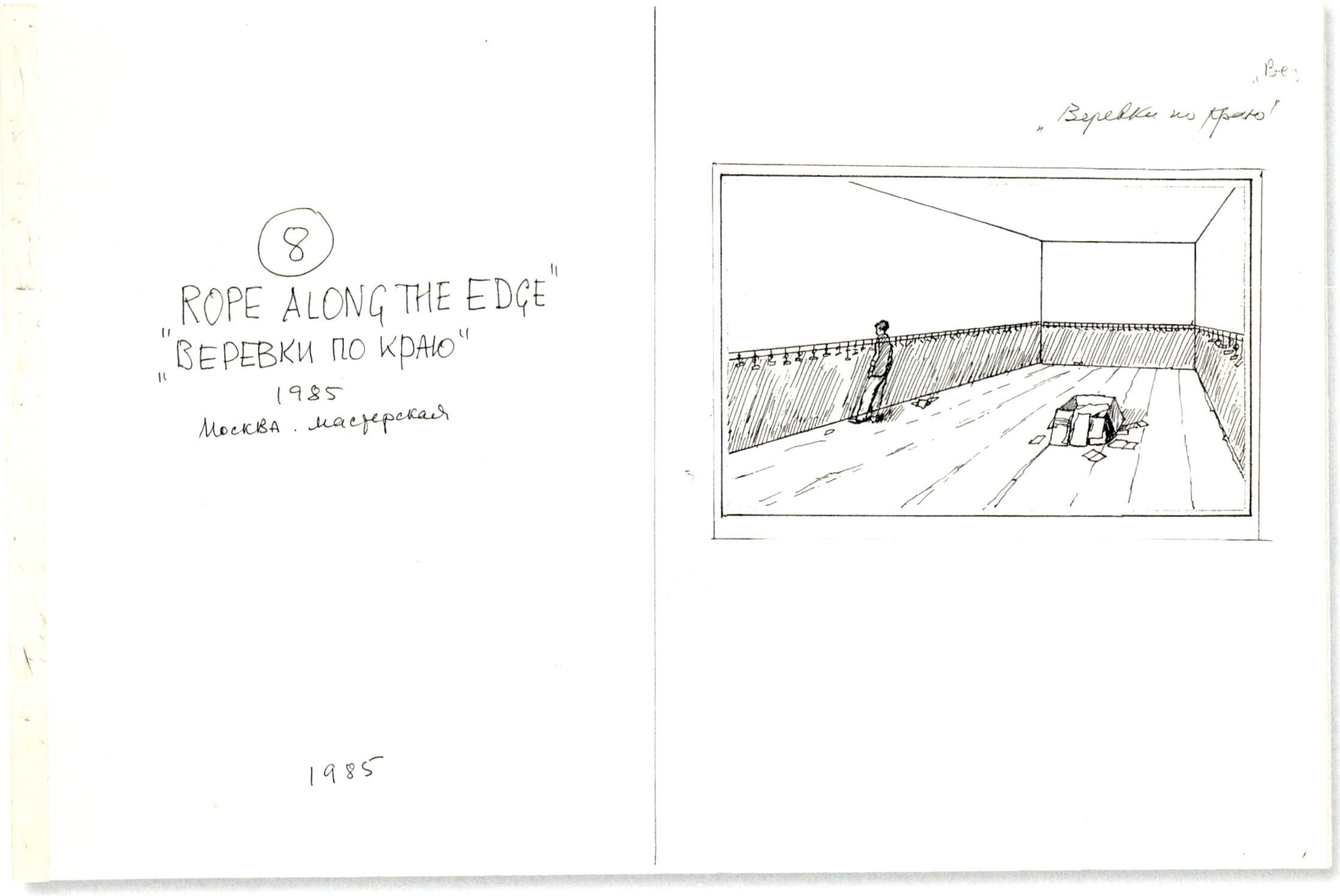

Ilya Kabakov
New York: published by the author
28 x 43.4 cm
12 photocopied pp. with 4 b/w ills.
quick bind
Schnellhefter
edition: 19 copies

thematic publication | *thematische Publikation*

layout by Ilya Kabakov | *Layout von Ilya Kabakov*

For the installation of the same name in Kabakov's studio in Moscow in 1985. Text by Ilya Kabakov; Russian, English.

Zur gleichnamigen Installation in Kabakovs Atelier in Moskau 1985. Text von Ilya Kabakov; russisch, englisch.

see also | *siehe auch* CRI, vol. 1, no. 8, pp. 88–93

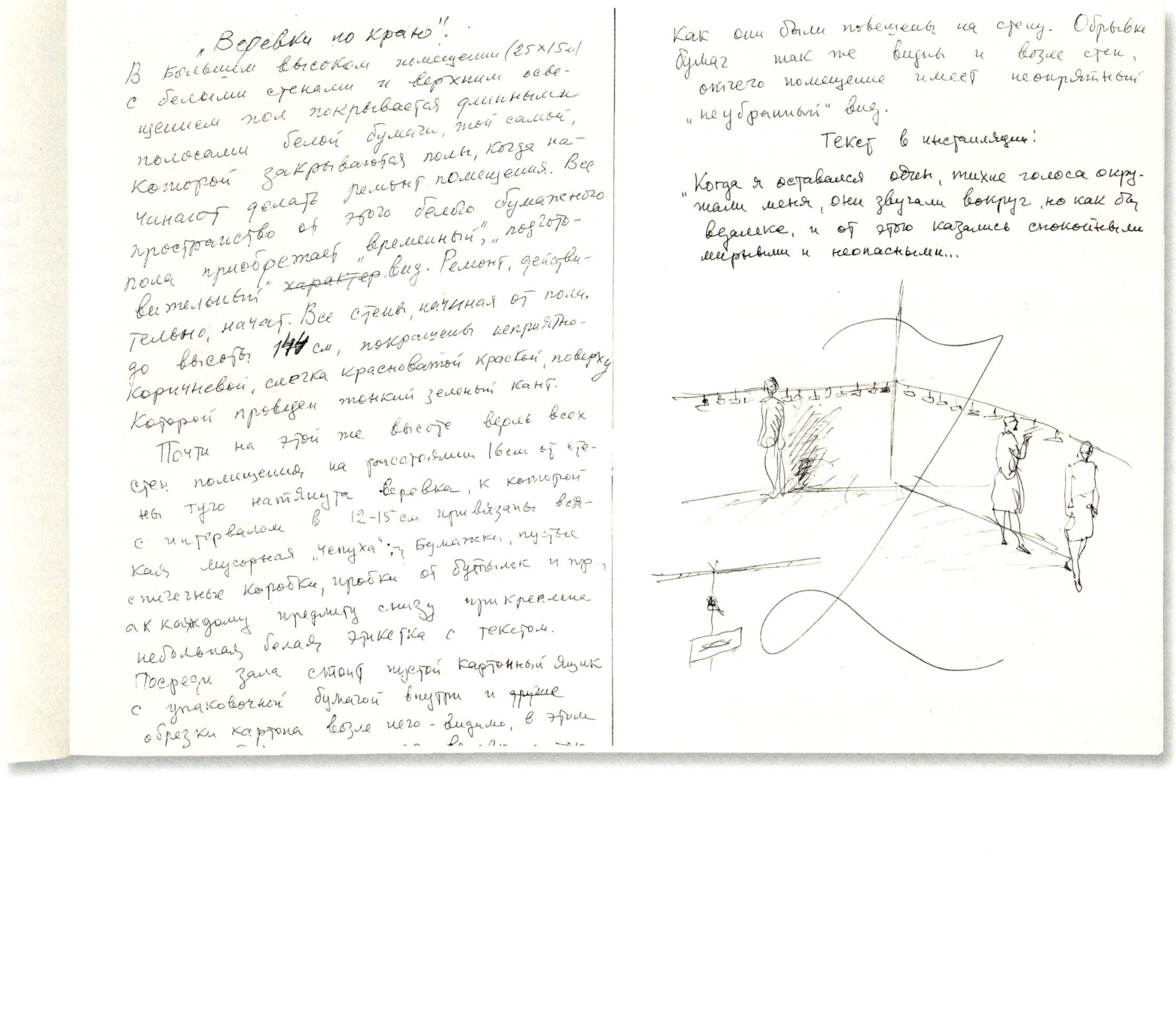

„Веревки по краю“.

В большом высоком помещении (25×15 м) с белыми стенами и верхним освещением пол покрывается длинными полосами белой бумаги, той самой, которой закрываются полы, когда начинают делать ремонт помещения. Все пространство от этого белого бумажного пола приобретает „временный“, „подготовительный“ ~~характер~~ вид. Ремонт, действительно, начат. Все стены, начиная от пола, до высоты 141 см, покрашены неприятно-коричневой, слегка красноватой краской, поверху которой проведен тонкий зеленый кант.

Почти на этой же высоте вдоль всех стен помещения на расстоянии 16 см от стены туго натянута веревка, к которой с интервалом в 12-15 см привязаны всякая мусорная „чепуха“: бумажки, пустые спичечные коробки, пробки от бутылок и пр., а к каждому предмету снизу прикреплена небольшая белая этикетка с текстом. Посреди зала стоит пустой картонный ящик с упаковочной бумагой внутри и ~~другие~~ обрезки картона возле него - видимо, в этом [illegible]

Как они были повешены на стену. Обрывки бумаг так же видны и возле стен, отчего помещение имеет неопрятный „неубранный“ вид.

Текст в инсталляции:

„Когда я оставался один, тихие голоса окружали меня, они звучали вокруг, но как бы вдалеке, и от этого казались спокойными мирными и неопасными...“

47 The Art of Flight. Dialogues About Fear, the Sacred White and the Soviet Garbage

Die Kunst des Fliehens. Dialoge über Angst, das heilige Weiss und den sowjetischen Müll

with Boris Groys | *mit Boris Groys*

1991 / 2007

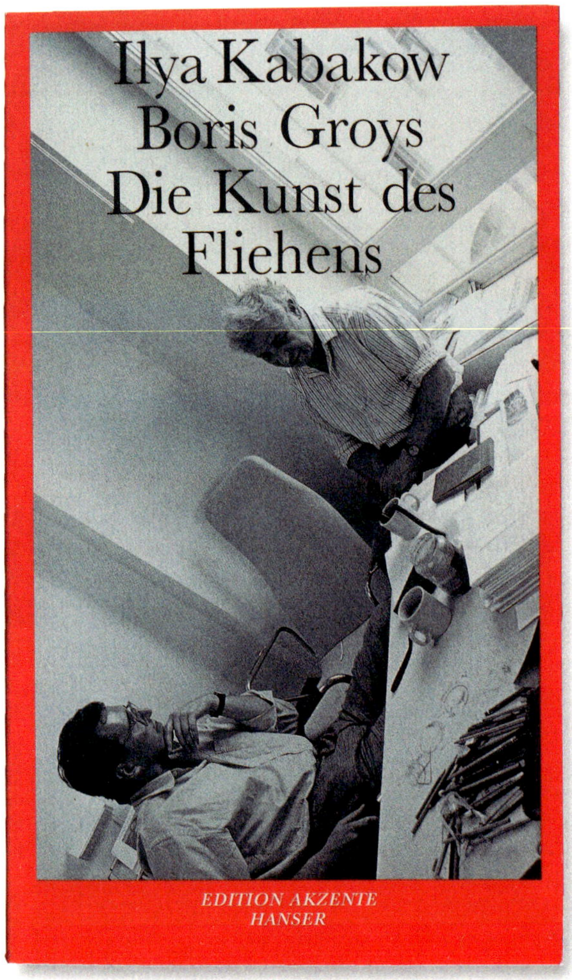

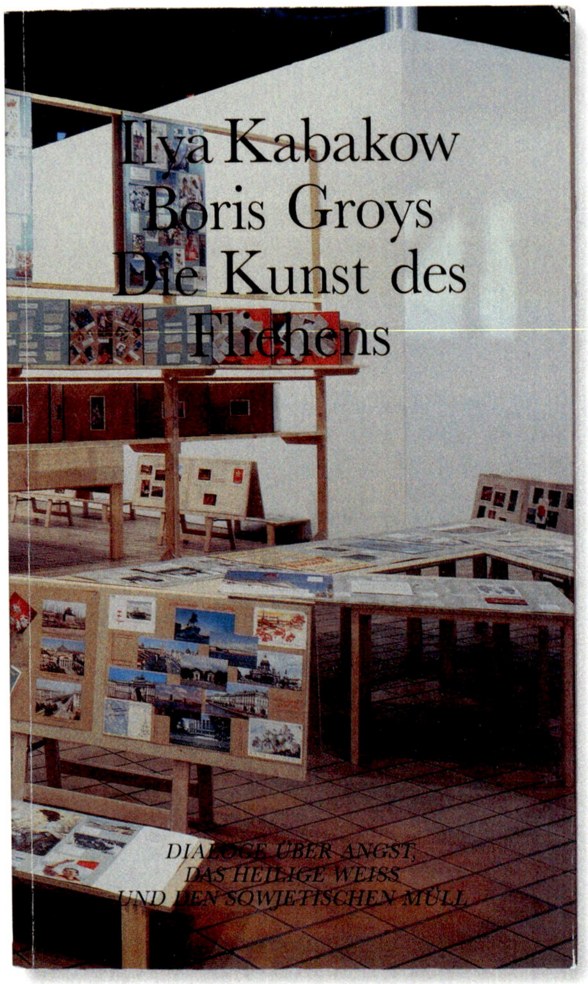

Michael Krüger
Munich/Vienna: Carl Hanser Verlag (Edition Akzente)
20 x 12 cm
133 pp. with 16 b/w ills.
adhesive binding, softback with flaps
Klebebindung, broschiert mit Umschlagklappen
second edition August 2007

thematic publication | *thematische Publikation*

layout by Ilya Kabakov | *Layout von Ilya Kabakov*

This book was published to coincide with Ilya Kabakov's acceptance of the Aachen Art Prize and with the exhibition of his installation »The Ship« in the ballroom of the Neue Galerie, Sammlung Ludwig, Aachen, which took place from September 30 to November 30, 1990. The dialogues conducted by Ilya Kabakov and Boris Groys, which are summarized in »The Art of Flight«, formed part of the installation »Exhibition of a Book« at the DAAD Galerie, Berlin, December 9, 1989 to January 28, 1990; German.

Die Publikation erschien zeitgleich mit der Verleihung des ‚Kunstpreis Aachen' an Ilya Kabakov und zur Ausstellung seiner Installation »Das Schiff« im Ballsaal, Neue Galerie, Sammlung Ludwig, Aachen, 30. September – 30. November 1990. Die unter dem Titel »Kunst des Fliehens« zusammengefassten Dialoge von Ilya Kabakov und Boris Groys sind Bestandteil der Installation »Ausstellung eines Buches«, DAAD-Galerie, Berlin, 9. Dezember 1989 – 28. Januar 1990; deutsch.

see also | *siehe auch* no. 27; no. 91

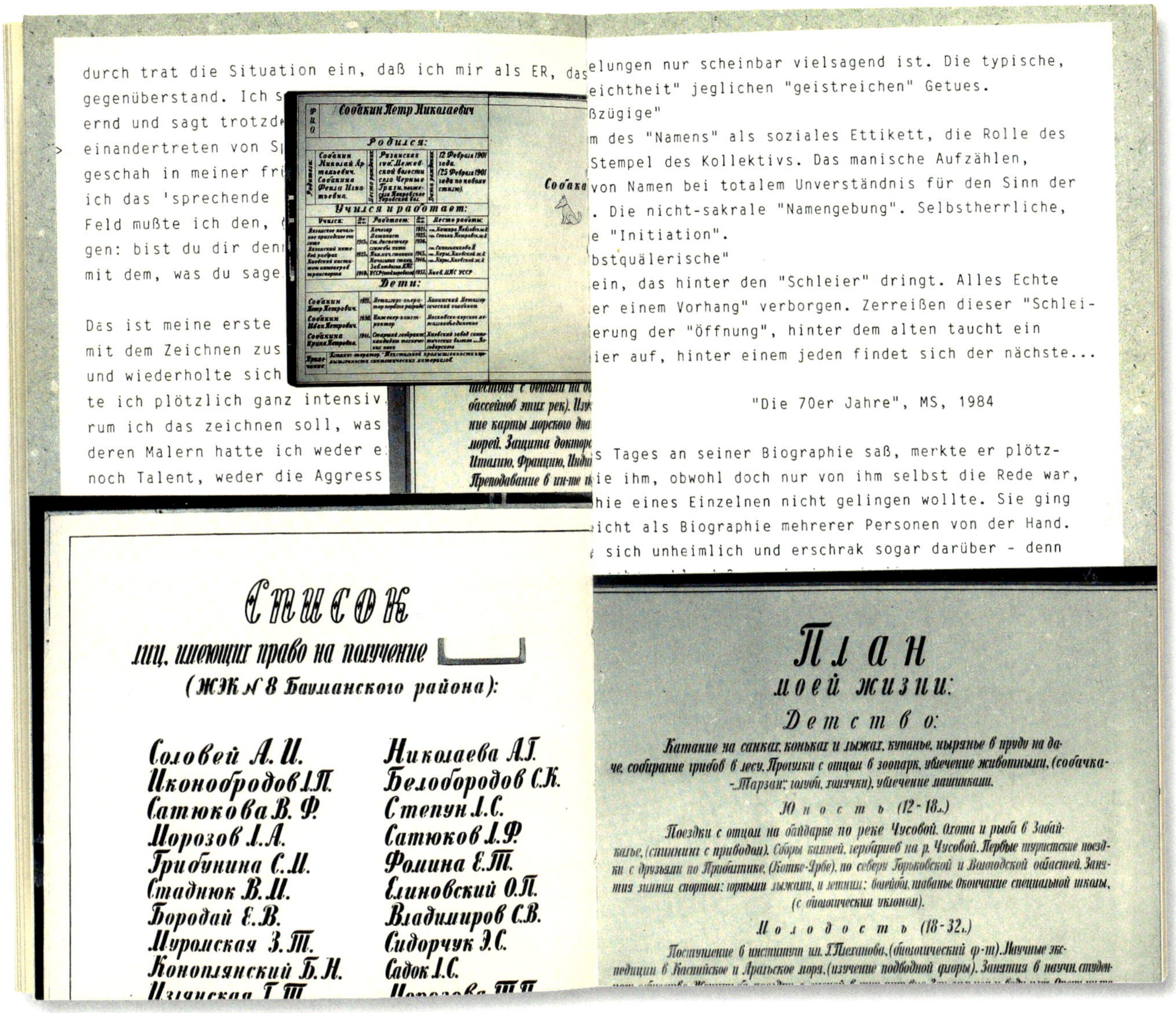

durch trat die Situation ein, daß ich mir als ER, das
gegenüberstand. Ich s
ernd und sagt trotzd
einandertreten von S
geschah in meiner fr
ich das 'sprechende
Feld mußte ich den,
gen: bist du dir den
mit dem, was du sage
Das ist meine erste
mit dem Zeichnen zus
und wiederholte sich
te ich plötzlich ganz intensiv
rum ich das zeichnen soll, was
deren Malern hatte ich weder e
noch Talent, weder die Aggress
Собакин Петр Николаевич
Родился:
Учился и работает:
Дети:
Собака
elungen nur scheinbar vielsagend ist. Die typische,
eichtheit" jeglichen "geistreichen" Getues.
ßzügige"
m des "Namens" als soziales Ettikett, die Rolle des
Stempel des Kollektivs. Das manische Aufzählen,
von Namen bei totalem Unverständnis für den Sinn der
. Die nicht-sakrale "Namengebung". Selbstherrliche,
e "Initiation".
bstquälerische"
ein, das hinter den "Schleier" dringt. Alles Echte
er einem Vorhang" verborgen. Zerreißen dieser "Schlei-
erung der "Öffnung", hinter dem alten taucht ein
ier auf, hinter einem jeden findet sich der nächste...
"Die 70er Jahre", MS, 1984
s Tages an seiner Biographie saß, merkte er plötz-
ie ihm, obwohl doch nur von ihm selbst die Rede war,
hie eines Einzelnen nicht gelingen wollte. Sie ging
icht als Biographie mehrerer Personen von der Hand.
sich unheimlich und erschrak sogar darüber - denn
Список
лиц, имеющих право на получение
(ЖЭК № 8 Бауманского района):
Соловей А. И.
Иконобродов І.П.
Сатюкова В. Ф.
Морозов І.А.
Грибунина С.И.
Стаднюк В.И.
Бородай Е.В.
Муромская З.Т.
Конопляский Б.Н.
Николаева А.Г.
Белобородов С.К.
Степун І.С.
Сатюков І.Ф.
Фомина Е.Т.
Елиновский О.П.
Владимиров С.В.
Сидорчук Э.С.
Садок І.С.
План
моей жизни:
Детство:
Катание на санках, коньках и лыжах, купанье, ныряние в пруду на даче, собирание грибов в лесу. Прогулки с отцом в зоопарк, увлечение животными, (собачка-„Тарзан", голуби, хомячки), увлечение машинками.
Юность (12-18.)
Поездки с отцом на байдарке по реке Чусовой. Охота и рыба в Забайкалье, (спиннинг с приводом). Сборы камней, гербариев на р. Чусовой. Первые туристские поездки с друзьями по Прибалтике, (Котке-Ярве), по северу Горьковской и Вологодской областей. Занятия зимним спортом: горными лыжами, и летним: борьбой, плаванье. Окончание специальной школы, (с биологическим уклоном).
Молодость (18-32.)
Поступление в институт им. Г.Плеханова, (биологический ф-т). Научные экспедиции в Каспийское и Аральское моря, (изучение подводной флоры). Занятия в научн. студен-

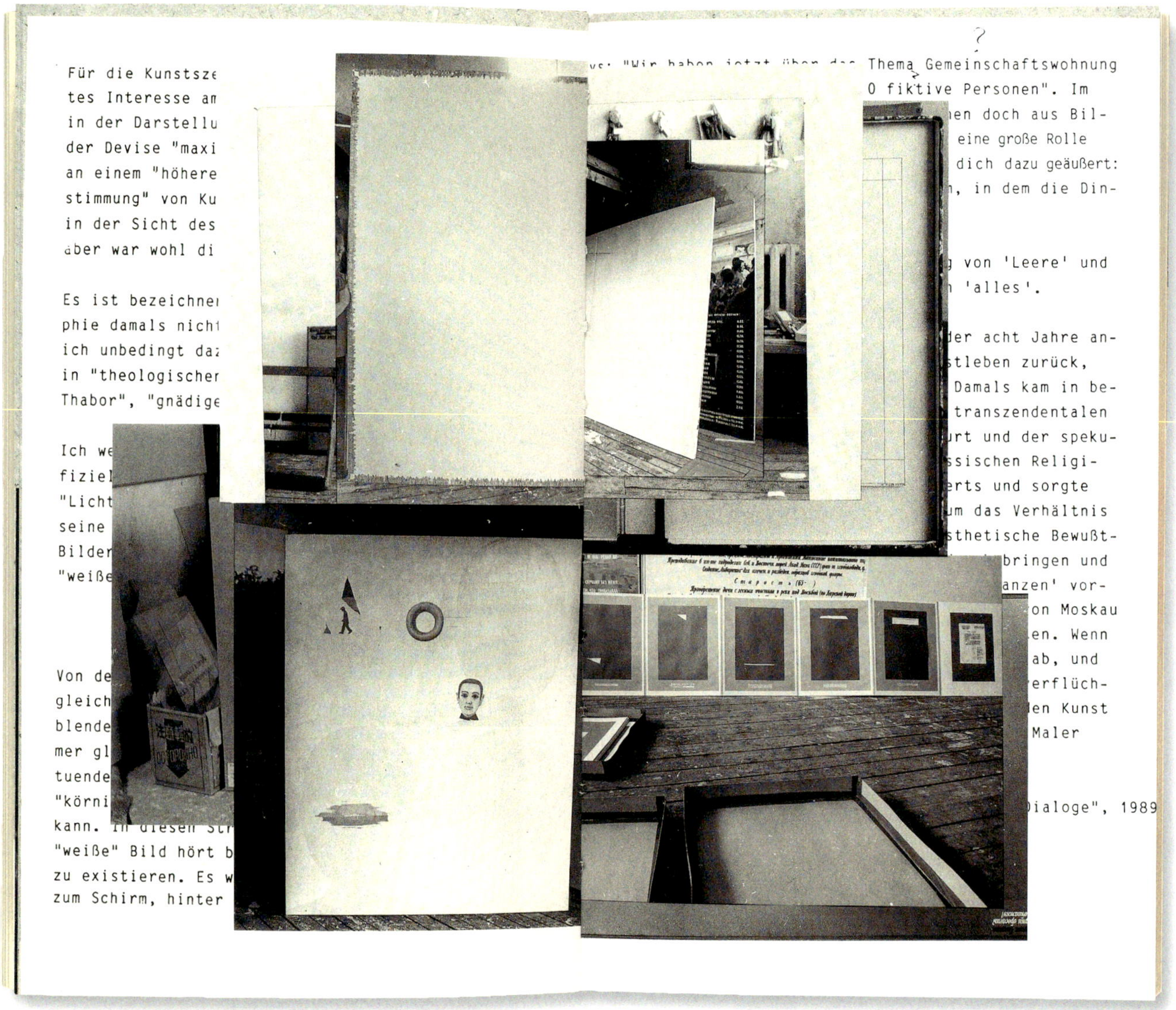
Für die Kunstsze
tes Interesse am
in der Darstellu
der Devise "maxi
an einem "höhere
stimmung" von Ku
in der Sicht des
aber war wohl di
Es ist bezeichne
phie damals nicht
ich unbedingt da
in "theologischer
Thabor", "gnädige
Ich we
fiziel
"Licht
seine
Bilder
"weiße
Von de
gleich
blende
mer gl
tuende
"körni
kann.
"weiße" Bild hört b
zu existieren. Es w
zum Schirm, hinter
Thema Gemeinschaftswohnung
0 fiktive Personen". Im
en doch aus Bil-
eine große Rolle
dich dazu geäußert:
, in dem die Din-
von 'Leere' und
'alles'.
der acht Jahre an-
tleben zurück,
Damals kam in be-
transzendentalen
rt und der speku-
ssischen Religi-
rts und sorgte
m das Verhältnis
thetische Bewußt-
bringen und
anzen' vor-
on Moskau
en. Wenn
ab, und
erflüch-
en Kunst
Maler
ialoge", 1989

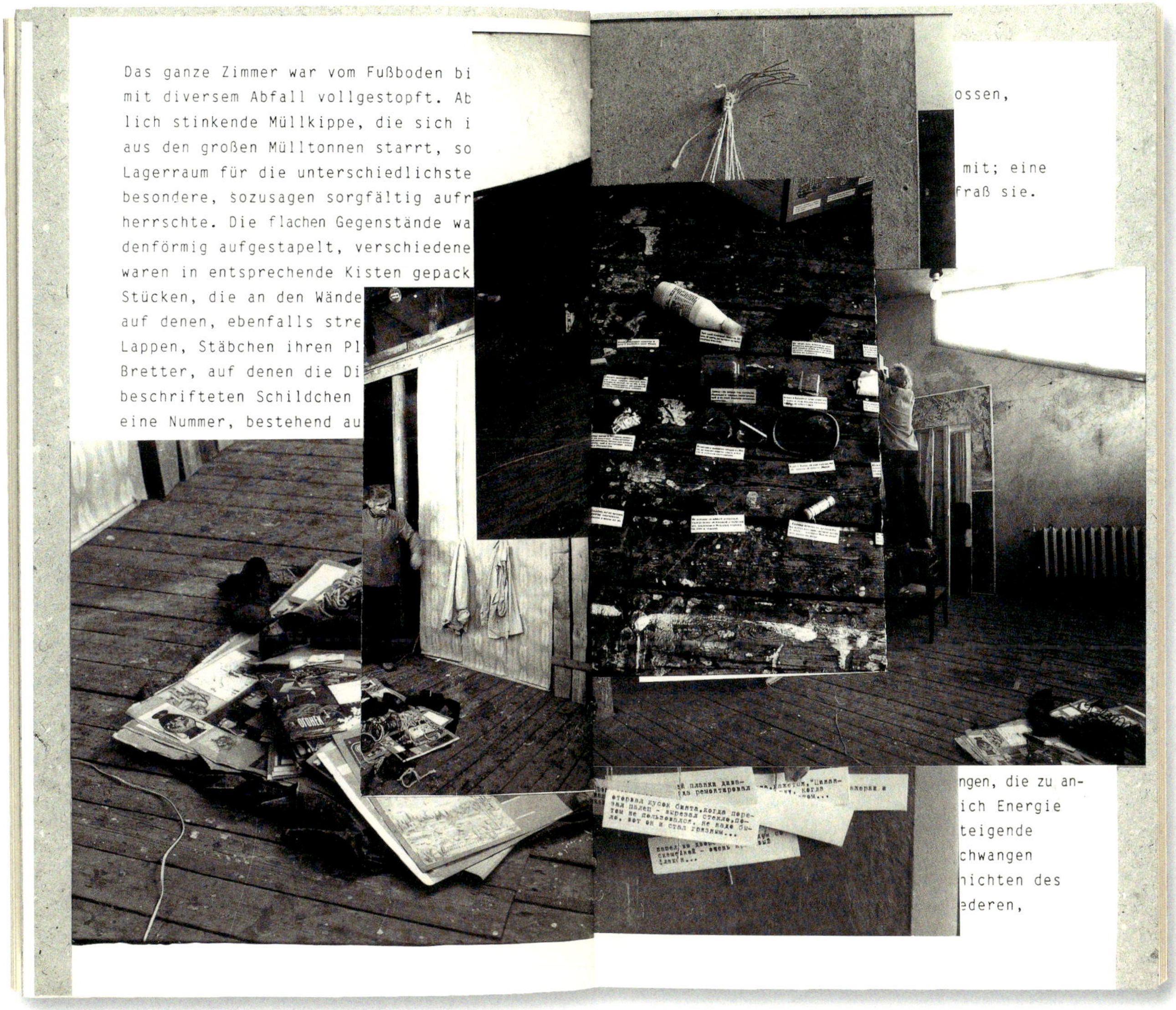
Das ganze Zimmer war vom Fußboden bi
mit diversem Abfall vollgestopft. Ab
lich stinkende Müllkippe, die sich i
aus den großen Mülltonnen starrt, so
Lagerraum für die unterschiedlichste
besondere, sozusagen sorgfältig aufr
herrschte. Die flachen Gegenstände wa
denförmig aufgestapelt, verschiedene
waren in entsprechende Kisten gepack
Stücken, die an den Wände
auf denen, ebenfalls stre
Lappen, Stäbchen ihren Pl
Bretter, auf denen die Di
beschrifteten Schildchen
eine Nummer, bestehend au
ossen,
mit; eine
fraß sie.
ngen, die zu an-
ich Energie
teigende
chwangen
ichten des
ederen,

48 The Man Who Flew Into His Picture | *Der Mann, der ins Bild flog*

1991

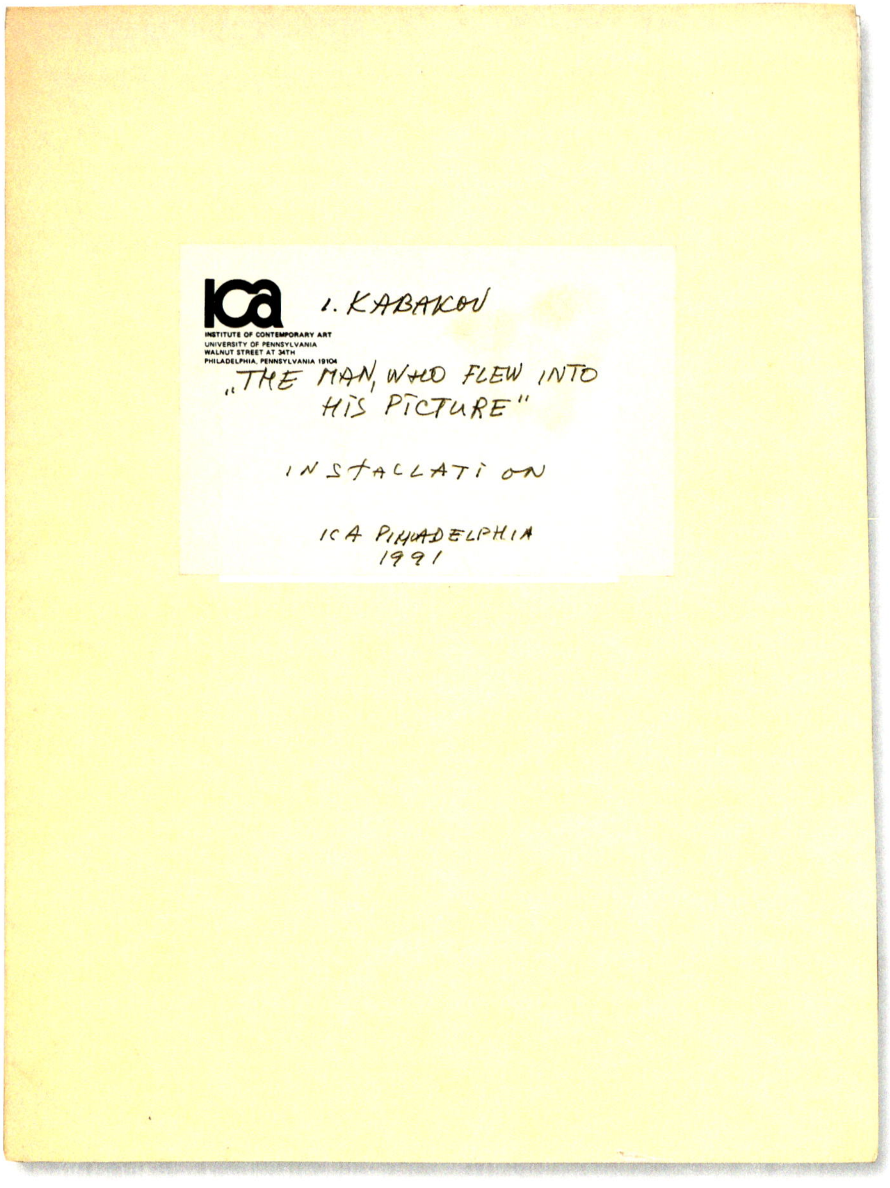

Institute of Contemporary Art, University of Pennsylvania
Philadelphia: Institute of Contemporary Art, University of Pennsylvania
28.8 x 22.4 cm
41 photocopied pp. with 37 b/w ills.
loose sheets, cardboard cover, label on the cover
lose Blätter, Kartonumschlag, Etikette auf dem Umschlag

exhibition catalogue | *Ausstellungskatalog*

layout by Ilya Kabakov | *Layout von Ilya Kabakov*

For the installation of the same name in the exhibition »The Devil on the Stairs: Looking Back on the Eighties« at the Institute of Contemporary Art, University of Pennsylvania, Philadelphia, October 4, 1990 to January 5, 1991 and at the Newport Harbor Art Museum, Newport Beach, CA, April 16 to June 21, 1992. Text by Ilya Kabakov; English.

Zur gleichnamigen Installation für die Ausstellung »The Devil on the Stairs: Looking Back on the Eighties«, Institute of Contemporary Art, University of Pennsylvania, Philadelphia, 4. Oktober 1990 – 5. Januar 1991 und Newport Harbor Art Museum, Newport Beach, CA, 16. April – 21. Juni 1992. Text von Ilya Kabakov; englisch.

see also | *siehe auch* no. 53; no. 54; CRI, vol. 1, no. 16, pp. 146–151; CRP, vol. 1, no. 49, pp. 101–102, no. 95, p. 169

6

THE MAN WHO FLEW INTO HIS PICTURE

He drew himself on the big white board, depicting himself as a small gray figure, barely discernible on the enormous board standing in front of him in the small room. He looks at himself, so small and plain, lost in the huge space of the empty white field, and a strange, surprising state envelops him . . .

The white board stops being just a white board and becomes for him at first a white fog, and then the fog disappears, dispersing, and the "white" at which he continues to look gradually turns into an enormous bright expanse pierced by an even, sparkling light. The light in this space simultaneously stands still and flows from some infinite distance, from some sort of good and wonderful source. He moves torward it, sitting in front of this magic screen. He really, in actual fact, sees before him an enormous, endless ocean of light, and at that moment he merges with the little, plain figure that he had drawn. But this figure changes, too. It stops being just a drawn image. Entirely alive and real (though only very small, many times smaller than he -- and he certainly knows this) the figure moves smoothly, quietly and uninterruptedly and moves away from him into the infinite depth from where the light is shining. And it quickly becomes completely indiscernible in the blinding depth.

But at the same time that he experiences all this, strange and completely contradictory feelings persist to bother him. At the same time that he is moving with all his soul and is following the departing figure, in a strange way understanding that he is also going there himself, the other half of his consciousness clearly realizes that he is sitting completely

5

THE MAN WHO FLEW INTO HIS PICTURE

He comes home from work fairly early, and eating supper quickly, he sits down on a chair in his lonely room across from a big board which is covered with white paint. A little to the left of the center of this board is a small figure of a person depicted in light-gray paint. He drew it himself sometime long ago. He casts out all of the day's thoughts and worries, moves the chair closer to the white board and gradually a strange spiritual state envelops him. It begins to seem to him that it is not the figure which is already drawn but he himself that, at first slowly and then faster and faster, flies into the white board, into the shining distance full of some sort of strange light . . .

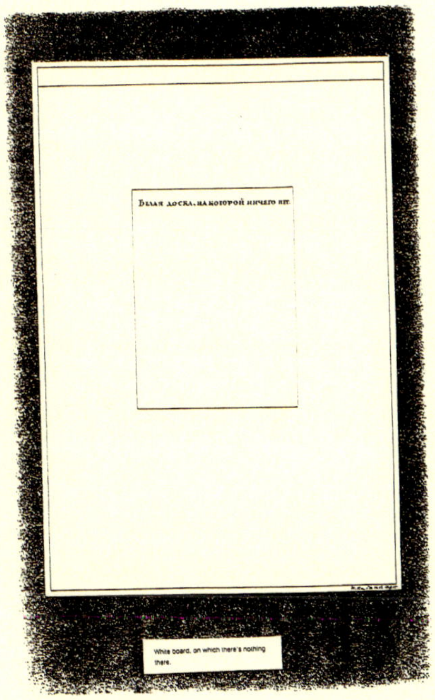

8

Let others speak. They fill up the room with their voices, their discordant noise sounds in one's ears, they are heard from outside and from within it. They speak so loudly and so clearly, that it is possible to write down their words and entire phrases on separate sheets of paper.

It's as though certain spoken phrases are relevant to his "painting."

49 The Ripped Off Landscape | *Heruntergerissene Landschaft*

1991

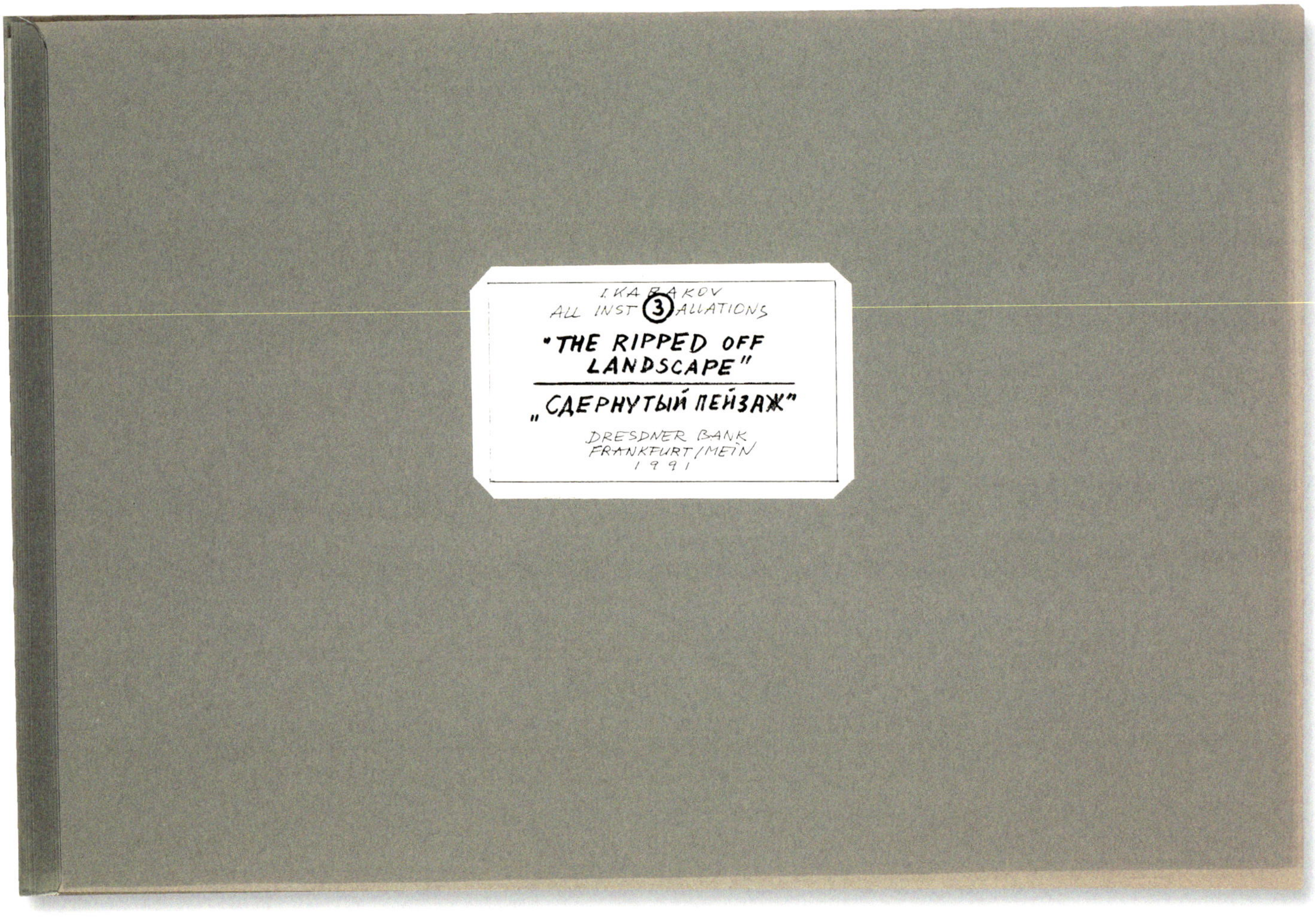

Ilya Kabakov
New York: published by the author
27.9 x 43.3 cm
17 photocopied pp. with 13 (4 color) ills.
quick bind, cardboard cover,
label on the cover
Schnellhefter, Kartonumschlag,
Etikette auf dem Umschlag
edition: 19 copies

thematic publication | *thematische Publikation*

layout by Ilya Kabakov | *Layout von Ilya Kabakov*

Documentation of the work of the same name in the Dresdner Bank collection, Frankfurt am Main. Texts by Ilya Kabakov. Dialogue between Joseph Backstein and Ilya Kabakov. »The Ripped Off Landscape« is part of the installation »Seven Exhibitions of a Painting«, 1990; English, Russian.

Dokumentation der gleichnamigen Arbeit in der Sammlung Dresdner Bank, Frankfurt am Main. Texte von Ilya Kabakov. Dialog von Josef Bakstein und Ilya Kabakov. »Heruntergerissene Landschaft« ist Teil der Installation »Sieben Ausstellungen eines Bildes«, 1990; englisch, russisch.

see also | *siehe auch* no. 32; CRI, vol. 1, no. 49, pp. 324–329; CRP, vol. 1, no. 45, p. 96, no. 93, p. 167

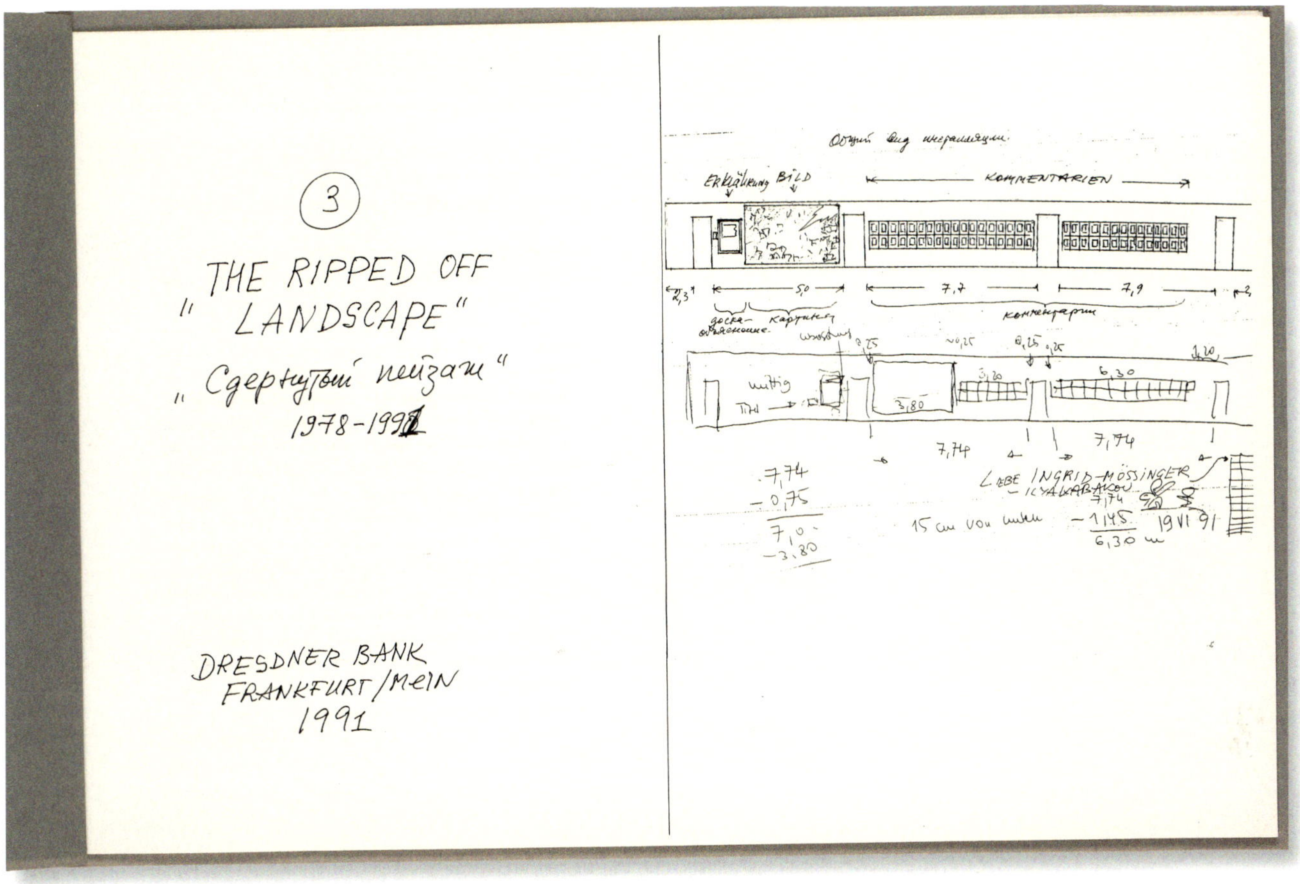

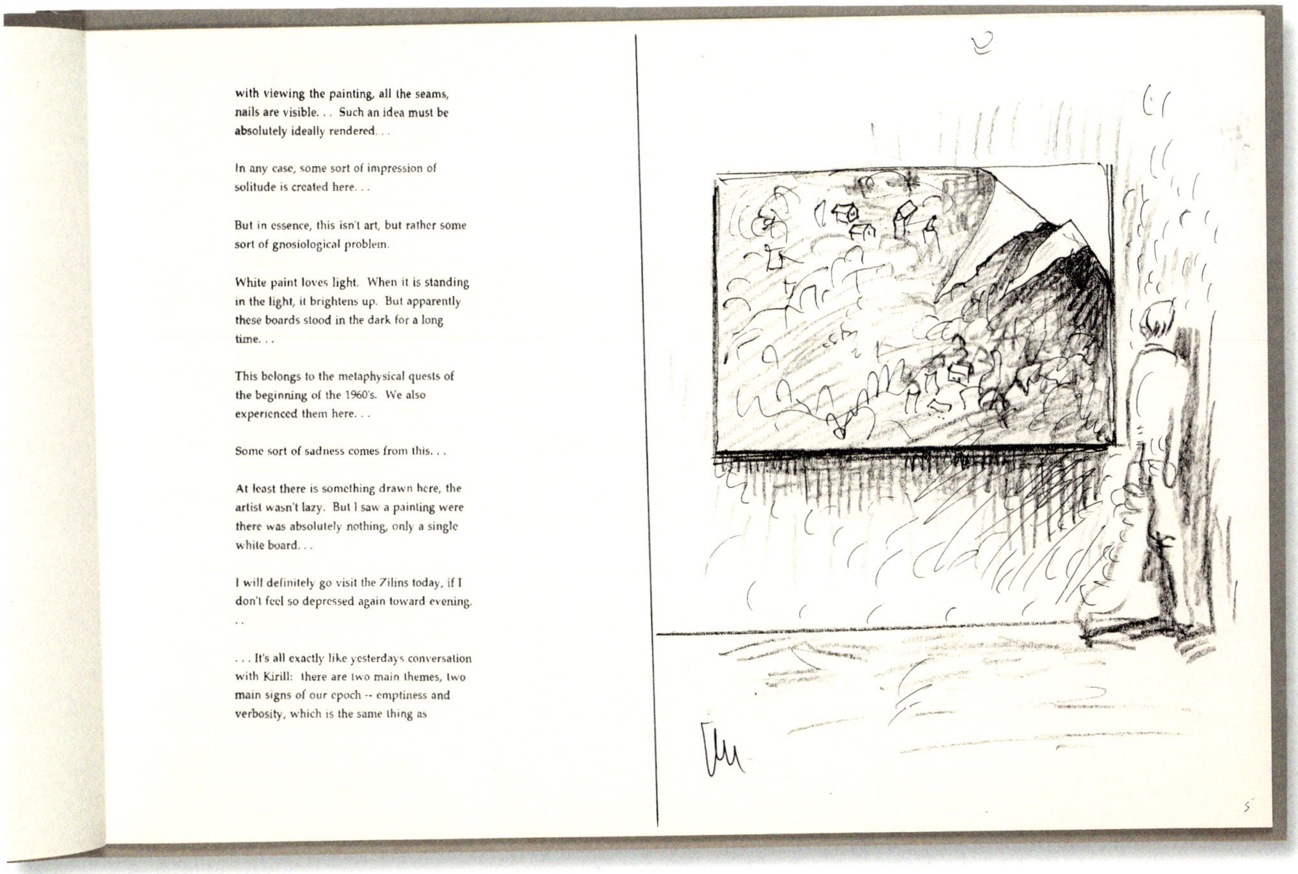
with viewing the painting, all the seams, nails are visible. . . Such an idea must be absolutely ideally rendered. . .

In any case, some sort of impression of solitude is created here. . .

But in essence, this isn't art, but rather some sort of gnosiological problem.

White paint loves light. When it is standing in the light, it brightens up. But apparently these boards stood in the dark for a long time. . .

This belongs to the metaphysical quests of the beginning of the 1960's. We also experienced them here. . .

Some sort of sadness comes from this. . .

At least there is something drawn here, the artist wasn't lazy. But I saw a painting were there was absolutely nothing, only a single white board. . .

I will definitely go visit the Zilins today, if I don't feel so depressed again toward evening. . .

. . . It's all exactly like yesterdays conversation with Kirill: there are two main themes, two main signs of our epoch -- emptiness and verbosity, which is the same thing as

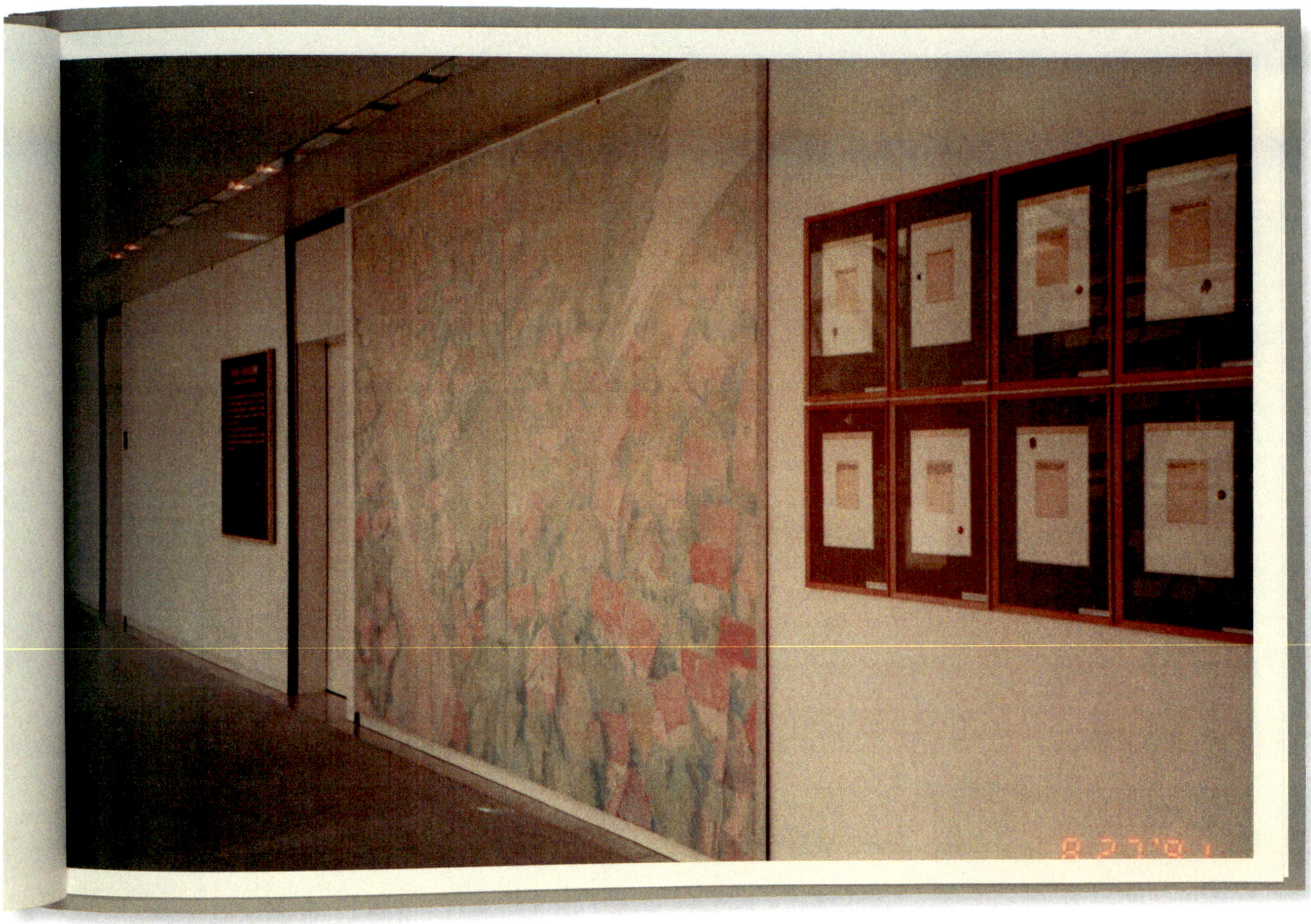

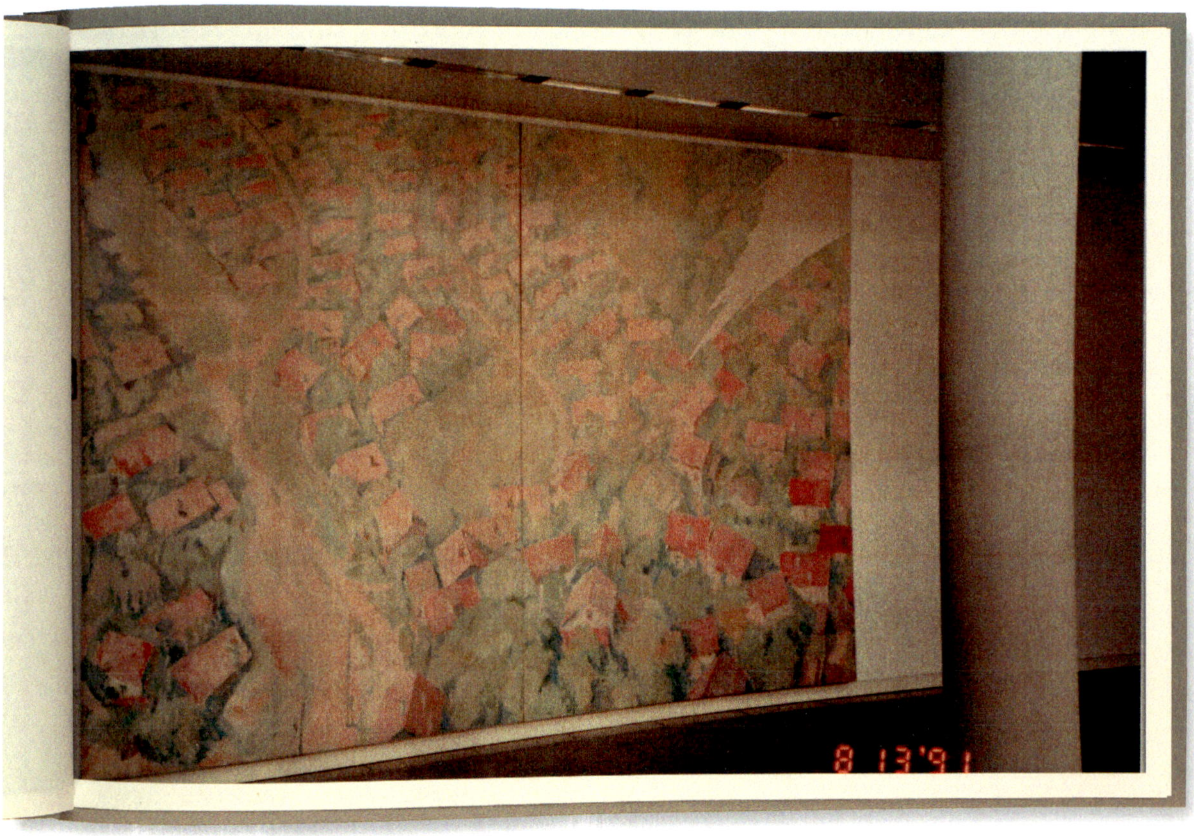
8 13'91

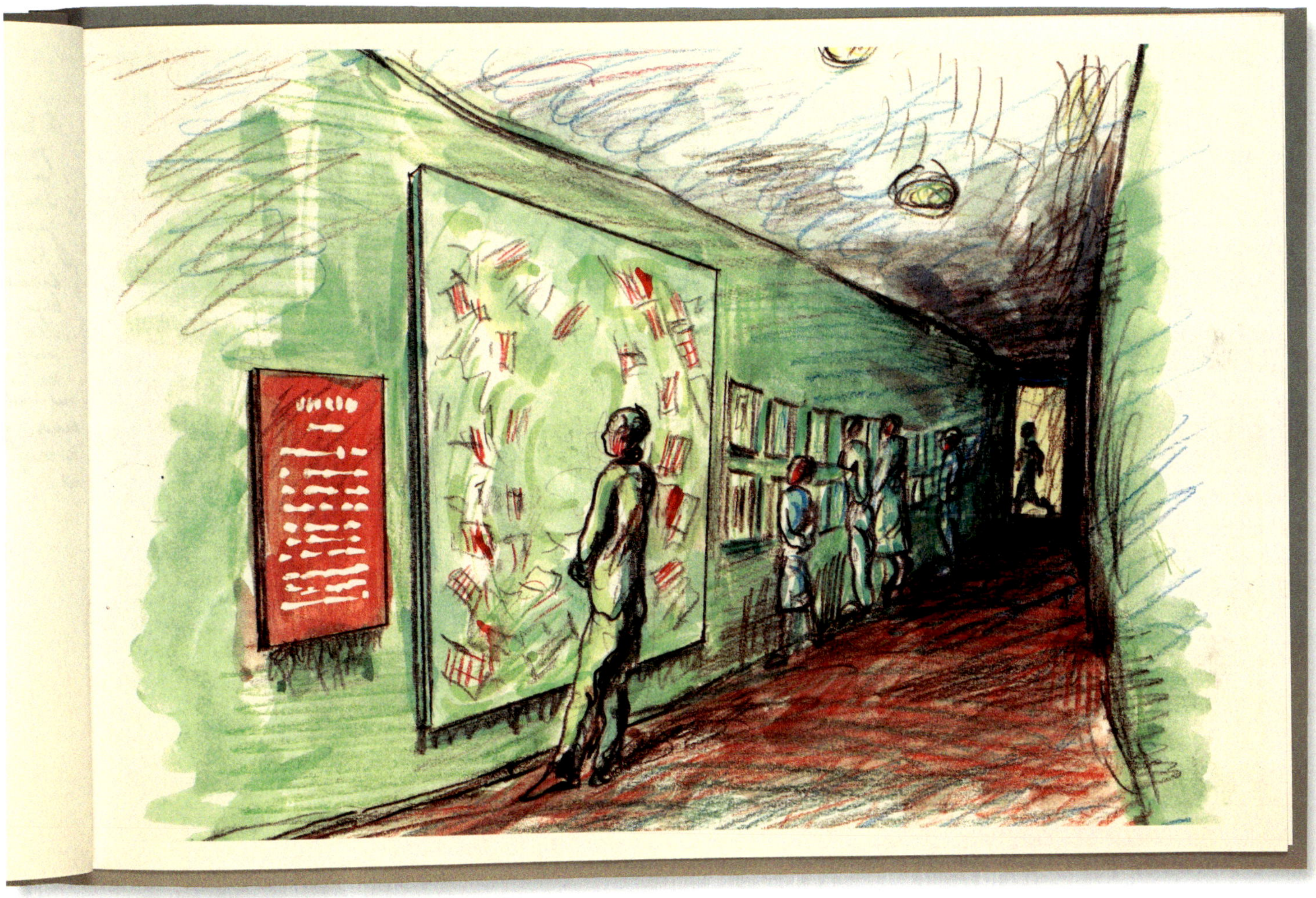

50 Life of Flies | *Das Leben der Fliegen*

1992

Kölnischer Kunstverein
Ostfildern bei Stuttgart: Edition Cantz
23.3 x 16.8 cm
271 pp. with 35 (9 color) ills.
stitchbound, quarter cloth, hardcover, blind blocking with label on the cover, front and back fly leaf with illustrations, with Sketch for Installation at the Kölnischer Kunstverein by Ilya Kabakov from 1991
Fadenheftung, Halbleinen, Blindprägung mit Etikette, Vorsatz vorne und hinten mit Illustration Skizze für Installation im Kölner Kunstverein von Ilya Kabakov von 1991

exhibition catalogue | *Ausstellungskatalog*

layout by Ilya Kabakov | *Layout von Ilya Kabakov*

For the installation of the same name at the Kölnischer Kunstverein, Cologne, February 2 to March 29, 1992. Fictitious academic treatise on the influence of flies on human civilization. Texts from the exhibition installation »The Fly with the Wings« and a dialogue between Boris Groys and Ilya Kabakov on »Installations«. The texts »On the Subject of the Local Language« and »The Ant« were published autonomously in 1982 and 1991 respectively; Russian, German, English.

Zur gleichnamigen Installation für den Kölnischen Kunstverein, Köln, 2. Februar – 29. März 1992. Fiktive wissenschaftliche Abhandlung über den Einfluss der Fliegen auf die menschliche Zivilisation. Texte aus der Ausstellungsinstallation »Fliege mit Flügeln« und ein Dialog von Boris Groys und Ilya Kabakov über »Installationen. Über die lokale Sprache« und »Die Ameise« erschienen 1982 bzw. 1991 als selbständige Texte; russisch, deutsch, englisch.

see also | *siehe auch* no. 8; no. 9; no. 33; no. 35; no. 36; no. 43; no. 44; no. 37; no. 38; no. 56; no. 134; CRI, vol. 1, no. 56, pp. 366–373; CRP, vol. 1, no. 161, pp. 251, 411

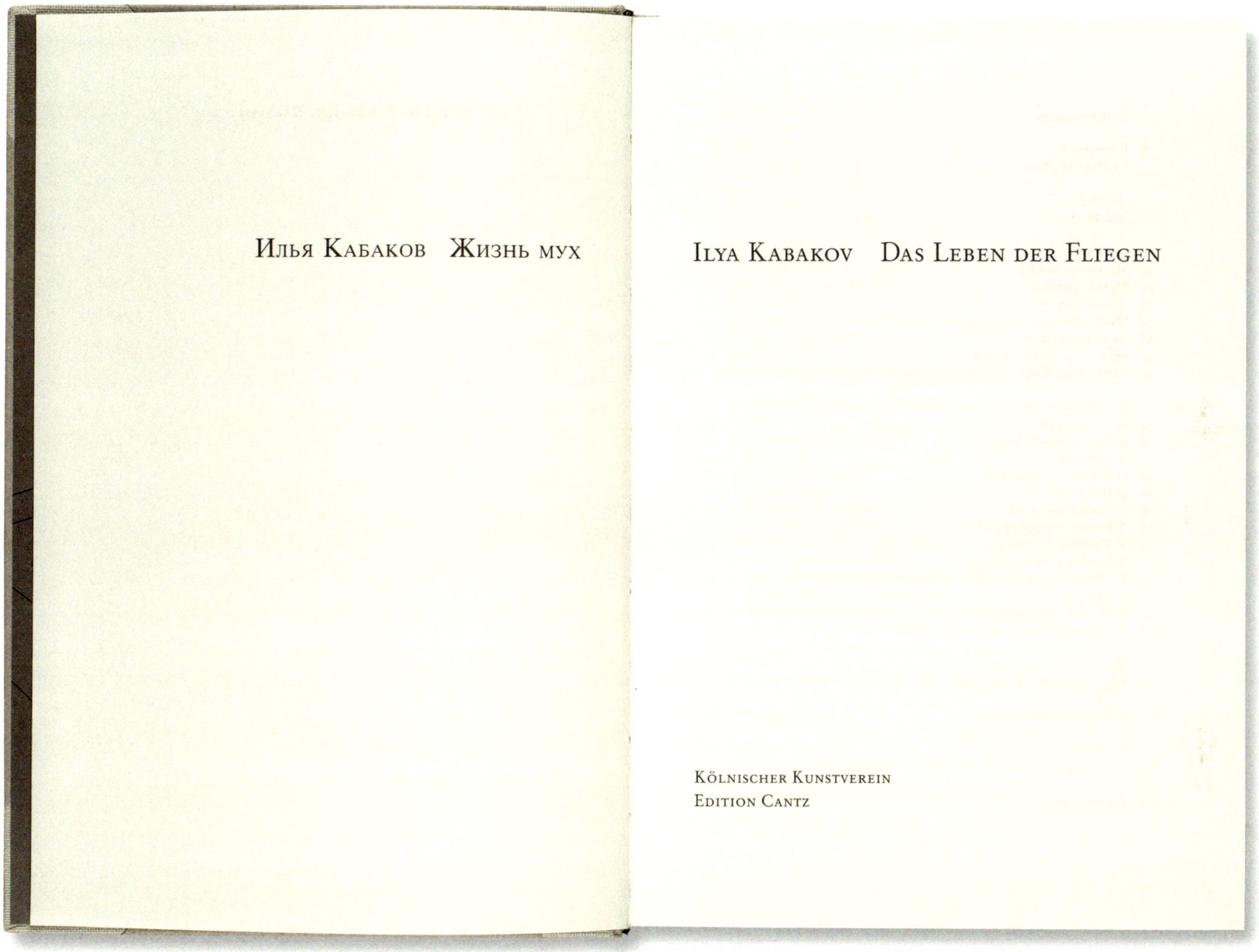
Илья Кабаков Жизнь мух
Ilya Kabakov Das Leben der Fliegen
Kölnischer Kunstverein
Edition Cantz

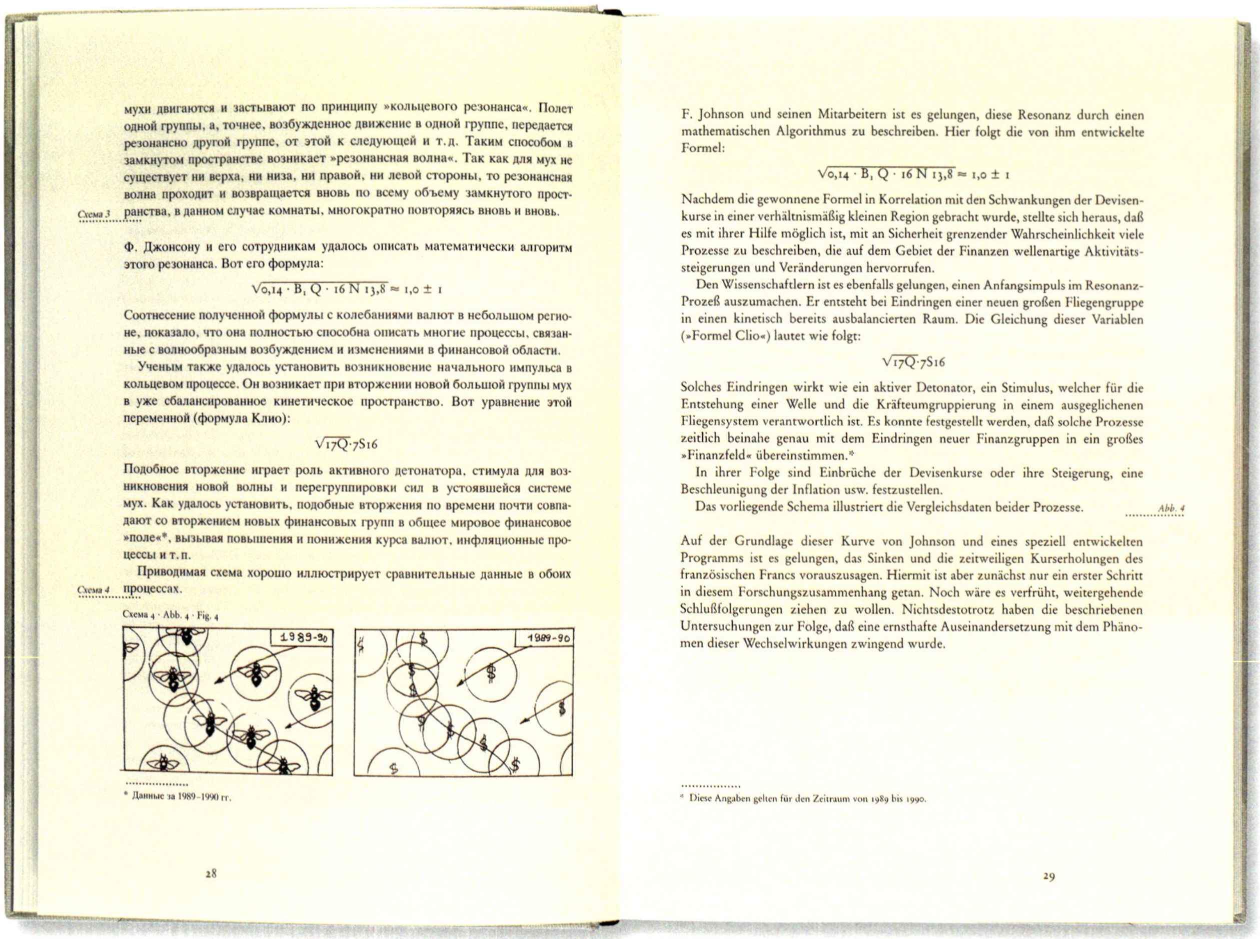

мухи двигаются и застывают по принципу »кольцевого резонанса«. Полет одной группы, а, точнее, возбужденное движение в одной группе, передается резонансно другой группе, от этой к следующей и т. д. Таким способом в замкнутом пространстве возникает »резонансная волна«. Так как для мух не существует ни верха, ни низа, ни правой, ни левой стороны, то резонансная волна проходит и возвращается вновь по всему объему замкнутого пространства, в данном случае комнаты, многократно повторяясь вновь и вновь. Схема 3

Ф. Джонсону и его сотрудникам удалось описать математически алгоритм этого резонанса. Вот его формула:

$$\sqrt{0{,}14 \cdot B_1\, Q \cdot 16\, N\, 13{,}8} \approx 1{,}0 \pm 1$$

Соотнесение полученной формулы с колебаниями валют в небольшом регионе, показало, что она полностью способна описать многие процессы, связанные с волнообразным возбуждением и изменениями в финансовой области.

Ученым также удалось установить возникновение начального импульса в кольцевом процессе. Он возникает при вторжении новой большой группы мух в уже сбалансированное кинетическое пространство. Вот уравнение этой переменной (формула Клио):

$$\sqrt{17Q} \cdot 7S16$$

Подобное вторжение играет роль активного детонатора, стимула для возникновения новой волны и перегруппировки сил в устоявшейся системе мух. Как удалось установить, подобные вторжения по времени почти совпадают со вторжением новых финансовых групп в общее мировое финансовое »поле«*, вызывая повышения и понижения курса валют, инфляционные процессы и т. п.

Приводимая схема хорошо иллюстрирует сравнительные данные в обоих процессах. Схема 4

Схема 4 · Abb. 4 · Fig. 4

1989-90

1989-90

* Данные за 1989–1990 гг.

28

F. Johnson und seinen Mitarbeitern ist es gelungen, diese Resonanz durch einen mathematischen Algorithmus zu beschreiben. Hier folgt die von ihm entwickelte Formel:

$$\sqrt{0{,}14 \cdot B_1\, Q \cdot 16\, N\, 13{,}8} \approx 1{,}0 \pm 1$$

Nachdem die gewonnene Formel in Korrelation mit den Schwankungen der Devisenkurse in einer verhältnismäßig kleinen Region gebracht wurde, stellte sich heraus, daß es mit ihrer Hilfe möglich ist, mit an Sicherheit grenzender Wahrscheinlichkeit viele Prozesse zu beschreiben, die auf dem Gebiet der Finanzen wellenartige Aktivitätssteigerungen und Veränderungen hervorrufen.

Den Wissenschaftlern ist es ebenfalls gelungen, einen Anfangsimpuls im Resonanz-Prozeß auszumachen. Er entsteht bei Eindringen einer neuen großen Fliegengruppe in einen kinetisch bereits ausbalancierten Raum. Die Gleichung dieser Variablen (»Formel Clio«) lautet wie folgt:

$$\sqrt{17Q} \cdot 7S16$$

Solches Eindringen wirkt wie ein aktiver Detonator, ein Stimulus, welcher für die Entstehung einer Welle und die Kräfteumgruppierung in einem ausgeglichenen Fliegensystem verantwortlich ist. Es konnte festgestellt werden, daß solche Prozesse zeitlich beinahe genau mit dem Eindringen neuer Finanzgruppen in ein großes »Finanzfeld« übereinstimmen.*

In ihrer Folge sind Einbrüche der Devisenkurse oder ihre Steigerung, eine Beschleunigung der Inflation usw. festzustellen.

Das vorliegende Schema illustriert die Vergleichsdaten beider Prozesse. Abb. 4

Auf der Grundlage dieser Kurve von Johnson und eines speziell entwickelten Programms ist es gelungen, das Sinken und die zeitweiligen Kurserholungen des französischen Francs vorauszusagen. Hiermit ist aber zunächst nur ein erster Schritt in diesem Forschungszusammenhang getan. Noch wäre es verfrüht, weitergehende Schlußfolgerungen ziehen zu wollen. Nichtsdestotrotz haben die beschriebenen Untersuchungen zur Folge, daß eine ernsthafte Auseinandersetzung mit dem Phänomen dieser Wechselwirkungen zwingend wurde.

* Diese Angaben gelten für den Zeitraum von 1989 bis 1990.

29

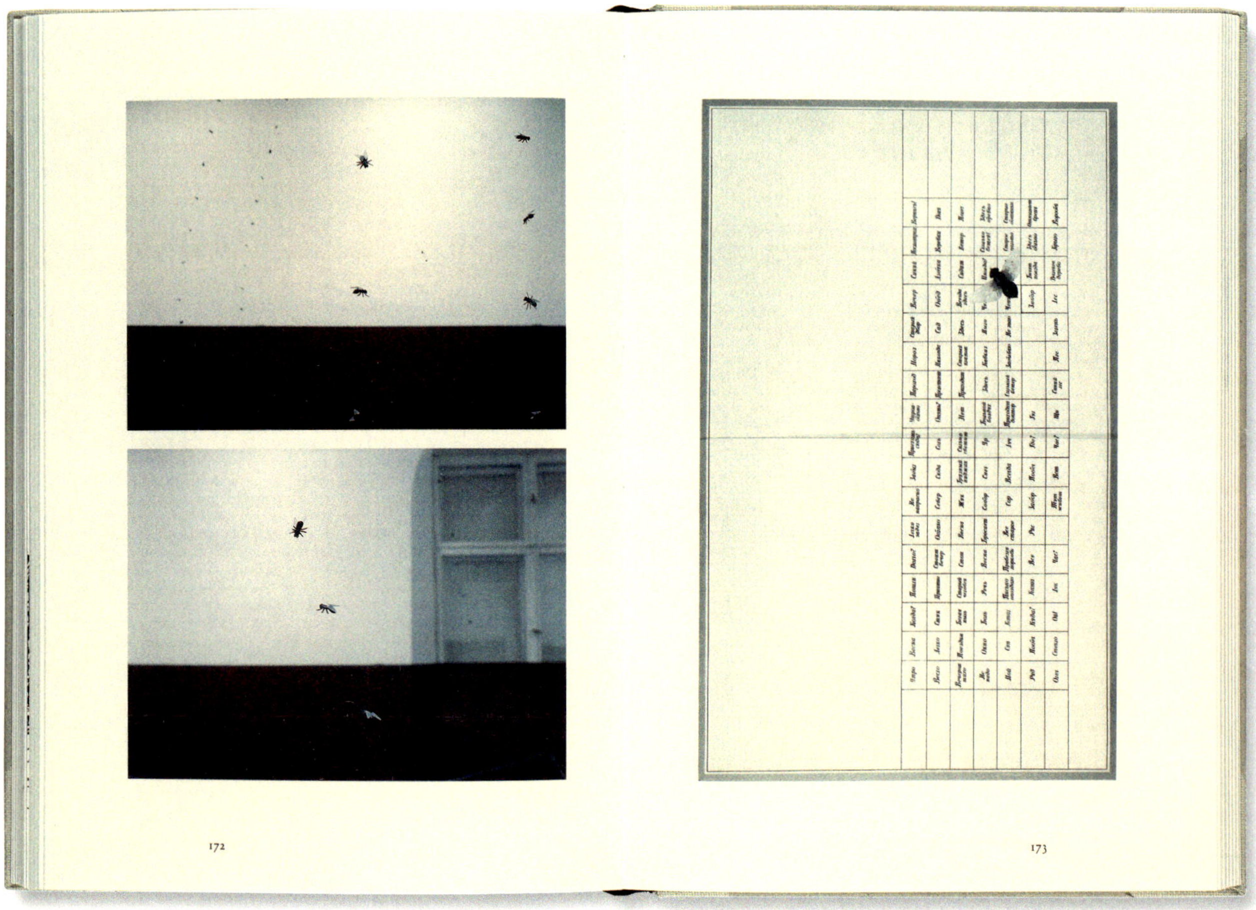

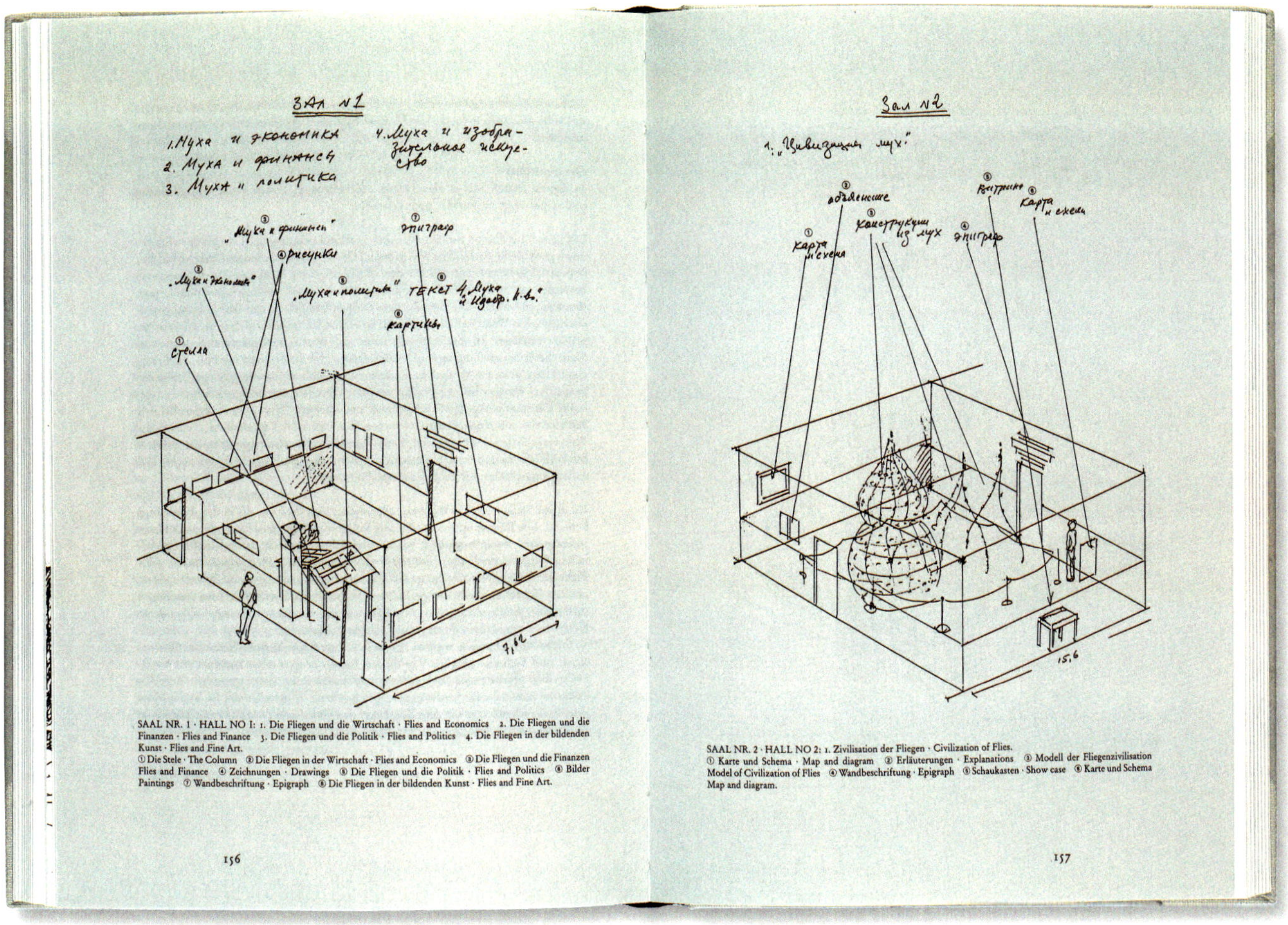
SAAL NR. 1 · HALL NO I: 1. Die Fliegen und die Wirtschaft · Flies and Economics 2. Die Fliegen und die Finanzen · Flies and Finance 3. Die Fliegen und die Politik · Flies and Politics 4. Die Fliegen in der bildenden Kunst · Flies and Fine Art.
① Die Stele · The Column ② Die Fliegen in der Wirtschaft · Flies and Economics ③ Die Fliegen und die Finanzen Flies and Finance ④ Zeichnungen · Drawings ⑤ Die Fliegen und die Politik · Flies and Politics ⑥ Bilder Paintings ⑦ Wandbeschriftung · Epigraph ⑧ Die Fliegen in der bildenden Kunst · Flies and Fine Art.
156
SAAL NR. 2 · HALL NO 2: 1. Zivilisation der Fliegen · Civilization of Flies.
① Karte und Schema · Map and diagram ② Erläuterungen · Explanations ③ Modell der Fliegenzivilisation Model of Civilization of Flies ④ Wandbeschriftung · Epigraph ⑤ Schaukasten · Show case ⑥ Karte und Schema Map and diagram.
157

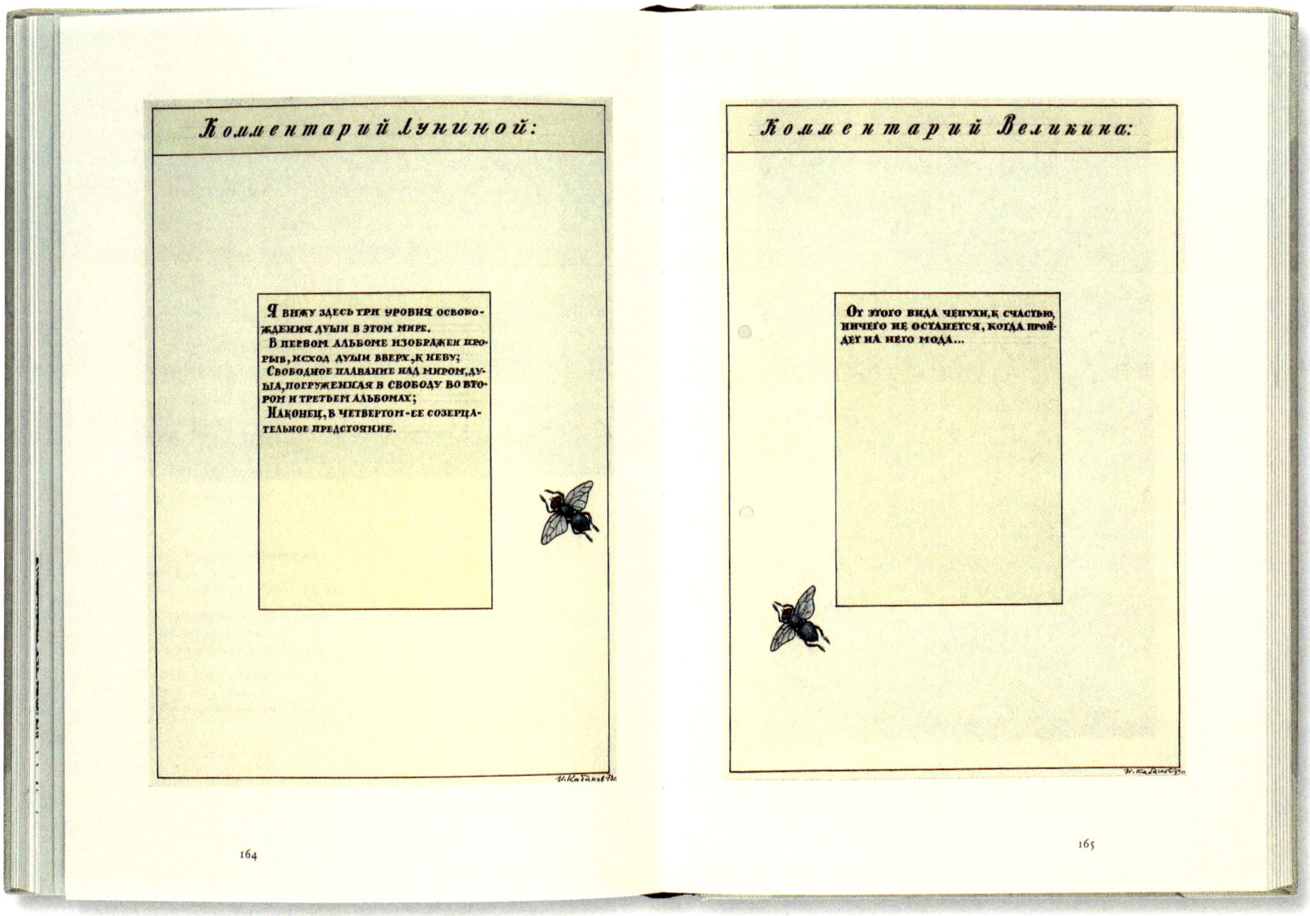
Комментарий Луниной:
Я вижу здесь три уровня освобождения души в этом мире.
В первом альбоме изображен прорыв, исход души вверх, к небу;
Свободное плавание над миром, душа, погруженная в свободу во втором и третьем альбомах;
Наконец, в четвертом - ее созерцательное предстояние.
164
Комментарий Великина:
От этого вида чепухи, к счастью, ничего не останется, когда пройдет на него мода...
165

51 Illustration as a Way to Survive | *Illustration als Mittel zum Überleben*

1992

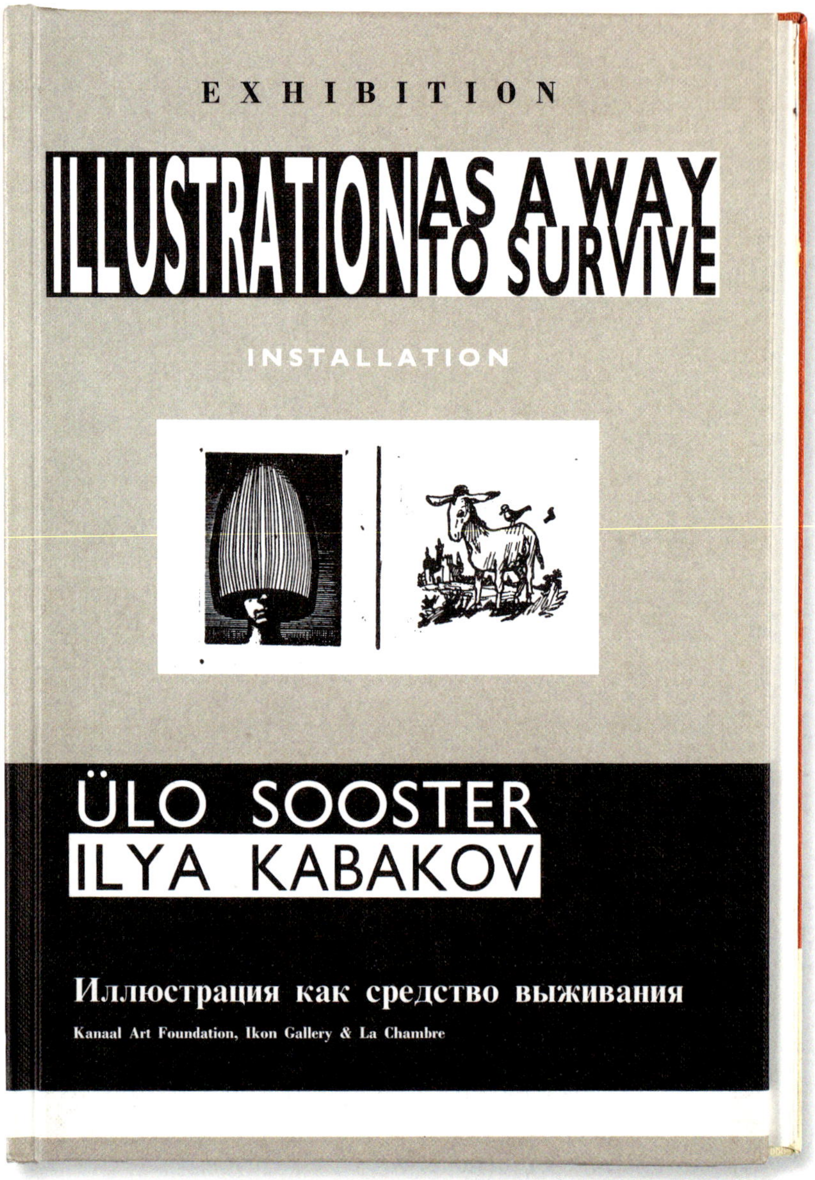

Kanaal Art Foundation, Kortrijk; Ikon Gallery, Birmingham
Kortrijk/Birmingham: Kanaal Art Foundation, Ikon Gallery
24.6 x 16.7 cm
30 pp. with 27 (21 color) ills.
concertina-folded brochure in hardcover
Leporello in Hardcover
edition: 500 signed, numbered, and dated copies

exhibition catalogue | *Ausstellungskatalog*

layout by Ilya Kabakov | *Layout von Ilya Kabakov*

For the installation of the same name at the Kanaal Art Foundation, Kortrijk, Belgium, October 10 to December 20, 1992; Ikon Gallery, Birmingham, April 14 to May 15, 1993; Centre for Contemporary Arts, Glasgow, July 24 to September 4, 1993; Museum of Israeli Art, Ramat Gan, September 2 to October 31, 1993; and Vancouver Art Gallery, Vancouver, April 13 to May 30, 1994. Texts by M. Catherine de Zegher, Boris Groys, Ilya Kabakov, and a dialogue between Joseph Backstein and Ilya Kabakov; Russian, English.

Zur gleichnamigen Installation, Kanaal Art Foundation, Kortrijk, Belgien, 10. Oktober – 20. Dezember 1992, Ikon Gallery, Birmingham, 14. April – 15. Mai 1993, Centre for Contemporary Arts, Glasgow, 24. Juli – 4. September 1993, Museum of Israeli Art, Ramat Gan, 2. September – 31. Oktober 1993, und Vancouver Art Gallery, Vancouver, 13. April – 30. Mai 1994. Texte von M. Catherine de Zegher, Boris Groys, Ilya Kabakov und ein Dialog von Josef Backstein und Ilya Kabakov; russisch, englisch.

see also | *siehe auch* CRI, vol. 1, no. 62, pp. 408–415

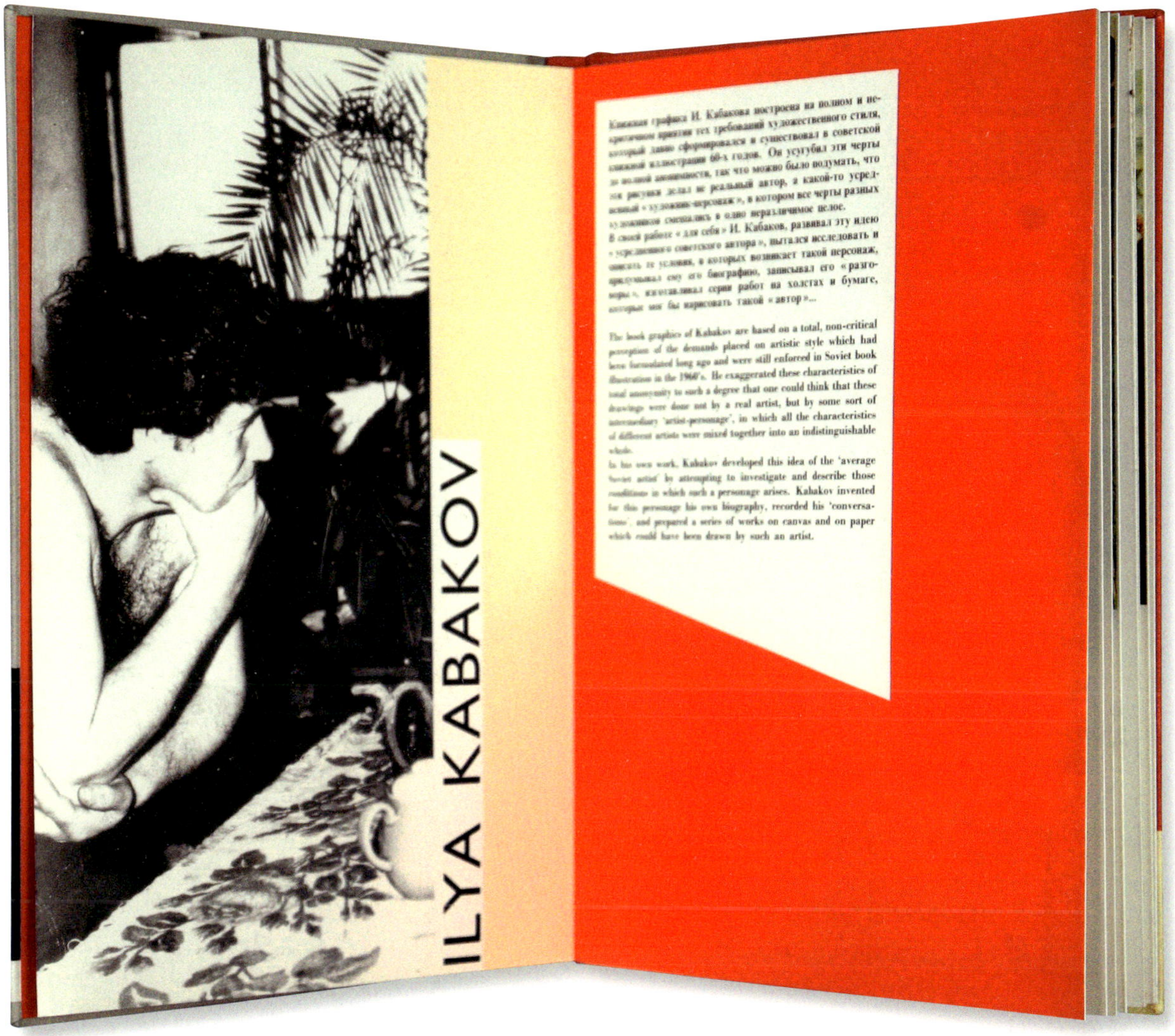
ILYA KABAKOV
Книжная графика И. Кабакова построена на полном и не-
критичном принятии тех требований художественного стиля,
который давно сформировался и существовал в советской
книжной иллюстрации 60-х годов. Он усугубил эти черты
до полной анонимности, так что можно было подумать, что
эти рисунки делал не реальный автор, а какой-то усред-
нённый « художник-персонаж », в котором все черты разных
художников смешались в одно неразличимое целое.
В своей работе « для себя » И. Кабаков, развивал эту идею
« усреднённого советского автора », пытался исследовать и
описать те условия, в которых возникает такой персонаж,
придумывал ему его биографию, записывал его « разго-
воры », изготавливал серии работ на холстах и бумаге,
которые мог бы нарисовать такой « автор »...
The book graphics of Kabakov are based on a total, non-critical
perception of the demands placed on artistic style which had
been formulated long ago and were still enforced in Soviet book
illustration in the 1960's. He exaggerated these characteristics of
total anonymity to such a degree that one could think that these
drawings were done not by a real artist, but by some sort of
intermediary 'artist-personage', in which all the characteristics
of different artists were mixed together into an indistinguishable
whole.
In his own work, Kabakov developed this idea of the 'average
Soviet artist' by attempting to investigate and describe those
conditions in which such a personage arises. Kabakov invented
for this personage his own biography, recorded his 'conversa-
tions', and prepared a series of works on canvas and on paper
which could have been drawn by such an artist.

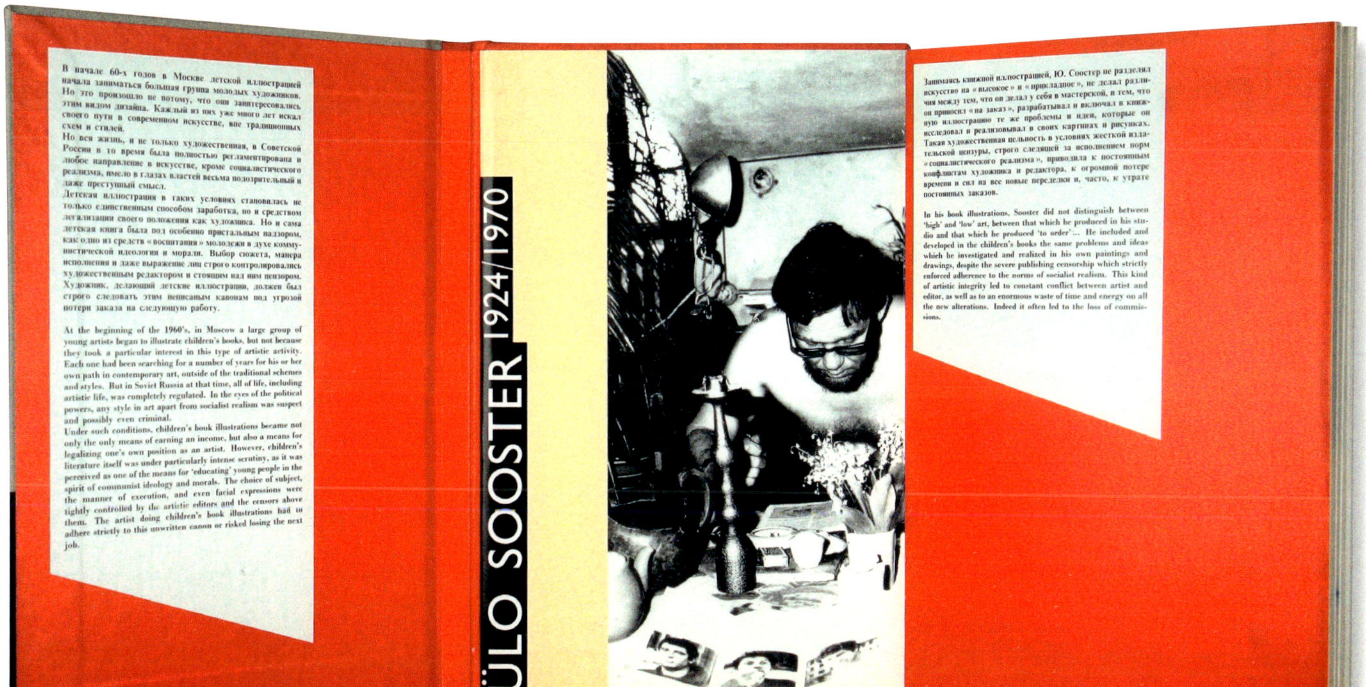
В начале 60-х годов в Москве детской иллюстрацией
начала заниматься большая группа молодых художников.
Но это произошло не потому, что они заинтересовались
этим видом дизайна. Каждый из них уже много лет искал
своего пути в современном искусстве, вне традиционных
схем и стилей.
Но вся жизнь, и не только художественная, в Советской
России в то время была полностью регламентирована и
любое направление в искусстве, кроме социалистического
реализма, имело в глазах властей весьма подозрительный и
даже преступный смысл.
Детская иллюстрация в таких условиях становилась не
только единственным способом заработка, но и средством
легализации своего положения как художника. Но и сама
детская книга была под особенно пристальным надзором,
как одно из средств « воспитания » молодежи в духе комму-
нистической идеологии и морали. Выбор сюжета, манера
исполнения и даже выражение лиц строго контролировались
художественным редактором и стоящим над ним цензором.
Художник, делающий детские иллюстрации, должен был
строго следовать этим неписаным канонам под угрозой
потери заказа на следующую работу.
At the beginning of the 1960's, in Moscow a large group of
young artists began to illustrate children's books, but not because
they took a particular interest in this type of artistic activity.
Each one had been searching for a number of years for his or her
own path in contemporary art, outside of the traditional schemes
and styles. But in Soviet Russia at that time, all of life, including
artistic life, was completely regulated. In the eyes of the political
powers, any style in art apart from socialist realism was suspect
and possibly even criminal.
Under such conditions, children's book illustrations became not
only the only means of earning an income, but also a means for
legalizing one's own position as an artist. However, children's
literature itself was under particularly intense scrutiny, as it was
perceived as one of the means for 'educating' young people in the
spirit of communist ideology and morals. The choice of subject,
the manner of execution, and even facial expressions were
tightly controlled by the artistic editors and the censors above
them. The artist doing children's book illustrations had to
adhere strictly to this unwritten canon or risked losing the next
job.
ÜLO SOOSTER 1924/1970
Занимаясь книжной иллюстрацией, Ю. Соостер не разделял
искусство на « высокое » и « прикладное », не делал разли-
чия между тем, что он делал у себя в мастерской, и тем, что
он приносил « на заказ », разрабатывал и включал в книж-
ную иллюстрацию те же проблемы и идеи, которые он
исследовал и реализовывал в своих картинах и рисунках.
Такая художественная цельность в условиях жесткой изда-
тельской цензуры, строго следящей за исполнением норм
« социалистического реализма », приводила к постоянным
конфликтам художника и редактора, к огромной потере
времени и сил на все новые переделки и, часто, к утрате
постоянных заказов.
In his book illustrations, Sooster did not distinguish between
'high' and 'low' art, between that which he produced in his stu-
dio and that which he produced 'to order'... He included and
developed in the children's books the same problems and ideas
which he investigated and realized in his own paintings and
drawings, despite the severe publishing censorship which strictly
enforced adherence to the norms of socialist realism. This kind
of artistic integrity led to constant conflict between artist and
editor, as well as to an enormous waste of time and energy on all
the new alterations. Indeed it often led to the loss of commis-
sions.

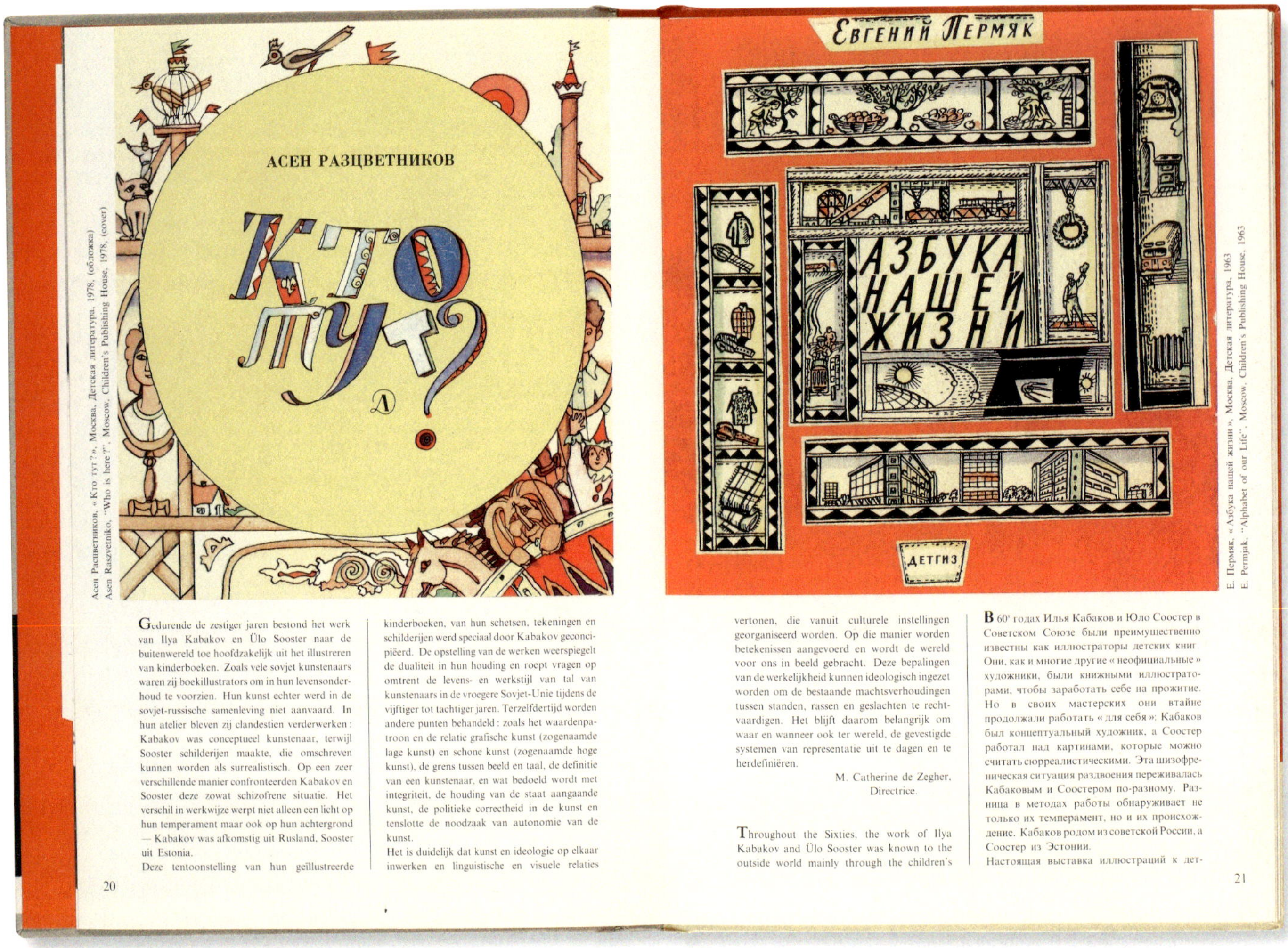

Асен Расцветников, « Кто тут? », Москва, Детская литература, 1978, (обложка)
Asen Raszvetniko, "Who is here?", Moscow, Children's Publishing House, 1978, (cover)

Е. Пермяк, « Азбука нашей жизни », Москва, Детская литература, 1963
E. Permjak, "Alphabet of our Life", Moscow, Children's Publishing House, 1963

Gedurende de zestiger jaren bestond het werk van Ilya Kabakov en Ülo Sooster naar de buitenwereld toe hoofdzakelijk uit het illustreren van kinderboeken. Zoals vele sovjet kunstenaars waren zij boekillustrators om in hun levensonderhoud te voorzien. Hun kunst echter werd in de sovjet-russische samenleving niet aanvaard. In hun atelier bleven zij clandestien verderwerken : Kabakov was conceptueel kunstenaar, terwijl Sooster schilderijen maakte, die omschreven kunnen worden als surrealistisch. Op een zeer verschillende manier confronteerden Kabakov en Sooster deze zowat schizofrene situatie. Het verschil in werkwijze werpt niet alleen een licht op hun temperament maar ook op hun achtergrond — Kabakov was afkomstig uit Rusland, Sooster uit Estonia.

Deze tentoonstelling van hun geïllustreerde kinderboeken, van hun schetsen, tekeningen en schilderijen werd speciaal door Kabakov geconcipiëerd. De opstelling van de werken weerspiegelt de dualiteit in hun houding en roept vragen op omtrent de levens- en werkstijl van tal van kunstenaars in de vroegere Sovjet-Unie tijdens de vijftiger tot tachtiger jaren. Terzelfdertijd worden andere punten behandeld : zoals het waardenpatroon en de relatie grafische kunst (zogenaamde lage kunst) en schone kunst (zogenaamde hoge kunst), de grens tussen beeld en taal, de definitie van een kunstenaar, en wat bedoeld wordt met integriteit, de houding van de staat aangaande kunst, de politieke correctheid in de kunst en tenslotte de noodzaak van autonomie van de kunst.

Het is duidelijk dat kunst en ideologie op elkaar inwerken en linguistische en visuele relaties vertonen, die vanuit culturele instellingen georganiseerd worden. Op die manier worden betekenissen aangevoerd en wordt de wereld voor ons in beeld gebracht. Deze bepalingen van de werkelijkheid kunnen ideologisch ingezet worden om de bestaande machtsverhoudingen tussen standen, rassen en geslachten te rechtvaardigen. Het blijft daarom belangrijk om waar en wanneer ook ter wereld, de gevestigde systemen van representatie uit te dagen en te herdefiniëren.

M. Catherine de Zegher,
Directrice.

Throughout the Sixties, the work of Ilya Kabakov and Ülo Sooster was known to the outside world mainly through the children's

В 60ᵉ годах Илья Кабаков и Юло Соостер в Советском Союзе были преимущественно известны как иллюстраторы детских книг. Они, как и многие другие « неофициальные » художники, были книжными иллюстраторами, чтобы заработать себе на прожитие. Но в своих мастерских они втайне продолжали работать « для себя »: Кабаков был концептуальный художник, а Соостер работал над картинами, которые можно считать сюрреалистическими. Эта шизофреническая ситуация раздвоения переживалась Кабаковым и Соостером по-разному. Разница в методах работы обнаруживает не только их темперамент, но и их происхождение. Кабаков родом из советской России, а Соостер из Эстонии.

Настоящая выставка иллюстраций к дет-

20

21

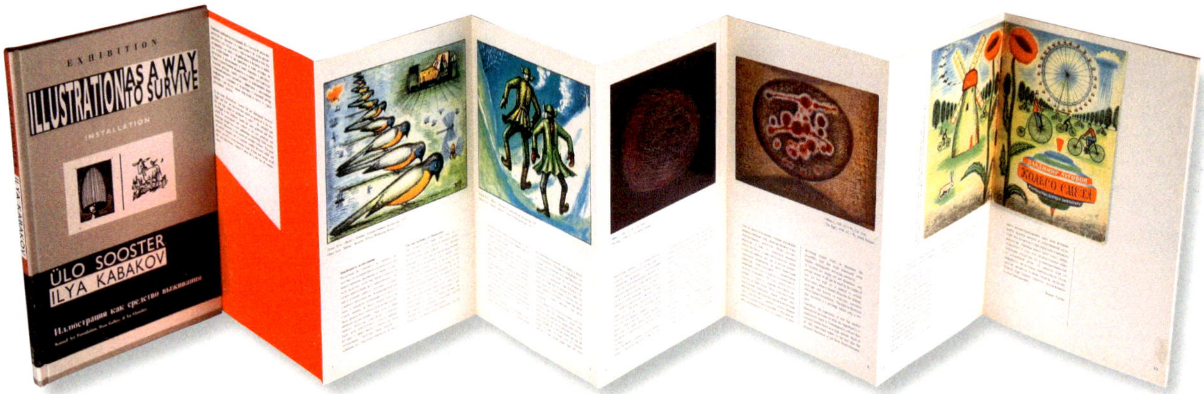

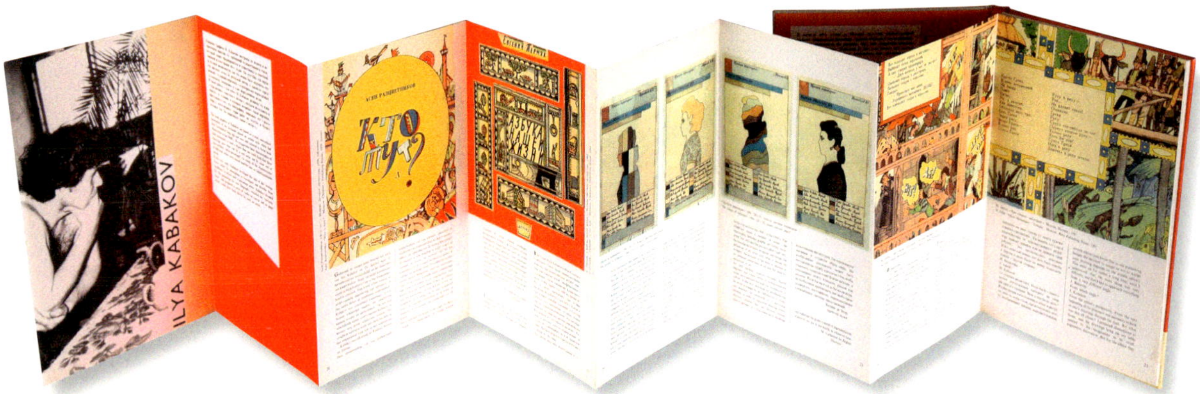

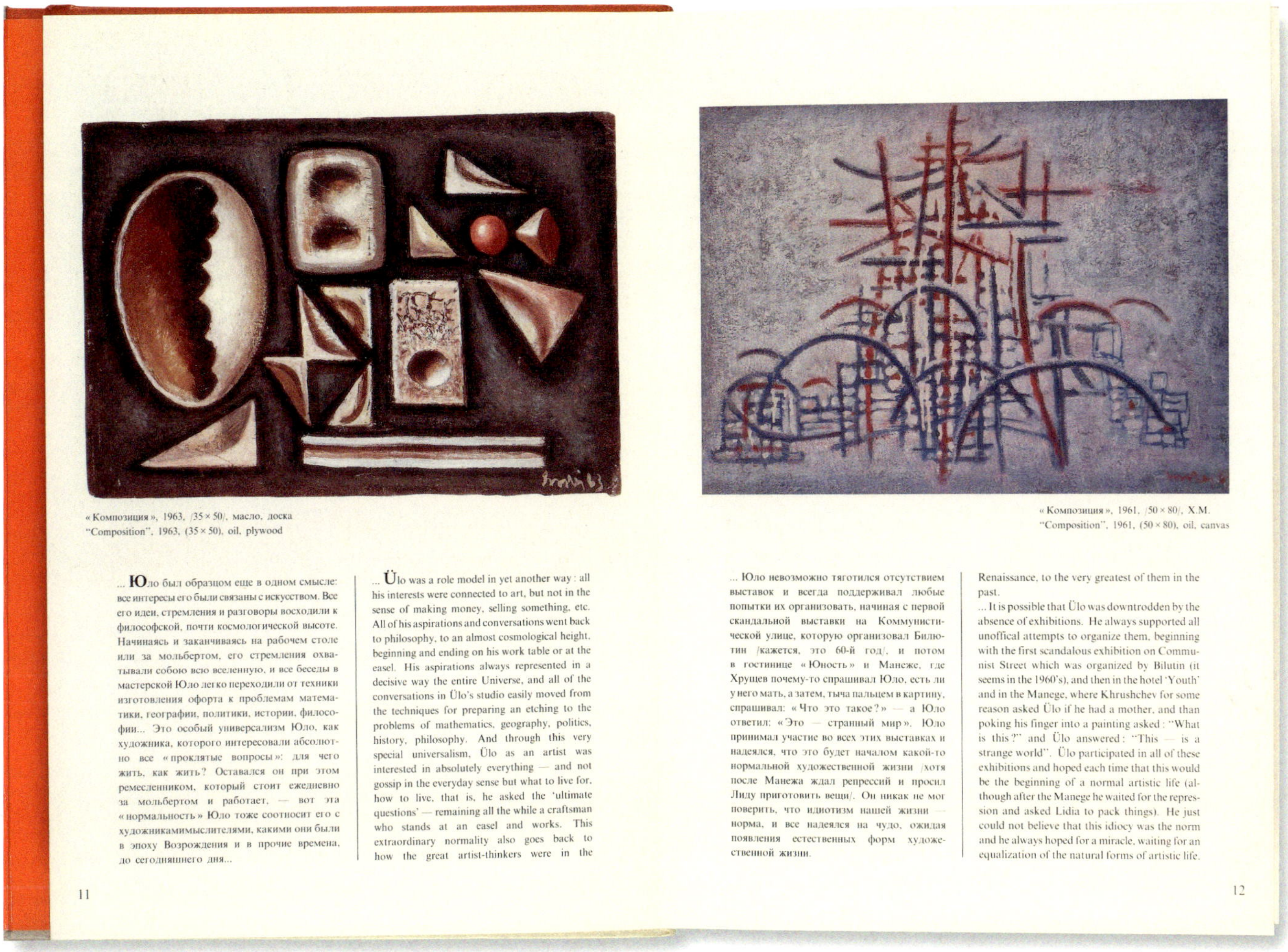

« Композиция », 1963, /35 × 50/, масло, доска
"Composition", 1963, (35 × 50), oil, plywood

« Композиция », 1961, /50 × 80/, Х.М.
"Composition", 1961, (50 × 80), oil, canvas

... Юло был образцом еще в одном смысле: все интересы его были связаны с искусством. Все его идеи, стремления и разговоры восходили к философской, почти космологической высоте. Начинаясь и заканчиваясь на рабочем столе или за мольбертом, его стремления охватывали собою всю вселенную, и все беседы в мастерской Юло легко переходили от техники изготовления офорта к проблемам математики, географии, политики, истории, философии... Это особый универсализм Юло, как художника, которого интересовали абсолютно все « проклятые вопросы »: для чего жить, как жить? Оставался он при этом ремесленником, который стоит ежедневно за мольбертом и работает, — вот эта « нормальность » Юло тоже соотносит его с художникамимыслителями, какими они были в эпоху Возрождения и в прочие времена, до сегодняшнего дня...

... Ülo was a role model in yet another way: all his interests were connected to art, but not in the sense of making money, selling something, etc. All of his aspirations and conversations went back to philosophy, to an almost cosmological height, beginning and ending on his work table or at the easel. His aspirations always represented in a decisive way the entire Universe, and all of the conversations in Ülo's studio easily moved from the techniques for preparing an etching to the problems of mathematics, geography, politics, history, philosophy. And through this very special universalism, Ülo as an artist was interested in absolutely everything — and not gossip in the everyday sense but what to live for, how to live, that is, he asked the 'ultimate questions' — remaining all the while a craftsman who stands at an easel and works. This extraordinary normality also goes back to how the great artist-thinkers were in the Renaissance, to the very greatest of them in the past.

11

... Юло невозможно тяготился отсутствием выставок и всегда поддерживал любые попытки их организовать, начиная с первой скандальной выставки на Коммунистической улице, которую организовал Билютин /кажется, это 60-й год/, и потом в гостинице « Юность » и Манеже, где Хрущев почему-то спрашивал Юло, есть ли у него мать, а затем, тыча пальцем в картину, спрашивал: « Что это такое? » — а Юло ответил: « Это — странный мир ». Юло принимал участие во всех этих выставках и надеялся, что это будет началом какой-то нормальной художественной жизни /хотя после Манежа ждал репрессий и просил Лиду приготовить вещи/. Он никак не мог поверить, что идиотизм нашей жизни — норма, и все надеялся на чудо, ожидая появления естественных форм художественной жизни.

... It is possible that Ülo was downtrodden by the absence of exhibitions. He always supported all unoffical attempts to organize them, beginning with the first scandalous exhibition on Communist Street which was organized by Bilutin (it seems in the 1960's), and then in the hotel 'Youth' and in the Manege, where Khrushchev for some reason asked Ülo if he had a mother, and than poking his finger into a painting asked: "What is this?" and Ülo answered: "This — is a strange world". Ülo participated in all of these exhibitions and hoped each time that this would be the beginning of a normal artistic life (although after the Manege he waited for the repression and asked Lidia to pack things). He just could not believe that this idiocy was the norm and he always hoped for a miracle, waiting for an equalization of the natural forms of artistic life.

12

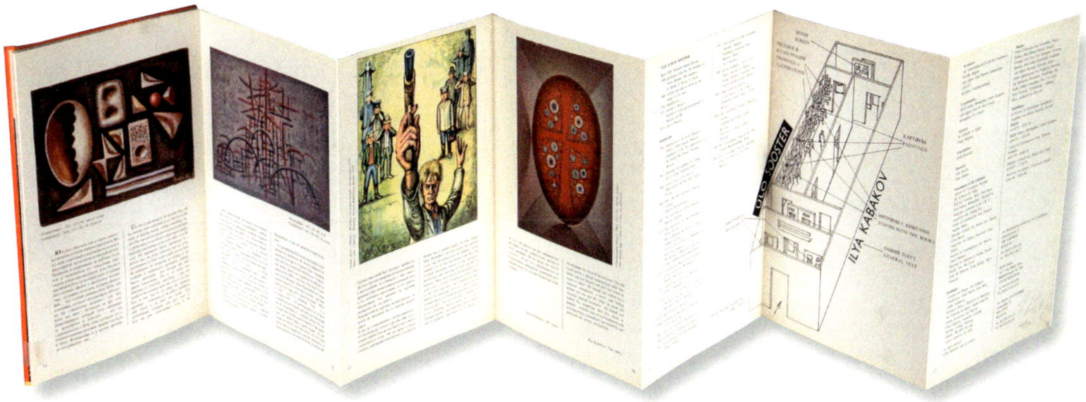

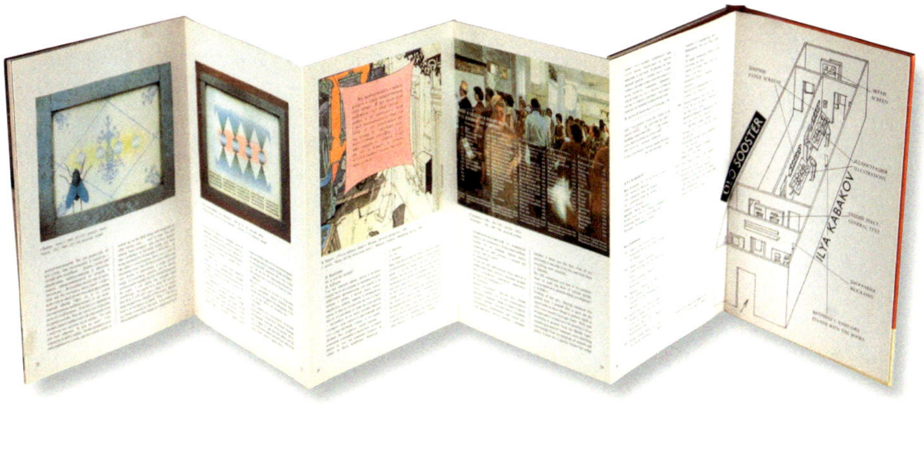

52 Ilya Kabakov | *Ilya Kabakov*

1992

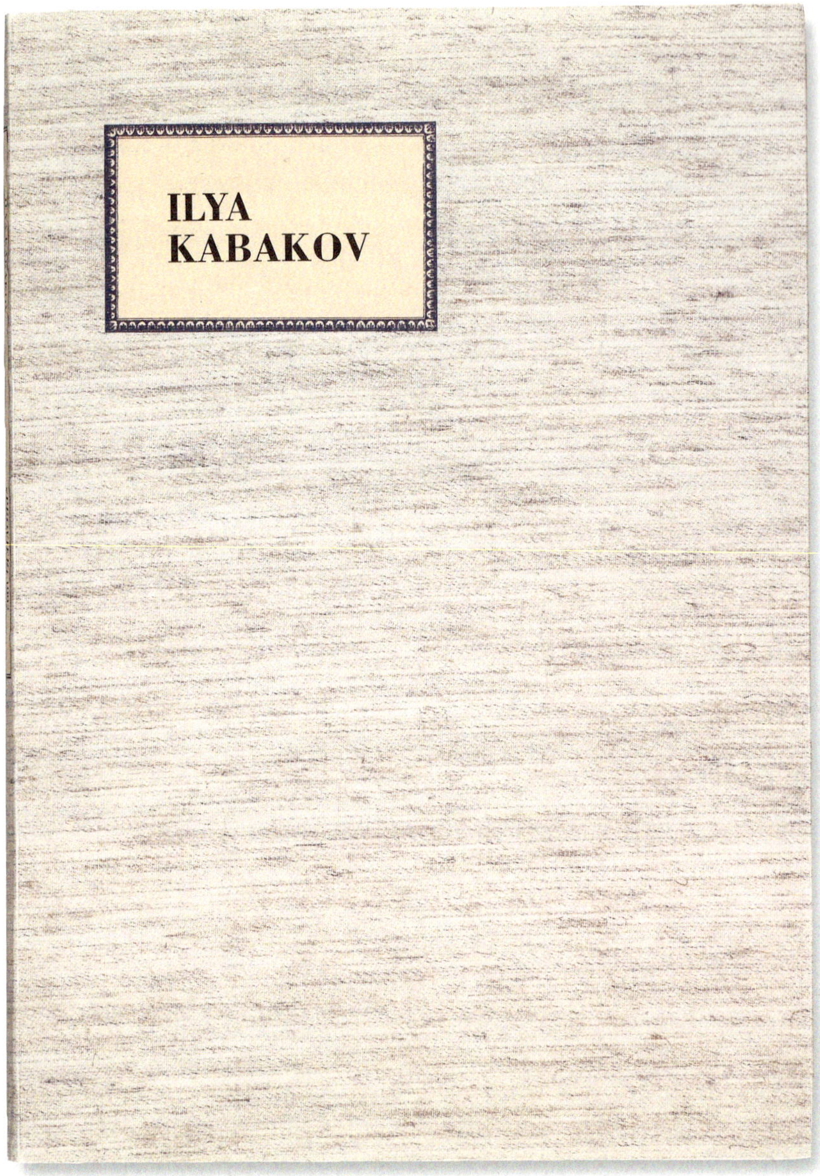

Galleria Sprovieri, Rom
Rome: Edizione Galleria Sprovieri (vol. 6)
29.6 x 21 cm
103 pp. with 29 (8 color) ills.
stitchbound, softback with flaps
Fadenheftung, broschiert mit Umschlagklappen

exhibition catalogue | *Ausstellungskatalog*

layout by Ilya Kabakov | *Layout von Ilya Kabakov*

For the exhibition of the same name at the Galleria Sprovieri, Rome, November 21, 1992 to January 21, 1993. Texts by Joseph Backstein, Ilya Kabakov, and Tatiana Polomochnykh. Dialogue between Boris Groys and Ilya Kabakov on »Russia on our Tails«; Italian, Russian.

Zur gleichnamigen Ausstellung, Galleria Sprovieri, Rom, 21. November 1992 – 21. Januar 1993. Texte von Josef Bakstein, Ilya Kabakov und Tatiana Polomochnykh. Dialog von Boris Groys und Ilya Kabakov über »Mit Russland im Nacken«; italienisch, russisch.

see also | *siehe auch*

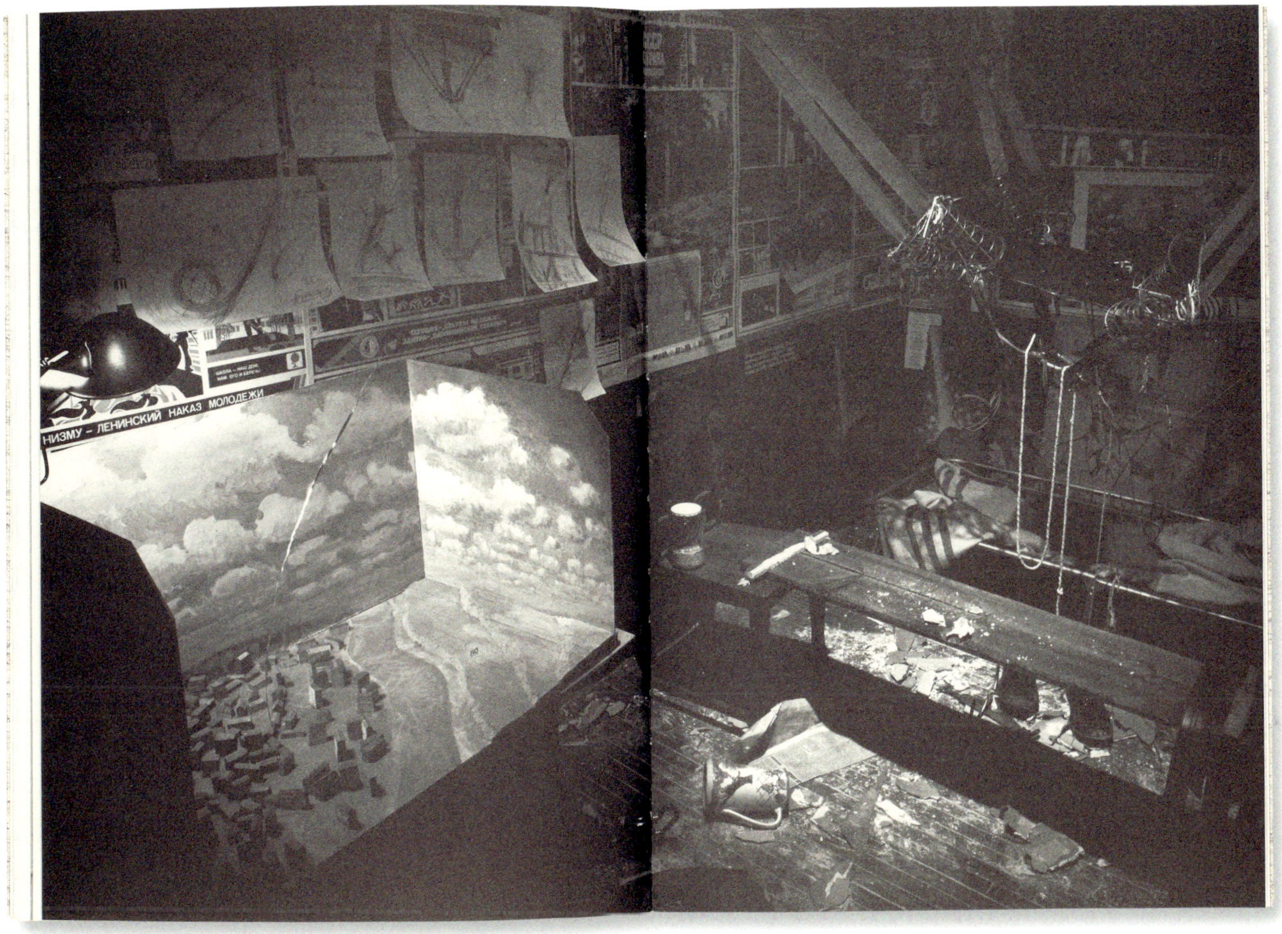
НИЗМУ – ЛЕНИНСКИЙ НАКАЗ МОЛОДЕЖИ

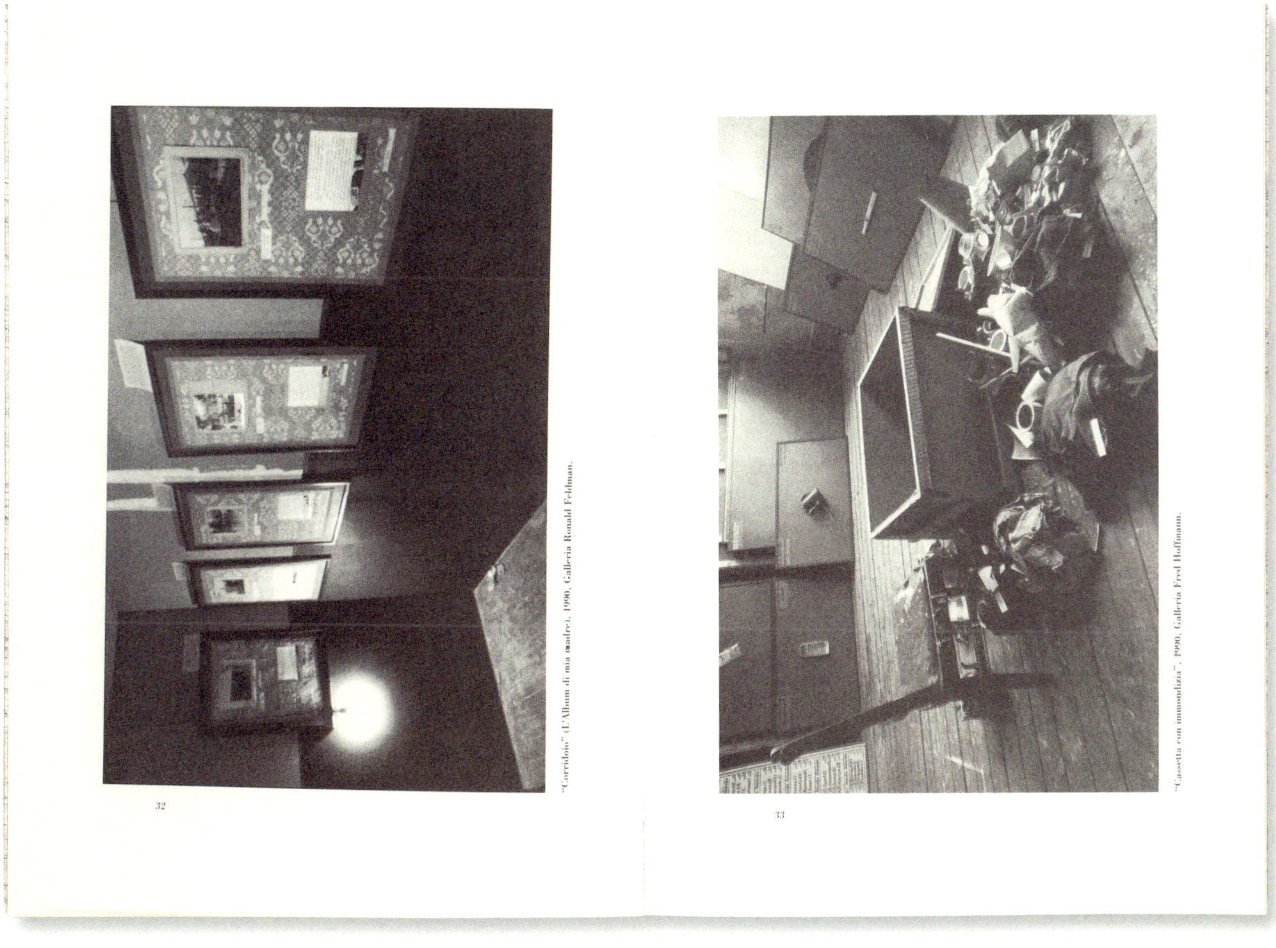
"Corridoio" (L'Album di mia madre), 1990, Galleria Ronald Feldman.
32
"Cassetta con immondizia", 1990, Galleria Fred Hoffmann.
33

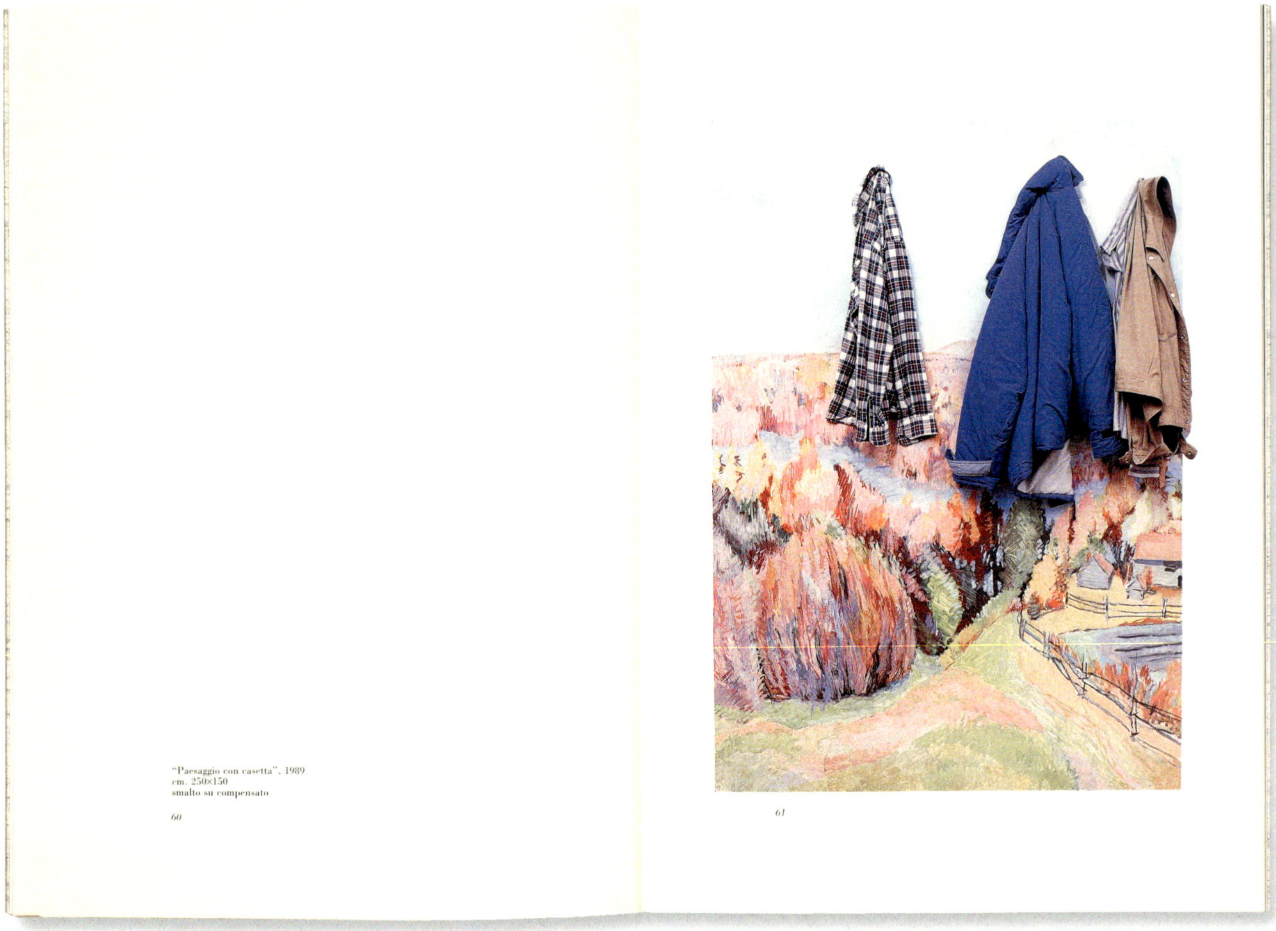
"Paesaggio con casetta". 1989
cm. 250×150
smalto su compensato
60
61

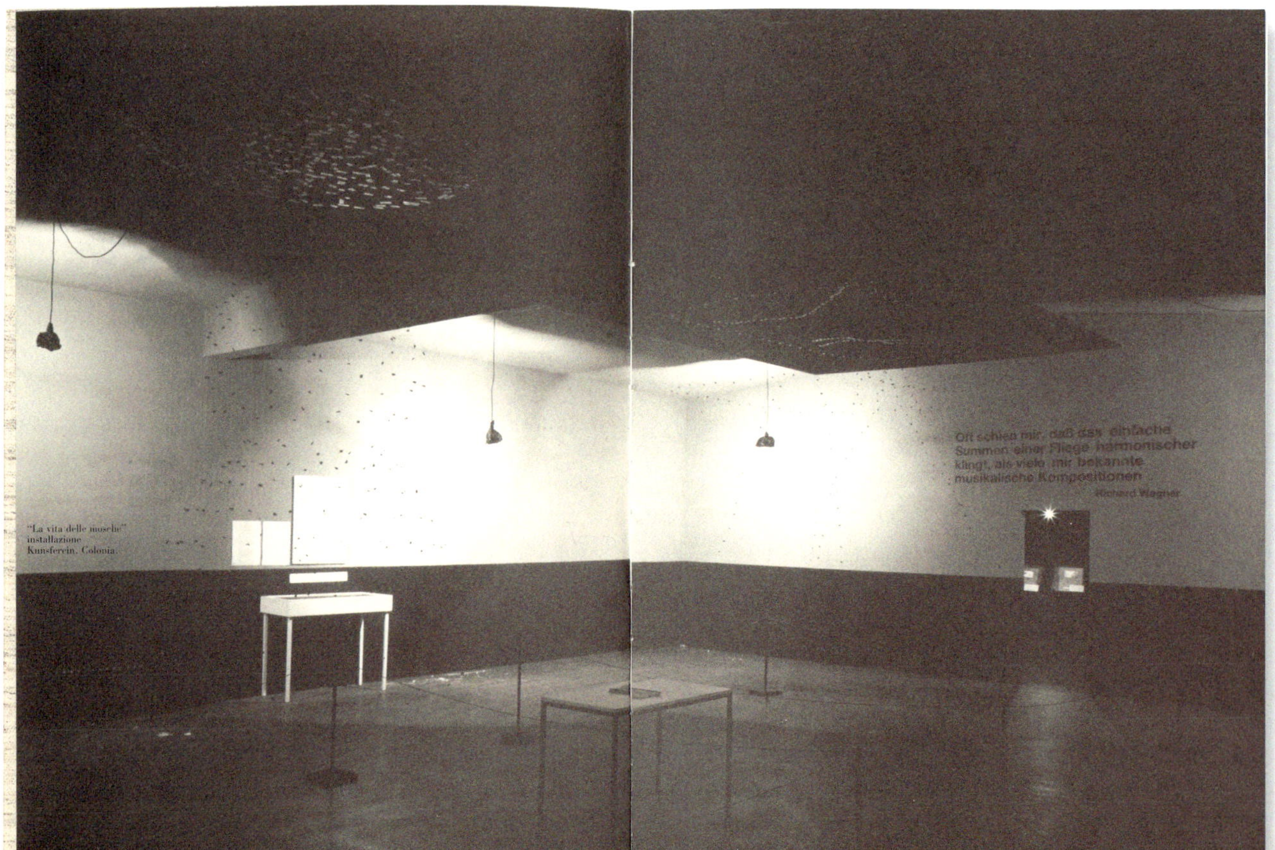
"La vita delle mosche"
installazione
Kunsferein. Colonia.
Oft schien mir, daß das einfache Summen einer Fliege harmonischer klingt, als viele mir bekannte musikalische Kompositionen
Richard Wagner

53 The Man Who Flew Into His Picture | *Der Mensch, der in das Bild flog*

1992

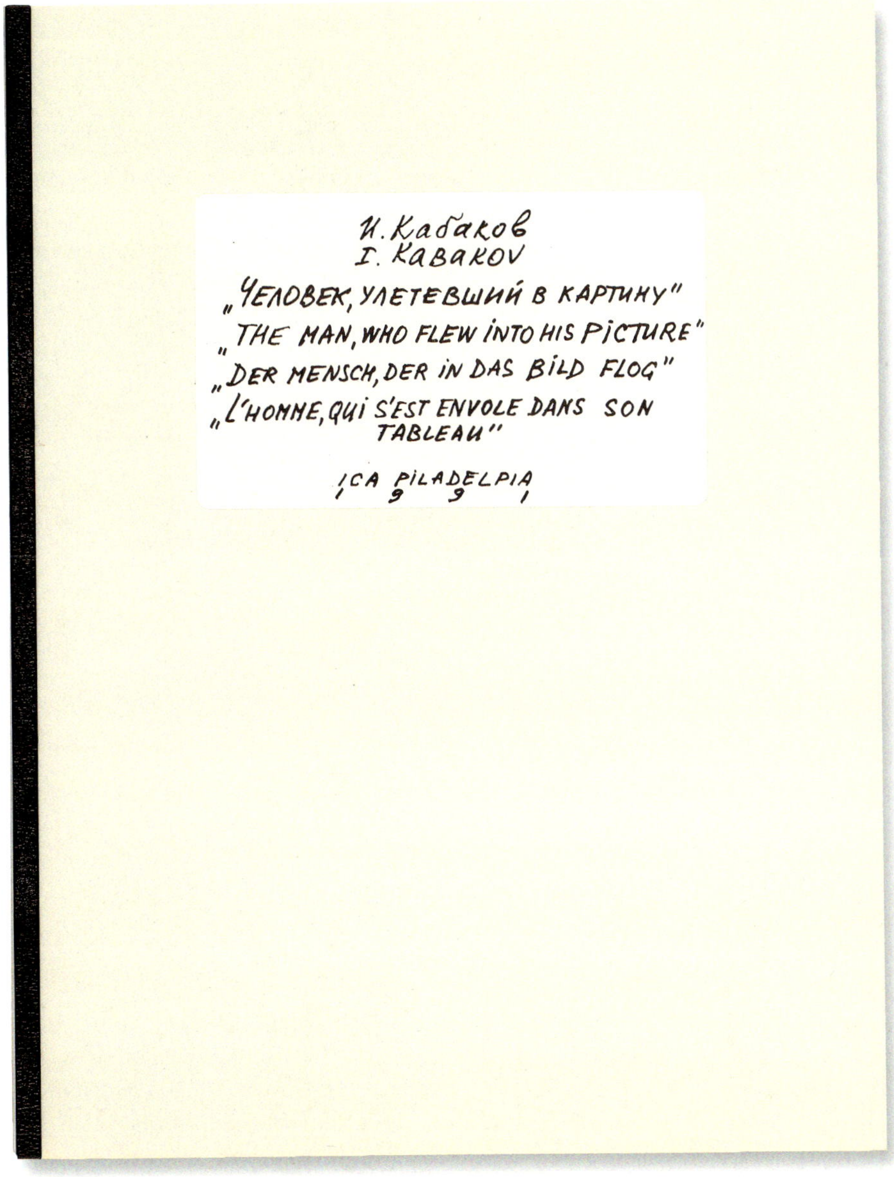

Ilya and Emilia Kabakov
New York: published by Ilya and Emilia Kabakov
27.9 x 21.5 cm
148 photocopied pp. with 41 (incl. 1 color foldout) ills.
quick bind, cardboard cover,
label on the cover
Schnellhefter, Kartonumschlag,
Etikette auf dem Umschlag
edition: 500 numbered copies with 5 including an original signed, numbered, and dated drawing by Ilya Kabakov from 1994

thematic publication | *thematische Publikation*

layout by Ilya Kabakov | *Layout von Ilya Kabakov*

Documentation of the installation of the same name for the exhibition »The Devil on the Stairs: Looking Back on the Eighties« at the Institute of Contemporary Art, University of Pennsylvania, Philadelphia, October 4, 1990 to January 5, 1991 and at the Newport Harbor Art Museum, Newport Beach, CA, April 16 to June 21, 1991. Dialogue between Joseph Backstein and Ilya Kabakov on »The Man Who Flew Into His Picture« and the first part of Sven Gundlakh's text »Hermetische Menschen« from »Sphäre der unbeweglichen Sterne«; Russian, English, German, French.

Dokumentation der gleichnamigen Installation für die Ausstellung »The Devil on the Stairs: Looking Back on the Eighties«, Institute of Contemporary Art, University of Pennsylvania, Philadelphia, 4. Oktober 1990 – 5. Januar 1991 und Newport Harbor Art Museum, Newport Beach, CA, 16. April – 21. Juni 1991. Dialog von Josef Bakstein und Ilya Kabakov über »Der Mensch, der in das

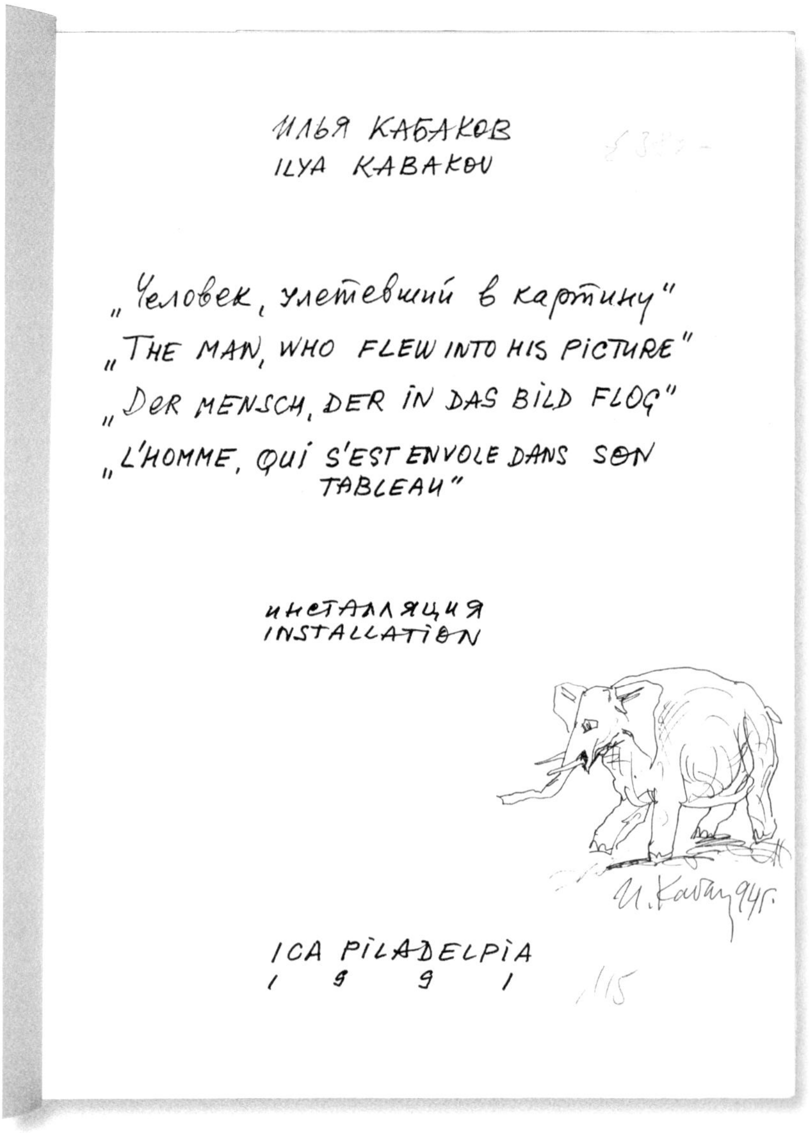

Bild flog« und der 1. Teil des Textes von Sven Gundlakh: »Hermetische Menschen« aus »Sphäre der unbeweglichen Sterne«; russisch, englisch, deutsch, französisch.

see also | *siehe auch* no. 48; no. 54; CRI, vol. 1, no. 16, pp. 146–151; CRP, vol. 1, no. 49, pp. 101–102, no. 95, p. 169

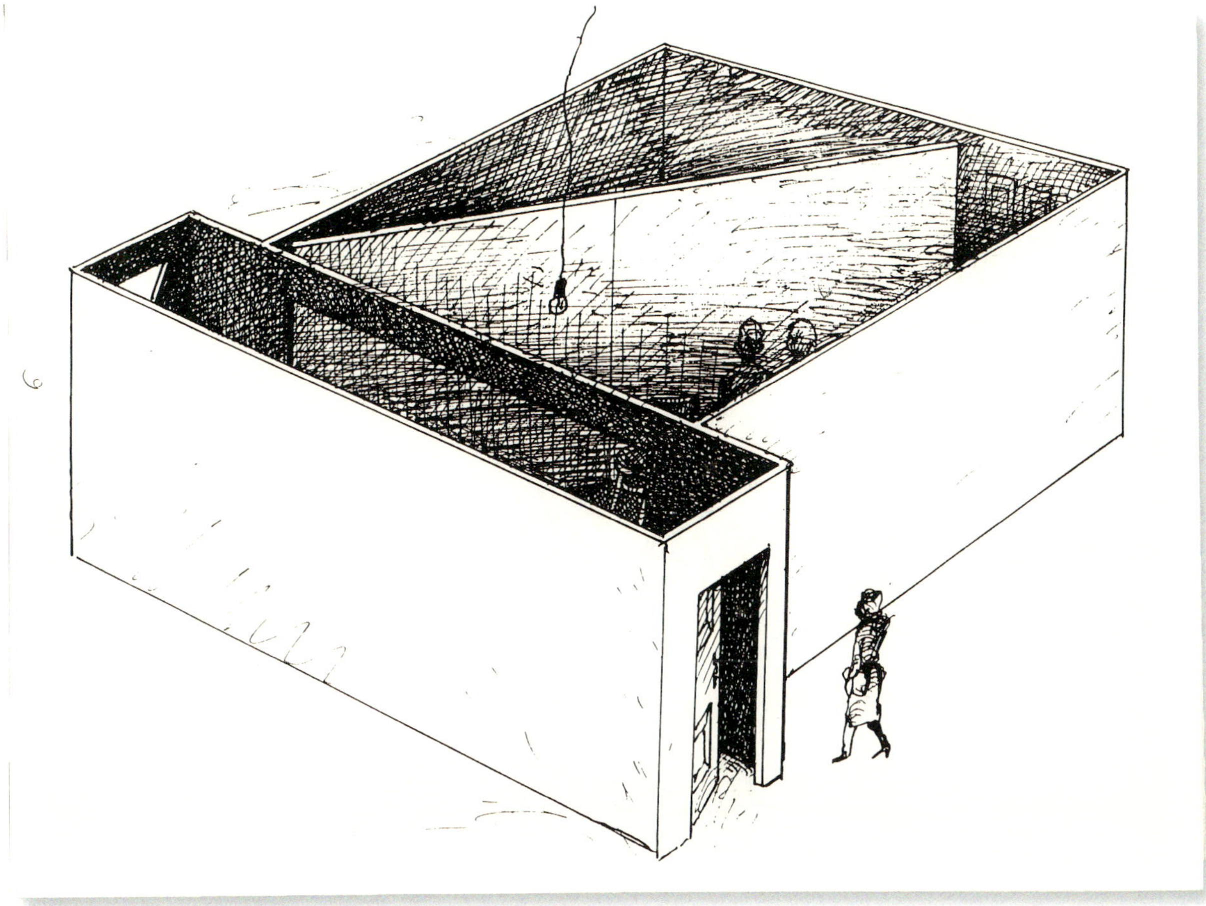

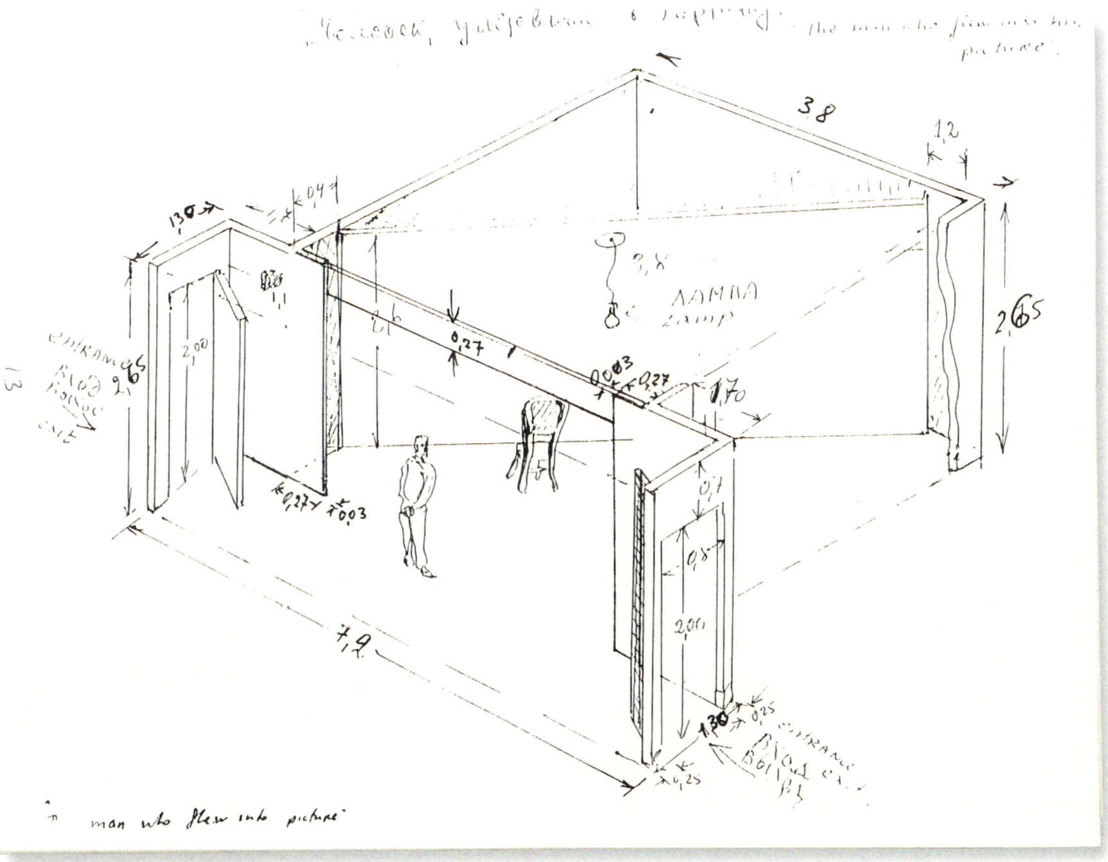
38
1,2
2,65
ЛАМПА
lamp
0,27
1,70
2,00
man who flew into picture

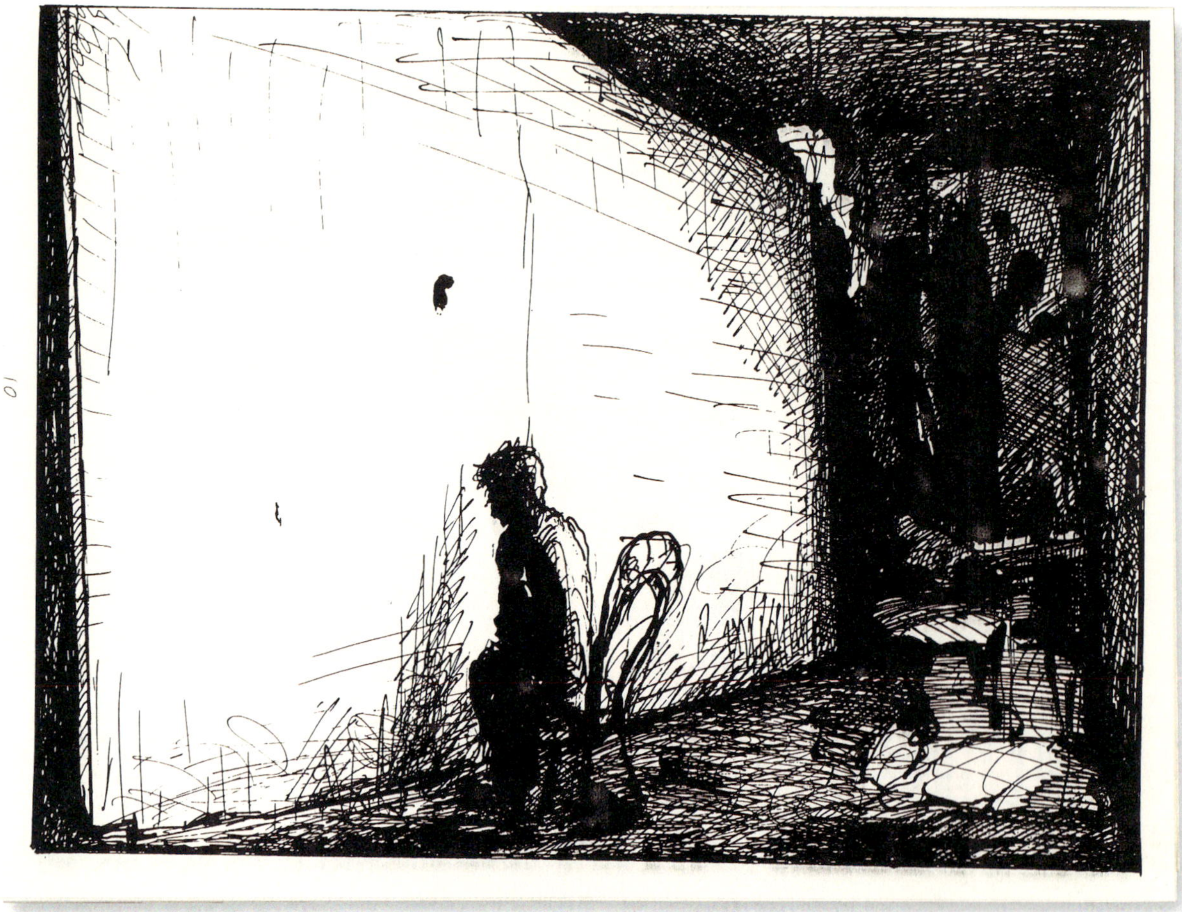

54 The Man Who Flew Into His Picture | *Der Mensch, der in das Bild flog*

1992

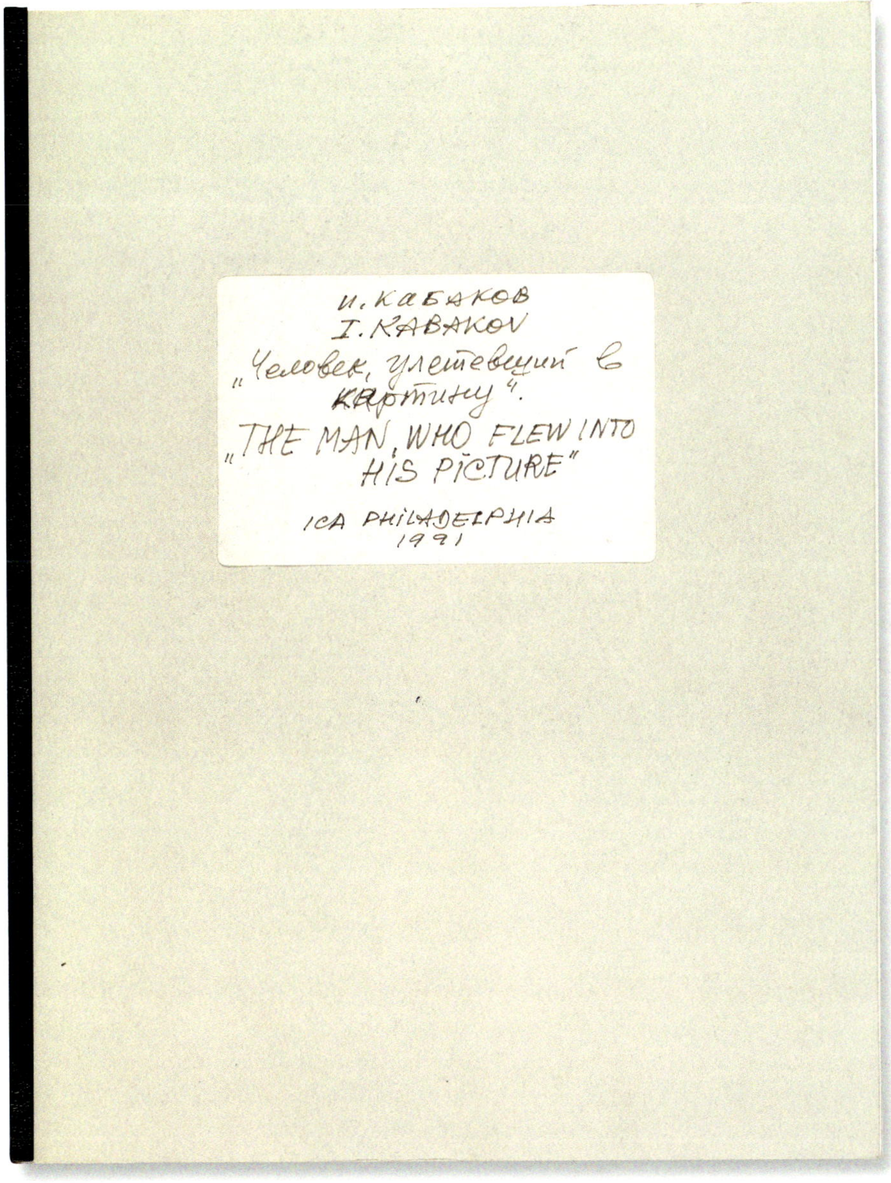

Ilya and Emilia Kabakov
New York: published by Ilya and Emilia Kabakov
27.9 x 21.6 cm
97 photocopied pp. with 40 (incl. 1 color foldout) ills.
quick bind, cardboard cover, label on the cover
Schnellhefter, Kartonumschlag, Etikette auf dem Umschlag
edition: 20 numbered copies

thematic publication | *thematische Publikation*

layout by Ilya Kabakov | *Layout von Ilya Kabakov*

Documentation of the installation of the same name for the exhibition »The Devil on the Stairs: Looking Back on the Eighties« at the Institute of Contemporary Art, University of Pennsylvania, Philadelphia, October 4, 1990 to January 5, 1991 and at the Newport Harbor Art Museum, Newport Beach, CA, April 16 to June 21, 1991. Dialogue between Joseph Backstein and Ilya Kabakov on »The Man Who Flew Into His Picture« and the first part of Sven Gundlakh's text »Hermetische Menschen« from »Sphäre der unbeweglichen Sterne«; Russian, English, German, French.

Dokumentation der gleichnamigen Installation für die Ausstellung »The Devil on the Stairs: Looking Back on the Eighties«, Institute of Contemporary Art, University of Pennsylvania, Philadelphia, 4. Oktober 1990 – 5. Januar 1991 und Newport Harbor Art Museum, Newport Beach, CA, 16. April – 21. Juni 1991. Dialog von Josef Bakstein und Ilya Kabakov über »Der Mensch, der in das Bild flog« und der 1. Teil des Textes von Sven

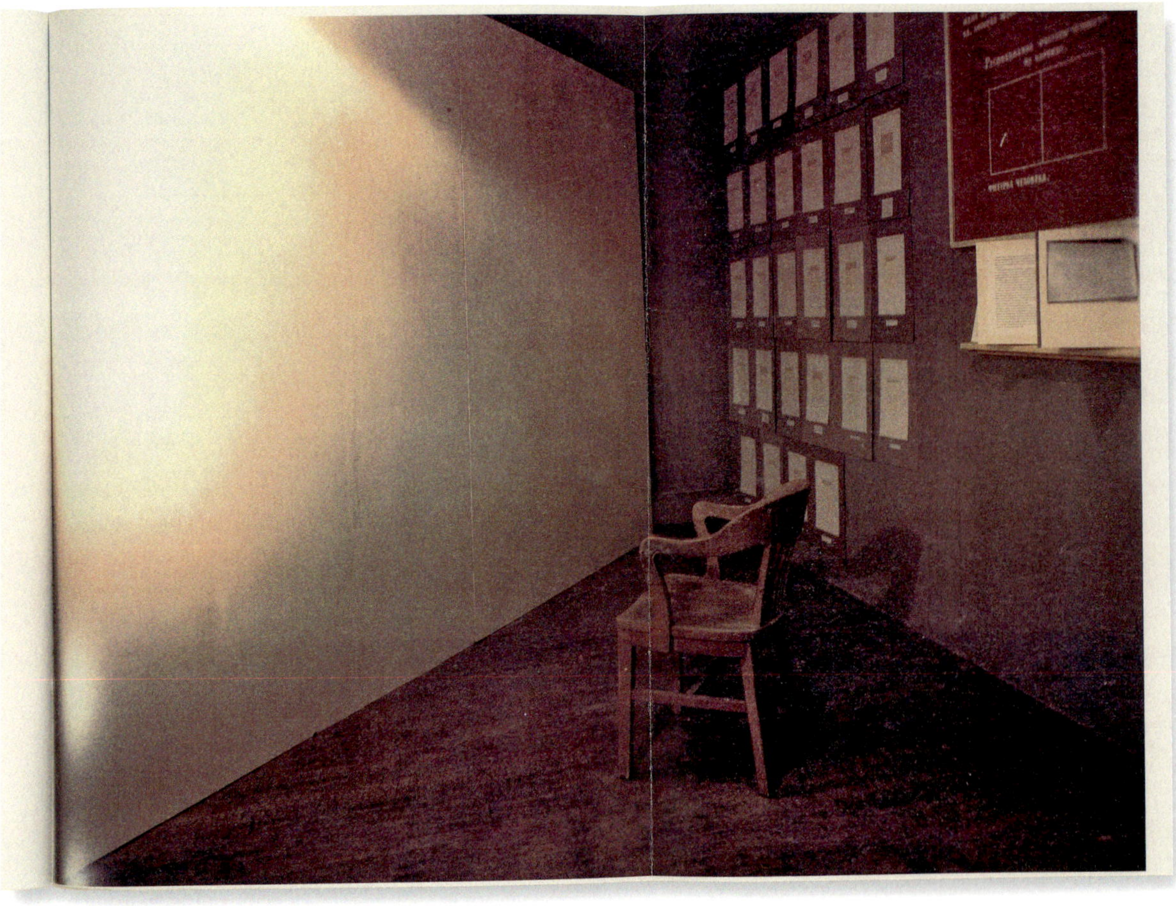

Gundlakh: »Hermetische Menschen« aus »Sphäre der unbeweglichen Sterne«; russisch, englisch, deutsch, französisch.

see also | *siehe auch* no. 48; no. 54; CRI, vol. 1, no. 16, pp. 146–151; CRP, vol. 1, no. 49, pp. 101–102, no. 95, p. 169

55 The Red Wagon | *Der rote Waggon*

1992

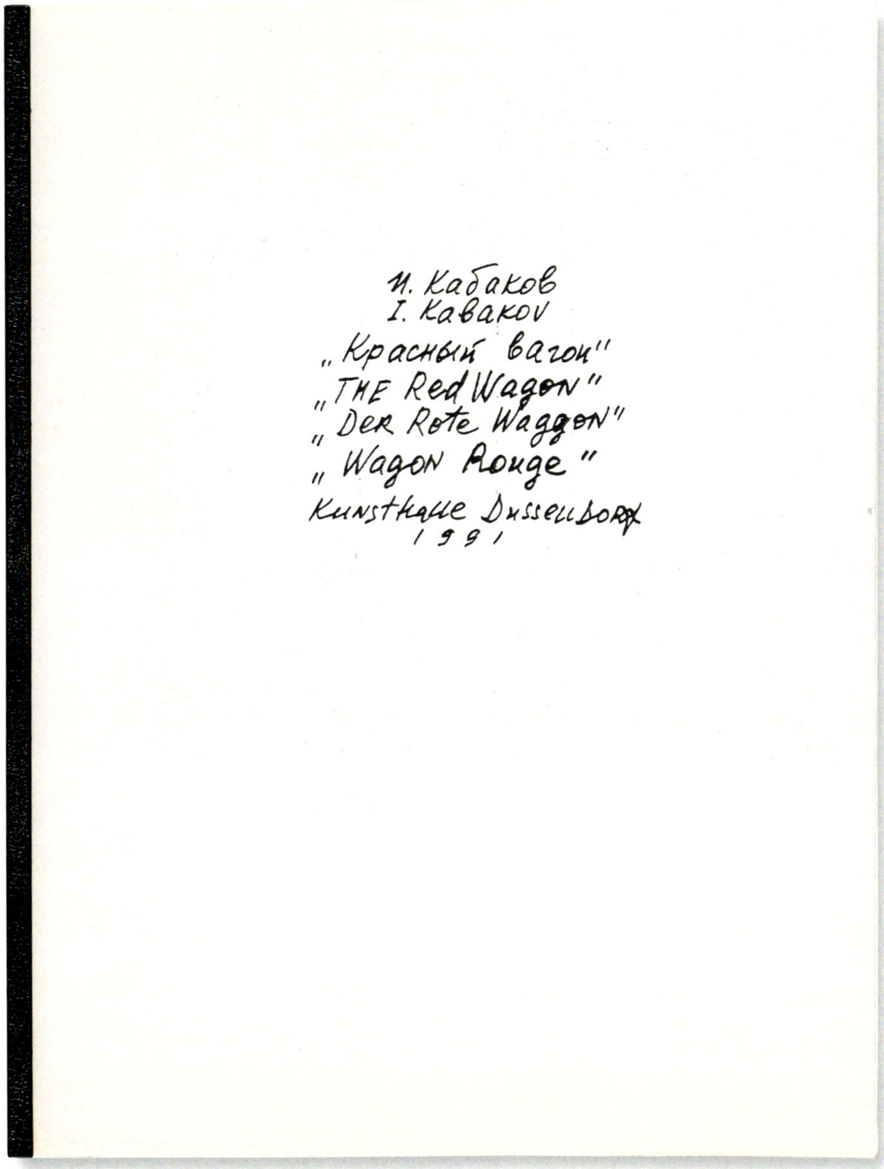

Ilya and Emilia Kabakov
New York: published by Ilya and Emilia Kabakov
28 x 21.5 cm
27 photocopied pp. with 4 b/w (foldouts) and 24 color (incl. 6 foldouts) ills.
quick bind, cardboard cover, label on the cover
Schnellhefter, Kartonumschlag, Etikette auf dem Umschlag
edition: 500 numbered copies with 5 including an original signed, numbered, and dated drawing by Ilya Kabakov from 1992

thematic publication | *thematische Publikation*

layout by Ilya Kabakov | *Layout von Ilya Kabakov*

Documentation of the installation of the same name for the exhibition »Soviet Art Around 1990: Binational«, Städtische Kunsthalle Düsseldorf, Düsseldorf, April 12 to June 2, 1991. Texts by Ilya Kabakov; Russian, English, German, French.

Dokumentation der gleichnamigen Installation für die Ausstellung »Sowjetische Kunst um 1990: Binationale«, Städtische Kunsthalle Düsseldorf, Düsseldorf, 12. April – 2. Juni 1991. Texte von Ilya Kabakov; russisch, englisch, deutsch, französisch.

see also | *siehe auch* no. 135; CRI, vol. 1, no. 42, pp. 290–295; CRP, vol. 1, nos. 165–181, pp. 255–265

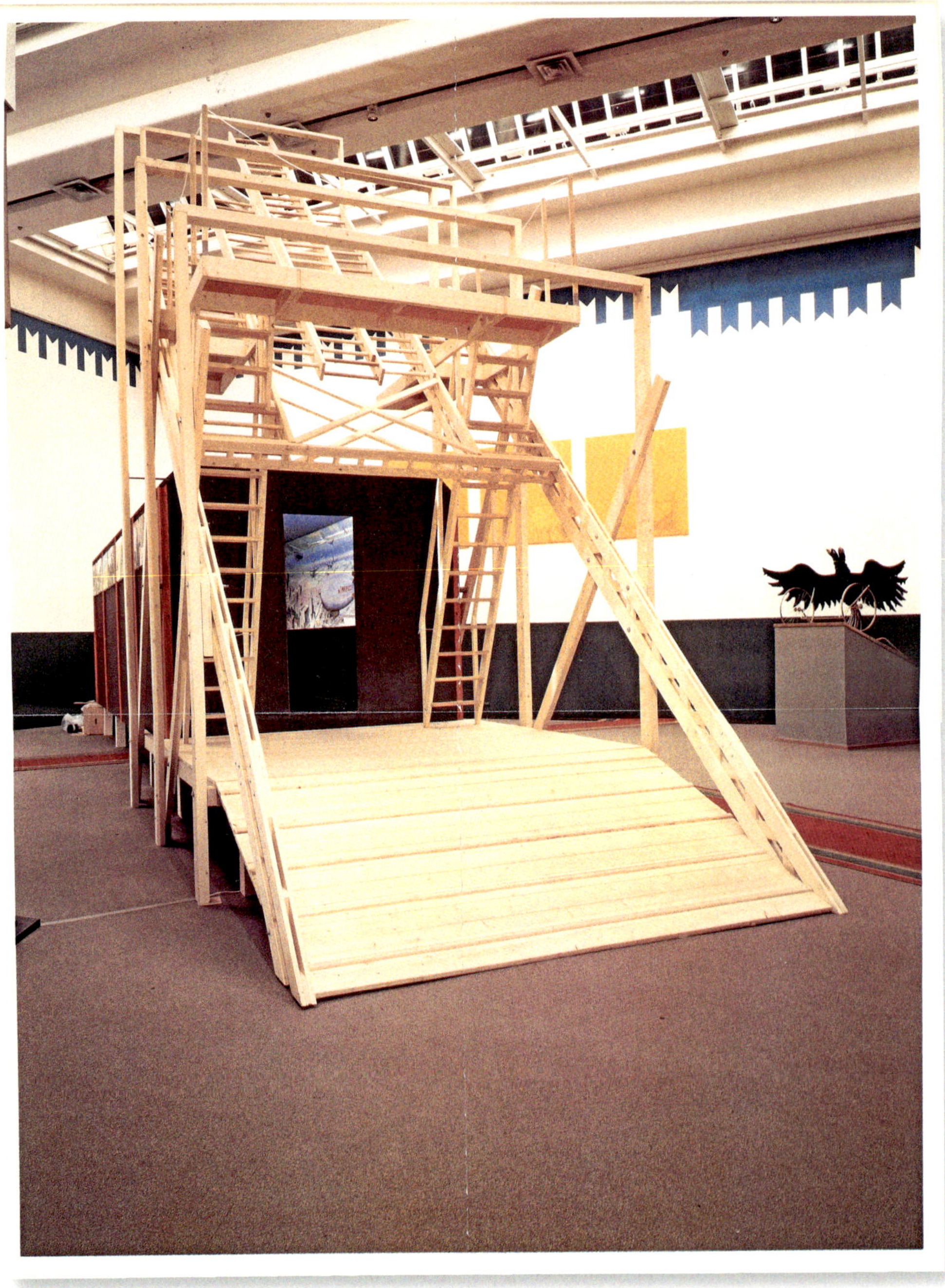

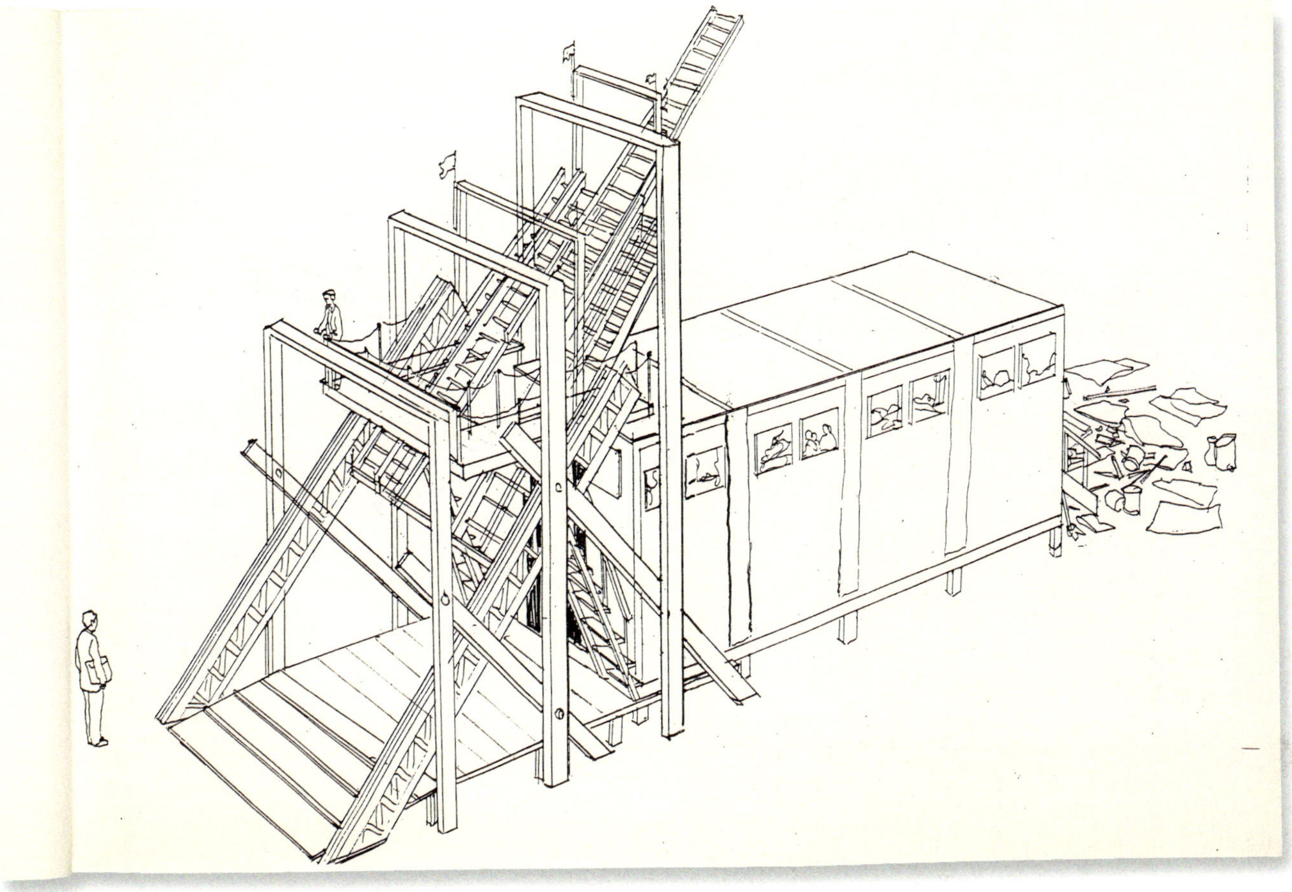

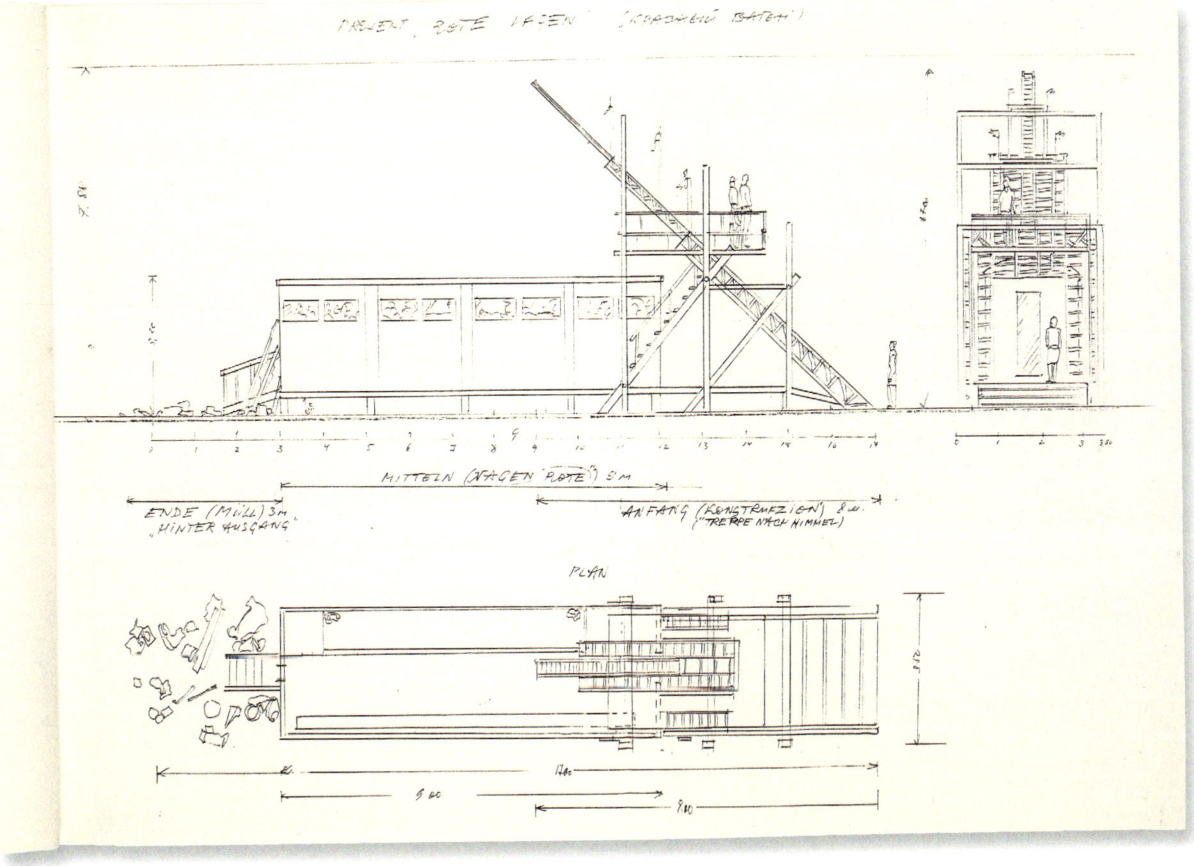
PROJEKT „ROTE VAGEN" (КРАСНЫЙ ВАГОН)
MITTELN (WAGEN „ROTE") 9 M
ENDE (MÜLL) 3 M
„HINTER AUSGANG"
ANFANG (KONSTRUKZION) 8 M
(„TREPPE NACH HIMMEL")
PLAN

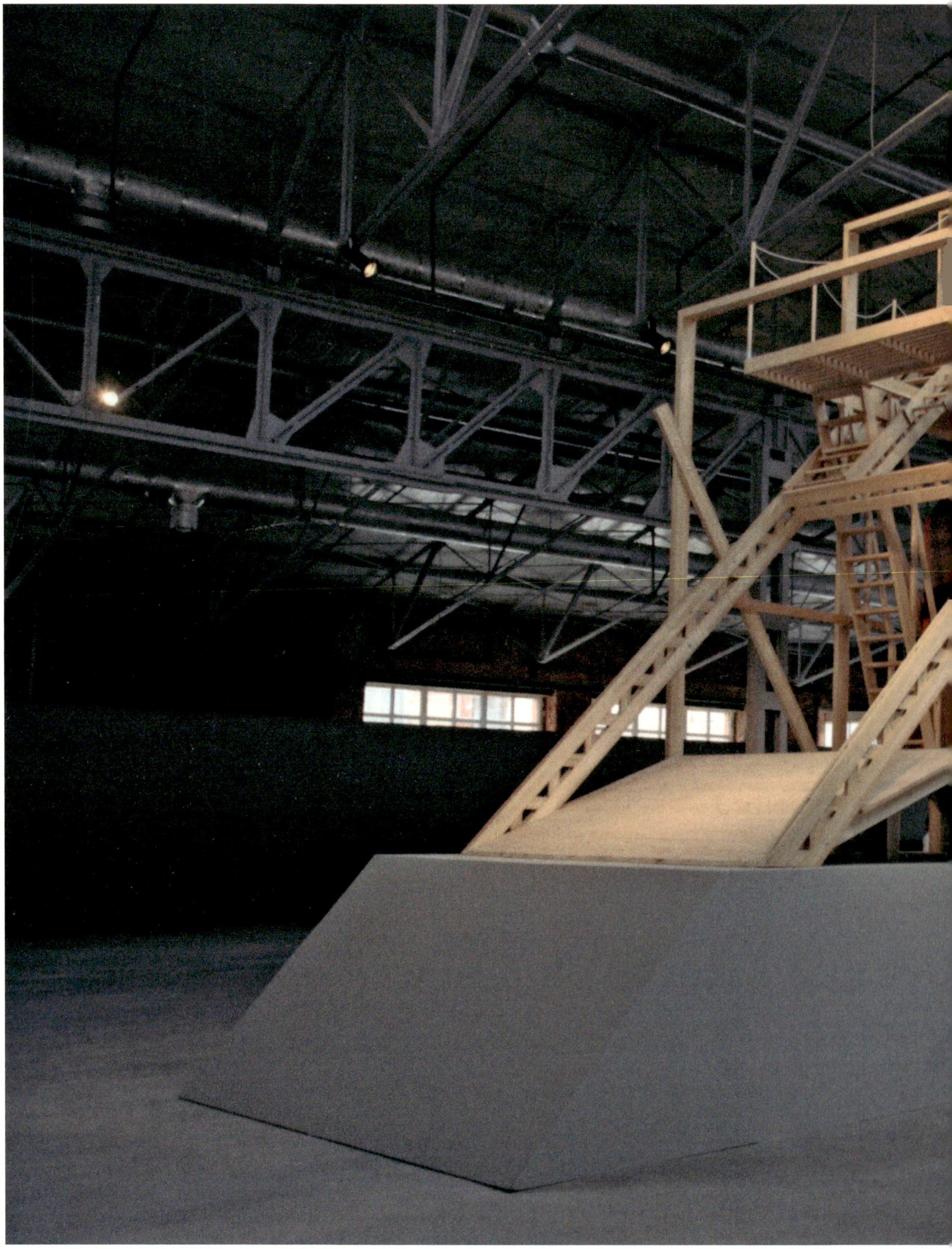

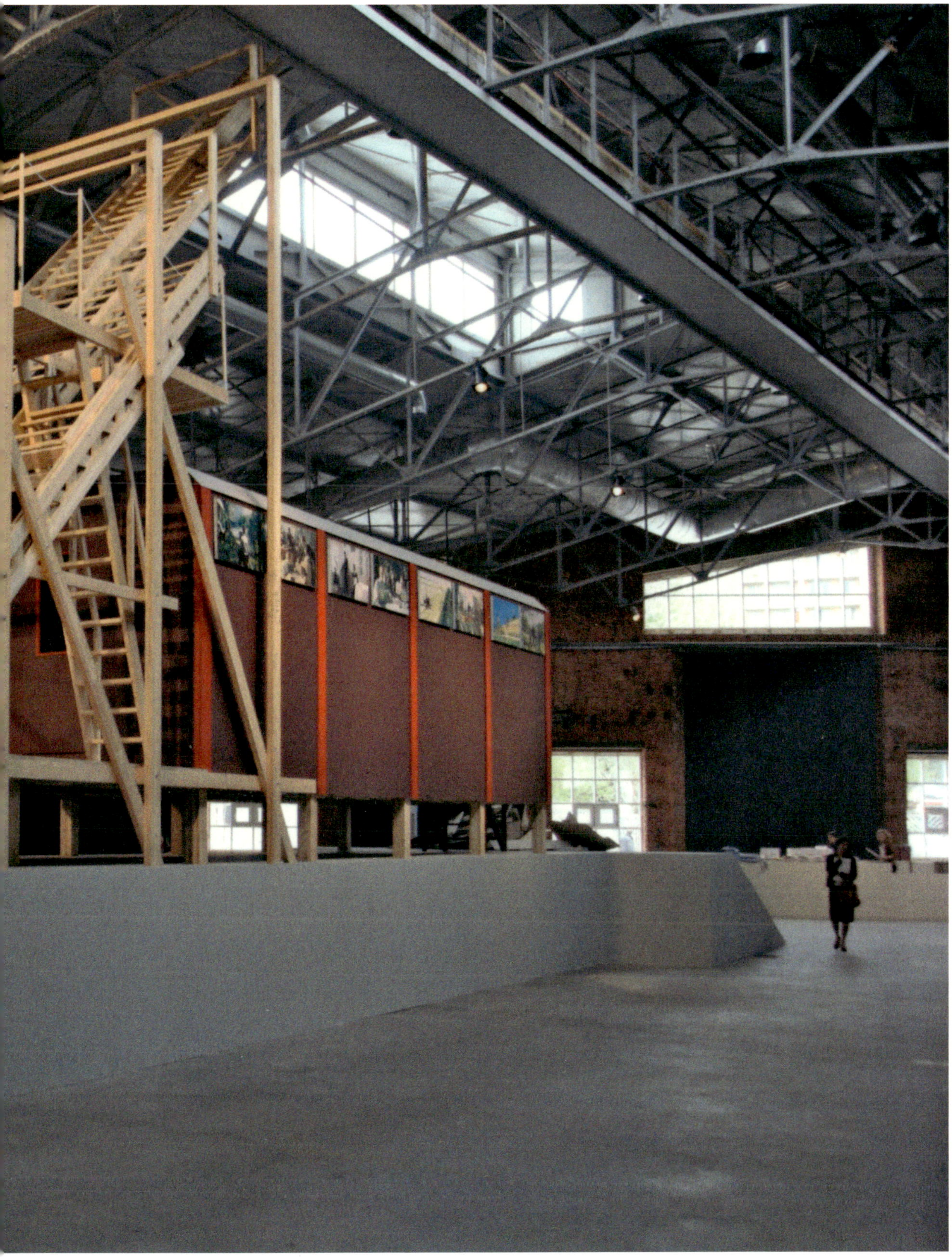

56 The Fly with the Wings | *Fliege mit Flügeln*

1992

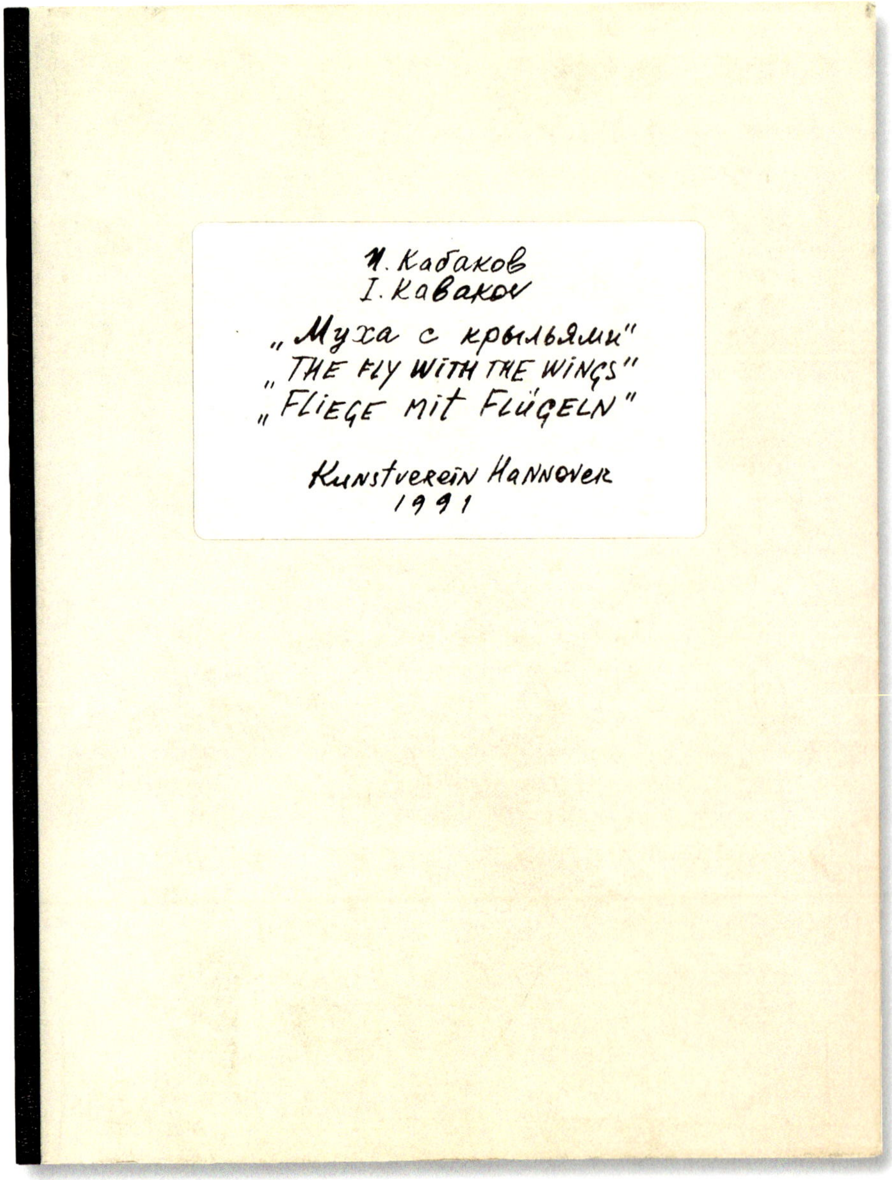

Ilya and Emilia Kabakov
New York: published by Ilya and Emilia Kabakov
27.9 x 21.5 cm
222 photocopied pp. with 11 b/w (incl. 2 foldouts) and 6 color ills.
quick bind, cardboard cover, label on the cover
Schnellhefter, Kartonumschlag, tikette auf dem Umschlag
edition: 500 numbered copies with 5 including an original signed, numbered, and dated drawing by Ilya Kabakov from 1992

thematic publication | *thematische Publikation*

layout by Ilya Kabakov | *Layout von Ilya Kabakov*

Documentation of the installation of the same name for the exhibition »Art, Europe: Soviet Union«, Kunstverein Hannover, Hanover, June 22 to August 25, 1991. Texts by Ilya Kabakov, which were published in 1992 as the chapter entitled »The Fly as a Subject and Basis for Philosophical Discourse« in the book »Life of Flies«; Russian, English, German.

Dokumentation der gleichnamigen Installation für die Ausstellung »Kunst, Europa: Sowjetunion«, Kunstverein Hannover, Hannover, 22. Juni – 25. August 1991. Texte von Ilya Kabakov, die 1992 unter dem Kapitel »Die Fliege als Ursache und Grundlage des philosophischen Diskurses« im Buch »Das Leben der Fliegen« publiziert wurden; russisch, englisch, deutsch.

see also | *siehe auch* no. 8; no. 9; no. 33; no. 43; no. 44; no. 37; no. 38; no. 50; no. 134; CRI, vol. 1, no. 3, pp. 60–65

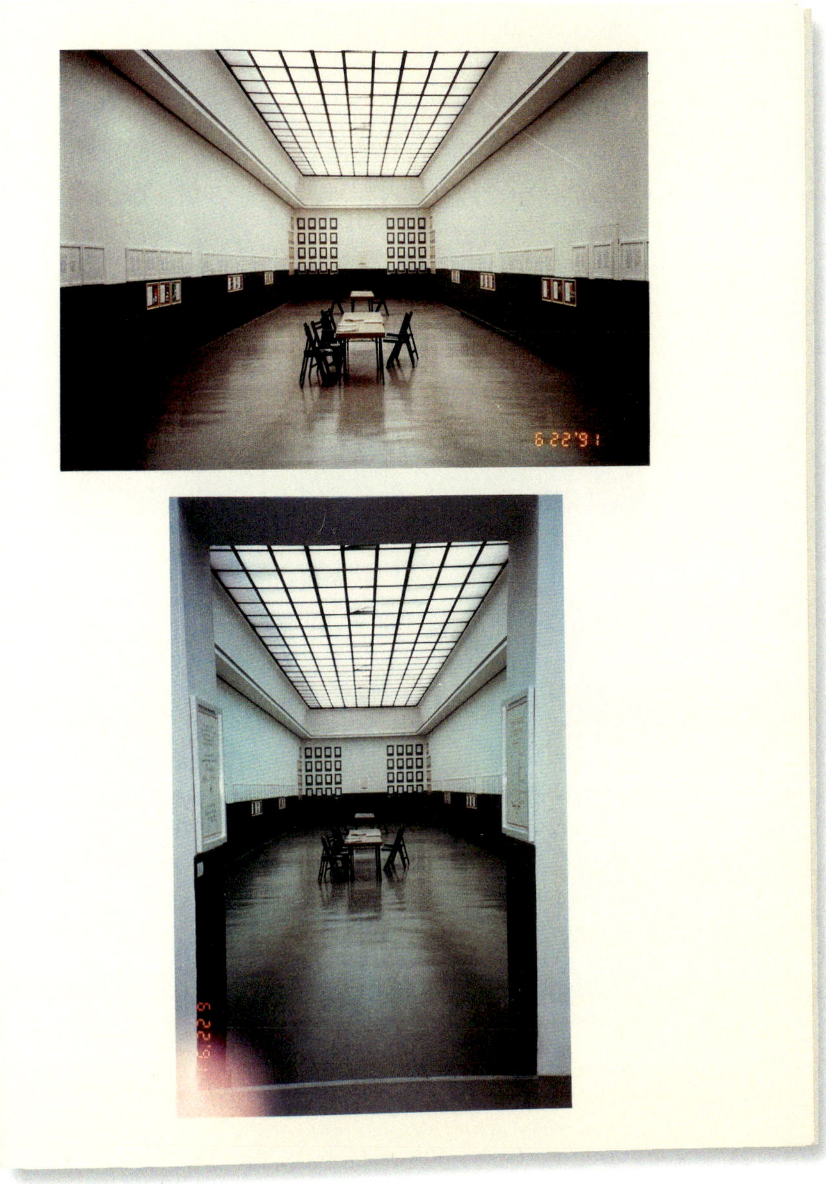
6 22 '91

57 Mental Institution or Institute of Creative Research

Das Irrenhaus oder Institut für kreative Forschungen

1992

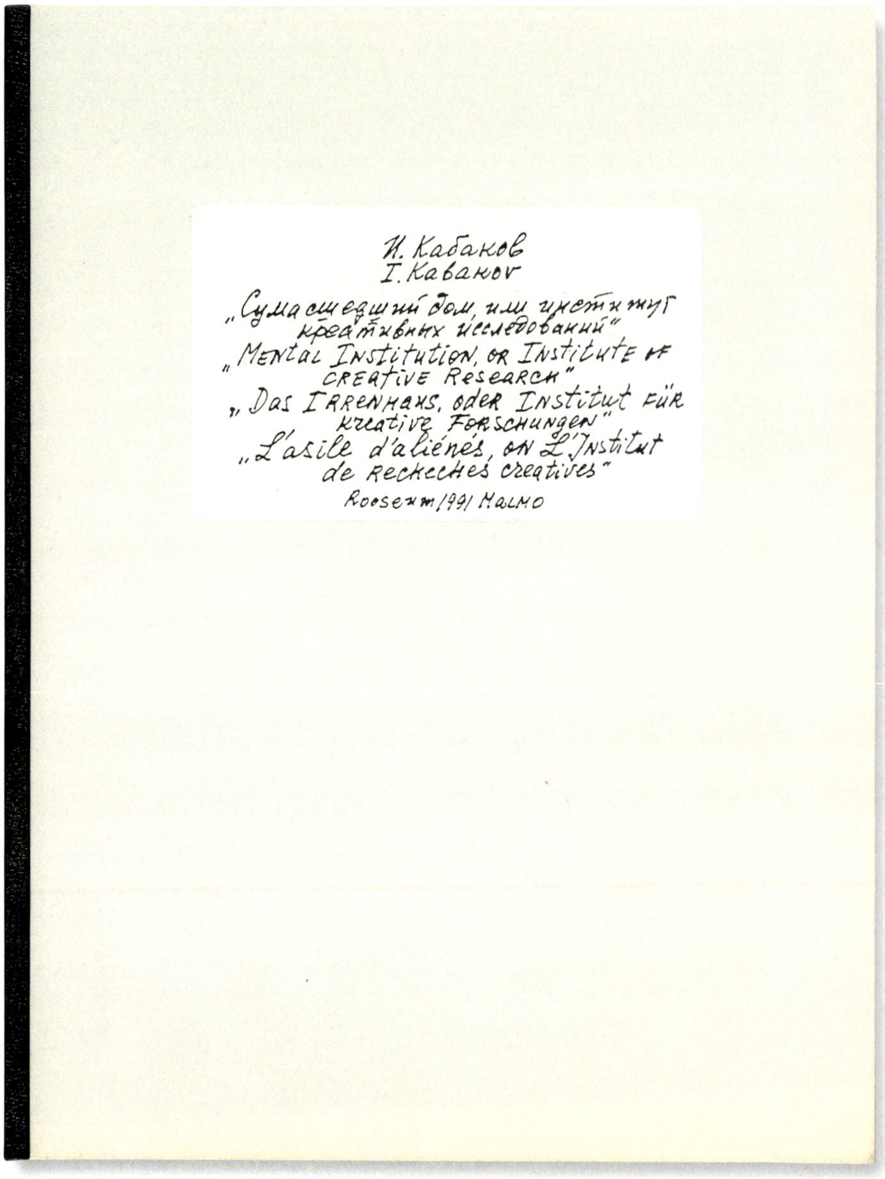

Ilya and Emilia Kabakov
New York: published by Ilya and Emilia Kabakov
27.9 x 21.5 cm
203 photocopied pp. with 68 (37 color) ills.
quick bind, cardboard cover,
label on the cover
Schnellhefter, Kartonumschlag,
Etikette auf dem Umschlag
edition: 500 numbered copies with 5 including an original signed, numbered, and dated drawing by Ilya Kabakov from 1992

thematic publication | *thematische Publikation*

layout by Ilya Kabakov | *Layout von Ilya Kabakov*

Documentation of the installation of the same name for the exhibition »Trans/Mission – Konst i interkulturell limbo«, Rooseum, Center for Contemporary Art, Malmö, August 26 to October 27, 1991. Texts by Ilya Kabakov; Russian, English, German, French.

Dokumentation der gleichnamigen Installation in der Ausstellung »Trans/Mission – Konst i interkulturell limbo«, Rooseum, Center for Contemporary Art, Malmö, 26. August – 27. Oktober 1991. Texte von Ilya Kabakov; russisch, englisch, deutsch, französisch.

see also | *siehe auch* no. 41; CRI, vol. 1, no. 50, pp. 330–335; CRP, vol. 1, no. 220, p. 290, nos. 222–224, pp. 292–294

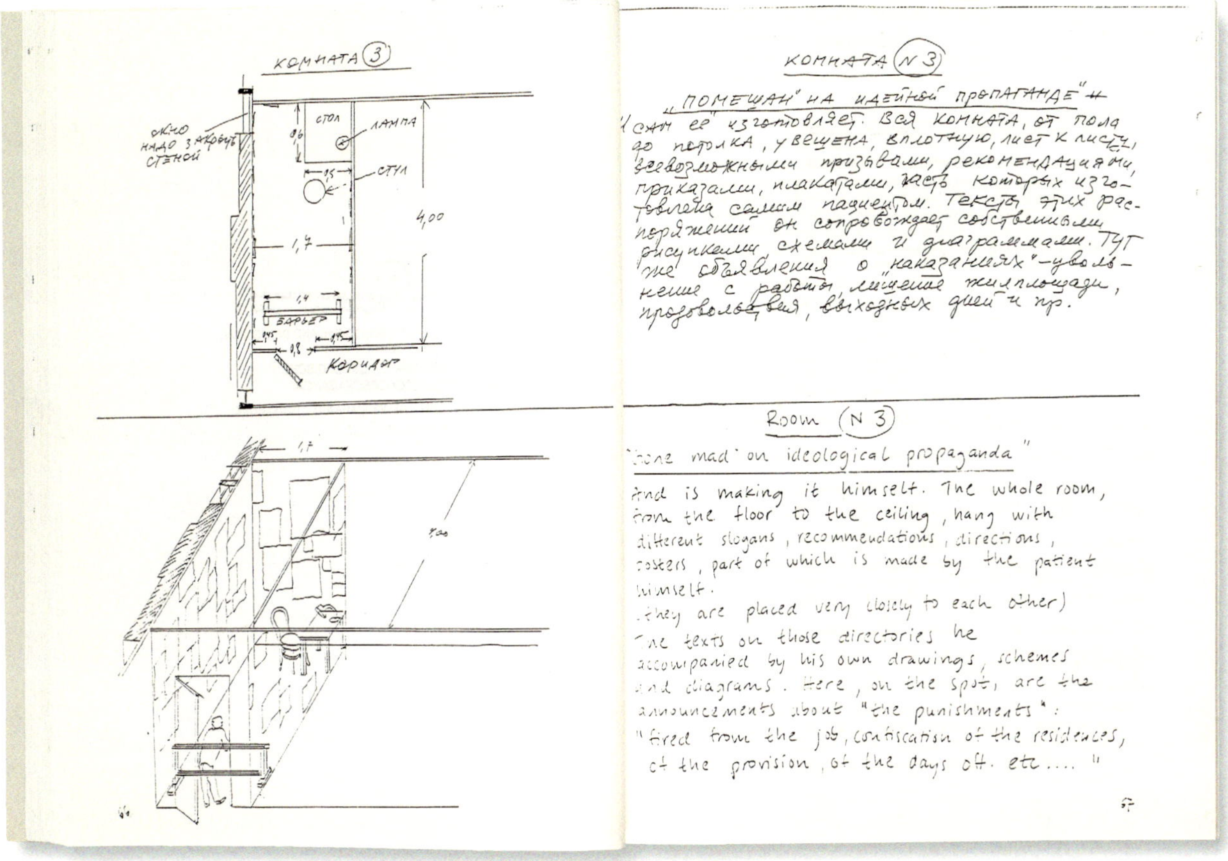
КОМНАТА (3)

КОМНАТА (N 3)

„ПОМЕШАН" НА ИДЕЙНОЙ ПРОПАГАНДЕ" и сам ее изготовляет. Вся комната, от пола до потолка, увешена, вплотную, лист к листу, всевозможными призывами, рекомендациями, приказами, плакатами, часть которых изготовлена самим пациентом. Тексты этих распоряжений он сопровождает собственными рисунками, схемами и диаграммами. Тут же объявления о „наказаниях"-увольнение с работы, лишение жилплощади, продовольствия, выходных дней и пр.

Room (N 3)

"Gone mad on ideological propaganda"

And is making it himself. The whole room, from the floor to the ceiling, hang with different slogans, recommendations, directions, posters, part of which is made by the patient himself.
(they are placed very closely to each other)
The texts on those directories he accompanied by his own drawings, schemes and diagrams. Here, on the spot, are the announcements about "the punishments":
"fired from the job, confiscation of the residences, of the provision, of the days off. etc...."

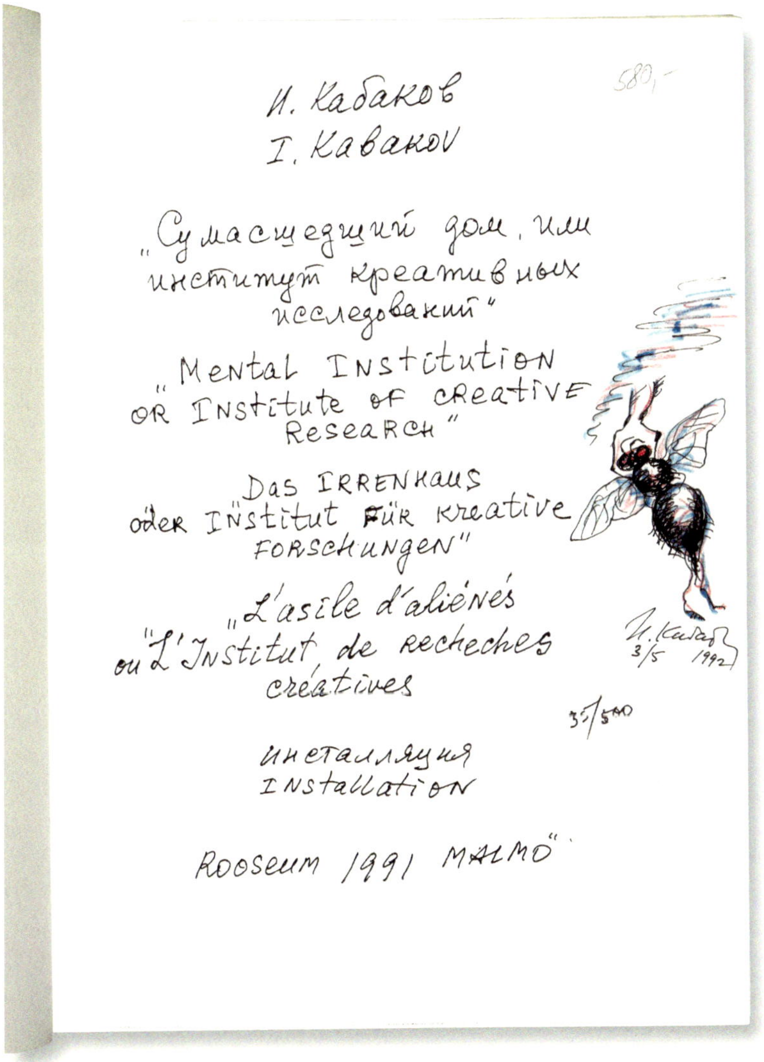
И. Кабаков
I. Kabakov

„Сумасшедший дом, или „институт креативных исследований"

„Mental Institution or "Institute of creative Research"

Das Irrenhaus oder "Institut für kreative Forschungen"

L'asile d'aliénés ou "L'Institut de recheches créatives

инсталляция
Installation

Rooseum 1991 Malmö

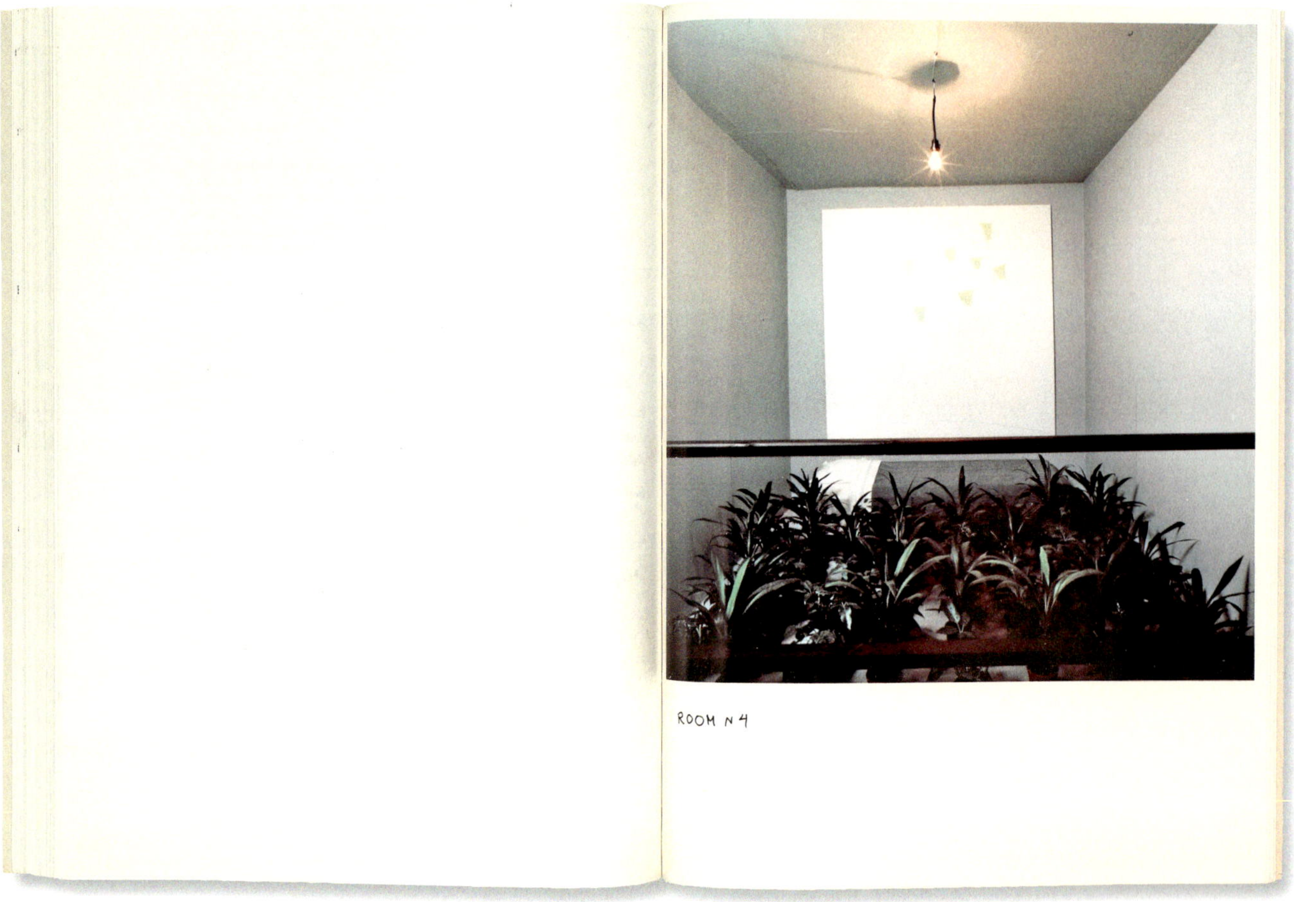
ROOM N 4

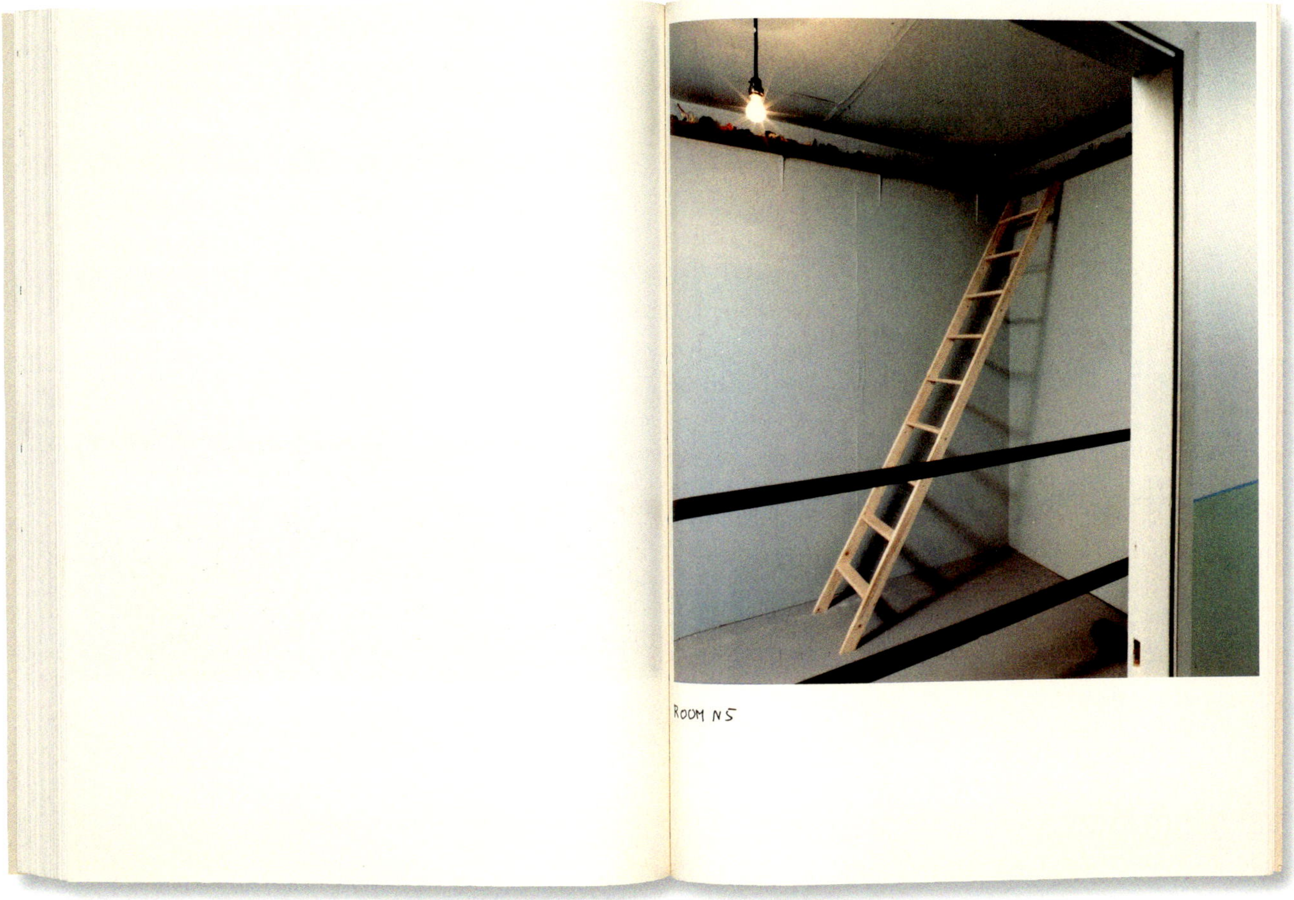
ROOM N5

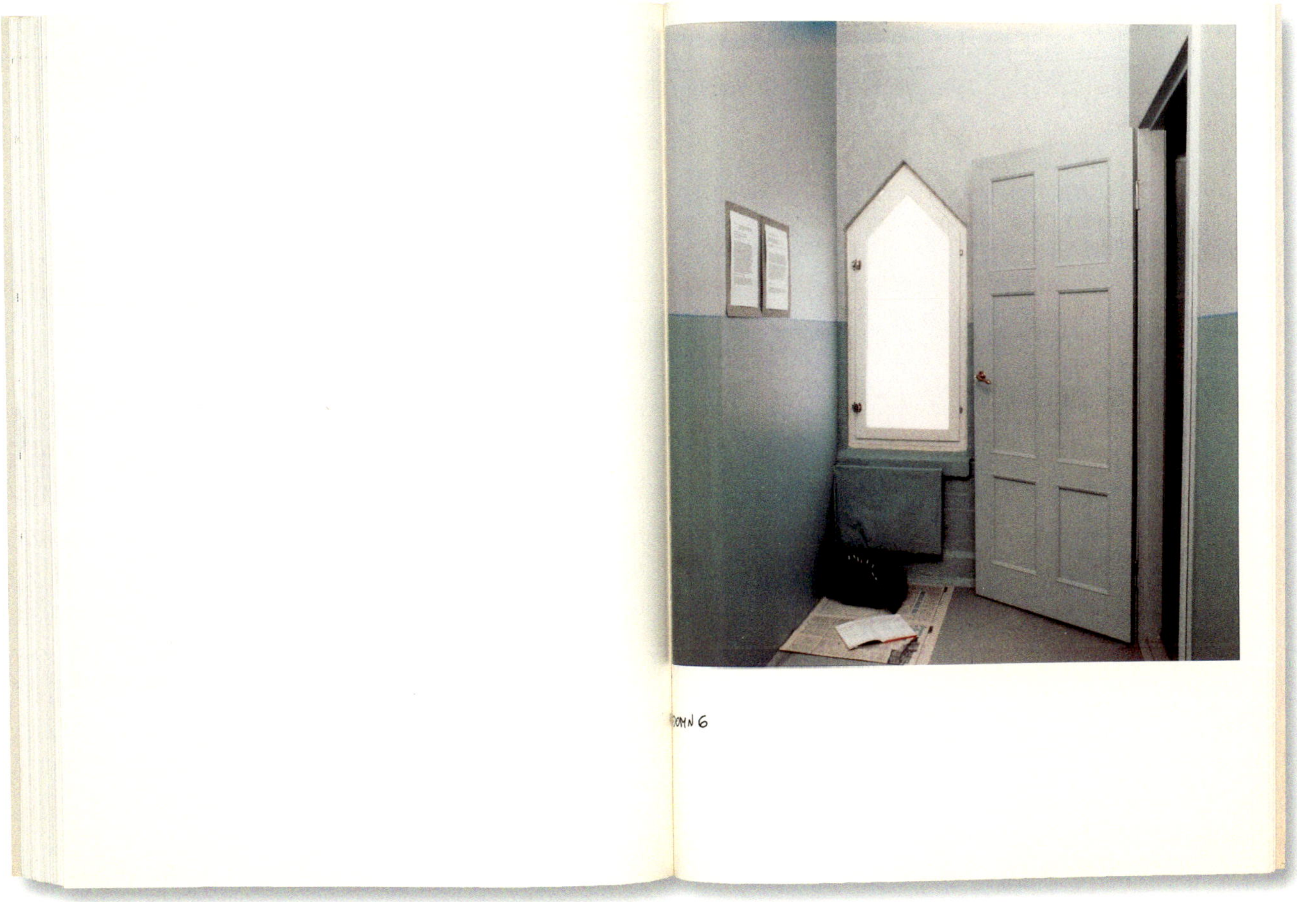
OOM N 6

58 We Are Leaving Here Forever! | *Wir gehen von hier für immer fort!*

1992

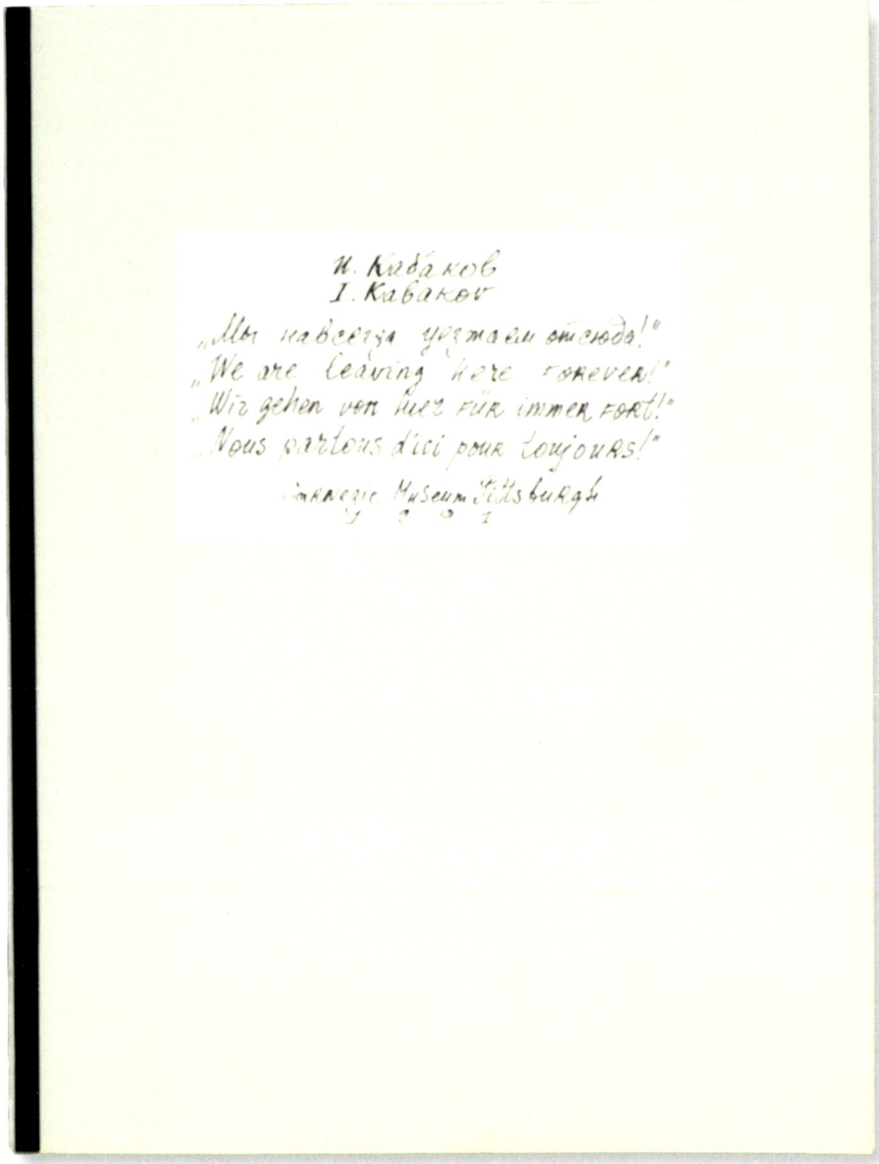

Ilya and Emilia Kabakov
New York: published by Ilya and Emilia Kabakov
28 x 21.5 cm
296 photocopied pp. with 174 b/w (incl. 15 foldouts) and 26 color (incl. 4 foldouts) ills.
quick bind, cardboard cover, label on the cover
Schnellhefter, Kartonumschlag, Etikette auf dem Umschlag
edition: 500 numbered copies with 5 including an original signed, numbered, and dated drawing by Ilya Kabakov from 1992

thematic publication | *thematische Publikation*

layout by Ilya Kabakov | *Layout von Ilya Kabakov*

Documentation of the installation of the same name for the Carnegie International 1991, Carnegie Museum of Art, Pittsburgh, October 19, 1991 to February 16, 1992. Texts by Ilya Kabakov; Russian, English, German, French.

Dokumentation der gleichnamigen Installation für die Carnegie International 1991, Carnegie Museum of Art, Pittsburgh, 19. Oktober 1991 – 16. Februar 1992. Texte von Ilya Kabakov; russisch, englisch, deutsch, französisch.

see also | *siehe auch* CRI, vol. 1, no. 54, pp. 354–359

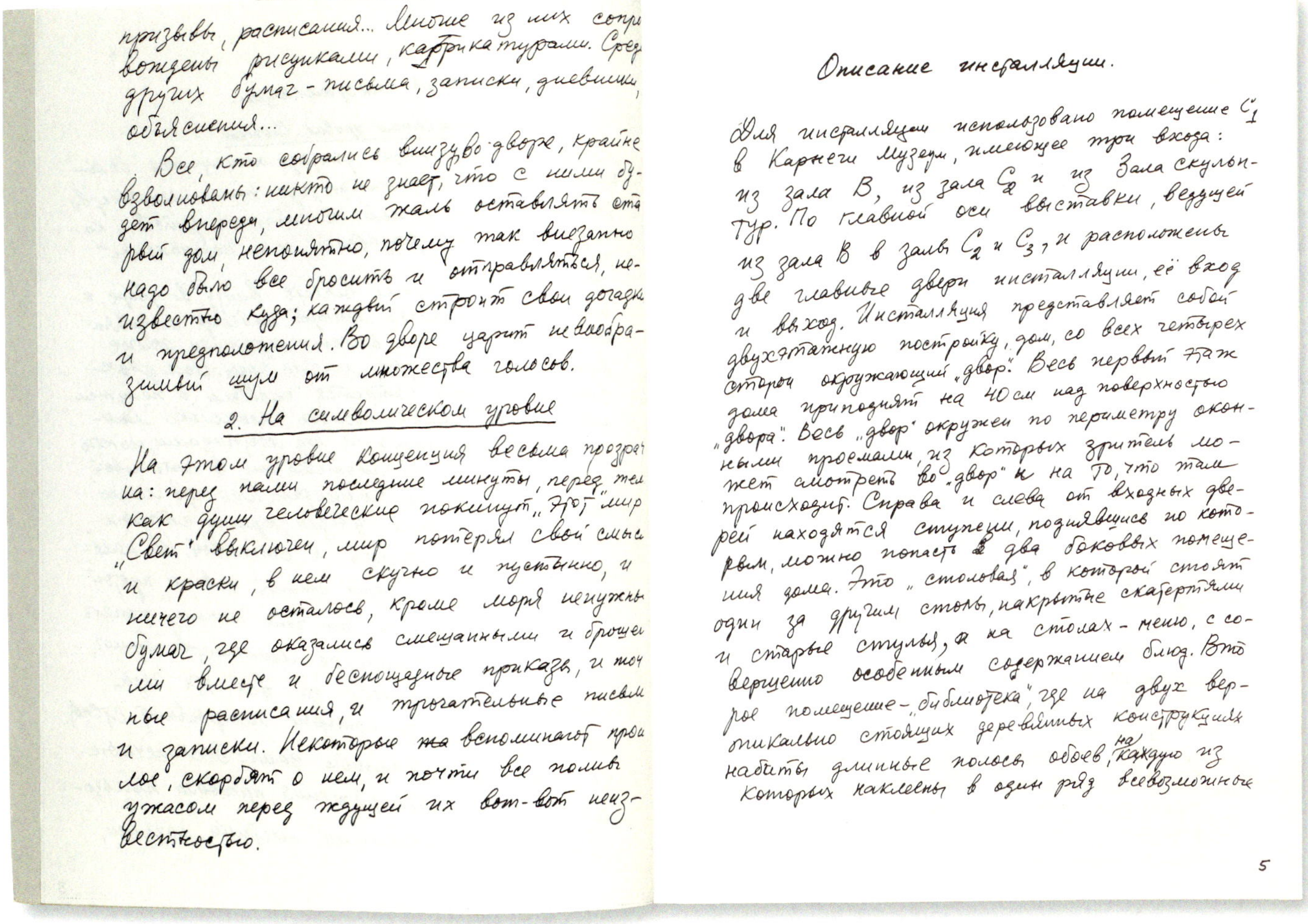

призывы, расписания... Многие из них сопр
вождены рисунками, карикатурами. Сред
других бумаг - письма, записки, дневники,
объяснения...

Все, кто собрались внизу во дворе, крайне
взволнованы: никто не знает, что с ними бу-
дет впереди, многим жаль оставлять ста
рый дом, непонятно, почему так внезапно
надо было все бросить и отправляться, не-
известно куда; каждый строит свои догадк
и предположения. Во дворе царит невообра-
зимый шум от множества голосов.

2. На символическом уровне

На этом уровне концепция весьма прозра
на: перед нами последние минуты, перед тем
как души человеческие покинут „этот" мир
„Свет" выключен, мир потерял свой смыс
и краски, в нем скучно и пустынно, и
ничего не осталось, кроме моря ненужны
бумаг, где оказались смешанными и брошен
ми вместе и беспощадные приказы, и точ
ные расписания, и трогательные письм
и записки. Некоторые ~~же~~ вспоминают прош
лое, скорбят о нем, и почти все полны
ужасом перед ждущей их вот-вот неиз-
вестностью.

Описание инсталляции.

Для инсталляции использовано помещение C_1
в Карнеги Музеум, имеющее три входа:
из зала B, из зала C_2 и из Зала скульп-
тур. По главной оси выставки, ведущей
из зала B в залы C_2 и C_3, и расположены
две главные двери инсталляции, её вход
и выход. Инсталляция представляет собой
двухэтажную постройку, дом, со всех четырех
сторон окружающий „двор". Весь первый этаж
дома приподнят на 40 см над поверхностью
„двора". Весь „двор" окружен по периметру окон-
ными проемами, из которых зритель мо-
жет смотреть во „двор" и на то, что там
происходит. Справа и слева от входных две-
рей находятся ступени, поднявшись по кото-
рым, можно попасть в два боковых помеще-
ния дома. Это „столовая", в которой стоят
один за другим столы, накрытые скатертями
и старые стулья, а на столах - меню, с со-
вершенно особенным содержанием блюд. Вто-
рое помещение - „библиотека", где на двух вер-
тикально стоящих деревянных конструкциях
набиты длинные полосы обоев, на каждую из
которых наклеены в один ряд всевозможные

5

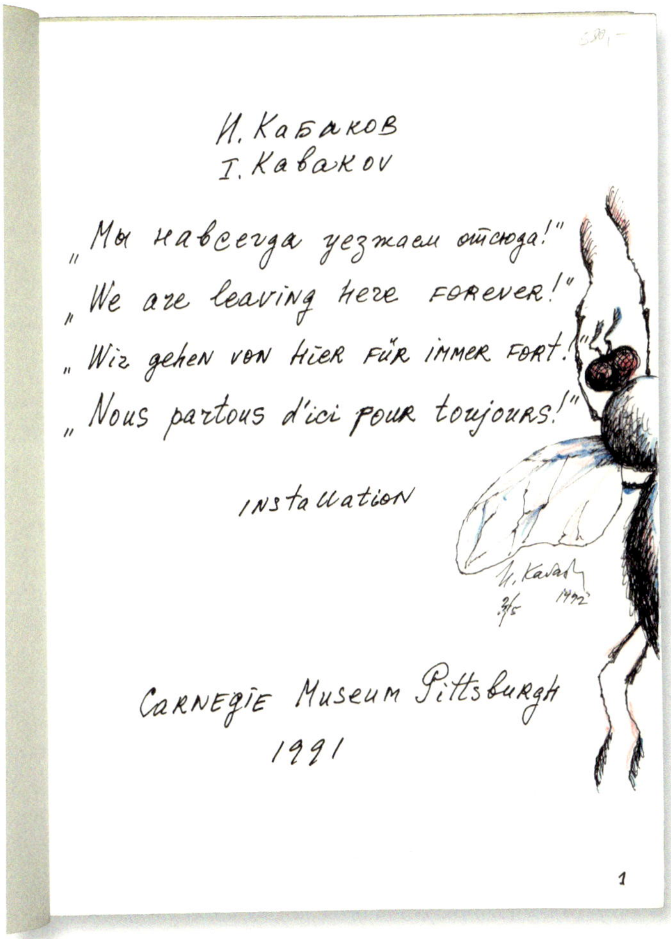

И. Кабаков
I. Kabakov

„Мы навсегда уезжаем отсюда!"
„We are leaving here FOREVER!"
„Wir gehen von hier für immer fort!"
„Nous partons d'ici pour toujours!"

installation

И. Кабаков
1992
3/5

Carnegie Museum Pittsburgh
1991

1

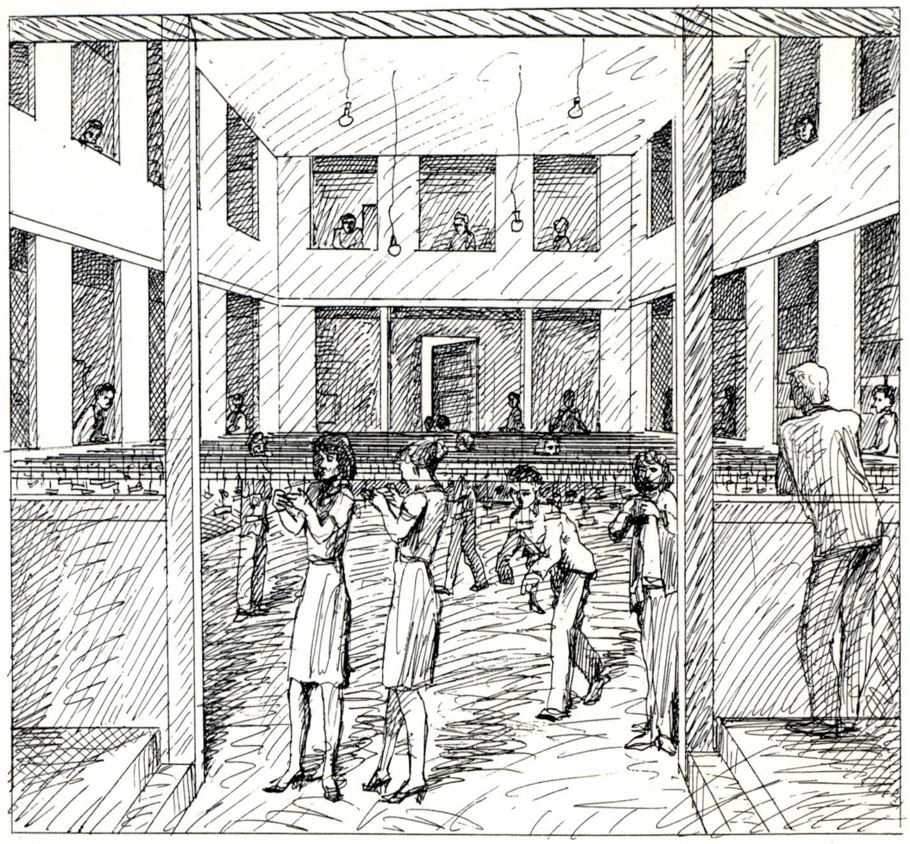

Вид со стороны входа из комнаты B и C,

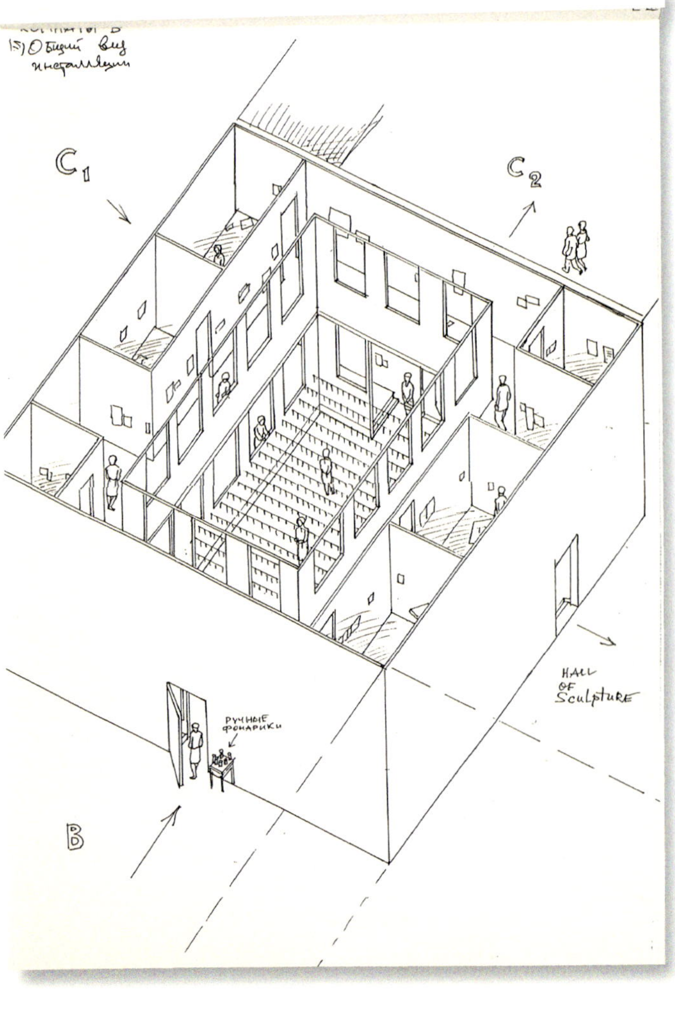

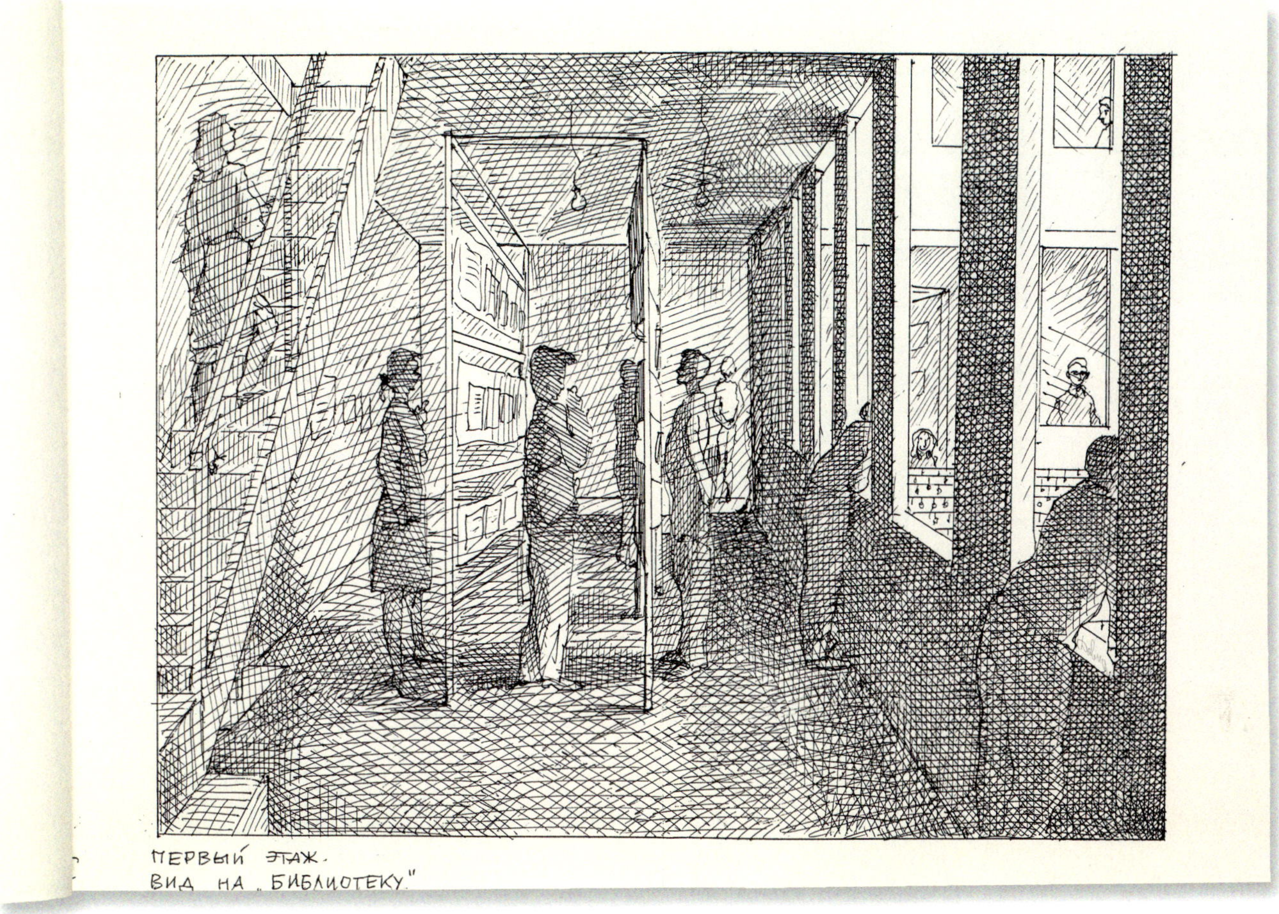
ПЕРВЫЙ ЭТАЖ.
ВИД НА „БИБЛИОТЕКУ"

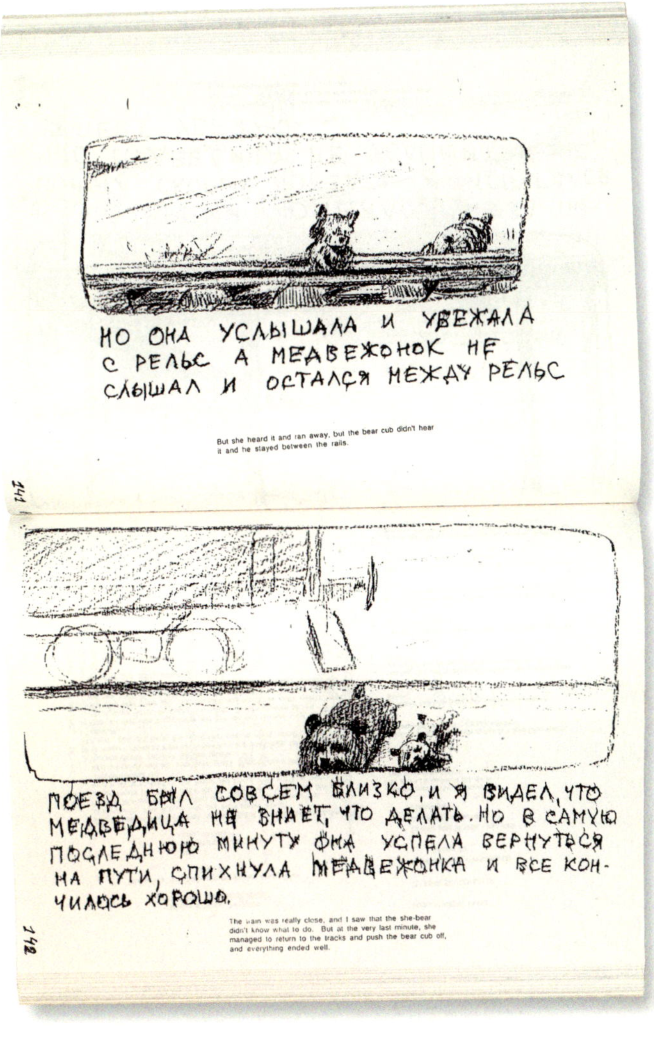
НО ОНА УСЛЫШАЛА И УБЕЖАЛА С РЕЛЬС А МЕДВЕЖОНОК НЕ СЛЫШАЛ И ОСТАЛСЯ МЕЖДУ РЕЛЬС
But she heard it and ran away, but the bear cub didn't hear it and he stayed between the rails.
141
ПОЕЗД БЫЛ СОВСЕМ БЛИЗКО, И Я ВИДЕЛ, ЧТО МЕДВЕДИЦА НЕ ЗНАЕТ, ЧТО ДЕЛАТЬ. НО В САМУЮ ПОСЛЕДНЮЮ МИНУТУ ОНА УСПЕЛА ВЕРНУТЬСЯ НА ПУТИ, СПИХНУЛА МЕДВЕЖОНКА И ВСЕ КОНЧИЛОСЬ ХОРОШО.
The train was really close, and I saw that the she-bear didn't know what to do. But at the very last minute, she managed to return to the tracks and push the bear cub off, and everything ended well.
142

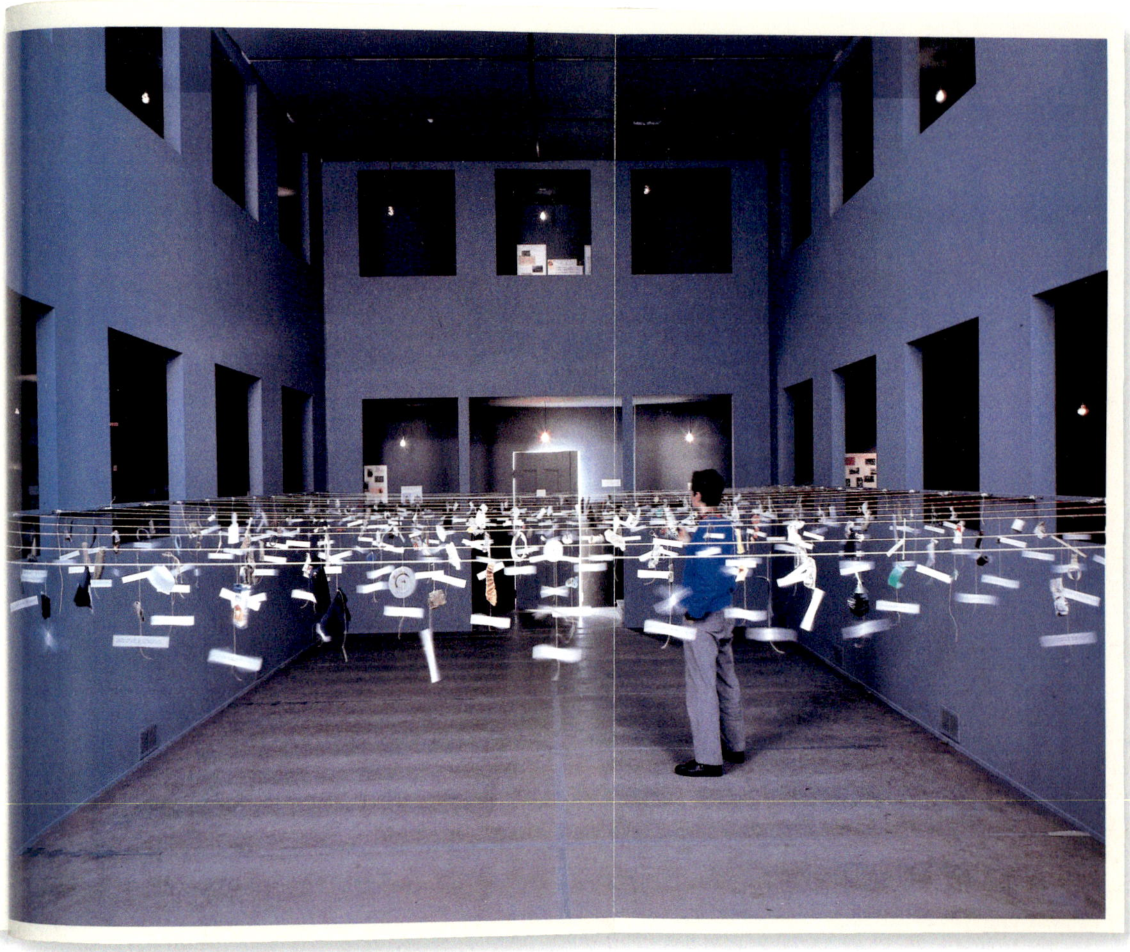

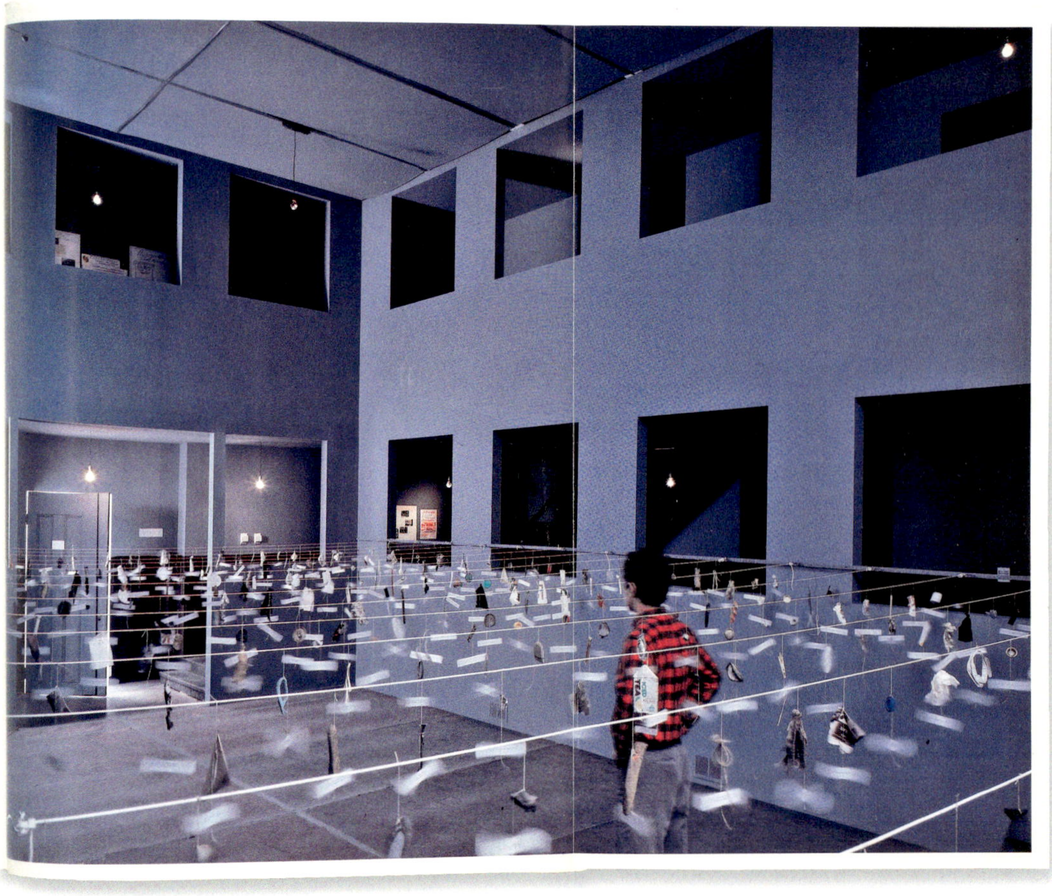

59 The Big Archive | *Das grosse Archiv*

1993

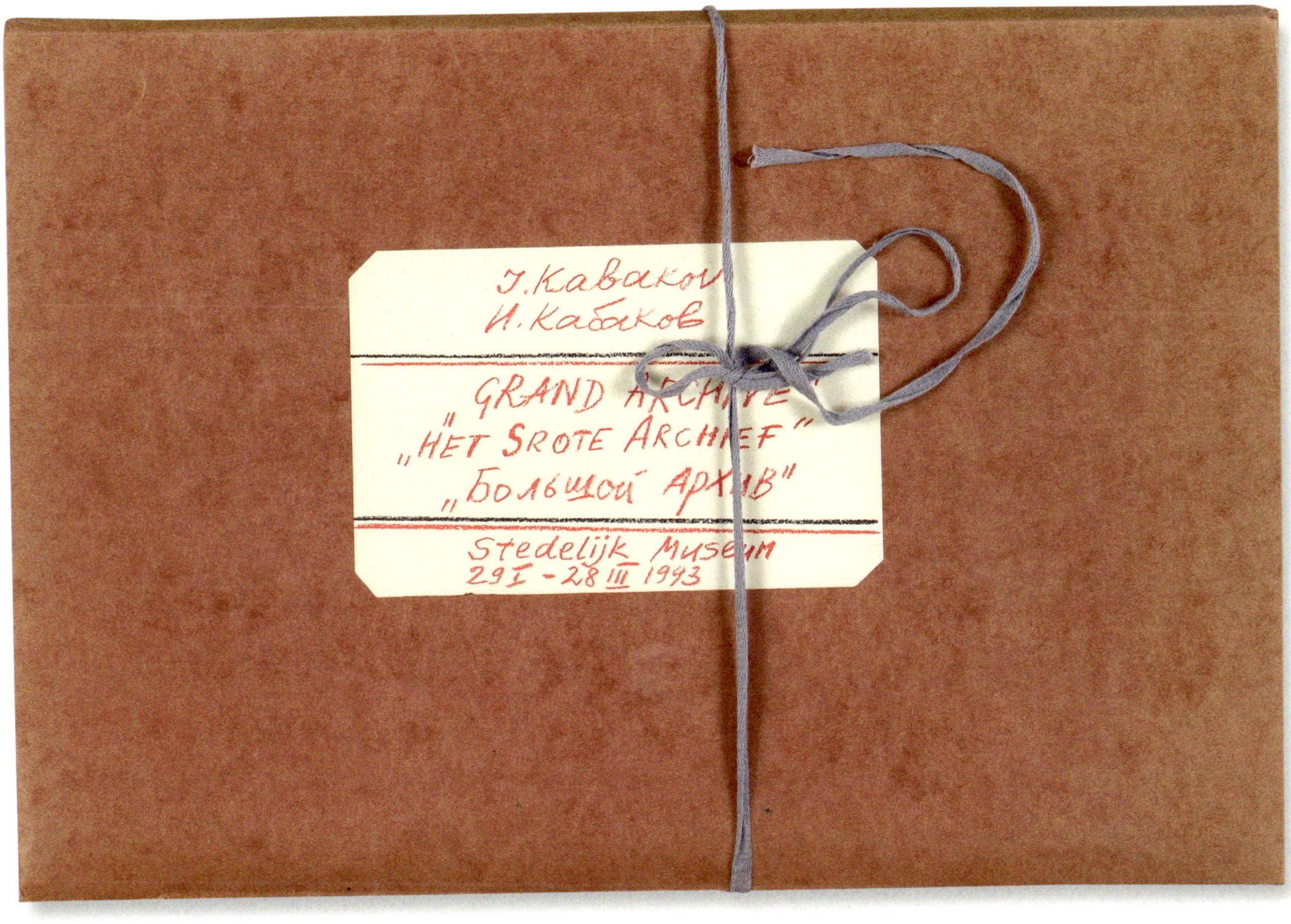

Stedelijk Museum
Amsterdam: Stedelijk Museum
outer folder bound together with a ribbon, 38 x 26.5 cm, label on the cover, 23 loose sheets of different size (2 b/w and 17 color ills.), staplebound
inner folder, 31 x 23.3 cm, with 64 (partly double-sided) photocopied sheets of different size (20 b/w and 25 color ills.), quick bind
äussere Mappe mit Band, 38 x 26,5 cm, Etikette auf dem Umschlag, 23 lose Blätter verschiedener Grösse (2 s/w und 17 farbige Illustrationen), Drahtheftung
innere Mappe, 31 x 23,3 cm, mit 64 (teilweise doppelseitigen) Fotokopien verschiedener Grösse (20 s/w und 25 farbige Illustrationen), Schnellhefter
edition: 1,000 copies

exhibition catalogue | *Ausstellungskatalog*

layout by Ilya Kabakov | *Layout von Ilya Kabakov*

For the installation of the same name at the Stedelijk Museum, Amsterdam, January 29 to March 28, 1993. Texts by Ilya Kabakov, including a text from the book »On the 'Total' Installation« and a fictitious certificate of good conduct from a museum director for the artist Ilya Kabakov; Dutch, Russian, English.

Zur gleichnamigen Installation, Stedelijk Museum, Amsterdam, 29. Januar – 28. März 1993. Texte von Ilya Kabakov, darunter ein Text aus dem Buch »Über die ‚totale' Installation« und ein fiktives Führungszeugnis eines Museumsdirektors über den Künstler Ilya Kabakov; niederländisch, russisch, englisch.

see also | *siehe auch* no. 83; CRI, vol. 1, no. 66, pp. 430–437

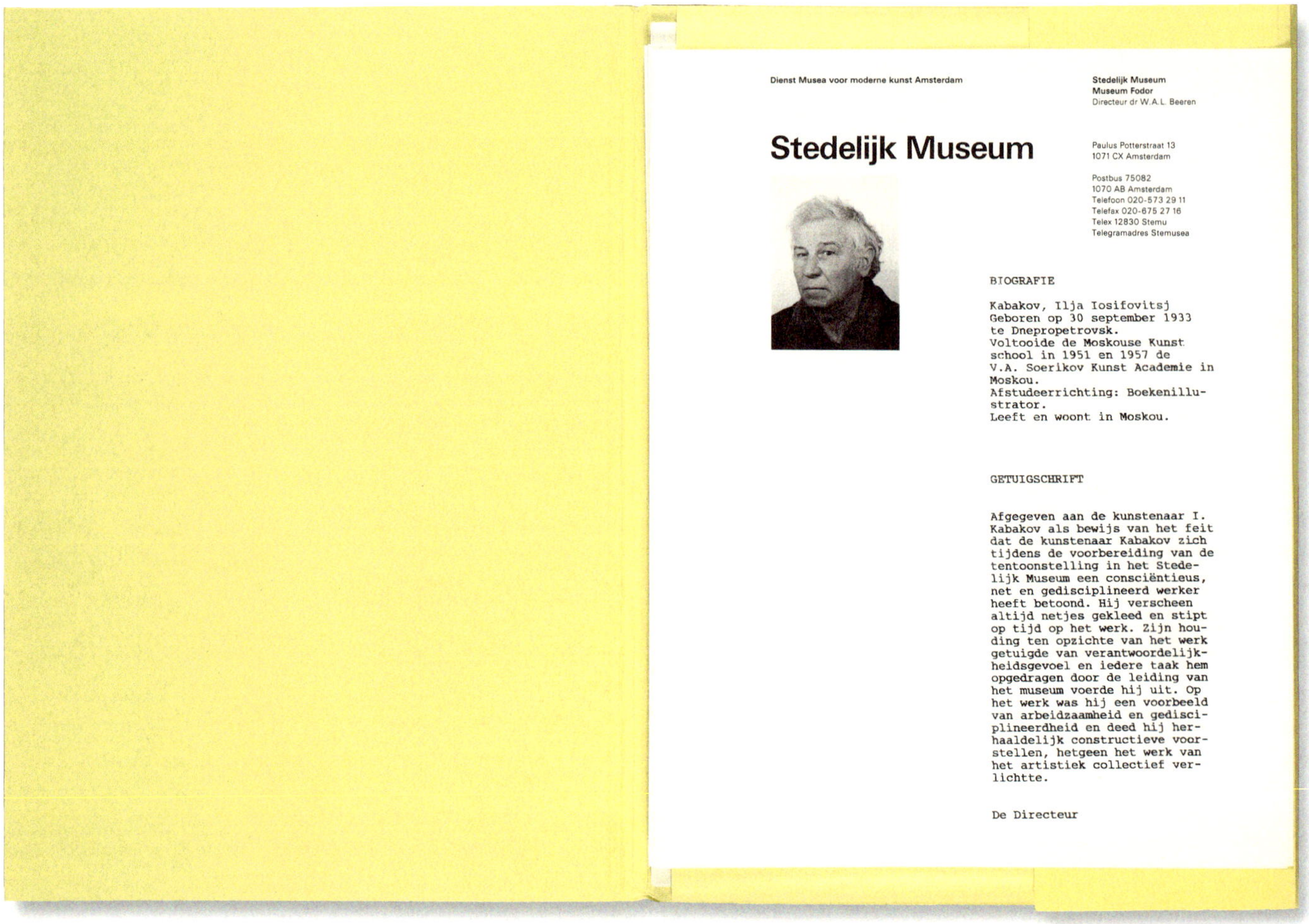

Dienst Musea voor moderne kunst Amsterdam

Stedelijk Museum
Museum Fodor
Directeur dr W.A.L. Beeren

Stedelijk Museum

Paulus Potterstraat 13
1071 CX Amsterdam

Postbus 75082
1070 AB Amsterdam
Telefoon 020-573 29 11
Telefax 020-675 27 16
Telex 12830 Stemu
Telegramadres Stemusea

BIOGRAFIE

Kabakov, Ilja Iosifovitsj
Geboren op 30 september 1933 te Dnepropetrovsk.
Voltooide de Moskouse Kunstschool in 1951 en 1957 de V.A. Soerikov Kunst Academie in Moskou.
Afstudeerrichting: Boekenillustrator.
Leeft en woont in Moskou.

GETUIGSCHRIFT

Afgegeven aan de kunstenaar I. Kabakov als bewijs van het feit dat de kunstenaar Kabakov zich tijdens de voorbereiding van de tentoonstelling in het Stedelijk Museum een consciëntieus, net en gedisciplineerd werker heeft betoond. Hij verscheen altijd netjes gekleed en stipt op tijd op het werk. Zijn houding ten opzichte van het werk getuigde van verantwoordelijkheidsgevoel en iedere taak hem opgedragen door de leiding van het museum voerde hij uit. Op het werk was hij een voorbeeld van arbeidzaamheid en gedisciplineerdheid en deed hij herhaaldelijk constructieve voorstellen, hetgeen het werk van het artistiek collectief verlichtte.

De Directeur

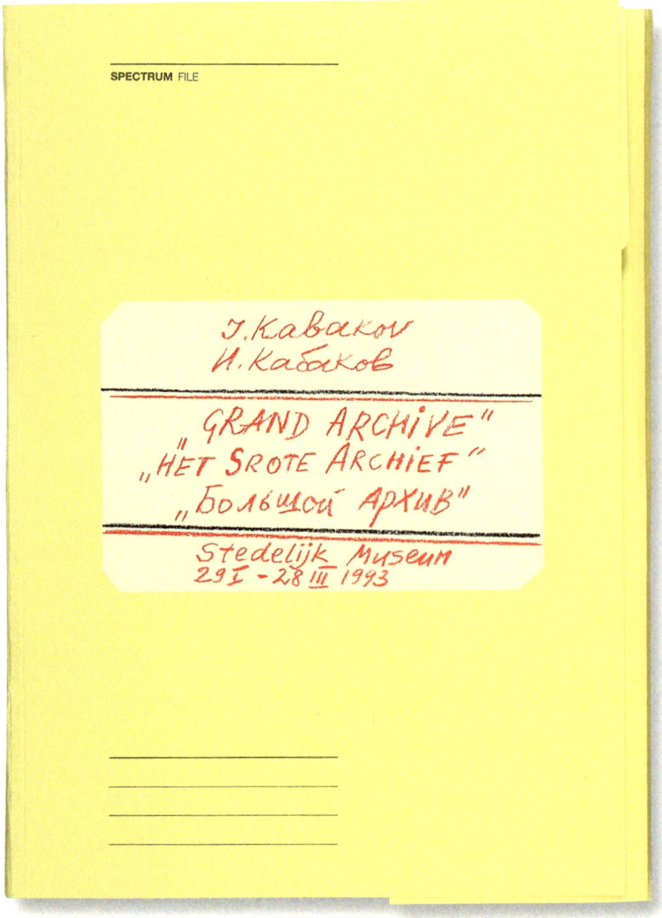

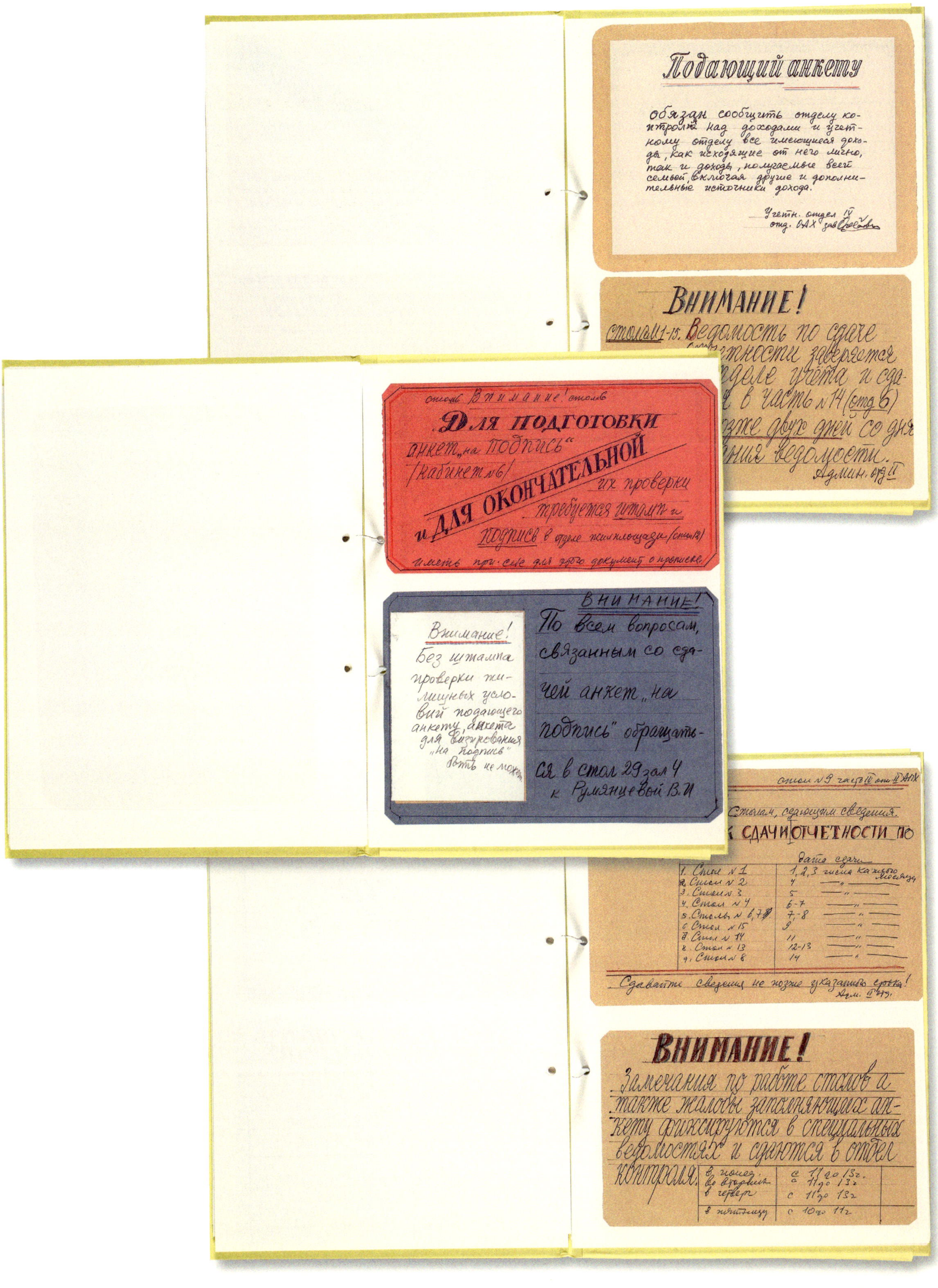
Подающий анкету
обязан сообщить отделу контроля над доходами и учетному отделу все имеющиеся доходы, как исходящие от него лично, так и доходы, получаемые всей семьей, включая другие и дополнительные источники дохода.
Учетн. отдел IV отд. ОАХ
ВНИМАНИЕ!
Столы 1-15. Ведомость по сдаче
в часть № 14 (отд 6)
Админ. отд II
Внимание!
Для подготовки анкет „на подпись" (кабинет № 6)
и для окончательной их проверки
требуется штамп и подпись в отделе жилплощади (стол № 12)
иметь при себе для этого документ о прописке
ВНИМАНИЕ!
По всем вопросам, связанным со сдачей анкет „на подпись" обращаться в стол 29 зал 4 к Румянцевой В.И
Внимание!
Без штампа проверки жилищных условий подающего анкету, анкета для визирования „на подпись" быть не может
Столам, сдающим сведения.
СДАЧИ ОТЧЕТНОСТИ ПО
Дата сдачи
1. Стол № 1 — 1, 2, 3 число каждого месяца
2. Стол № 2 — 4
3. Стол № 3 — 5
4. Стол № 4 — 6-7
5. Столы № 6, 7, 8 — 7-8
6. Стол № 15 — 9
7. Стол № 14 — 11
8. Стол № 13 — 12-13
9. Стол № 8 — 14
Сдавайте сведения не позже указанных сроков!
ВНИМАНИЕ!
Замечания по работе столов а также жалобы заполняющих анкету фиксируются в специальных ведомостях и сдаются в отдел контроля.
в понед. с 11 до 13 ч.
во вторник с 11 до 13 ч.
в четверг с 11 до 13 ч.
в пятницу с 10 до 11 ч.

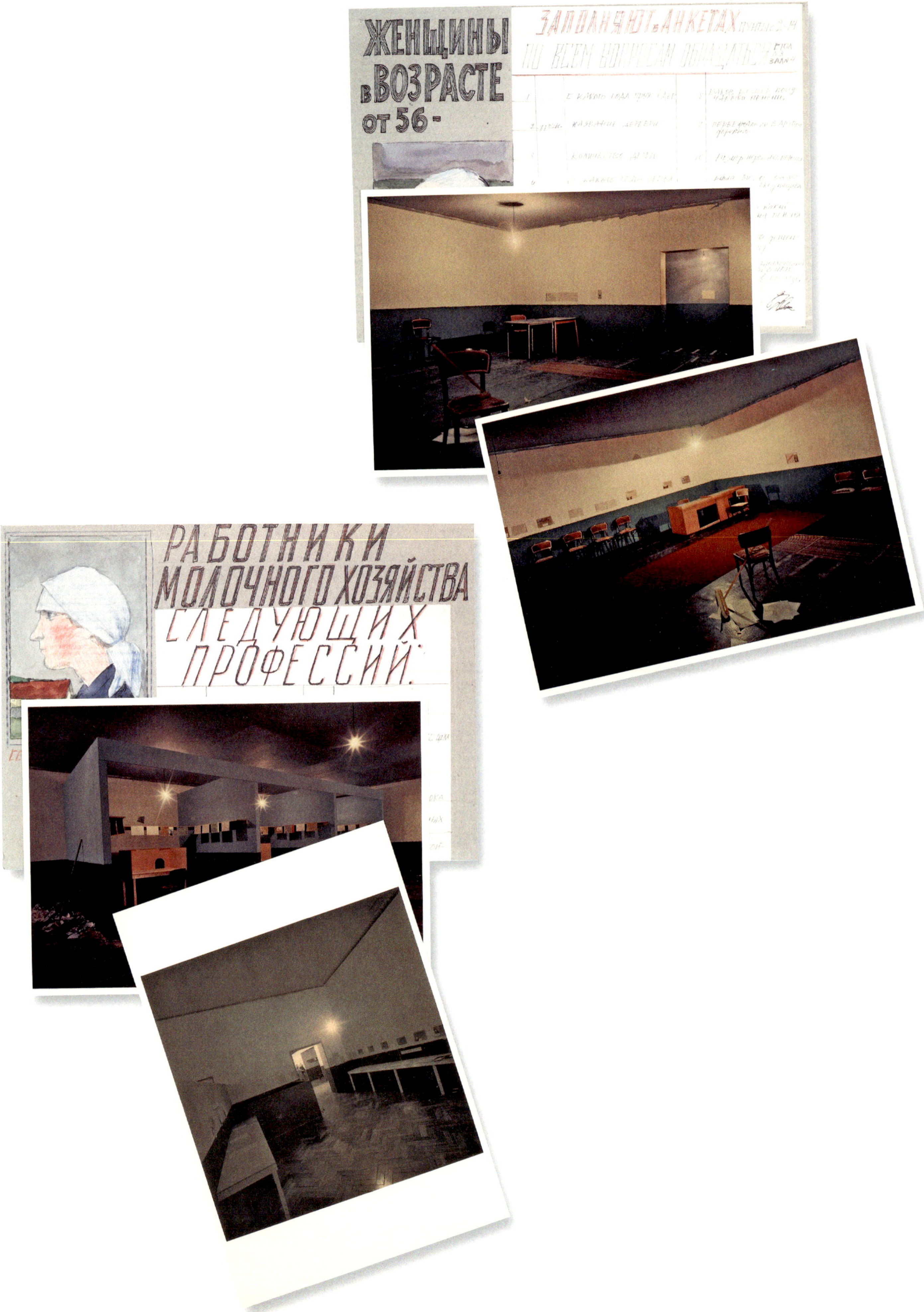
ЖЕНЩИНЫ
в ВОЗРАСТЕ
от 56-
ЗАПОЛНЯЮТ в АНКЕТАХ
ПО ВСЕМ ВОПРОСАМ ОБРАЩАТЬСЯ
РАБОТНИКИ
МОЛОЧНОГО ХОЗЯЙСТВА
СЛЕДУЮЩИХ
ПРОФЕССИЙ:

60 The Red Pavilion | *Der rote Pavillon*

1993

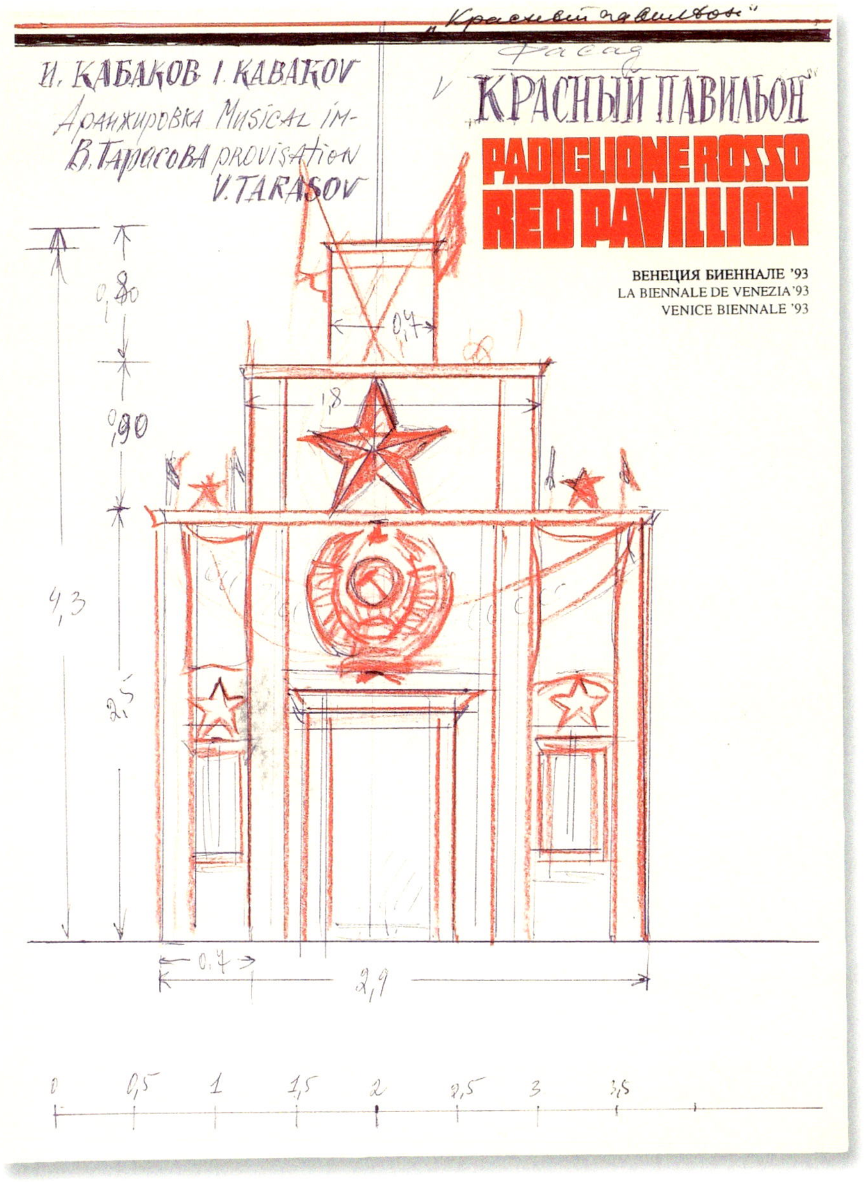

Ilya Kabakov
New York: published by the author
56 x 43 / 28 x 21.5 cm
DIN A2 poster, folded to DIN A4 with 6 color ills.
DIN A2 Poster, gefaltet auf DIN A4 Format mit 6 farbigen Illustrationen

exhibition catalogue | *Ausstellungskatalog*

layout by Ilya Kabakov | *Layout von Ilya Kabakov*

For the installation of the same name at the 45th Biennale, Venice, June 14 to September 14, 1993. Text by Ilya Kabakov; Russian, Italian, English.

Zur gleichnamigen Installation für die 45. Biennale, Venedig, 14. Juni – 14. September 1993. Text von Ilya Kabakov; russisch, italienisch, englisch.

see also | *siehe auch* no. 78; CRI, vol. 1, no. 70, pp. 454–459

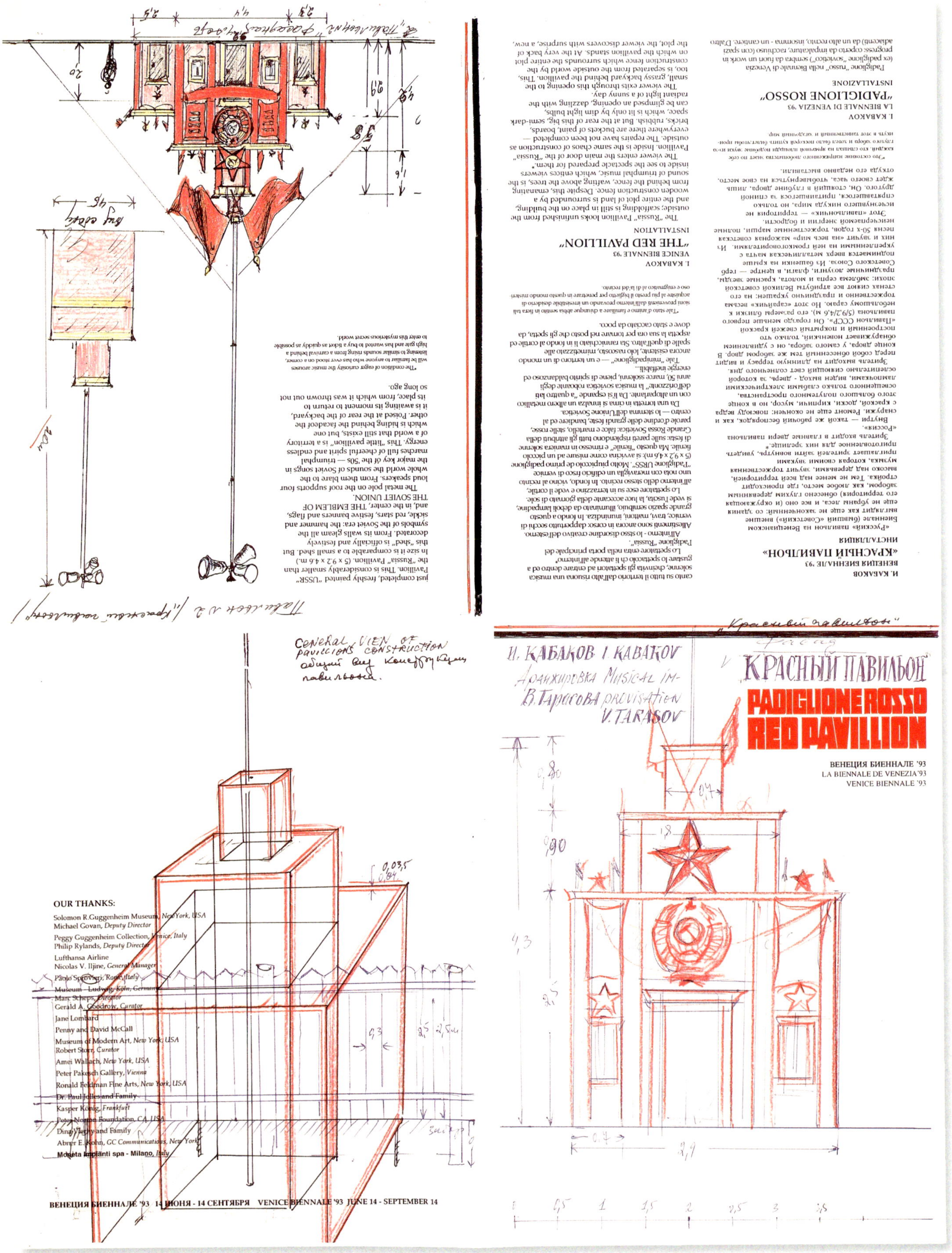

И. КАБАКОВ
ВЕНЕЦИЯ БИЕННАЛЕ '93
«КРАСНЫЙ ПАВИЛЬОН»
ИНСТАЛЛЯЦИЯ

«Русский» павильон на Венецианском Биеннале (бывший «Советский») внешне выглядит как еще не законченный: со здания еще не убраны леса, и все оно (и окружающая его территория) обнесено глухим деревянным забором, как любое место, где происходит стройка. Тем не менее над всей территорией, высоко над деревьями, звучит торжественная музыка, которая своими звуками приглашает зрителей зайти вовнутрь, увидеть приготовленное для них зрелище.*

Зритель входит в главные двери павильона «Россия».

Внутри — такой же рабочий беспорядок, как и снаружи. Ремонт еще не окончен: повсюду ведра с краской, доски, кирпичи, мусор, но в конце этого большого полутемного пространства, освещенного только слабыми электрическими лампочками, виден выход - дверь, за которой ослепительно сияющий свет солнечного дня.

Зритель выходит на длинную террасу и видит перед собой обнесенный тем же забором двор. В конце двора, у самого забора, он с удивлением обнаруживает новенький, только что построенный и покрытый свежей краской «Павильон СССР». Он гораздо меньше первого павильона (5/9,2/4,6 м), его размеры близки к небольшому сараю. Но этот «сарайчик» весьма торжественно и празднично украшен: на его стенах сияют все атрибуты Великой советской эпохи: эмблема серпа и молота, красные звезды, праздничные лозунги, флаги, в центре — герб Советского Союза. Из башенки на крыше поднимается вверх металлическая мачта с укрепленными на ней громкоговорителями. Из них и звучит «на весь мир» мажорная советская песня 50-х годов, торжественные марши, полные неисчерпаемой энергии и бодрости.

Этот «павильончик» — территория не исчезнувшего никуда мира, но только спрятавшегося, притаившегося за спиной другого. Он, стоящий в глубине двора, лишь ждет своего часа, чтобывернуться на свое место, откуда его недавно выставили.

*Это состояние напряженного любопытства знает по себе каждый, кто слышал на ярмачной площади подобные звуки из-за глухого забора и хотел было поскорей купить билет,чтобы проникуть в этот таинственный и загадочный мир.

I. KABAKOV
LA BIENNALE DI VENEZIA '93
"PADIGLIONE ROSSO"
INSTALLAZIONE

Padiglione "russo" nella Biennale di Venezia (ex padiglione "sovietico") sembra da fuori un work in progress: coperto da impalcature, racchiuso (con spazi adiacenti) da un alto recnto, insomma - un cantiere. D'altro canto su tutto il terrtorio dall'alto risuona una musica solenne, cheinvita gli spettatori ad entrare dentro ed a gustare lo spettacolo ch li attende all'interno*

Lo spettatore entra nella porta principale del Padiglione "Russia".

All'interno - lo stsso disordine creativo dell'esterno. Allestimenti sono ancora in corso: dappertutto secchi di vernice, travi, mattoni, inunindiza. In fondo a questo grande spazio semibuio, illuminato da deboli lampadine, si vede l'uscita, la luce accecante della giornato di sole.

Lo spettatore esce su in terrazzino e vede il cortile, all'interno dello stesso recinto. In fondo, vicino al recinto uno nota con meraviglla un edificio frsco di vernice "Padiglione URSS". Molto piupiccolo de primo padiglione (5 x 9,2 x 4,6 m): si avvicina come misure ad un piccolo fienile. Ma questo "fienile" e rimesso in maniera solenne di festa: sulle pareti risplendono tutti gli attributi della Grande Rossa Sovietica: falce e martello, stelle rosse, parole d'ordine delle grandi feste, bandiere ed al centro — lo stemma dell'Unione Sovietica.

Da una torretta in cima si innalza un albero metallico con un altoparlante. Da li'si espande "a quattro lati dell'orizzonte" la musica sovietica roboante degli anni 50, marce ssolenni, piene di spirito baldanzoso ed energie ineffabili...

Tale "minipadiglione" — e un terrtoro di un mondo ancora esistente, lolo nascosto, mimetizzato alle spalle di quell'altro. Sta rannicchiato li in fondo al cortile ed aspetta la sua ora per tornare nel posto che gli spetta, da dove e stato cacciato da poco.

*Tale stato d'animo e familiare a chiunque abbia sentito in fiera tali sioni provenienti dalli'interno provando un irresistibile desiderio di acquistre al piu presto il biglietto per penetrare in questo mondo misterioso e enigmatico al di la'del recinto.

I. KABAKOV
VENICE BIENNALE '93
"THE RED PAVILLION"
INSTALLATION

The "Russia" Pavillion looks unfinished from the outside; scaffolding is still in place on the building, and the entire plot of land is surrounded by a wooden construction fence. Despite this, emanating from behind the fence, wafting above the trees, is the sound of triumphal music, which entices viewers inside to see the spectacle prepared for them.*

The viewer enters the main door of the "Russia" Pavillion. Inside is the same chaos of construction as outside. The repairs have not been completed — everywhere there are buckets of paint, boards, bricks, rubbish. But at the rear of this big, semi-dark space, which is lit only by dim light bulbs, can be glimpsed an opening, dazzling with the radiant light of a sunny day.

The viewer exits through this opening to the small, grassy backyard behind the pavillion. This, too, is separated from the outside world by the construction fence which surrounds the entire plot on which the pavillion stands. At the very back of the plot, the viewer discovers with surprise, a new, just completed, freshly painted "USSR" Pavillion. This is considerably smaller than the "Russia" Pavillion. (5 x 9.2 x 4.6 m.) In size it is comparable to a small shed. But this "shed" is officially and festively decorated. From its walls gleam all the symbols of the Soviet era: the hammer and sickle, red stars, festive banners and flags, and, in the center, THE EMBLEM OF THE SOVIET UNION.

The metal pole on the roof supports four loud speakers. From them blare to the whole world the sounds of Soviet songs in the major key of the '50s — triumphal marches full of cheerful spirit and endless energy. This "little pavillion" is a territory of a world that still exists, but one which is hiding behind the facadeof the other. Poised at the rear of the backyard, it is awaiting its moment to return to its place, from which it was thrown out not so long ago.

*The condition of eager curiosity the music arouses will be familiar to anyone who has ever stood on a corner, listening to similar sounds rising from a carnival behind a high gate and has wanted to buy a ticket as quickly as possible to enter this mysterious secret world.

OUR THANKS:
Solomon R.Guggenheim Museum, New York, USA
Michael Govan, Deputy Director
Peggy Guggenheim Collection, Venice, Italy
Philip Rylands, Deputy Director
Lufthansa Airline
Nicolas V. Iljine, General Manager
Paolo Sprovieri, Rome, Italy
Museum Ludwig, Koln, Germany
Marc Scheps, Director
Gerald A. Goodrow, Curator
Jane Lombard
Penny and David McCall
Museum of Modern Art, New York, USA
Robert Storr, Curator
Amei Wallach, New York, USA
Peter Pakesch Gallery, Vienna
Ronald Feldman Fine Arts, New York, USA
Dr. Paul Jolles and Family
Kasper König, Frankfurt
Peter Norton Foundation, CA, USA
[illegible] and Family
Abner E. Kohn, GC Communications, New York
Moneta Impianti spa - Milano, Italy

ВЕНЕЦИЯ БИЕННАЛЕ '93 14 ИЮНЯ - 14 СЕНТЯБРЯ VENICE BIENNALE '93 JUNE 14 - SEPTEMBER 14

И. КАБАКОВ I. KABAKOV
Аранжировка Musical im-
В. Тарасова provisation
V. TARASOV

КРАСНЫЙ ПАВИЛЬОН
PADIGLIONE ROSSO
RED PAVILLION

ВЕНЕЦИЯ БИЕННАЛЕ '93
LA BIENNALE DE VENEZIA '93
VENICE BIENNALE '93

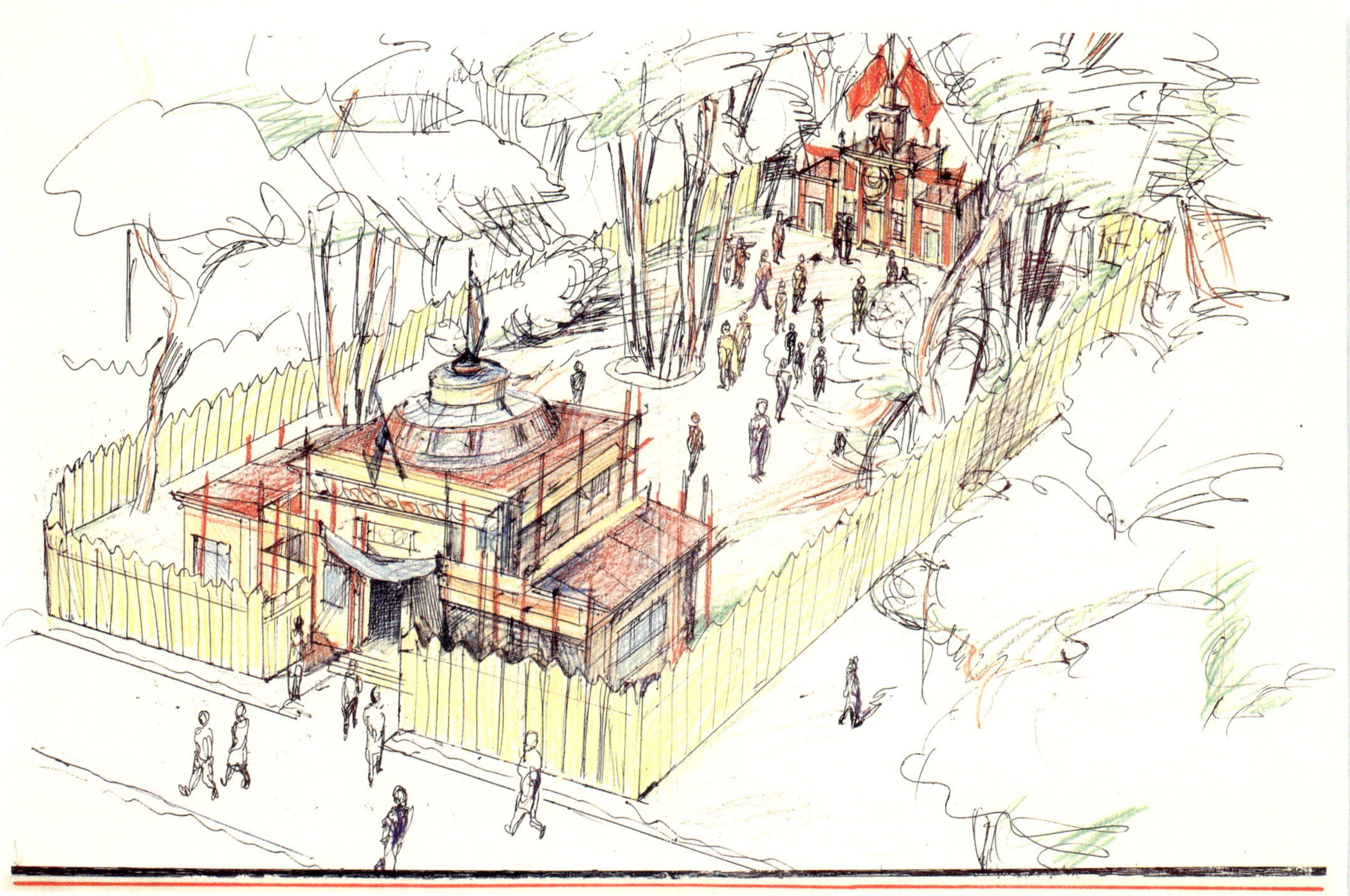

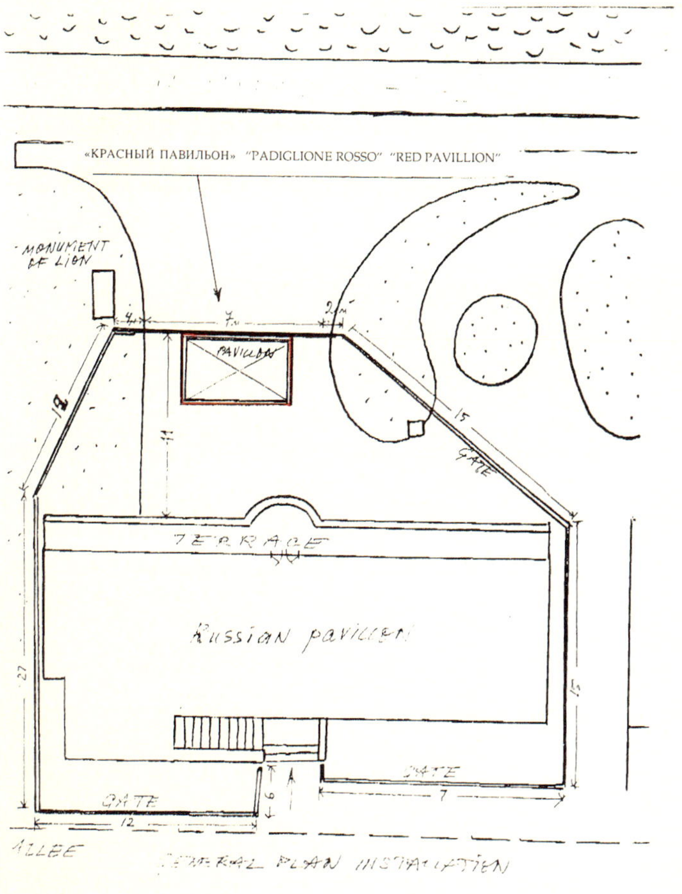

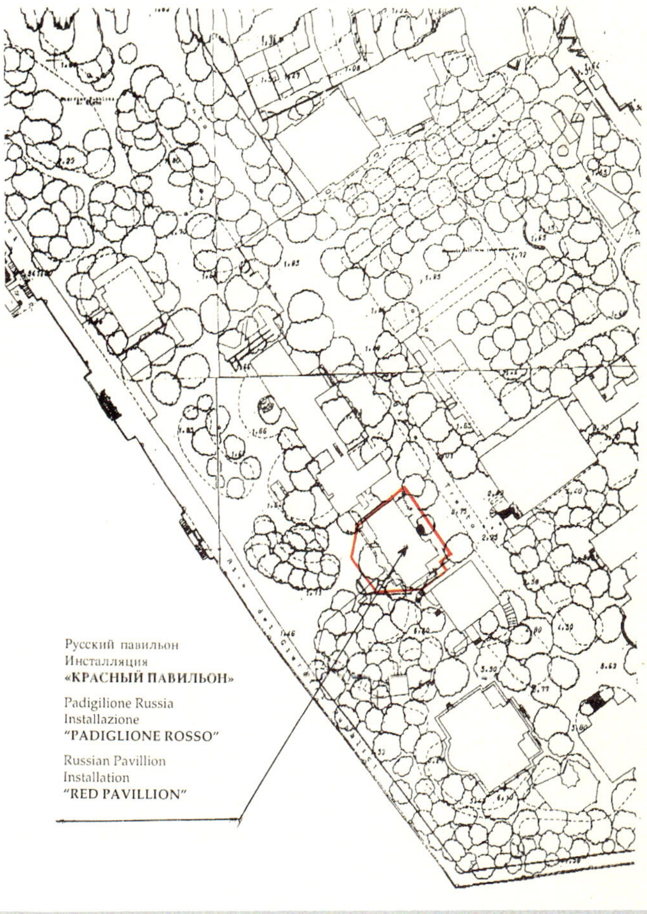

Русский павильон
Инсталляция
«КРАСНЫЙ ПАВИЛЬОН»

Padigilione Russia
Installazione
"PADIGLIONE ROSSO"

Russian Pavillion
Installation
"RED PAVILLION"

61 Incident at the Museum or Water Music | *Zwischenfall im Museum oder Wassermusik*

with Vladimir Tarasov | *mit Vladimir Tarasov*

1993

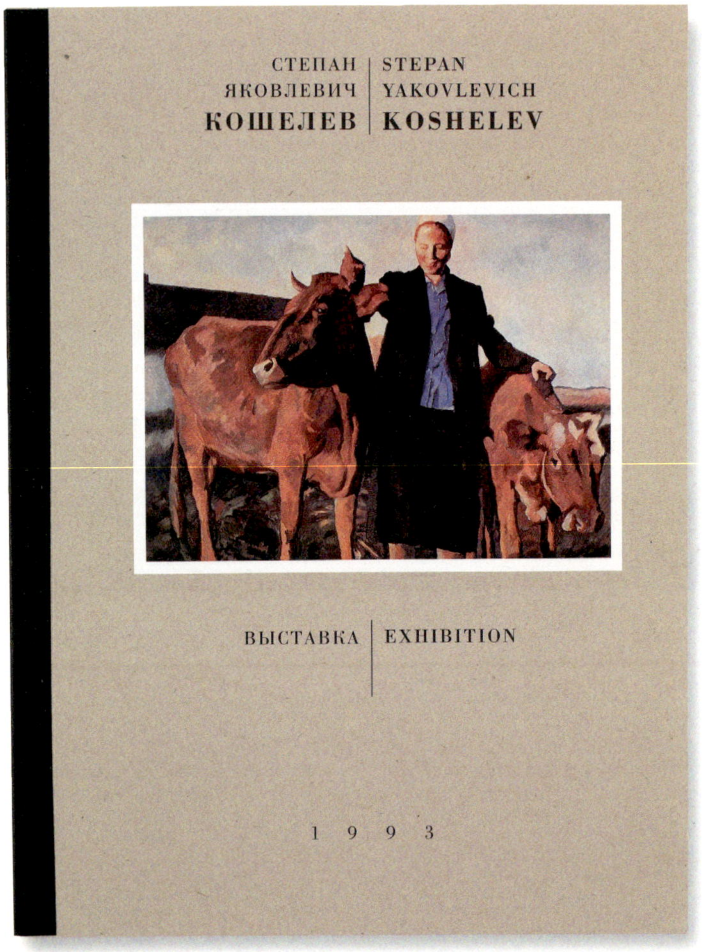

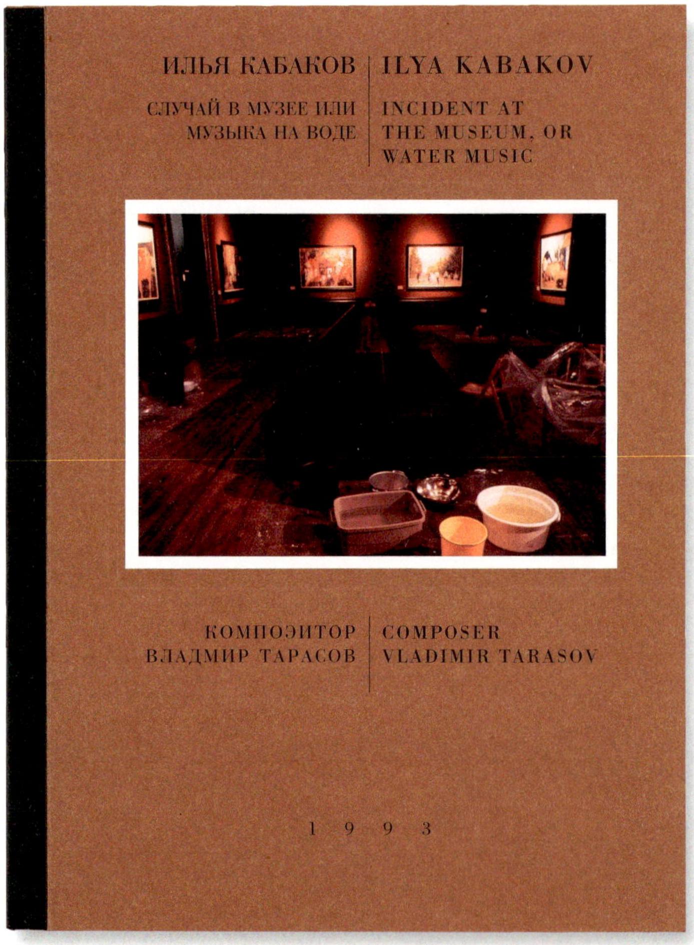

Stepan Yakovlevich Koshelev
Stefan Jakowlewitsch Koschelew
1993
Museum of Contemporary Art Chicago
Chicago: Museum of Contemporary Art Chicago
30.4 x 22.9 cm
vol. 1, [25] pp. with 11 (6 color) ills.
vol. 2, [26] pp. with 18 (14 color) ills.
softback, blind blocking with label, in cardboard slipcase
broschiert, Blindprägung mit Etikette, im Kartonschuber

exhibition catalogue | *Ausstellungskatalog*

layout by Ilya Kabakov | *Layout von Ilya Kabakov*

For the installation of the same name at the Museum of Contemporary Art Chicago, Chicago, July 10 to September 21, 1993; vol. 1: texts by Ilya Kabakov and a dialogue between Joseph Backstein and Ilya Kabakov; vol. 2: texts by Ilya Kabakov on the fictitious artist Koshelev; English, Russian.

Zur gleichnamigen Installation, Museum of Contemporary Art Chicago, Chicago, 10. Juli – 21. September 1993. Bd. 1 Texte von Ilya Kabakov und ein Dialog von Josef Bakstein und Ilya Kabakov; Bd. 2 Texte von Ilya Kabakov über den fiktiven Künstler Koschelew; englisch, russisch.

see also | *siehe auch* no. 124; CRI, vol. 1, no. 60, pp. 394–401; CRP, vol. 1, nos. 225–238, pp. 295–308

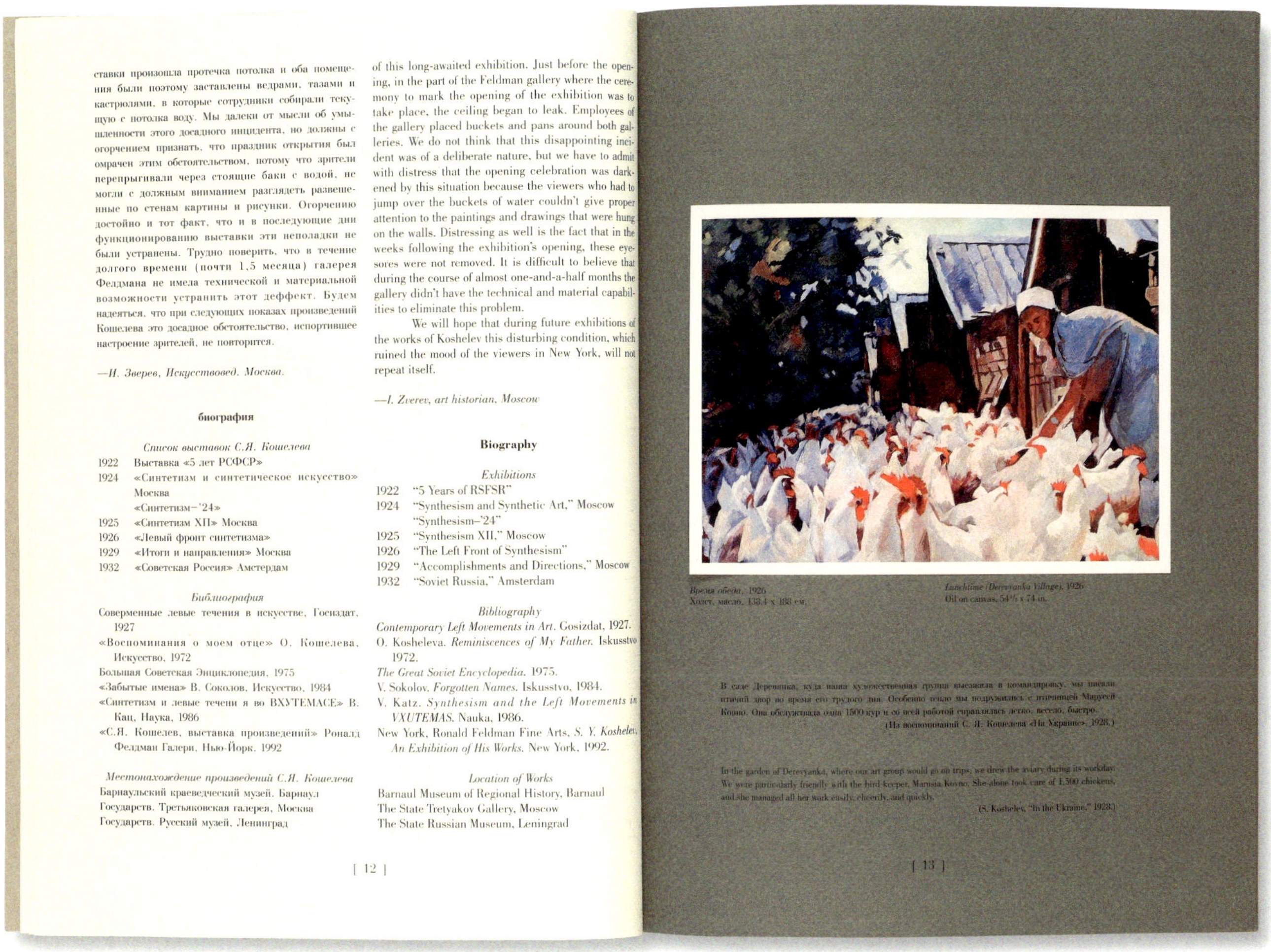

ставки произошла протечка потолка и оба помещения были поэтому заставлены ведрами, тазами и кастрюлями, в которые сотрудники собирали текущую с потолка воду. Мы далеки от мысли об умышленности этого досадного инцидента, но должны с огорчением признать, что праздник открытия был омрачен этим обстоятельством, потому что зрители перепрыгивали через стоящие баки с водой, не могли с должным вниманием разглядеть развешенные по стенам картины и рисунки. Огорчению достойно и тот факт, что и в последующие дни функционированию выставки эти неполадки не были устранены. Трудно поверить, что в течение долгого времени (почти 1,5 месяца) галерея Фелдмана не имела технической и материальной возможности устранить этот деффект. Будем надеяться, что при следующих показах произведений Кошелева это досадное обстоятельство, испортившее настроение зрителей, не повторится.

—И. Зверев, Искуствовед. Москва.

биография

Список выставок С.Я. Кошелева

1922 Выставка «5 лет РСФСР»
1924 «Синтетизм и синтетическое искусство» Москва
«Синтетизм–'24»
1925 «Синтетизм XII» Москва
1926 «Левый фронт синтетизма»
1929 «Итоги и направления» Москва
1932 «Советская Россия» Амстердам

Библиография

Соверменные левые течения в искусстве, Госиздат, 1927
«Воспоминания о моем отце» О. Кошелева, Искусство, 1972
Большая Советская Энциклопедия, 1975
«Забытые имена» В. Соколов, Искусство, 1984
«Синтетизм и левые течени я во ВХУТЕМАСЕ» В. Кац, Наука, 1986
«С.Я. Кошелев, выставка произведений» Роналд Фелдман Галери, Нью-Йорк, 1992

Местонахождение произведений С.Я. Кошелева

Барнаульский краеведческий музей, Барнаул
Государств. Третьяковская галерея, Москва
Государств. Русский музей, Ленинград

of this long-awaited exhibition. Just before the opening, in the part of the Feldman gallery where the ceremony to mark the opening of the exhibition was to take place, the ceiling began to leak. Employees of the gallery placed buckets and pans around both galleries. We do not think that this disappointing incident was of a deliberate nature, but we have to admit with distress that the opening celebration was darkened by this situation because the viewers who had to jump over the buckets of water couldn't give proper attention to the paintings and drawings that were hung on the walls. Distressing as well is the fact that in the weeks following the exhibition's opening, these eyesores were not removed. It is difficult to believe that during the course of almost one-and-a-half months the gallery didn't have the technical and material capabilities to eliminate this problem.

We will hope that during future exhibitions of the works of Koshelev this disturbing condition, which ruined the mood of the viewers in New York, will not repeat itself.

—I. Zverev, art historian, Moscow

Biography

Exhibitions

1922 "5 Years of RSFSR"
1924 "Synthesism and Synthetic Art," Moscow
"Synthesism–'24"
1925 "Synthesism XII," Moscow
1926 "The Left Front of Synthesism"
1929 "Accomplishments and Directions," Moscow
1932 "Soviet Russia," Amsterdam

Bibliography

Contemporary Left Movements in Art. Gosizdat, 1927.
O. Kosheleva. *Reminiscences of My Father*. Iskusstvo 1972.
The Great Soviet Encyclopedia. 1975.
V. Sokolov. *Forgotten Names*. Iskusstvo, 1984.
V. Katz. *Synthesism and the Left Movements in VXUTEMAS*. Nauka, 1986.
New York, Ronald Feldman Fine Arts, *S. Y. Koshelev, An Exhibition of His Works*. New York, 1992.

Location of Works

Barnaul Museum of Regional History, Barnaul
The State Tretyakov Gallery, Moscow
The State Russian Museum, Leningrad

[12]

Время обеда, 1926
Холст, масло, 138,4 x 188 см.

Lunchtime (Derevyanka Village), 1926
Oil on canvas, 54½ x 74 in.

В саде Деревянка, куда наша художественная группа выезжала в командировку, мы писали птичий двор во время его трудого дня. Особенно тесно мы подружились с птичницей Марусей Ковно. Она обслужтвала одна 1500 кур и со всей работой справлялась легко, весело, быстро.
(Из восномнаний С. Я. Кошелева «На Украине», 1928.)

In the garden of Derevyanka, where our art group would go on trips, we drew the aviary during its workday. We were particularly friendly with the bird-keeper, Marusia Kovno. She alone took care of 1,500 chickens, and she managed all her work easily, cheerily, and quickly.
(S. Koshelev, "In the Ukraine," 1928.)

[13]

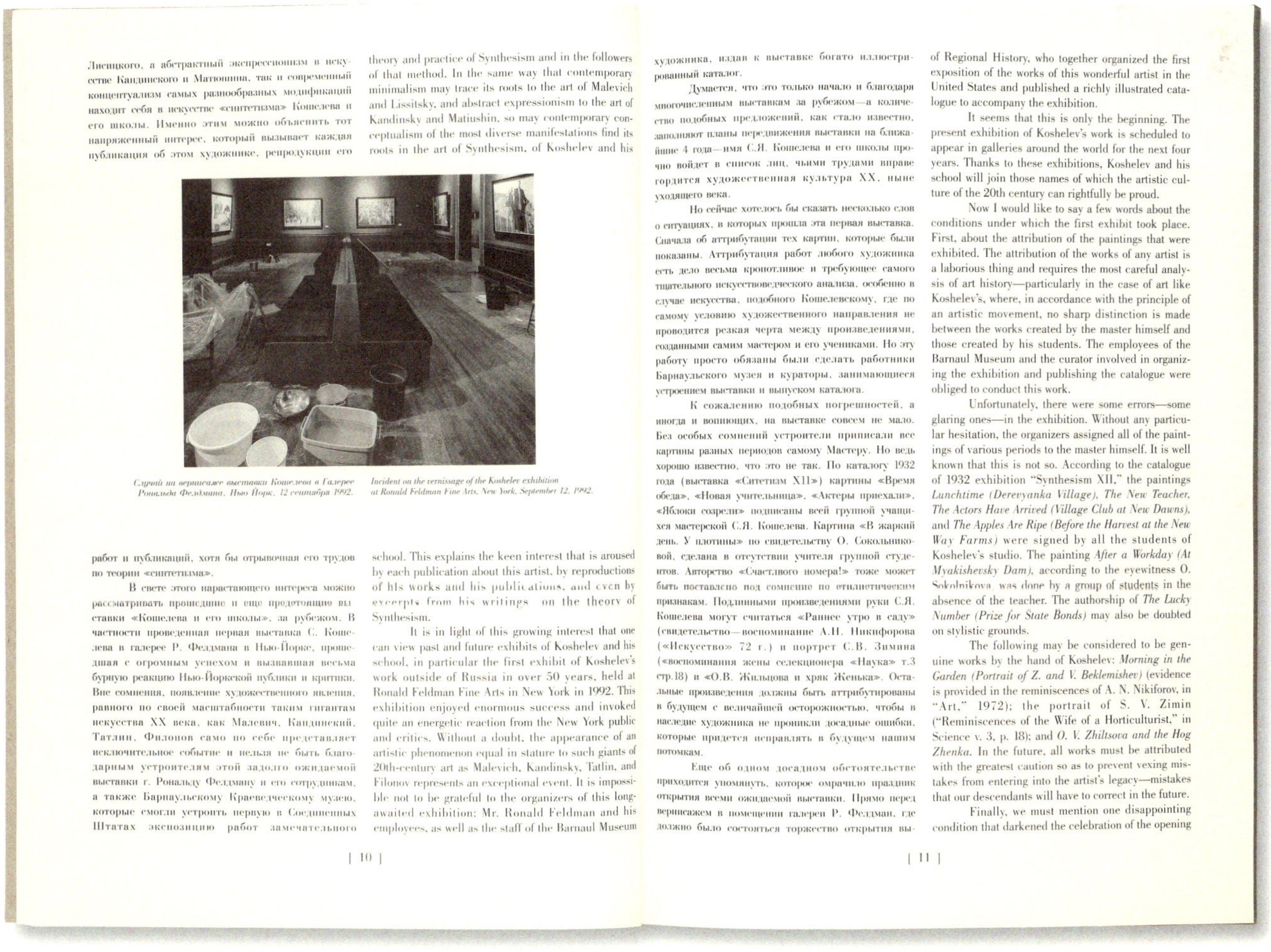

Лисицкого, а абстрактный экспрессионизм в искусстве Кандинского и Матюшина, так и современный концептуализм самых разнообразных модификаций находит себя в искусстве «синтетизма» Кошелева и его школы. Именно этим можно объяснить тот напряженный интерес, который вызывает каждая публикация об этом художнике, репродукции его работ и публикаций, хотя бы отрывочная его трудов по теории «синтетизма».

В свете этого нарастающего интереса можно рассматривать прошедшие и еще предстоящие выставки «Кошелева и его школы», за рубежом. В частности проведенная первая выставка С. Кошелева в галерее Р. Фелдмана в Нью-Йорке, прошедшая с огромным успехом и вызвавшая весьма бурную реакцию Нью-Йоркской публики и критики. Вне сомнения, появление художественного явления, равного по своей масштабности таким гигантам искусства XX века, как Малевич, Кандинский, Татлин, Филонов само по себе представляет исключительное событие и нельзя не быть благодарным устроителям этой задолго ожидаемой выставки г. Рональду Фелдману и его сотрудникам, а также Барнаульскому Краеведческому музею, которые смогли устроить первую в Соединенных Штатах экспозицию работ замечательного

theory and practice of Synthesism and in the followers of that method. In the same way that contemporary minimalism may trace its roots to the art of Malevich and Lissitsky, and abstract expressionism to the art of Kandinsky and Matiushin, so may contemporary conceptualism of the most diverse manifestations find its roots in the art of Synthesism, of Koshelev and his school. This explains the keen interest that is aroused by each publication about this artist, by reproductions of his works and his publications, and even by excerpts from his writings on the theory of Synthesism.

It is in light of this growing interest that one can view past and future exhibits of Koshelev and his school, in particular the first exhibit of Koshelev's work outside of Russia in over 50 years, held at Ronald Feldman Fine Arts in New York in 1992. This exhibition enjoyed enormous success and invoked quite an energetic reaction from the New York public and critics. Without a doubt, the appearance of an artistic phenomenon equal in stature to such giants of 20th-century art as Malevich, Kandinsky, Tatlin, and Filonov represents an exceptional event. It is impossible not to be grateful to the organizers of this long-awaited exhibition: Mr. Ronald Feldman and his employees, as well as the staff of the Barnaul Museum

Случай на вернисаже выставки Кошелева в Галерее Рональда Фелдмана, Нью Йорк, 12 сентября 1992.

Incident on the vernissage of the Koshelev exhibition at Ronald Feldman Fine Arts, New York, September 12, 1992.

[10]

художника, издав к выставке богато иллюстрированный каталог.

Думается, что это только начало и благодаря многочисленным выставкам за рубежом—а количество подобных предложений, как стало известно, заполняют планы передвижения выставки на ближайшие 4 года—имя С.Я. Кошелева и его школы прочно войдет в список лиц, чьими трудами вправе гордится художественная культура XX, ныне уходящего века.

Но сейчас хотелось бы сказать несколько слов о ситуациях, в которых прошла эта первая выставка. Сначала об аттрибутации тех картин, которые были показаны. Аттрибутация работ любого художника есть дело весьма кропотливое и требующее самого тщательного искусствоведческого анализа, особенно в случае искусства, подобного Кошелевскому, где по самому условию художественного направления не проводится резкая черта между произведениями, созданными самим мастером и его учениками. Но эту работу просто обязаны были сделать работники Барнаульского музея и кураторы, занимающиеся устроением выставки и выпуском каталога.

К сожалению подобных погрешностей, а иногда и вопиющих, на выставке совсем не мало. Без особых сомнений устроители приписали все картины разных периодов самому Мастеру. Но ведь хорошо известно, что это не так. По каталогу 1932 года (выставка «Ситетизм X11») картины «Время обеда», «Новая учительница», «Актеры приехали», «Яблоки созрели» подписаны всей группой учащихся мастерской С.Я. Кошелева. Картина «В жаркий день. У плотины» по свидетельству О. Сокольниковой, сделана в отсутствии учителя группой студентов. Авторство «Счастливого номера!» тоже может быть поставлено под сомнение по стилистическим признакам. Подлинными произведениями руки С.Я. Кошелева могут считаться «Раннее утро в саду» (свидетельство—воспоминание А.Н. Никифорова («Искусство» 72 г.) и портрет С.В. Зимина («воспоминания жены селекционера «Наука» т.3 стр.18) и «О.В. Жильцова и хряк Женька». Остальные произведения должны быть аттрибутированы в будущем с величайшей осторожностью, чтобы в наследие художника не проникли досадные ошибки, которые придется исправлять в будущем нашим потомкам.

Еще об одном досадном обстоятельстве приходится упомянуть, которое омрачило праздник открытия всеми ожидаемой выставки. Прямо перед вернисажем в помещении галереи Р. Фелдман, где должно было состояться торжество открытия вы-

of Regional History, who together organized the first exposition of the works of this wonderful artist in the United States and published a richly illustrated catalogue to accompany the exhibition.

It seems that this is only the beginning. The present exhibition of Koshelev's work is scheduled to appear in galleries around the world for the next four years. Thanks to these exhibitions, Koshelev and his school will join those names of which the artistic culture of the 20th century can rightfully be proud.

Now I would like to say a few words about the conditions under which the first exhibit took place. First, about the attribution of the paintings that were exhibited. The attribution of the works of any artist is a laborious thing and requires the most careful analysis of art history—particularly in the case of art like Koshelev's, where, in accordance with the principle of an artistic movement, no sharp distinction is made between the works created by the master himself and those created by his students. The employees of the Barnaul Museum and the curator involved in organizing the exhibition and publishing the catalogue were obliged to conduct this work.

Unfortunately, there were some errors—some glaring ones—in the exhibition. Without any particular hesitation, the organizers assigned all of the paintings of various periods to the master himself. It is well known that this is not so. According to the catalogue of 1932 exhibition "Synthesism XII," the paintings *Lunchtime (Derevyanka Village)*, *The New Teacher*, *The Actors Have Arrived (Village Club at New Dawns)*, and *The Apples Are Ripe (Before the Harvest at the New Way Farms)* were signed by all the students of Koshelev's studio. The painting *After a Workday (At Myakishevsky Dam)*, according to the eyewitness O. Sokolnikova, was done by a group of students in the absence of the teacher. The authorship of *The Lucky Number (Prize for State Bonds)* may also be doubted on stylistic grounds.

The following may be considered to be genuine works by the hand of Koshelev: *Morning in the Garden (Portrait of Z. and V. Beklemishev)* (evidence is provided in the reminiscences of A. N. Nikiforov, in "Art," 1972); the portrait of S. V. Zimin ("Reminiscences of the Wife of a Horticulturist," in Science v. 3, p. 18); and *O. V. Zhiltsova and the Hog Zhenka*. In the future, all works must be attributed with the greatest caution so as to prevent vexing mistakes from entering into the artist's legacy—mistakes that our descendants will have to correct in the future.

Finally, we must mention one disappointing condition that darkened the celebration of the opening

[11]

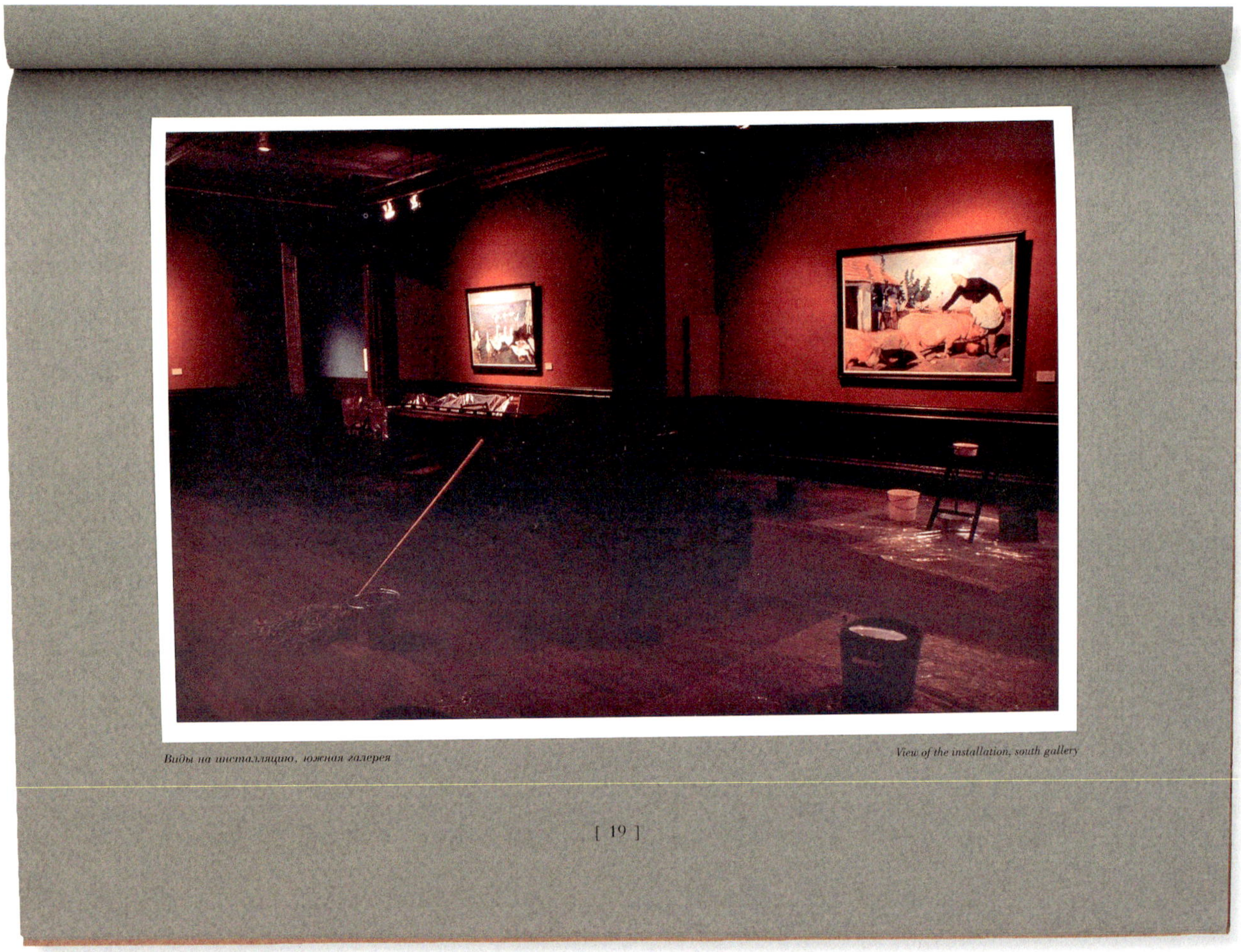

Виды на инсталляцию, южная галерея

View of the installation, south gallery

[19]

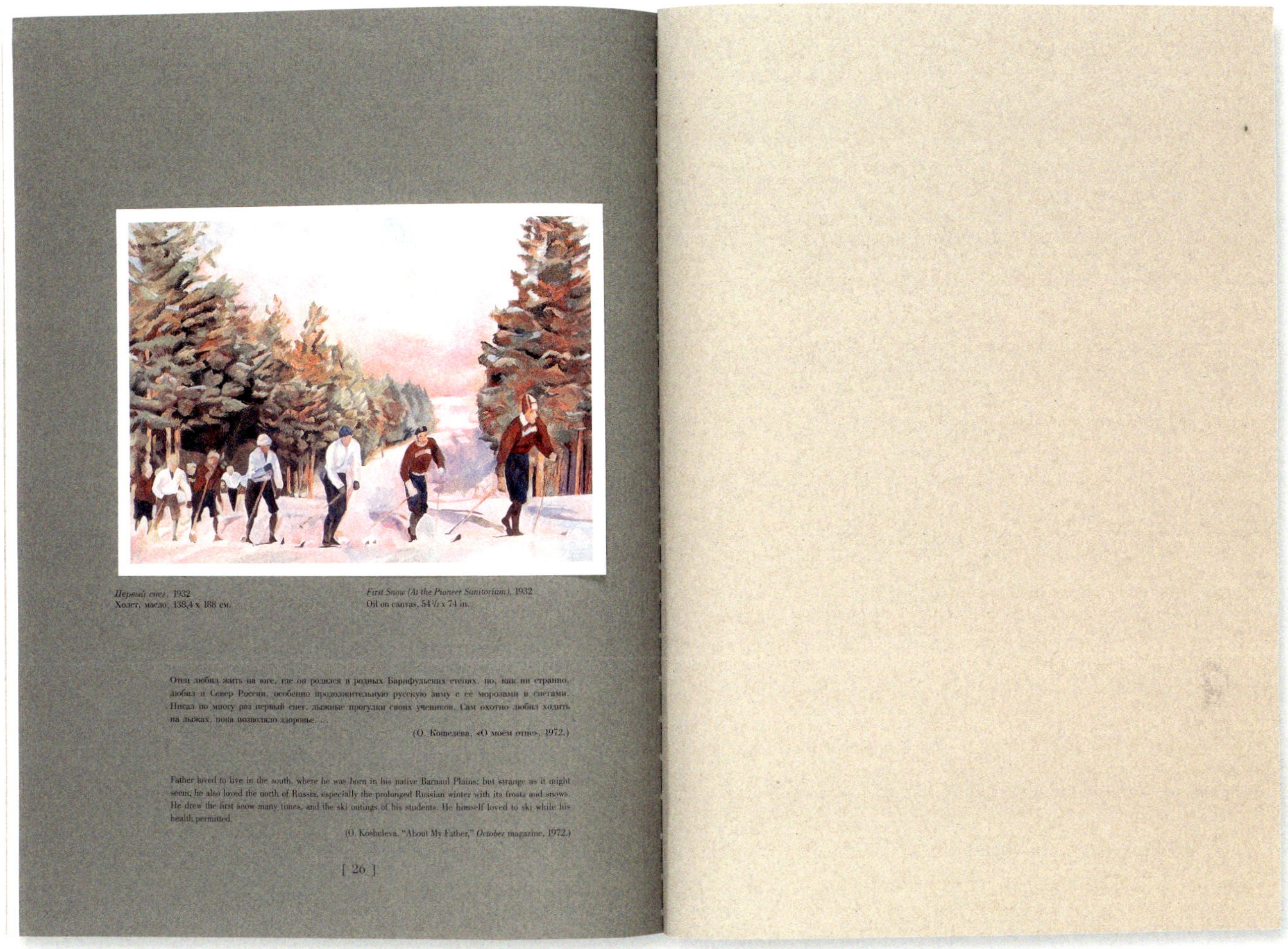
Первый снег, 1932
Холст, масло, 138,4 x 188 см.
First Snow (At the Pioneer Sanitorium), 1932
Oil on canvas, 54½ x 74 in.
Отец любил жить на юге, где он родился в родных Барнаульских степях, но, как ни странно, любил и Север России, особенно продолжительную русскую зиму с её морозами и снегами. Писал по многу раз первый снег, лыжные прогулки своих учеников. Сам охотно любил ходить на лыжах, пока позволяло здоровье. . .
(О. Кошелева, «О моём отце», 1972.)
Father loved to live in the south, where he was born in his native Barnaul Plains; but strange as it might seem, he also loved the north of Russia, especially the prolonged Russian winter with its frosts and snows. He drew the first snow many times, and the ski outings of his students. He himself loved to ski while his health permitted.
(O. Kosheleva, "About My Father," October magazine, 1972.)
[26]

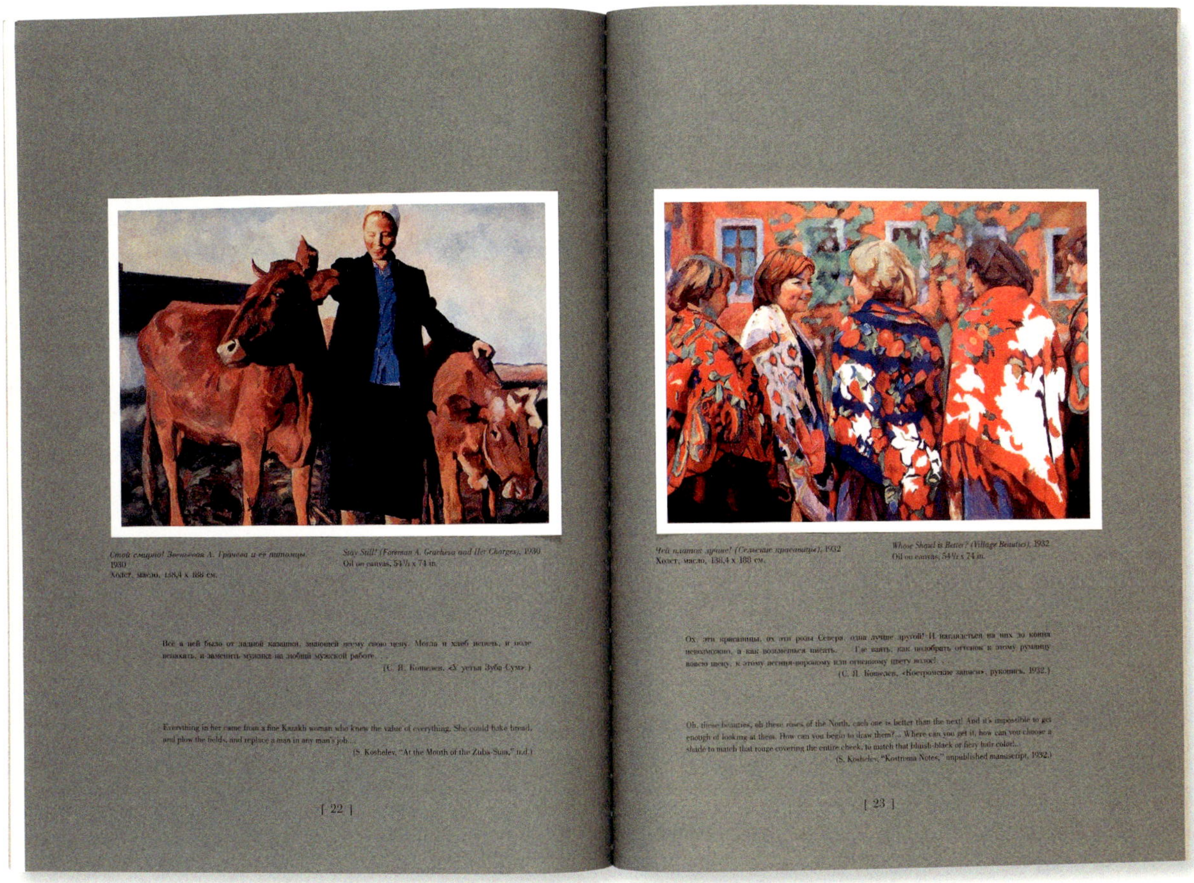
1930
Stay Still! (Foreman A. Gracheva and Her Charges), 1930
Oil on canvas, 54½ x 74 in.
Everything in her came from a fine Kazakh woman who knew the value of everything. She could bake bread, and plow the fields, and replace a man in any man's job…
(S. Koshelev, "At the Mouth of the Zuba-Sum," n.d.)
[22]
Холст, масло, 138,4 x 188 см.
Whose Shawl is Better? (Village Beauties), 1932
Oil on canvas, 54½ x 74 in.
Oh, these beauties, oh these roses of the North, each one is better than the next! And it's impossible to get enough of looking at them. How can you begin to draw them?.. Where can you get it, how can you choose a shade to match that rouge covering the entire cheek, to match that bluish-black or fiery hair color!..
(S. Koshelev, "Kostroma Notes," unpublished manuscript, 1932.)
[23]

62 NOMA or the Moscow Conceptual Circle

NOMA oder Der Kreis der Moskauer Konzeptualisten

1993

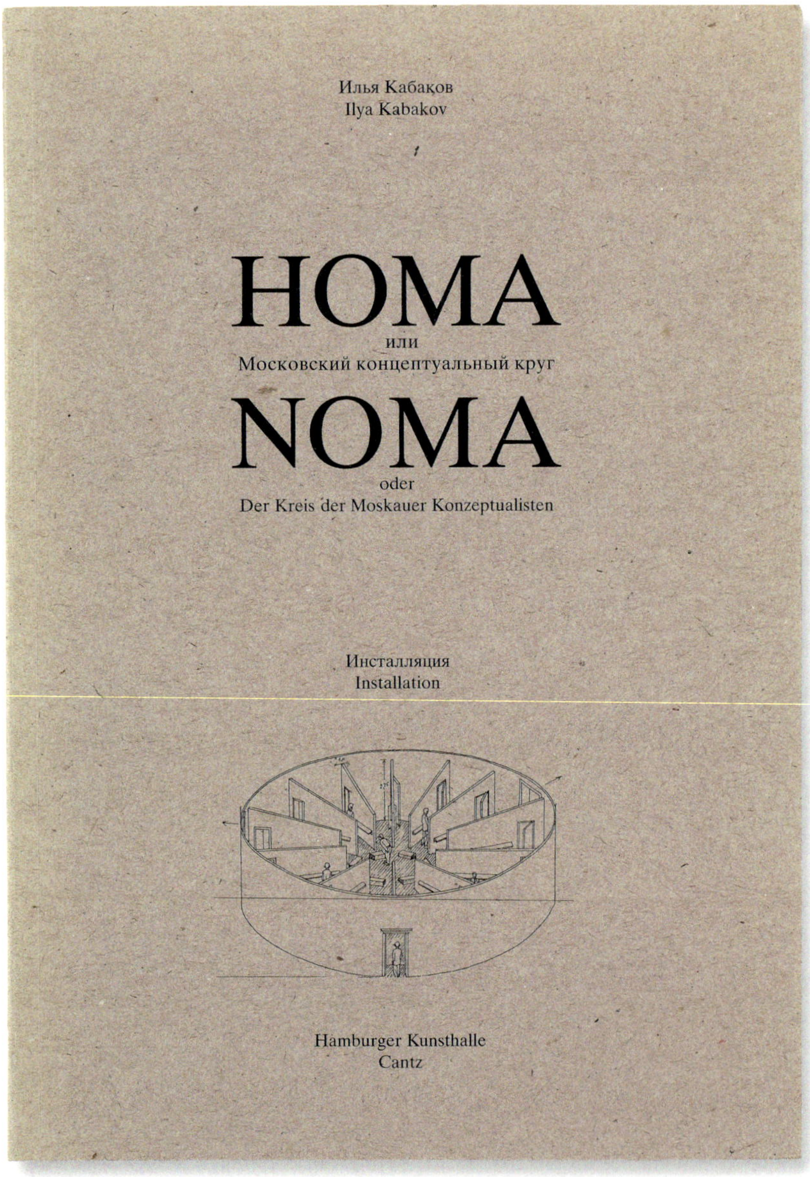

Hamburger Kunsthalle
Ostfildern bei Stuttgart: Cantz Verlag
24 x 17 cm
191 pp. with 71 b/w ills.
stitchbound, softback
Fadenheftung, broschiert

exhibition catalogue | *Ausstellungskatalog*

layout by Ilya Kabakov | *Layout von Ilya Kabakov*

For the installation of the same name in the Domed Hall, Hamburger Kunsthalle, Hamburg, December 10, 1993 to February 6, 1994.

Texts by Nikita Alexeyev, Joseph Backstein, Boris Groys, Ilya Kabakov, Yuri Leiderman, Andrei Monastyrski, Pavel Pepperstein, Dimitri Prigov, Lev Rubinstein, Uwe M. Schneede, Vladimir Sorokin, Vadim Zakharov, and a dialogue between Boris Groys and Ilya Kabakov on »NOMA«, which was also published in the book »The Art of Installation«, 1996; Russian, German.

Zur gleichnamigen Installation Kuppelsaal, Hamburger Kunsthalle, Hamburg, 10. Dezember 1993 – 6. Februar 1994.

Texte von Nikita Alexejev, Josef Bakstein, Boris Groys, Ilya Kabakov, Juri Leiderman, Andrej Monastyrskij, Pavel Pepperstein, Dimitrij Prigov, Lev Rubinstein, Uwe M. Schneede, Vladimir Sorokin, Vadim Zakharov, und ein Dialog von Boris Groys und Ilya Kabakov über »NOMA«, der auch im Buch »Die Kunst der Installation«, 1996, publiziert wurde; russisch, deutsch.

see also | *siehe auch* no. 91; CRI, vol. 1, no. 76, pp. 486–491

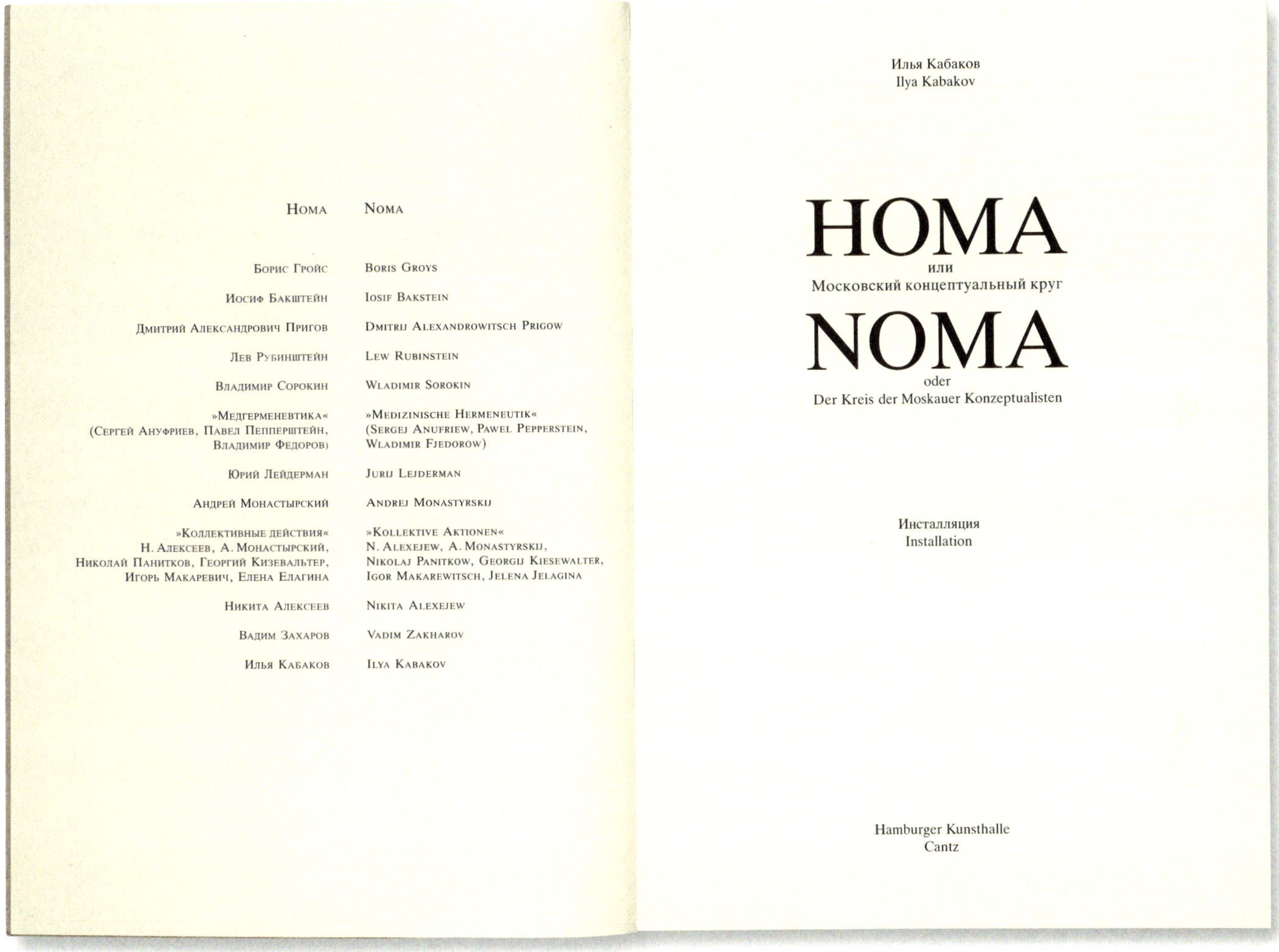

Нома	Noma
Борис Гройс	Boris Groys
Иосиф Бакштейн	Iosif Bakstein
Дмитрий Александрович Пригов	Dmitrij Alexandrowitsch Prigow
Лев Рубинштейн	Lew Rubinstein
Владимир Сорокин	Wladimir Sorokin
»Медгерменевтика« (Сергей Ануфриев, Павел Пепперштейн, Владимир Федоров)	»Medizinische Hermeneutik« (Sergej Anufriew, Pawel Pepperstein, Wladimir Fjedorow)
Юрий Лейдерман	Jurij Lejderman
Андрей Монастырский	Andrej Monastyrskij
»Коллективные действия« Н. Алексеев, А. Монастырский, Николай Панитков, Георгий Кизевальтер, Игорь Макаревич, Елена Елагина	»Kollektive Aktionen« N. Alexejew, A. Monastyrskij, Nikolaj Panitkow, Georgij Kiesewalter, Igor Makarewitsch, Jelena Jelagina
Никита Алексеев	Nikita Alexejew
Вадим Захаров	Vadim Zakharov
Илья Кабаков	Ilya Kabakov

Илья Кабаков
Ilya Kabakov

НОМА
или
Московский концептуальный круг
NOMA
oder
Der Kreis der Moskauer Konzeptualisten

Инсталляция
Installation

Hamburger Kunsthalle
Cantz

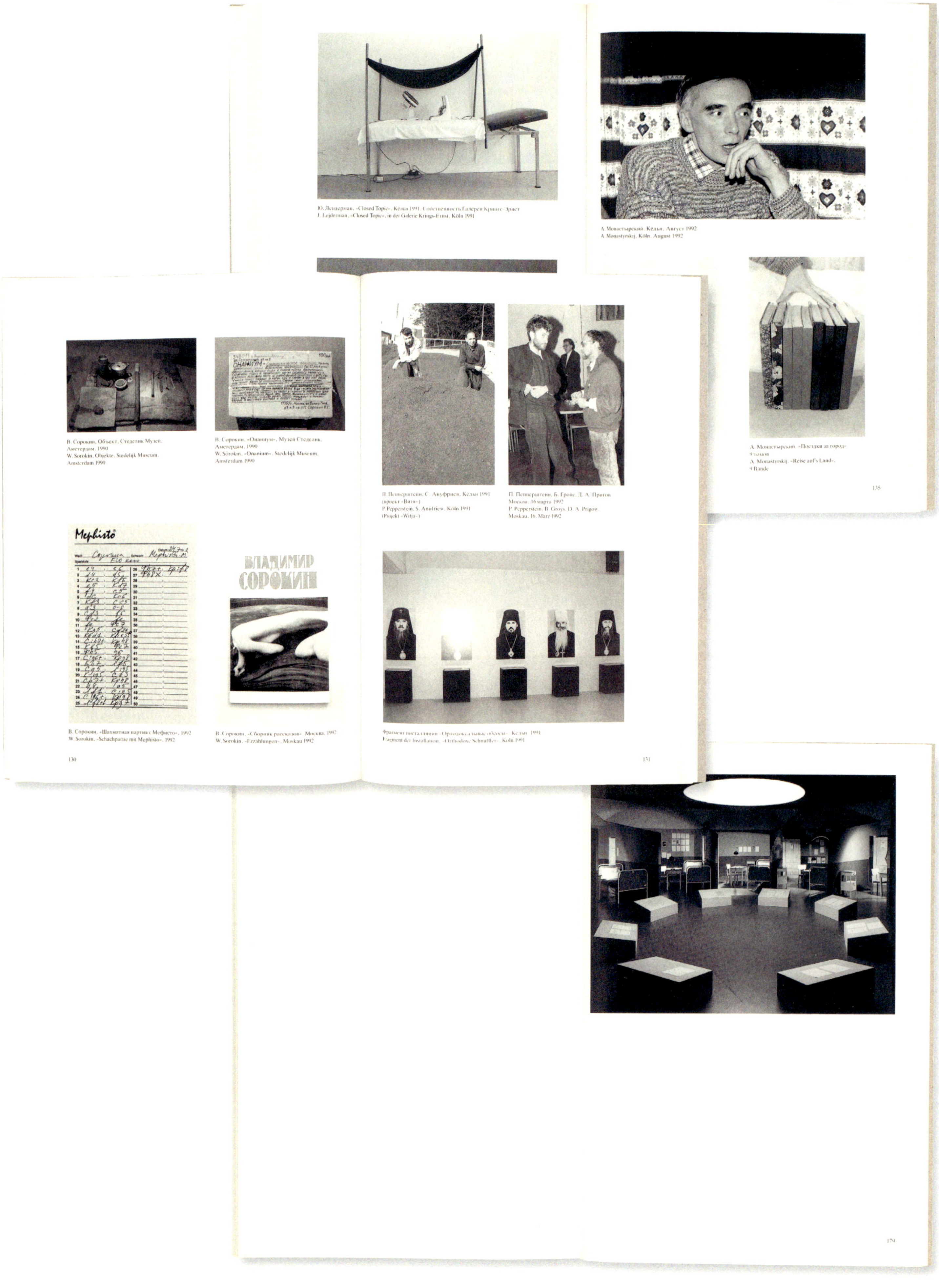
Ю. Лейдерман, «Closed Topic», Кёльн 1991. Собственность Галереи Крингс-Эрнст
J. Lejderman, «Closed Topic», in der Galerie Krings-Ernst, Köln 1991
А. Монастырский. Кёльн, Август 1992
A. Monastyrskij, Köln, August 1992
В. Сорокин, Объект, Стеделик Музей, Амстердам, 1990
W. Sorokin, Objekte, Stedelijk Museum, Amsterdam 1990
ОНАНИУМ
В. Сорокин, «Онаниум», Музей Стеделик, Амстердам, 1990
W. Sorokin, «Onanium», Stedelijk Museum, Amsterdam 1990
П. Пепперштейн, С. Ануфриев, Кёльн 1991 (проект «Витя»)
P. Pepperstein, S. Anufriew, Köln 1991 (Projekt «Witja»)
П. Пепперштейн, Б. Гройс, Д. А. Пригов Москва, 16 марта 1992
P. Pepperstein, B. Groys, D. A. Prigow, Moskau, 16. März 1992
А. Монастырский, «Поездки за город» 9 томов
A. Monastyrskij, «Reise auf's Land», 9 Bände
135
Mephisto
В. Сорокин, «Шахматная партия с Мефисто», 1992
W. Sorokin, «Schachpartie mit Mephisto», 1992
ВЛАДИМИР СОРОКИН
В. Сорокин, «Сборник рассказов», Москва, 1992
W. Sorokin, «Erzählungen», Moskau 1992
Фрагмент инсталляции «Ортодоксальные обсосы». Кельн 1991
Fragment der Installation «Orthodoxe Schnüffler». Köln 1991
130

63 The Man Who Flew Into Space | *Der Mensch, der in den Kosmos flog*

1993

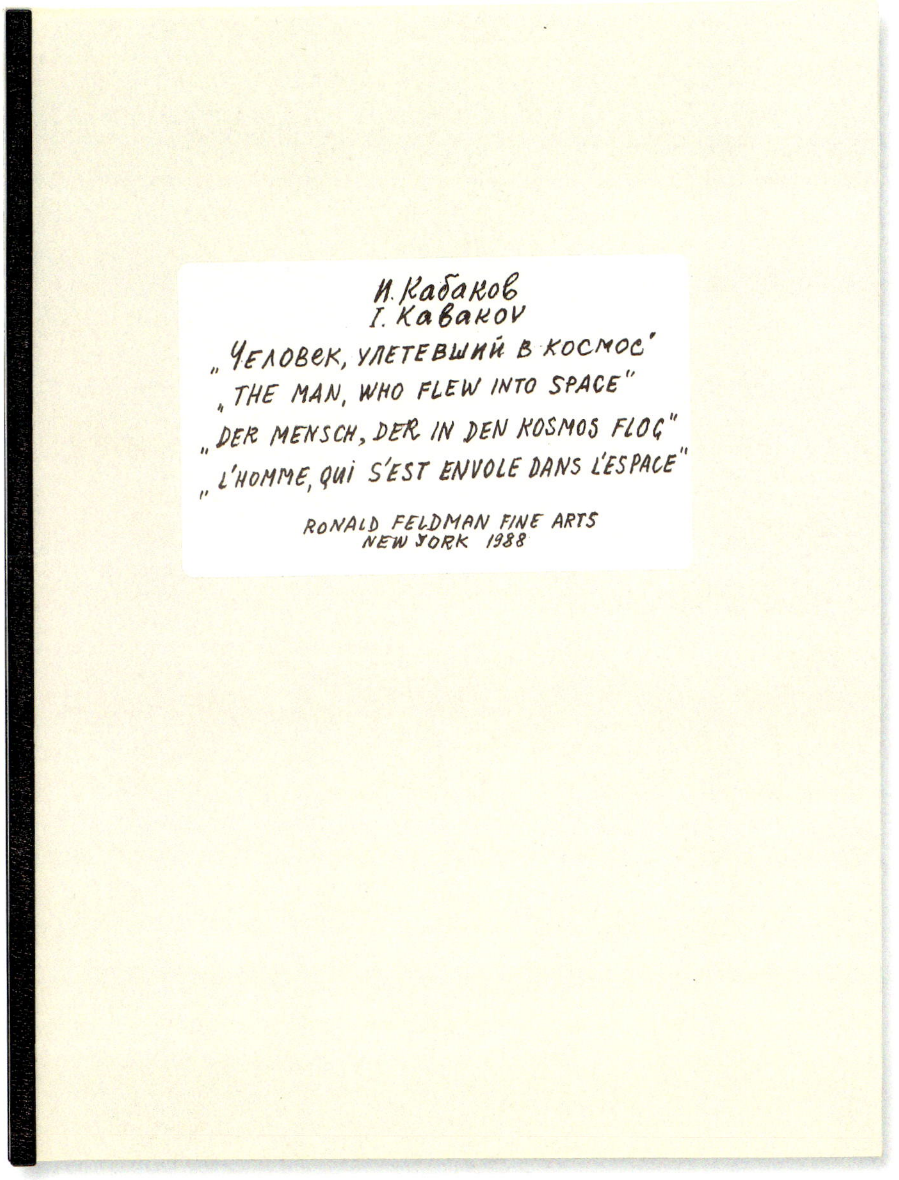

Ilya and Emilia Kabakov
New York: published by Ilya and Emilia Kabakov
27.9 x 21.5 cm
83 photocopied pp. with 5 b/w (incl. 4 foldouts) and 16 color (incl. 4 foldouts) ills.
quick bind, cardboard cover, label on the cover
Schnellhefter, Kartonumschlag, Etikette auf dem Umschlag
edition: 500 numbered copies with 5 including an original signed, numbered, and dated drawing by Ilya Kabakov from 1994

thematic publication | *thematische Publikation*

layout by Ilya Kabakov | *Layout von Ilya Kabakov*

For the documentation of the installation of the same name for the exhibition »10 Characters«, Ronald Feldman Fine Arts Gallery, New York, April 30 to June 4, 1988. Texts by Ilya Kabakov. Dialogue between Joseph Backstein and Ilya Kabakov on the installation; Russian, English, German, French.

Zur Dokumentation der gleichnamigen Installation in der Ausstellung »10 Charaktere«, Galerie Ronald Feldman Fine Arts, New York, 30. April – 4. Juni 1988. Texte von Ilya Kabakov. Dialog von Josef Bakstein und Ilya Kabakov über die Installation; russisch, englisch, deutsch, französisch.

see also | *siehe auch* no. 22; no. 76; CRI, vol. 1, no. 9, pp. 94–101; CRP, vol. 1, no. 114, pp. 196–197

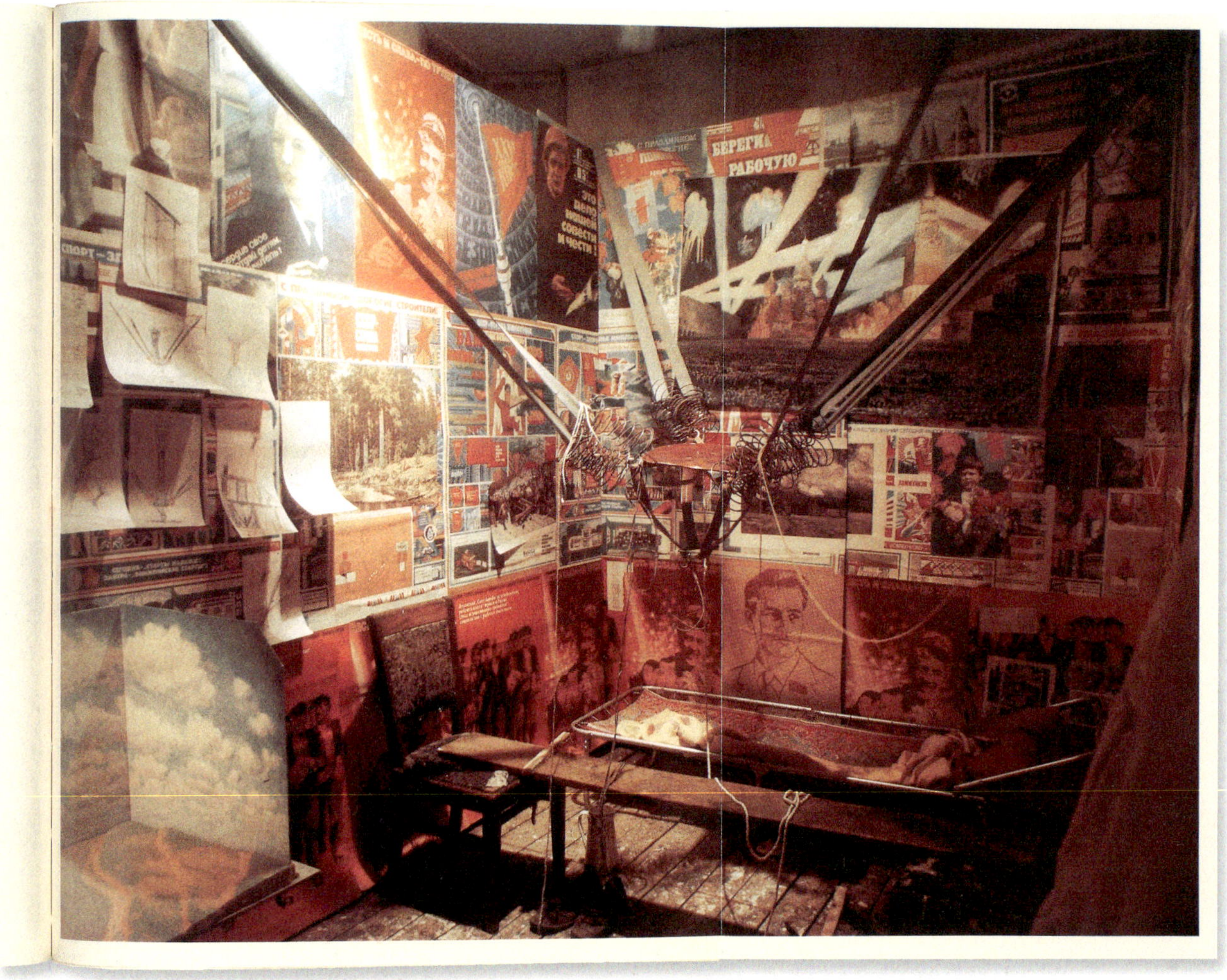

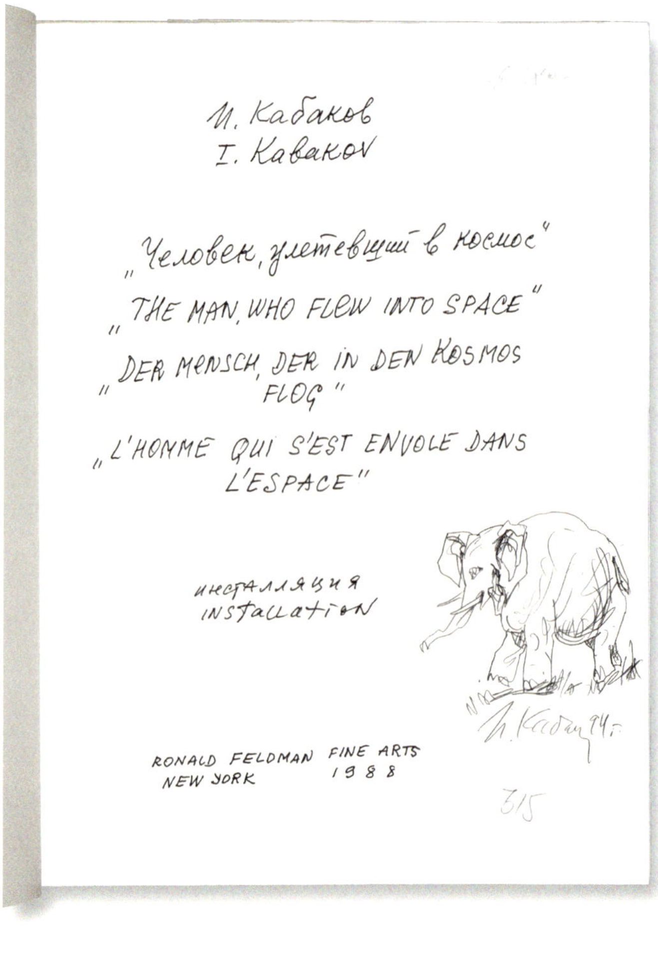
И. Кабаков
I. Kabakov

„Человек, улетевший в космос"

„THE MAN, WHO FLEW INTO SPACE"

„DER MENSCH, DER IN DEN KOSMOS FLOG"

„L'HOMME QUI S'EST ENVOLE DANS L'ESPACE"

инсталляция
installation

RONALD FELDMAN FINE ARTS
NEW YORK 1988

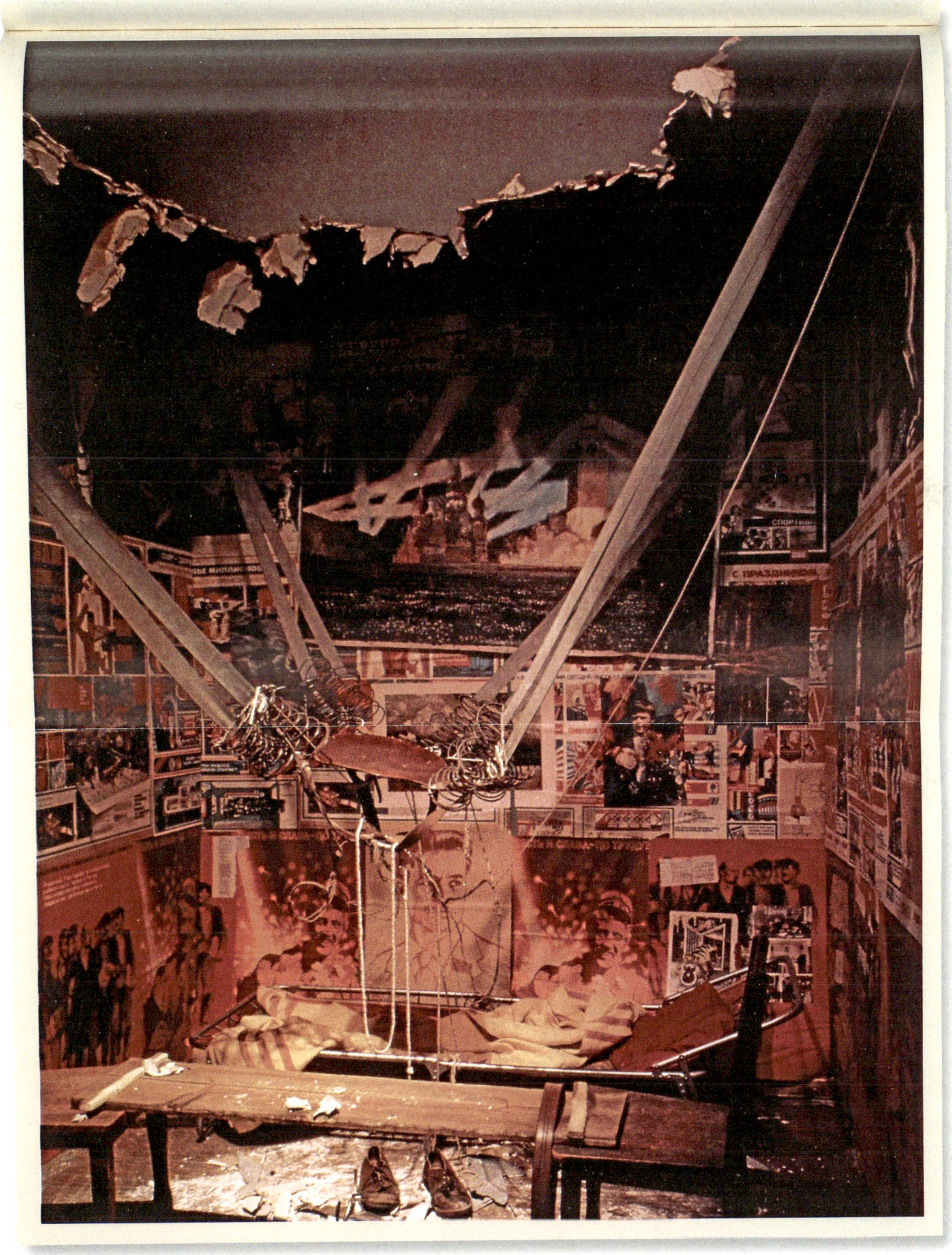
С ПРАЗДНИКОМ

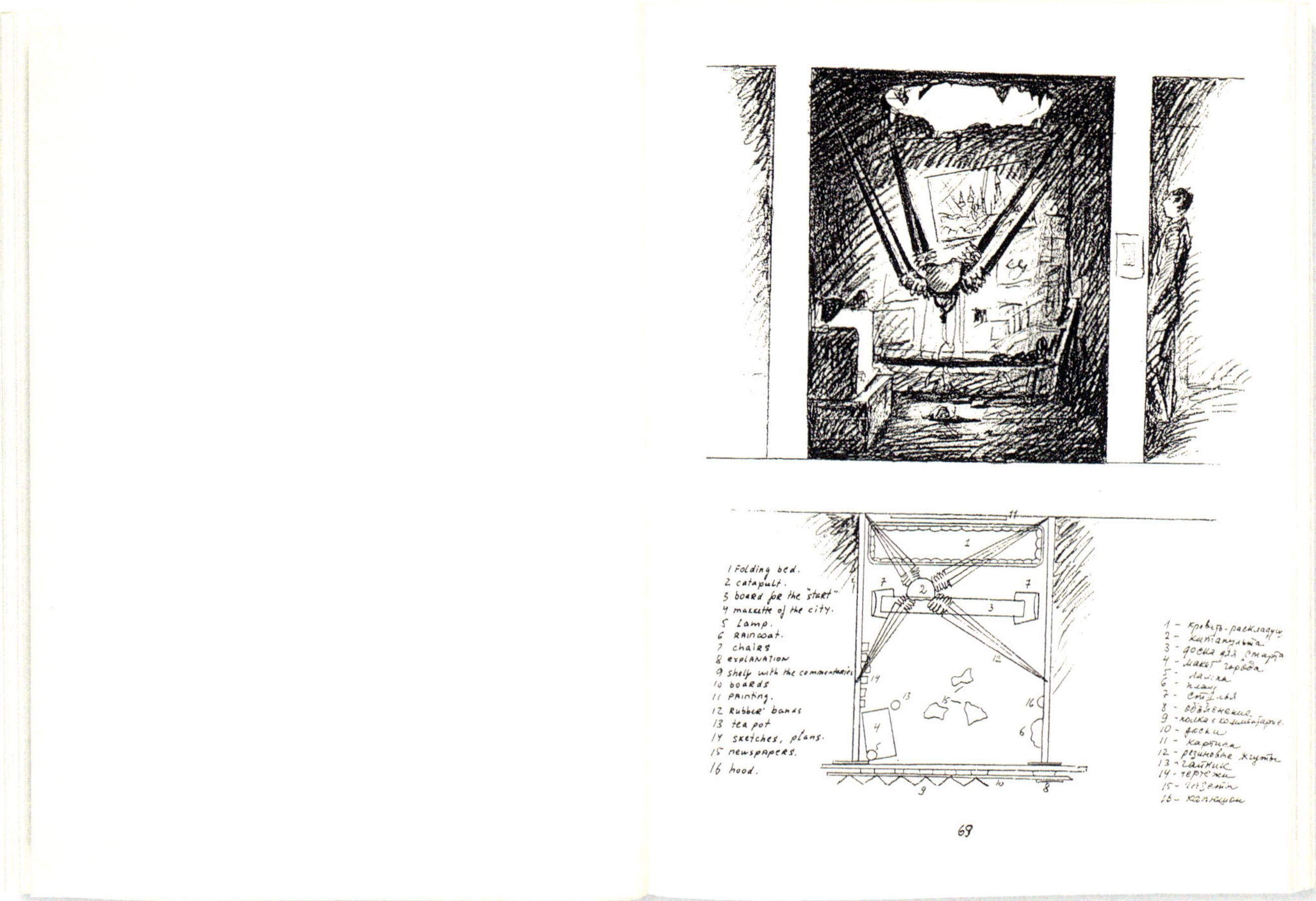
1 Folding bed.
2 catapult.
3 board for the "start"
4 maquette of the city.
5 Lamp.
6 Raincoat.
7 chairs
8 explanation
9 shelf with the commentaries
10 boards
11 painting.
12 Rubber bands
13 tea pot
14 sketches, plans.
15 newspapers.
16 hood.
69

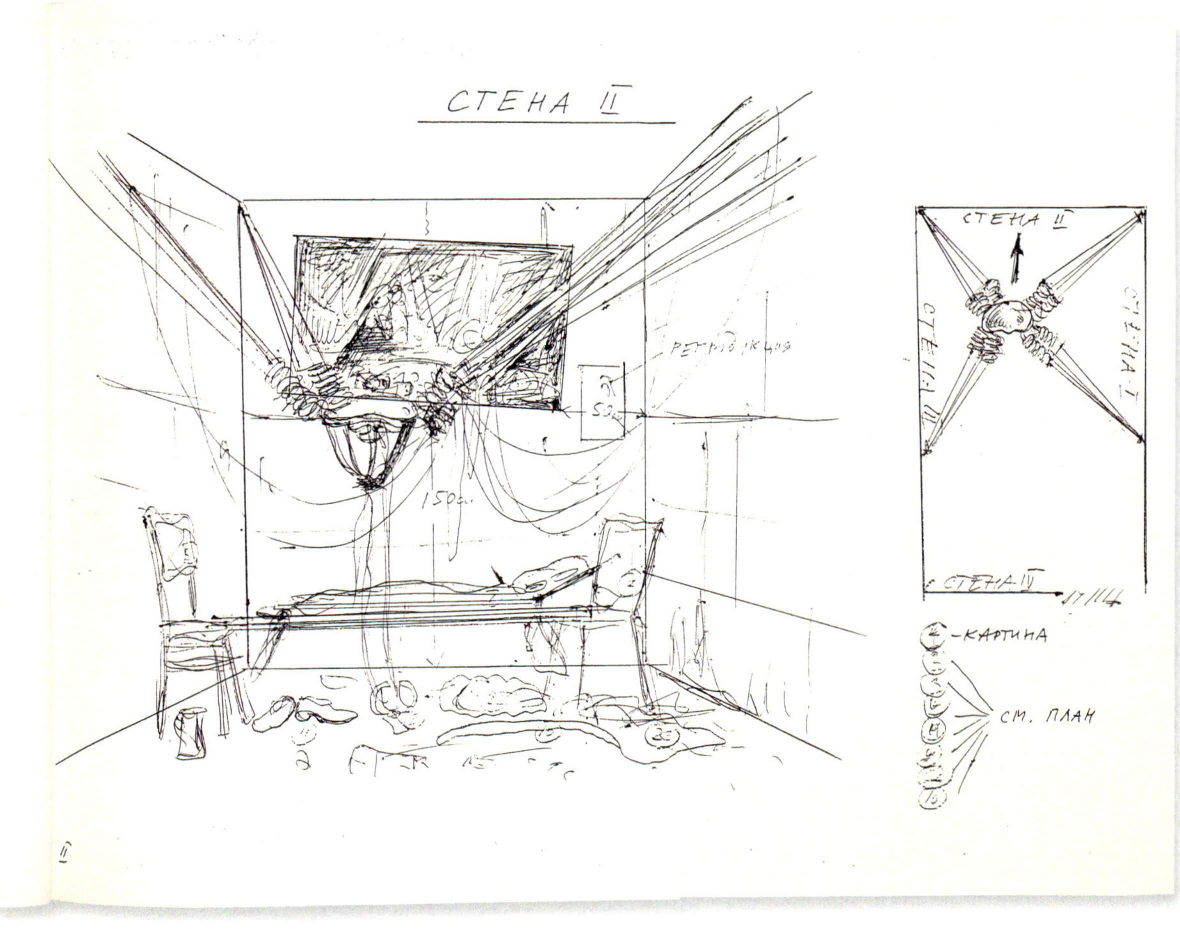
СТЕНА II
150
СТЕНА II
СТЕНА IV
-КАРТИНА
СМ. ПЛАН

64 **Targets** | *Die Zielscheiben*

1993

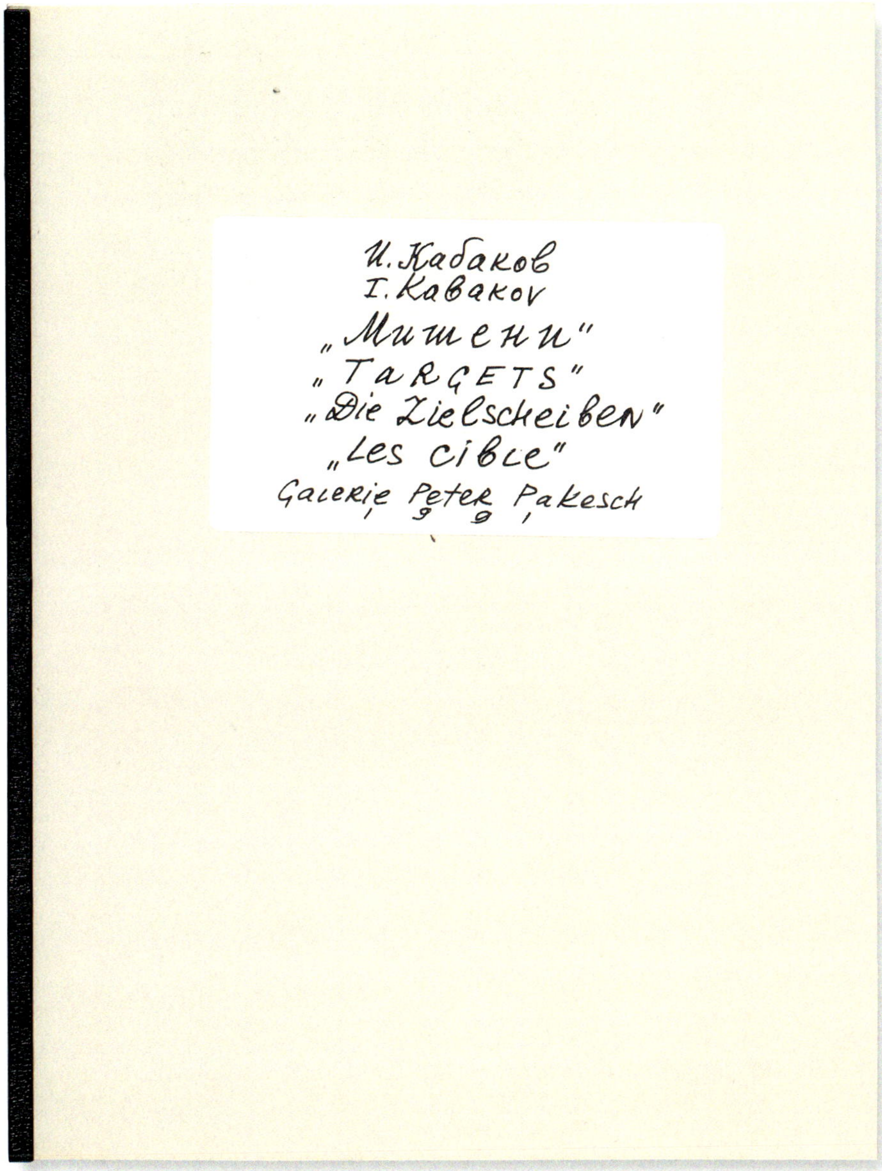

Ilya and Emilia Kabakov
New York: published by Ilya and Emilia Kabakov
27.9 x 21.5 cm
109 photocopied pp. with 9 (incl. 4 color foldouts) ills.
quick bind, cardboard cover, label on the cover
Schnellhefter, Kartonumschlag, Etikette auf dem Umschlag
edition: 500 numbered copies with 5 including an original signed, numbered, and dated drawing by Ilya Kabakov from 1994

thematic publication | *thematische Publikation*

layout by Ilya Kabakov | *Layout von Ilya Kabakov*

For the documentation of the installation of the same name at the Galerie Peter Pakesch, Vienna, February 12 to March 16, 1991. Texts by Ilya Kabakov. Dialogue between Boris Groys and Ilya Kabakov on »Targets«; Russian, English, German, French.

Zur Dokumentation der gleichnamigen Installation, Galerie Peter Pakesch, Wien, 12. Februar – 16. März 1991. Texte von Ilya Kabakov. Dialog von Boris Groys und Ilya Kabakov über »Zielscheiben«; russisch, englisch, deutsch, französisch.

see also | *siehe auch* CRI, vol. 1, no. 41, pp. 284–289; CRP, vol. 1, nos. 162–164, pp. 252–254

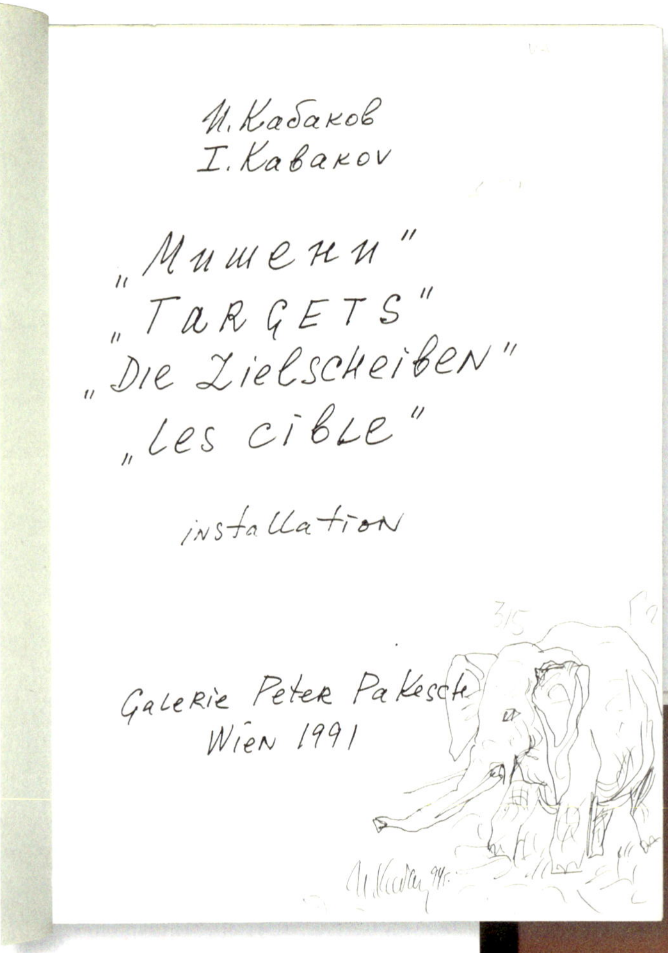
И. Кабаков
I. Kabakov
„Мишени"
„Targets"
„Die Zielscheiben"
„les cible"
installation
Galerie Peter Pakesch
Wien 1991

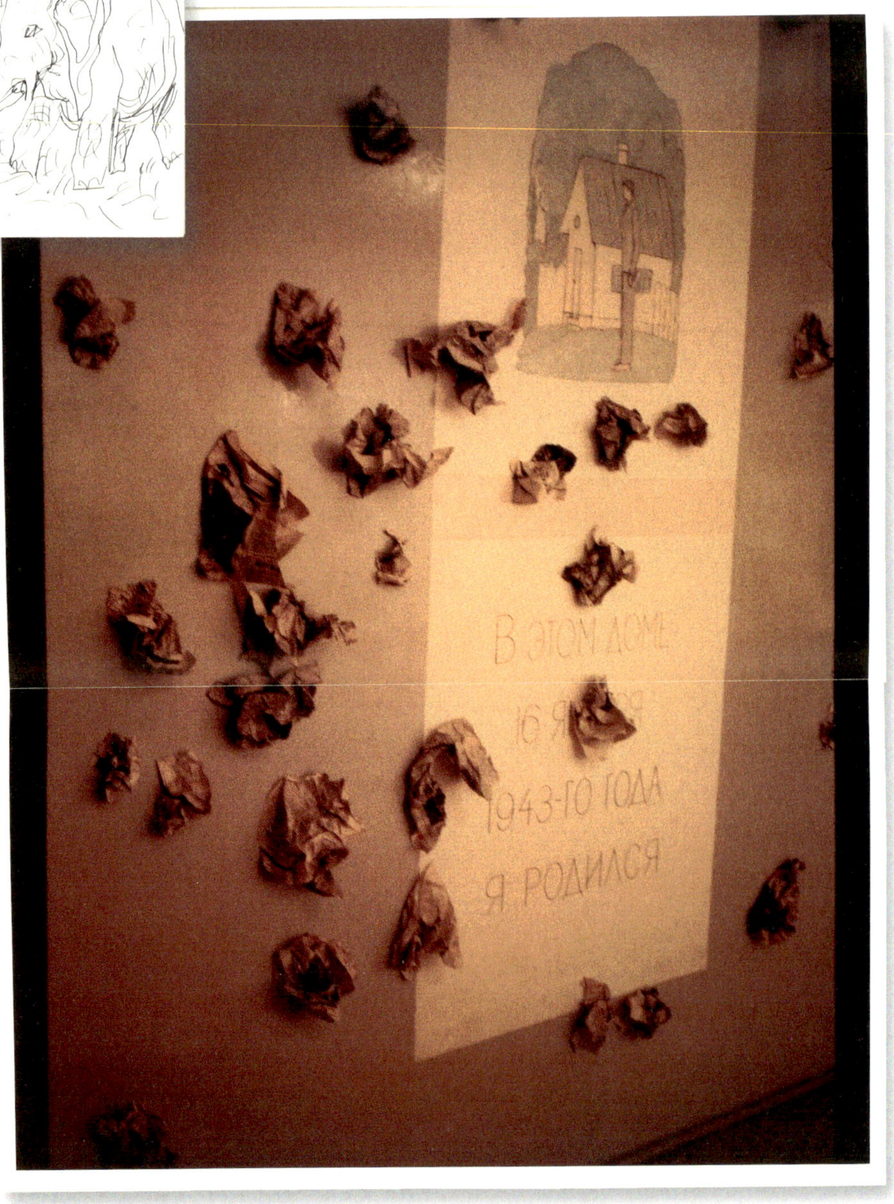
В ЭТОМ ДОМЕ
1943-ГО ГОДА
Я РОДИЛСЯ

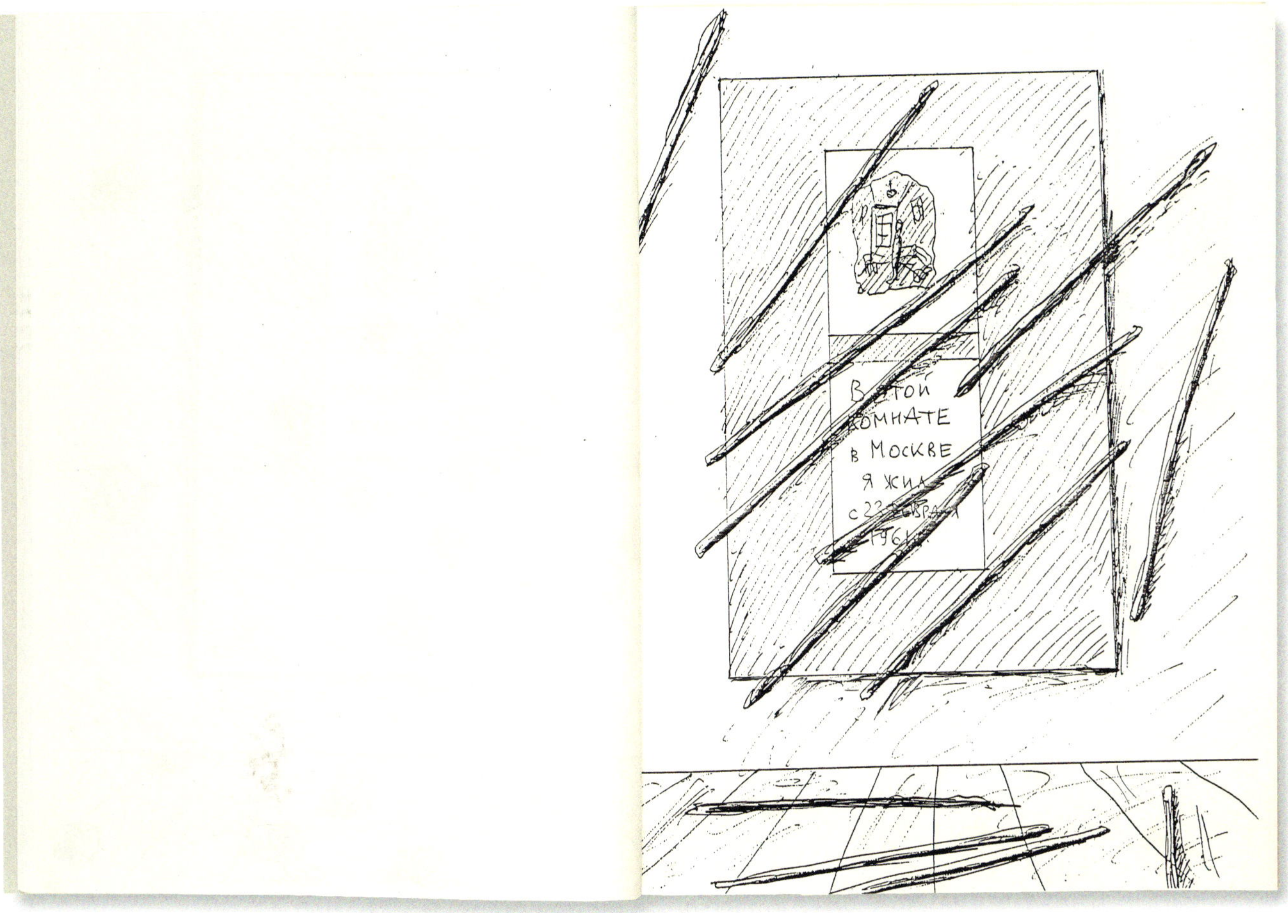
в Москве
я жил

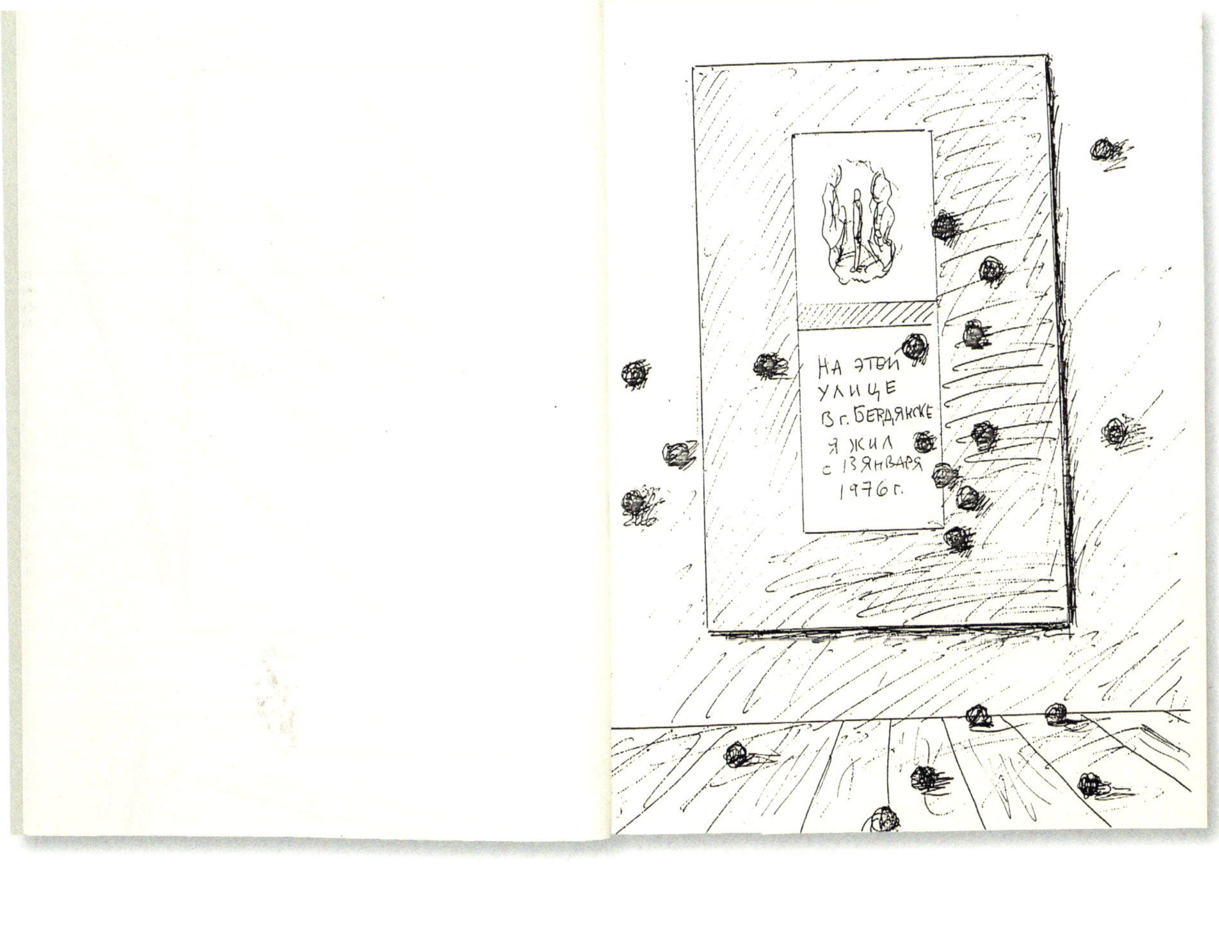
На этой
улице
в г. Бердянске
я жил
с 13 января
1976 г.

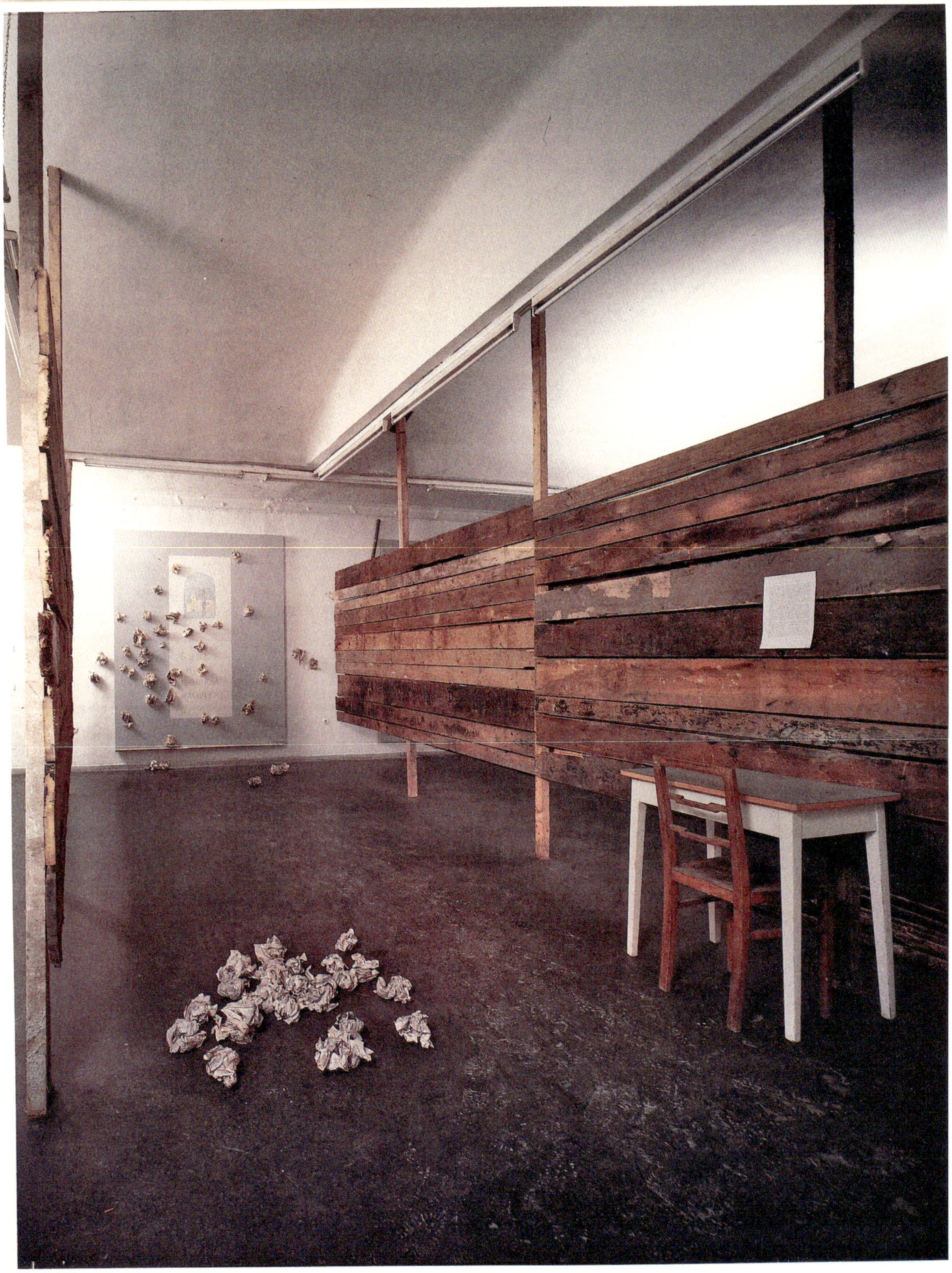

65 The Bridge | *Die Brücke*

1993

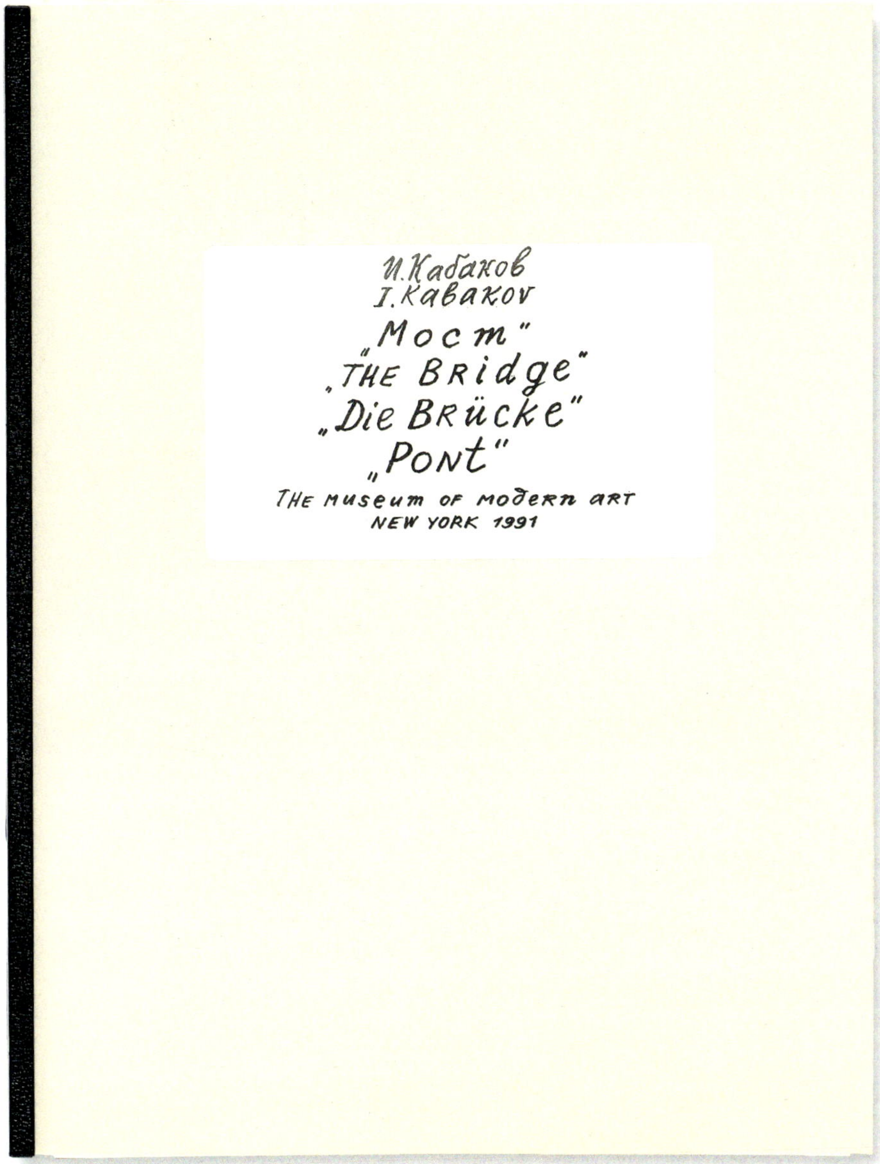

Ilya and Emilia Kabakov
New York: published by Ilya and Emilia Kabakov
27.9 x 21.5 cm
133 photocopied pp. with 5 b/w (foldouts) and 15 color (incl. 3 foldouts) ills.
quick bind, cardboard cover, label on the cover
Schnellhefter, Kartonumschlag, Etikette auf dem Umschlag
edition: 500 numbered copies with 5 including an original signed, numbered, and dated drawing by Ilya Kabakov from 1994

thematic publication | *thematische Publikation*

layout by Ilya Kabakov | *Layout von Ilya Kabakov*

For the documentation of the installation of the same name for the exhibition »Dislocations«, Museum of Modern Art, New York, October 20, 1991 to January 7, 1992. Text by Ilya Kabakov. Dialogue between Boris Groys and Ilya Kabakov on the installation; Russian, English, German, French.

Zur Dokumentation der gleichnamigen Installation für die Ausstellung »Dislocations«, Museum of Modern Art, New York, 20. Oktober 1991 – 7. Januar 1992. Text von Ilya Kabakov. Dialog von Boris Groys und Ilya Kabakov über die Installation; russisch, englisch, deutsch, französisch.

see also | *siehe auch* CRI, vol. 1, no. 53, pp. 346–353

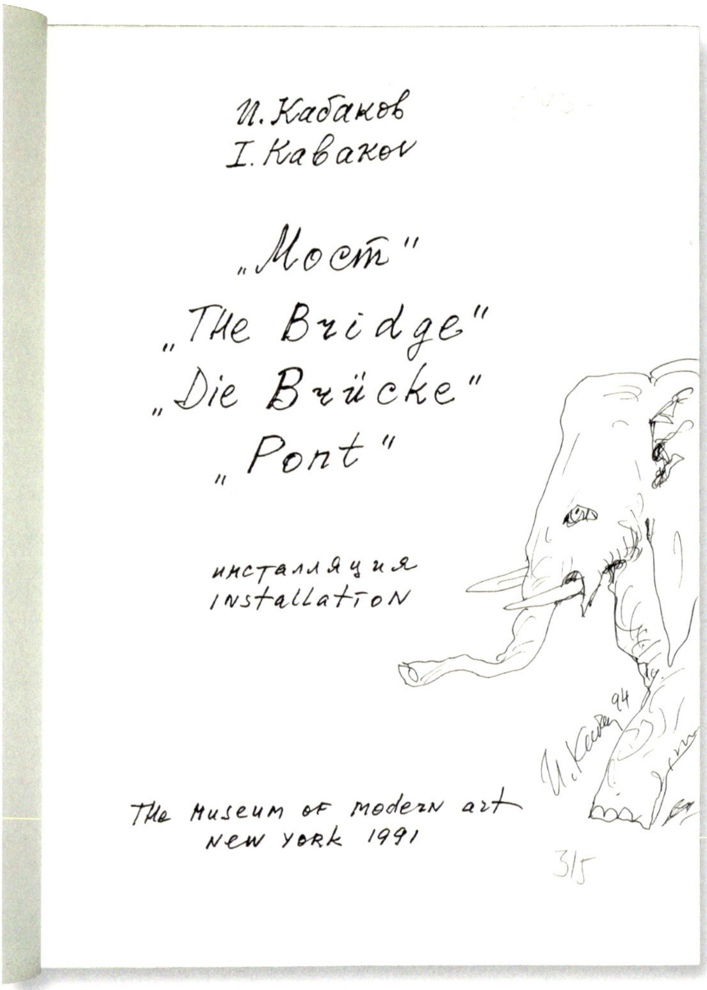
И. Кабаков
I. Kabakov

„Мост“
„The Bridge“
„Die Brücke“
„Pont“

инсталляция
installation

The Museum of Modern Art
New York 1991

И. Кабаков 94

3/5

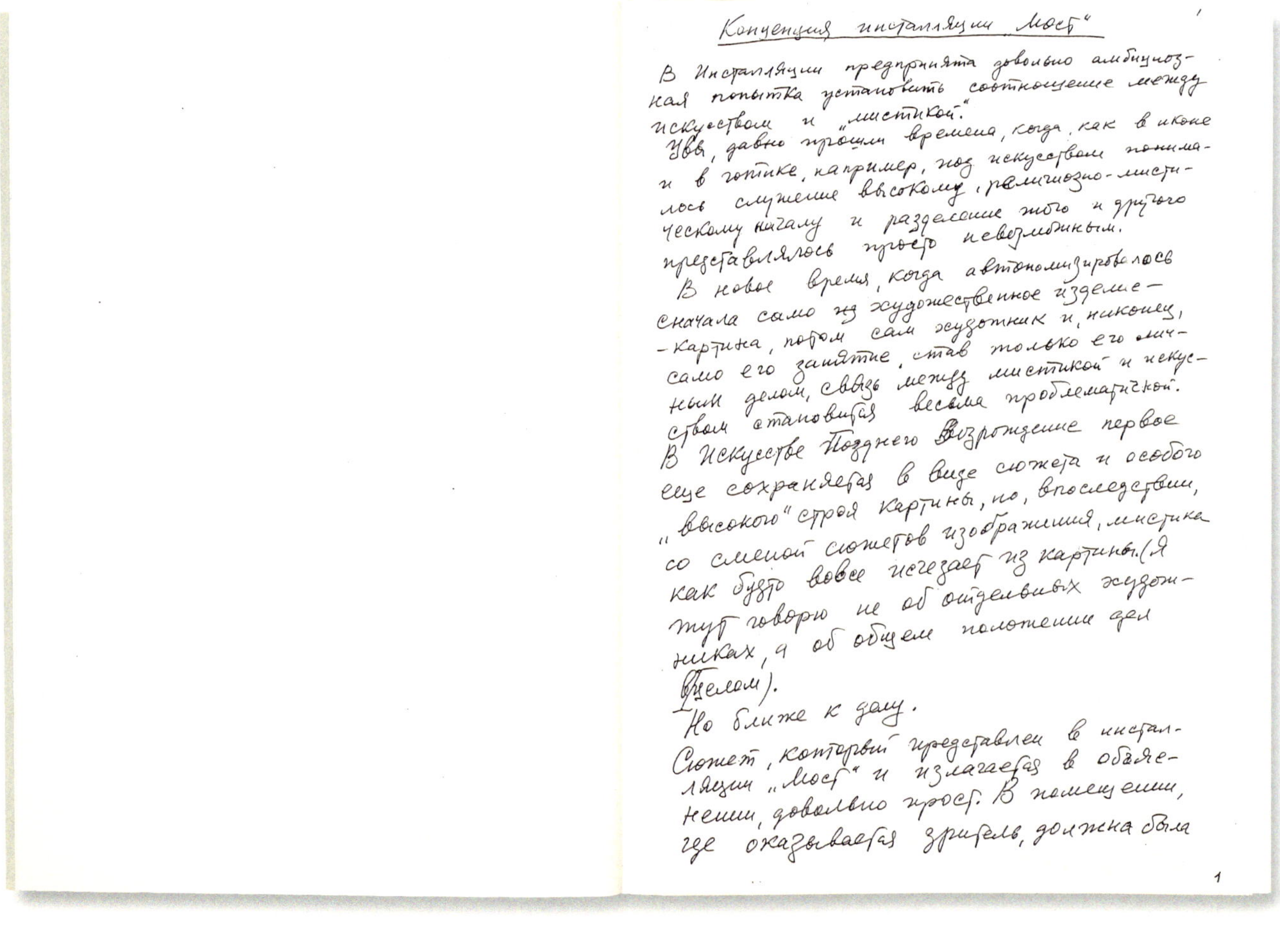
Концепция инсталляции „Мост“

В Инсталляции предпринята довольно амбициоз-
ная попытка установить соотношение между
искусством и „мистикой“.
Увы, давно прошли времена, когда, как в иконе
и в готике, например, под искусством понима-
лось служение высокому, религиозно-мисти-
ческому началу и разделение того и другого
представлялось просто невозможным.
В новое время, когда автономизировалось
сначала само из художественное изделие —
- картина, потом сам художник и, наконец,
само его занятие, став только его лич-
ным делом, связь между мистикой и искус-
ством становится весьма проблематичной.
В Искусстве Позднего Возрождения первое
еще сохраняется в виде сюжета и особого
„высокого“ строя картины, но, впоследствии,
со сменой сюжетов изображения, мистика
как будто вовсе исчезает из картины. (Я
тут говорю не об отдельных худож-
никах, а об общем положении дел
в целом).
Но ближе к делу.
Сюжет, который представлен в инстал-
ляции „Мост“ и излагается в объяс-
нении, довольно прост. В помещении,
где оказывается зритель, должна была

1

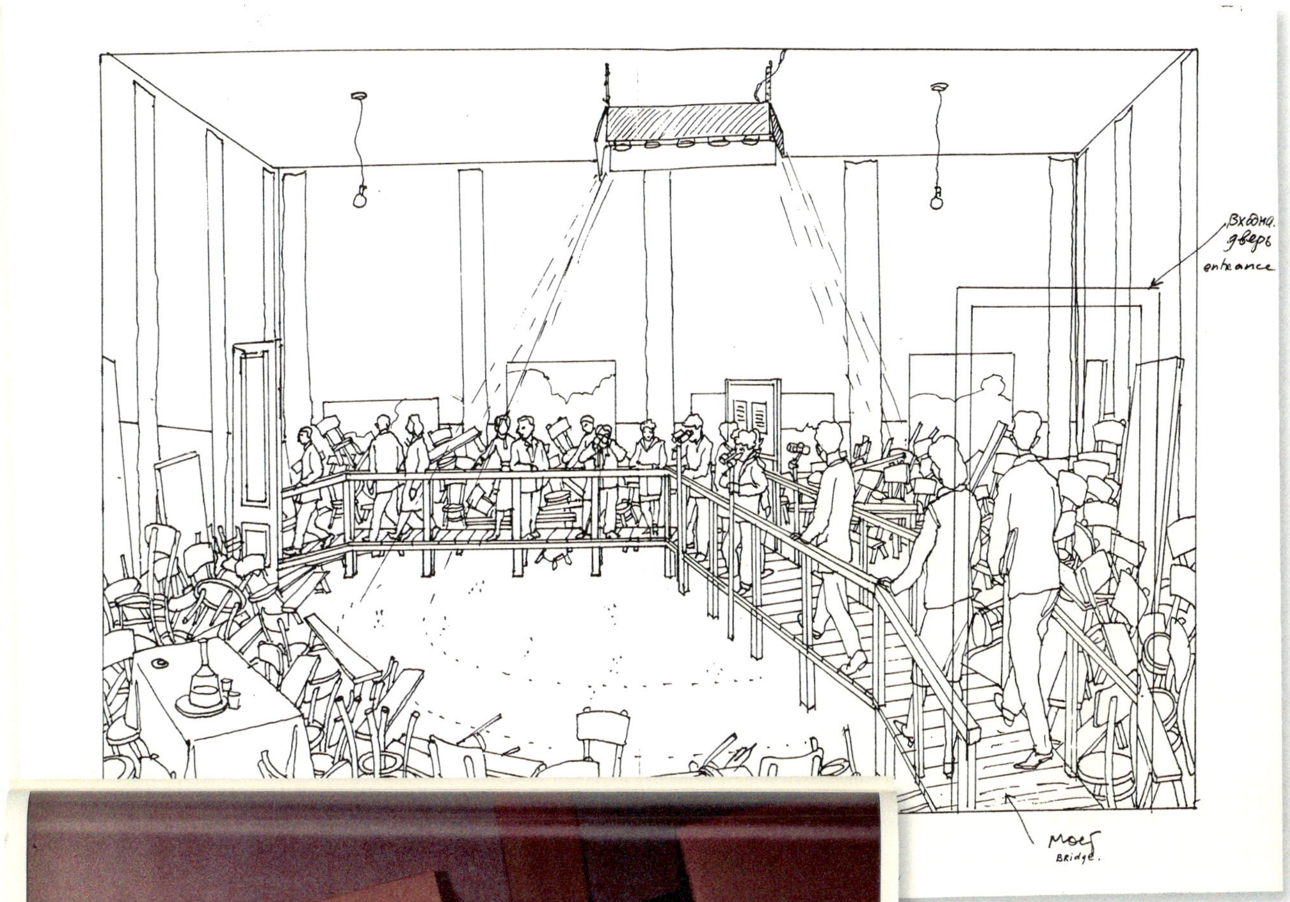
Входна.
дверь
entrance
Мост
Bridge.

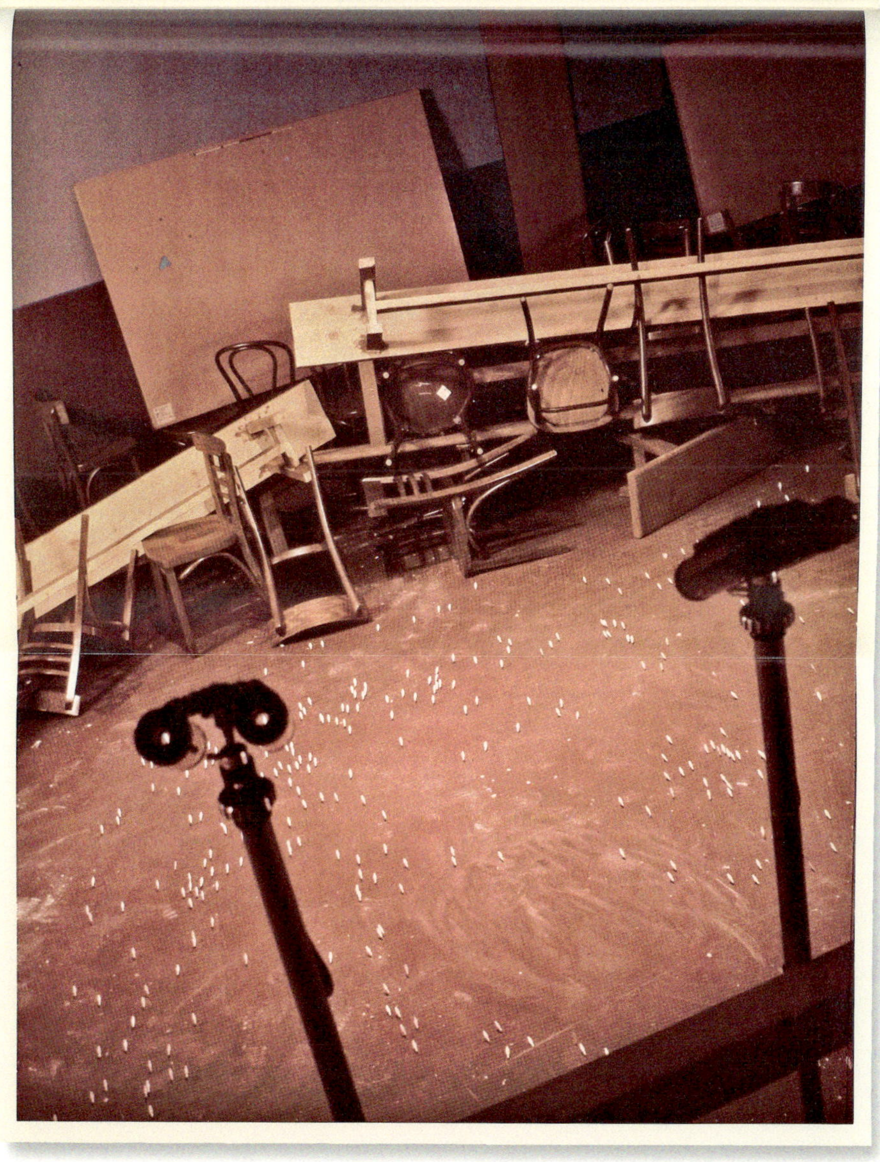

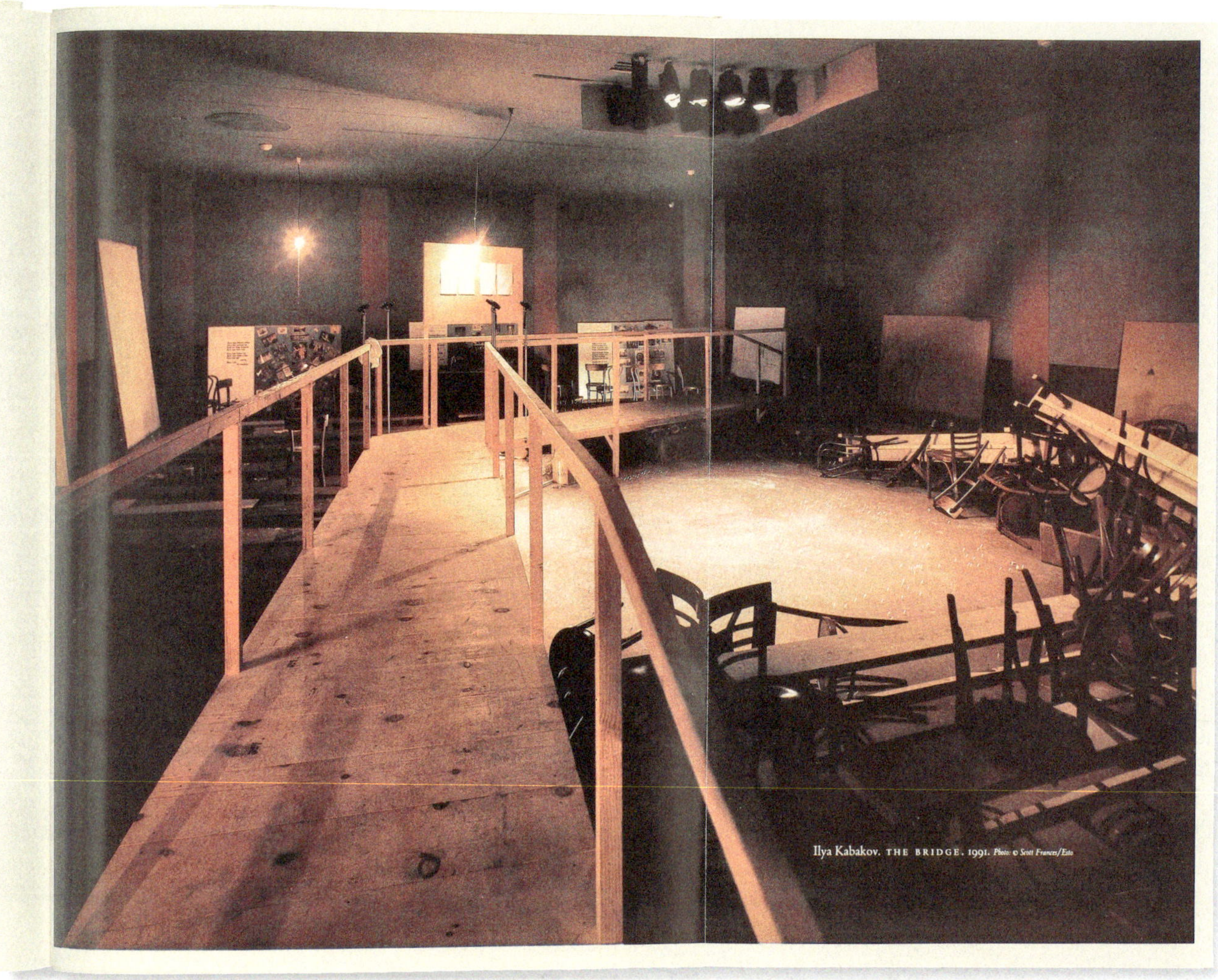
Ilya Kabakov. THE BRIDGE. 1991. Photo: © Scott Frances/Esto

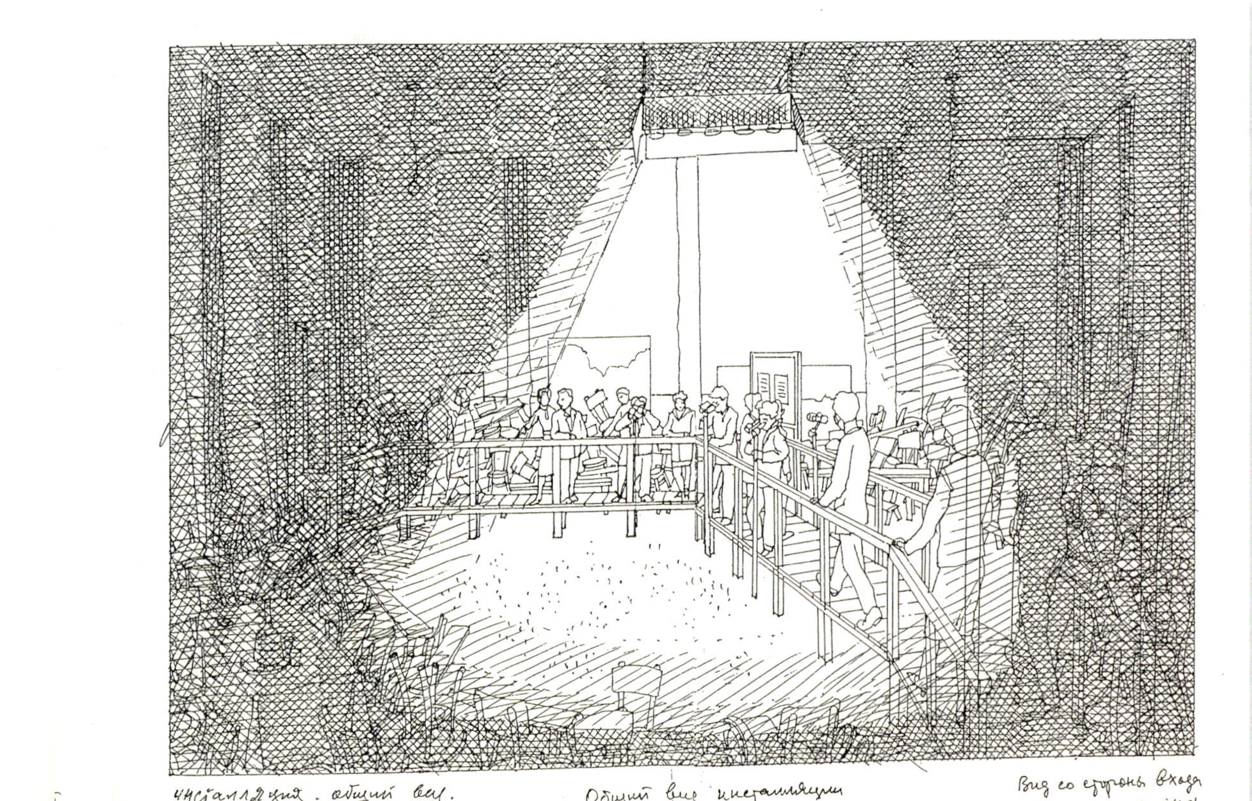
Инсталляция. общий вид.
installation. General view.
Общий вид инсталляции „Мост"
Вид со стороны входа
view from the side of entrance.

66 In the Communal Kitchen: New Documents and Materials

In der Gemeinschaftsküche: Neue Dokumente und Materialien

1993

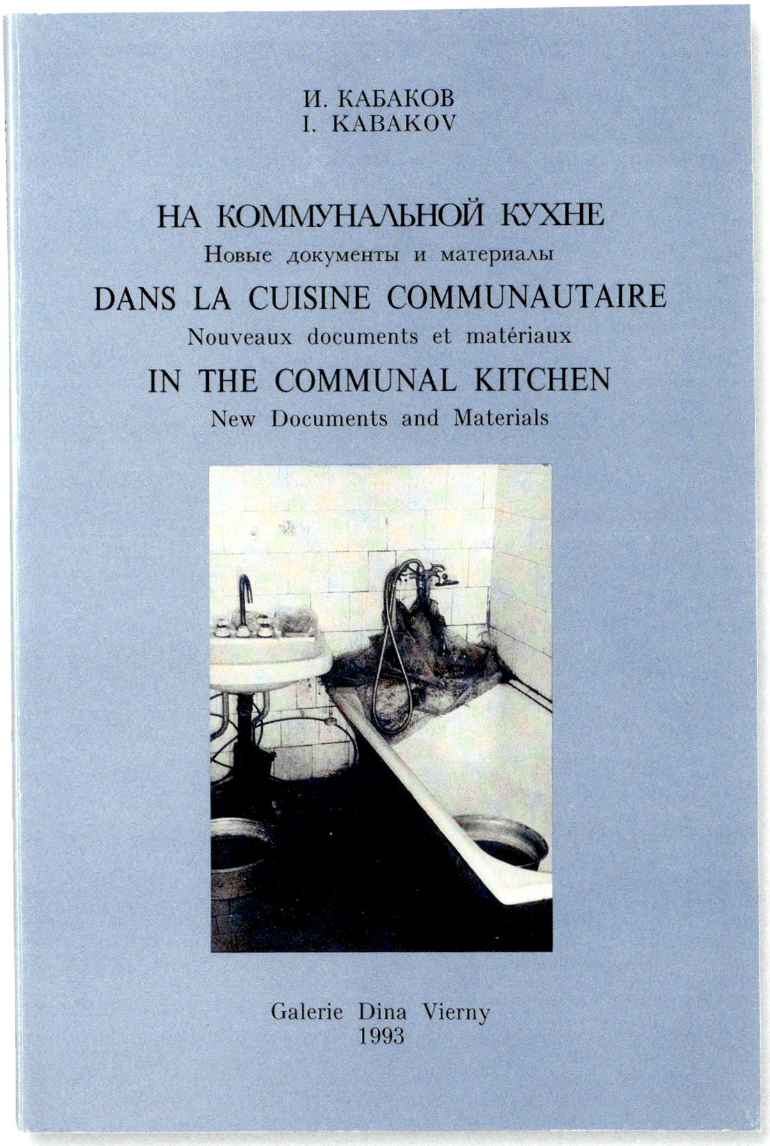

Luc Derycke
Paris: Galerie Dina Vierny
21.6 x 14.1 cm
203 pp. with 55 (5 color) ills.
adhesive binding, softback
Klebebindung, broschiert

thematic publication | *thematische Publikation*

layout by Ilya Kabakov | *Layout von Ilya Kabakov*

For the exhibition »Nouveaux Documents«, Galerie Dina Vierny, Paris, May 20 to July 18, 1992. Text by Ilya Kabakov; Russian, French, English.

Zur Ausstellung »Nouveaux Documents«, Galerie Dina Vierny, Paris, 20. Mai – 18. Juli 1992. Text von Ilya Kabakov; russisch, französisch, englisch.

see also | *siehe auch* CRI, vol. 1, no. 58, pp. 380–387

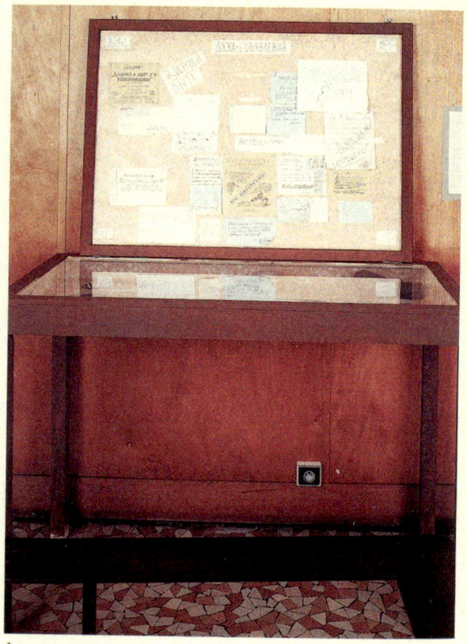

Фрагмент экспозиции в галерее Дины Верни. Зал №2
Détail de l'exposition à la galerie Dina Vierny. Salle №2
Fragment of the exposition in the Dina Vierny Gallery. Hall №2

НА КОММУНАЛЬНОЙ КУХНЕ
DANS LA CUISINE COMMUNAUTAIRE
IN THE COMMUNAL KITCHEN

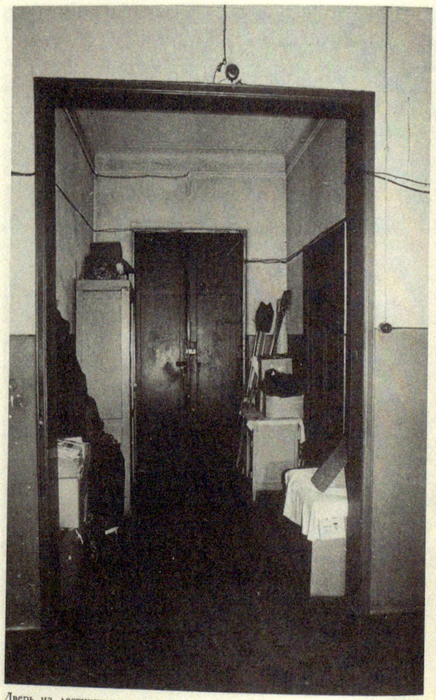

Дверь на лестничную площадку
Porte sur palier
Door onto the stairwell landing

22

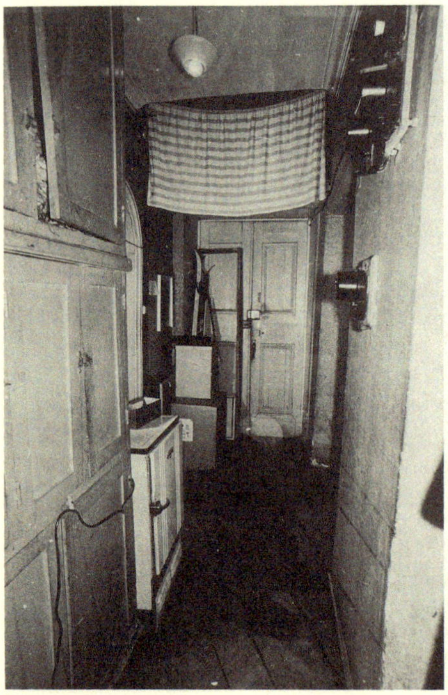

Коридор коммунальной квартиры.
Couloir d'appartement communautaire.
Corridor of a communal apartment.

23

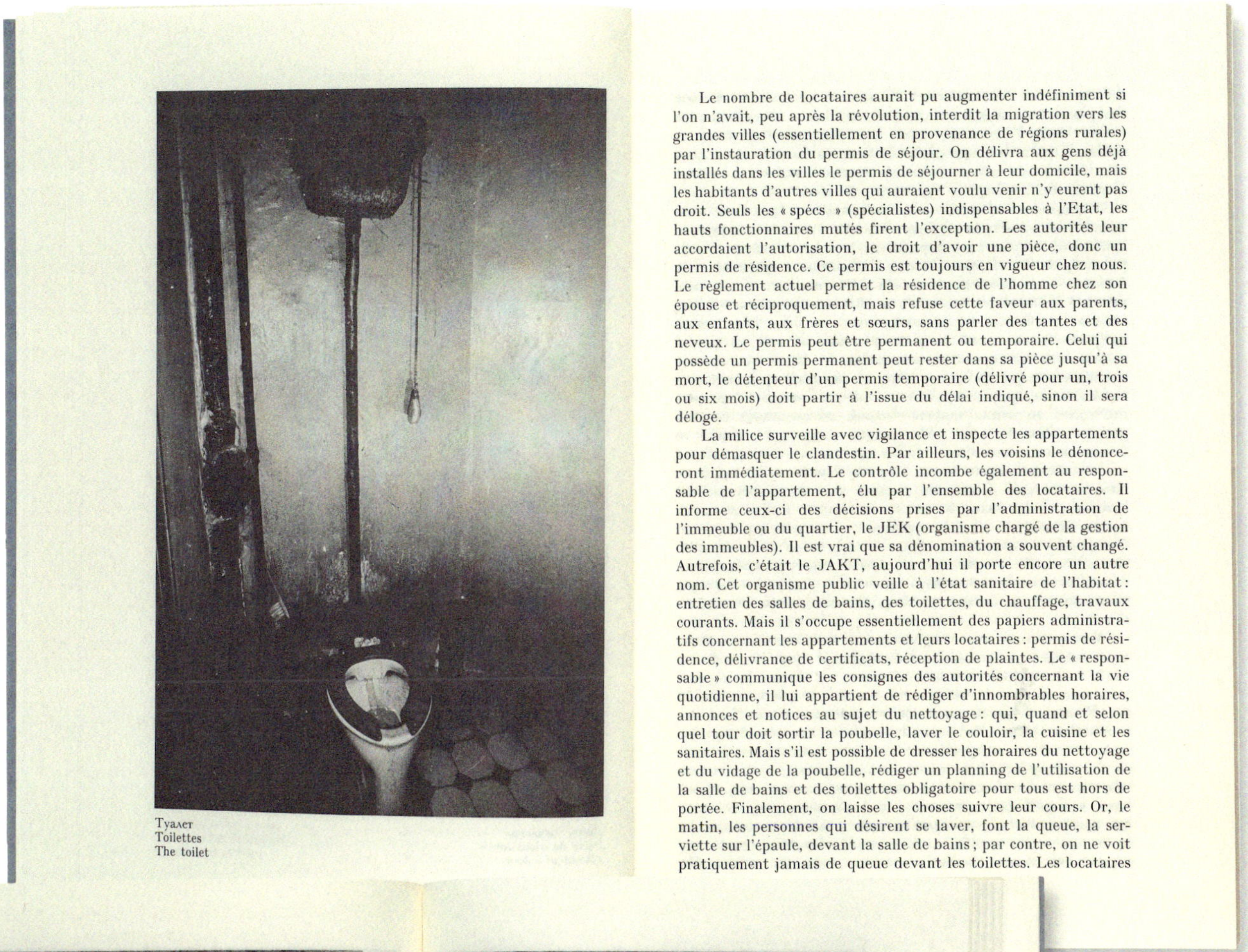

Туалет
Toilettes
The toilet

Le nombre de locataires aurait pu augmenter indéfiniment si l'on n'avait, peu après la révolution, interdit la migration vers les grandes villes (essentiellement en provenance de régions rurales) par l'instauration du permis de séjour. On délivra aux gens déjà installés dans les villes le permis de séjourner à leur domicile, mais les habitants d'autres villes qui auraient voulu venir n'y eurent pas droit. Seuls les « spécs » (spécialistes) indispensables à l'Etat, les hauts fonctionnaires mutés firent l'exception. Les autorités leur accordaient l'autorisation, le droit d'avoir une pièce, donc un permis de résidence. Ce permis est toujours en vigueur chez nous. Le règlement actuel permet la résidence de l'homme chez son épouse et réciproquement, mais refuse cette faveur aux parents, aux enfants, aux frères et sœurs, sans parler des tantes et des neveux. Le permis peut être permanent ou temporaire. Celui qui possède un permis permanent peut rester dans sa pièce jusqu'à sa mort, le détenteur d'un permis temporaire (délivré pour un, trois ou six mois) doit partir à l'issue du délai indiqué, sinon il sera délogé.

La milice surveille avec vigilance et inspecte les appartements pour démasquer le clandestin. Par ailleurs, les voisins le dénonceront immédiatement. Le contrôle incombe également au responsable de l'appartement, élu par l'ensemble des locataires. Il informe ceux-ci des décisions prises par l'administration de l'immeuble ou du quartier, le JEK (organisme chargé de la gestion des immeubles). Il est vrai que sa dénomination a souvent changé. Autrefois, c'était le JAKT, aujourd'hui il porte encore un autre nom. Cet organisme public veille à l'état sanitaire de l'habitat : entretien des salles de bains, des toilettes, du chauffage, travaux courants. Mais il s'occupe essentiellement des papiers administratifs concernant les appartements et leurs locataires : permis de résidence, délivrance de certificats, réception de plaintes. Le « responsable » communique les consignes des autorités concernant la vie quotidienne, il lui appartient de rédiger d'innombrables horaires, annonces et notices au sujet du nettoyage : qui, quand et selon quel tour doit sortir la poubelle, laver le couloir, la cuisine et les sanitaires. Mais s'il est possible de dresser les horaires du nettoyage et du vidage de la poubelle, rédiger un planning de l'utilisation de la salle de bains et des toilettes obligatoire pour tous est hors de portée. Finalement, on laisse les choses suivre leur cours. Or, le matin, les personnes qui désirent se laver, font la queue, la serviette sur l'épaule, devant la salle de bains ; par contre, on ne voit pratiquement jamais de queue devant les toilettes. Les locataires

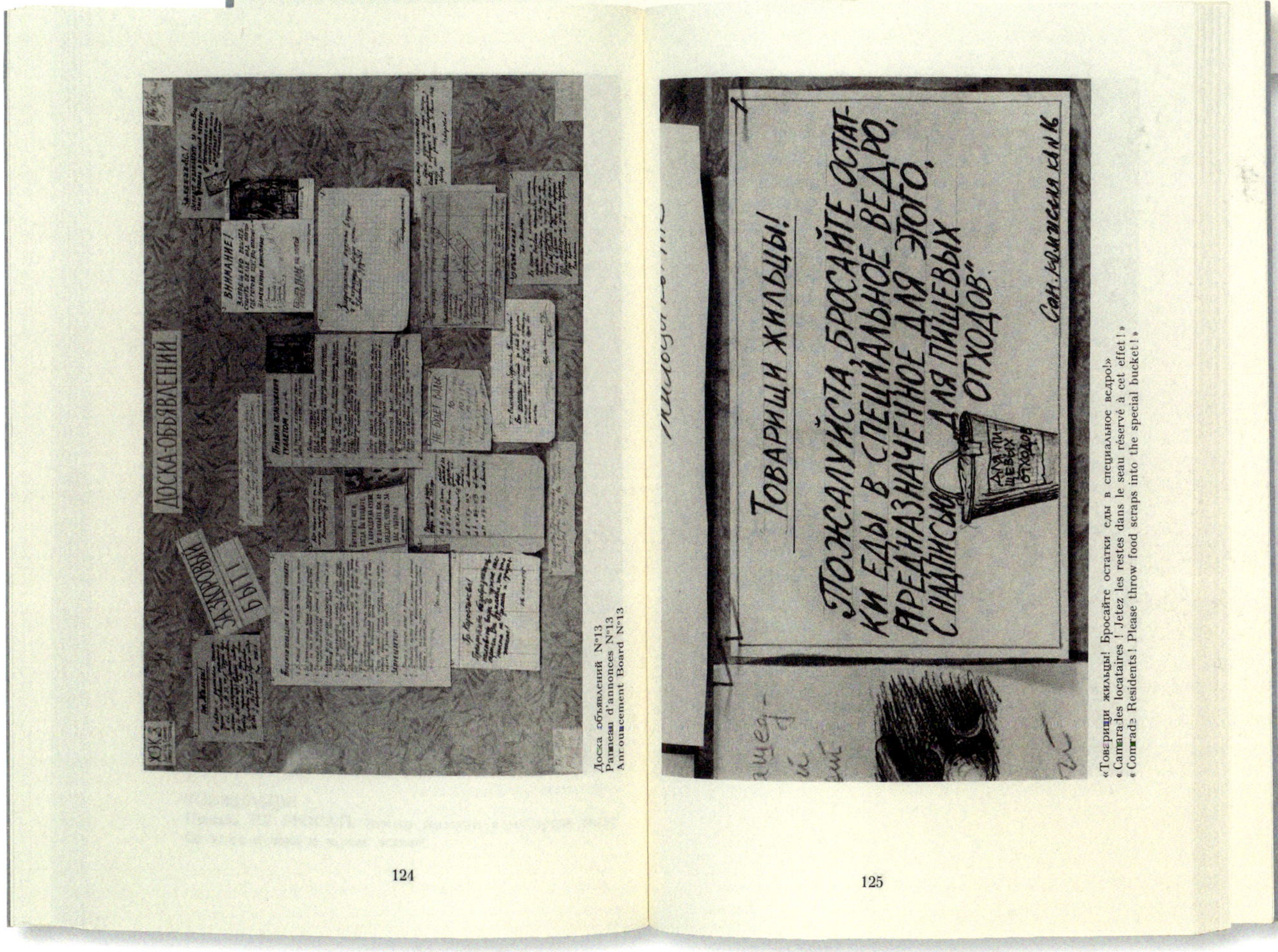

Доска объявлений №13
Panneau d'annonces №13
Announcement Board №13

«Товарищи жильцы! Бросайте остатки еды в специальное ведро!»
« Camarades locataires ! Jetez les restes dans le seau réservé à cet effet ! »
« Comrades Residents! Please throw food scraps into the special bucket! »

124

125

67 The Toilet | *Die Toilette*

1993

Ilya and Emilia Kabakov
New York: published by Ilya and Emilia Kabakov
27.9 x 21.5 cm
67 photocopied pp. with 14 b/w (incl. 4 foldouts) and 24 color (incl. 4 foldouts) ills.
quick bind, cardboard cover, label on the cover
Schnellhefter, Kartonumschlag, Etikette auf dem Umschlag
edition: 500 numbered copies with 5 including an original signed, numbered, and dated drawing by Ilya Kabakov from 1994

thematic publication | *thematische Publikation*

layout by Ilya Kabakov | *Layout von Ilya Kabakov*

Documentation of the installation of the same name for Documenta IX, Kassel, June 13 to September 20, 1992. Text by Ilya Kabakov. Dialogue between Boris Groys and Ilya Kabakov on »The Toilet«, which was also published in the book »The Art of Installation«, 1996; Russian, English, German.

Dokumentation der gleichnamigen Installation für die Documenta IX, Kassel, 13. Juni – 20. September 1992. Text von Ilya Kabakov. Dialog von Boris Groys und Ilya Kabakov über »Die Toilette«, der auch im Buch »Die Kunst der Installation«, 1996 erschien; russisch, englisch, deutsch.

see also | *siehe auch* no. 91; no. 135; CRI, vol. 1, no. 59, pp. 388–393

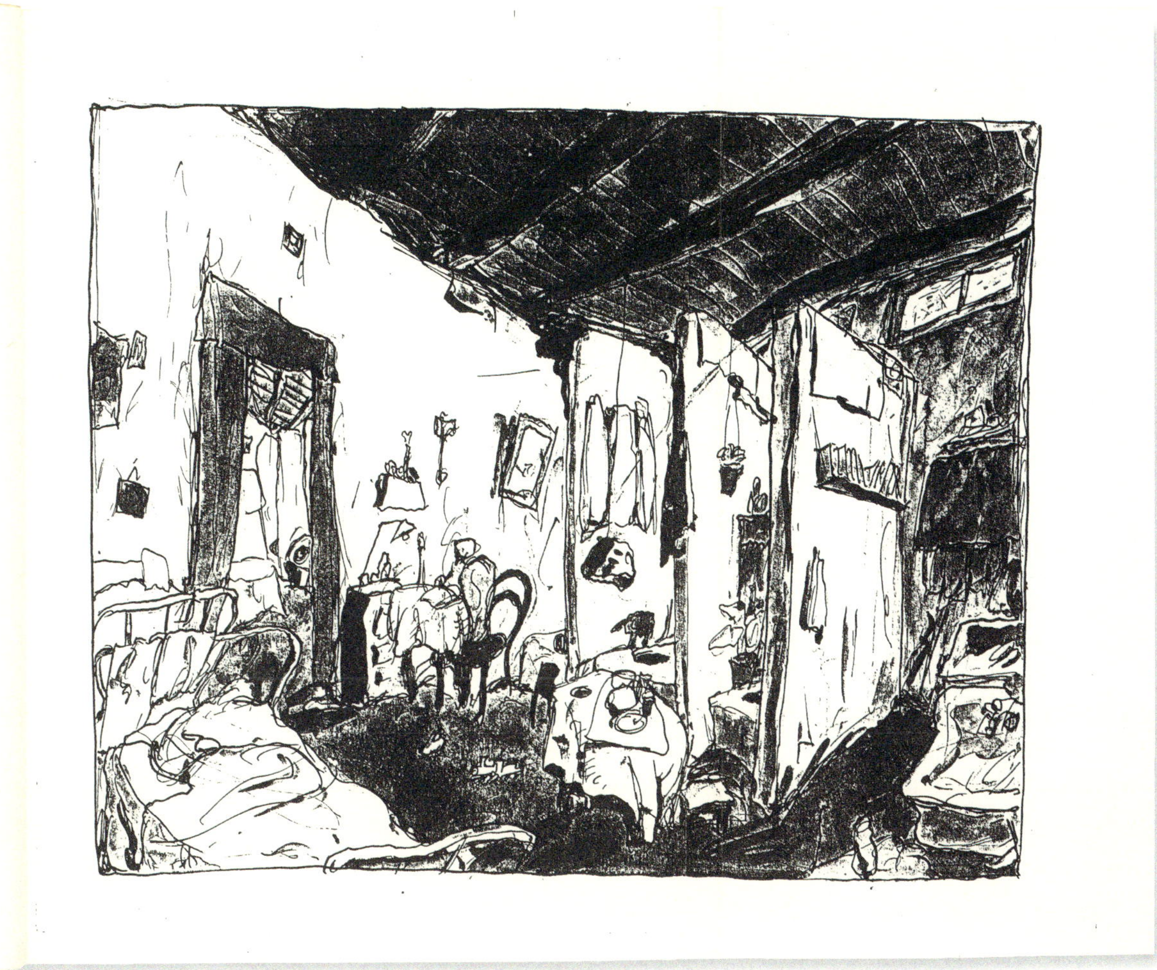

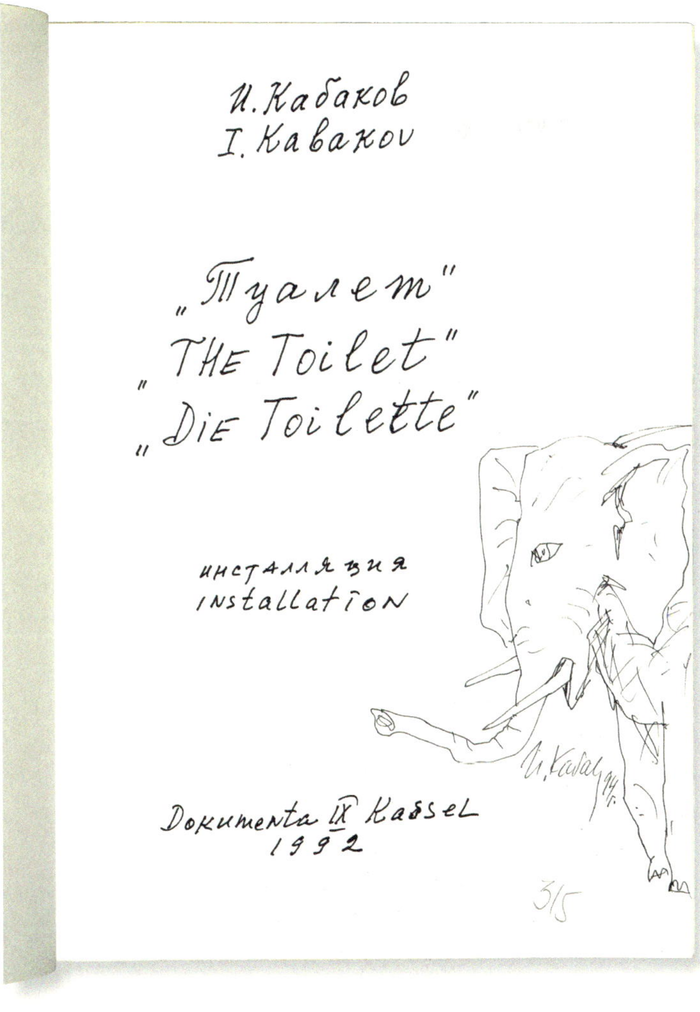

И. Кабаков
I. Kabakov
„Туалет"
„THE Toilet"
„Die Toilette"
инсталляция
installation
Dokumenta IX Kassel
1992
3/5

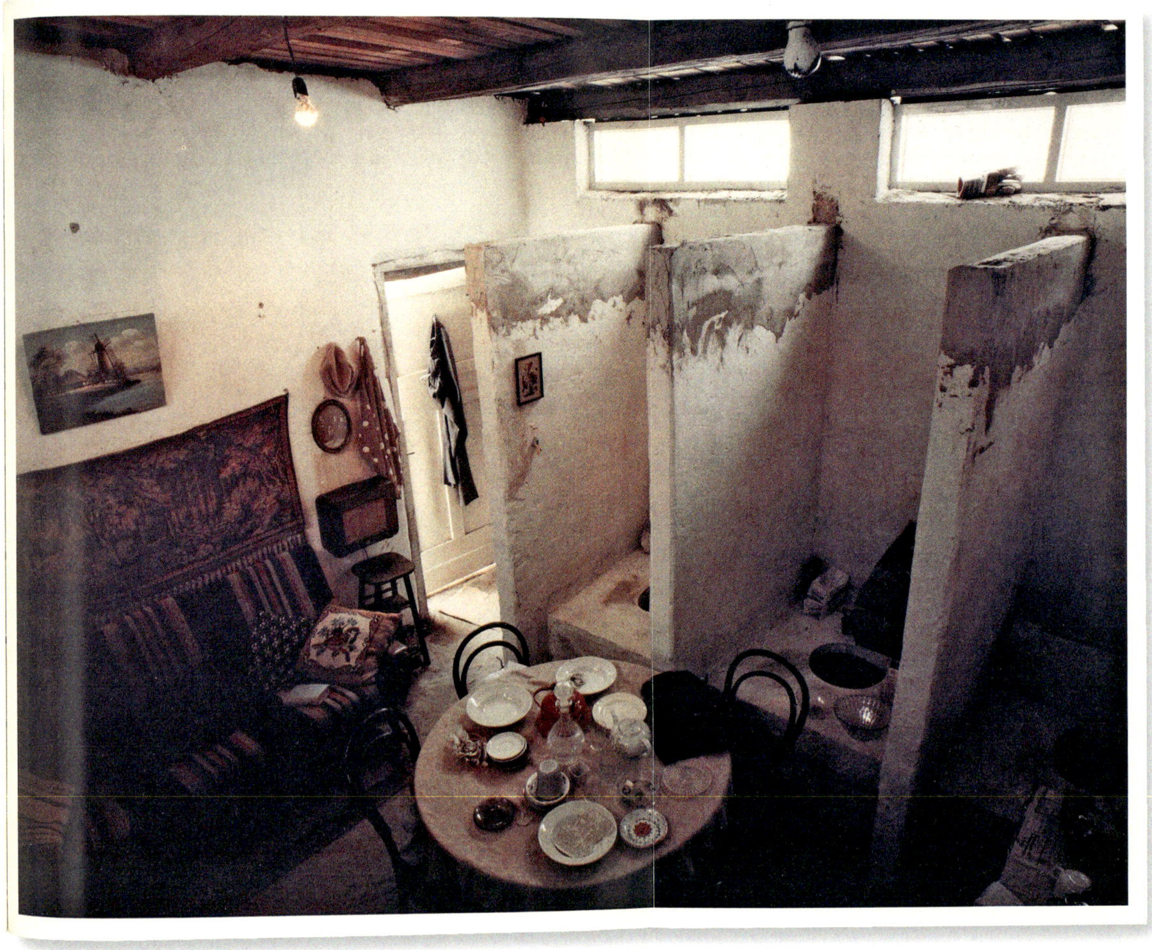

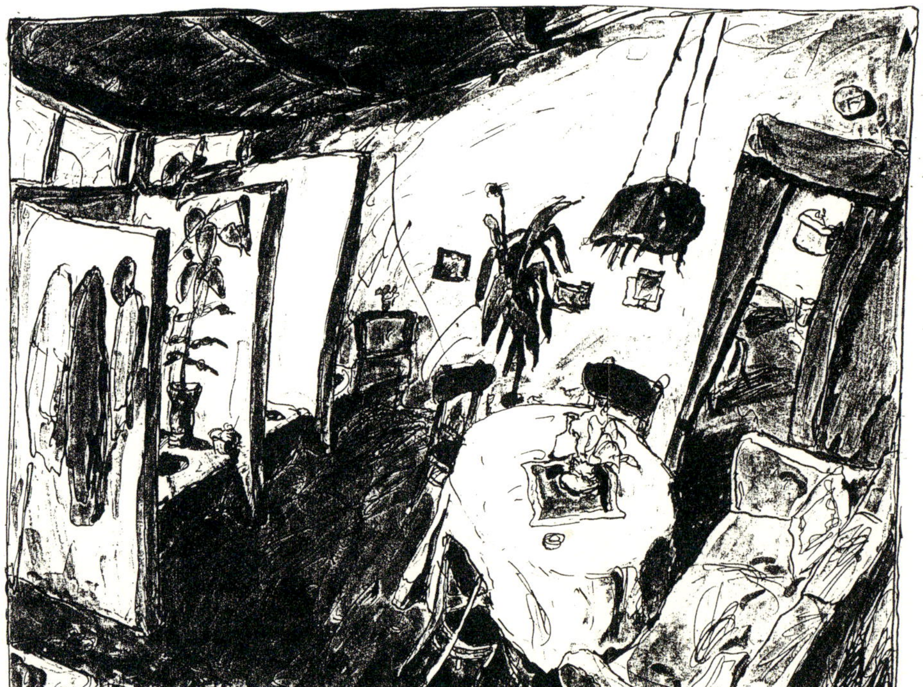

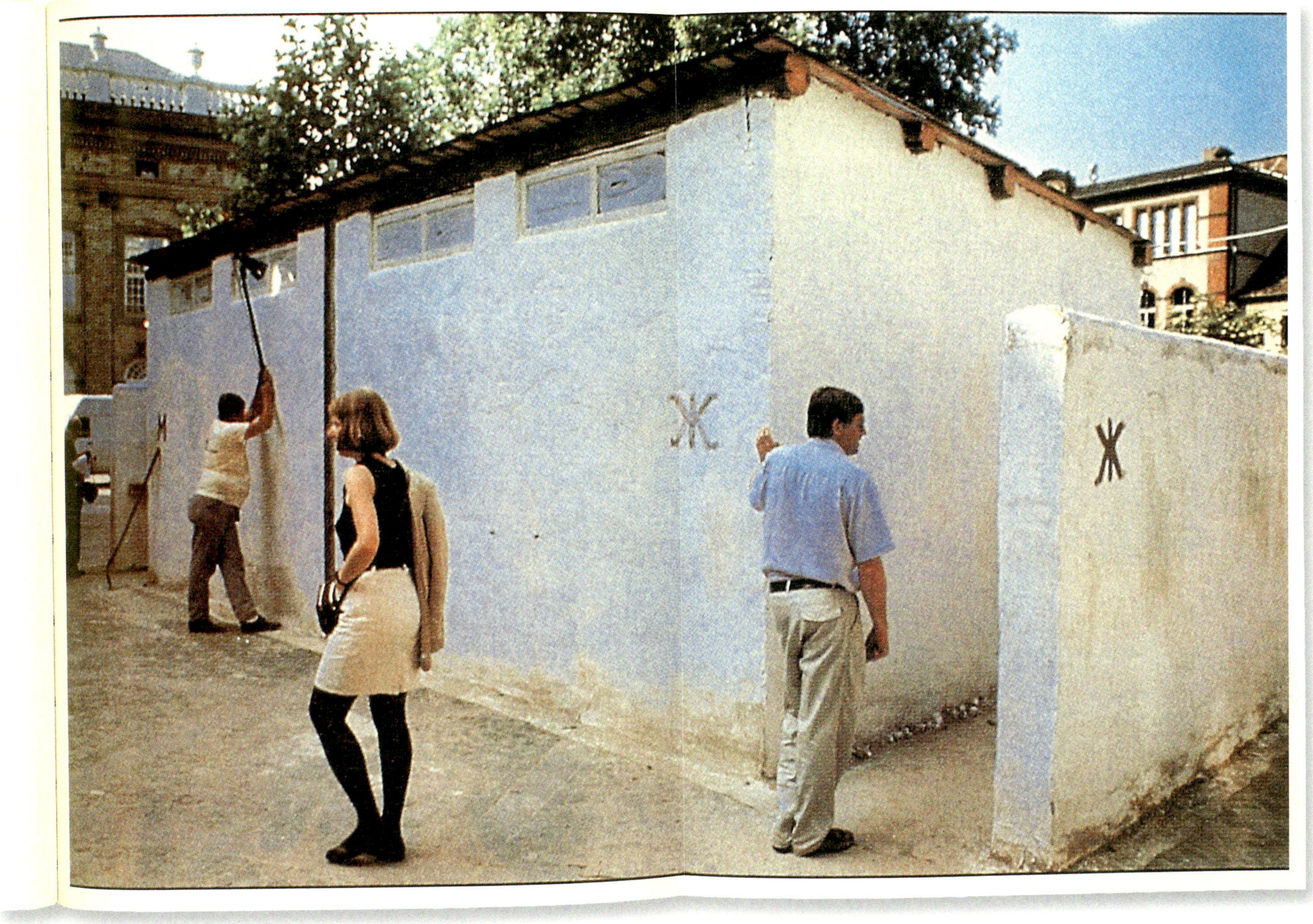

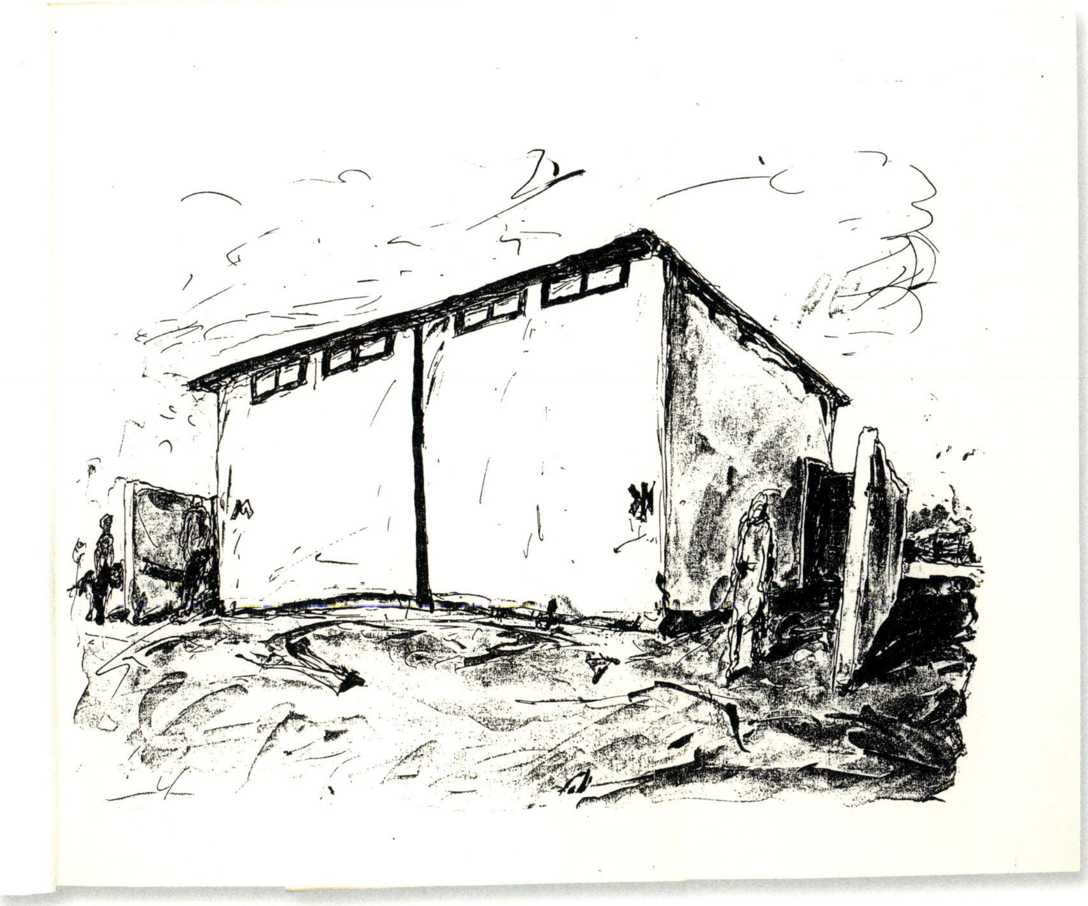

68 5 Albums | *5 Alben*

1994

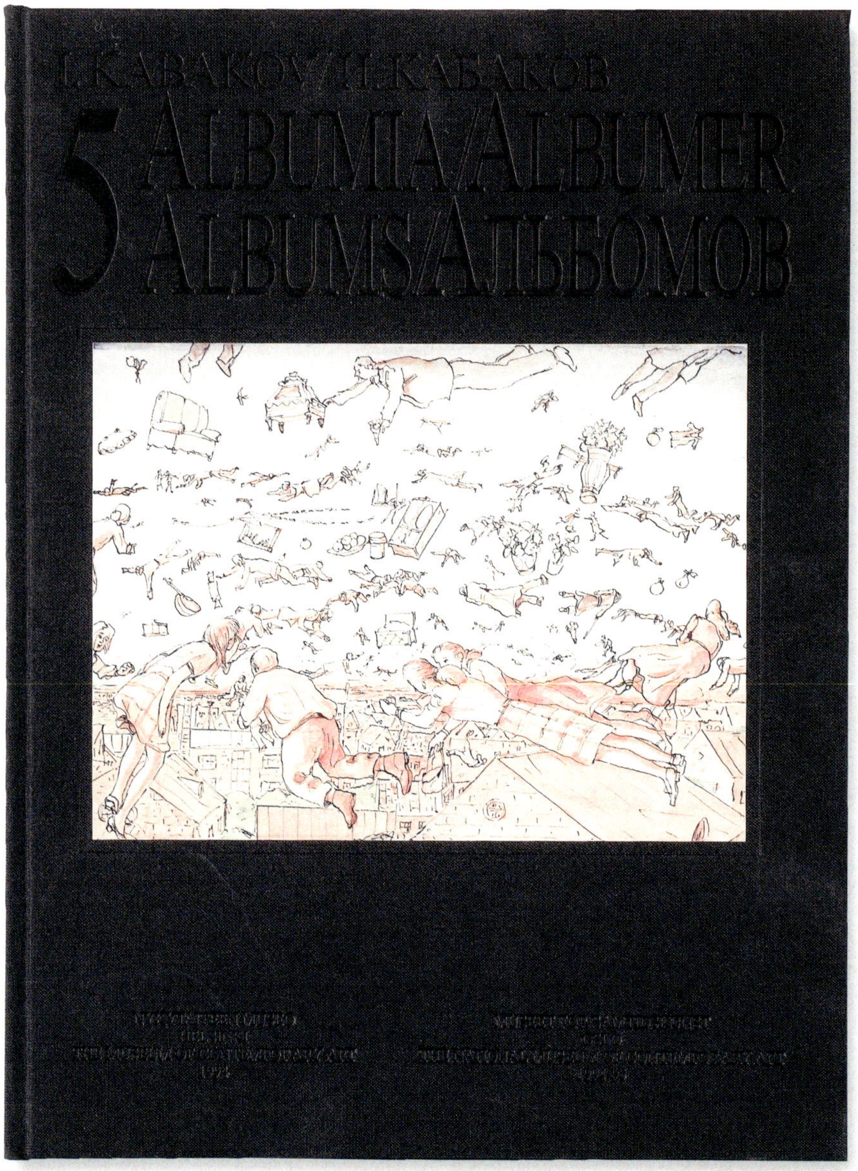

Kiasma Nykytaiteen Museo, Helsinki; Museet for Samtidskunst, Oslo
Helsinki: Artprint
31 x 23.5 cm
242 pp. with 227 (219 color) ills.
stitchbound, clothbound, blind blocking with label
Fadenheftung, Leinen, Blindprägung mit Etikette

thematic publication | *thematische Publikation*

layout by Ilya Kabakov | *Layout von Ilya Kabakov*

For the installation »The Operating Room (Mother and Son)« at the Kiasma Nykytaiteen Museo, Helsinki, February 3 to April 10, 1994 and the Museet for Samtidskunst, Oslo, October 8, 1994 to January 8, 1995. Texts by Boris Groys and Ilya Kabakov; Finnish, Norwegian, English, Russian.

Zur Installation »Operationssaal (Mutter und Sohn)«, Kiasma Nykytaiteen Museo, Helsinki, 3. Februar – 10. April 1994 und Museet for Samtidskunst, Oslo, 8. Oktober 1994 – 8. Januar 1995. Texte von Boris Groys und Ilya Kabakov; finnisch, norwegisch, englisch, russisch.

see also | *siehe auch* no. 3; no. 21; no. 100; CRI, vol. 2, no. 78, pp. 28–33

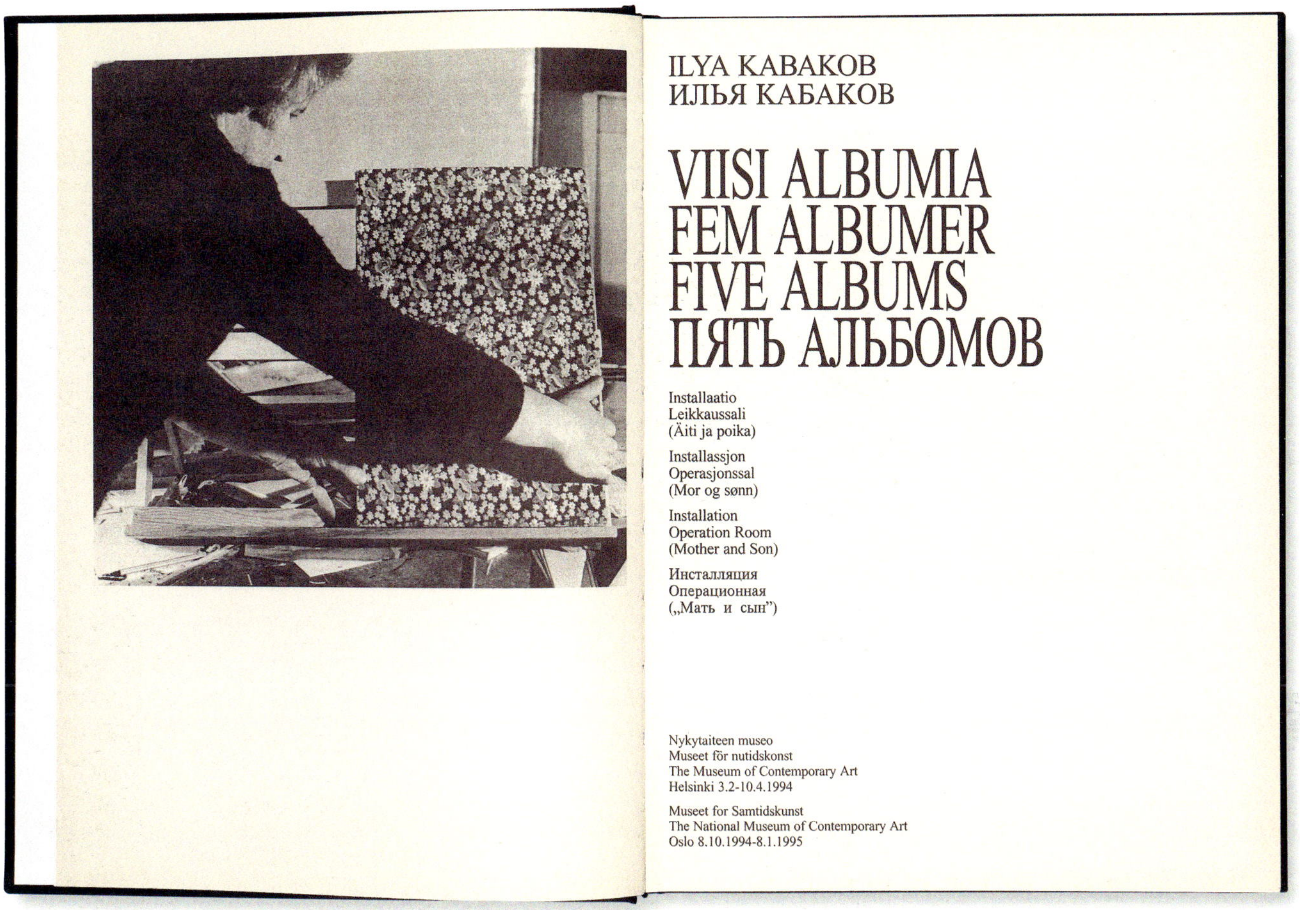

ILYA KABAKOV
ИЛЬЯ КАБАКОВ

VIISI ALBUMIA
FEM ALBUMER
FIVE ALBUMS
ПЯТЬ АЛЬБОМОВ

Installaatio
Leikkaussali
(Äiti ja poika)

Installassjon
Operasjonssal
(Mor og sønn)

Installation
Operation Room
(Mother and Son)

Инсталляция
Операционная
(„Мать и сын")

Nykytaiteen museo
Museet för nutidskonst
The Museum of Contemporary Art
Helsinki 3.2-10.4.1994

Museet for Samtidskunst
The National Museum of Contemporary Art
Oslo 8.10.1994-8.1.1995

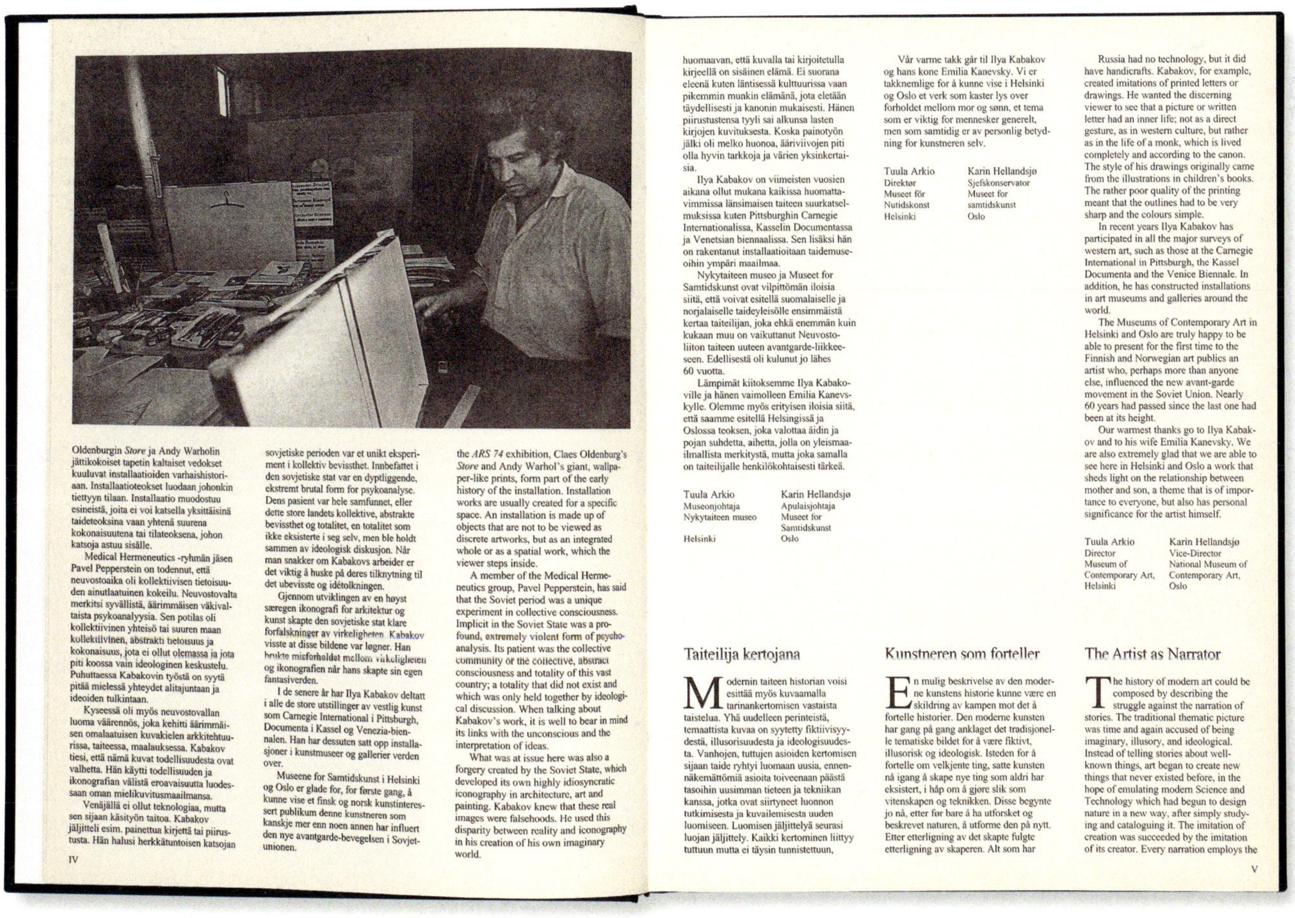

Oldenburgin *Store* ja Andy Warholin jättikokoiset tapetin kaltaiset vedokset kuuluvat installaatioiden varhaishistoriaan. Installaatioteokset luodaan johonkin tiettyyn tilaan. Installaatio muodostuu esineistä, joita ei voi katsella yksittäisinä taideteoksina vaan yhtenä suurena kokonaisuutena tai tilateoksena, johon katsoja astuu sisälle.

Medical Hermeneutics -ryhmän jäsen Pavel Pepperstein on todennut, että neuvostoaika oli kollektiivisen tietoisuuden ainutlaatuinen kokeilu. Neuvostovalta merkitsi syvällistä, äärimmäisen väkivaltaista psykoanalyysia. Sen potilas oli kollektiivinen yhteisö tai suuren maan kollektiivinen, abstrakti tietoisuus ja kokonaisuus, jota ei ollut olemassa ja jota piti koossa vain ideologinen keskustelu. Puhuttaessa Kabakovin työstä on syytä pitää mielessä yhteydet alitajuntaan ja ideoiden tulkintaan.

Kyseessä oli myös neuvostovallan luoma väärennös, joka kehitti äärimmäisen omalaatuisen kuvakielen arkkitehtuurissa, taiteessa, maalauksessa. Kabakov tiesi, että nämä kuvat todellisuudesta ovat valhetta. Hän käytti todellisuuden ja ikonografian välistä eroavaisuutta luodessaan oman mielikuvitusmaailmansa.

Venäjällä ei ollut teknologiaa, mutta sen sijaan käsityön taitoa. Kabakov jäljitteli esim. painettua kirjettä tai piirustusta. Hän halusi herkkätuntoisen katsojan

IV

sovjetiske perioden var et unikt eksperiment i kollektiv bevissthet. Innbefattet i den sovjetiske stat var en dyptliggende, ekstremt brutal form for psykoanalyse. Dens pasient var hele samfunnet, eller dette store landets kollektive, abstrakte bevissthet og totalitet, en totalitet som ikke eksisterte i seg selv, men ble holdt sammen av ideologisk diskusjon. Når man snakker om Kabakovs arbeider er det viktig å huske på deres tilknytning til det ubevisste og idétolkningen.

Gjennom utviklingen av en høyst særegen ikonografi for arkitektur og kunst skapte den sovjetiske stat klare forfalskninger av virkeligheten. Kabakov visste at disse bildene var løgner. Han brukte misforholdet mellom virkeligheten og ikonografien når hans skapte sin egen fantasiverden.

I de senere år har Ilya Kabakov deltatt i alle de store utstillinger av vestlig kunst som Carnegie International i Pittsburgh, Documenta i Kassel og Venezia-biennalen. Han har dessuten satt opp installasjoner i kunstmuseer og gallerier verden over.

Museene for Samtidskunst i Helsinki og Oslo er glade for, for første gang, å kunne vise et finsk og norsk kunstinteressert publikum denne kunstneren som kanskje mer enn noen annen har influert den nye avantgarde-bevegelsen i Sovjetunionen.

the *ARS 74* exhibition, Claes Oldenburg's *Store* and Andy Warhol's giant, wallpaper-like prints, form part of the early history of the installation. Installation works are usually created for a specific space. An installation is made up of objects that are not to be viewed as discrete artworks, but as an integrated whole or as a spatial work, which the viewer steps inside.

A member of the Medical Hermeneutics group, Pavel Pepperstein, has said that the Soviet period was a unique experiment in collective consciousness. Implicit in the Soviet State was a profound, extremely violent form of psychoanalysis. Its patient was the collective community or the collective, abstract consciousness and totality of this vast country; a totality that did not exist and which was only held together by ideological discussion. When talking about Kabakov's work, it is well to bear in mind its links with the unconscious and the interpretation of ideas.

What was at issue here was also a forgery created by the Soviet State, which developed its own highly idiosyncratic iconography in architecture, art and painting. Kabakov knew that these real images were falsehoods. He used this disparity between reality and iconography in his creation of his own imaginary world.

huomaavan, että kuvalla tai kirjoitetulla kirjeellä on sisäinen elämä. Ei suorana eleenä kuten läntisessä kulttuurissa vaan pikemmin munkin elämänä, jota eletään täydellisesti ja kanonin mukaisesti. Hänen piirustustensa tyyli sai alkunsa lasten kirjojen kuvituksesta. Koska painotyön jälki oli melko huonoa, ääriviivojen piti olla hyvin tarkkoja ja värien yksinkertaisia.

Ilya Kabakov on viimeisten vuosien aikana ollut mukana kaikissa huomattavimmissa länsimaisen taiteen suurkatselmuksissa kuten Pittsburghin Carnegie Internationalissa, Kasselin Documentassa ja Venetsian biennaalissa. Sen lisäksi hän on rakentanut installaatioitaan taidemuseoihin ympäri maailmaa.

Nykytaiteen museo ja Museet for Samtidskunst ovat vilpittömän iloisia siitä, että voivat esitellä suomalaiselle ja norjalaiselle taideyleisölle ensimmäistä kertaa taiteilijan, joka ehkä enemmän kuin kukaan muu on vaikuttanut Neuvostoliiton taiteen uuteen avantgarde-liikkeeseen. Edellisestä oli kulunut jo lähes 60 vuotta.

Lämpimät kiitoksemme Ilya Kabakoville ja hänen vaimolleen Emilia Kanevskylle. Olemme myös erityisen iloisia siitä, että saamme esitellä Helsingissä ja Oslossa teoksen, joka valottaa äidin ja pojan suhdetta, aihetta, jolla on yleismaailmallista merkitystä, mutta joka samalla on taiteilijalle henkilökohtaisesti tärkeä.

Tuula Arkio
Museonjohtaja
Nykytaiteen museo
Helsinki

Karin Hellandsjø
Apulaisjohtaja
Museet for
Samtidskunst
Oslo

Vår varme takk går til Ilya Kabakov og hans kone Emilia Kanevsky. Vi er takknemlige for å kunne vise i Helsinki og Oslo et verk som kaster lys over forholdet mellom mor og sønn, et tema som er viktig for mennesker generelt, men som samtidig er av personlig betydning for kunstneren selv.

Tuula Arkio
Direktør
Museet för
Nutidskonst
Helsinki

Karin Hellandsjø
Sjefskonservator
Museet for
samtidskunst
Oslo

Russia had no technology, but it did have handicrafts. Kabakov, for example, created imitations of printed letters or drawings. He wanted the discerning viewer to see that a picture or written letter had an inner life; not as a direct gesture, as in western culture, but rather as in the life of a monk, which is lived completely and according to the canon. The style of his drawings originally came from the illustrations in children's books. The rather poor quality of the printing meant that the outlines had to be very sharp and the colours simple.

In recent years Ilya Kabakov has participated in all the major surveys of western art, such as those at the Carnegie International in Pittsburgh, the Kassel Documenta and the Venice Biennale. In addition, he has constructed installations in art museums and galleries around the world.

The Museums of Contemporary Art in Helsinki and Oslo are truly happy to be able to present for the first time to the Finnish and Norwegian art publics an artist who, perhaps more than anyone else, influenced the new avant-garde movement in the Soviet Union. Nearly 60 years had passed since the last one had been at its height.

Our warmest thanks go to Ilya Kabakov and to his wife Emilia Kanevsky. We are also extremely glad that we are able to see here in Helsinki and Oslo a work that sheds light on the relationship between mother and son, a theme that is of importance to everyone, but also has personal significance for the artist himself.

Tuula Arkio
Director
Museum of
Contemporary Art,
Helsinki

Karin Hellandsjø
Vice-Director
National Museum of
Contemporary Art,
Oslo

Taiteilija kertojana

Modernin taiteen historian voisi esittää myös kuvaamalla tarinankertomisen vastaista taistelua. Yhä uudelleen perinteistä, temaattista kuvaa on syytetty fiktiivisyydestä, illusorisuudesta ja ideologisuudesta. Vanhojen, tuttujen asioiden kertomisen sijaan taide ryhtyi luomaan uusia, ennennäkemättömiä asioita toiveenaan päästä tasoihin uusimman tieteen ja tekniikan kanssa, jotka ovat siirtyneet luonnon tutkimisesta ja kuvailemisesta uuden luomiseen. Luomisen jäljittelyä seurasi luojan jäljittely. Kaikki kertominen liittyy tuttuun mutta ei täysin tunnistettuun,

Kunstneren som forteller

En mulig beskrivelse av den moderne kunstens historie kunne være en skildring av kampen mot det å fortelle historier. Den moderne kunsten har gang på gang anklaget det tradisjonelle tematiske bildet for å være fiktivt, illusorisk og ideologisk. Isteden for å fortelle om velkjente ting, satte kunsten nå igang å skape nye ting som aldri har eksistert, i håp om å gjøre slik som vitenskapen og teknikken. Disse begynte jo nå, etter før bare å ha utforsket og beskrevet naturen, å utforme den på nytt. Etter etterligning av det skapte fulgte etterligning av skaperen. Alt som har

The Artist as Narrator

The history of modern art could be composed by describing the struggle against the narration of stories. The traditional thematic picture was time and again accused of being imaginary, illusory, and ideological. Instead of telling stories about well-known things, art began to create new things that never existed before, in the hope of emulating modern Science and Technology which had begun to design nature in a new way, after simply studying and cataloguing it. The imitation of creation was succeeded by the imitation of its creator. Every narration employs the

V

6
ISÄ TULI TÖISTÄ
FAREN KOM FRA JOBBEN
FATHER CAME HOME FROM WORK
Отец пришел с работы.
7
MARGARITA LVOVNA SAAPUI
MARGARITA LVOVNA ER KOMMET
MARGARITA LVOVNA CAME OVER
Маргарита Львовна пришла.
8
9

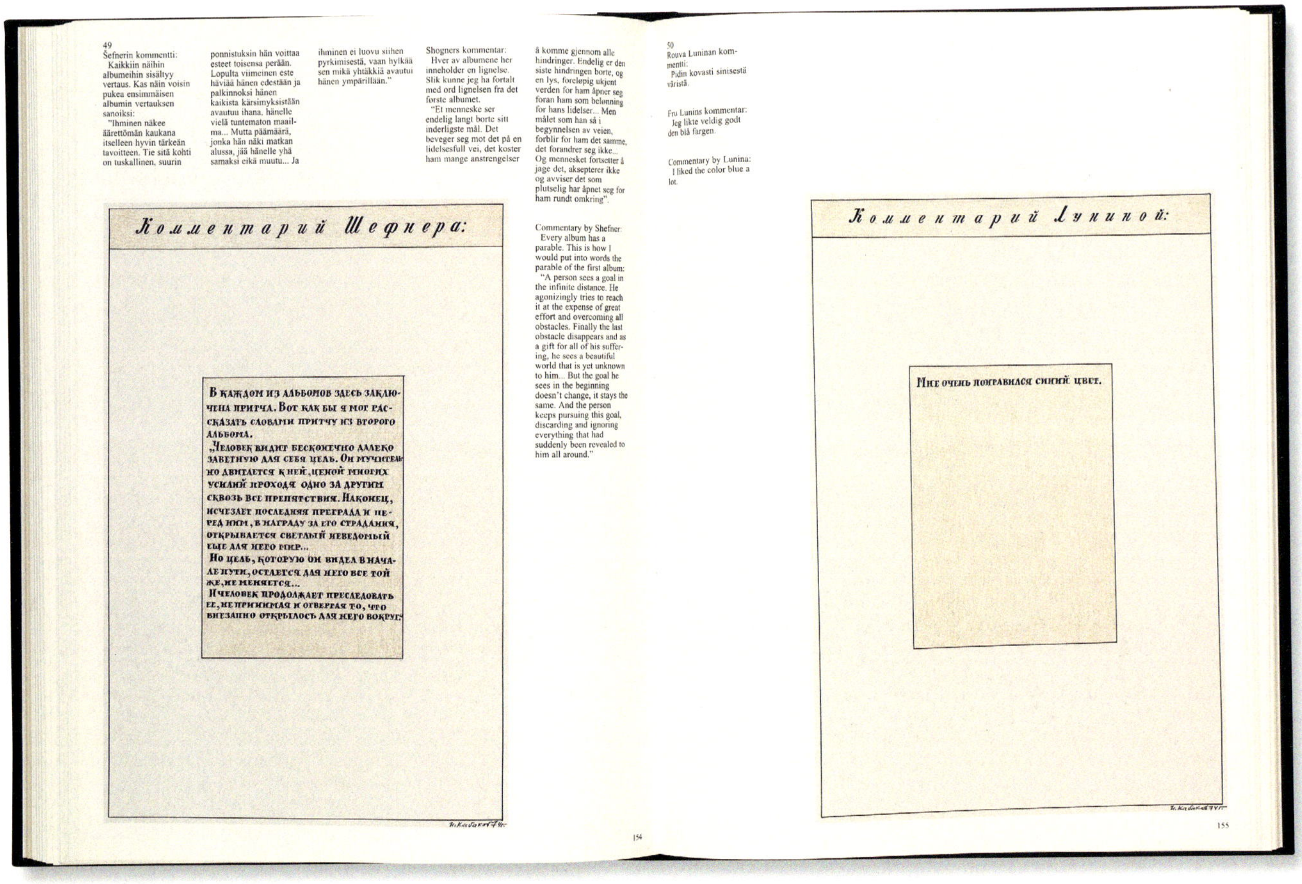
49
Šefnerin kommentti:
Kaikkiin näihin albumeihin sisältyy vertaus. Kas näin voisin pukea ensimmäisen albumin vertauksen sanoiksi:
"Ihminen näkee äärettömän kaukana itselleen hyvin tärkeän tavoitteen. Tie sitä kohti on tuskallinen, suurin ponnistuksin hän voittaa esteet toisensa perään. Lopulta viimeinen este häviää hänen edestään ja palkinnoksi hänen kaikista kärsimyksistään avautuu ihana, hänelle vielä tuntematon maailma... Mutta päämäärä, jonka hän näki matkan alussa, jää hänelle yhä samaksi eikä muutu... Ja ihminen ei luovu siihen pyrkimisestä, vaan hylkää sen mikä yhtäkkiä avautui hänen ympärillään."
Shogners kommentar:
Hver av albumene her inneholder en lignelse. Slik kunne jeg ha fortalt med ord lignelsen fra det første albumet.
"Et menneske ser endelig langt borte sitt inderligste mål. Det beveger seg mot det på en lidelsesfull vei, det koster ham mange anstrengelser å komme gjennom alle hindringer. Endelig er den siste hindringen borte, og en lys, foreløpig ukjent verden for ham åpner seg foran ham som belønning for hans lidelser... Men målet som han så i begynnelsen av veien, forblir for ham det samme, det forandrer seg ikke... Og mennesket fortsetter å jage det, aksepterer ikke og avviser det som plutselig har åpnet seg for ham rundt omkring".
Commentary by Shefner:
Every album has a parable. This is how I would put into words the parable of the first album:
"A person sees a goal in the infinite distance. He agonizingly tries to reach it at the expense of great effort and overcoming all obstacles. Finally the last obstacle disappears and as a gift for all of his suffering, he sees a beautiful world that is yet unknown to him... But the goal he sees in the beginning doesn't change, it stays the same. And the person keeps pursuing this goal, discarding and ignoring everything that had suddenly been revealed to him all around."
Комментарий Шефнера:
В каждом из альбомов здесь заключена притча. Вот как бы я мог рассказать словами притчу из второго альбома.
„Человек видит бесконечно далеко заветную для себя цель. Он мучительно двигается к ней, ценой многих усилий проходя одно за другим сквозь все препятствия. Наконец, исчезает последняя преграда и перед ним, в награду за его страдания, открывается светлый неведомый еще для него мир...
Но цель, которую он видел в начале пути, остается для него все той же, не меняется...
И человек продолжает преследовать ее, не принимая и отвергая то, что внезапно открылось для него вокруг.
154
50
Rouva Luninan kommentti:
Pidin kovasti sinisestä väristä.
Fru Lunins kommentar:
Jeg likte veldig godt den blå fargen.
Commentary by Lunina:
I liked the color blue a lot.
Комментарий Луниной:
Мне очень понравился синий цвет.
155

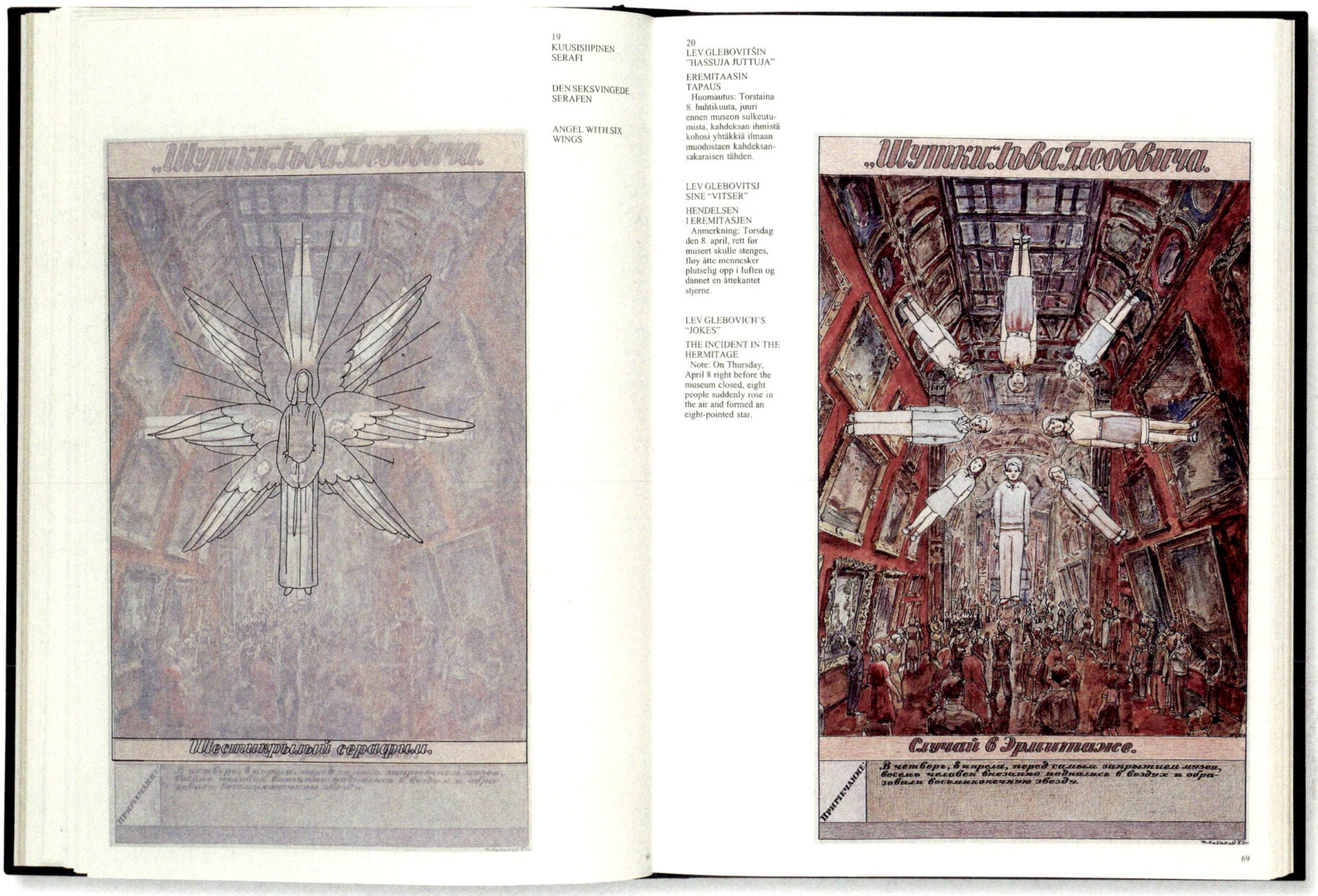
"Шутки Льва Глебовича."
Шестикрылый серафим.
Случай в Эрмитаже.
19
KUUSISIIPINEN
SERAFI
DEN SEKSVINGEDE
SERAFEN
ANGEL WITH SIX
WINGS
20
LEV GLEBOVITŠIN
"HASSUJA JUTTUJA"
EREMITAASIN
TAPAUS
Huomautus: Torstaina 8. huhtikuuta, juuri ennen museon sulkeutumista, kahdeksan ihmistä kohosi yhtäkkiä ilmaan muodostaen kahdeksansakaraisen tähden.
LEV GLEBOVITSJ
SINE "VITSER"
HENDELSEN
I EREMITASJEN
Anmerkning: Torsdag den 8. april, rett før museet skulle stenges, fløy åtte mennesker plutselig opp i luften og dannet en åttekantet stjerne.
LEV GLEBOVICH'S
"JOKES"
THE INCIDENT IN THE
HERMITAGE
Note: On Thursday, April 8 right before the museum closed, eight people suddenly rose in the air and formed an eight-pointed star.
69

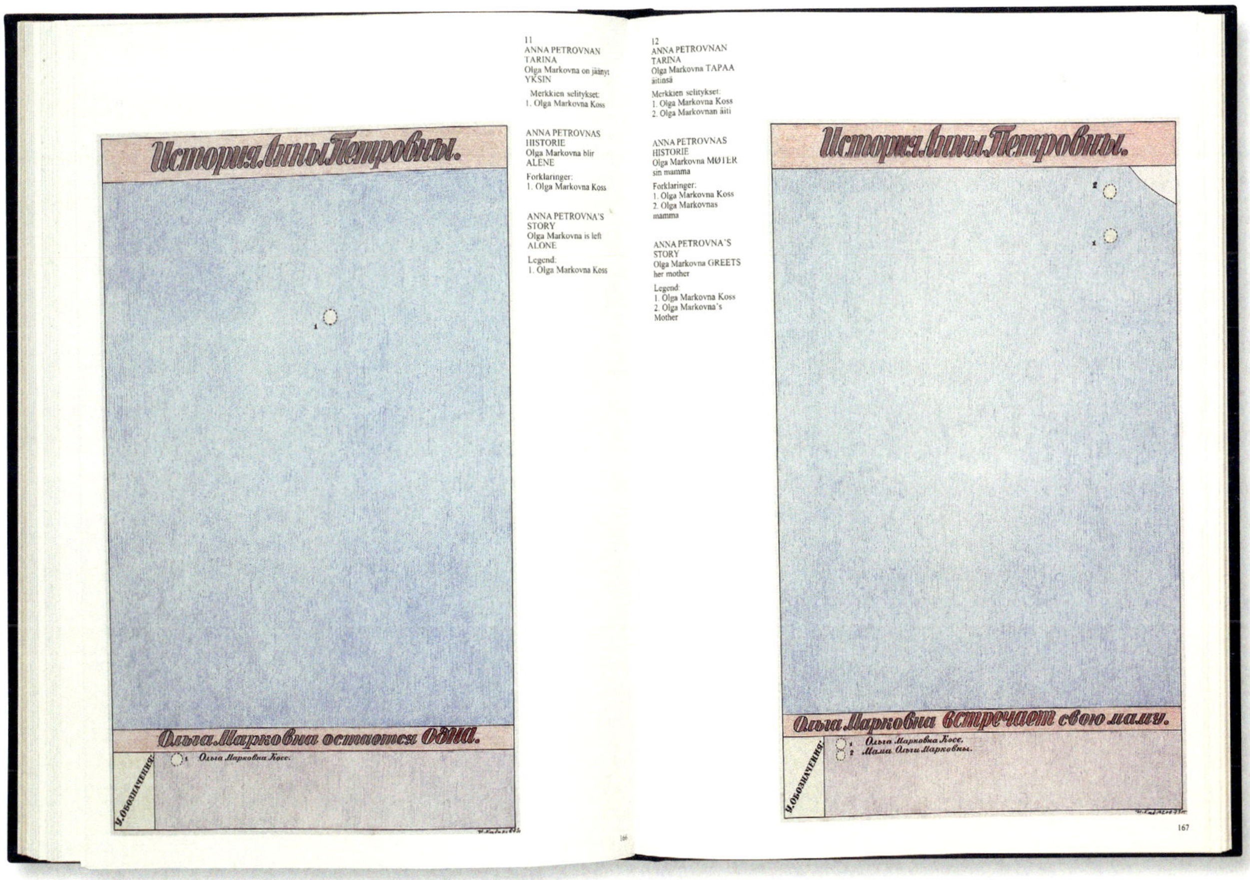
История Анны Петровны.
Ольга Марковна остается одна.
История Анны Петровны.
Ольга Марковна встречает свою маму.
11
ANNA PETROVNAN
TARINA
Olga Markovna on jäänyt
YKSIN
Merkkien selitykset:
1. Olga Markovna Koss
ANNA PETROVNAS
HISTORIE
Olga Markovna blir
ALENE
Forklaringer:
1. Olga Markovna Koss
ANNA PETROVNA'S
STORY
Olga Markovna is left
ALONE
Legend:
1. Olga Markovna Koss
12
ANNA PETROVNAN
TARINA
Olga Markovna TAPAA
äitinsä
Merkkien selitykset:
1. Olga Markovna Koss
2. Olga Markovnan äiti
ANNA PETROVNAS
HISTORIE
Olga Markovna MØTER
sin mamma
Forklaringer:
1. Olga Markovna Koss
2. Olga Markovnas
mamma
ANNA PETROVNA'S
STORY
Olga Markovna GREETS
her mother
Legend:
1. Olga Markovna Koss
2. Olga Markovna's
Mother
167

69 The Artist's Despair or The Conspiracy of the Untalented

Die Verzweiflung des Künstlers oder die Verschwörung der Untalentierten

1994

Ilya Kabakov
Berlin: Wewerka & Weiss Galerie
29.7 x 21 cm
11 photocopied pp. with 4 b/w ills.
stapled, cardboard cover, label on the cover
Drahtheftung, Kartonumschlag, Etikette auf dem Umschlag

exhibition catalogue | *Ausstellungskatalog*

layout by Ilya Kabakov | *Layout von Ilya Kabakov*

For the installation of the same name at the Galerie Barbara Weiss, Berlin, March 2 to April 22, 1994. Text by Ilya Kabakov; German, Russian.

Zur gleichnamigen Installation, Galerie Barbara Weiss, Berlin, 2. März – 22. April 1994. Text von Ilya Kabakov; deutsch, russisch.

see also | *siehe auch* CRI, vol. 2, no. 79, pp. 34–39; CRP, vol. 1, nos. 182–184, pp. 266–269

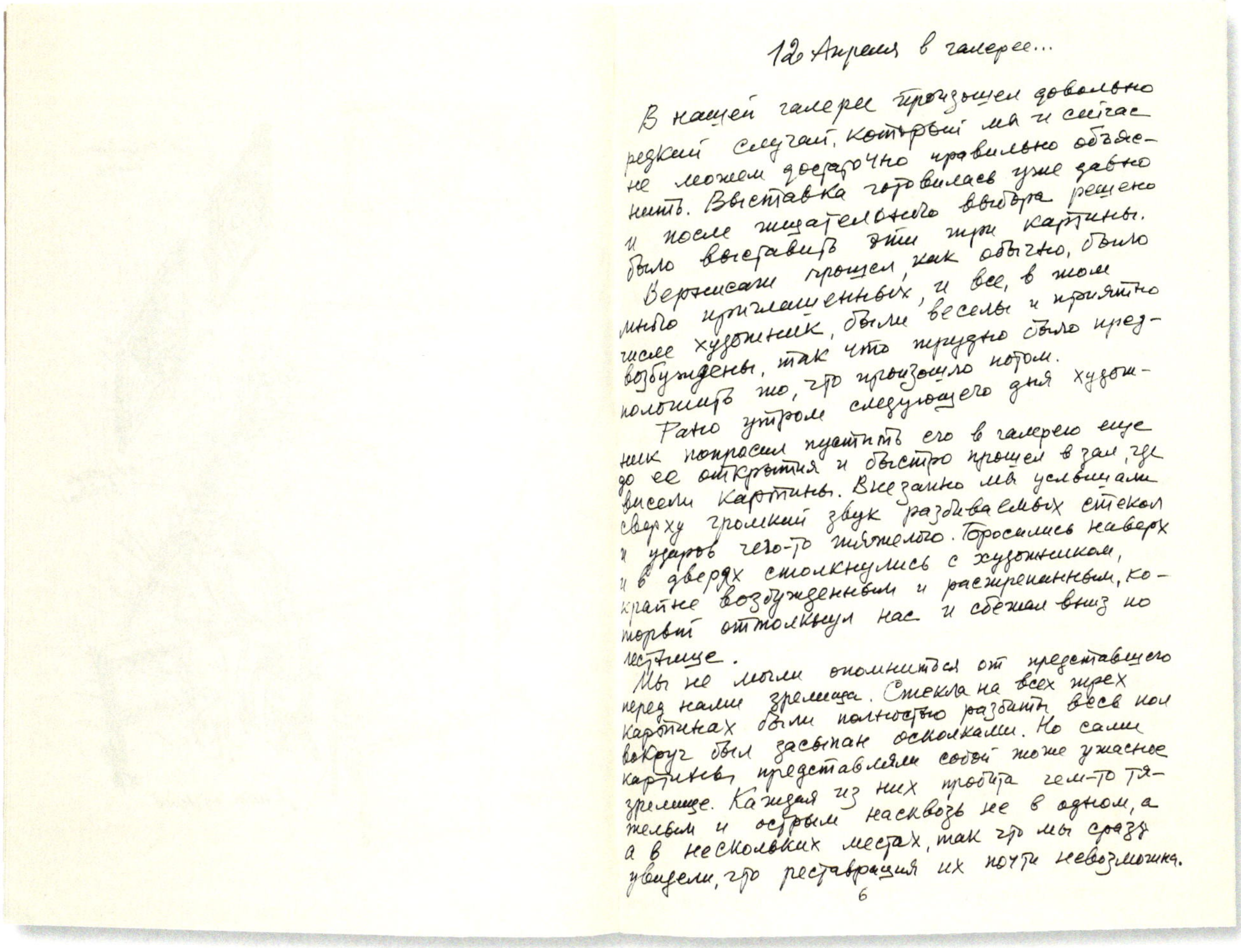

12 Апреля в галерее...

В нашей галерее произошел довольно
редкий случай, который мы и сейчас
не можем достаточно правильно объяс-
нить. Выставка готовилась уже давно
и после тщательного выбора решено
было выставить эти три картины.
Вернисаж прошел, как обычно, было
много приглашенных, и все, в том
числе художник, были веселы и приятно
возбуждены, так что трудно было пред-
положить то, что произошло потом.
Рано утром следующего дня худож-
ник попросил пустить его в галерею еще
до ее открытия и быстро прошел в зал, где
висели картины. Внезапно мы услышали
сверху громкий звук разбиваемых стекол
и ударов чего-то тяжелого. Бросились наверх
и в дверях столкнулись с художником,
крайне возбужденным и расстроенным, ко-
торый оттолкнул нас и сбежал вниз по
лестнице.
Мы не могли опомниться от представшего
перед нами зрелища. Стекла на всех трех
картинах были полностью разбиты, весь пол
вокруг был засыпан осколками. Но сами
картины представляли собой тоже ужасное
зрелище. Каждая из них пробита чем-то тя-
желым и острым насквозь не в одном, а
в нескольких местах, так что мы сразу
увидели, что реставрация их почти невозможна.
6

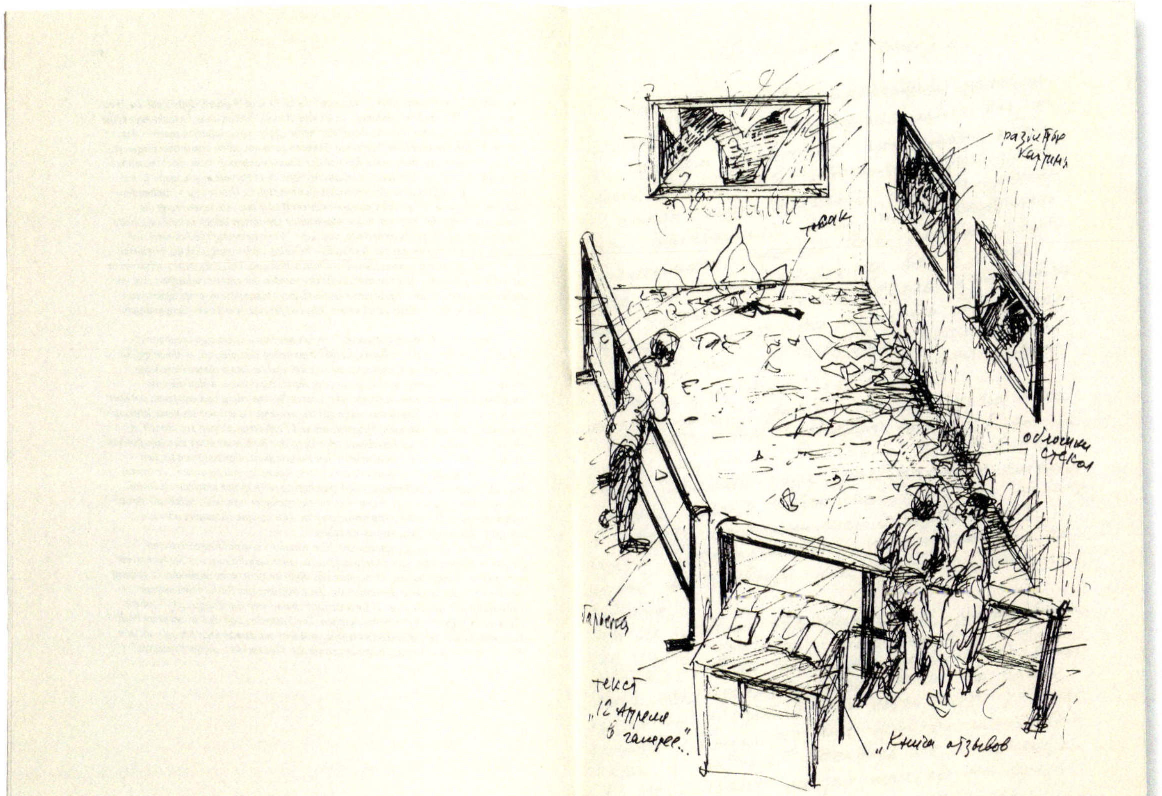

70 The Boat of My Life, My Mother's Album, The Underground Golden River

Das Boot meines Lebens, Album meiner Mutter, Der goldene unterirdische Fluss

1994

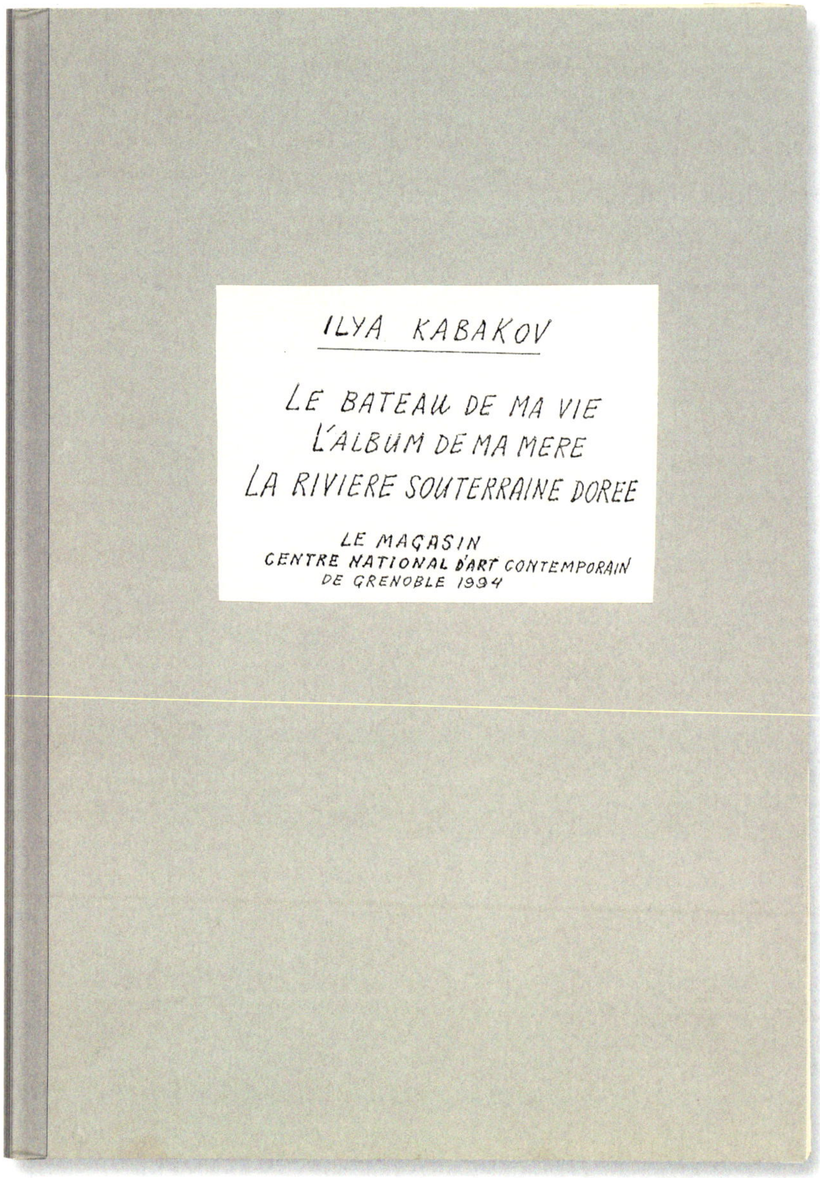

Ilya Kabakov
Grenoble: Magasin. Centre National d'Art Contemporain
29.8 x 21.3 cm
43 (partly double-sided) photocopied pp. with 13 b/w ills.
quick bind, cardboard cover, label on the cover
Schnellhefter, Kartonumschlag, Etikette auf dem Umschlag

exhibition catalogue | *Ausstellungskatalog*

layout by Ilya Kabakov | *Layout von Ilya Kabakov*

For the installations of the same name at Magasin, Centre National d'Art Contemporain, Grenoble, April 17 to July 17, 1994. Installation texts by Ilya Kabakov; French.

Zu den gleichnamigen Installationen, Magasin. Centre National d'Art Contemporain, Grenoble, 17. April – 17. Juli 1994. Texte der Installation von Ilya Kabakov; französisch.

see also | *siehe auch* no. 79; no. 84; CRI, vol. 1, no. 11, pp. 108–113, no. 36, pp. 254–259, no. 72, pp. 464–469

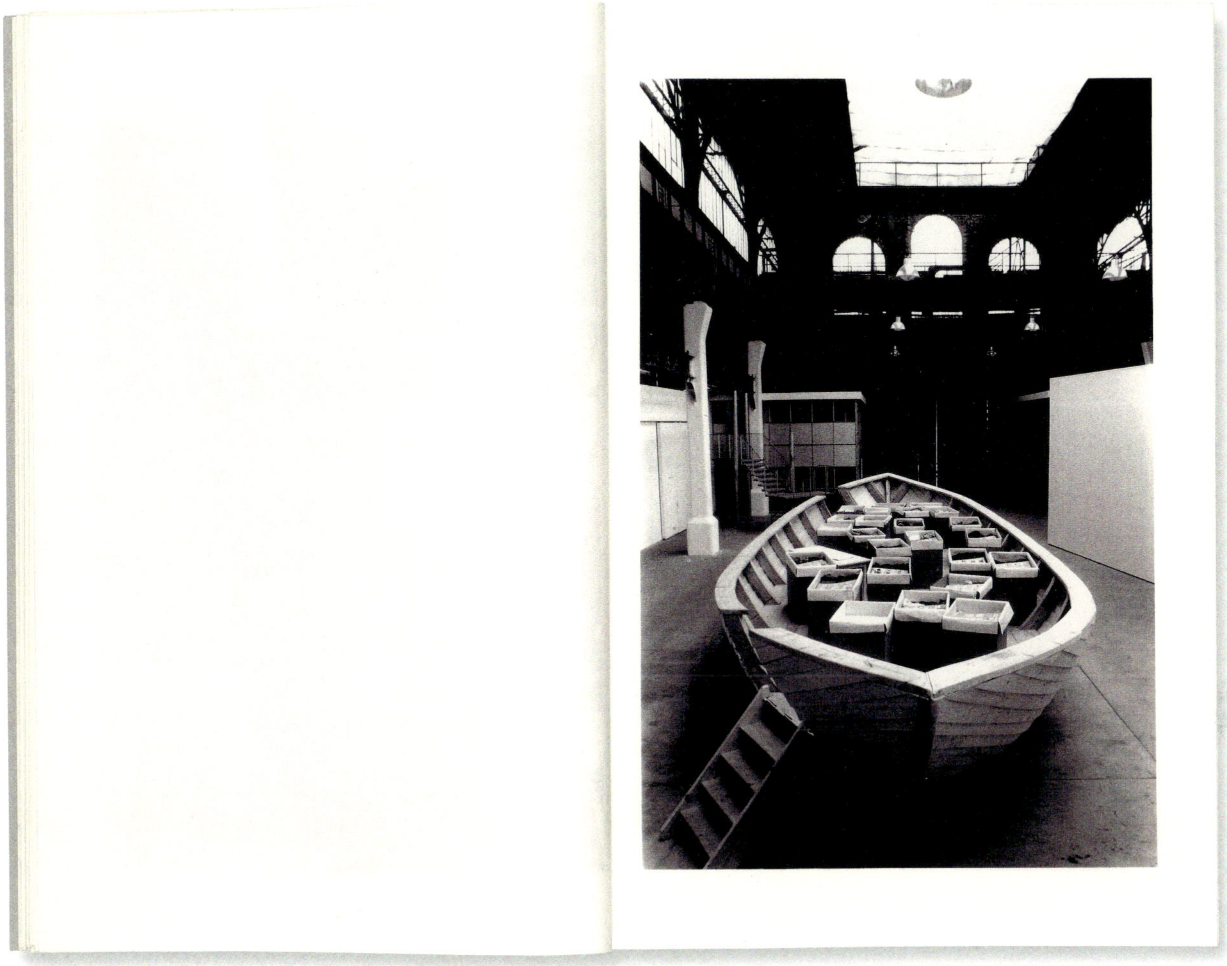

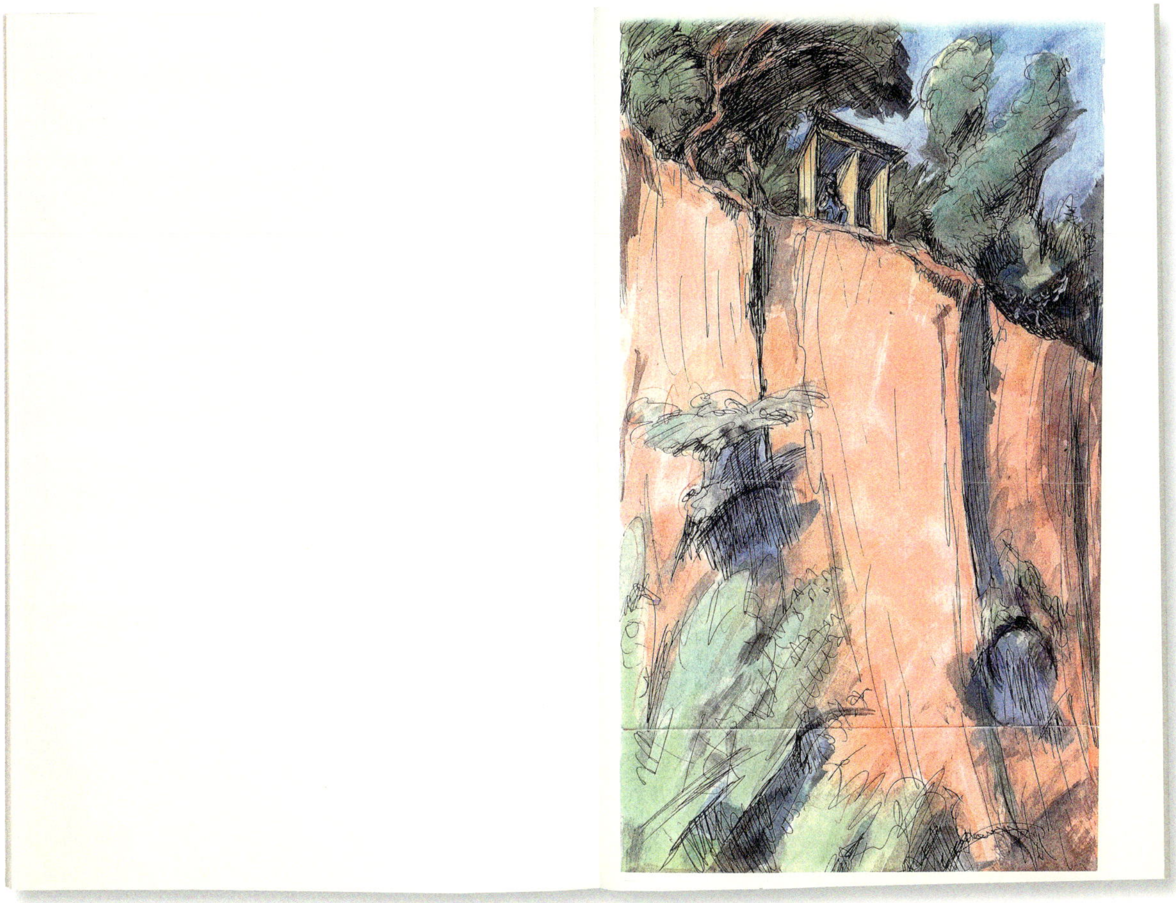

71 Unrealized Projects | *Nicht ausgeführte Projekte*

1994

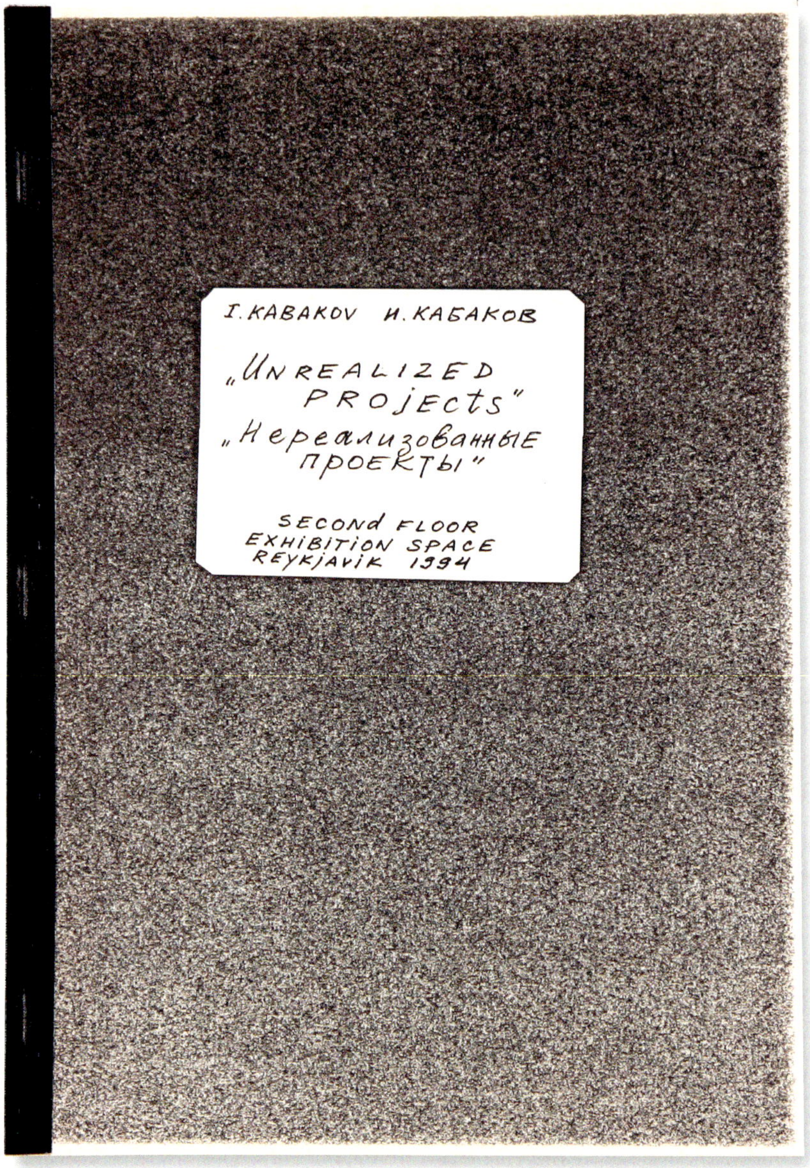

Ilya Kabakov
Reykjavik: Second Floor Exhibition Space
29.7 x 21.3 cm
42 photocopied pp. with 9 (6 color) ills.
stapled, adhesive binding, paper cover, label on the cover
Drahtheftung, Klebebindung, Papierumschlag, Etikette auf dem Umschlag

exhibition catalogue | *Ausstellungskatalog*

layout by Ilya Kabakov | *Layout von Ilya Kabakov*

For the installation of the same name at Önur Hæd Sýningarsalur/Second Floor Exhibition Space, Reykjavik, June 4 to July 31, 1994. Text by Ilya Kabakov; Icelandic, English, Russian.

Zur gleichnamigen Installation, Önur Hæd Sýningarsalur / Second Floor Exhibition Space, Reykjavik, 4. Juni – 31. Juli 1994. Text von Ilya Kabakov; isländisch, englisch, russisch.

see also | *siehe auch* no. 85; CRI, vol. 2, no. 82, pp. 52–59

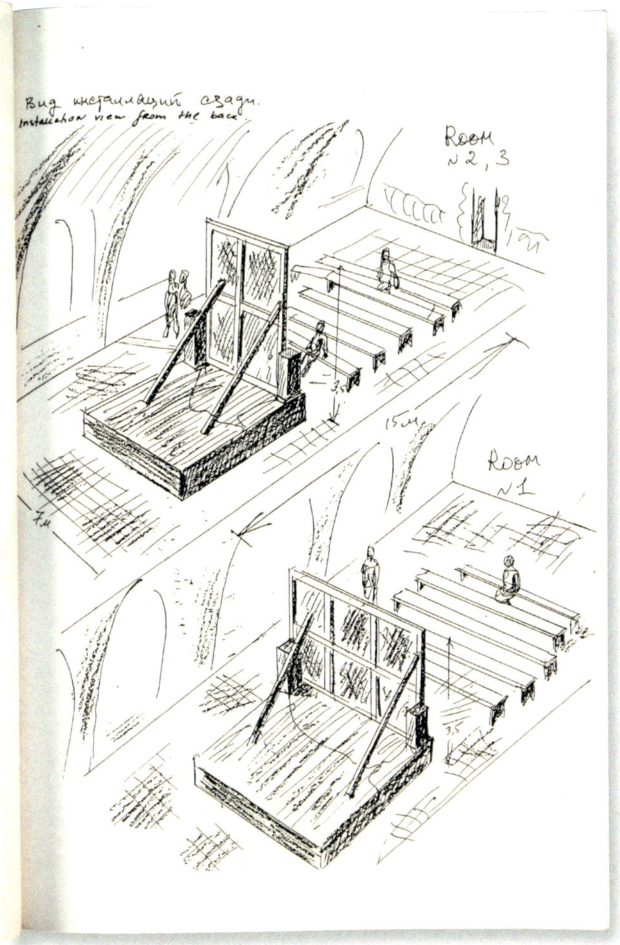
Вид инсталляций сзади.
Installation view from the back.
Room N 2, 3
Room N 1

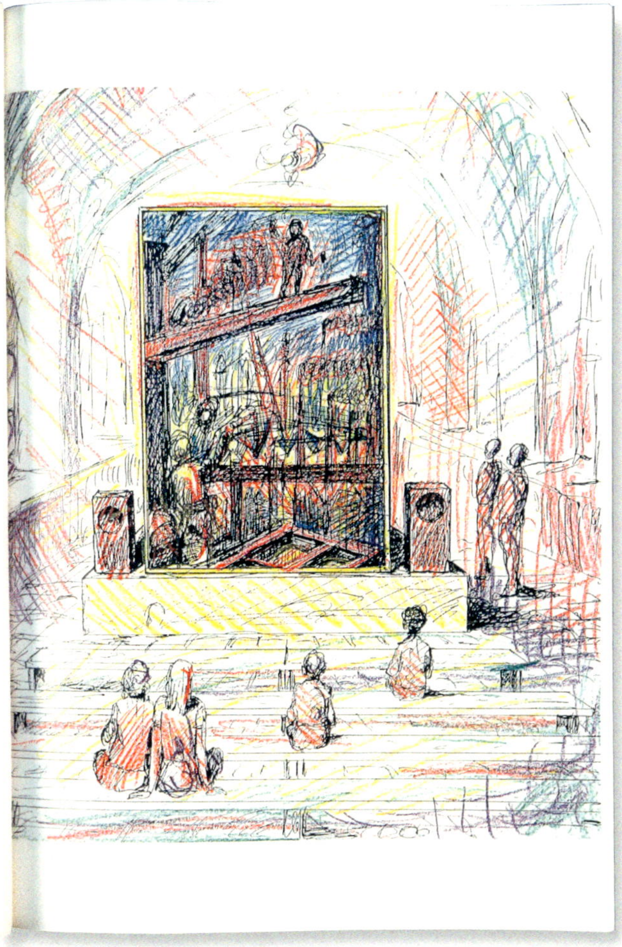

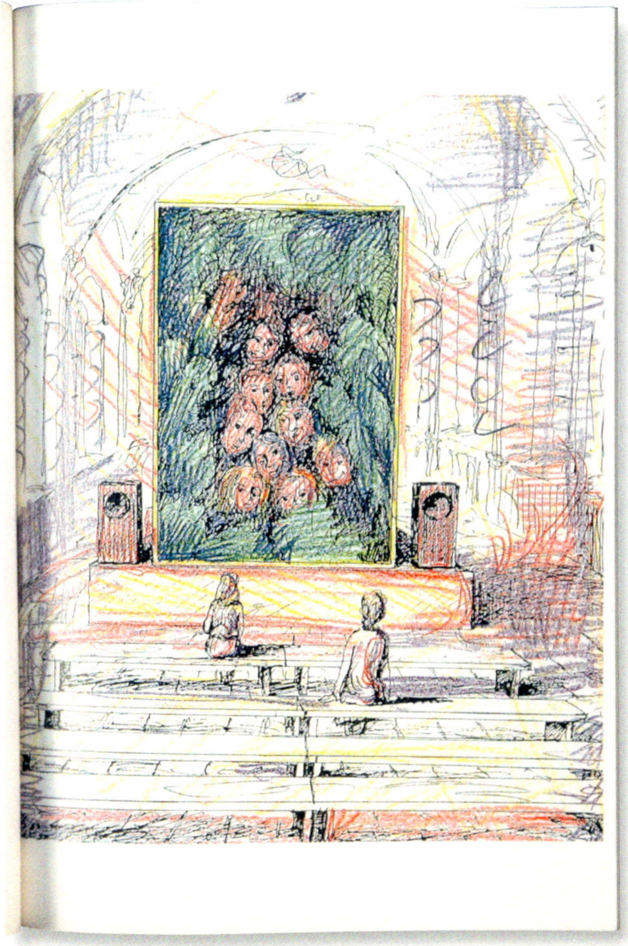

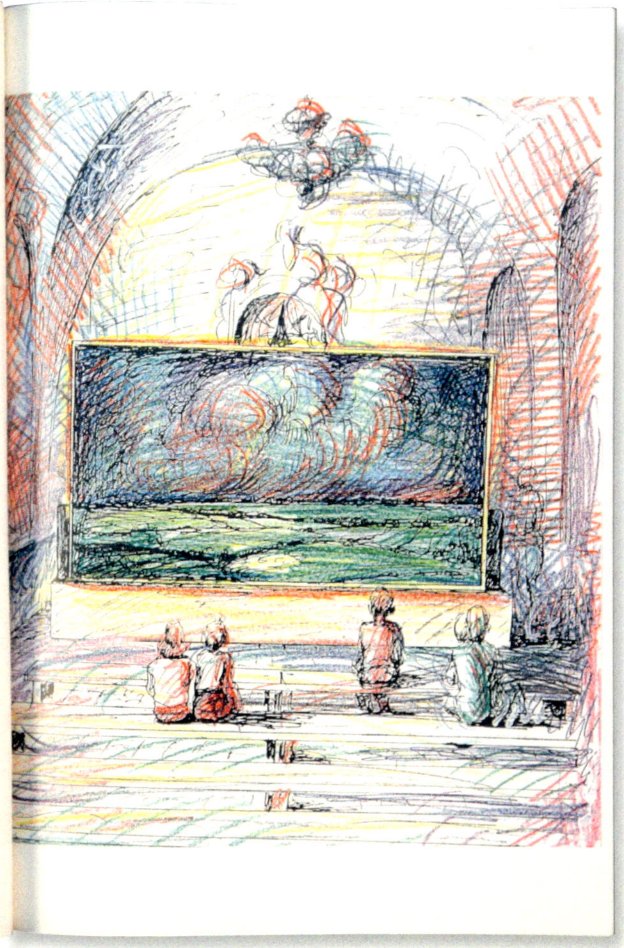

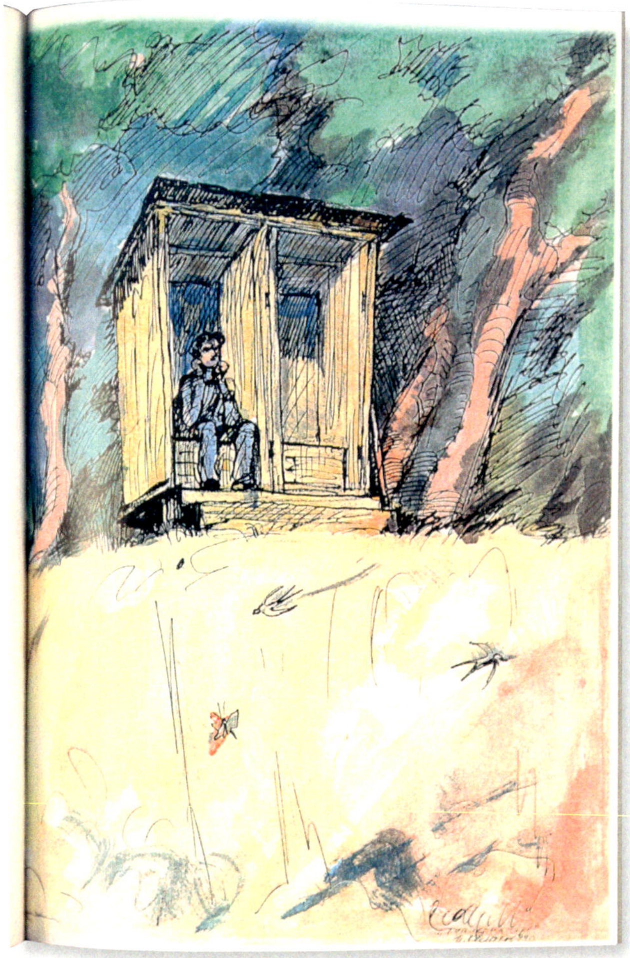

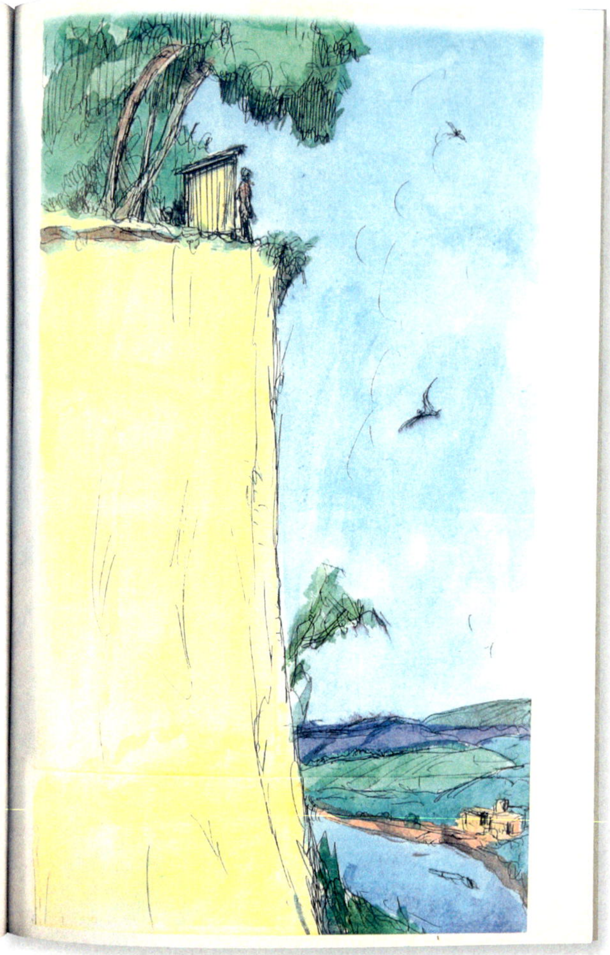

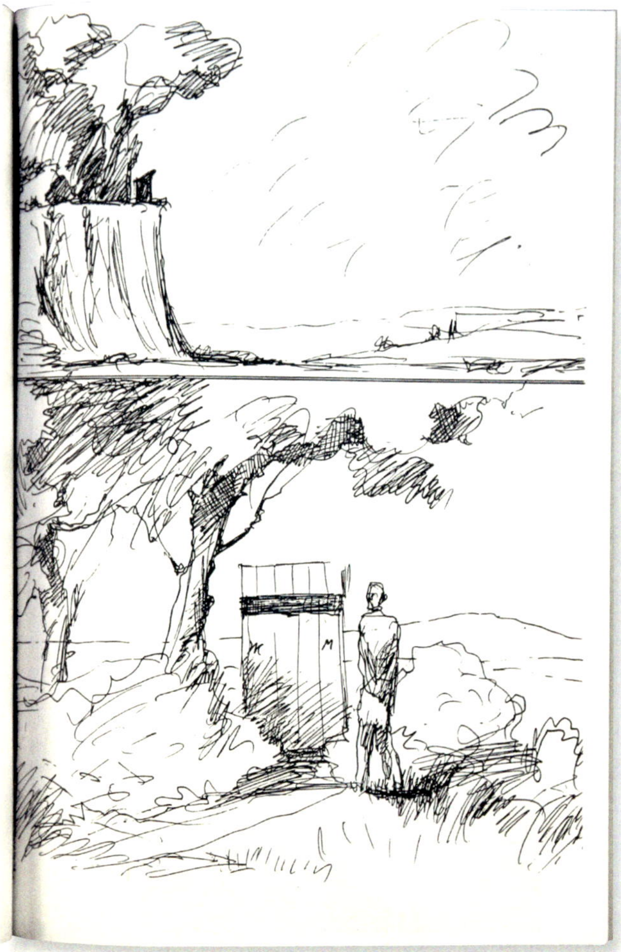

72 A Story About a Culturally Relocated Person

Erzählung von einem kulturell Verschleppten

1994

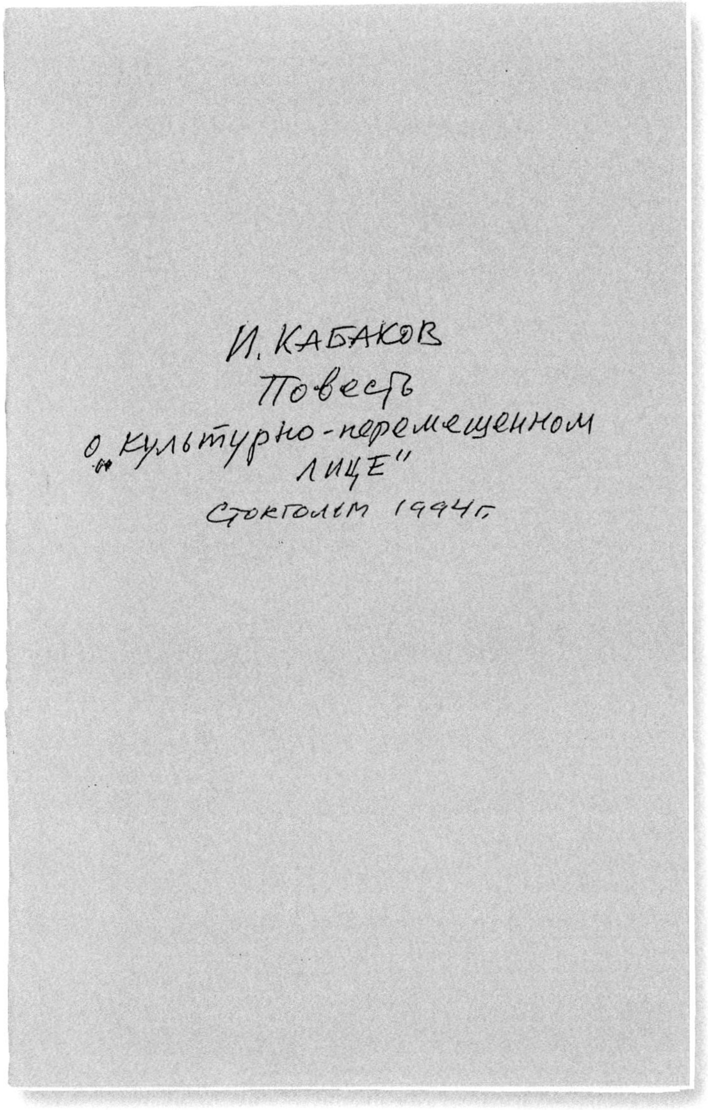

Ilya Kabakov
New York: published by the author
21.6 x 14.1 cm
23 photocopied pp.
stapled, cardboard cover
Drahtheftung, Kartonumschlag

thematic publication | *thematische Publikation*

layout by Ilya Kabakov | *Layout von Ilya Kabakov*

Text for Ilya Kabakov's lecture at the 28th IAAC/AICA Congress, Stockholm, September 22, 1994; Russian.

Text für den Vortrag von Ilya Kabakov am 28. IAAC / AICA Kongress, Stockholm, 22. September 1994; russisch.

see also | *siehe auch* no. 73

2

Нынешняя ситуация напоминает только что рассказанную один к одному: зал молчит, и я сам должен догадаться, почему я здесь. Я должен догадаться, что во мне такого типического.

И я, как мне кажется, догадался. Я «перемещённое лицо». Я, воспитанный и окончательно сформированный в одном культурном регионе, достаточно долго, вот уже 6 лет, живу в другом. Моё «культурное» прошлое сталкивается с моим «культурным» настоящим. Научившись плавать в одном озере, я, захлёбываясь, барахтаюсь в новом море, хотя состав воды в нём совсем иной. Сегодня таких барахтающихся, то выныривающих на поверхность, то вновь уходящих под воду, десятки, если не сотни. И в этом смысле я так понимаю тему, о которой я должен сейчас говорить, так я понимаю этот «выбор» -- я должен рассказать, что чувствует такое «культурно-перемещённое лицо», как в его сознании преломляются и взаимодействуют оба культурных слоя, как и в чём это сказывается на результатах его работы.

При этом рассказе я буду испытывать определённое удовольствие, укоренненое, видимо, в одном обстоятельстве -- уже весьма личного свойства. Приятно чувствовать себя так называемой индивидуальностью, но не менее, если не более, приятно выдать и выставить свою индивидуальность, не как нечто исключительное, а как раз наоборот -- как весьма характерное и типическое. Психоаналитик легко обнаружил бы в этом результат саморепрессии человека, воспитанного в тоталитарном обществе -- следует согласиться с его проницательностью.

Приступим. В духе старинной бюрократической, то есть организующей традиции, о чём можно только пожалеть сегодня после

3

распада Советской державы, мы сформулируем план предстоящего изложения:

Сначала мы коснёмся ситуации, когда «перемещённое лицо» ещё не начало «своё перемещение», но у него уже существует «Образ Запада» и сформировался тот набор «ожиданий» и претензий, с которым он выезжает и который он, этому «Западу», будет предъявлять.

Далее мы коснёмся двух тенденций, так сказать двух стратегий, которые, конечно, связаны между собой, но которые можно выделить и рассмотреть отдельно: первую мы назовём «идеалистической», склонной к широким художественным обобщениям и спекуляциям; вторую «практической», более связанную с материальными аспектами художественной деятельности на «Западе», которые выбирает «перемещённое лицо».

Далее коснёмся априорных, и как правило, роковых ошибок в этих, казалось хорошо и заблаговременно «фундированных» гипотезах о «Западном художественном мире»;

В конце -- это и будет основная часть доклада -- мы попробуем поговорить о действительных результатах этой «конвергенции», этого соединения двух культур, о реальных и абсолютно нереальных возможностях в подобной ситуации.

При этом изложении я буду занимать позицию пациента, озабоченного лишь тем, чтобы как можно точнее описать симптомы этого процесса.

На «Западе» «перемещённое культурное лицо», как правило, оказывается добровольно, и как бы не был внезапен или постепеннен этот переезд, «лицо» внутренне задолго подготавливается к этому и, естественно, не может предварительно не сформировать образ того мира, в котором ему предстоит оказаться. Этот образ существовал и существует

4

до сих пор, (думаю, что и будет существовать) на территории русско-советского мира образца 70х - начала 80х годов, но мне кажется, что подобная картина видна из любой страны -- и её «реалистичность» при всём разнообразии контуров остаётся такой-же.

Основой такого образа служит представление о строгой иерархичности, пирамидальности западного артмира. Существует одна, самая важная в этом смысле страна, в ней главный её город, а в нём самая главная галерея или группа галерей. Почему именно на вершине и в центре артмира стоит галерея, а не что-нибудь другое, я скажу несколько позже. Директор или директора таких галерей без ума от любви к искусству, ищут беспрерывно «настоящее» искусство и «настоящих» художников. Но найти и то и другое, при всём том, что западный мир огромен, не так просто. В основном всё, что там делается -- скучно, бездарно и неинтересно, судя по репродукциям из журналов и каталогов. И это, конечно, очень хорошо для того, кто туда сейчас отправляется -- на таком фоне его будет легче заметить и «взять».

Соответственно такому образу выстраивается и система «ожиданий», выстраивается стратегия поведения после высадки на желанную территорию. Основа этих ожиданий -- попадание если не в самую лучшую, «главную», то во всяком случае в «очень хорошую» галерею. К этому моменту информация о главной стране и главном городе уже собрана и, разумеется, о всех лучших и главных галереях в нём. С этой мечтой о попадании в «хорошую», «очень хорошую» галерею связаны все остальные мечты, вся основная программа уже до самого конца жизни художника: относительное материальное благополучие, успешные выставки и третье -- затаённое -- постепенное, шаг за шагом, распространение известности художника в мире. Всё это, повторяю, связано только с «уровнем» галереи. «Хорошая» галерея

5

осуществит это быстрее и лучше, не очень хорошая -- медленней и хуже, и «самая главная» -- буквально сразу. И всё это, разумеется, связано с именем директора галереи, некоторые из этих имён звучат прямо легендарно. Раньше я коротко сказал об образах этих директоров дышащих только воздухом искусства, ищущих кого бы поскорей поднять на поверхность «мировых гениев» -- кстати, воспоминания и самоописания самих директоров ~~из них~~ живописуют именно такой портрет. ~~образ~~. В проектах «ожиданий» переезжающего им уготованна роль заботливого и трепетного отца, пекущегося «денно и нощно» о выращивании гениального ребёнка, взявшегося не только выполнять и реализировать его мечты, но и все остальные материальные заботы: легализацию его в новой стране обитания, ведение всех его житейских и бумажных дел в новых незнакомых условиях и -- основное -- постоянное снабжение его деньгами от продажи его картин. В этом чудесном проекте художник видит для себя лишь одно «святое» дело -- создавать произведения искусства, всё остальное -- дело «хорошей» галереи, в которой всё работает в автоматическом режиме, в изначально давно заданном ритме: выставка, успех, продажа картин коллекционерам, выставка, успех, продажа картин музеям и т.д. уже до конца. В этой композиции особенно важное место уделено всё тому же директору, пламенной и страстной его заинтересованности в расширении «успеха» «своего» художника -- впрочем, это и вполне логично: чем больше и чаще удачи сына, тем большие доходы получит «отец», и больше будет его радость от так заботливо вскормленного и направленного таланта. Если же собирающееся переместиться «лицо» не просто прекрасный художник и талант, а принципиальный «модернист», «знает и принимает» западное искусство и хочет в нём поучаствовать, он исполнен тех же ожиданий: реализовать свои идеи и концепты, которые

73 A Story About a Culturally Relocated Person

Erzählung von einem kulturell Verschleppten

1994

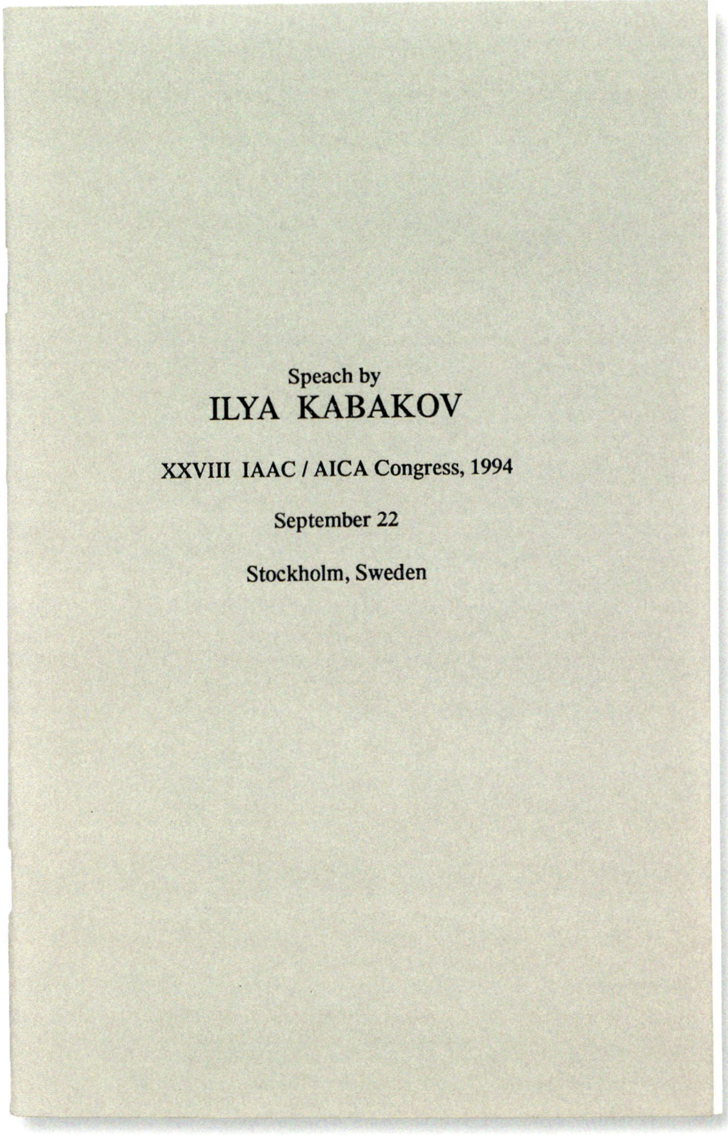

Ilya Kabakov
New York: published by the author
21.6 x 14.1 cm
26 photocopied pp.
stapled, cardboard cover
Drahtheftung, Kartonumschlag

thematic publication | *thematische Publikation*

layout by Ilya Kabakov | *Layout von Ilya Kabakov*

Text for Ilya Kabakov's lecture at the 28th IAAC/AICA Congress, Stockholm, September 22, 1994; English.

Text für den Vortrag von Ilya Kabakov am 28. IAAC / AICA Kongress, Stockholm, 22. September 1994; englisch.

see also | *siehe auch* no. 72

1

I. Kabakov

"A Story about a Culturally Relocated Person"

Speech

The circumstances of my appearance at this podium are fairly remarkable. Not thinking or even contemplating such a thing, I unexpectedly receive the news that I am supposed to speak at this congress and that I have been "chosen" to do so. This situation instantly reminded me of an episode from my childhood, from my school days.

My classmates and I were racing around during the break between classes, textbooks and notebooks were flying all over the place, when suddenly the teacher appeared and announced that I was being summoned immediately to the director's office. When I opened the tall, leather-covered door, I saw before me what we call a "Senior Pedagogical Council": the entire core teaching staff was sitting at a long table, a bit farther was the director himself and the counselor of the academic program. My appearance was met with total silence. Finally the director asked: "Kabakov, can't you guess why we summoned you?" I was silent, shifting from one foot to the other. "We wanted to speak about your hooliganism." Thoughts rushed into my head with frightening speed. First of all, Sidorov and Pokrass were in our class and they were much worse than I, and secondly, as far as I could recall, I hadn't done anything at all during the past week. . . The director continued: "Don't worry, you haven't

4

During my speech I will assume the position of a patient obsessed with only one thing: how to describe the symptoms of this process most accurately.

As a rule, a "relocated cultural person" winds up in the "West" voluntarily, and no matter how sudden or gradual this relocation is, the "person" has been preparing internally for it for a long time, and naturally he can't help but form an image beforehand of that world in which he will find himself. This image existed and exists until today (I think that it will exist also) on the territory of the Russian-Soviet world of the 1970's-beginning of the 1980's, but it seems to me that a similar picture is visible from any country, and its "realisticness" remains the same despite all the diversity of the contours.

The notion that the Western art world is hierarchical, that it has a pyramidal quality, serves as the base of this image. In this sense there exists one most important country, the main city in it, and the most important gallery or group of galleries in that city. I'll speak a bit later about why the gallery and not something else is precisely at the top and in the center of the art world. The director or directors of such galleries are crazed with their love of art, they are continually searching for "genuine" art and "genuine" artists. But to find both of these, given the fact that the Western world is enormous, is not so easy. For the most part, judging by the reproductions in journals and catalogues, what is done there is boring, third-rate and uninteresting. And this, of course, is very good for the one who is now heading there -- it will be easier to notice and "take" him against such a background.

5

In accordance with such an image, a system of "expectations" is devised, along with a strategy of behavior after arriving in the desired territory. The base of these expectations is getting into if not the very best, "main" gallery, then at least into a "very good" gallery. By that time, information has already been gathered about the main country and the main city and, of course, about all the best and main galleries in it. With this dream of getting into a "good," "very good" gallery are connected all the other dreams, the entire fundamental program to the very end of the artist's life: relative material prosperity, successful exhibits and thirdly, -- the cherished -- gradual, step by step, dissemination of the artist's fame throughout the world. All of this, I repeat, is connected only with the "level" of the gallery. A "good" gallery will achieve this more quickly and better, a not so good one, more slowly and worse, and "the main" one -- literally immediately. And all of this, naturally, is connected with the name of the director of the gallery. A few of these names sound downright legendary. Earlier I spoke briefly about the images of these directors breathing only the air of art, searching for someone to promote instantaneously to the top of "world geniuses"; incidentally, the memoirs and self-descriptions of the directors themselves paint just such an image. In his plans of "expectations," the relocating person prepares for these directors the role of the caring and anxious father, toiling "day and night" over the rearing of this genius child, a father who has taken it upon himself not only to fulfill and realize all of his child's dreams, but to take care of all the other material concerns as well: the legalization of his status in the country of residence, the conduct of all of his everyday and legal affairs in these

74 SHEK No. 8, Baumann – District, City of Moscow

SHEK No. 8, Baumann – Bezirk, Stadt Moskau

1994

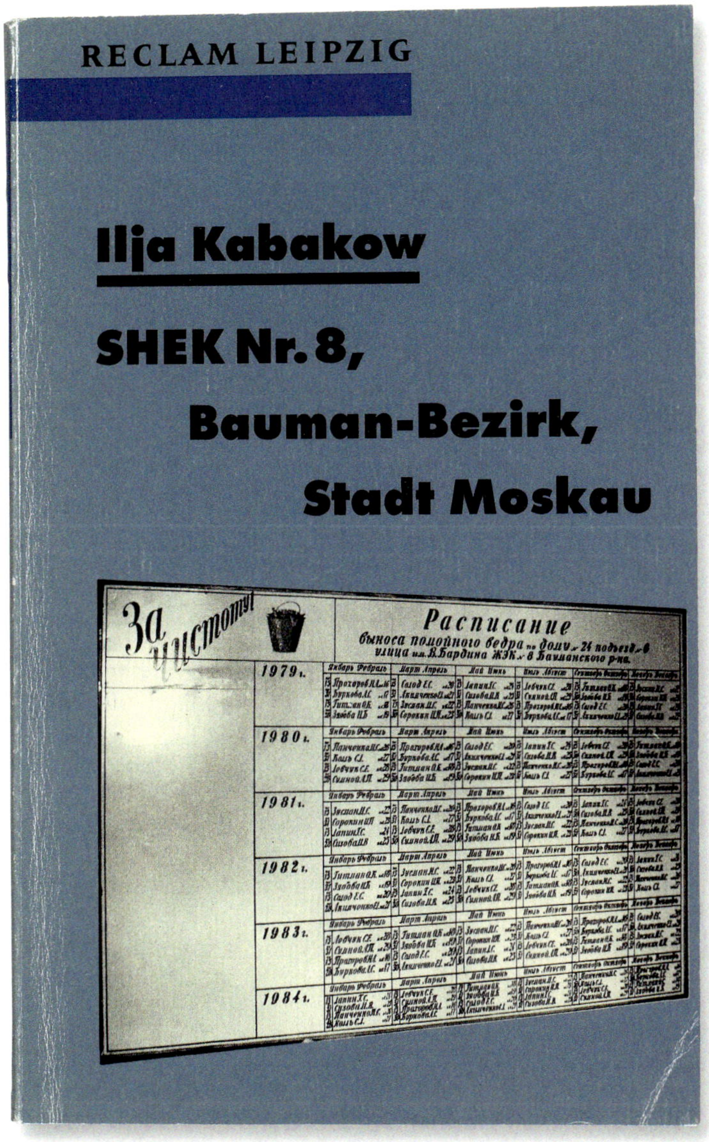

Günter Hirt, Sascha Wonders
Leipzig: Reclam (Reclam Bibliothek, vol. 1489)
18.4 x 11.6 cm
203 pp. with 38 b/w ills.
stitchbound, softback
Fadenheftung, broschiert

thematic publication | *thematische Publikation*

idea by Ilya Kabakov | *Idee von Ilya Kabakov*

A book portraying proponents of Moscow conceptualism and fictitious artists in the form of a fictitious propaganda pamphlet from the "SHEK," the residential management authority in a small urban residential area.

Texts by Erik Bulatov, Ilya Kabakov, Oleg Vassilyev, and a dialogue between Erik Bulatov and Boris Groys on »The Existential Space in the Picture«; German.

Ein Buch mit Vertretern des Moskauer Konzeptualismus und fiktiven Künstlern in Form einer fiktiven Propagandabroschüre des „SHEK", der Wohnungsverwaltung eines kleinen städtischen Wohnbereichs.

Texte von Erik Bulatov, Ilya Kabakov, Oleg Wassiljew und ein Dialog von Erik Bulatov und Boris Groys über »Der existentielle Raum des Bildes«; deutsch.

see also | *siehe auch* no. 5

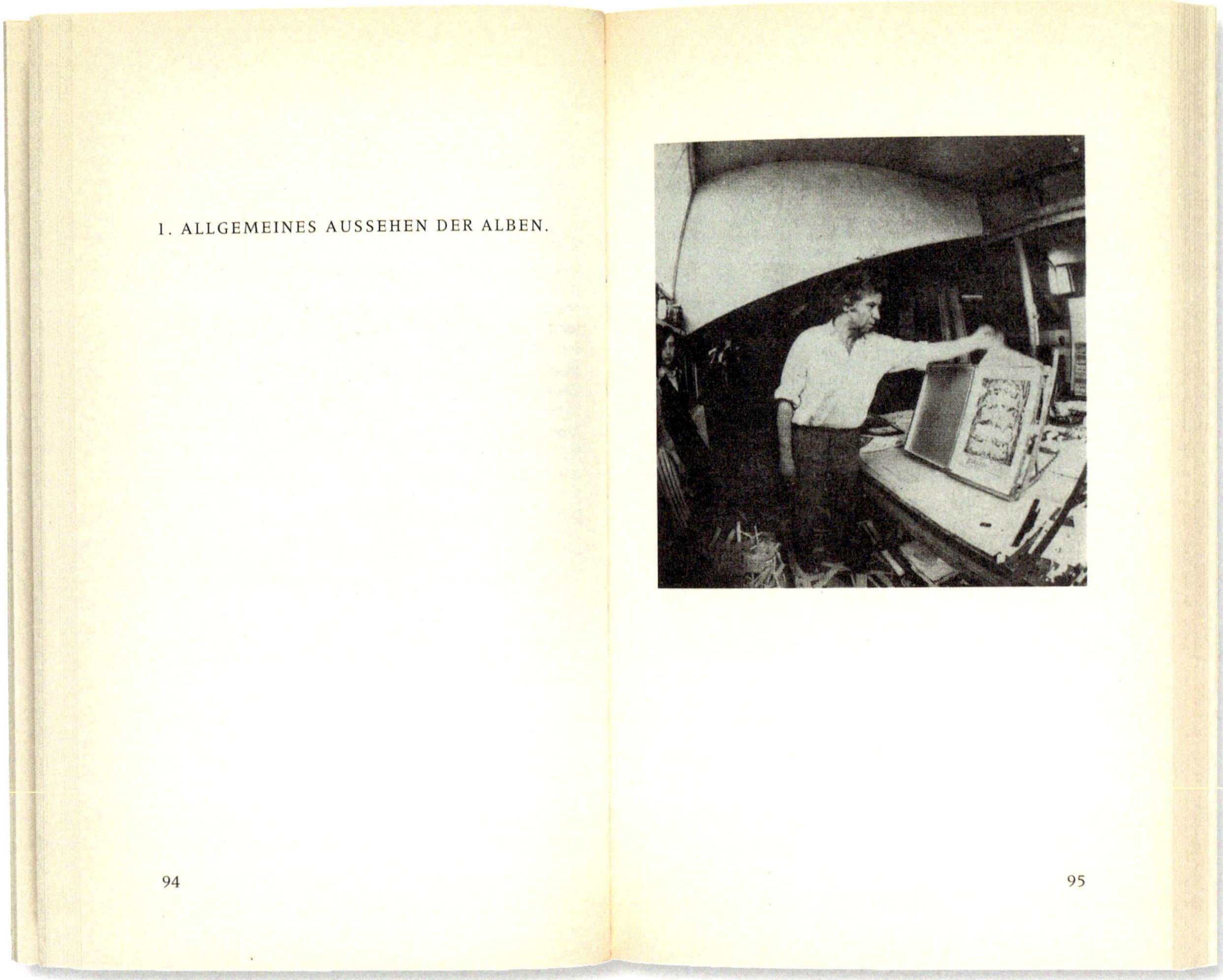
1. ALLGEMEINES AUSSEHEN DER ALBEN.
94
95

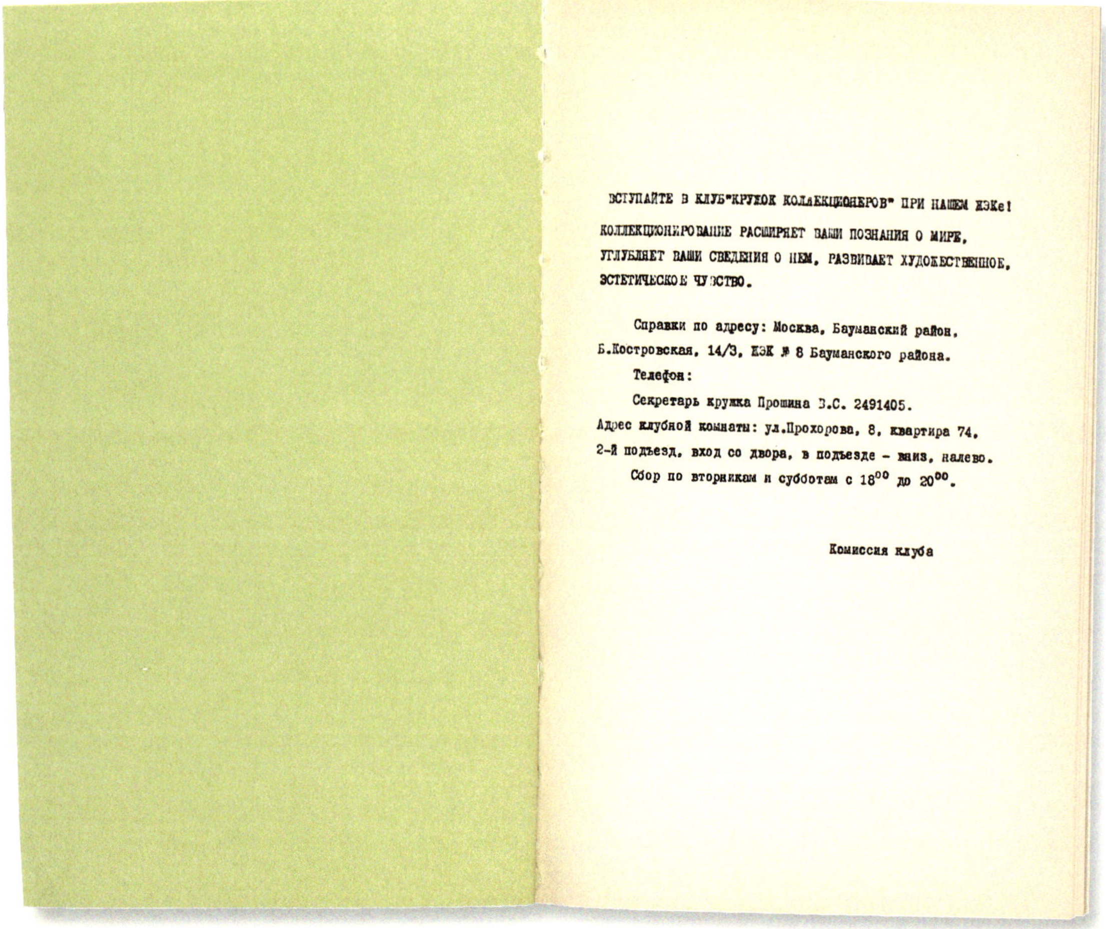
ВСТУПАЙТЕ В КЛУБ"КРУЖОК КОЛЛЕКЦИОНЕРОВ" ПРИ НАШЕМ ЖЭКе!
КОЛЛЕКЦИОНИРОВАНИЕ РАСШИРЯЕТ ВАШИ ПОЗНАНИЯ О МИРЕ,
УГЛУБЛЯЕТ ВАШИ СВЕДЕНИЯ О НЕМ, РАЗВИВАЕТ ХУДОЖЕСТВЕННОЕ,
ЭСТЕТИЧЕСКОЕ ЧУВСТВО.
Справки по адресу: Москва, Бауманский район,
Б.Костровская, 14/3, ЖЭК № 8 Бауманского района.
Телефон:
Секретарь кружка Прошина В.С. 2491405.
Адрес клубной комнаты: ул.Прохорова, 8, квартира 74,
2-й подъезд, вход со двора, в подъезде - вниз, налево.
Сбор по вторникам и субботам с 18⁰⁰ до 20⁰⁰.
Комиссия клуба

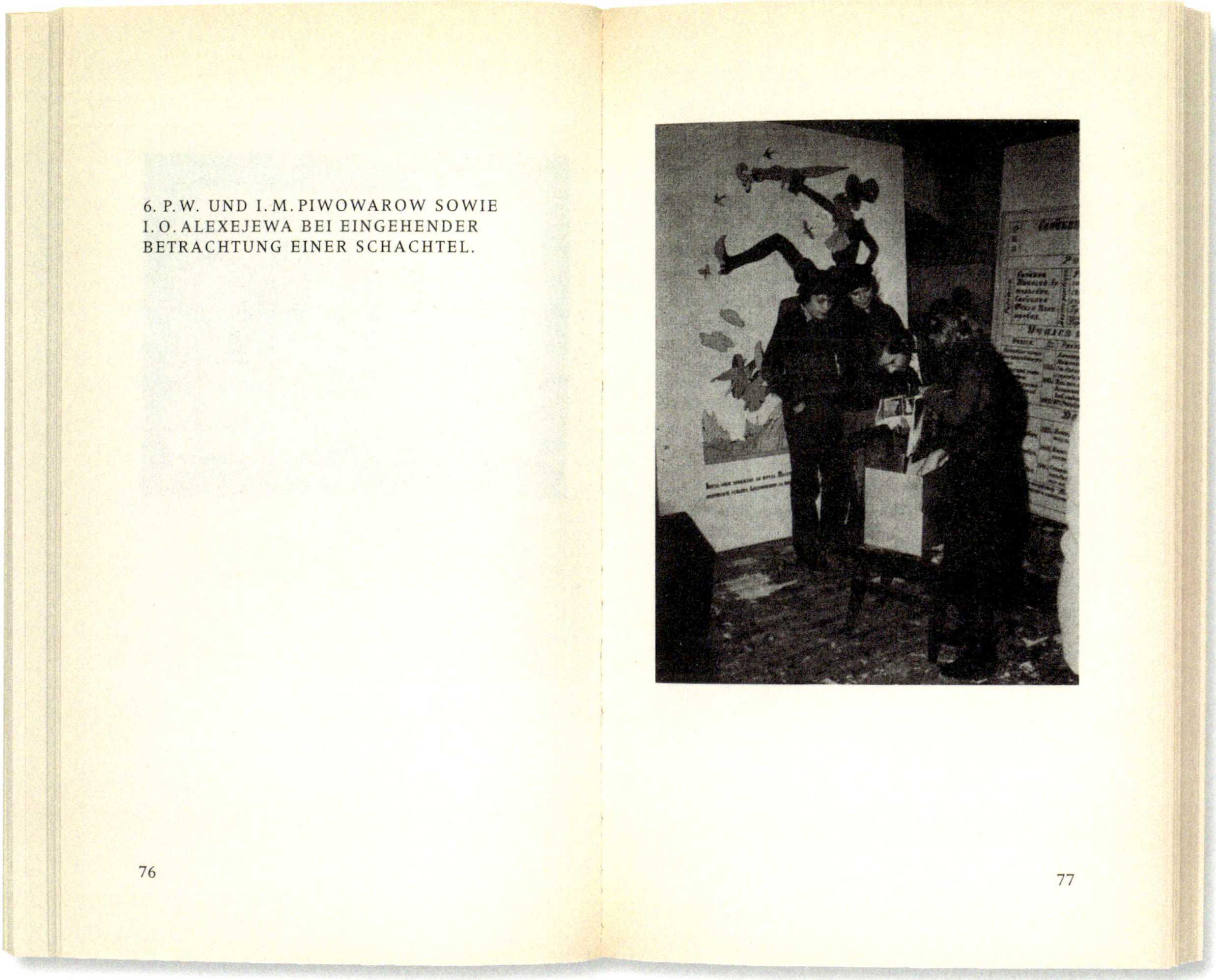

6. P.W. UND I.M. PIWOWAROW SOWIE
I.O. ALEXEJEWA BEI EINGEHENDER
BETRACHTUNG EINER SCHACHTEL.

76

77

75 The Communal Kitchen | *Die Gemeinschaftsküche*

1994

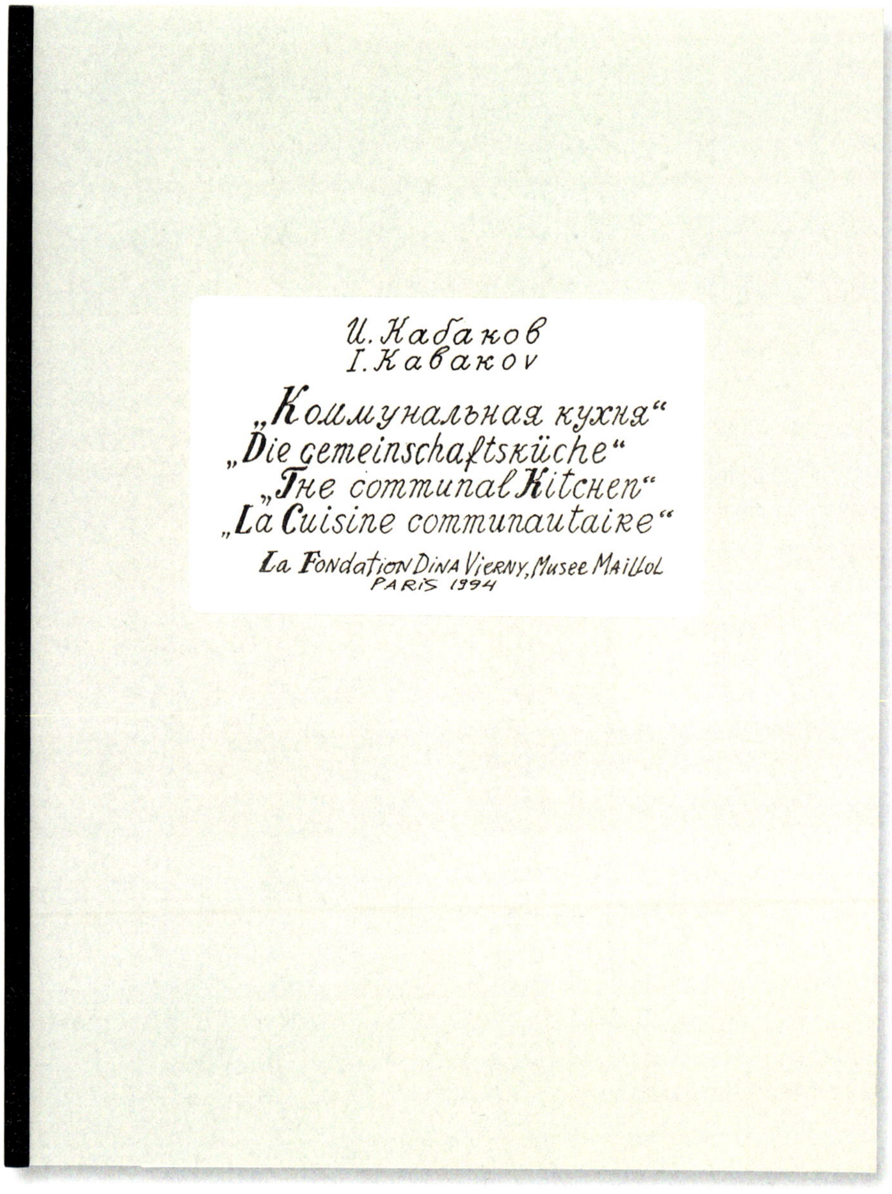

Ilya and Emilia Kabakov
New York: published by Ilya and Emilia Kabakov
27.9 x 21.5 cm
311 photocopied pp. with 8 b/w (incl. 1 foldout) and 5 color (foldouts) ills.
quick bind, paper cover, label on the cover
Schnellhefter, Papierumschlag, Etikette auf dem Umschlag
edition: 500 numbered copies

thematic publication | *thematische Publikation*

layout by Ilya Kabakov | *Layout von Ilya Kabakov*

Documentation of the installation of the same name at the Fondation Dina Vierny, Musée Maillol, Paris. Texts by Ilya Kabakov; Russian, German, English.

Dokumentation der gleichnamigen Installation, Fondation Dina Vierny, Musée Maillol, Paris. Texte von Ilya Kabakov; russisch, deutsch, englisch.

see also | *siehe auch* CRI, vol. 1, no. 48, pp. 318–323; CRP, vol. 1, nos. 185–216, pp. 270–286

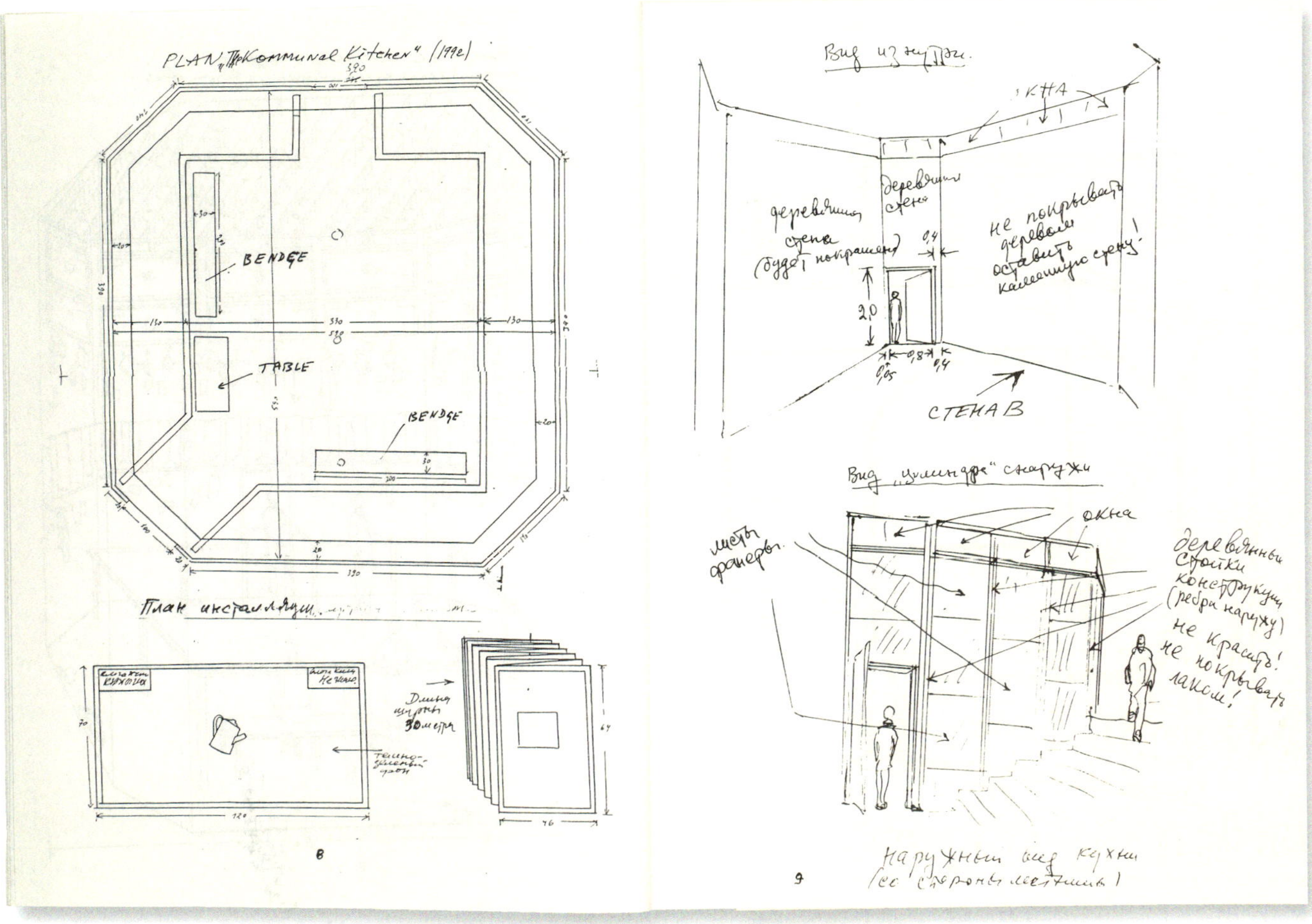
BENDGE
TABLE
BENDGE
План инсталляции
8
СТЕНА В
окна
9

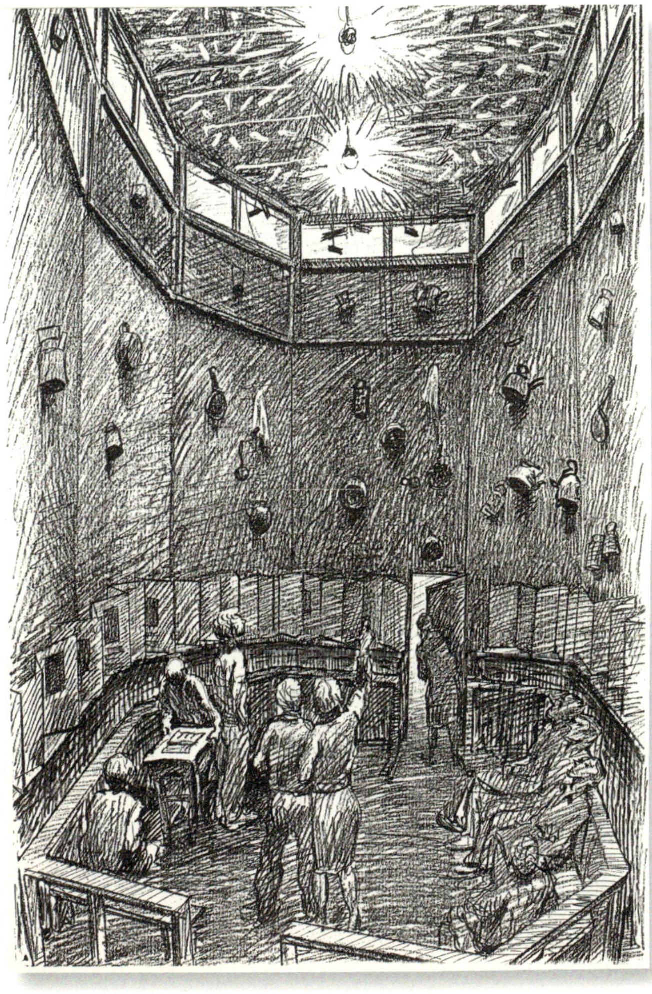

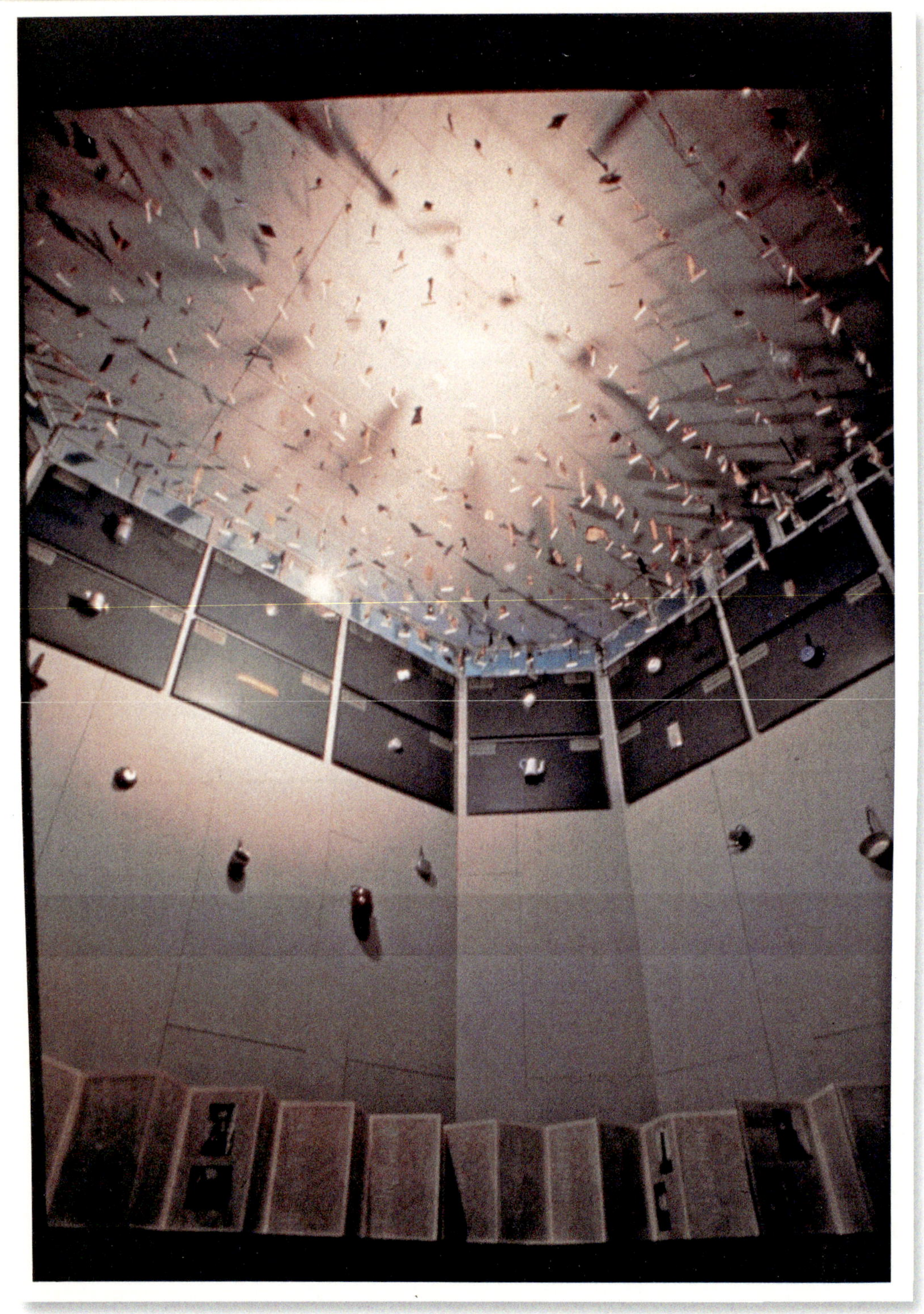

76 10 Characters | *10 Personagen*

1994

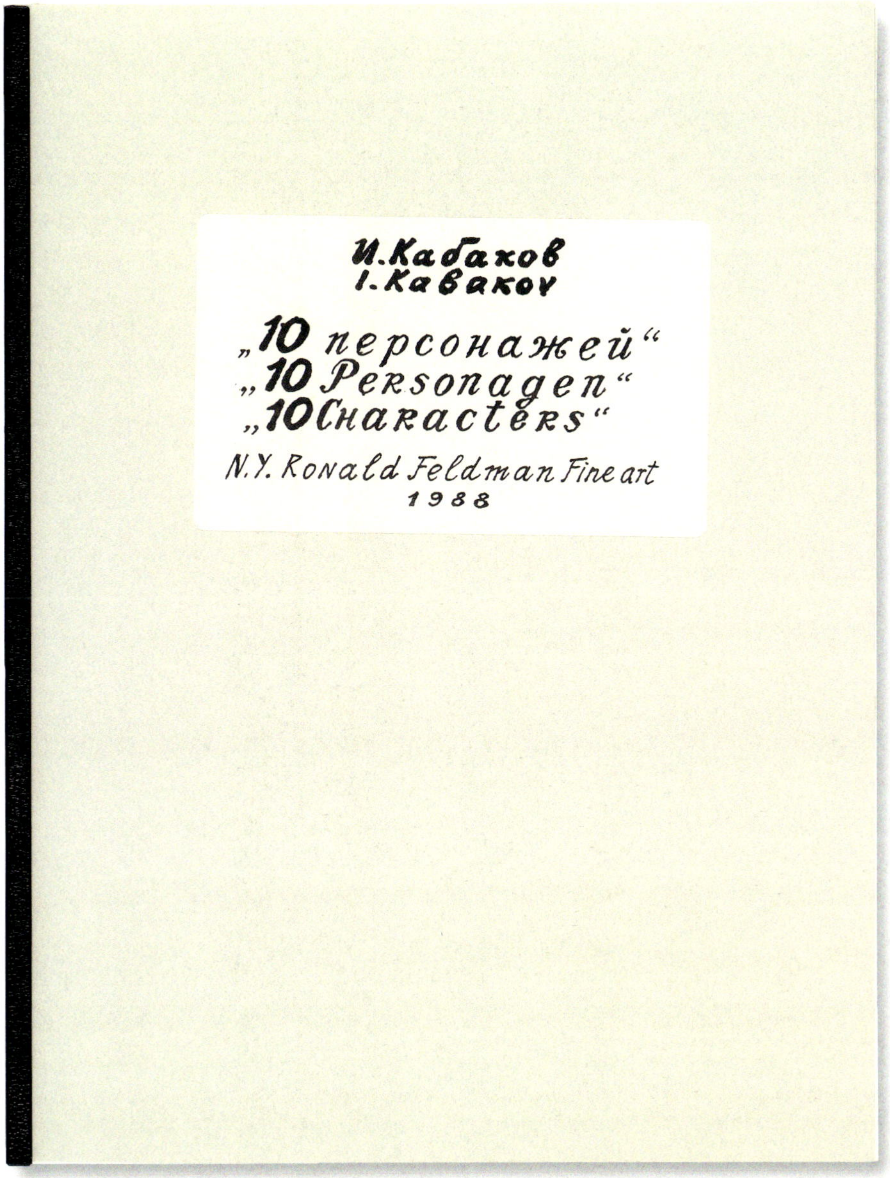

New York: published by Ilya and Emilia Kabakov
27.9 x 21.5 cm
239 photocopied pp. with 84 (incl. 13 color foldouts) ills.
quick bind, cardboard cover, label on the cover
Schnellhefter, Kartonumschlag, Etikette auf dem Umschlag
edition: 500 numbered copies

thematic publication | *thematische Publikation*

layout by Ilya Kabakov | *Layout von Ilya Kabakov*

Documentation of the installation of the same name at the Ronald Feldman Fine Arts Gallery, New York, April 30 to June 4, 1988. Text by Ilya Kabakov; Russian, German, English.

Dokumentation der gleichnamigen Installation, Galerie Ronald Feldman Fine Arts, New York, 30. April – 4. Juni 1988. Text von Ilya Kabakov; russisch, deutsch, englisch.

see also | *siehe auch* no. 22; no. 25; no. 48; no. 53; no. 54; no. 63; no. 89; CRI, vol. 1, no. 15, pp. 132–145; CRP, vol. 1, no. 49, pp.101–102, no. 57, pp. 114–115, no. 67, p. 132, no. 73, pp. 141–142, no. 114, pp. 196–197, nos. 128–129, pp. 213–214

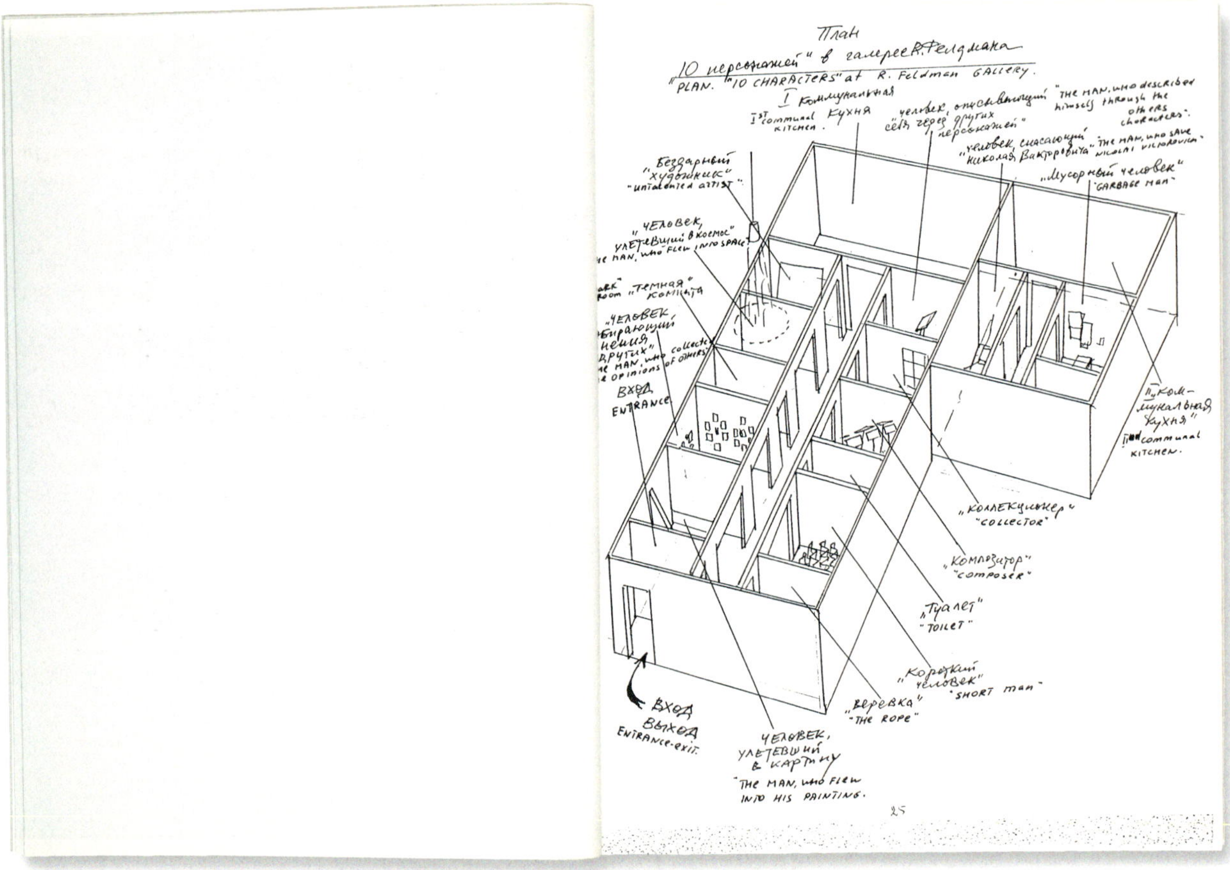
План
„10 персонажей" в галерее R. Фелдмана
"PLAN. "10 CHARACTERS" at R. Feldman GALLERY.
I Коммунальная Кухня
Ist communal KITCHEN.
человек, описывающий себя через других персонажей"
"THE MAN, who described himself through the others characters".
„человек, спасающий Николая Викторовича" "THE MAN, who SAVE NIKOLAI VIKTOROVICH".
„Мусорный человек" "GARBAGE MAN"
„Бездарный художник" "untalented artist".
„человек, улетевший в космос" ...HE MAN, who FLEW INTO SPACE
„Темная" комната
„человек, ...нения других"
...HE MAN, who collected ...E opinions OF OTHERS
ВХОД ENTRANCE
„коммунальная кухня" communal KITCHEN.
„коллекционер" "collector"
„композитор" "composer"
„Туалет" "toilet"
„Короткий человек" "SHORT man"
„Веревка" "THE ROPE"
ВХОД ВЫХОД ENTRANCE-EXIT.
человек, улетевший в картину
"THE MAN, who FLEW INTO HIS PAINTING.
25

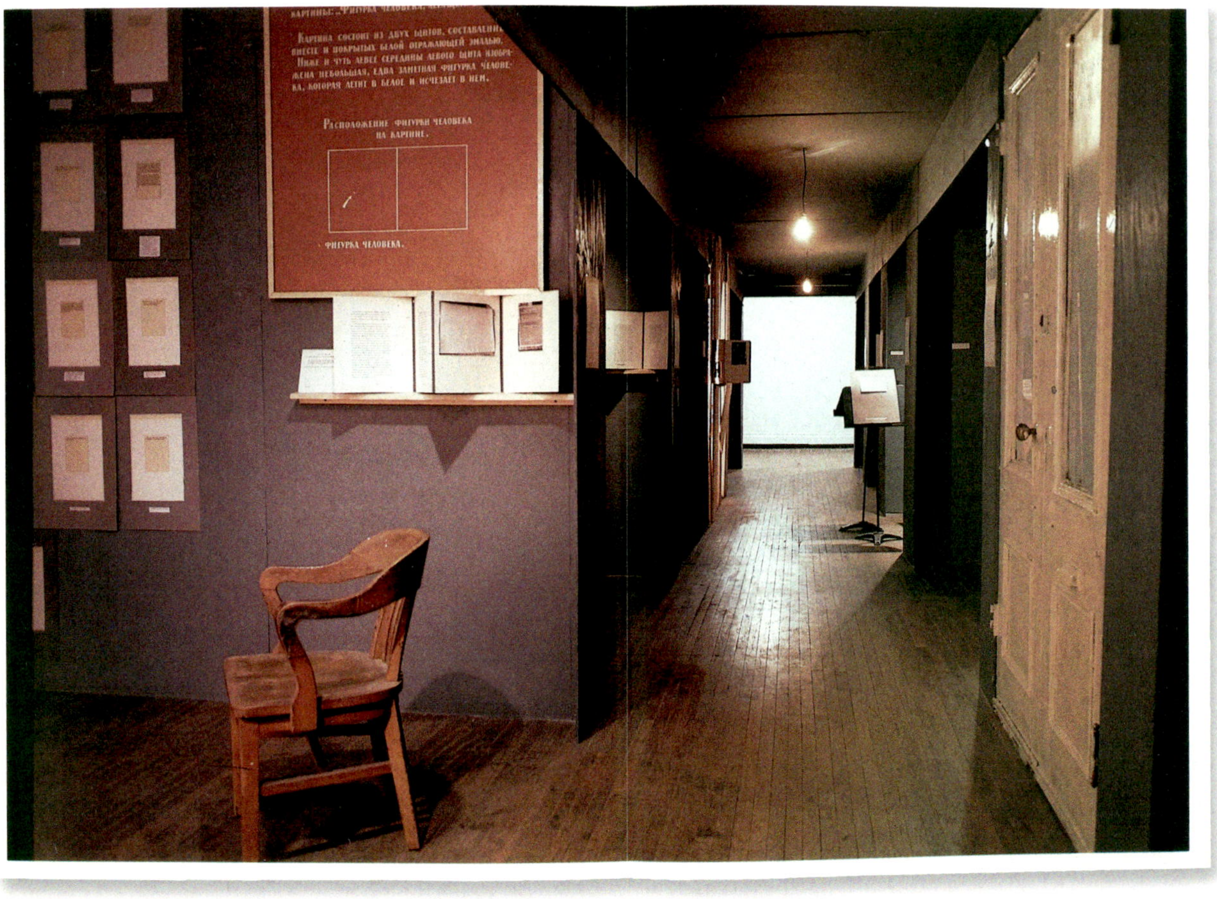
Расположение фигурки человека на картине.
Фигурка человека.

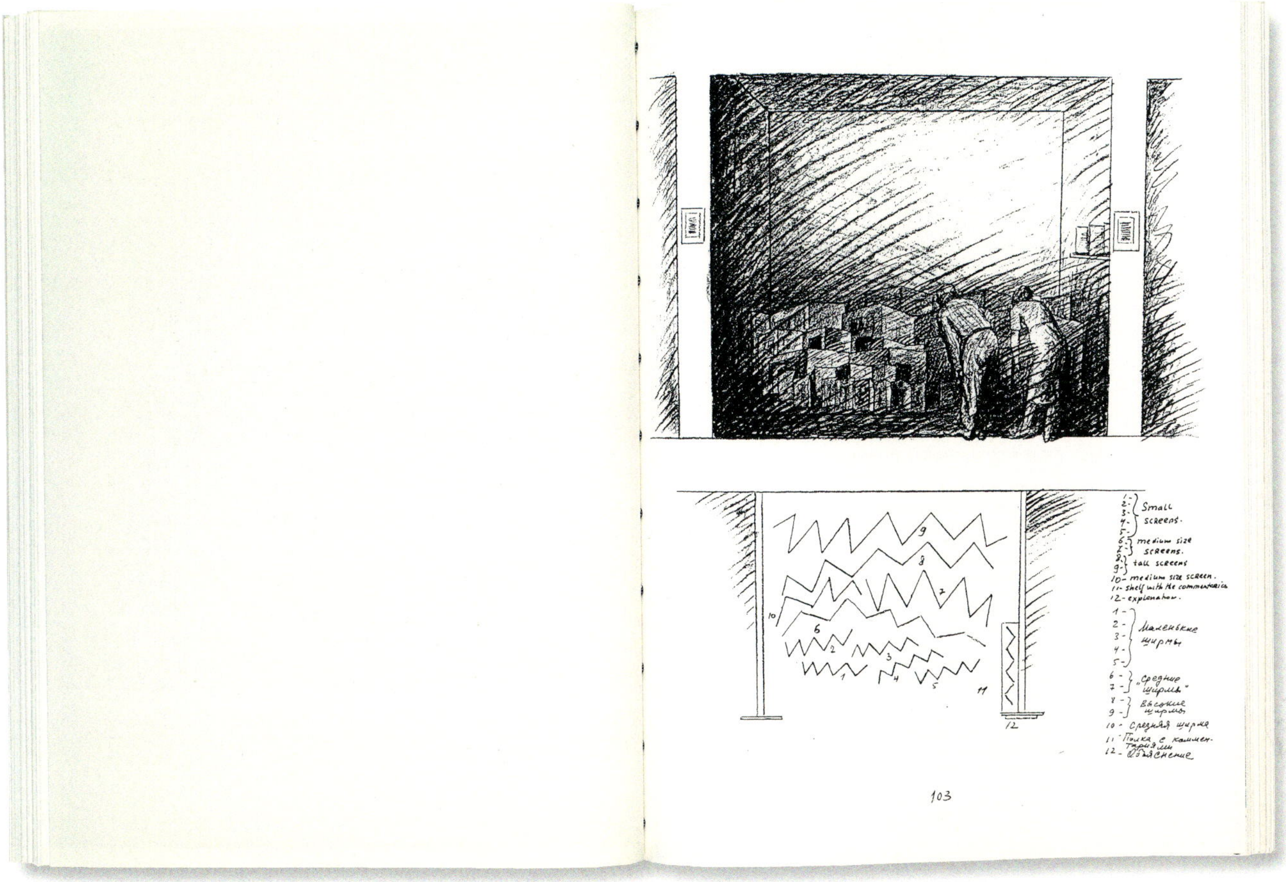
1- 2- 3- 4- 5- Small screens.
6- 7- medium size screens.
8- 9- tall screens
10- medium size screen.
11- shelf with the commentaries
12- explanation.
1- 2- 3- 4- 5- Маленькие ширмы
6- 7- „Средние ширмы"
8- 9- Высокие ширмы
10- Средняя ширма
11- Полка с комментариями
12- Объяснение
103

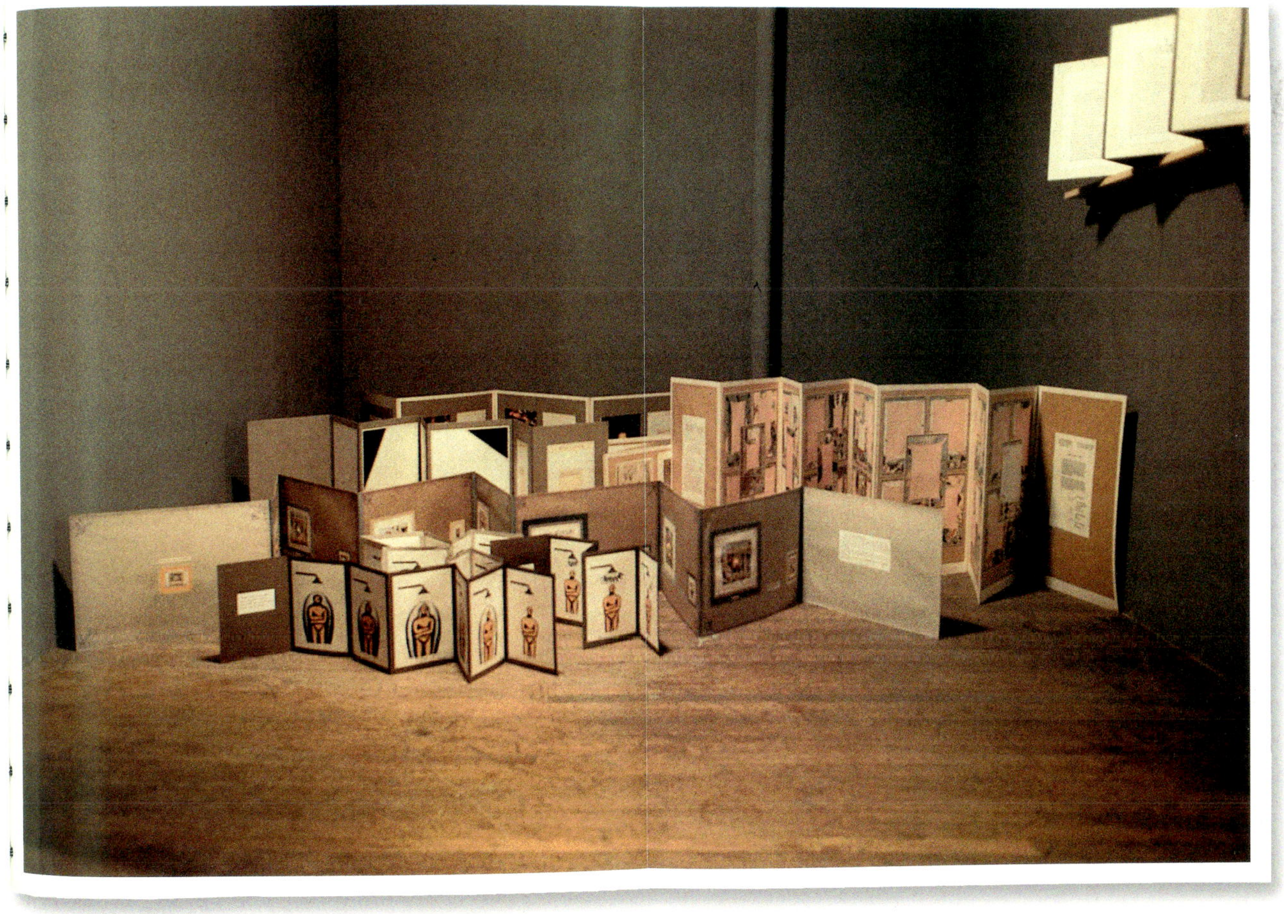

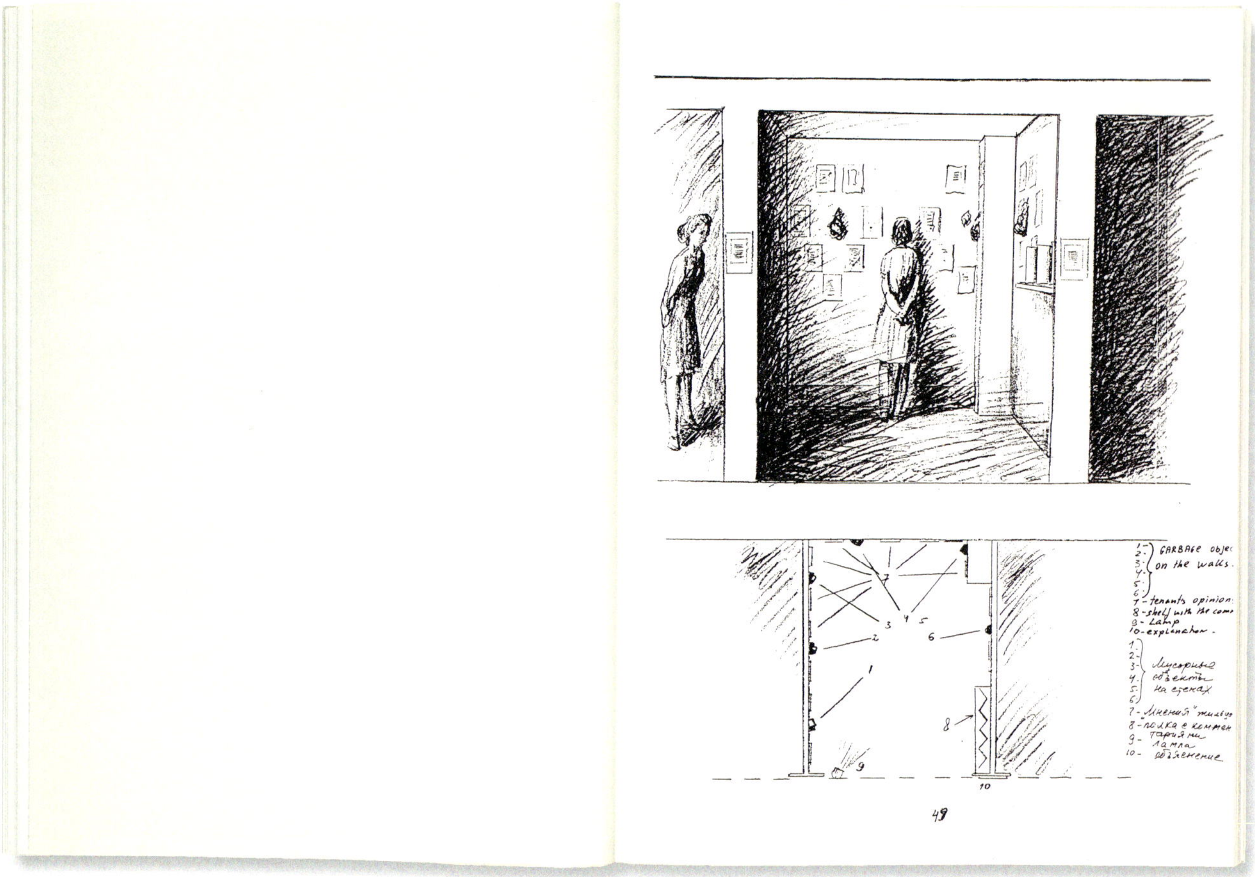
1-
2-
3-
4-
5-
6- GARBAGE objec
on the walls.
7 - tenants opinion:
8 - shelf with the comm
9 - Lamp
10 - explanation.
1-
2-
3-
4-
5-
6- Мусорные
на стенах
8 - полка с коммен
9 - лампа
10
49

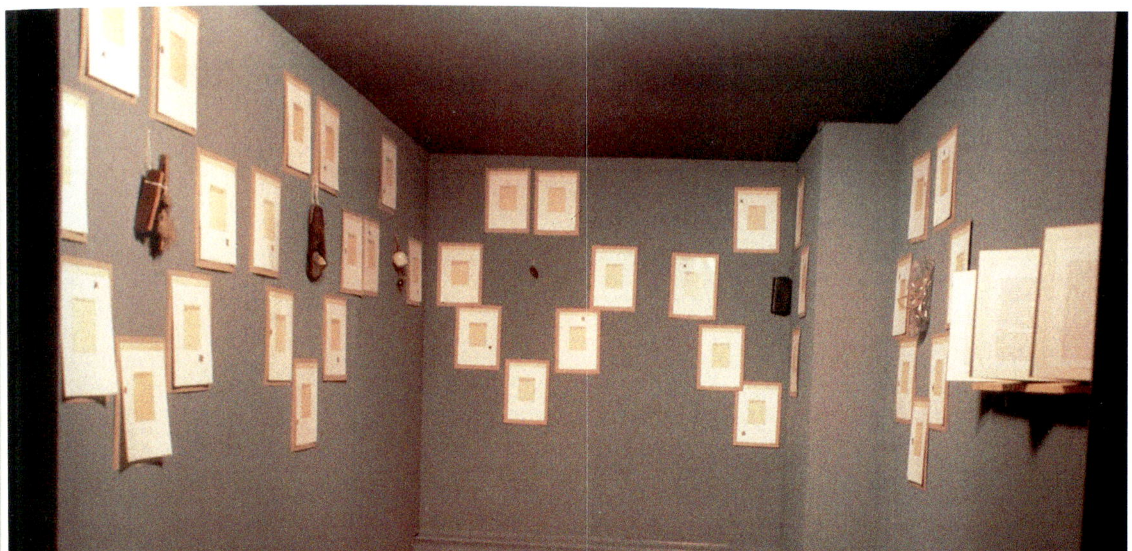

77 The Unhung Painting | *Unaufgehängtes Bild*

1994

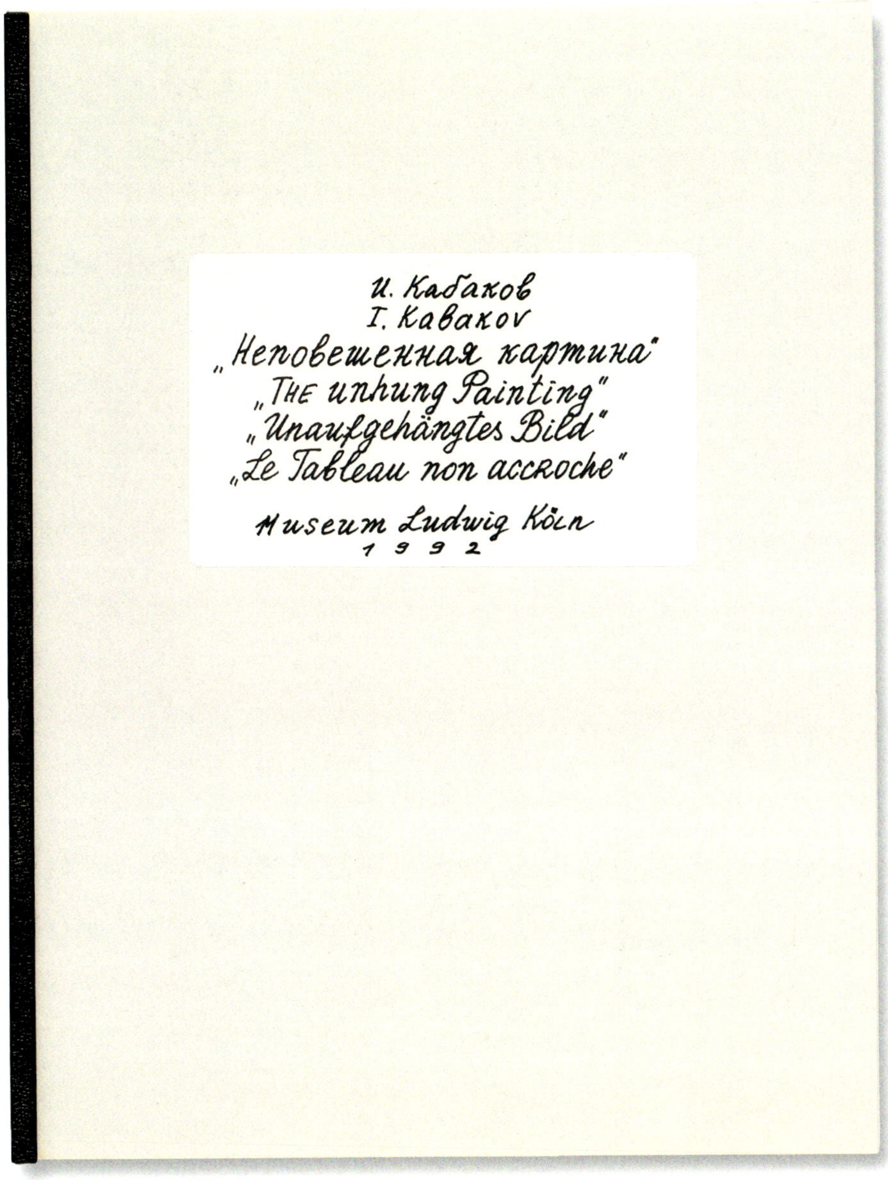

Ilya and Emilia Kabakov
New York: published by Ilya and Emilia Kabakov
27.9 x 21.5 cm
78 photocopied pp. with 45 (9 color incl. 5 foldouts) ills.
quick bind, cardboard cover, label on the cover
Schnellhefter, Kartonumschlag, Etikette auf dem Umschlag
edition: 500 numbered copies with 5 including an original signed, numbered, and dated drawing by Ilya Kabakov from 1994

thematic publication | *thematische Publikation*

layout by Ilya Kabakov | *Layout von Ilya Kabakov*

Documentation of the 1992 installation of the same name in the Museum Ludwig collection, Cologne. Texts by Ilya Kabakov and a dialogue between Boris Groys and Ilya Kabakov on »The Unhung Painting«, which was also published in the book »The Art of Installation«, 1996; Russian, English, German, French.

Dokumentation der gleichnamigen Installation von 1992, Sammlung Museum Ludwig, Köln. Texte von Ilya Kabakov und ein Dialog von Boris Groys und Ilya Kabakov über »Das unaufgehängte Bild«, der auch im Buch »Die Kunst der Installation«, 1996 erschien; russisch, englisch, deutsch, französisch.

see also | *siehe auch* no. 91; CRI, vol. 1, no. 64, pp. 420–425; CRP, vol. 1, no. 72, pp. 139–140

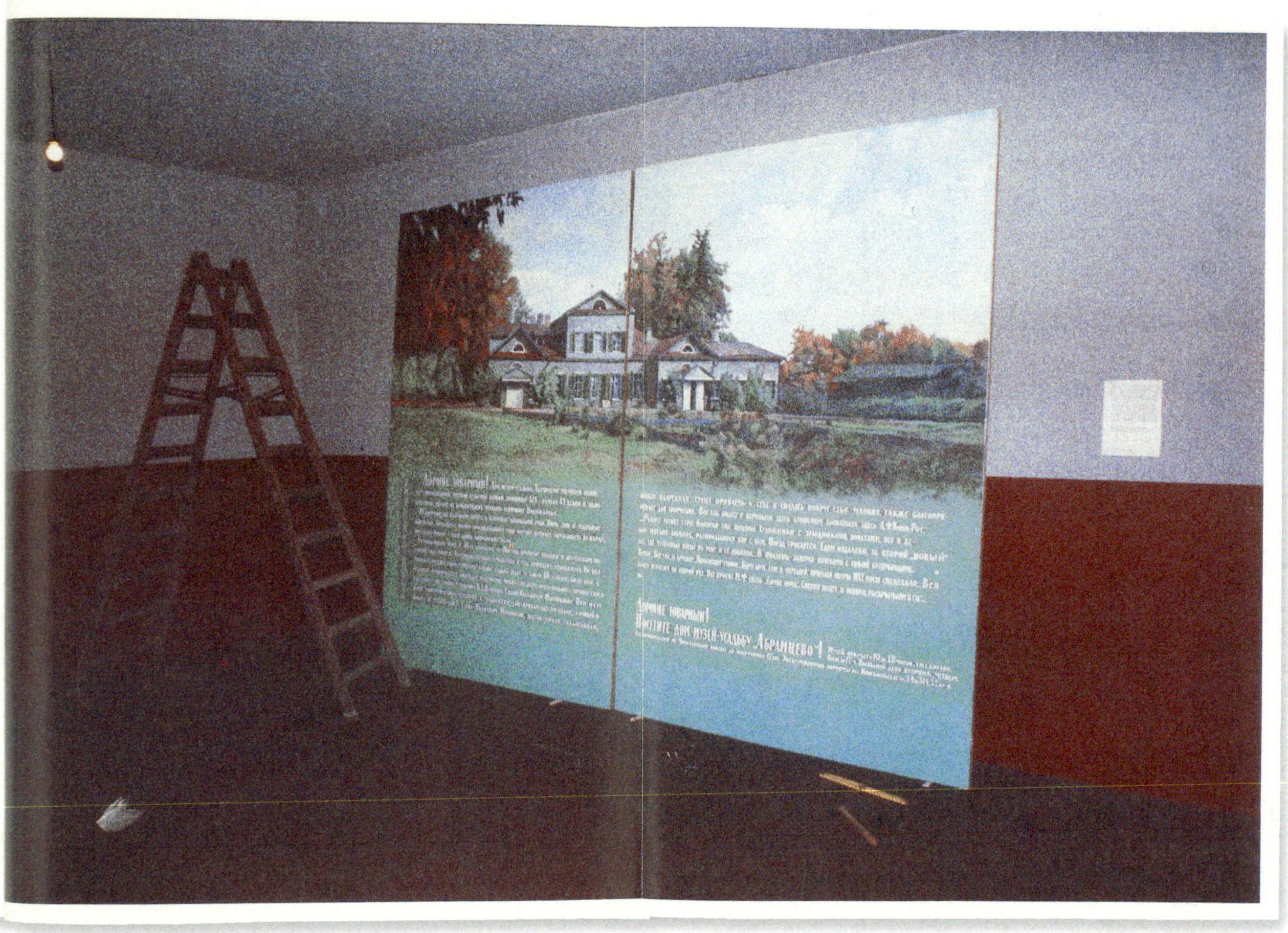
Дорогие товарищи!
Посетите дом-музей-усадьбу „Абрамцево“!

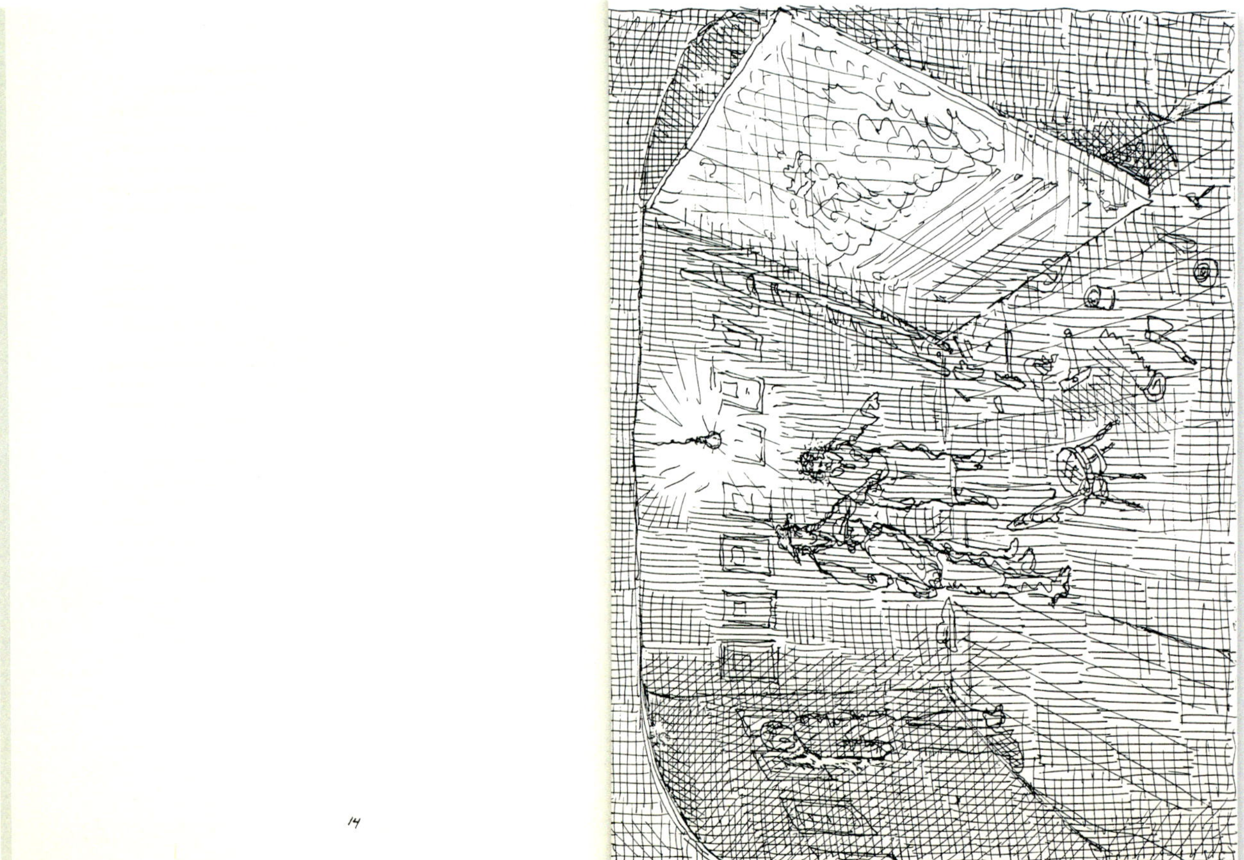
14

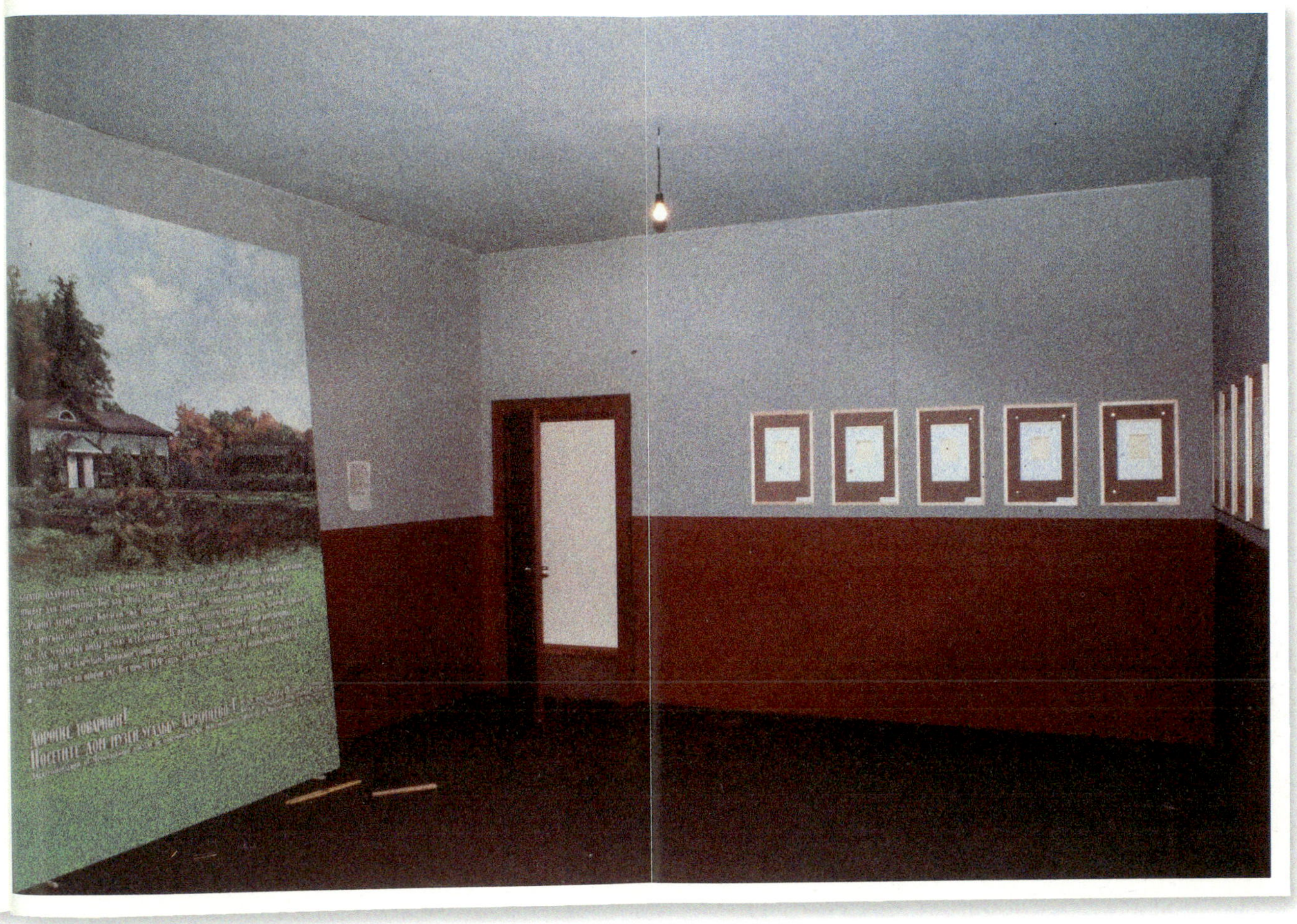

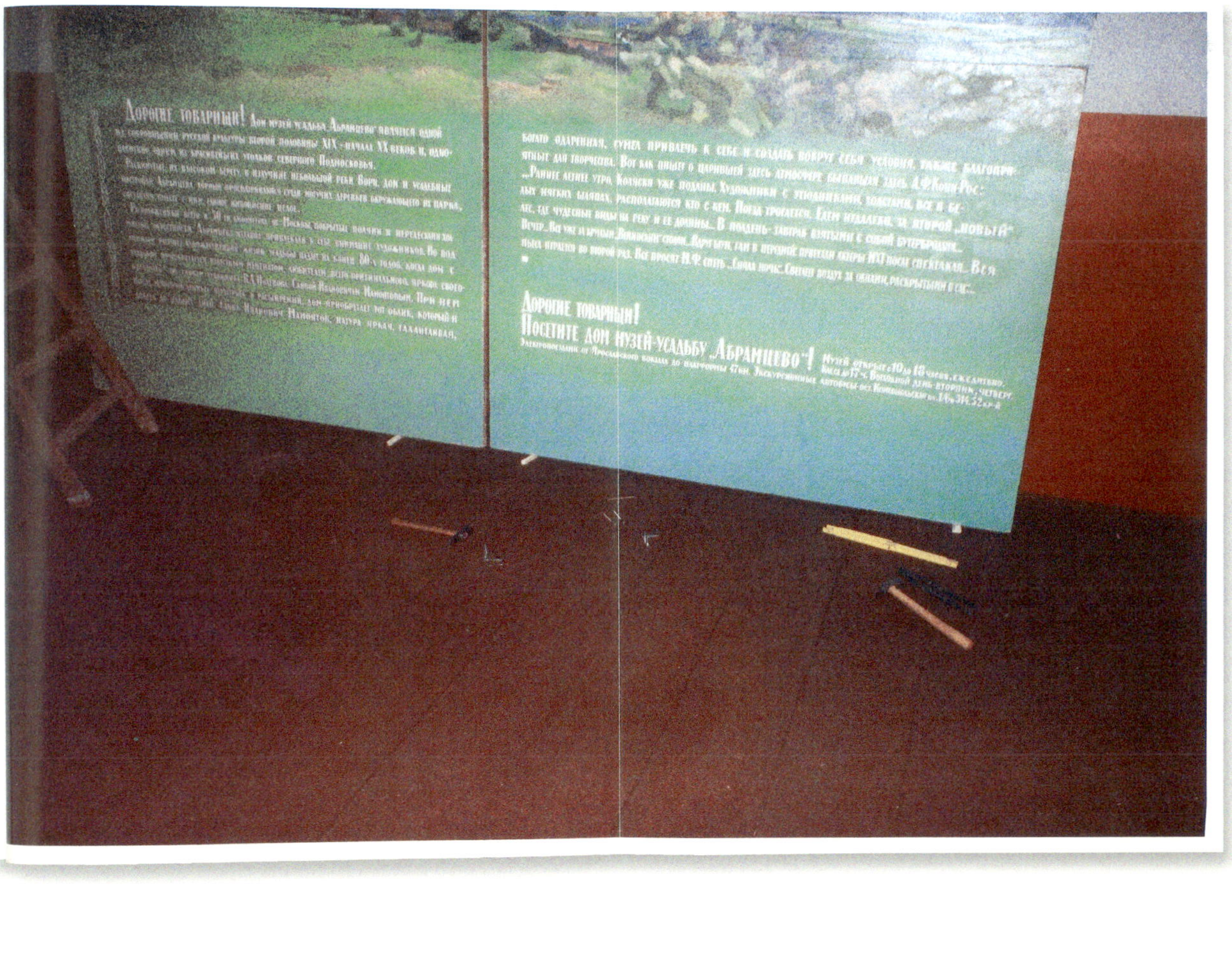
Дорогие товарищи!
Посетите дом музей-усадьбу „Абрамцево"!

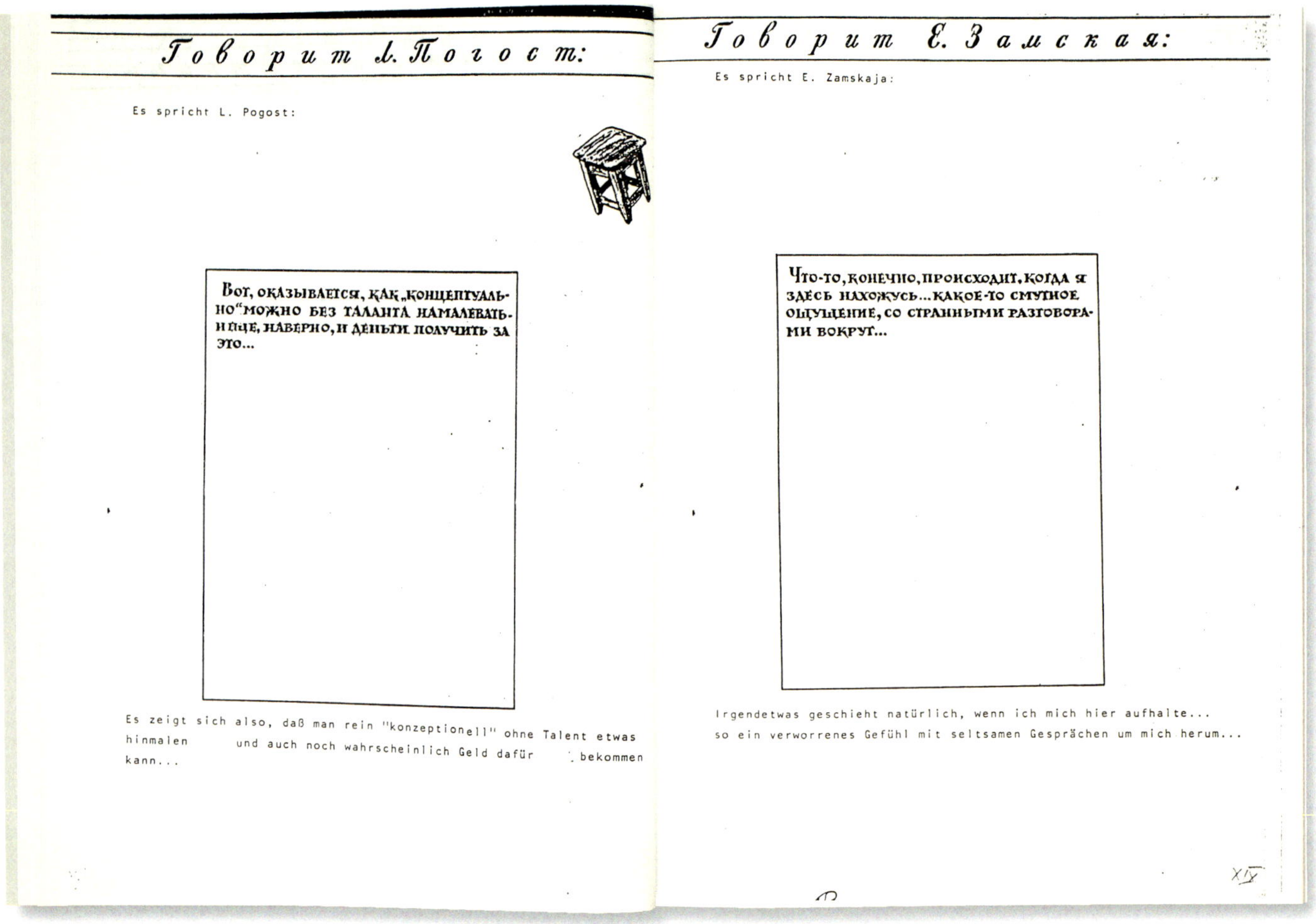
Говорит Л. Погост:
Es spricht L. Pogost:
Вот, оказывается, как „концептуально“ можно без таланта намалевать-нечто, наверно, и деньги получить за это...
Es zeigt sich also, daß man rein "konzeptionell" ohne Talent etwas hinmalen und auch noch wahrscheinlich Geld dafür bekommen kann...
Говорит Е. Замская:
Es spricht E. Zamskaja:
Что-то, конечно, происходит, когда я здесь нахожусь... какое-то смутное ощущение, со странными разговорами вокруг...
Irgendetwas geschieht natürlich, wenn ich mich hier aufhalte...
so ein verworrenes Gefühl mit seltsamen Gesprächen um mich herum...
XIV

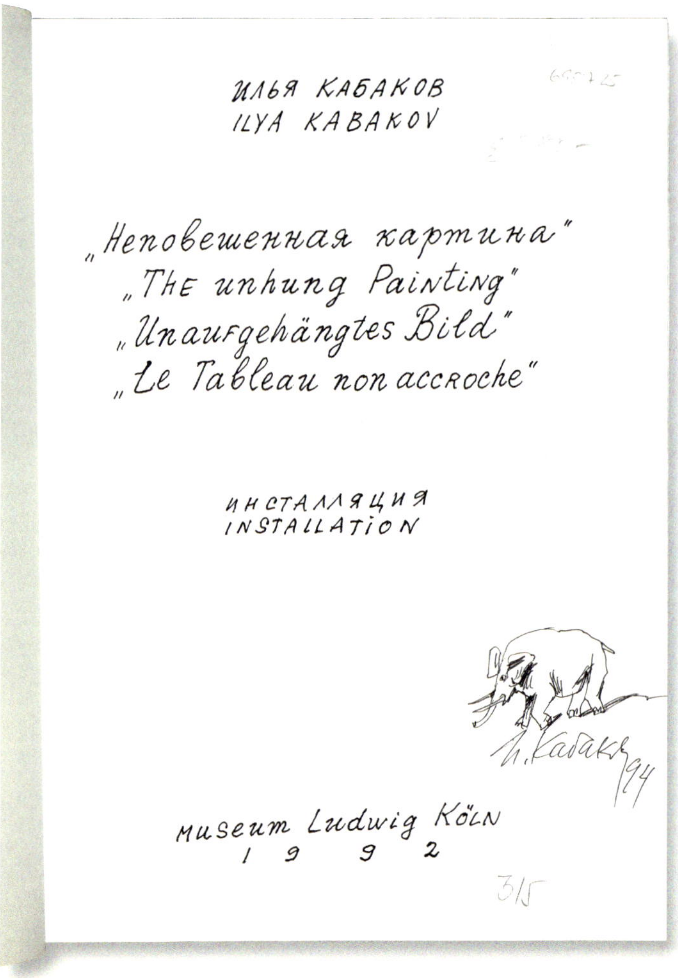
ИЛЬЯ КАБАКОВ
ILYA KABAKOV
„Неповешенная картина"
„The unhung Painting"
„Unaufgehängtes Bild"
„Le Tableau non accroche"
ИНСТАЛЛЯЦИЯ
INSTALLATION
И. Кабаков 94
Museum Ludwig Köln
1 9 9 2
315

78 The Red Pavilion | *Roter Pavillon*

1994

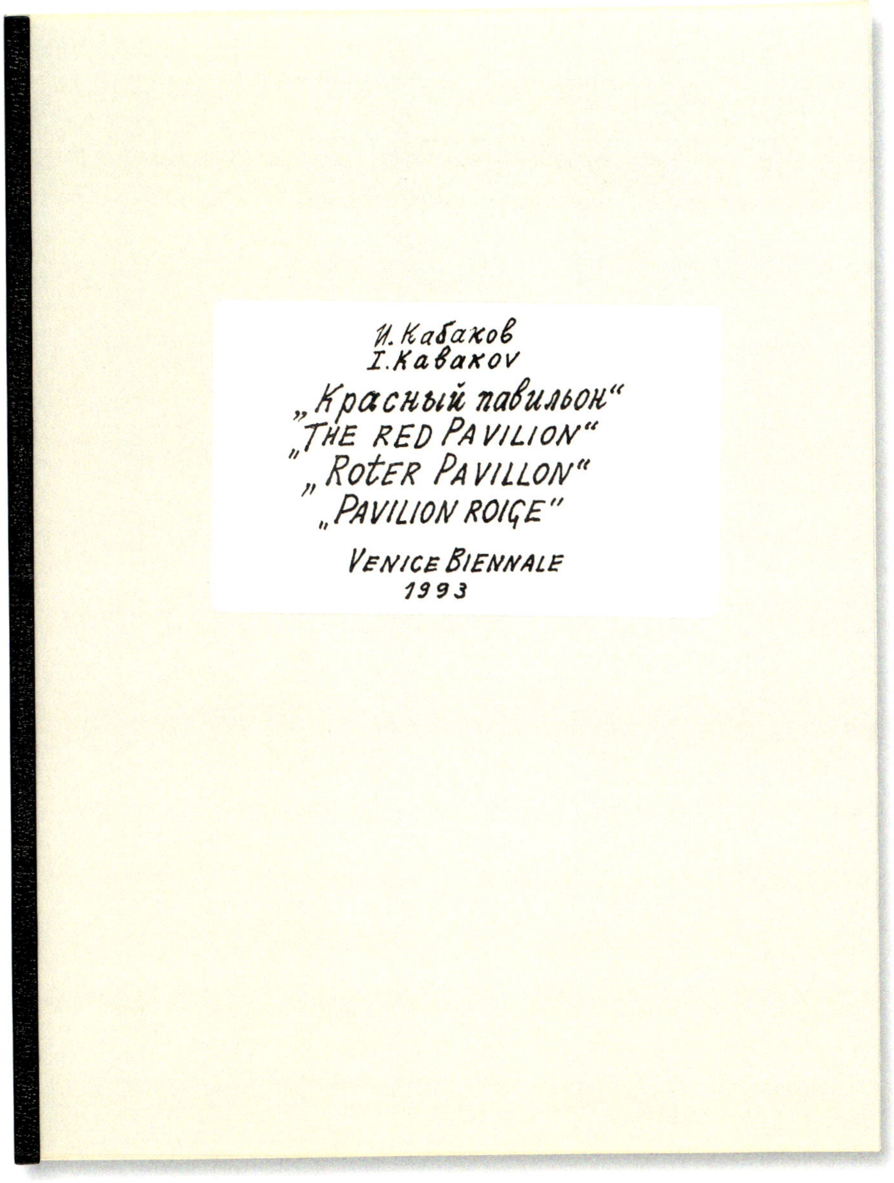

Ilya and Emilia Kabakov
New York: published by Ilya and Emilia Kabakov
27.9 x 21.5 cm
92 photocopied pp. with 16 b/w (incl. 4 foldouts) and 21 color (incl. 5 foldouts) ills.
quick bind, cardboard cover, label on the cover
Schnellhefter, Kartonumschlag, Etikette auf dem Umschlag
edition: 500 numbered copies with 5 including an original signed and dated drawing by Ilya Kabakov from 1994

thematic publication | *thematische Publikation*

layout by Ilya Kabakov | *Layout von Ilya Kabakov*

Documentation of the installation of the same name in cooperation with the composer Vladimir Tarasov at the 45th Biennale, Venice, June 14 to September 14, 1993. Texts by Ilya Kabakov and a dialogue between Boris Groys and Ilya Kabakov on »The Biennale«, which was also published in 1996 in the book »The Art of Installation«; Russian, English, German, French.

Dokumentation der gleichnamigen Installation in Zusammenarbeit mit dem Komponisten Vladimir Tarasov, 45. Biennale, Venedig, 14. Juni – 14. September 1993. Texte von Ilya Kabakov und ein Dialog von Boris Groys und Ilya Kabakov über »Die Biennale«, der 1996 auch im Buch »Die Kunst der Installation« erschien; russisch, englisch, deutsch, französisch.

see also | *siehe auch* no. 60; no. 91; CRI, vol. 1, no. 70, pp. 454–459

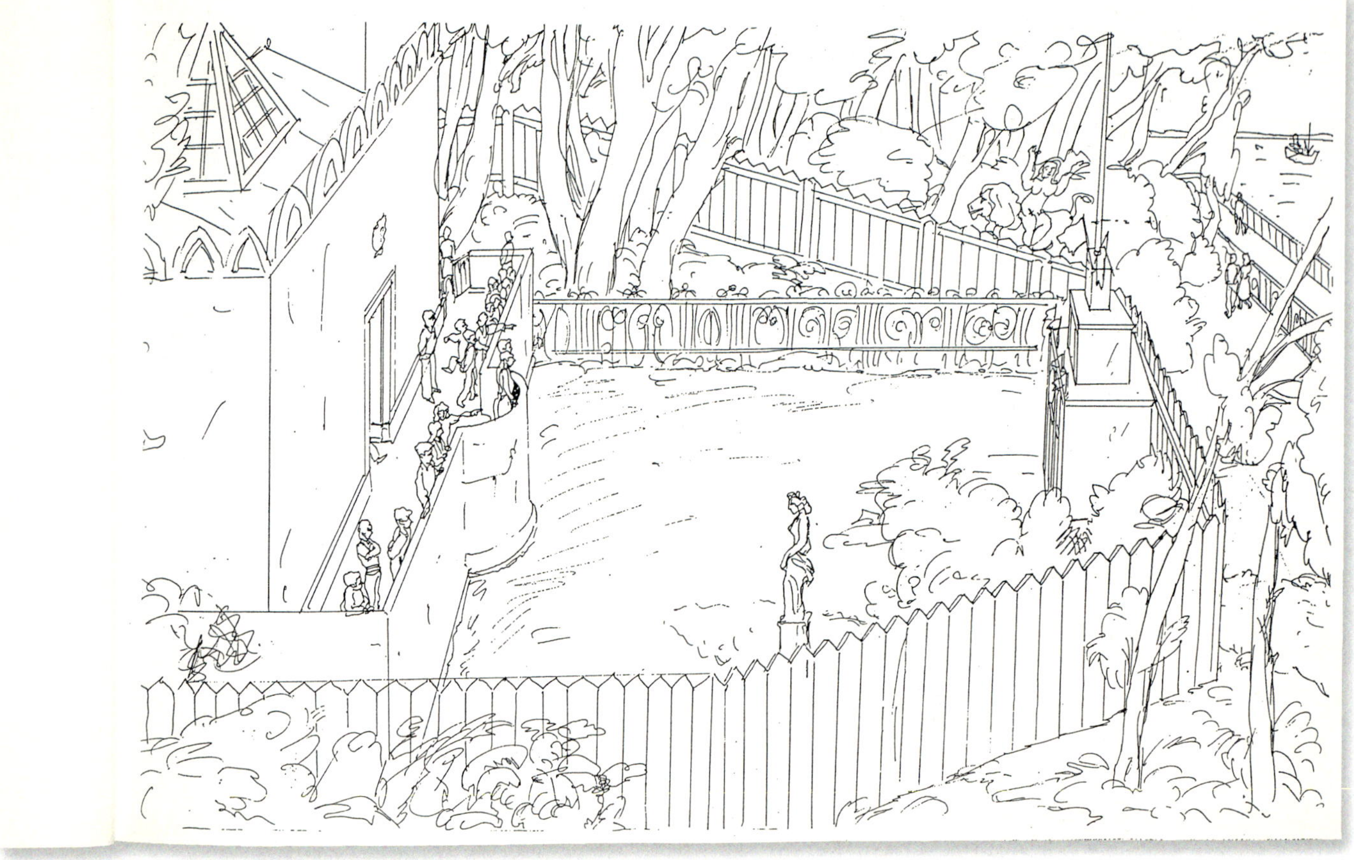

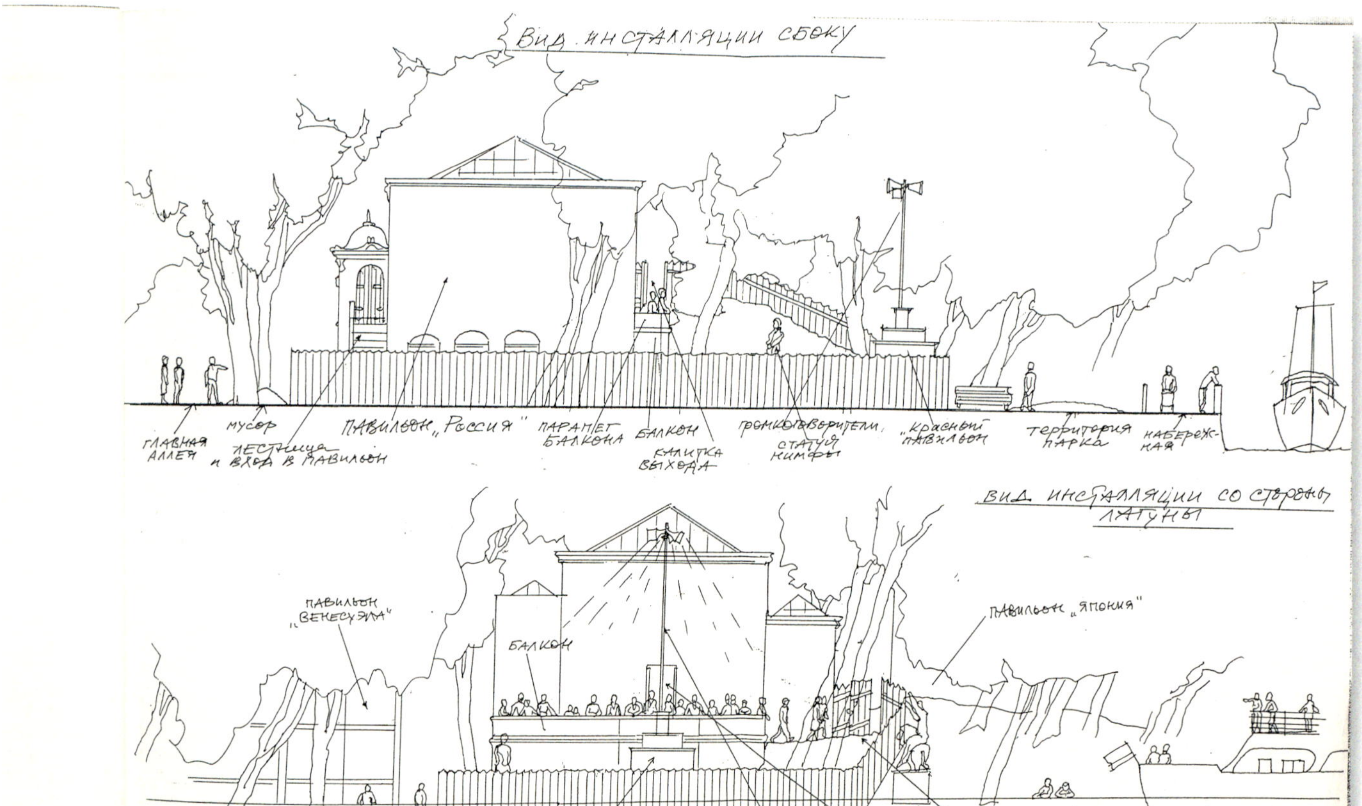
ВИД ИНСТАЛЛЯЦИИ СБОКУ
ГЛАВНАЯ АЛЛЕЯ
МУСОР
ЛЕСТНИЦА И ВХОД В ПАВИЛЬОН
ПАВИЛЬОН „РОССИЯ"
ПАРАПЕТ БАЛКОНА
БАЛКОН
КАЛИТКА ВЫХОДА
ГРОМКОГОВОРИТЕЛИ
СТАТУЯ НИМФЫ
„КРАСНЫЙ ПАВИЛЬОН"
ТЕРРИТОРИЯ ПАРКА
НАБЕРЕЖНАЯ
ВИД ИНСТАЛЛЯЦИИ СО СТОРОНЫ ЛАГУНЫ
ПАВИЛЬОН „ВЕНЕСУЭЛА"
БАЛКОН
ПАВИЛЬОН „ЯПОНИЯ"
НАБЕРЕЖНАЯ
ЗАБОР
„КРАСНЫЙ ПАВИЛЬОН"
МАЧТА
ДВЕРЬ ИЗ ПАВИЛЬОНА НА БАЛКОН
КАЛИТКА. ВЫХОД

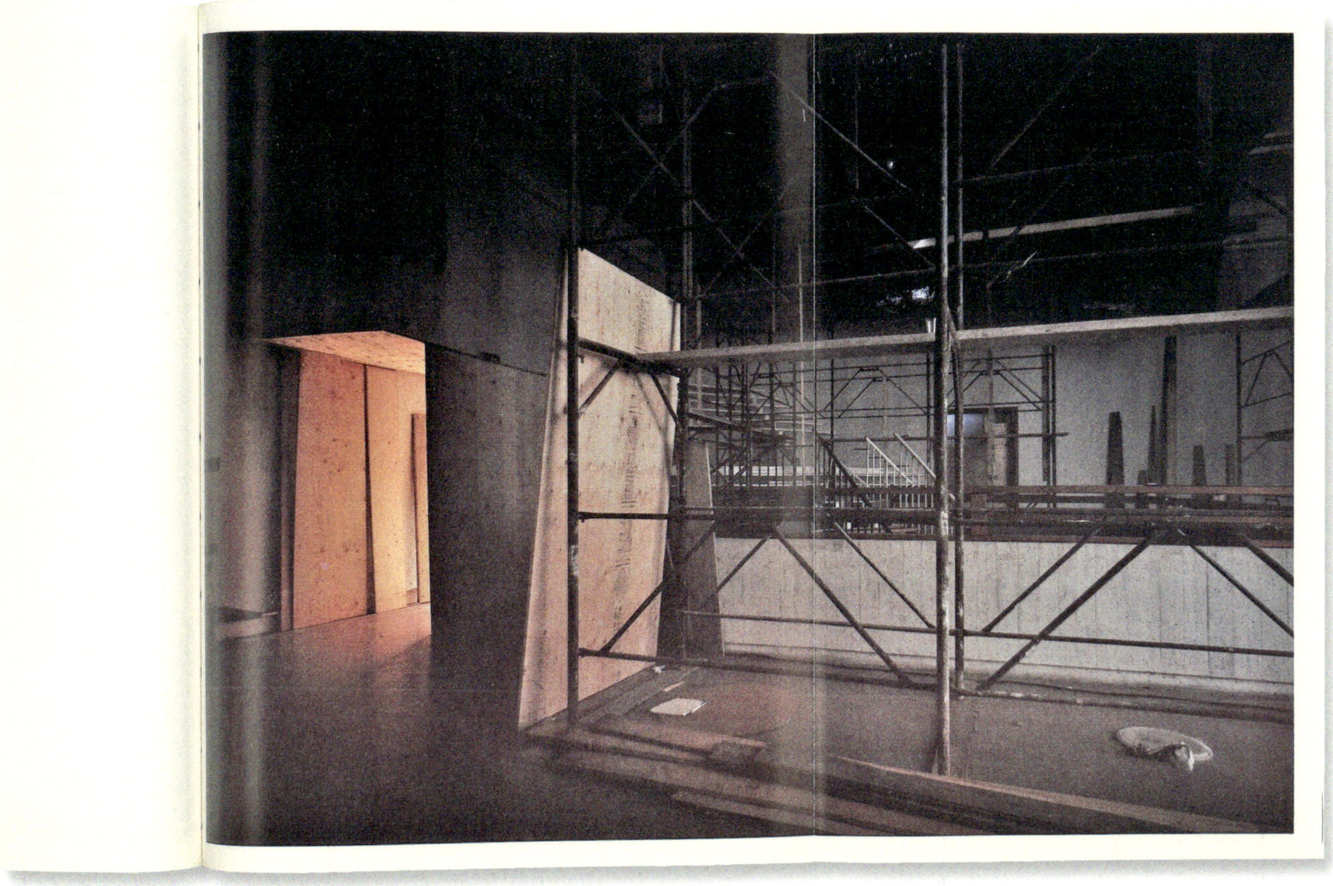

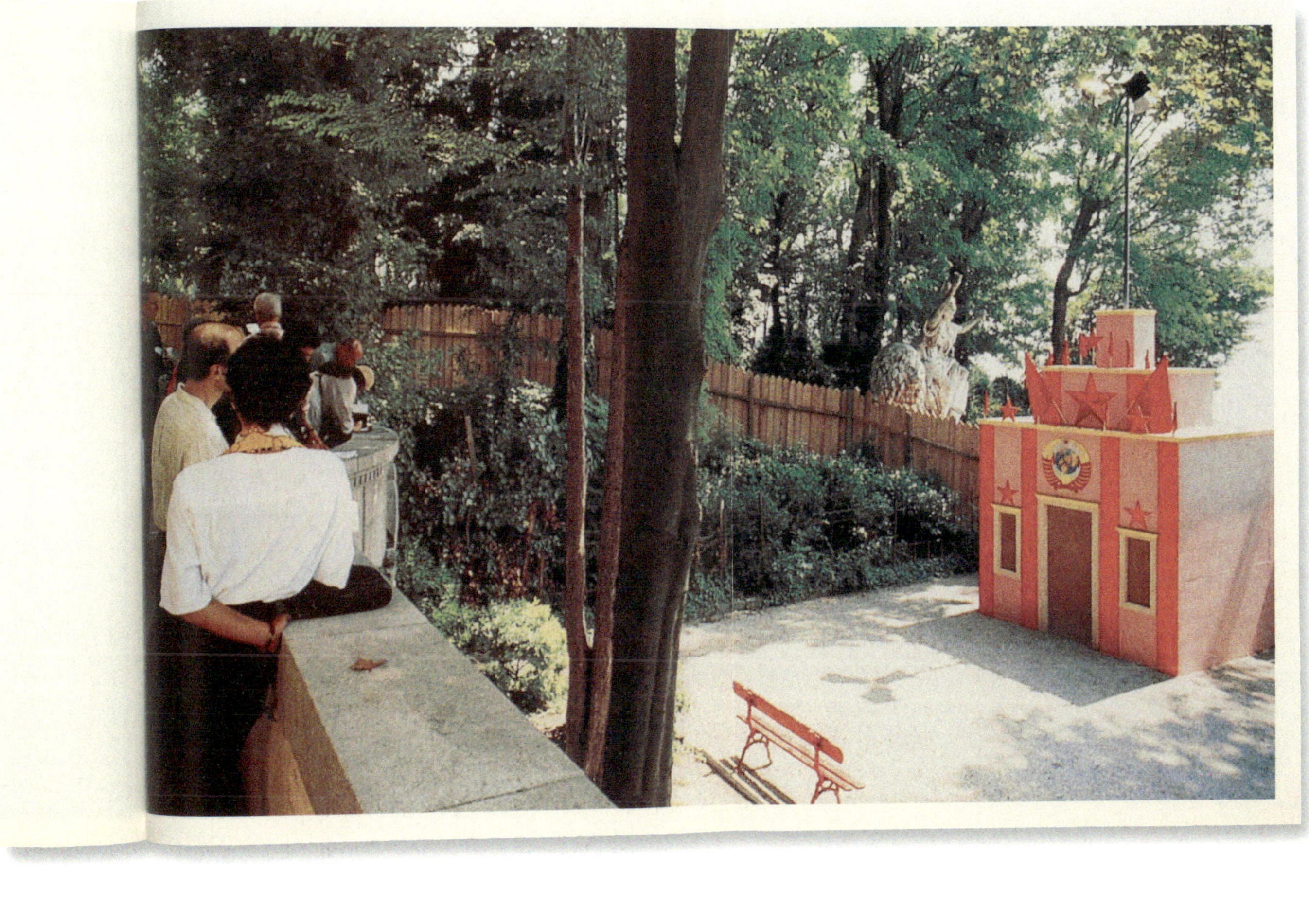

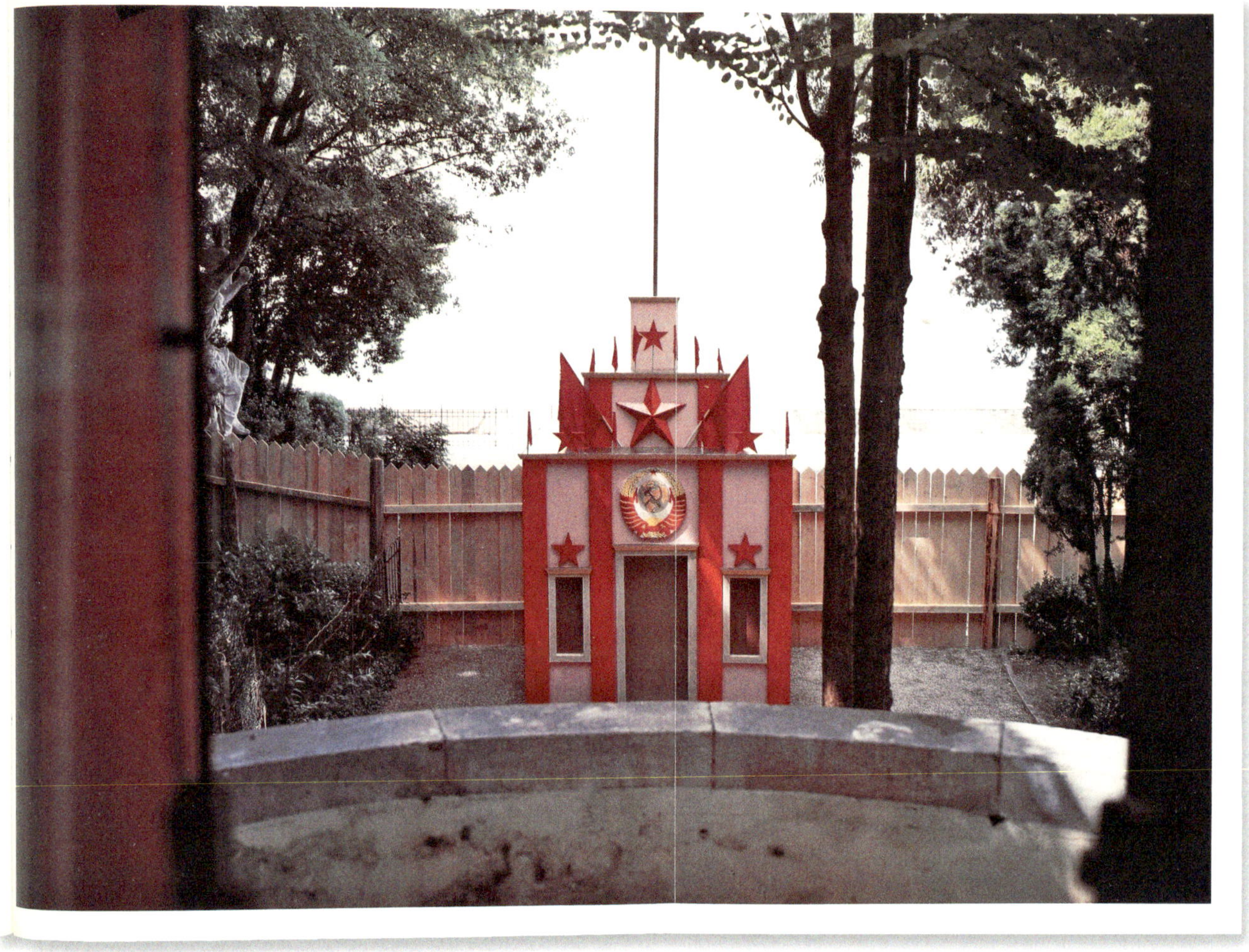

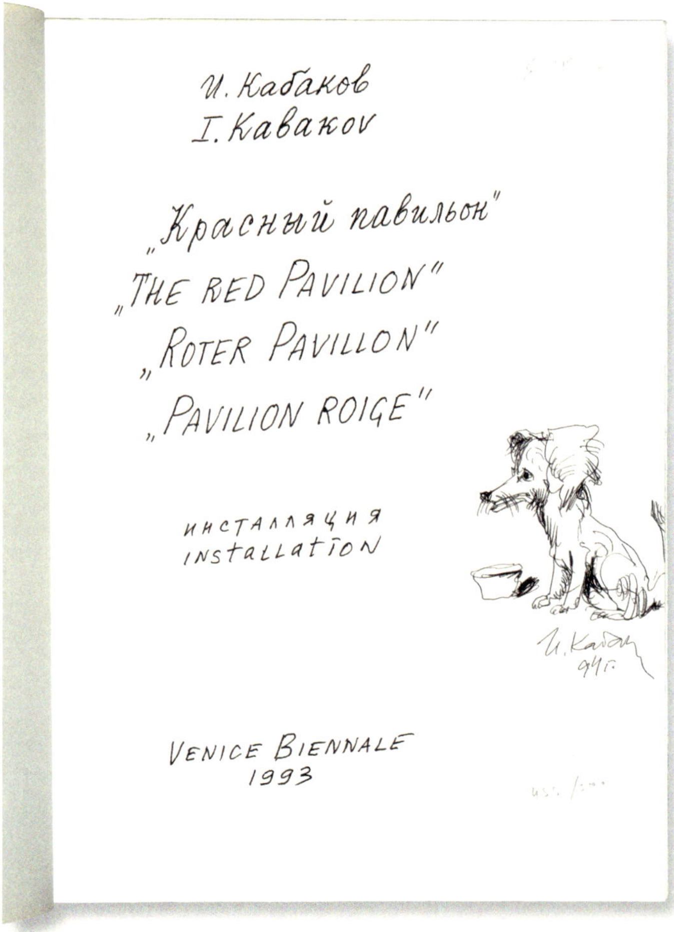
И. Кабаков
I. Kabakov

„Красный павильон"
„The Red Pavilion"
„Roter Pavillon"
„Pavilion Roige"

инсталляция
installation

Venice Biennale
1993

79 The Boat of My Life | *Das Boot meines Lebens*

1994

Ilya and Emilia Kabakov
New York: published by Ilya and Emilia Kabakov
27.9 x 21.5 cm
183 photocopied pp. with 18 (10 color incl. 4 foldouts) ills.
quick bind, cardboard cover, label on the cover
Schnellhefter, Kartonumschlag, Etikette auf dem Umschlag
edition: 500 numbered copies

thematic publication | *thematische Publikation*

layout by Ilya Kabakov | *Layout von Ilya Kabakov*

Documentation of the installation of the same name at the Salzburger Kunstverein, Salzburg, August 11 to October 13, 1993. Texts by Ilya Kabakov; Russian, English, German, French.

Dokumentation der gleichnamigen Installation, Salzburger Kunstverein, Salzburg, 11. August – 13. Oktober 1993. Texte von Ilya Kabakov; russisch, englisch, deutsch, französisch.

see also | *siehe auch* no. 70; CRI, vol. 1, no. 72, pp. 464–469

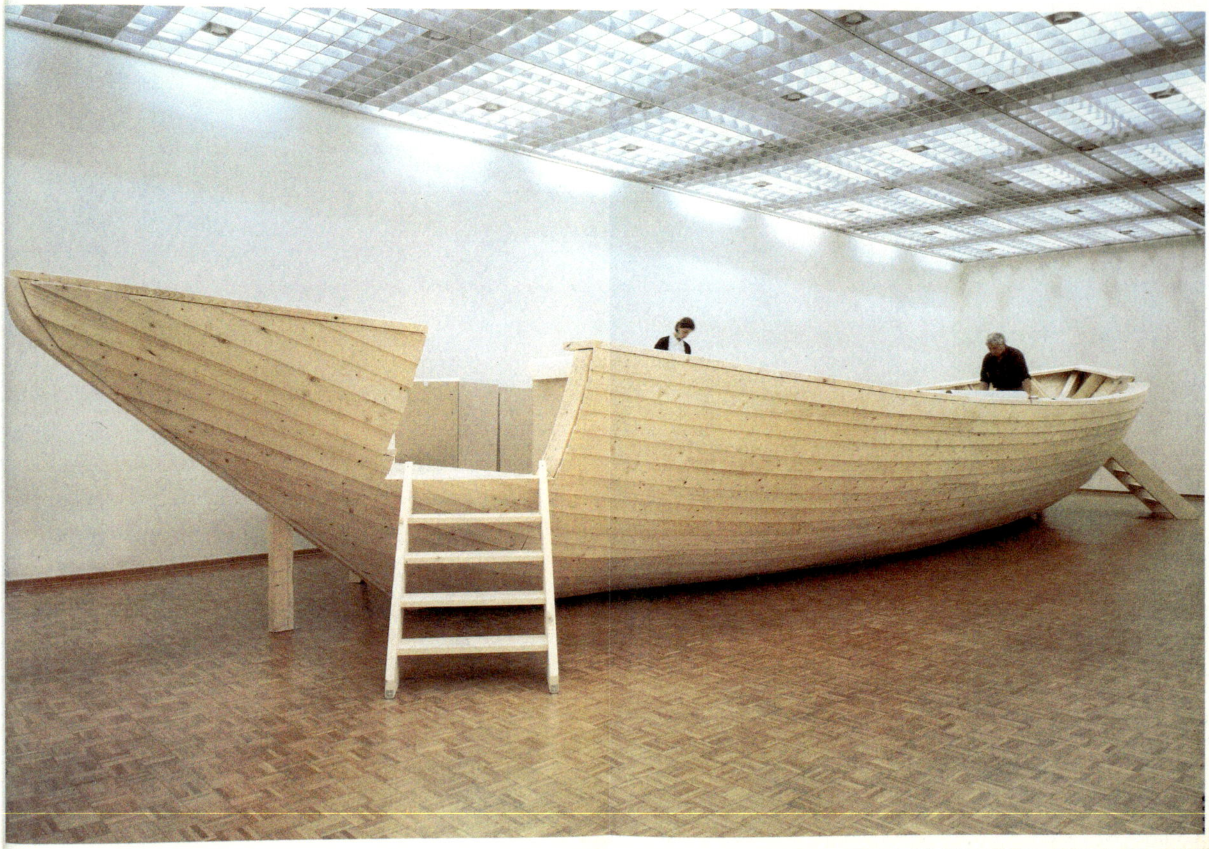

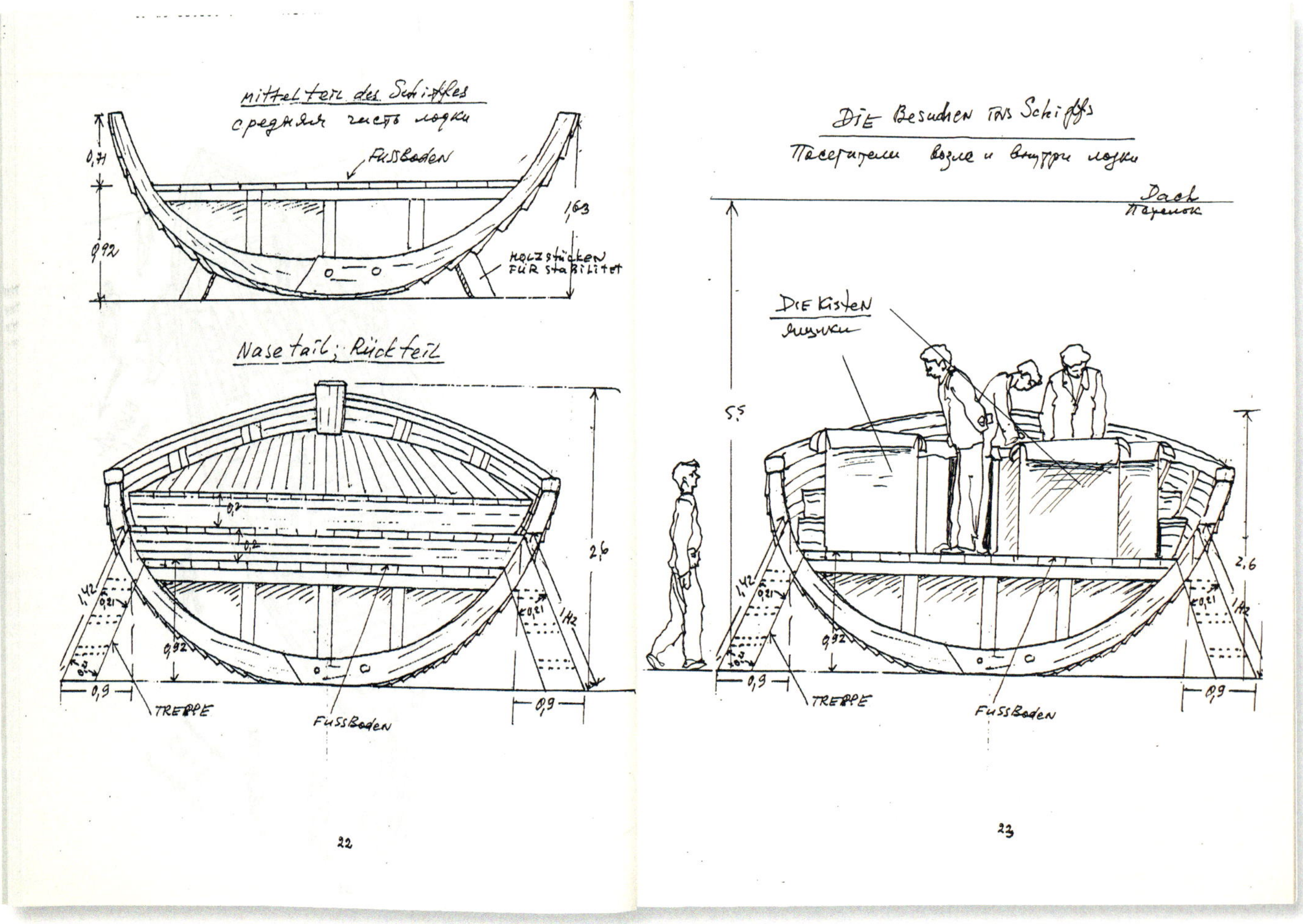
mittelteil des Schiffes
средняя часть лодки
Fussboden
0,71
0,92
1,63
Holzstücken für Stabilität
Nase teil; Rückteil
0,2
0,2
2,6
1,42
0,21
0,92
0,9
Treppe
Fussboden
0,9
22
Die Besucher des Schiffs
Посетители возле и внутри лодки
Dach
Die Kisten
ящики
5,5
2,6
1,42
0,21
0,92
0,9
Treppe
Fussboden
0,9
23

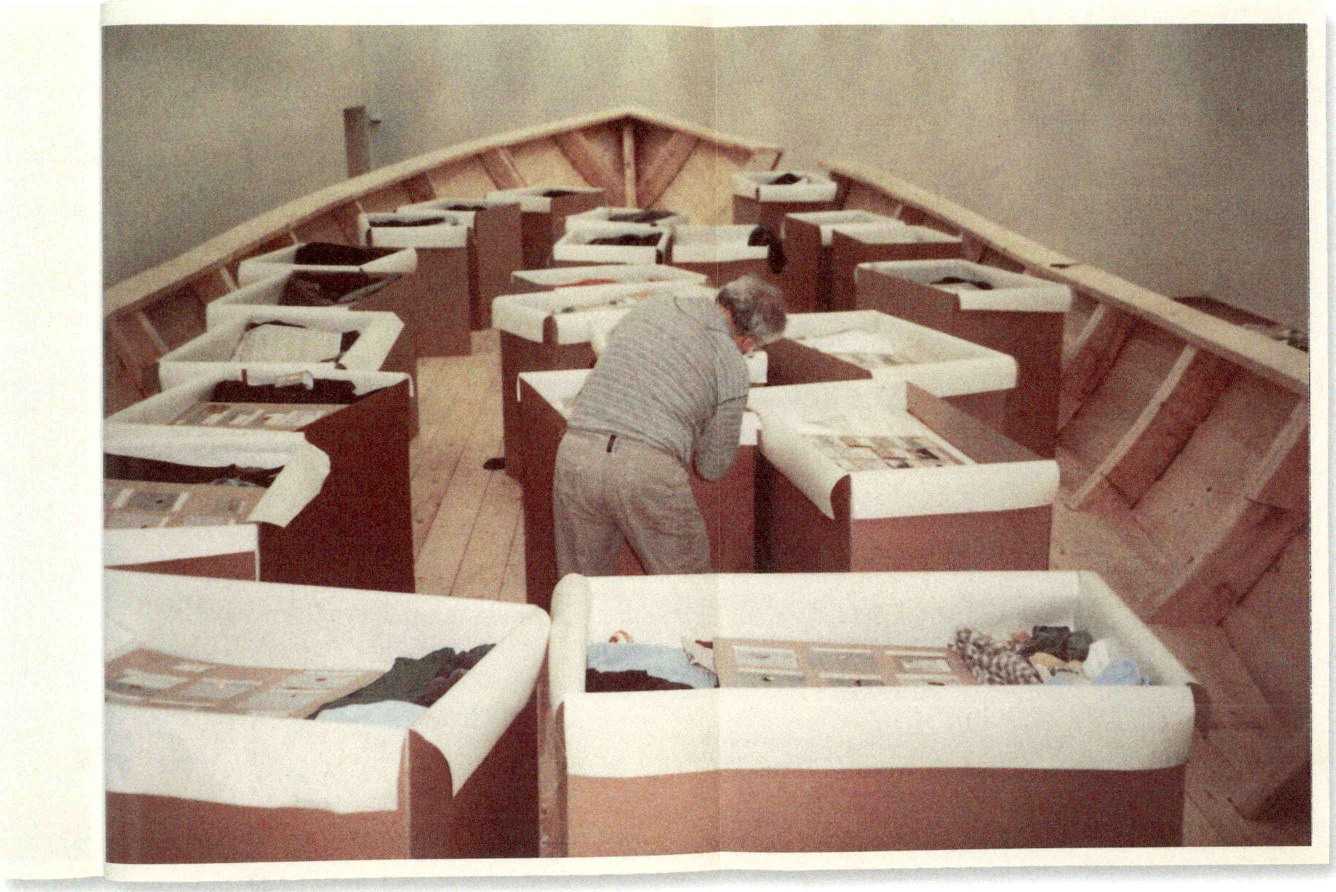

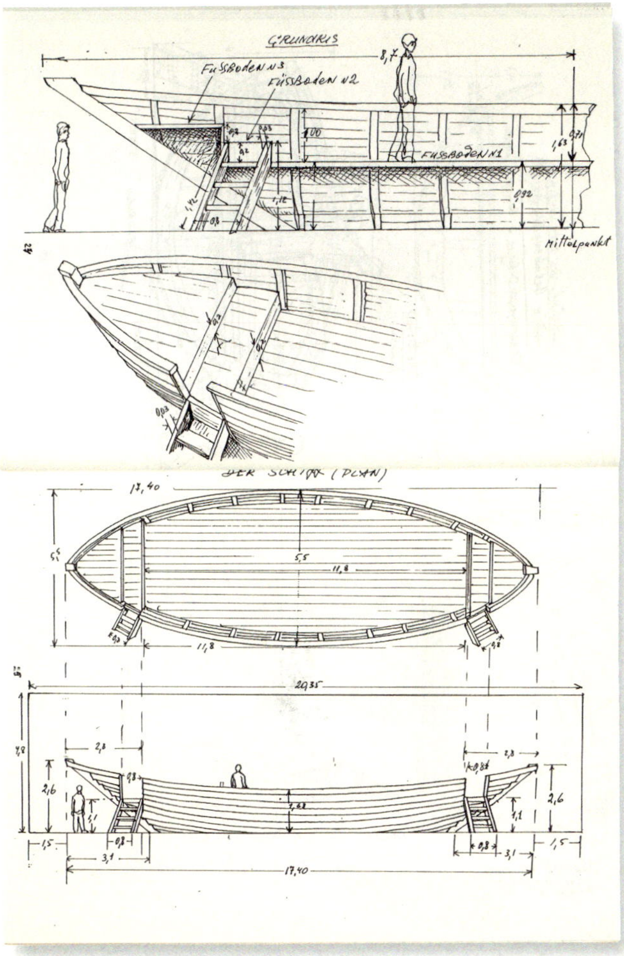
GRUNDRISS
FUSSBODEN N3
FUSSBODEN N2
FUSSBODEN N1
Mittelpunkt
DER SCHIFF (PLAN)

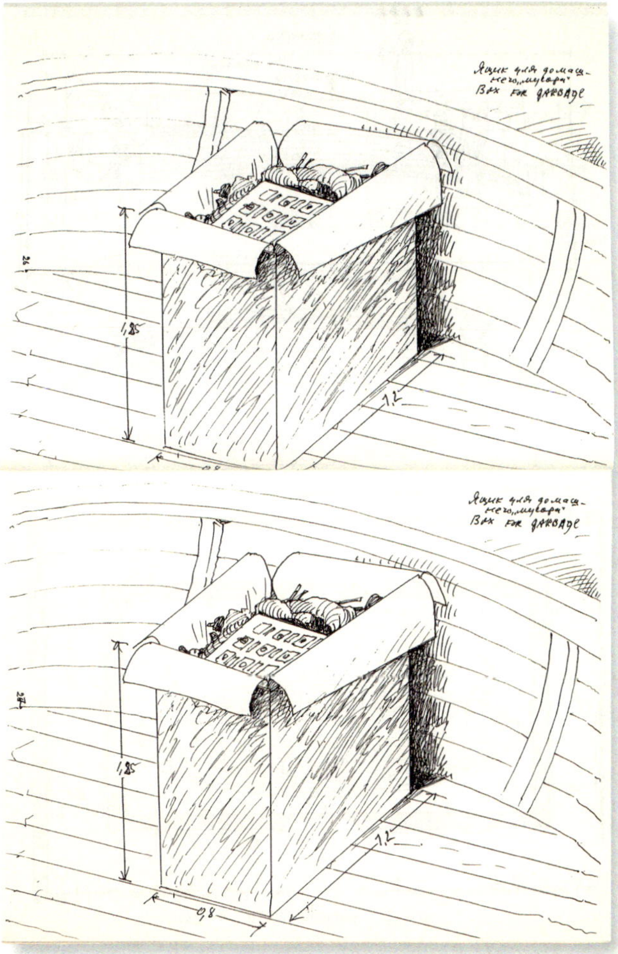
BOX FOR GARBAGE
BOX FOR GARBAGE

80 Installations 1983–1995 | *Installationen 1983–1995*

1995

Centre national d'art et de culture Georges Pompidou Paris: Centre national d'art et de culture Georges Pompidou
30.6 x 24 cm
259 pp. with 336 (272 color) ills.
stitchbound, clothbound, blind blocking with label
Fadenheftung, Leinen, Blindprägung mit Etikette

exhibition catalogue | *Ausstellungskatalog*

idea by Ilya Kabakov | *Idee von Ilya Kabakov*

For the installation »We Live Here« at the Forum des Centre national d'art et de culture Georges Pompidou, Paris, May 17 to September 4, 1995. Texts by François Barré, Boris Groys, Ilya Kabakov, Jean-Hubert Martin, Robert Storr, and a dialogue between Ilya Kabakov and Nadine Pouillon on »The Museum: Temple or Garbage Pit?« Catalogue of Kabakov's installations from 1983 to 1995; French.

Zur Installation »Wir leben hier«, Forum des Centre national d'art et de culture Georges Pompidou, Paris, 17. Mai – 4. September 1995. Texte von François Barré, Boris Groys, Ilya Kabakov, Jean-Hubert Martin, Robert Storr und ein Dialog von Ilya Kabakov und Nadine Pouillon über »Das Museum: Tempel oder Müllgrube?« Verzeichnis der Kabakov-Installationen von 1983 bis 1995; französisch.

see also | *siehe auch*

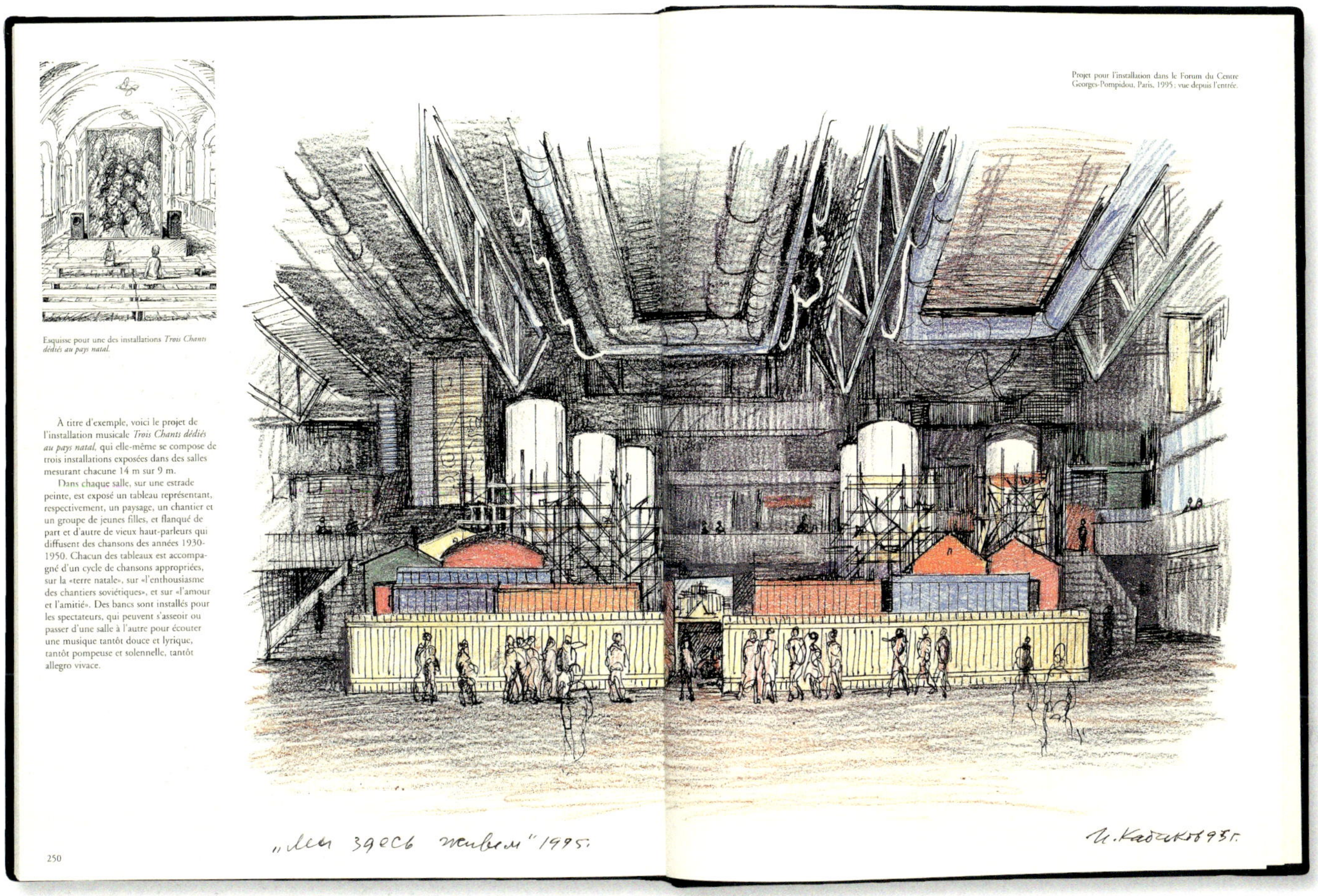

Esquisse pour une des installations *Trois Chants dédiés au pays natal.*

À titre d'exemple, voici le projet de l'installation musicale *Trois Chants dédiés au pays natal,* qui elle-même se compose de trois installations exposées dans des salles mesurant chacune 14 m sur 9 m.

Dans chaque salle, sur une estrade peinte, est exposé un tableau représentant, respectivement, un paysage, un chantier et un groupe de jeunes filles, et flanqué de part et d'autre de vieux haut-parleurs qui diffusent des chansons des années 1930-1950. Chacun des tableaux est accompagné d'un cycle de chansons appropriées, sur la «terre natale», sur «l'enthousiasme des chantiers soviétiques», et sur «l'amour et l'amitié». Des bancs sont installés pour les spectateurs, qui peuvent s'asseoir ou passer d'une salle à l'autre pour écouter une musique tantôt douce et lyrique, tantôt pompeuse et solennelle, tantôt allegro vivace.

Projet pour l'installation dans le Forum du Centre Georges-Pompidou, Paris, 1995 ; vue depuis l'entrée.

250

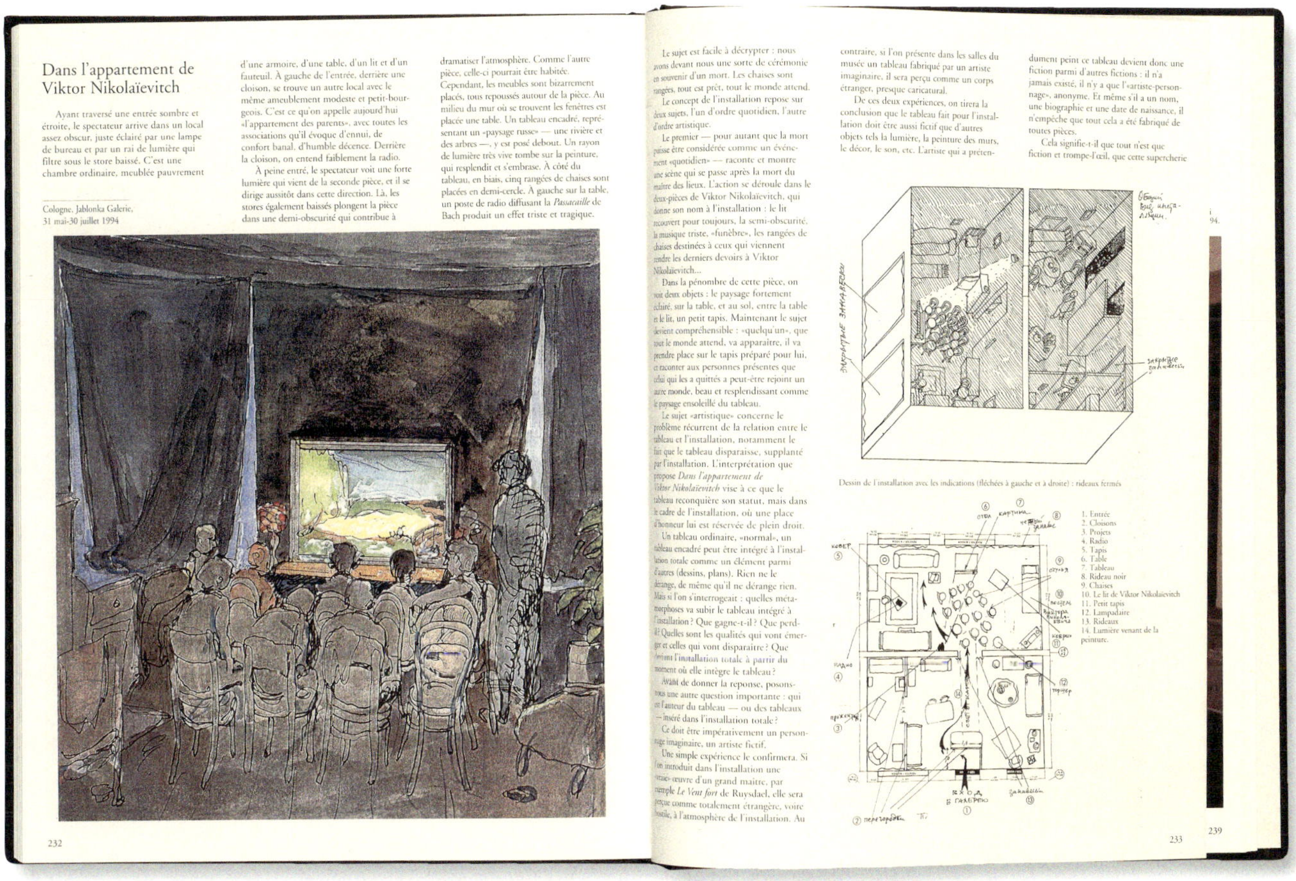

Dans l'appartement de Viktor Nikolaïevitch

Ayant traversé une entrée sombre et étroite, le spectateur arrive dans un local assez obscur, juste éclairé par une lampe de bureau et par un rai de lumière qui filtre sous le store baissé. C'est une chambre ordinaire, meublée pauvrement d'une armoire, d'une table, d'un lit et d'un fauteuil. À gauche de l'entrée, derrière une cloison, se trouve un autre local avec le même ameublement modeste et petit-bourgeois. C'est ce qu'on appelle aujourd'hui «l'appartement des parents», avec toutes les associations qu'il évoque d'ennui, de confort banal, d'humble décence. Derrière la cloison, on entend faiblement la radio.

À peine entré, le spectateur voit une forte lumière qui vient de la seconde pièce, et il se dirige aussitôt dans cette direction. Là, les stores également baissés plongent la pièce dans une demi-obscurité qui contribue à dramatiser l'atmosphère. Comme l'autre pièce, celle-ci pourrait être habitée. Cependant, les meubles sont bizarrement placés, tous repoussés autour de la pièce. Au milieu du mur où se trouvent les fenêtres est placée une table. Un tableau encadré, représentant un «paysage russe» — une rivière et des arbres —, y est posé debout. Un rayon de lumière très vive tombe sur la peinture, qui resplendit et s'embrase. À côté du tableau, en biais, cinq rangées de chaises sont placées en demi-cercle. À gauche sur la table, un poste de radio diffusant la *Passacaille* de Bach produit un effet triste et tragique.

Cologne, Jablonka Galerie,
31 mai-30 juillet 1994

232

Le sujet est facile à décrypter : nous avons devant nous une sorte de cérémonie en souvenir d'un mort. Les chaises sont rangées, tout est prêt, tout le monde attend.

Le concept de l'installation repose sur deux sujets, l'un d'ordre quotidien, l'autre d'ordre artistique.

Le premier — pour autant que la mort puisse être considérée comme un événement «quotidien» — raconte et montre une scène qui se passe après la mort du maître des lieux. L'action se déroule dans le deux-pièces de Viktor Nikolaïevitch, qui donne son nom à l'installation : le lit recouvert pour toujours, la semi-obscurité, la musique triste, «funèbre», les rangées de chaises destinées à ceux qui viennent rendre les derniers devoirs à Viktor Nikolaïevitch...

Dans la pénombre de cette pièce, on voit deux objets : le paysage fortement éclairé, sur la table, et au sol, entre la table et le lit, un petit tapis. Maintenant le sujet devient compréhensible : «quelqu'un», que tout le monde attend, va apparaître, il va prendre place sur le tapis préparé pour lui, et raconter aux personnes présentes que celui qui les a quittés a peut-être rejoint un autre monde, beau et resplendissant comme le paysage ensoleillé du tableau.

Le sujet «artistique» concerne le problème récurrent de la relation entre le tableau et l'installation, notamment le fait que le tableau disparaisse, supplanté par l'installation. L'interprétation que propose *Dans l'appartement de Viktor Nikolaïevitch* vise à ce que le tableau reconquière son statut, mais dans le cadre de l'installation, où une place d'honneur lui est réservée de plein droit.

Un tableau ordinaire, «normal», un tableau encadré peut être intégré à l'installation totale comme un élément parmi d'autres (dessins, plans). Rien ne le dérange, de même qu'il ne dérange rien. Mais si l'on s'interrogeait : quelles métamorphoses va subir le tableau intégré à l'installation ? Que gagne-t-il ? Que perd-il ? Quelles sont les qualités qui vont émerger et celles qui vont disparaître ? Que devient l'installation totale à partir du moment où elle intègre le tableau ?

Avant de donner la reponse, posons-nous une autre question importante : qui est l'auteur du tableau — ou des tableaux — inséré dans l'installation totale ?

Ce doit être impérativement un personnage imaginaire, un artiste fictif.

Une simple expérience le confirmera. Si l'on introduit dans l'installation une «vraie» œuvre d'un grand maître, par exemple *Le Vent fort* de Ruysdael, elle sera perçue comme totalement étrangère, voire hostile, à l'atmosphère de l'installation. Au contraire, si l'on présente dans les salles du musée un tableau fabriqué par un artiste imaginaire, il sera perçu comme un corps étranger, presque caricatural.

De ces deux expériences, on tirera la conclusion que le tableau fait pour l'installation doit être aussi fictif que d'autres objets tels la lumière, la peinture des murs, le décor, le son, etc. L'artiste qui a prétendument peint ce tableau devient donc une fiction parmi d'autres fictions : il n'a jamais existé, il n'y a que l'«artiste-personnage», anonyme. Et même s'il a un nom, une biographie et une date de naissance, il n'empêche que tout cela a été fabriqué de toutes pièces.

Cela signifie-t-il que tout n'est que fiction et trompe-l'œil, que cette supercherie

Dessin de l'installation avec les indications (fléchées à gauche et à droite) : rideaux fermés

1. Entrée
2. Cloisons
3. Projets
4. Radio
5. Tapis
6. Table
7. Tableau
8. Rideau noir
9. Chaises
10. Le lit de Viktor Nikolaïevitch
11. Petit tapis
12. Lampadaire
13. Rideaux
14. Lumière venant de la peinture.

233

239

produisait la même impression que les autres : une impression d'absurdité, d'incongruité, à la fois drôle et sinistre.

Quelques mots du personnage central de la série : sa couleur — que j'ai recherchée longtemps, en tant que «créateur». Je finis par trouver : c'était une couleur «de ménage» extrêmement répandue chez nous, une teinture que l'on utilise pour les toitures et les planchers (d'où son nom «teinture de plancher») et que l'on trouve dans les quincailleries.

Cependant, à mon avis, cette teinture a un sens «onthologique».

La couleur de notre pays et de notre vie m'apparaît en gris, et celle du pouvoir en rouge. Si l'on mélange les deux, on obtient cette «*color*» dont j'ai recouvert mes «œuvres».

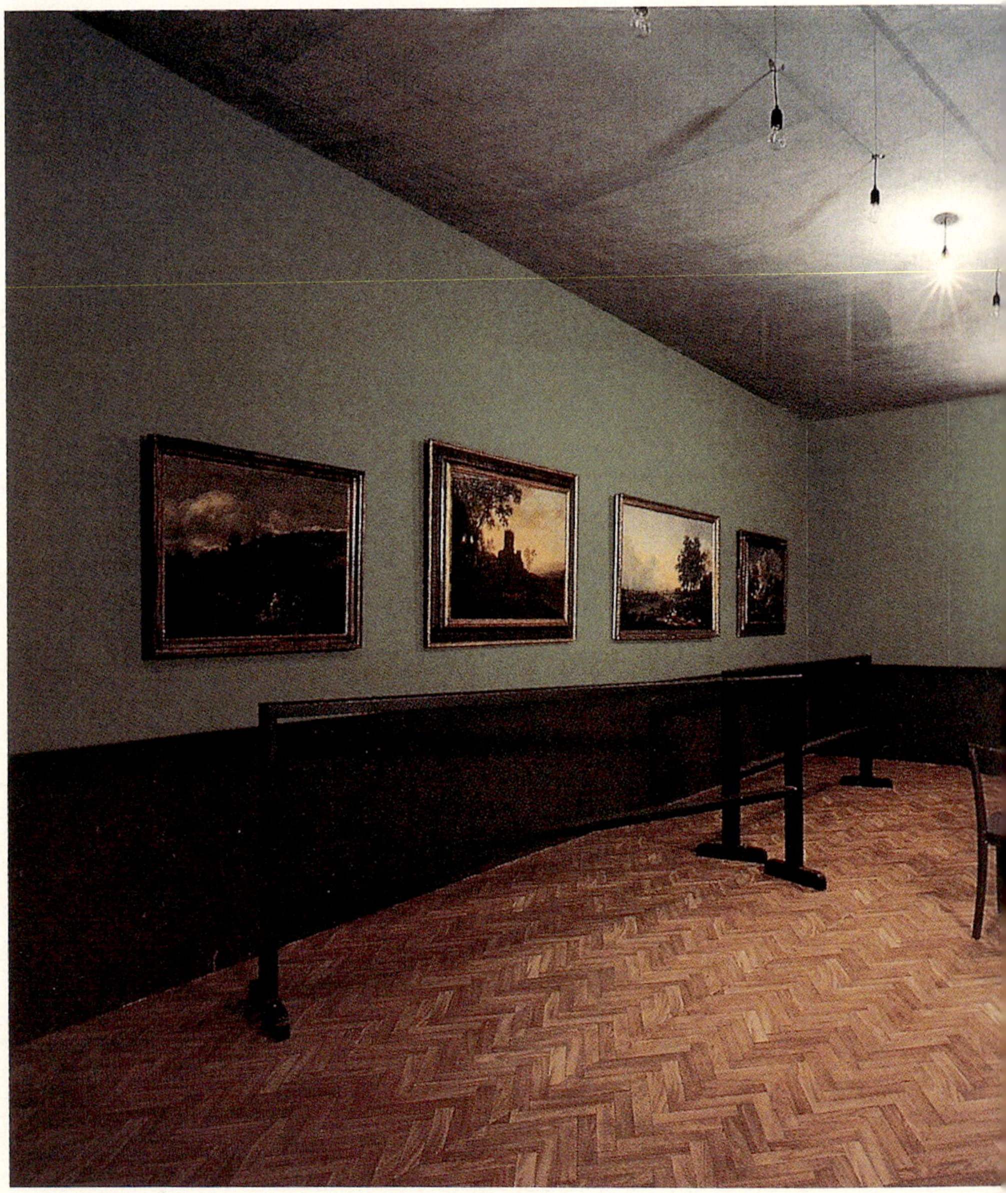

Vue de l'installation exposée à l'Akademie der bildenden Künste, Vienne, 1992.

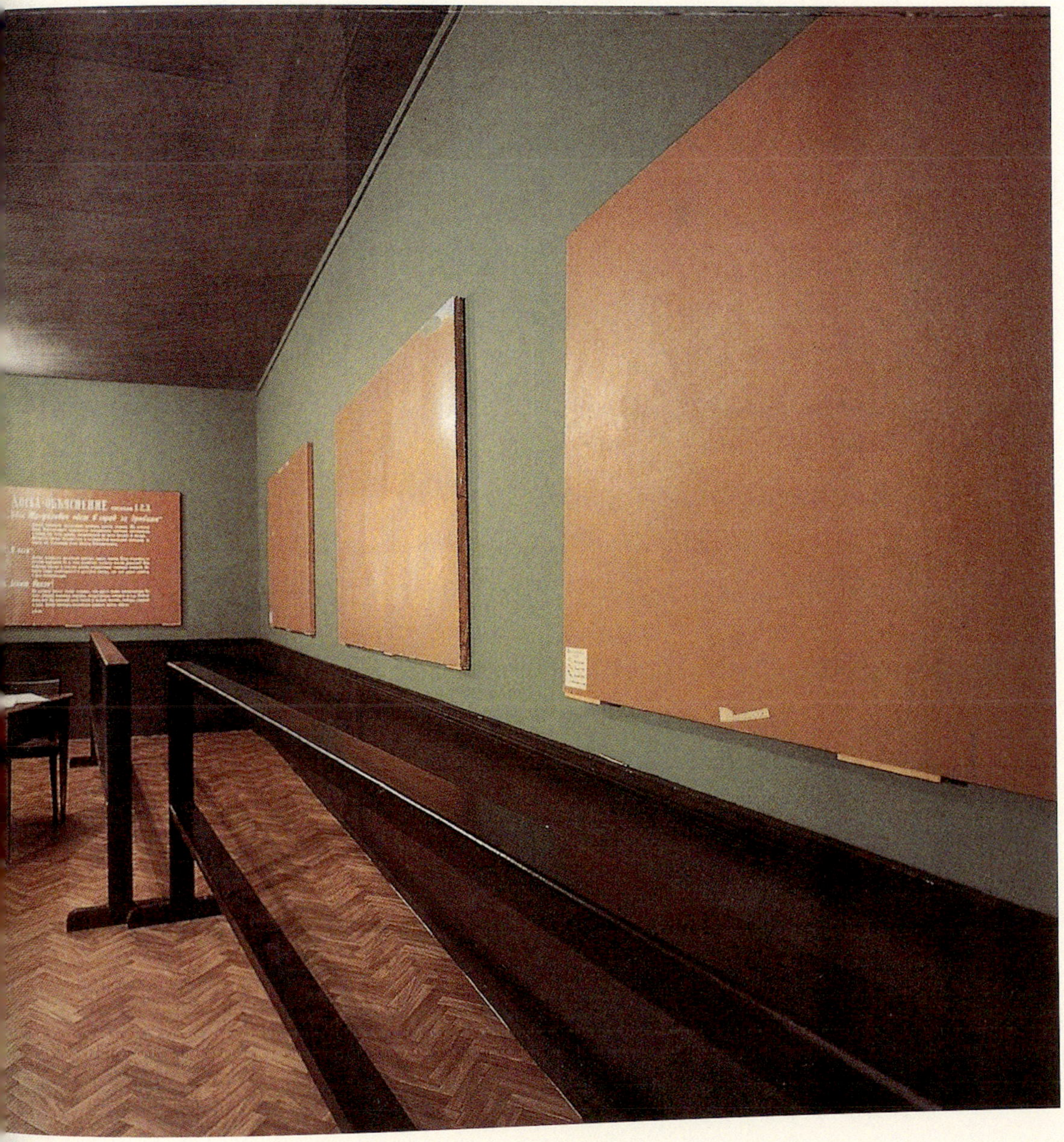

81 The Rope of Life and Other Installations

Das Seil des Lebens und andere Installationen

1995

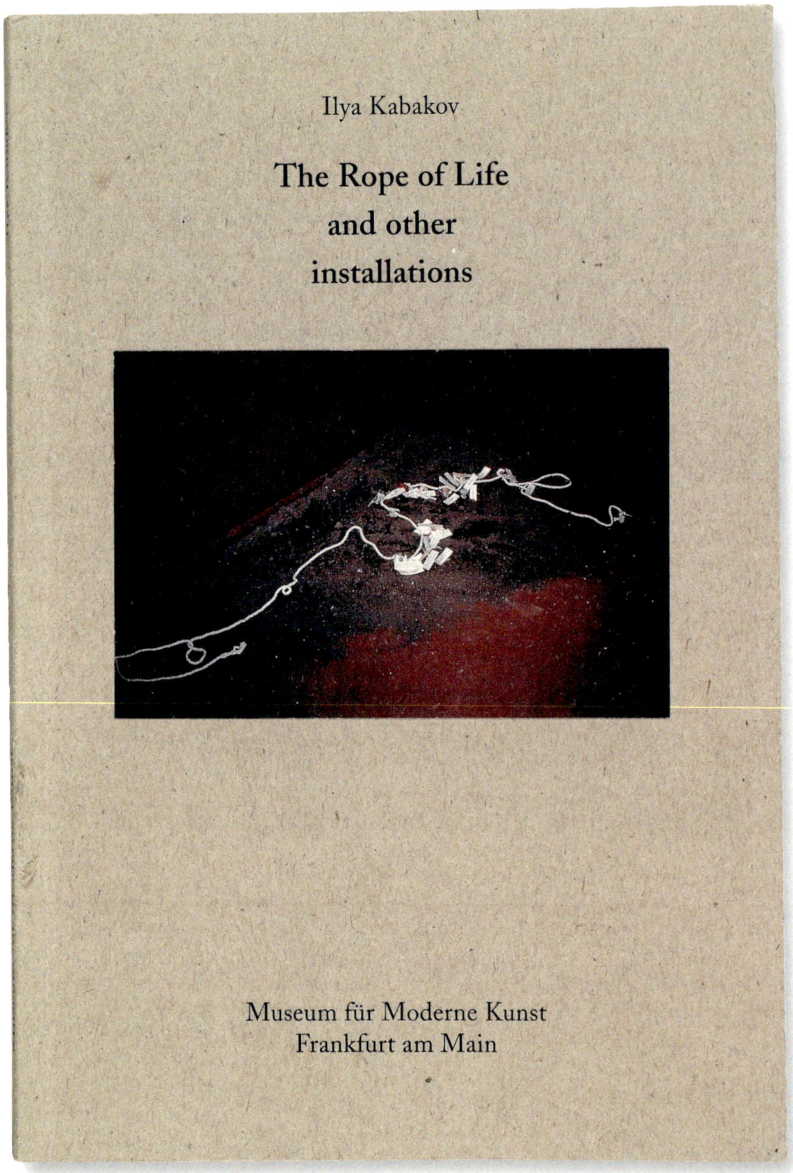

Museum für Moderne Kunst,
Frankfurt am Main
Frankfurt am Main: Museum für Moderne Kunst
22 x 15 cm
155 pp. with 34 (10 color) ills.
stitchbound, softback
Fadenheftung, broschiert

exhibition catalogue | *Ausstellungskatalog*

layout by Ilya Kabakov | *Layout von Ilya Kabakov*

For the exhibition »Szenenwechsel VIII« at the Museum für Moderne Kunst, Frankfurt am Main, June 23, 1995 to January 14, 1996. Texts by Ilya Kabakov. Documentation of the installation »The Rope of Life, Along the Margins, Box with Garbage«, and »In the Corner«; German, English.

Zur Ausstellung »Szenenwechsel VIII«, Museum für Moderne Kunst, Frankfurt am Main, 23. Juni 1995 – 14. Januar 1996. Texte von Ilya Kabakov. Dokumentation der Installation »Das Seil des Lebens, Am Rande, Kiste mit Müll« und »In der Ecke«; deutsch, englisch.

see also | *siehe auch* no. 30; no. 31; no. 46; CRI, vol. 1, nos. 7–8, pp. 82–93, no. 13, pp. 120–125, no. 32, pp. 234–237

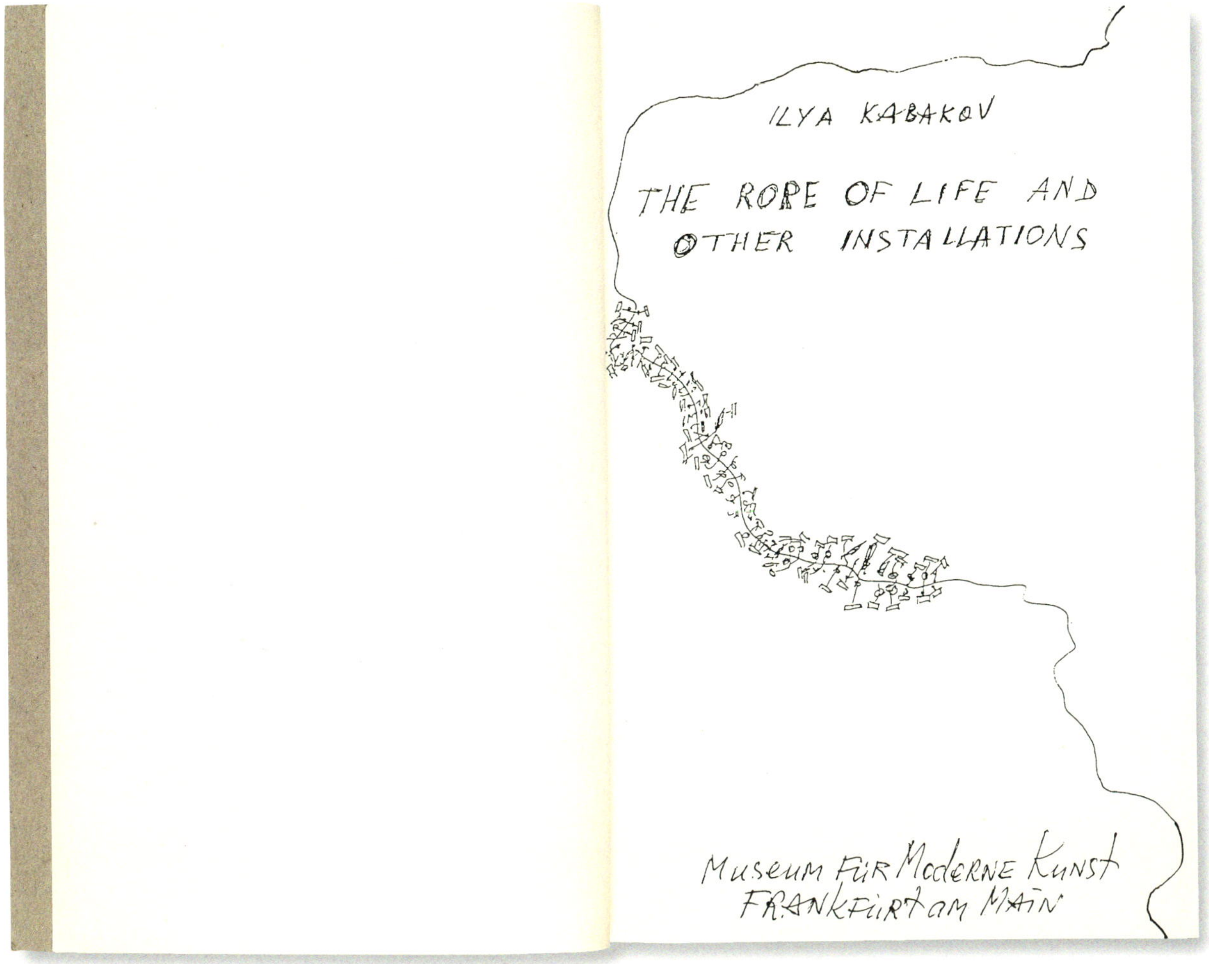
ILYA KABAKOV
THE ROPE OF LIFE AND OTHER INSTALLATIONS
Museum Für Moderne Kunst
FRANKFURT am MAIN

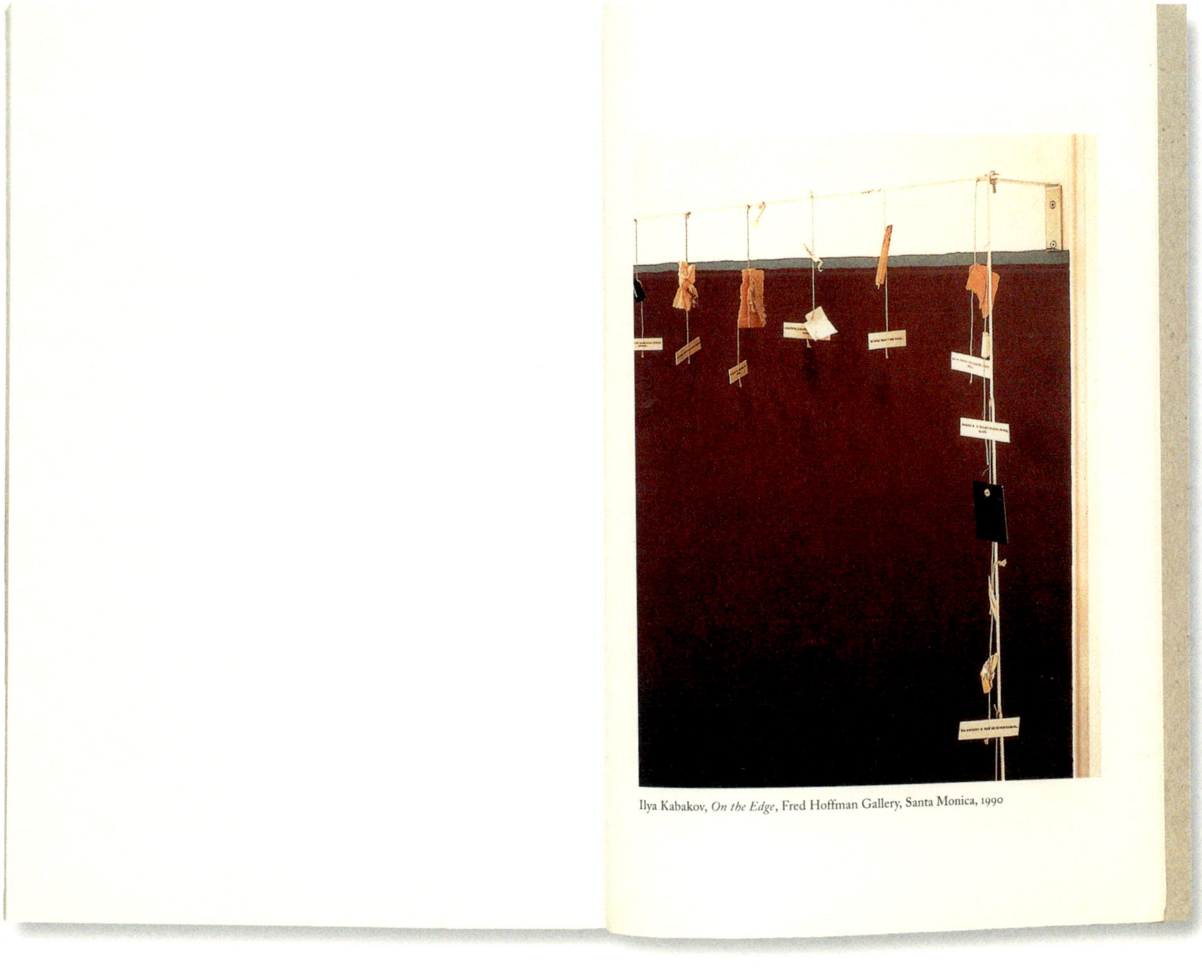
Ilya Kabakov, *On the Edge*, Fred Hoffman Gallery, Santa Monica, 1990

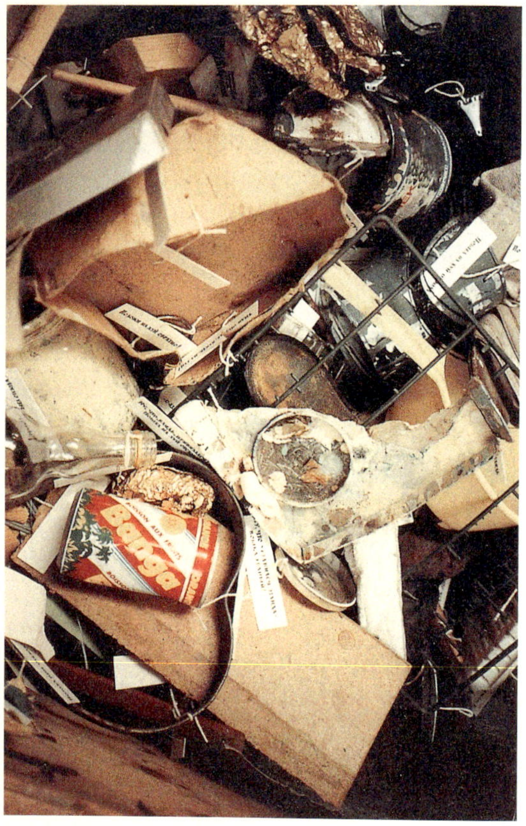

Ilya Kabakov, *Box with Garbage*, Fred Hoffman Gallery, Santa Monica, 1990

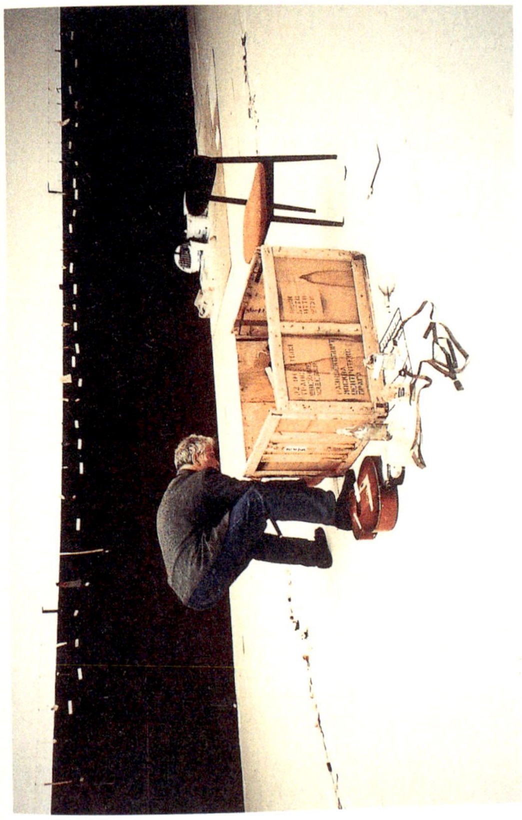

Ilya Kabakov, *Box with Garbage*, Stedelijk Museum, Amsterdam, 1990

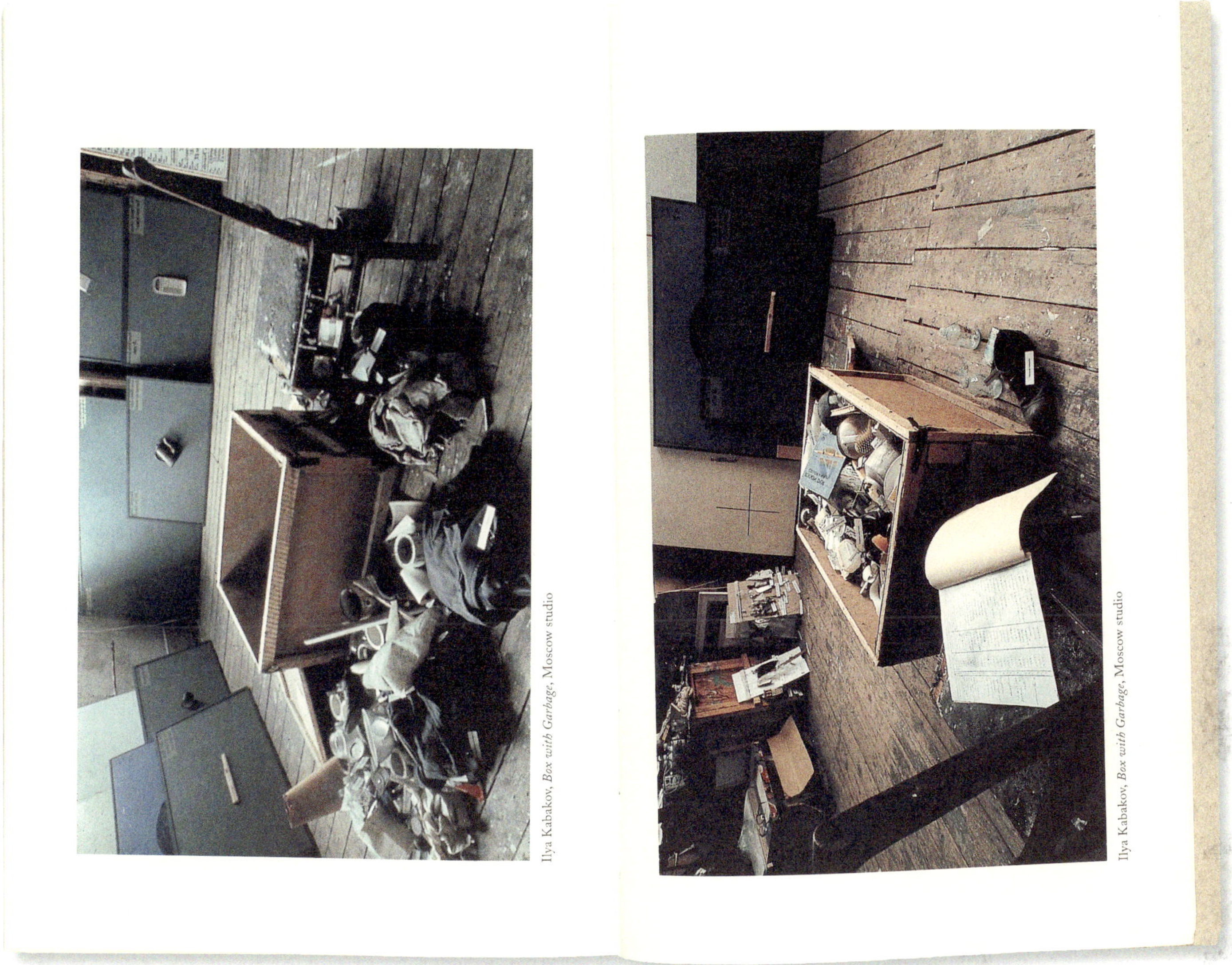
Ilya Kabakov, *Box with Garbage*, Moscow studio
Ilya Kabakov, *Box with Garbage*, Moscow studio

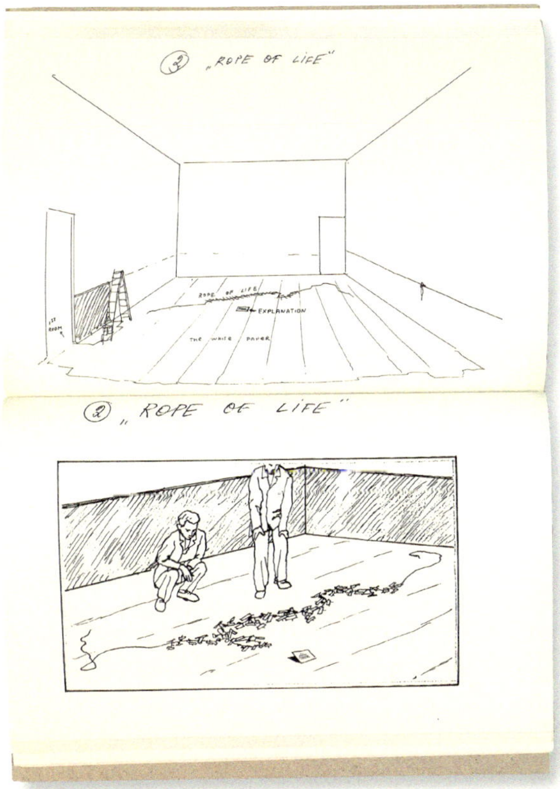
② „ROPE OF LIFE"
② „ROPE OF LIFE"

82 Flies (In the Communal Kitchen): A Musical Phantasmagoria

Fliegen (In der Gemeinschaftsküche). Eine musikalische Phantasmagorie

with Vladimir Tarasov | *mit Vladimir Tarasov*

1995

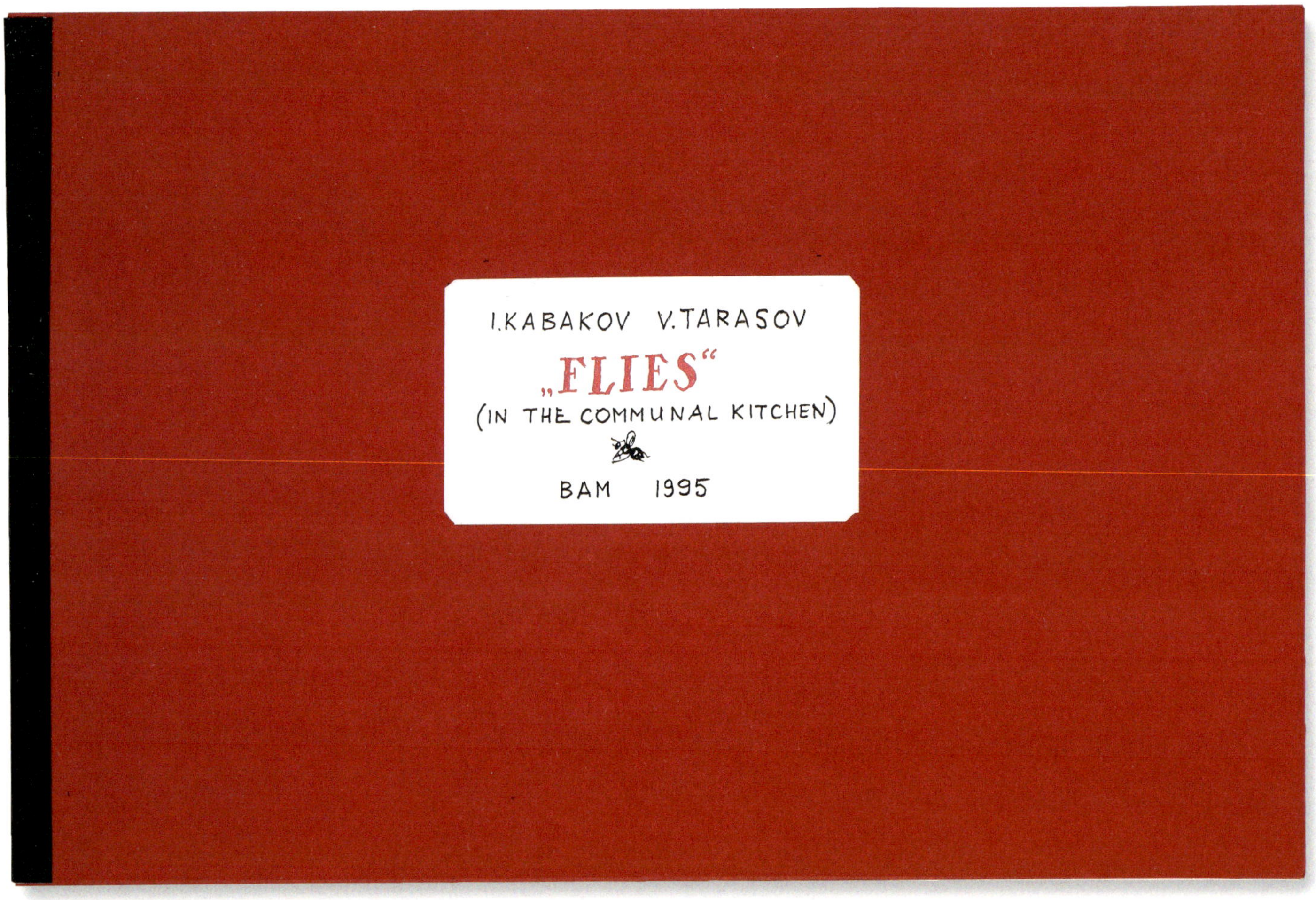

Ilya Kabakov
New York: published by the author
28.2 x 43.5 cm
44 photocopied pp. (3 foldouts) with 27 (19 color) ills.
adhesive binding, cardboard cover, label on the cover
Klebebindung, Kartonumschlag, Etikette auf dem Umschlag
edition: 100 copies

libretto | *Libretto*

layout by Ilya Kabakov | *Layout von Ilya Kabakov*

Libretto for the play »Flies (In the Communal Kitchen): A Musical Phantasmagoria« for the series »Artists in Action« as part of the 'Next Wave Festival', BAM, Brooklyn Academy of Music, Majestic Theater, New York, October 26 to 28, 1995, in cooperation with David Dorfman (choreography) and Vladimir Tarasov (percussion). Libretto and notation by Ilya Kabakov; English, Russian.

Libretto des Theaterstücks »Fliegen (In der Kommunalküche). Eine musikalische Phantasmagorie« für die Serie »Artists in Action« während dem ‚Next Wave Festival', BAM, Brooklyn Academy of Music, Majestic Theater, New York, 26. – 28. Oktober 1995, in Zusammenarbeit mit David Dorfman (Tanz) und Vladimir Tarasov. Libretto und Notation von Ilya Kabakov und Notation von Vladimir Tarasov (Schlagzeug); englisch, russisch.

see also | *siehe auch* no. 134

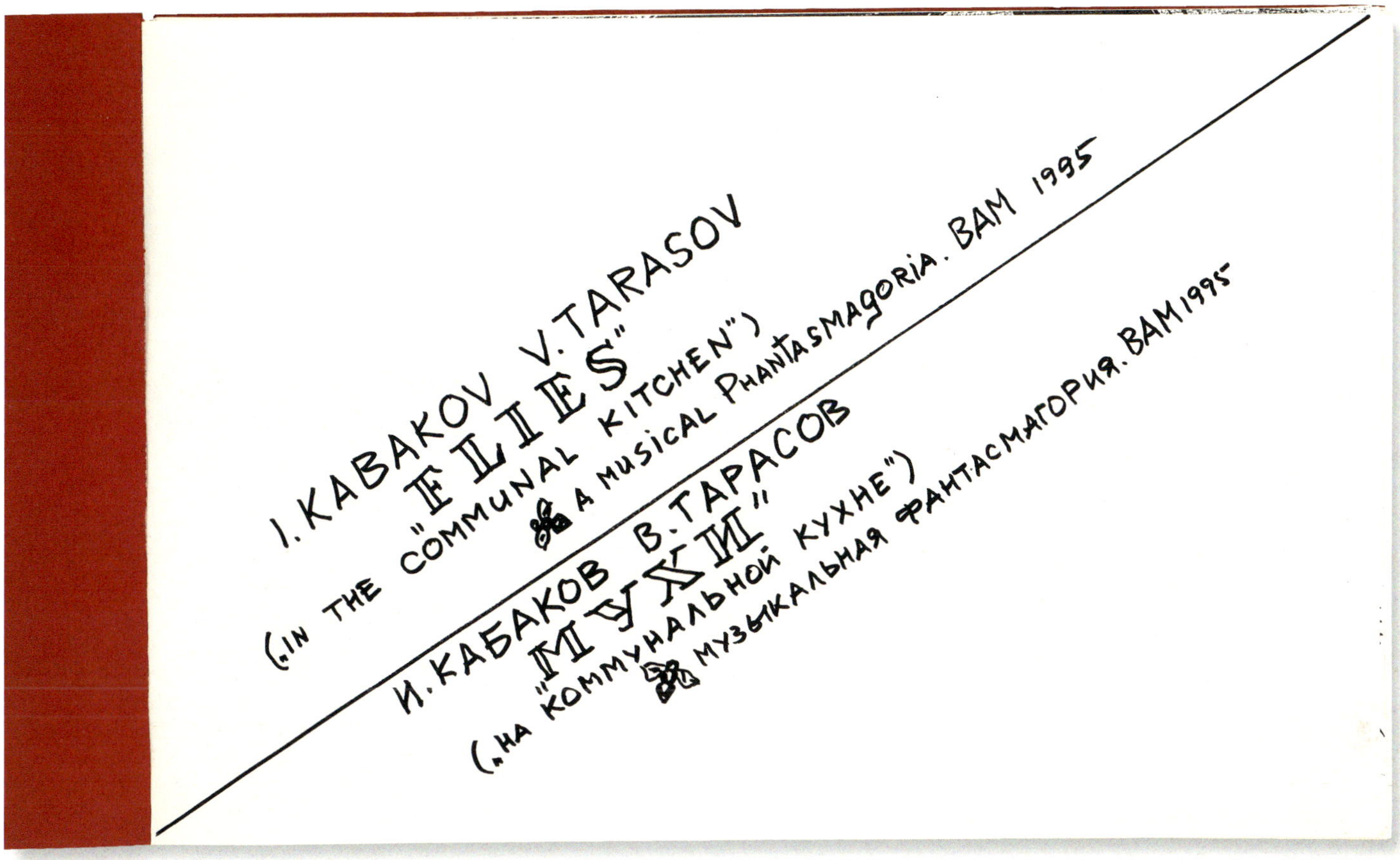
I. KABAKOV V. TARASOV
"FLIES"
("IN THE "COMMUNAL KITCHEN")
A MUSICAL PHANTASMAGORIA. BAM 1995
И. КАБАКОВ В. ТАРАСОВ
"МУХИ"
(„НА "КОММУНАЛЬНОЙ КУХНЕ")
МУЗЫКАЛЬНАЯ ФАНТАСМАГОРИЯ. BAM 1995

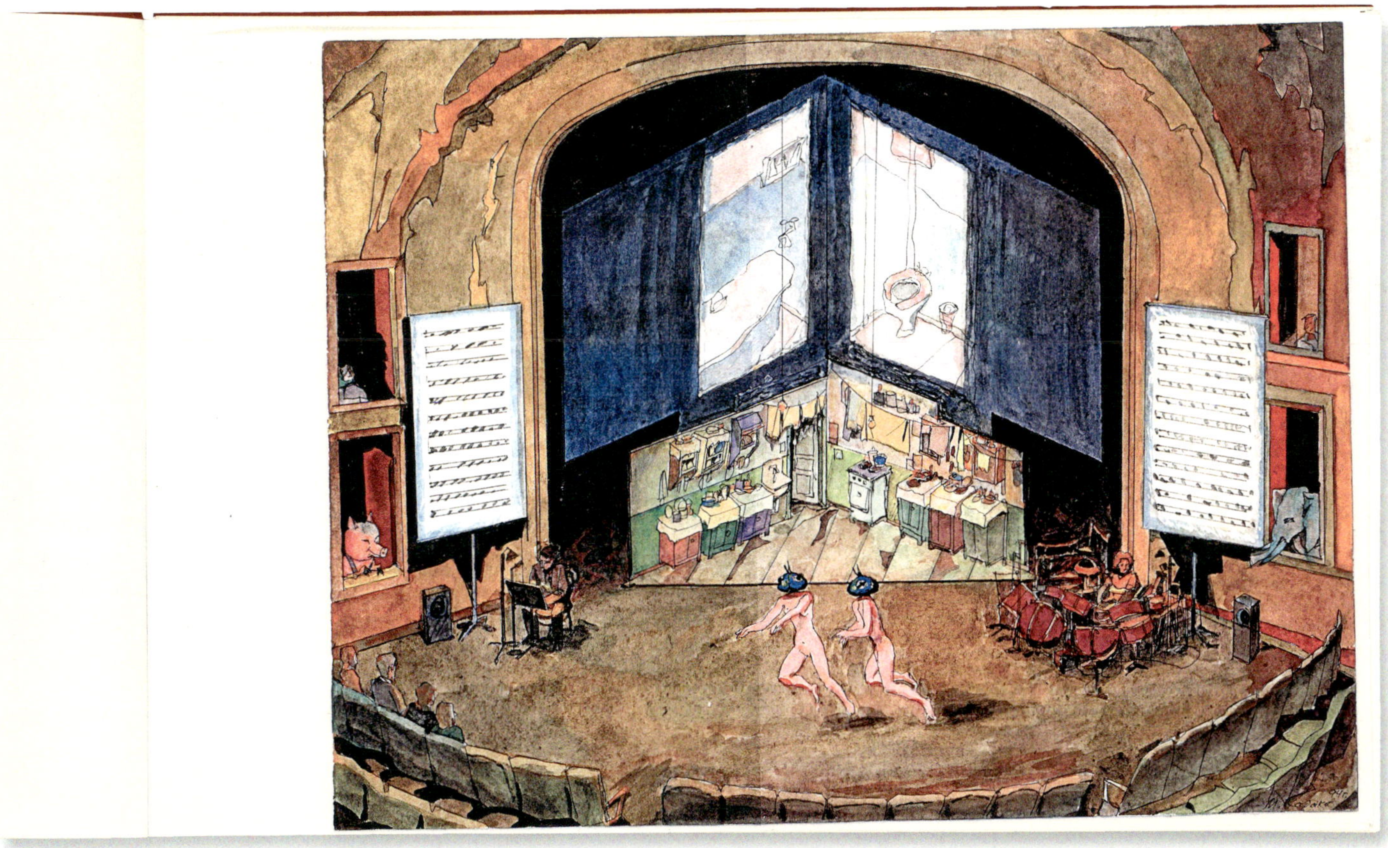

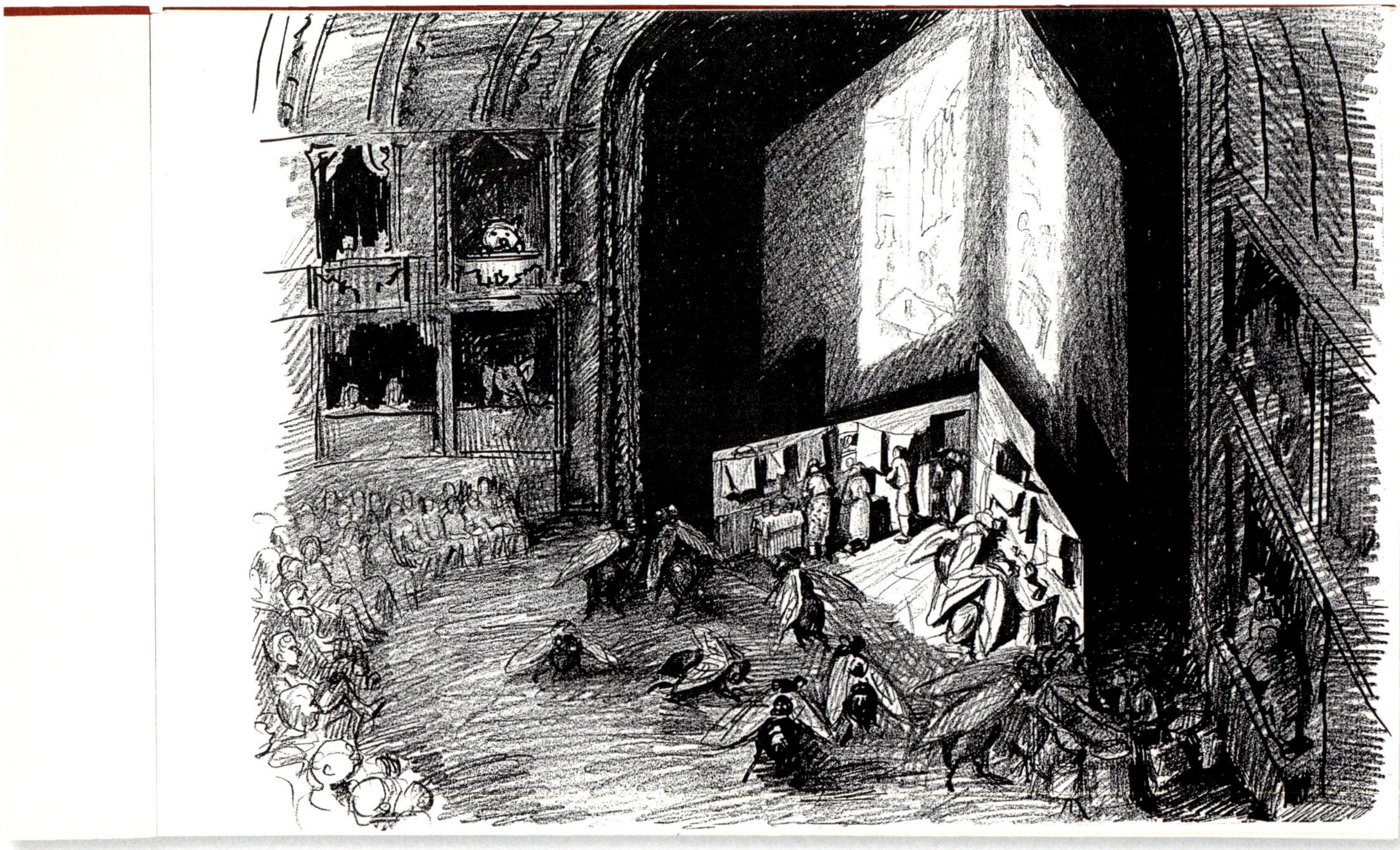

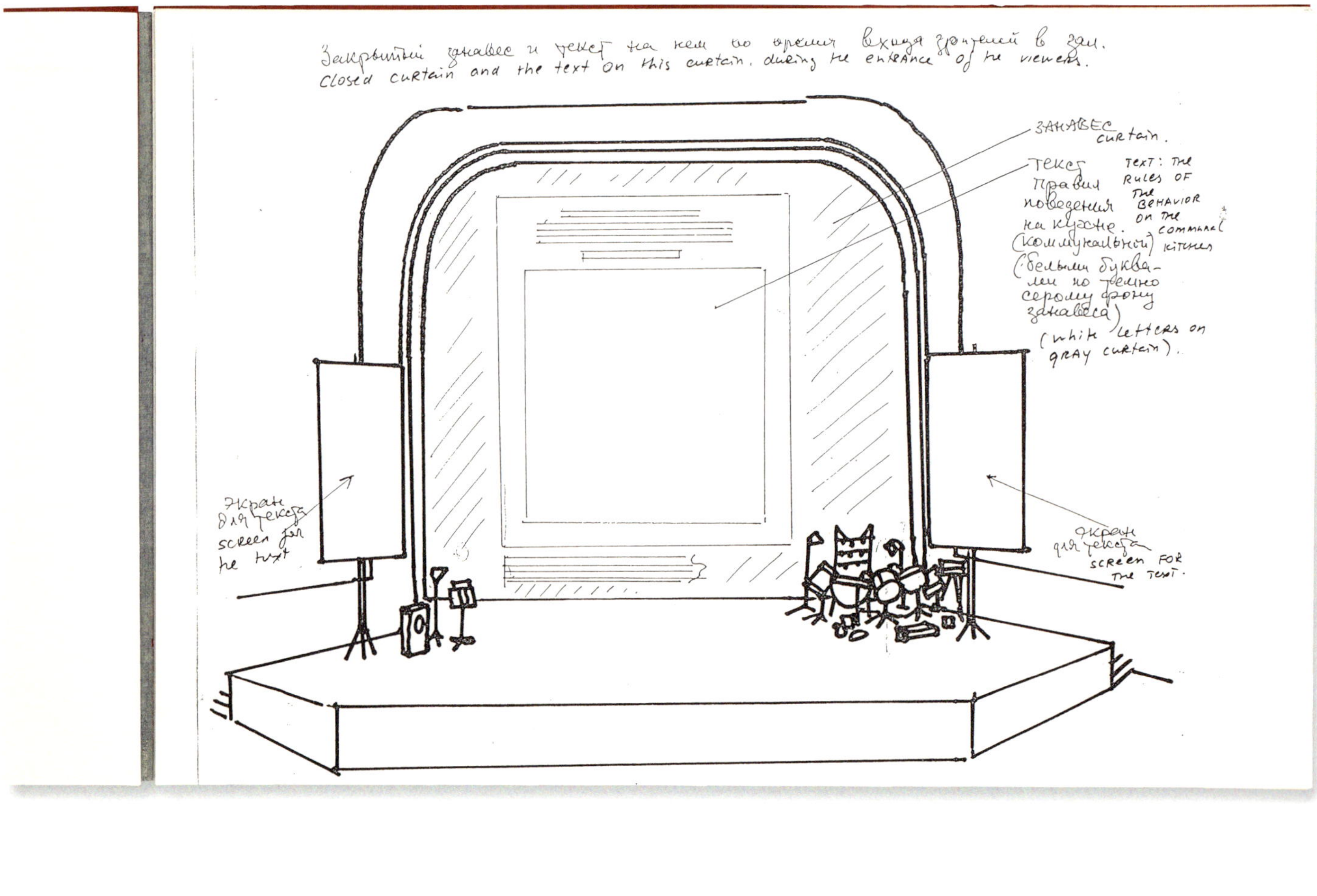
Закрытый занавес и текст на нем во время входа зрителей в зал.
Closed curtain and the text on this curtain. during he entrance of he viewers.
ЗАНАВЕС curtain.
Текст Правил поведения на кухне. (коммунальной) (белыми буквами по темно серому фону занавеса)
TEXT: THE RULES OF THE BEHAVIOR ON THE communal kitchen
(whit letters on gray curtain).
Экран для текста screen for he text
Экран для текста screen FOR THE TEXT.

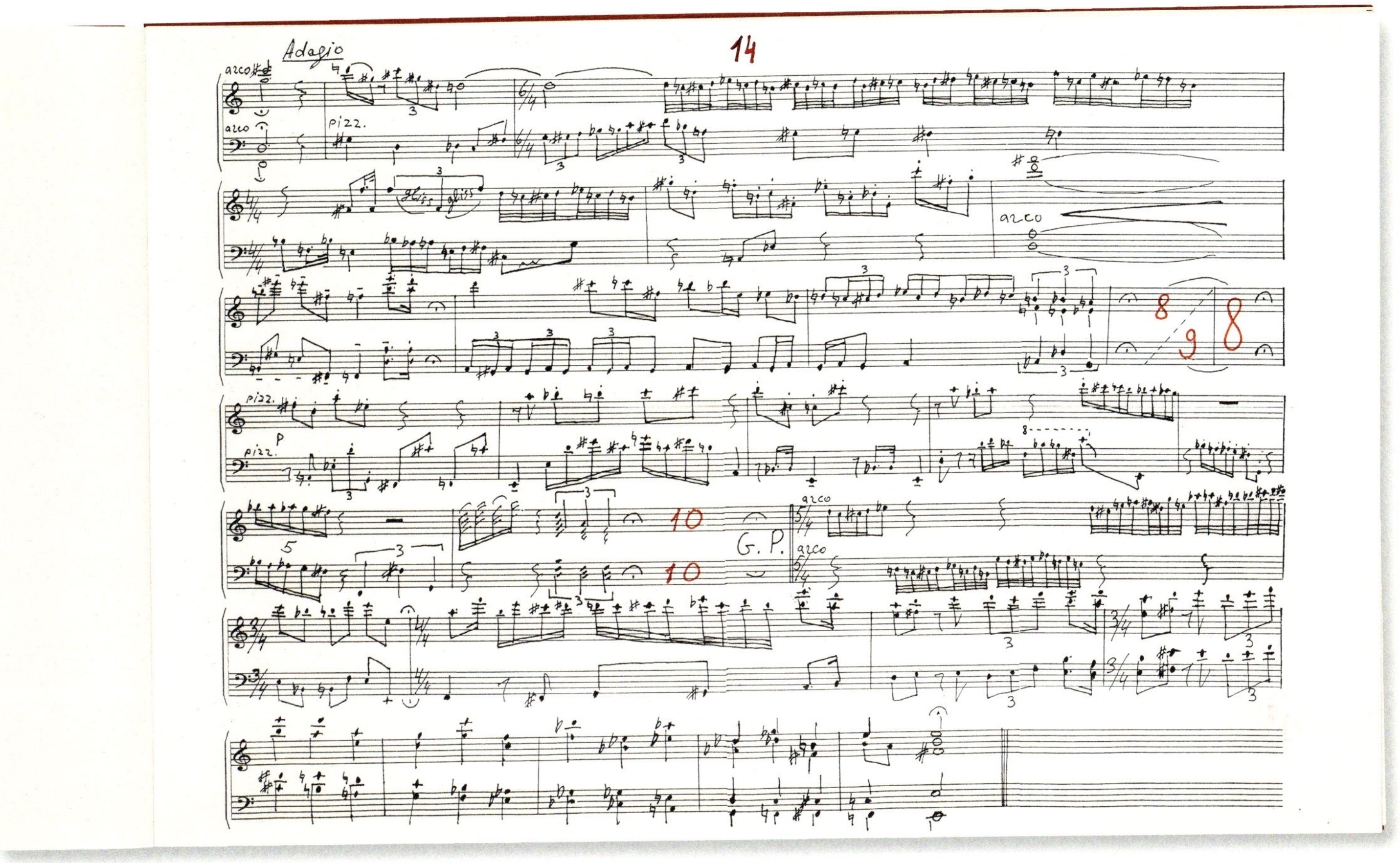
14
Adagio
arco
arco
pizz.
gliss.
gliss.
arco
pizz.
pizz.
p
8
9
8
10
10
G. P.
arco
arco

83 On the "Total" Installation | *Über die „totale" Installation*

1995

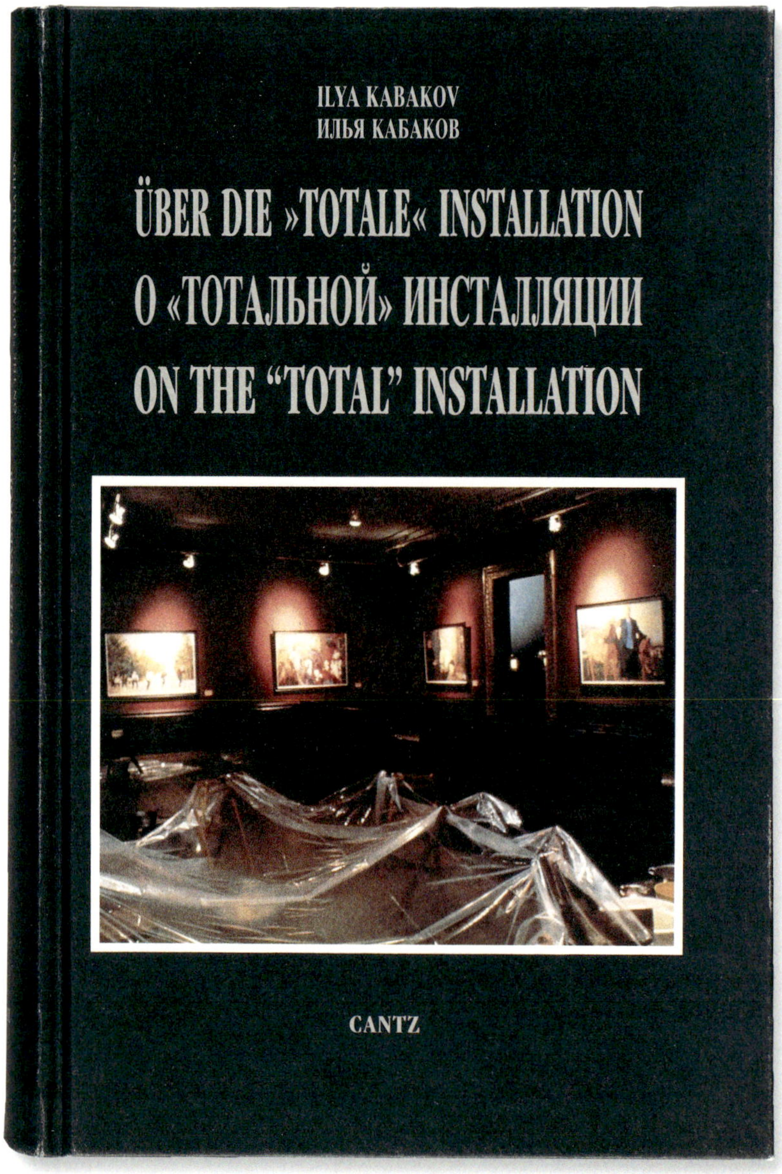

Ilya Kabakov
Ostfildern: Cantz Verlag
23.3 x 15.8 cm
398 pp. with 74 (16 color) ills.
stitchbound, hardcover
Fadenheftung, Hardcover

thematic publication | *thematische Publikation*

idea by Ilya Kabakov | *Idee von Ilya Kabakov*

The book is based on a fifteen-part series of lectures delivered by Ilya Kabakov on his installation concept during the 1992–93 winter semester at the Städelschule, Frankfurt am Main; German, Russian, English.

Das Buch basiert auf einer fünfzehnteiligen Vorlesungsreihe von Ilya Kabakov über sein Installationskonzept im Wintersemester 1992/93 an der Städelschule, Frankfurt am Main; deutsch, russisch, englisch.

see also | *siehe auch* no. 133

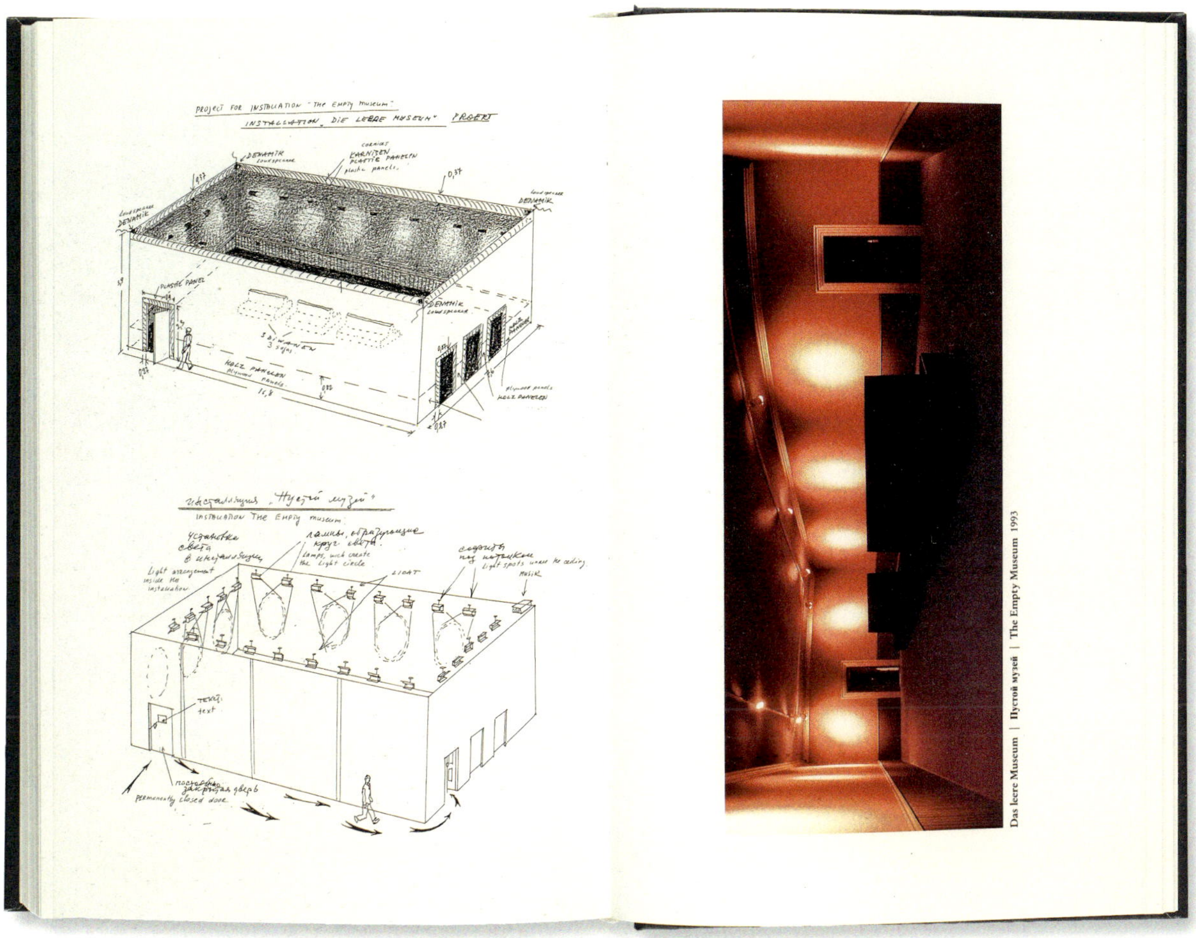

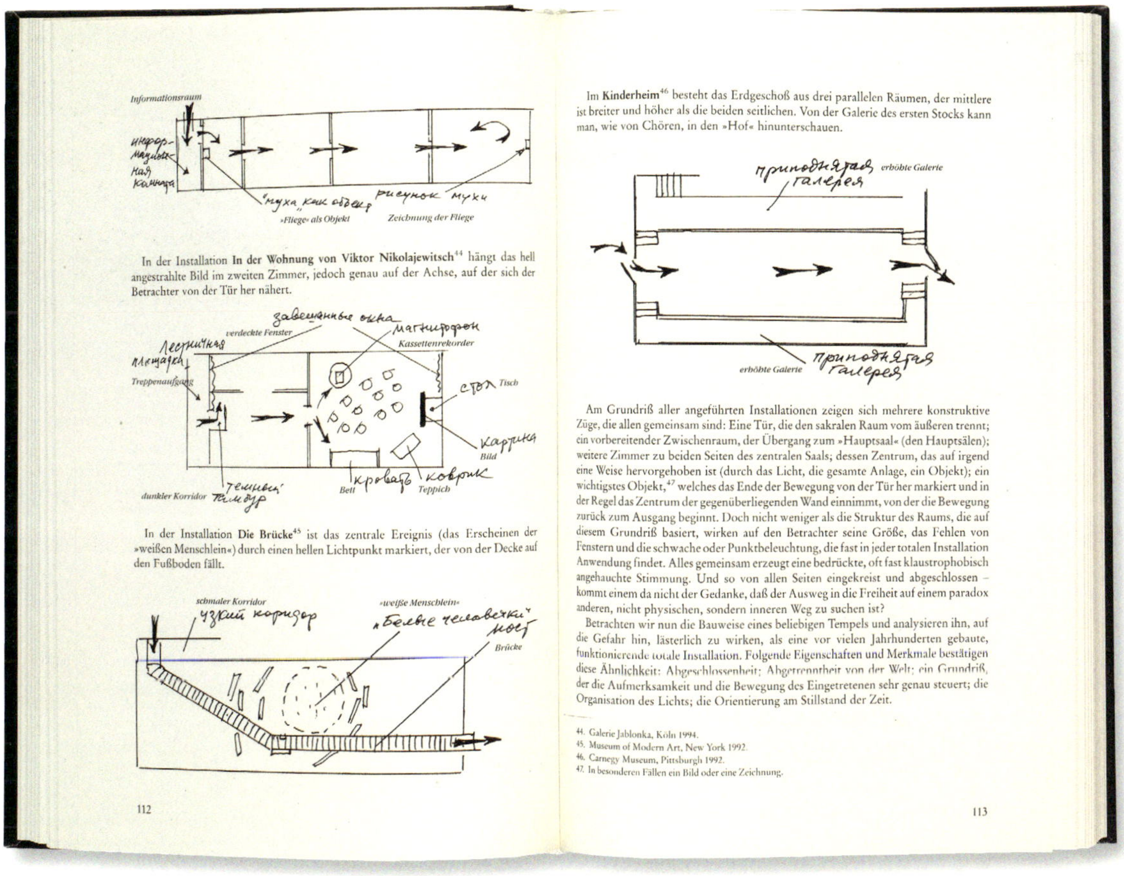
Informationsraum

»Fliege« als Objekt

Zeichnung der Fliege

In der Installation **In der Wohnung von Viktor Nikolajewitsch**[44] hängt das hell angestrahlte Bild im zweiten Zimmer, jedoch genau auf der Achse, auf der sich der Betrachter von der Tür her nähert.

verdeckte Fenster

Kassettenrekorder

Treppenaufgang

Tisch

Bild

Bett

Teppich

dunkler Korridor

In der Installation **Die Brücke**[45] ist das zentrale Ereignis (das Erscheinen der »weißen Menschlein«) durch einen hellen Lichtpunkt markiert, der von der Decke auf den Fußboden fällt.

schmaler Korridor

»weiße Menschlein«

Brücke

112

Im **Kinderheim**[46] besteht das Erdgeschoß aus drei parallelen Räumen, der mittlere ist breiter und höher als die beiden seitlichen. Von der Galerie des ersten Stocks kann man, wie von Chören, in den »Hof« hinunterschauen.

erhöhte Galerie

erhöhte Galerie

Am Grundriß aller angeführten Installationen zeigen sich mehrere konstruktive Züge, die allen gemeinsam sind: Eine Tür, die den sakralen Raum vom äußeren trennt; ein vorbereitender Zwischenraum, der Übergang zum »Hauptsaal« (den Hauptsälen); weitere Zimmer zu beiden Seiten des zentralen Saals; dessen Zentrum, das auf irgend eine Weise hervorgehoben ist (durch das Licht, die gesamte Anlage, ein Objekt); ein wichtigstes Objekt,[47] welches das Ende der Bewegung von der Tür her markiert und in der Regel das Zentrum der gegenüberliegenden Wand einnimmt, von der die Bewegung zurück zum Ausgang beginnt. Doch nicht weniger als die Struktur des Raums, die auf diesem Grundriß basiert, wirken auf den Betrachter seine Größe, das Fehlen von Fenstern und die schwache oder Punktbeleuchtung, die fast in jeder totalen Installation Anwendung findet. Alles gemeinsam erzeugt eine bedrückte, oft fast klaustrophobisch angehauchte Stimmung. Und so von allen Seiten eingekreist und abgeschlossen – kommt einem da nicht der Gedanke, daß der Ausweg in die Freiheit auf einem paradox anderen, nicht physischen, sondern inneren Weg zu suchen ist?

Betrachten wir nun die Bauweise eines beliebigen Tempels und analysieren ihn, auf die Gefahr hin, lästerlich zu wirken, als eine vor vielen Jahrhunderten gebaute, funktionierende totale Installation. Folgende Eigenschaften und Merkmale bestätigen diese Ähnlichkeit: Abgeschlossenheit; Abgetrenntheit von der Welt; ein Grundriß, der die Aufmerksamkeit und die Bewegung des Eingetretenen sehr genau steuert; die Organisation des Lichts; die Orientierung am Stillstand der Zeit.

44. Galerie Jablonka, Köln 1994.
45. Museum of Modern Art, New York 1992.
46. Carnegy Museum, Pittsburgh 1992.
47. In besonderen Fällen ein Bild oder eine Zeichnung.

113

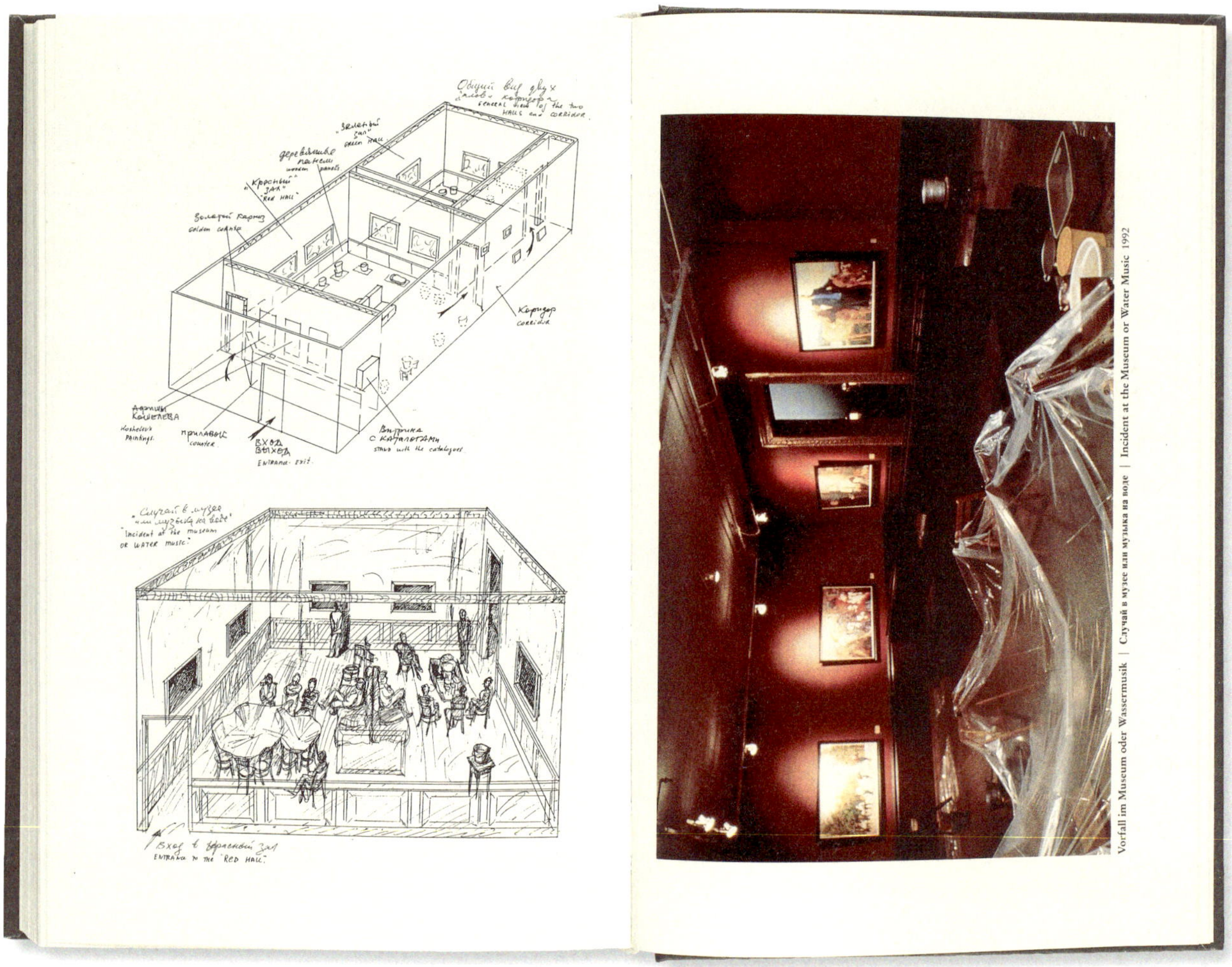
Vorfall im Museum oder Wassermusik | Случай в музее или музыка на воде | Incident at the Museum or Water Music 1992

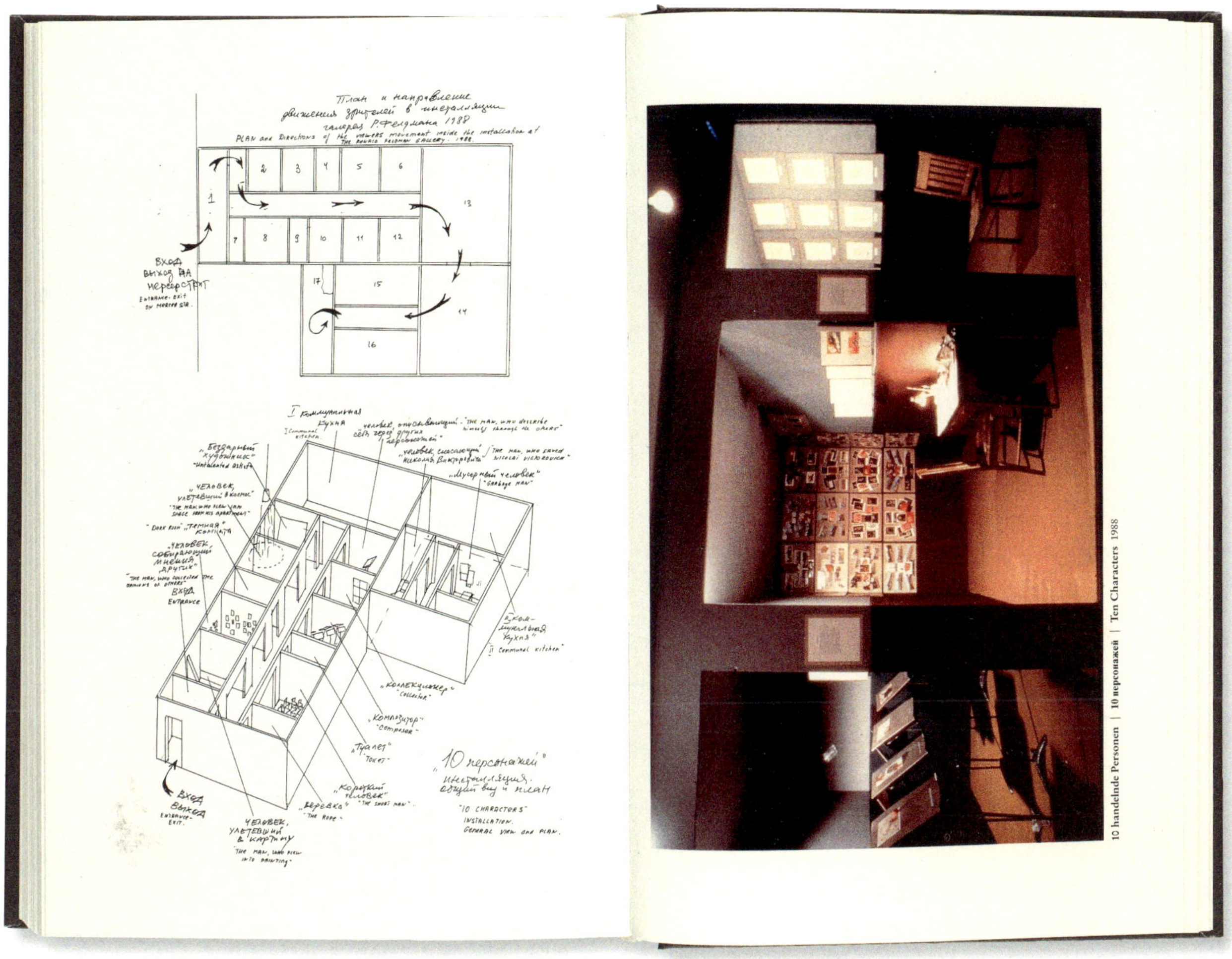

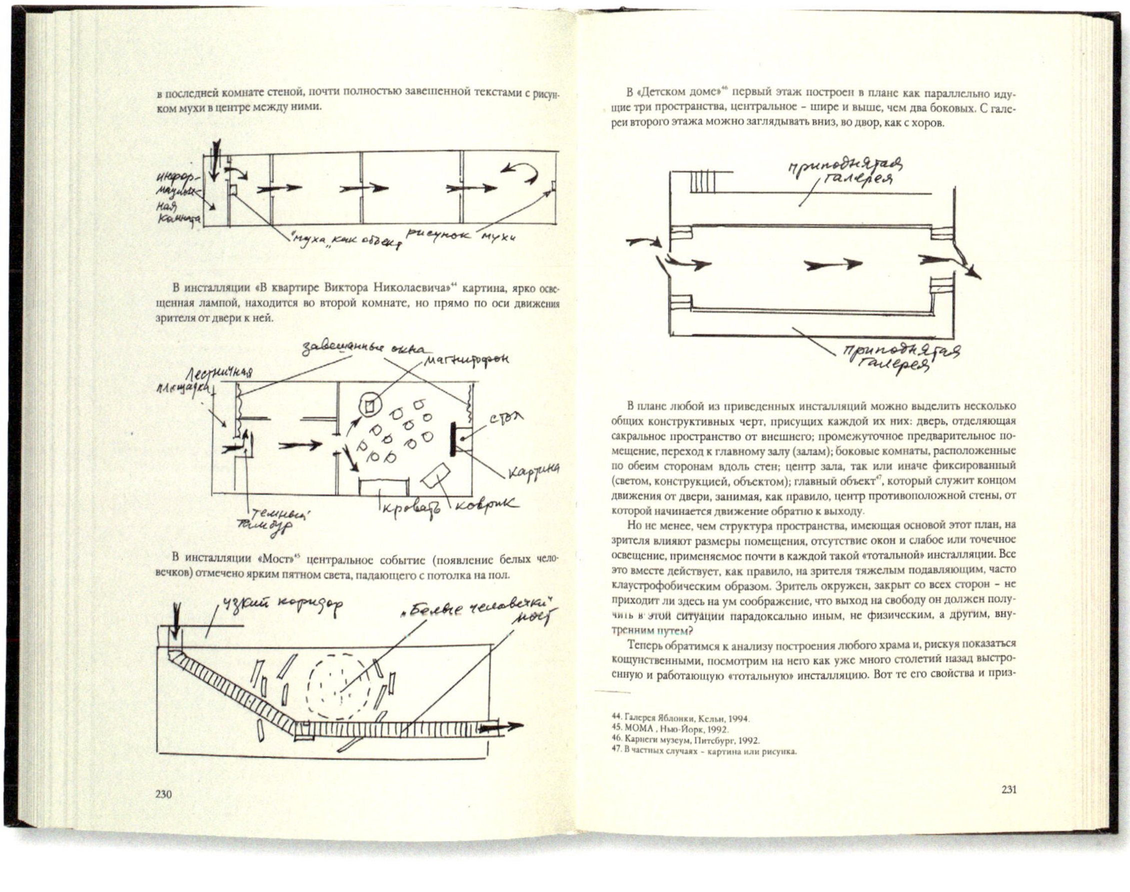
в последней комнате стеной, почти полностью завешенной текстами с рисунком мухи в центре между ними.

В инсталляции «В квартире Виктора Николаевича»[44] картина, ярко освещенная лампой, находится во второй комнате, но прямо по оси движения зрителя от двери к ней.

В инсталляции «Мост»[45] центральное событие (появление белых человечков) отмечено ярким пятном света, падающего с потолка на пол.

230

В «Детском доме»[46] первый этаж построен в плане как параллельно идущие три пространства, центральное – шире и выше, чем два боковых. С галереи второго этажа можно заглядывать вниз, во двор, как с хоров.

В плане любой из приведенных инсталляций можно выделить несколько общих конструктивных черт, присущих каждой их них: дверь, отделяющая сакральное пространство от внешнего; промежуточное предварительное помещение, переход к главному залу (залам); боковые комнаты, расположенные по обеим сторонам вдоль стен; центр зала, так или иначе фиксированный (светом, конструкцией, объектом); главный объект[47], который служит концом движения от двери, занимая, как правило, центр противоположной стены, от которой начинается движение обратно к выходу.

Но не менее, чем структура пространства, имеющая основой этот план, на зрителя влияют размеры помещения, отсутствие окон и слабое или точечное освещение, применяемое почти в каждой такой «тотальной» инсталляции. Все это вместе действует, как правило, на зрителя тяжелым подавляющим, часто клаустрофобическим образом. Зритель окружен, закрыт со всех сторон – не приходит ли здесь на ум соображение, что выход на свободу он должен получить в этой ситуации парадоксально иным, не физическим, а другим, внутренним путем?

Теперь обратимся к анализу построения любого храма и, рискуя показаться кощунственными, посмотрим на него как уже много столетий назад выстроенную и работающую «тотальную» инсталляцию. Вот те его свойства и приз-

44. Галерея Яблонки, Кельн, 1994.
45. МОМА , Нью-Йорк, 1992.
46. Карнеги музеум, Питсбург, 1992.
47. В частных случаях – картина или рисунка.

231

84 **My Mother's Album** | *Album meiner Mutter*

1995

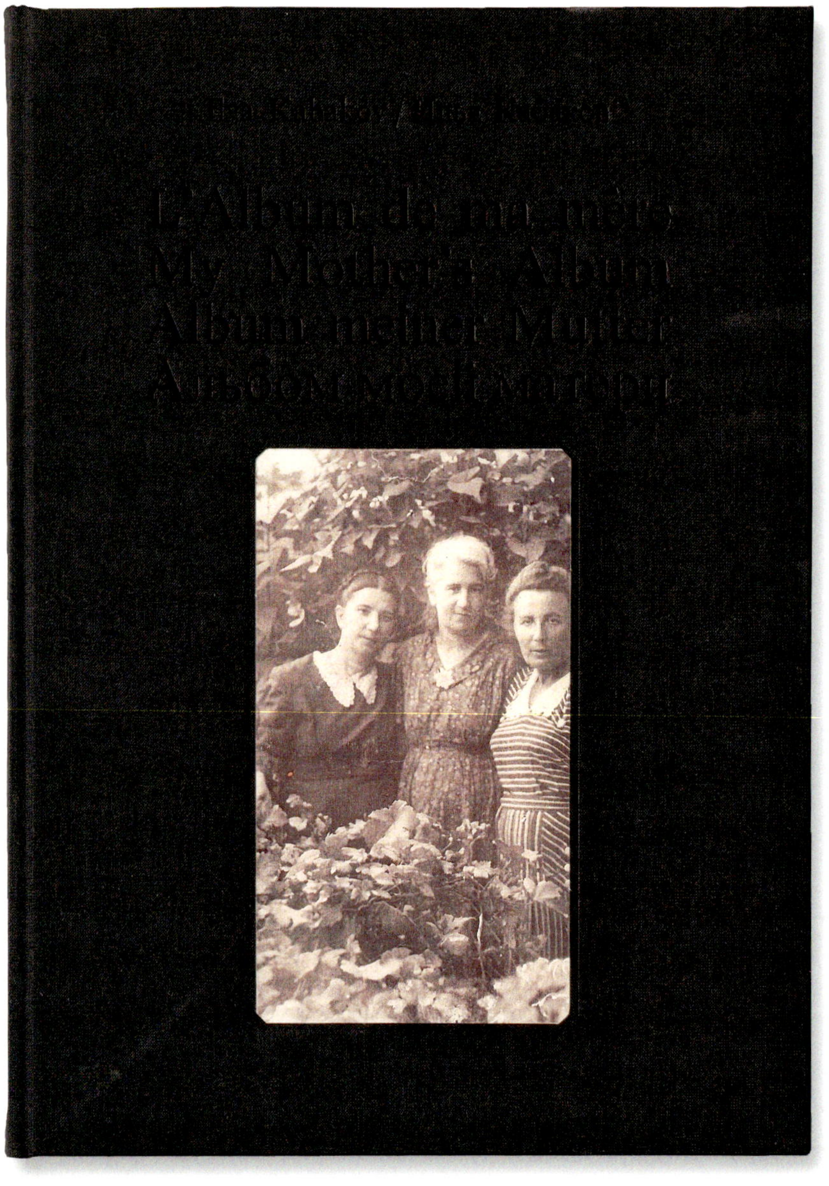

Ilya Kabakov
Paris: Flies France
34 x 24.6 cm
264 pp. with 151 (144 color) ills.
stitchbound, clothbound, blind blocking with label
Fadenheftung, Leinen, Blindprägung mit Etikette

thematic publication | *thematische Publikation*

layout by Ilya Kabakov | *Layout von Ilya Kabakov*

Autobiographical notes by Beyla Soloduchina (1902–1988), Ilya Kabakov's mother. The album is part of the installation »Mother and Son«, which is documented in the book; French, English, German, Russian.

Autobiografische Aufzeichnungen von Bejla Soloduchina (1902–1988), der Mutter Ilya Kabakovs. Das Album ist Teil der Installation »Mutter und Sohn«, die im Buch dokumentiert ist; französisch, englisch, deutsch, russisch.

see also | *siehe auch* no. 70; CRI, vol. 1, no. 36, pp. 254–259

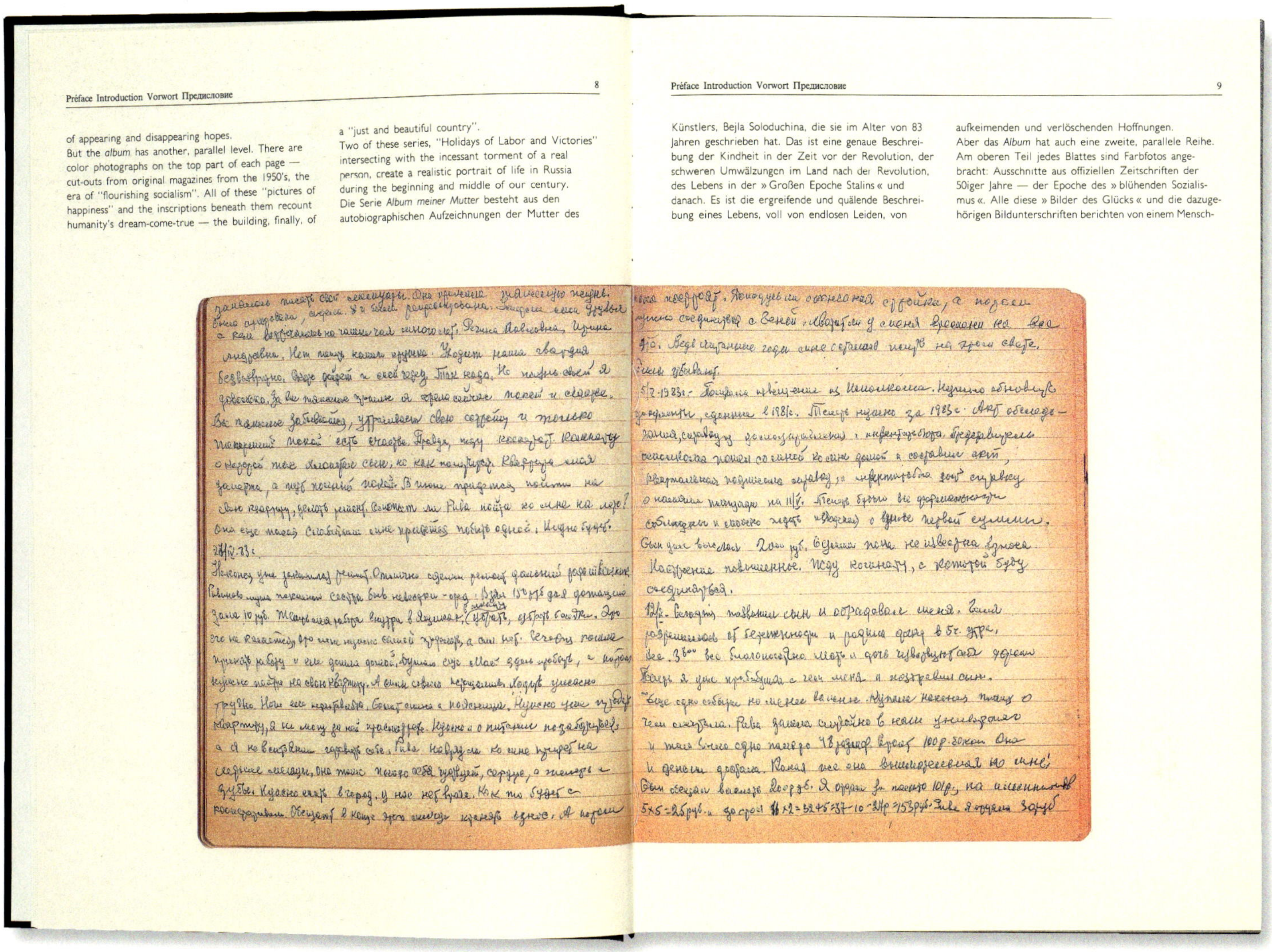

Préface Introduction Vorwort Предисловие 8

of appearing and disappearing hopes.
But the *album* has another, parallel level. There are color photographs on the top part of each page — cut-outs from original magazines from the 1950's, the era of "flourishing socialism". All of these "pictures of happiness" and the inscriptions beneath them recount humanity's dream-come-true — the building, finally, of a "just and beautiful country".
Two of these series, "Holidays of Labor and Victories" intersecting with the incessant torment of a real person, create a realistic portrait of life in Russia during the beginning and middle of our century.
Die Serie *Album meiner Mutter* besteht aus den autobiographischen Aufzeichnungen der Mutter des

Préface Introduction Vorwort Предисловие 9

Künstlers, Bejla Soloduchina, die sie im Alter von 83 Jahren geschrieben hat. Das ist eine genaue Beschreibung der Kindheit in der Zeit vor der Revolution, der schweren Umwälzungen im Land nach der Revolution, des Lebens in der »Großen Epoche Stalins« und danach. Es ist die ergreifende und quälende Beschreibung eines Lebens, voll von endlosen Leiden, von aufkeimenden und verlöschenden Hoffnungen.
Aber das *Album* hat auch eine zweite, parallele Reihe. Am oberen Teil jedes Blattes sind Farbfotos angebracht: Ausschnitte aus offiziellen Zeitschriften der 50iger Jahre — der Epoche des »blühenden Sozialismus«. Alle diese »Bilder des Glücks« und die dazugehörigen Bildunterschriften berichten von einem Mensch-

1.

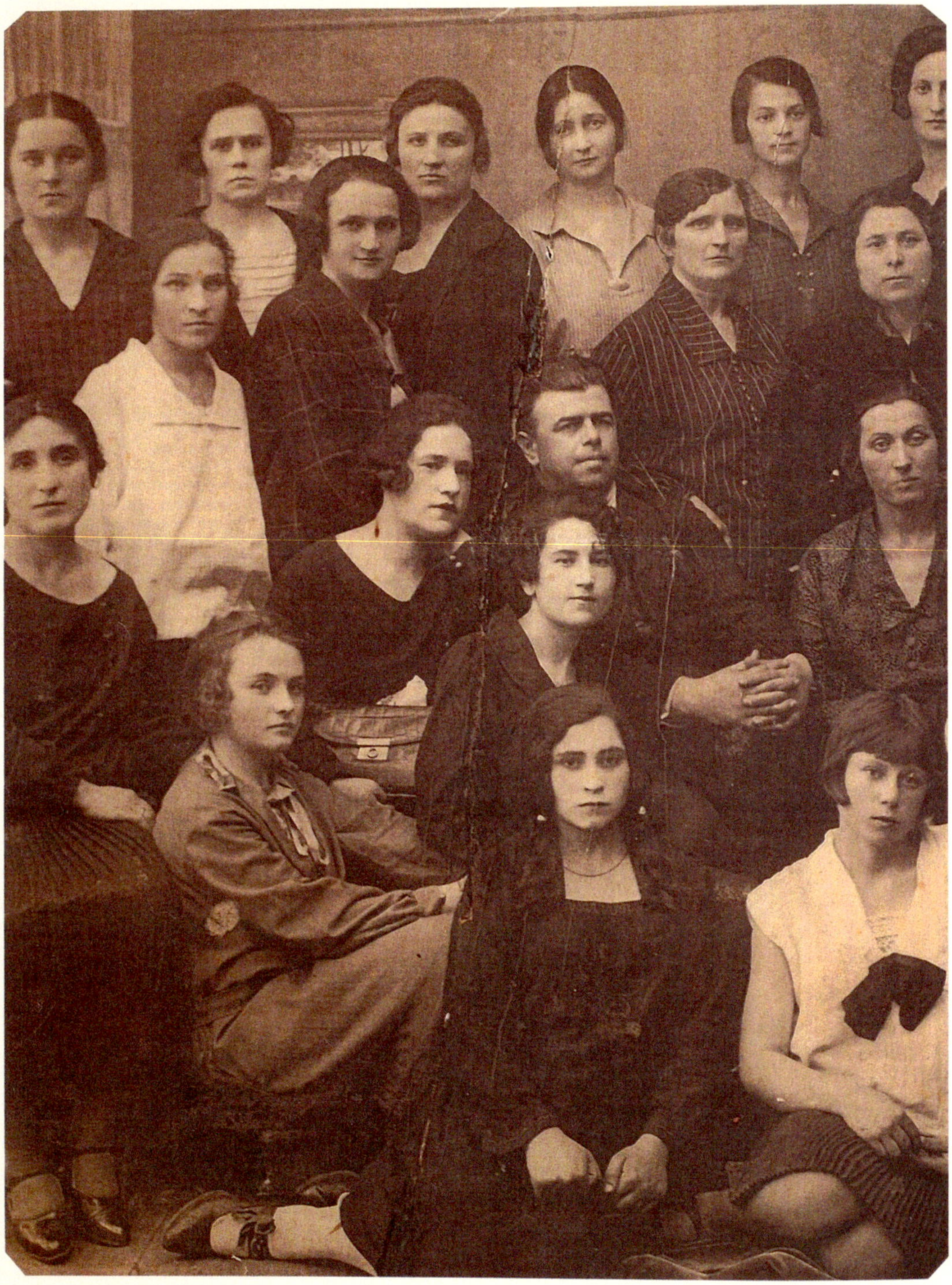

2.

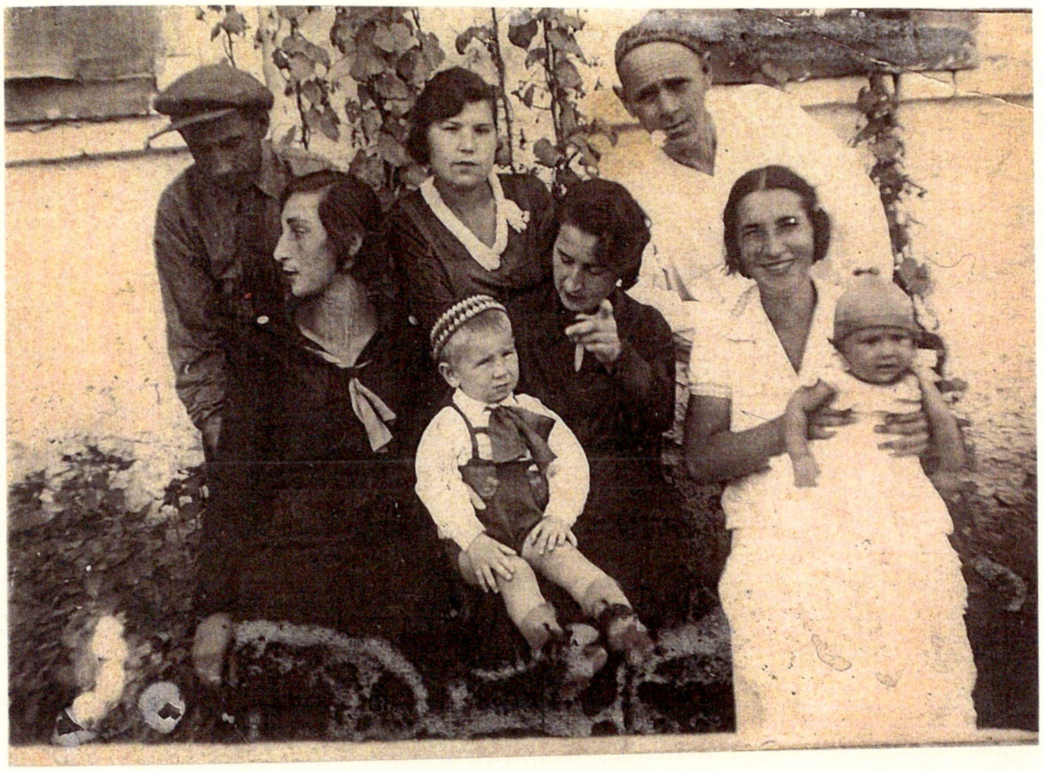

1.
1920. Marioupol. Promotion d'école du travail (ancien gymnase de filles de Marioupol). Au centre B. Y. Solodoukhina.
Mariupol, 1920. A group of graduates from the labor school (formerly Mariupol Women's Gymnasium). In the center B. Yu. Solodukhina.
1920 Mariupol. Gruppenbild der Absolventinnen der Arbeiterschule (früher: Mariupoler Mädchengymnasium). In der Mitte: B. Ju. Soloduchina
1920 Мариуполь. Группа выпускников трудовой школы (б. Мариупольская женская гимназия). В центре: Б.Ю.Солодухина

2.
Août 1935. Marioupol. Assis: première à droite Riva Youlievna Blékher avec son fils, B. Y. Solodoukhina avec son fils. Debout: à droite Y. G. Blékher.
August 1935, Mariupol. Sitting: first from the right — Riva Yulevna Blekher and son, B. Yu. Solodukhina and son; standing: from the right — Yu. G. Blekher.
August 1935, Mariupol. Sitzend, von rechts, Riva Juljevna Blecher mit Sohn, B. Ju. Soloduchina mit Sohn; stehend: rechts Ju. G. Blecher.
Август 1935 г. Г.Мариуполь. Сидят: первая справа Рива Юльевна Блехер с сыном, Б.Ю.Солодухина с сыном; стоят: справа Ю.Г.Блехер.

3.
1922. Photo d'identité.
1922. A photo for an ID card.
1922, Paßbild.
1922 г. Фото для пропуска

3.

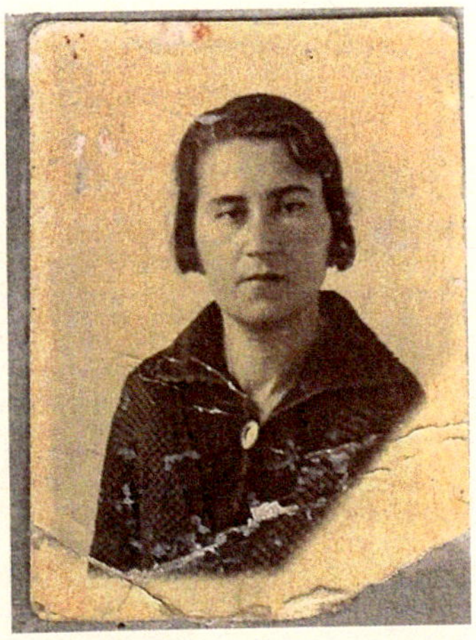

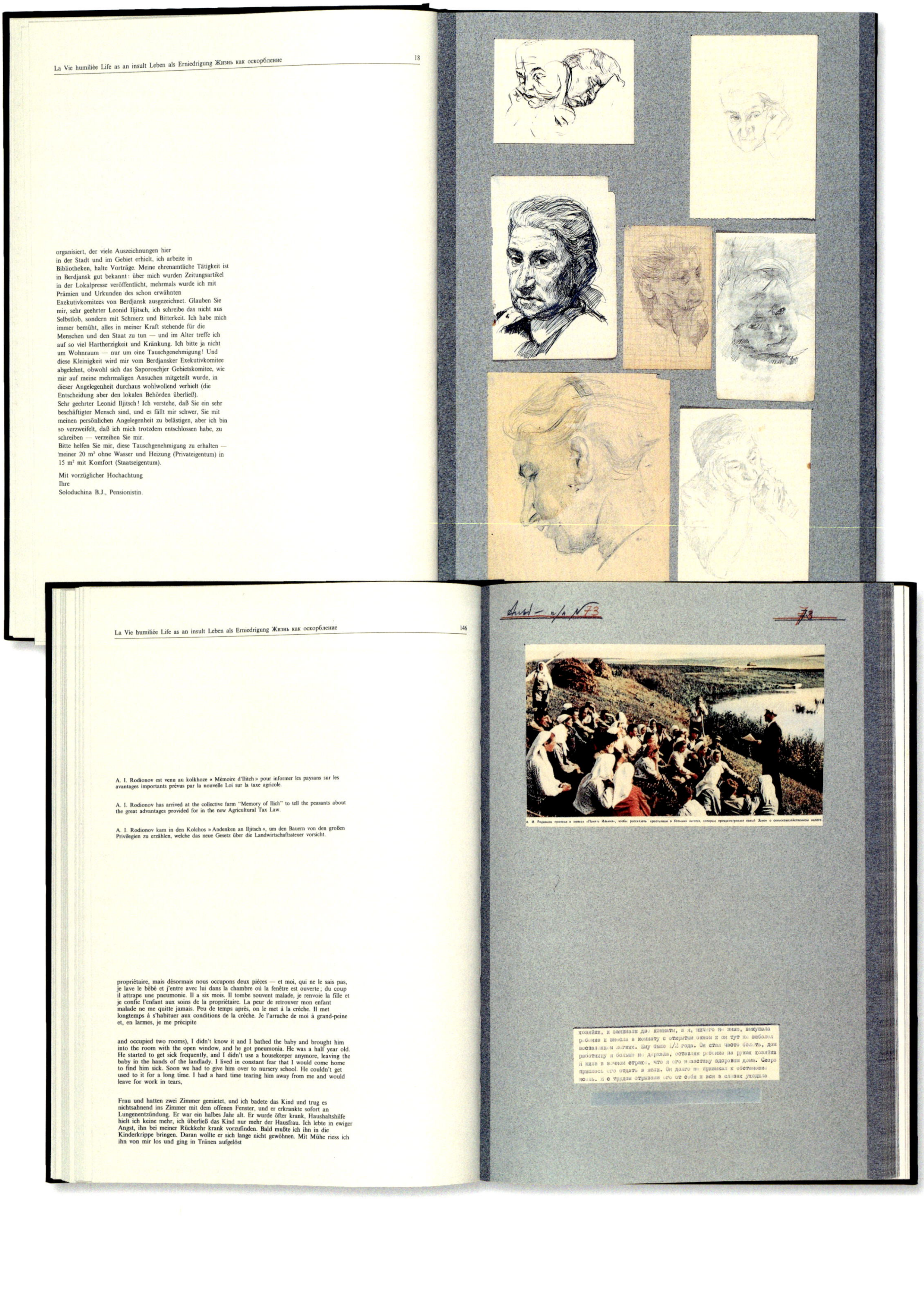

La Vie humiliée Life as an insult Leben als Erniedrigung Жизнь как оскорбление 18

organisiert, der viele Auszeichnungen hier
in der Stadt und im Gebiet erhielt, ich arbeite in
Bibliotheken, halte Vorträge. Meine ehrenamtliche Tätigkeit ist
in Berdjansk gut bekannt: über mich wurden Zeitungsartikel
in der Lokalpresse veröffentlicht, mehrmals wurde ich mit
Prämien und Urkunden des schon erwähnten
Exekutivkomitees von Berdjansk ausgezeichnet. Glauben Sie
mir, sehr geehrter Leonid Iljitsch, ich schreibe das nicht aus
Selbstlob, sondern mit Schmerz und Bitterkeit. Ich habe mich
immer bemüht, alles in meiner Kraft stehende für die
Menschen und den Staat zu tun — und im Alter treffe ich
auf so viel Hartherzigkeit und Kränkung. Ich bitte ja nicht
um Wohnraum — nur um eine Tauschgenehmigung! Und
diese Kleinigkeit wird mir vom Berdjansker Exekutivkomitee
abgelehnt, obwohl sich das Saporoschjer Gebietskomitee, wie
mir auf meine mehrmaligen Ansuchen mitgeteilt wurde, in
dieser Angelegenheit durchaus wohlwollend verhielt (die
Entscheidung aber den lokalen Behörden überließ).
Sehr geehrter Leonid Iljitsch! Ich verstehe, daß Sie ein sehr
beschäftigter Mensch sind, und es fällt mir schwer, Sie mit
meinen persönlichen Angelegenheit zu belästigen, aber ich bin
so verzweifelt, daß ich mich trotzdem entschlossen habe, zu
schreiben — verzeihen Sie mir.
Bitte helfen Sie mir, diese Tauschgenehmigung zu erhalten —
meiner 20 m² ohne Wasser und Heizung (Privateigentum) in
15 m² mit Komfort (Staatseigentum).

Mit vorzüglicher Hochachtung
Ihre
Soloduchina B.J., Pensionistin.

La Vie humiliée Life as an insult Leben als Erniedrigung Жизнь как оскорбление 146

A. I. Rodionov est venu au kolkhoze « Mémoire d'Ilitch » pour informer les paysans sur les avantages importants prévus par la nouvelle Loi sur la taxe agricole.

A. I. Rodionov has arrived at the collective farm "Memory of Ilich" to tell the peasants about the great advantages provided for in the new Agricultural Tax Law.

A. I. Rodionov kam in den Kolchos » Andenken an Iljitsch «, um den Bauern von den großen Privilegien zu erzählen, welche das neue Gesetz über die Landwirtschaftssteuer vorsicht.

propriétaire, mais désormais nous occupons deux pièces — et moi, qui ne le sais pas, je lave le bébé et j'entre avec lui dans la chambre où la fenêtre est ouverte; du coup il attrape une pneumonie. Il a six mois. Il tombe souvent malade, je renvoie la fille et je confie l'enfant aux soins de la propriétaire. La peur de retrouver mon enfant malade ne me quitte jamais. Peu de temps après, on le met à la crèche. Il met longtemps à s'habituer aux conditions de la crèche. Je l'arrache de moi à grand-peine et, en larmes, je me précipite

and occupied two rooms), I didn't know it and I bathed the baby and brought him into the room with the open window, and he got pneumonia. He was a half year old. He started to get sick frequently, and I didn't use a housekeeper anymore, leaving the baby in the hands of the landlady. I lived in constant fear that I would come home to find him sick. Soon we had to give him over to nursery school. He couldn't get used to it for a long time. I had a hard time tearing him away from me and would leave for work in tears,

Frau und hatten zwei Zimmer gemietet, und ich badete das Kind und trug es nichtsahnend ins Zimmer mit dem offenen Fenster, und er erkrankte sofort an Lungenentzündung. Er war ein halbes Jahr alt. Er wurde öfter krank, Haushaltshilfe hielt ich keine mehr, ich überließ das Kind nur mehr der Hausfrau. Ich lebte in ewiger Angst, ihn bei meiner Rückkehr krank vorzufinden. Bald mußte ich ihn in die Kinderkrippe bringen. Daran wollte er sich lange nicht gewöhnen. Mit Mühe riess ich ihn von mir los und ging in Tränen aufgelöst

хозяйки, и занимали две комнаты, а я, ничего не зная, викупала
ребенка и внесла в комнату с открытым окном и он тут же заболел
воспалением легких. Ему было 1/2 года. Он стал часто болеть, дом
работницу я больше не держала, оставляя ребенка на руках хозяйки
Я жила в вечном страхе, что я его не застану здоровым дома. Скоро
пришлось его отдать в ясли. Он долго не привыкал к обстановке
яслей. Я с трудом отрывала его от себя и вся в слезах уходила

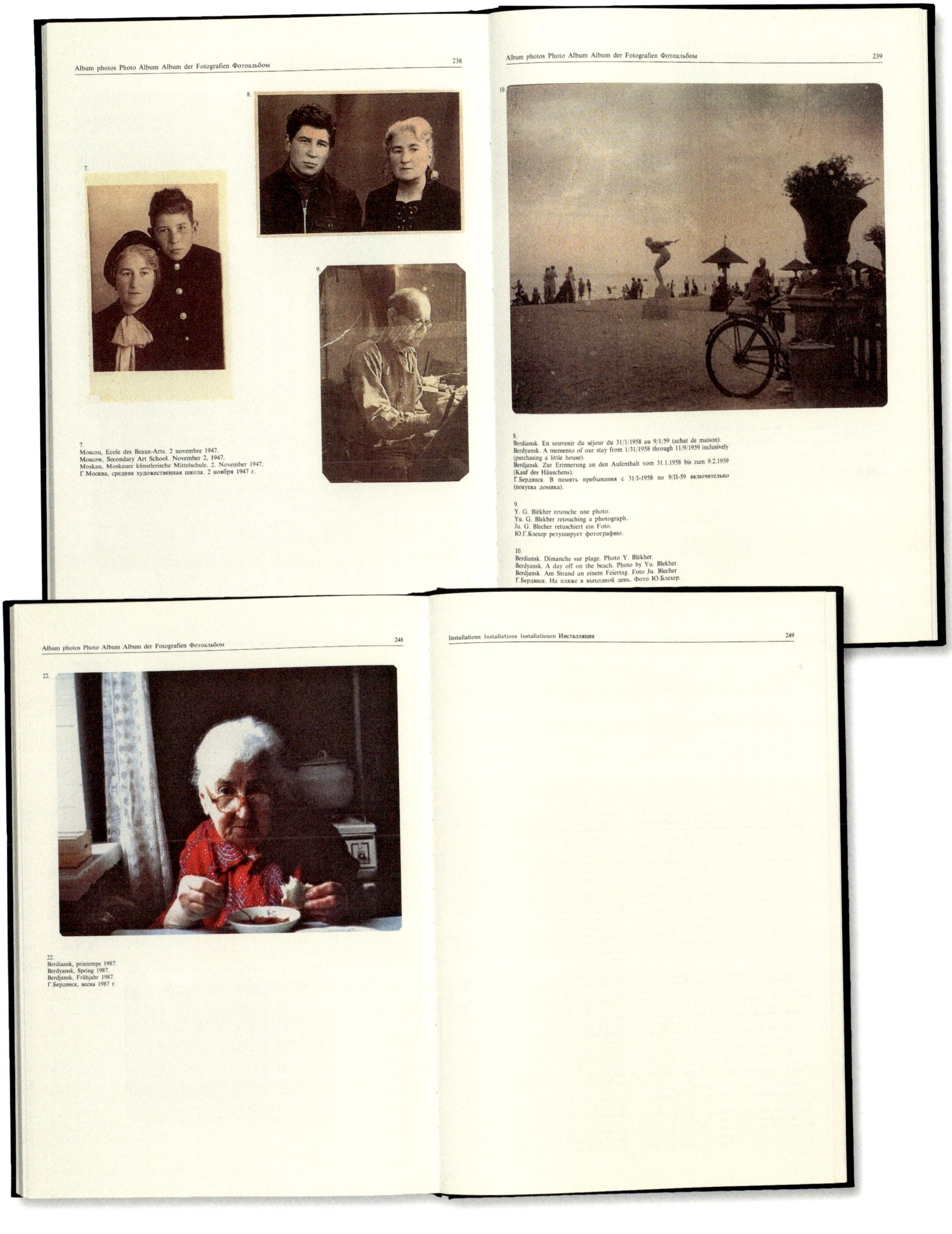

Album photos Photo Album Album der Fotografien Фотоальбом 238

7.
Moscou, Ecole des Beaux-Arts. 2 novembre 1947.
Moscow, Secondary Art School. November 2, 1947.
Moskau, Moskauer künstlerische Mittelschule. 2. November 1947.
Г.Москва, средняя художественная школа. 2 ноября 1947 г.

Album photos Photo Album Album der Fotografien Фотоальбом 239

8.
Berdiansk. En souvenir du séjour du 31/1/1958 au 9/1/59 (achat de maison).
Berdyansk. A memento of our stay from 1/31/1958 through 11/9/1959 inclusively (purchasing a little house).
Berdjansk. Zur Erinnerung an den Aufenthalt vom 31.1.1958 bis zum 9.2.1959 (Kauf des Häuschens).
Г.Бердянск. В память пребывания с 31/I-1958 по 9/II-59 включительно (покупка домика).

9.
Y. G. Blékher retouche une photo.
Yu. G. Blekher retouching a photograph.
Ju. G. Blecher retuschiert ein Foto.
Ю.Г.Блехер ретуширует фотографию.

10.
Berdiansk. Dimanche sur plage. Photo Y. Blékher.
Berdyansk. A day off on the beach. Photo by Yu. Blekher.
Berdjansk. Am Strand an einem Feiertag. Foto Ju. Blecher
Г.Бердянск. На пляже в выходной день. Фото Ю.Блехер.

Album photos Photo Album Album der Fotografien Фотоальбом 248

22.
Berdiansk, printemps 1987.
Berdyansk, Spring 1987.
Berdjansk, Frühjahr 1987.
Г.Бердянск, весна 1987 г.

Installations Installations Installationen Инсталляции 249

85 Unrealized Projects | *Nicht ausgeführte Projekte*

1995

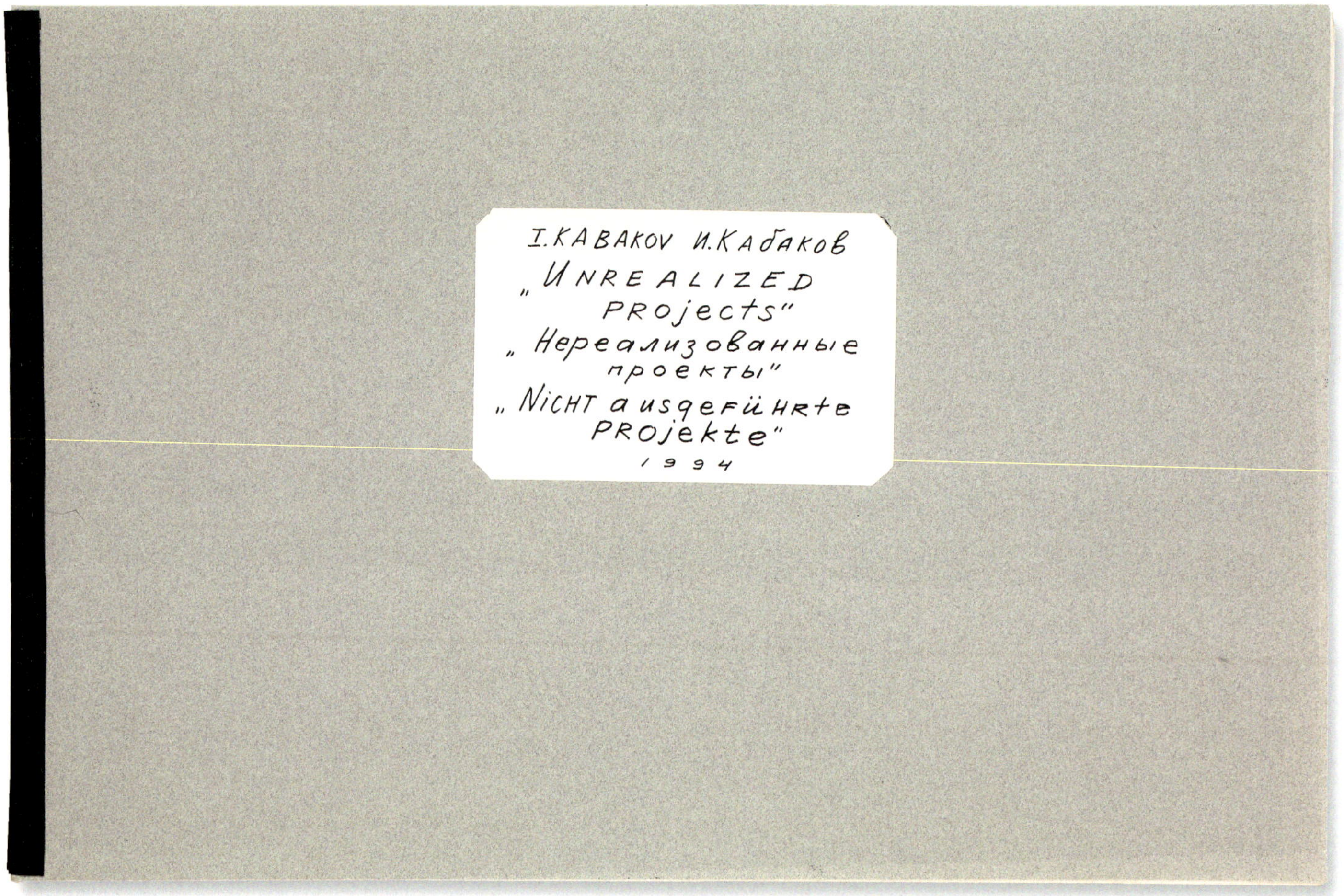

Ilya and Emilia Kabakov
New York: published by Ilya and Emilia Kabakov
27.9 x 43.4 cm
103 photocopied pp. (4 foldouts) with 84 (28 color) ills.
quick bind, paper cover, label on the cover
Schnellhefter, Papierumschlag, Etikette auf dem Umschlag
edition: 120 copies

thematic publication | *thematische Publikation*

layout by Ilya Kabakov | *Layout von Ilya Kabakov*

Documentation of the installation. Texts by Ilya Kabakov; Russian, English.

Dokumentation der Installation. Texte von Ilya Kabakov; russisch, englisch.

see also | *siehe auch* no. 71; CRI, vol. 2, no. 82, pp. 52–59

it interacts well with the gold of the cupola of "Seccession". The green color is the color of the basket and all four figures and it corresponds to the color of the green park while at the same time it is different from it.

But just what are these green "figures" and why are they throwing golden apples?

II. The Concept of the Installation

Here, beyond a doubt, is a reworking of a well-known theme from the Bible -- about paradise and paradise apples and about a serpent. In our installation the golden cupola of "Seccession" assumes the role of the garden of paradise and the park near it; the "golden" apples -- the apples in the basket and around it, and the role of the serpent, more precisely, of "serpents", is performed by the four terrible half-figures (each of them has its own name: "Electric", "Raymon", "Sobatik", and "Dush"). The installation belongs to the type of "disconnected" installations with its own internal drama: at first the viewer sees only one part of it, and then in search of meaning discovers another one in a place which is often unexpected. Thus, the viewer, having seen the scattered apples, sees neither a meaning nor a reason for why they are here, but only having raised his head, so to speak having changed the "horizon of vision", does he discover for himself the reason for their appearance. But we know that the serpent-tempter was also not visible (understood) by Adam and Eve until a certain time. Hence, the installation easily reveals its theme: Before taking the "golden apples", you must not only carefully look

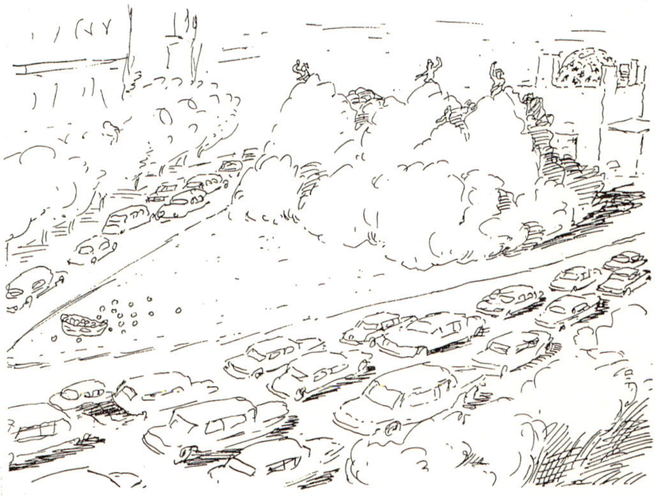

42

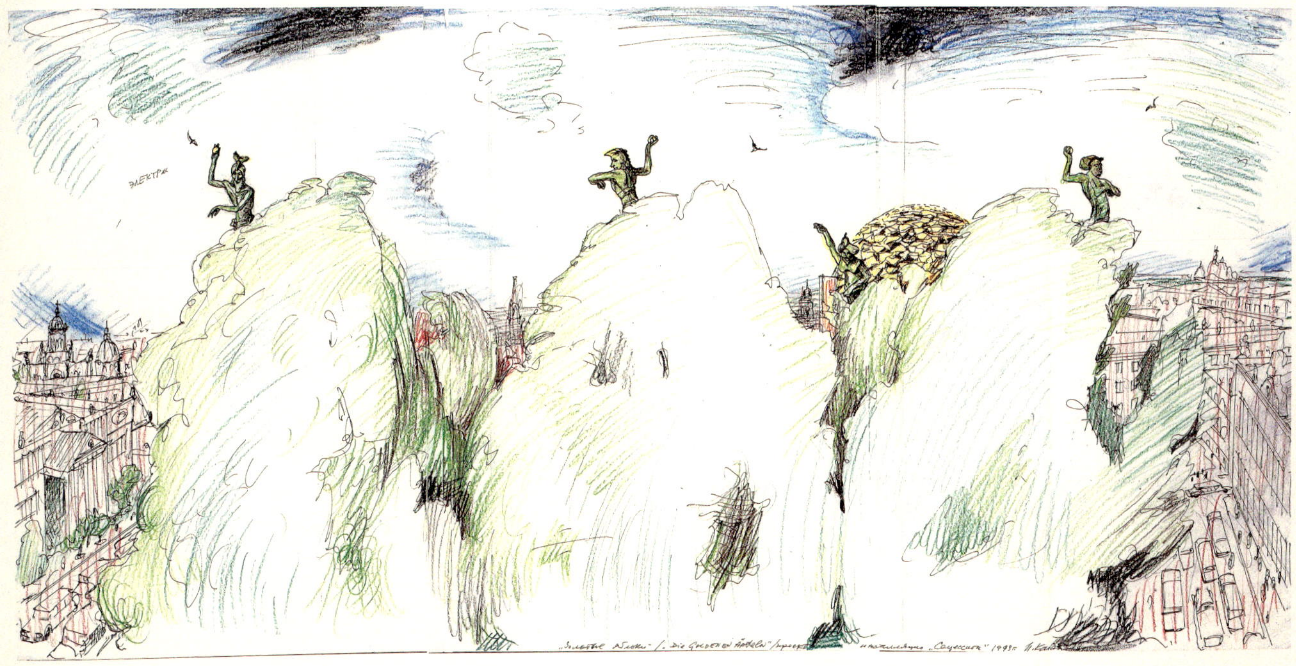

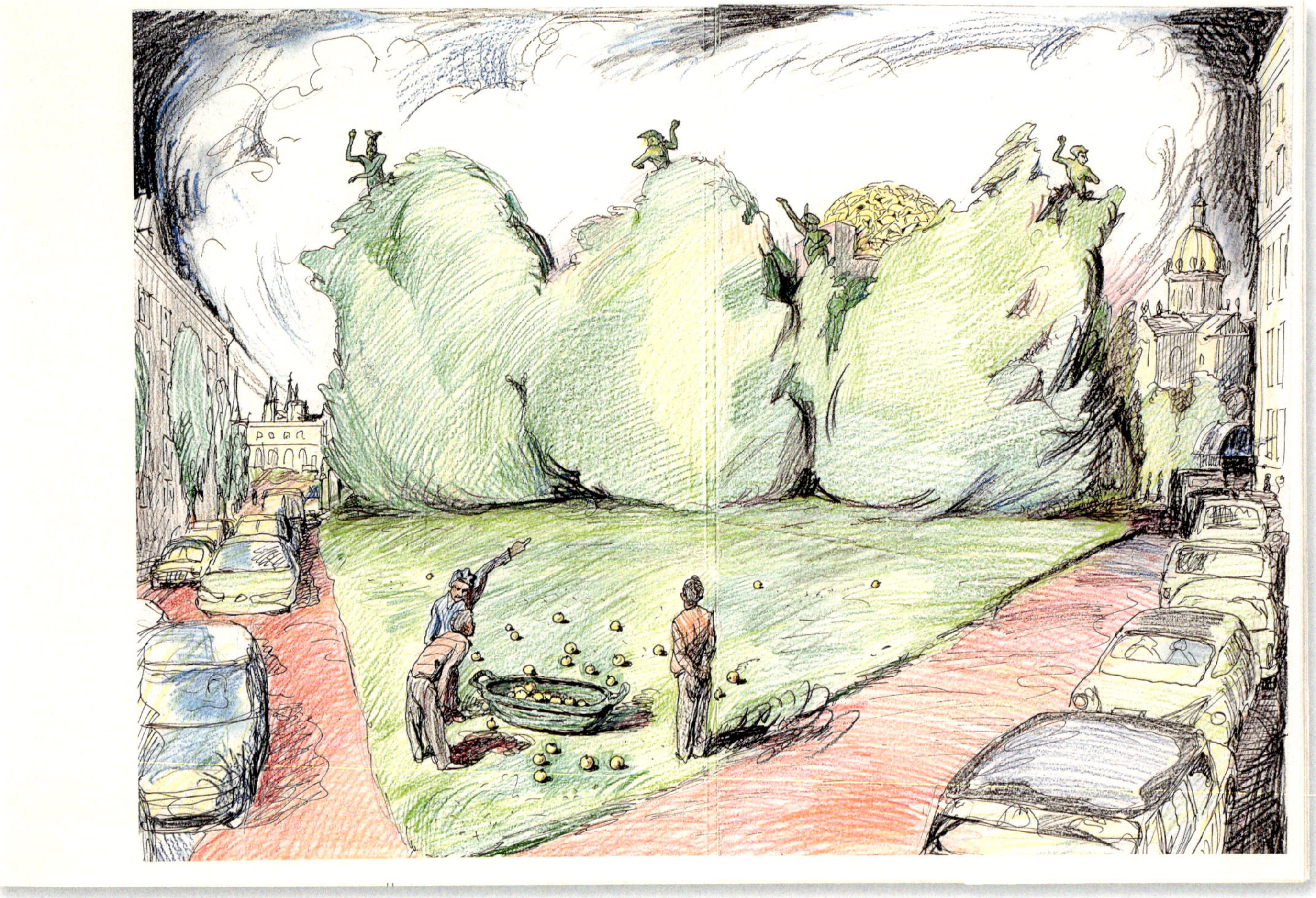

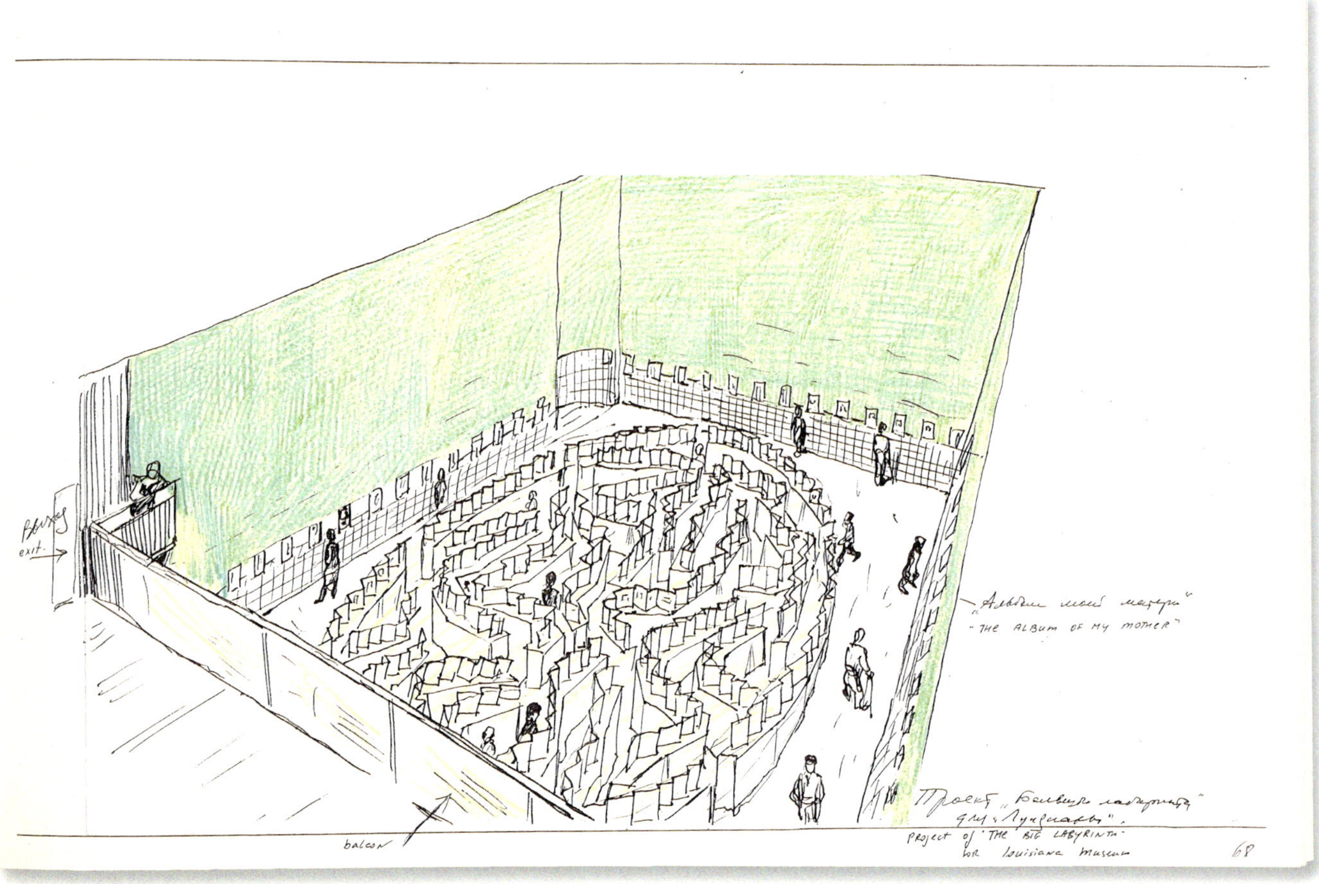
exit
„Альбом моей матери"
"THE ALBUM OF MY MOTHER"
balcon
PROJECT OF "THE BIG LABYRINTH"
for Louisiana Museum
68

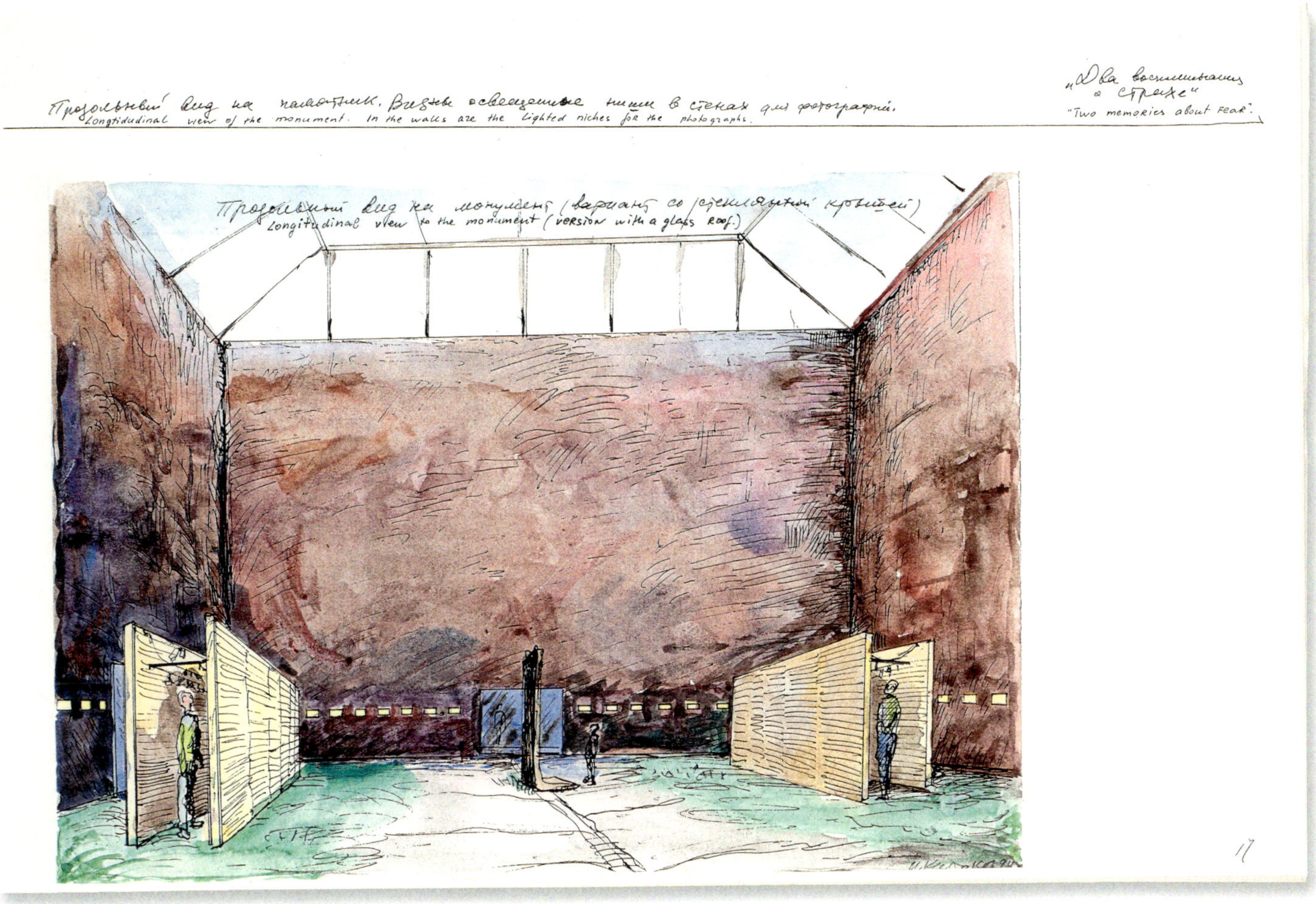
Longtidudinal view of the monument. In the walls are the lighted niches for the photographs.
"Two memories about Fear".
Longitudinal view to the monument (version with a glass roof.)
17

86 The Reading Room | *Der Lesesaal*

1996

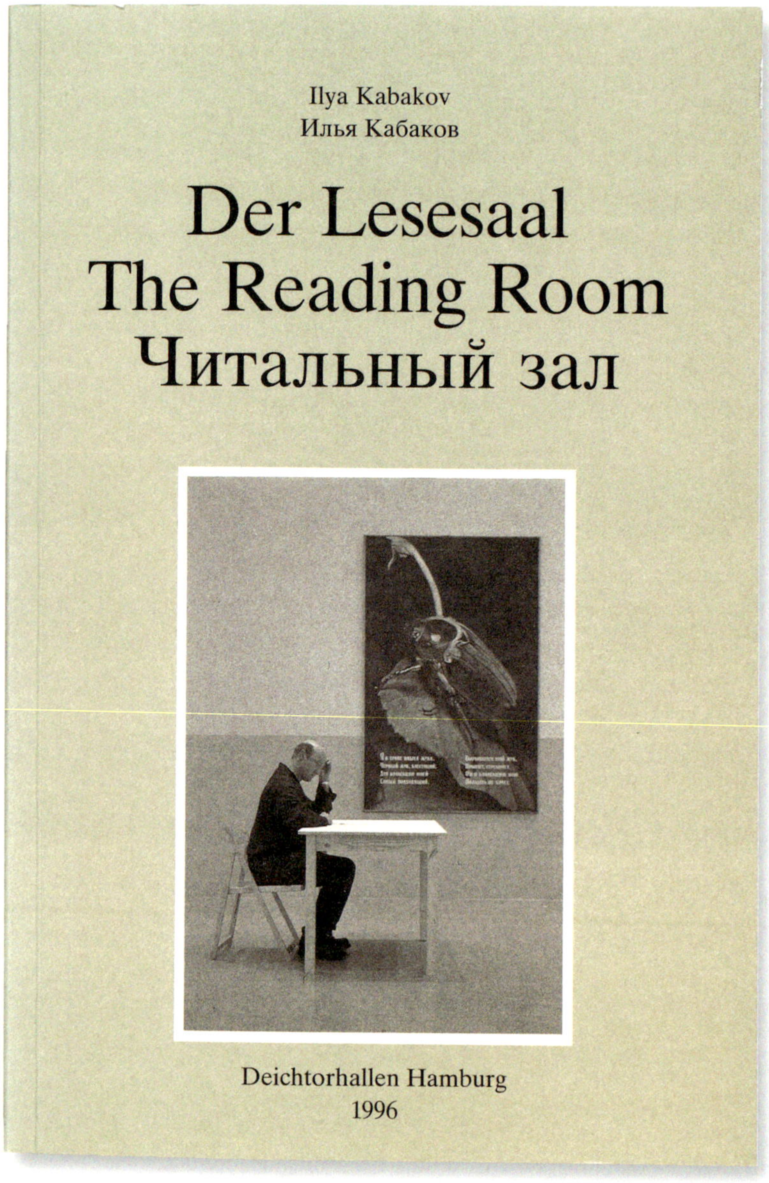

Deichtorhallen Hamburg
Hamburg: Deichtorhallen
23 x 15.5 cm
87 pp. with 30 b/w ills.
stitchbound, softback
Fadenheftung, broschiert

exhibition catalogue | *Ausstellungskatalog*

layout by Ilya Kabakov | *Layout von Ilya Kabakov*

For the installation of the same name for the exhibition »Ilya Kabakov: Der Lesesaal, Bilder, Leporellos und Zeichnungen« at the Deichtorhallen, Hamburg, April 19 to July 28, 1996. Texts by Ilya Kabakov; German, English, Russian.

Zur gleichnamigen Installation für die Ausstellung »Ilya Kabakov. Der Lesesaal. Bilder, Leporellos und Zeichnungen«, Deichtorhallen, Hamburg, 19. April – 28. Juli 1996. Texte von Ilya Kabakov; deutsch, englisch und russisch.

see also | *siehe auch* CRI, vol. 2, no. 90, pp. 98–103

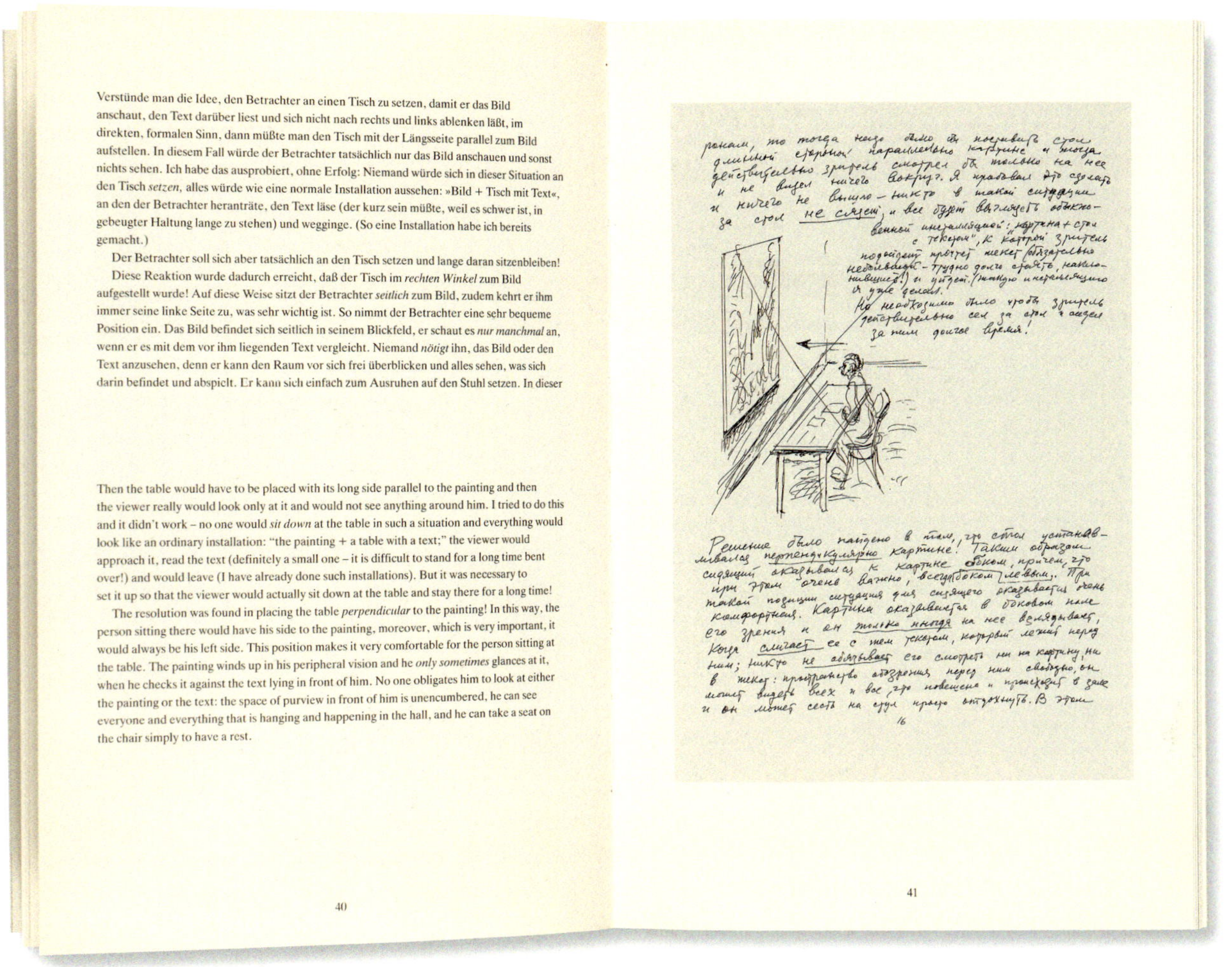

Verstünde man die Idee, den Betrachter an einen Tisch zu setzen, damit er das Bild anschaut, den Text darüber liest und sich nicht nach rechts und links ablenken läßt, im direkten, formalen Sinn, dann müßte man den Tisch mit der Längsseite parallel zum Bild aufstellen. In diesem Fall würde der Betrachter tatsächlich nur das Bild anschauen und sonst nichts sehen. Ich habe das ausprobiert, ohne Erfolg: Niemand würde sich in dieser Situation an den Tisch *setzen*, alles würde wie eine normale Installation aussehen: »Bild + Tisch mit Text«, an den der Betrachter heranträte, den Text läse (der kurz sein müßte, weil es schwer ist, in gebeugter Haltung lange zu stehen) und wegginge. (So eine Installation habe ich bereits gemacht.)

Der Betrachter soll sich aber tatsächlich an den Tisch setzen und lange daran sitzenbleiben!

Diese Reaktion wurde dadurch erreicht, daß der Tisch im *rechten Winkel* zum Bild aufgestellt wurde! Auf diese Weise sitzt der Betrachter *seitlich* zum Bild, zudem kehrt er ihm immer seine linke Seite zu, was sehr wichtig ist. So nimmt der Betrachter eine sehr bequeme Position ein. Das Bild befindet sich seitlich in seinem Blickfeld, er schaut es *nur manchmal* an, wenn er es mit dem vor ihm liegenden Text vergleicht. Niemand *nötigt* ihn, das Bild oder den Text anzusehen, denn er kann den Raum vor sich frei überblicken und alles sehen, was sich darin befindet und abspielt. Er kann sich einfach zum Ausruhen auf den Stuhl setzen. In dieser

Then the table would have to be placed with its long side parallel to the painting and then the viewer really would look only at it and would not see anything around him. I tried to do this and it didn't work – no one would *sit down* at the table in such a situation and everything would look like an ordinary installation: "the painting + a table with a text;" the viewer would approach it, read the text (definitely a small one – it is difficult to stand for a long time bent over!) and would leave (I have already done such installations). But it was necessary to set it up so that the viewer would actually sit down at the table and stay there for a long time!

The resolution was found in placing the table *perpendicular* to the painting! In this way, the person sitting there would have his side to the painting, moreover, which is very important, it would always be his left side. This position makes it very comfortable for the person sitting at the table. The painting winds up in his peripheral vision and he *only sometimes* glances at it, when he checks it against the text lying in front of him. No one obligates him to look at either the painting or the text: the space of purview in front of him is unencumbered, he can see everyone and everything that is hanging and happening in the hall, and he can take a seat on the chair simply to have a rest.

40

рокам, что тогда надо было бы поставить стол
длинной стороной параллельно картине и тогда
действительно зритель смотрел бы только на нее
и не видел ничего вокруг. Я пробовал это сделать
и ничего не вышло – никто в такой ситуации
за стол не сядет, и все будет выглядеть обыкно-
венной инсталляцией: „картина + стол
с текстом", к которой зритель
подойдет прочтет текст (обязательно
небольшой – трудно долго стоять, накло-
нившись!) и уйдет. (такую инсталляцию
я уже делал.
Но необходимо было чтобы зритель
действительно сел за стол и сидел
за ним долгое время!

Решение было найдено в том, что стол устанав-
ливался перпендикулярно картине! Таким образом
сидящий оказывался к картине боком, причем, что
при этом очень важно, всегда боком левым. При
такой позиции ситуация для сидящего оказывается очень
комфортной. Картина оказывается в боковом поле
его зрения и он только иногда на нее взглядывает,
когда сличает ее с тем текстом, который лежит перед
ним; никто не обязывает его смотреть ни на картину, ни
в текст: пространство обозрения перед ним свободно, он
может видеть всех и все, что повешено и происходит в зале
и он может сесть на стул просто отдохнуть. В этом

16

41

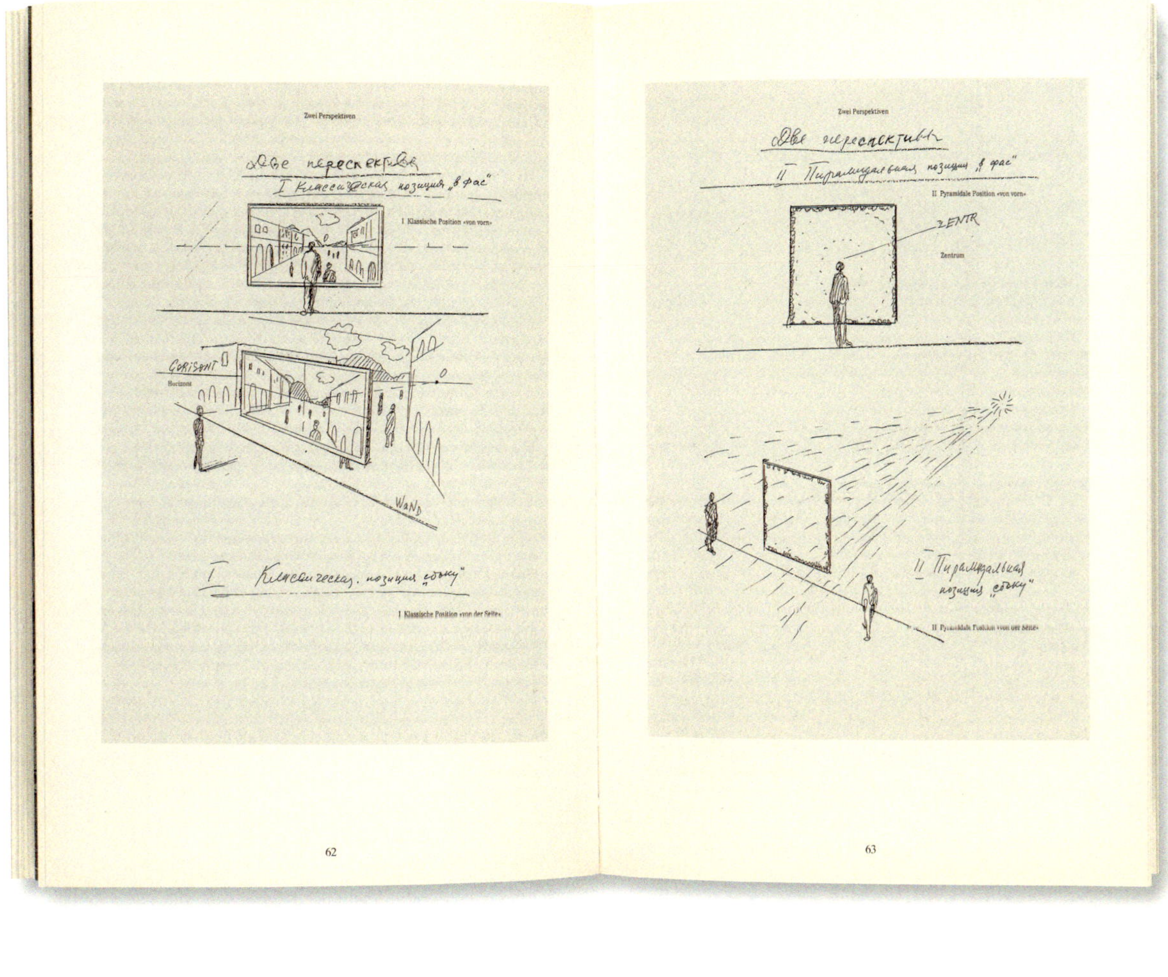

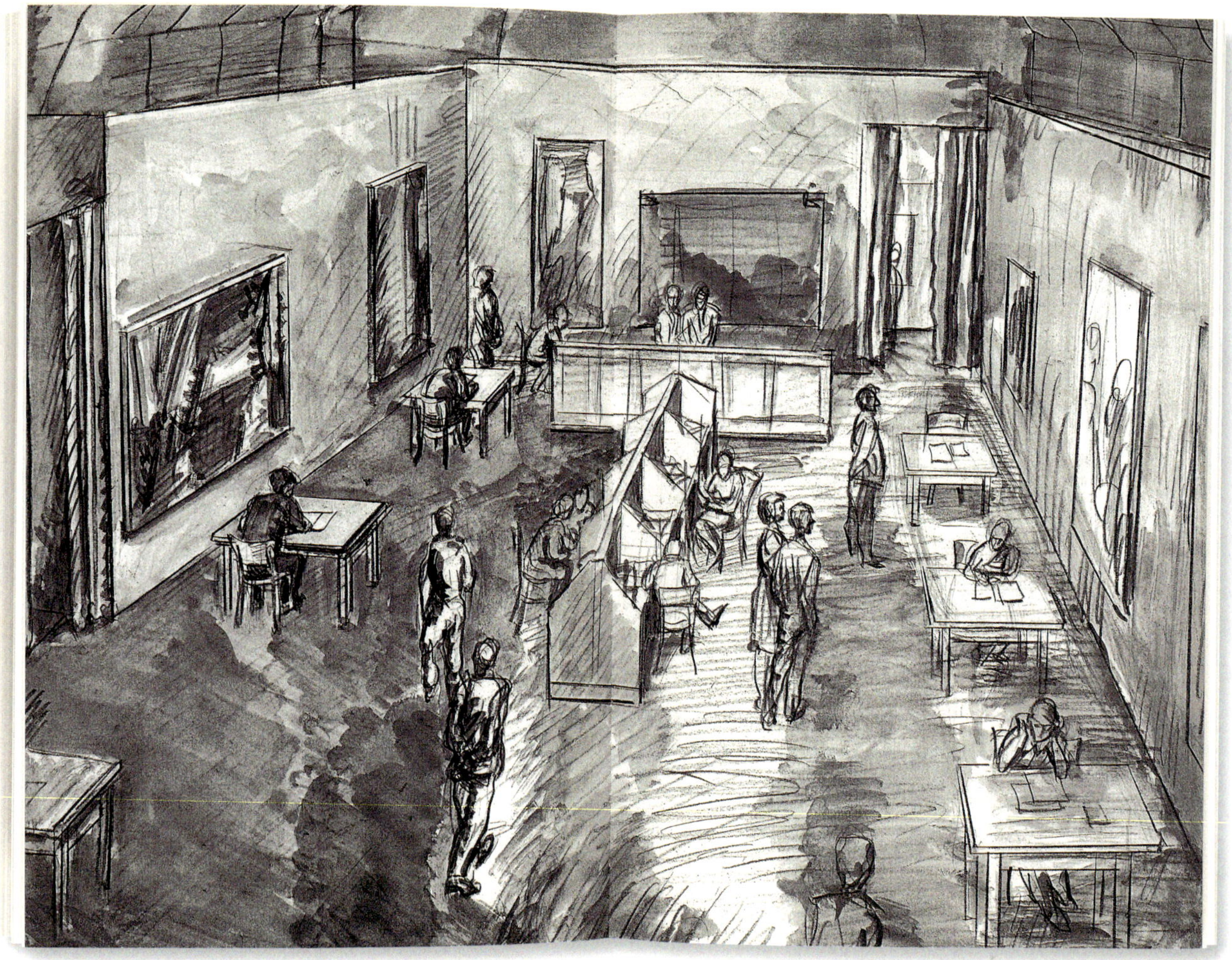

In jedem dieser abgetrennten Räume stehen Tische, aber nicht so wie in den »allgemeinen« Lesesälen der Bibliotheken, wo alle nebeneinander und einander gegenüber an langen Tischen sitzen, sondern so, wie sie in den Sälen für Forschungsarbeit aufgestellt sind. Jeder Tisch steht für sich, und an jedem kann nur eine Person arbeiten. Der Abstand zwischen ihnen ist so bemessen, daß man sich nicht gegenseitig »stört«. Jeder Tisch steht unter einem Bild. In jedem Saal befinden sich so viele Tische wie Bilder an den Wänden.

Die Tische und Stühle sind aus hellem Holz gefertigt.

Sie stehen entlang den Wänden. In der Raummitte sind ein etwas längerer Tisch und ein pultähnliches Möbel aufgestellt.

Rather these are the kinds of tables that are usually arranged in halls intended for special "scholarly" work: each table stands alone, only one person can study at it. Furthermore, the tables stand at a significant distance from one another so as not to "bother" anyone. Each one of these tables stands under a painting. There are as many paintings in the hall as there are tables. The tables are made of light wood, the chairs are also wooden and of the same color.

All of this is arranged along the walls. Another table, an authentic one, is placed in the center, along with something resembling in appearance a unique kind of podium.

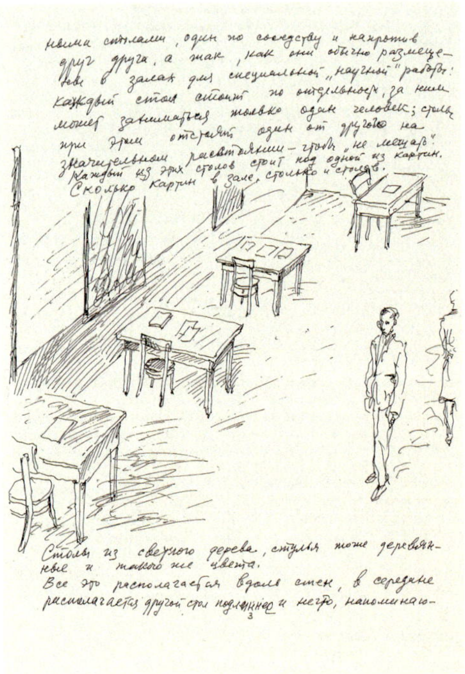

14

15

87 On the Roof | *Auf dem Dach*

1996

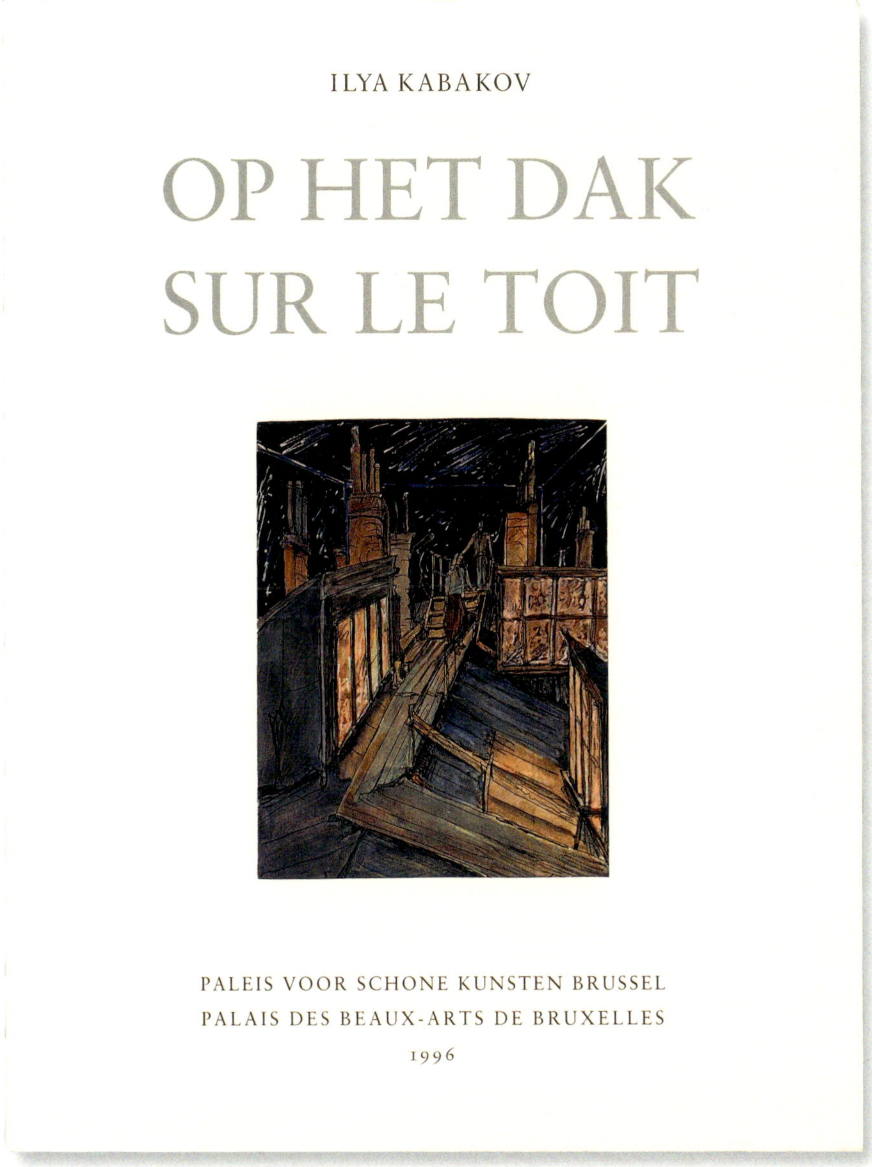

Paleis voor Schone Kunsten, Brussel/Palais des Beaux-Arts, Bruxelles
Brussels: Paleis voor Schone Kunsten/Palais des Beaux-Arts
29.4 x 22.4 cm
175 pp. with 260 (10 color) ills.
stitchbound, softback
Fadenheftung, broschiert

exhibition catalogue | *Ausstellungskatalog*

layout by Ilya Kabakov | *Layout von Ilya Kabakov*

For the installation of the same name at the Paleis voor Schone Kunsten / Palais des Beaux-Arts, Brussels, June 7 to September 8, 1996. Texts by Piet Coessens and Ilya Kabakov; Flemish, French.

Zur gleichnamigen Installation, Paleis voor Schone Kunsten, Brussel / Palais des Beaux-Arts, Bruxelles, 7. Juni – 8. September 1996. Texte von Piet Coessens und Ilya Kabakov; flämisch, französisch.

see also | *siehe auch* no. 93; CRI, vol. 2, no. 100, pp. 150–155

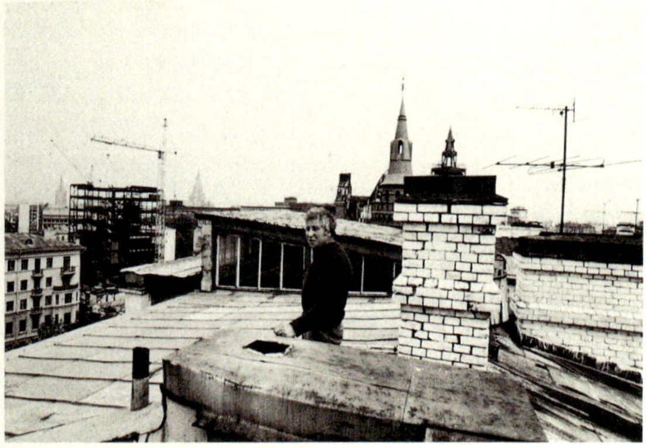

ILYA KABAKOV

OP HET DAK
SUR LE TOIT

INSTALLATIE
INSTALLATION

PALEIS VOOR SCHONE KUNSTEN BRUSSEL
PALAIS DES BEAUX-ARTS DE BRUXELLES
1996

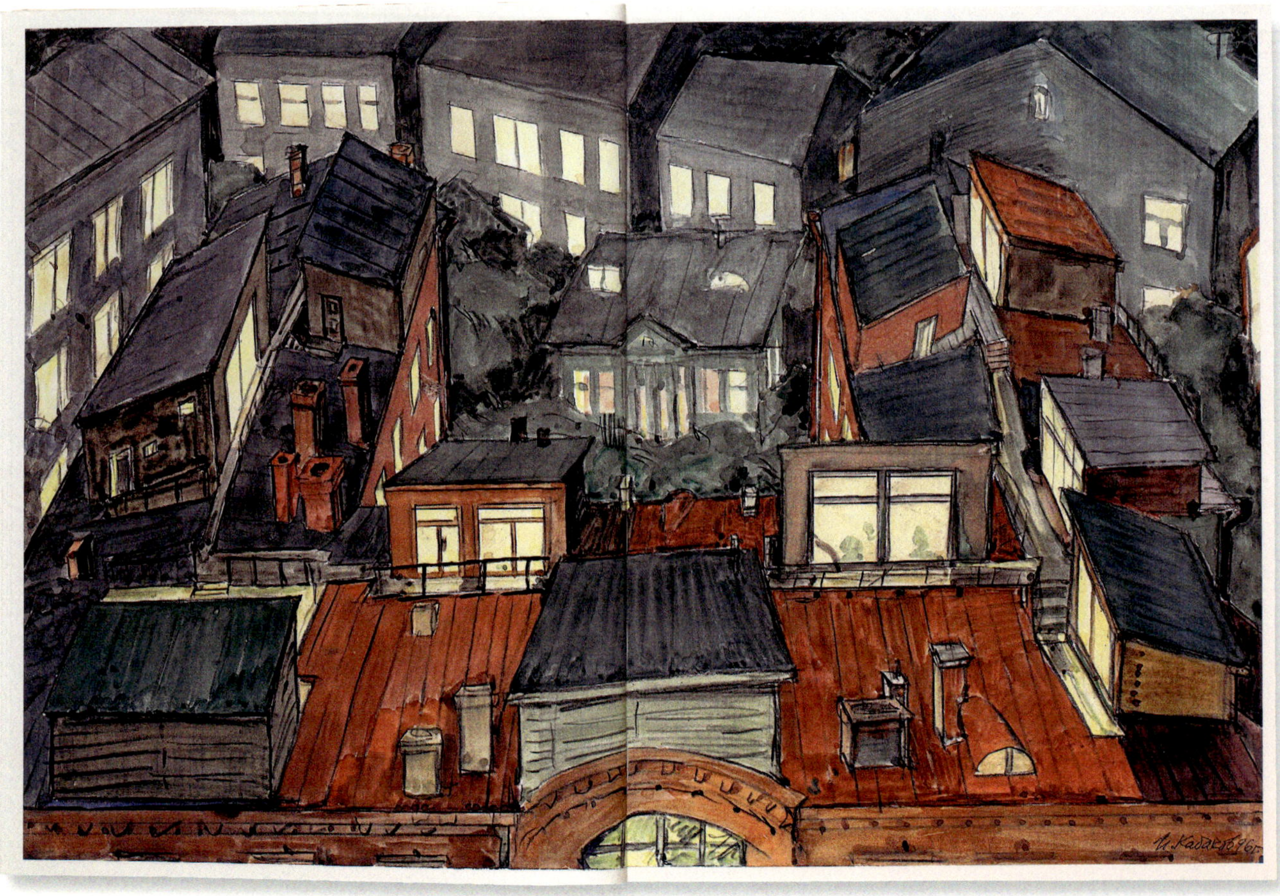

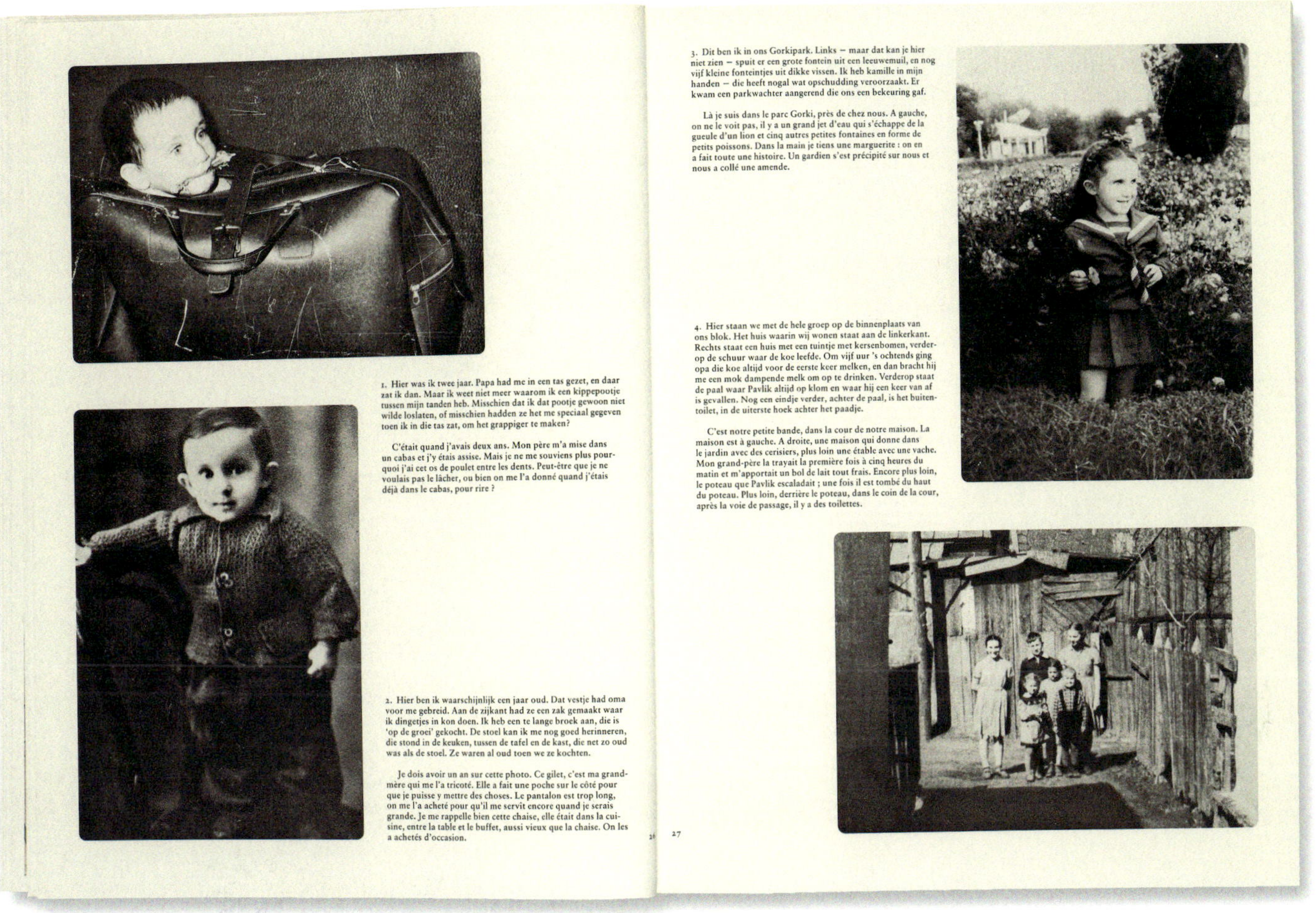

1. Hier was ik twee jaar. Papa had me in een tas gezet, en daar zat ik dan. Maar ik weet niet meer waarom ik een kippepootje tussen mijn tanden heb. Misschien dat ik dat pootje gewoon niet wilde loslaten, of misschien hadden ze het me speciaal gegeven toen ik in die tas zat, om het grappiger te maken?

C'était quand j'avais deux ans. Mon père m'a mise dans un cabas et j'y étais assise. Mais je ne me souviens plus pourquoi j'ai cet os de poulet entre les dents. Peut-être que je ne voulais pas le lâcher, ou bien on me l'a donné quand j'étais déjà dans le cabas, pour rire ?

2. Hier ben ik waarschijnlijk een jaar oud. Dat vestje had oma voor me gebreid. Aan de zijkant had ze een zak gemaakt waar ik dingetjes in kon doen. Ik heb een te lange broek aan, die is 'op de groei' gekocht. De stoel kan ik me nog goed herinneren, die stond in de keuken, tussen de tafel en de kast, die net zo oud was als de stoel. Ze waren al oud toen we ze kochten.

Je dois avoir un an sur cette photo. Ce gilet, c'est ma grand-mère qui me l'a tricoté. Elle a fait une poche sur le côté pour que je puisse y mettre des choses. Le pantalon est trop long, on me l'a acheté pour qu'il me servît encore quand je serais grande. Je me rappelle bien cette chaise, elle était dans la cuisine, entre la table et le buffet, aussi vieux que la chaise. On les a achetés d'occasion.

26

3. Dit ben ik in ons Gorkipark. Links – maar dat kan je hier niet zien – spuit er een grote fontein uit een leeuwemuil, en nog vijf kleine fonteintjes uit dikke vissen. Ik heb kamille in mijn handen – die heeft nogal wat opschudding veroorzaakt. Er kwam een parkwachter aangerend die ons een bekeuring gaf.

Là je suis dans le parc Gorki, près de chez nous. A gauche, on ne le voit pas, il y a un grand jet d'eau qui s'échappe de la gueule d'un lion et cinq autres petites fontaines en forme de petits poissons. Dans la main je tiens une marguerite : on en a fait toute une histoire. Un gardien s'est précipité sur nous et nous a collé une amende.

4. Hier staan we met de hele groep op de binnenplaats van ons blok. Het huis waarin wij wonen staat aan de linkerkant. Rechts staat een huis met een tuintje met kersenbomen, verderop de schuur waar de koe leefde. Om vijf uur 's ochtends ging opa die koe altijd voor de eerste keer melken, en dan bracht hij me een mok dampende melk om op te drinken. Verderop staat de paal waar Pavlik altijd op klom en waar hij een keer van af is gevallen. Nog een eindje verder, achter de paal, is het buitentoilet, in de uiterste hoek achter het paadje.

C'est notre petite bande, dans la cour de notre maison. La maison est à gauche. A droite, une maison qui donne dans le jardin avec des cerisiers, plus loin une étable avec une vache. Mon grand-père la trayait la première fois à cinq heures du matin et m'apportait un bol de lait tout frais. Encore plus loin, le poteau que Pavlik escaladait ; une fois il est tombé du haut du poteau. Plus loin, derrière le poteau, dans le coin de la cour, après la voie de passage, il y a des toilettes.

27

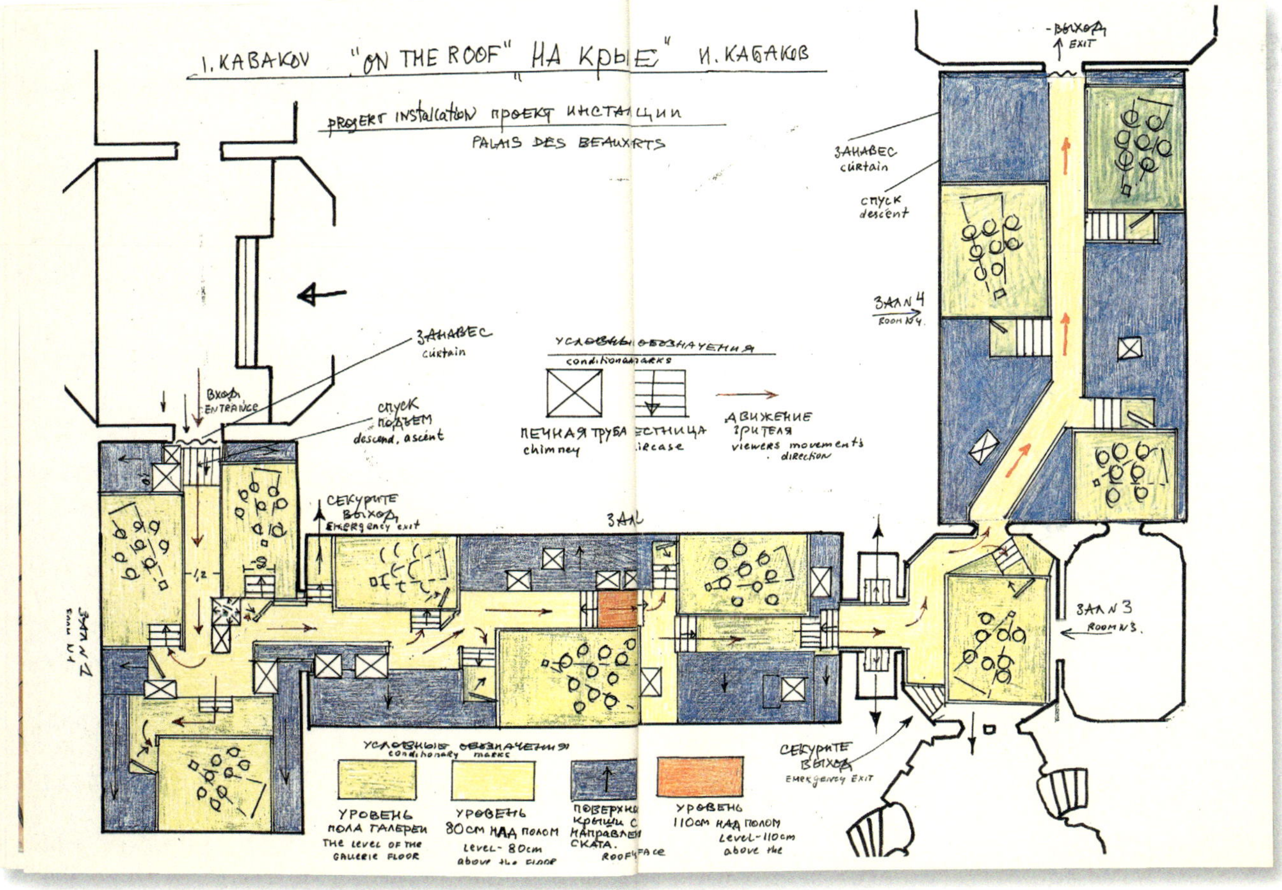

88 1964–1983: The Ship | *1964–1983. Das Schiff*

1996

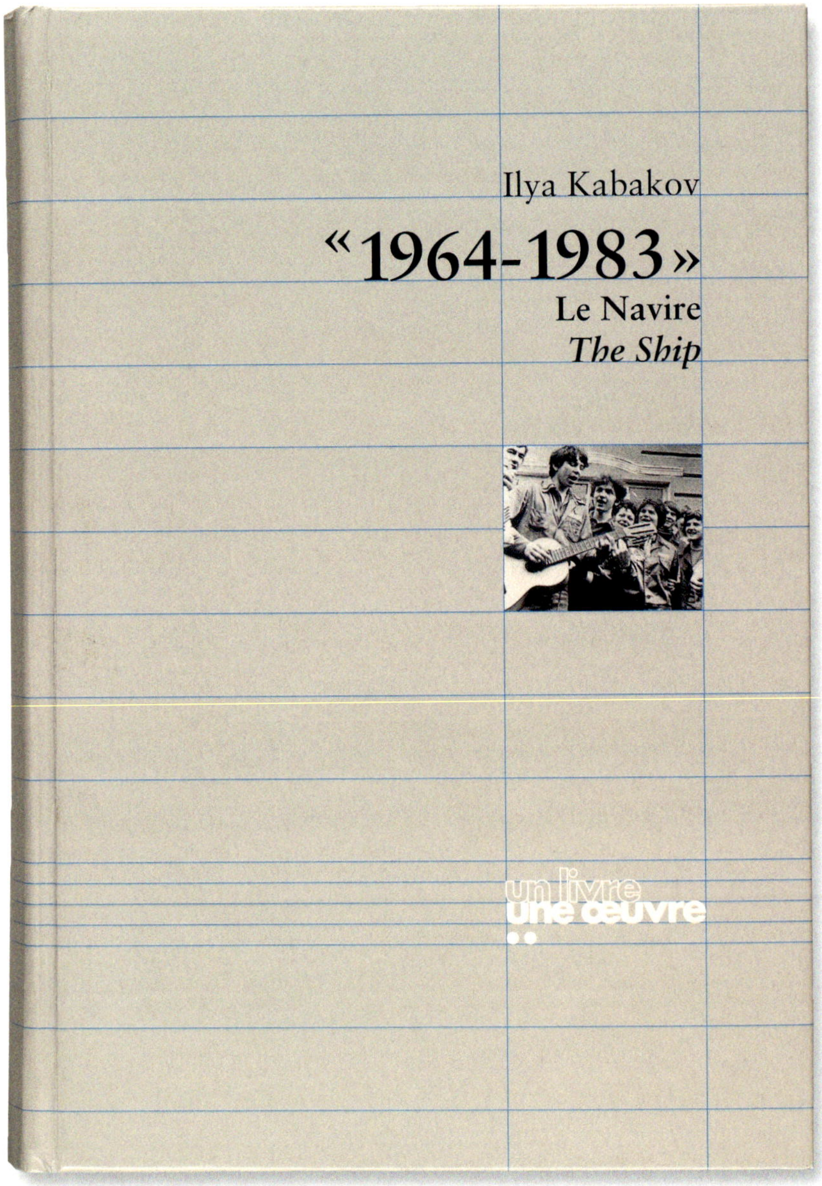

Musée d'Art Contemporain, Lyon
Lyon: Musée d'Art Contemporain
(un livre/une œuvre)
17.9 x 12.7 cm
472 pp. with 67 (46 color) ills.
stitchbound, hardcover, bookmark
Fadenheftung, Hardcover, Lesezeichen

exhibition catalogue | *Ausstellungskatalog*

idea by Ilya Kabakov | *Idee von Ilya Kabakov*

Texts for the installation »The Ship«, which have been part of the collection of the Musée d'Art Contemporain, Lyon since 1989. Texts by Ilya Kabakov and Thierry Raspail; French, English.

Texte der Installation »Das Schiff«, seit 1989 in der Sammlung des Musée d'Art Contemporain, Lyon. Texte von Ilya Kabakov und Thierry Raspail; französisch, englisch.

see also | *siehe auch* no. 26; CRI, vol. 1, no. 10, pp. 102–107

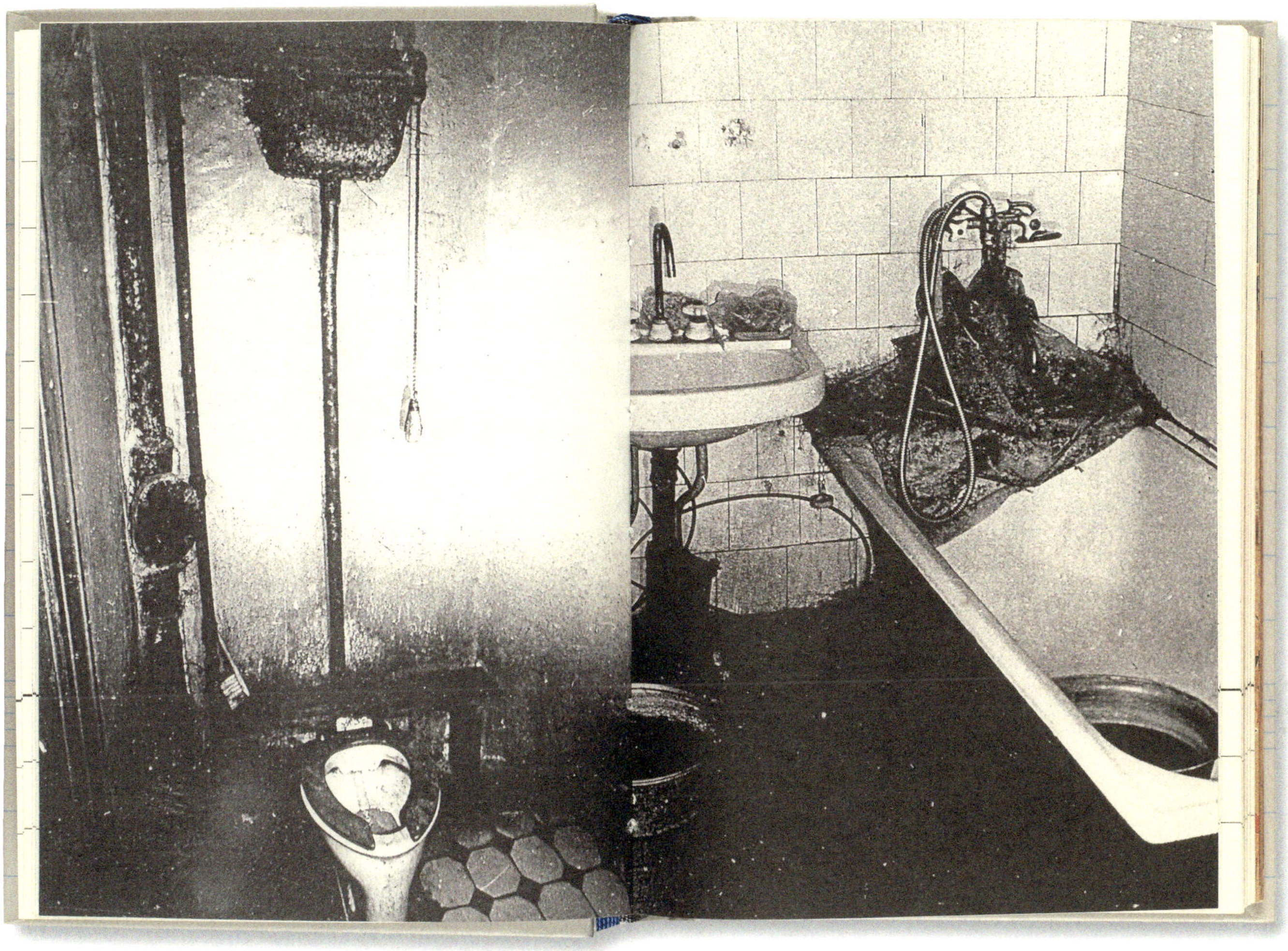

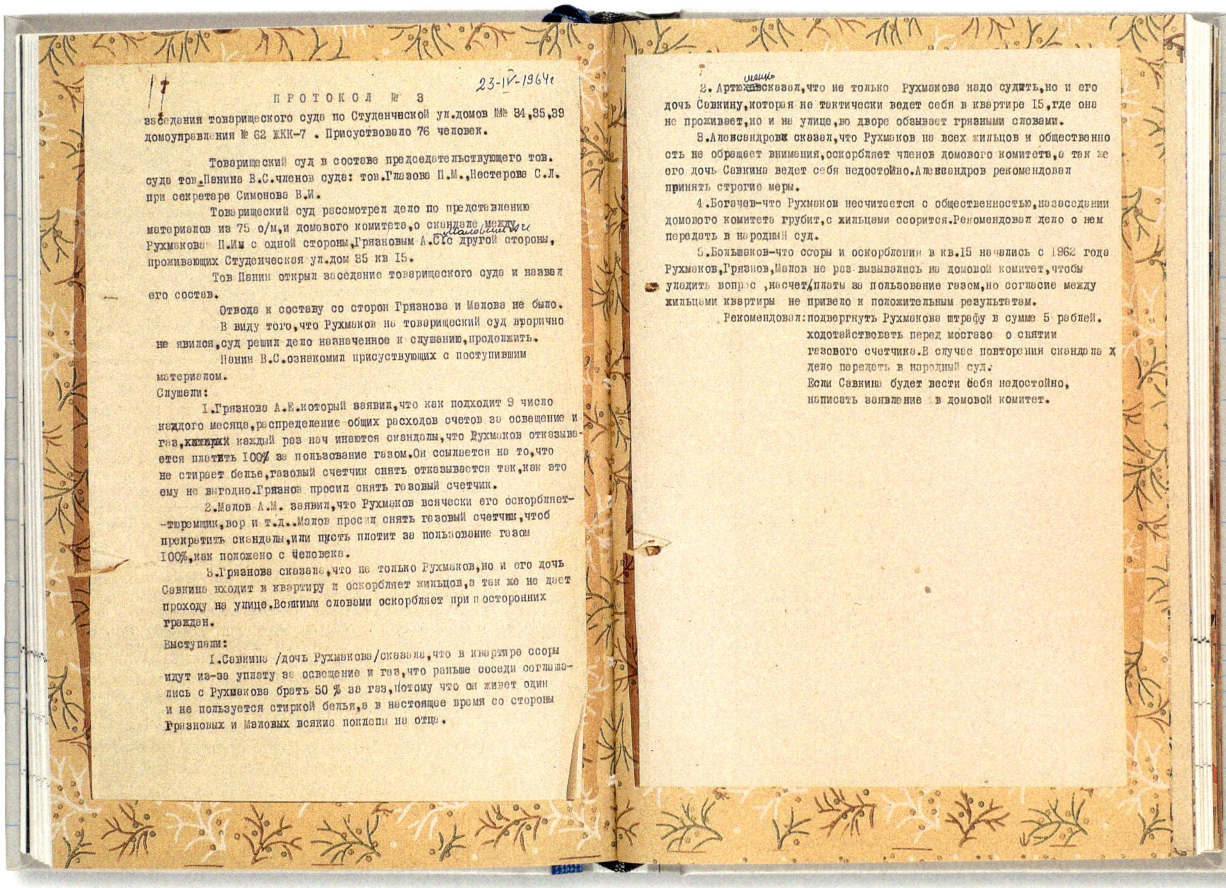
17 23-IV-1964г

ПРОТОКОЛ № 3

заседения товарищеского суда по Студенчиской ул.домов №№ 34,35,39 домоуправления № 62 ЖКК-7. Присуствовало 76 человек.

Товарищеский суд в составе председательствующего тов. суда тов.Панина В.С.членов суда: тов.Глазова П.М.,Нестерова С.Л. при секретаре Симонова В.И.

Товарищеский суд рассмотрел дело по представлению материалов из 75 о/м,и домового комитета,о скандале между Рухмаковым П.И. с одной стороны,Грязновым А.С. Маловым с другой стороны, проживающих Студенческая ул.дом 35 кв 15.

Тов Панин открыл заседание товарищеского суда и назвал его состав.

Отвода к составу со сторон Грязнова и Малова не было.

В виду того,что Рухмаков на товарищеский суд вторично не явился,суд решил дело назначенное к слушанию,продолжить.

Панин В.С.ознакомил присуствующих с поступившим материалом.

Слушали:

I.Грязнова А.Е.который заявил,что как подходит 9 число каждого месяца,распределение общих расходов счетов за освещение и газ, каждый раз начинаются скандалы,что Рухмаков отказывается платить 100% за пользование газом.Он ссылается на то,что не стирает белье,газовый счетчик снять отказывается так,как это ему не выгодно.Грязнов просил снять газовый счетчик.

2.Малов А.М. заявил,что Рухмаков всячески его оскорбляет-тюремщик,вор и т.д..Малов просил снять газовый счетчик,чтоб прекратить скандалы,или пусть платит за пользование газом 100%,как положено с человека.

3.Грязнова сказала,что не только Рухмаков,но и его дочь Савкина входит в квартиру и оскорбляет жильцов,а так же не дает проходу на улице.Всякими словами оскорбляет при посторонних граждан.

Выступали:

I.Савкина /дочь Рухмакова/сказала,что в квартире ссоры идут из-за уплату за освещение и газ,что раньше соседи соглашались с Рухмакова брать 50 % за газ,потому что он живет один и не пользуется стиркой белья,а в настоящее время со стороны Грязновых и Маловых всякие поклепы на отца.

2.Артюшенко сказал,что не только Рухмакова надо судить,но и его дочь Савкину,которая не тактически ведет себя в квартире 15,где она не проживает,но и на улице,во дворе обзывает грязными словами.

3.Александров сказал,что Рухмаков на всех жильцов и общественность не обращает внимания,оскорбляет членов домового комитета,а так же его дочь Савкина ведет себя недостойно.Александров рекомендовал принять строгие меры.

4.Богачев-что Рухмаков несчитается с общественностью,на заседании домового комитета грубит,с жильцами ссорится.Рекомендовал дело о нем передать в народный суд.

5.Большаков-что ссоры и оскорбления в кв.15 начались с 1962 года Рухмаков,Грязнов,Малов не раз вызывались на домовой комитет,чтобы уладить вопрос ,насчет/платы за пользование газом,но согласие между жильцами квартиры не привело к положительным результатам.

Рекомендовал: подвергнуть Рухмакова штрафу в сумме 5 раблей.
ходотайствовать перед мосгазо о снятии газового счетчика.В случае повторения скандала дело передать в народный суд.
Если Савкина будет вести себя недостойно, написать заявление в домовой комитет.

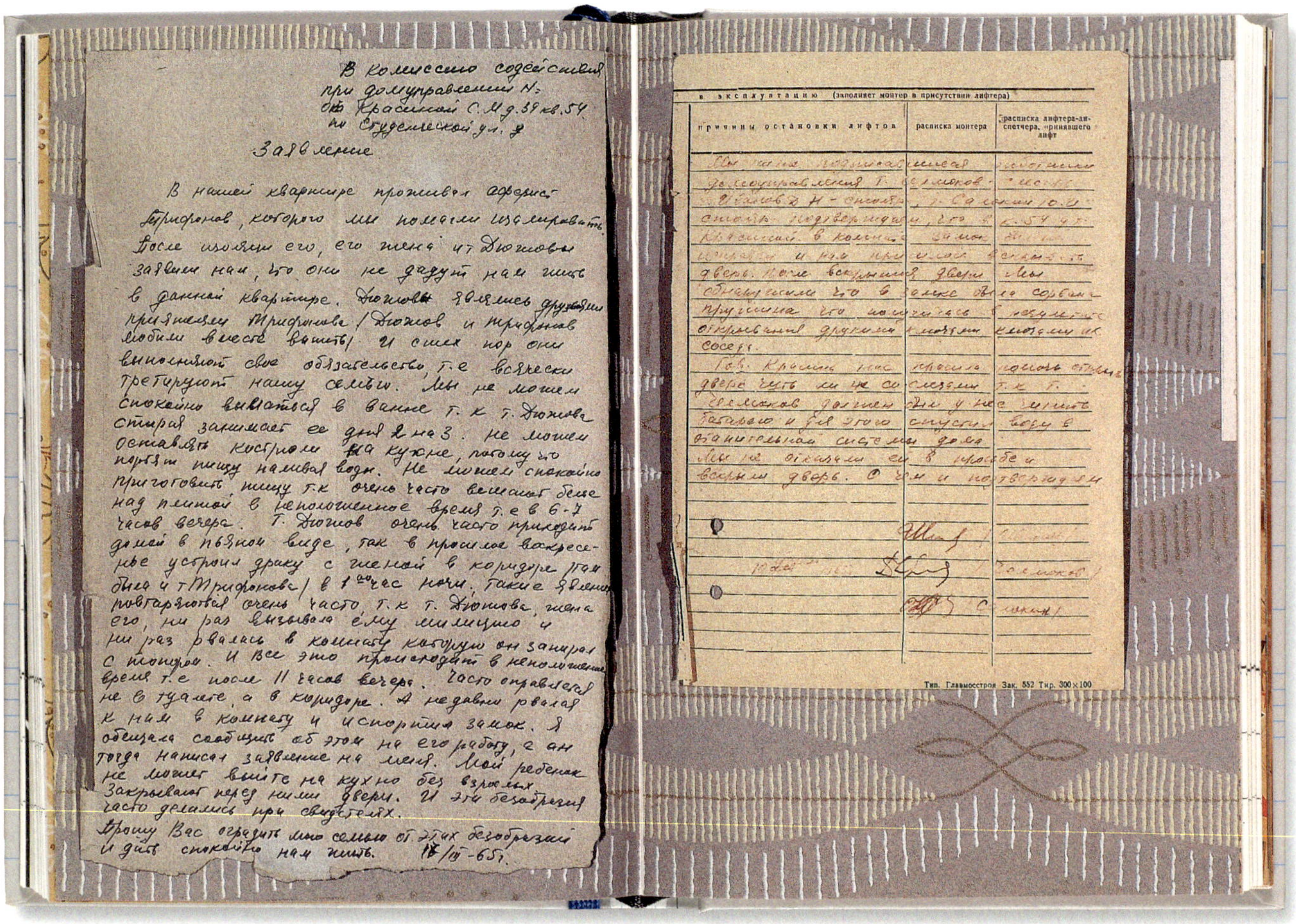

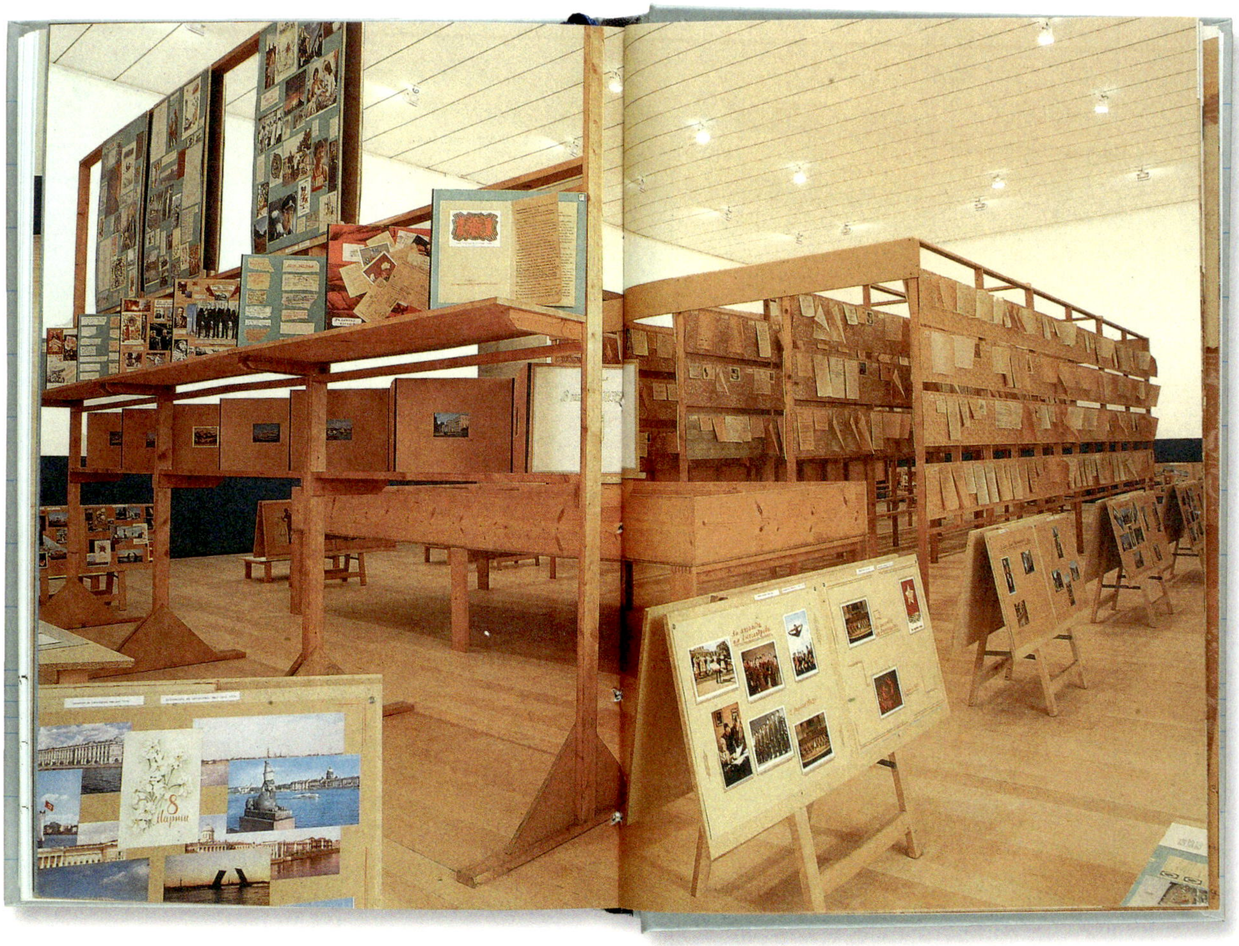

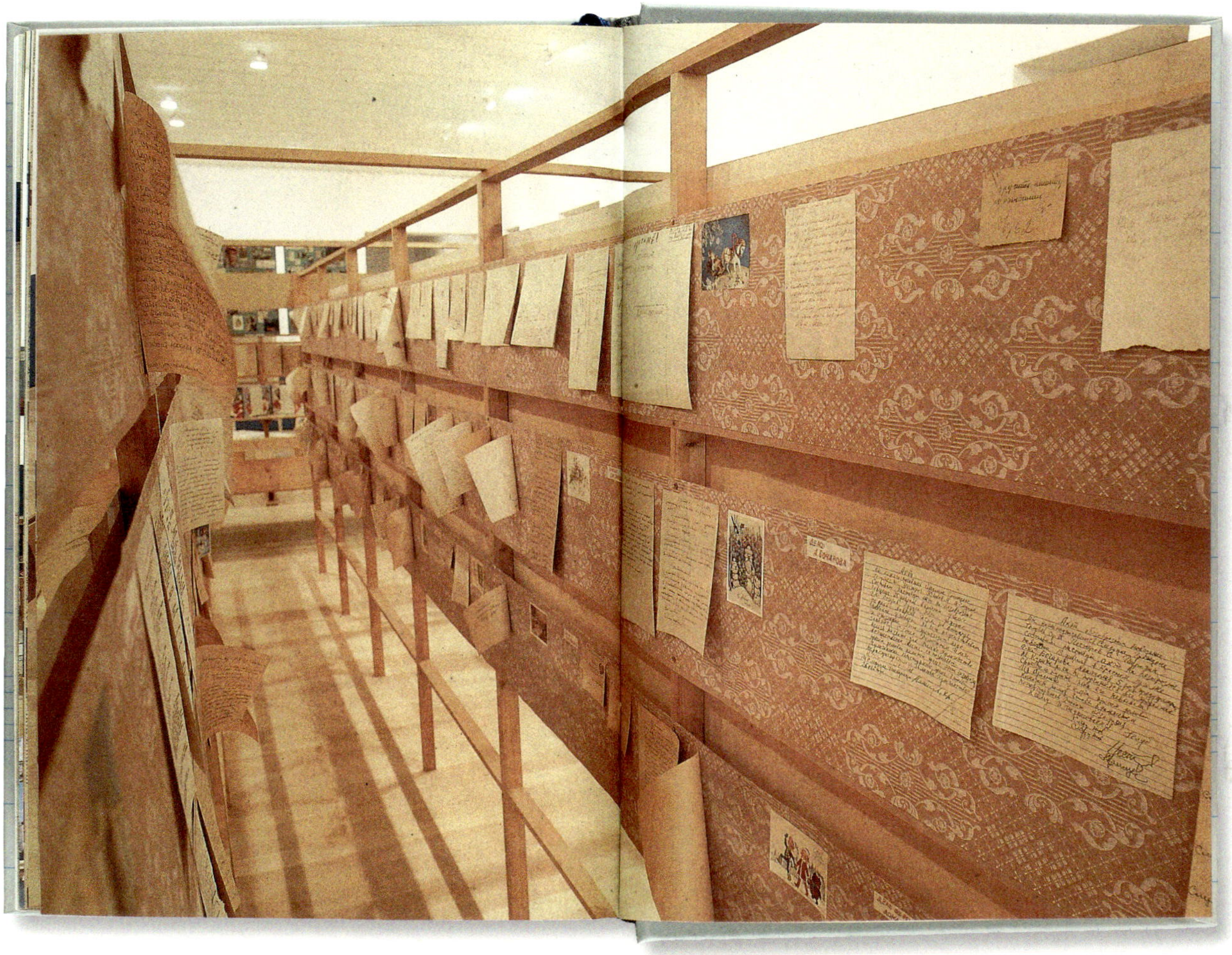

89 The Garbage Man | *Der Müllmensch*

1996

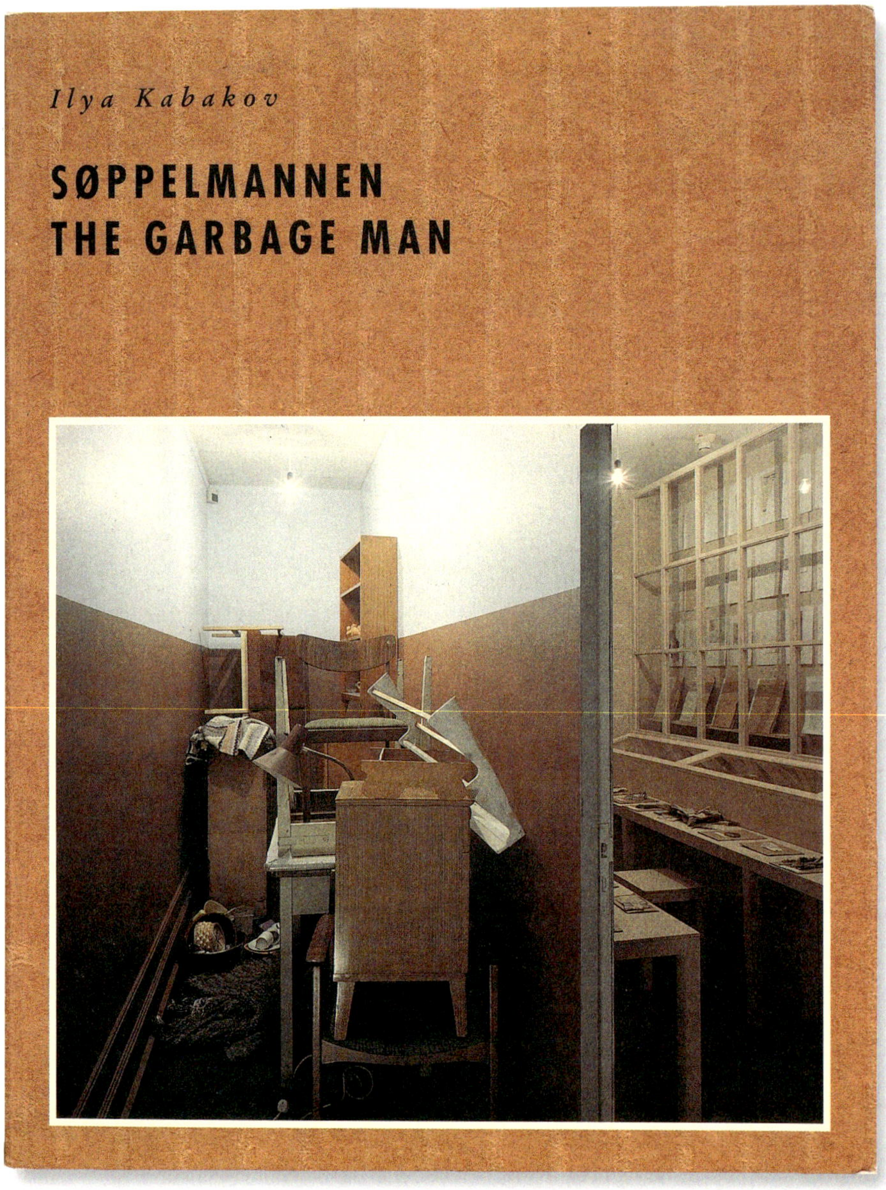

Museet for Samtidskunst, Oslo
Oslo: Museet for Samtidskunst (no. 1)
22 x 17 cm
191 pp. with 57 (30 color) ills.
adhesive binding, softback
Klebebindung, broschiert

exhibition catalogue | *Ausstellungskatalog*

layout by Ilya Kabakov | *Layout von Ilya Kabakov*

For the installation of the same name at the Museet for Samtidskunst, Oslo, since 1995. Texts by Boris Groys, Karin Hellandsjø, Ilya Kabakov, and a dialogue between Boris Groys and Ilya Kabakov on »Garbage«; Norwegian, English.

Zur gleichnamigen Installation, Museet for Samtidskunst, Oslo, seit 1995. Texte von Boris Groys, Karin Hellandsjø, Ilya Kabakov und ein Dialog von Boris Groys und Ilya Kabakov über »Müll«; norwegisch, englisch.

see also | *siehe auch* CRI, vol. 1, no. 21, pp. 174–181

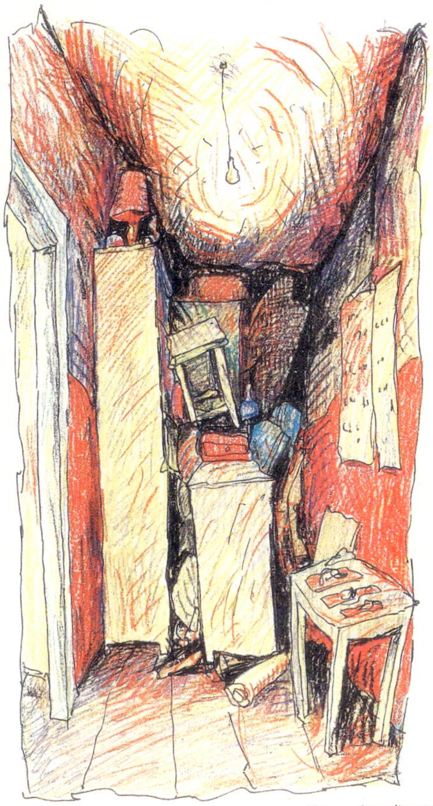

Skisse av det tredje rommet.
Scetch of the third room.

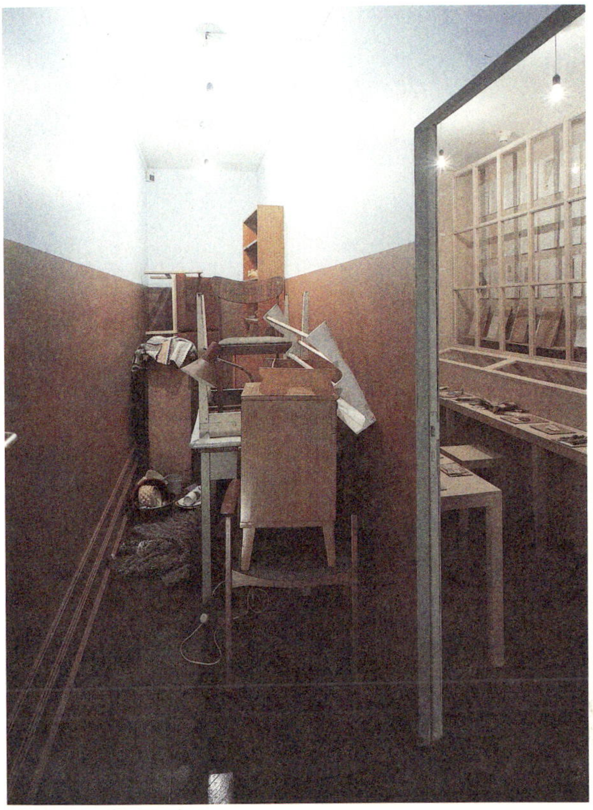

Det første rommet, fra inngangsdøren.
The first room, from the entrance door.

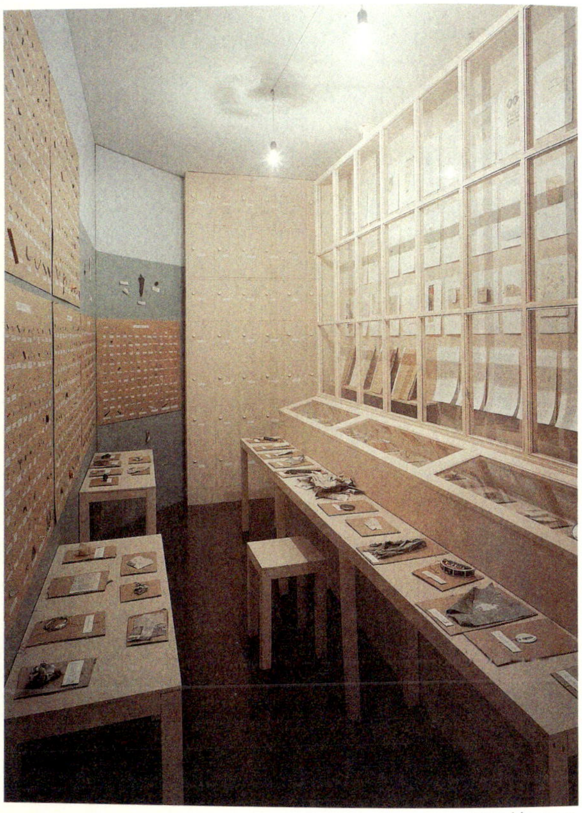

Første del av rom to.
The first part of the second room.

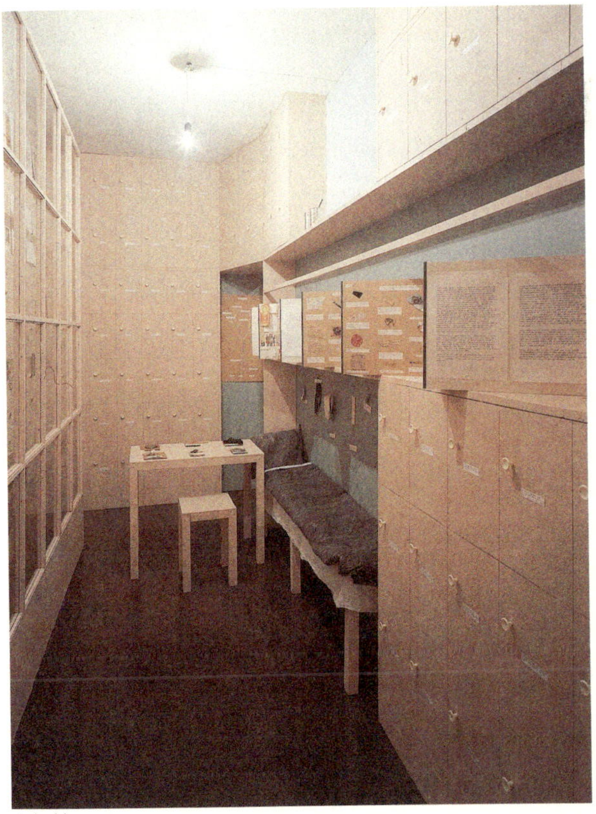

Andre del av rom to.
The second part of the second room.

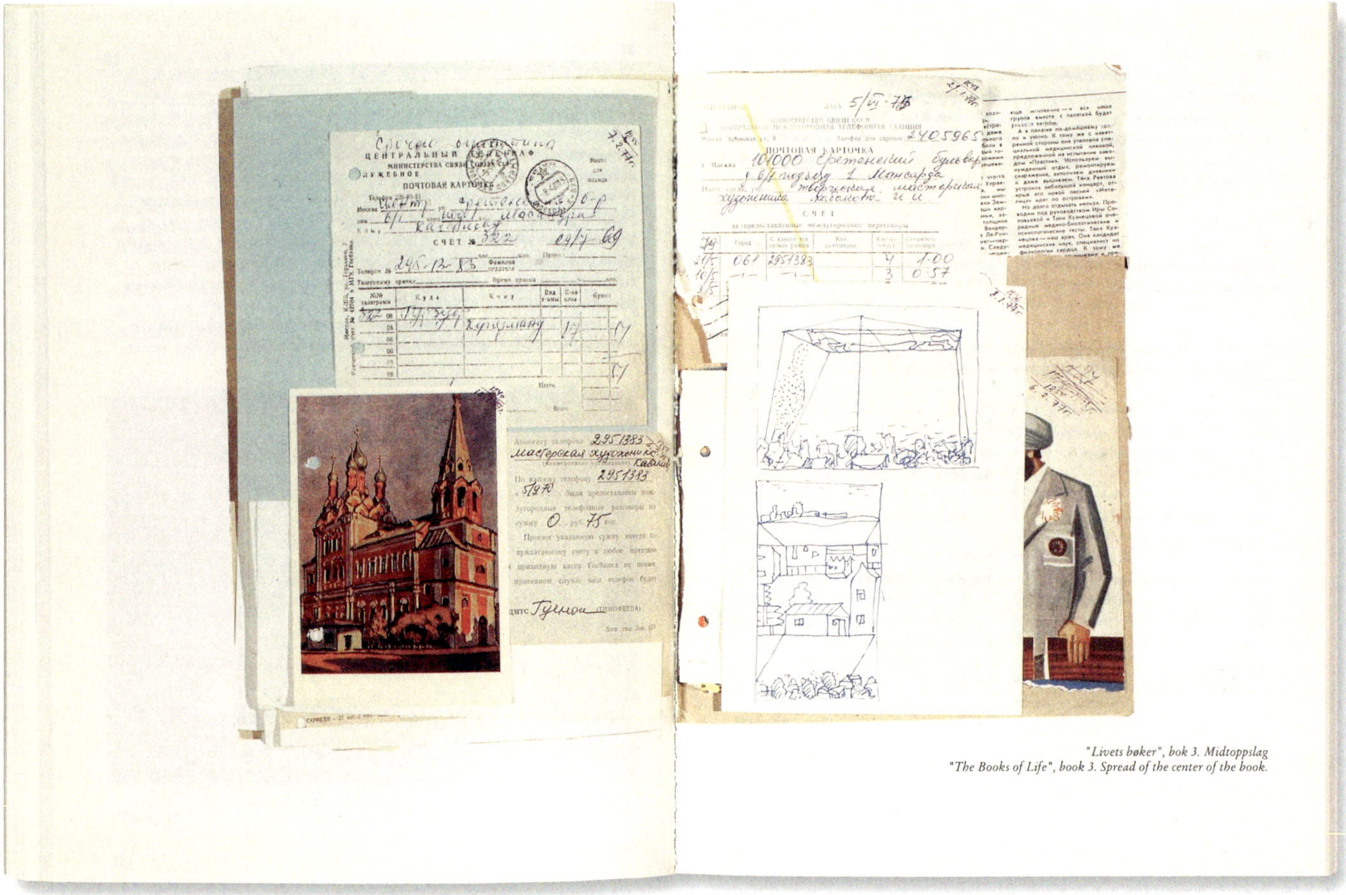

"Livets bøker", bok 3. Midtoppslag
"The Books of Life", book 3. Spread of the center of the book.

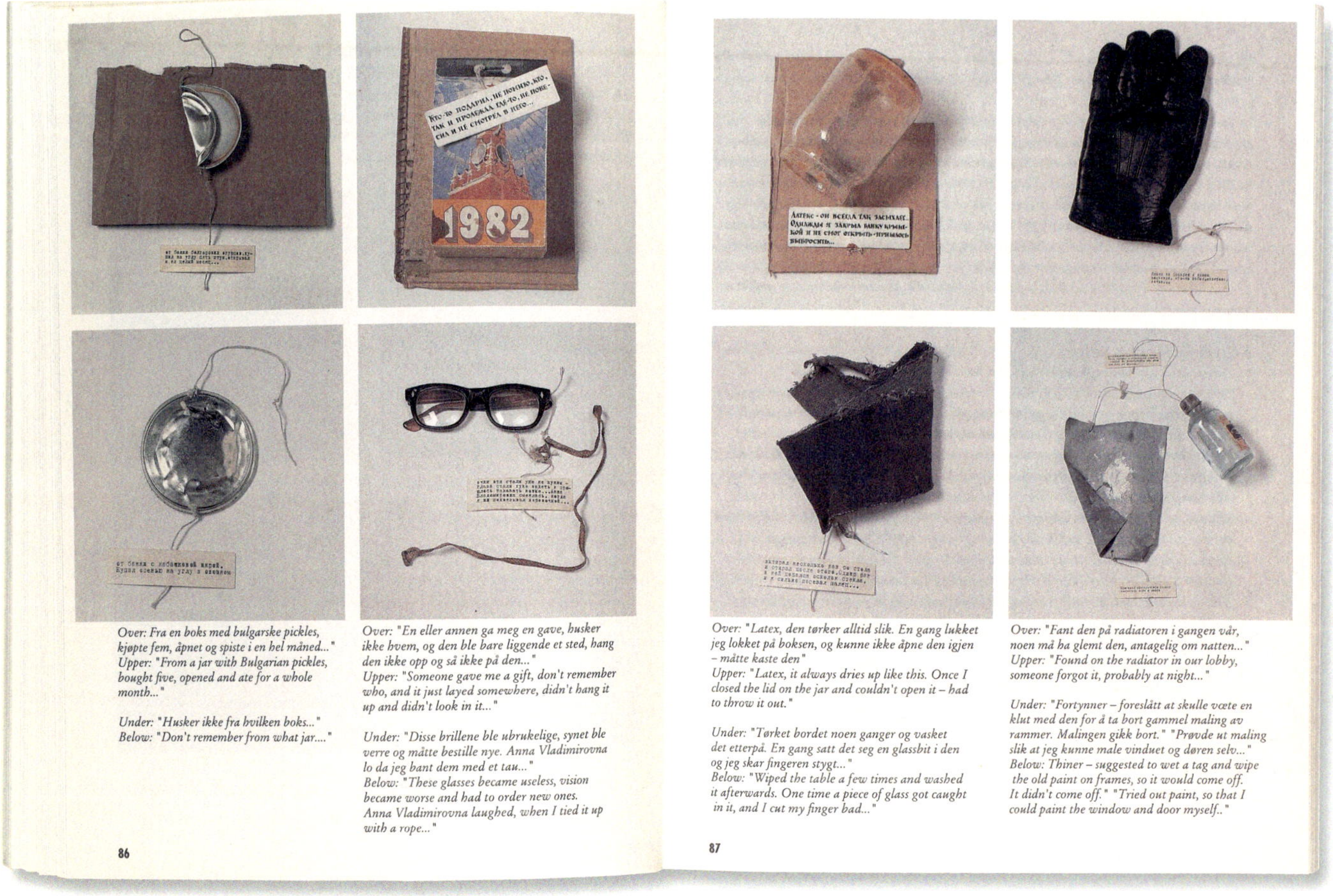

Over: Fra en boks med bulgarske pickles, kjøpte fem, åpnet og spiste i en hel måned..."
Upper: "From a jar with Bulgarian pickles, bought five, opened and ate for a whole month..."

Under: "Husker ikke fra hvilken boks..."
Below: "Don't remember from what jar...."

Over: "En eller annen ga meg en gave, husker ikke hvem, og den ble bare liggende et sted, hang den ikke opp og så ikke på den..."
Upper: "Someone gave me a gift, don't remember who, and it just layed somewhere, didn't hang it up and didn't look in it..."

Under: "Disse brillene ble ubrukelige, synet ble verre og måtte bestille nye. Anna Vladimirovna lo da jeg bant dem med et tau..."
Below: "These glasses became useless, vision became worse and had to order new ones. Anna Vladimirovna laughed, when I tied it up with a rope..."

86

Over: "Latex, den tørker alltid slik. En gang lukket jeg lokket på boksen, og kunne ikke åpne den igjen – måtte kaste den"
Upper: "Latex, it always dries up like this. Once I closed the lid on the jar and couldn't open it – had to throw it out."

Under: "Tørket bordet noen ganger og vasket det etterpå. En gang satt det seg en glassbit i den og jeg skar fingeren stygt..."
Below: "Wiped the table a few times and washed it afterwards. One time a piece of glass got caught in it, and I cut my finger bad..."

Over: "Fant den på radiatoren i gangen vår, noen må ha glemt den, antagelig om natten..."
Upper: "Found on the radiator in our lobby, someone forgot it, probably at night..."

Under: "Fortynner – foreslått at skulle væte en klut med den for å ta bort gammel maling av rammer. Malingen gikk bort." "Prøvde ut maling slik at jeg kunne male vinduet og døren selv..."
Below: Thiner – suggested to wet a tag and wipe the old paint on frames, so it would come off. It didn't come off." "Tried out paint, so that I could paint the window and door myself.."

87

90 Music on the Water | *Musik auf dem Wasser*

with Vladimir Tarasov | *mit Vladimir Tarasov*

1996

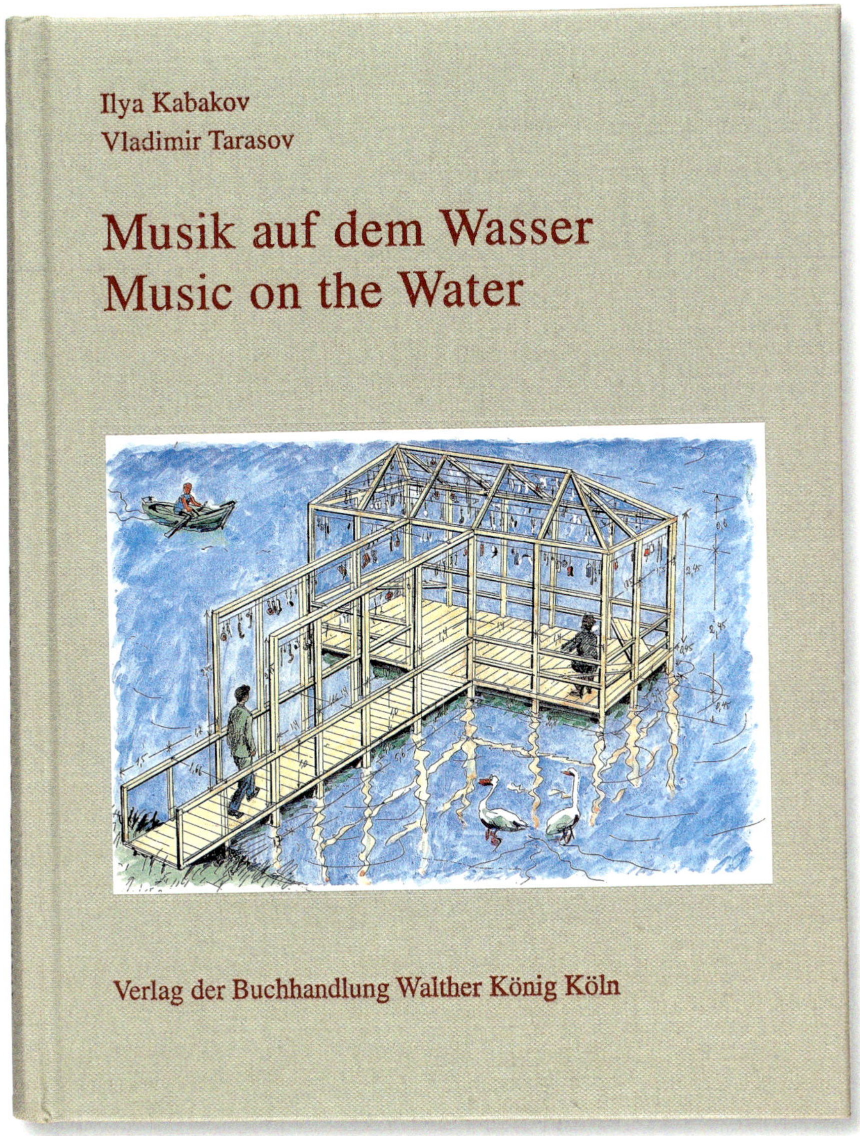

Rainer Haarmann
Cologne: Verlag der Buchhandlung Walther König
22.6 x 17.6 cm
159 pp. with 68 (63 color) ills.
stitchbound, clothbound, blind blocking with label
Fadenheftung, Leinen, Blindprägung mit Etikette
edition: limited edition of 20 signed and numbered copies with a drawing by Ilya Kabakov

exhibition catalogue | *Ausstellungskatalog*

layout by Ilya Kabakov | *Layout von Ilya Kabakov*

For the installation of the same name at the park of the Landeskulturzentrum Salzau, Schleswig-Holstein, Germany. Texts by Thomas Deecke, Rainer Haarmann, Ilya Kabakov, and Vladimir Tarasov; German, English.

Zur gleichnamigen Installation, Park des Landeskulturzentrum Salzau, Schleswig-Holstein, Deutschland. Texte von Thomas Deecke, Rainer Haarmann, Ilya Kabakov und Vladimir Tarasov; deutsch, englisch.

see also | *siehe auch* CRI, vol. 2, no. 97, pp. 136–141

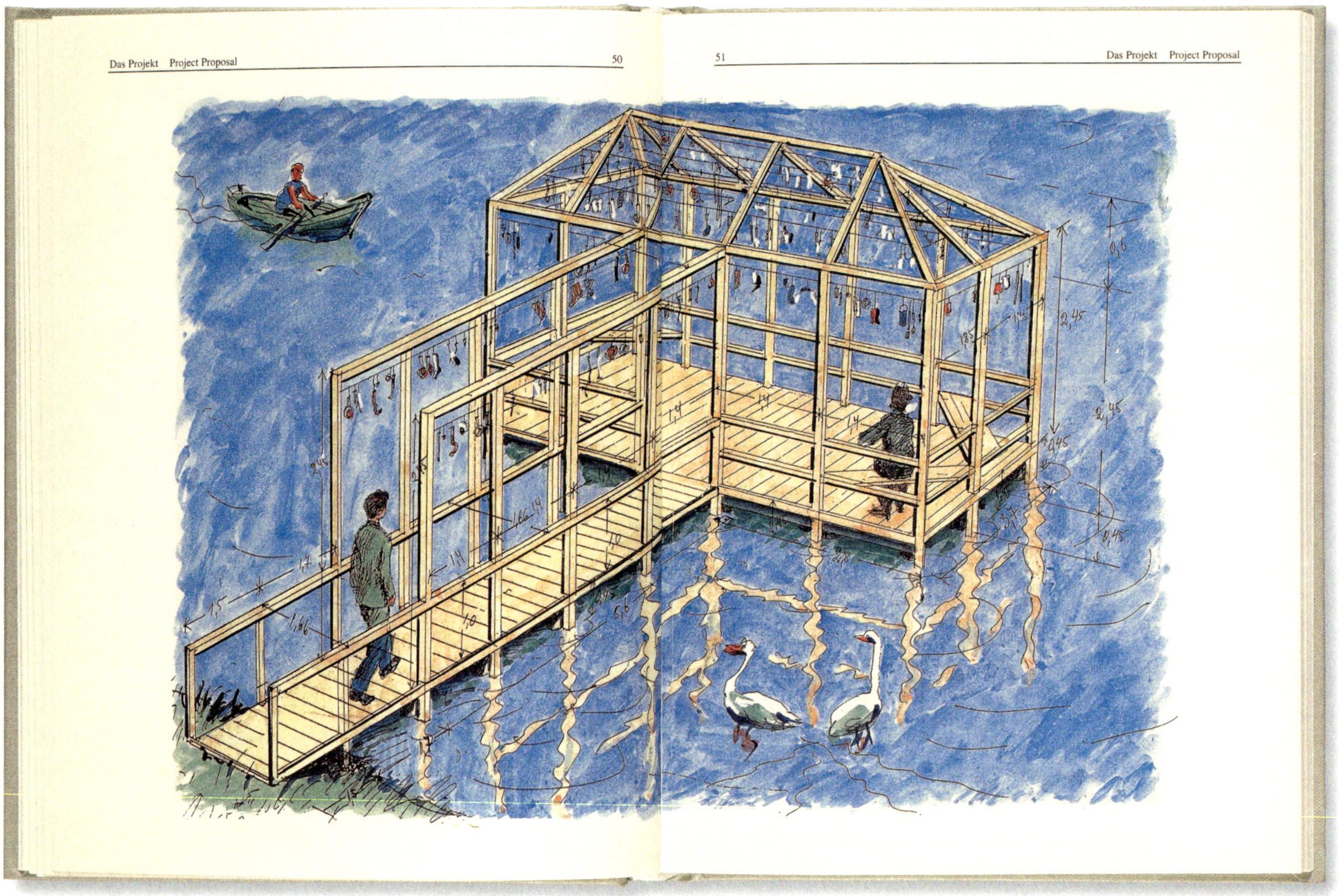

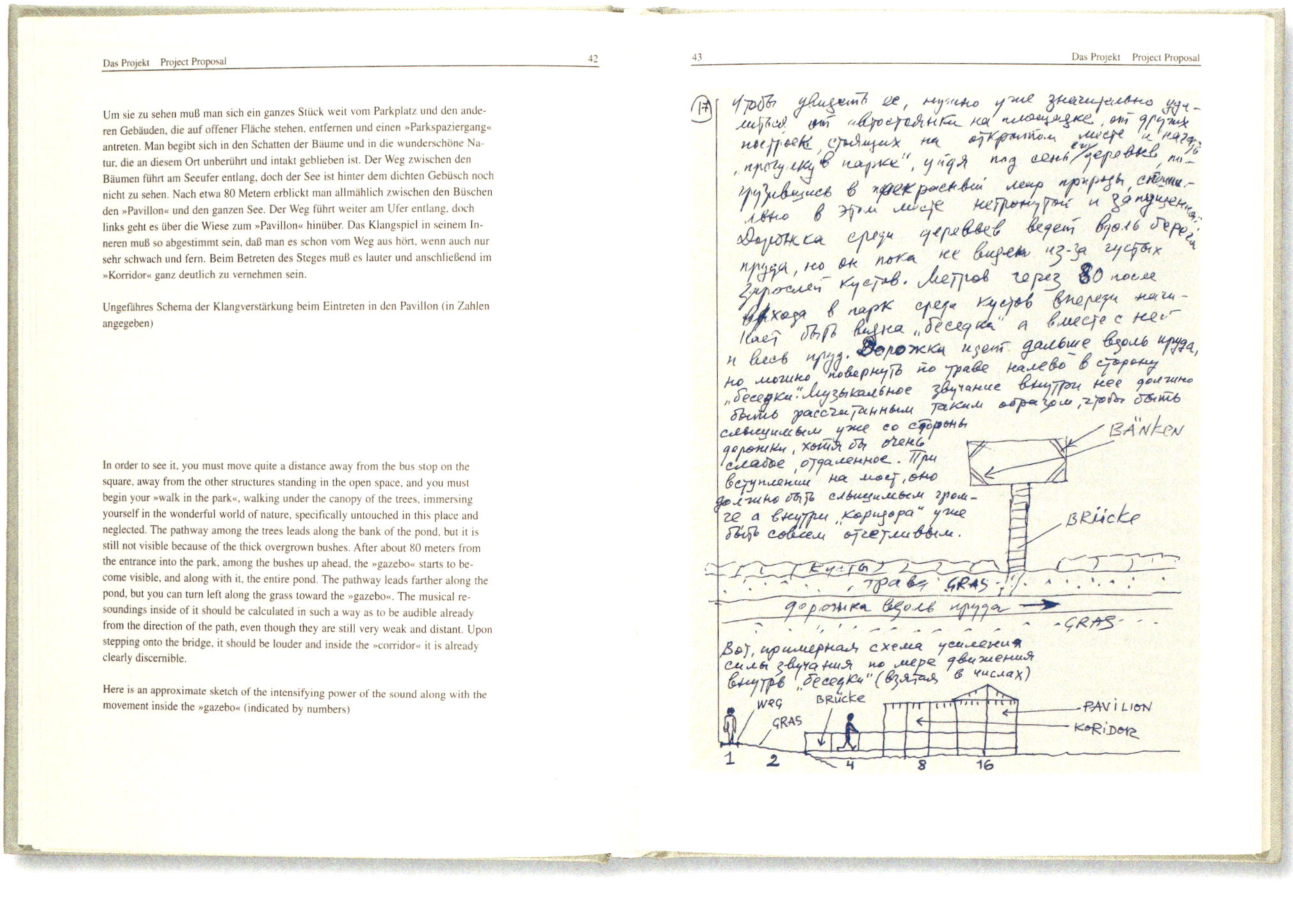

Das Projekt Project Proposal 42

Um sie zu sehen muß man sich ein ganzes Stück weit vom Parkplatz und den anderen Gebäuden, die auf offener Fläche stehen, entfernen und einen »Parkspaziergang« antreten. Man begibt sich in den Schatten der Bäume und in die wunderschöne Natur, die an diesem Ort unberührt und intakt geblieben ist. Der Weg zwischen den Bäumen führt am Seeufer entlang, doch der See ist hinter dem dichten Gebüsch noch nicht zu sehen. Nach etwa 80 Metern erblickt man allmählich zwischen den Büschen den »Pavillon« und den ganzen See. Der Weg führt weiter am Ufer entlang, doch links geht es über die Wiese zum »Pavillon« hinüber. Das Klangspiel in seinem Inneren muß so abgestimmt sein, daß man es schon vom Weg aus hört, wenn auch nur sehr schwach und fern. Beim Betreten des Steges muß es lauter und anschließend im »Korridor« ganz deutlich zu vernehmen sein.

Ungefähres Schema der Klangverstärkung beim Eintreten in den Pavillon (in Zahlen angegeben)

In order to see it, you must move quite a distance away from the bus stop on the square, away from the other structures standing in the open space, and you must begin your »walk in the park«, walking under the canopy of the trees, immersing yourself in the wonderful world of nature, specifically untouched in this place and neglected. The pathway among the trees leads along the bank of the pond, but it is still not visible because of the thick overgrown bushes. After about 80 meters from the entrance into the park, among the bushes up ahead, the »gazebo« starts to become visible, and along with it, the entire pond. The pathway leads farther along the pond, but you can turn left along the grass toward the »gazebo«. The musical resoundings inside of it should be calculated in such a way as to be audible already from the direction of the path, even though they are still very weak and distant. Upon stepping onto the bridge, it should be louder and inside the »corridor« it is already clearly discernible.

Here is an approximate sketch of the intensifying power of the sound along with the movement inside the »gazebo« (indicated by numbers)

43 Das Projekt Project Proposal

(17) Чтобы увидеть ее, нужно уже значительно удалиться от автостоянки на площадке, от других построек, стоящих на открытом месте и начать „прогулку в парке", уйдя под сень деревьев, погрузившись в прекрасный мир природы, специально в этом месте нетронутой и запущенной. Дорожка среди деревьев ведет вдоль берега пруда, но он пока не виден из-за густых заросших кустов. Метров через 80 после входа в парк среди кустов впереди начинает быть видна „беседка" а вместе с ней и весь пруд. Дорожка идет дальше вдоль пруда, но можно повернуть по траве налево в сторону „беседки". Музыкальное звучание внутри нее должно быть рассчитанным таким образом, чтобы быть слышимым уже со стороны дорожки, хотя бы очень слабое, отдаленное. При вступлении на мост, оно должно быть слышимым громче а внутри „коридора" уже быть совсем отчетливым.

Вот, примерная схема усиления силы звучания по мере движения внутрь „беседки" (взятая в числах)

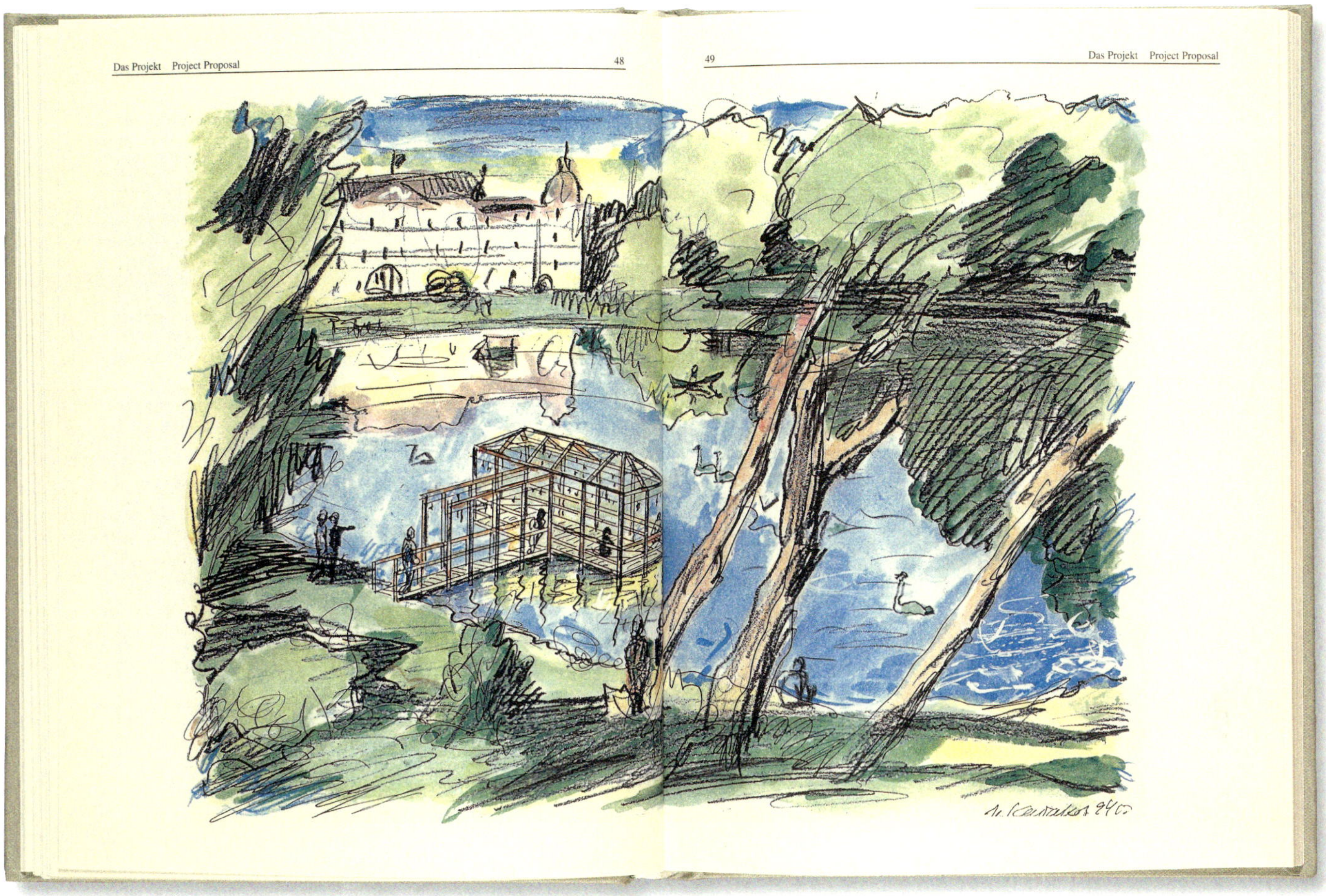

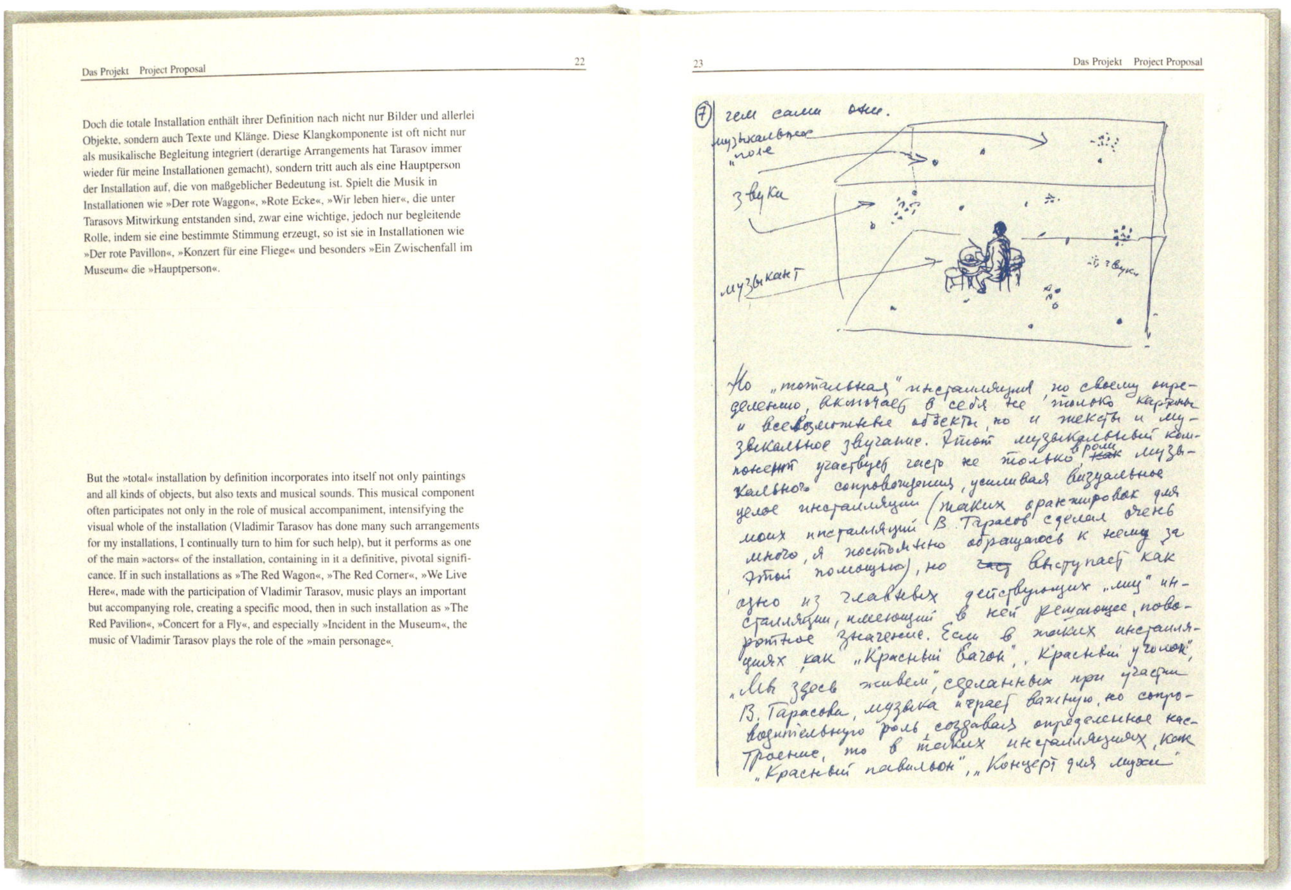

Doch die totale Installation enthält ihrer Definition nach nicht nur Bilder und allerlei Objekte, sondern auch Texte und Klänge. Diese Klangkomponente ist oft nicht nur als musikalische Begleitung integriert (derartige Arrangements hat Tarasov immer wieder für meine Installationen gemacht), sondern tritt auch als eine Hauptperson der Installation auf, die von maßgeblicher Bedeutung ist. Spielt die Musik in Installationen wie »Der rote Waggon«, »Rote Ecke«, »Wir leben hier«, die unter Tarasovs Mitwirkung entstanden sind, zwar eine wichtige, jedoch nur begleitende Rolle, indem sie eine bestimmte Stimmung erzeugt, so ist sie in Installationen wie »Der rote Pavillon«, »Konzert für eine Fliege« und besonders »Ein Zwischenfall im Museum« die »Hauptperson«.

But the »total« installation by definition incorporates into itself not only paintings and all kinds of objects, but also texts and musical sounds. This musical component often participates not only in the role of musical accompaniment, intensifying the visual whole of the installation (Vladimir Tarasov has done many such arrangements for my installations, I continually turn to him for such help), but it performs as one of the main »actors« of the installation, containing in it a definitive, pivotal significance. If in such installations as »The Red Wagon«, »The Red Corner«, »We Live Here«, made with the participation of Vladimir Tarasov, music plays an important but accompanying role, creating a specific mood, then in such installation as »The Red Pavilion«, »Concert for a Fly«, and especially »Incident in the Museum«, the music of Vladimir Tarasov plays the role of the »main personage«.

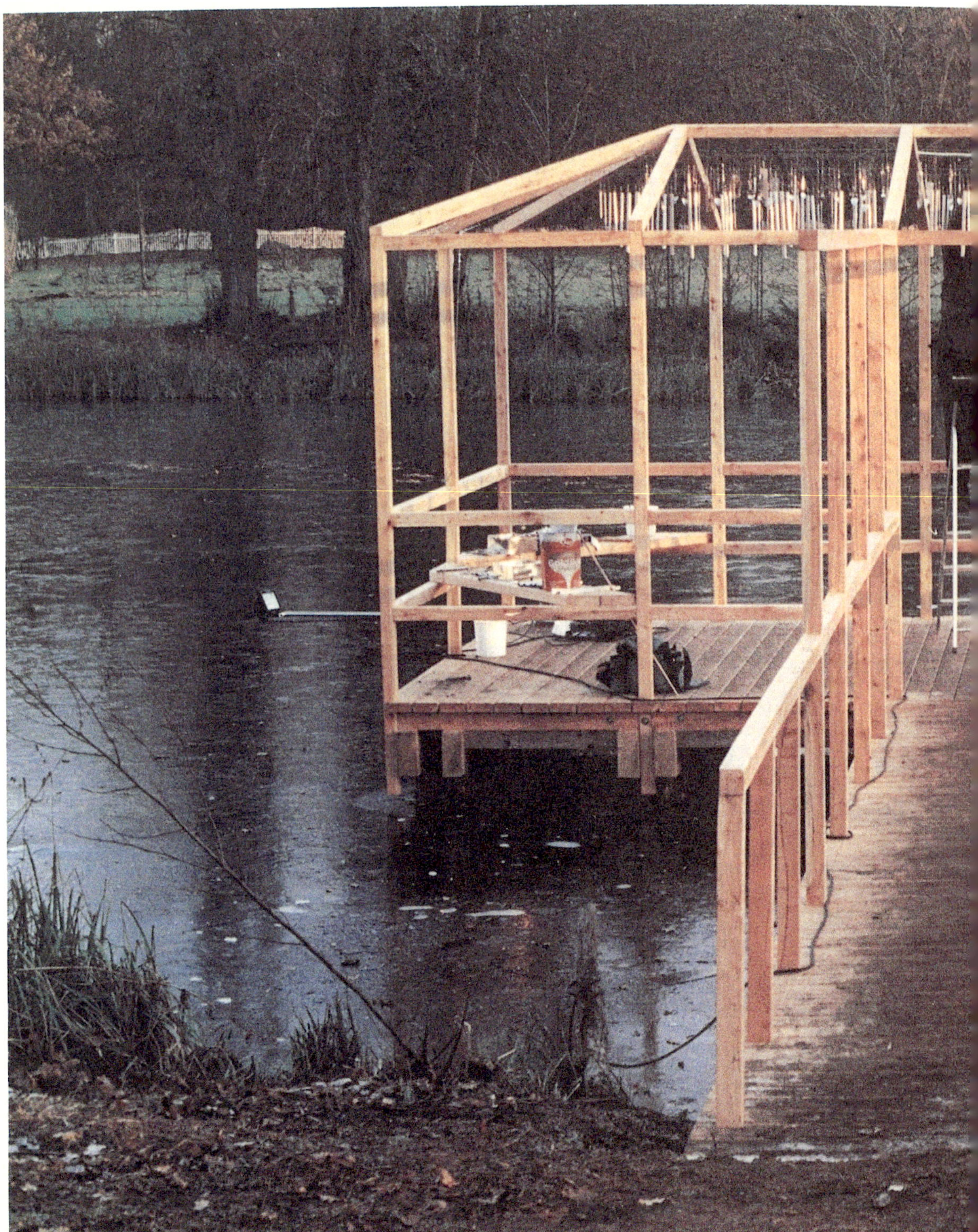

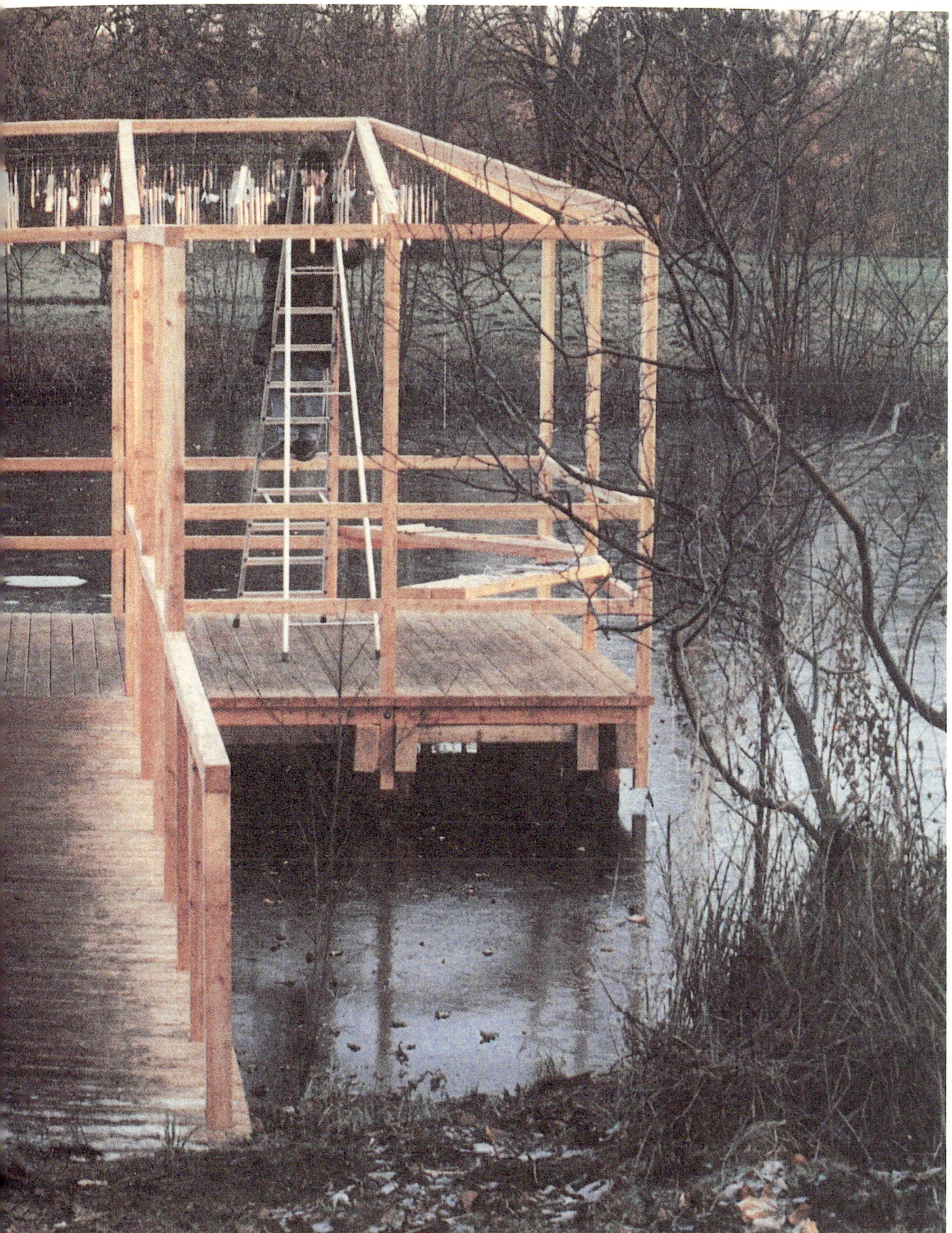

91 The Art of Installation | *Die Kunst der Installation*

with Boris Groys | *mit Boris Groys*

1996

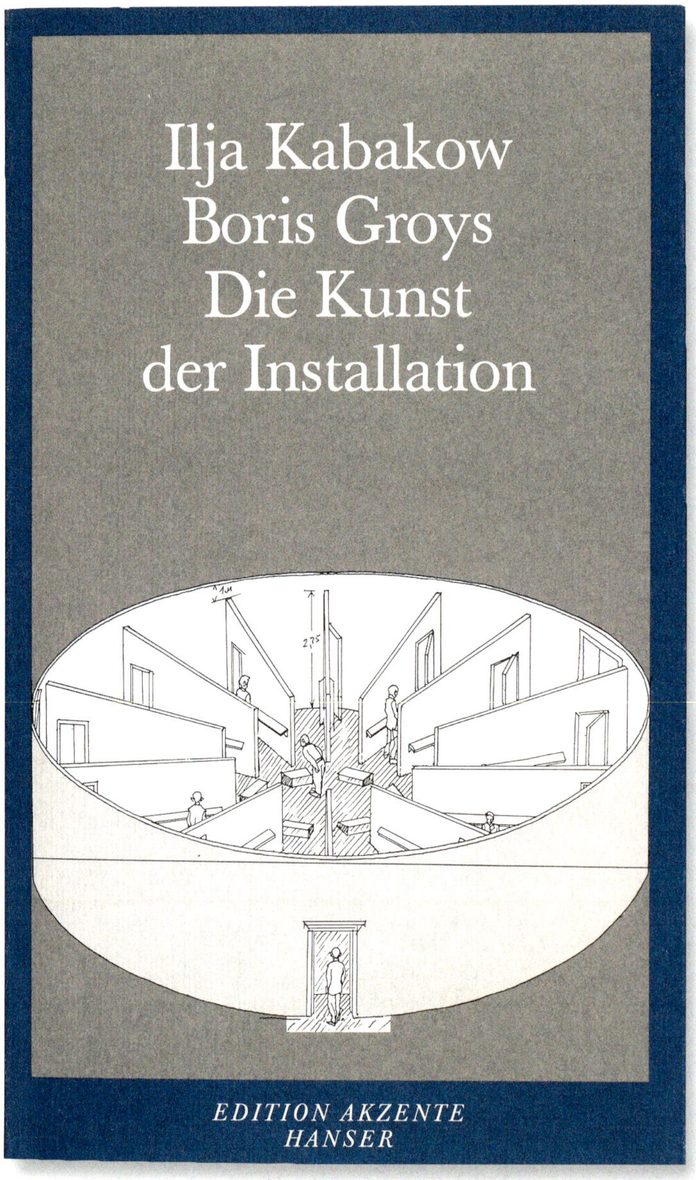

Michael Krüger
Munich/Vienna: Carl Hanser Verlag
(Edition Akzente)
20 x 12.1 cm
176 pp. with 30 b/w ills.
adhesive binding, softback with flaps
Klebebindung, broschiert mit Umschlagklappen

thematic publication | *thematische Publikation*

Dialogue between Boris Groys and Ilya Kabakov on »The Art of Installation«. Foreword by Boris Groys; German.

Dialog von Boris Groys und Ilya Kabakov über »Die Kunst der Installation«. Vorwort von Boris Groys; deutsch.

see also | *siehe auch* no. 47

uninteressant ist. Der Anlaß dieser Erzählung ist freilich ebenso uninteressant. So sind wir gleichsam gefangen in einer geschlossenen Spirale, wo man uns an der Nase herumführt und wir nicht mehr ein noch aus wissen. Der eine sagt: »Nein, geh zu dem da, der wird dir alles erzählen«, der andere dagegen: »Wieso bist du zu mir gekommen? Der dort hat doch das ganze Geld.« Der Besucher gerät in einen Teufelskreis, in eine Pattsituation.

G. Als ich die Installation betrachtete und die Texte las, war mein erster Eindruck: Die Besucher, die dort hereinkommen, sind alle vom gleichen Schlag. Es waren keine zufälligen Besucher, sondern schon bestimmte Typen ...

K. Wieso? Es konnten doch alle durch die Tür eintreten.

G. Aber nicht alle konnten diese Tür finden. Zum Beispiel habe ich sie erst nicht gefunden. Ich kam eigentlich, um ...

K. War die Tür geschlossen oder nicht?

G. Die Tür war geschlossen. Dabei habe ich sie gar nicht erwartet, weil unmittelbar daneben Künstler eines absolut anderen Typs ausgestellt sind. Theoretisch habe ich mir natürlich vorgestellt, daß diese Installation mit den anderen russischen Künstlern verbunden sein wird, die im Museum Ludwig vertreten sind. Aber eine solche Verbindung gab es nicht. Die ganze Hängung demonstrierte die westliche Kunstgeschichte des 20. Jahrhunderts, und ich folgte ihr. Meine Frau Natascha hat der Hängung hingegen weniger Aufmerksamkeit geschenkt als ich, sie wußte nur, daß es irgendwo eine Tür und dahinter deine Installation geben soll. So war es dann auch. Sie ging dorthin, wo ich nie hingegangen wäre, dann öffnete sie eine Tür, und dort war tatsächlich deine Installation.

K. Entschuldige, daß ich dich unterbreche. War die Tür fest geschlossen? Hast du keinen Ausgang gesehen, als du drin warst?

G. Als wir reingingen, ließen wir die Tür halb offenstehen. Ich will nur sagen, daß ich dieses Zimmer nicht ge-

86

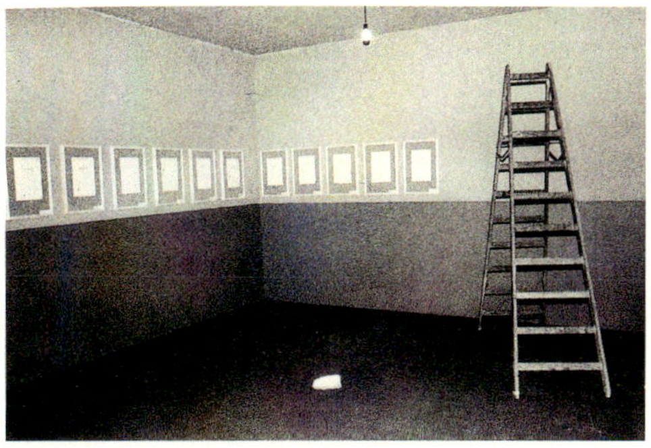

Installation »Das nicht aufgehängte Bild«. Die Wand mit den Kommentaren. Museum Ludwig, Köln 1992

Die Treppe und das Bild »Abramtsewo«

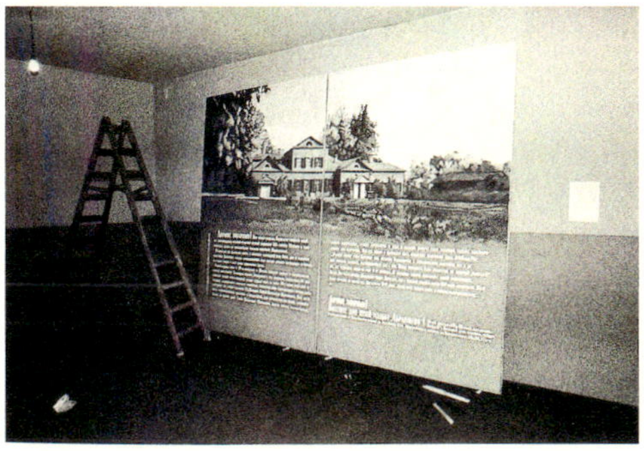

87

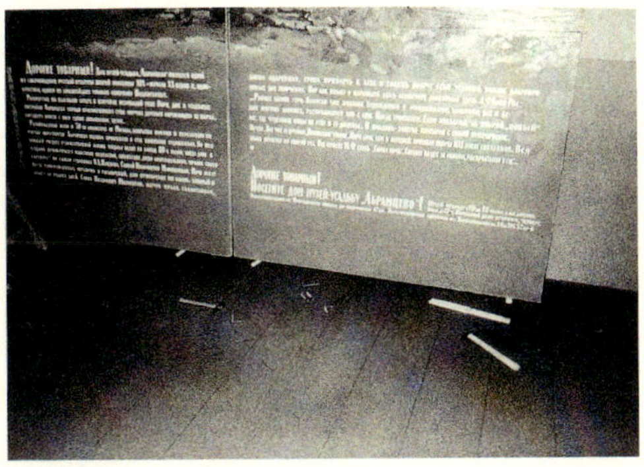

Fragment

Die Wand mit der Ausgangstür

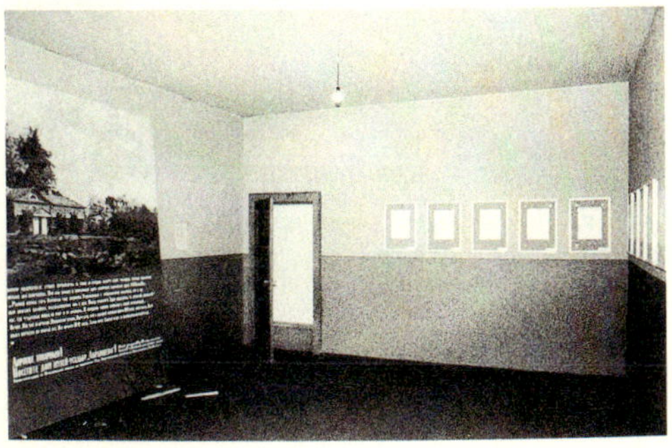

90

funden hätte, weil ich einer gewissen Logik der Kunstgeschichte folgte, so wie ich sie mir vorstelle. Ehrlich gesagt, ließ mich diese Logik ein Zimmer wie deines nicht erwarten. Ich glaube, daß die Leute, die dort reinkommen, etwas seltsam sind. Das Museum war gut besucht, aber solange ich im Raum mit deiner Installation stand, kamen nur wenige Leute herein. Und diese wenigen waren alle etwas seltsam. Manche trugen zum Beispiel Rucksäcke, was schon einiges aussagt.

Jemand, der mit einem Rucksack ins Museum geht, ist auch in seiner Wahrnehmung so etwas wie ein Wanderer. Es waren Leute mit einem Reise- oder Wanderungshabitus; man sah, wie gerne sie schwer erreichbare Felsen erklimmen und in Höhlen kriechen. Und da sie schon eine bestimmte Sorte von Mensch waren, führten sie sich auch entsprechend auf. Es ist mir aufgefallen, daß fast jeder der wenigen Besucher in diesem Raum auf die gleiche Weise agierte. Auf dem Fußboden waren einzelne Müllbrocken befestigt. Die erste Reaktion dieser Menschen bestand darin, daß sie mit aller Kraft versuchten, diese Brocken mit den Füßen vom Fußboden abzuschlagen und sie aus der Mitte in die Zimmerecken zu schleudern. Das schafften sie nicht. Dann versuchten sie es erneut, mit kräftigen Fußschlägen, einen Müllbrocken abzubrechen und wegzuwerfen. Das ging aber wieder nicht. Nun betrachteten sie diesen Müllbrocken aufmerksam und vergewisserten sich, daß er eigens befestigt worden war. Erst dann hoben sie die Augen vom Fußboden und sahen sich im Zimmer um.

Interessant ist die Rolle des Zentrums. Die Menschen betraten den Raum, und das erste, worauf sie aufmerksam wurden, war seine Mitte und die Unordnung dort. Da sie keine Ordnung wiederherstellen konnten, waren sie frustriert, was zur Folge hatte, daß sie sich nun umschauten.

K. Aber nicht umgekehrt ...

G. Aber nicht umgekehrt. Das war das erste interessante Experiment. Das zweite Experiment war das mit den

91

92 On Ülo Sooster's Paintings | *Über Ülo Soosters Gemälde*

1996

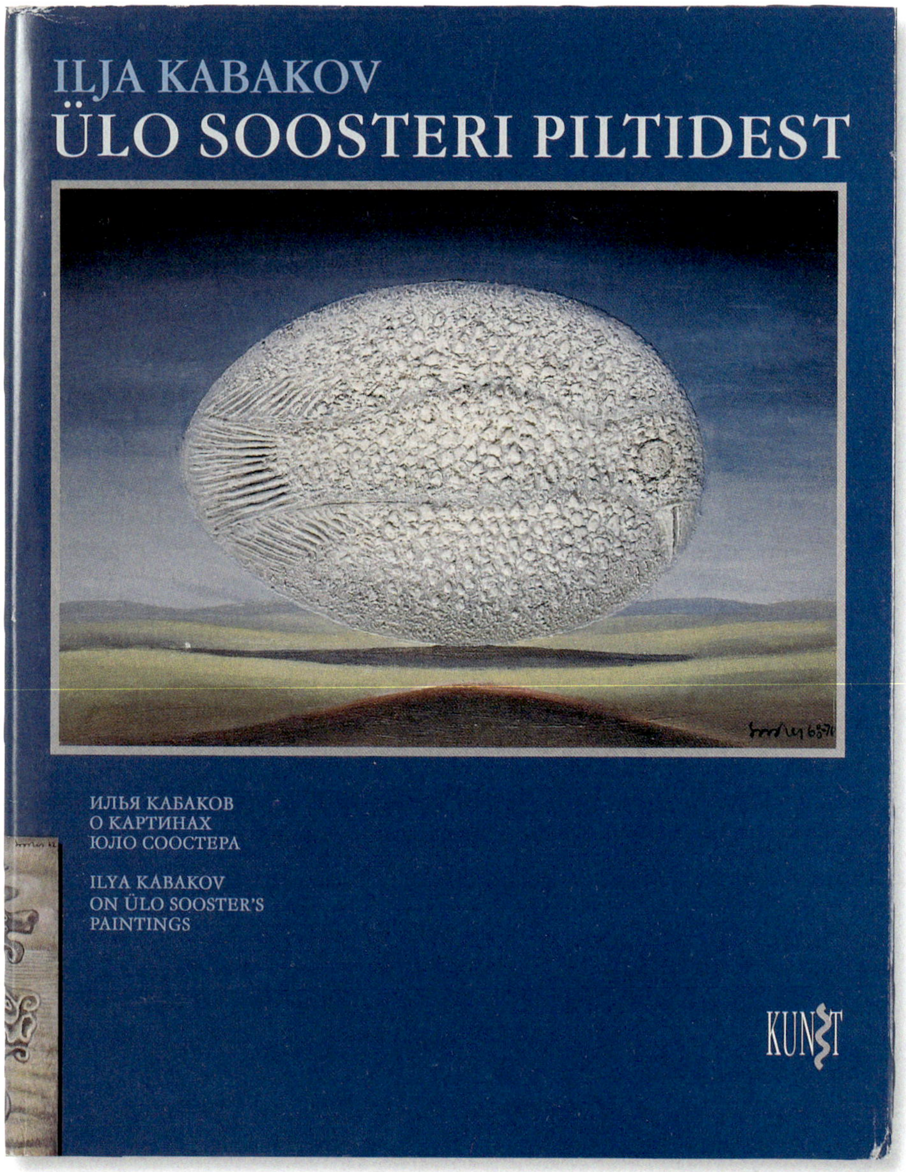

Ilya Kabakov
Tallinn: Kirjastus "Kunst"
26.7 x 21 cm
208 pp. with 288 (35 color) ills.
adhesive binding, hardcover with blind blocking, dust jacket
Klebebindung, Hardcover mit Blindprägung, Schutzumschlag

thematic publication | *thematische Publikation*

layout by Ilya Kabakov | *Layout von Ilya Kabakov*

Monograph on the painter Ülo Sooster (1924–1970). Texts by Ilya Kabakov and Reet Varblane; Estonian, Russian, English.

Monografie über den Maler Ülo Sooster (1924–1970). Texte von Ilya Kabakov und Reet Varblane; estnisch, russisch, englisch.

see also | *siehe auch*

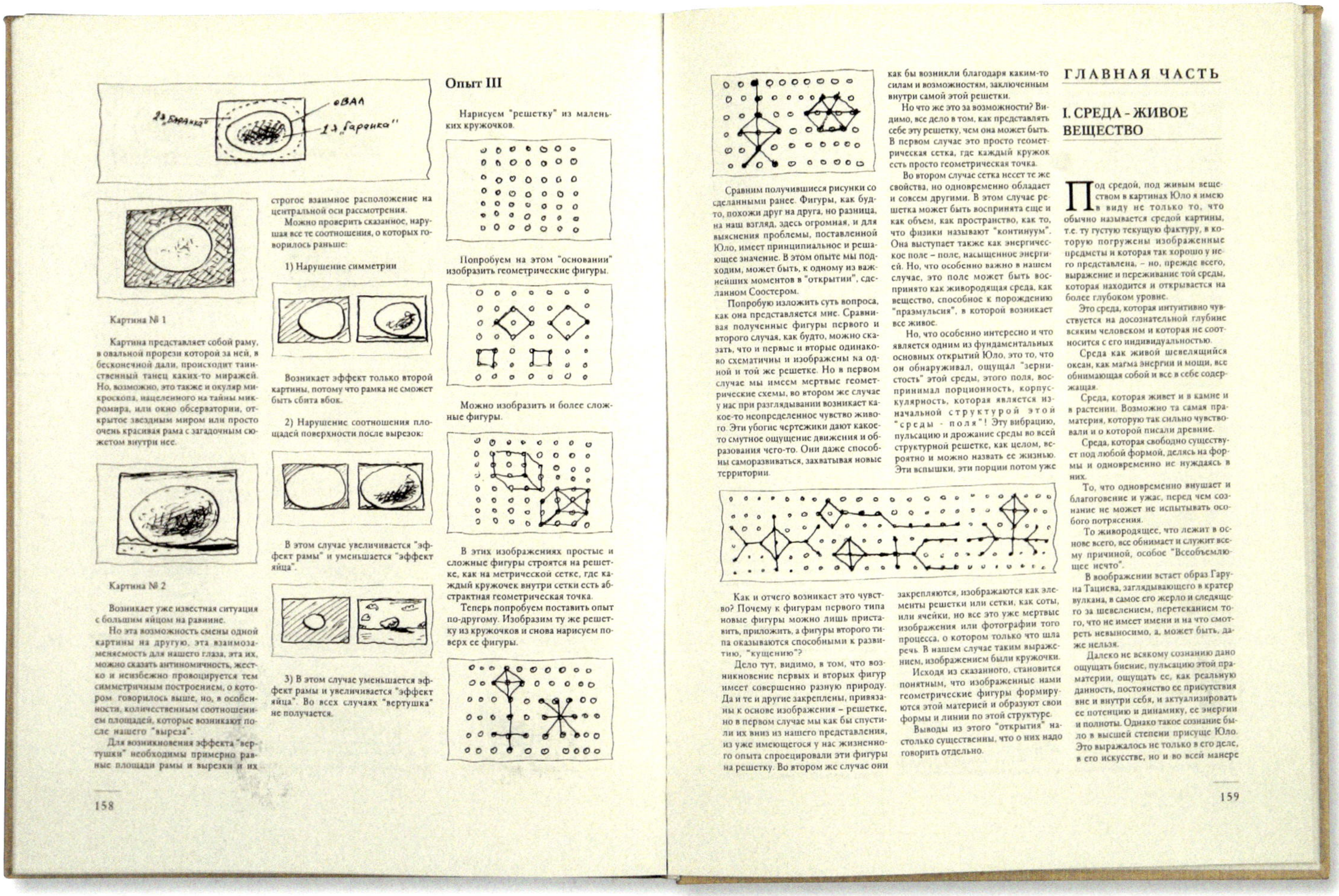

строгое взаимное расположение на центральной оси рассмотрения.

Можно проверить сказанное, нарушая все те соотношения, о которых говорилось раньше:

1) Нарушение симметрии

Возникает эффект только второй картины, потому что рамка не сможет быть сбита вбок.

2) Нарушение соотношения площадей поверхности после вырезок:

В этом случае увеличивается "эффект рамы" и уменьшается "эффект яйца".

3) В этом случае уменьшается эффект рамы и увеличивается "эффект яйца". Во всех случаях "вертушка" не получается.

Картина № 1

Картина представляет собой раму, в овальной прорези которой за ней, в бесконечной дали, происходит таинственный танец каких-то миражей. Но, возможно, это также и окуляр микроскопа, нацеленного на тайны микромира, или окно обсерватории, открытое звездным миром или просто очень красивая рама с загадочным сюжетом внутри нее.

Картина № 2

Возникает уже известная ситуация с большим яйцом на равнине.

Но эта возможность смены одной картины на другую, эта взаимозаменяемость для нашего глаза, эта их, можно сказать антиномичность, жестко и неизбежно провоцируется тем симметричным построением, о котором говорилось выше, но, в особенности, количественным соотношением площадей, которые возникают после нашего "выреза".

Для возникновения эффекта "вертушки" необходимы примерно равные площади рамы и вырезки и их

Опыт III

Нарисуем "решетку" из маленьких кружочков.

Попробуем на этом "основании" изобразить геометрические фигуры.

Можно изобразить и более сложные фигуры.

В этих изображениях простые и сложные фигуры строятся на решетке, как на метрической сетке, где каждый кружочек внутри сетки есть абстрактная геометрическая точка.

Теперь попробуем поставить опыт по-другому. Изобразим ту же решетку из кружочков и снова нарисуем поверх ее фигуры.

158

Сравним получившиеся рисунки со сделанными ранее. Фигуры, как будто, похожи друг на друга, но разница, на наш взгляд, здесь огромная, и для выяснения проблемы, поставленной Юло, имеет принципиальное и решающее значение. В этом опыте мы подходим, может быть, к одному из важнейших моментов в "открытии", сделанном Соостером.

Попробую изложить суть вопроса, как она представляется мне. Сравнивая полученные фигуры первого и второго случая, как будто, можно сказать, что и первые и вторые одинаково схематичны и изображены на одной и той же решетке. Но в первом случае мы имеем мертвые геометрические схемы, во втором же случае у нас при разглядывании возникает какое-то неопределенное чувство живого. Эти убогие чертежики дают какое-то смутное ощущение движения и образования чего-то. Они даже способны саморазвиваться, захватывая новые территории.

как бы возникли благодаря каким-то силам и возможностям, заключенным внутри самой этой решетки.

Но что же это за возможности? Видимо, все дело в том, как представлять себе эту решетку, чем она может быть. В первом случае это просто геометрическая сетка, где каждый кружок есть просто геометрическая точка.

Во втором случае сетка несет те же свойства, но одновременно обладает и совсем другими. В этом случае решетка может быть воспринята еще и как объем, как пространство, как то, что физики называют "континуум". Она выступает также как энергическое поле – поле, насыщенное энергией. Но, что особенно важно в нашем случае, это поле может быть воспринято как живородящая среда, как вещество, способное к порождению "праэмульсия", в которой возникает все живое.

Но, что особенно интересно и что является одним из фундаментальных основных открытий Юло, это то, что он обнаруживал, ощущал "зернистость" этой среды, этого поля, воспринимал порционность, корпускулярность, которая является изначальной структурой этой "среды - поля"! Эту вибрацию, пульсацию и дрожание среды во всей структурной решетке, как целом, вероятно и можно назвать ее жизнью. Эти вспышки, эти порции потом уже

Как и отчего возникает это чувство? Почему к фигурам первого типа новые фигуры можно лишь приставить, приложить, а фигуры второго типа оказываются способными к развитию, "кущению"?

Дело тут, видимо, в том, что возникновение первых и вторых фигур имеет совершенно разную природу. Да и те и другие закреплены, привязаны к основе изображения – решетке, но в первом случае мы как бы спустили их вниз из нашего представления, из уже имеющегося у нас жизненного опыта спроецировали эти фигуры на решетку. Во втором же случае они

закрепляются, изображаются как элементы решетки или сетки, как соты, или ячейки, но все это уже мертвые изображения или фотографии того процесса, о котором только что шла речь. В нашем случае таким выражением, изображением были кружочки.

Исходя из сказанного, становится понятным, что изображенные нами геометрические фигуры формируются этой материей и образуют свои формы и линии по этой структуре.

Выводы из этого "открытия" настолько существенны, что о них надо говорить отдельно.

ГЛАВНАЯ ЧАСТЬ

I. СРЕДА - ЖИВОЕ ВЕЩЕСТВО

Под средой, под живым веществом в картинах Юло я имею в виду не только то, что обычно называется средой картины, т.е. ту густую текущую фактуру, в которую погружены изображенные предметы и которая так хорошо у него представлена, – но, прежде всего, выражение и переживание той среды, которая находится и открывается на более глубоком уровне.

Это среда, которая интуитивно чувствуется на досознательной глубине всяким человеком и которая не соотносится с его индивидуальностью.

Среда как живой шевелящийся океан, как магма энергии и мощи, все обнимающая собой и все в себе содержащая.

Среда, которая живет и в камне и в растении. Возможно та самая праматерия, которую так сильно чувствовали и о которой писали древние.

Среда, которая свободно существует под любой формой, делясь на формы и одновременно не нуждаясь в них.

То, что одновременно внушает и благоговение и ужас, перед чем сознание не может не испытывать особого потрясения.

То живородящее, что лежит в основе всего, все обнимает и служит всему причиной, особое "Всеобъемлющее нечто".

В воображении встает образ Гаруна Тациева, заглядывающего в кратер вулкана, в самое его жерло и следящего за шевелением, перетеканием того, что не имеет имени и на что смотреть невыносимо, а, может быть, даже нельзя.

Далеко не всякому сознанию дано ощущать биение, пульсацию этой праматерии, ощущать ее, как реальную данность, постоянство ее присутствия вне и внутри себя, и актуализировать ее потенцию и динамику, ее энергии и полноты. Однако такое сознание было в высшей степени присуще Юло. Это выражалось не только в его деле, в его искусстве, но и во всей манере

159

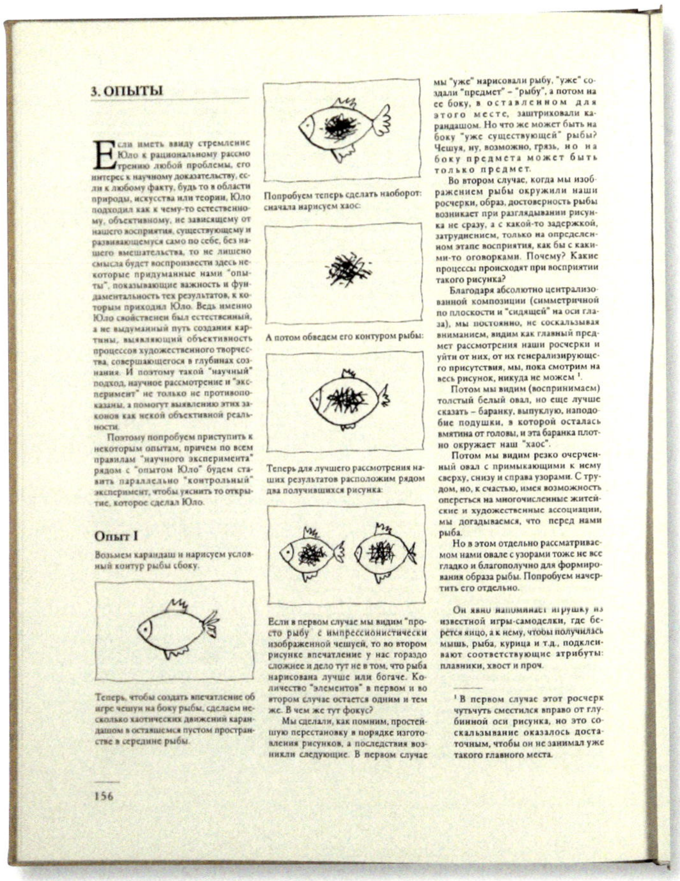

3. ОПЫТЫ

Если иметь ввиду стремление Юло к рациональному рассмотрению любой проблемы, его интерес к научному доказательству, если к любому факту, будь то в области природы, искусства или теории, Юло подходил как к чему-то естественному, объективному, не зависящему от нашего восприятия, существующему и развивающемуся само по себе, без нашего вмешательства, то не лишено смысла будет воспроизвести здесь некоторые придуманные нами "опыты", показывающие важность и фундаментальность тех результатов, к которым приходил Юло. Ведь именно Юло свойственен был естественный, а не выдуманный путь создания картины, выявляющий объективность процессов художественного творчества, совершающегося в глубинах сознания. И поэтому такой "научный" подход, научное рассмотрение и "эксперимент" не только не противопоказаны, а помогут выявлению этих законов как некой объективной реальности.

Поэтому попробуем приступить к некоторым опытам, причем по всем правилам "научного эксперимента" рядом с "опытом Юло" будем ставить параллельно "контрольный" эксперимент, чтобы уяснить то открытие, которое сделал Юло.

Опыт I

Возьмем карандаш и нарисуем условный контур рыбы сбоку.

Теперь, чтобы создать впечатление об игре чешуи на боку рыбы, сделаем несколько хаотических движений карандашом в оставшемся пустом пространстве в середине рыбы.

Попробуем теперь сделать наоборот: сначала нарисуем хаос:

А потом обведем его контуром рыбы:

Теперь для лучшего рассмотрения наших результатов расположим рядом два получившихся рисунка:

Если в первом случае мы видим "просто рыбу" с импрессионистически изображенной чешуей, то во втором рисунке впечатление у нас гораздо сложнее и дело тут не в том, что рыба нарисована лучше или богаче. Количество "элементов" в первом и во втором случае остается одним и тем же. В чем же тут фокус?

Мы сделали, как помним, простейшую перестановку в порядке изготовления рисунков, а последствия возникли следующие. В первом случае мы "уже" нарисовали рыбу, "уже" создали "предмет" – "рыбу", а потом на ее боку, в оставленном для этого месте, заштриховали карандашом. Но что же может быть на боку "уже существующей" рыбы? Чешуя, ну, возможно, грязь, но на боку предмета может быть только предмет.

Во втором случае, когда мы изображением рыбы окружили наши росчерки, образ, достоверность рыбы возникает при разглядывании рисунка не сразу, а с какой-то задержкой, затруднением, только на определенном этапе восприятия, как бы с какими-то оговорками. Почему? Какие процессы происходят при восприятии такого рисунка?

Благодаря абсолютно централизованной композиции (симметричной по плоскости и "сидящей" на оси глаза), мы постоянно, не соскальзывая вниманием, видим как главный предмет рассмотрения наши росчерки и уйти от них, от их генерализирующего присутствия, мы, пока смотрим на весь рисунок, никуда не можем [1].

Потом мы видим (воспринимаем) толстый белый овал, но еще лучше сказать – баранку, выпуклую, наподобие подушки, в которой осталась вмятина от головы, и эта баранка плотно окружает наш "хаос".

Потом мы видим резко очерченный овал с примыкающими к нему сверху, снизу и справа узорами. С трудом, но, к счастью, имея возможность опереться на многочисленные житейские и художественные ассоциации, мы догадываемся, что перед нами рыба.

Но в этом отдельно рассматриваемом нами овале с узорами тоже не все гладко и благополучно для формирования образа рыбы. Попробуем начертить его отдельно.

Он явно напоминает игрушку из известной игры-самоделки, где берется яйцо, а к нему, чтобы получилась мышь, рыба, курица и т.д., подклеивают соответствующие атрибуты: плавники, хвост и проч.

[1] В первом случае этот росчерк чутьчуть сместился вправо от глубинной оси рисунка, но это соскальзывание оказалось достаточным, чтобы он не занимал уже такого главного места.

156

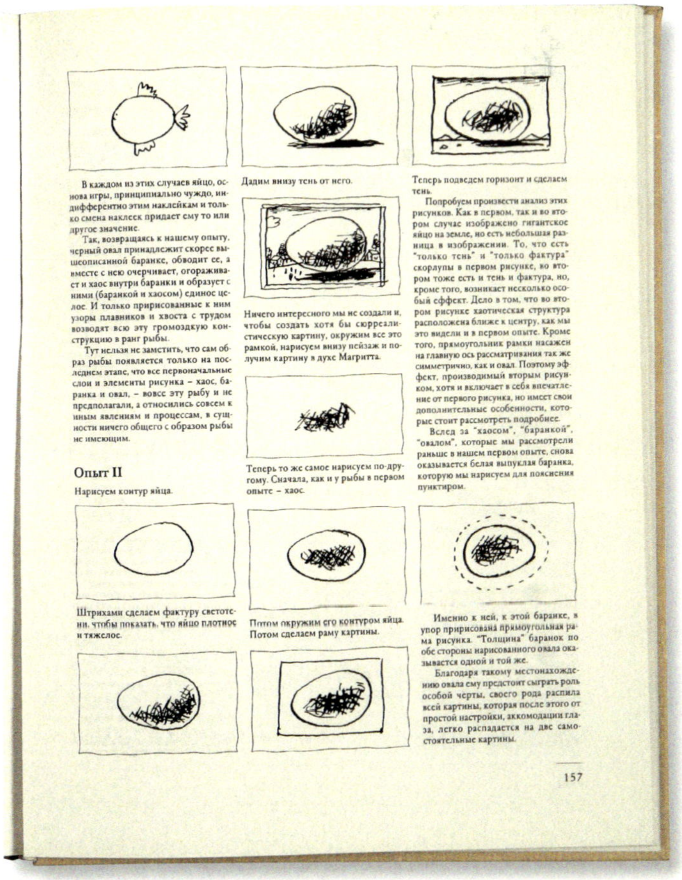

В каждом из этих случаев яйцо, основа игры, принципиально чуждо, индифферентно этим наклейкам и только смена наклеек придает ему то или другое значение.

Так, возвращаясь к нашему опыту, черный овал принадлежит скорее вышеописанной баранке, обводит ее, а вместе с нею очерчивает, огораживает и хаос внутри баранки и образует с ними (баранкой и хаосом) единое целое. И только пририсованные к ним узоры плавников и хвоста с трудом возводят всю эту громоздкую конструкцию в ранг рыбы.

Тут нельзя не заметить, что сам образ рыбы появляется только на последнем этапе, что все первоначальные слои и элементы рисунка – хаос, баранка и овал, – вовсе эту рыбу и не предполагали, а относились совсем к иным явлениям и процессам, в сущности ничего общего с образом рыбы не имеющим.

Опыт II

Нарисуем контур яйца.

Штрихами сделаем фактуру светотени, чтобы показать, что яйцо плотное и тяжелое.

Дадим внизу тень от него.

Ничего интересного мы не создали и, чтобы создать хотя бы сюрреалистическую картину, окружим все это рамкой, нарисуем внизу пейзаж и получим картину в духе Магритта.

Теперь то же самое нарисуем по-другому. Сначала, как и у рыбы в первом опыте – хаос.

Потом окружим его контуром яйца. Потом сделаем раму картины.

Теперь подведем горизонт и сделаем тень.

Попробуем произвести анализ этих рисунков. Как в первом, так и во втором случае изображено гигантское яйцо на земле, но есть небольшая разница в изображении. То, что есть "только тень" и "только фактура" скорлупы в первом рисунке, во втором тоже есть и тень и фактура, но, кроме того, возникает несколько особый эффект. Дело в том, что во втором рисунке хаотическая структура расположена ближе к центру, как мы это видели и в первом опыте. Кроме того, прямоугольник рамки насажен на главную ось рассматривания так же симметрично, как и овал. Поэтому эффект, производимый вторым рисунком, хотя и включает в себя впечатление от первого рисунка, но имеет свои дополнительные особенности, которые стоит рассмотреть подробнее.

Вслед за "хаосом", "баранкой", "овалом", которые мы рассмотрели раньше в нашем первом опыте, снова оказывается белая выпуклая баранка, которую мы нарисуем для пояснения пунктиром.

Именно к ней, к этой баранке, в упор пририсована прямоугольная рама рисунка. "Толщина" баранок по обе стороны нарисованного овала оказывается одной и той же.

Благодаря такому местонахождению овала ему предстоит сыграть роль особой черты, своего рода распила всей картины, которая после этого от простой настройки, аккомодации глаза, легко распадается на две самостоятельные картины.

157

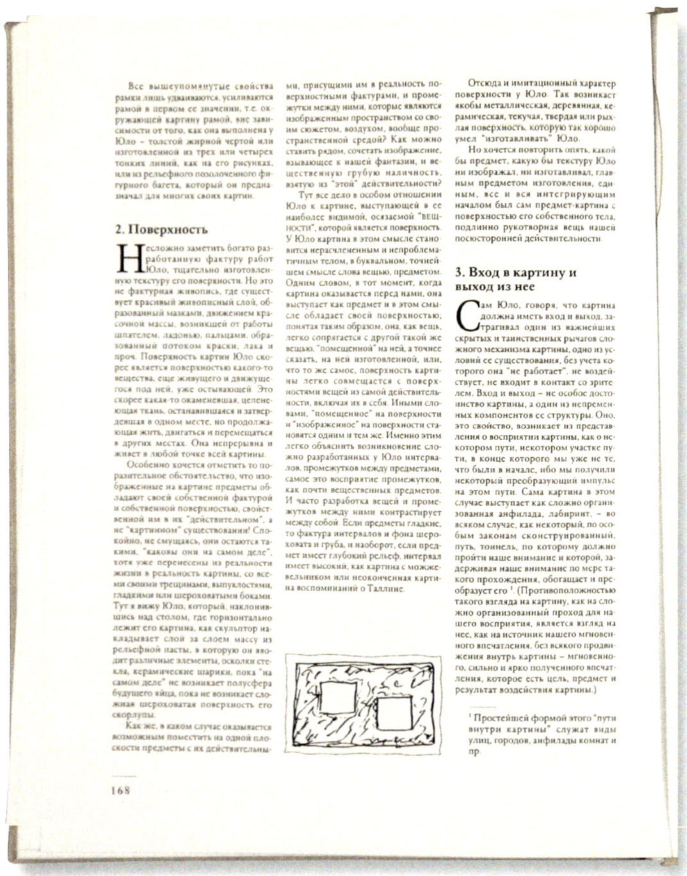

Все вышеупомянутые свойства рамки лишь удваиваются, усиливаются рамой в первом ее значении, т.е. окружающей картину рамой, вне зависимости от того, как она выполнена у Юло – толстой жирной чертой или изготовленной из трех или четырех тонких линий, как на его рисунках, или из рельефного позолоченного фигурного багета, который он предназначал для многих своих картин.

2. Поверхность

Несложно заметить богато разработанную фактуру работ Юло, тщательно изготовленную текстуру его поверхности. Но это не фактурная живопись, где существует красивый живописный слой, образованный мазками, движением красочной массы, возникшей от работы шпателем, ладонью, пальцами, образованный потоком краски, лака и проч. Поверхность картин Юло скорее является поверхностью какого-то вещества, еще живущего и движущегося под ней, уже остывающей. Это скорее какая-то окаменевшая, цепенеющая ткань, остановившаяся и затвердевшая в одном месте, но продолжающая жить, двигаться и перемещаться в других местах. Она непрерывна и живет в любой точке всей картины.

Особенно хочется отметить то поразительное обстоятельство, что изображенные на картине предметы обладают своей собственной фактурой и собственной поверхностью, свойственной им в их "действительном", а не "картинном" существовании! Спокойно, не смущаясь, они остаются такими, "каковы они на самом деле", хотя уже перенесены из реальности жизни в реальность картины, со всеми своими трещинами, выпуклостями, гладкими или шероховатыми боками. Тут я вижу Юло, который, наклонившись над столом, где горизонтально лежит его картина, как скульптор накладывает слой за слоем массу из рельефной пасты, в которую он вводит различные элементы, осколки стекла, керамические шарики, пока "на самом деле" не возникает полусфера будущего яйца, пока не возникает сложная шероховатая поверхность его скорлупы.

Как же, в каком случае оказывается возможным поместить на одной плоскости предметы с их действительными, присущими им в реальность поверхностными фактурами, и промежутки между ними, которые являются изображенным пространством со своим сюжетом, воздухом, вообще пространственной средой? Как можно ставить рядом, сочетать изображение, взывающее к нашей фантазии, и вещественную грубую наличность, взятую из "этой" действительности?

Тут все дело в особом отношении Юло к картине, выступающей в ее наиболее видимой, осязаемой "вещности", которой является поверхность. У Юло картина в этом смысле становится нерасчлененным и непроблематичным телом, в буквальном, точнейшем смысле слова вещью, предметом. Одним словом, в тот момент, когда картина оказывается перед нами, она выступает как предмет и в этом смысле обладает своей поверхностью; понятая таким образом, она, как вещь, легко сопрягается с другой такой же вещью, "помещенной" на ней, а точнее сказать, на ней изготовленной, или, что то же самое, поверхность картины легко совмещается с поверхностями вещей из самой действительности, включая их в себя. Иными словами, "помещенное" на поверхности и "изображенное" на поверхности становятся одним и тем же. Именно этим легко объяснить возникновение сложно разработанных у Юло интервалов, промежутков между предметами, самое это восприятие промежутков, как почти вещественных предметов. И часто разработка вещей и промежутков между ними контрастирует между собой. Если предметы гладкие, то фактура интервалов и фона шероховата и груба, и наоборот, если предмет имеет глубокий рельеф, интервал имеет высокий, как картина с можжевельником или неоконченная картина воспоминаний о Таллине.

Отсюда и имитационный характер поверхности у Юло. Так возникает якобы металлическая, деревянная, керамическая, текучая, твердая или рыхлая поверхность, которую так хорошо умел "изготавливать" Юло.

Но хочется повторить опять, какой бы предмет, какую бы текстуру Юло ни изображал, ни изготавливал, главным предметом изготовления, единым, все и вся интегрирующим началом был сам предмет-картина с поверхностью его собственного тела, подлинно рукотворная вещь нашей посюсторонней действительности.

3. Вход в картину и выход из нее

Сам Юло, говоря, что картина должна иметь вход и выход, затрагивал один из важнейших скрытых и таинственных рычагов сложного механизма картины, одно из условий ее существования, без учета которого она "не работает", не воздействует, не входит в контакт со зрителем. Вход и выход – не особое достоинство картины, а один из непременных компонентов ее структуры. Оно, это свойство, возникает из представления о восприятии картины, как о некотором пути, некотором участке пути, в конце которого мы уже не те, что были в начале, ибо мы получили некоторый преобразующий импульс на этом пути. Сама картина в этом случае выступает как сложно организованная анфилада, лабиринт, – во всяком случае, как некоторый, по особым законам сконструированный, путь, тоннель, по которому должно пройти наше внимание и которой, задерживая наше внимание по мере такого прохождения, обогащает и преобразует его [1]. (Противоположностью такого взгляда на картину, как на сложно организованный проход для нашего восприятия, является взгляд на нее, как на источник нашего мгновенного впечатления, без всякого продвижения внутрь картины – мгновенного, сильно и ярко полученного впечатления, которое есть цель, предмет и результат воздействия картины.)

[1] Простейшей формой этого "пути внутри картины" служат виды улиц, городов, анфилады комнат и пр.

168

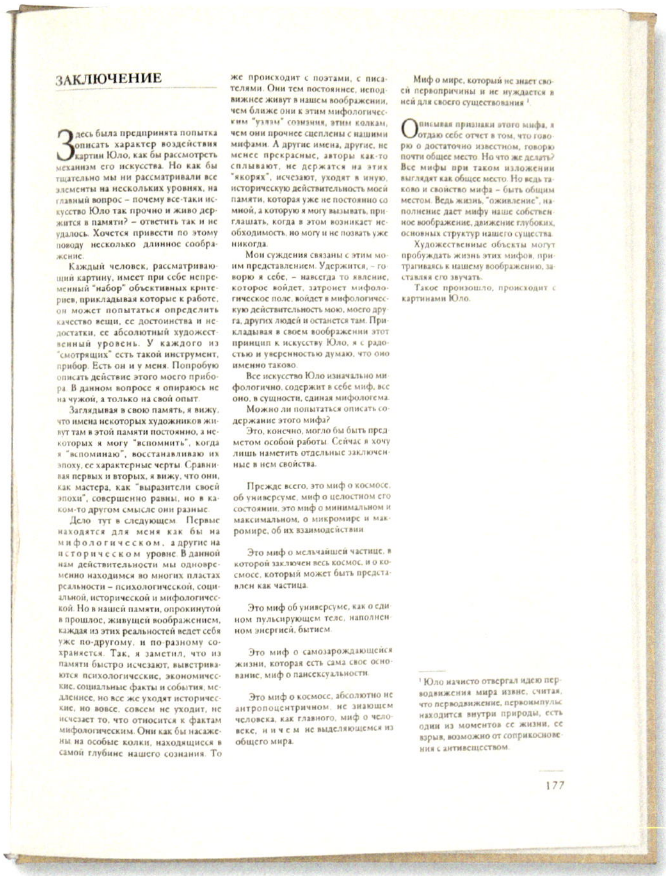

ЗАКЛЮЧЕНИЕ

Здесь была предпринята попытка описать характер воздействия картин Юло, как бы рассмотреть механизм его искусства. Но как бы тщательно мы ни рассматривали все элементы на нескольких уровнях, на главный вопрос – почему все-таки искусство Юло так прочно и живо держится в памяти? – ответить так и не удалось. Хочется привести по этому поводу несколько длинное соображение.

Каждый человек, рассматривающий картину, имеет при себе непременный "набор" объективных критериев, прикладывая которые к работе, он может попытаться определить качество вещи, ее достоинства и недостатки, ее абсолютный художественный уровень. У каждого из "смотрящих" есть такой инструмент, прибор. Есть он и у меня. Попробую описать действие этого моего прибора. В данном вопросе я опираюсь не на чужой, а только на свой опыт.

Заглядывая в свою память, я вижу, что имена некоторых художников живут там в этой памяти постоянно, а некоторых я могу "вспомнить", когда я "вспоминаю", восстанавливаю их эпоху, ее характерные черты. Сравнивая первых и вторых, я вижу, что они, как мастера, как "выразители своей эпохи", совершенно равны, но в каком-то другом смысле они разные.

Дело тут в следующем. Первые находятся для меня как бы на мифологическом, а другие на историческом уровне. В данной нам действительности мы одновременно находимся во многих пластах реальности – психологической, социальной, исторической и мифологической. Но в нашей памяти, опрокинутой в прошлое, живущей воображением, каждая из этих реальностей ведет себя уже по-другому, и по-разному сохраняется. Так, я заметил, что из памяти быстро исчезают, выветриваются психологические, экономические, социальные факты и события, медленнее, но все же уходят исторические, но вовсе, совсем не уходит, не исчезает то, что относится к фактам мифологическим. Они как бы насажены на особые колки, находящиеся в самой глубине нашего сознания. То же происходит с поэтами, с писателями. Они тем постояннее, неподвижнее живут в нашем воображении, чем ближе они к этим мифологическим "узлам" сознания, этим колкам, чем они прочнее сцеплены с нашими мифами. А другие имена, другие, не менее прекрасные, авторы как-то сплывают, не держатся на этих "якорях", исчезают, уходят в иную, историческую действительность моей памяти, которая уже не постоянно со мной, а которую я могу вызывать, приглашать, когда в этом возникает необходимость, но могу и не позвать уже никогда.

Мои суждения связаны с этим моим представлением. Удержится, – говорю я себе, – навсегда то явление, которое войдет, затронет мифологическое поле, войдет в мифологическую действительность мою, моего друга, других людей и останется там. Прикладывая в своем воображении этот принцип к искусству Юло, я с радостью и уверенностью думаю, что оно именно таково.

Все искусство Юло изначально мифологично, содержит в себе миф, все оно, в сущности, единая мифологема.

Можно ли попытаться описать содержание этого мифа?

Это, конечно, могло бы быть предметом особой работы. Сейчас я хочу лишь наметить отдельные заключенные в нем свойства.

Прежде всего, это миф о космосе, об универсуме, миф о целостном его состоянии, это миф о минимальном и максимальном, о микромире и макромире, об их взаимодействии.

Это миф о мельчайшей частице, в которой заключен весь космос, и о космосе, который может быть представлен как частица.

Это миф об универсуме, как о едином пульсирующем теле, наполненном энергией, бытием.

Это миф о самозарождающейся жизни, которая есть сама свое основание, миф о пансексуальности.

Это миф о космосе, абсолютно не антропоцентричном, не знающем человека, как главного, миф о человеке, н и ч е м не выделяющемся из общего мира.

Миф о мире, который не знает своей первопричины и не нуждается в ней для своего существования [1].

Описывая признаки этого мифа, я отдаю себе отчет в том, что говорю о достаточно известном, говорю почти общее место. Но что же делать? Все мифы при таком изложении выглядят как общее место. Но ведь таково и свойство мифа – быть общим местом. Ведь жизнь, "оживление", наполнение дает мифу наше собственное воображение, движение глубоких, основных структур нашего существа.

Художественные объекты могут пробуждать жизнь этих мифов, притрагиваясь к нашему воображению, заставляя его звучать.

Такое произошло, происходит с картинами Юло.

[1] Юло начисто отвергал идею перводвижения мира извне, считая, что перводвижение, первоимпульс находится внутри природы, есть один из моментов ее жизни, ее взрыв, возможно от соприкосновения с антивеществом.

177

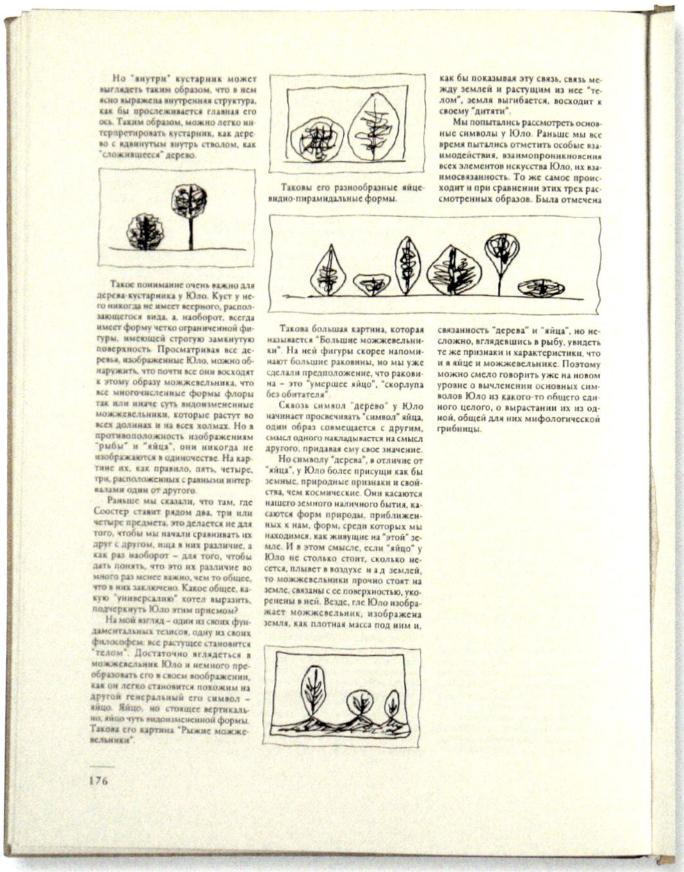

Но "внутри" кустарник может выглядеть таким образом, что в нем ясно выражена внутренняя структура, как бы прослеживается главная его ось. Таким образом, можно легко интерпретировать кустарник, как дерево с вдвинутым внутрь стволом, как "сложившееся" дерево.

Такое понимание очень важно для дерева-кустарника у Юло. Куст у него никогда не имеет веерного, расползающегося вида, а, наоборот, всегда имеет форму четко ограниченной фигуры, имеющей строгую замкнутую поверхность. Просматривая все деревья, изображенные Юло, можно обнаружить, что почти все они восходят к этому образу можжевельника, что все многочисленные формы флоры так или иначе суть видоизмененные можжевельники, которые растут во всех долинах и на всех холмах. Но в противоположность изображениям "рыбы" и "яйца", они никогда не изображаются в одиночестве. На картине их, как правило, пять, четыре, три, расположенных с равными интервалами один от другого.

Раньше мы сказали, что там, где Соостер ставит рядом два, три или четыре предмета, это делается не для того, чтобы мы начали сравнивать их друг с другом, ища в них различие, а как раз наоборот – для того, чтобы дать понять, что это их различие во много раз менее важно, чем то общее, что в них заключено. Какое общее, какую "универсалию" хотел выразить, подчеркнуть Юло этим приемом?

На мой взгляд – один из своих фундаментальных тезисов, одну из своих философем: все растущее становится "телом". Достаточно вглядеться в можжевельник Юло и немного преобразовать его в своем воображении, как он легко становится похожим на другой генеральный его символ – яйцо. Яйцо, но стоящее вертикально, яйцо чуть видоизмененной формы. Такова его картина "Рыжие можжевельники".

Таковы его разнообразные яйцевидно-пирамидальные формы.

Такова большая картина, которая называется "Большие можжевельники". На ней фигуры скорее напоминают большие раковины, но мы уже сделали предположение, что раковина – это "умершее яйцо", "скорлупа без обитателя".

Сквозь символ "дерево" у Юло начинает просвечивать "символ" яйца, один образ совмещается с другим, смысл одного накладывается на смысл другого, придавая ему свое значение.

Но символу "дерева", в отличие от "яйца", у Юло более присущи как бы земные, природные признаки и свойства, чем космические. Они касаются нашего земного наличного бытия, касаются форм природы, приближенных к нам, форм, среди которых мы находимся, как живущие на "этой" земле. И в этом смысле, если "яйцо" у Юло не столько стоит, сколько несется, плывет в воздухе над землей, то можжевельники прочно стоят на земле, связаны с ее поверхностью, укоренены в ней. Везде, где Юло изображает можжевельник, изображена земля, как плотная масса под ним и, как бы показывая эту связь, связь между землей и растущим из нее "телом", земля выгибается, восходит к своему "дитяти".

Мы попытались рассмотреть основные символы у Юло. Раньше мы все время пытались отметить особые взаимодействия, взаимопроникновения всех элементов искусства Юло, их взаимосвязанность. То же самое происходит и при сравнении этих трех рассмотренных образов. Была отмечена связанность "дерева" и "яйца", но несложно, вглядевшись в рыбу, увидеть те же признаки и характеристики, что и в яйце и можжевельнике. Поэтому можно смело говорить уже на новом уровне о вычленении основных символов Юло из какого-то общего единого целого, о вырастании их из одной, общей для них мифологической грибницы.

176

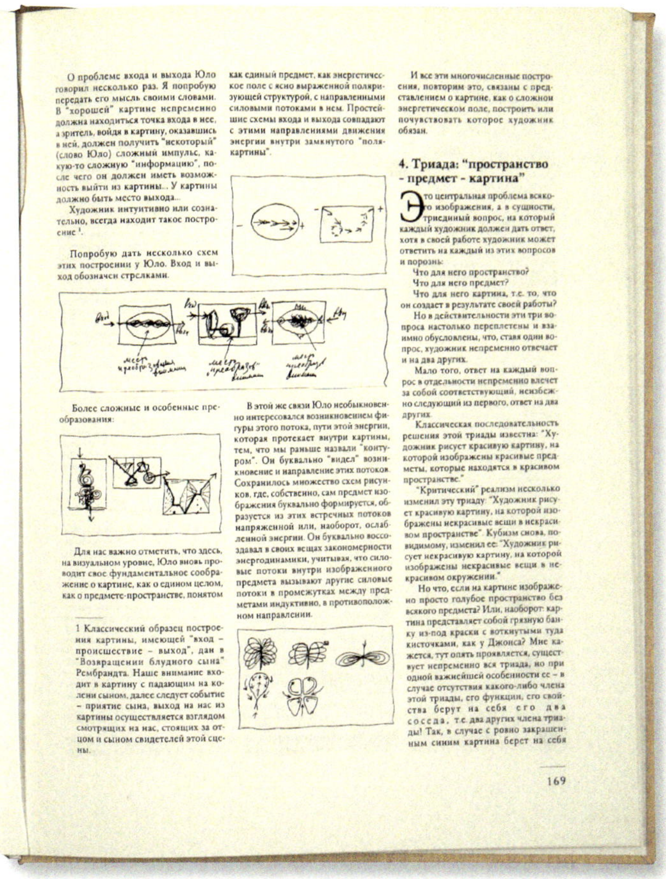

О проблеме входа и выхода Юло говорил несколько раз. Я попробую передать его мысль своими словами. В "хорошей" картине непременно должна находиться точка входа в нее, а зритель, войдя в картину, оказавшись в ней, должен получить "некоторый" (слово Юло) сложный импульс, какую-то сложную "информацию", после чего он должен иметь возможность выйти из картины... У картины должно быть место выхода...

Художник интуитивно или сознательно, всегда находит такое построение [1].

Попробую дать несколько схем этих построении у Юло. Вход и выход обозначен стрелками.

Более сложные и особенные преобразования:

Для нас важно отметить, что здесь, на визуальном уровне, Юло вновь проводит свое фундаментальное соображение о картине, как о едином целом, как о предмете-пространстве, понятом как единый предмет, как энергетическое поле с ясно выраженной поляризующей структурой, с направленными силовыми потоками в нем. Простейшие схемы входа и выхода совпадают с этими направлениями движения энергии внутри замкнутого "поля-картины".

В этой же связи Юло необыкновенно интересовался возникновением фигуры этого потока, пути этой энергии, которая протекает внутри картины, тем, что мы раньше назвали "контуром". Он буквально "видел" возникновение и направление этих потоков. Сохранилось множество схем рисунков, где, собственно, сам предмет изображения буквально формируется, образуется из этих встречных потоков напряженной или, наоборот, ослабленной энергии. Он буквально воссоздавал в своих вещах закономерности энергодинамики, учитывая, что силовые потоки внутри изображенного предмета вызывают другие силовые потоки в промежутках между предметами индуктивно, в противоположном направлении.

И все эти многочисленные построения, повторим это, связаны с представлением о картине, как о сложном энергетическом поле, построить или почувствовать которое художник обязан.

4. Триада: "пространство - предмет - картина"

Это центральная проблема всякого изображения, а в сущности, триединый вопрос, на который каждый художник должен дать ответ, хотя в своей работе художник может ответить на каждый из этих вопросов и порознь:

Что для него пространство?

Что для него предмет?

Что для него картина, т.е. то, что он создает в результате своей работы?

Но в действительности эти три вопроса настолько переплетены и взаимно обусловлены, что, ставя один вопрос, художник непременно отвечает и на два других.

Мало того, ответ на каждый вопрос в отдельности непременно влечет за собой соответствующий, неизбежно следующий из первого, ответ на два других.

Классическая последовательность решения этой триады известна: "Художник рисует красивую картину, на которой изображены красивые предметы, которые находятся в красивом пространстве."

"Критический" реализм несколько изменил эту триаду: "Художник рисует красивую картину, на которой изображены некрасивые вещи в некрасивом пространстве". Кубизм снова, по-видимому, изменил ее: "Художник рисует некрасивую картину, на которой изображены некрасивые вещи в некрасивом окружении."

Но что, если на картине изображено просто голубое пространство без всякого предмета? Или, наоборот: картина представляет собой грязную банку из-под краски с воткнутыми туда кисточками, как у Джонса? Мне кажется, тут опять проявляется, существует непременно вся триада, но при одной важнейшей особенности ее – в случае отсутствия какого-либо члена этой триады, его функции, его свойства берут на себя его два соседа, т.е. два других члена триады! Так, в случае с ровно закрашенным синим картина берет на себя

1 Классический образец построения картины, имеющей "вход – происшествие – выход", дан в "Возвращении блудного сына" Рембрандта. Наше внимание входит в картину с падающим на колени сыном, далее следует событие – приятие сына, выход на нас из картины осуществляется взглядом смотрящих на нас, стоящих за отцом и сыном свидетелей этой сцены.

169

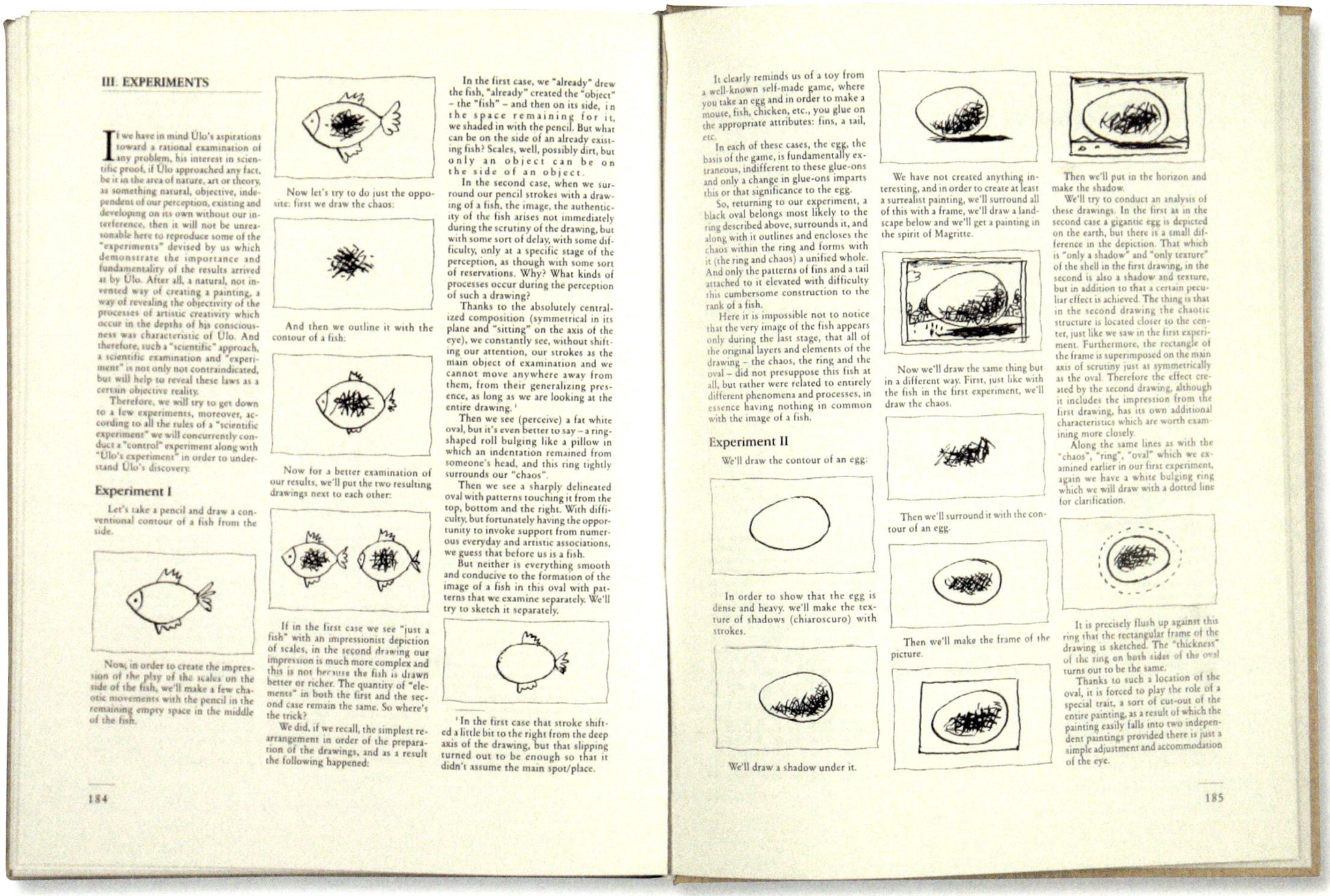

III. EXPERIMENTS

If we have in mind Ülo's aspirations toward a rational examination of any problem, his interest in scientific proof, if Ülo approached any fact, be it in the area of nature, art or theory, as something natural, objective, independent of our perception, existing and developing on its own without our interference, then it will not be unreasonable here to reproduce some of the "experiments" devised by us which demonstrate the importance and fundamentality of the results arrived at by Ülo. After all, a natural, not invented way of creating a painting, a way of revealing the objectivity of the processes of artistic creativity which occur in the depths of his consciousness was characteristic of Ülo. And therefore, such a "scientific" approach, a scientific examination and "experiment" is not only not contraindicated, but will help to reveal these laws as a certain objective reality.

Therefore, we will try to get down to a few experiments, moreover, according to all the rules of a "scientific experiment" we will concurrently conduct a "control" experiment along with "Ülo's experiment" in order to understand Ülo's discovery.

Experiment I

Let's take a pencil and draw a conventional contour of a fish from the side.

Now, in order to create the impression of the play of the scales on the side of the fish, we'll make a few chaotic movements with the pencil in the remaining empty space in the middle of the fish.

Now let's try to do just the opposite: first we draw the chaos:

And then we outline it with the contour of a fish:

Now for a better examination of our results, we'll put the two resulting drawings next to each other:

If in the first case we see "just a fish" with an impressionist depiction of scales, in the second drawing our impression is much more complex and this is not because the fish is drawn better or richer. The quantity of "elements" in both the first and the second case remain the same. So where's the trick?

We did, if we recall, the simplest rearrangement in order of the preparation of the drawings, and as a result the following happened:

In the first case, we "already" drew the fish, "already" created the "object" – the "fish" – and then on its side, in the space remaining for it, we shaded in with the pencil. But what can be on the side of an already existing fish? Scales, well, possibly dirt, but only an object can be on the side of an object.

In the second case, when we surround our pencil strokes with a drawing of a fish, the image, the authenticity of the fish arises not immediately during the scrutiny of the drawing, but with some sort of delay, with some difficulty, only at a specific stage of the perception, as though with some sort of reservations. Why? What kinds of processes occur during the perception of such a drawing?

Thanks to the absolutely centralized composition (symmetrical in its plane and "sitting" on the axis of the eye), we constantly see, without shifting our attention, our strokes as the main object of examination and we cannot move anywhere away from them, from their generalizing presence, as long as we are looking at the entire drawing.[1]

Then we see (perceive) a fat white oval, but it's even better to say – a ring-shaped roll bulging like a pillow in which an indentation remained from someone's head, and this ring tightly surrounds our "chaos".

Then we see a sharply delineated oval with patterns touching it from the top, bottom and the right. With difficulty, but fortunately having the opportunity to invoke support from numerous everyday and artistic associations, we guess that before us is a fish.

But neither is everything smooth and conducive to the formation of the image of a fish in this oval with patterns that we examine separately. We'll try to sketch it separately.

[1] In the first case that stroke shifted a little bit to the right from the deep axis of the drawing, but that slipping turned out to be enough so that it didn't assume the main spot/place.

184

It clearly reminds us of a toy from a well-known self-made game, where you take an egg and in order to make a mouse, fish, chicken, etc., you glue on the appropriate attributes: fins, a tail, etc.

In each of these cases, the egg, the basis of the game, is fundamentally extraneous, indifferent to these glue-ons and only a change in glue-ons imparts this or that significance to the egg.

So, returning to our experiment, a black oval belongs most likely to the ring described above, surrounds it, and along with it outlines and encloses the chaos within the ring and forms with it (the ring and chaos) a unified whole. And only the patterns of fins and a tail attached to it elevated with difficulty this cumbersome construction to the rank of a fish.

Here it is impossible not to notice that the very image of the fish appears only during the last stage, that all of the original layers and elements of the drawing – the chaos, the ring and the oval – did not presuppose this fish at all, but rather were related to entirely different phenomena and processes, in essence having nothing in common with the image of a fish.

Experiment II

We'll draw the contour of an egg:

In order to show that the egg is dense and heavy, we'll make the texture of shadows (chiaroscuro) with strokes.

We'll draw a shadow under it.

We have not created anything interesting, and in order to create at least a surrealist painting, we'll surround all of this with a frame, we'll draw a landscape below and we'll get a painting in the spirit of Magritte.

Now we'll draw the same thing but in a different way. First, just like with the fish in the first experiment, we'll draw the chaos.

Then we'll surround it with the contour of an egg.

Then we'll make the frame of the picture.

Then we'll put in the horizon and make the shadow.

We'll try to conduct an analysis of these drawings. In the first as in the second case a gigantic egg is depicted on the earth, but there is a small difference in the depiction. That which is "only a shadow" and "only texture" of the shell in the first drawing, in the second is also a shadow and texture, but in addition to that a certain peculiar effect is achieved. The thing is that in the second drawing the chaotic structure is located closer to the center, just like we saw in the first experiment. Furthermore, the rectangle of the frame is superimposed on the main axis of scrutiny just as symmetrically as the oval. Therefore the effect created by the second drawing, although it includes the impression from the first drawing, has its own additional characteristics which are worth examining more closely.

Along the same lines as with the "chaos", "ring", "oval" which we examined earlier in our first experiment, again we have a white bulging ring which we will draw with a dotted line for clarification.

It is precisely flush up against this ring that the rectangular frame of the drawing is sketched. The "thickness" of the ring on both sides of the oval turns out to be the same.

Thanks to such a location of the oval, it is forced to play the role of a special trait, a sort of cut-out of the entire painting, as a result of which the painting easily falls into two independent paintings provided there is just a simple adjustment and accommodation of the eye.

185

93 On the Roof | *Auf dem Dach*

1997

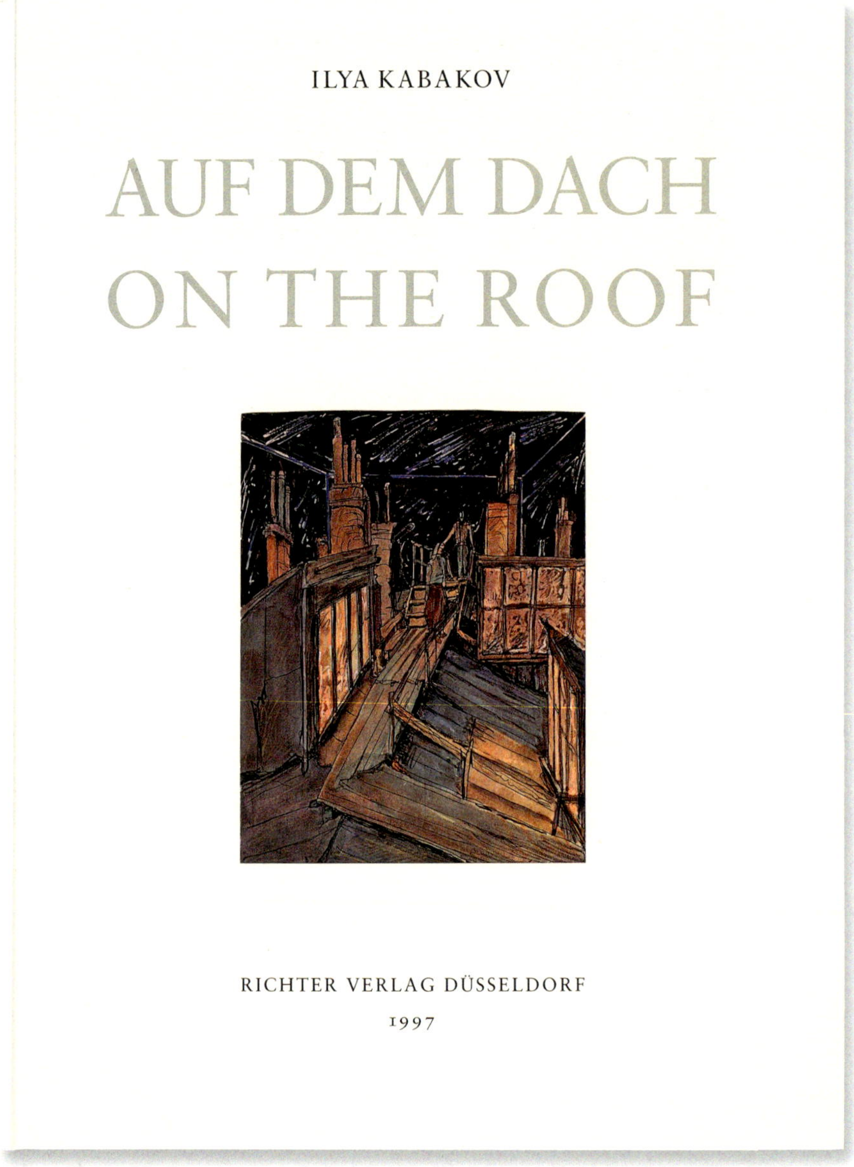

Catherine Robberechts
Düsseldorf: Richter Verlag
30 x 23 cm
191 pp. with 260 (9 color) ills.
stitchbound, hardcover
Fadenheftung, Hardcover

thematic publication | *thematische Publikation*

layout by Ilya Kabakov | *Layout von Ilya Kabakov*

Documentation of the installation of the same name at the Paleis voor Schone Kunsten / Palais des Beaux-Arts, Brussels, June 7 to September 8, 1996. Texts by Piet Coessens and Ilya Kabakov; German, English, Russian.

Dokumentation der gleichnamigen Installation, Paleis voor Schone Kunsten, Brussel / Palais des Beaux-Arts, Bruxelles, 7. Juni – 8. September 1996. Texte von Piet Coessens und Ilya Kabakov; deutsch, englisch, russisch.

see also | *siehe auch* no. 87; CRI, vol. 2, no. 100, pp. 150–155

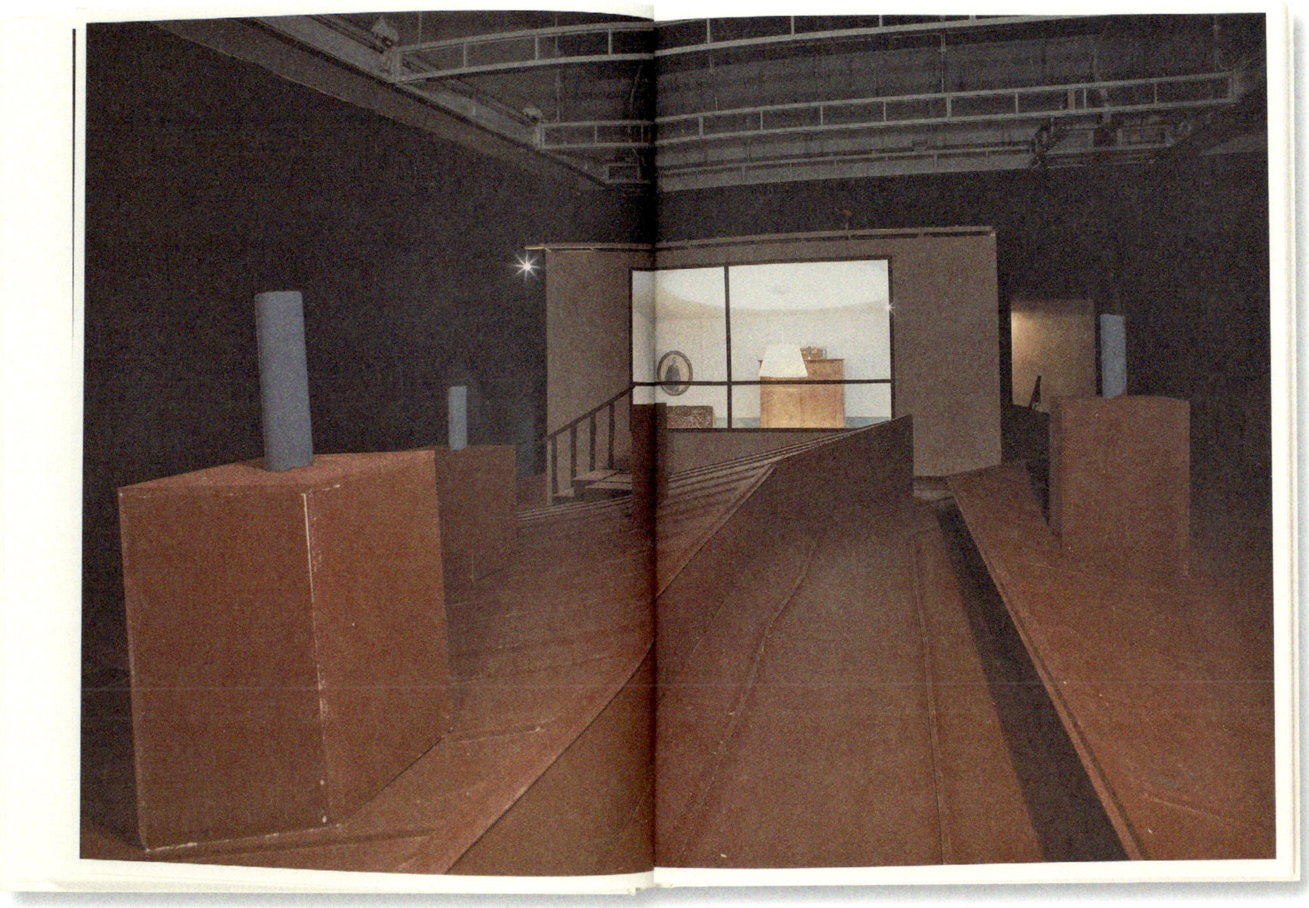

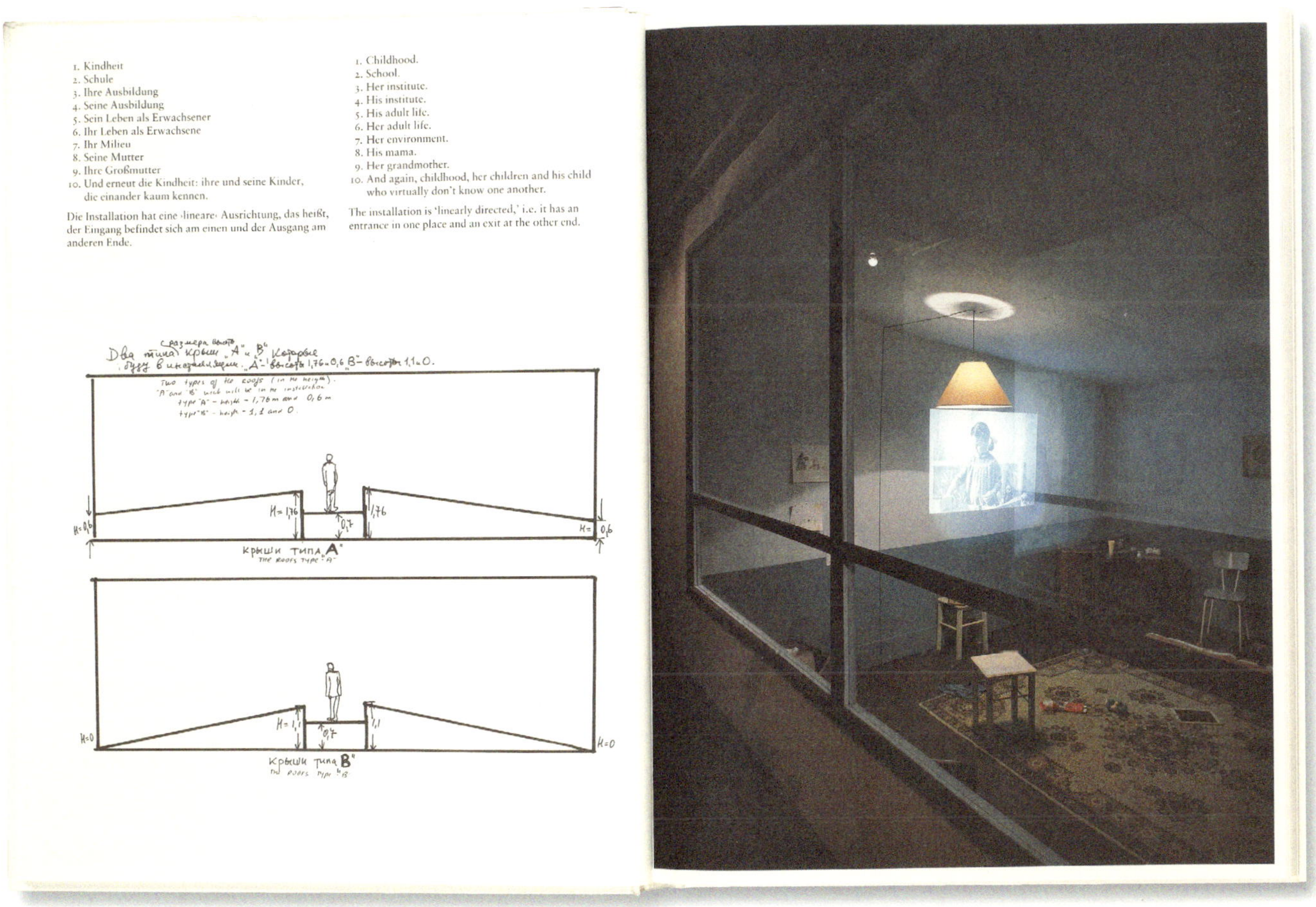
1. Kindheit
2. Schule
3. Ihre Ausbildung
4. Seine Ausbildung
5. Sein Leben als Erwachsener
6. Ihr Leben als Erwachsene
7. Ihr Milieu
8. Seine Mutter
9. Ihre Großmutter
10. Und erneut die Kindheit: ihre und seine Kinder, die einander kaum kennen.
Die Installation hat eine ›lineare‹ Ausrichtung, das heißt, der Eingang befindet sich am einen und der Ausgang am anderen Ende.
1. Childhood.
2. School.
3. Her institute.
4. His institute.
5. His adult life.
6. Her adult life.
7. Her environment.
8. His mama.
9. Her grandmother.
10. And again, childhood, her children and his child who virtually don't know one another.
The installation is 'linearly directed,' i.e. it has an entrance in one place and an exit at the other end.
H=1,76
1,76
0,7
H=0,6
КРЫШИ ТИПА „A“
THE ROOFS TYPE „A“
H=1,1
1,1
0,7
H=0
КРЫШИ ТИПА „B“

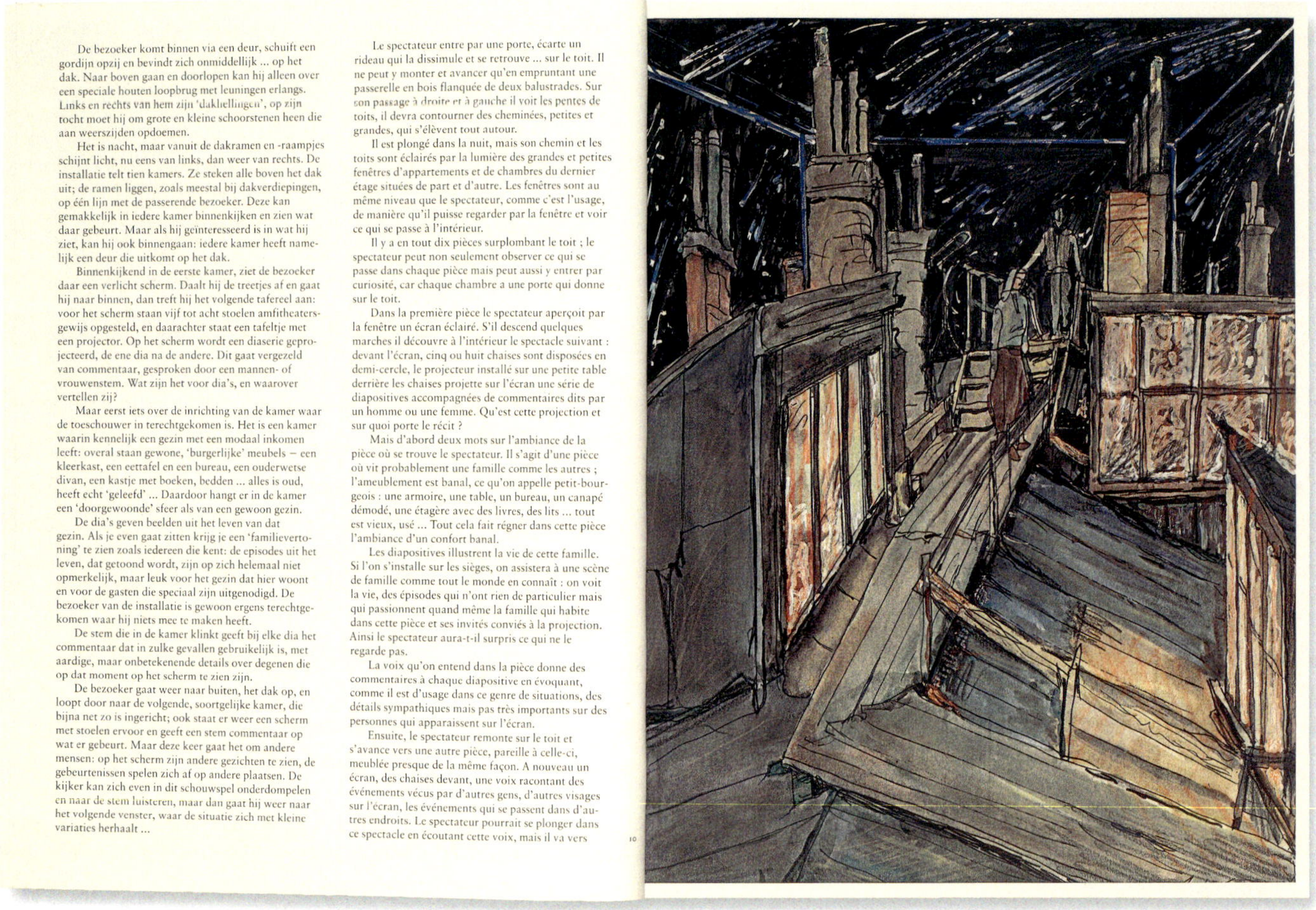

De bezoeker komt binnen via een deur, schuift een gordijn opzij en bevindt zich onmiddellijk ... op het dak. Naar boven gaan en doorlopen kan hij alleen over een speciale houten loopbrug met leuningen erlangs. Links en rechts van hem zijn 'dakhellingen', op zijn tocht moet hij om grote en kleine schoorstenen heen die aan weerszijden opdoemen.

Het is nacht, maar vanuit de dakramen en -raampjes schijnt licht, nu eens van links, dan weer van rechts. De installatie telt tien kamers. Ze steken alle boven het dak uit; de ramen liggen, zoals meestal bij dakverdiepingen, op één lijn met de passerende bezoeker. Deze kan gemakkelijk in iedere kamer binnenkijken en zien wat daar gebeurt. Maar als hij geïnteresseerd is in wat hij ziet, kan hij ook binnengaan: iedere kamer heeft namelijk een deur die uitkomt op het dak.

Binnenkijkend in de eerste kamer, ziet de bezoeker daar een verlicht scherm. Daalt hij de treetjes af en gaat hij naar binnen, dan treft hij het volgende tafereel aan: voor het scherm staan vijf tot acht stoelen amfitheatersgewijs opgesteld, en daarachter staat een tafeltje met een projector. Op het scherm wordt een diaserie geprojecteerd, de ene dia na de andere. Dit gaat vergezeld van commentaar, gesproken door een mannen- of vrouwenstem. Wat zijn het voor dia's, en waarover vertellen zij?

Maar eerst iets over de inrichting van de kamer waar de toeschouwer in terechtgekomen is. Het is een kamer waarin kennelijk een gezin met een modaal inkomen leeft: overal staan gewone, 'burgerlijke' meubels – een kleerkast, een eettafel en een bureau, een ouderwetse divan, een kastje met boeken, bedden ... alles is oud, heeft echt 'geleefd' ... Daardoor hangt er in de kamer een 'doorgewoonde' sfeer als van een gewoon gezin.

De dia's geven beelden uit het leven van dat gezin. Als je even gaat zitten krijg je een 'familievertoning' te zien zoals iedereen die kent: de episodes uit het leven, dat getoond wordt, zijn op zich helemaal niet opmerkelijk, maar leuk voor het gezin dat hier woont en voor de gasten die speciaal zijn uitgenodigd. De bezoeker van de installatie is gewoon ergens terechtgekomen waar hij niets mee te maken heeft.

De stem die in de kamer klinkt geeft bij elke dia het commentaar dat in zulke gevallen gebruikelijk is, met aardige, maar onbetekenende details over degenen die op dat moment op het scherm te zien zijn.

De bezoeker gaat weer naar buiten, het dak op, en loopt door naar de volgende, soortgelijke kamer, die bijna net zo is ingericht; ook staat er weer een scherm met stoelen ervoor en geeft een stem commentaar op wat er gebeurt. Maar deze keer gaat het om andere mensen: op het scherm zijn andere gezichten te zien, de gebeurtenissen spelen zich af op andere plaatsen. De kijker kan zich even in dit schouwspel onderdompelen en naar de stem luisteren, maar dan gaat hij weer naar het volgende venster, waar de situatie zich met kleine variaties herhaalt ...

Le spectateur entre par une porte, écarte un rideau qui la dissimule et se retrouve ... sur le toit. Il ne peut y monter et avancer qu'en empruntant une passerelle en bois flanquée de deux balustrades. Sur son passage à droite et à gauche il voit les pentes de toits, il devra contourner des cheminées, petites et grandes, qui s'élèvent tout autour.

Il est plongé dans la nuit, mais son chemin et les toits sont éclairés par la lumière des grandes et petites fenêtres d'appartements et de chambres du dernier étage situées de part et d'autre. Les fenêtres sont au même niveau que le spectateur, comme c'est l'usage, de manière qu'il puisse regarder par la fenêtre et voir ce qui se passe à l'intérieur.

Il y a en tout dix pièces surplombant le toit ; le spectateur peut non seulement observer ce qui se passe dans chaque pièce mais peut aussi y entrer par curiosité, car chaque chambre a une porte qui donne sur le toit.

Dans la première pièce le spectateur aperçoit par la fenêtre un écran éclairé. S'il descend quelques marches il découvre à l'intérieur le spectacle suivant : devant l'écran, cinq ou huit chaises sont disposées en demi-cercle, le projecteur installé sur une petite table derrière les chaises projette sur l'écran une série de diapositives accompagnées de commentaires dits par un homme ou une femme. Qu'est cette projection et sur quoi porte le récit ?

Mais d'abord deux mots sur l'ambiance de la pièce où se trouve le spectateur. Il s'agit d'une pièce où vit probablement une famille comme les autres ; l'ameublement est banal, ce qu'on appelle petit-bourgeois : une armoire, une table, un bureau, un canapé démodé, une étagère avec des livres, des lits ... tout est vieux, usé ... Tout cela fait régner dans cette pièce l'ambiance d'un confort banal.

Les diapositives illustrent la vie de cette famille. Si l'on s'installe sur les sièges, on assistera à une scène de famille comme tout le monde en connaît : on voit la vie, des épisodes qui n'ont rien de particulier mais qui passionnent quand même la famille qui habite dans cette pièce et ses invités conviés à la projection. Ainsi le spectateur aura-t-il surpris ce qui ne le regarde pas.

La voix qu'on entend dans la pièce donne des commentaires à chaque diapositive en évoquant, comme il est d'usage dans ce genre de situations, des détails sympathiques mais pas très importants sur des personnes qui apparaissent sur l'écran.

Ensuite, le spectateur remonte sur le toit et s'avance vers une autre pièce, pareille à celle-ci, meublée presque de la même façon. A nouveau un écran, des chaises devant, une voix racontant des événements vécus par d'autres gens, d'autres visages sur l'écran, les événements qui se passent dans d'autres endroits. Le spectateur pourrait se plonger dans ce spectacle en écoutant cette voix, mais il va vers

10

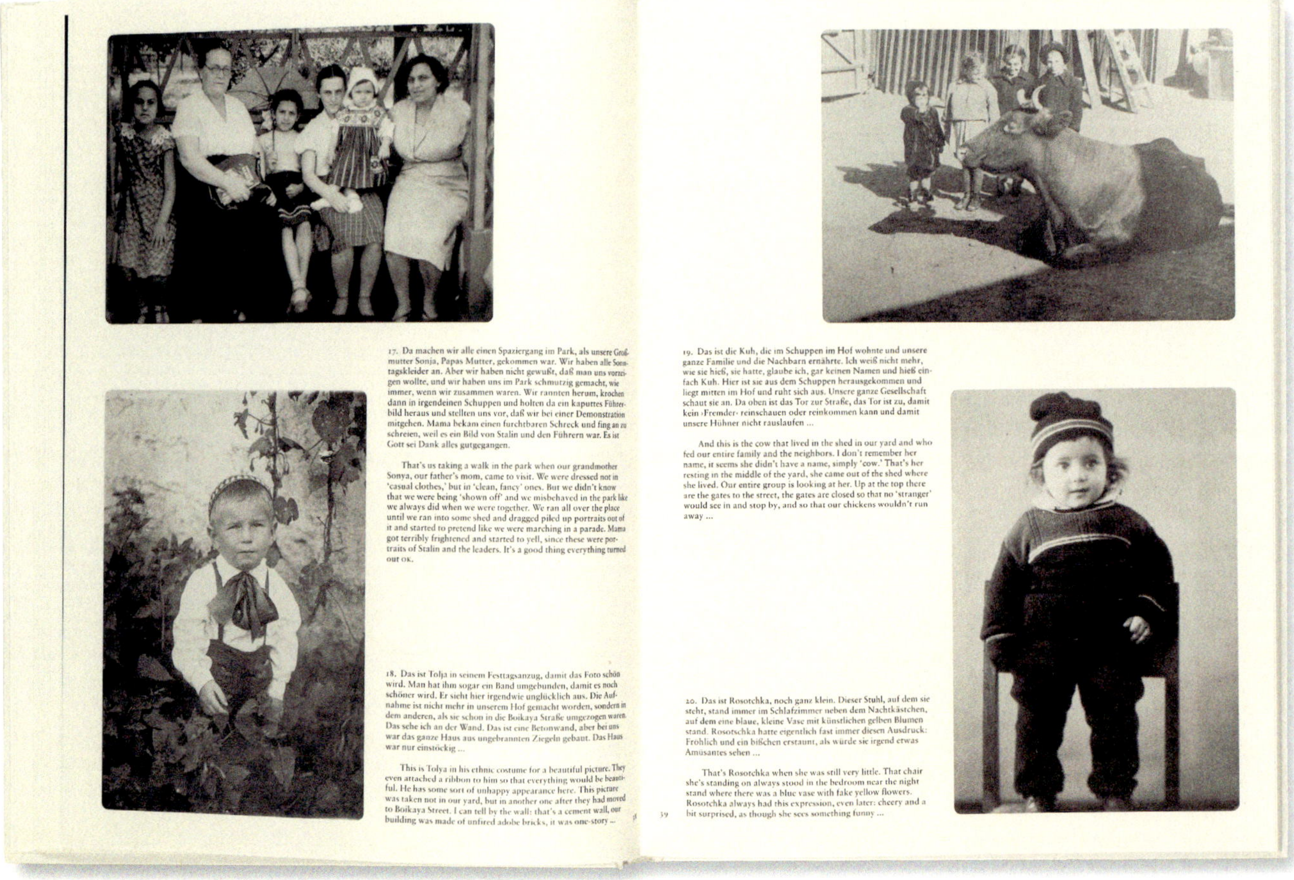

17. Da machen wir alle einen Spaziergang im Park, als unsere Großmutter Sonja, Papas Mutter, gekommen war. Wir haben alle Sonntagskleider an. Aber wir haben nicht gewußt, daß man uns vorzeigen wollte, und wir haben uns im Park schmutzig gemacht, wie immer, wenn wir zusammen waren. Wir rannten herum, krochen dann in irgendeinen Schuppen und holten da ein kaputtes Führerbild heraus und stellten uns vor, daß wir bei einer Demonstration mitgehen. Mama bekam einen furchtbaren Schreck und fing an zu schreien, weil es ein Bild von Stalin und den Führern war. Es ist Gott sei Dank alles gutgegangen.

That's us taking a walk in the park when our grandmother Sonya, our father's mom, came to visit. We were dressed not in 'casual clothes,' but in 'clean, fancy' ones. But we didn't know that we were being 'shown off' and we misbehaved in the park like we always did when we were together. We ran all over the place until we ran into some shed and dragged piled up portraits out of it and started to pretend like we were marching in a parade. Mama got terribly frightened and started to yell, since these were portraits of Stalin and the leaders. It's a good thing everything turned out OK.

18. Das ist Tolja in seinem Festtagsanzug, damit das Foto schön wird. Man hat ihm sogar ein Band umgebunden, damit es noch schöner wird. Er sieht hier irgendwie unglücklich aus. Die Aufnahme ist nicht mehr in unserem Hof gemacht worden, sondern in dem anderen, als sie schon in die Boikaya Straße umgezogen waren. Das sehe ich an der Wand. Das ist eine Betonwand, aber bei uns war das ganze Haus aus ungebrannten Ziegeln gebaut. Das Haus war nur einstöckig ...

This is Tolya in his ethnic costume for a beautiful picture. They even attached a ribbon to him so that everything would be beautiful. He has some sort of unhappy appearance here. This picture was taken not in our yard, but in another one after they had moved to Boikaya Street. I can tell by the wall: that's a cement wall, our building was made of unfired adobe bricks, it was one-story ...

19. Das ist die Kuh, die im Schuppen im Hof wohnte und unsere ganze Familie und die Nachbarn ernährte. Ich weiß nicht mehr, wie sie hieß, sie hatte, glaube ich, gar keinen Namen und hieß einfach Kuh. Hier ist sie aus dem Schuppen herausgekommen und liegt mitten im Hof und ruht sich aus. Unsere ganze Gesellschaft schaut sie an. Da oben ist das Tor zur Straße, das Tor ist zu, damit kein ›Fremder‹ reinschauen oder reinkommen kann und damit unsere Hühner nicht rauslaufen ...

And this is the cow that lived in the shed in our yard and who fed our entire family and the neighbors. I don't remember her name, it seems she didn't have a name, simply 'cow.' That's her resting in the middle of the yard, she came out of the shed where she lived. Our entire group is looking at her. Up at the top there are the gates to the street, the gates are closed so that no 'stranger' would see in and stop by, and so that our chickens wouldn't run away ...

20. Das ist Rosotchka, noch ganz klein. Dieser Stuhl, auf dem sie steht, stand immer im Schlafzimmer neben dem Nachtkästchen, auf dem eine blaue, kleine Vase mit künstlichen gelben Blumen stand. Rosotschka hatte eigentlich fast immer diesen Ausdruck: Fröhlich und ein bißchen erstaunt, als würde sie irgend etwas Amüsantes sehen ...

That's Rosotchka when she was still very little. That chair she's standing on always stood in the bedroom near the night stand where there was a blue vase with fake yellow flowers. Rosotchka always had this expression, even later: cheery and a bit surprised, as though she sees something funny ...

39

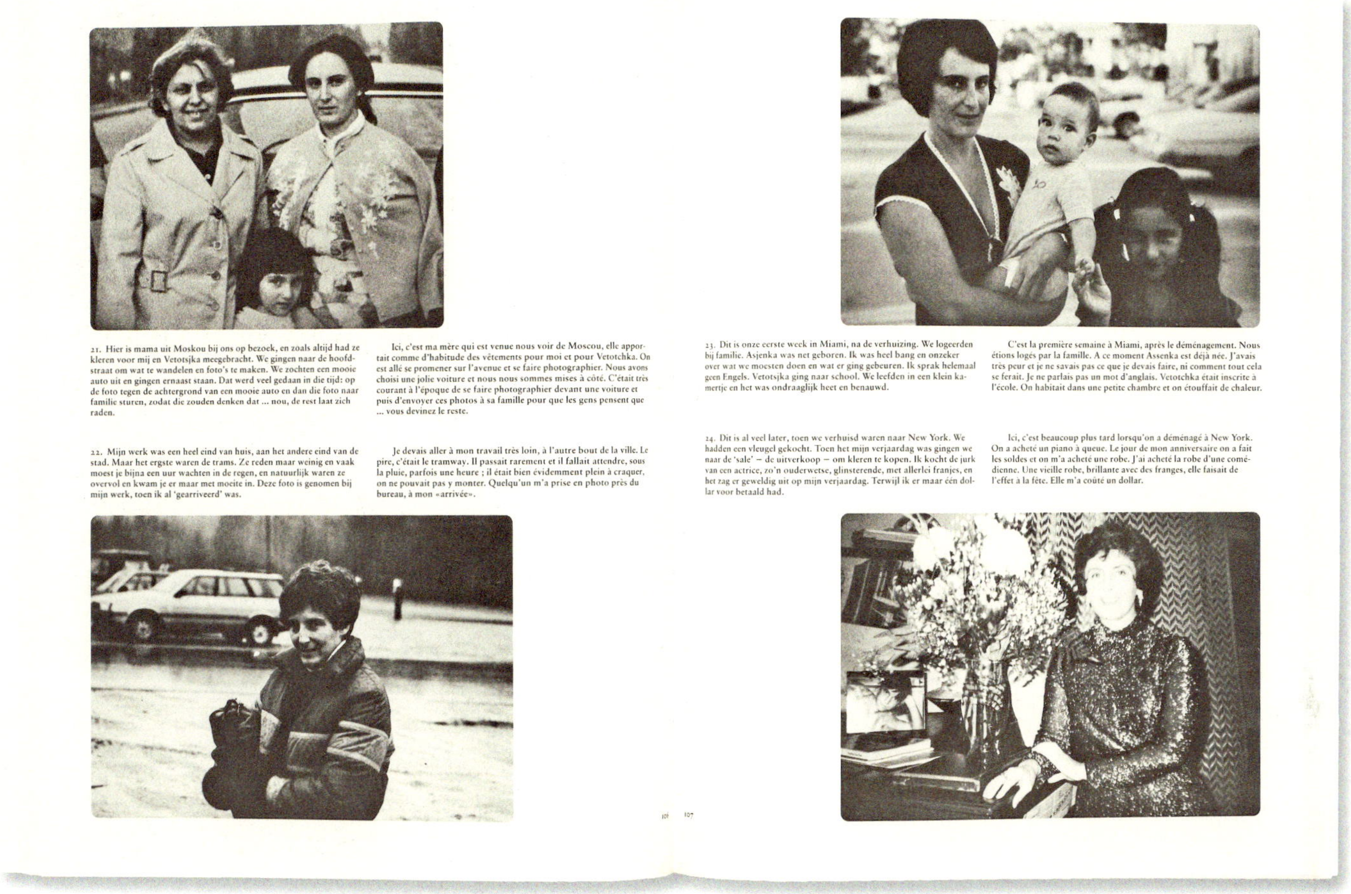

21. Hier is mama uit Moskou bij ons op bezoek, en zoals altijd had ze kleren voor mij en Vetotsjka meegebracht. We gingen naar de hoofdstraat om wat te wandelen en foto's te maken. We zochten een mooie auto uit en gingen ernaast staan. Dat werd veel gedaan in die tijd: op de foto tegen de achtergrond van een mooie auto en dan die foto naar familie sturen, zodat die zouden denken dat ... nou, de rest laat zich raden.

Ici, c'est ma mère qui est venue nous voir de Moscou, elle apportait comme d'habitude des vêtements pour moi et pour Vetotchka. On est allé se promener sur l'avenue et se faire photographier. Nous avons choisi une jolie voiture et nous nous sommes mises à côté. C'était très courant à l'époque de se faire photographier devant une voiture et puis d'envoyer ces photos à sa famille pour que les gens pensent que ... vous devinez le reste.

22. Mijn werk was een heel eind van huis, aan het andere eind van de stad. Maar het ergste waren de trams. Ze reden maar weinig en vaak moest je bijna een uur wachten in de regen, en natuurlijk waren ze overvol en kwam je er maar met moeite in. Deze foto is genomen bij mijn werk, toen ik al 'gearriveerd' was.

Je devais aller à mon travail très loin, à l'autre bout de la ville. Le pire, c'était le tramway. Il passait rarement et il fallait attendre, sous la pluie, parfois une heure ; il était bien évidemment plein à craquer, on ne pouvait pas y monter. Quelqu'un m'a prise en photo près du bureau, à mon «arrivée».

23. Dit is onze eerste week in Miami, na de verhuizing. We logeerden bij familie. Asjenka was net geboren. Ik was heel bang en onzeker over wat we moesten doen en wat er ging gebeuren. Ik sprak helemaal geen Engels. Vetotsjka ging naar school. We leefden in een klein kamertje en het was ondraaglijk heet en benauwd.

C'est la première semaine à Miami, après le déménagement. Nous étions logés par la famille. A ce moment Assenka est déjà née. J'avais très peur et je ne savais pas ce que je devais faire, ni comment tout cela se ferait. Je ne parlais pas un mot d'anglais. Vetotchka était inscrite à l'école. On habitait dans une petite chambre et on étouffait de chaleur.

24. Dit is al veel later, toen we verhuisd waren naar New York. We hadden een vleugel gekocht. Toen het mijn verjaardag was gingen we naar de 'sale' – de uitverkoop – om kleren te kopen. Ik kocht de jurk van een actrice, zo'n ouderwetse, glinsterende, met allerlei franjes, en het zag er geweldig uit op mijn verjaardag. Terwijl ik er maar één dollar voor betaald had.

Ici, c'est beaucoup plus tard lorsqu'on a déménagé à New York. On a acheté un piano à queue. Le jour de mon anniversaire on a fait les soldes et on m'a acheté une robe. J'ai acheté la robe d'une comédienne. Une vieille robe, brillante avec des franges, elle faisait de l'effet à la fête. Elle m'a coûté un dollar.

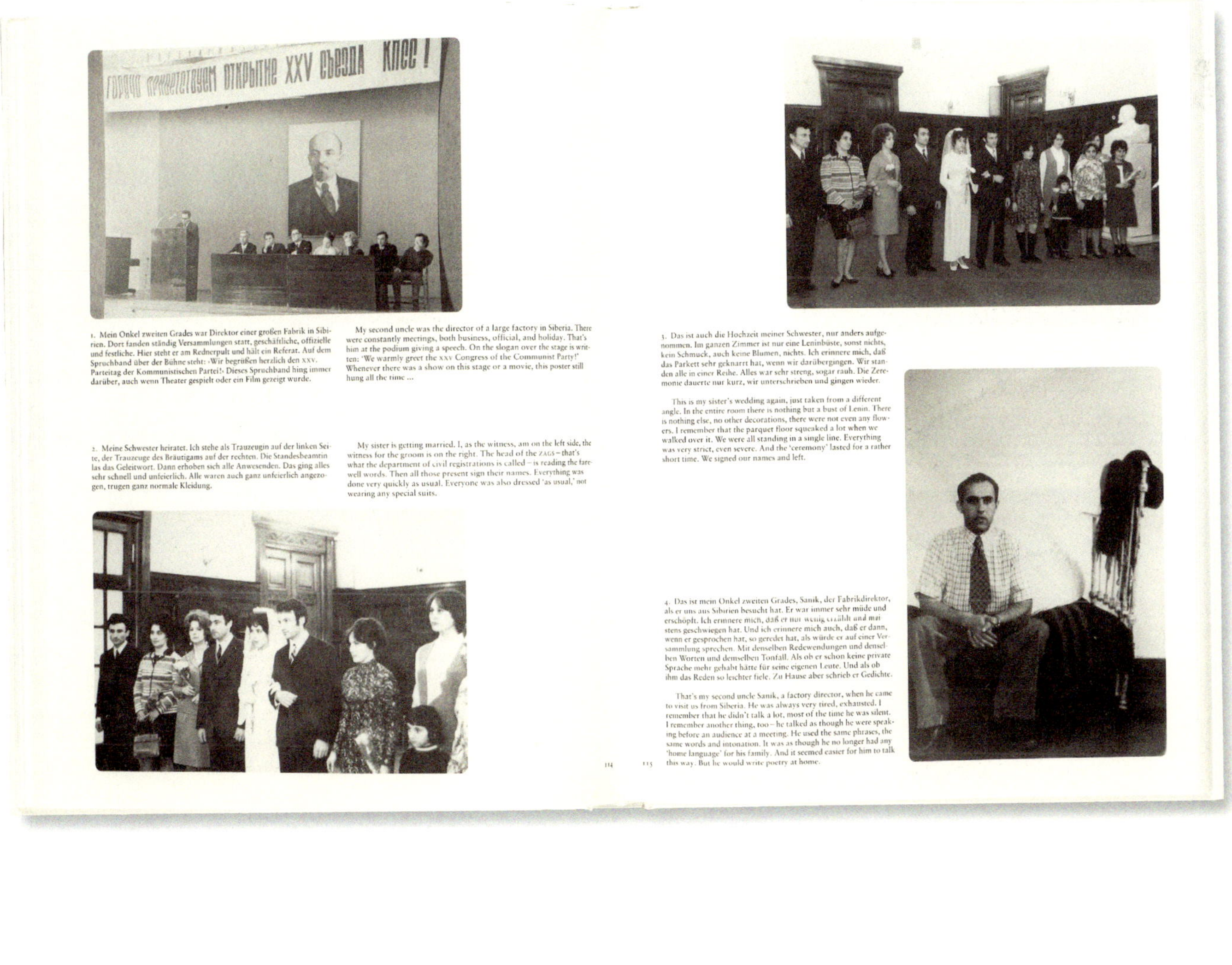

1. Mein Onkel zweiten Grades war Direktor einer großen Fabrik in Sibirien. Dort fanden ständig Versammlungen statt, geschäftliche, offizielle und festliche. Hier steht er am Rednerpult und hält ein Referat. Auf dem Spruchband über der Bühne steht: ›Wir begrüßen herzlich den XXV. Parteitag der Kommunistischen Partei!‹ Dieses Spruchband hing immer darüber, auch wenn Theater gespielt oder ein Film gezeigt wurde.

My second uncle was the director of a large factory in Siberia. There were constantly meetings, both business, official, and holiday. That's him at the podium giving a speech. On the slogan over the stage is written: 'We warmly greet the XXV Congress of the Communist Party!' Whenever there was a show on this stage or a movie, this poster still hung all the time ...

2. Meine Schwester heiratet. Ich stehe als Trauzeugin auf der linken Seite, der Trauzeuge des Bräutigams auf der rechten. Die Standesbeamtin las das Geleitwort. Dann erhoben sich alle Anwesenden. Das ging alles sehr schnell und unfeierlich. Alle waren auch ganz unfeierlich angezogen, trugen ganz normale Kleidung.

My sister is getting married. I, as the witness, am on the left side, the witness for the groom is on the right. The head of the ZAGS – that's what the department of civil registrations is called – is reading the farewell words. Then all those present sign their names. Everything was done very quickly as usual. Everyone was also dressed 'as usual,' not wearing any special suits.

114

3. Das ist auch die Hochzeit meiner Schwester, nur anders aufgenommen. Im ganzen Zimmer ist nur eine Leninbüste, sonst nichts, kein Schmuck, auch keine Blumen, nichts. Ich erinnere mich, daß das Parkett sehr geknarrt hat, wenn wir darübergingen. Wir standen alle in einer Reihe. Alles war sehr streng, sogar rauh. Die Zeremonie dauerte nur kurz, wir unterschrieben und gingen wieder.

This is my sister's wedding again, just taken from a different angle. In the entire room there is nothing but a bust of Lenin. There is nothing else, no other decorations, there were not even any flowers. I remember that the parquet floor squeaked a lot when we walked over it. We were all standing in a single line. Everything was very strict, even severe. And the 'ceremony' lasted for a rather short time. We signed our names and left.

4. Das ist mein Onkel zweiten Grades, Sanik, der Fabrikdirektor, als er uns aus Sibirien besucht hat. Er war immer sehr müde und erschöpft. Ich erinnere mich, daß er nur wenig erzählt und meistens geschwiegen hat. Und ich erinnere mich auch, daß er dann, wenn er gesprochen hat, so geredet hat, als würde er auf einer Versammlung sprechen. Mit denselben Redewendungen und denselben Worten und demselben Tonfall. Als ob er schon keine private Sprache mehr gehabt hätte für seine eigenen Leute. Und als ob ihm das Reden so leichter fiele. Zu Hause aber schrieb er Gedichte.

That's my second uncle Sanik, a factory director, when he came to visit us from Siberia. He was always very tired, exhausted. I remember that he didn't talk a lot, most of the time he was silent. I remember another thing, too – he talked as though he were speaking before an audience at a meeting. He used the same phrases, the same words and intonation. It was as though he no longer had any 'home language' for his family. And it seemed easier for him to talk this way. But he would write poetry at home.

115

94 Tennis Game | *Das Tennisspiel*

with Pavel Pepperstein | *mit Pavel Pepperstein*

1997

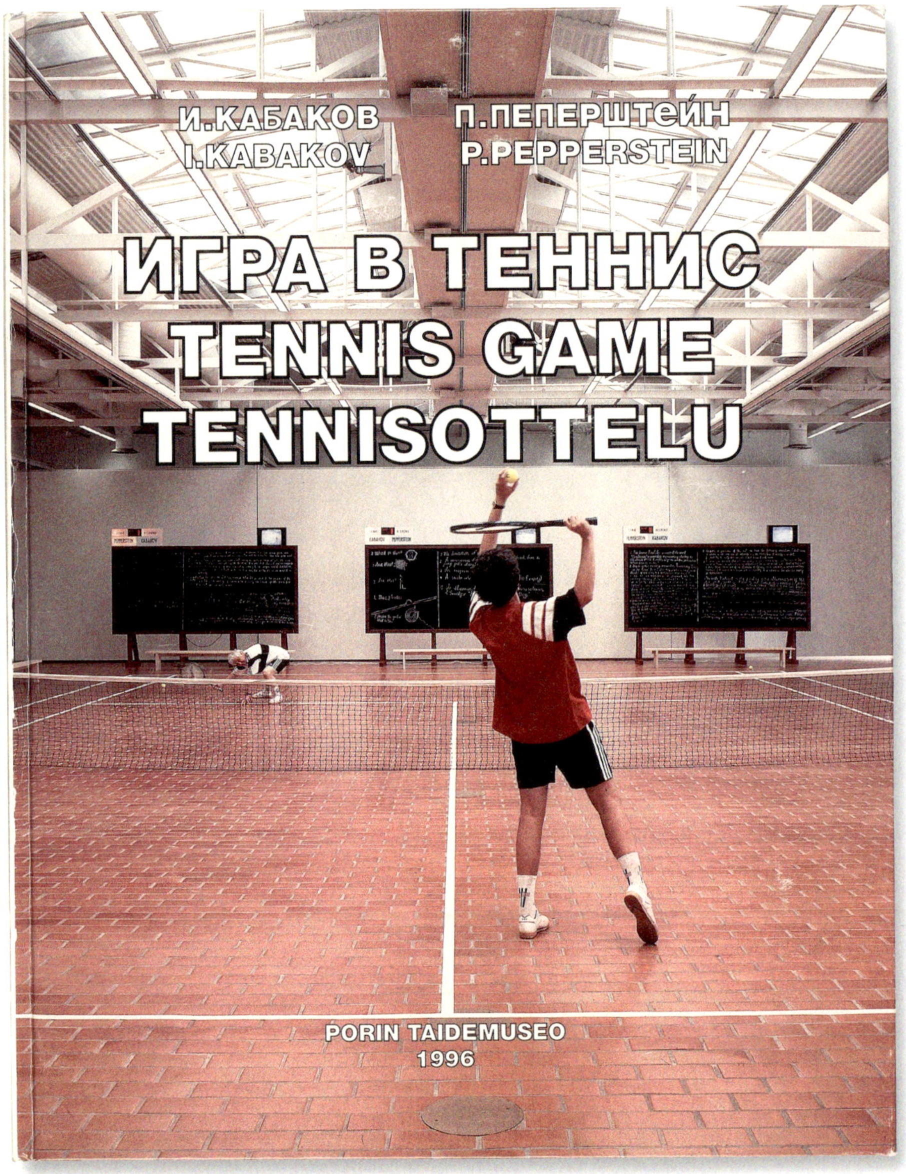

Jari-Pekka Vanhala
Pori: Porin Taidemuseo Publications (no. 36)
29.5 x 23.5 cm
81 pp. with 70 (10 color) ills.
stitchbound, hardcover, illustration »The Tennis Game« by Ilya Kabakov on front flyleaf
Fadenheftung, Hardcover, Illustration »The Tennis Game« von Ilya Kabakov auf dem Vorsatz vorne

exhibition catalogue | *Ausstellungskatalog*

layout by Ilya Kabakov | *Layout von Ilya Kabakov*

Documentation of the installation of the same name at the Paleis voor Schone Kunsten / Palais des Beaux-Arts, Brussels, June 7 to September 8, 1996. Texts by Piet Coessens and Ilya Kabakov; German, English, Russian.

Dokumentation der gleichnamigen Installation, Paleis voor Schone Kunsten, Brussel / Palais des Beaux-Arts, Bruxelles, 7. Juni – 8. September 1996. Texte von Piet Coessens und Ilya Kabakov; deutsch, englisch, russisch.

see also | *siehe auch* no. 135; CRI, vol. 2, no. 95, pp. 126–131

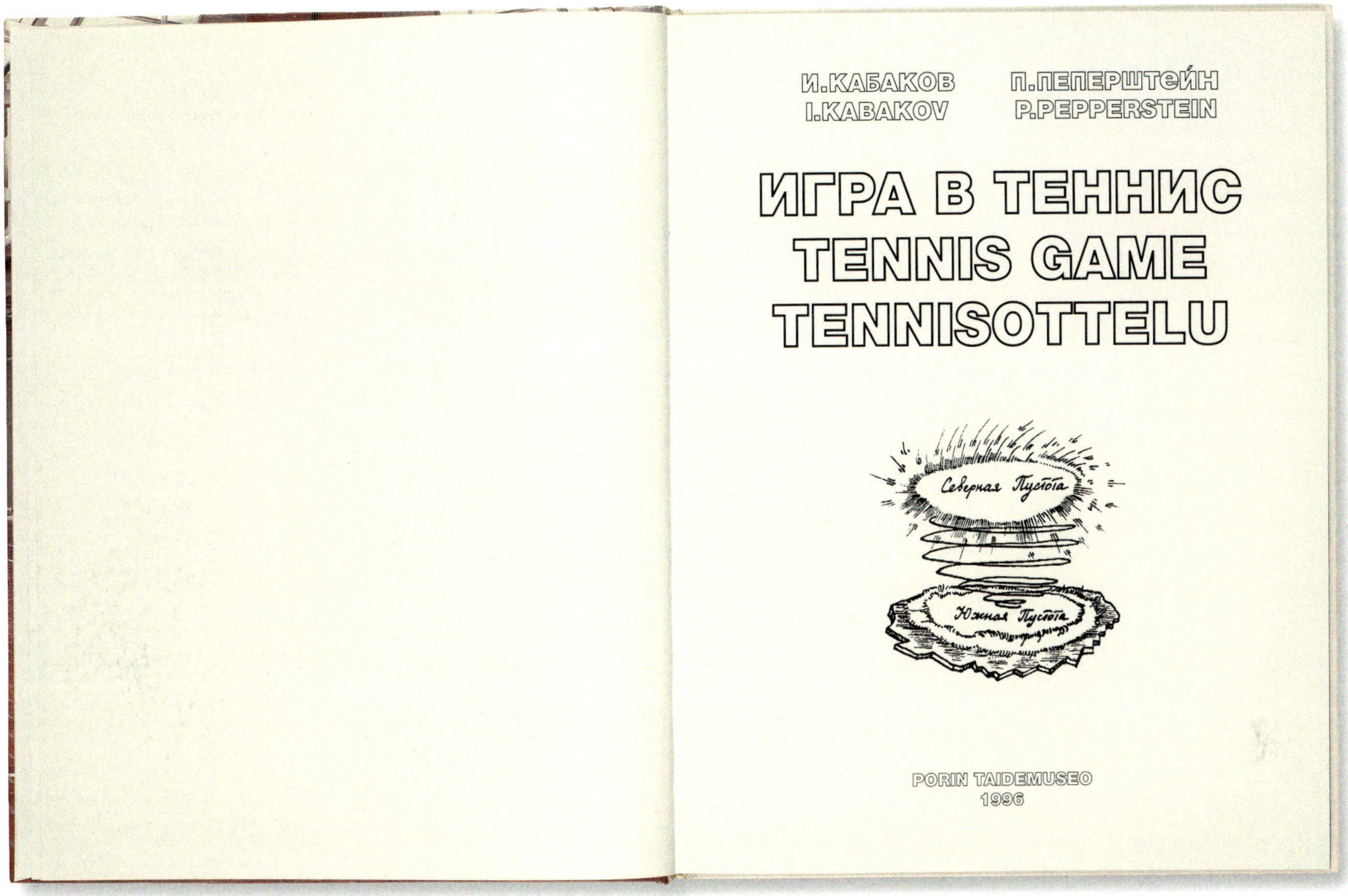
И.КАБАКОВ
I.KABAKOV
П.ПЕПЕРШТЕЙН
P.PEPPERSTEIN
ИГРА В ТЕННИС
TENNIS GAME
TENNISOTTELU
Северная Пустота
Южная Пустота
PORIN TAIDEMUSEO
1996

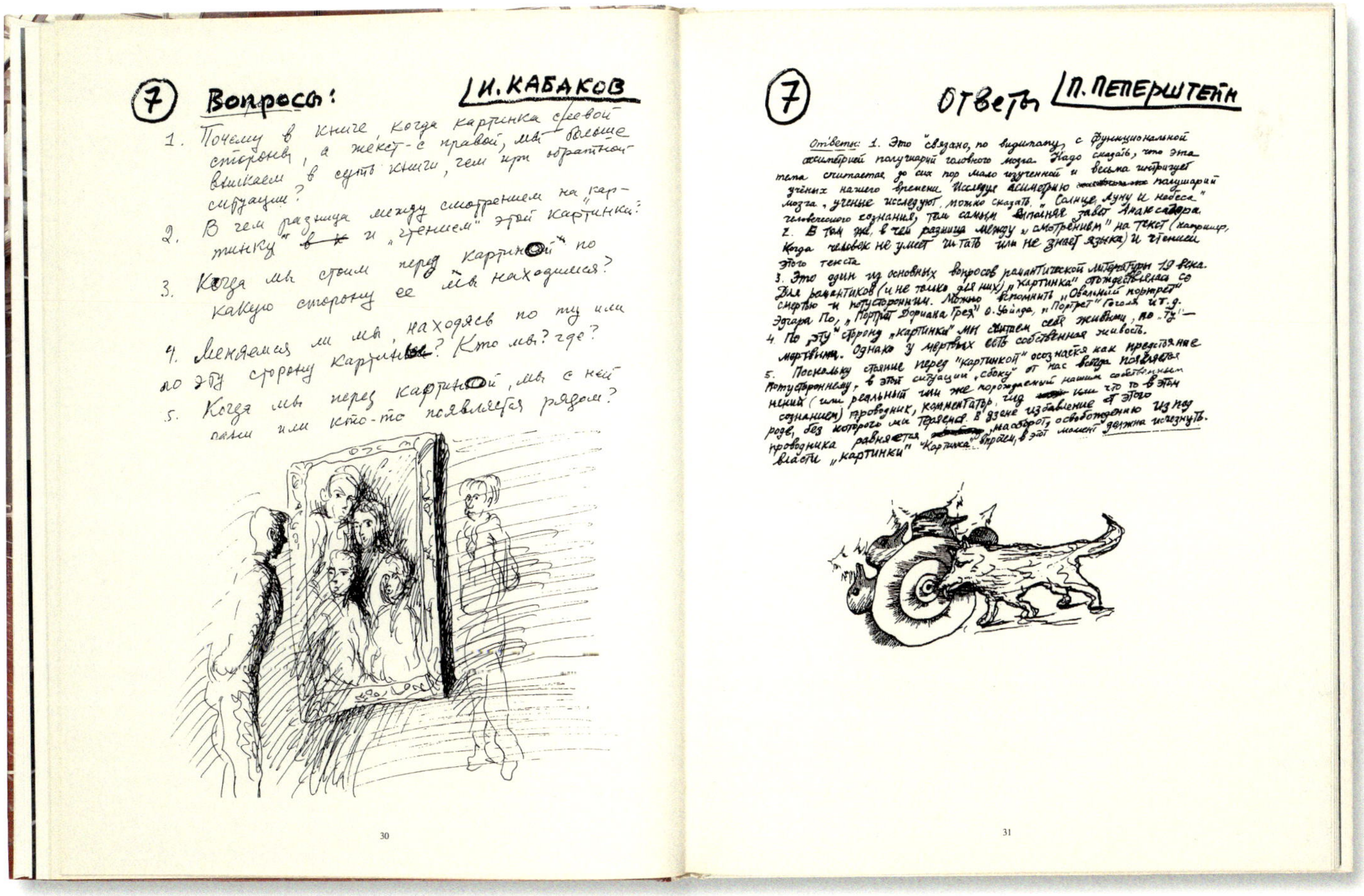
7 Вопросы: И. КАБАКОВ
7 Ответы П. ПЕПЕРШТЕЙН
30
31

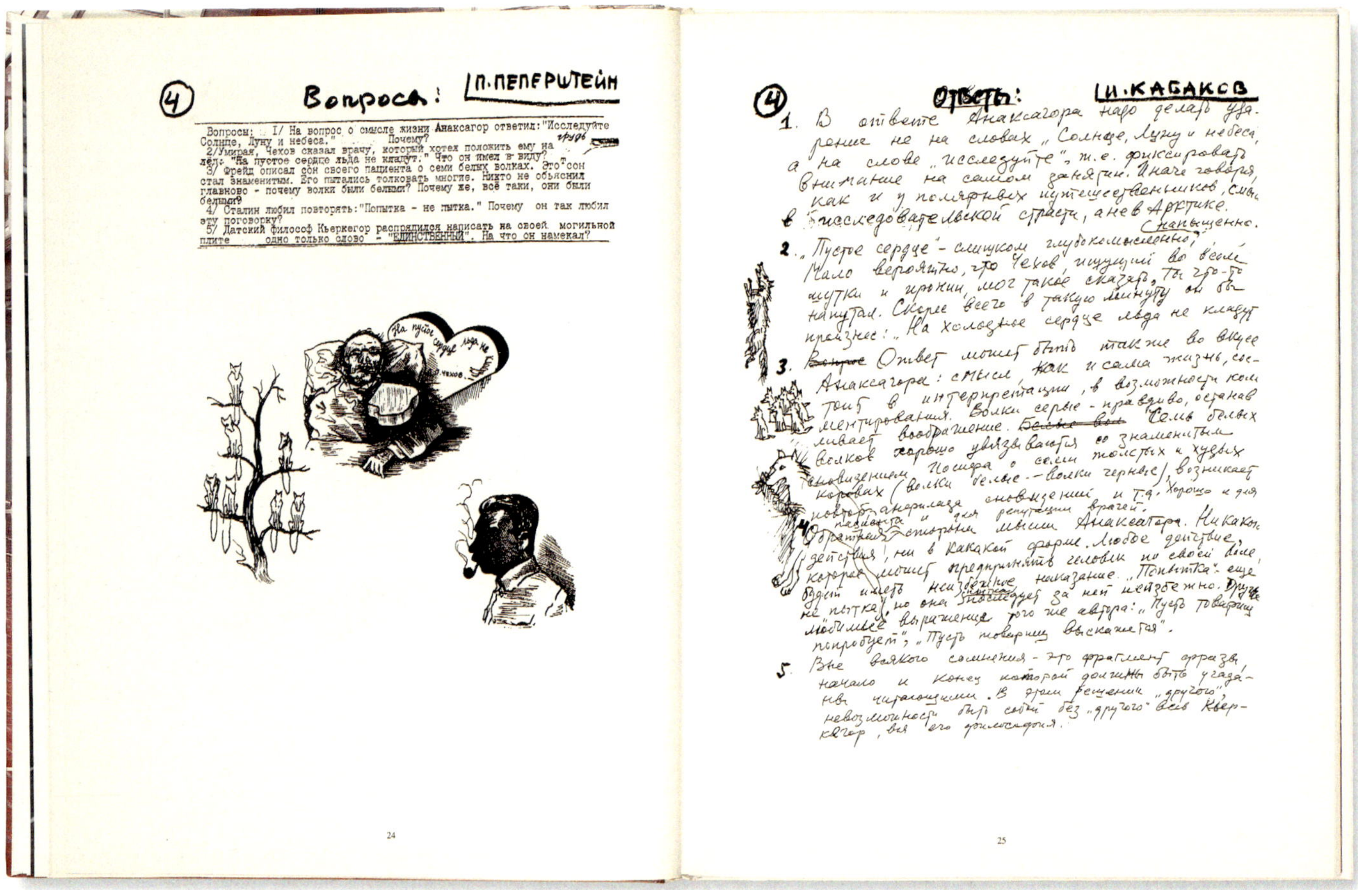
4
Вопроса: П.ПЕПЕРШТЕЙН
Вопросы: I/ На вопрос о смысле жизни Анаксагор ответил:"Исследуйте Солнце, Луну и небеса." Почему?
2/Умирая, Чехов сказал врачу, который хотел положить ему на грудь лёд: "На пустое сердце льда не кладут." Что он имел в виду?
3/ Фрейд описал сон своего пациента о семи белых волках. Этот сон стал знаменитым. Его пытались толковать многие. Никто не объяснил главново - почему волки были белыми? Почему же, всё таки, они были белыми?
4/ Сталин любил повторять:"Попытка - не пытка." Почему он так любил эту поговорку?
5/ Датский философ Кьеркегор распорядился написать на своей могильной плите одно только слово - "ЕДИНСТВЕННЫЙ". На что он намекал?
На пустое сердце льда не
4
Ответы: И.КАБАКОВ
24
25

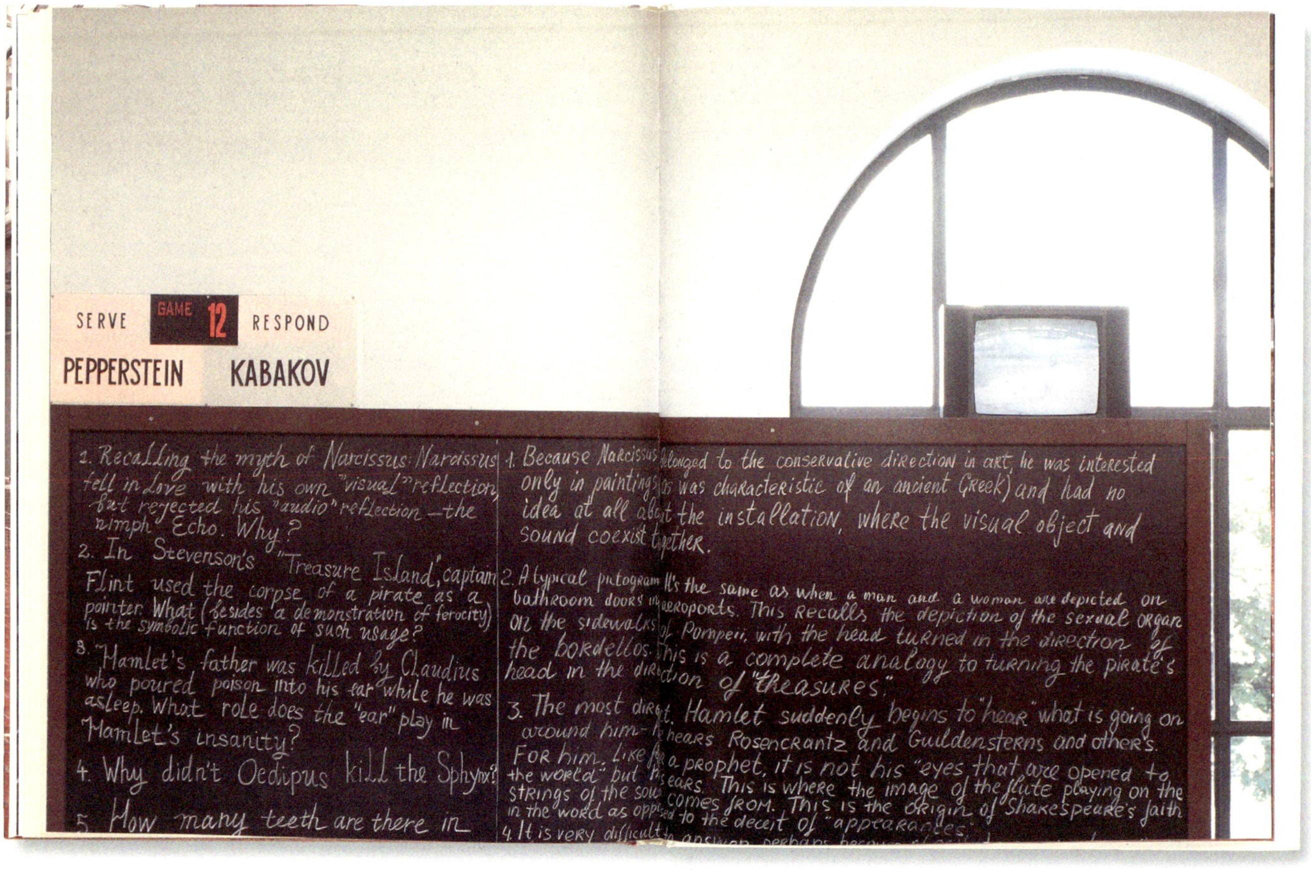
SERVE
GAME 12
RESPOND
PEPPERSTEIN
KABAKOV
1. Recalling the myth of Narcissus: Narcissus fell in love with his own "visual" reflection, but rejected his "audio" reflection – the nimph Echo. Why?
2. In Stevenson's "Treasure Island", captain Flint used the corpse of a pirate as a pointer. What (besides a demonstration of ferocity) is the symbolic function of such usage?
3. "Hamlet's father was killed by Claudius who poured poison into his ear while he was asleep. What role does the "ear" play in "Hamlet's insanity?
4. Why didn't Oedipus kill the Sphynx?
5. How many teeth are there in
1. Because Narcissus belonged to the conservative direction in art, he was interested only in paintings (as was characteristic of an ancient Greek) and had no idea at all about the installation, where the visual object and sound coexist together.
2. A typical pictogram. It's the same as when a man and a woman are depicted on bathroom doors in aeroports. This recalls the depiction of the sexual organ on the sidewalks of Pompeii, with the head turned in the direction of the bordellos. This is a complete analogy to turning the pirate's head in the direction of "theasures".
3. The most direct. Hamlet suddenly begins to "hear" what is going on around him – he hears Rosencrantz and Guildensterns and other's. For him, like for a prophet, it is not his "eyes that are opened to the world" but his ears. This is where the image of the flute playing on the strings of the soul comes from. This is the origin of Shakespeare's faith in the word as opposed to the deceit of "appearances".
4. It is very difficult to answer

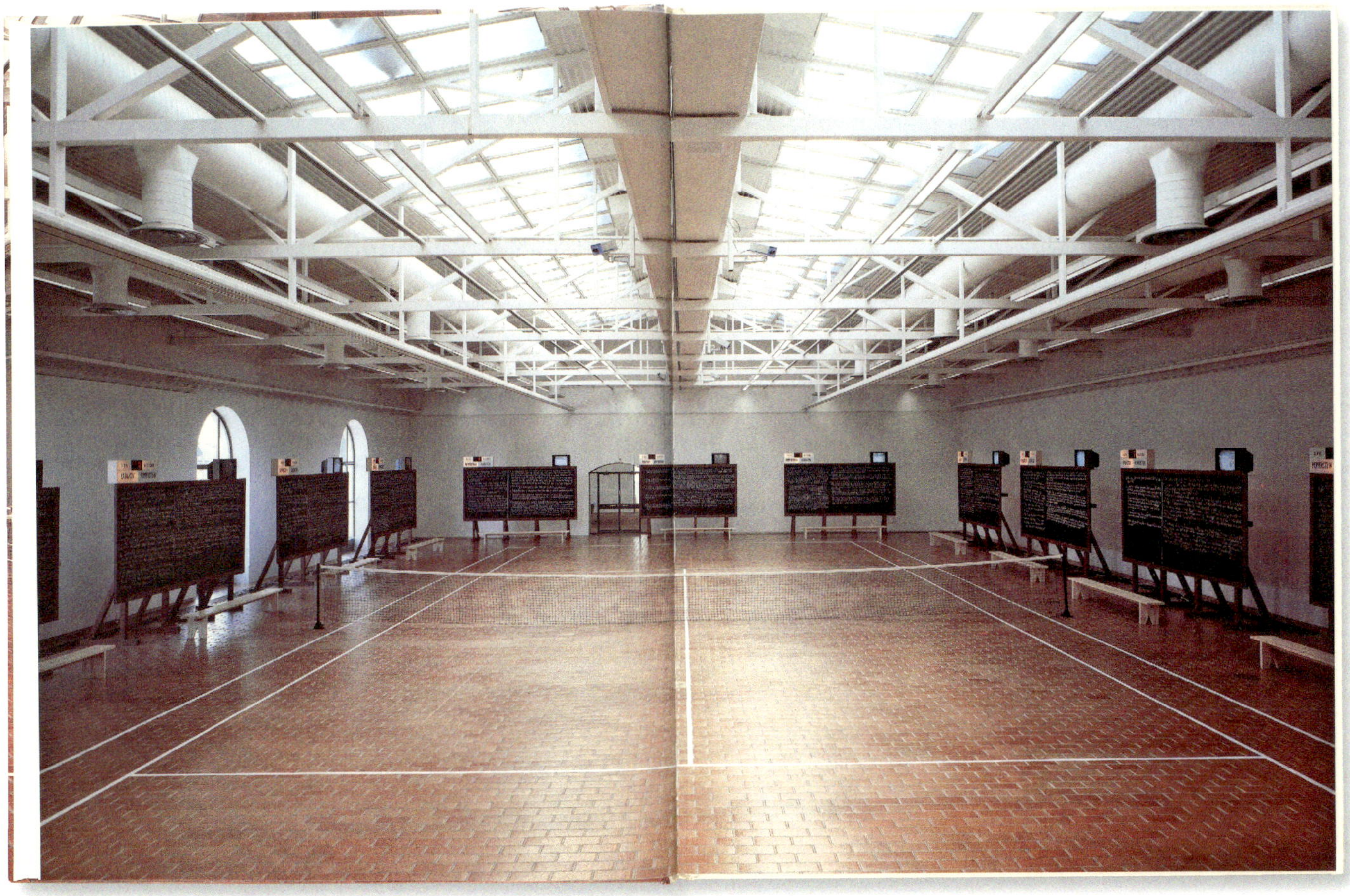

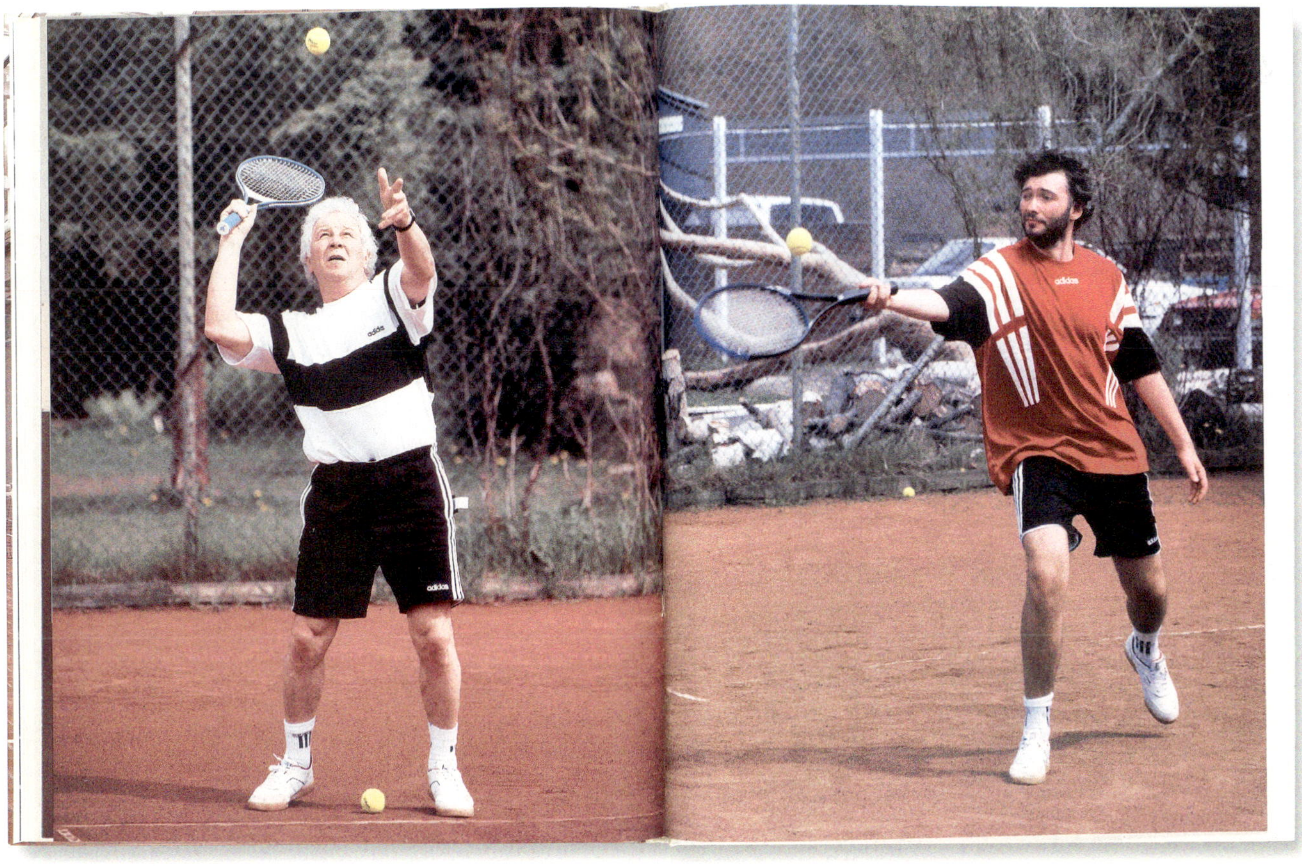

95 The Palace of Projects: 1995–1998 | *Der Palast der Projekte. 1995–1998*

1998

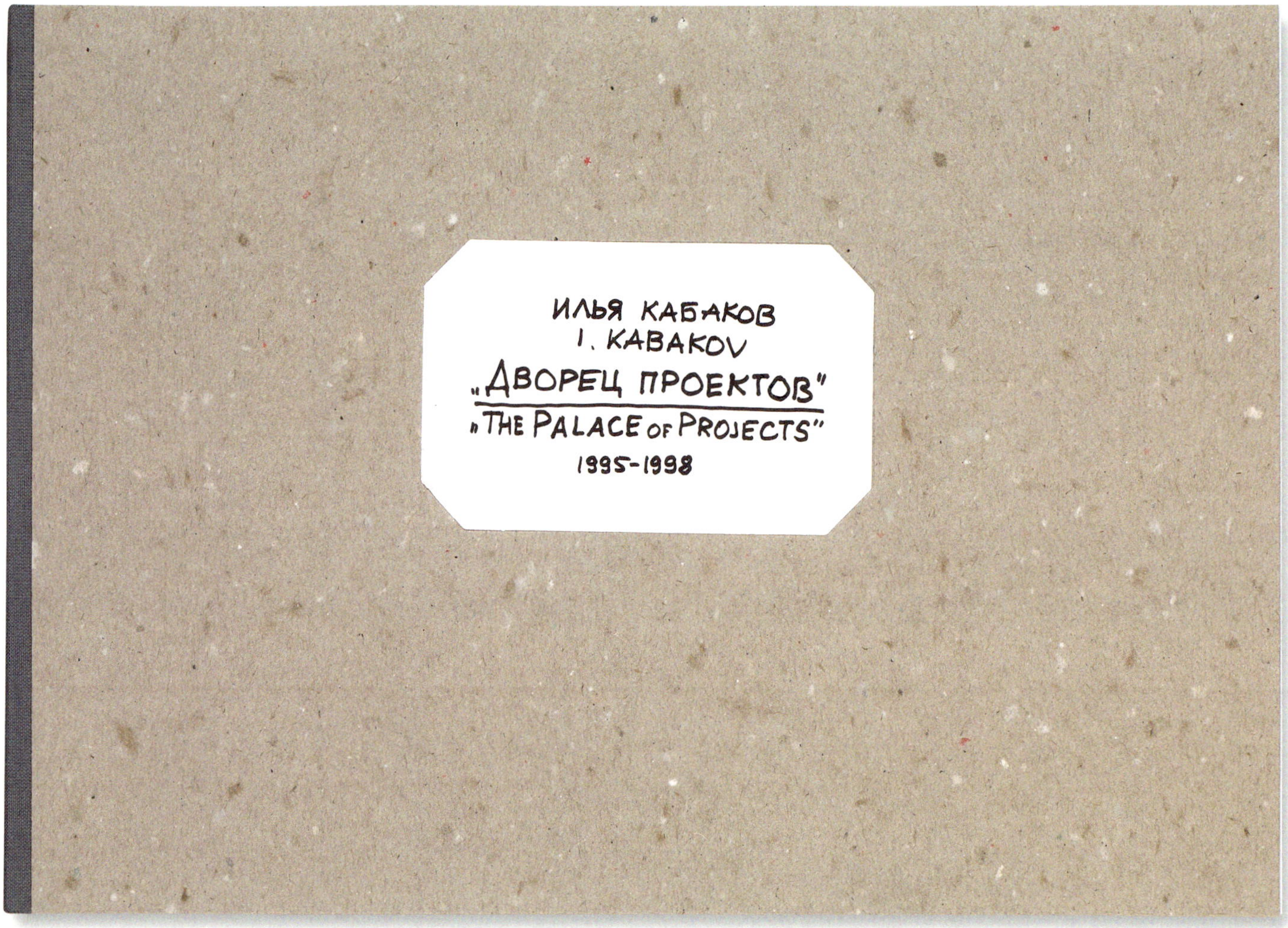

Artangel, London; Museo Nacional Centro de Arte Reina Sofía, Madrid
London: Artangel
20.4 x 29.8 cm
[287] pp. with 136 (67 color) ills.
stitchbound, quarter cloth binding, blind blocking with label
Fadenheftung, Halbleinen, Blindprägung mit Etikette

exhibition catalogue | *Ausstellungskatalog*

layout by Ilya Kabakov | *Layout von Ilya Kabakov*

For the installation of the same name. »Artangel Project« series of exhibitions, Roundhouse, London, March 24 to May 10, 1998; Upper Campfield Market, Manchester, May 23 to August 16, 1998; and Museo Nacional Centro de Arte Reina Sofía, Palacio de Cristal, Madrid, December 10, 1998 to April 30, 1999 (see separate catalogue, no. 103). Texts by Ilya Kabakov; Russian, English.

Zur gleichnamigen Installation. »Artangel Project«-Ausstellungsreihe, Roundhouse, London, 24. März – 10. Mai 1998, Upper Campfield Market, Manchester, 23. Mai – 16. August 1998, Museo Nacional Centro de Arte Reina Sofía, Palacio de Cristal, Madrid, 10. Dezember 1998 – 30. April 1999 (siehe den separaten Katalog, Nr. 103). Texte von Ilya Kabakov; russisch, englisch.

see also | *siehe auch* no. 98; no. 101; no. 102; no. 117; CRI, vol. 2, no. 117, pp. 244–251; CRP, vol. 1, nos. 279–289, pp. 350–360

Н. Саломаткин, шофер
г. Кишинев

„Невысокий полет над землей"

Человеческая мысль о возможности свободного полета над землей как правило связывалась с различными вариантами тех или других воздушных аппаратов, механических крыльев, в последнее время с реактивными двигателями и ракетами — и, одновременно, среди этих проектов исчезающе мало проектов полетов безо всяких приспособлений, полетов низко и высоко над землей с малой или большой скоростью просто так "нормального" человеческого существа в его простом физическом существовании. И тем не менее это ему так же свойственно как ходить, есть и т.п. Подтверждение этому — постоянная готовность и желание каждого человека к такому „естественному" полету. Но все дело, на которое раньше не было обращено внимание, не в самом только человеке, а в той ситуации, точнее специальном поле, которое формируется вокруг человека (или которое формирует он сам) и которое „держит" его в воздухе и направляет его в нем. Это поле должно быть очень сильно энергетически заряжено, а готовый отправиться в полет, сам „летчик" должен хорошо и активно коммуницировать и воспринимать его. Вот простой опыт, который подтвердит и продемонстрирует вам правоту этого положения, позволит вам самому проверить его на практике.

Отправьтесь в лес с двумя вашими близкими друзьями и запаситесь при этом тонкими металлическими стержнями высотой около 2 м. Выбрав небольшую лужайку, воткните стержни в землю на расстоянии 4-5 друг от друга, так, чтобы они образовали неширокий коридор, образованный двумя "полумесяцами" обращенными верхушками „дуг" друг к другу. Попросите друзей занять противоположную позицию по обе стороны „коридора" и в центре этих „дуг". Теперь попросите их обоих как более сосредоточенно думать о чем-то одном, например о теме вчерашнего разговора. Этот разговор и вам хорошо известен. Сосредоточьтесь на нем.

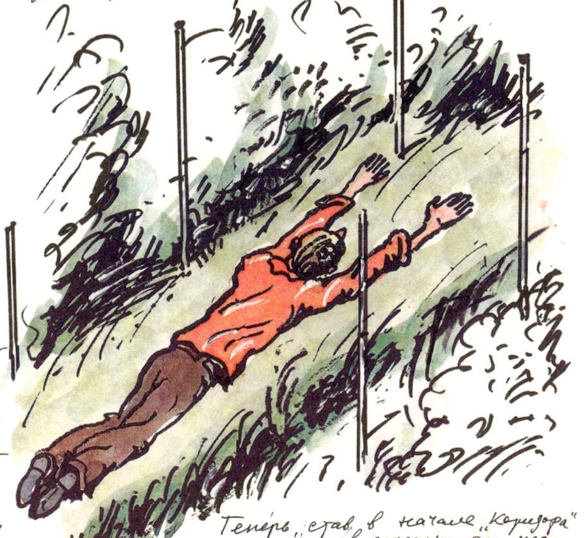

Теперь, став в начале „коридора" разбегитесь и в середине его постарайтесь прыгнуть, а потом вытянуть ноги. Вы, к своему удивлению увидите, что сможете пролететь небольшое расстояние. Причина — в мощном энергетическом поле, образованном вашими друзьями, в которое включились и вы. Металлические стержни лишь усилили его концентрацию

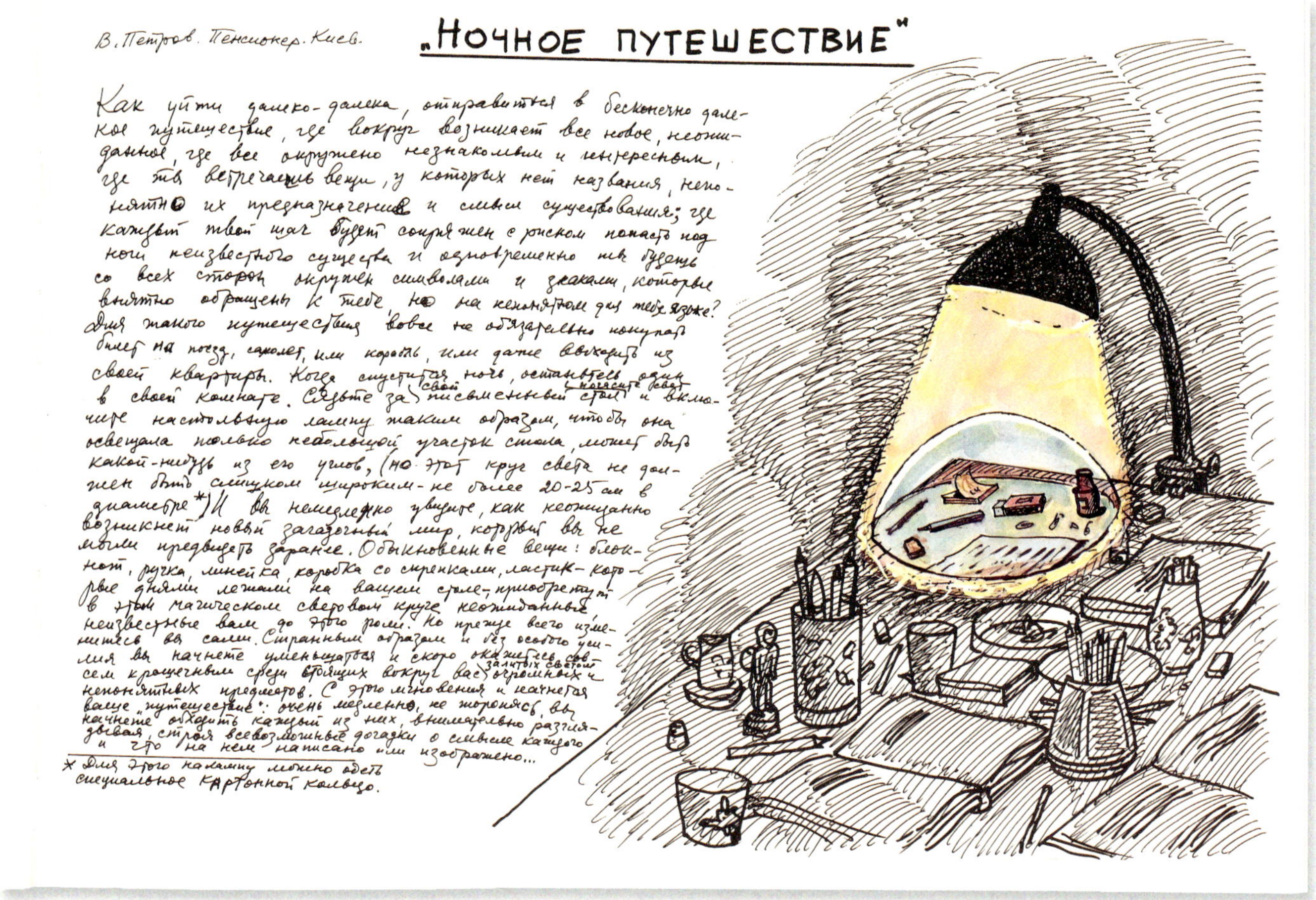
В. Петров. Пенсионер. Киев.
„Ночное путешествие“
Как уйти далеко-далеко, отправиться в бесконечно далекое путешествие, где вокруг возникает все новое, неожиданное, где все окружено незнакомым и интересным, где ты встречаешь вещи, у которых нет названия, непонятно их предназначение и смысл существования; где каждый твой шаг будет сопряжен с риском попасть под ноги неизвестного существа и одновременно ты будешь со всех сторон окружен символами и знаками, которые внятно обращены к тебе, но на непонятном для тебя языке?
Для такого путешествия вовсе не обязательно покупать билет на поезд, самолет, или корабль, или даже выходить из своей квартиры. Когда опустится ночь, останьтесь один в своей комнате. Сядьте за свой письменный стол (погасите свет) и включите настольную лампу таким образом, чтобы она освещала только небольшой участок стола, может быть какой-нибудь из его углов, (но этот круг света не должен быть слишком широким - не более 20-25 см в диаметре*) И вы немедленно увидите, как неожиданно возникнет новый загадочный мир, который вы не могли предвидеть заранее. Обыкновенные вещи: блокнот, ручка, линейка, коробка со скрепками, ластик - которые днями лежали на вашем столе, приобретут в этом магическом световом круге неожиданные, неизвестные вам до этого роли. Но прежде всего изменитесь вы сами. Странным образом и без особого усилия вы начнете уменьшаться и скоро окажетесь совсем крошечным среди стоящих вокруг вас (залитых светом) огромных и непонятных предметов. С этого мгновения и начнется ваше „путешествие“: очень медленно, не торопясь, вы начнете обходить каждый из них, внимательно разглядывая, строя всевозможные догадки о смысле каждого и что на нем написано или изображено...
* Для этого на лампу можно одеть специальное картонное кольцо.

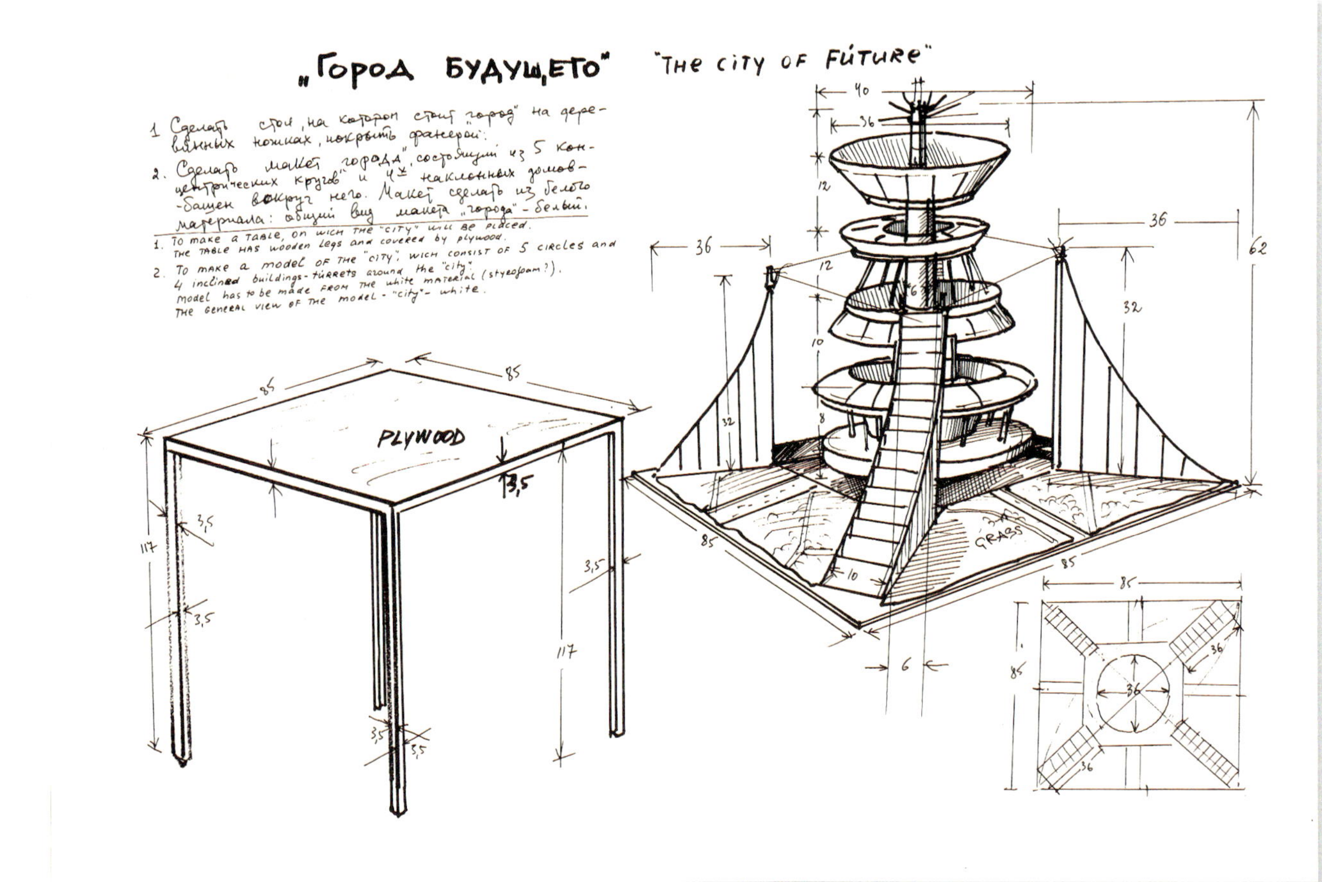
„Город будущего“
"The city of fúture"
1 Сделать стол, на котором стоит „город“ на деревянных ножках, покрыть фанерой.
2. Сделать макет „города“, состоящий из 5 концентрических кругов“ и 4ˣ наклонных домов-башен вокруг него. Макет сделать из белого материала: общий вид макета „города“ - белый.
1. To make a table, on wich the "city" will be placed. The table has wooden legs and covered by plywood.
2. To make a model of the "city", wich consist of 5 circles and 4 inclined buildings-túrrets around the "city". model has to be made from the white material (styrofoam?). The general view of the model - "city" - white.
PLYWOOD
GRASS
85
117
3,5
40
36
12
62
32
10
6

Г. Лисянский Артист г. Одесса

„Искусство будущего"

Искусство будущего, скорее всего, будет многомерным и, одновременно, соединением в новое единое пространство многих, прежне разрозненных пространств и миров. При этом каждое из них, включаясь в общее единство, будет продолжать существовать по собственным законам, как бы не зная, в каком новом единстве ему предназначено оказаться. Тем самым это новое целое окажется в новом измерение – и зритель, сохраняя наблюдения за прошлыми более „низкими" уровнями, „способен будет оказаться в, так сказать, следующей степени понимания или, другими словами, от двух и трехмерных объектов он перейдет к созерцанию четырехмерного пространства. В нашем примере – сочетание трехмерной скульптуры возле двухмерной картины (где помещена та же скульптура) и комментария к ним обоим, повешенное рядом – способно создать то „поле", о котором идет речь.

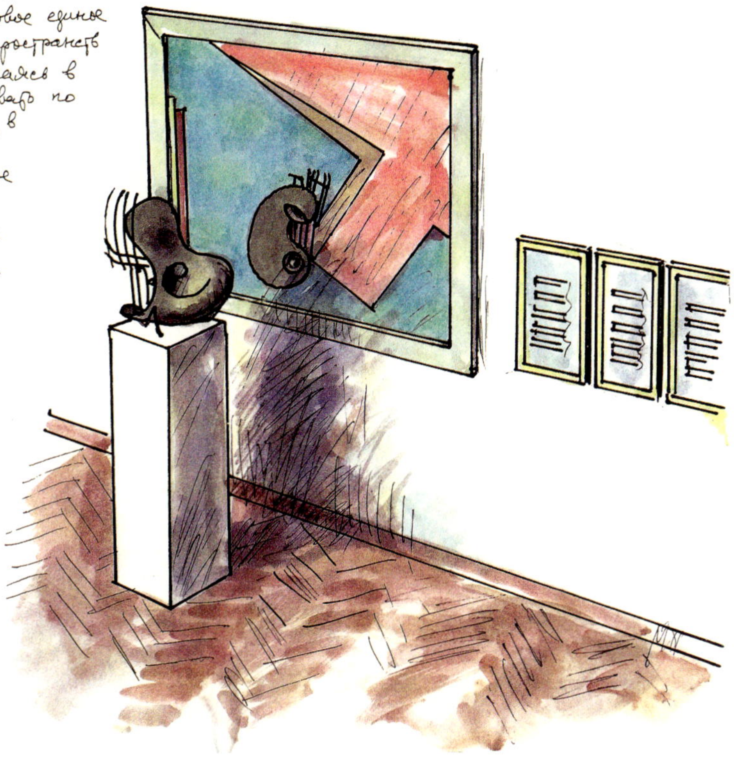

„Встреча с ангелом"

1. Построить низкий постамент в виде рамы (черный полированный цвет) и в него положить изготовленный из гипса макет ландшафта (поля, леса, реки, домики, берег моря и т.п.)
2. Сделать из светлого металла лестницу (H=115) состоящую из трех частей: нижняя (26см) напоминающая треножник; средняя, трехгранная с поворотом вдоль центральной оси; и верхняя, имеющая вид простой лестницы.
3. На верху лестницы укрепить фигурку человечка, сделанную из гипса.
4. С потолка на прозрачной нитке из пластика (тонкая леска) опустить фигурку ангела. Раскрасить белой, золотой (волосы) краской. Высота ангела от ландшафта – 133.

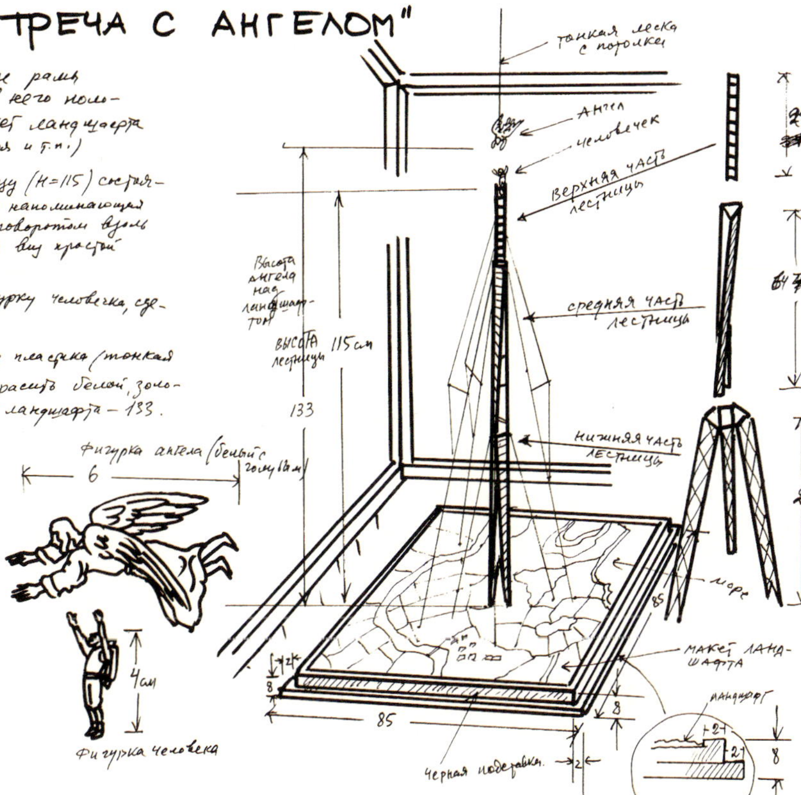

96 16 Installations | *16 Installationen*

1998

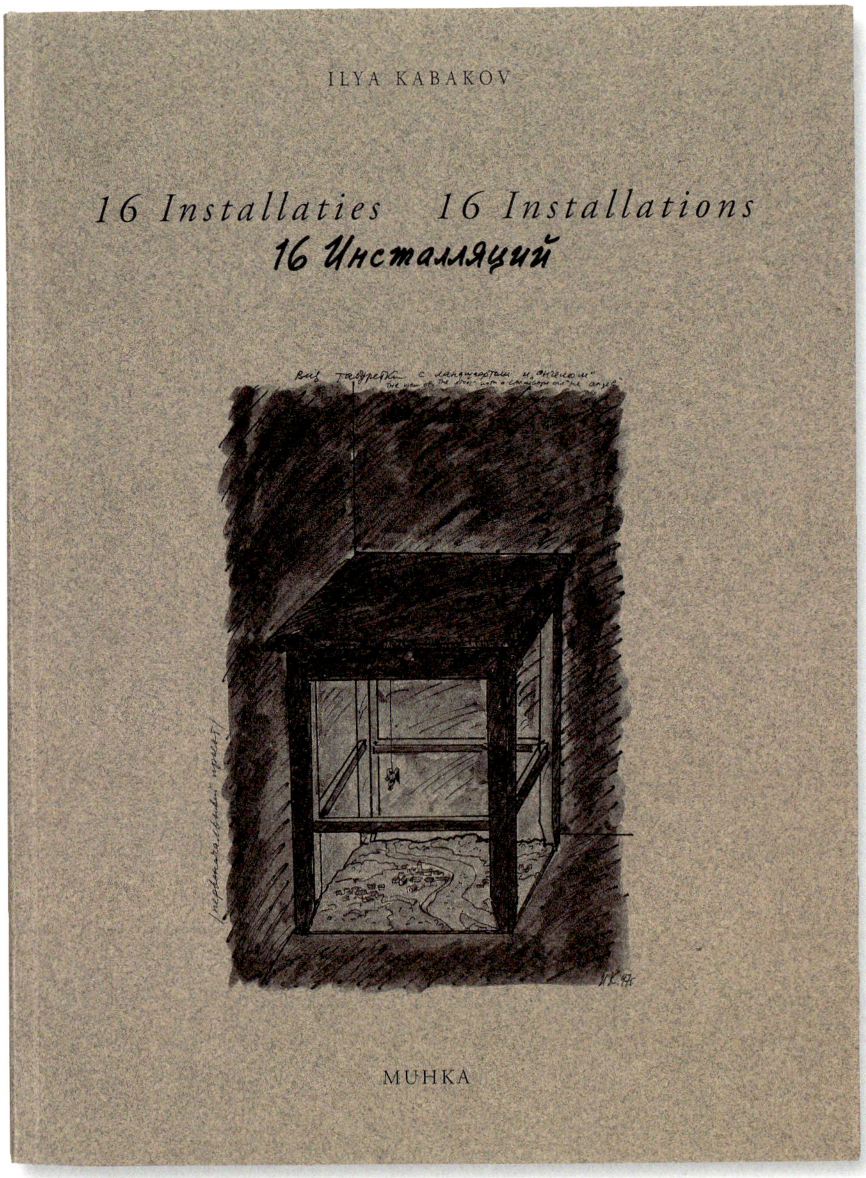

Museum van Hedendaagse Kunst Antwerpen
Antwerp: MUHKA
28 x 21.2 cm
165 pp. with 71 (21 color) ills.
stitchbound, softback with flaps
Fadenheftung, broschiert mit Umschlagklappen
edition: 1,500 copies

exhibition catalogue | *Ausstellungskatalog*

layout by Ilya Kabakov | *Layout von Ilya Kabakov*

For the installation of the same name at the MUHKA, Museum van Hedendaagse Kunst Antwerpen, Antwerp, April 17 to August 23, 1998. Texts by Florent Bex and Ilya Kabakov; Dutch, English.

Zur gleichnamigen Installation, MUHKA, Museum van Hedendaagse Kunst Antwerpen, Antwerpen, 17. April – 23. August 1998. Texte von Florent Bex und Ilya Kabakov; niederländisch, englisch.

see also | *siehe auch* CRI, vol. 2, no. 118, pp. 252–257

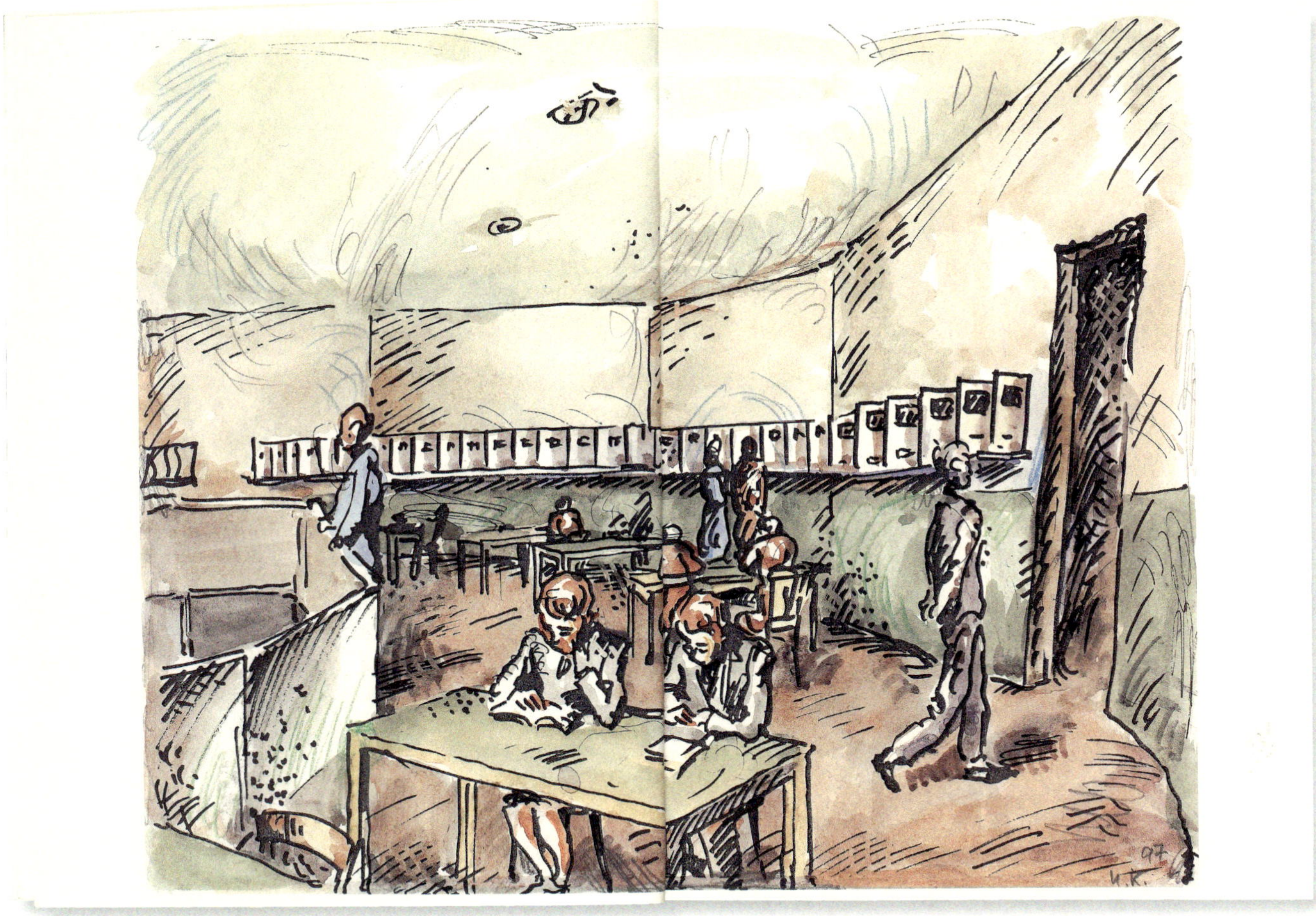

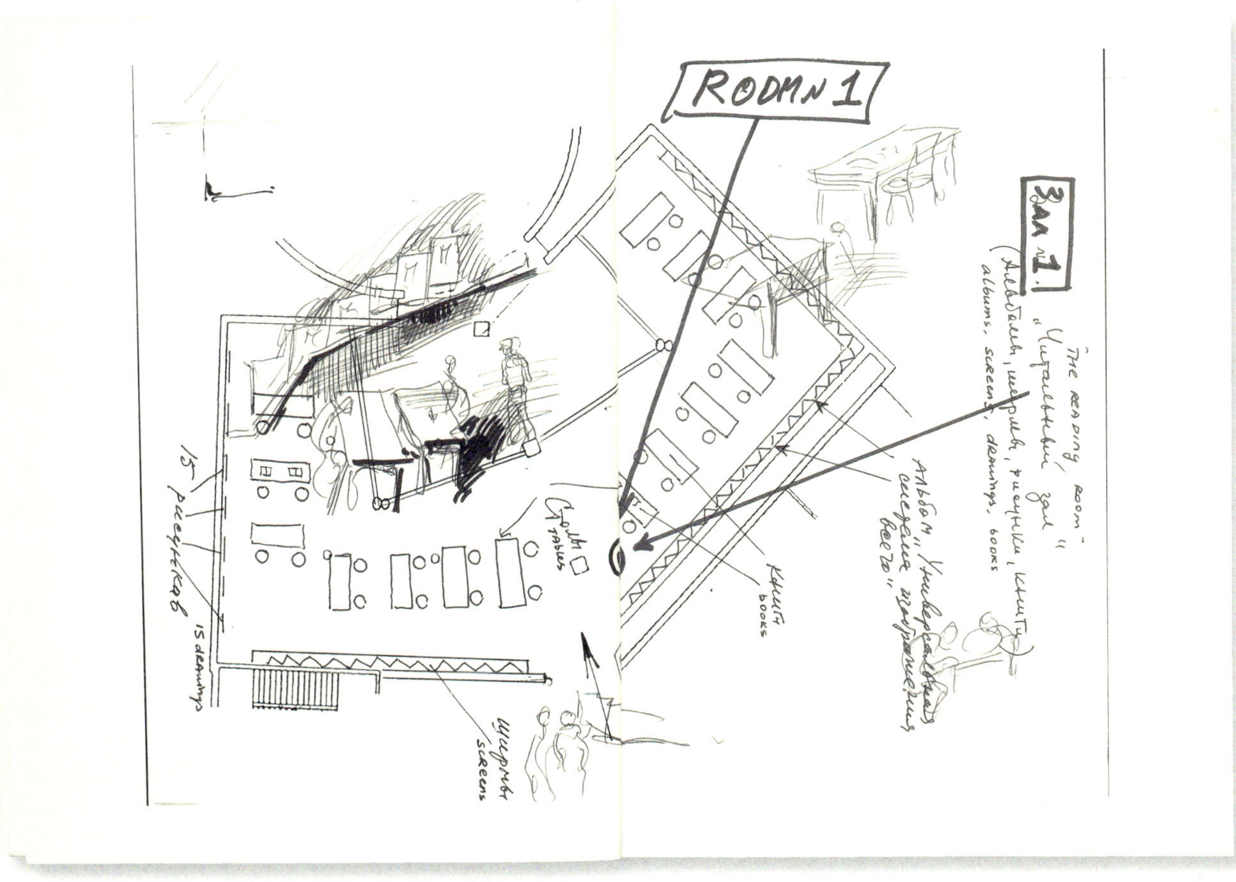

ROOM N 1

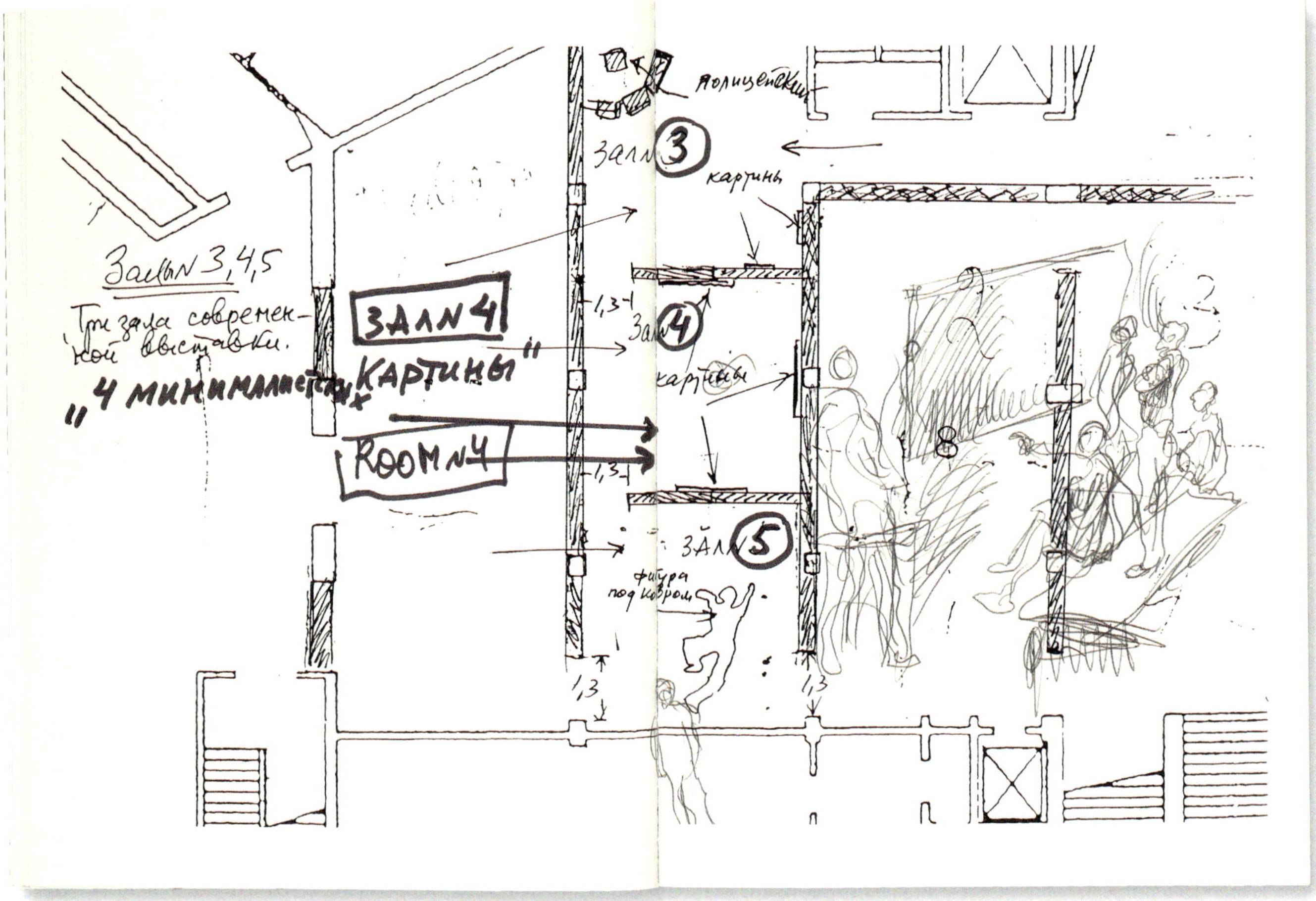
полицейские
Зал N 3
картины
Залы N 3,4,5
Три зала современной выставки.
ЗАЛ N 4
„4 минималистов"
КАРТИНЫ"
ROOM N 4
Зал N 4
картины
ЗАЛ N 5
фигура под ковром
1,3

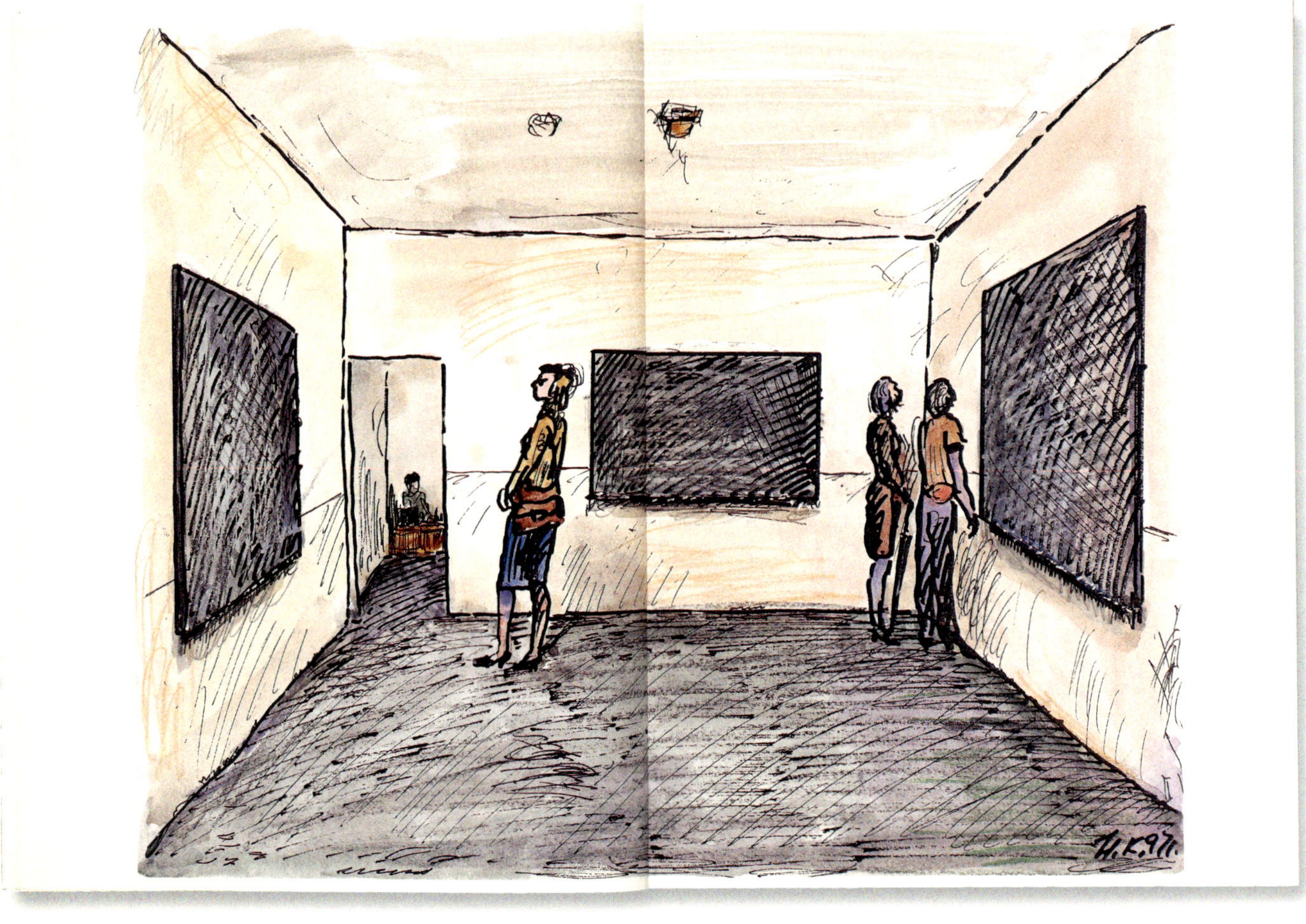
И.К.97.

Zaal nr. 4
'Vier minimale schilderijen'

Deze zaal stelt een tentoonstelling voor van vier schilderijen, gerealiseerd in het klassieke minimalistische idioom: ze zijn monochroom en hebben een saaie, grijze kleur en uiteraard bevatten ze hoegenaamd geen afbeelding van wat dan ook, ze zijn dof en zacht van aard... Onverwachts stelt de toeschouwer vast dat de donkergrijze vierkanten die hier hangen uit hetzelfde materiaal vervaardigd zijn als de vloerbekleding waarop hij wandelt. Hetzelfde materiaal werd gebruikt zowel om de vloer te bedekken als om deze schilderijen te produceren.

Room N° 4
'Four Minimalist Paintings'

The hall represents an exposition of four paintings of the classical minimalist type: they are a monochrome, dull grey colour, and naturally there is no depiction whatsoever on them, their manner is matt, soft. . . Unexpectedly the viewer discovers that these hanging dark grey squares are made of the same material as the floor he is walking upon-one and the same material was used for both the floor and the making of these paintings.

36

Зал № 4

„Четыре минималистских картины"

1. Зал представляет экспозицию четырех картин „классического" минималистского типа: они одноцветны, тускло серого цвета, на них нет, естественно, никакого изображения, их фактура ~~на~~ матовая, мягкая... Внезапно зритель обнаруживает, что эти висящие темносерые прямоугольники сделаны из того же материала, что и пол, по которому он ходит — один и тот же материал пошел и на пол, и на изготовление этих картин.
2. Все 4-ре картины и доски, на которые будут натянуты куски ковра для пола, должны ~~быть~~ изготовлены в Антверпене.

Ориентировочные размеры картин: 140×270 см

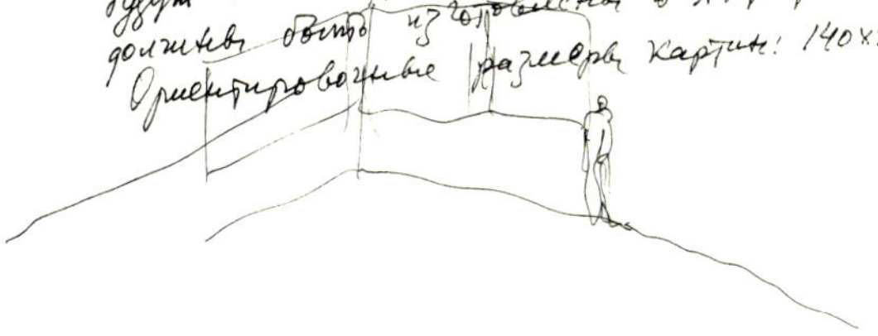

37

97 Treatment with Memories | *Behandlung mit Erinnerungen*

1998

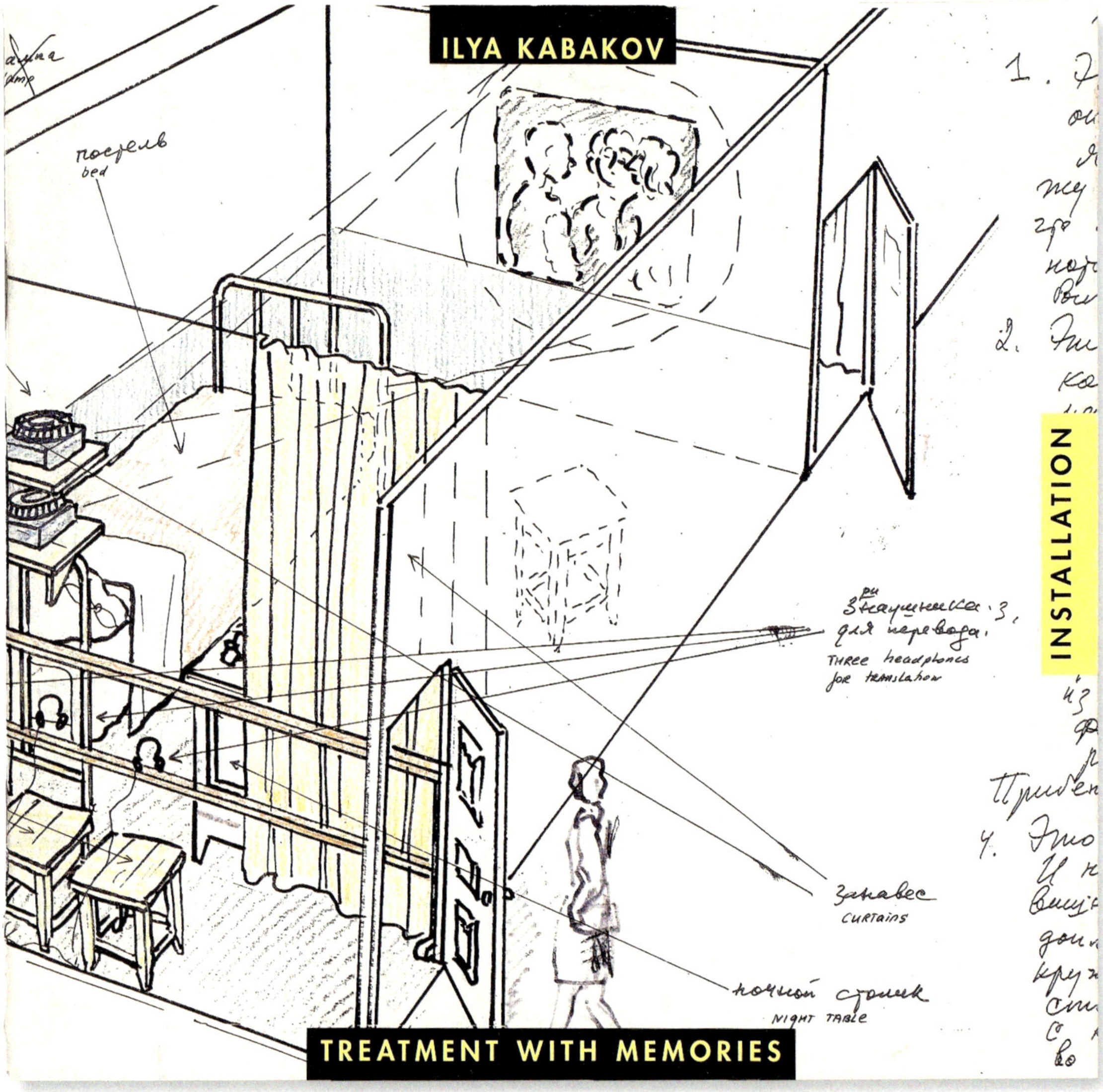

Friedegund Weidemann
Berlin: Nationalgalerie im Hamburger Bahnhof, Museum für Gegenwart – Staatliche Museen zu Berlin, Preussischer Kulturbesitz
20 x 21 cm
35 pp. with 18 (4 color) ills.
stapled, softback with flaps
Drahtheftung, broschiert mit Umschlagklappen

exhibition catalogue | *Ausstellungskatalog*

layout by Ilya Kabakov | *Layout von Ilya Kabakov*

For the installation of the same name at the Nationalgalerie im Hamburger Bahnhof, Museum für Gegenwart, Berlin, May 15 to August 30, 1998. Texts by Ilya and Emilia Kabakov, Dieter Scholz, and Friedegund Weidemann; German.

Zur gleichnamigen Installation, Nationalgalerie im Hamburger Bahnhof, Museum für Gegenwart, Berlin, 15. Mai – 30. August 1998. Texte von Ilya und Emilia Kabakov, Dieter Scholz und Friedegund Weidemann; deutsch.

see also | *siehe auch* CRI, vol. 2, no. 107, pp. 188–193

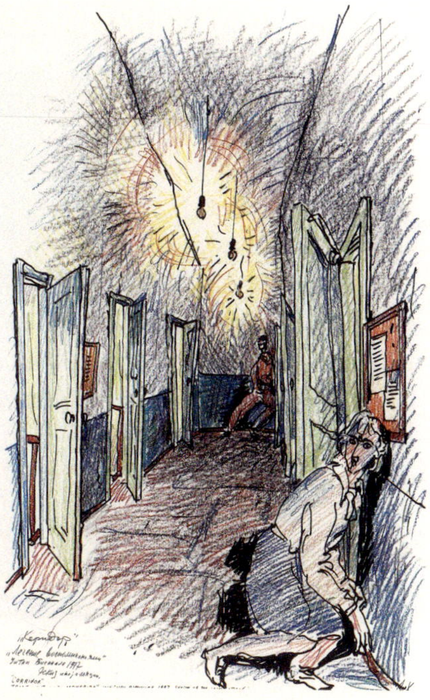

Korridor der Installation.
Zeichnung von Ilya Kabakov

Atmosphäre im Raum spirituellen Charakter zu verleihen. Nackte Glühlampen, in der oberen Hälfte schwarz gestrichen, geben ein gedämpftes, neutrales Licht; punktuelle Lichtquellen setzen Akzente und erzeugen in ihrer Menge den Eindruck vieler Welten. Der Einzelbeleuchtung kommt bei Kabakov zugleich ein metaphysischer Aspekt zu, sie "leuchtet ... das Gedächtnis aus, hebt es aus der ... Finsternis des Vergessens". Bei dem Betrachter als Akteur und ausschließlichem Bezugspunkt der totalen Installation soll eine Zwiespältigkeit der Wahrnehmung zwischen der inszenierten Künstlichkeit und der Wiedererkennbarkeit des Vertrauten entstehen. Er muß in den Zustand einer "Halbillusion" versetzt werden. Angezogen und abgestossen zugleich möge er sich fühlen, Neugierde und Scheu sollen gleichermaßen erwachen. Die Türen sind halboffen, die Atmosphäre im ärmlichen und tristen Raum ist trübe und unangenehm, dennoch eigenartig sinnlich und meditativ durch Musik oder Sprache mit Bild, die einem langsamen Rhythmus folgen. Unsichtbar steuernd führt eine theatergleiche Dramaturgie den Besucher wie eine Marionette durch die Installation, damit seine Aufmerksamkeit nicht erlischt, denn das wäre das Ende der totalen Installation. Einen Zustand "zerstreuter Konzentration" wünscht der Künstler zu erhalten. Der Zeit kommt ebenfalls eine Hauptrolle in dieser Szene zu, Vergangenheit, Gegenwart und Zukunft treten an verschiedenen Stellen, verbunden mit verschiedenen Gegenständen, auf. Ilya Kabakov will den sein installatives Theater Erlebenden in eine psychische Spannung versetzen: Momentan und heftig sollen ihm die Lasten des eigenen Lebens unbezwingbar erscheinen, doch zugleich vermöge er einen Anstoß spüren, sich von seinen Lasten zu befreien. Diese gebrochenen Empfindungen verbinden sich im Idealfall zu einem Zustand des Wachtraumes. Man fühlt sich wie der Leser von Tolstois Romanen in das Geschehen schicksalhaft eingebunden und dennoch fremd und unbehaglich.
Für den Hamburger Bahnhof, nahe der berühmten Charité, hat Ilya Kabakov in Zusammenarbeit mit seiner Frau Emilia die Installation "Treatment With Memories" (Heilung mit Erinnerungen) entworfen.
Aus der sowjetischen Literatur kennen wir hervorragende Beispiele der Verbindung von Kunst und Therapie: Im Werk V. Nabukovs, A. Tarkovskis u. a. nimmt das in Sprache geronnene Erinnern zum Zwecke der Läuterung einen expliziten Platz ein. Vor fünfzig Jahren heilte der Schriftsteller

9

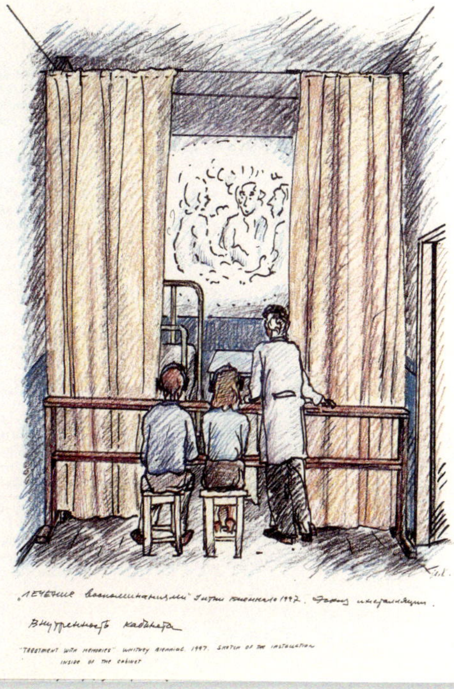

Betrachter der Diaprojektion
im Krankenzimmer.
Zeichnung von Ilya Kabakov

M. Soschtschenko mit der Autobiographie "Schlüssel des Glücks" durch kathartisches Sich-Erinnern selbst seine schwere Depression. Kabakov, der 1989 als Stipendiat des DAAD in Berlin weilte, kennt aus eigenem Erleben die problematische Situation der Stadt. Unmittelbar nach dem Fall der Mauer beteiligte er sich an der internationalen Ausstellung "Die Endlichkeit der Freiheit. Berlin 1990" mit einer Installation, die ebenfalls Erinnerungen aufrief, kollektive Erinnerungen an die permanente, unterschwellige Angst. Hier, an einer der Nahtstellen zwischen Ost und West, dicht hinter dem ehemaligen "Schutzwall", hat das Erinnern der noch schmerzenden Wunden und Verletzungen durch die Teilung der Stadt und des Landes und ihre "Heilung" aktuell-symbolische Bedeutung.
So schlug der Kunstbeirat der Bundesregierung vor, den in diesem Jahr mit dem Kaiserring Goslar geehrten Künstler einzuladen, gegenüber dem Hamburger Bahnhof, an der östlichen Uferpromenade hinter dem Wirtschaftsministerium (dem ehemaligen Regierungskrankenhaus), eine permanente Installation zu schaffen, die für allezeit an die Beklemmungen des Lebens auf beiden Seiten dieser Stadt vor dem Fall der Mauer erinnern soll.
Über drei Säle im Westflügel des Erdgeschosses im Hamburger Bahnhof entwickelt sich die Installation, die in Architektur und Mobiliar ein russisches Krankenhaus assoziiert. In dieser, zuvor in veränderter Form auf der Whitney-Biennale 1997 in New York gezeigten, wie in anderen Installationen bezieht sich Kabakov auf authentische und erdachte Vorgänge. Hier erfand er eine psychiatrische Klinik in Saratow im Jahre 1992, die ein kabakovscher Charakter, Dr. V. N. Lublin, leitet. Sechs zimmergroße, spärlich beleuchtete Räume, durch einen schmalen Gang verbunden, werden zum Ort der Begegnung mit der ungewöhnlichen "Heilbehandlung". Der Besucher tritt durch eine schmale alte Tür und befindet sich in einem engen Korridor, der seinen "öffentlichen" Charakter durch ein häßliches Paneel verrät. Von ihm aus gelangt er durch sechs leicht angelehnte Türen nacheinander in die Krankenzimmer. In den Räumen, deren Wände ebenfalls in einen lichten oberen Teil und einen dunklen Sockel gegliedert sind, findet er jeweils ein altes Metallbett und einen Nachttisch vor sowie - etwas verdeckt - Geräte für eine Vorführung. Vor jedem Zimmer laden drei Hocker zum Platznehmen ein. Die Darbietung erfolgt hinter einer Distanz gebietenden Barriere durch einen halboffenen

11

gen eine vom umgebenden Raum gesonderte Welt. Sie wollen das Bildhafte in universaler Modellhaftigkeit, ihre Entstehung und Form ist eng mit dem Theater und dem Bild im Sinne von "Weltbild" verbunden.
Kabakovs großes Thema ist die Gesellschaft der ehemaligen Sowjetunion. Er karikiert den offiziellen Kunststil "Sozialistischer Realismus" mit den banalen Mitteln der Installation und symbolisiert das bedrückende Klima dieser geschlossenen Gesellschaft durch klaustrophobische Räume. Aus seiner Absicht, das Alltägliche zum Mythos zu erheben, entwickelte er die Notwendigkeit der geschlossenen Installation. In fünfzehn Lektionen, basierend auf einem Zyklus von Vorlesungen 1992 bis 1993 an der Städelschule in Frankfurt am Main, erarbeitete der Künstler Theorie und Typologie der "totalen Installation".
Ihre Wirkung beruht auf schlichten Alltagsmaterialien in einem niedrigen sozialen Milieu, die durch die Umgebung der Installation eine sakrale Aura erhalten. Den Weg durch die streng konstruierte, fast suprematistische Form der Installation sollte man mit einem "Spaziergang durch Lissitzkys 'Proun'" vergleichen. Jener Weg führt durch vollständig bearbeitete, einfache, gut erkennbare soziale Räume wie Schulen, Krankenhäuser, kommunale Wohnungen, deren Benutzer nur gerade eben nicht anwesend sind. Durch herumliegende, gewöhnliche Gegenstände herrscht eine lebendige Unordnung, die menschliche Gegenwart verrät. Zudem vertreten die Gegenstände die Schauspieler in dieser Inszenierung. Es ist Kabakov wichtig, daß immer ein vorbereitender Raum vorhanden ist, der den Übergang aus der umgebenden Welt, in der sich die totale Installation befindet, beispielsweise dem Museum, in die innere Welt der Installation bildet. Dabei erfüllt auch die Tür als Eingang und Ausgang der Welten in Form, Farbe und Stellung eine wichtige Aufgabe. Gewöhnliche, alte Türen von schmutzigweißer Farbe sollen es sein. Die Wände bilden die Ränder der Innenwelt der Installation und grenzen sie von der Außenwelt ab. Ihr Gleichnischarakter als vollständiges, geschlossenes "Modell der Welt" verbietet Fenster. Die Decke versinnbildlicht den Himmel, der Fußboden die Erde, lebendig mit herumliegenden Zeichen aktiven Lebens; dagegen wäre ein sauberer Fußboden ein Zeichen des Todes. Der Beleuchtung kommt bei der mythisierenden Verfremdung des Alltäglichen eine besondere Bedeutung zu, sie ist eines der wichtigsten Mittel, um der

6

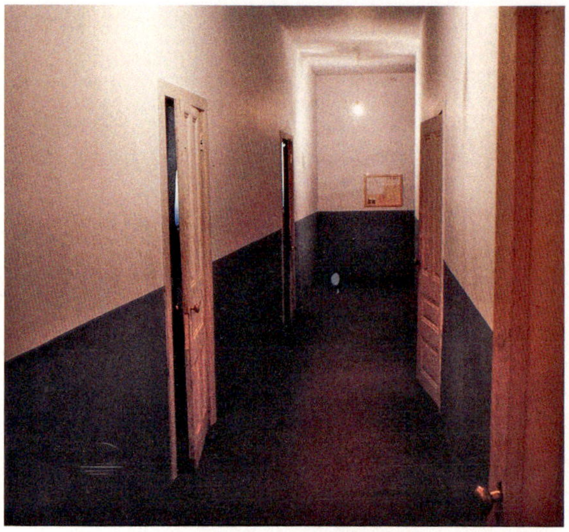

Blick in den Korridor der Installation

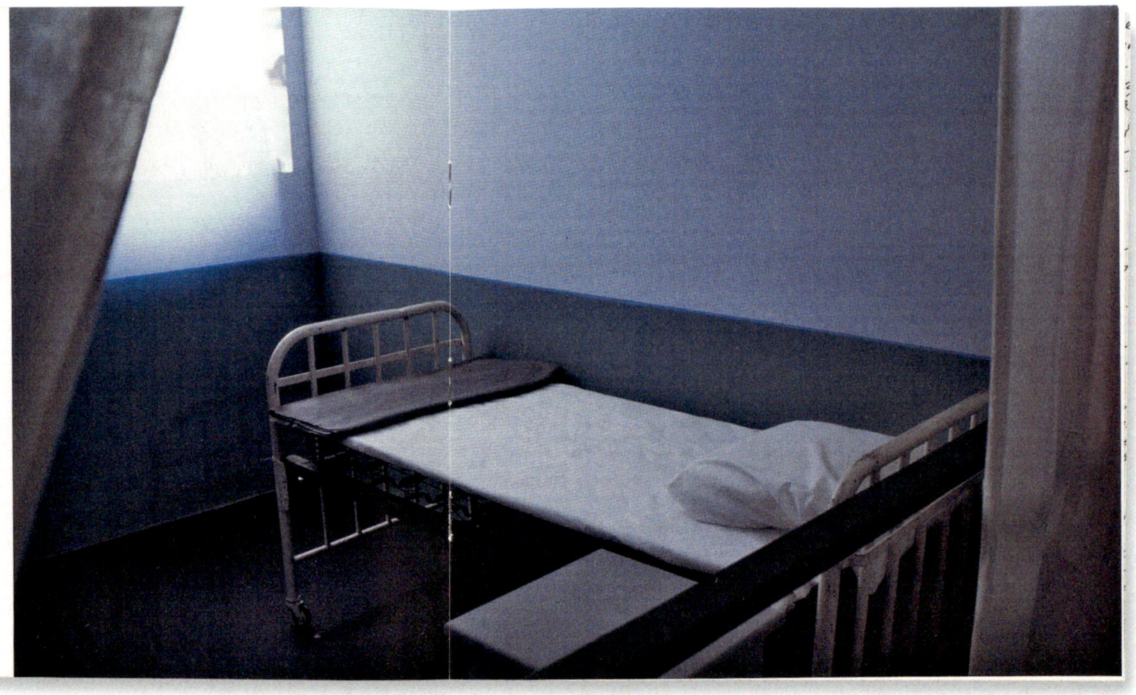

Ein Krankenzimmer in der Installation

98 The Palace of Projects: 1995–1998 | *Der Palast der Projekte. 1995–1998*

1998

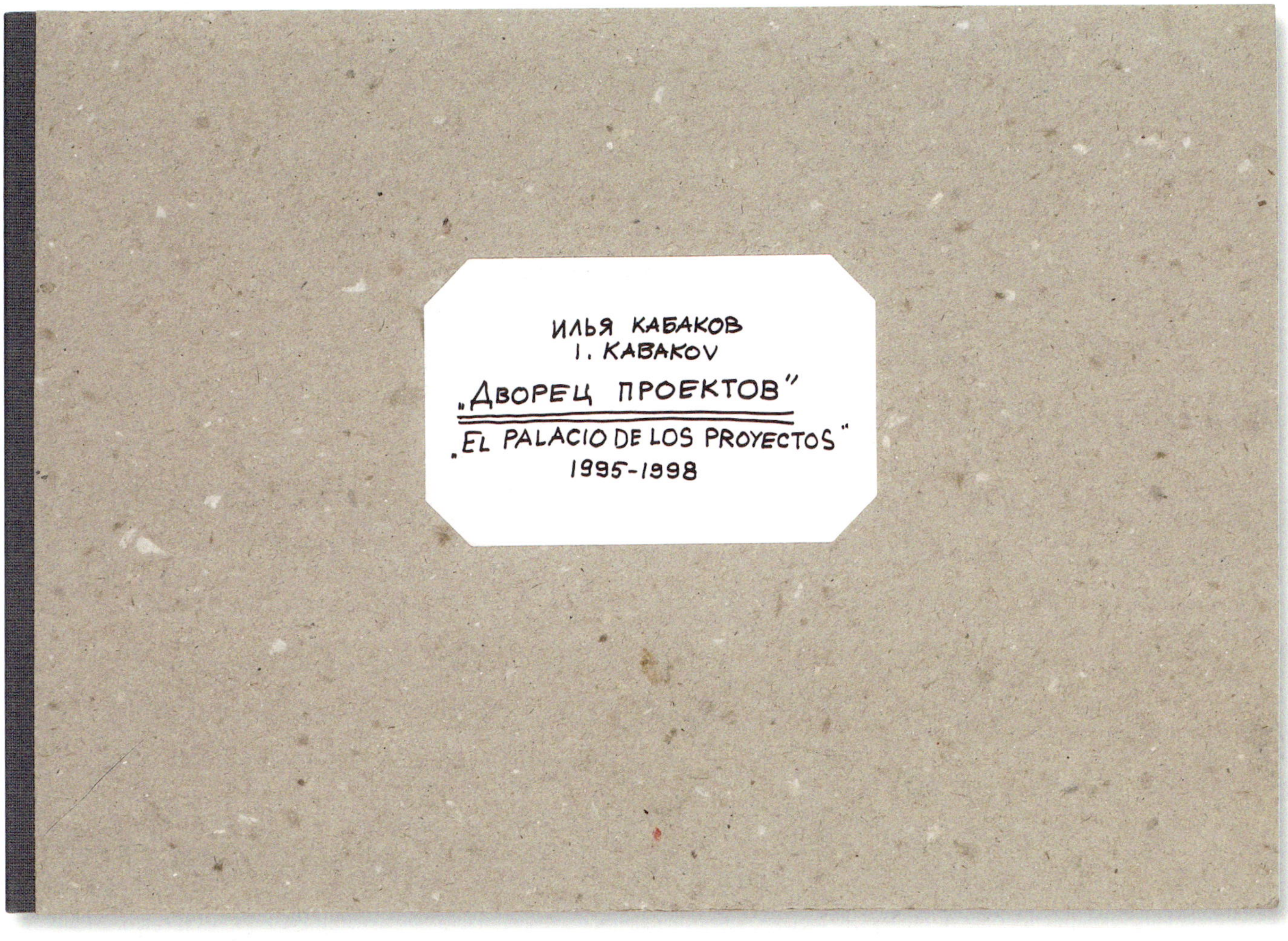

Museo Nacional Centro de Arte Reina Sofía, Madrid; Artangel, London
Madrid/London: Museo Nacional Centro de Arte Reina Sofía, Artangel
20.4 x 29.8 cm
[289] pp. with 136 (67 color) ills.
stitchbound, quarter cloth binding, label on the cover
Fadenheftung, Halbleinen, Etikette auf dem Umschlag

exhibition catalogue | *Ausstellungskatalog*

layout by Ilya Kabakov | *Layout von Ilya Kabakov*

For the installation of the same name at the Museo Nacional Centro de Arte Reina Sofía, Palacio de Cristal, Madrid, December 10, 1998 to April 30, 1999. Texts by Ilya Kabakov; Russian, Spanish.

Zur gleichnamigen Installation, Museo Nacional Centro de Arte Reina Sofía, Palacio de Cristal, Madrid, 10. Dezember 1998 – 30. April 1999. Texte von Ilya Kabakov; russisch, spanisch.

see also | *siehe auch* no. 95; no. 101; no. 102; no. 117; CRI, vol. 2, no. 117, pp. 244–251; CRP, vol. 1, nos. 279–289, pp. 350–360

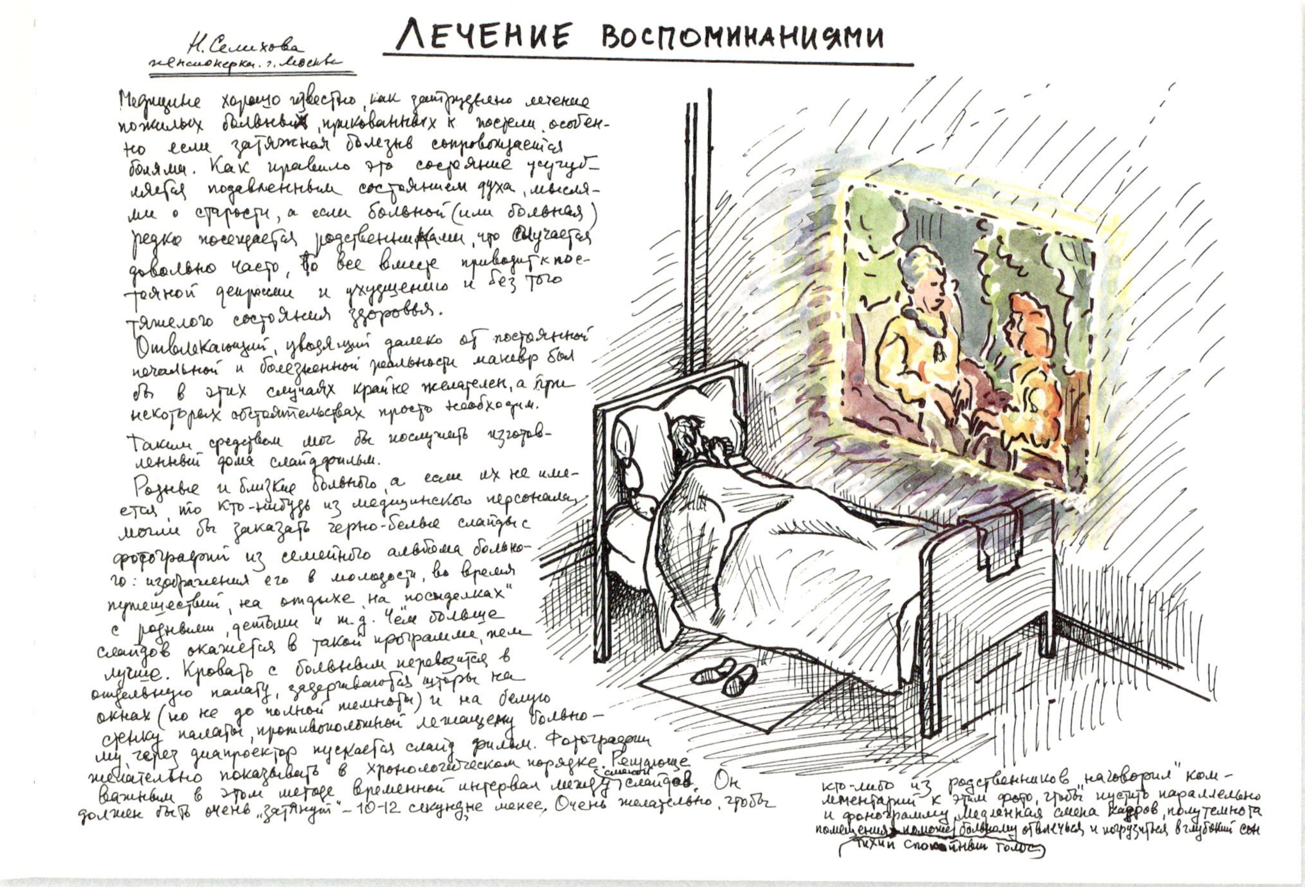
ЛЕЧЕНИЕ ВОСПОМИНАНИЯМИ
Н. Семихова
пенсионерка. г. Москва
Медицине хорошо известно, как затруднено лечение пожилых больных, прикованных к постели, особенно если затяжная болезнь сопровождается болями. Как правило это состояние усугубляется подавленным состоянием духа, мыслями о старости, а если больной (или больная) редко посещается родственниками, что случается довольно часто, то все вместе приводит к постоянной депрессии и ухудшению и без того тяжелого состояния здоровья.
Отвлекающий, уводящий далеко от постоянной печальной и болезненной реальности маневр был бы в этих случаях крайне желателен, а при некоторых обстоятельствах просто необходим.
Таким средством мог бы послужить изготовленный дома слайдфильм.
Родные и близкие больного, а если их не имеется, то кто-нибудь из медицинского персонала, могли бы заказать черно-белые слайды с фотографий из семейного альбома больного: изображения его в молодости, во время путешествий, на отдыхе, на „посиделках" с родными, детьми и т.д. Чем больше слайдов окажется в такой программе, тем лучше. Кровать с больным перевозится в отдельную палату, задергиваются шторы на окнах (но не до полной темноты) и на белую стенку палаты, противоположной лежащему больному, через диапроектор пускается слайд фильм. Фотографии желательно показывать в хронологическом порядке. Решающе важным в этом методе временной интервал между сменой слайдов. Он должен быть очень „затянут" – 10-12 секунд, не менее. Очень желательно, чтобы кто-либо из родственников „наговорил" комментарии к этим фото, чтобы пустить параллельно и фонограмму. Медленная смена кадров, полутемнота помещения, помогает больному отвлечься и погрузиться в глубокий сон
тихий спокойный голос

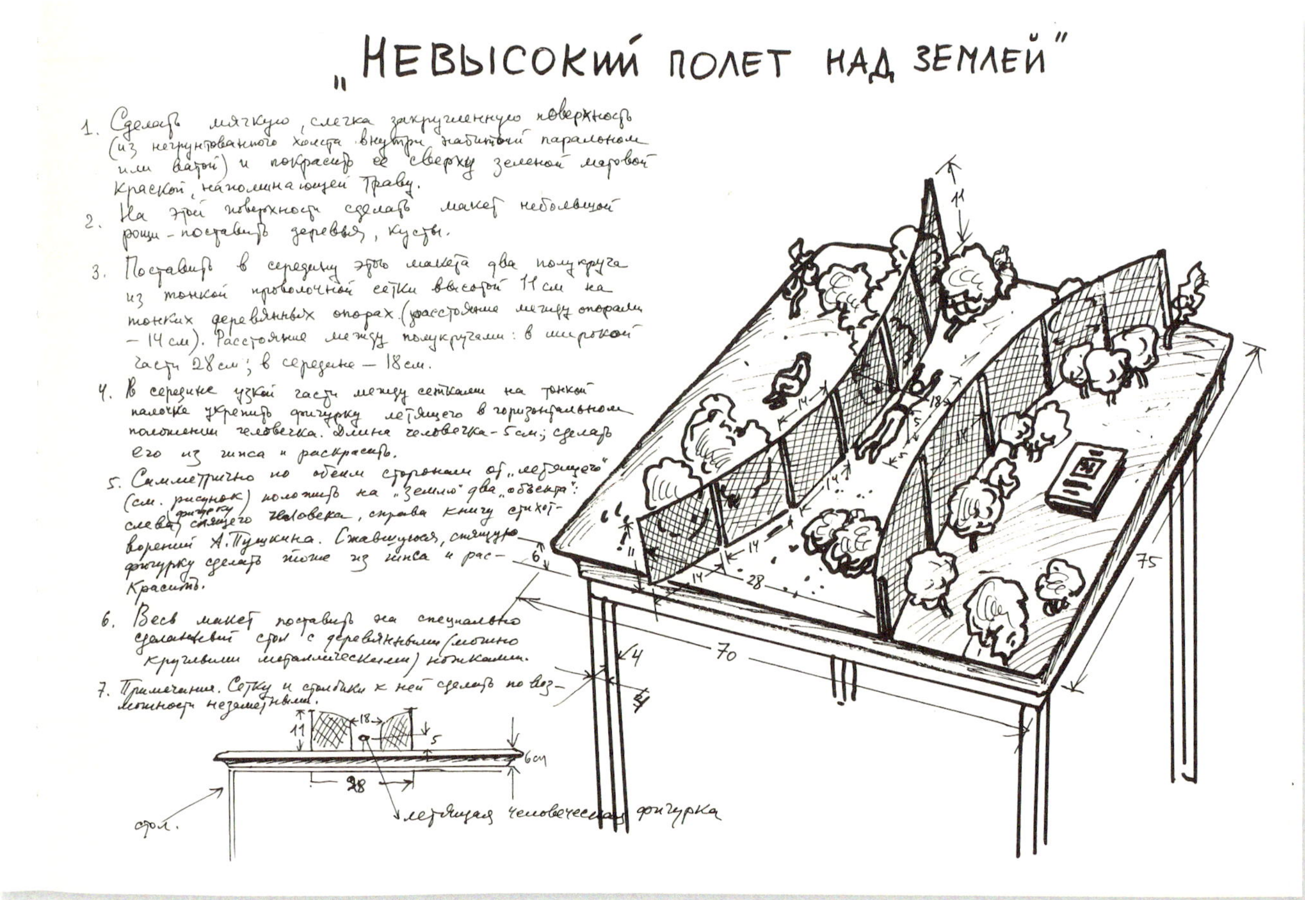
„НЕВЫСОКИЙ ПОЛЕТ НАД ЗЕМЛЕЙ"
1. Сделать мягкую, слегка закругленную поверхность (из негрунтованного холста внутри набитой паралоном или ватой) и покрасить ее сверху зеленой матовой краской, напоминающей траву.
2. На этой поверхности сделать макет небольшой рощи – поставить деревья, кусты.
3. Поставить в середину этого макета два полукруга из тонкой проволочной сетки высотой 11 см на тонких деревянных опорах. (расстояние между опорами – 14 см). Расстояние между полукругами: в широкой части 28 см; в середине – 18 см.
4. В середине узкой части между сетками на тонкой палочке укрепить фигурку летящего в горизонтальном положении человечка. Длина человечка – 5 см; сделать его из гипса и раскрасить.
5. Симметрично по обеим сторонам от „летящего" (см. рисунок) положить на „землю" два „объекта": слева фигурку спящего человека, справа книгу стихотворений А. Пушкина. Сжавшуюся, спящую фигурку сделать тоже из гипса и раскрасить.
6. Весь макет поставить на специально сделанный стол с деревянными (можно круглыми металлическими) ножками.
7. Примечание. Сетку и столбики к ней сделать по возможности незаметными.
11
18
14
28
6
4
70
75
5
6 см
стол
летящая человеческая фигурка

Постоянная поляризация двух энергий

Л. Стахович Скрипач
г. Москва

Хорошо известно уже с древних времен, что энергии (раньше их называли „влияния") бывают верхние и нижние, имеющие происхождение или в верхней сфере, окружающей нашу Землю, или относятся к нижнему, иными словами, подземному миру. Уровень поверхности земли и все что располагается на этом уровне: дома, вещи, растения и сам человек подвержены влияниям обоих этих сил, действующих в разных, противоположных направлениях: вверх, к воздуху, к небу, и, наоборот, идущих вниз, уходя глубоко под землю.

Параллельное существование, действие обеих энергий одновременно создают подчас мучительные, стрессовые состояния у обитателей жизни на поверхности Земли, тем более, что никто из них самостоятельно не в силах самостоятельно отделить в своей постоянной практике одно от другого, хотя отлично понимают их разницу (в этом месте говорится, конечно о людях). Что же касается мертвой природы то подобно разделение и вовсе выглядит невозможным.

Проект „поляризации" предлагает несложное, но эффективное средство разделения двух указанных энергий в местах проживания и работы людей, там, где они вынуждены проводить большую часть своего времени. Предлагается связать вместе (бечевкой) 28-30 деревянных палочек и такое же количество больших металлических гвоздей связать металлической проволокой. После чего, подойдя к стене дома, где проживает ваша семья или где вы работаете, закопать в землю возле стен приготовленные таким образом пачки из дерева и металла, следя за тем, чтобы верхняя часть пачек осталась незакрытой. Закапывать их следует таким образом, чтобы металлическая пачка оказалась под небольшим углом к деревянной и, одновременно, очень плотно к ней прижата — деревянная должна немного войти в нее. Такое их положение объясняется тем, что обе энергии действуют в тесном соседстве а разница наклона связана с различной направленностью двух энергий: светлая энергия, уходящая вверх не совпадает по оси с энергией, направленной вниз, к центру Земли. Нужно так же иметь в виду окружить такими пачками нужно весь периметр дома поэтому изготовить их надо 6-8 пар.

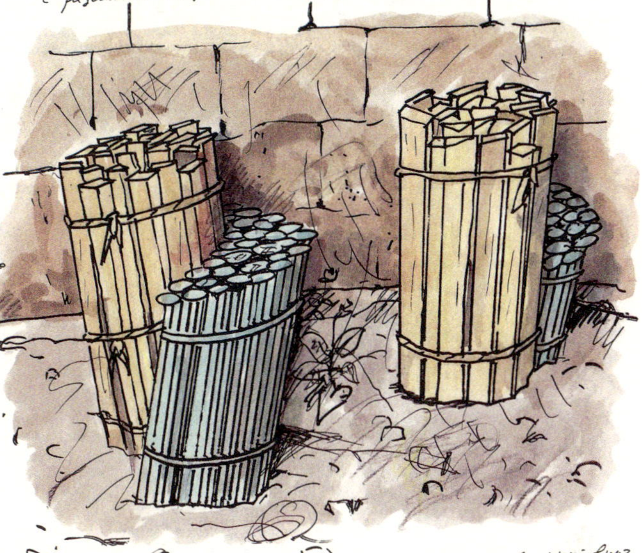

В. Стотаров
Пенсионер
г. Ленинград

Прорытие каналов по всей стране

Лучшими из проектов (государственного масштаба) можно считать такие, в которых принимает участие как можно большее число людей, но в пределе который может занять большую часть трудового населения страны. Одним из важнейших результатов осуществления такого проекта, помимо прямой экономической пользы его, можно считать вовлеченность и энтузиазм людей, выполняющих сообща какое-либо дело. Растворенность и соучастие в грандиозном проекте заставляет целеустремленно работать над его осуществлением, где каждый осознает и считает себя необходимой частицей в выполнении грандиозного целого.

Прорытие каналов на большой части территории страны пример как раз такого проекта, дающий большую отдачу как экономического, так и — а это не менее, если не более важно — психологического характера.

Для этого требуется немного. Следует расчертить (по карте) симметричные квадраты (разумеется речь идет о равнинных районах, горные попрежнему служат источниками водопитания равнин) и вдоль этих квадратов провести под прямыми углами, на равном расстоянии линии каналов. Насосные станции в местах пересечения этих линий позволят держать одинаковый уровень воды по все территории страны.

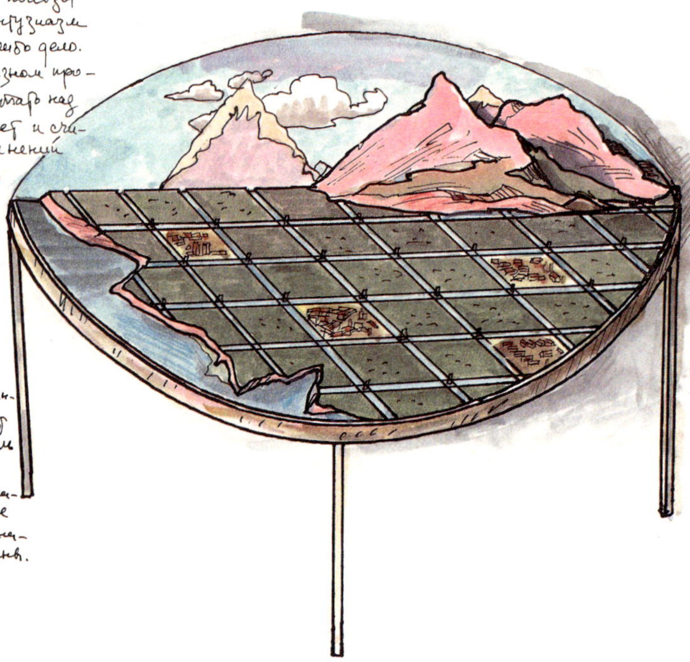

99 The Hospital: Five Confessions | *Das Krankenhaus: Fünf Bekenntnisse*

1997

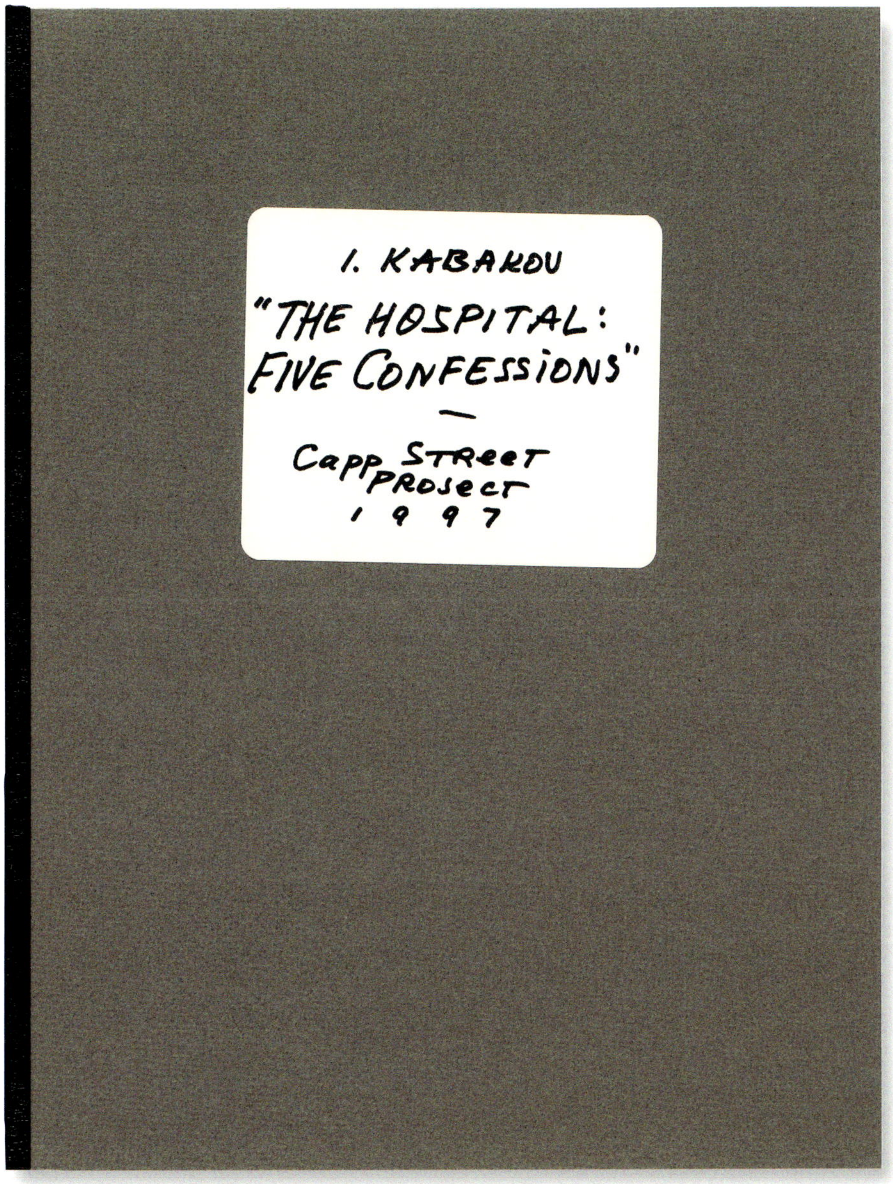

Ilya and Emilia Kabakov
New York: published by Ilya and Emilia Kabakov
28.1 x 22 cm
28 (partly double-sided) photocopied pp. with 16 (4 color) ills.
quick bind, cardboard cover, label on the cover
Schnellhefter, Kartonumschlag, Etikette auf dem Umschlag
edition: 20 copies include an original signed, numbered, and dated drawing by Ilya Kabakov from 1997

exhibition catalogue | *Ausstellungskatalog*

layout by Ilya Kabakov | *Layout von Ilya Kabakov*

Documentation of the installation of the same name at the Capp Street Project, CCA Wattis Institute for Contemporary Arts, San Francisco, October 30, 1997 to January 31, 1998. Texts by Ilya Kabakov in the form of fictitious dialogues between a doctor and his patient; English.

Dokumentation der gleichnamigen Installation, Capp Street Project, CCA Wattis Institute for Contemporary Arts, San Francisco, 30. Oktober 1997 – 31. Januar 1998. Texte von Ilya Kabakov als fiktive Dialoge von Arzt und Patient; englisch.

see also | *siehe auch* CRI, vol. 2, no. 114, pp. 230–235

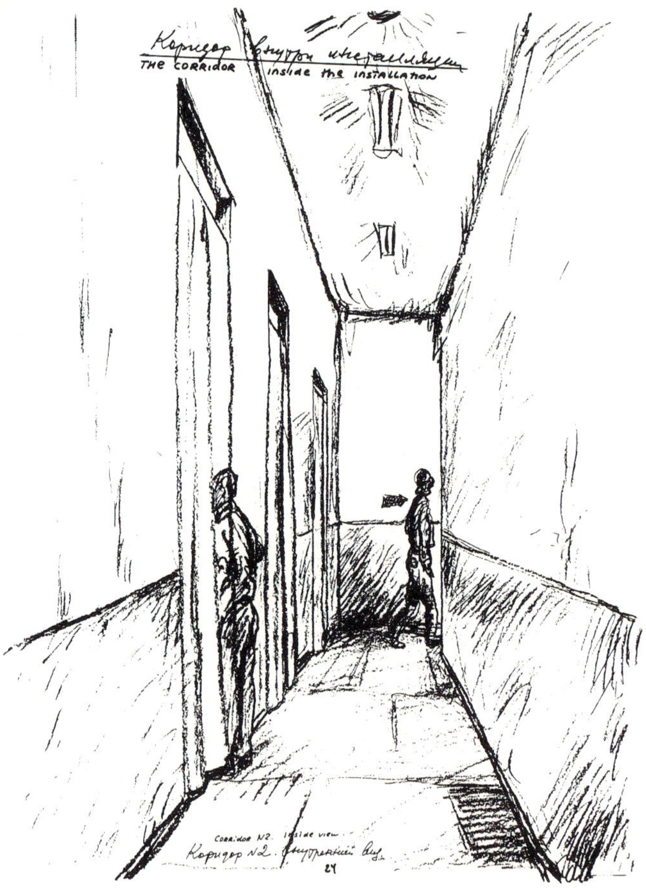
THE CORRIDOR inside the INSTALLATION
Corridor N2. inside view
24

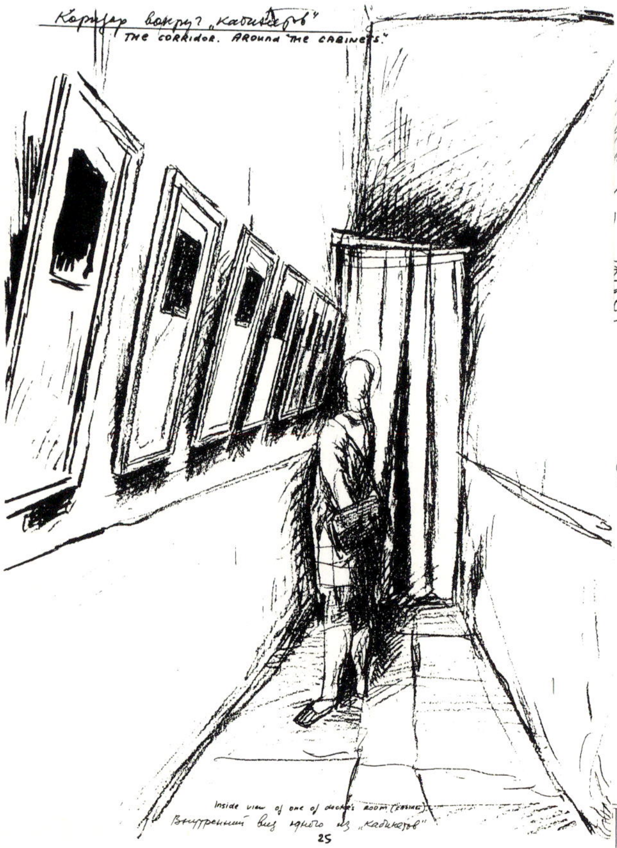
THE CORRIDOR. AROUND "THE CABINETS."
25

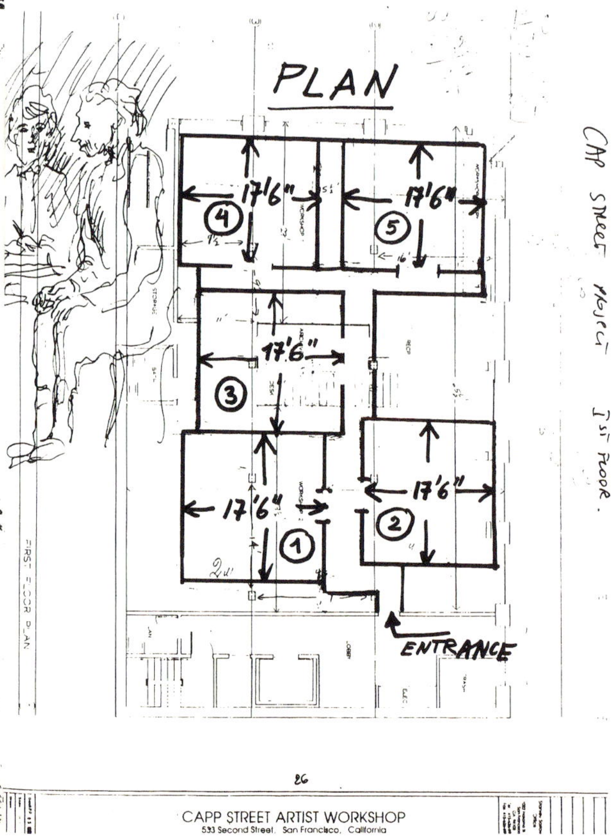
PLAN
17'6"
4
5
3
1
2
ENTRANCE
FIRST FLOOR PLAN
1st FLOOR.
26
CAPP STREET ARTIST WORKSHOP
533 Second Street, San Francisco, California

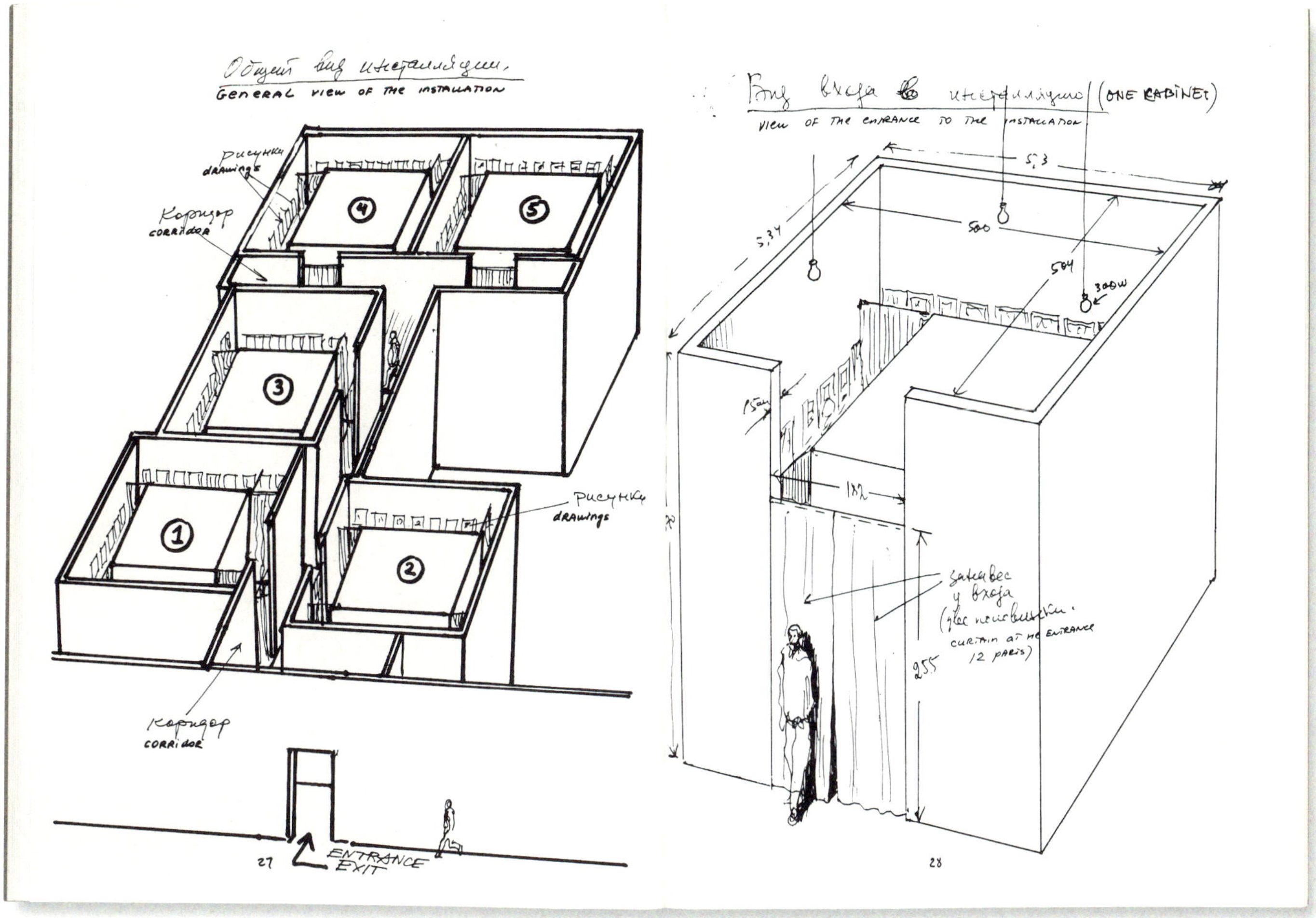

Общий вид инсталляции,
GENERAL VIEW OF THE INSTALLATION
Рисунки
drawings
Коридор
CORRIDOR
Рисунки
drawings
Коридор
CORRIDOR
ENTRANCE
EXIT
27
Вид входа в инсталляцию (ONE CABINET)
VIEW OF THE ENTRANCE TO THE INSTALLATION
5,3
500
504
300W
Занавес у входа
CURTAIN AT THE ENTRANCE
255
28

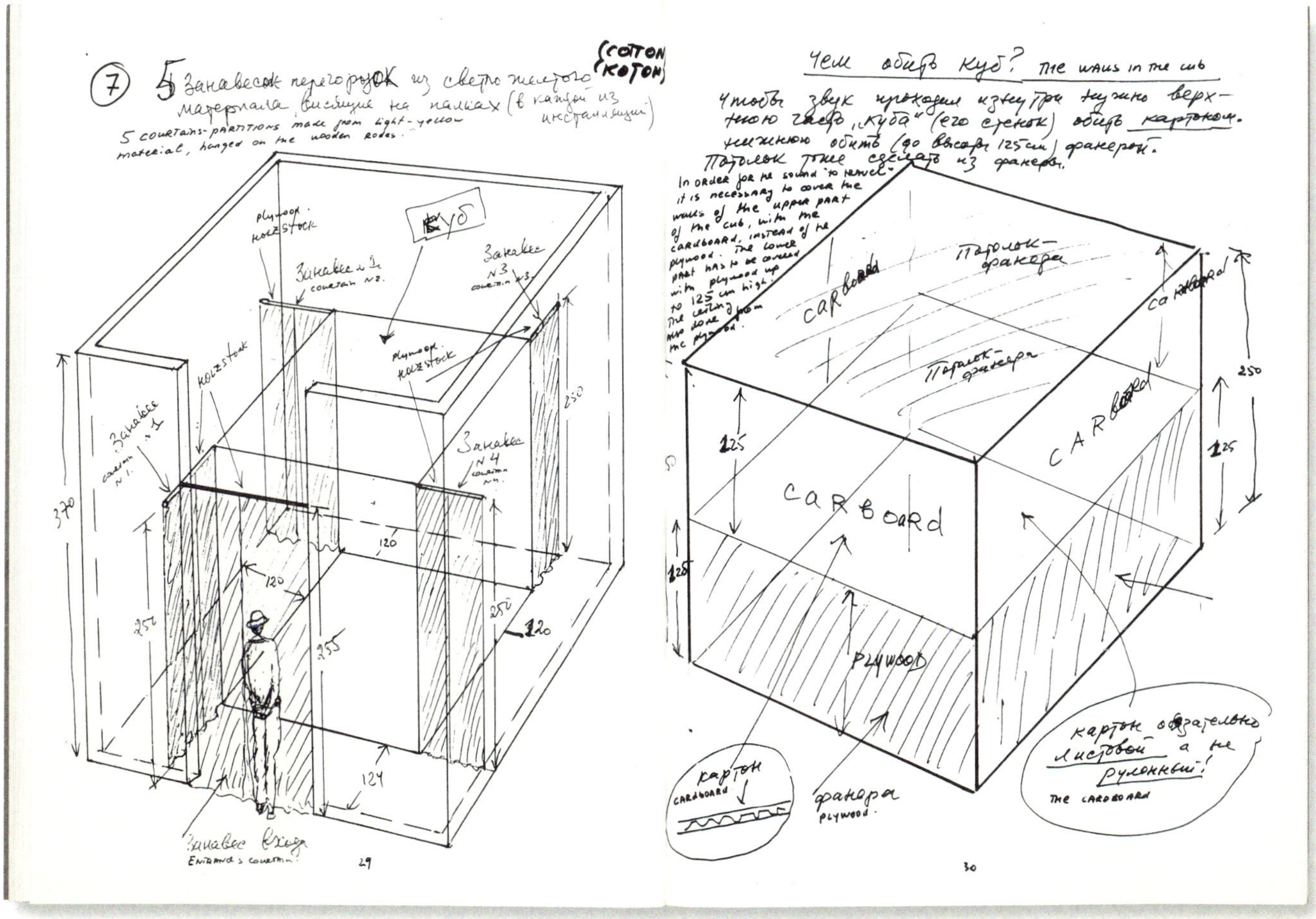

(COTTON KOTOH)
5 COURTAINS-PARTITIONS MAKE FROM LIGHT-YELLOW MATERIAL, HANGED ON THE WOODEN RODES.
Куб
370
250
120
124
255
29
Чем обить куб? THE WALLS IN THE CUB
CARBOARD
PLYWOOD
картон
CARDBOARD
фанера
PLYWOOD
125
250
30

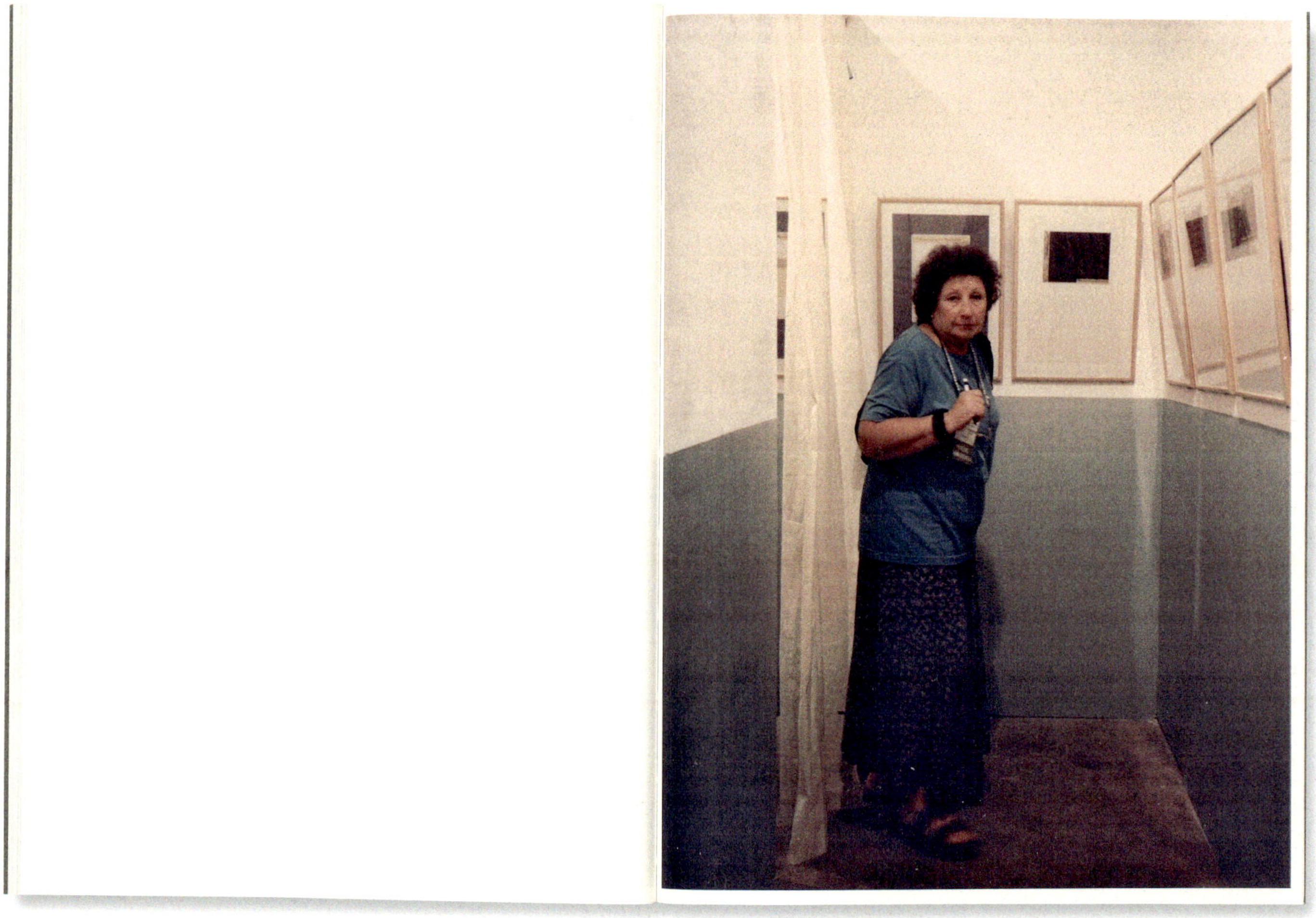

100 5 Albums: Second Book | *5 Alben. Zweites Buch*

1998

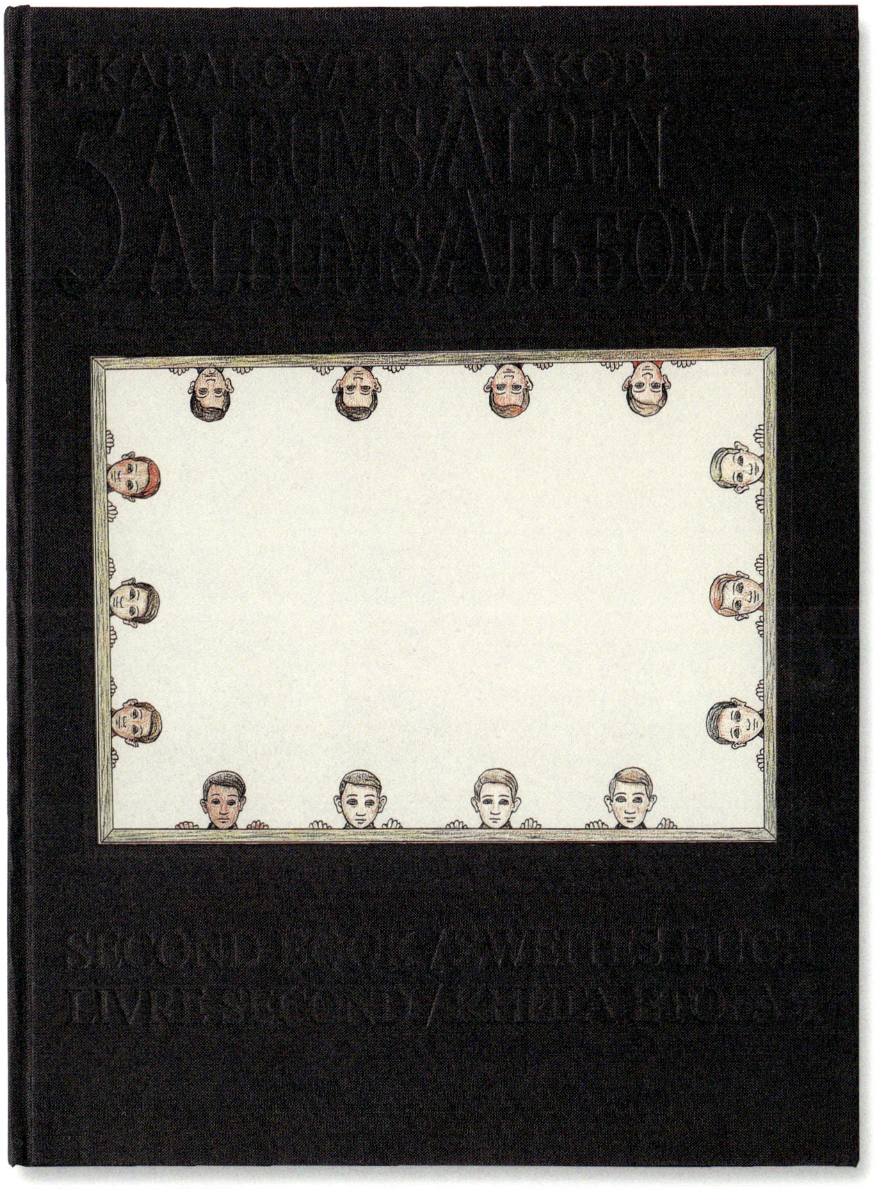

Emilia Kabakov, Maaretta Jaukkuri
Helsinki: Artprint
31 x 23.5 cm
282 pp. (incl. 9 foldouts) with 249 (241 color) ills.
stitchbound, clothbound, blind blocking with label
Fadenheftung, Leinen, Blindprägung mit Etikette

thematic publication | *thematische Publikation*

layout by Ilya Kabakov | *Layout von Ilya Kabakov*

Second part of the album series »10 Characters«. Texts by Ilya Kabakov; English, German, French.

Zweiter Teil der Albumserie »10 Personen«. Texte von Ilya Kabakov; englisch, deutsch, französisch.

see also | *siehe auch* no. 3; no. 16; no. 21; no. 68

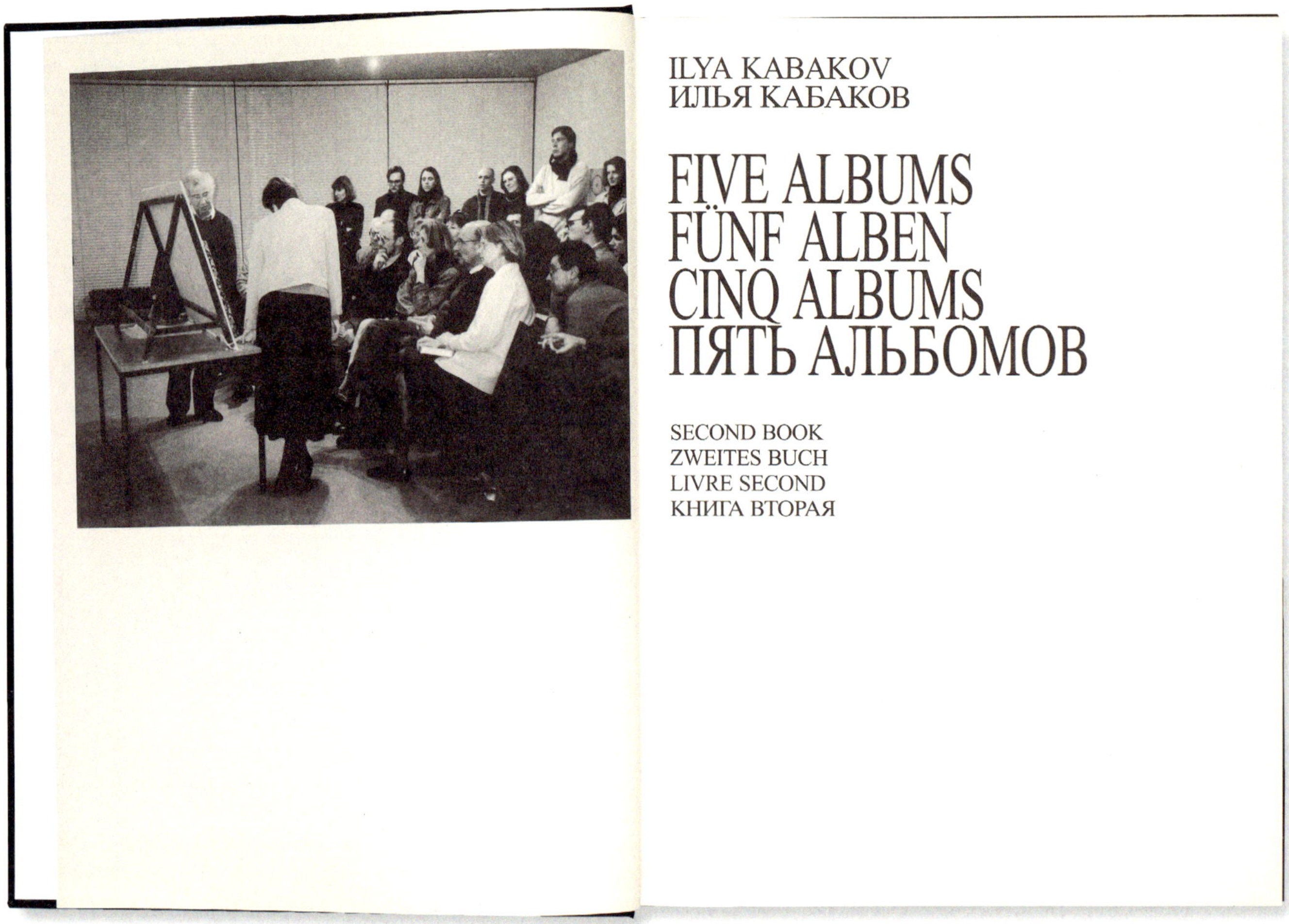

ILYA KABAKOV
ИЛЬЯ КАБАКОВ

FIVE ALBUMS
FÜNF ALBEN
CINQ ALBUMS
ПЯТЬ АЛЬБОМОВ

SECOND BOOK
ZWEITES BUCH
LIVRE SECOND
КНИГА ВТОРАЯ

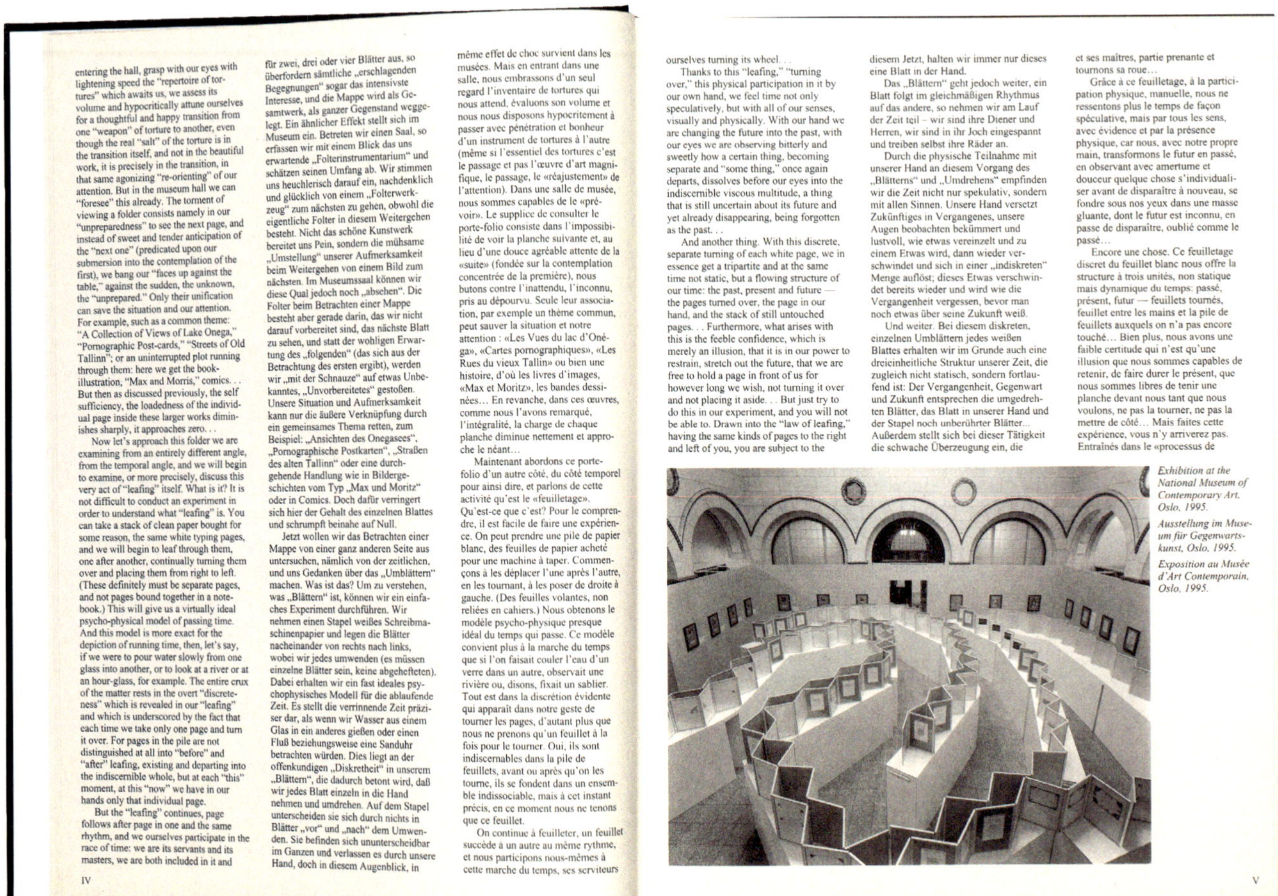

entering the hall, grasp with our eyes with lightening speed the "repertoire of tortures" which awaits us, we assess its volume and hypocritically attune ourselves for a thoughtful and happy transition from one "weapon" of torture to another, even though the real "salt" of the torture is in the transition itself, and not in the beautiful work, it is precisely in the transition, in that same agonizing "re-orienting" of our attention. But in the museum hall we can "foresee" this already. The torment of viewing a folder consists namely in our "unpreparedness" to see the next page, and instead of sweet and tender anticipation of the "next one" (predicated upon our submersion into the contemplation of the first), we bang our "faces up against the table," against the sudden, the unknown, the "unprepared." Only their unification can save the situation and our attention. For example, such as a common theme: "A Collection of Views of Lake Onega," "Pornographic Post-cards," "Streets of Old Tallinn"; or an uninterrupted plot running through them: here we get the book-illustration, "Max and Morris," comics. . . But then as discussed previously, the self sufficiency, the loadedness of the individual page inside these larger works diminishes sharply, it approaches zero. . .

Now let's approach this folder we are examining from an entirely different angle, from the temporal angle, and we will begin to examine, or more precisely, discuss this very act of "leafing" itself. What is it? It is not difficult to conduct an experiment in order to understand what "leafing" is. You can take a stack of clean paper bought for some reason, the same white typing pages, and we will begin to leaf through them, one after another, continually turning them over and placing them from right to left. (These definitely must be separate pages, and not pages bound together in a notebook.) This will give us a virtually ideal psycho-physical model of passing time. And this model is more exact for the depiction of running time, then, let's say, if we were to pour water slowly from one glass into another, or to look at a river or at an hour-glass, for example. The entire crux of the matter rests in the overt "discreteness" which is revealed in our "leafing" and which is underscored by the fact that each time we take only one page and turn it over. For pages in the pile are not distinguished at all into "before" and "after" leafing, existing and departing into the indiscernible whole, but at each "this" moment, at this "now" we have in our hands only that individual page.

But the "leafing" continues, page follows after page in one and the same rhythm, and we ourselves participate in the race of time: we are its servants and its masters, we are both included in it and

für zwei, drei oder vier Blätter aus, so überfordern sämtliche „erschlagenden Begegnungen" sogar das intensivste Interesse, und die Mappe wird als Gesamtwerk, als ganzer Gegenstand weggelegt. Ein ähnlicher Effekt stellt sich im Museum ein. Betreten wir einen Saal, so erfassen wir mit einem Blick das uns erwartende „Folterinstrumentarium" und schätzen seinen Umfang ab. Wir stimmen uns heuchlerisch darauf ein, nachdenklich und glücklich von einem „Folterwerkzeug" zum nächsten zu gehen, obwohl die eigentliche Folter in diesem Weitergehen besteht. Nicht das schöne Kunstwerk bereitet uns Pein, sondern die mühsame „Umstellung" unserer Aufmerksamkeit beim Weitergehen von einem Bild zum nächsten. Im Museumssaal können wir diese Qual jedoch noch „absehen". Die Folter beim Betrachten einer Mappe besteht aber gerade darin, das wir nicht darauf vorbereitet sind, das nächste Blatt zu sehen, und statt der wohligen Erwartung des „folgenden" (das sich aus der Betrachtung des ersten ergibt), werden wir „mit der Schnauze" auf etwas Unbekanntes, „Unvorbereitetes" gestoßen. Unsere Situation und Aufmerksamkeit kann nur die äußere Verknüpfung durch ein gemeinsames Thema retten, zum Beispiel: „Ansichten des Onegasees", „Pornographische Postkarten", „Straßen des alten Tallinn" oder eine durchgehende Handlung wie in Bildergeschichten vom Typ „Max und Moritz" oder in Comics. Doch dafür verringert sich hier der Gehalt des einzelnen Blattes und schrumpft beinahe auf Null.

Jetzt wollen wir das Betrachten einer Mappe von einer ganz anderen Seite aus untersuchen, nämlich von der zeitlichen, und uns Gedanken über das „Umblättern" machen. Was ist das? Um zu verstehen, was „Blättern" ist, können wir ein einfaches Experiment durchführen. Wir nehmen einen Stapel weißes Schreibmaschinenpapier und legen die Blätter nacheinander von rechts nach links, wobei wir jedes umwenden (es müssen einzelne Blätter sein, keine abgehefteten). Dabei erhalten wir ein fast ideales psychophysisches Modell für die ablaufende Zeit. Es stellt die verrinnende Zeit präziser dar, als wenn wir Wasser aus einem Glas in ein anderes gießen oder einen Fluß beziehungsweise eine Sanduhr betrachten würden. Dies liegt an der offenkundigen „Diskretheit" in unserem „Blättern", die dadurch betont wird, daß wir jedes Blatt einzeln in die Hand nehmen und umdrehen. Auf dem Stapel unterscheiden sie sich durch nichts in Blätter „vor" und „nach" dem Umwenden. Sie befinden sich ununterscheidbar im Ganzen und verlassen es durch unsere Hand, doch in diesem Augenblick, in

même effet de choc survient dans les musées. Mais en entrant dans une salle, nous embrassons d'un seul regard l'inventaire de tortures qui nous attend, évaluons son volume et nous nous disposons hypocritement à passer avec pénétration et bonheur d'un instrument de tortures à l'autre (même si l'essentiel des tortures c'est le passage et pas l'œuvre d'art magnifique, le passage, le «réajustement» de l'attention). Dans une salle de musée, nous sommes capables de le «prévoir». Le supplice de consulter le porte-folio consiste dans l'impossibilité de voir la planche suivante et, au lieu d'une douce agréable attente de la «suite» (fondée sur la contemplation concentrée de la première), nous butons contre l'inattendu, l'inconnu, pris au dépourvu. Seule leur association, par exemple un thème commun, peut sauver la situation et notre attention : «Les Vues du lac d'Onéga», «Cartes pornographiques», «Les Rues du vieux Tallin» ou bien une histoire, d'où les livres d'images, «Max et Moritz», les bandes dessinées… En revanche, dans ces œuvres, comme nous l'avons remarqué, l'intégralité, la charge de chaque planche diminue nettement et approche le néant…

Maintenant abordons ce porte-folio d'un autre côté, du côté temporel pour ainsi dire, et parlons de cette activité qu'est le «feuilletage». Qu'est-ce que c'est? Pour le comprendre, il est facile de faire une expérience. On peut prendre une pile de papier blanc, des feuilles de papier acheté pour une machine à taper. Commençons à les déplacer l'une après l'autre, en les tournant, à les poser de droite à gauche. (Des feuilles volantes, non reliées en cahiers.) Nous obtenons le modèle psycho-physique presque idéal du temps qui passe. Ce modèle convient plus à la marche du temps que si l'on faisait couler l'eau d'un verre dans un autre, observait une rivière ou, disons, fixait un sablier. Tout est dans la discrétion évidente qui apparaît dans notre geste de tourner les pages, d'autant plus que nous ne prenons qu'un feuillet à la fois pour le tourner. Oui, ils sont indiscernables dans la pile de feuillets, avant ou après qu'on les tourne, ils se fondent dans un ensemble indissociable, mais à cet instant précis, en ce moment nous ne tenons que ce feuillet.

On continue à feuilleter, un feuillet succède à un autre au même rythme, et nous participons nous-mêmes à cette marche du temps, ses serviteurs

IV

ourselves turning its wheel. . .

Thanks to this "leafing," "turning over," this physical participation in it by our own hand, we feel time not only speculatively, but with all of our senses, visually and physically. With our hand we are changing the future into the past, with our eyes we are observing bitterly and sweetly how a certain thing, becoming separate and "some thing," once again departs, dissolves before our eyes into the indiscernible viscous multitude, a thing that is still uncertain about its future and yet already disappearing, being forgotten as the past. . .

And another thing. With this discrete, separate turning of each white page, we in essence get a tripartite and at the same time not static, but a flowing structure of our time: the past, present and future — the pages turned over, the page in our hand, and the stack of still untouched pages. . . Furthermore, what arises with this is the feeble confidence, which is merely an illusion, that it is in our power to restrain, stretch out the future, that we are free to hold a page in front of us for however long we wish, not turning it over and not placing it aside. . . But just try to do this in our experiment, and you will not be able to. Drawn into the "law of leafing," having the same kinds of pages to the right and left of you, you are subject to the

diesem Jetzt, halten wir immer nur dieses eine Blatt in der Hand.

Das „Blättern" geht jedoch weiter, ein Blatt folgt im gleichmäßigen Rhythmus auf das andere, so nehmen wir am Lauf der Zeit teil – wir sind ihre Diener und Herren, wir sind in ihr Joch eingespannt und treiben selbst ihre Räder an.

Durch die physische Teilnahme mit unserer Hand an diesem Vorgang des „Blätterns" und „Umdrehens" empfinden wir die Zeit nicht nur spekulativ, sondern mit allen Sinnen. Unsere Hand versetzt Zukünftiges in Vergangenes, unsere Augen beobachten bekümmert und lustvoll, wie etwas vereinzelt und zu einem Etwas wird, dann wieder verschwindet und sich in einer „indiskreten" Menge auflöst; dieses Etwas verschwindet bereits wieder und wird wie die Vergangenheit vergessen, bevor man noch etwas über seine Zukunft weiß.

Und weiter. Bei diesem diskreten, einzelnen Umblättern jedes weißen Blattes erhalten wir im Grunde auch eine dreieinheitliche Struktur unserer Zeit, die zugleich nicht statisch, sondern fortlaufend ist: Der Vergangenheit, Gegenwart und Zukunft entsprechen die umgedrehten Blätter, das Blatt in unserer Hand und der Stapel noch unberührter Blätter... Außerdem stellt sich bei dieser Tätigkeit die schwache Überzeugung ein, die

et ses maîtres, partie prenante et tournons sa roue…

Grâce à ce feuilletage, à la participation physique, manuelle, nous ne ressentons plus le temps de façon spéculative, mais par tous les sens, avec évidence et par la présence physique, car nous, avec notre propre main, transformons le futur en passé, en observant avec amertume et douceur quelque chose s'individualiser avant de disparaître à nouveau, se fondre sous nos yeux dans une masse gluante, dont le futur est inconnu, en passe de disparaître, oublié comme le passé…

Encore une chose. Ce feuilletage discret du feuillet blanc nous offre la structure à trois unités, non statique mais dynamique du temps: passé, présent, futur — feuillets tournés, feuillet entre les mains et la pile de feuillets auxquels on n'a pas encore touché… Bien plus, nous avons une faible certitude qui n'est qu'une illusion que nous sommes capables de retenir, de faire durer le présent, que nous sommes libres de tenir une planche devant nous tant que nous voulons, ne pas la tourner, ne pas la mettre de côté… Mais faites cette expérience, vous n'y arriverez pas. Entraînés dans le «processus de

Exhibition at the National Museum of Contemporary Art, Oslo, 1995.

Ausstellung im Museum für Gegenwartskunst, Oslo, 1995.

Exposition au Musée d'Art Contemporain, Oslo, 1995.

V

14
Some, laughing, depict "RECEIVING GUESTS", they gather furniture, pour tea, the "guests" bow, hang up their hats, they repeat everything that they always did down below.

Manche spielen lachend „WIR HABEN GÄSTE", stellen Möbel zusammen, schenken Tee ein, die „Gäste" verbeugen sich, hängen die Hüte auf und wiederholen all das, was sie auch unten immer tun.

Certains miment en riant «L'ACCUEIL DES INVITÉS»: ils rassemblent des meubles, offrent du thé, les «invités» font la révérence, suspendent leurs chapeaux, répètent tous les gestes qu'ils ont toujours faits en bas.

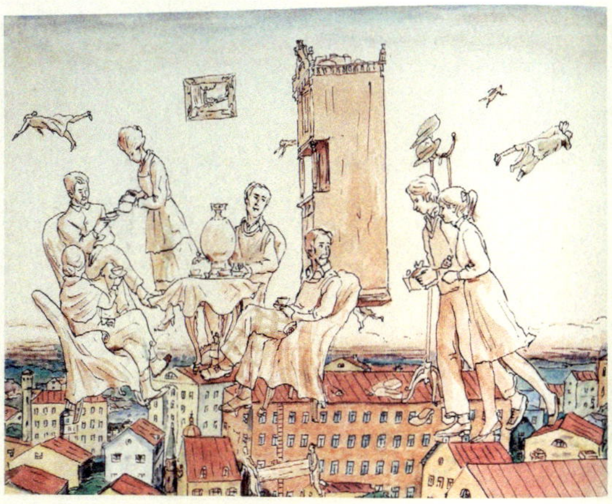

88

15
"IN THE EVENING" everybody is already down below, on the darkening earth. But those still returning from far-off travels can be seen in the last rays, carrying things from foreign places, with objects whose purpose is often completely unclear to them.

„ABENDS" sind alle wieder unten, auf der dunkelnden Erde. Aber in den letzten Strahlen sieht man noch die Heimkehrer von Fernreisen, mit Erzeugnissen aus fremden Regionen, Gegenständen, deren Bestimmung ihnen oft nicht ganz klar ist.

«LE SOIR», tous sont déjà en bas, sur la terre qui s'obscurcit. On voit encore dans les derniers rayons lumineux ceux qui rentrent de voyages lointains et qui rapportent de pays étrangers des produits et des objets dont ils ne connaissent pas vraiment la fonction.

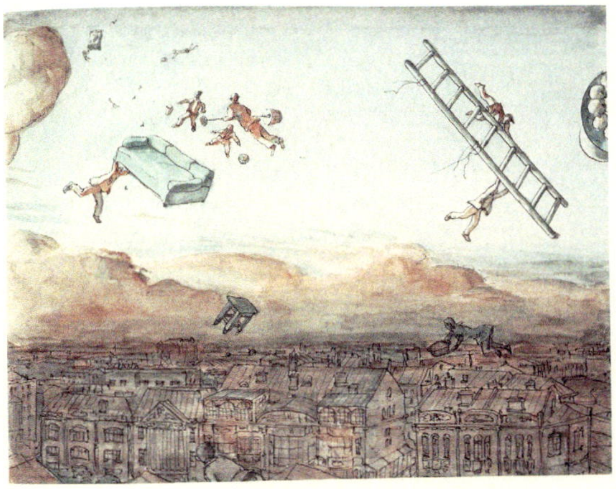

89

16
"ON SUNDAYS" the air is particularly crowded with people, and it is even bustling from the "fliers" headed in various directions, hurrying out of town and simply talking, it is crowded from the innumerable sacks, gifts and purchases.

„SONNTAGS" ist es in der Luft besonders voll und eng; es geht sogar geschäftig zu, weil viele in verschiedene Richtungen fliegen, aus der Stadt hinauseilen oder sich einfach unterhalten und zahllose Tragetüten, Geschenke und Einkäufe bei sich haben.

«LE DIMANCHE», l'air est particulièrement animé, encombré et même soumis à l'excitation des passants volant dans tous les sens, revenant de la ville avec précipitation et discutant simplement des cadeaux et des achats qu'ils ramènent dans d'innombrables sacs en papier.

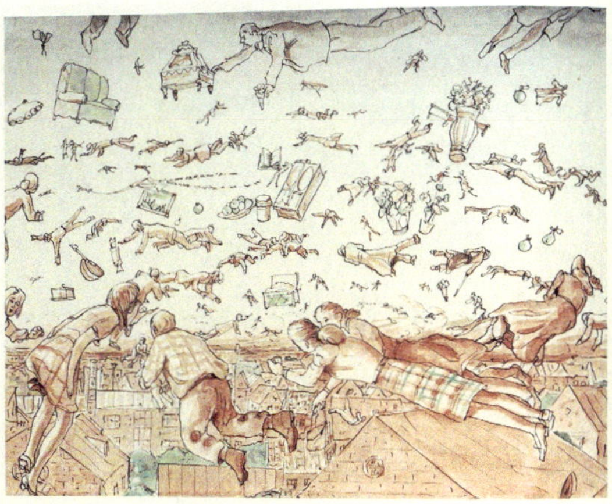

90

17
During "Big Holidays", everybody "SOLEMNLY HOLDING HANDS" forms an enormous resounding ring. They slowly revolve and a slow, orderly choral drifts about in the morning air (the holiday begins at six o'clock in the morning), it is a multi-voiced chorus of women's, men's and children's voices.

Während der „Großen Festlichkeiten" bilden alle, „SICH FEIERLICH an den Händen HALTEND", riesige klingende Kreise. Sie drehen sich langsam, und in der Morgenluft (das Fest beginnt um sechs Uhr morgens) erschallt ein getragener, wohlklingender Choral, ein vielstimmiger Chor von Frauen-, Männer- und Kinderstimmen.

«LORS DES GRANDES FÊTES», ils forment tous de grands cercles bruyants, et se tiennent «SOLENNELLEMENT» par la main. Ils tournent lentement et, dans l'air du matin (la fête commence à six heures du matin), s'élève un cantique harmonieux, un chœur à plusieures voix, de femmes, d'hommes et d'enfants.

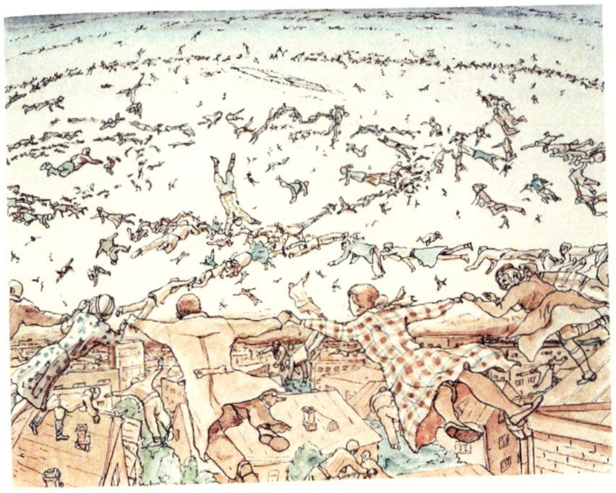

91

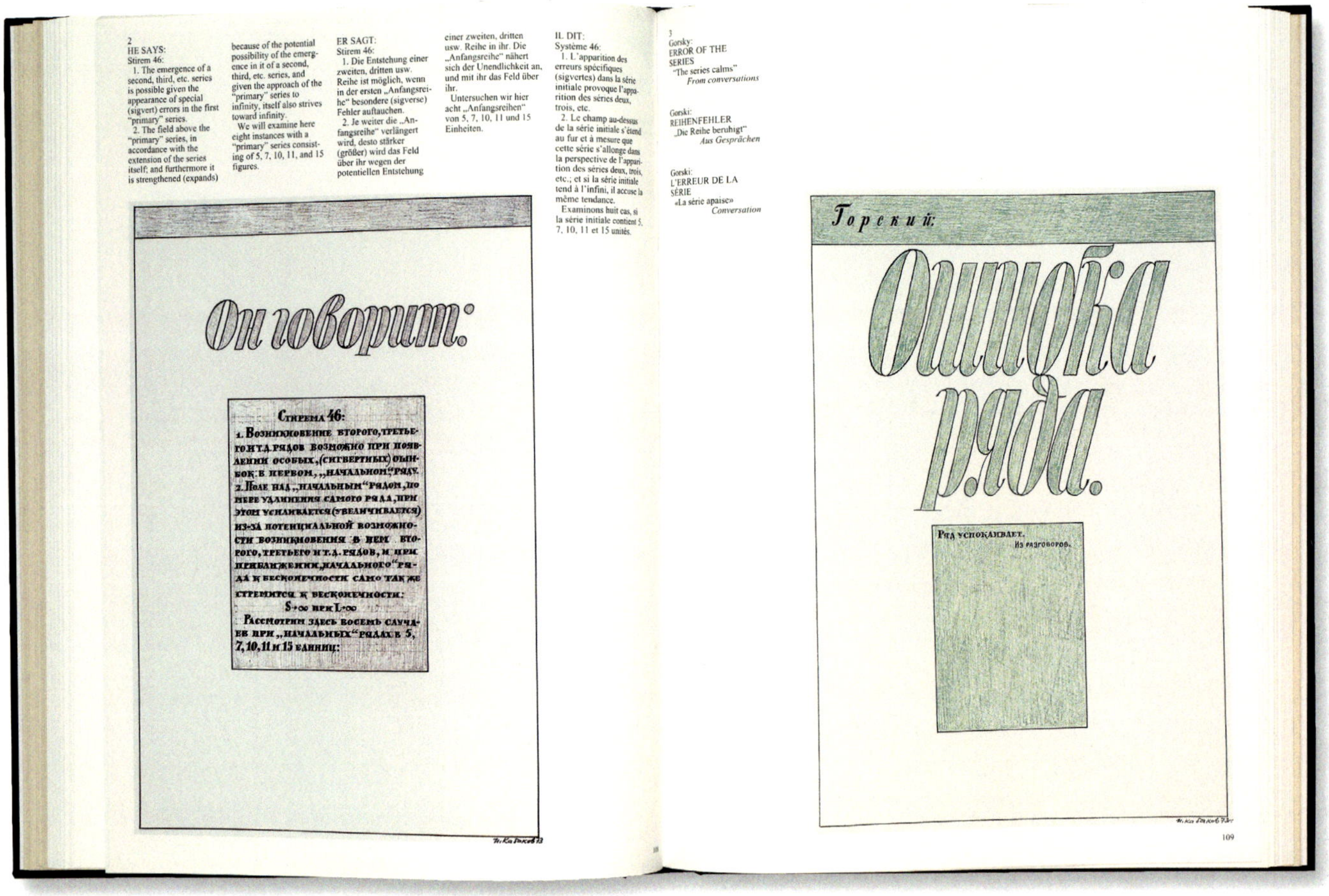
2
HE SAYS:
Stirem 46:
1. The emergence of a second, third, etc. series is possible given the appearance of special (sigvert) errors in the first "primary" series.
2. The field above the "primary" series, in accordance with the extension of the series itself; and furthermore it is strengthened (expands) because of the potential possibility of the emergence in it of a second, third, etc. series, and given the approach of the "primary" series to infinity, itself also strives toward infinity.
We will examine here eight instances with a "primary" series consisting of 5, 7, 10, 11, and 15 figures.
ER SAGT:
Stirem 46:
1. Die Entstehung einer zweiten, dritten usw. Reihe ist möglich, wenn in der ersten „Anfangsreihe" besondere (sigverse) Fehler auftauchen.
2. Je weiter die „Anfangsreihe" verlängert wird, desto stärker (größer) wird das Feld über ihr wegen der potentiellen Entstehung einer zweiten, dritten usw. Reihe in ihr. Die „Anfangsreihe" nähert sich der Unendlichkeit an, und mit ihr das Feld über ihr.
Untersuchen wir hier acht „Anfangsreihen" von 5, 7, 10, 11 und 15 Einheiten.
IL DIT:
Système 46:
1. L'apparition des erreurs spécifiques (sigvertes) dans la série initiale provoque l'apparition des séries deux, trois, etc.
2. Le champ au-dessus de la série initiale s'étend au fur et à mesure que cette série s'allonge dans la perspective de l'apparition des séries deux, trois, etc.; et si la série initiale tend à l'infini, il accuse la même tendance.
Examinons huit cas, si la série initiale contient 5, 7, 10, 11 et 15 unités.
Он говорит:
3
Gorsky:
ERROR OF THE SERIES
"The series calms"
From conversations
Gorski:
REIHENFEHLER
„Die Reihe beruhigt"
Aus Gesprächen
Gorski:
L'ERREUR DE LA SÉRIE
«La série apaise»
Conversation
Горский:
Ошибка ряда.
Ряд успокаивает.
Из разговоров.
109

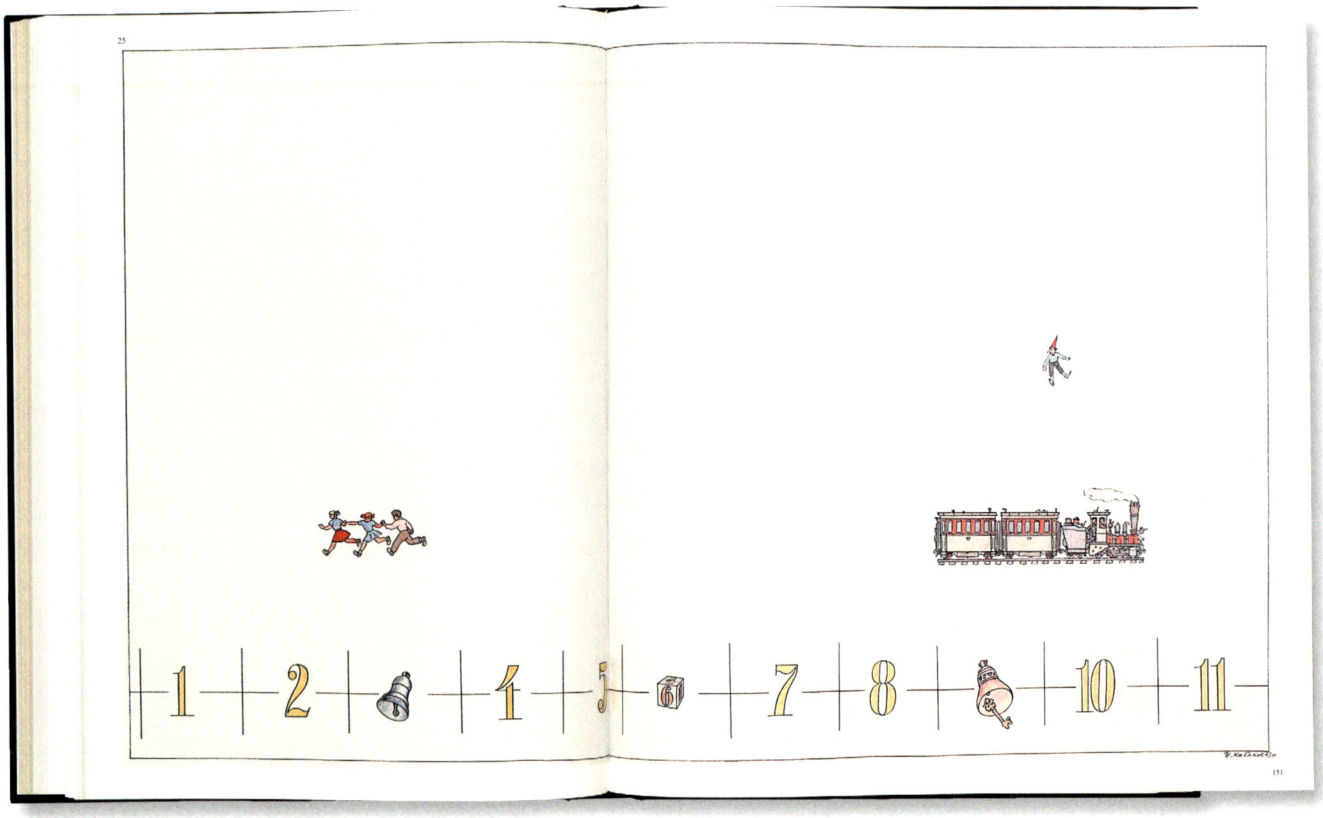
25
1
2
4
5
6
7
8
10
11
151

101 The Palace of Projects. 1995–1996. Part I | *Der Palast der Projekte. 1995–1996. Teil I*

1998

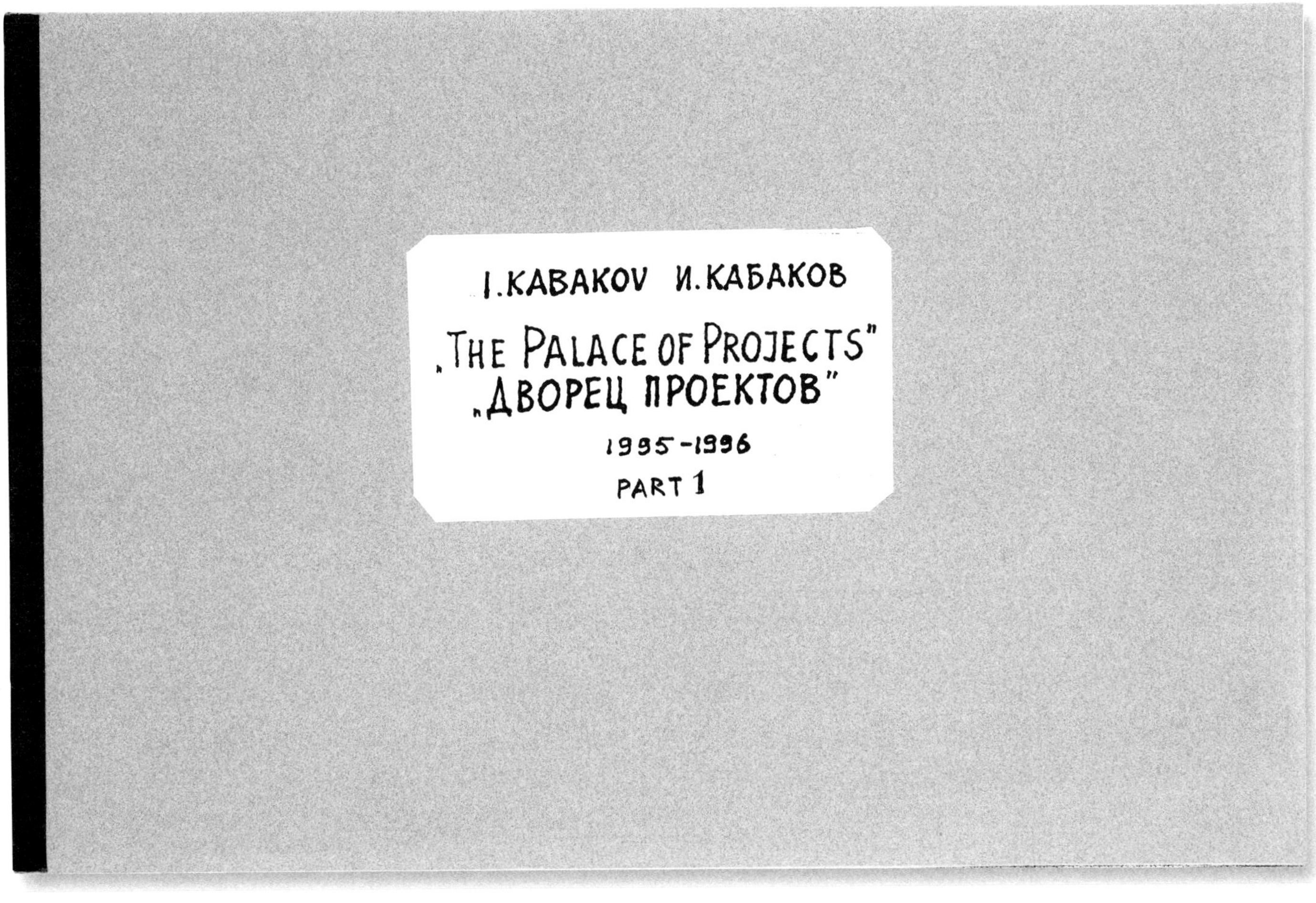

Ilya Kabakov
New York: published by the author
27.9 x 43.3 cm
103 photocopied (partly numbered) pp. with 67 b/w ills.
adhesive binding, paper cover, label on the cover
Klebebindung, Papierumschlag, Etikette auf dem Umschlag
edition: 2 copies

thematic publication | *thematische Publikation*

layout by Ilya Kabakov | *Layout von Ilya Kabakov*

For the installation »The Palace of Projects«. Texts by Ilya and Emilia Kabakov; English, Russian.

Zur Installation »Palast der Projekte«. Texte von Ilya und Emilia Kabakov; englisch und russisch.

see also | *siehe auch* no. 95; no. 102; no. 117; CRI, vol. 2, no. 117, pp. 244–251; CRP, vol. 1, nos. 279–289, pp. 350–360

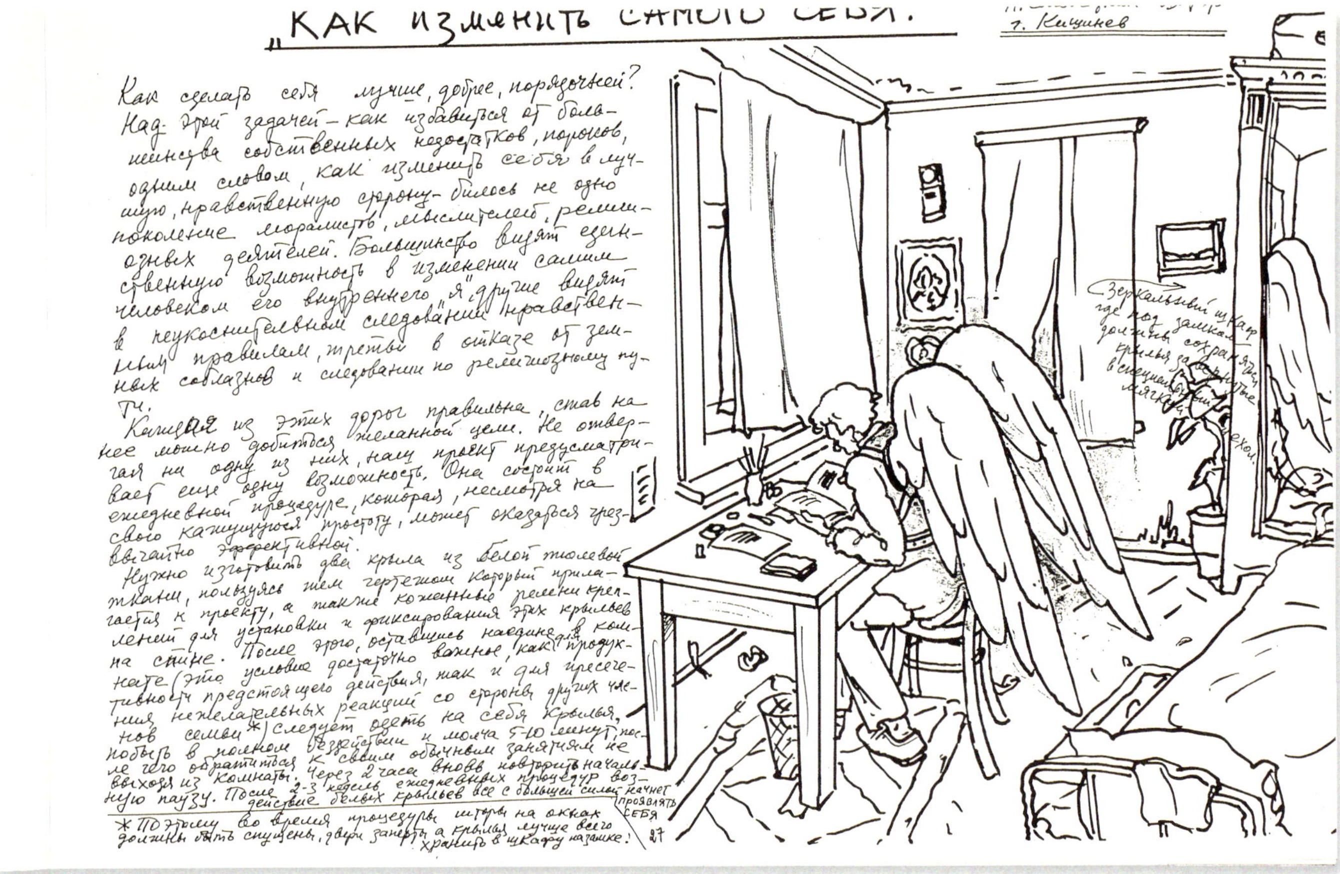

„КАК ИЗМЕНИТЬ САМОГО СЕБЯ"

г. Кишинев

Как сделать себя лучше, добрее, порядочней?
Над этой задачей – как избавиться от боль-
шинства собственных недостатков, пороков,
одним словом, как изменить себя в луч-
шую, нравственную сторону – билось не одно
поколение моралистов, мыслителей, религи-
озных деятелей. Большинство видят един-
ственную возможность в изменении самим
человеком его внутреннего „я", другие видят
в неукоснительном следовании нравствен-
ным правилам, третьи в отказе от зем-
ных соблазнов и следовании по религиозному пу-
ти.
Каждая из этих дорог правильна, став на
нее можно добиться желанной цели. Не отвер-
гая ни одну из них, наш проект предусматри-
вает еще одну возможность. Она состоит в
ежедневной процедуре, которая, несмотря на
свою кажущуюся простоту, может оказаться чрез-
вычайно эффективной.
Нужно изготовить два крыла из белой тюлевой
ткани, пользуясь тем чертежом который прила-
гается к проекту, а также кожанные ремни креп-
лений для установки и фиксирования этих крыльев
на спине. После этого, оставшись наедине в ком-
нате (это условие достаточно важное, как для продук-
тивности предстоящего действия, так и для пресече-
ния нежелательных реакций со стороны других чле-
нов семьи*) следует одеть на себя крылья,
побыть в полном бездействии и молча 5-10 минут, пос-
ле чего обратиться к своим обычным занятиям не
выходя из комнаты. Через 2 часа вновь повторить началь-
ную паузу. После 2-3 недель ежедневных процедур воз-
действие белых крыльев все с большей силой начнет
проявлять себя

* Поэтому во время процедуры шторы на окнах
должны быть спущены, двери заперты, а крылья лучше всего
хранить в шкафу на замке!

27

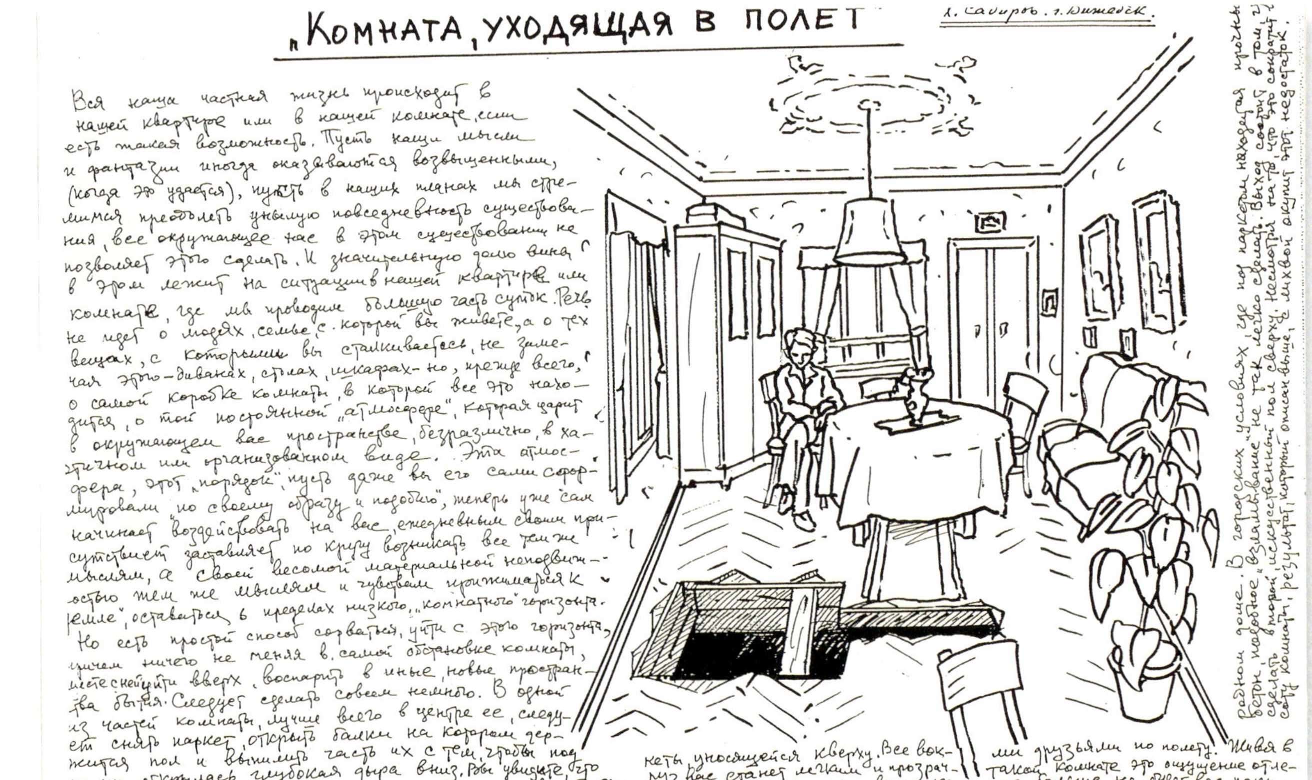

„КОМНАТА, УХОДЯЩАЯ В ПОЛЕТ"

Вся наша частная жизнь происходит в
нашей квартире или в нашей комнате, если
есть такая возможность. Пусть наши мысли
и фантазии иногда оказываются возвышенными,
(когда это удается), пусть в наших планах мы стре-
мимся преодолеть унылую повседневность существова-
ния, все окружающее нас в этом существовании не
позволяет этого сделать. И значительную долю вины
в этом лежит на ситуации в нашей квартире или
комнате, где мы проводим большую часть суток. Речь
не идет о людях, семье, с которой вы живете, а о тех
вещах, с которыми вы сталкиваетесь, не заме-
чая этого – диванах, столах, шкафах – но, прежде всего,
о самой коробке комнаты, в которой все это нахо-
дится, о той постоянной „атмосфере", которая царит
в окружающем вас пространстве, безразлично, в ха-
отичном или организованном виде. Эта атмос-
фера, этот „порядок", пусть даже вы его сами сфор-
мировали „по своему образу и подобию", теперь уже сам
начинает воздействовать на вас, ежедневным своим при-
сутствием заставляет по кругу возникать все тем же
мыслям, а своей весомой материальной неподвиж-
ностью тем же мыслям и чувствам прижиматься к
„земле", оставаться в пределах низкого „комнатного" горизонта.
Но есть простой способ сорваться, уйти с этого горизонта,
причем ничего не меняя в самой обстановке комнаты,
вместе с ней уйти вверх, воспарить в иные, новые простран-
ства бытия. Следует сделать совсем немного. В одной
из частей комнаты, лучше всего в центре ее, следу-
ет снять паркет, открыть балки на которых дер-
жится пол и вынимать часть их с тем, чтобы под
ними открылась глубокая дыра вниз. Вы увидите, что
все вокруг вас внезапно преобразилось. В присутствии бездны,
оказавшейся внизу, комната, до сих пор казавшейся столь
прочной, приобретет свойства кабины воздушного шара или ра-
кеты, уносящейся кверху. Все вок-
руг вас станет легким и прозрач-
ным, и даже тяжелые вещи, ка-
завшиеся столь неподвижными,
станут вашими близкими и легки-
ми друзьями по полету. Живя в
такой комнате это ощущение отле-
та больше не будет вас поки-
дать.
Разумеется, речь здесь идет о заго-
родном доме. В городских условиях, где под паркетом находится прочный
бетон, подобное „взламывание" не так легко сделать. Выход состоит в том, чтобы
сделать второй, искусственный пол сверху, несмотря на то, что это сократит
высоту комнаты, результат, который окажется выше, с лихвой окупит этот недостаток.

35

СОСРЕДОТОЧЕННОСТЬ В ШКАФУ

В. Корнейчук.
Писатель
г. Улан-Удэ

Огромное количество проблем, которые касаются
возможности концентрировать свое постоянное вни-
мание, особенно когда это касается не отдыха,
а какой-нибудь важной, продуктивной работы
(особенно над разработкой сложного проекта) —
возникает в семье, если в ней существует недоста-
ток жилплощади или, даже когда имеется отдель-
ная комната для работы, в ней из-за постоянно доносящегося
шума также невозможно сосредоточиться.
Проект предусматривает место такой концентрации
внимания в платяном шкафу. В пользу такого решения могут быть
выдвинуты следующие аргументы:

1. Шкаф внутри комнаты может создать дополнительную
звуковую изоляцию.
2. Пространство внутри шкафа, небольшое по сравнению с
любой комнатой, и где нет отвлекающих побочных
объектов, более чем комната, концентрирует внимание на
предмете разработки.
3. Определенный дискомфорт стимулирует креативный
процесс, как контраст к реальной повседневной жизни
как противопоставление несчастности, трагичности, экстремальности нормальному существованию.
4. Установление в шкафу автономного освещения (лампы 25 w)
позволяет полностью изменить время сна и бодрствования,
отключиться от времени и ритма жизни семьи, создать
свой распорядок, удобный для работы.
5. Если запастись всем необходимым для длительного
пребывания в шкафу — едой, водой, радиоприемником, кни-
гами — то, пользуясь „внутришкафной" ситуацией и по
согласованию с другими членами семьи — кроме продук-
тивной длительной творческой деятельности можно за-
няться медитацией и проводить другие эксперименты, нахо-
дясь внутри капсулы космического корабля и при этом
не испытывая все превратности полета в космос.

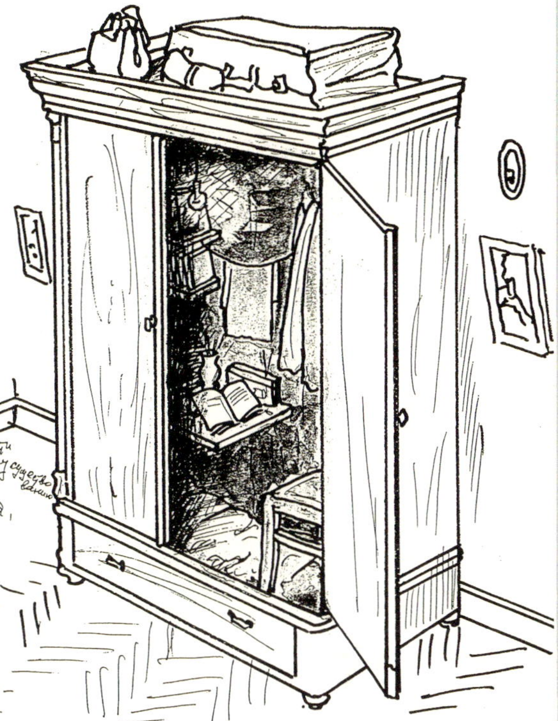

67

„Встречи с прошлым"

Г. Собакина Преподава-
тельница музыки
г. Серпухов.

Во многих странах сегодня — то ли благодаря
обилию товаров, то ли благодаря дешевому их про-
изводству, — общая мода носить только новые вещи:
одежду, обувь; но то же самое происходит и
с вещами домашнего быта: новая мебель, но-
вая посуда и так вплоть до новой квартиры,
нового дома... При этом все старое безжалостно
выбрасывается, заменяется часто и только потому, что
оно просто „старое", немодное. Но при этой, такой
быстрой замене старого на новое мало кто заме-
чает, что вместе со старыми вещами выбрас-
вается на свалку и наша прошлая жизнь, то!
что мы знали, переживали, чувствовали в нашем.
прошлом, все, что с этими вещами для нас было.
связано, а вместе с такими воспоминаниями теряем;
утрачиваем окончательно и всю нашу жизнь.
Проект, который можно назвать „Встречи с прошлым"
как раз и предполагает сочетать нашу сегодняшнюю
страсть к новому и важность для нашего полноцен-
ного существования таких старых вещей. Нужно сде-
лать в комнате специальную загородку, чтобы она не
мешала новой мебели, пристроить её к стене. Ящик следует
периодически наполнять вещами, в которых уже отпала
необходимость или они оказались сломанными: ножки от
стульев, старые пальто, пакеты, сумки, старые книги —
все, с чем связаны наши воспоминания, что мы хотели
ли бы удержать в нашей памяти. Когда приходили бы ваши
гости вы, беря в руки какую-нибудь старую вещь (ящик должен
быть постоянно открыт), могли бы увлеченно рассказать, что свя-
зано для вас с этой вещью, припомнив дату и обстоятельства. Тем
самым вся прошлая жизнь была бы рядом с вами, а ваши друзья,

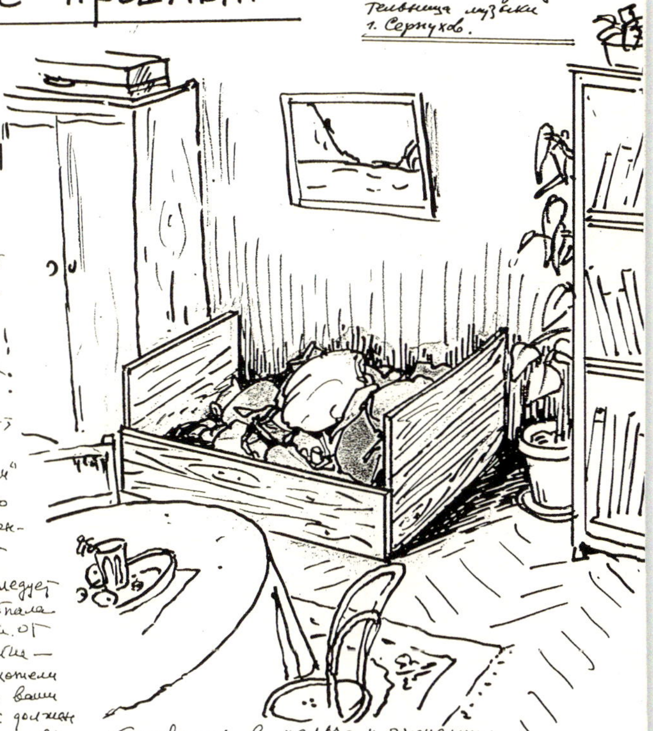

убедившись в пользе и значении
такого „Мемориала", сами бы пришли к
решению создать у себя дома такой же
„музей".

39

102 The Palace of Projects. 1995–1996. Part II | *Der Palast der Projekte. 1995–1996. Teil II*

1998

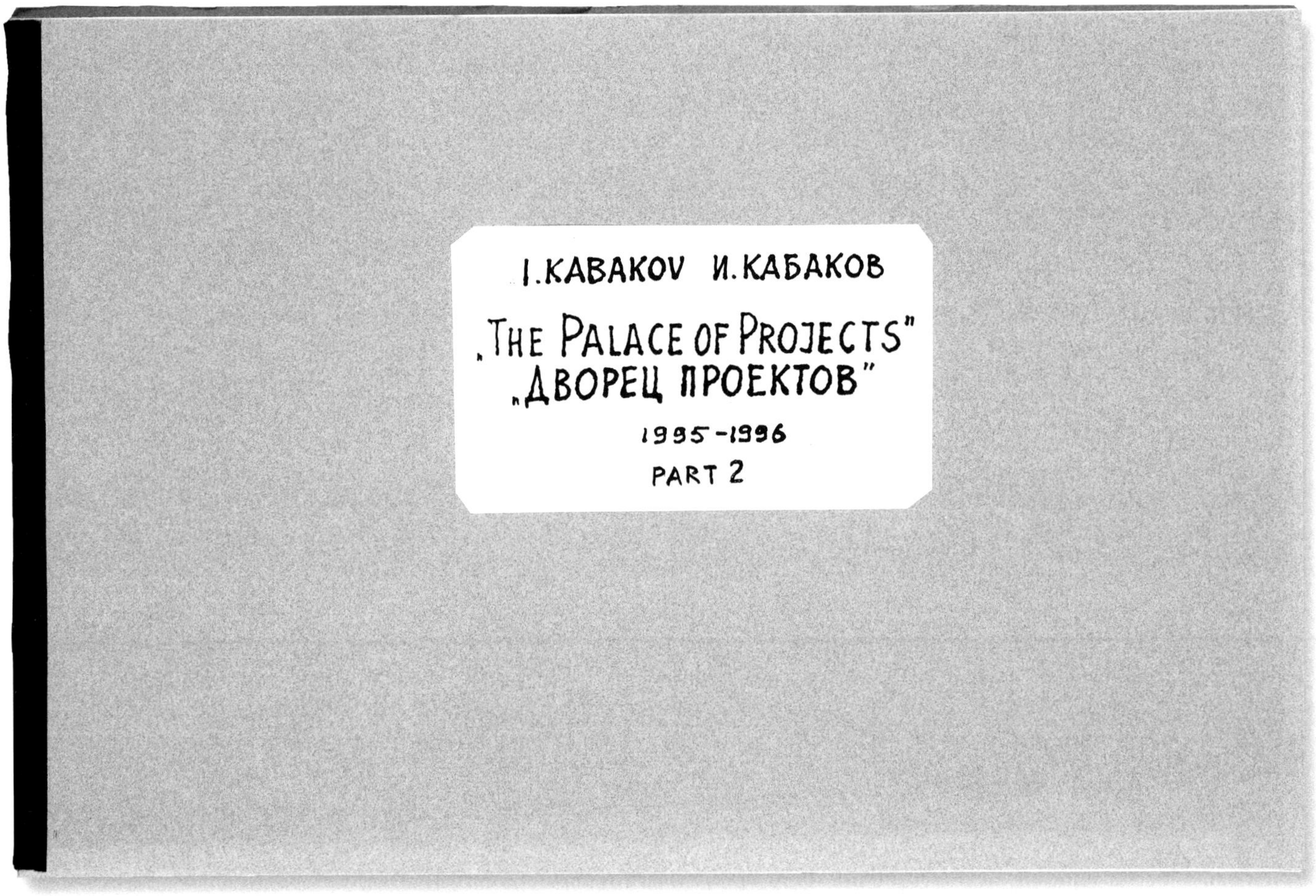

Ilya Kabakov
New York: published by Ilya and Emilia Kabakov
27.9 x 43.3 cm
117 photocopied pp. with 76 b/w ills.
adhesive binding, paper cover, label on the cover
Klebebindung, Papierumschlag, Etikette auf dem Umschlag
edition: 2 copies

thematic publication | *thematische Publikation*

layout by Ilya Kabakov | *Layout von Ilya Kabakov*

For the installation »The Palace of Projects«. Texts by Ilya and Emilia Kabakov; English, Russian.

Zur Installation »Palast der Projekte«. Texte von Ilya und Emilia Kabakov; englisch und russisch.

see also | *siehe auch* no. 95; no. 101; no. 117; CRI, vol. 2, no. 117, pp. 244–251; CRP, vol. 1, nos. 279–289, pp. 350–360

„РАССКАЗ О БЕЛЫХ ЧЕЛОВЕЧКАХ"

Е. Снегирева. Учительница. г. Кзыл-Орда.

Этот проект, о котором пойдет рассказ ниже, можно было бы кратко назвать: „О пользе истерии". Сразу же надо сказать, что речь идет здесь не о клинической форме истерии, а о тех периодических припадках слез, тоски, беспричинного глубокого отчаяния и горя, которые свойственны больным или склонным к истерии людям. Имеется в виду использования полезного, так сказать „здорового" зерна, которое находится внутри, как бы странно это ни звучало, любой болезни, в нашем случае истерии. Врачами давно установлено, что причиной истерии служит несовместимость самой глубины нашего существа, то, что обычно в просторечии называют „душой", с обстоятельствами существования человека на „этом свете", в более глубоком смысле — несогласие, непонимание души, почему она оказалась на „этом свете", почему, зачем она должна была воплотиться в эту свою „земную" жизнь. Это острое переживание своей непричастности, посторонности всему реальному, которое каждый раз обостряется в критических обстоятельствах и служит причиной часто роковых симптомов истерии.

Но с другой стороны „встреча" с собственной „душой", открытой и незащищенной, для человека очень полезна, дает возможность вернуться к „самому себе", к своему центру, к тому небольшому незащищенному „я", который внутри каждого из нас и есть то „настоящее", что мы собой представляем. И есть простой способ этого „возвращения". Возьмите небольшой лист бумаги. И начинайте, не задумываясь, писать рассказ о „белых человечках": как они выглядят, где вы их видели. Неважно, что на первых порах это покажется вам нелепо и смешно. Скоро вы увидите, что писать становится все легче, ваше воображение легко будет подсказывать вам все обстоятельства. Неудивительно: ваша душа, которая и есть „белый человечек" внутри вас, сама всплывет в ваше сознание и будет дальше диктовать ваш текст.

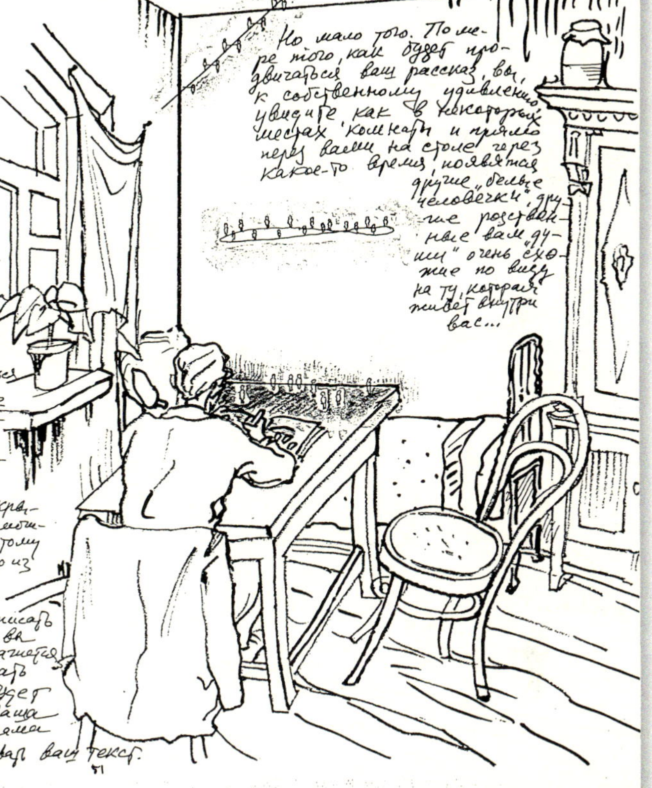

Но мало того. По мере того, как будет продвигаться ваш рассказ, вы, к собственному удивлению, увидите, как в некоторых местах комнаты и прямо перед вами на столе через какое-то время появятся другие „белые человечки", другие родственные вам „души", очень схожие по виду на ту, которая живет внутри вас...

51

ПРОЕКТ ОСТАВИТЬ ПАМЯТНИК О СЕБЕ

Р. Седов спортсмен чемпион по бегу. г. Ворошилов.

У каждого человека вполне естественное желание оставить по себе какой-нибудь памятник, и, конечно, чтобы он, по крайней мере, выполнил три условия: не мог бы исчезнуть за короткое время из-за непрочности материала, или из-за погодных или социальных катаклизмов; второе, — был в тоже время достаточно величественен и грандиозен, производил бы впечатление; и, конечно, третье условие: чтобы памятник носил отпечаток личности того, кому этот памятник поставлен, его неповторимой индивидуальности, а не только различным абстрактным идеям с которыми он соотносил себя в жизни.

Проект горного памятника, описанный ниже, удовлетворяет всем этим требованиям и добавляет еще одно свойство — его очень трудно повторить, он уникален в своем замысле и, вне сомнения, может быть рассмотрен и принят личностью не только сознающей свою уникальность и исключительность но и желающую и после своей смерти остаться вдали от шума людского, замкнуться и вечно пребывать среди величественного и недоступного людям ландшафта.

В недоступной горной местности разыскивается высокая расщелина между скал с каменным широким уступом внизу. С обеих ног того, кто хочет установить памятник, снимается гипсовый слепок до высоты голени, который и послужит моделью. После этого бригада взрывателей и каменотесов повторяет сначала в подошве скалы форму обеих ступней, пользуясь большим, но точным повторением модели, а затем в верхней части каменной расселины повторяет боковые части голени и задние части икр. После окончания этих скульптурных работ и полировки камня возникает эффект стоящей, и продавившей камень гигантской фигуры, которая затем ушла в неизвестном направлении.

Нет никаких сомнений, что в скором времени об этом будут распространятся легенды и это место окажется целью паломничества, тем более желанным, чем оно более будет недоступным.

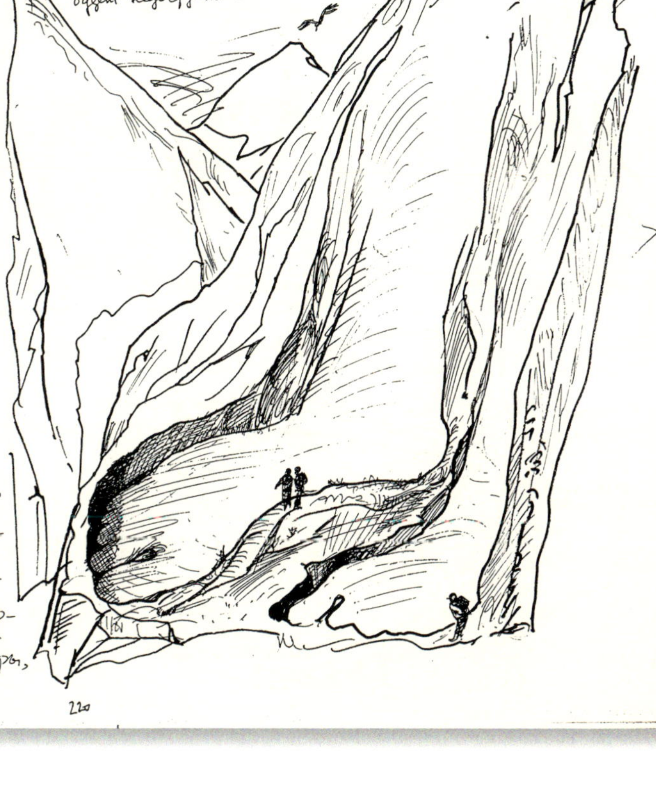

220

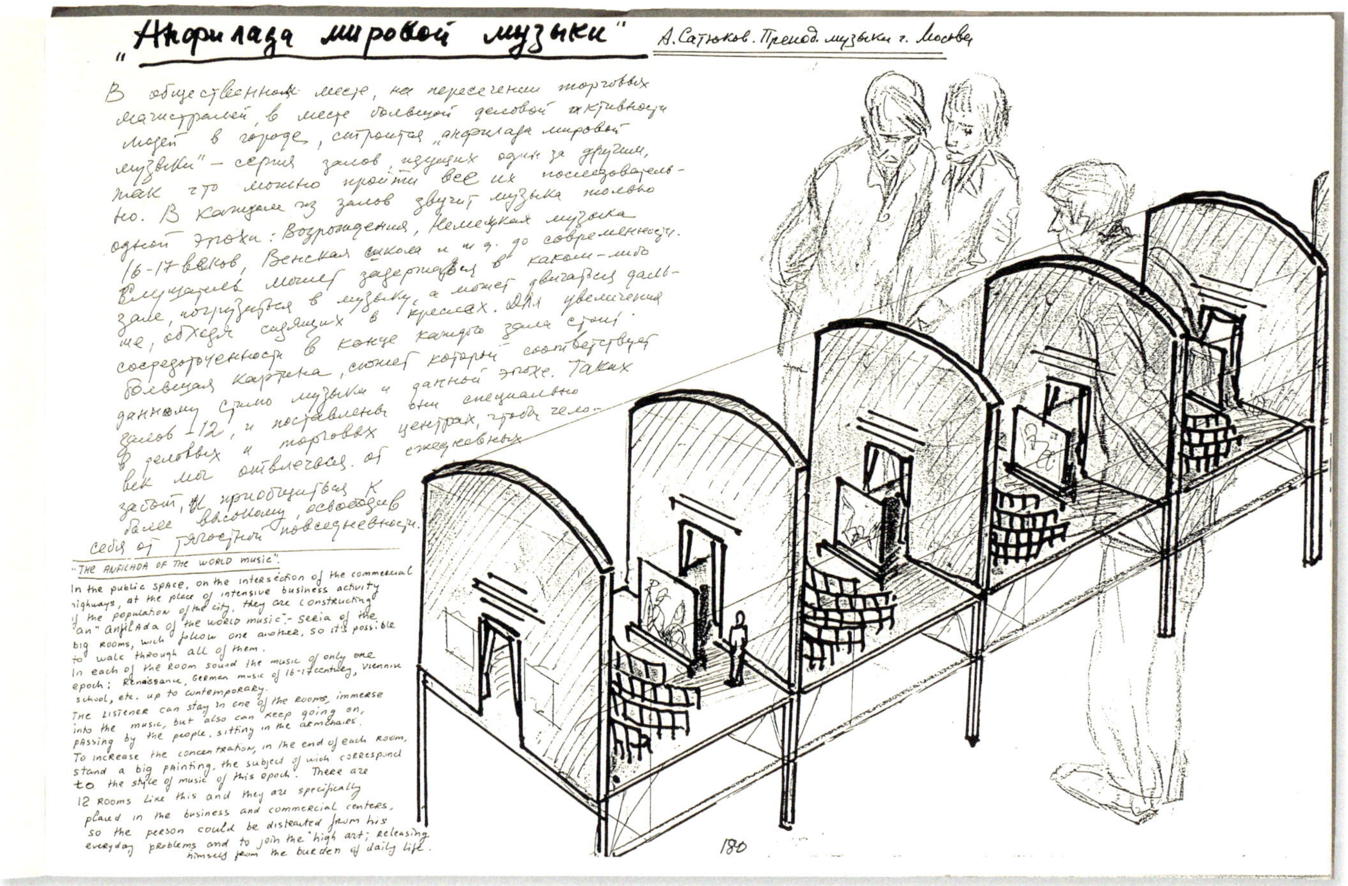
„Анфилада мировой музыки"
А. Сатюков. Препод. музыки г. Москва
В общественном месте, на пересечении торговых
магистралей, в месте большой деловой активности
людей в городе, строится „анфилада мировой
музыки" – серия залов, идущих один за другим,
так что можно пройти все их последователь-
но. В каждом из залов звучит музыка только
одной эпохи: Возрождения, Немецкая музыка
16-17 веков, Венская школа и т. д. до современности.
Слушатель может задержаться в каком-либо
зале, погрузиться в музыку, а может двигаться даль-
ше, обходя сидящих в креслах. Для увеличения
сосредоточенности в конце каждого зала стоит
большая картина, сюжет которой соответствует
данному стилю музыки и данной эпохе. Таких
залов 12, и поставлены они специально
в деловых и торговых центрах, чтобы чело-
век мог отвлечься от ежедневных
забот, и приобщиться к
более высокому, освободив
себя от тягостной повседневности.
"THE ANFILADA OF THE WORLD music".
In the public space, on the intersection of the commercial
highways, at the place of intensive business activity
of the population of the city, they are constructing
an "anfilada of the world music" - seria of the
big rooms, wich folow one another, so it's possible
to walk through all of them.
In each of the room sound the music of only one
epoch: Renaissance, German music of 16-17 century, viennise
school, etc. up to contemporary.
The listener can stay in one of the rooms, immerse
into the music, but also can keep going on,
passing by the people, sitting in the armchairs.
To increase the concentration, in the end of each room,
stand a big painting, the subject of wich correspond
to the style of music of this epoch. There are
12 rooms like this and they are specifically
placed in the business and commercial centers,
so the person could be distracted from his
everyday problems and to join the "high art; releasing
himself from the burden of daily life.
180

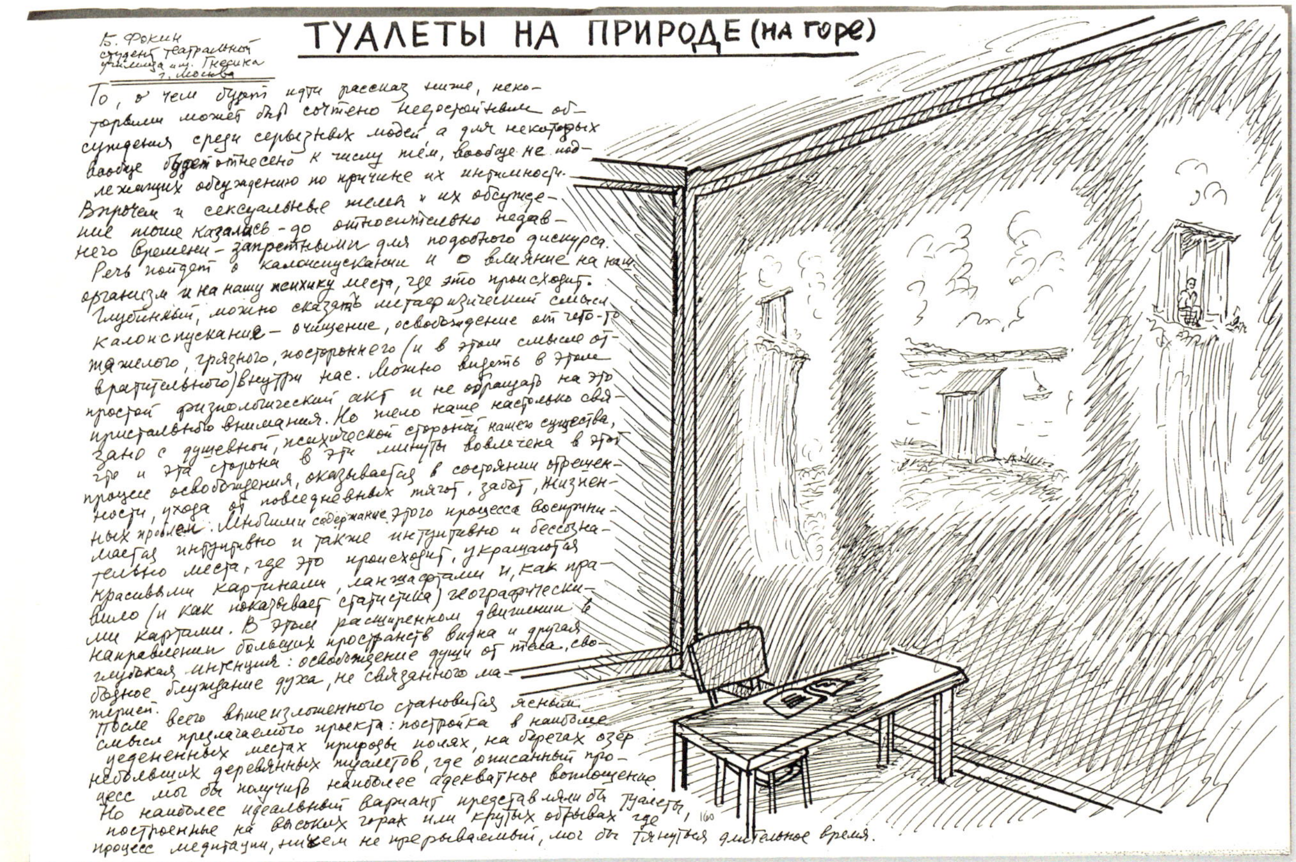
ТУАЛЕТЫ НА ПРИРОДЕ (на горе)
Б. Фокин
студент театрального
училища им. Щукина
г. Москва
То, о чем будет идти рассказ ниже, неко-
торыми может быть сочтено недостойным об-
суждения среди серьезных людей, а для некоторых
вообще будет отнесено к числу тем, вообще не под-
лежащих обсуждению по причине их интимности.
Впрочем и сексуальные темы и их обсужде-
ние тоже казались - до относительно недав-
него времени - запретными для подобного дискурса.
Речь пойдет о калоиспускании и о влияние на наш
организм и на нашу психику места, где это происходит.
Глубинный, можно сказать метафизический смысл
калоиспускания - очищение, освобождение от чего-то
тяжелого, грязного, постороннего (и в этом смысле от-
вратительного) внутри нас. Можно видеть в этом
простой физиологический акт и не обращать на это
пристального внимания. Но тело наше настолько свя-
зано с душевной, психической стороной нашего существа,
что и эта сторона в эти минуты вовлечена в этот
процесс освобождения, оказываеться в состоянии отрешен-
ности, ухода от повседневных тягот, забот, жизнен-
ных проблем. Многими содержание этого процесса воспрini-
мается интуитивно и также интуитивно и бессозна-
тельно места, где это происходит, украшаются
красивыми картинами, ландшафтами и, как пра-
вило (и как показывает статистика) географически-
ми картами. В этом расширенном движении в
направлении больших пространств видна и другая
глубокая интенция: освобождение души от тела, сво-
бодное блуждание духа, не связанного ма-
терией. После всего вышеизложенного становиться ясным
смысл предлагаемого проекта: постройка в наиболее
уединенных местах природы полях, на берегах озер
небольших деревянных туалетов, где описанный про-
цесс мог бы получить наиболее адекватное воплощение.
Но наиболее идеальный вариант представляли бы туалеты,
построенные на высоких горах или крутых обрывах где
процесс медитации, ничем не прерываемый, мог бы тянуться длительное время.
160

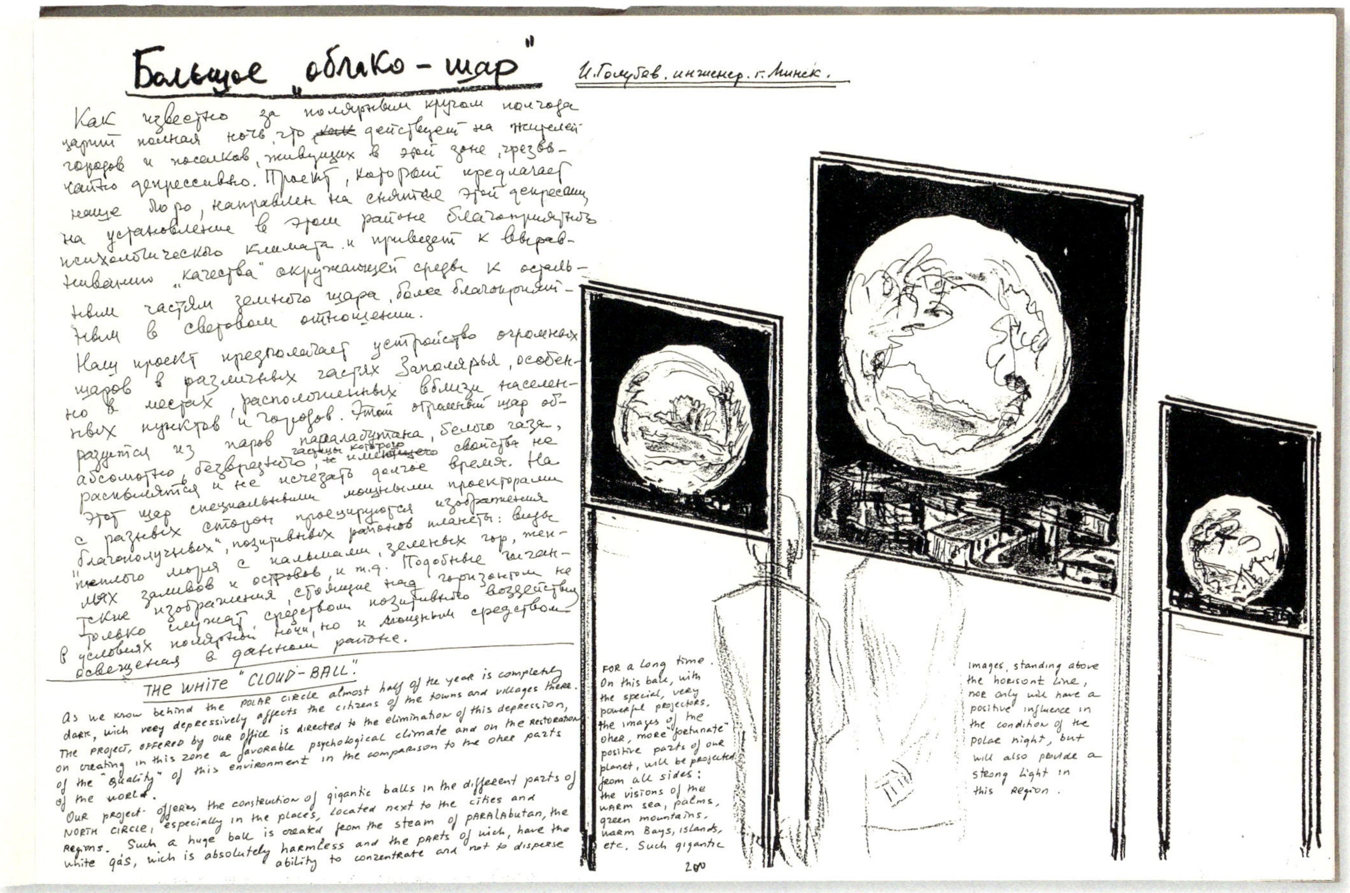

Большое „облако-шар"

И. Голубев. инженер. г. Минск.

Как известно за полярным кругом полгода
царит полная ночь, что ~~как~~ действует на жителей
городов и поселков, живущих в этой зоне, чрезвы-
чайно депрессивно. Проект, который предлагает
наше бюро, направлен на снятие этой депрессии,
на установление в этом районе благоприятного
психологического климата и приведет к вырав-
ниванию „качества" окружающей среды к осталь-
ным частям земного шара, более благоприят-
ным в световом отношении.

Наш проект предполагает устройство огромных
шаров в различных частях Заполярья, особен-
но в местах расположенных вблизи населен-
ных пунктов и городов. Этот огромный шар об-
разуется из паров паралабутана, белого газа,
абсолютно безвредного, частицы которого ~~не имеющего~~ свойства не
рассеиваться и не исчезать долгое время. На
этот шар специальными мощными проекторами
с разных сторон проецируются изображения
„благополучных", позитивных районов планеты: виды
теплого моря с пальмами, зеленых гор, теп-
лых заливов и островов, и т.д. Подобные гиган-
тские изображения, стоящие над горизонтом не
только служат средством позитивного воздействия
в условиях полярной ночи, но и мощным средством
освещения в данном районе.

THE WHITE "CLOUD-BALL".

As we know behind the POLAR CIRCLE almost half of the year is completely dark, wich very depressively affects the citizens of the towns and villages there. The project, offered by our office is directed to the elimination of this depression, on creating in this zone a favorable psychological climate and on the restoration of the "quality" of this environment in the comparison to the other parts of the world.

Our project offers the construction of gigantic balls in the different parts of NORTH CIRCLE, especially in the places, located next to the cities and regions. Such a huge ball is created from the steam of PARALAbutan, the white gas, wich is absolutely harmless and the parts of wich, have the ability to concentrate and not to disperse for a long time. On this ball, with the special, very powerful projectors, the images of the other, more "fortunate" positive parts of our planet, will be projected from all sides: the visions of the warm sea, palms, green mountains, warm Bays, islands, etc. Such gigantic images, standing above the horisont line, not only will have a positive influence in the condition of the polar night, but will also provide a strong light in this region.

200

103 Old Bridge | *Alte Brücke*

1998

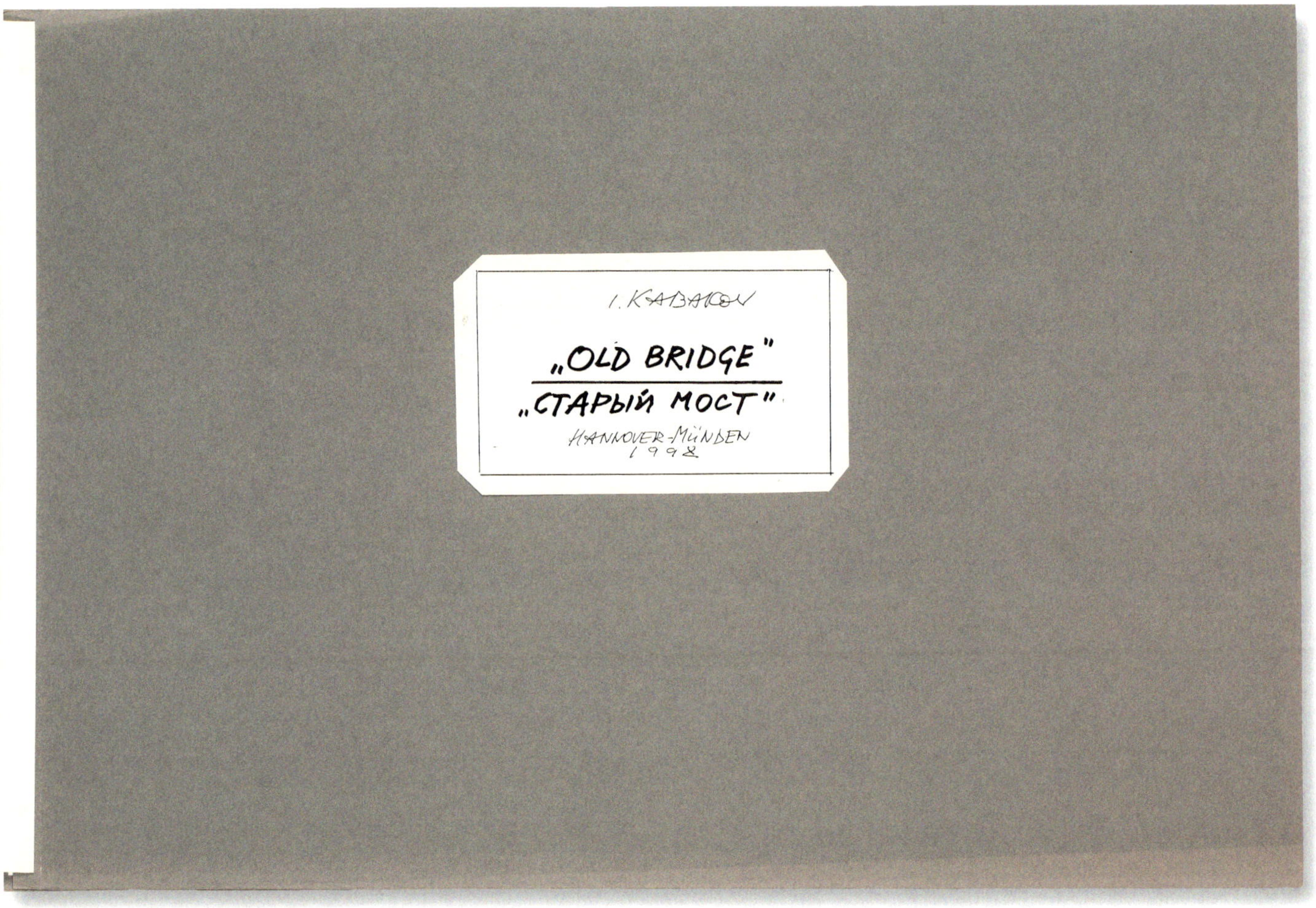

Ilya Kabakov
New York: published by the author
27.9 x 43.3 cm
9 photocopied pp. with 7 (3 color) ills.
quick bind, paper cover, label on the cover
Schnellhefter, Kartonumschlag, Etikette auf dem Umschlag
edition: 2 copies

thematic publication | *thematische Publikation*

layout by Ilya Kabakov | *Layout von Ilya Kabakov*

Documentation of the installation of the same name in the exhibition »3 Räume – 3 Flüsse«, Hannoversch Münden, Germany, October 12 to November 30, 2000. Texts by Ilya Kabakov; Russian, English.

Dokumentation der gleichnamigen Installation zur Ausstellung »3 Räume – 3 Flüsse«, Hannoversch Münden, Deutschland, 12. Oktober – 30. November 2000. Texte von Ilya Kabakov; russisch, englisch.

see also | *siehe auch* CRI, vol. 2, no. 137, pp. 334–339

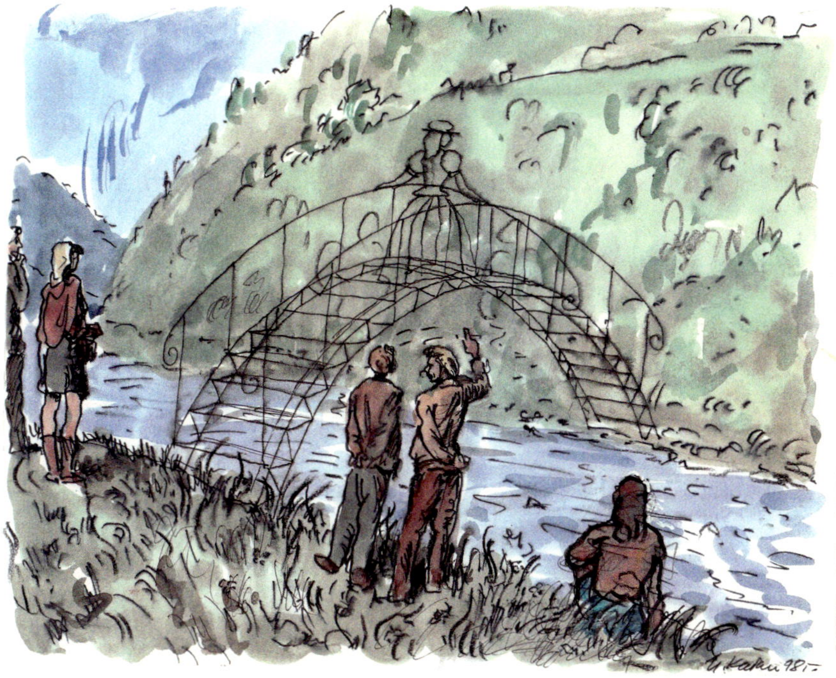

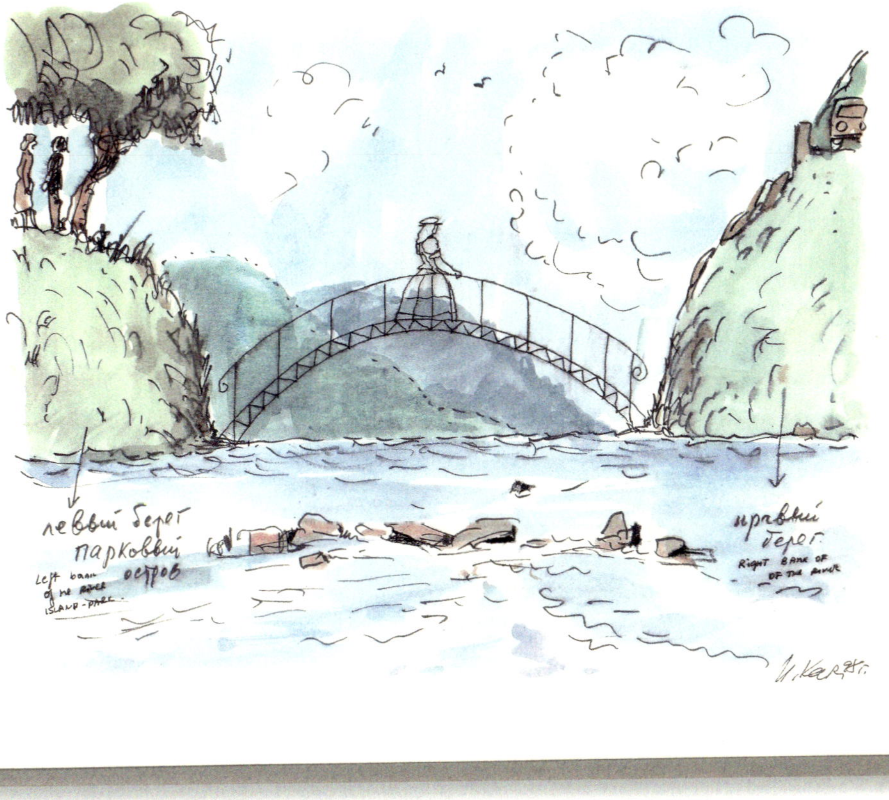
левый берег
парковый остров
Left bank
ISLAND-PARK
правый берег
RIGHT BANK OF
OF THE RIVER

104 Monument to a Lost Civilization | *Denkmal für eine untergegangene Zivilisation*

with Emilia Kabakov | *mit Emilia Kabakov*

1999

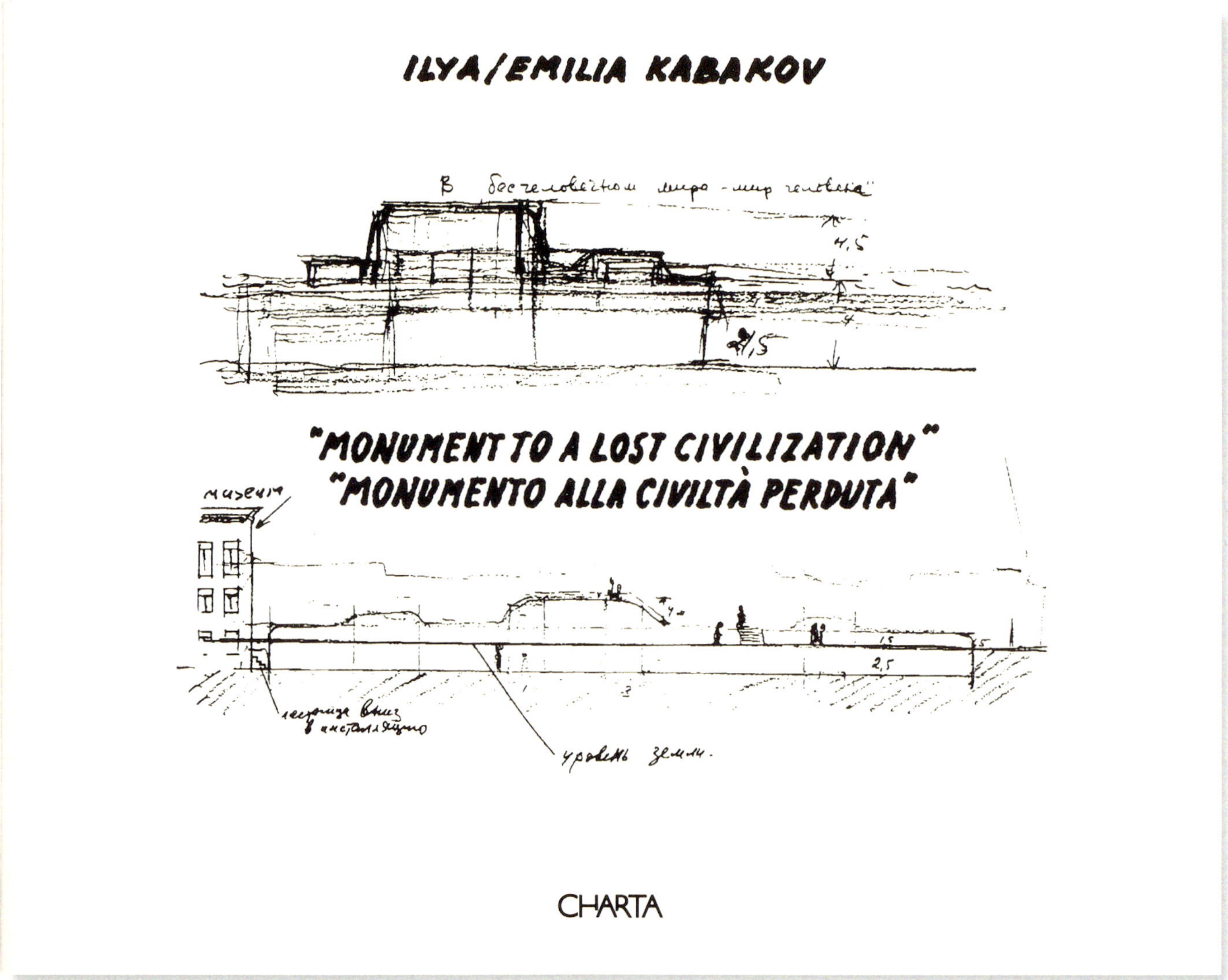

Chiara Bertola, Paolo Falcone
Milan: Charta
21 x 27 cm
247 pp. with 180 (137 color) ills.
stitchbound, softback
Fadenheftung, broschiert

exhibition catalogue | *Ausstellungskatalog*

layout by Ilya Kabakov | *Layout von Ilya Kabakov*

Documentation of the installation of the same name at Cantieri Culturali alla Zisa, Palermo, April 16 to June 27, 1999. Texts by Chiara Bertola, Ilya Kabakov, and Bianca Tarozzi, and a dialogue between Paolo Falcone and Ilya and Emilia Kabakov; Italian, English.

Dokumentation der gleichnamigen Installation, Cantieri Culturali alla Zisa, Palermo, 16. April – 27. Juni 1999. Texte von Chiara Bertola, Ilya Kabakov und Bianca Tarozzi sowie ein Dialog von Paolo Falcone mit Ilya und Emilia Kabakov; italienisch, englisch.

see also | *siehe auch* CRI, vol. 2, no. 141, pp. 356–363

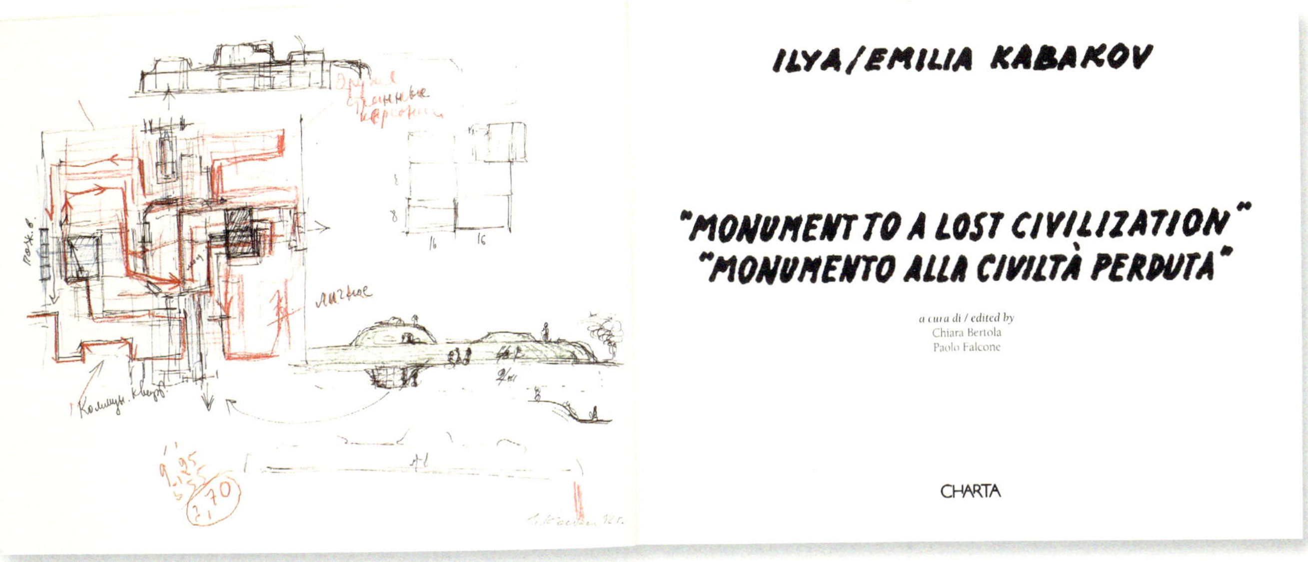

ILYA/EMILIA KABAKOV

"MONUMENT TO A LOST CIVILIZATION"
"MONUMENTO ALLA CIVILTÀ PERDUTA"

a cura di / edited by
Chiara Bertola
Paolo Falcone

CHARTA

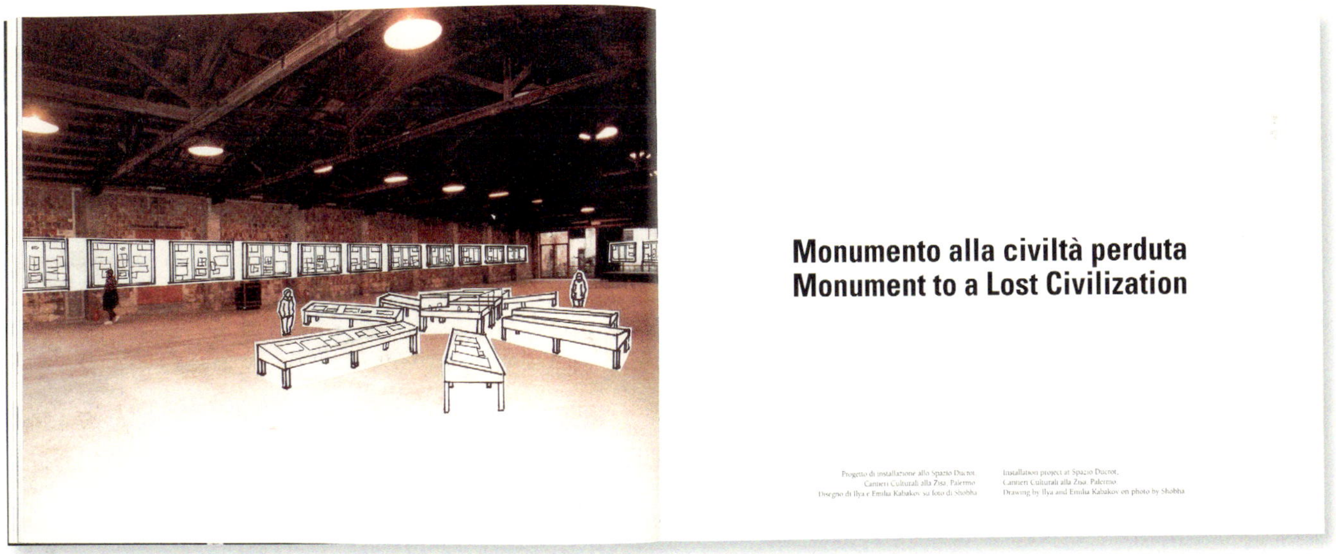

Monumento alla civiltà perduta
Monument to a Lost Civilization

Progetto di installazione allo Spazio Ducrot,
Cantieri Culturali alla Zisa, Palermo
Disegno di Ilya e Emilia Kabakov su foto di Shobha

Installation project at Spazio Ducrot,
Cantieri Culturali alla Zisa, Palermo
Drawing by Ilya and Emilia Kabakov on photo by Shobha

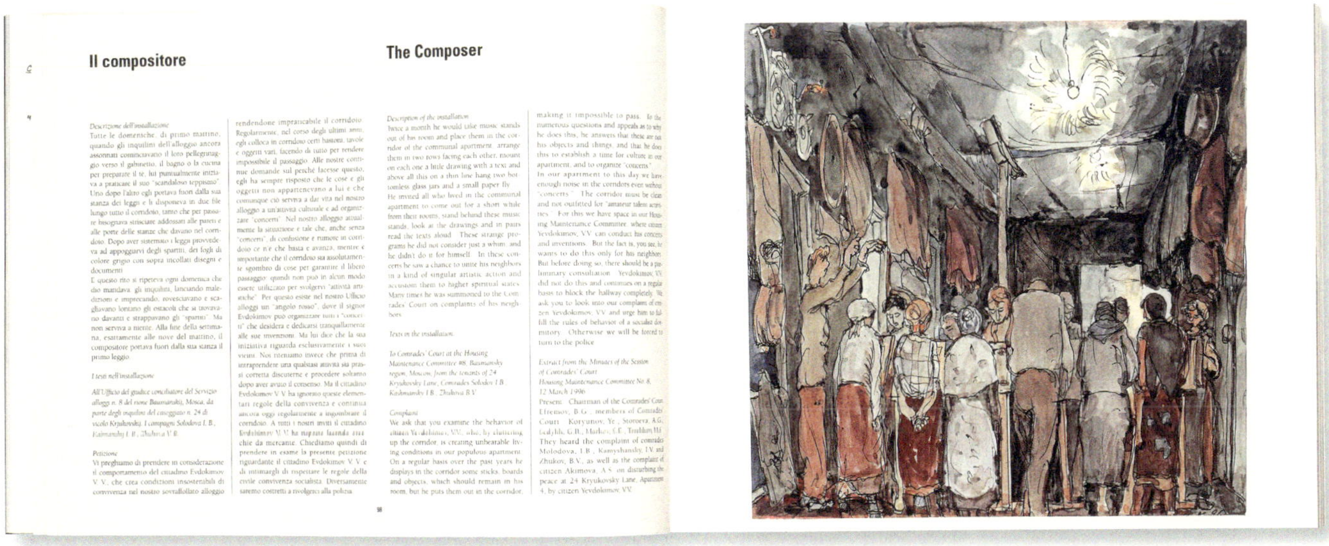

Il compositore

The Composer

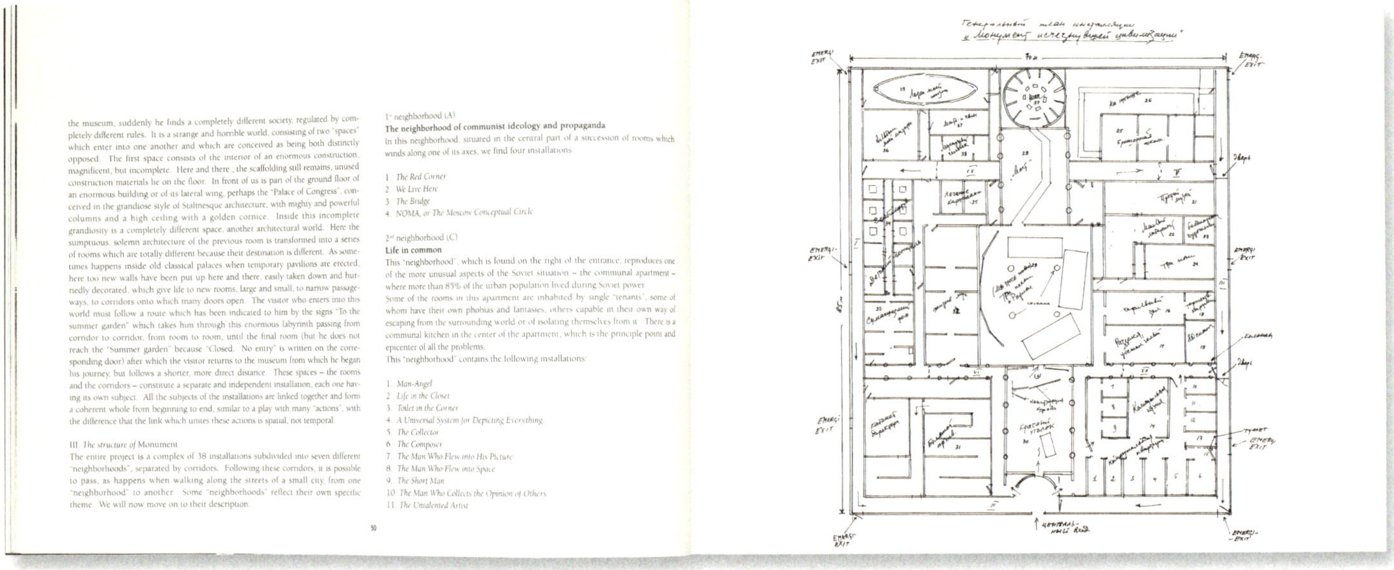

the museum, suddenly he finds a completely different society, regulated by completely different rules. It is a strange and horrible world, consisting of two "spaces" which enter into one another and which are conceived as being both distinctly opposed. The first space consists of the interior of an enormous construction, magnificent, but incomplete. Here and there, the scaffolding still remains, unused construction materials lie on the floor. In front of us is part of the ground floor of an enormous building or of its lateral wing, perhaps the "Palace of Congress", conceived in the grandiose style of Stalinesque architecture, with mighty and powerful columns and a high ceiling with a golden cornice. Inside this incomplete grandiosity is a completely different space, another architectural world. Here the sumptuous, solemn architecture of the previous room is transformed into a series of rooms which are totally different because their destination is different. As sometimes happens inside old classical palaces when temporary pavilions are erected, here too new walls have been put up here and there, easily taken down and hurriedly decorated, which give life to new rooms, large and small, to narrow passageways, to corridors onto which many doors open. The visitor who enters into this world must follow a route which has been indicated to him by the signs "To the summer garden" which takes him through this enormous labyrinth passing from corridor to corridor, from room to room, until the final room (but he does not reach the "Summer garden" because "Closed. No entry" is written on the corresponding door) after which the visitor returns to the museum from which he began his journey, but follows a shorter, more direct distance. These spaces – the rooms and the corridors – constitute a separate and independent installation, each one having its own subject. All the subjects of the installations are linked together and form a coherent whole from beginning to end, similar to a play with many "actions", with the difference that the link which unites these actions is spatial, not temporal.

III. *The structure of* Monument
The entire project is a complex of 38 installations subdivided into seven different "neighborhoods", separated by corridors. Following these corridors, it is possible to pass, as happens when walking along the streets of a small city, from one "neighborhood" to another. Some "neighborhoods" reflect their own specific theme. We will now move on to their description.

1st neighborhood (A)
The neighborhood of communist ideology and propaganda
In this neighborhood, situated in the central part of a succession of rooms which winds along one of its axes, we find four installations

1. *The Red Corner*
2. *We Live Here*
3. *The Bridge*
4. *NOMA, or The Moscow Conceptual Circle*

2nd neighborhood (C)
Life in common
This "neighborhood", which is found on the right of the entrance, reproduces one of the more unusual aspects of the Soviet situation – the communal apartment – where more than 85% of the urban population lived during Soviet power.
Some of the rooms in this apartment are inhabited by single "tenants", some of whom have their own phobias and fantasies, others capable in their own way of escaping from the surrounding world or of isolating themselves from it. There is a communal kitchen in the center of the apartment, which is the principle point and epicenter of all the problems.
This "neighborhood" contains the following installations:

1. *Man-Angel*
2. *Life in the Closet*
3. *Toilet in the Corner*
4. *A Universal System for Depicting Everything*
5. *The Collector*
6. *The Composer*
7. *The Man Who Flew into His Picture*
8. *The Man Who Flew into Space*
9. *The Short Man*
10. *The Man Who Collects the Opinion of Others*
11. *The Untalented Artist*

50

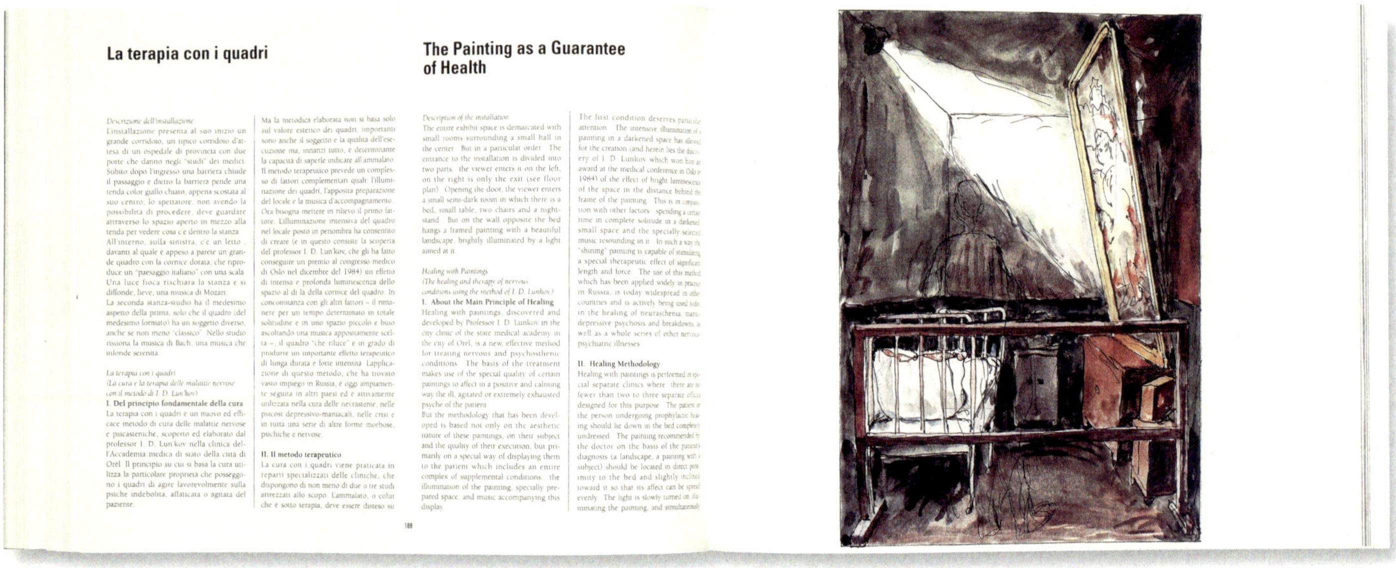

La terapia con i quadri

Descrizione dell'installazione
L'installazione presenta al suo inizio un grande corridoio, un tipico corridoio d'attesa di un ospedale di provincia con due porte che danno negli "studi" dei medici. Subito dopo l'ingresso una barriera chiude il passaggio e dietro la barriera pende una tenda color giallo chiaro, appena scostata al suo centro; lo spettatore, non avendo la possibilità di procedere, deve guardare attraverso lo spazio aperto in mezzo alla tenda per vedere cosa c'è dentro la stanza.
All'interno, sulla sinistra, c'è un letto, davanti al quale è appeso a parete un grande quadro con la cornice dorata, che riproduce un "paesaggio italiano" con una scala. Una luce fioca rischiara la stanza e si diffonde, lieve, una musica di Mozart.
La seconda stanza-studio ha il medesimo aspetto della prima, solo che il quadro (del medesimo formato) ha un soggetto diverso, anche se non meno "classico". Nello studio risuona la musica di Bach, una musica che infonde serenità.

La terapia con i quadri
(La cura e la terapia delle malattie nervose con il metodo di I. D. Lun'kov)
I. Del principio fondamentale della cura
La terapia con i quadri è un nuovo ed efficace metodo di cura delle malattie nervose e psicasteniche, scoperto ed elaborato dal professor I. D. Lun'kov nella clinica dell'Accademia medica di stato della città di Orël. Il principio su cui si basa la cura utilizza la particolare proprietà che posseggono i quadri di agire favorevolmente sulla psiche indebolita, affaticata o agitata del paziente.
Ma la metodica elaborata non si basa solo sul valore estetico dei quadri, importanti sono anche il soggetto e la qualità dell'esecuzione ma, innanzi tutto, è determinante la capacità di saperle indicare all'ammalato. Il metodo terapeutico prevede un complesso di fattori complementari quali: l'illuminazione dei quadri, l'apposita preparazione del locale e la musica d'accompagnamento. Ora bisogna mettere in rilievo il primo fattore. L'illuminazione intensiva del quadro nel locale posto in penombra ha consentito di creare (e in questo consiste la scoperta del professor I. D. Lun'kov, che gli ha fatto conseguire un premio al congresso medico di Oslo nel dicembre del 1984) un effetto di intensa e profonda luminescenza dello spazio al di là della cornice del quadro. In concomitanza con gli altri fattori – il rimanere per un tempo determinato in totale solitudine e in uno spazio piccolo e buio ascoltando una musica appositamente scelta –, il quadro "che riluce" è in grado di produrre un importante effetto terapeutico di lunga durata e forte intensità. L'applicazione di questo metodo, che ha trovato vasto impiego in Russia, è oggi ampiamente seguita in altri paesi ed è attivamente utilizzata nella cura delle nevrastenie, nelle psicosi depressivo-maniacali, nelle crisi e in tutta una serie di altre forme morbose, psichiche e nervose.

II. Il metodo terapeutico
La cura con i quadri viene praticata in reparti specializzati delle cliniche, che dispongono di non meno di due o tre studi attrezzati allo scopo. L'ammalato, o colui che è sotto terapia, deve essere disteso su

The Painting as a Guarantee of Health

Description of the installation:
The entire exhibit space is demarcated with small rooms surrounding a small hall in the center. But in a particular order. The entrance to the installation is divided into two parts: the viewer enters it on the left, on the right is only the exit (see floor plan). Opening the door, the viewer enters a small semi-dark room in which there is a bed, small table, two chairs and a night-stand. But on the wall opposite the bed hangs a framed painting with a beautiful landscape, brightly illuminated by a light aimed at it.

Healing with Paintings
(The healing and therapy of nervous conditions using the method of I. D. Lunkov)
I. About the Main Principle of Healing
Healing with paintings, discovered and developed by Professor I. D. Lunkov in the city clinic of the state medical academy in the city of Orel, is a new, effective method for treating nervous and psychosthenic conditions. The basis of the treatment makes use of the special quality of certain paintings to affect in a positive and calming way the ill, agitated or extremely exhausted psyche of the patient.
But the methodology that has been developed is based not only on the aesthetic nature of these paintings, on their subject and the quality of their execution, but primarily on a special way of displaying them to the patient which includes an entire complex of supplemental conditions: the illumination of the painting, specially prepared space, and music accompanying this display.
The first condition deserves particular attention. The intensive illumination of a painting in a darkened space has allowed for the creation (and herein lies the discovery of I. D. Lunkov which won him an award at the medical conference in Oslo in 1984) of the effect of bright luminescence of the space in the distance behind the frame of the painting. This is in conjunction with other factors: spending a certain time in complete solitude in a darkened small space and the specially selected music resounding in it. In such a way the "shining" painting is capable of stimulating a special therapeutic effect of significant length and force. The use of this method which has been applied widely in practice in Russia, is today widespread in other countries and is actively being used today in the healing of neurasthenia, manic-depressive psychosis and breakdowns as well as a whole series of other nervous-psychiatric illnesses.

II. Healing Methodology
Healing with paintings is performed in special separate clinics where there are no fewer than two to three separate offices designed for this purpose. The patient or the person undergoing prophylactic healing should lie down in the bed completely undressed. The painting recommended by the doctor on the basis of the patient's diagnosis (a landscape, a painting with a subject) should be located in direct proximity to the bed and slightly inclined toward it so that its affect can be spread evenly. The light is slowly turned on, illuminating the painting, and simultaneously

188

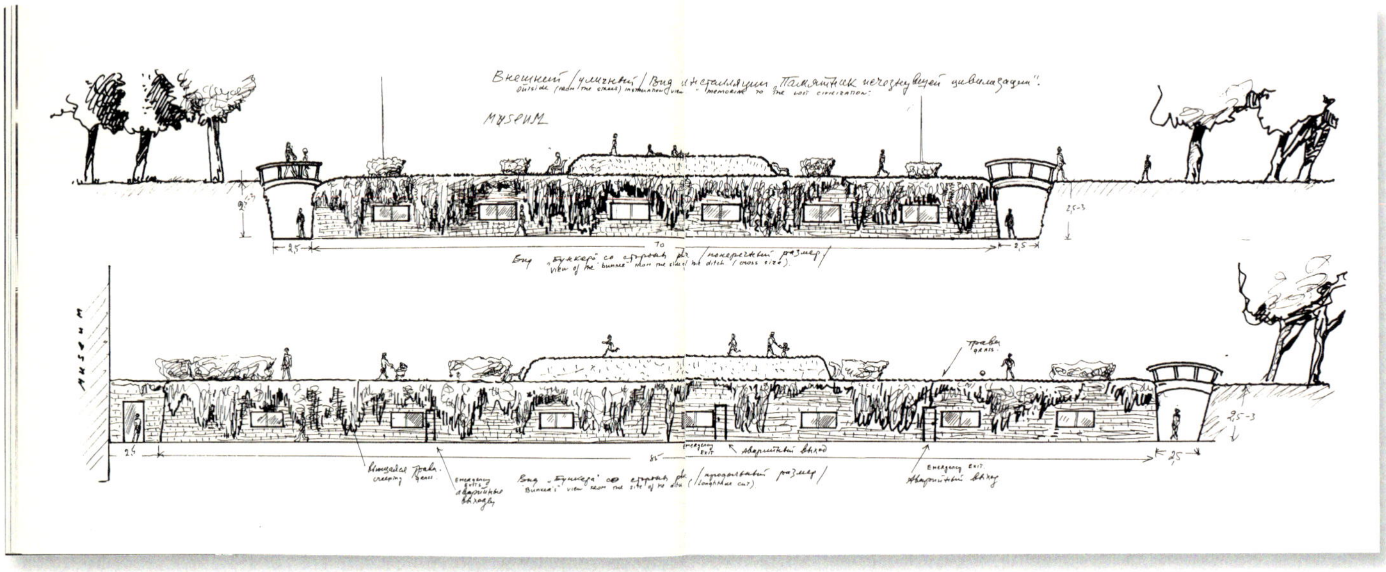

105 The Old Reading Room | *Der alte Lesesaal*

1999

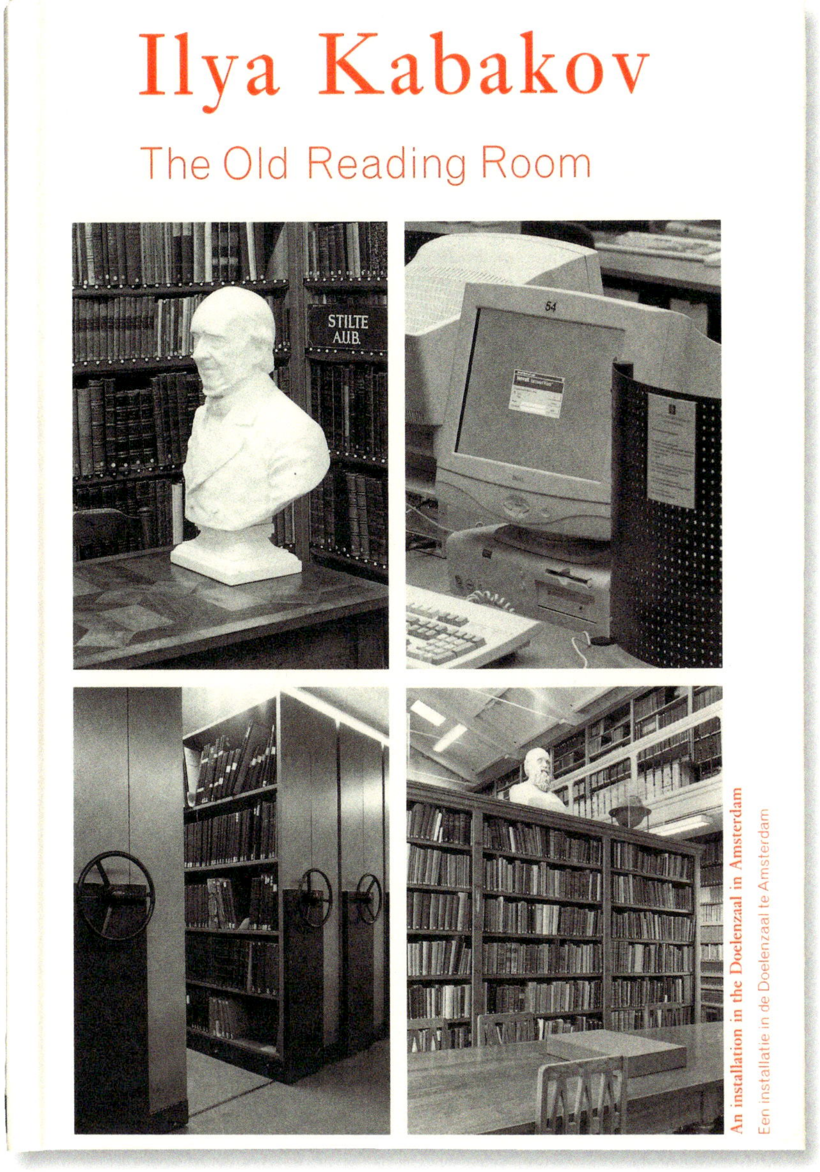

Bibliotheek van de Universiteit van Amsterdam
Amsterdam: Vossiuspers AUP
23.4 x 16.7 cm
35 [+ 21] pp. with 15 (10 color) ills.
stitchbound, hardcover
Fadenheftung, Hardcover

exhibition catalogue | *Ausstellungskatalog*

layout by Ilya Kabakov | *Layout von Ilya Kabakov*

For the installation of the same name at the Universiteit van Amsterdam, Universiteitsbibliotheek, Doelenzaal, Amsterdam, July 8 to August 6, 1999. Text by Ilya Kabakov, and a dialogue between Boris Groys and Ilya Kabakov on »The Library as Installation«; English, Dutch.

Zur gleichnamigen Installation, Universiteit van Amsterdam, Universiteitsbibliotheek, Doelenzaal, Amsterdam, 8. Juli – 6. August 1999. Text von Ilya Kabakov und ein Dialog von Boris Groys und Ilya Kabakov über »Die Bibliothek als Installation«; englisch, niederländisch.

see also | *siehe auch* CRI, vol. 2, no. 143, pp. 370–375

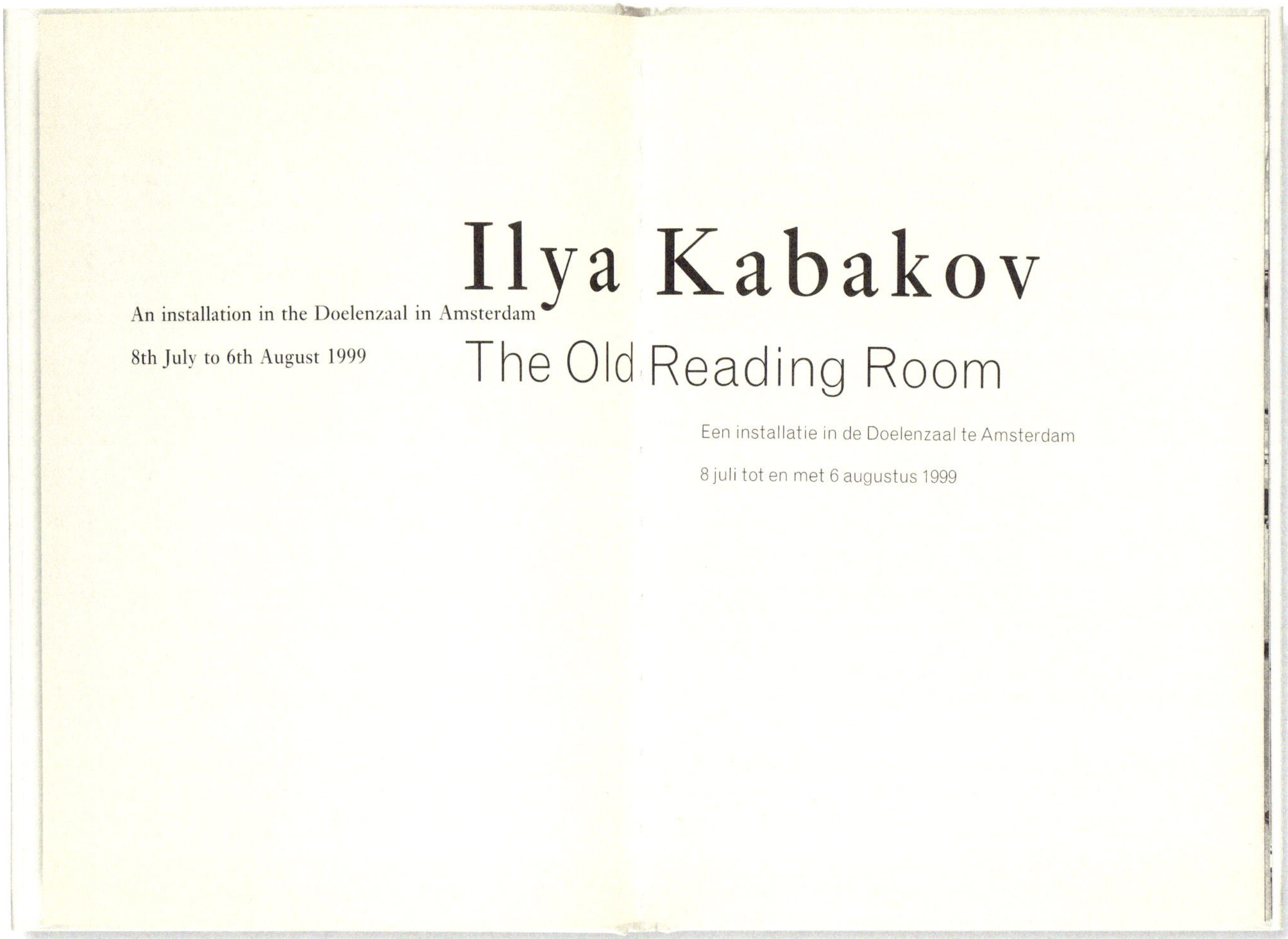

Ilya Kabakov

An installation in the Doelenzaal in Amsterdam

8th July to 6th August 1999

The Old Reading Room

Een installatie in de Doelenzaal te Amsterdam

8 juli tot en met 6 augustus 1999

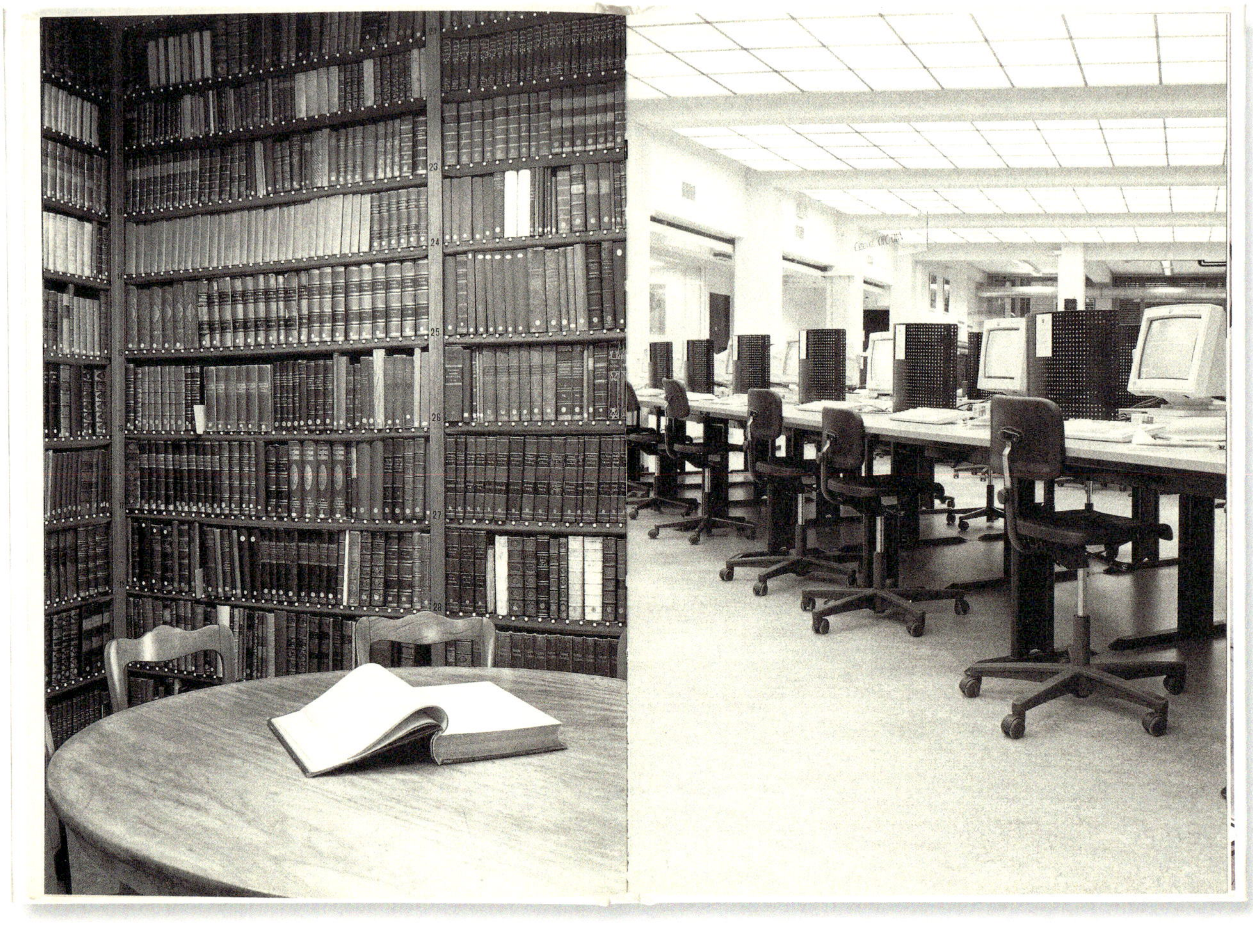

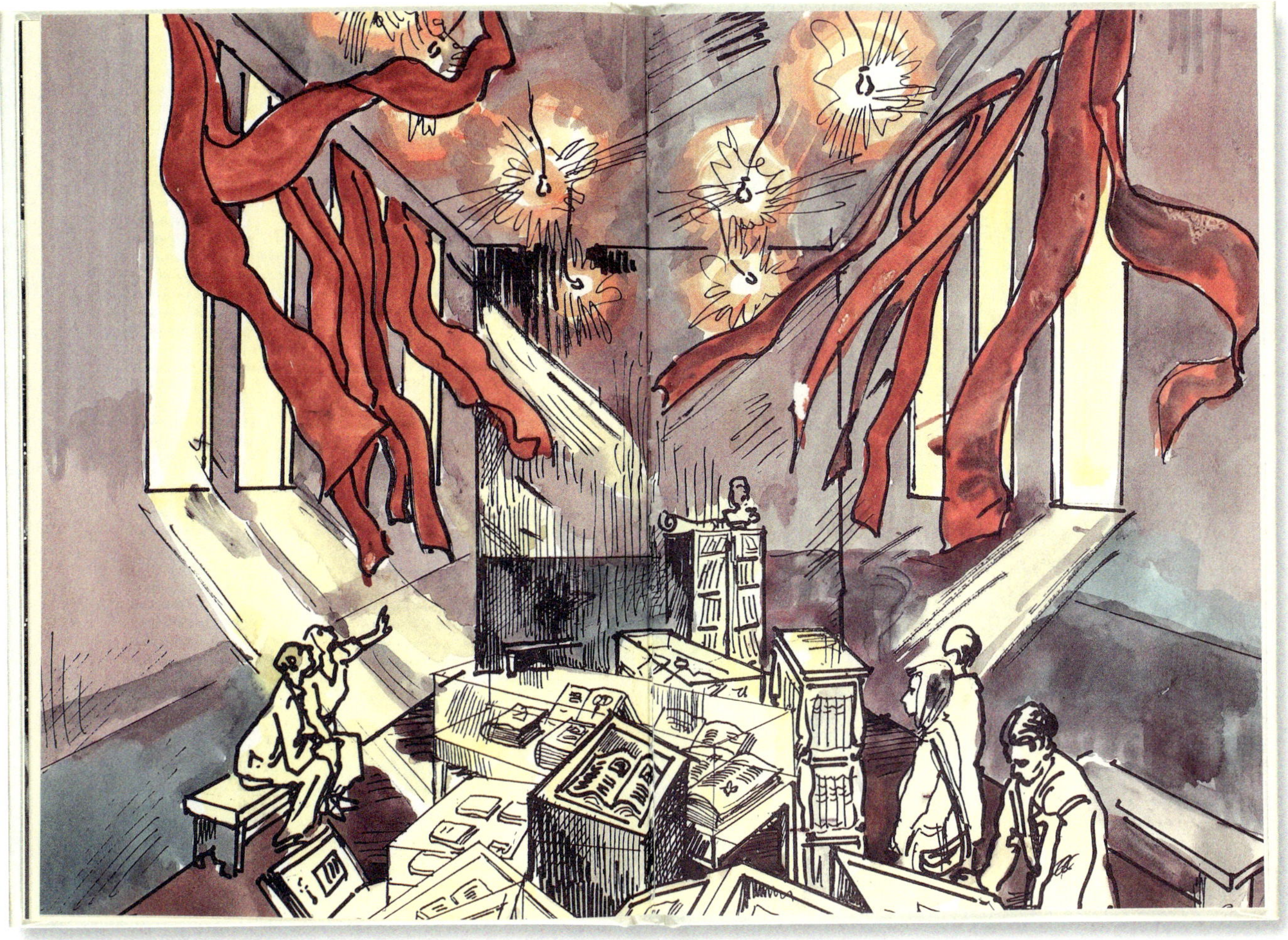

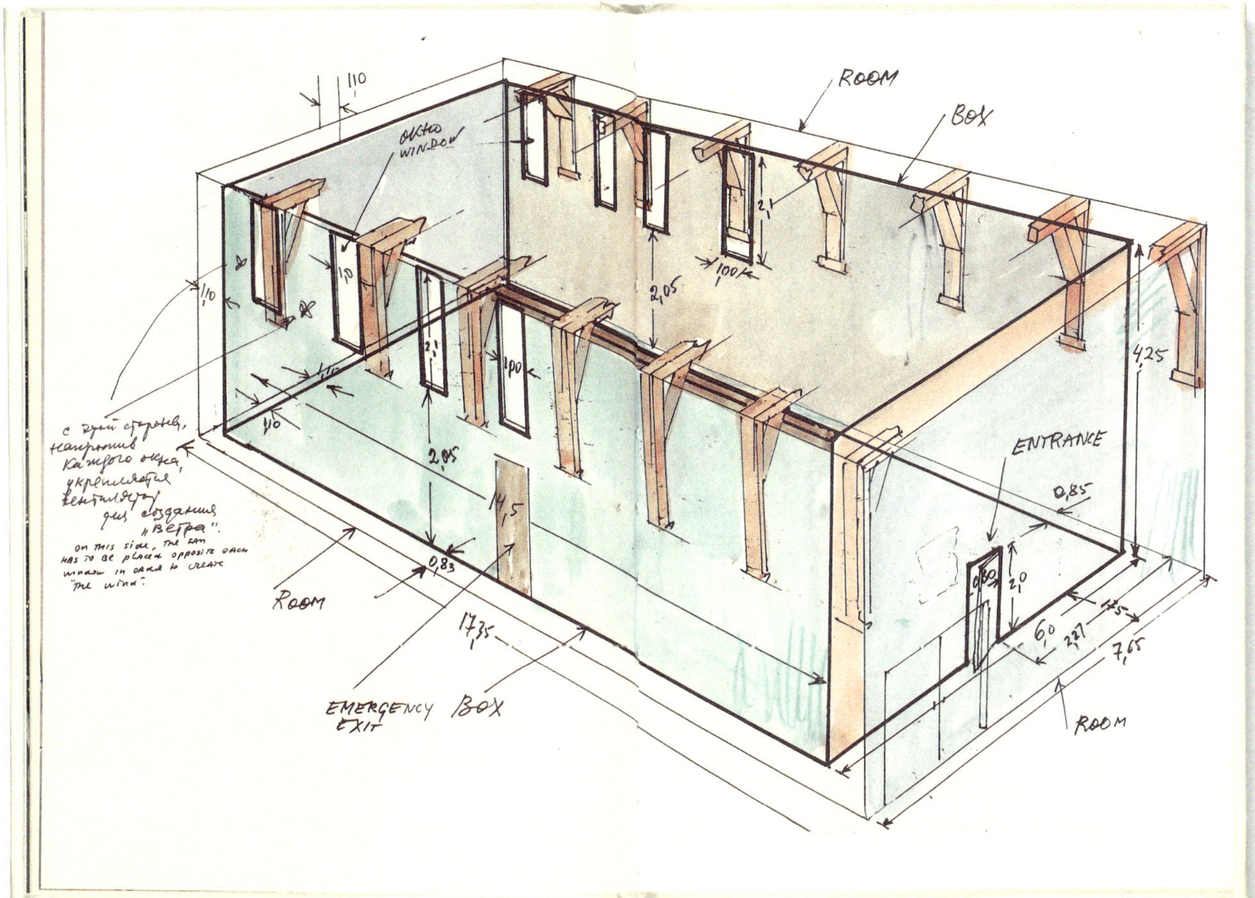
ROOM
BOX
WINDOW
ENTRANCE
ROOM
EMERGENCY EXIT
BOX
ROOM
ON THIS SIDE, THE FAN HAS TO BE PLACED OPPOSITE EACH WINDOW IN ORDER TO CREATE "THE WIND".
14,5
17,35
4,25
7,65
2,05
0,85
0,83

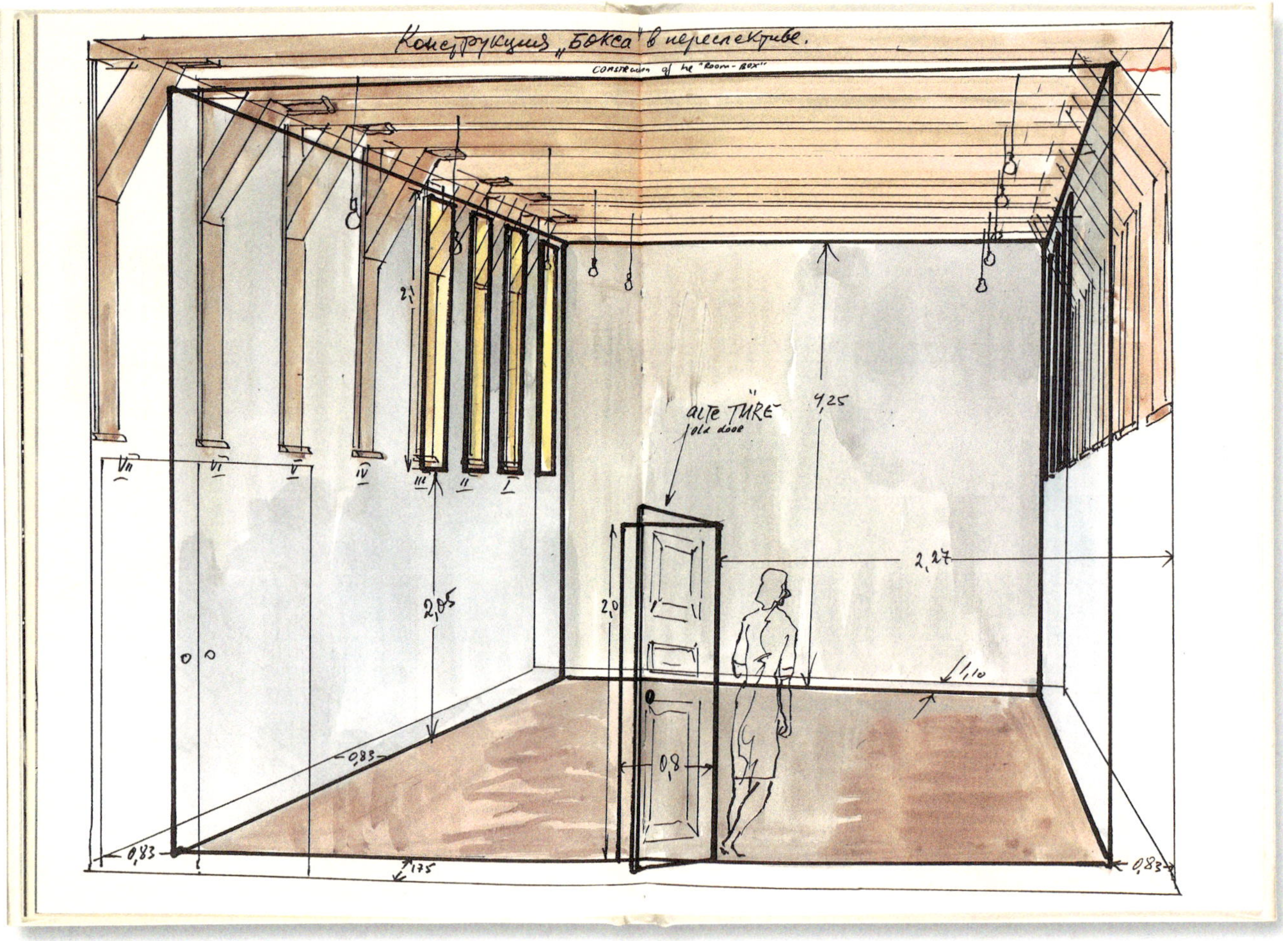
Конструкция „бокса" в перспективе.
ALTE TÜRE
old door
4,25
2,27
2,05
2,0
0,83
0,8
1,75
0,83

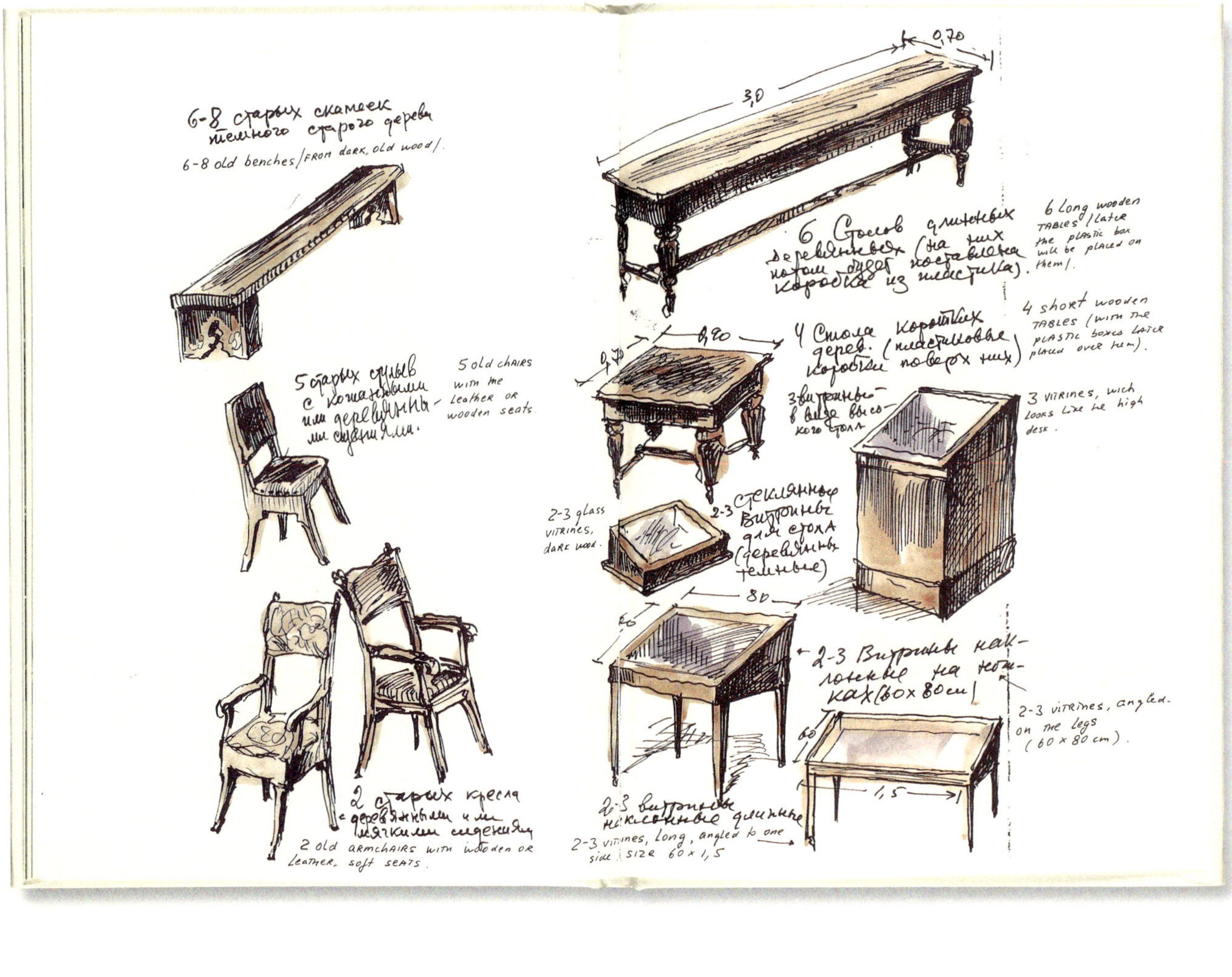
6-8 старых скамеек темного старого дерева
6-8 old benches /FROM dark, old wood/.
5 старых стульев с кожаными или деревянными сиденьями.
5 old chairs with the leather or wooden seats.
3,0
0,70
6 столов длинных деревянных (на них потом будет поставлена коробка из пластика).
6 Long wooden TABLES / Later the plastic box will be placed on them /.
4 стола коротких дерев. (пластиковые коробки поверх них)
4 short wooden TABLES (with the plastic boxes Later placed over them).
3 витрины в виде высокого стола
3 vitrines, wich looks like the high desk.
2-3 стеклянные витрины для стола (деревянные темные)
2-3 glass vitrines, dark wood.
80
2-3 витрины наклонные на ножках (60×80 см)
2-3 vitrines, angled. on the legs (60 x 80 cm).
2 старых кресла с деревянными или мягкими сидениями
2 old armchairs with wooden or leather soft seats.
2-3 витрины наклонные длинные
2-3 vitrines, long, angled to one side size 60 x 1,5
1,5

106 Life and Creativity of Charles Rosenthal (1898–1933)

Leben und Werk von Charles Rosenthal (1898–1933)

1999

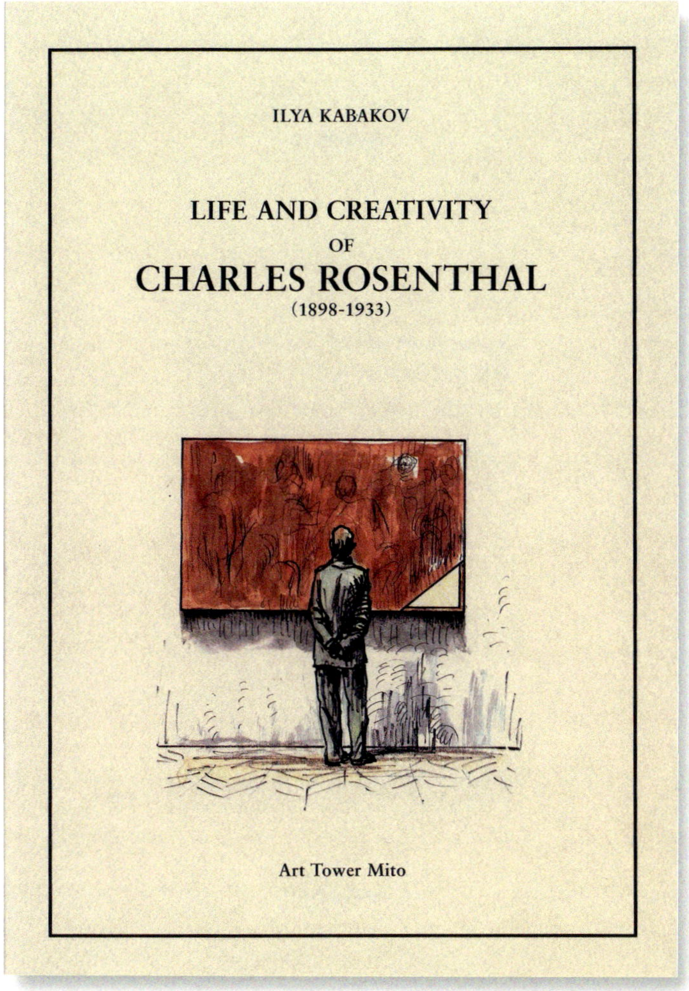

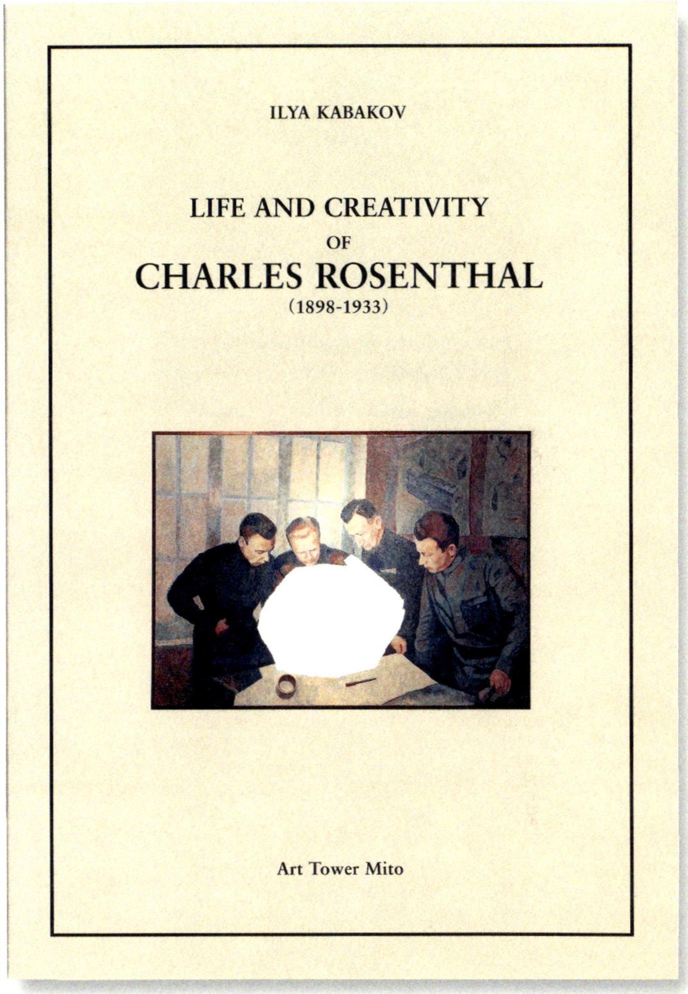

Eriko Osaka
Mito: Contemporary Art Center, Art Tower Mito
29.7 x 21 cm
vol. 1 (no. 44), 115 pp. with 47 (35 color) ills.
vol. 2 (no. 45), 79 pp. with 68 (63 color) ills.
stitchbound, softback
Fadenheftung, broschiert

exhibition catalogue | *Ausstellungskatalog*

layout by Ilya Kabakov | *Layout von Ilya Kabakov*

Documentation of the installation of the same name at the Contemporary Art Center, Art Tower Mito, Mito, Japan, August 7 to November 3, 1999. Volume 1: texts by Ilya Kabakov and Robert Storr; designs for the five exhibition spaces of fictitious artist Charles Rosenthal. Volume 2: text by Eriko Osaka and a dialogue between Ilya Kabakov and Yusuke Nakahara; photographic documentation of all exhibition spaces (five belonging to Charles Rosenthal, two belonging to Ilya Kabakov). Kabakov's installation »The Artist's Archive« was exhibited in the last space; Japanese, English.

Dokumentation der gleichnamigen Installation, Contemporary Art Center, Art Tower Mito, Mito, Japan, 7. August – 3. November 1999. Band 1 Texte von Ilya Kabakov und Robert Storr. Entwürfe zu den fünf Räumen des fiktiven Künstlers Charles Rosenthal. Band 2 Text von Eriko Osaka und ein Dialog von Ilya Kabakov und Yusuke Nakahara. Fotodokumentation aller Ausstellungsräume (fünf von Charles Rosenthal, zwei von Ilya Kabakov). Im letzten Raum wurde Kabakovs Installation »Das Künstlerarchiv« gezeigt; japanisch, englisch.

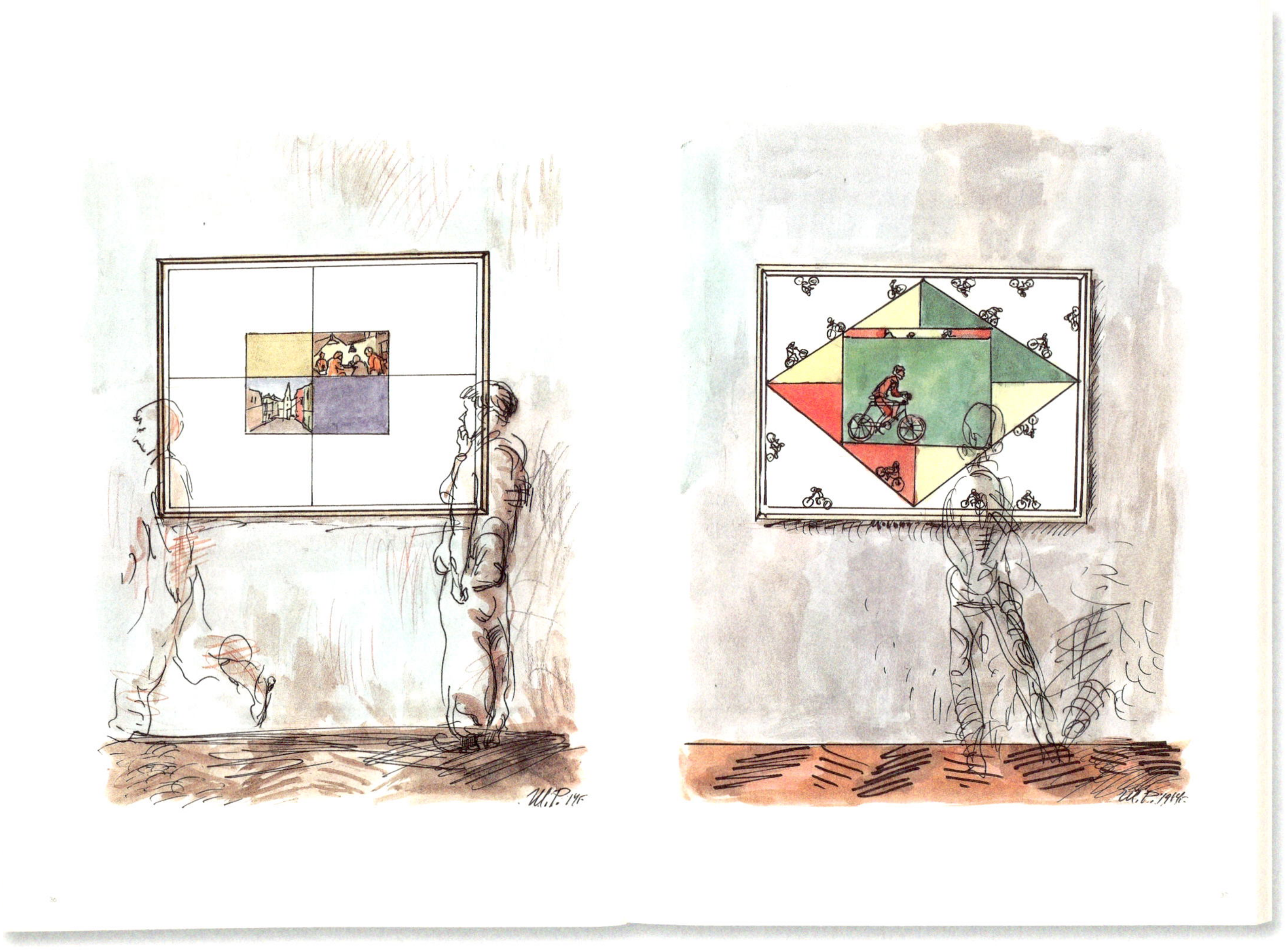

see also | *siehe auch* no. 125; no. 132; CRI, vol. 2, no. 144, pp. 376–385; CRP, vol. 1, no. 264, p. 335; CRP, vol. 2, nos. 304–309, pp. 21–26, nos. 311–314, pp. 28–31, nos. 317–318, pp. 34–35, nos. 321–328, pp. 40–47, nos. 336–340, pp. 55–63, nos. 342–343, pp. 65–66, nos. 345–346, pp. 68–69, nos. 348–349, pp. 71–72, nos. 351–352, pp. 74–75, no. 355, p. 78, nos. 357–373, pp. 80–91

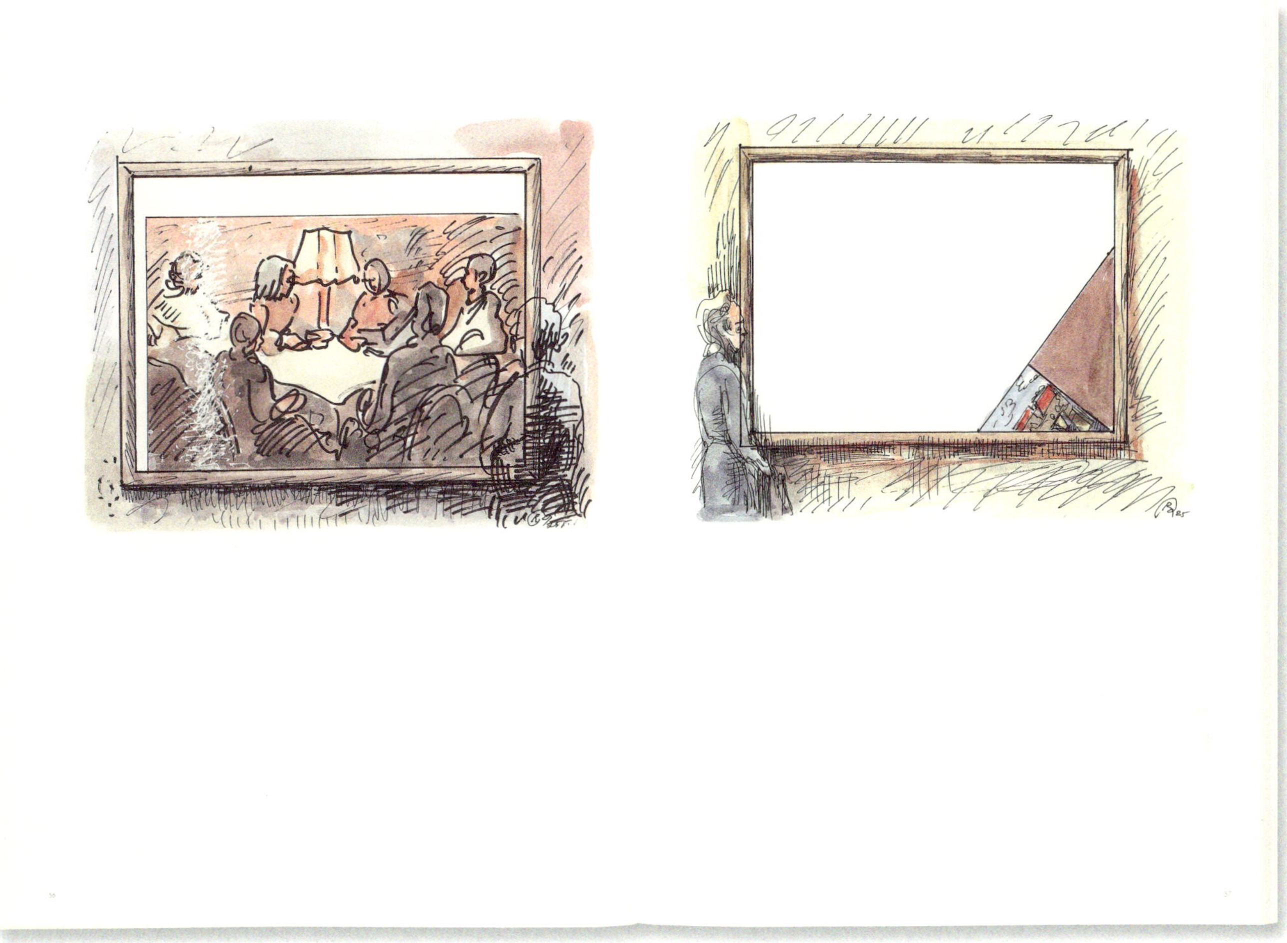

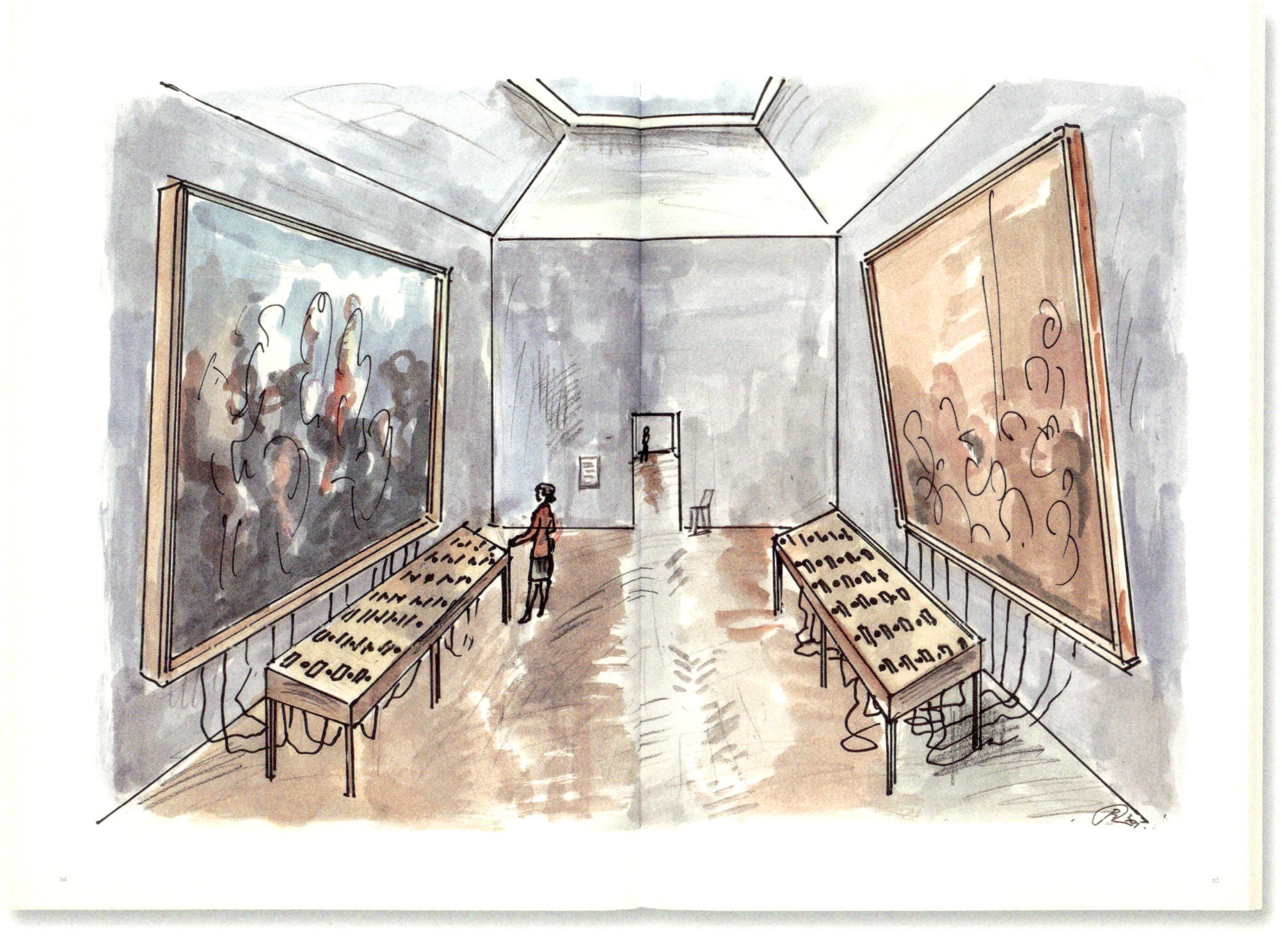

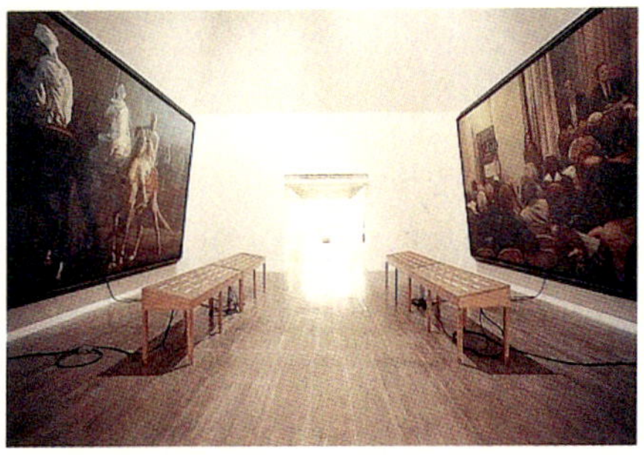

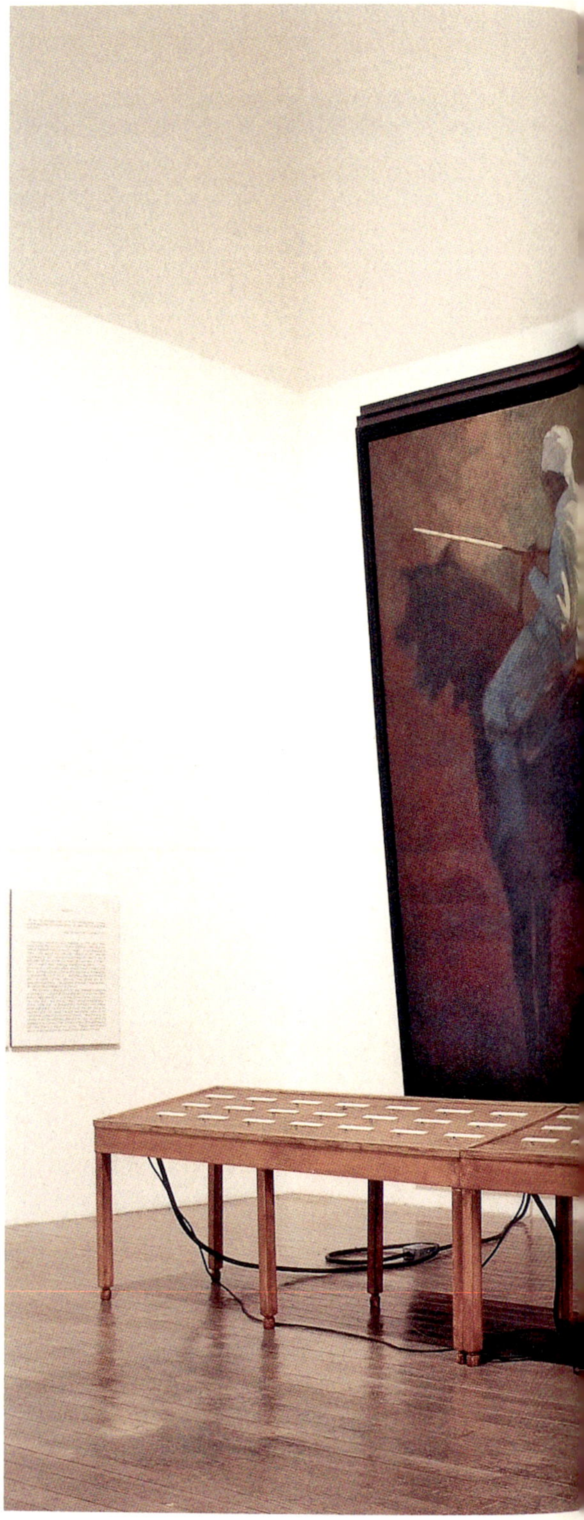

騎手たち The Riders 1931-32

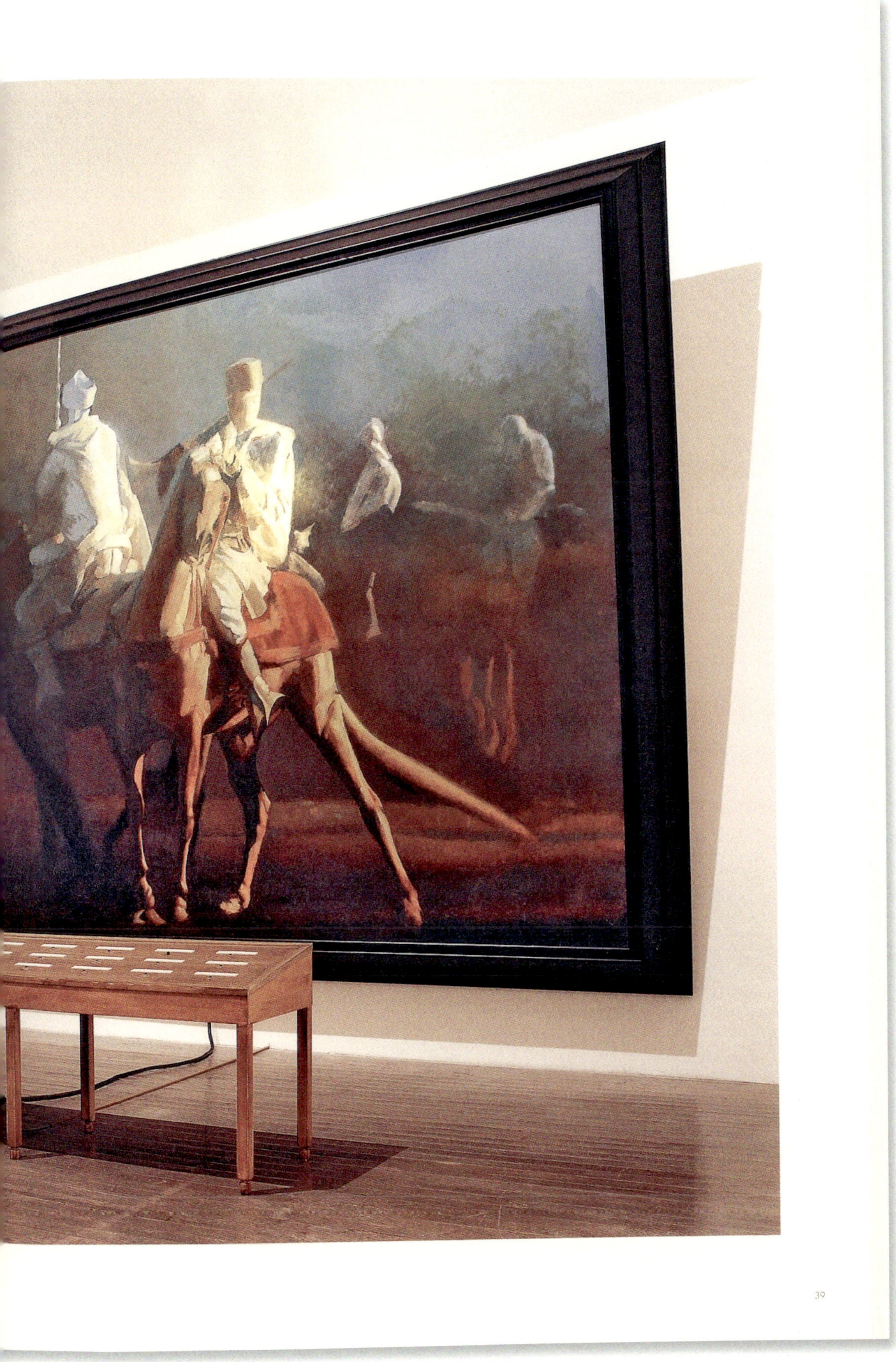

107 The Sixties and the Seventies: Notes About Unofficial Life in Moscow

Die 60er und 70er Jahre. Aufzeichnungen über das inoffizielle Leben in Moskau

1999

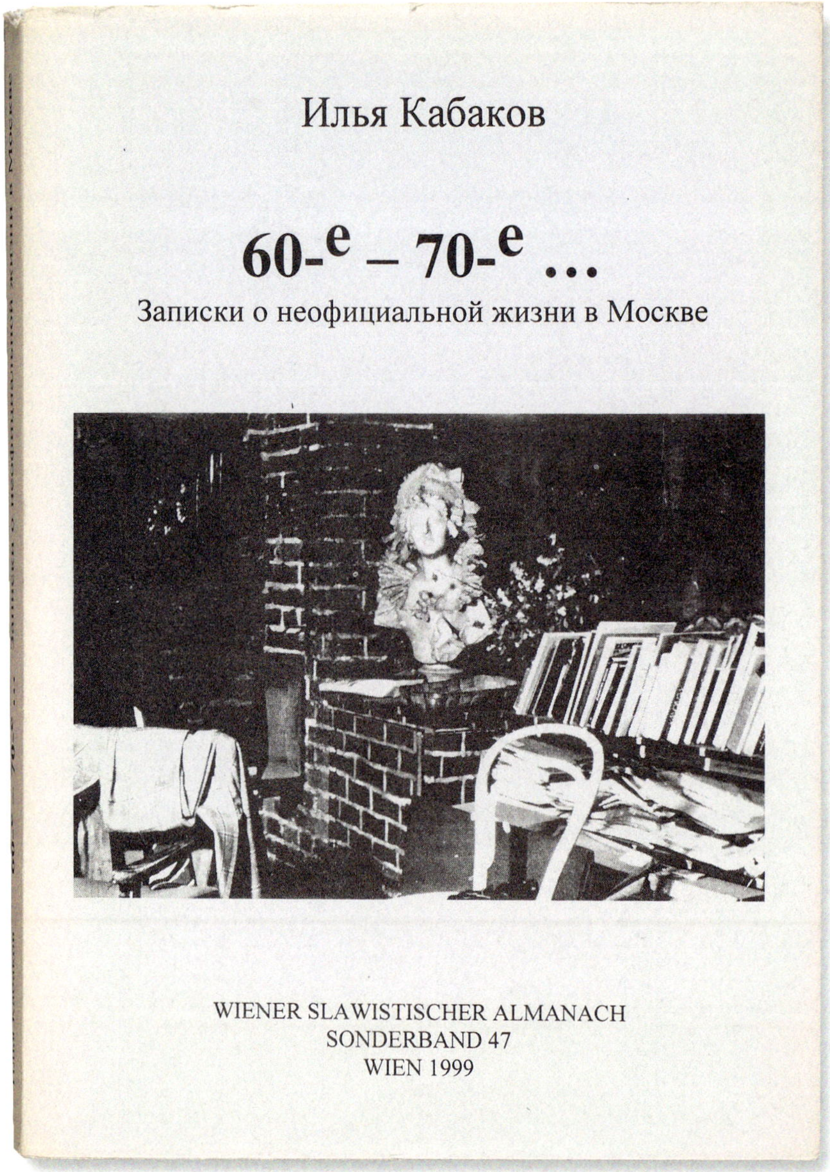

Aage A. Hansen-Löve
Vienna/Munich: Wiener Slawistischer Almanach (literary series; special vol. 47)
20.8 x 15 cm
267 pp. with 1 b/w ill.
adhesive binding, softback with dust jacket
Klebebindung, broschiert mit Schutzumschlag

exhibition catalogue | *Ausstellungskatalog*

concept by Ilya Kabakov | *Konzept von Ilya Kabakov*

Ilya Kabakov depicts his own artistic development within the context of the unofficial art scene in Moscow in the 1960s and 1970s. Texts by Erik Bulatov, Boris Groys, Ilya Kabakov, and Oleg Vassilyev; Russian.

Ilya Kabakov schildert den eigenen künstlerischen Werdegang im Kontext der inoffiziellen Kunst in Moskau in den 1960er- und 1970er-Jahren. Texte von Erik Bulatov, Boris Groys, Ilya Kabakov und Oleg Wassiljew; russisch.

see also | *siehe auch* no. 14; no. 116; no. 131; no. 136

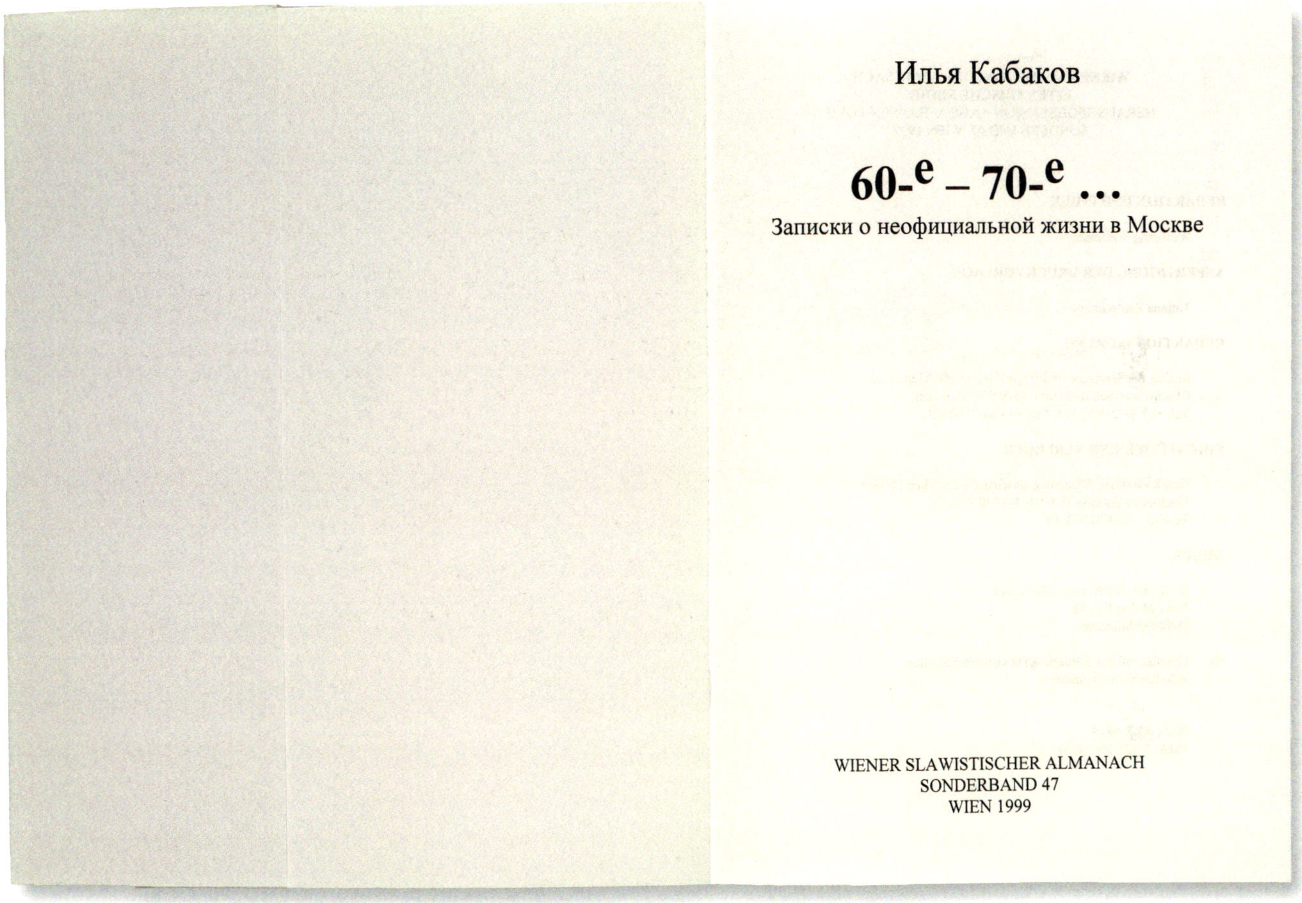

Илья Кабаков

60-е – 70-е …

Записки о неофициальной жизни в Москве

WIENER SLAWISTISCHER ALMANACH
SONDERBAND 47
WIEN 1999

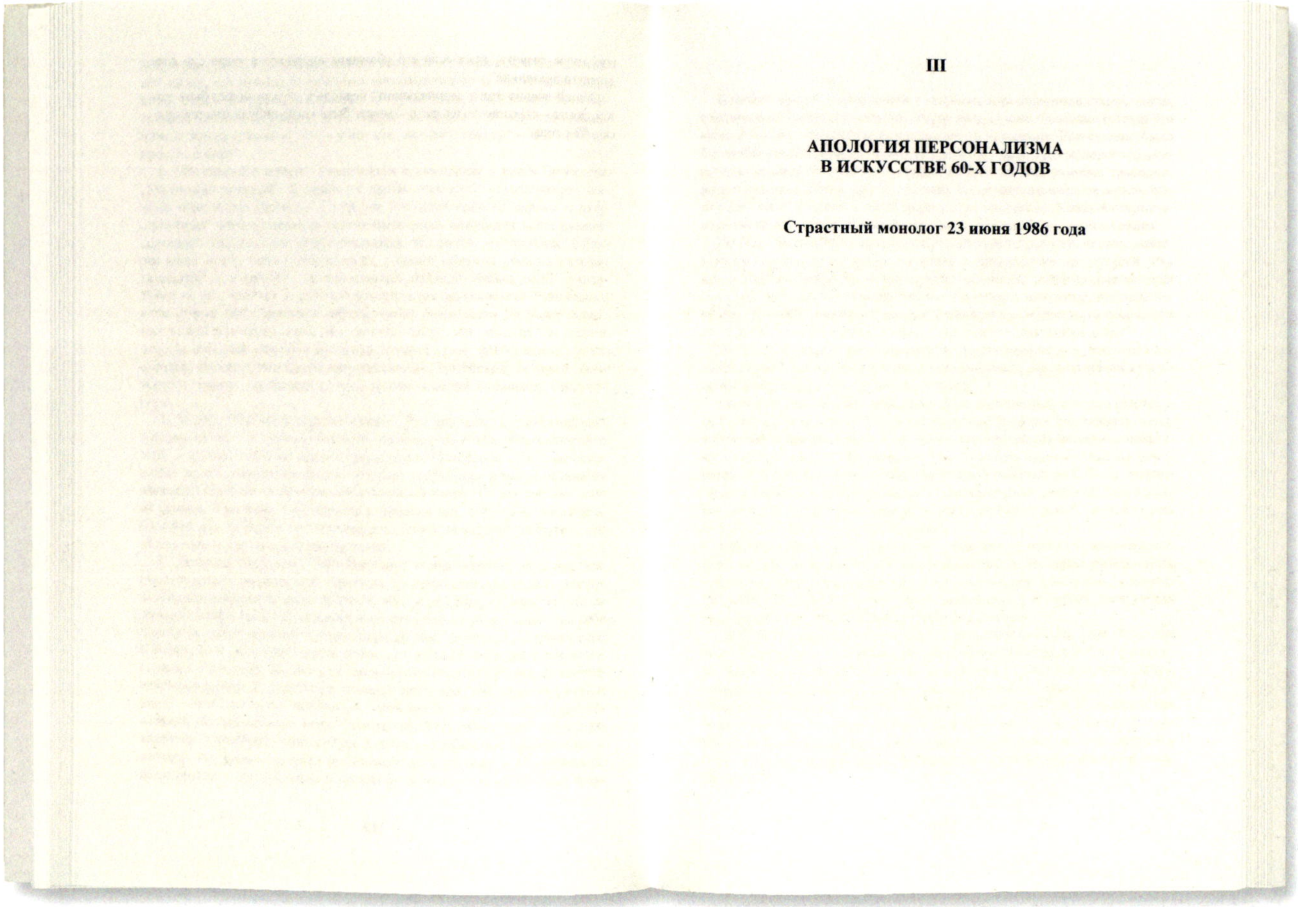

III

АПОЛОГИЯ ПЕРСОНАЛИЗМА
В ИСКУССТВЕ 60-Х ГОДОВ

Страстный монолог 23 июня 1986 года

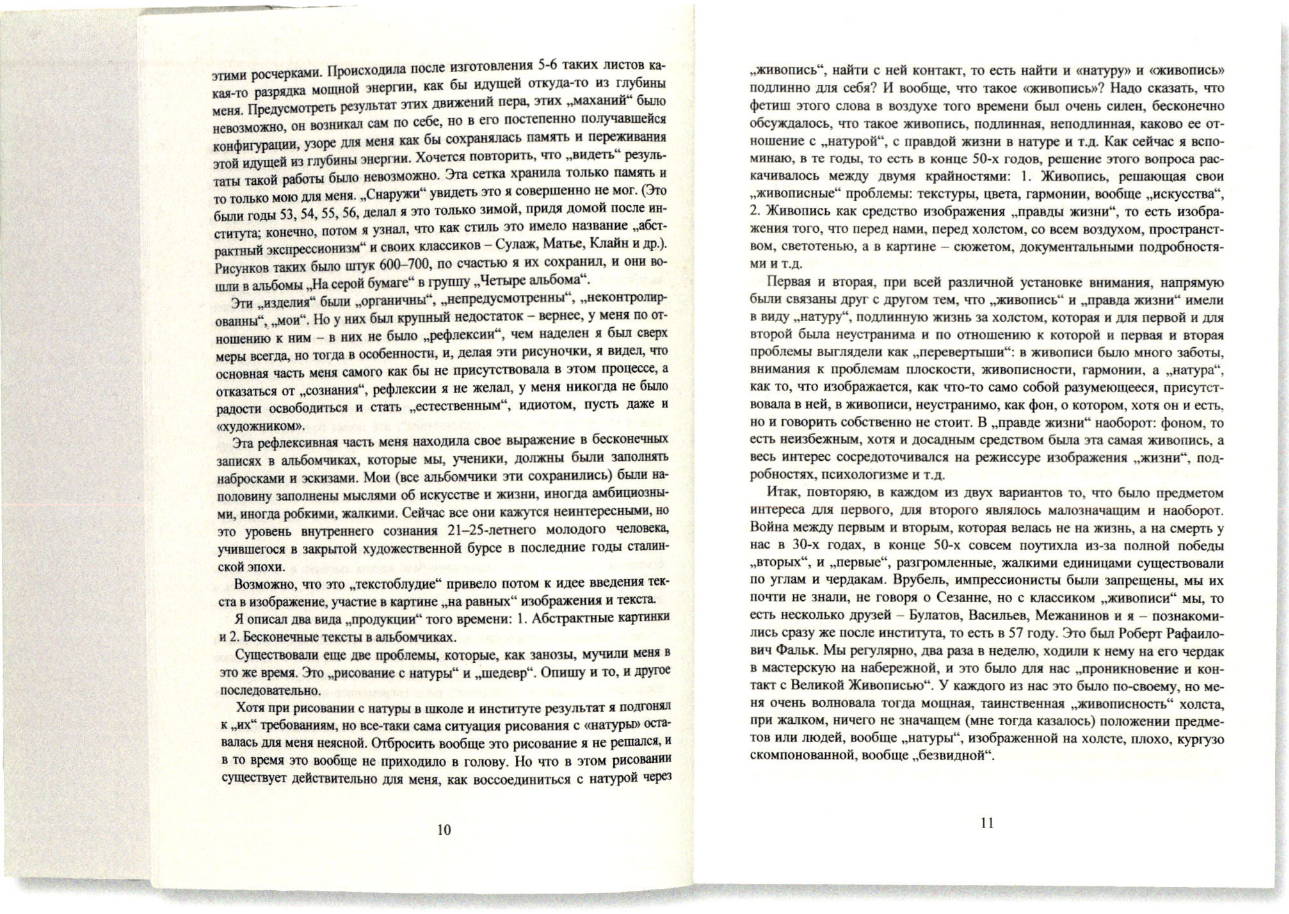

этими росчерками. Происходила после изготовления 5-6 таких листов какая-то разрядка мощной энергии, как бы идущей откуда-то из глубины меня. Предусмотреть результат этих движений пера, этих „маханий" было невозможно, он возникал сам по себе, но в его постепенно получавшейся конфигурации, узоре для меня как бы сохранялась память и переживания этой идущей из глубины энергии. Хочется повторить, что „видеть" результаты такой работы было невозможно. Эта сетка хранила только память и то только мою для меня. „Снаружи" увидеть это я совершенно не мог. (Это были годы 53, 54, 55, 56, делал я это только зимой, придя домой после института; конечно, потом я узнал, что как стиль это имело название „абстрактный экспрессионизм" и своих классиков – Сулаж, Матье, Клайн и др.). Рисунков таких было штук 600–700, по счастью я их сохранил, и они вошли в альбомы „На серой бумаге" в группу „Четыре альбома".

Эти „изделия" были „органичны", „непредусмотренны", „неконтролированны", „мои". Но у них был крупный недостаток – вернее, у меня по отношению к ним – в них не было „рефлексии", чем наделен я был сверх меры всегда, но тогда в особенности, и, делая эти рисуночки, я видел, что основная часть меня самого как бы не присутствовала в этом процессе, а отказаться от „сознания", рефлексии я не желал, у меня никогда не было радости освободиться и стать „естественным", идиотом, пусть даже и «художником».

Эта рефлексивная часть меня находила свое выражение в бесконечных записях в альбомчиках, которые мы, ученики, должны были заполнять набросками и эскизами. Мои (все альбомчики эти сохранились) были наполовину заполнены мыслями об искусстве и жизни, иногда амбициозными, иногда робкими, жалкими. Сейчас все они кажутся неинтересными, но это уровень внутреннего сознания 21–25-летнего молодого человека, учившегося в закрытой художественной бурсе в последние годы сталинской эпохи.

Возможно, что это „текстоблудие" привело потом к идее введения текста в изображение, участие в картине „на равных" изображения и текста.

Я описал два вида „продукции" того времени: 1. Абстрактные картинки и 2. Бесконечные тексты в альбомчиках.

Существовали еще две проблемы, которые, как занозы, мучили меня в это же время. Это „рисование с натуры" и „шедевр". Опишу и то, и другое последовательно.

Хотя при рисовании с натуры в школе и институте результат я подгонял к „их" требованиям, но все-таки сама ситуация рисования с «натуры» оставалась для меня неясной. Отбросить вообще это рисование я не решался, и в то время это вообще не приходило в голову. Но что в этом рисовании существует действительно для меня, как воссоединиться с натурой через

10

„живопись", найти с ней контакт, то есть найти и «натуру» и «живопись» подлинно для себя? И вообще, что такое «живопись»? Надо сказать, что фетиш этого слова в воздухе того времени был очень силен, бесконечно обсуждалось, что такое живопись, подлинная, неподлинная, каково ее отношение с „натурой", с правдой жизни в натуре и т.д. Как сейчас я вспоминаю, в те годы, то есть в конце 50-х годов, решение этого вопроса раскачивалось между двумя крайностями: 1. Живопись, решающая свои „живописные" проблемы: текстуры, цвета, гармонии, вообще „искусства", 2. Живопись как средство изображения „правды жизни", то есть изображения того, что перед нами, перед холстом, со всем воздухом, пространством, светотенью, а в картине – сюжетом, документальными подробностями и т.д.

Первая и вторая, при всей различной установке внимания, напрямую были связаны друг с другом тем, что „живопись" и „правда жизни" имели в виду „натуру", подлинную жизнь за холстом, которая и для первой и для второй была неустранима и по отношению к которой и первая и вторая проблемы выглядели как „перевертыши": в живописи было много заботы, внимания к проблемам плоскости, живописности, гармонии, а „натура", как то, что изображается, как что-то само собой разумеющееся, присутствовала в ней, в живописи, неустранимо, как фон, о котором, хотя он и есть, но и говорить собственно не стоит. В „правде жизни" наоборот: фоном, то есть неизбежным, хотя и досадным средством была эта самая живопись, а весь интерес сосредоточивался на режиссуре изображения „жизни", подробностях, психологизме и т.д.

Итак, повторяю, в каждом из двух вариантов то, что было предметом интереса для первого, для второго являлось малозначащим и наоборот. Война между первым и вторым, которая велась не на жизнь, а на смерть у нас в 30-х годах, в конце 50-х совсем поутихла из-за полной победы „вторых", и „первые", разгромленные, жалкими единицами существовали по углам и чердакам. Врубель, импрессионисты были запрещены, мы их почти не знали, не говоря о Сезанне, но с классиком „живописи" мы, то есть несколько друзей – Булатов, Васильев, Межанинов и я – познакомились сразу же после института, то есть в 57 году. Это был Роберт Рафаилович Фальк. Мы регулярно, два раза в неделю, ходили к нему на его чердак в мастерскую на набережной, и это было для нас „проникновение и контакт с Великой Живописью". У каждого из нас это было по-своему, но меня очень волновала тогда мощная, таинственная „живописность" холста, при жалком, ничего не значащем (мне тогда казалось) положении предметов или людей, вообще „натуры", изображенной на холсте, плохо, кургузо скомпонованной, вообще „безвидной".

11

108 50 Installations | *50 Installationen*

2000

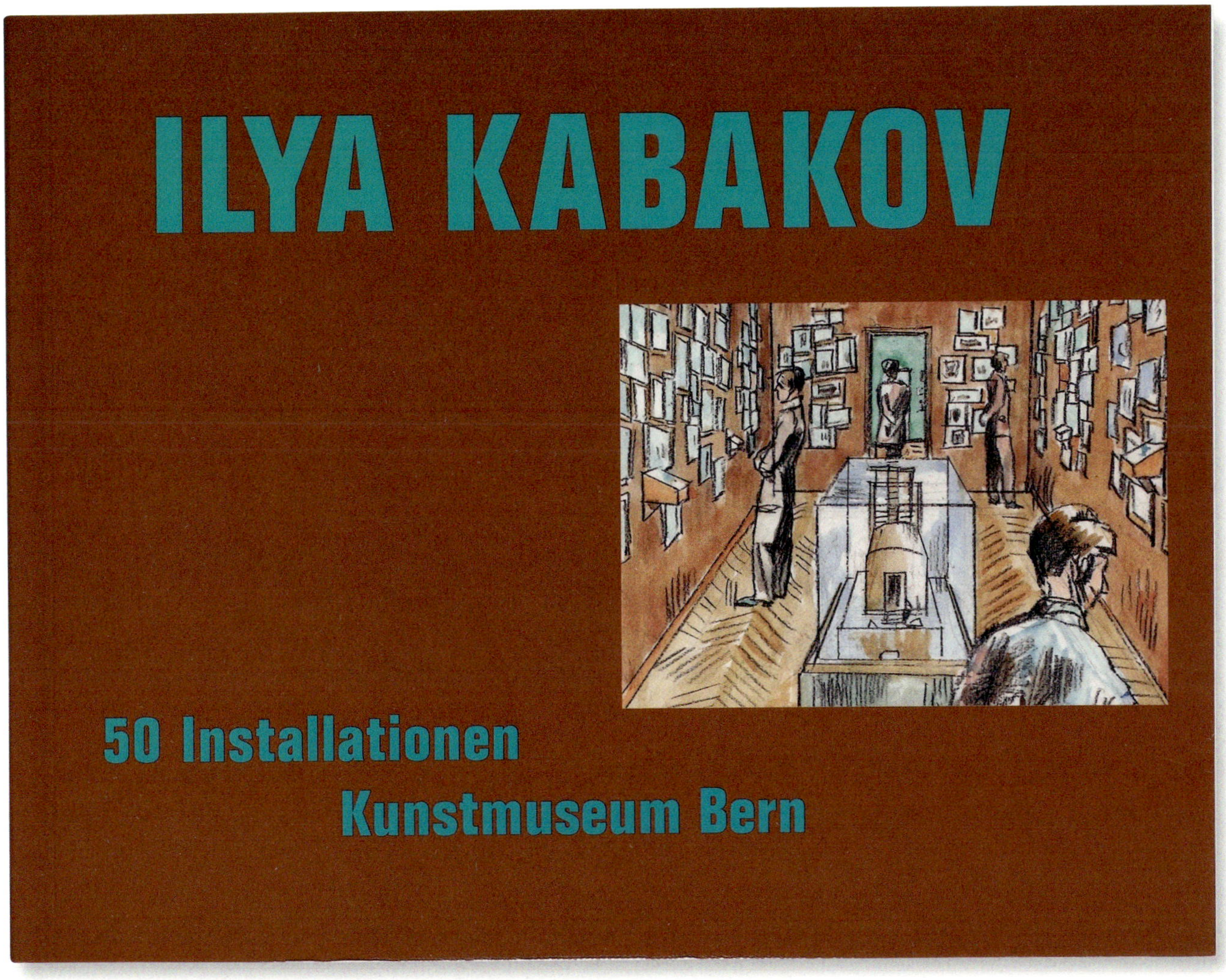

Kunstmuseum Bern
Bern: Kunstmuseum Bern
17 x 22 cm
119 pp. with 50 (26 color) ills.
stitchbound, softback
Fadenheftung, broschiert

exhibition catalogue | *Ausstellungskatalog*

layout by Ilya Kabakov | *Layout von Ilya Kabakov*

For the installation of the same name at the Kunstmuseum Bern, Bern, April 7 to June 25, 2000. Texts by Ralf Beil, Ilya Kabakov, and Toni Stooss; German.

Zur gleichnamigen Installation, Kunstmuseum Bern, Bern, 7. April – 25. Juni 2000. Texte von Ralf Beil, Ilya Kabakov und Toni Stooss; deutsch.

see also | *siehe auch* no. 113; CRI, vol. 2, no. 152, pp. 420–425

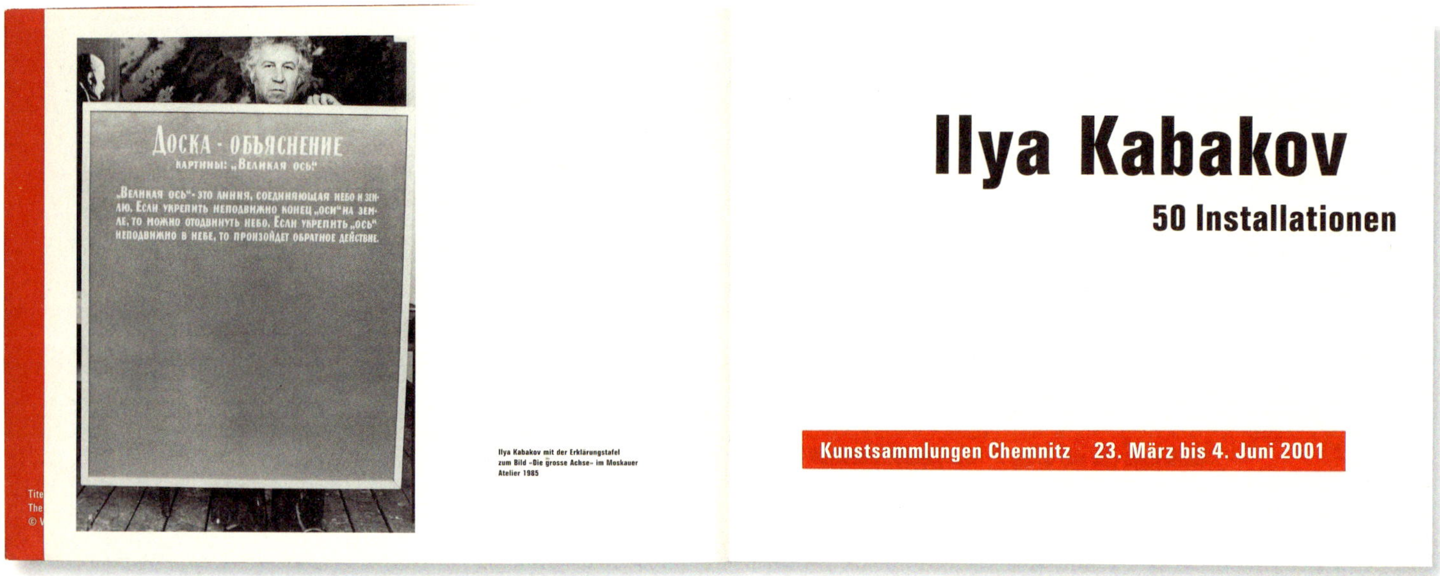

Ilya Kabakov mit der Erklärungstafel zum Bild «Die grosse Achse» im Moskauer Atelier 1985

Ilya Kabakov

50 Installationen

Kunstsammlungen Chemnitz 23. März bis 4. Juni 2001

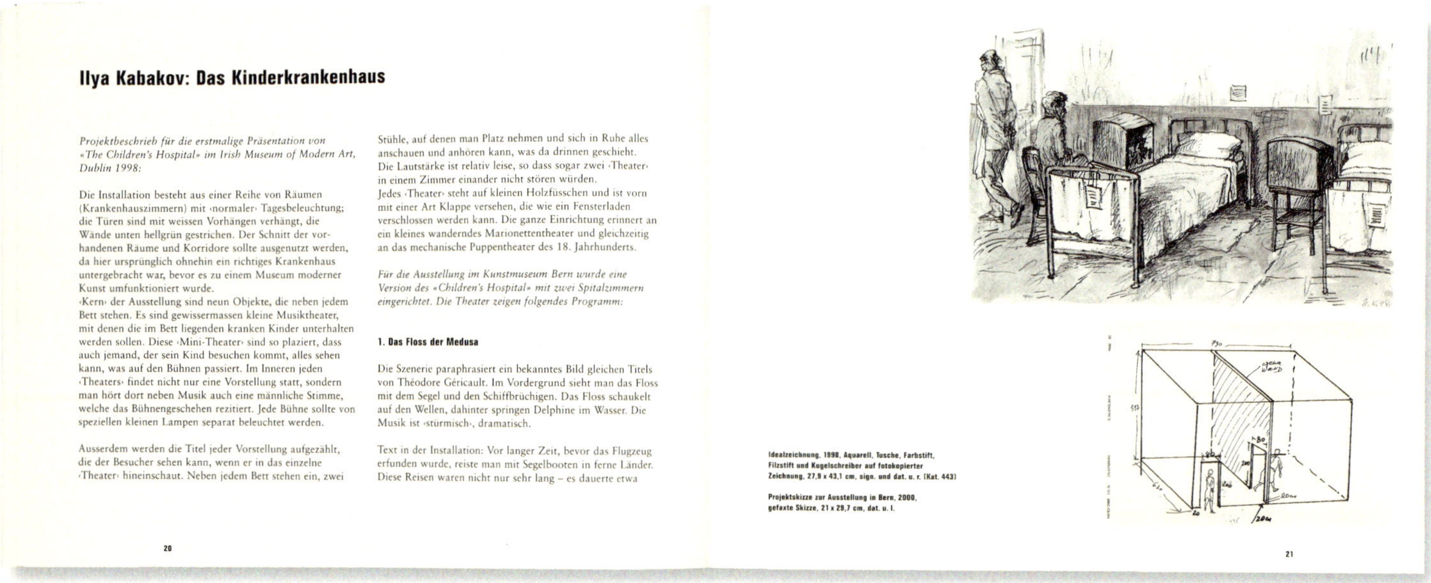

Ilya Kabakov: Das Kinderkrankenhaus

Projektbeschrieb für die erstmalige Präsentation von «The Children's Hospital» im Irish Museum of Modern Art, Dublin 1998:

Die Installation besteht aus einer Reihe von Räumen (Krankenhauszimmern) mit ‹normaler› Tagesbeleuchtung; die Türen sind mit weissen Vorhängen verhängt, die Wände unten hellgrün gestrichen. Der Schnitt der vorhandenen Räume und Korridore sollte ausgenutzt werden, da hier ursprünglich ohnehin ein richtiges Krankenhaus untergebracht war, bevor es zu einem Museum moderner Kunst umfunktioniert wurde.
‹Kern› der Ausstellung sind neun Objekte, die neben jedem Bett stehen. Es sind gewissermassen kleine Musiktheater, mit denen die im Bett liegenden kranken Kinder unterhalten werden sollen. Diese ‹Mini-Theater› sind so plaziert, dass auch jemand, der sein Kind besuchen kommt, alles sehen kann, was auf den Bühnen passiert. Im Inneren jeden ‹Theaters› findet nicht nur eine Vorstellung statt, sondern man hört dort neben Musik auch eine männliche Stimme, welche das Bühnengeschehen rezitiert. Jede Bühne sollte von speziellen kleinen Lampen separat beleuchtet werden.

Ausserdem werden die Titel jeder Vorstellung aufgezählt, die der Besucher sehen kann, wenn er in das einzelne ‹Theater› hineinschaut. Neben jedem Bett stehen ein, zwei Stühle, auf denen man Platz nehmen und sich in Ruhe alles anschauen und anhören kann, was da drinnen geschieht.
Die Lautstärke ist relativ leise, so dass sogar zwei ‹Theater› in einem Zimmer einander nicht stören würden.
Jedes ‹Theater› steht auf kleinen Holzfüsschen und ist vorn mit einer Art Klappe versehen, die wie ein Fensterladen verschlossen werden kann. Die ganze Einrichtung erinnert an ein kleines wanderndes Marionettentheater und gleichzeitig an das mechanische Puppentheater des 18. Jahrhunderts.

Für die Ausstellung im Kunstmuseum Bern wurde eine Version des «Children's Hospital» mit zwei Spitalzimmern eingerichtet. Die Theater zeigen folgendes Programm:

1. Das Floss der Medusa

Die Szenerie paraphrasiert ein bekanntes Bild gleichen Titels von Théodore Géricault. Im Vordergrund sieht man das Floss mit dem Segel und den Schiffbrüchigen. Das Floss schaukelt auf den Wellen, dahinter springen Delphine im Wasser. Die Musik ist ‹stürmisch›, dramatisch.

Text in der Installation: Vor langer Zeit, bevor das Flugzeug erfunden wurde, reiste man mit Segelbooten in ferne Länder. Diese Reisen waren nicht nur sehr lang – es dauerte etwa

20

Idealzeichnung, 1998, Aquarell, Tusche, Farbstift, Filzstift und Kugelschreiber auf fotokopierter Zeichnung, 27,9 x 43,1 cm, sign. und dat. u. r. (Kat. 443)

Projektskizze zur Ausstellung in Bern, 2000, gefaxte Skizze, 21 x 29,7 cm, dat. u. l.

21

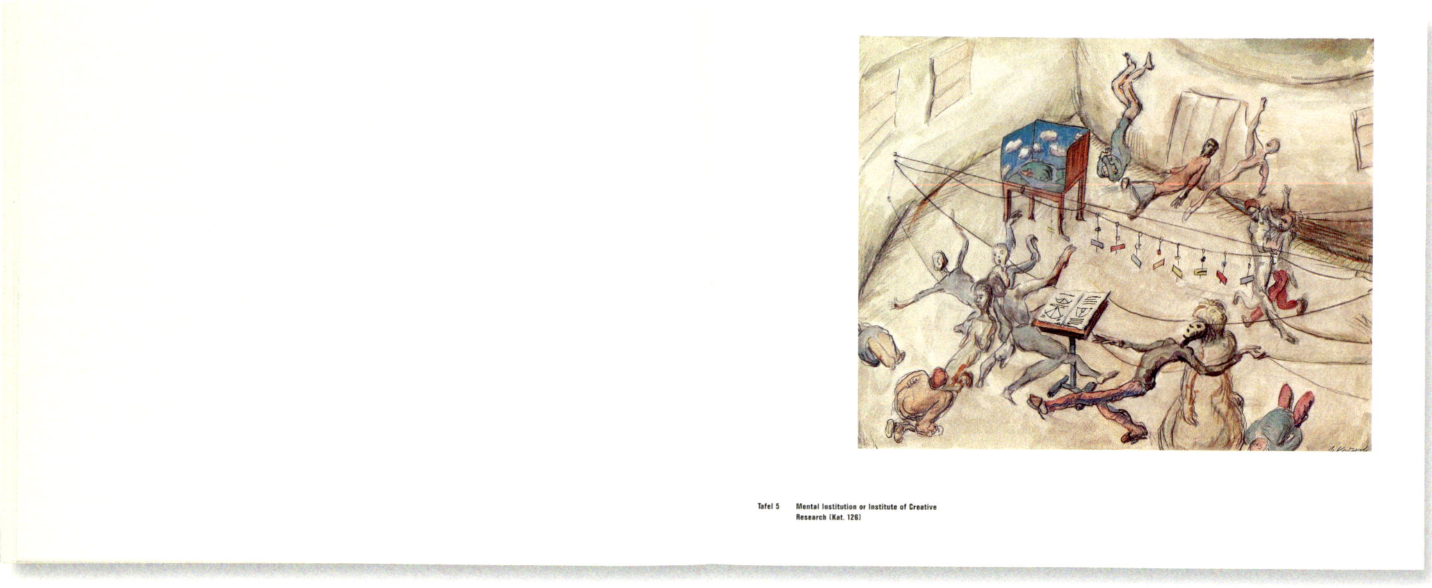

Tafel 5 Mental Institution or Institute of Creative Research (Kat. 126)

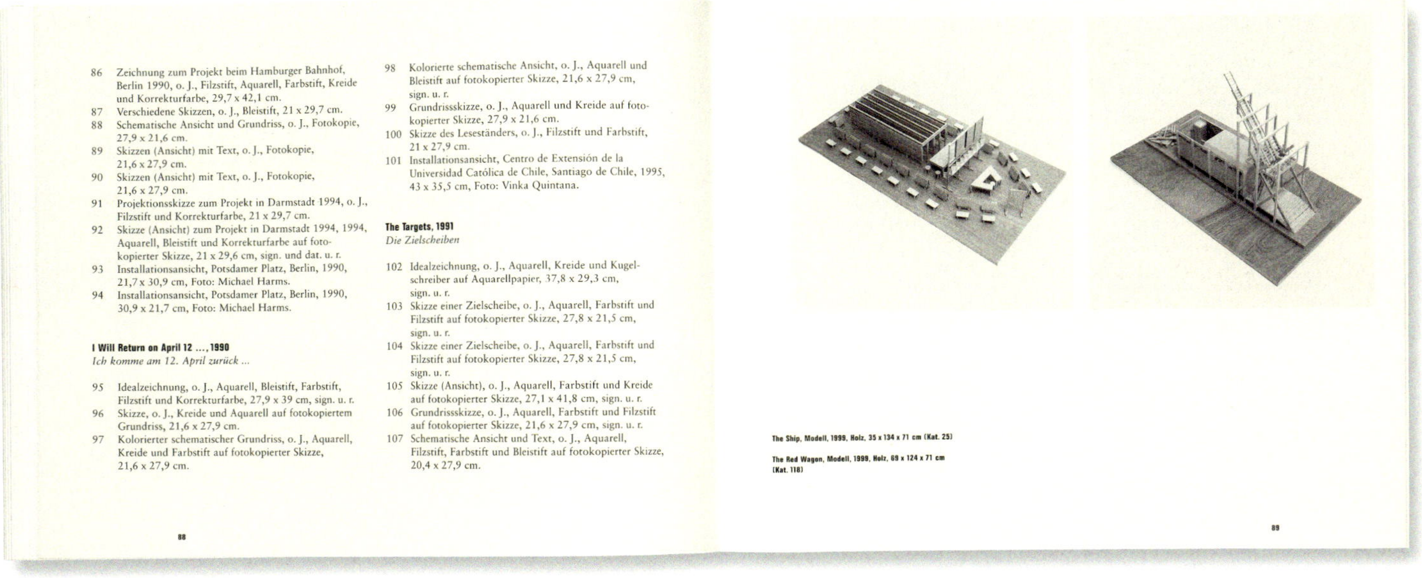

86 Zeichnung zum Projekt beim Hamburger Bahnhof, Berlin 1990, o. J., Filzstift, Aquarell, Farbstift, Kreide und Korrekturfarbe, 29,7 x 42,1 cm.
87 Verschiedene Skizzen, o. J., Bleistift, 21 x 29,7 cm.
88 Schematische Ansicht und Grundriss, o. J., Fotokopie, 27,9 x 21,6 cm.
89 Skizzen (Ansicht) mit Text, o. J., Fotokopie, 21,6 x 27,9 cm.
90 Skizzen (Ansicht) mit Text, o. J., Fotokopie, 21,6 x 27,9 cm.
91 Projektionsskizze zum Projekt in Darmstadt 1994, o. J., Filzstift und Korrekturfarbe, 21 x 29,7 cm.
92 Skizze (Ansicht) zum Projekt in Darmstadt 1994, 1994, Aquarell, Bleistift und Korrekturfarbe auf fotokopierter Skizze, 21 x 29,6 cm, sign. und dat. u. r.
93 Installationsansicht, Potsdamer Platz, Berlin, 1990, 21,7 x 30,9 cm, Foto: Michael Harms.
94 Installationsansicht, Potsdamer Platz, Berlin, 1990, 30,9 x 21,7 cm, Foto: Michael Harms.

I Will Return on April 12 ..., 1990
Ich komme am 12. April zurück ...

95 Idealzeichnung, o. J., Aquarell, Bleistift, Farbstift, Filzstift und Korrekturfarbe, 27,9 x 39 cm, sign. u. r.
96 Skizze, o. J., Kreide und Aquarell auf fotokopiertem Grundriss, 21,6 x 27,9 cm.
97 Kolorierter schematischer Grundriss, o. J., Aquarell, Kreide und Farbstift auf fotokopierter Skizze, 21,6 x 27,9 cm.
98 Kolorierte schematische Ansicht, o. J., Aquarell und Bleistift auf fotokopierter Skizze, 21,6 x 27,9 cm, sign. u. r.
99 Grundrissskizze, o. J., Aquarell und Kreide auf fotokopierter Skizze, 27,9 x 21,6 cm.
100 Skizze des Leseständers, o. J., Filzstift und Farbstift, 21 x 27,9 cm.
101 Installationsansicht, Centro de Extensión de la Universidad Católica de Chile, Santiago de Chile, 1995, 43 x 35,5 cm, Foto: Vinka Quintana.

The Targets, 1991
Die Zielscheiben

102 Idealzeichnung, o. J., Aquarell, Kreide und Kugelschreiber auf Aquarellpapier, 37,8 x 29,3 cm, sign. u. r.
103 Skizze einer Zielscheibe, o. J., Aquarell, Farbstift und Filzstift auf fotokopierter Skizze, 27,8 x 21,5 cm, sign. u. r.
104 Skizze einer Zielscheibe, o. J., Aquarell, Farbstift und Filzstift auf fotokopierter Skizze, 27,8 x 21,5 cm, sign. u. r.
105 Skizze (Ansicht), o. J., Aquarell, Farbstift und Kreide auf fotokopierter Skizze, 27,1 x 41,8 cm, sign. u. r.
106 Grundrissskizze, o. J., Aquarell, Farbstift und Filzstift auf fotokopierter Skizze, 21,6 x 27,9 cm, sign. u. r.
107 Schematische Ansicht und Text, o. J., Aquarell, Filzstift, Farbstift und Bleistift auf fotokopierter Skizze, 20,4 x 27,9 cm.

88

The Ship, Modell, 1999, Holz, 35 x 134 x 71 cm (Kat. 25)

The Red Wagon, Modell, 1999, Holz, 69 x 124 x 71 cm (Kat. 118)

89

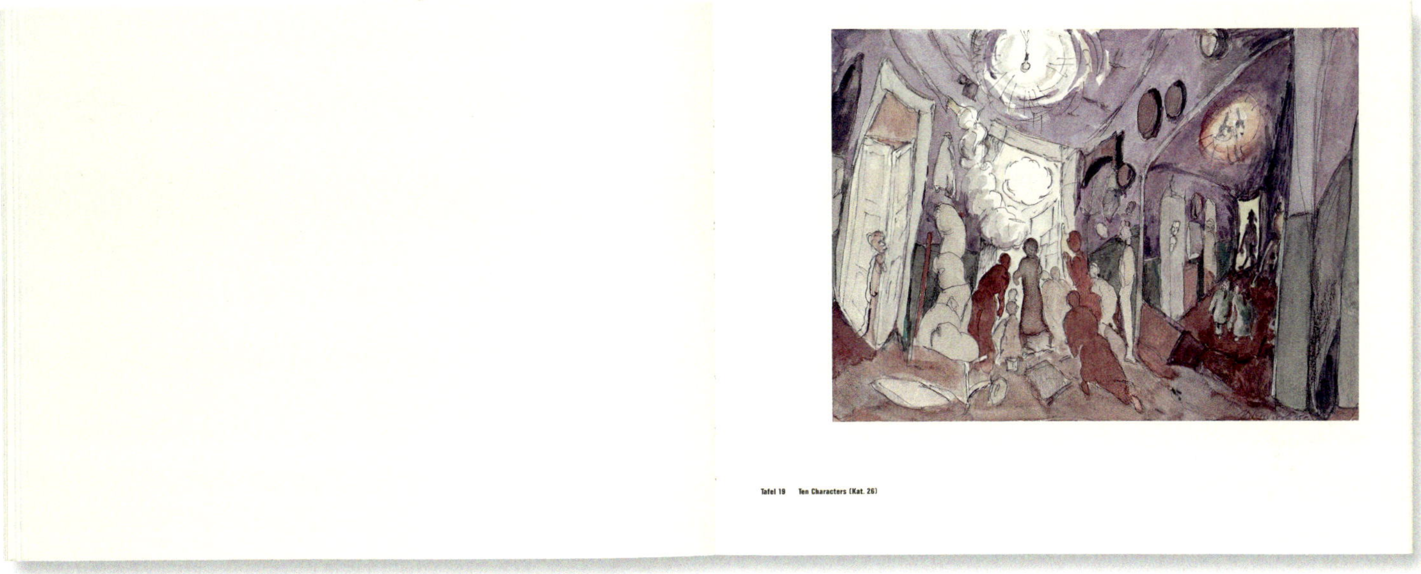

Tafel 19 Ten Characters (Kat. 26)

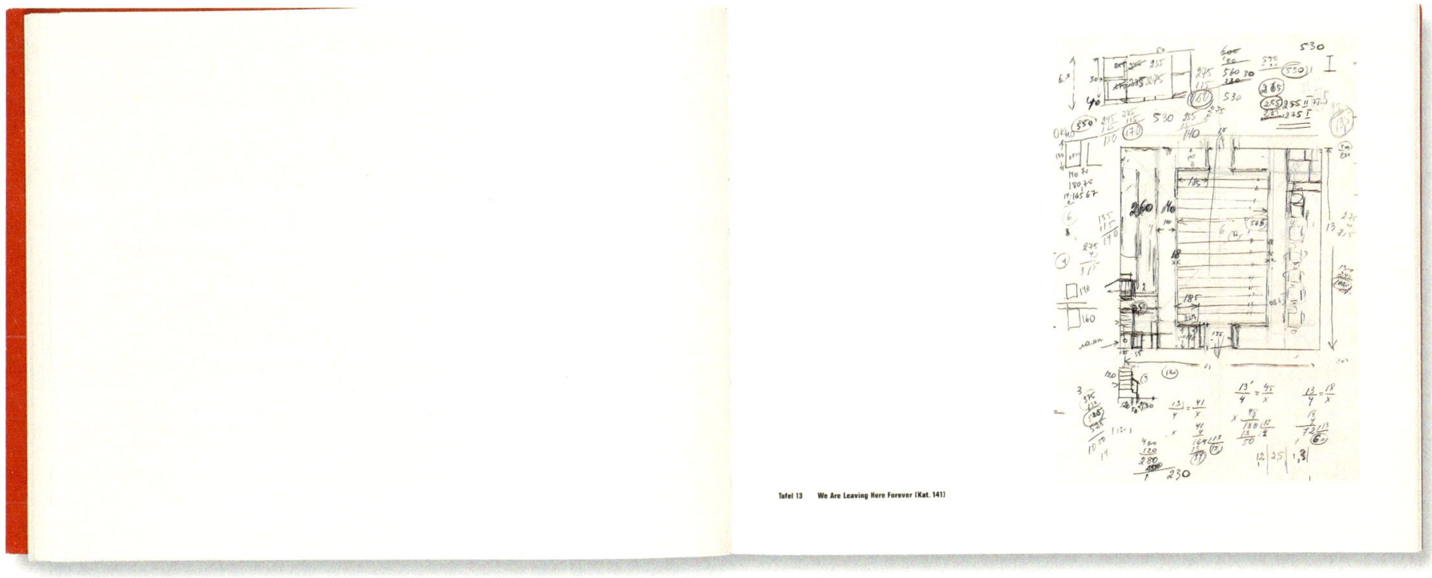

Tafel 13 We Are Leaving Here Forever (Kat. 141)

109 The Rice Fields | *Die Reisfelder*

2000

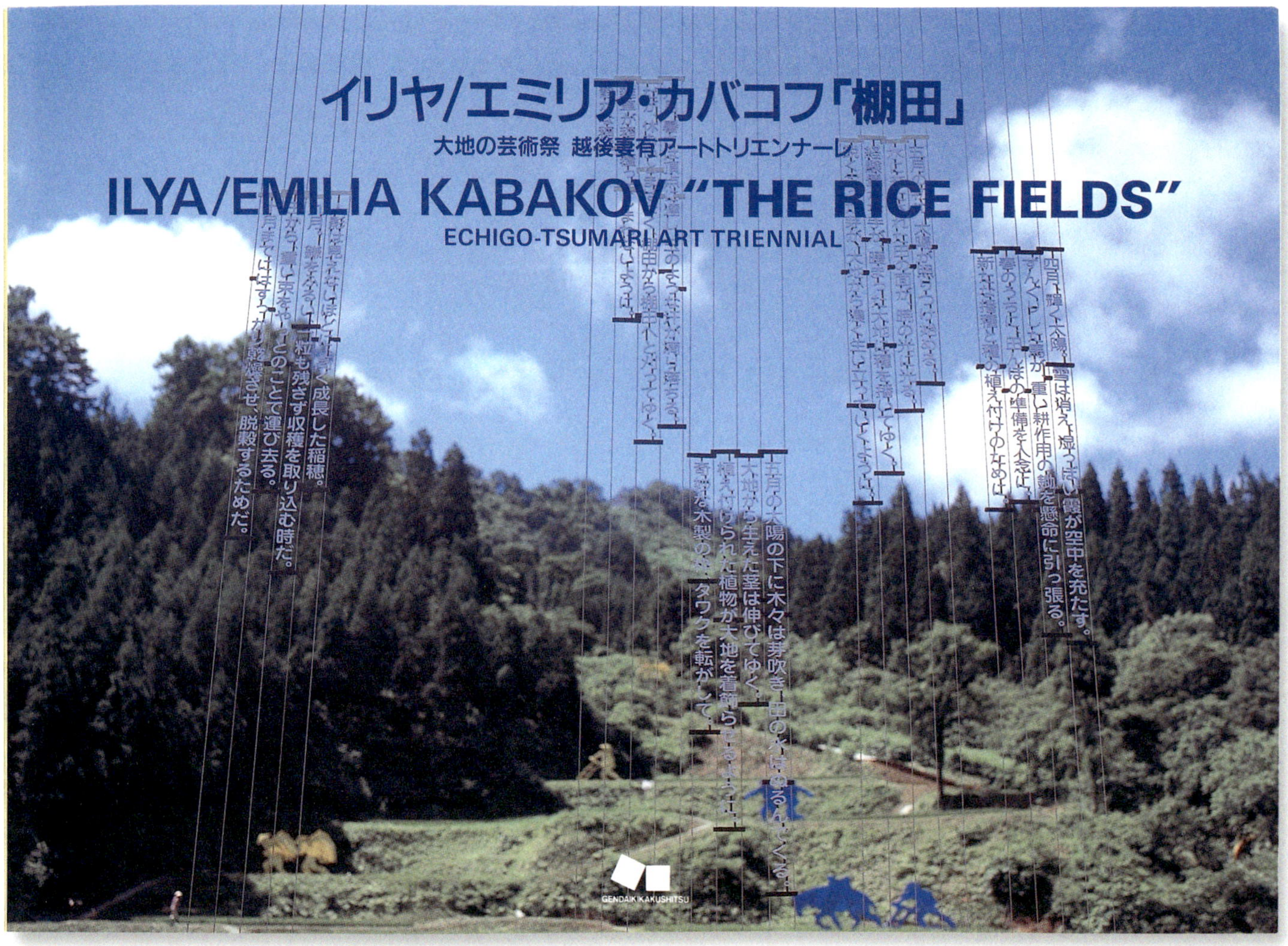

Fram Kitagawa
Tokyo: Gendaikikakushitsu Publishers
21 x 30 cm
80 pp. with 77 (25 color) ills.
adhesive binding, softback with flaps
Klebebindung, broschiert mit Umschlag-klappen

exhibition catalogue | *Ausstellungskatalog*

layout by Ilya Kabakov | *Layout von Ilya Kabakov*

Documentation of the installation of the same name at the First Echigo-Tsumari Art Triennial, Niigata Prefecture, Japan, July 20 to September 10, 2000. Texts by Ilya and Emilia Kabakov; Japanese, English.

Dokumentation der gleichnamigen Installation, 1. Echigo – Tsumari Art Triennial, Präfektur Niigata, Japan, 20. Juli – 10. September 2000. Texte von Ilya und Emilia Kabakov; japanisch, englisch.

see also | *siehe auch* CRI, vol. 2, no. 153, pp. 426–431

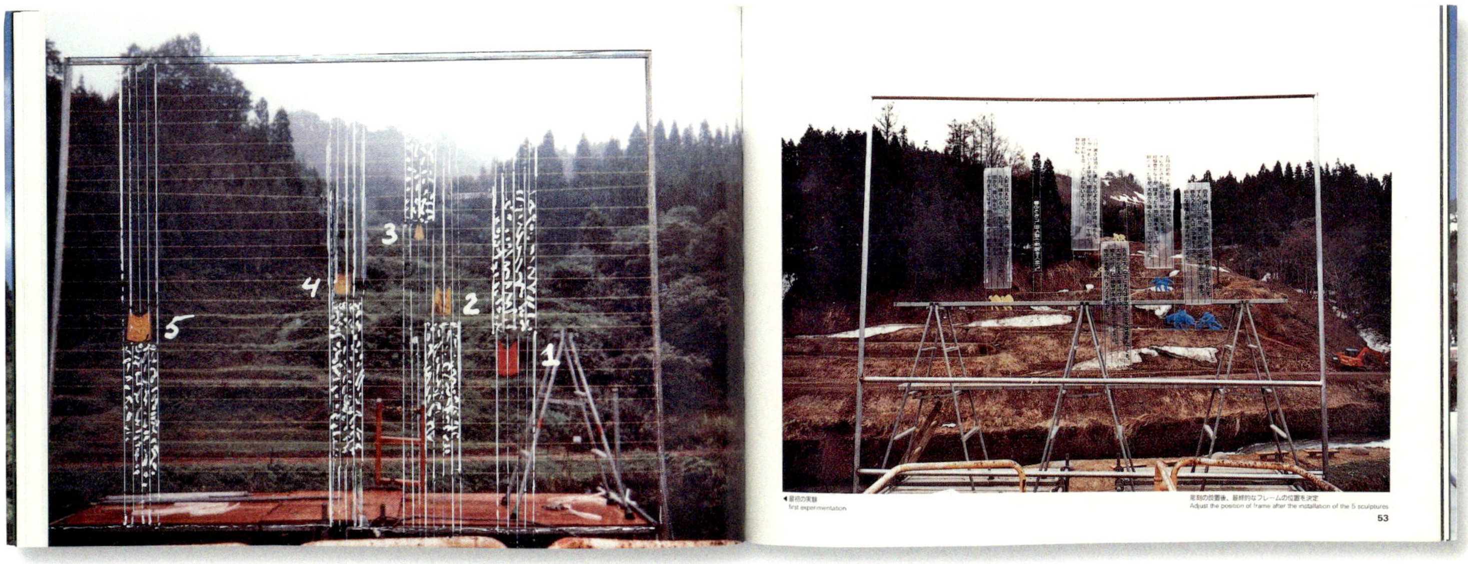
5
4
3
2
1
First experimentation
Adjust the position of frame after the installation of the 5 sculptures
53

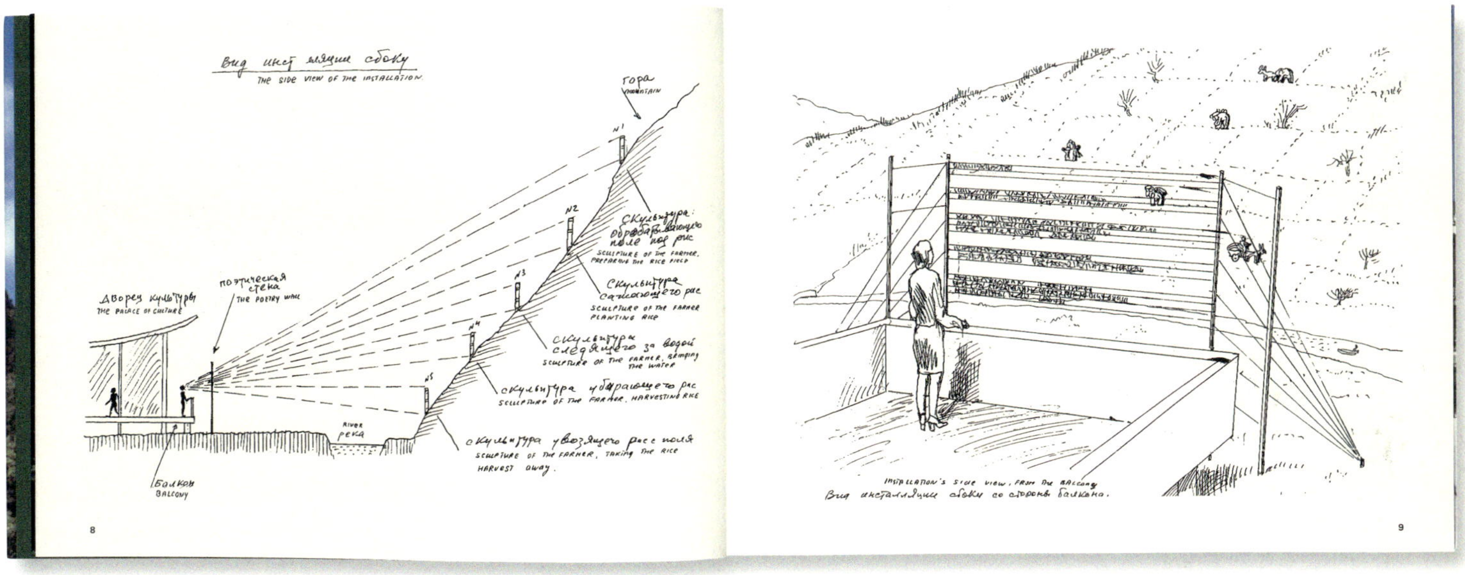
THE SIDE VIEW OF THE INSTALLATION
MOUNTAIN
THE PALACE OF CULTURE
THE POETRY WALL
SCULPTURE OF THE FARMER, PREPARING THE RICE FIELD
SCULPTURE OF THE FARMER PLANTING RICE
SCULPTURE OF THE FARMER, KEEPING THE WATER
SCULPTURE OF THE FARMER, HARVESTING RICE
SCULPTURE OF THE FARMER, TAKING THE RICE HARVEST AWAY
RIVER
BALCONY
8
INSTALLATION'S SIDE VIEW. FROM THE BALCONY
9

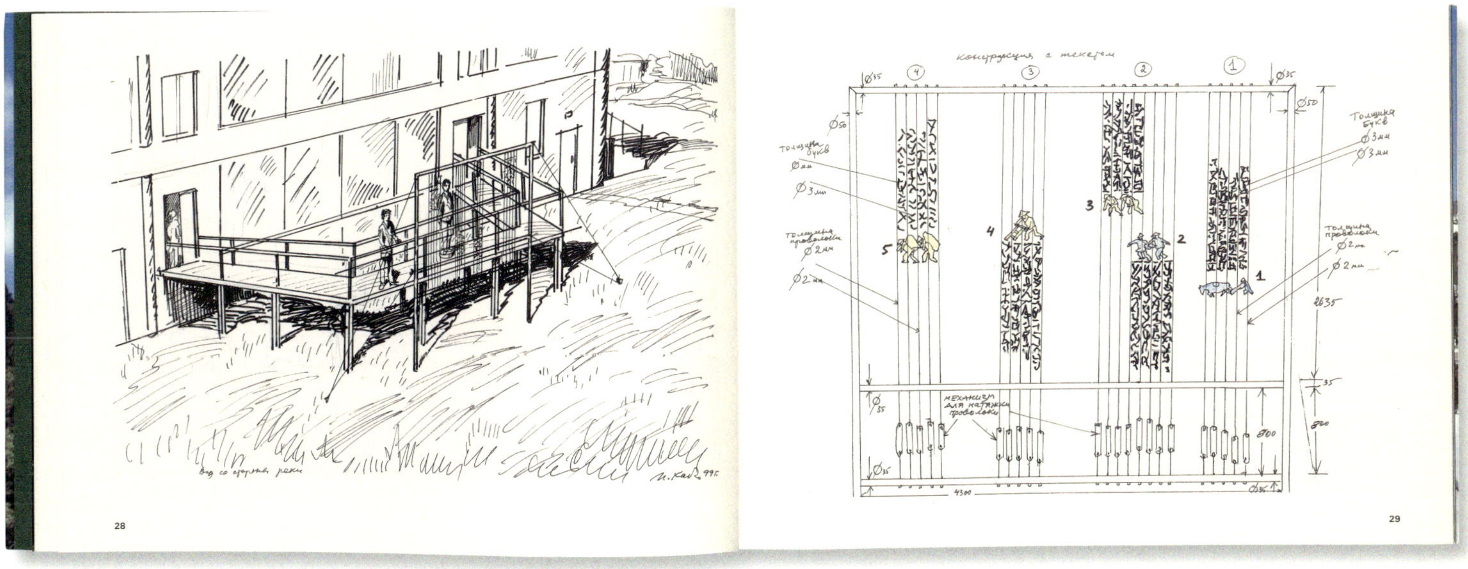
28
5
4
3
2
1
4300
29

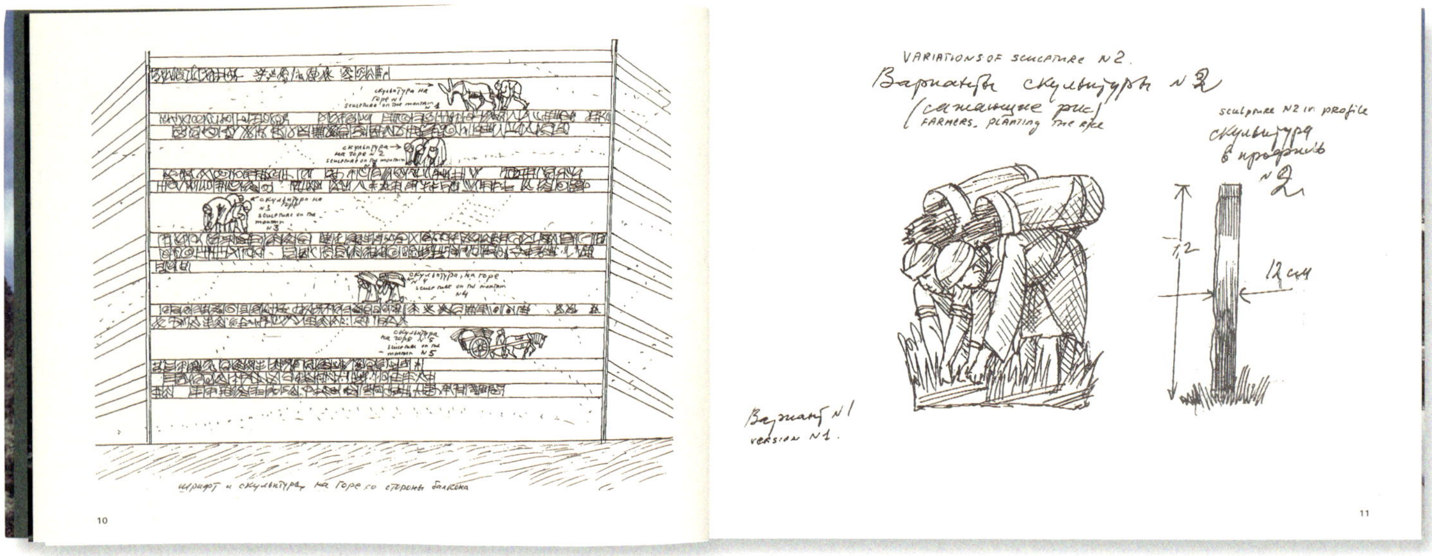
VARIATIONS OF SCULPTURE N2.
Варианты скульптуры N 2
(сажающие рис)
FARMERS, PLANTING THE RICE
sculpture N2 in profile
скульптура в профиль N 2
1,2
12 см
Вариант N 1
version N1.
10
11

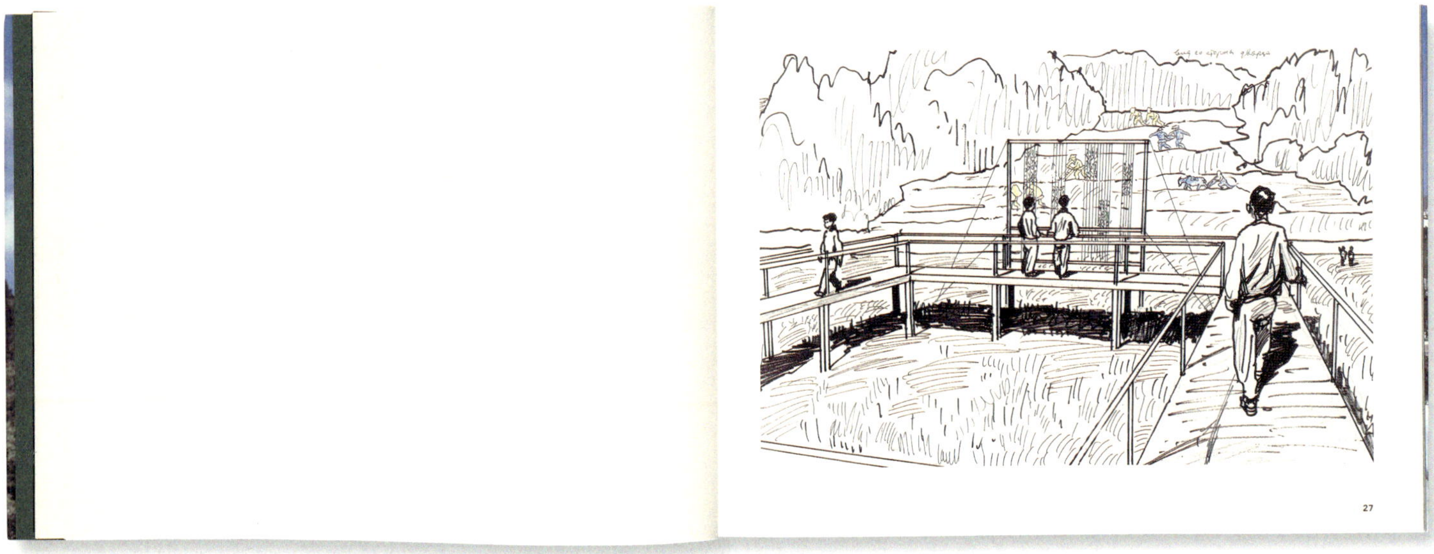
27

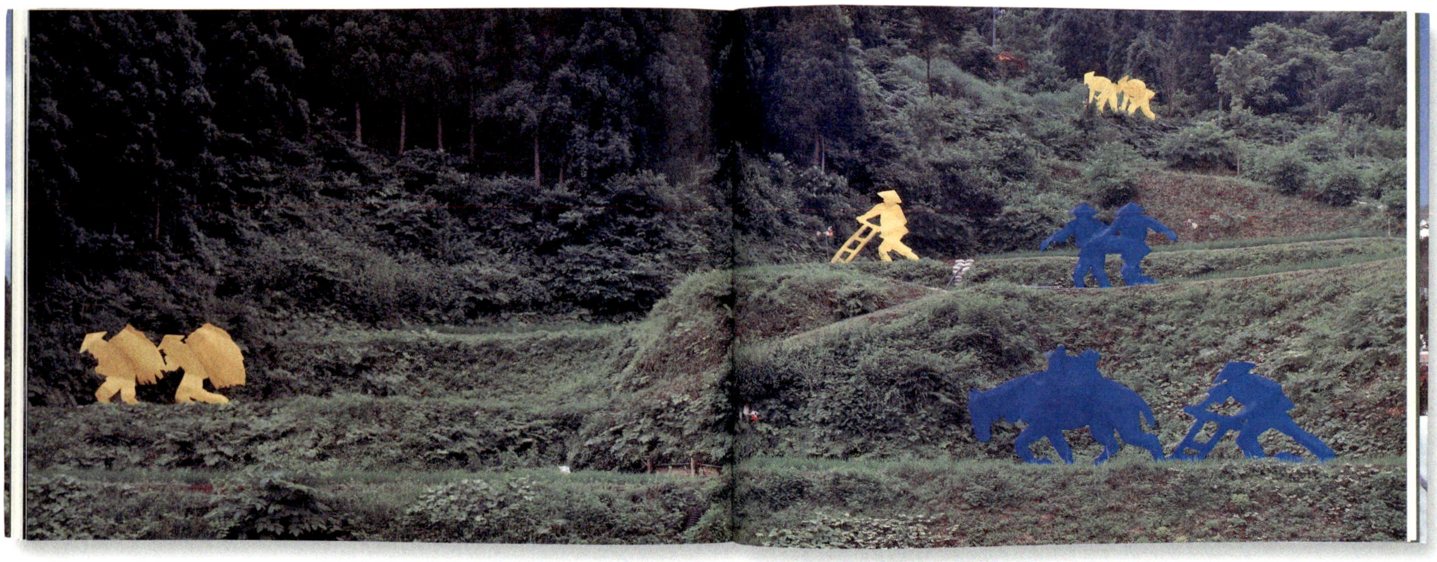

110 School No. 6 | *Schule No. 6*

2000

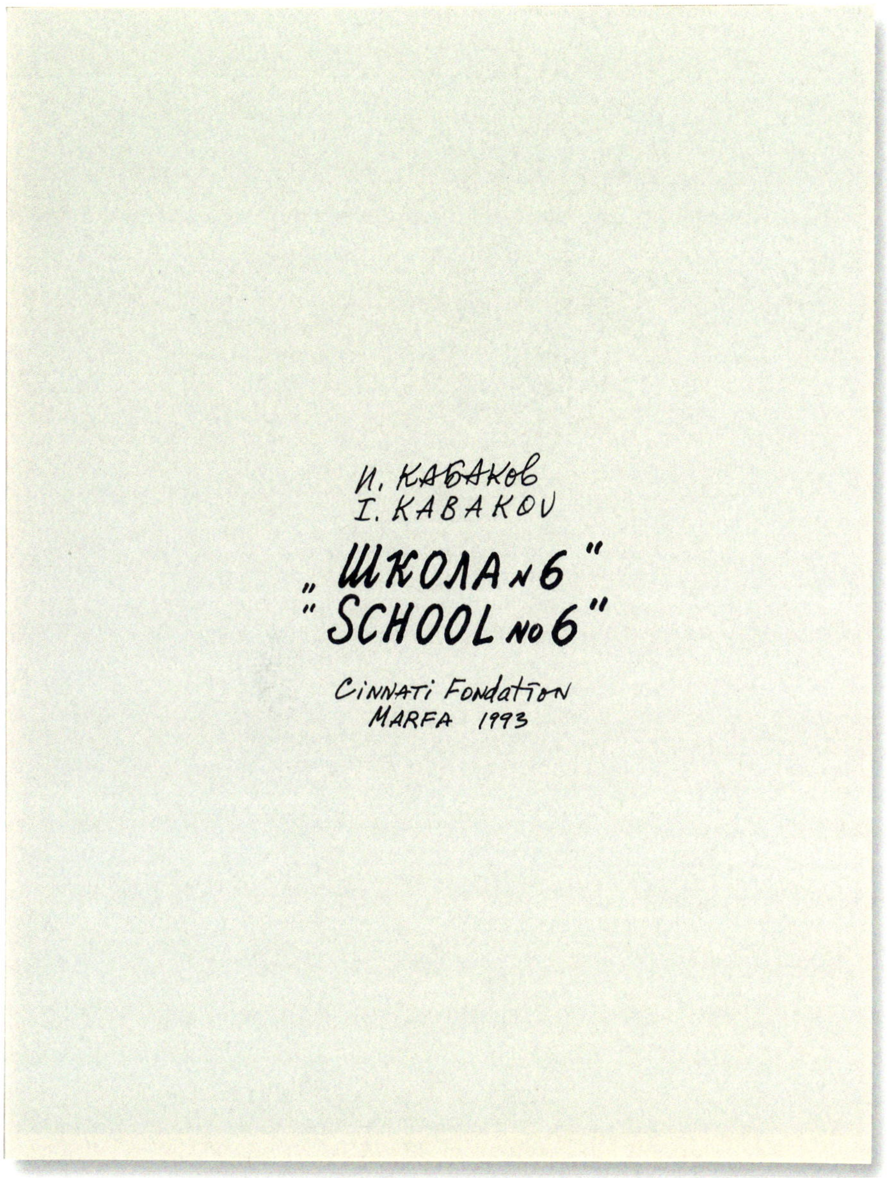

Ilya and Emilia Kabakov
New York: published by Ilya and Emilia Kabakov
27.5 x 21.2 cm
34 photocopied pp. with 24 (incl. 8 color foldouts) ills.
adhesive binding, cardboard cover, label on the cover
Klebebindung, Kartonumschlag, Etikette auf dem Umschlag
edition: 250 numbered copies

thematic publication | *thematische Publikation*

layout by Ilya Kabakov | *Layout von Ilya Kabakov*

Documentation of the installation »The Deserted School or School No. 6« from 1993 for the Chinati Foundation, Marfa, TX. Texts by Ilya and Emilia Kabakov; English, Russian.

Dokumentation der Installation »Die verlassene Schule oder Schule Nr. 6« von 1993 für die Chinati Foundation, Marfa, TX. Texte von Ilya und Emilia Kabakov; englisch, russisch.

see also | *siehe auch* CRI, vol. 1, no. 75, pp. 478–485

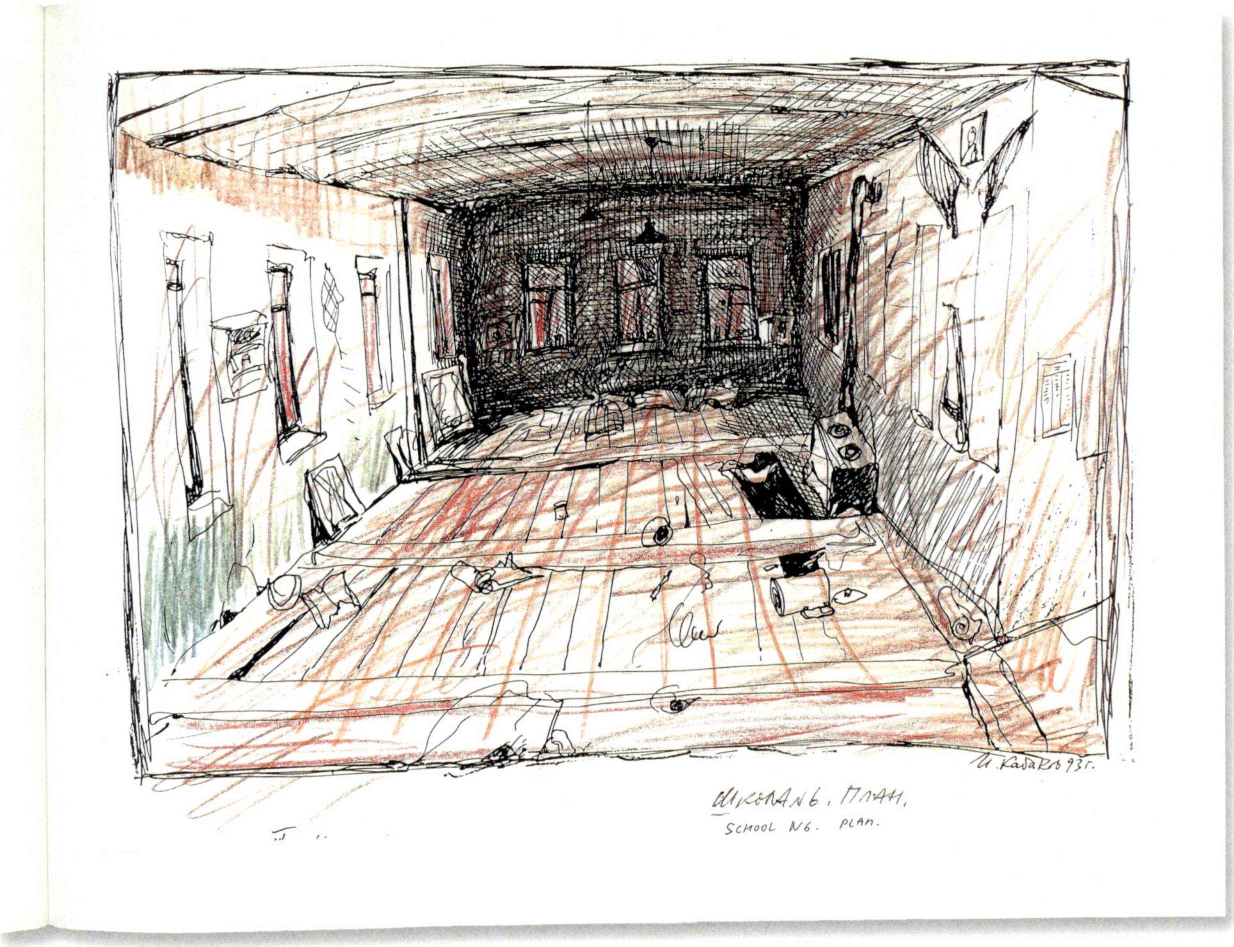
И. Кабаков 93 г.
Школа N6. План.
SCHOOL N6. PLAN.

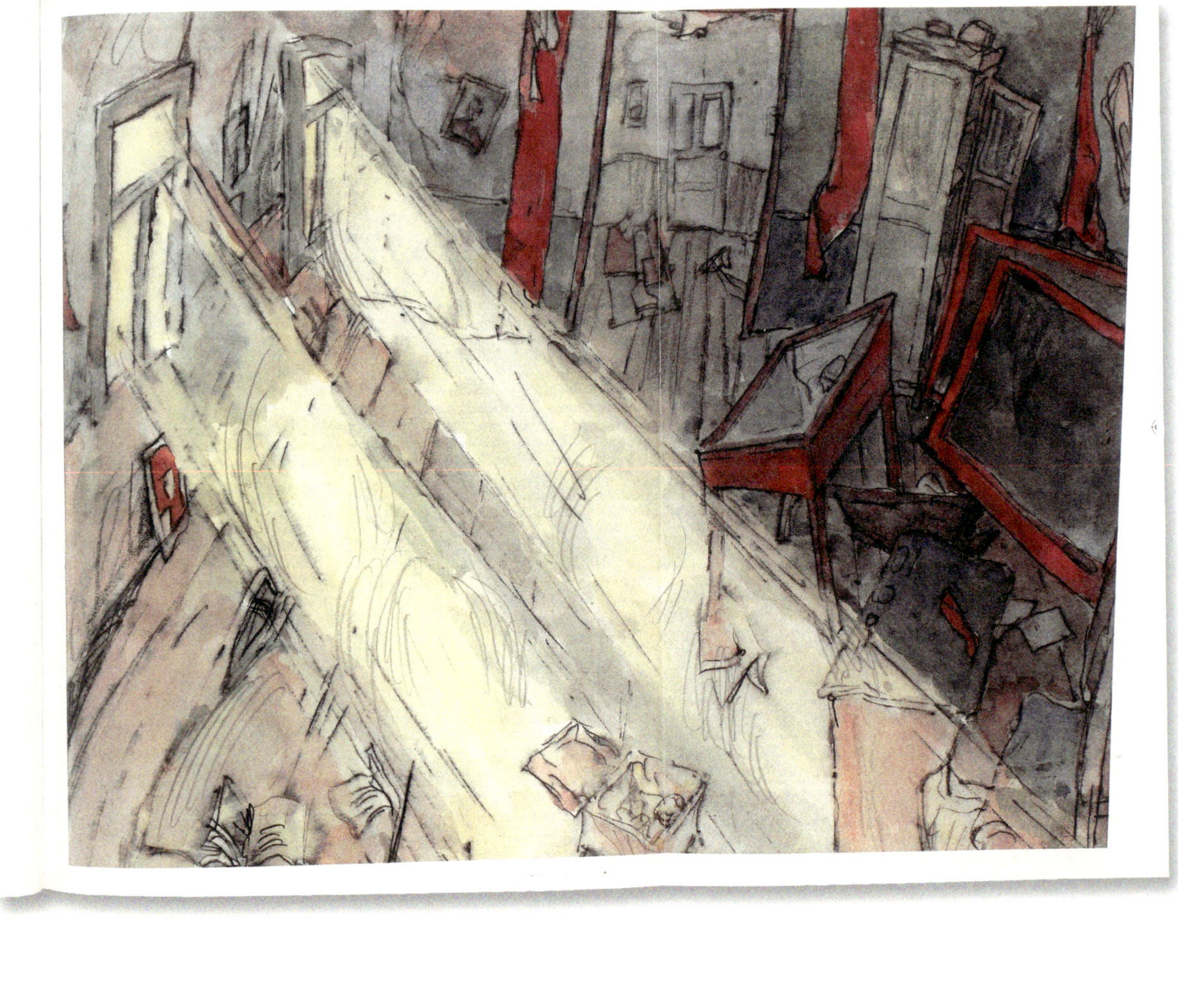

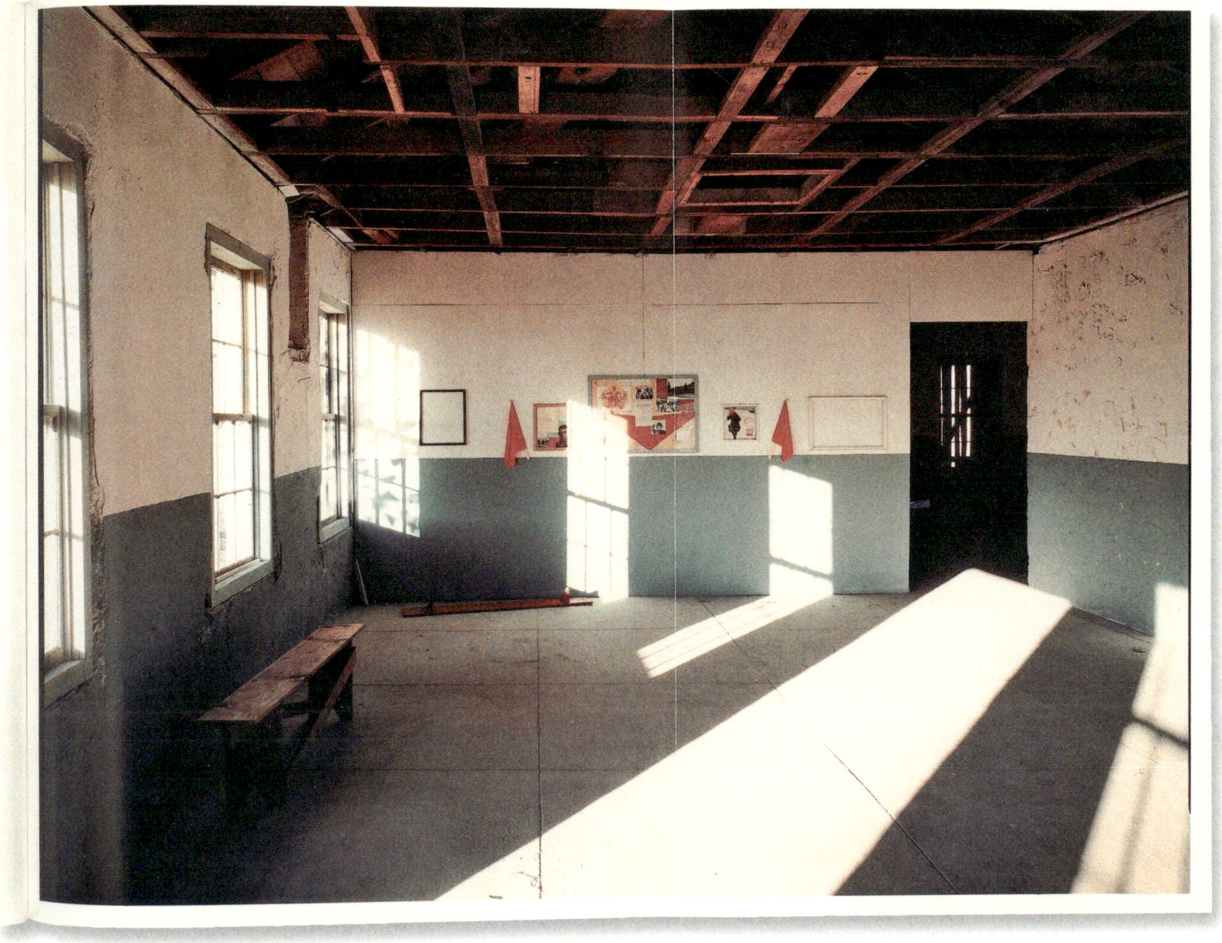

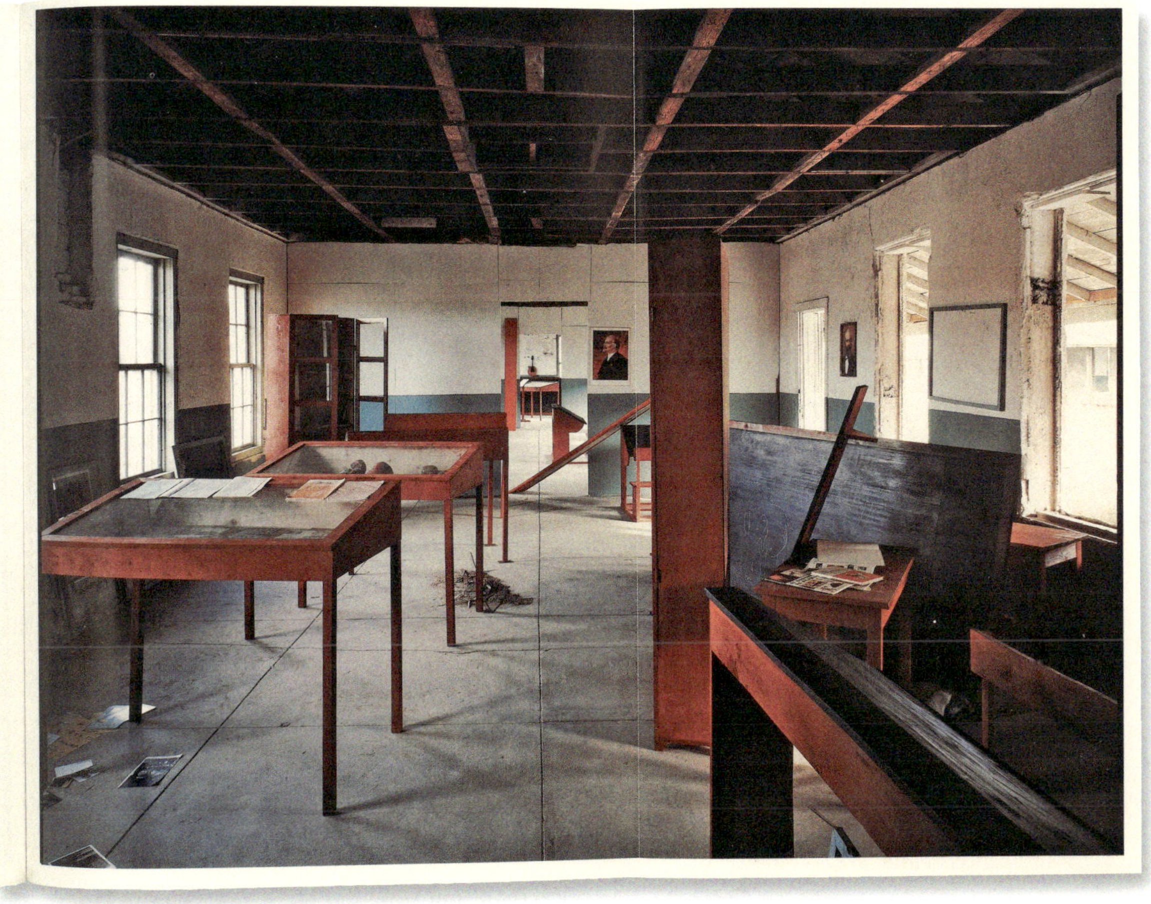

111 The Text as the Basis of Visual Expression | *Der Text als Grundlage des Visuellen*

2000

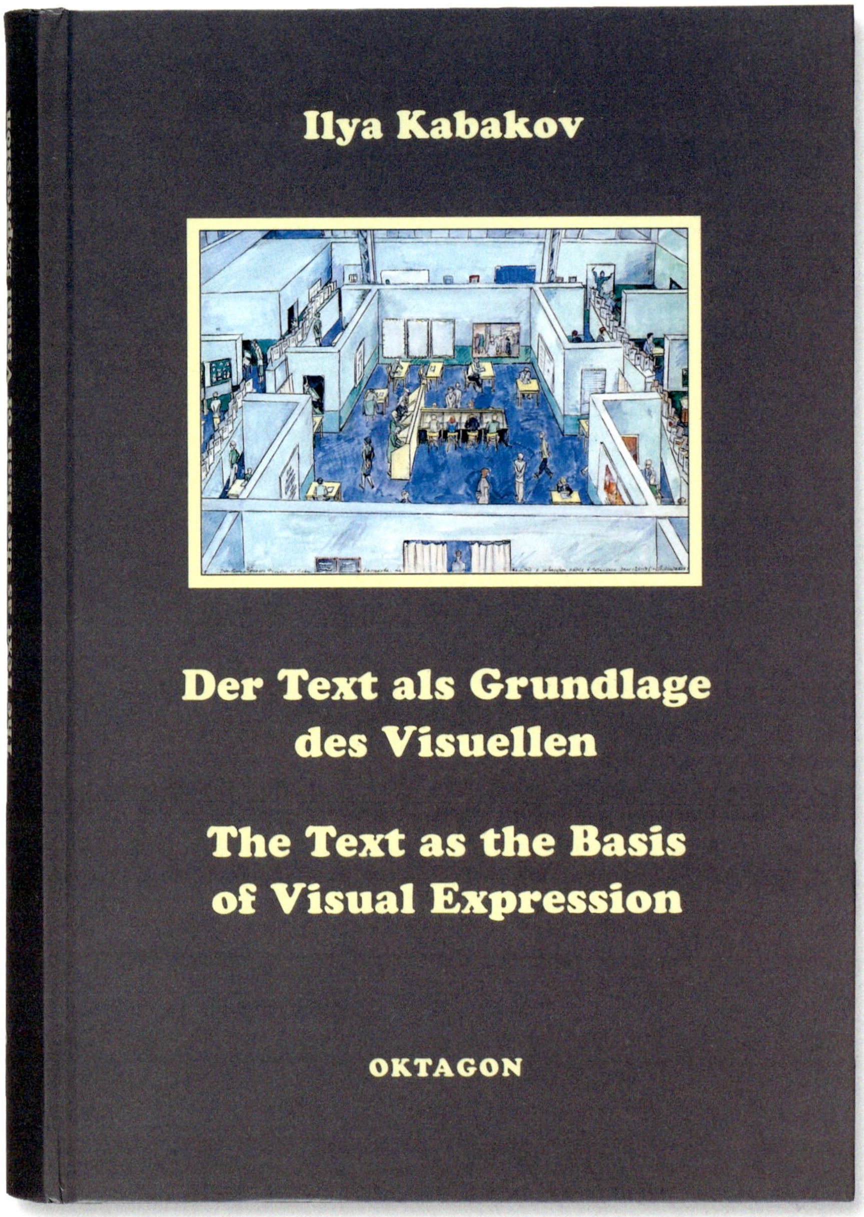

Zdenek Felix
Cologne: Oktagon
23.7 x 17.3 cm
404 pp. with 110 b/w ills.
stitchbound, versions in hardcover and softback
Fadenheftung, Fassungen in Hardcover und broschiert
edition: a limited edition of the book includes an original drawing in color by Ilya Kabakov, numbered 1-17

thematic publication | *thematische Publikation*

layout by Ilya Kabakov | *Layout von Ilya Kabakov*

Ilya Kabakov debates the role of the text in the various media-drawing, album, painting, and installation. Texts by Ilya Kabakov and Zdenek Felix; German.

Ilya Kabakov erörtert die Rolle des Textes in den verschiedenen Medien Zeichnung, Album, Bild und Installation. Texte von Ilya Kabakov und Zdenek Felix; deutsch.

see also | *siehe auch*

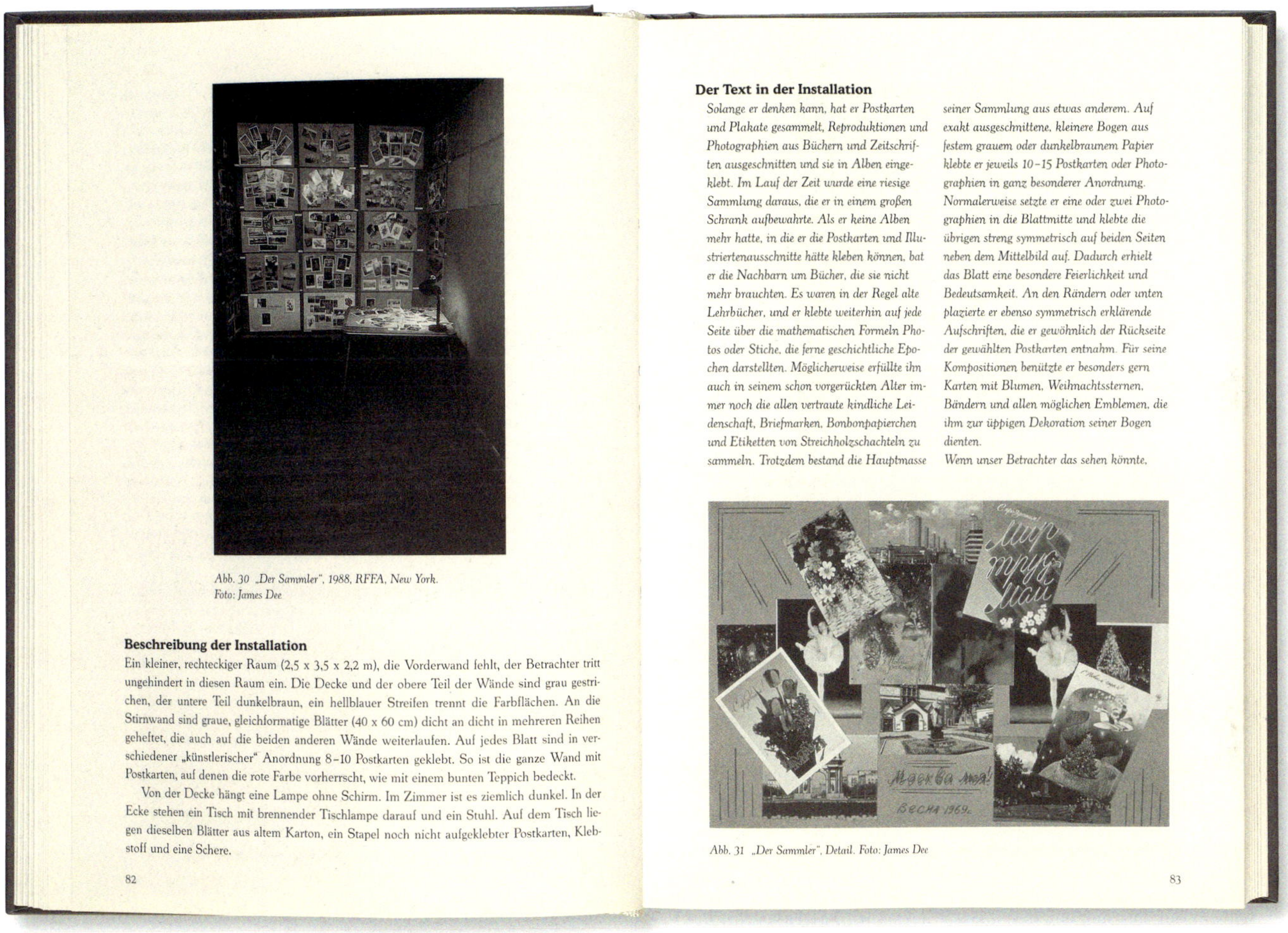

Abb. 30 „Der Sammler", 1988, RFFA, New York.
Foto: James Dee

Beschreibung der Installation

Ein kleiner, rechteckiger Raum (2,5 x 3,5 x 2,2 m), die Vorderwand fehlt, der Betrachter tritt ungehindert in diesen Raum ein. Die Decke und der obere Teil der Wände sind grau gestrichen, der untere Teil dunkelbraun, ein hellblauer Streifen trennt die Farbflächen. An die Stirnwand sind graue, gleichformatige Blätter (40 x 60 cm) dicht an dicht in mehreren Reihen geheftet, die auch auf die beiden anderen Wände weiterlaufen. Auf jedes Blatt sind in verschiedener „künstlerischer" Anordnung 8–10 Postkarten geklebt. So ist die ganze Wand mit Postkarten, auf denen die rote Farbe vorherrscht, wie mit einem bunten Teppich bedeckt.

Von der Decke hängt eine Lampe ohne Schirm. Im Zimmer ist es ziemlich dunkel. In der Ecke stehen ein Tisch mit brennender Tischlampe darauf und ein Stuhl. Auf dem Tisch liegen dieselben Blätter aus altem Karton, ein Stapel noch nicht aufgeklebter Postkarten, Klebstoff und eine Schere.

82

Der Text in der Installation

Solange er denken kann, hat er Postkarten und Plakate gesammelt, Reproduktionen und Photographien aus Büchern und Zeitschriften ausgeschnitten und sie in Alben eingeklebt. Im Lauf der Zeit wurde eine riesige Sammlung daraus, die er in einem großen Schrank aufbewahrte. Als er keine Alben mehr hatte, in die er die Postkarten und Illustriertenausschnitte hätte kleben können, bat er die Nachbarn um Bücher, die sie nicht mehr brauchten. Es waren in der Regel alte Lehrbücher, und er klebte weiterhin auf jede Seite über die mathematischen Formeln Photos oder Stiche, die ferne geschichtliche Epochen darstellten. Möglicherweise erfüllte ihn auch in seinem schon vorgerückten Alter immer noch die allen vertraute kindliche Leidenschaft, Briefmarken, Bonbonpapierchen und Etiketten von Streichholzschachteln zu sammeln. Trotzdem bestand die Hauptmasse seiner Sammlung aus etwas anderem. Auf exakt ausgeschnittene, kleinere Bogen aus festem grauem oder dunkelbraunem Papier klebte er jeweils 10–15 Postkarten oder Photographien in ganz besonderer Anordnung. Normalerweise setzte er eine oder zwei Photographien in die Blattmitte und klebte die übrigen streng symmetrisch auf beiden Seiten neben dem Mittelbild auf. Dadurch erhielt das Blatt eine besondere Feierlichkeit und Bedeutsamkeit. An den Rändern oder unten plazierte er ebenso symmetrisch erklärende Aufschriften, die er gewöhnlich der Rückseite der gewählten Postkarten entnahm. Für seine Kompositionen benützte er besonders gern Karten mit Blumen, Weihnachtssternen, Bändern und allen möglichen Emblemen, die ihm zur üppigen Dekoration seiner Bogen dienten.

Wenn unser Betrachter das sehen könnte,

Abb. 31 „Der Sammler", Detail. Foto: James Dee

83

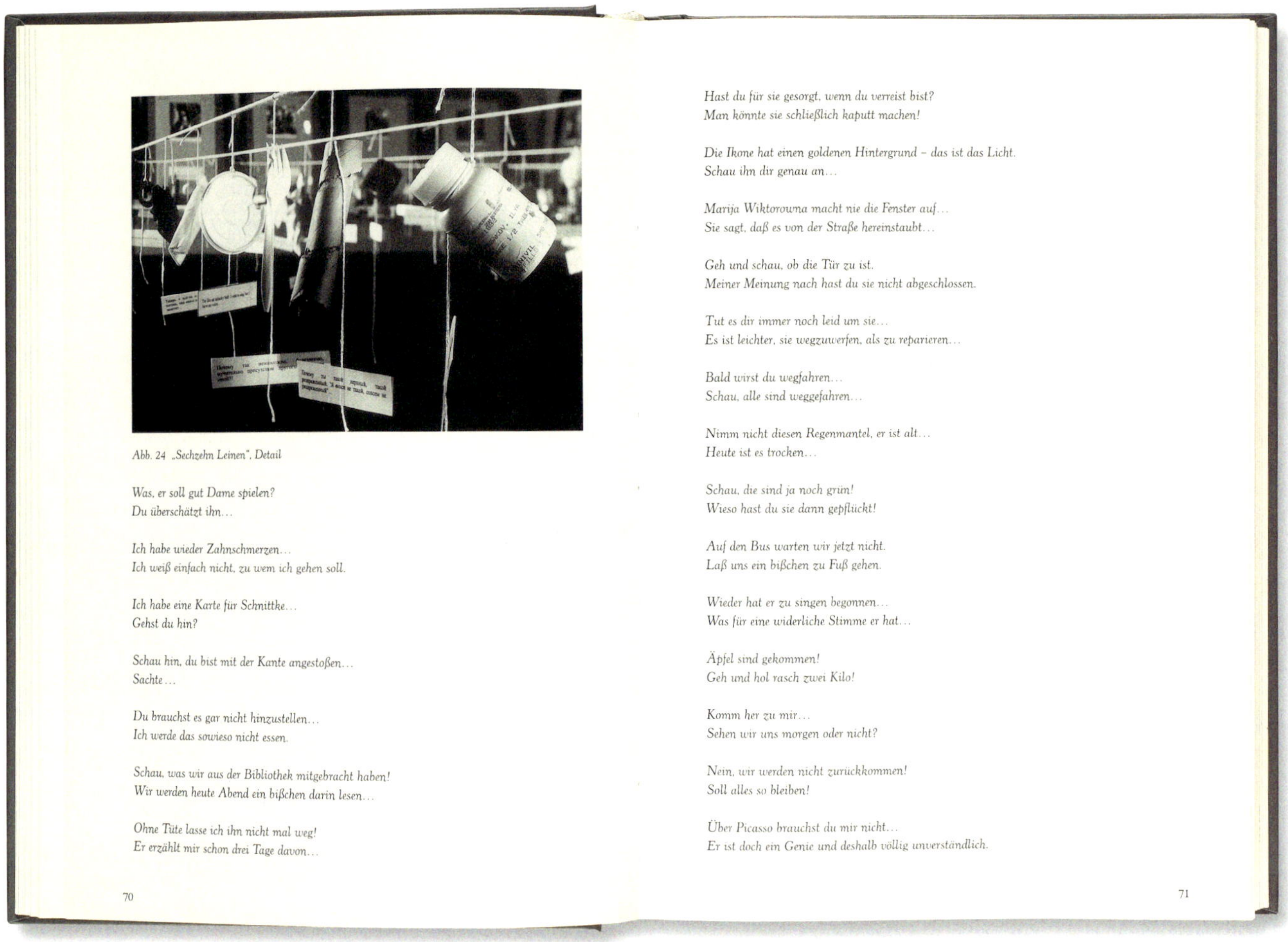

Abb. 24 „Sechzehn Leinen". Detail

Was, er soll gut Dame spielen?
Du überschätzt ihn…

Ich habe wieder Zahnschmerzen…
Ich weiß einfach nicht, zu wem ich gehen soll.

Ich habe eine Karte für Schnittke…
Gehst du hin?

Schau hin, du bist mit der Kante angestoßen…
Sachte…

Du brauchst es gar nicht hinzustellen…
Ich werde das sowieso nicht essen.

Schau, was wir aus der Bibliothek mitgebracht haben!
Wir werden heute Abend ein bißchen darin lesen…

Ohne Tüte lasse ich ihn nicht mal weg!
Er erzählt mir schon drei Tage davon…

70

Hast du für sie gesorgt, wenn du verreist bist?
Man könnte sie schließlich kaputt machen!

Die Ikone hat einen goldenen Hintergrund – das ist das Licht.
Schau ihn dir genau an…

Marija Wiktorowna macht nie die Fenster auf…
Sie sagt, daß es von der Straße hereinstaubt…

Geh und schau, ob die Tür zu ist.
Meiner Meinung nach hast du sie nicht abgeschlossen.

Tut es dir immer noch leid um sie…
Es ist leichter, sie wegzuwerfen, als zu reparieren…

Bald wirst du wegfahren…
Schau, alle sind weggefahren…

Nimm nicht diesen Regenmantel, er ist alt…
Heute ist es trocken…

Schau, die sind ja noch grün!
Wieso hast du sie dann gepflückt!

Auf den Bus warten wir jetzt nicht.
Laß uns ein bißchen zu Fuß gehen.

Wieder hat er zu singen begonnen…
Was für eine widerliche Stimme er hat…

Äpfel sind gekommen!
Geh und hol rasch zwei Kilo!

Komm her zu mir…
Sehen wir uns morgen oder nicht?

Nein, wir werden nicht zurückkommen!
Soll alles so bleiben!

Über Picasso brauchst du mir nicht…
Er ist doch ein Genie und deshalb völlig unverständlich.

71

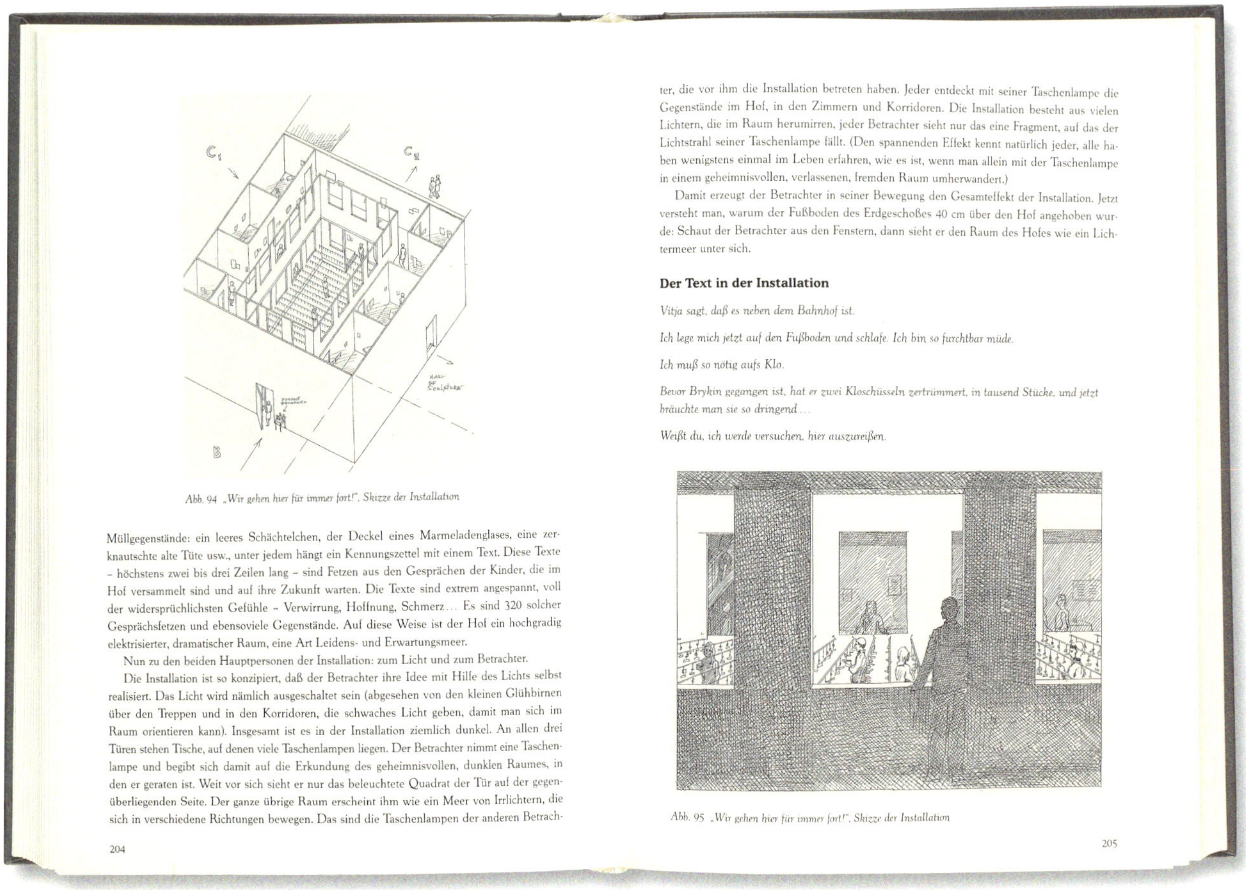

Abb. 94 *„Wir gehen hier für immer fort!". Skizze der Installation*

Müllgegenstände: ein leeres Schächtelchen, der Deckel eines Marmeladenglases, eine zerknautschte alte Tüte usw., unter jedem hängt ein Kennungszettel mit einem Text. Diese Texte – höchstens zwei bis drei Zeilen lang – sind Fetzen aus den Gesprächen der Kinder, die im Hof versammelt sind und auf ihre Zukunft warten. Die Texte sind extrem angespannt, voll der widersprüchlichsten Gefühle – Verwirrung, Hoffnung, Schmerz… Es sind 320 solcher Gesprächsfetzen und ebensoviele Gegenstände. Auf diese Weise ist der Hof ein hochgradig elektrisierter, dramatischer Raum, eine Art Leidens- und Erwartungsmeer.

Nun zu den beiden Hauptpersonen der Installation: zum Licht und zum Betrachter.

Die Installation ist so konzipiert, daß der Betrachter ihre Idee mit Hilfe des Lichts selbst realisiert. Das Licht wird nämlich ausgeschaltet sein (abgesehen von den kleinen Glühbirnen über den Treppen und in den Korridoren, die schwaches Licht geben, damit man sich im Raum orientieren kann). Insgesamt ist es in der Installation ziemlich dunkel. An allen drei Türen stehen Tische, auf denen viele Taschenlampen liegen. Der Betrachter nimmt eine Taschenlampe und begibt sich damit auf die Erkundung des geheimnisvollen, dunklen Raumes, in den er geraten ist. Weit vor sich sieht er nur das beleuchtete Quadrat der Tür auf der gegenüberliegenden Seite. Der ganze übrige Raum erscheint ihm wie ein Meer von Irrlichtern, die sich in verschiedene Richtungen bewegen. Das sind die Taschenlampen der anderen Betrachter, die vor ihm die Installation betreten haben. Jeder entdeckt mit seiner Taschenlampe die Gegenstände im Hof, in den Zimmern und Korridoren. Die Installation besteht aus vielen Lichtern, die im Raum herumirren, jeder Betrachter sieht nur das eine Fragment, auf das der Lichtstrahl seiner Taschenlampe fällt. (Den spannenden Effekt kennt natürlich jeder, alle haben wenigstens einmal im Leben erfahren, wie es ist, wenn man allein mit der Taschenlampe in einem geheimnisvollen, verlassenen, fremden Raum umherwandert.)

Damit erzeugt der Betrachter in seiner Bewegung den Gesamteffekt der Installation. Jetzt versteht man, warum der Fußboden des Erdgeschoßes 40 cm über den Hof angehoben wurde: Schaut der Betrachter aus den Fenstern, dann sieht er den Raum des Hofes wie ein Lichtermeer unter sich.

204

Der Text in der Installation

Vitja sagt, daß es neben dem Bahnhof ist.

Ich lege mich jetzt auf den Fußboden und schlafe. Ich bin so furchtbar müde.

Ich muß so nötig aufs Klo.

Bevor Brykin gegangen ist, hat er zwei Kloschüsseln zertrümmert, in tausend Stücke, und jetzt bräuchte man sie so dringend…

Weißt du, ich werde versuchen, hier auszureißen.

Abb. 95 *„Wir gehen hier für immer fort!". Skizze der Installation*

205

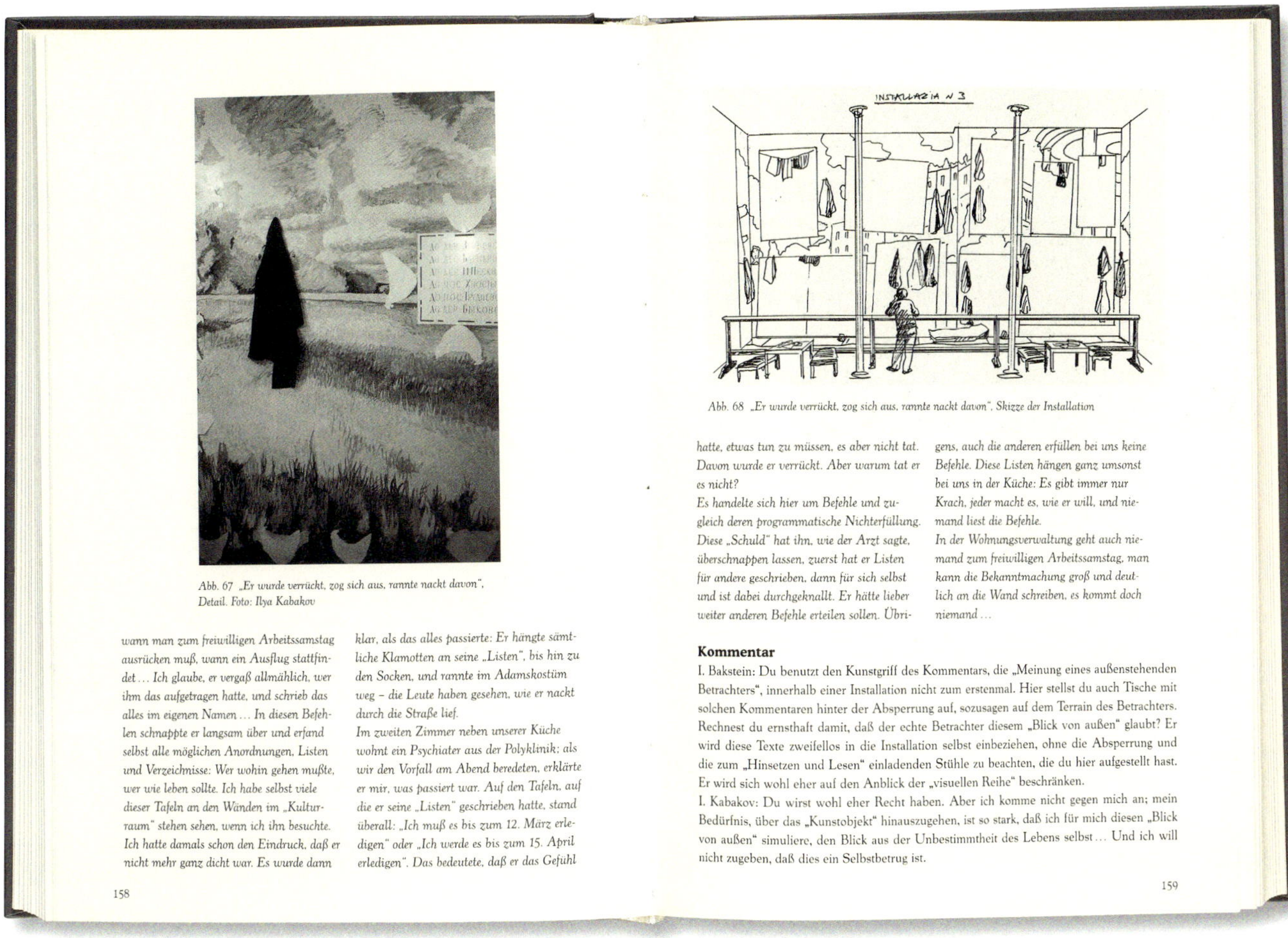

Abb. 67 „Er wurde verrückt, zog sich aus, rannte nackt davon", Detail. Foto: Ilya Kabakov

wann man zum freiwilligen Arbeitssamstag ausrücken muß, wann ein Ausflug stattfindet … Ich glaube, er vergaß allmählich, wer ihm das aufgetragen hatte, und schrieb das alles im eigenen Namen … In diesen Befehlen schnappte er langsam über und erfand selbst alle möglichen Anordnungen, Listen und Verzeichnisse: Wer wohin gehen mußte, wer wie leben sollte. Ich habe selbst viele dieser Tafeln an den Wänden im „Kulturraum" stehen sehen, wenn ich ihn besuchte. Ich hatte damals schon den Eindruck, daß er nicht mehr ganz dicht war. Es wurde dann klar, als das alles passierte: Er hängte sämtliche Klamotten an seine „Listen", bis hin zu den Socken, und rannte im Adamskostüm weg – die Leute haben gesehen, wie er nackt durch die Straße lief.

Im zweiten Zimmer neben unserer Küche wohnt ein Psychiater aus der Polyklinik; als wir den Vorfall am Abend beredeten, erklärte er mir, was passiert war. Auf den Tafeln, auf die er seine „Listen" geschrieben hatte, stand überall: „Ich muß es bis zum 12. März erledigen" oder „Ich werde es bis zum 15. April erledigen". Das bedeutete, daß er das Gefühl

158

Abb. 68 „Er wurde verrückt, zog sich aus, rannte nackt davon". Skizze der Installation

hatte, etwas tun zu müssen, es aber nicht tat. Davon wurde er verrückt. Aber warum tat er es nicht?

Es handelte sich hier um Befehle und zugleich deren programmatische Nichterfüllung. Diese „Schuld" hat ihn, wie der Arzt sagte, überschnappen lassen, zuerst hat er Listen für andere geschrieben, dann für sich selbst und ist dabei durchgeknallt. Er hätte lieber weiter anderen Befehle erteilen sollen. Übrigens, auch die anderen erfüllen bei uns keine Befehle. Diese Listen hängen ganz umsonst bei uns in der Küche: Es gibt immer nur Krach, jeder macht es, wie er will, und niemand liest die Befehle.

In der Wohnungsverwaltung geht auch niemand zum freiwilligen Arbeitssamstag, man kann die Bekanntmachung groß und deutlich an die Wand schreiben, es kommt doch niemand …

Kommentar

I. Bakstein: Du benutzt den Kunstgriff des Kommentars, die „Meinung eines außenstehenden Betrachters", innerhalb einer Installation nicht zum erstenmal. Hier stellst du auch Tische mit solchen Kommentaren hinter der Absperrung auf, sozusagen auf dem Terrain des Betrachters. Rechnest du ernsthaft damit, daß der echte Betrachter diesem „Blick von außen" glaubt? Er wird diese Texte zweifellos in die Installation selbst einbeziehen, ohne die Absperrung und die zum „Hinsetzen und Lesen" einladenden Stühle zu beachten, die du hier aufgestellt hast. Er wird sich wohl eher auf den Anblick der „visuellen Reihe" beschränken.

I. Kabakov: Du wirst wohl eher Recht haben. Aber ich komme nicht gegen mich an; mein Bedürfnis, über das „Kunstobjekt" hinauszugehen, ist so stark, daß ich für mich diesen „Blick von außen" simuliere, den Blick aus der Unbestimmtheit des Lebens selbst … Und ich will nicht zugeben, daß dies ein Selbstbetrug ist.

159

112 We Live Here | *Wir leben hier*

2000

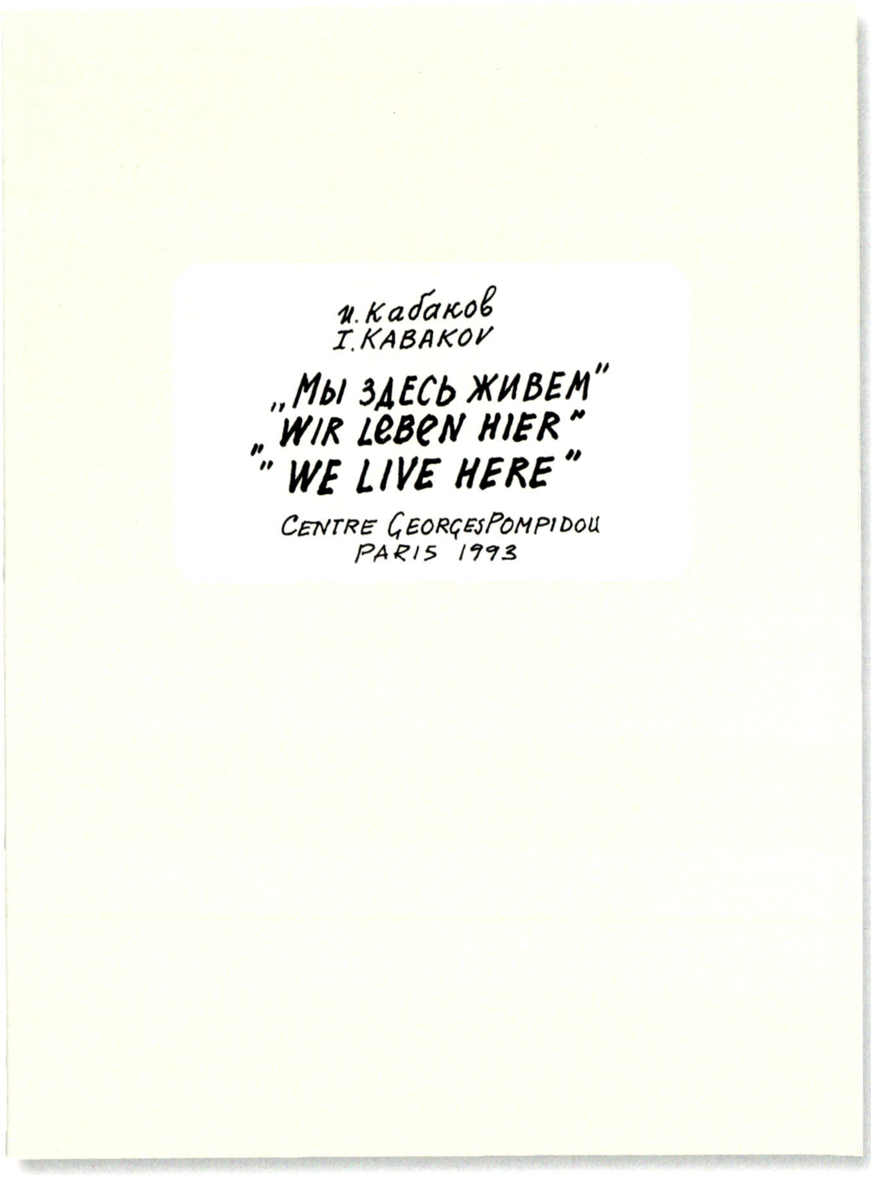

Ilya and Emilia Kabakov
New York: published by Ilya and Emilia Kabakov
27.2 x 20.9 cm
80 photocopied pp. with 35 b/w (incl. 4 foldouts) and 10 color (incl. 8 foldouts) ills.
adhesive binding, cardboard cover, label on the cover
Klebebindung, Kartonumschlag, Etikette auf dem Umschlag
edition: 250 numbered copies

thematic publication | *thematische Publikation*

layout by Ilya Kabakov | *Layout von Ilya Kabakov*

Documentation of the installation of the same name in the exhibition »C'est ici que nous vivons«, Centre national d'art et de culture Georges Pompidou, Paris, May 16 to September 4, 1995. Text by Ilya Kabakov and a dialogue between Boris Groys and Ilya Kabakov on the installation »We Live Here«; Russian, English, German.

Dokumentation der gleichnamigen Installation in der Ausstellung »C'est ici que nous vivons«, Centre national d'art et de culture Georges Pompidou, Paris, 16. Mai – 4. September 1995. Text von Ilya Kabakov und ein Dialog von Boris Groys und Ilya Kabakov über die Installation »Wir leben hier«; russisch, englisch, deutsch.

see also | *siehe auch* CRI, vol. 2, no. 86, pp. 76–83; CRP, vol. 1, nos. 259–262, pp. 330–333

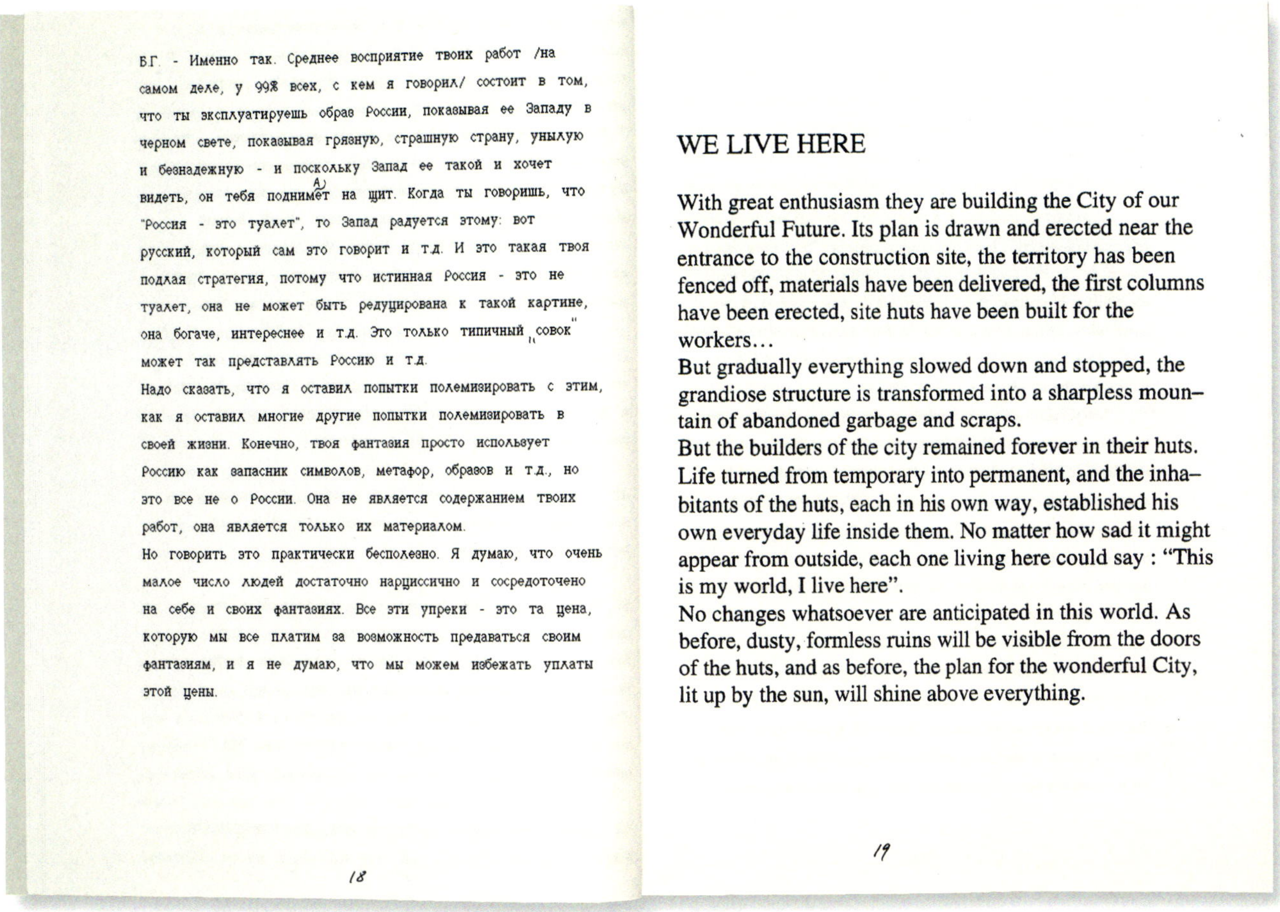

Б.Г. - Именно так. Среднее восприятие твоих работ /на самом деле, у 99% всех, с кем я говорил/ состоит в том, что ты эксплуатируешь образ России, показывая ее Западу в черном свете, показывая грязную, страшную страну, унылую и безнадежную - и поскольку Запад ее такой и хочет видеть, он тебя поднимет на щит. Когда ты говоришь, что "Россия - это туалет", то Запад радуется этому: вот русский, который сам это говорит и т.д. И это такая твоя подлая стратегия, потому что истинная Россия - это не туалет, она не может быть редуцирована к такой картине, она богаче, интереснее и т.д. Это только типичный „совок" может так представлять Россию и т.д.

Надо сказать, что я оставил попытки полемизировать с этим, как я оставил многие другие попытки полемизировать в своей жизни. Конечно, твоя фантазия просто использует Россию как запасник символов, метафор, образов и т.д., но это все не о России. Она не является содержанием твоих работ, она является только их материалом.

Но говорить это практически бесполезно. Я думаю, что очень малое число людей достаточно нарциссично и сосредоточено на себе и своих фантазиях. Все эти упреки - это та цена, которую мы все платим за возможность предаваться своим фантазиям, и я не думаю, что мы можем избежать уплаты этой цены.

18

WE LIVE HERE

With great enthusiasm they are building the City of our Wonderful Future. Its plan is drawn and erected near the entrance to the construction site, the territory has been fenced off, materials have been delivered, the first columns have been erected, site huts have been built for the workers…

But gradually everything slowed down and stopped, the grandiose structure is transformed into a sharpless mountain of abandoned garbage and scraps.

But the builders of the city remained forever in their huts. Life turned from temporary into permanent, and the inhabitants of the huts, each in his own way, established his own everyday life inside them. No matter how sad it might appear from outside, each one living here could say : "This is my world, I live here".

No changes whatsoever are anticipated in this world. As before, dusty, formless ruins will be visible from the doors of the huts, and as before, the plan for the wonderful City, lit up by the sun, will shine above everything.

19

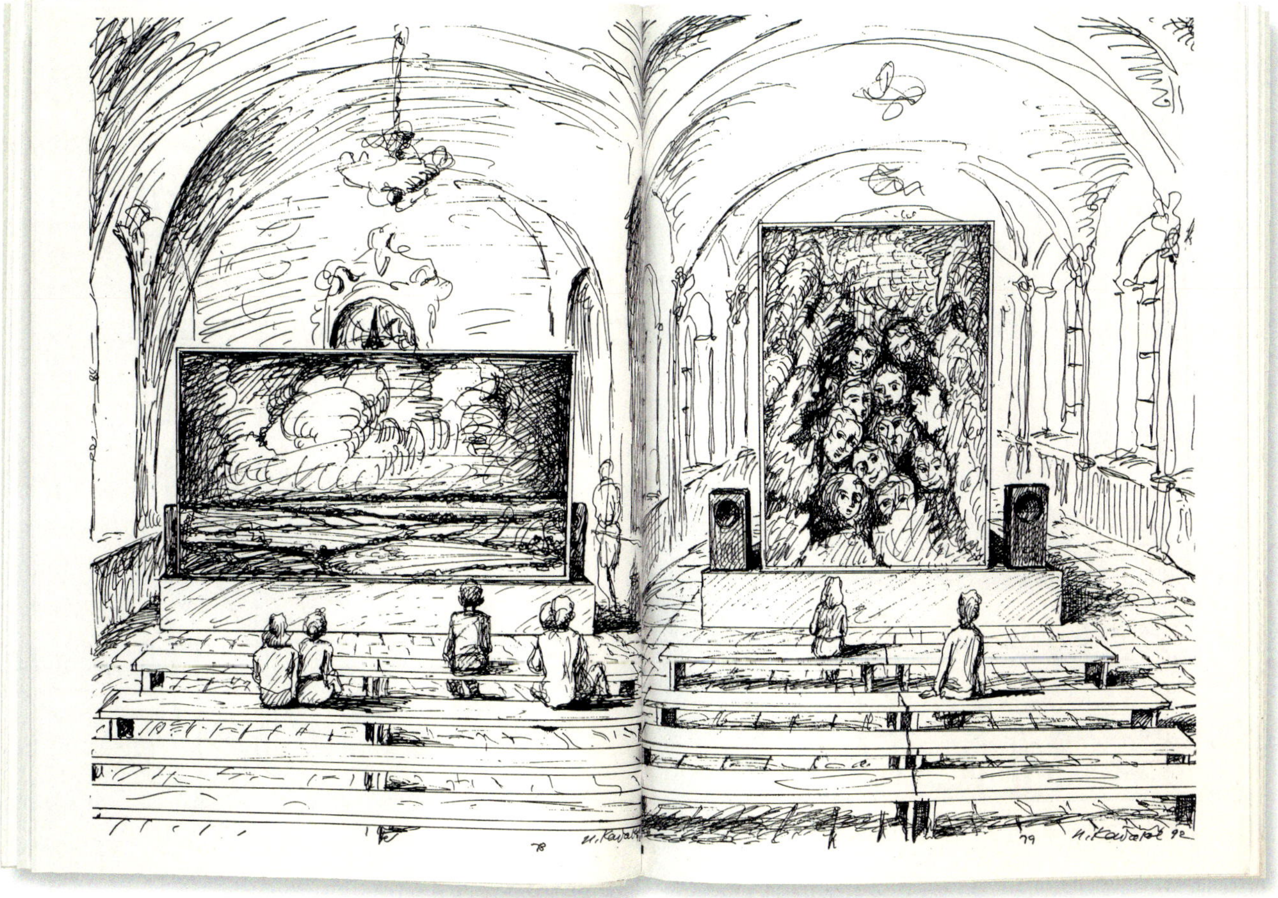

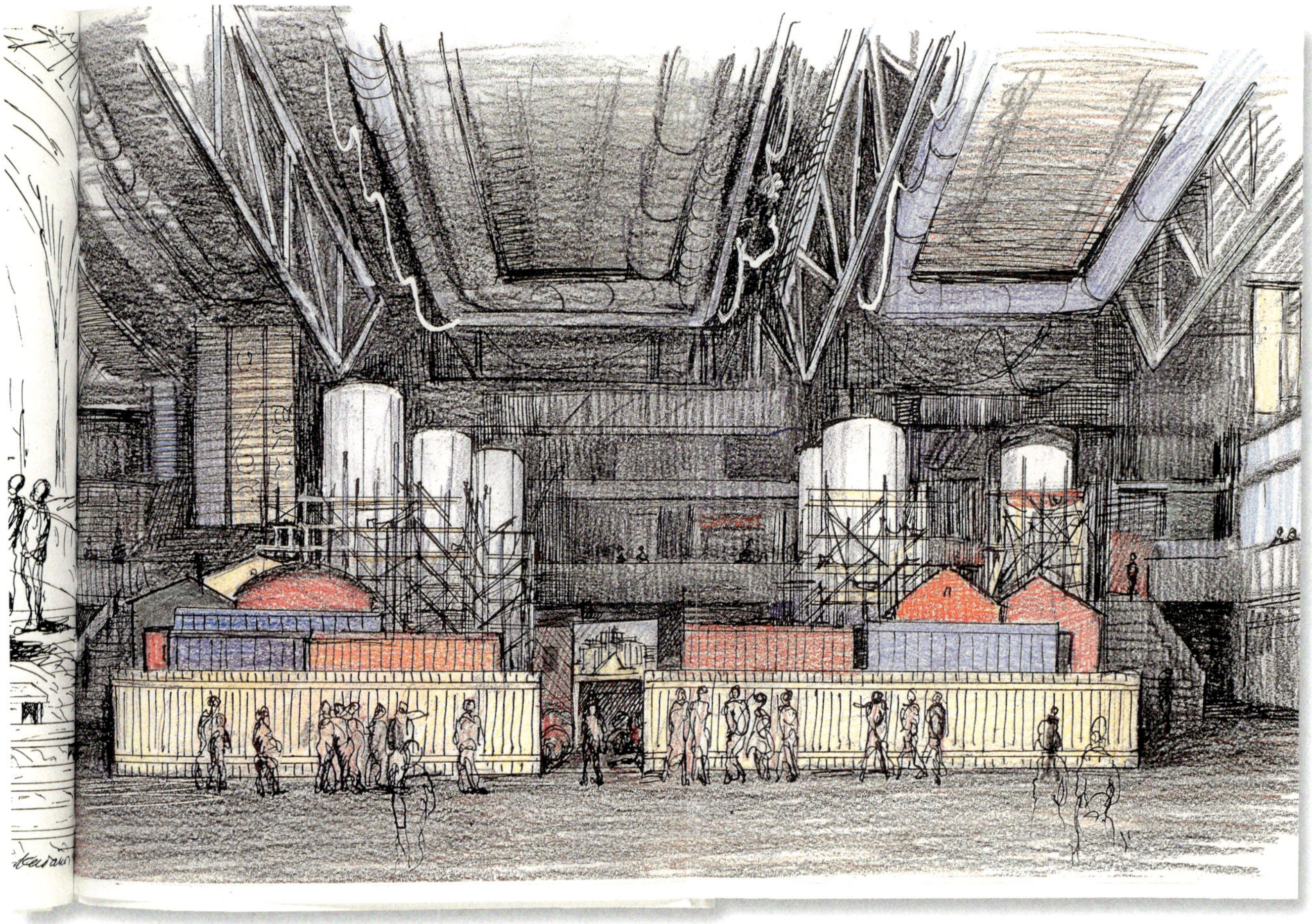

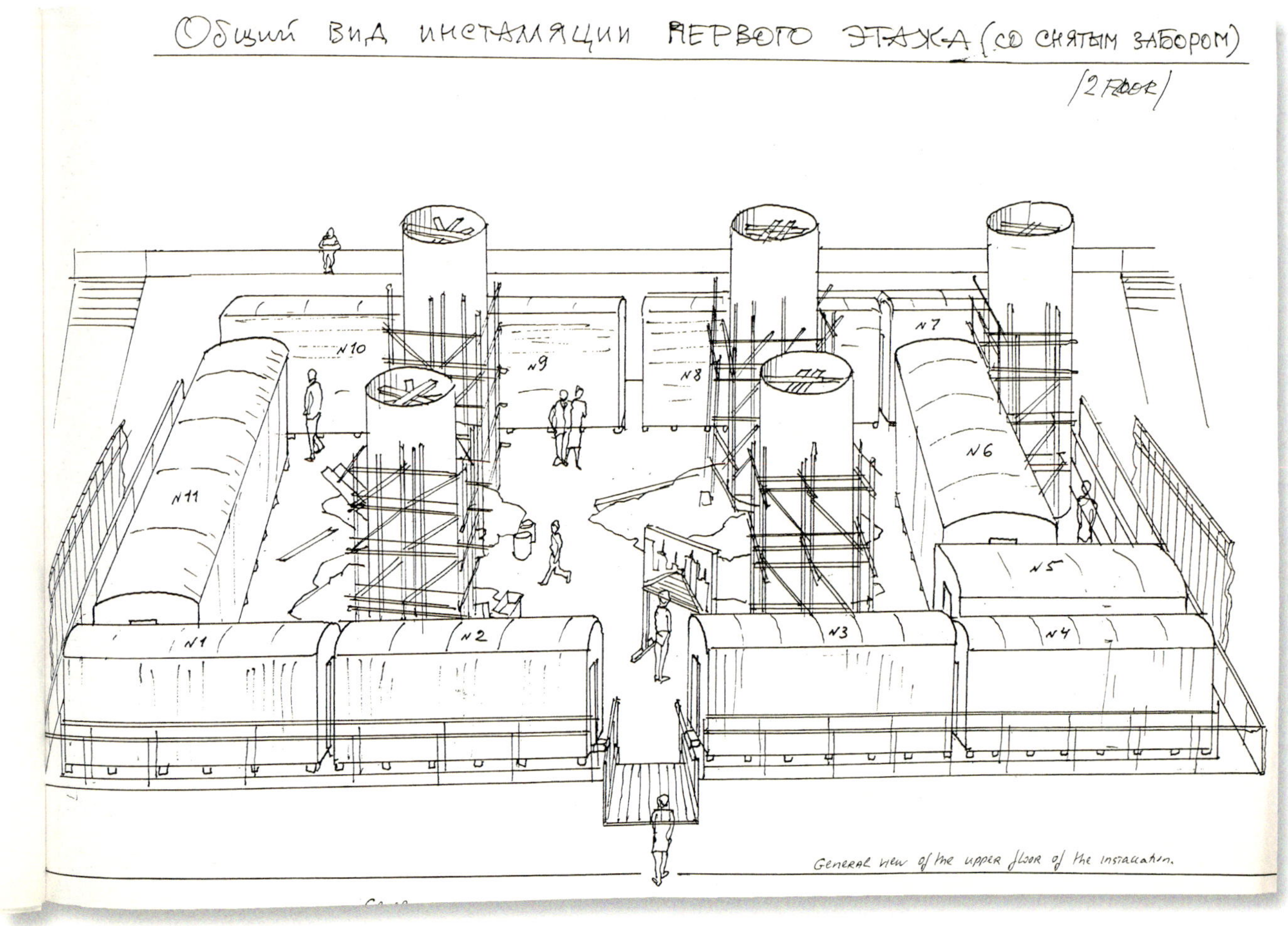
Общий вид инсталляции первого этажа (со снятым забором)
(2 floor)
N1
N2
N3
N4
N5
N6
N7
N8
N9
N10
N11
General view of the upper floor of the installation.

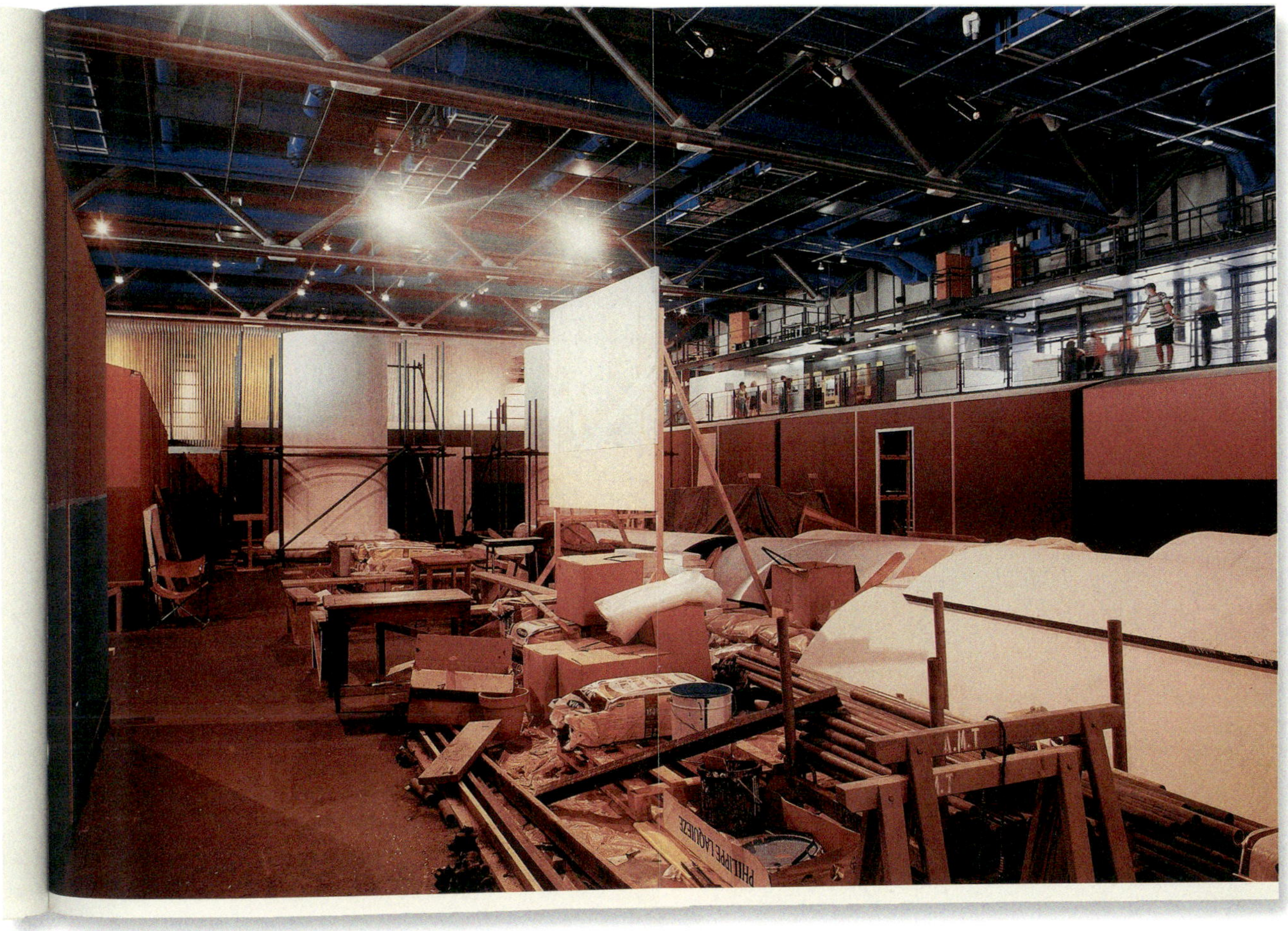
PHILIPPE LAQUIEZE
A.M.T

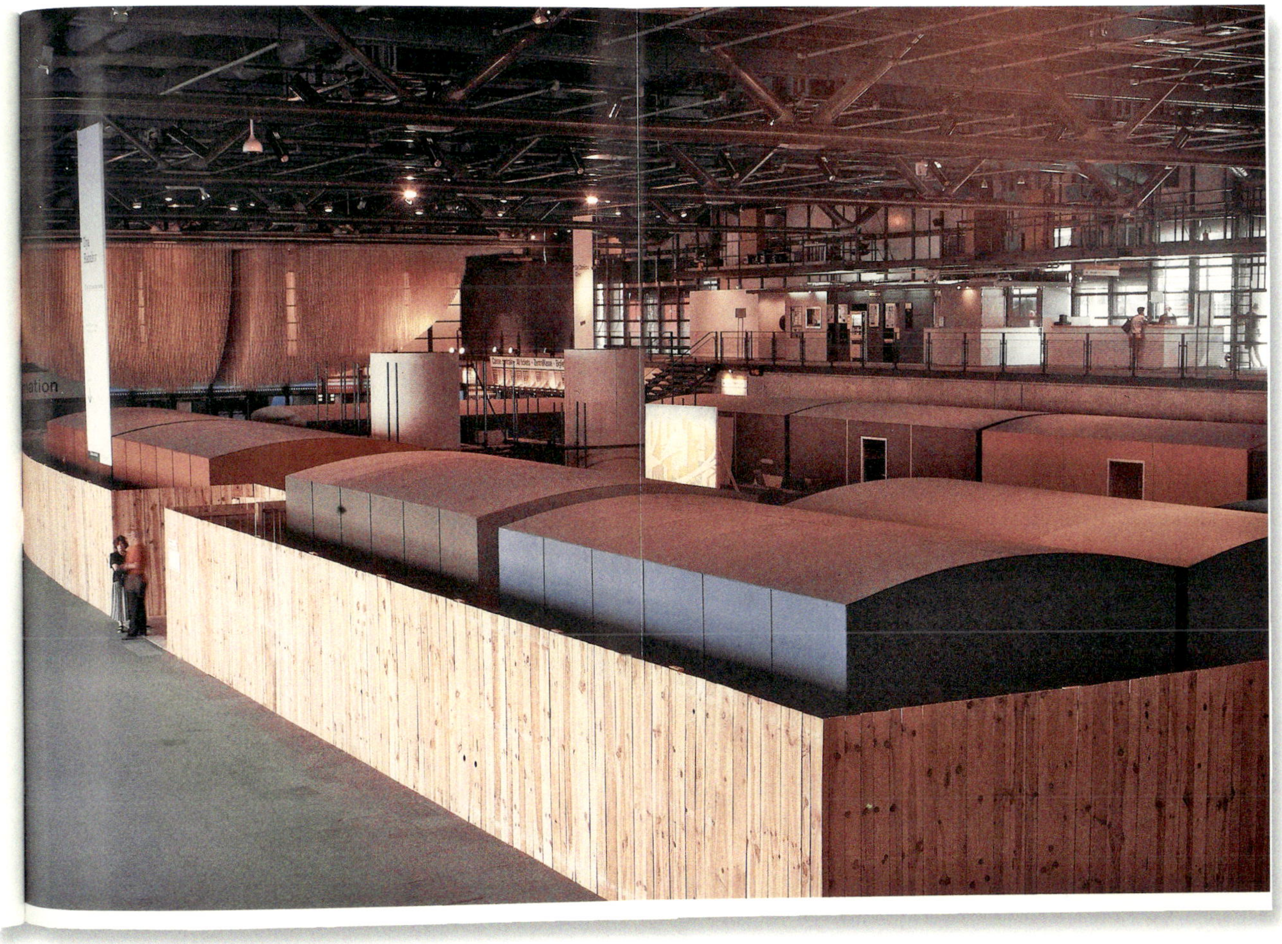

113 50 Installations | *50 Installationen*

2001

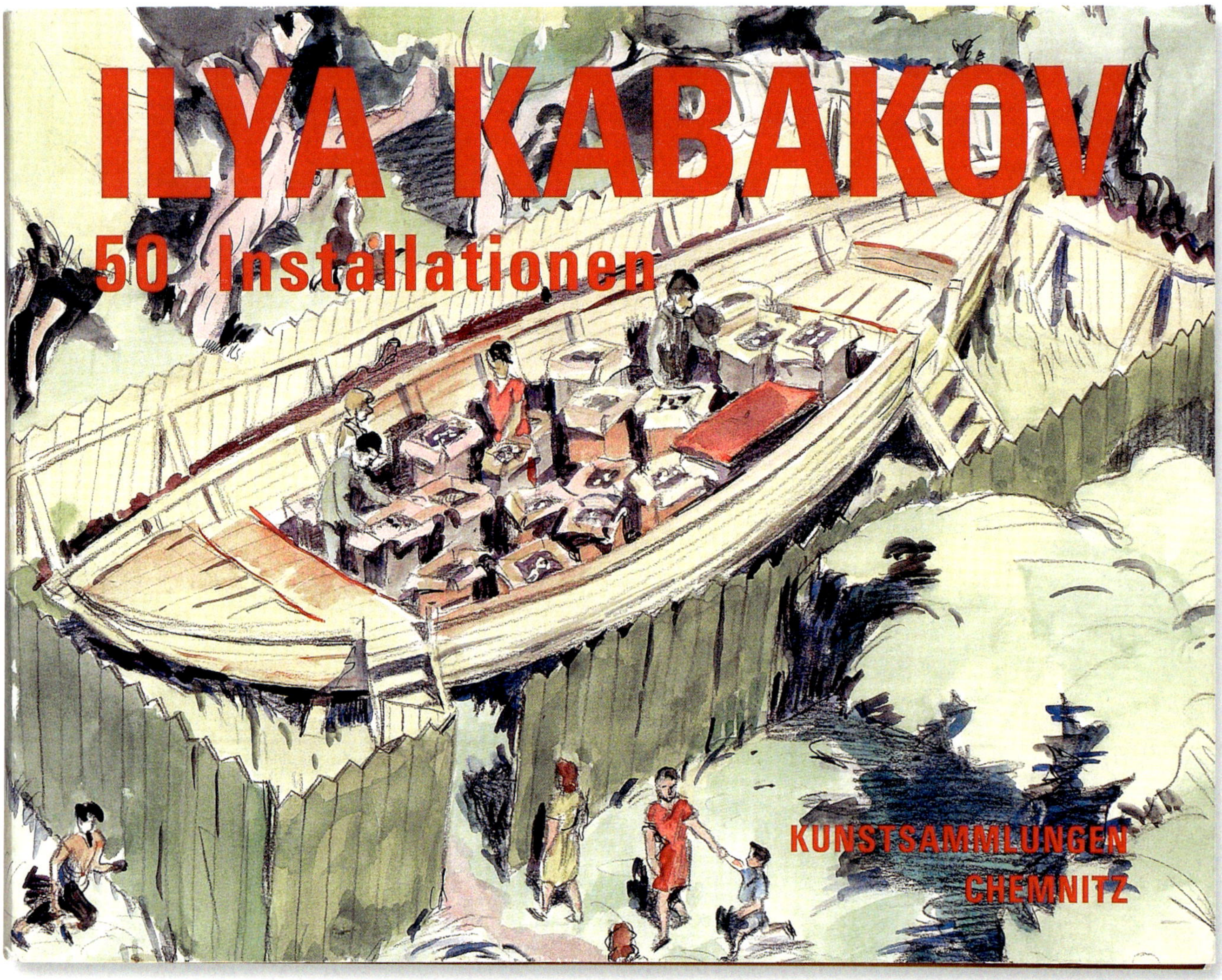

Kunstmuseum Bern
Bern: Kunstmuseum Bern
17 x 22 cm
119 pp. with 50 (26 color) ills.
stitchbound, softback with dust jacket
Fadenheftung, broschiert mit Schutzumschlag

exhibition catalogue | *Ausstellungskatalog*

layout by Ilya Kabakov | *Layout von Ilya Kabakov*

For the installation of the same name at the Kunstsammlungen Chemnitz, Chemnitz, March 23 to June 4, 2001. Texts by Ralf Beil, Ilya Kabakov, and Toni Stooss; German.

Zur gleichnamigen Installation, Kunstsammlungen Chemnitz, Chemnitz, 23. März – 4. Juni 2001. Texte von Ralf Beil, Ilya Kabakov und Toni Stooss; deutsch.

see also | *siehe auch* no. 108; CRI, vol. 2, no. 152, pp. 420–425

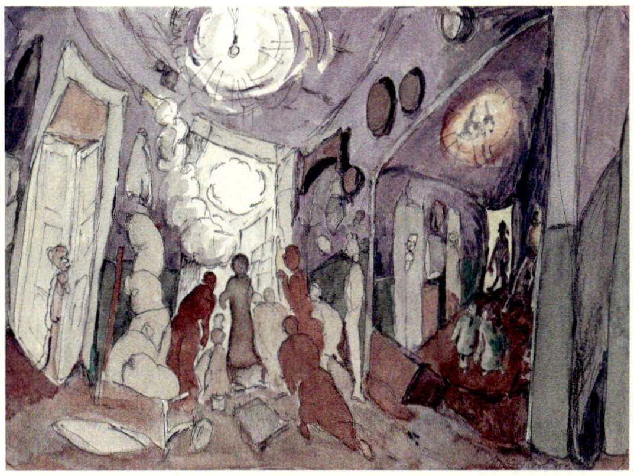

Tafel 19 Ten Characters (Kat. 26)

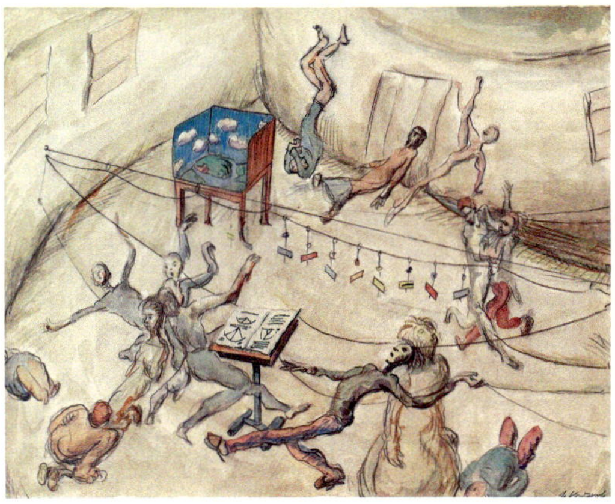

Tafel 5 Mental Institution or Institute of Creative Research (Kat. 126)

114 Public Projects or The Spirit of a Place

Öffentliche Projekte oder Der Geist eines Orts

2001

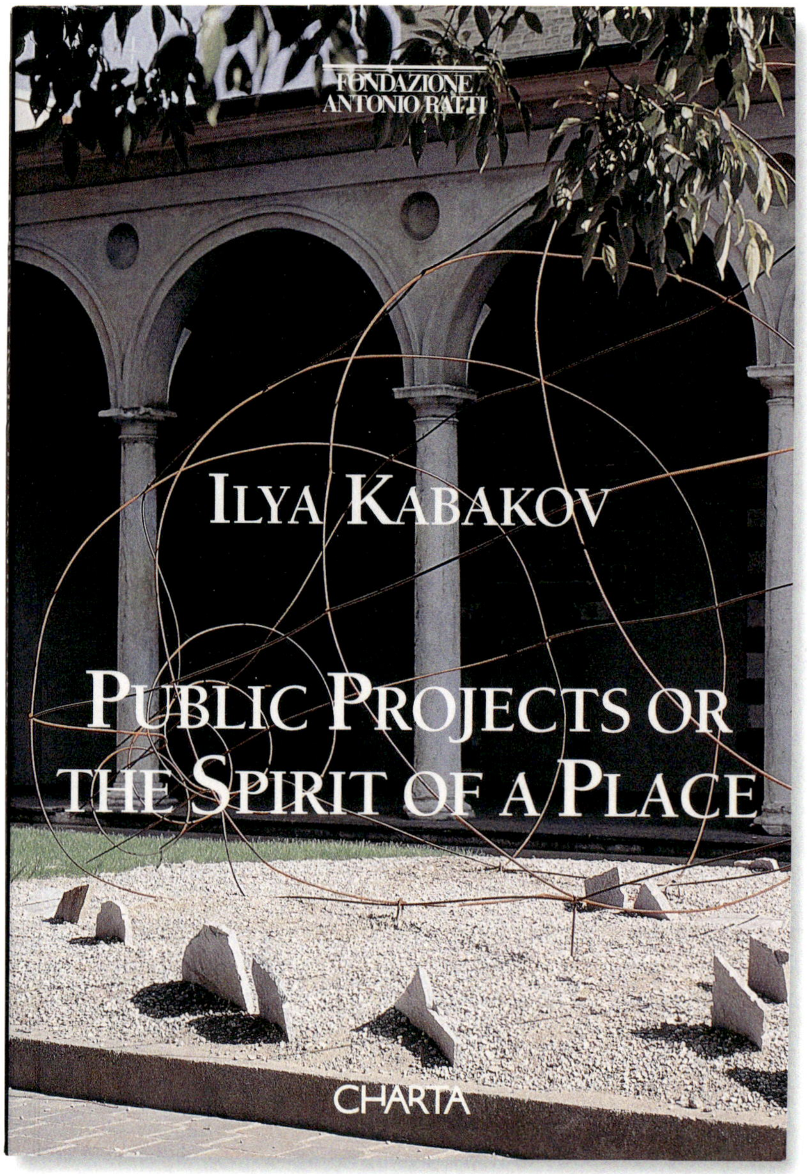

Fondazione Antonio Ratti, Como (Advanced Course in Visual Arts Publications; 5)
Milan: Charta
21 x 14.5 cm
370 pp. with 144 color ills.
stitchbound, softback with flaps
Fadenheftung, broschiert mit Umschlagklappen

thematic publication | *thematische Publikation*

layout by Ilya Kabakov | *Layout von Ilya Kabakov*

The book is based on a series of six lectures delivered by Ilya and Emilia Kabakov on their public projects at the Fondazione Antonio Ratti, Como, July 3 to 24, 2000. Texts by Boris Groys, Giairo Daghini, Giacinto Di Pietrantonio, Ilya Kabakov, and Angela Vettese; Italian, English.

Das Buch basiert auf der sechsteiligen Vorlesungsreihe von Ilya und Emilia Kabakov über ihre Projekte im öffentlichen Raum an der Fondazione Antonio Ratti, Como, 3. – 24. Juli 2000. Texte von Boris Groys, Giairo Daghini, Giacinto Di Pietrantonio, Ilya Kabakov und Angela Vettese; italienisch, englisch.

see also | *siehe auch*

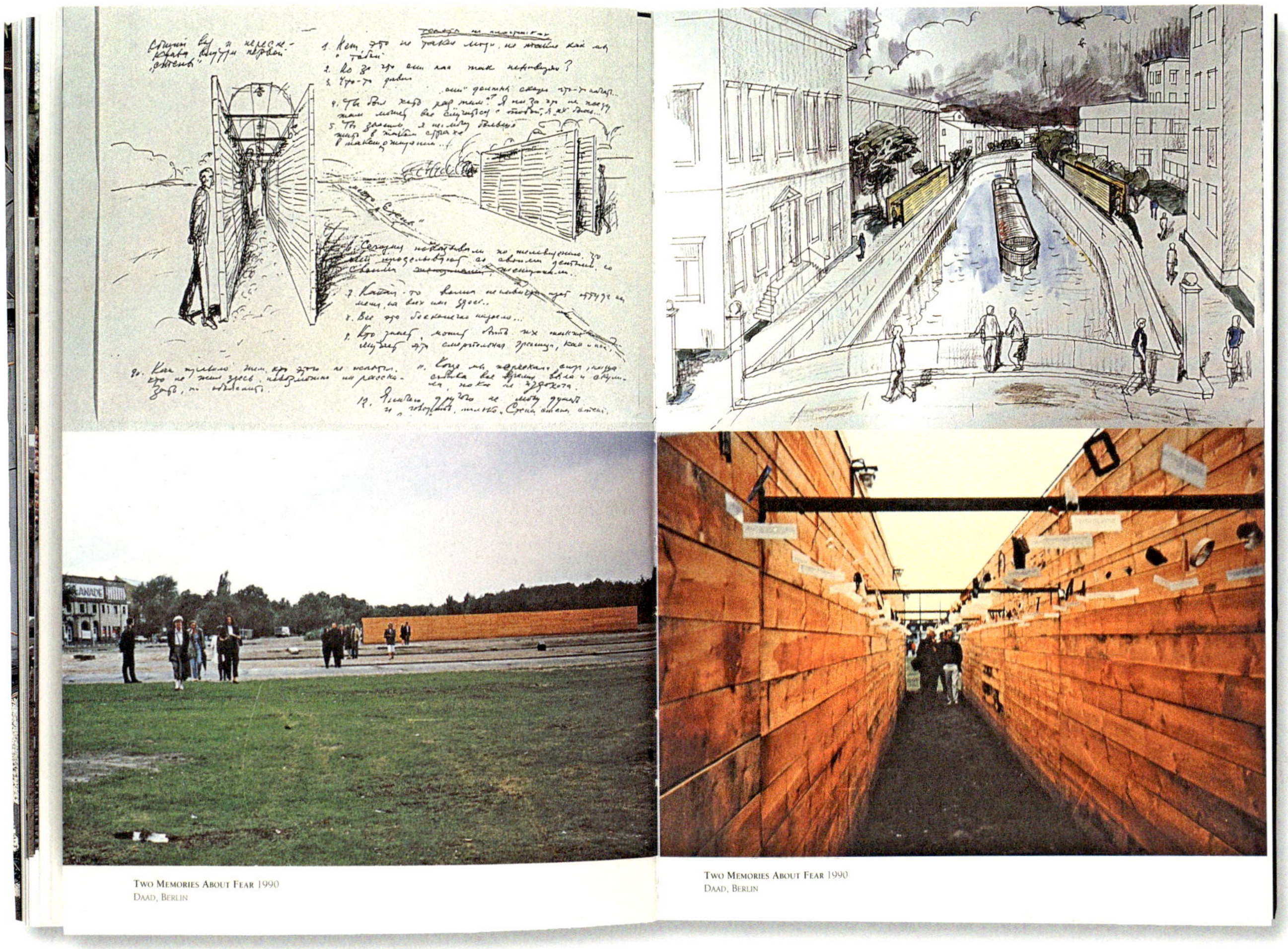
Two Memories About Fear 1990
Daad, Berlin
Two Memories About Fear 1990
Daad, Berlin

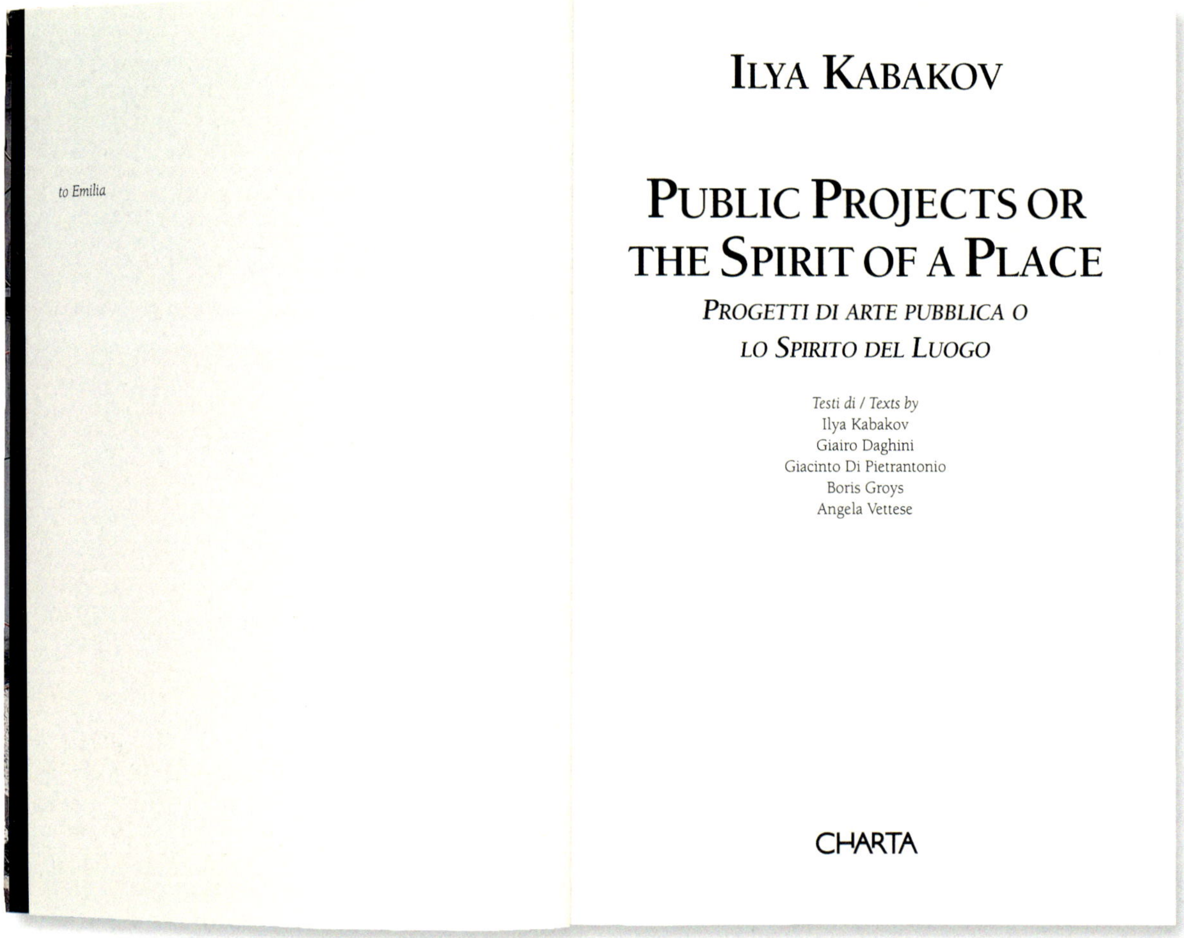

to Emilia

ILYA KABAKOV

PUBLIC PROJECTS OR THE SPIRIT OF A PLACE

PROGETTI DI ARTE PUBBLICA O LO SPIRITO DEL LUOGO

Testi di / Texts by
Ilya Kabakov
Giairo Daghini
Giacinto Di Pietrantonio
Boris Groys
Angela Vettese

CHARTA

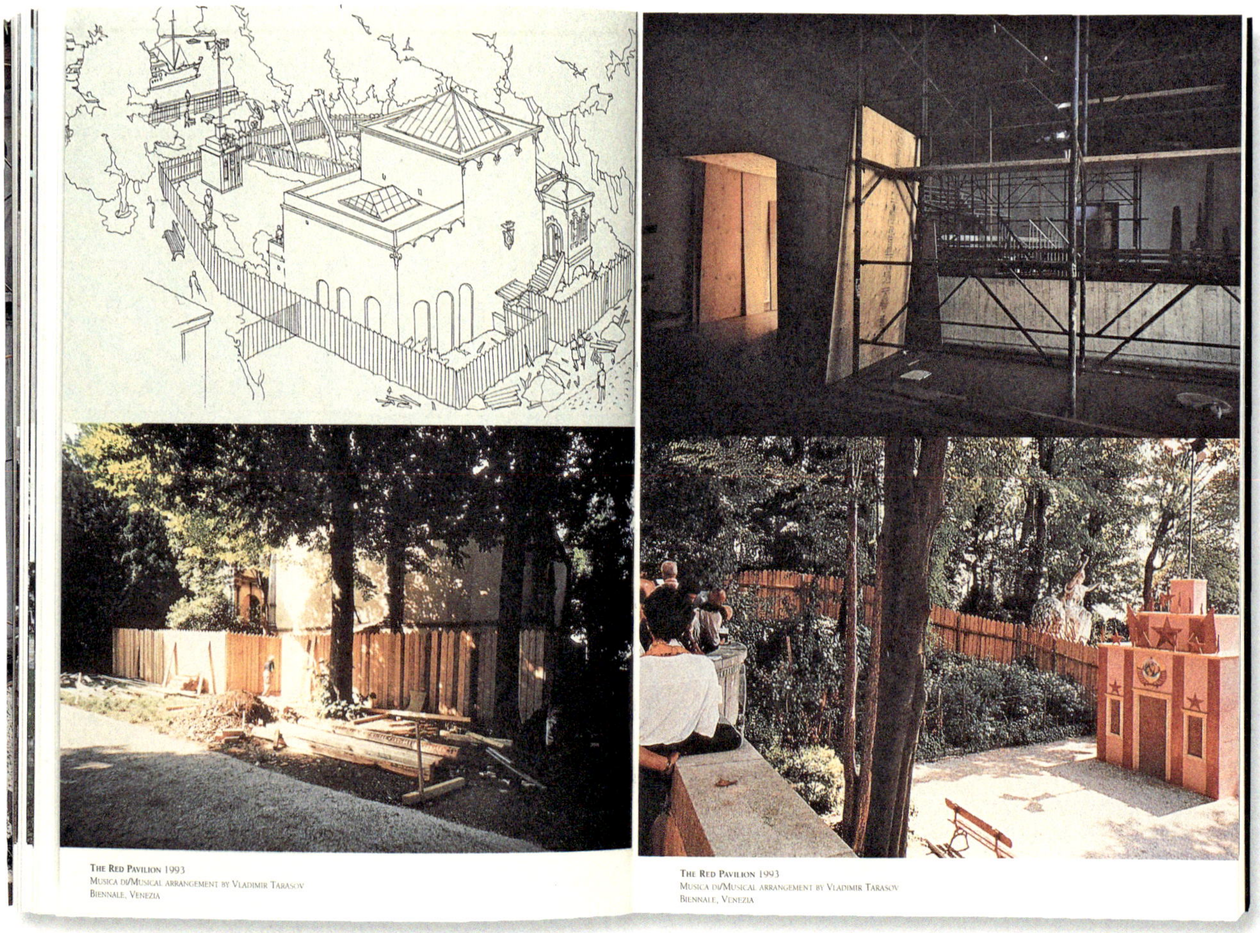

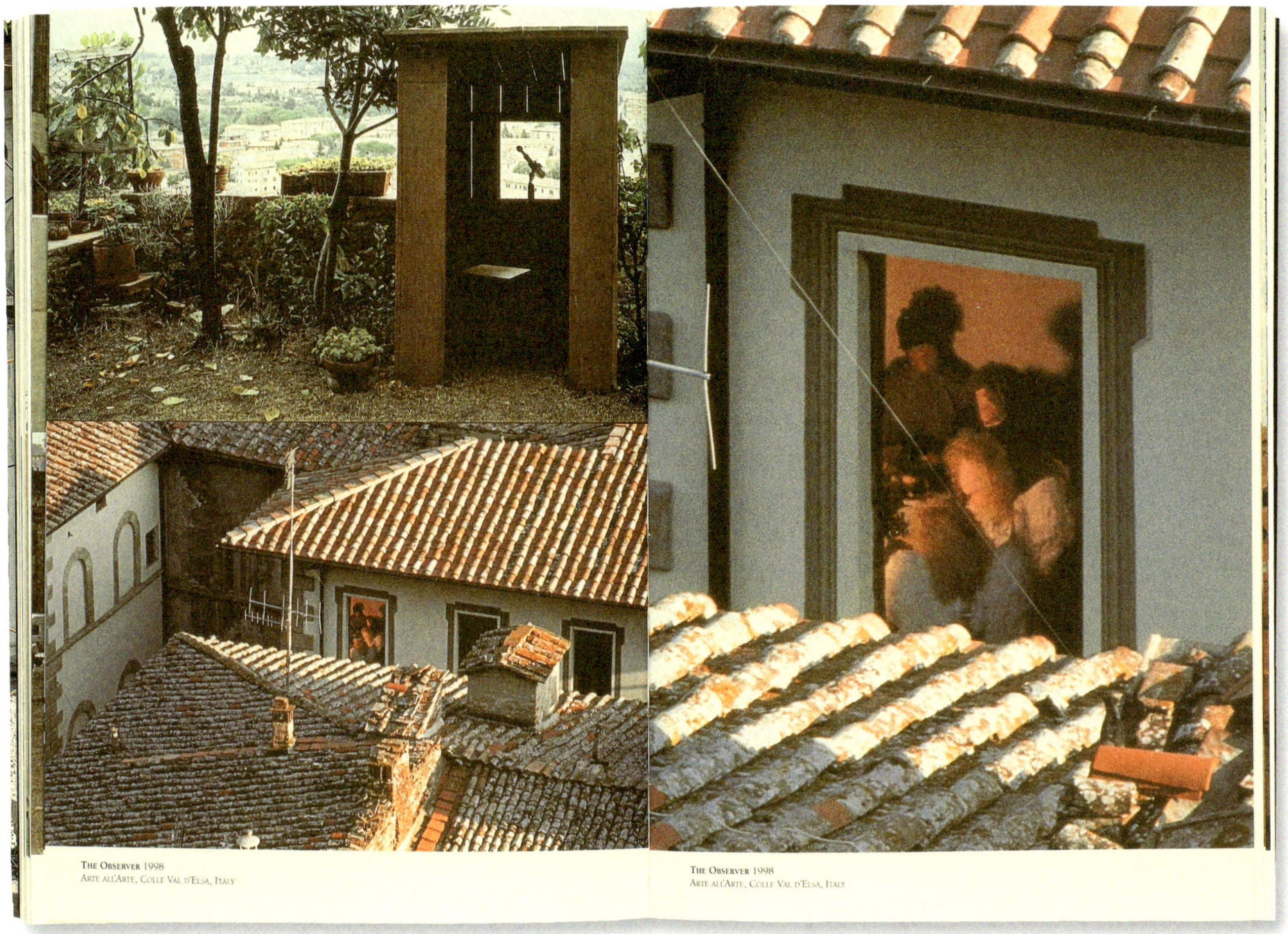
The Observer 1998
Arte all'Arte, Colle Val d'Elsa, Italy
The Observer 1998
Arte all'Arte, Colle Val d'Elsa, Italy

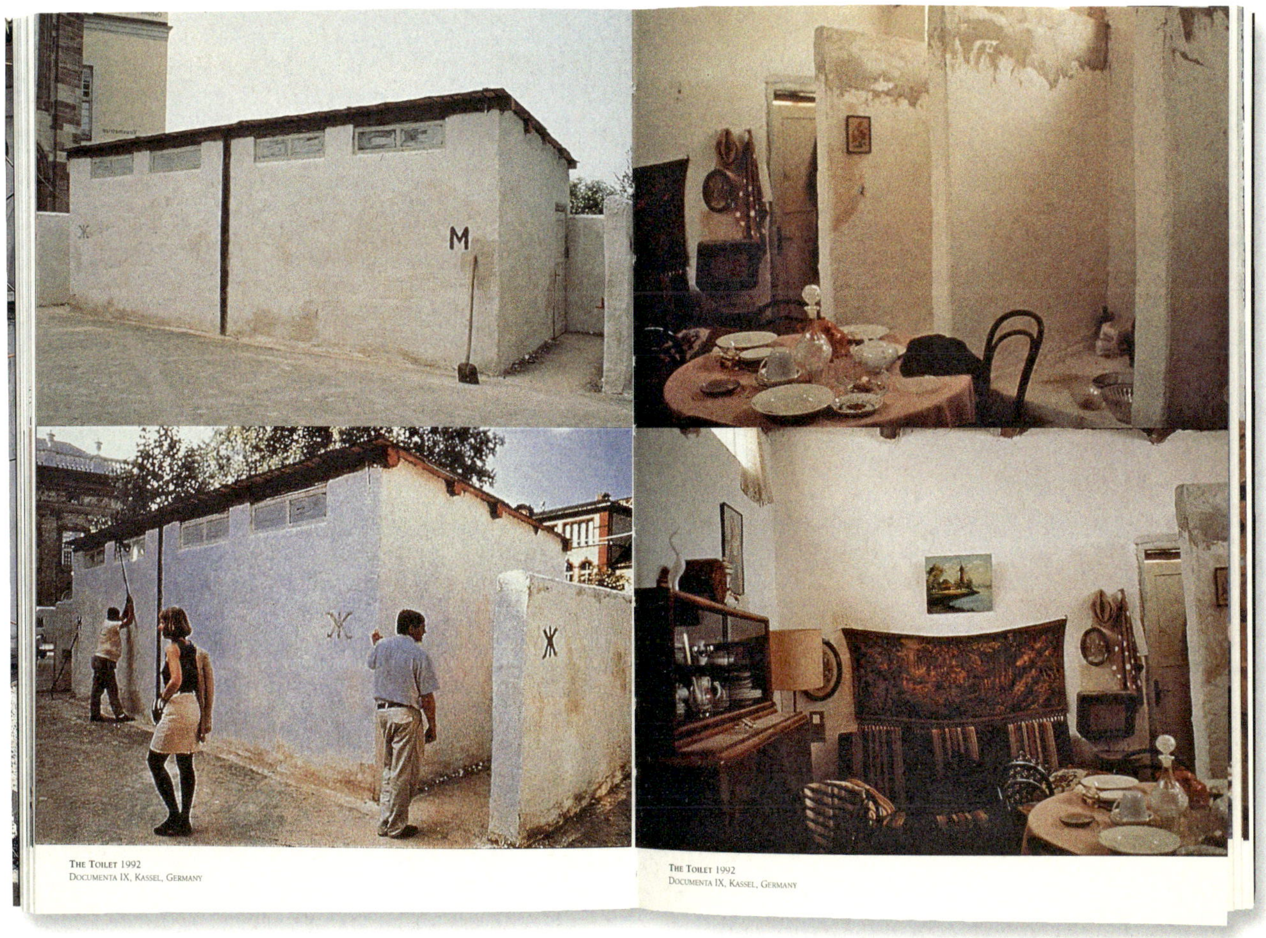
Ж
M
Ж
Ж
The Toilet 1992
Documenta IX, Kassel, Germany
The Toilet 1992
Documenta IX, Kassel, Germany

115 20 Ways to Get an Apple Listening to the Music of Mozart

20 Methoden, an einen Apfel heranzukommen, während man Mozart hört

with Emilia Kabakov | *mit Emilia Kabakov*

2001

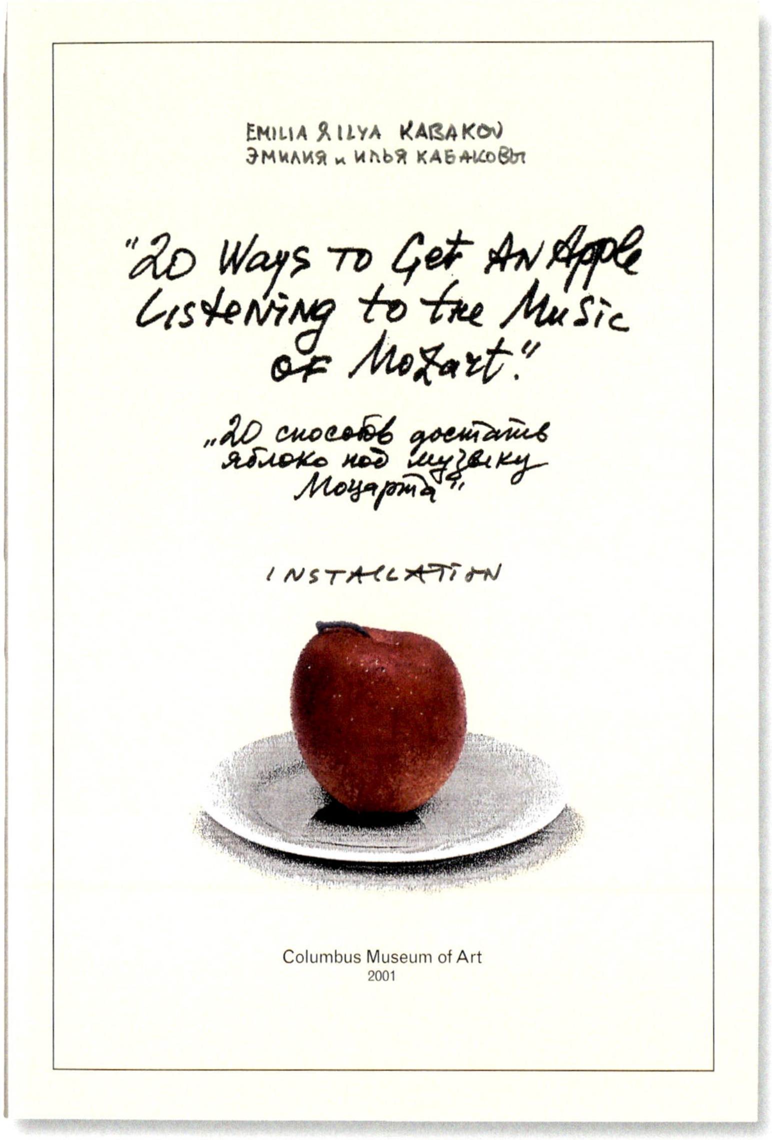

Columbus Museum of Art
Columbus: Columbus Museum of Art
30.4 x 21 cm
[120] pp. with 61 (47 color) ills.
adhesive binding, softback
Klebebindung, broschiert

exhibition catalogue | *Ausstellungskatalog*

layout by Ilya Kabakov | *Layout von Ilya Kabakov*

For the installation of the same name from 2001 at the Columbus Museum of Art, Columbus, OH. Texts by Ilya and Emilia Kabakov; English, Russian.

Zur gleichnamigen Installation von 2001, Columbus Museum of Art, Columbus, OH. Texte von Ilya und Emilia Kabakov; englisch, russisch.

see also | *siehe auch* CRI, vol. 2, no. 109, pp. 200–205

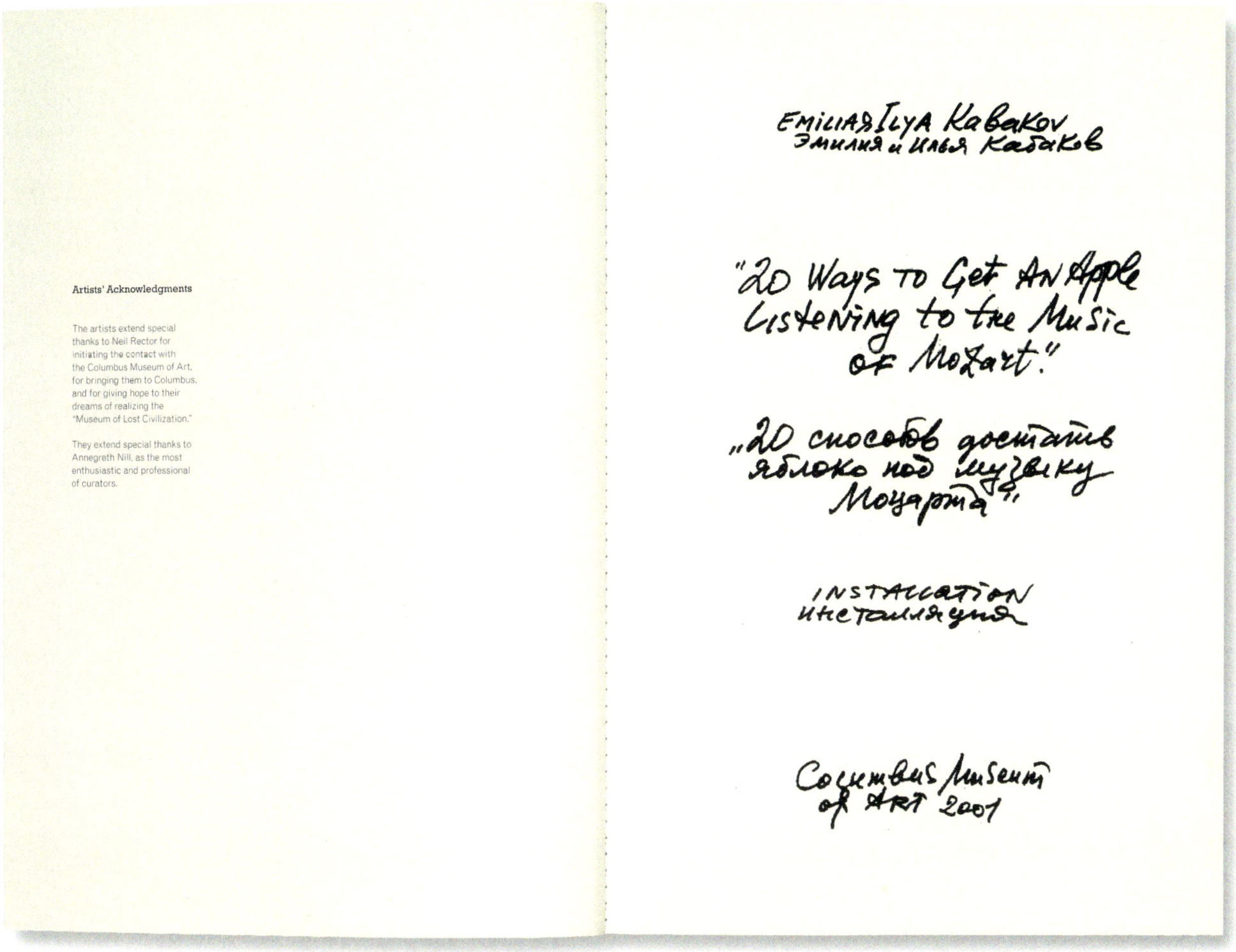

Artists' Acknowledgments

The artists extend special thanks to Neil Rector for initiating the contact with the Columbus Museum of Art, for bringing them to Columbus, and for giving hope to their dreams of realizing the "Museum of Lost Civilization."

They extend special thanks to Annegreth Nill, as the most enthusiastic and professional of curators.

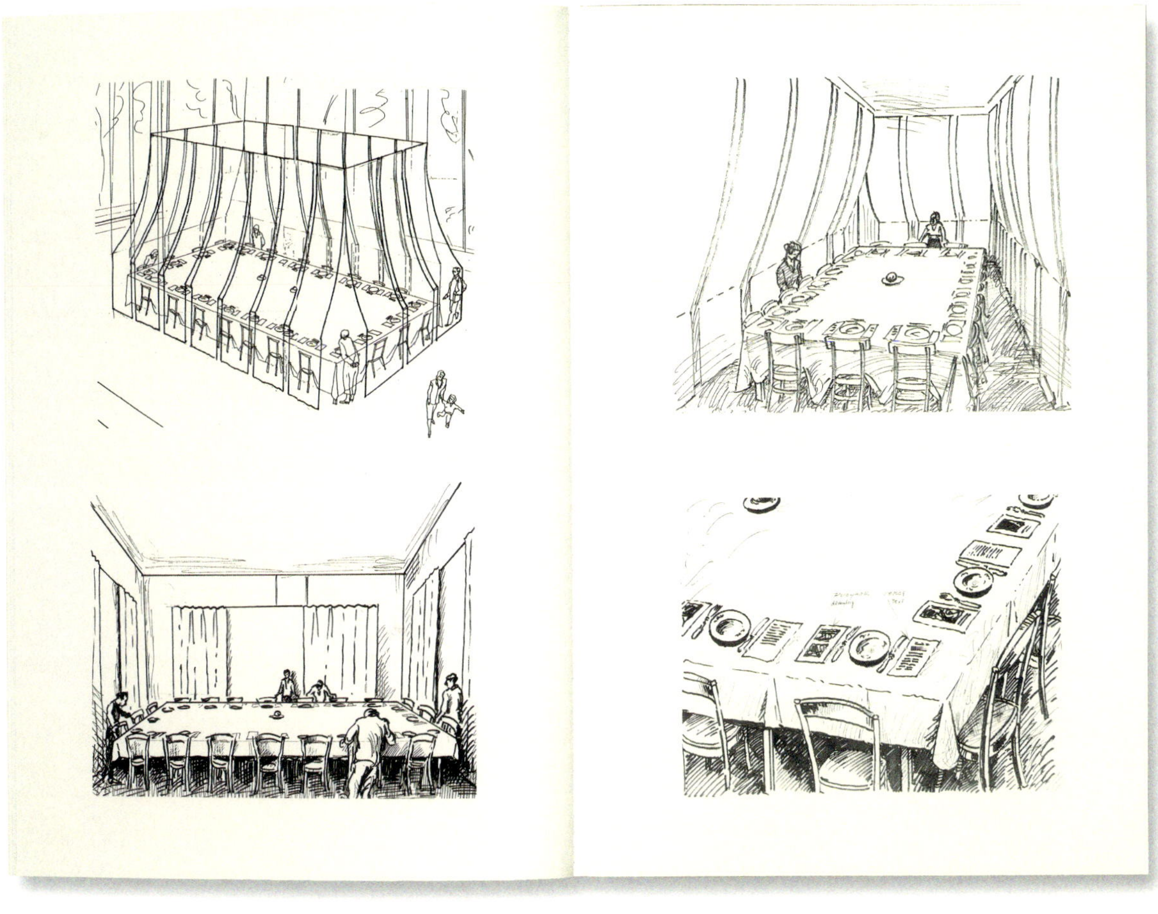

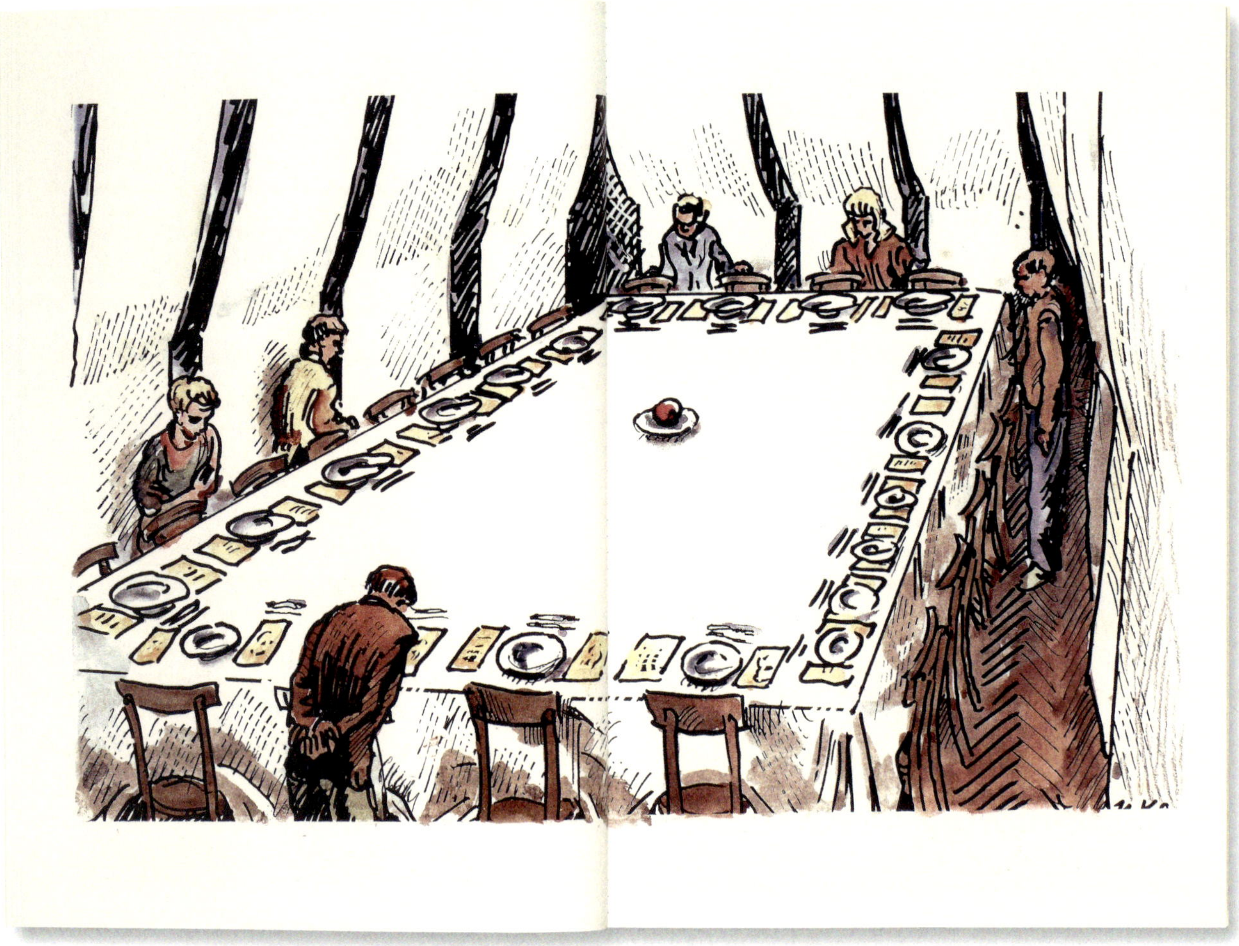

Кажется сейчас как раз тот случай, когда мне придется просить о не совсем обыкновенной помощи, к которой я прибегал в исключительных случаях – и эта помощь всегда приходила, совершалось то, что сделать, казалось бы, было невозможно. Я часто оказывался в безвыходном положении, не знал, что делать. В такие минуты я звал своего ангела и умолял его: „Помоги, сделай так, чтобы у меня это получилось!" И внезапно в голове возникало решение или, что удивительнее, происходило то, что по реальным причинам совершиться никак не могло. И сейчас я, кажется, поступлю таким же образом. Попрошу „Его" со всей силой моего желания и уверен – не знаю каким способом – но яблоко, к удивлению других, окажется на моей тарелке!

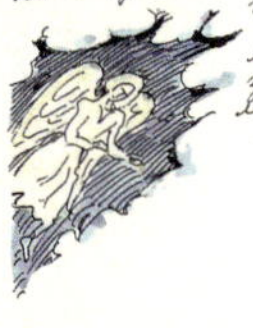

It seems that this is just the kind of instance when I will have to ask for the usual kind of help that I would turn to in extreme cases -- and this help would always come, whatever seemed impossible would always happen.

I often found myself in hopeless situations. I didn't know what to do. At such moments, I would call my angel and beg him: "Help, please make it so that I am able to do this!" And suddenly the solution would arise in my head, or which is even more amazing, something would happen that couldn't possibly take place for normal reasons.

And it seems that I will now act in the same way. I will ask "Him" with all the strength of my desire and I am certain -- I don't know how -- but the apple, to the surprise of the others, will wind up on my plate.

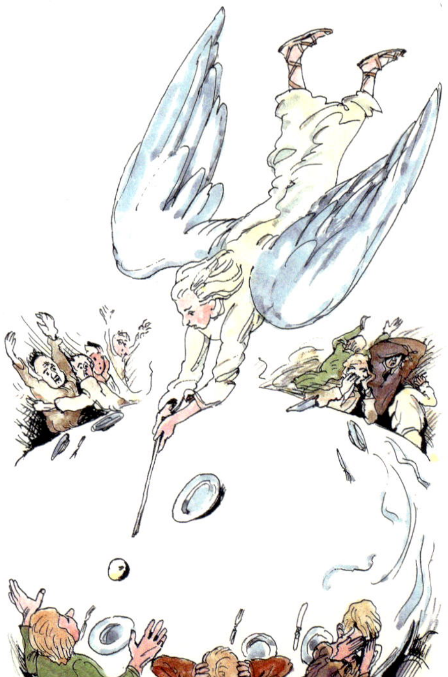

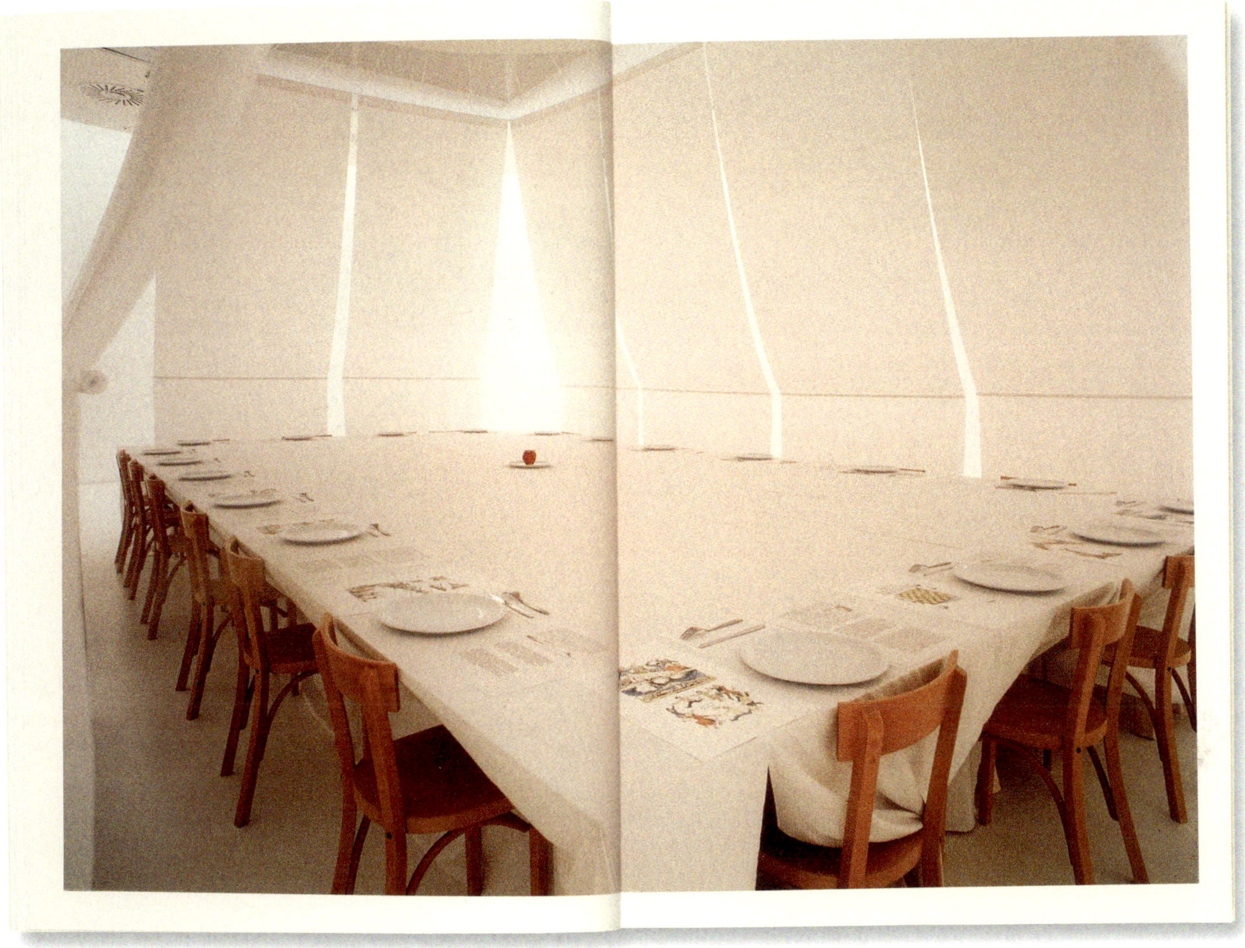

116 The Sixties and the Seventies: Notes About Unofficial Life in Moscow

Die 60er und 70er Jahre. Aufzeichnungen über das inoffizielle Leben in Moskau

2001

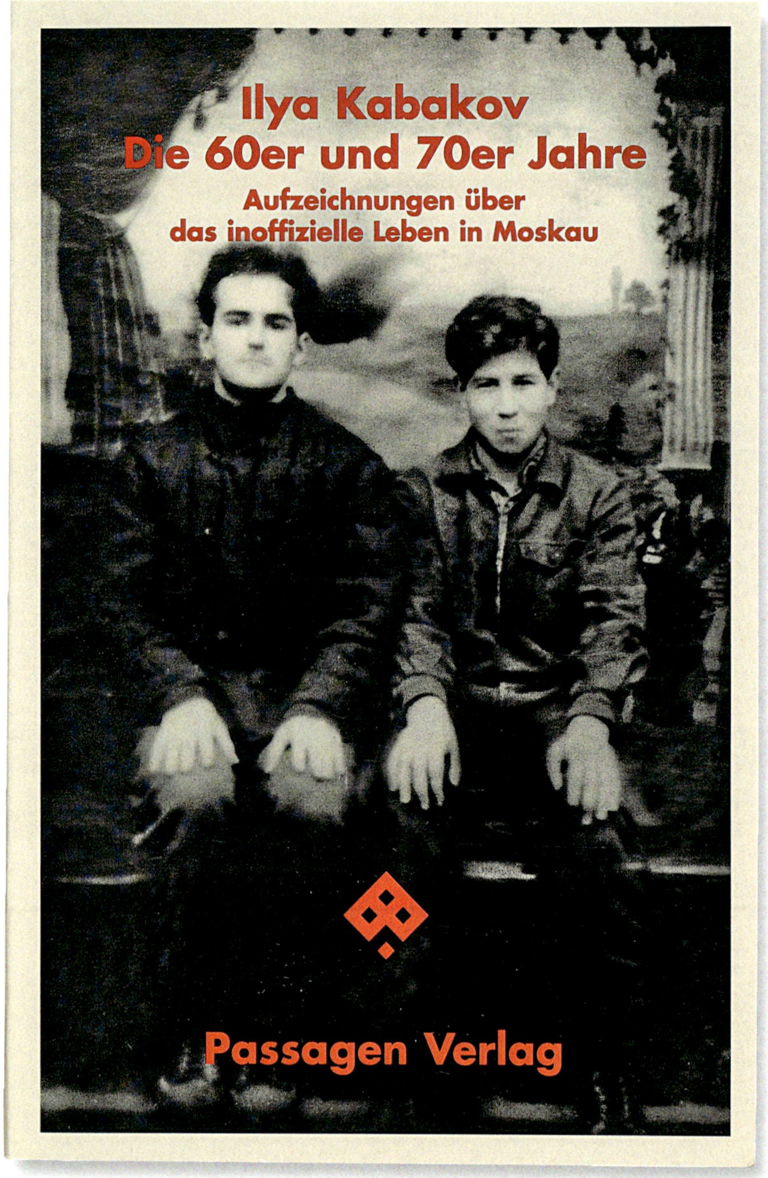

Peter Engelmann
Vienna: Passagen Verlag
23.4 x 15.5 cm
349 pp. with 46 b/w ills.
stitchbound, softback
Fadenheftung, broschiert

thematic publication | *thematische Publikation*

Ilya Kabakov depicts his own artistic development within the context of the unofficial art scene in Moscow in the 1960s and 1970s. The first edition was published in Russian in 1999. Texts by Erik Bulatov, Boris Groys, Ilya Kabakov, and Oleg Vassilyev; German.

Ilya Kabakov schildert den eigenen künstlerischen Werdegang im Kontext der inoffiziellen Kunst in Moskau in den 1960er- und 1970er-Jahren. Die Erstausgabe erschien russisch 1999. Texte von Erik Bulatov, Boris Groys, Ilya Kabakov und Oleg Wassiljew; deutsch.

see also | *siehe auch* no. 14; no. 107; no. 131; no. 136

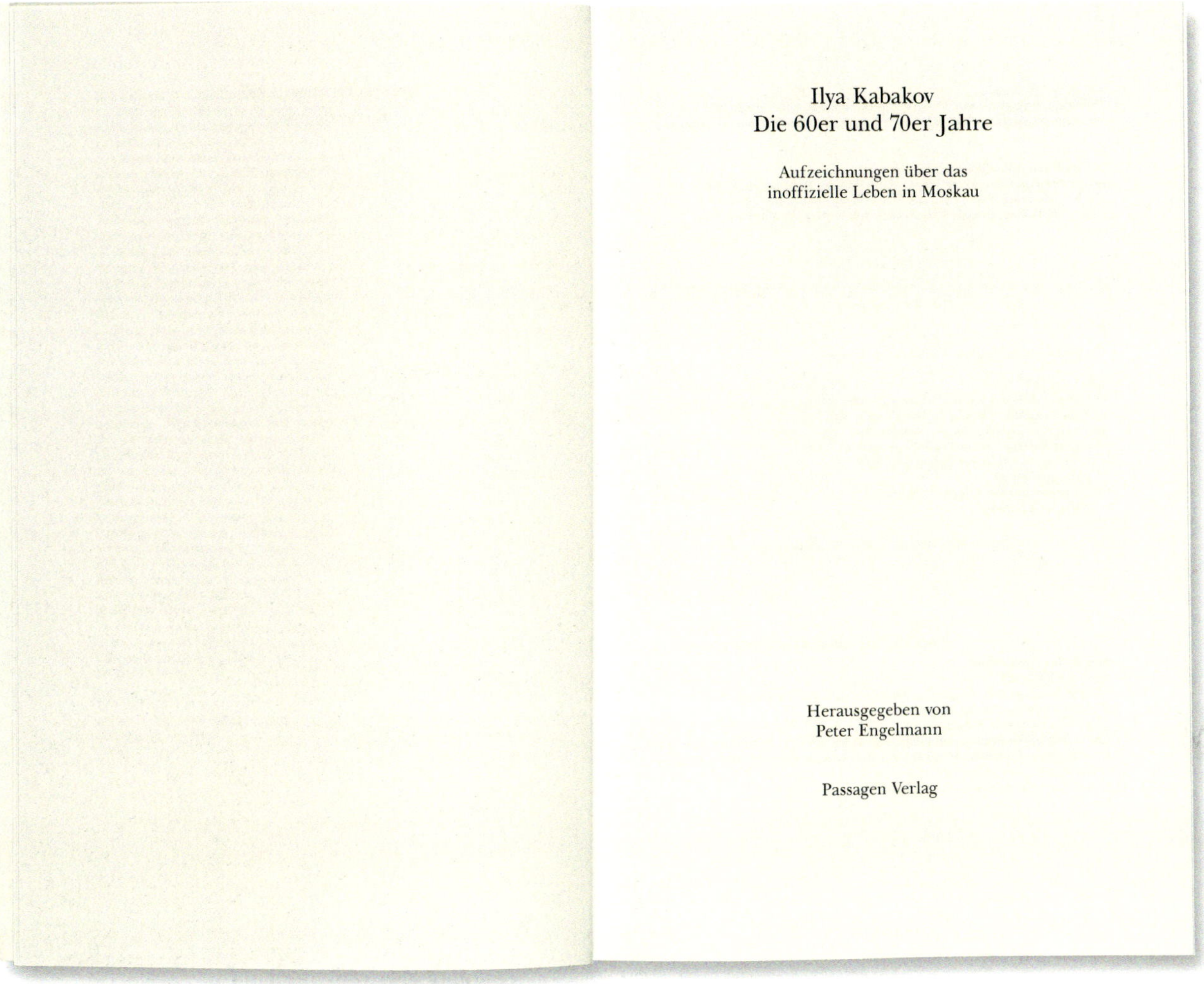

Ilya Kabakov
Die 60er und 70er Jahre

Aufzeichnungen über das
inoffizielle Leben in Moskau

Herausgegeben von
Peter Engelmann

Passagen Verlag

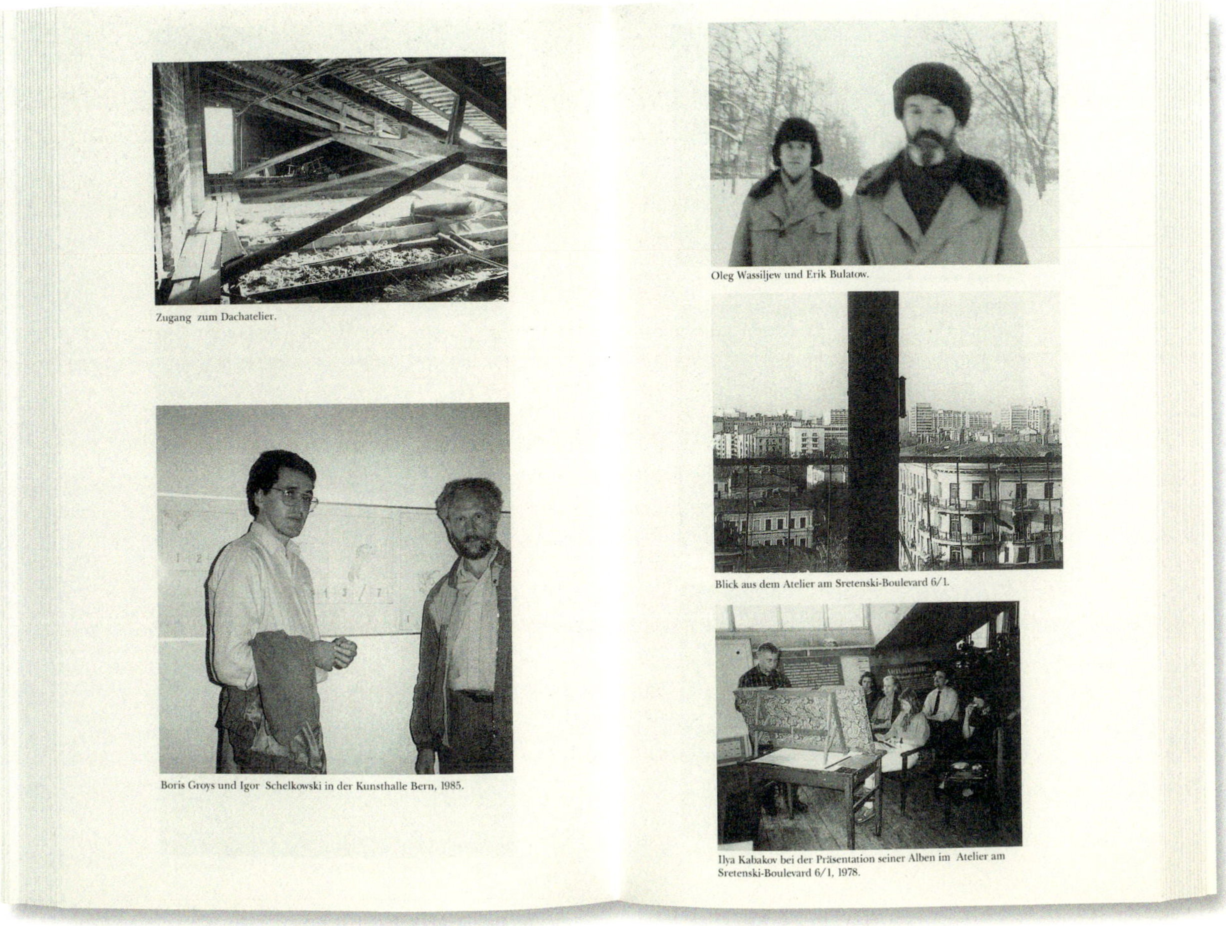

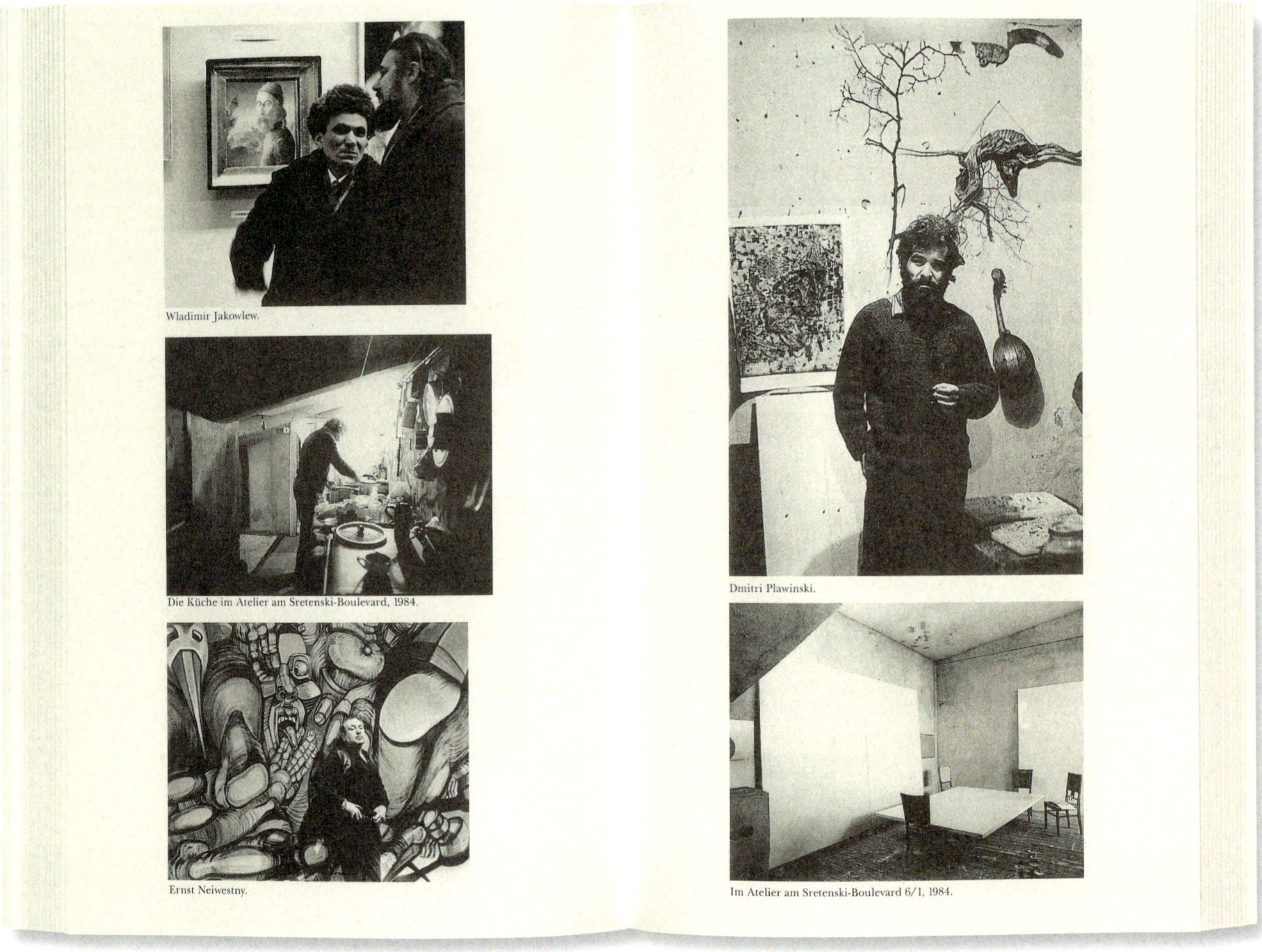
Wladimir Jakowlew.
Die Küche im Atelier am Sretenski-Boulevard, 1984.
Ernst Neiwestny.
Dmitri Plawinski.
Im Atelier am Sretenski-Boulevard 6/1, 1984.

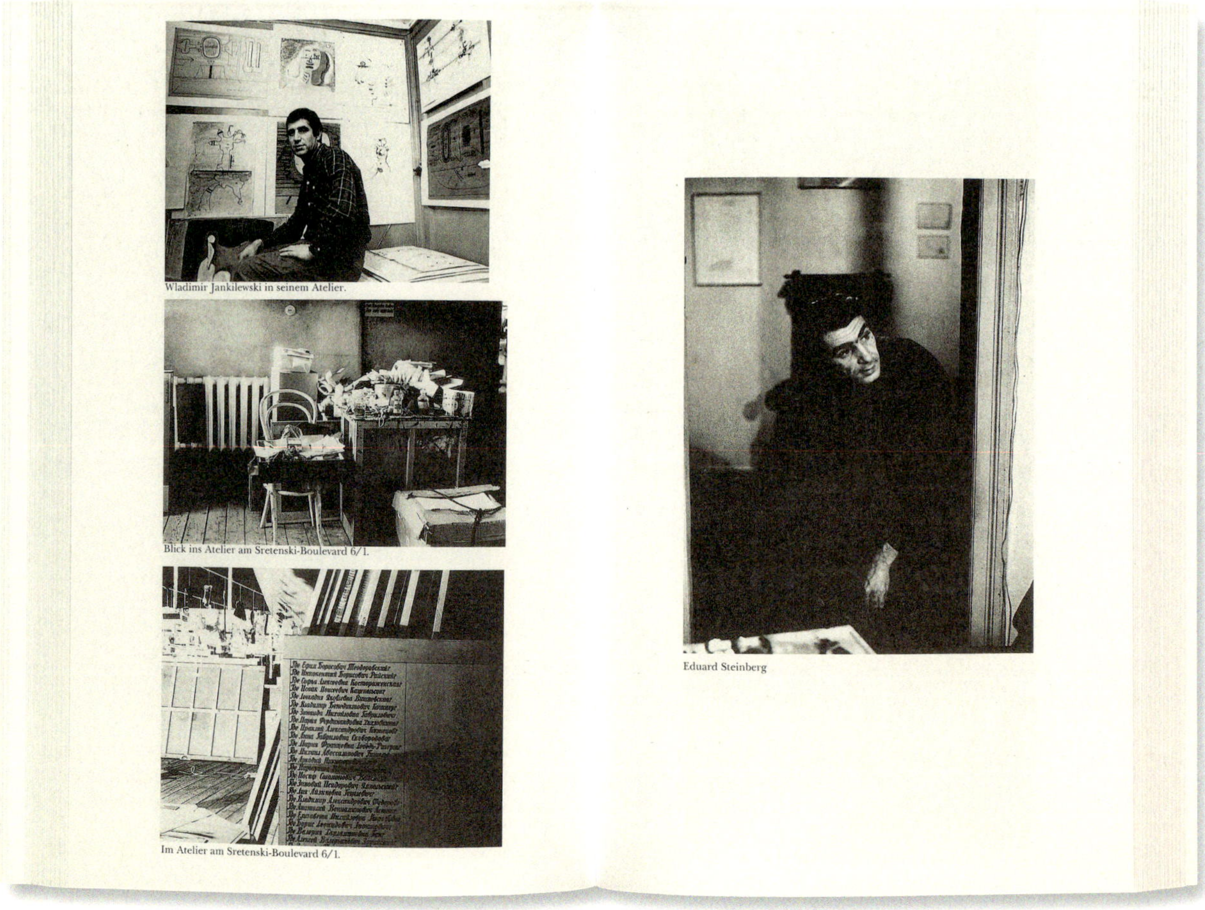
Wladimir Jankilewski in seinem Atelier.
Blick ins Atelier am Sretenski-Boulevard 6/1.
Im Atelier am Sretenski-Boulevard 6/1.
Eduard Steinberg

117 The Palace of Projects | *Der Palast der Projekte*

with Emilia Kabakov | *mit Emilia Kabakov*

2001

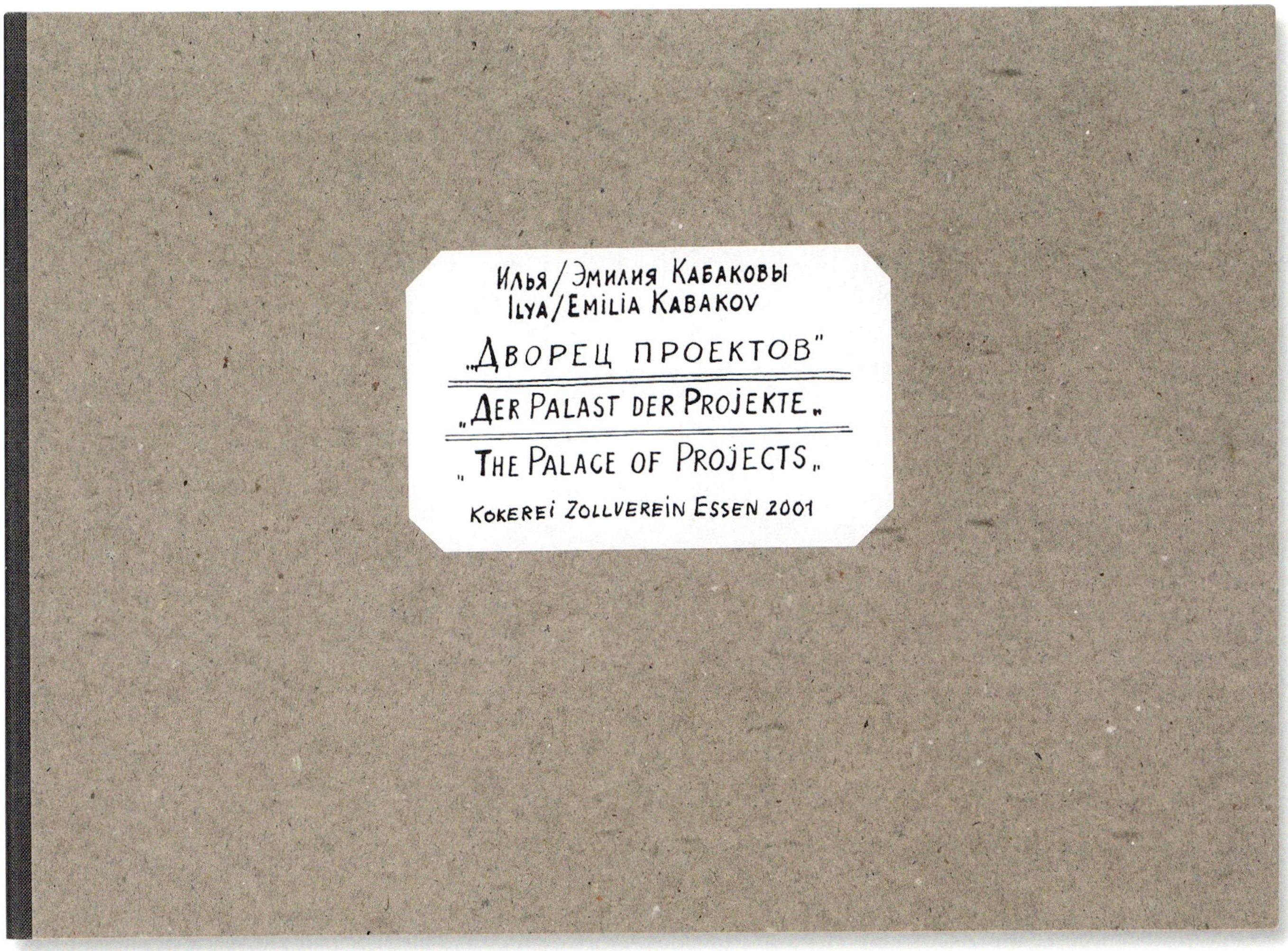

Stiftung Industriedenkmalpflege und Geschichtskultur
Düsseldorf: Richter Verlag
22.4 x 31.4 cm
[440] pp. with 310 (227 color) ills.
stitchbound, quarter cloth binding, label on the cover
Fadenheftung, Halbleinen, Etikette auf dem Umschlag

exhibition catalogue | *Ausstellungskatalog*

layout by Ilya Kabakov | *Layout von Ilya Kabakov*

Documentation of the permanent installation from 2001 in the salt store on the grounds of the Zollverein Coking Plant, Essen. Texts by Ilya Kabakov and Wolfgang Roters; German, English, Russian.

Dokumentation der permanenten Installation von 2001 im Salzlager auf dem Gelände der Kokerei Zollverein, Essen. Texte von Ilya Kabakov und Wolfgang Roters; deutsch, englisch, russisch.

see also | *siehe auch* no. 95; no. 98; no. 101; no. 102; CRI, vol. 2, no. 117, pp. 244–251; CRP, vol. 1, nos. 279–289, pp. 350–360

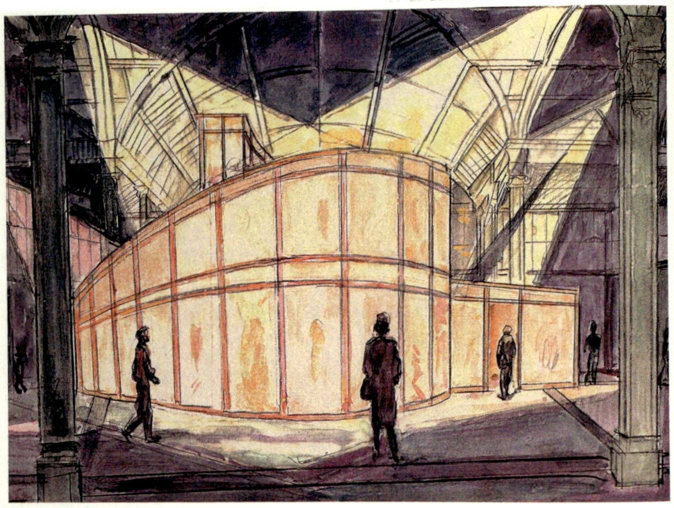

Илья/Эмилия Кабаковы
Ilya/Emilia Kabakov

„Дворец проектов"

„Der Palast der Projekte"

„The Palace of Projects"

Kokerei Zollverein
Essen 2001

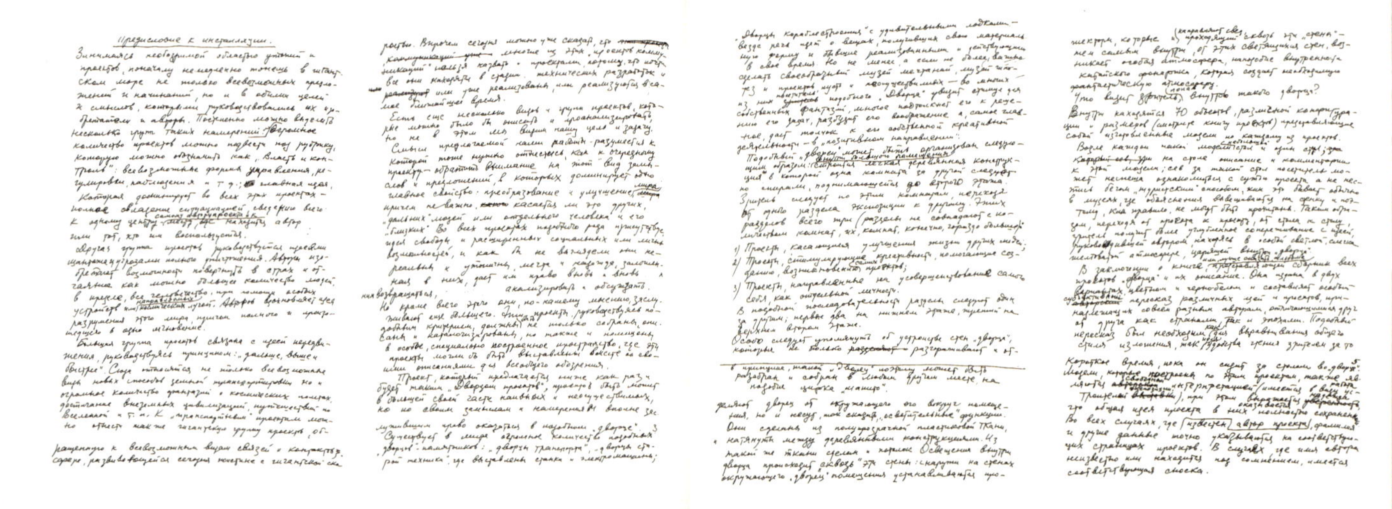
Предисловие к инсталляции.

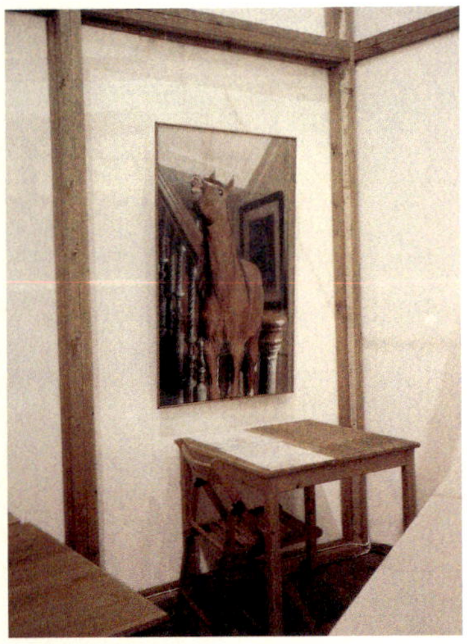

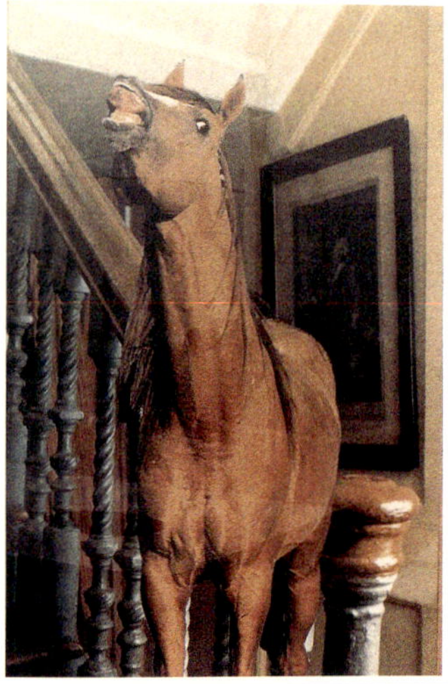

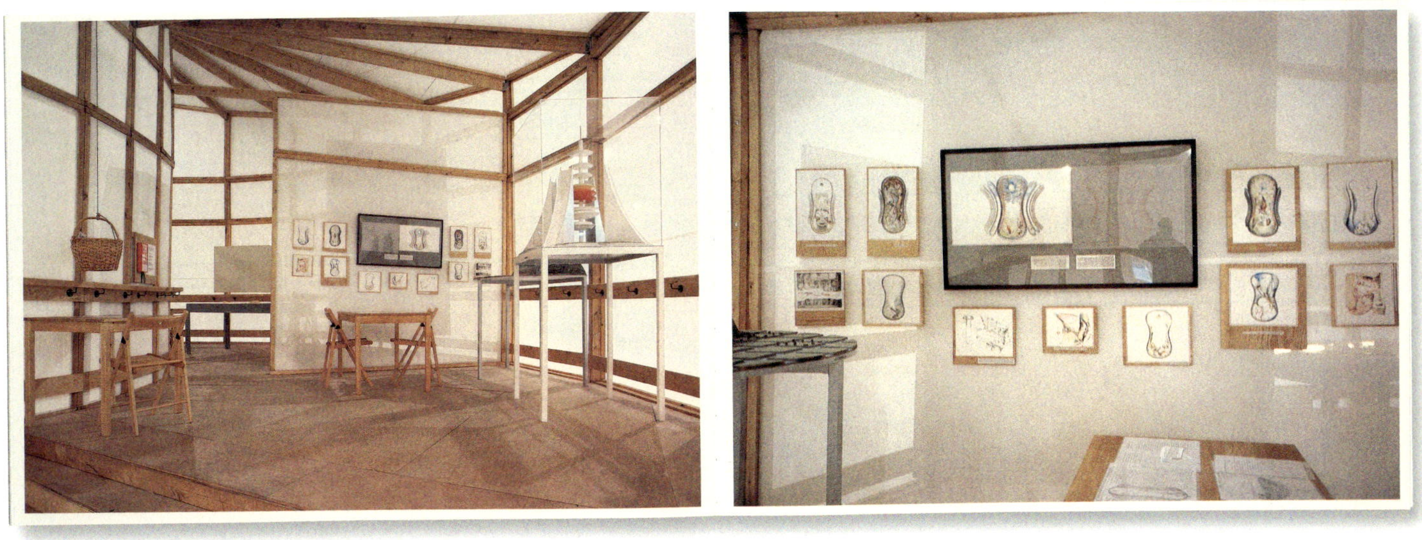

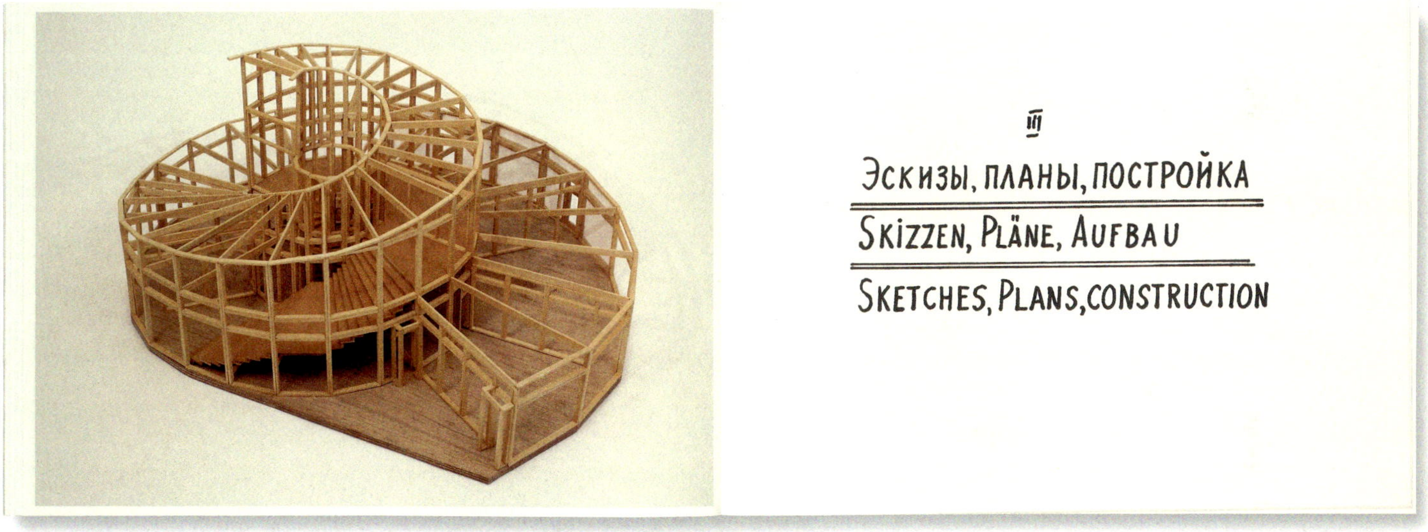

Эскизы, планы, постройка
Skizzen, Pläne, Aufbau
Sketches, Plans, construction

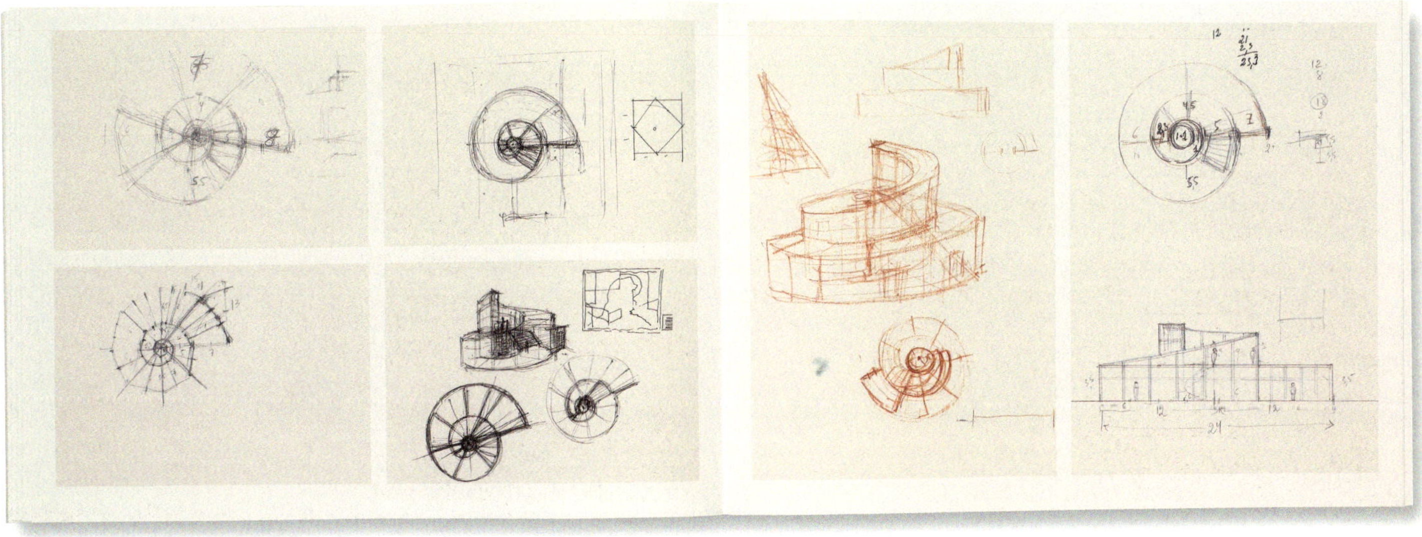

118 A Universal System for Depicting Everything

Universalsystem zur Darstellung von allem

2002

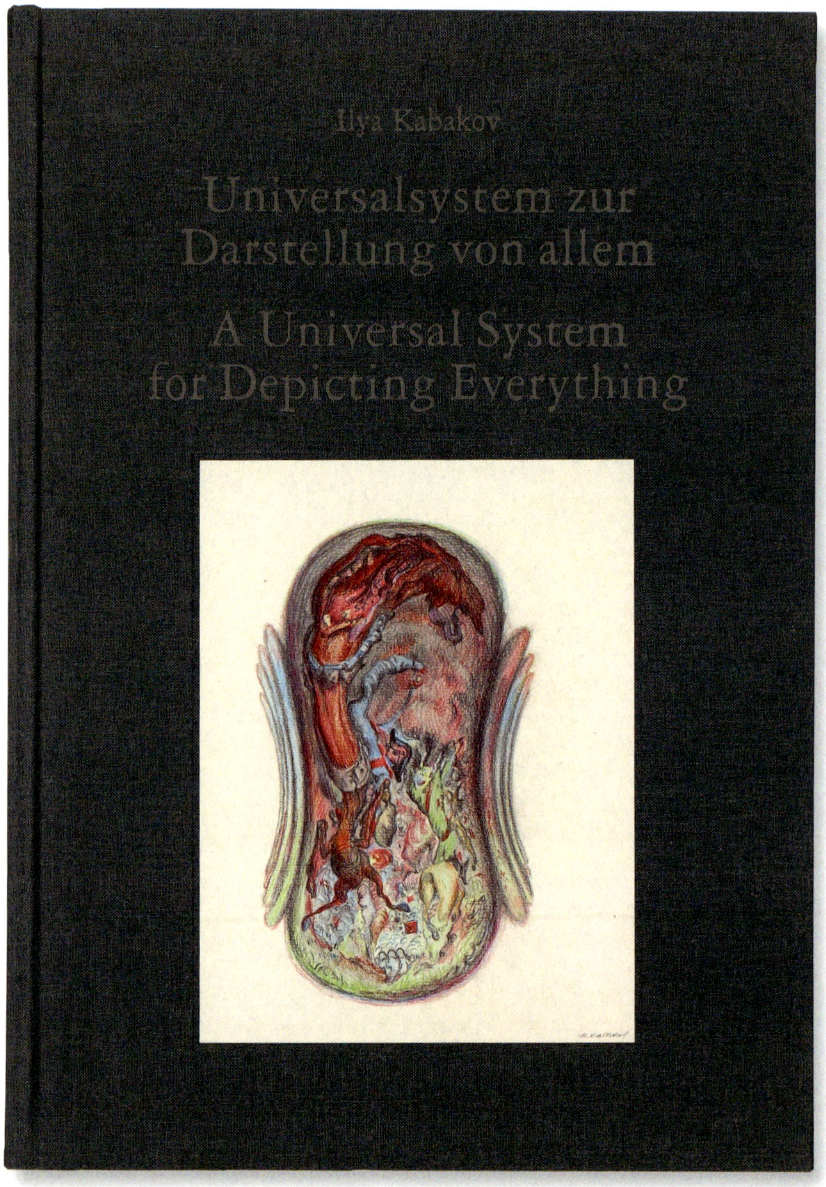

Werner Meyer, Kunsthalle Göppingen
Düsseldorf: Richter Verlag
34 x 24.3 cm
213 pp. with 80 (71 color incl. 1 foldout) ills.
stitchbound, clothbound, blind blocking with label
Fadenheftung, Leinen, Blindprägung mit Etikette

exhibition catalogue | *Ausstellungskatalog*

layout by Ilya Kabakov | *Layout von Ilya Kabakov*

Documentation of the installation of the same name at the Kunsthalle Göppingen, Göppingen, February 12 to March 31, 2002. Texts by Ilya Kabakov, and a dialogue between Boris Groys and Ilya Kabakov on the album »A Universal System for Depicting Everything«; German, English.

Dokumentation zur gleichnamigen Installation, Kunsthalle Göppingen, Göppingen, 12. Februar – 31. März 2002. Texte von Ilya Kabakov und ein Dialog von Boris Groys und Ilya Kabakov über das Album »Universalsystem zur Darstellung von allem«; deutsch, englisch.

see also | *siehe auch*

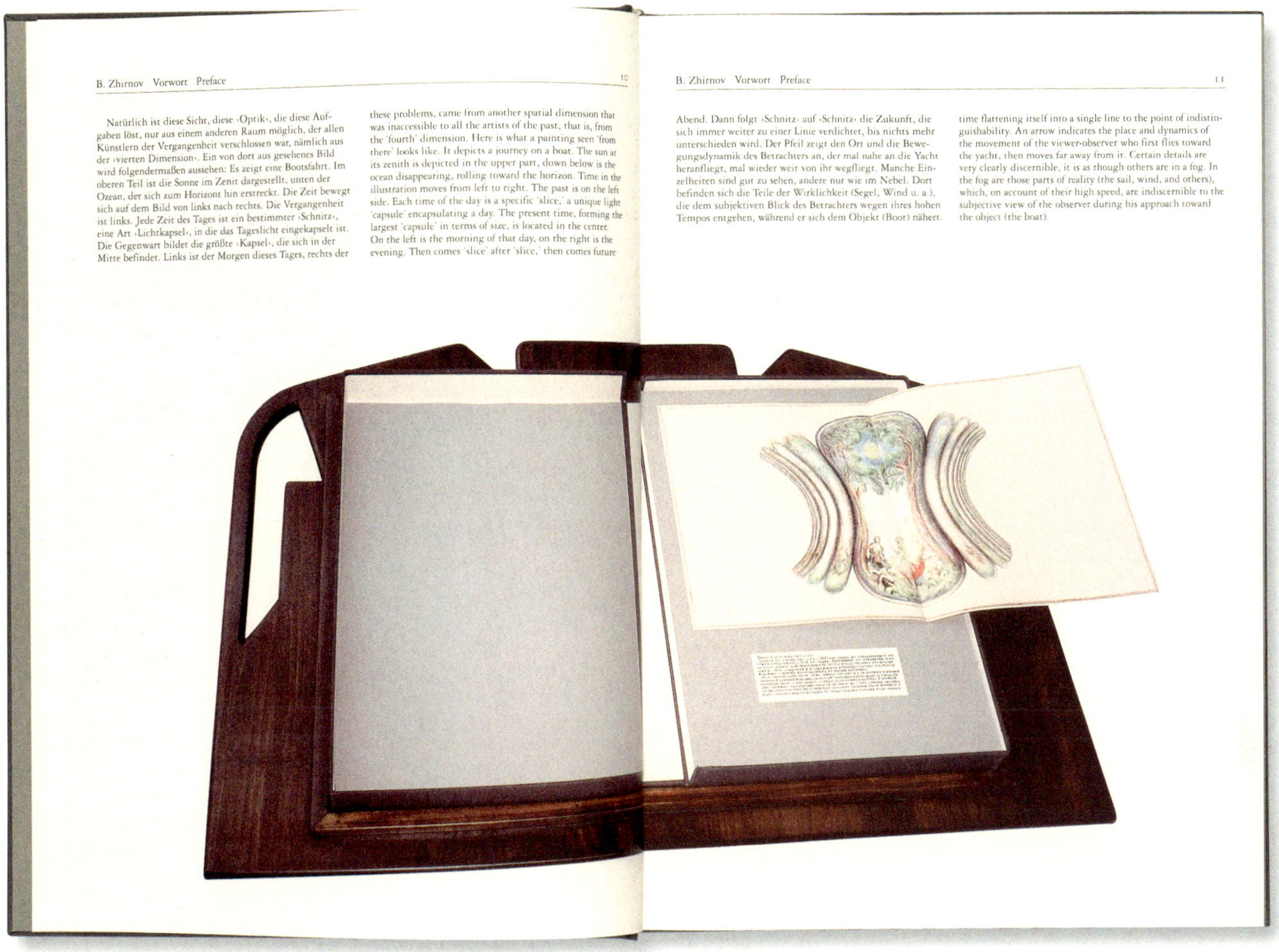
B. Zhirnov Vorwort Preface 10
Natürlich ist diese Sicht, diese ›Optik‹, die diese Aufgaben löst, nur aus einem anderen Raum möglich, der allen Künstlern der Vergangenheit verschlossen war, nämlich aus der ›vierten Dimension‹. Ein von dort aus gesehenes Bild wird folgendermaßen aussehen: Es zeigt eine Bootsfahrt. Im oberen Teil ist die Sonne im Zenit dargestellt, unten der Ozean, der sich zum Horizont hin erstreckt. Die Zeit bewegt sich auf dem Bild von links nach rechts. Die Vergangenheit ist links. Jede Zeit des Tages ist ein bestimmter ›Schnitz‹, eine Art ›Lichtkapsel‹, in die das Tageslicht eingekapselt ist. Die Gegenwart bildet die größte ›Kapsel‹, die sich in der Mitte befindet. Links ist der Morgen dieses Tages, rechts der
these problems, came from another spatial dimension that was inaccessible to all the artists of the past, that is, from the 'fourth' dimension. Here is what a painting seen 'from there' looks like. It depicts a journey on a boat. The sun at its zenith is depicted in the upper part, down below is the ocean disappearing, rolling toward the horizon. Time in the illustration moves from left to right. The past is on the left side. Each time of the day is a specific 'slice,' a unique light 'capsule' encapsulating a day. The present time, forming the largest 'capsule' in terms of size, is located in the center. On the left is the morning of that day, on the right is the evening. Then comes 'slice' after 'slice,' then comes future
B. Zhirnov Vorwort Preface 11
Abend. Dann folgt ›Schnitz‹ auf ›Schnitz‹ die Zukunft, die sich immer weiter zu einer Linie verdichtet, bis nichts mehr unterschieden wird. Der Pfeil zeigt den Ort und die Bewegungsdynamik des Betrachters an, der mal nahe an die Yacht heranfliegt, mal wieder weit von ihr wegfliegt. Manche Einzelheiten sind gut zu sehen, andere nur wie im Nebel. Dort befinden sich die Teile der Wirklichkeit (Segel, Wind u. a.), die dem subjektiven Blick des Betrachters wegen ihres hohen Tempos entgehen, während er sich dem Objekt (Boot) nähert.
time flattening itself into a single line to the point of indistinguishability. An arrow indicates the place and dynamics of the movement of the viewer-observer who first flies toward the yacht, then moves far away from it. Certain details are very clearly discernible, it is as though others are in a fog. In the fog are those parts of reality (the sail, wind, and others), which, on account of their high speed, are indiscernible to the subjective view of the observer during his approach toward the object (the boat).

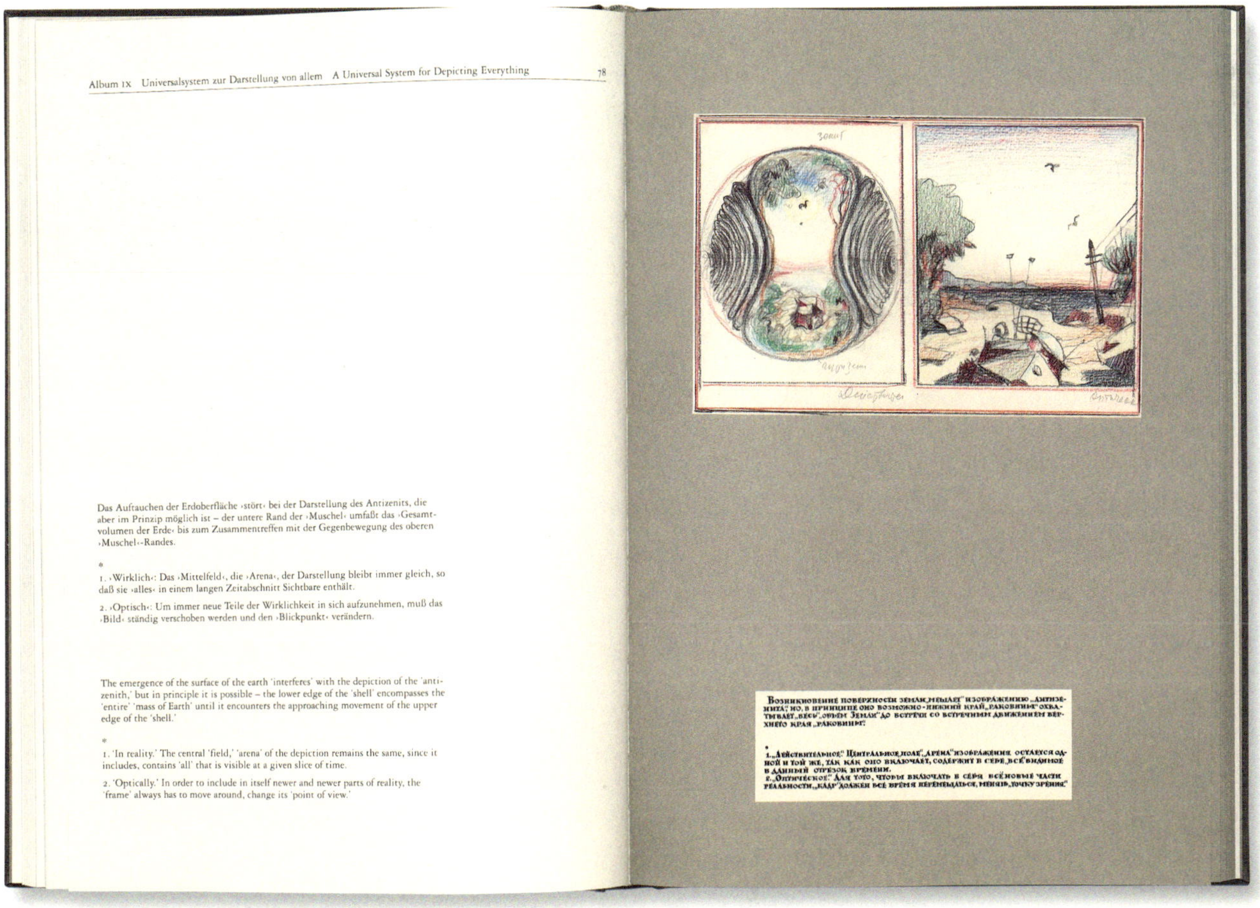
Album IX Universalsystem zur Darstellung von allem A Universal System for Depicting Everything 78
Das Auftauchen der Erdoberfläche ›stört‹ bei der Darstellung des Antizenits, die aber im Prinzip möglich ist – der untere Rand der ›Muschel‹ umfaßt das ›Gesamtvolumen der Erde‹ bis zum Zusammentreffen mit der Gegenbewegung des oberen ›Muschel‹-Randes.
*
1. ›Wirklich‹: Das ›Mittelfeld‹, die ›Arena‹, der Darstellung bleibt immer gleich, so daß sie ›alles‹ in einem langen Zeitabschnitt Sichtbare enthält.
2. ›Optisch‹: Um immer neue Teile der Wirklichkeit in sich aufzunehmen, muß das ›Bild‹ ständig verschoben werden und den ›Blickpunkt‹ verändern.
The emergence of the surface of the earth 'interferes' with the depiction of the 'anti-zenith,' but in principle it is possible – the lower edge of the 'shell' encompasses the 'entire' 'mass of Earth' until it encounters the approaching movement of the upper edge of the 'shell.'
*
1. 'In reality.' The central 'field,' 'arena' of the depiction remains the same, since it includes, contains 'all' that is visible at a given slice of time.
2. 'Optically.' In order to include in itself newer and newer parts of reality, the 'frame' always has to move around, change its 'point of view.'

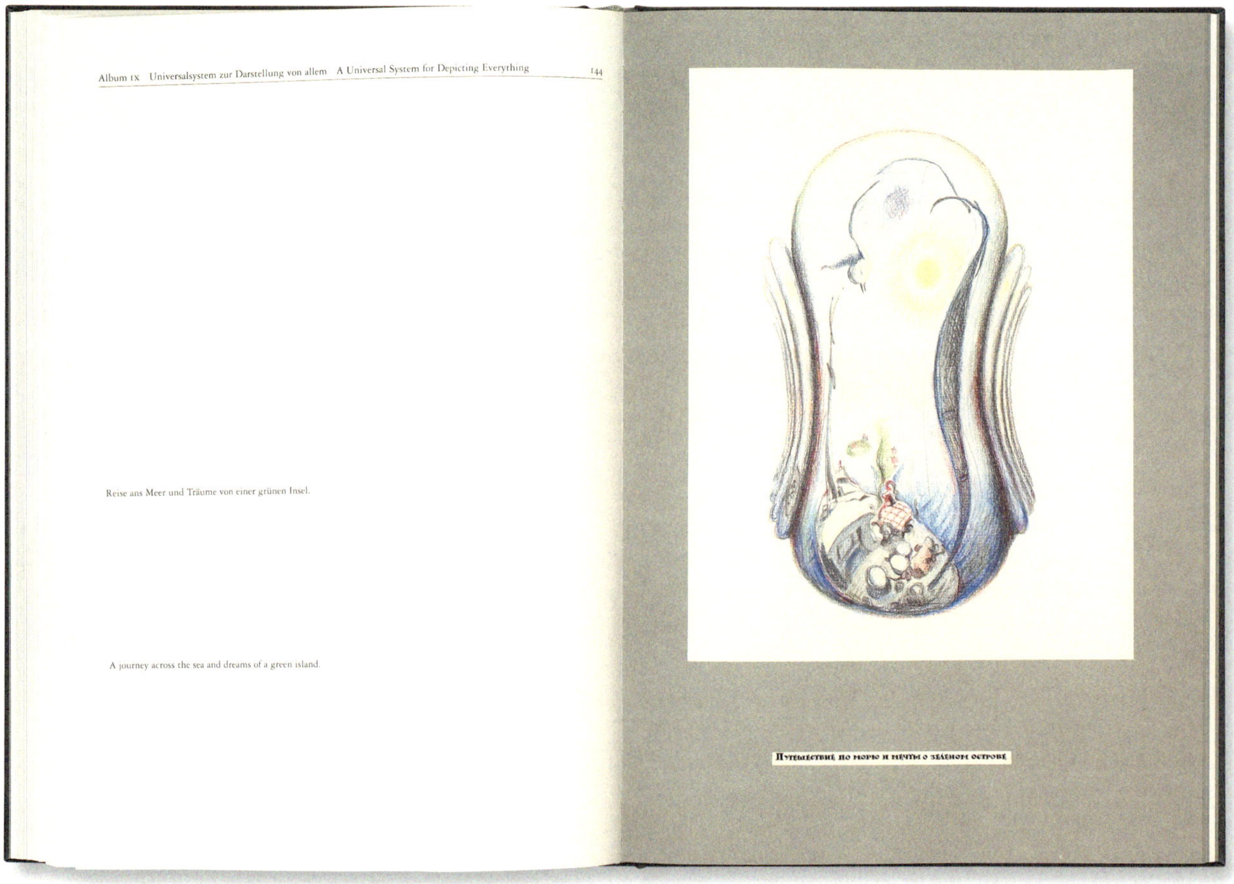
Album IX Universalsystem zur Darstellung von allem A Universal System for Depicting Everything 144
Reise ans Meer und Träume von einer grünen Insel.
A journey across the sea and dreams of a green island.
Путешествие по морю и мечты о зелёном острове

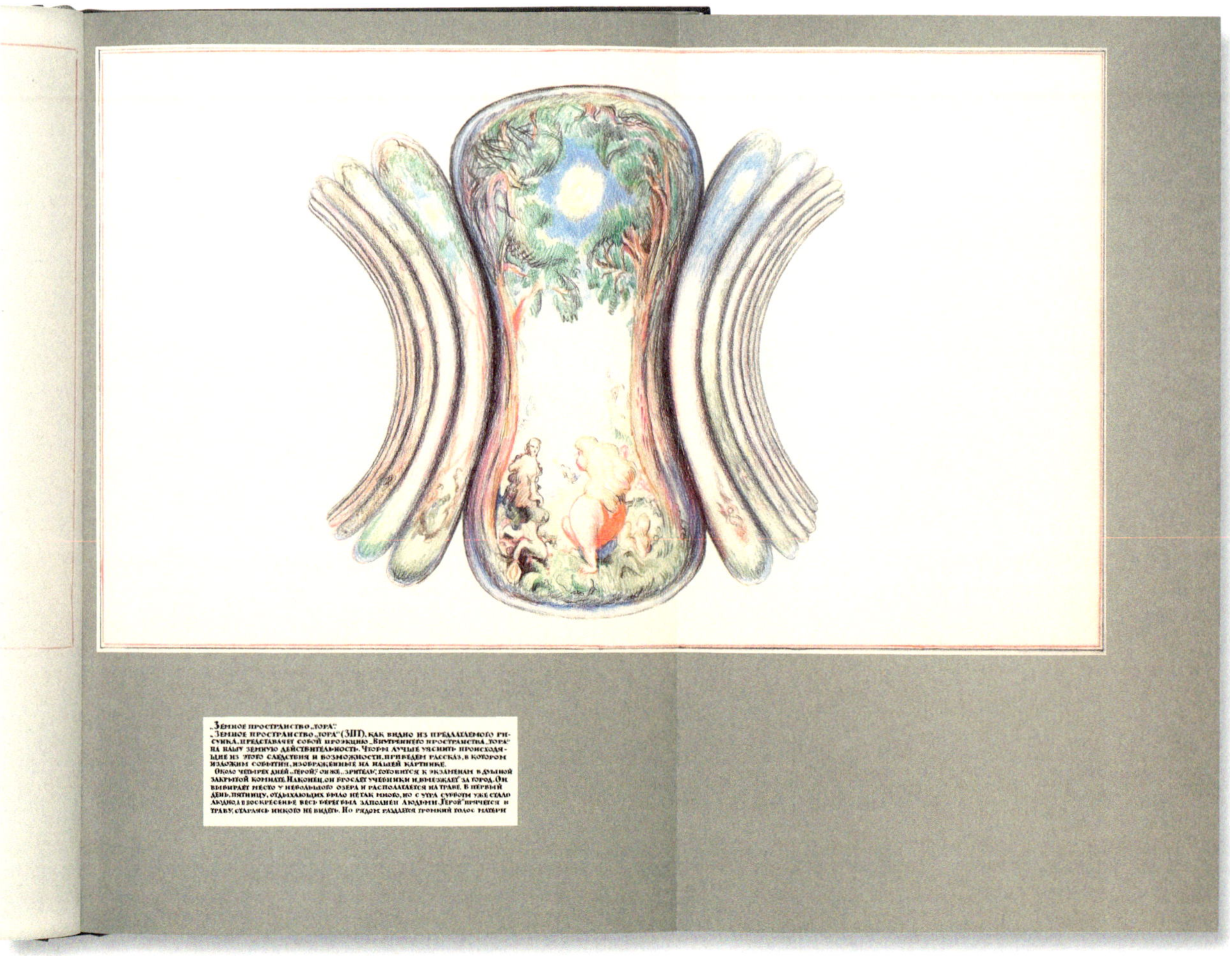
„Земное пространство „тора"
„Земное пространство „тора" (ЗПТ), как видно из предлагаемого рисунка, представляет собой проекцию „Внутреннего пространства „тора" на нашу земную действительность. Чтобы лучше уяснить происходящие из этого следствия и возможности, приведём рассказ, в котором изложим события, изображённые на нашей картинке.
Около четырёх дней „герой", он же „зритель", готовится к экзаменам в душной закрытой комнате. Наконец, он бросает учебники и выезжает за город. Он выбирает место у небольшого озера и располагается на траве. В первый день, пятницу, отдыхающих было не так много, но с утра субботы уже стало людно, а в воскресенье весь берег был заполнен людьми. „Герой" прячется в траву, стараясь никого не видеть. Но рядом раздаётся громкий голос матери

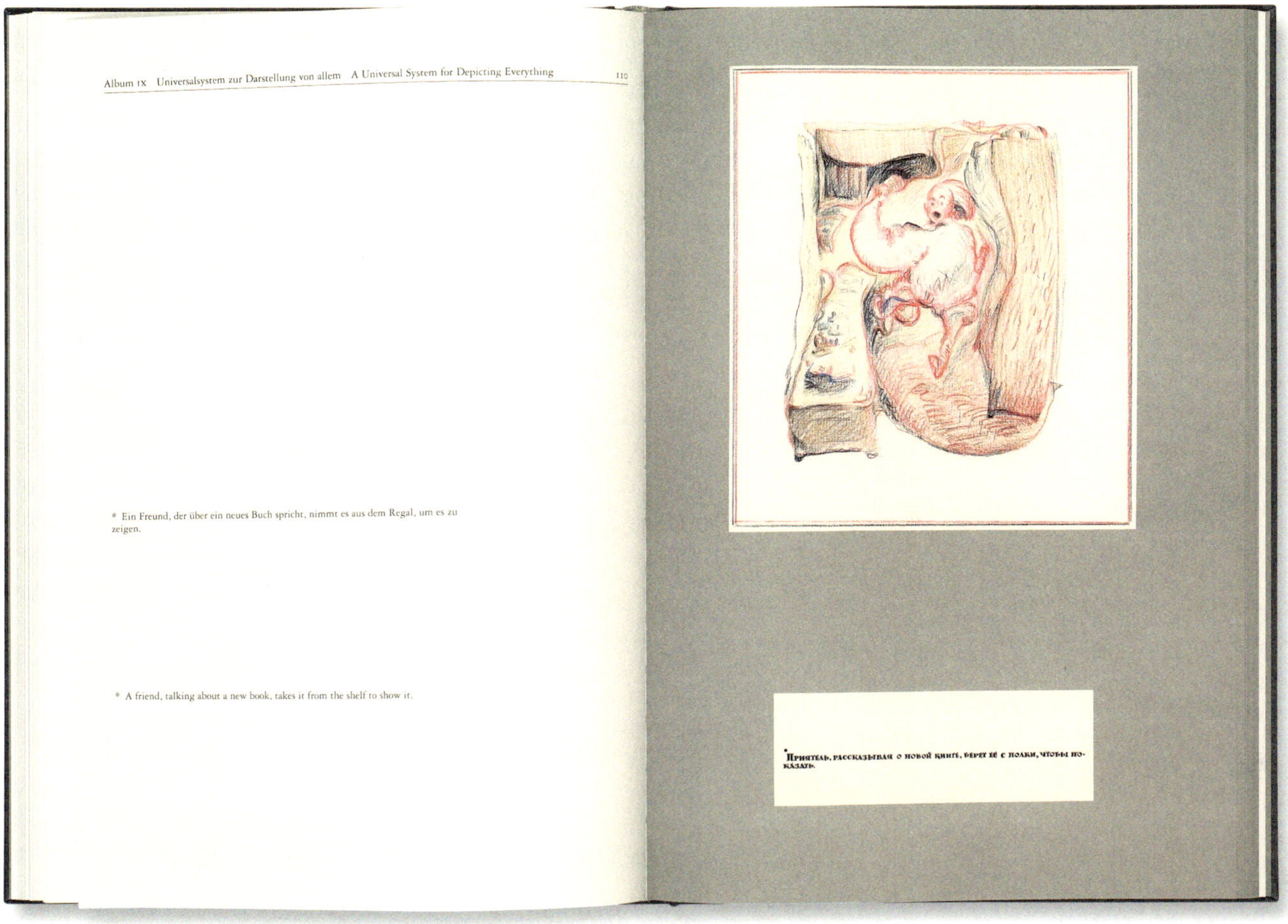
Album IX Universalsystem zur Darstellung von allem A Universal System for Depicting Everything 110

* Ein Freund, der über ein neues Buch spricht, nimmt es aus dem Regal, um es zu zeigen.

* A friend, talking about a new book, takes it from the shelf to show it.

* Приятель, рассказывая о новой книге, берет её с полки, чтобы показать.

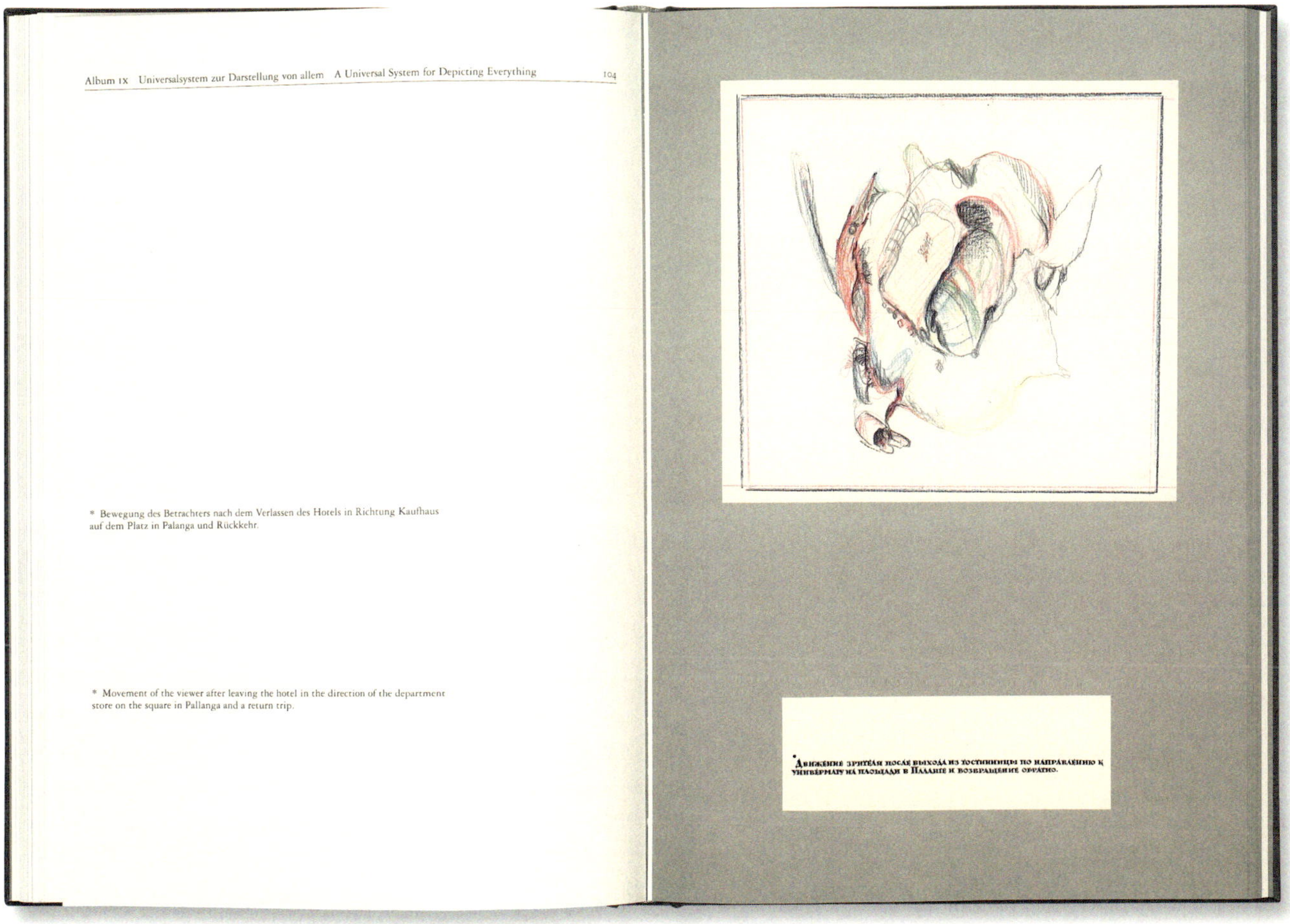
Album IX Universalsystem zur Darstellung von allem A Universal System for Depicting Everything 104

* Bewegung des Betrachters nach dem Verlassen des Hotels in Richtung Kaufhaus auf dem Platz in Palanga und Rückkehr.

* Movement of the viewer after leaving the hotel in the direction of the department store on the square in Pallanga and a return trip.

* Движение зрителя после выхода из гостиницы по направлению к универмагу на площади в Паланге и возвращение обратно.

119 Not Everyone Will Be Taken Into the Future

Nicht jedermann wird in die Zukunft mitgenommen

with Emilia Kabakov | *mit Emilia Kabakov*

2002

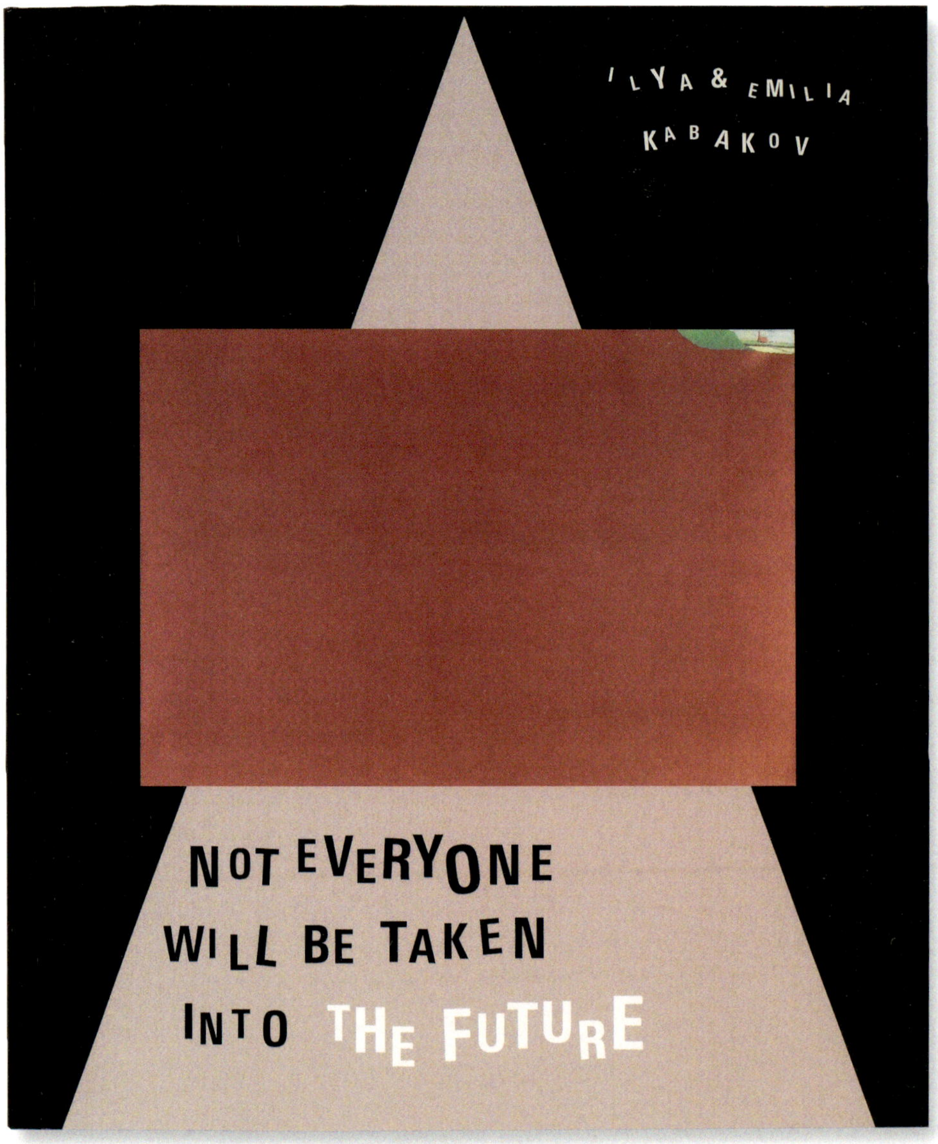

Galerie Thaddaeus Ropac, Salzburg/Paris; Galerie im Traklhaus, Salzburg; Internationale Sommerakademie für Bildende Kunst, Salzburg
Salzburg/Paris: Galerie Thaddaeus Ropac
27.9 x 23.5 cm
[49] pp. with 44 (27 color) ills.
adhesive binding, softback
Klebebindung, broschiert

exhibition catalogue | *Ausstellungskatalog*

layout by Ilya Kabakov | *Layout von Ilya Kabakov*

For the installation of the same name, originally for the 49th Biennale, Venice, June 10 to November 4, 2001. Galerie im Traklhaus, Salzburg, August 8 to September 14, 2002; Galerie Thaddaeus Ropac, Paris, November 22, 2002 to January 7, 2003. Texts by Lóránd Hegyi and Ilya Kabakov, and a dialogue between Ilya Kabakov and Barbara Wally on »Not Everyone Will Be Taken Into the Future«; German, English, Russian.

Zur gleichnamigen Installation, ursprünglich für die 49. Biennale, Venedig, 10. Juni – 4. November 2001. Galerie im Traklhaus, Salzburg, 8. August – 14. September 2002, und Galerie Thaddaeus Ropac, Paris, 22. November 2002 – 7. Januar 2003. Texte von Lóránd Hegyi und Ilya Kabakov und ein Dialog von Ilya Kabakov und Barbara Wally über »Nicht jedermann wird in die Zukunft mitgenommen«; deutsch, englisch, russisch.

see also | *siehe auch* CRP, vol. 2, nos. 381–392, pp. 100–111

Ilya Kabakov / 2001

NICHT JEDER WIRD IN DIE ZUKUNFT AUFGENOMMEN

Die Installation ist einem brandaktuellen Problem der Gegenwartskunst gewidmet: Was geschieht mit dem Künstler und seinen Arbeiten, wenn sie der jüngsten und sogar der ferneren Vergangenheit angehören? Wie wird sie der neue, künftige Betrachter, der neue Kritiker, Kurator oder Sammler nach einer gewissen Zeit sehen?
Dieses Problem wird in unserem Bewußtsein derzeit von der beherrschenden Forderung nach Aktualität überlagert. Man muß um jeden Preis zeitgenössisch sein. Die Forderung, heute zu sein, klingt um ein Vielfaches lauter als die Frage: Was geschieht morgen mit diesen Arbeiten?
Jeder Künstler ist persönlich mit diesem Problem konfrontiert. Geht es ihm darum, wie seine Arbeiten heute ankommen, oder möchte er, daß sie auch morgen noch »leben«? Und worin besteht der Unterschied?

Beschreibung der Installation
Beim Betreten des Raumes sieht der Besucher einen Zaun und eine Brücke. Um zu sehen, was sich hinter dem Zaun befindet, muß er die Brücke hinaufsteigen. Von der Brücke aus sieht er in der Mitte ein Stück des »letzten Waggons«, der von zwei hölzernen Bahnsteigen abzufahren scheint. Auf dem einen »Bahnsteig« liegen weggeworfene Bilder und Zeichnungen herum. Auch auf der Erde sieht man Bilder liegen. Über die Fensterscheibe des Waggons läuft eine rote Leuchtschrift (im Geist von Jenny Holzer): »Nicht jeder wird in die Zukunft aufgenommen.« Der von links nach rechts laufende Text wird ständig auf englisch und italienisch wiederholt.

1. Den Blick von der Brücke faßt der Besucher als Blick aus der Vogelperspektive auf, das heißt, aus einem anderen Raum und aus einer anderen Zeit, nämlich aus der Zukunft, denn der Zug ist ja schon abgefahren.

2. Die Bilder und Illustrationen stammen vom Autor der Installation, in der es keine an eine fremde Adresse gerichtete Kritik gibt. Dadurch wird die Situation auf den Autor selbst bezogen.

Technisches Problem
Die gesamte Installation ist aus Holz gefertigt, der Waggon besteht aus Blech.

Übersetzung aus dem Russischen: Annelore Nitschke

Biennale Venedig / 2001 / Gesamtansicht
Venice Biennale / 2001 / general view
Foto: Dirk Pauwels

Ilya Kabakov / 2001

NOT EVERYONE WILL BE TAKEN INTO THE FUTURE

This installation is dedicated to the problem that is very topical for the situation in the contemporary art world today: What will happen to artists and their works in the very near, and not so near future? How will they be accepted and understood by the new viewer of the future, the new art critic, the new collector, the new curator?
In our mind, this problem today is masked by the dominant reality, the demand to be »contemporary« no matter what! The demand »to exist today« overwhelms the question: What will happen to these works tomorrow?
This is a personal problem for every artist: What is more important, to have his works understood and accepted today, or to wish for them to live into »tomorrow«, and what is the difference?

Description of the Installation
The viewer, upon entering the space, encounters a fence and a bridge. In order to be able to see what is behind this fence, he has to go and walk onto the bridge. From the bridge he sees, in the center, a fragment of »The Last Train Car«, which is »leaving« from two wooden platforms (trucks). Paintings and rolls of drawings are on one of these platforms. The same kinds of paintings are also lying scattered on the ground. On the train car we see a running electronic text (in red, in Jenny Holzer's style) that reads: »Not everyone will be taken into the future«. The text, running from left to right, is repeated in different languages: English, Italian.

1. The viewer's point of view from the bridge is that of a bird in flight, i.e., it is a view from »another space«, from the future, because the train has already left.

2. The paintings and the images on them belong to the authors of the installation. There is »no critical escapade aimed at anyone in particular«. This is the problem of the authors themselves.

Translation: Cynthia Martin

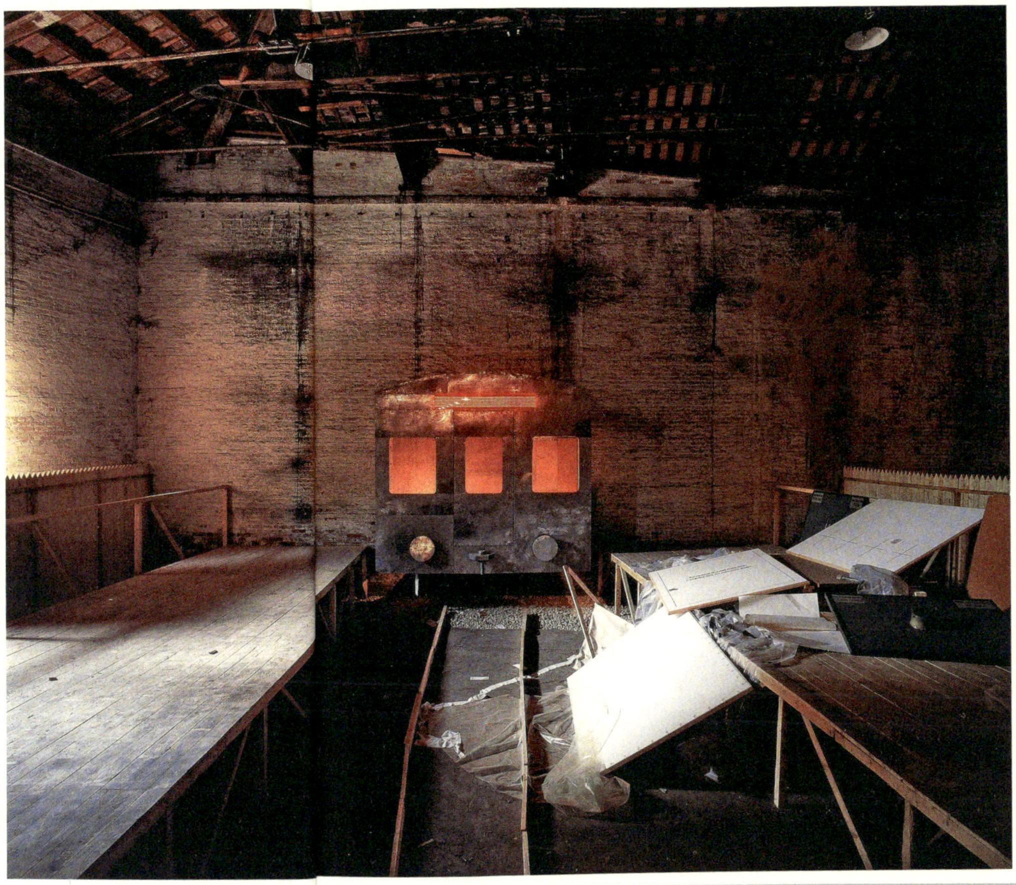

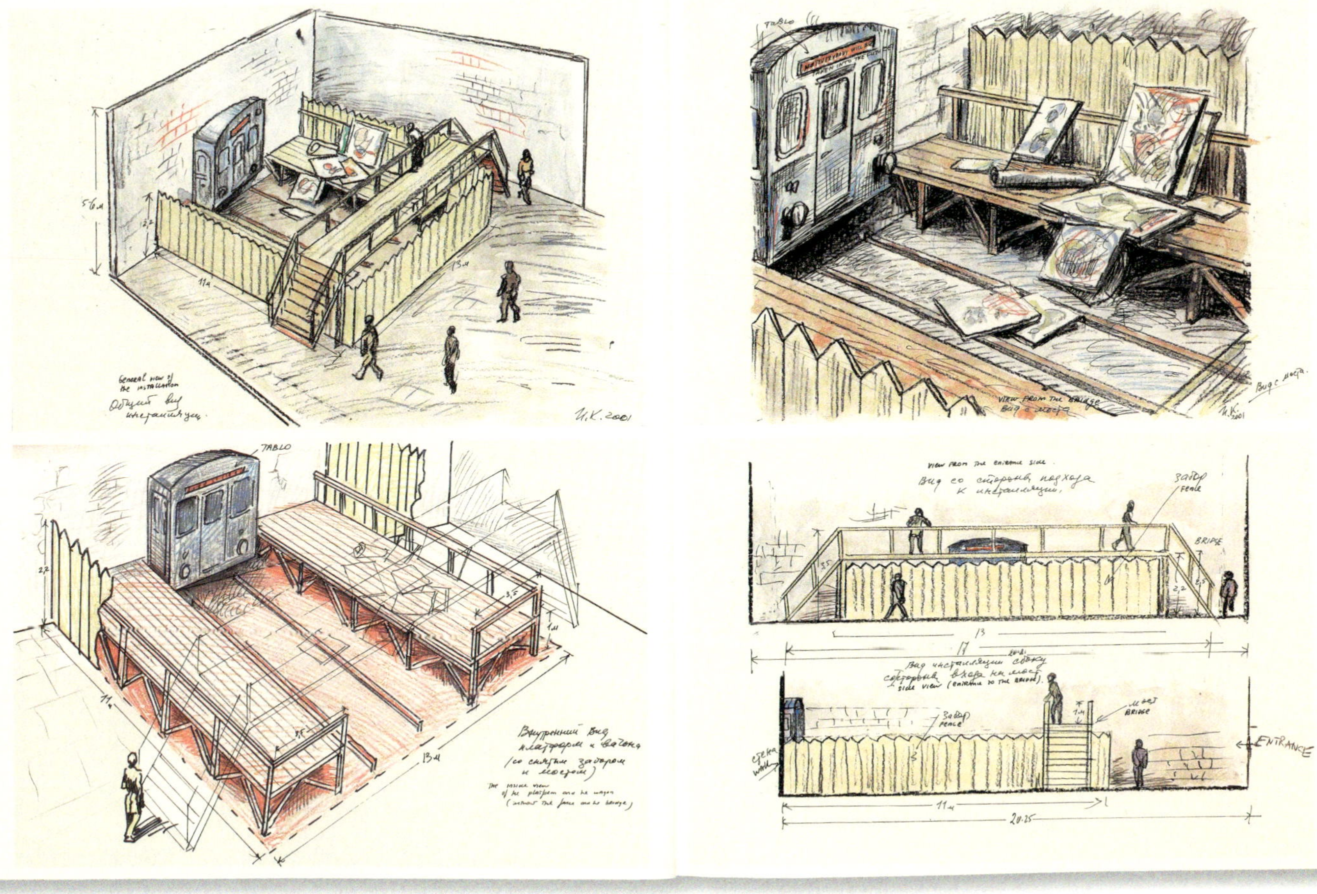

Modell der Installation / 2001
Holz / 94 x 113 x 39 cm
Foto: Gil Amiaga

BW Ich will noch einmal auf den doch sehr provozierenden Titel der Installation: »not everyone will be taken into the future« zurückkommen. Hier wird doch ein Selektionsmechanismus angesprochen, ein Filter, der die einen von den anderen scheidet. Es bedeutet, dass nur wenige die Zukunft erreichen und sehr viele davon ausgeschlossen werden. Das erinnert an göttliche Eingriffe, wie sie in den Mythen vorkommen. Ich denke an Noah, der vom biblischen Gott auserwählt wird, die Sintflut zu überleben, und als einziger mit seiner Sippe inklusive Tierbestand die Zukunft erreicht. Alle anderen werden durch eine Katastrophe vernichtet. In Ihrer Installation bildet der Waggon den Selektionsmechanismus. Wer darf einsteigen, wer mit diesem Waggon mitfahren?

IK Die Frage ist auch, wer verkauft die Tickets? Wer steuert den Waggon? Wer ist der Zugführer? Ich glaube, dass die Museen dabei eine wichtige Rolle spielen und zwar die internationalen Museen für klassische und moderne Kunst. In den letzten 100 Jahren waren die Museen massiver Kritik ausgesetzt: Museen sind schlecht, sind tot, sind korrupt und so weiter. Trotzdem, die Museen werden bleiben und nehmen eine wichtige und gute Entwicklung. Natürlich gibt es auch negative Seiten, dennoch: Das Museum ist die letzte und beste Institution, die wir derzeit für die bildende Kunst haben. Das Museum funktioniert heute wie eine Religion – die Religion der Kultur. Die Leute kommen ins Museum wegen dieser Begegnung – sie erwarten eine Empfindung, eine Erhöhung, eine Anleitung durch die Kunst. Dabei ist es egal, ob das alte oder neue Kunst ist. Die Leute kommen wie zum Essen: Essen für die Seele, für den Intellekt.

BW Wenn man beobachtet, auf welchem Wege heute Kunstwerke ins Museum kommen, so spiegeln die Stationen Prozesse der (Schatten-) Wirtschaft wider. Das Werk wird auf seinem Weg aus dem Atelier ins Museum erst zur Ware, dann zum Spekulationsobjekt, zur Verlustabschreibung, zum Katalysator für Geldwäsche, um dann – vielleicht vom ökonomischen Kontext befreit – in der Schausammlung, wahrscheinlicher aber im Depot zu landen. Das »vielleicht« bezieht sich auf die zunehmende Privatisierung öffentlicher Museen, die zu einer erneuten »Kapitalisierung« der Sammlungsobjekte führt.

IK Diese Vorgänge stören mich nicht. Das Geld, ob und wie lange ein Werk gezeigt oder in das Depot verfrachtet wird – ohne diesen

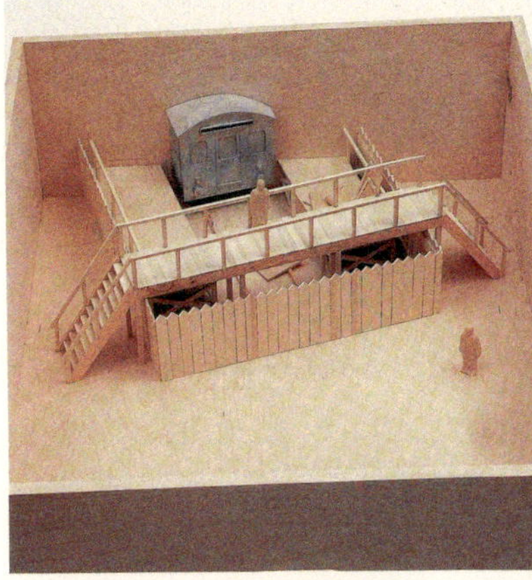

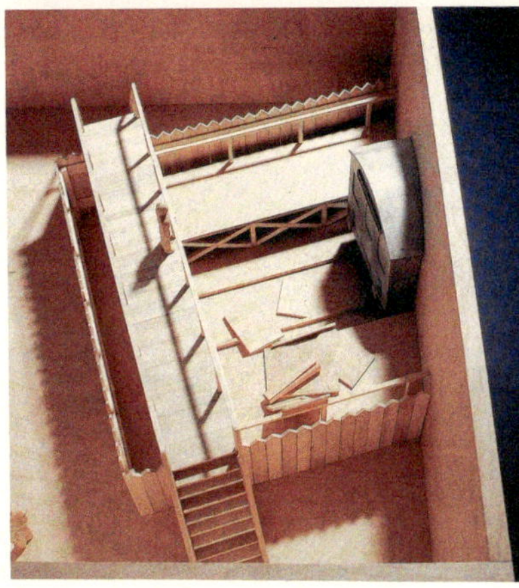

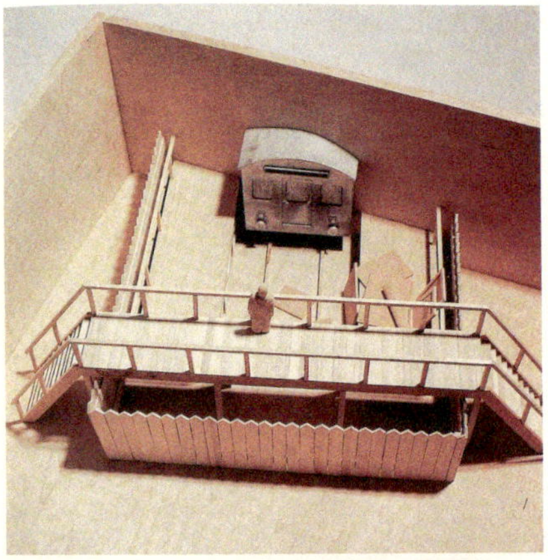

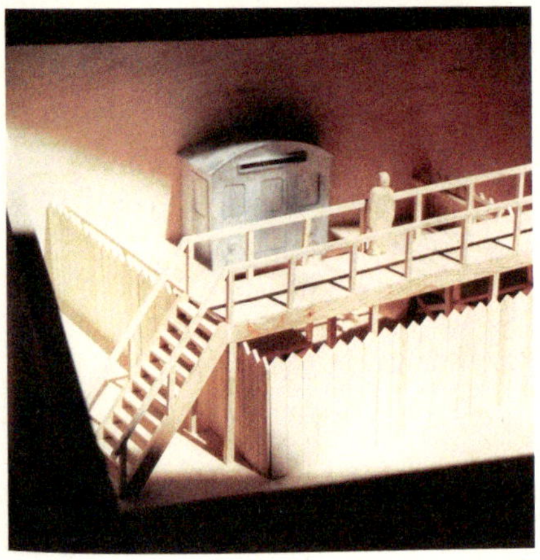

model of the installation / 2001
wood / 37 x 44.5 x 15.4 inches

IDEALZEICHNUNGEN >>
Filzstift, Bleistift, Buntstifte und Deckweiß auf Papier, teilweise aquarelliert / 2001
je 28 x 43.2 cm

IDEAL DRAWINGS
felt pen, pencil, crayons, opaque white and watercolour on paper / 2001
each 11 x 17 inches

trophe. In your installation, the wagon represents the selection mechanism. Who is allowed to enter; who may ride in it?

IK The question is also: who steers the wagon, who is the driver? Will the future of the artist still be the museum? During the past hundred years, museums have been subjected to massive criticism – museums are a bad idea, they are dead, corrupt, and so on. Nevertheless, museums are here to stay, and they show an important and valuable development. There are of course negative aspects, but even so, they are the best institution that we have for the fine arts. A museum today functions like a church. People visit museums and expect to gain enhanced emotional experience and guidance through art. And it is unimportant whether this is old or new art. People come as they would to a meal – to find food for the soul, for the intellect.

BW When one looks at the way works of art get into museums these days, the stages reflect processes of the (black) economy. On its way from the studio to the museum, the work becomes first a commodity, then an object of speculation, a depreciation allowance, a catalyst for money-laundering, and finally – perhaps now liberated from its economic context – lands in a public collection, or more probably in a depot. »Perhaps« refers here to the increasing privatisation of public museums, which leads to a renewed »capitalisation« of the objects in the collection.

IK These processes do not worry me – I see them as mere technical matters. The money, or how long a work remains on display, how long it lies in the depot – these are concerns of the materialistic aspect of art history. Without this aspect there is no art, no artists. But this is only one side of the question; the other is the mythological, spiritual and intellectual side of the artwork. There exists a special kind of energy, a special kind of spiritual and intellectual information, the so-called aura of the artwork. Artists create this aura by conveying a message in their work. I would compare art history to a train, where each artist is a station which takes up a fixed period in the timetable. The station marks a particular place and a particular time. There is a main track of art history, and there are side-tracks. From the contemporary point of view, art history looks like a vast ocean with no islands – everything floats, but nevertheless, the track is still there.

absolut geniale Arbeiten. Bei Nachbauten fehlt diese Aura, sie sind sinnlos geworden.

BW Wie ordnen Sie die im Kontext einer Installation entstandenen Zeichnungen, Skizzen, Pläne und Modelle zu? Sind sie Bestandteil der Installation oder autonome Arbeiten?

IK Sie sind nicht Teil der Installation, sondern eine Art Ersatz. Diese Arbeiten sind für die »Wiederherstellung des Gedächtnisses« bestimmt und für Leute, die sich intensiver und gründlicher für Installationen interessieren. Das ist wie beim tragischen Schicksal der Architektur, besonders der großen russischen Architekten, wie Melnikov oder Leonidov. Der Fall Melnikov ist ganz typisch. Seine Bauten sind nur sechs Jahre lang realisiert worden, aber danach lebte er noch 55 Jahre. Neben den ganz wenigen realen Bauten sind nur Pläne, Skizzen und Zeichnungen von ihm übrig geblieben, jedoch keine Modelle. Doch die Leute, die seine Arbeit kennen und lieben, können aus den Plänen und Skizzen die Projekte und die dahinter stehenden Visionen verstehen. Dasselbe gilt für viele andere Architekten, auch für meinen Lieblingsarchitekten, den italienischen Futuristen Sant'Elia. Er hat überhaupt nichts gebaut, trotzdem war er großartig. In diesem Kontext sind auch meine Zeichnungen, Skizzen, Texte und Modelle zu verstehen. Selbst falls ich manche Installationen nicht realisieren kann, bleiben diese vielleicht als Ersatz für zukünftige »archäologische« Recherchen übrig.

BW Heißt das, dass die jeweiligen Skizzen, Zeichnungen, Texte und Pläne grundsätzlich vor den Installationen entstanden sind?

IK Beide Fälle sind möglich. Viele Zeichnungen sind vorab entstanden, aber einige auch erst nach der Realisierung, sozusagen für die zukünftigen Leser und Betrachter.

BW Ihren Zeichnungen und den in ihrer Präzision wie Architekturzeichnungen anmutenden Skizzen entnehme ich etwas, was mich immer wieder verblüfft: Nämlich wie präzise Sie den Weg des Betrachters durch die Installation oder durch die Ausstellung vorherplanen. Sie ziehen jeden Schritt, den Blickwinkel, die Perspektive, die Ermüdung, in Betracht. Ich kenne keinen anderen Künstler, der sich in ähnlich intensiver Weise mit dem Ausstellungsbesucher, dem Betrachter seiner Arbeit auseinandersetzt. Ich würde sogar sagen, ich kenne keinen anderen Künstler, der den

»THE FLY«
Öl auf Leinwand / oil on canvas / 2001
205 x 155 cm / 80.7 x 61 inches

BW From your drawings and the sketches, which in their precision look like architectural drawings, I gather something that never ceases to amaze me: namely, how precisely you plan in advance the path the viewer will take through the installation or the exhibition. You take into account his every step, his angle of view, his perspective, his possible fatigue. I know no other artist who concerns himself so intensively with the people visiting the exhibition, with the person viewing his work. I would even say, I know no other artist who takes the viewer so seriously, and programmes him for the installation.

IK That is a good point, for this subject is essential for me. Another thing that is very important is dialogue and critical discussion, as for example with Boris Groys. Correspondingly important is the publication of these reflections and discussions – which is why I aim at having a publication to accompany every installation. I tend to collect more and more material about the installations, to do more and more documentation. On the one hand out of a fear that the installations themselves may one day no longer exist; but on the other, also with regard to the viewer. There is the standpoint of the »modern« artist, who says: »I am the prophet, the genius; the others are profane, idiots. I work for God, my ideals and my talent. I am not interested in how you, the viewer, react to it. You have to understand me; you come to me, not I to you.« My standpoint is exactly the opposite. For me, the viewer plays the principal role, he is an intelligent person who recognises and grasps everything. He is a connoisseur, and perfectly capable of placing my work within his knowledge of art history, judging it in the anonymity of the museums, and therefore always considering it within the context of art history.

BW The genre of the installation prevents the viewer's taking up a static frontal position, as he would do to look at a picture, and forces him to move around in the room – on a more or less prescribed route. Physically and mentally, he covers a certain distance. In the case of the installation »Not everyone will be taken into the future«, the viewer enters a rather obscure room, has to go up a rough wooden staircase and comes to a halt on a bridge leading at right angles over a railway, because it is not until there that he recognises a visual goal – some ten metres away stands a wagon, lit up in red, which has stopped in the middle of his route. Does this convey an atmosphere

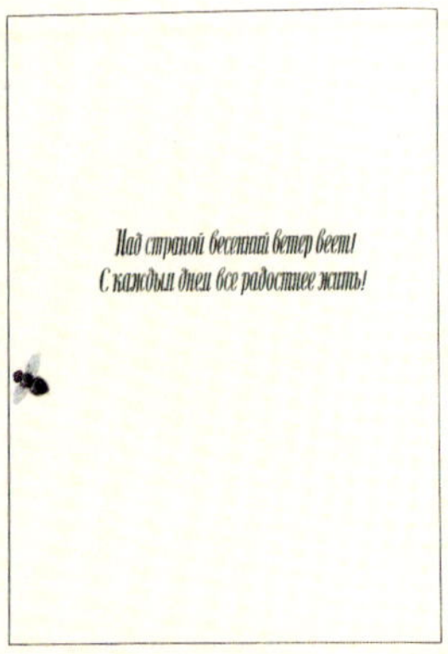

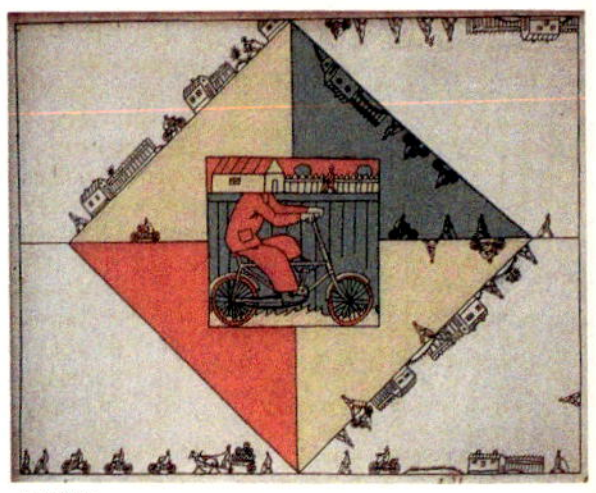

»THE CYCLIST«
Öl auf Leinwand / oil on canvas / 2001
153 x 207 cm / 60.2 x 81.5 inches

»BY THE EDGE«
Öl auf Leinwand / oil on canvas / 2001
250 x 163 cm / 98.4 x 64.2 inches

120 A Utopian City or A Monument Inside a Monument

Eine utopische Stadt oder Ein Denkmal innerhalb eines Denkmals

with Emilia Kabakov | *mit Emilia Kabakov*

2002

Ilya and Emilia Kabakov
New York: published by Ilya and Emilia Kabakov
28 x 43.5 cm
86 photocopied pp. with 54 (44 color) ills.
quick bind, paper cover, label on the cover
Schnellhefter, Papierumschlag, Etikette auf dem Umschlag
edition: 2 copies

thematic publication | *thematische Publikation*

layout by Ilya Kabakov | *Layout von Ilya Kabakov*

For the installation of the same name at the Zollverein Coking Plant, Essen. Texts by Ilya and Emilia Kabakov; Russian, English.

Zur gleichnamigen Installation für die Kokerei Zollverein, Essen. Texte von Ilya und Emilia Kabakov; russisch, englisch.

scc also | *siehe auch* no. 126

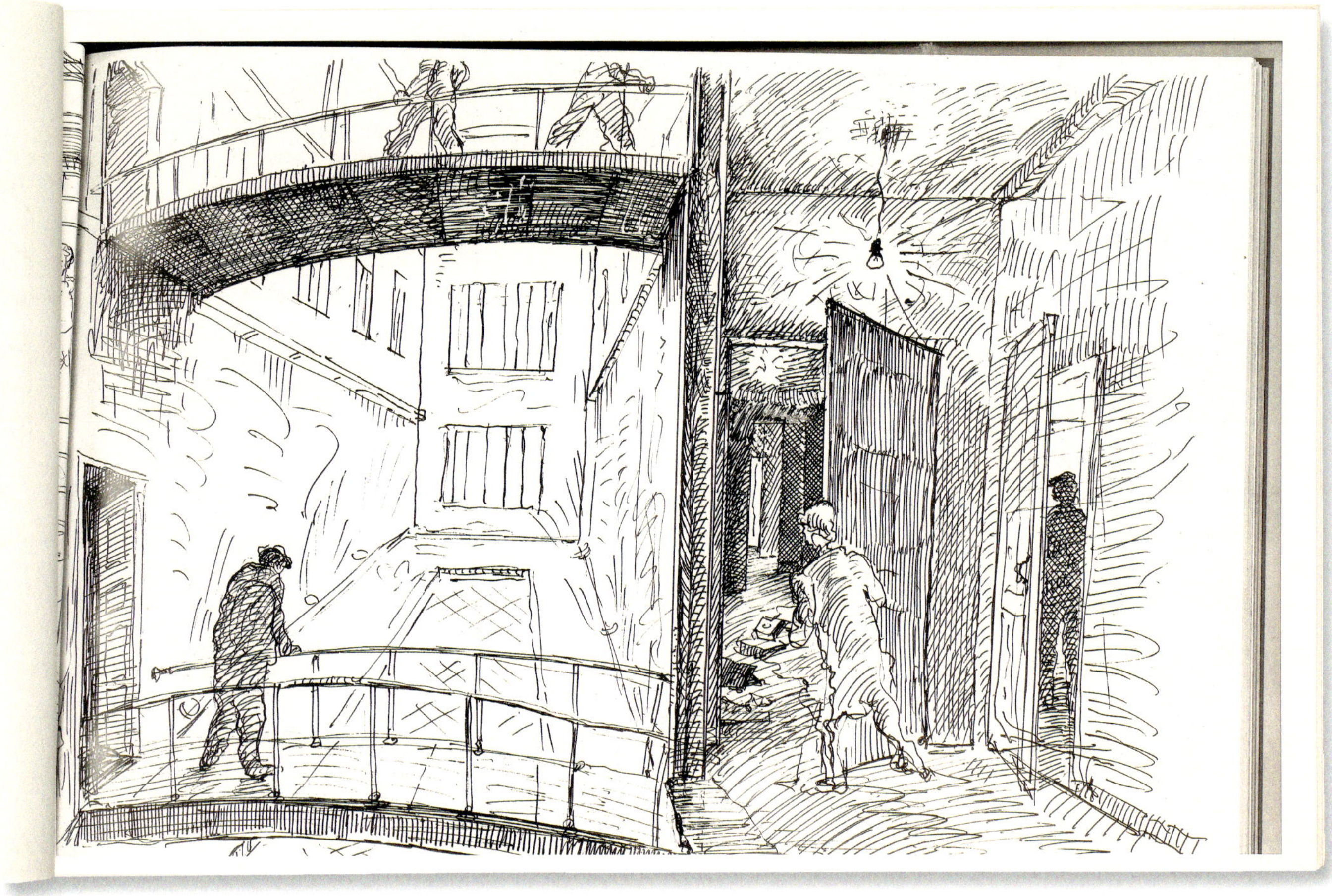

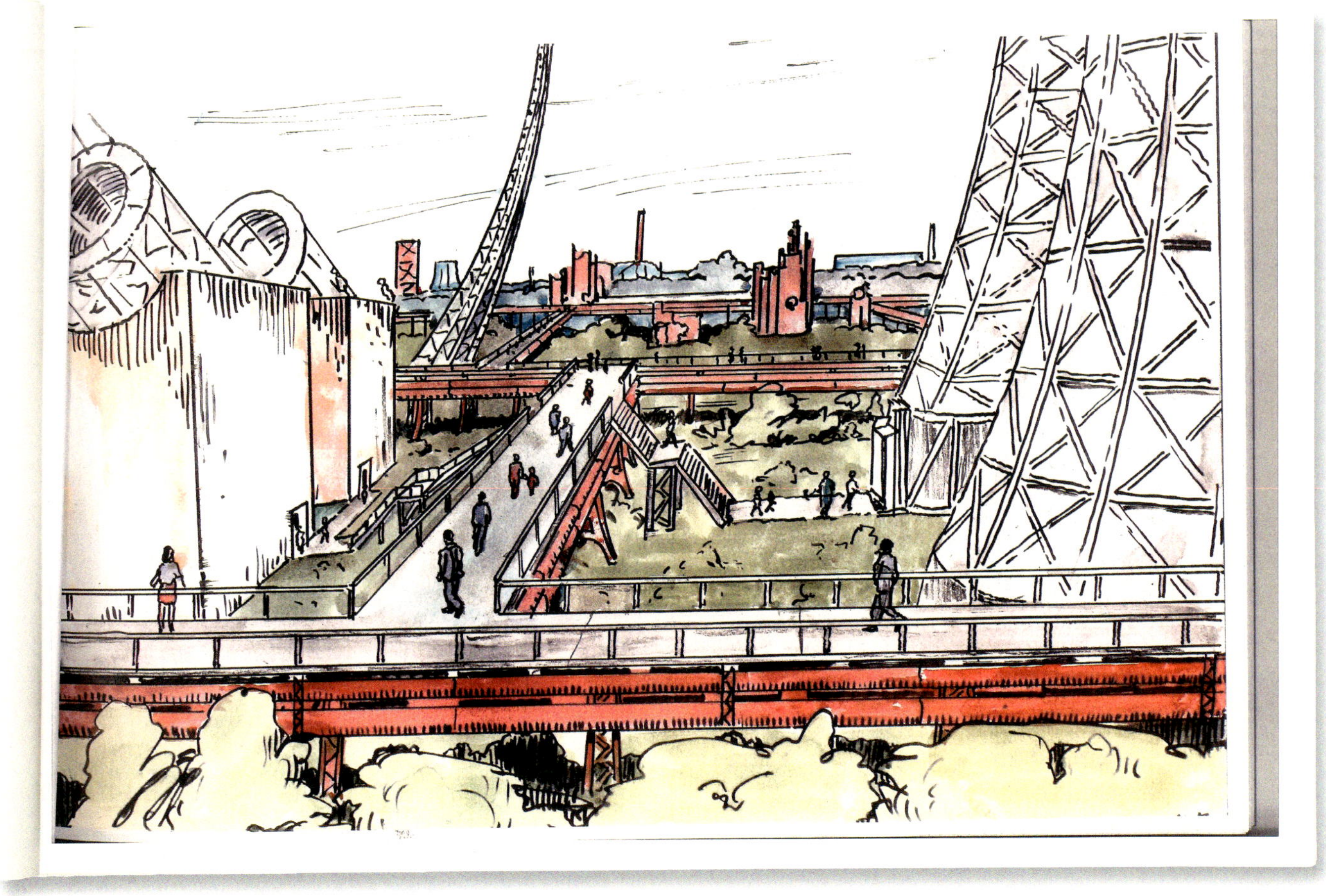

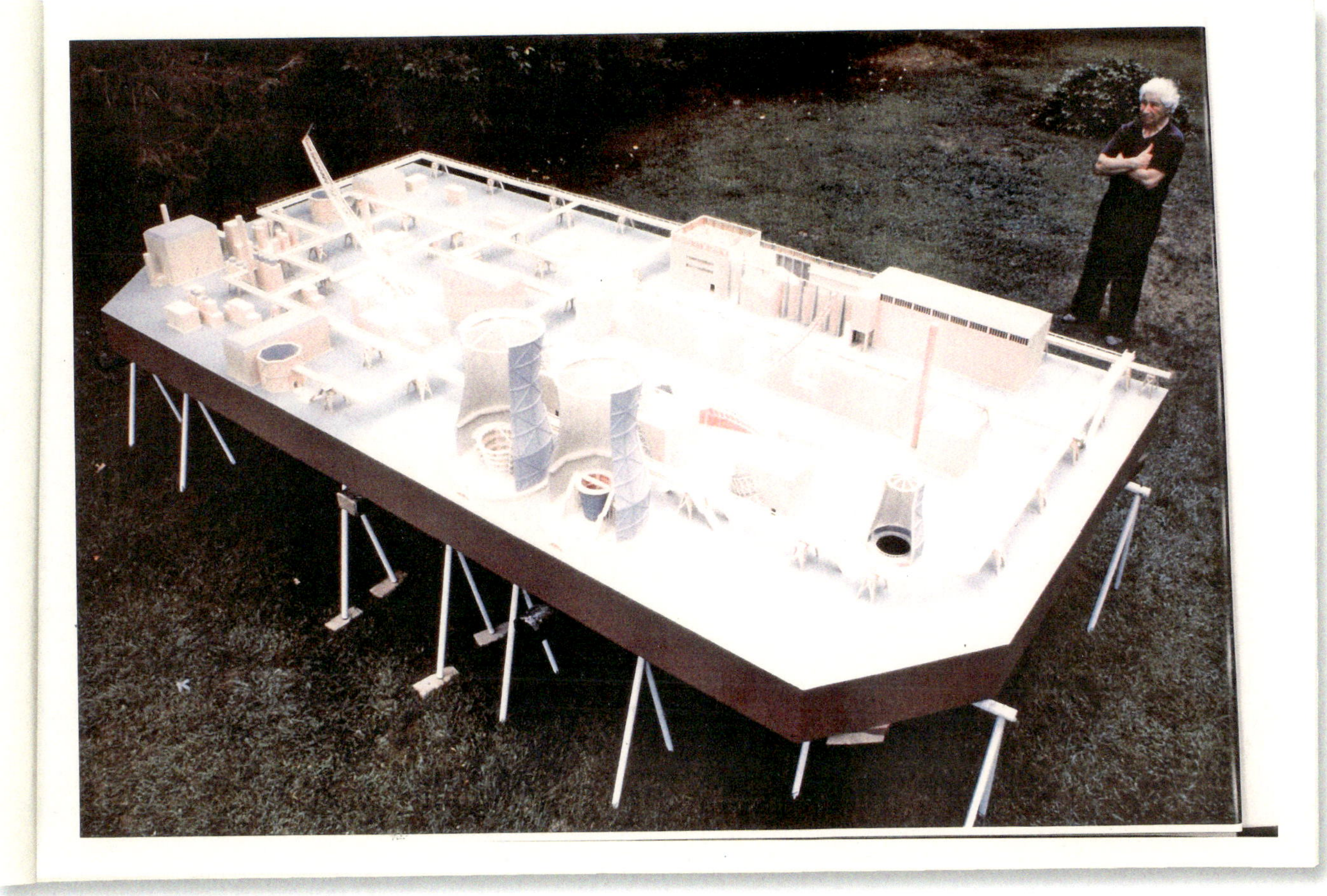

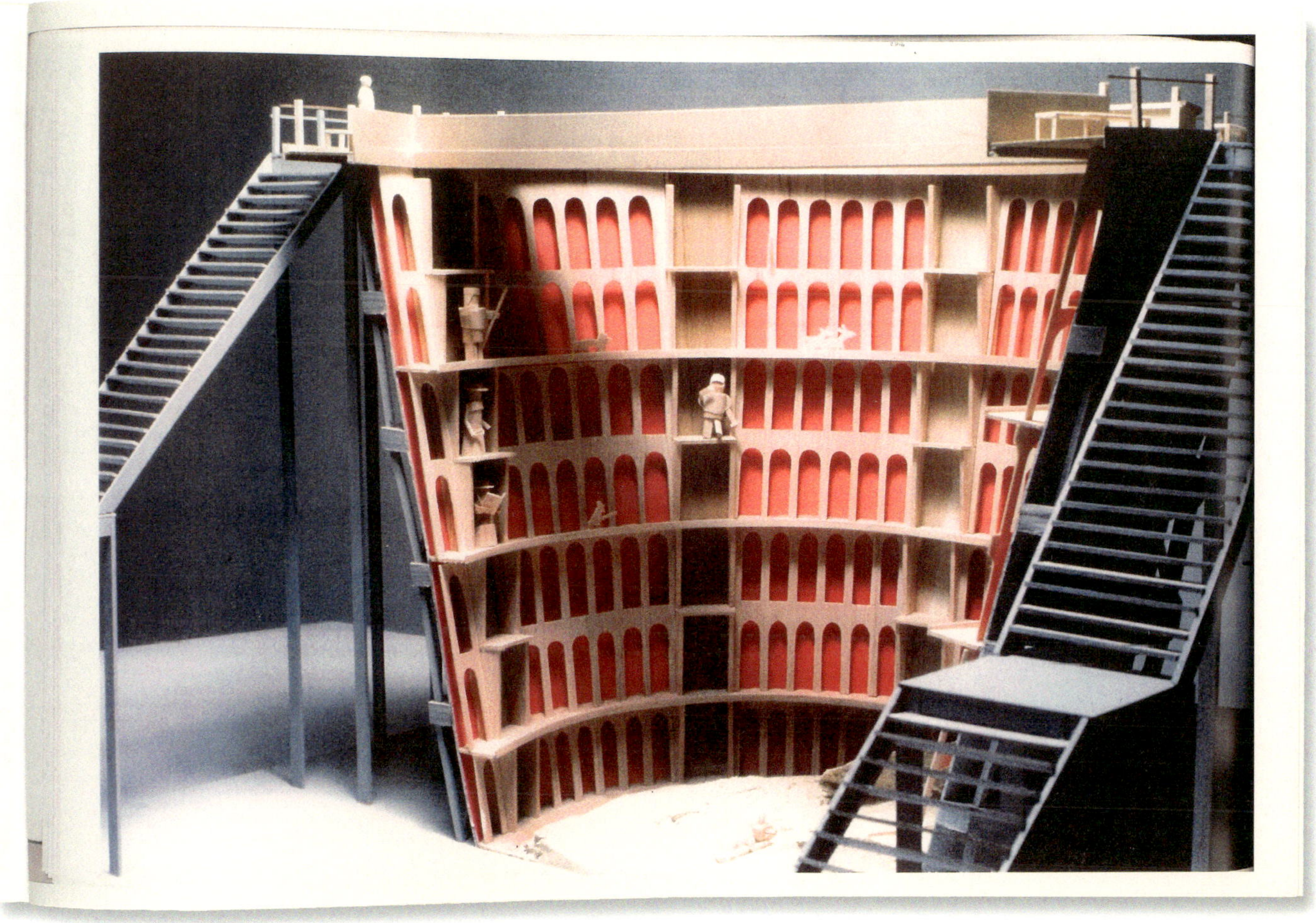

121 Center of Cosmic Energy | *Zentrum der kosmischen Energie*

with Emilia Kabakov | *mit Emilia Kabakov*

2003

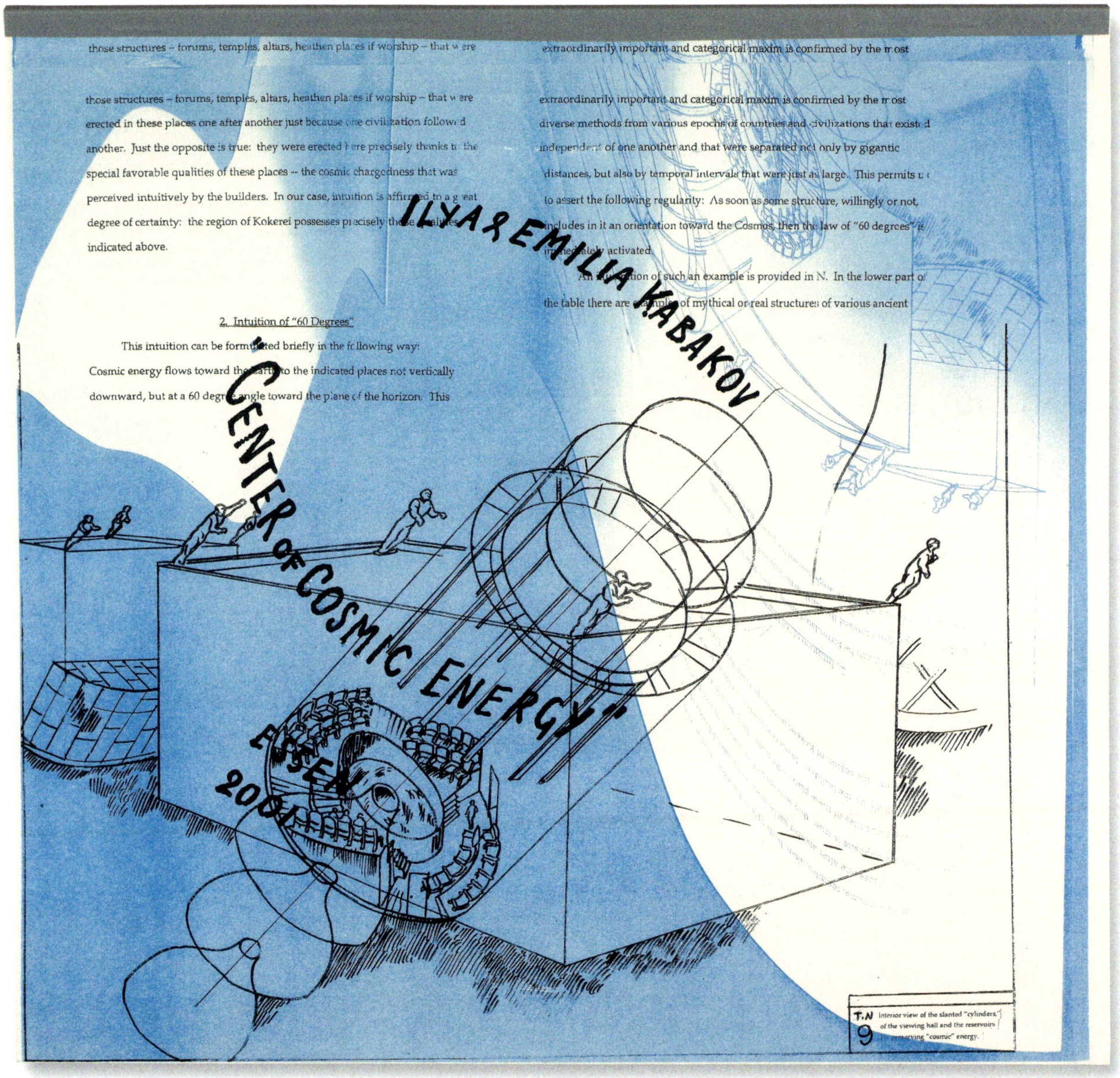

Ilya and Emilia Kabakov
Düsseldorf: Galerie Clara Maria Sels
28.3 x 30.5 cm
[55] pp. with 24 b/w ills.
stapled, cardboard cover
Drahtheftung, Kartonumschlag

exhibition catalogue | *Ausstellungskatalog*

layout by Ilya Kabakov | *Layout von Ilya Kabakov*

For the exhibition of the same name at the Clara Maria Sels Galerie, Düsseldorf, April 29 to July 12, 2003. Texts by Ilya and Emilia Kabakov; English.

Zur gleichnamigen Ausstellung, Clara Maria Sels Galerie, Düsseldorf, 29. April – 12. Juli 2003. Texte von Ilya und Emilia Kabakov; englisch.

see also | *siehe auch* no. 120; no. 126

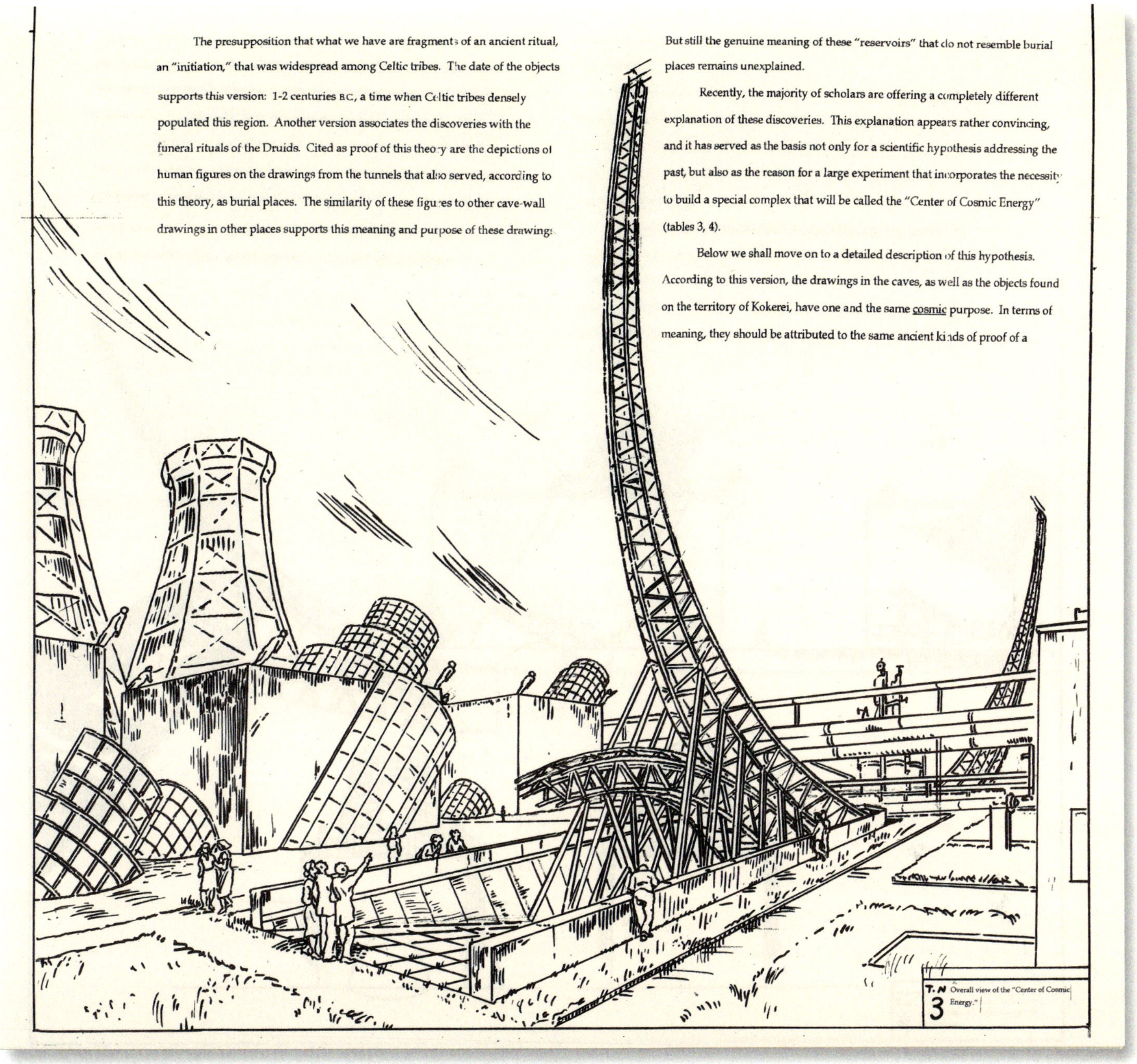

The presupposition that what we have are fragments of an ancient ritual, an "initiation," that was widespread among Celtic tribes. The date of the objects supports this version: 1-2 centuries BC, a time when Celtic tribes densely populated this region. Another version associates the discoveries with the funeral rituals of the Druids. Cited as proof of this theory are the depictions of human figures on the drawings from the tunnels that also served, according to this theory, as burial places. The similarity of these figures to other cave-wall drawings in other places supports this meaning and purpose of these drawings.

But still the genuine meaning of these "reservoirs" that do not resemble burial places remains unexplained.

Recently, the majority of scholars are offering a completely different explanation of these discoveries. This explanation appears rather convincing, and it has served as the basis not only for a scientific hypothesis addressing the past, but also as the reason for a large experiment that incorporates the necessity to build a special complex that will be called the "Center of Cosmic Energy" (tables 3, 4).

Below we shall move on to a detailed description of this hypothesis. According to this version, the drawings in the caves, as well as the objects found on the territory of Kokerei, have one and the same cosmic purpose. In terms of meaning, they should be attributed to the same ancient kinds of proof of a

T. N 3 Overall view of the "Center of Cosmic Energy."

sensitive. This is precisely what is generally known and widespread under the understanding of "intuition," the cognitive capacities of which have attracted attention only very recently.

This capacity of human intuition is "set in motion" in the most serious way in the concept behind the creation of a "Center," and will serve as one of the main methods to be used here, along with other scientific methodology conducted in the Center's experimental work.

II. Four Intuitions

Before enumerating these four intuitions and revealing the content of each of them, a few words should be said about the nature of "intuition" itself and how it differs from fantasy, even though the character of their emergence in the imagination is identical and the nature of both of them is rather similar.

The nature of fantasies, no matter how convincing these fantasies might

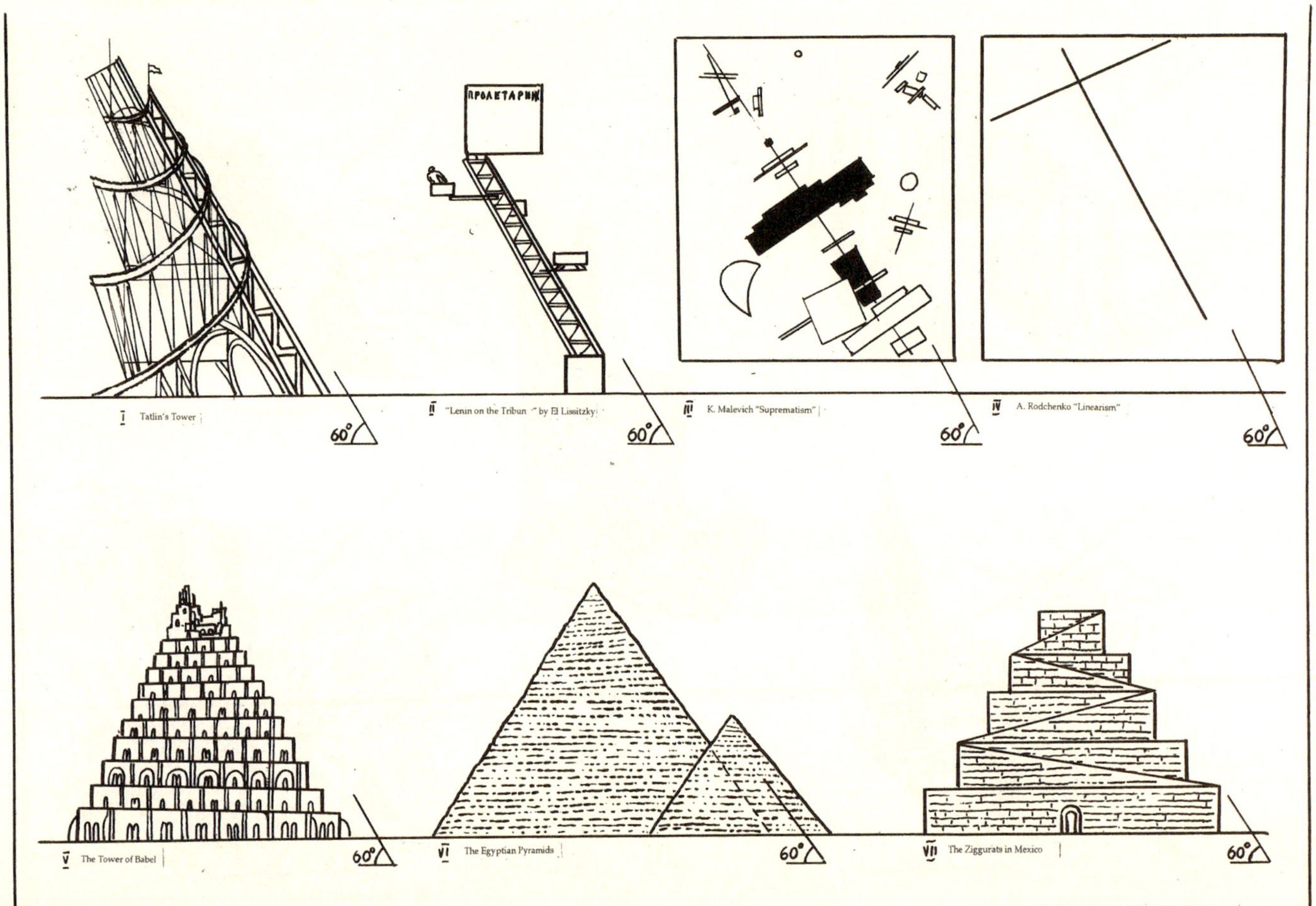

T. N 5 Projects and Structures Made Taking into Account the 60 Degree angle (the angle of Cosmic Energy)

Often confirmation of such "correctness" requires significant time. And this occurs particularly often in those instances that involve intuitively discovered facts or knowledge.

1. Intuition of "Place"

This intuition presumptively speaks about the fact that certain places or our planet for some reason are especially sensitive and perceptive to the reception of cosmic energy, at the same time that the majority of other places maintain their neutrality toward it. In these places it is as though a very high energy charge is present constantly, that most often does not coincide and is no connected with favorable climatic conditions in these regions. Moreover, these places are most often found in an especially "unfavorable" climate. In all probability, there is a sufficient quantity of such places on Earth, but they have not all been discovered yet. The human organism, his psyche, actively reacts

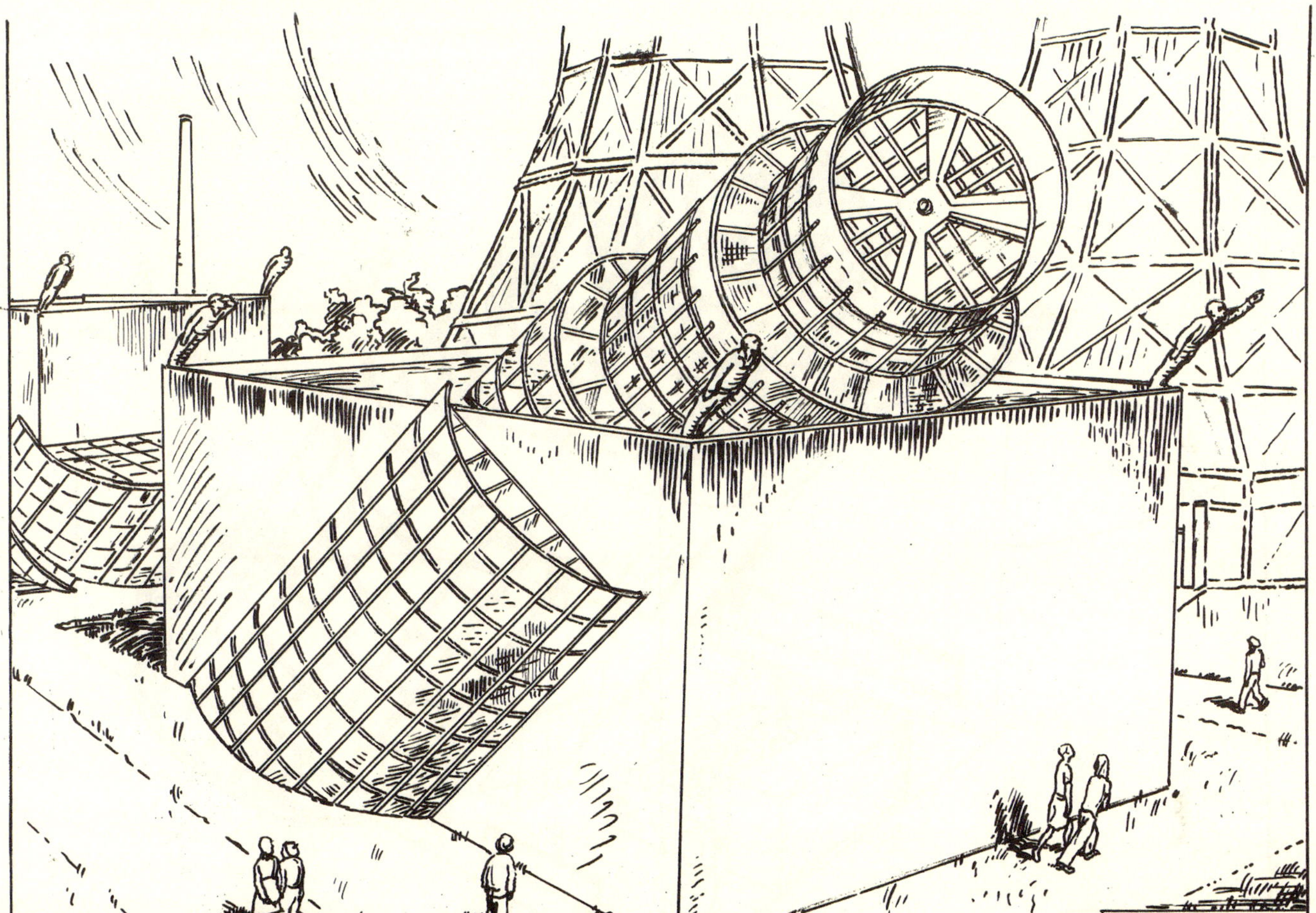

T.N 7 Exterior view of the central building (building No. 1).

122 Where Is Our Place? | *Wo ist unser Standort?*

with Emilia Kabakov | *mit Emilia Kabakov*

2003

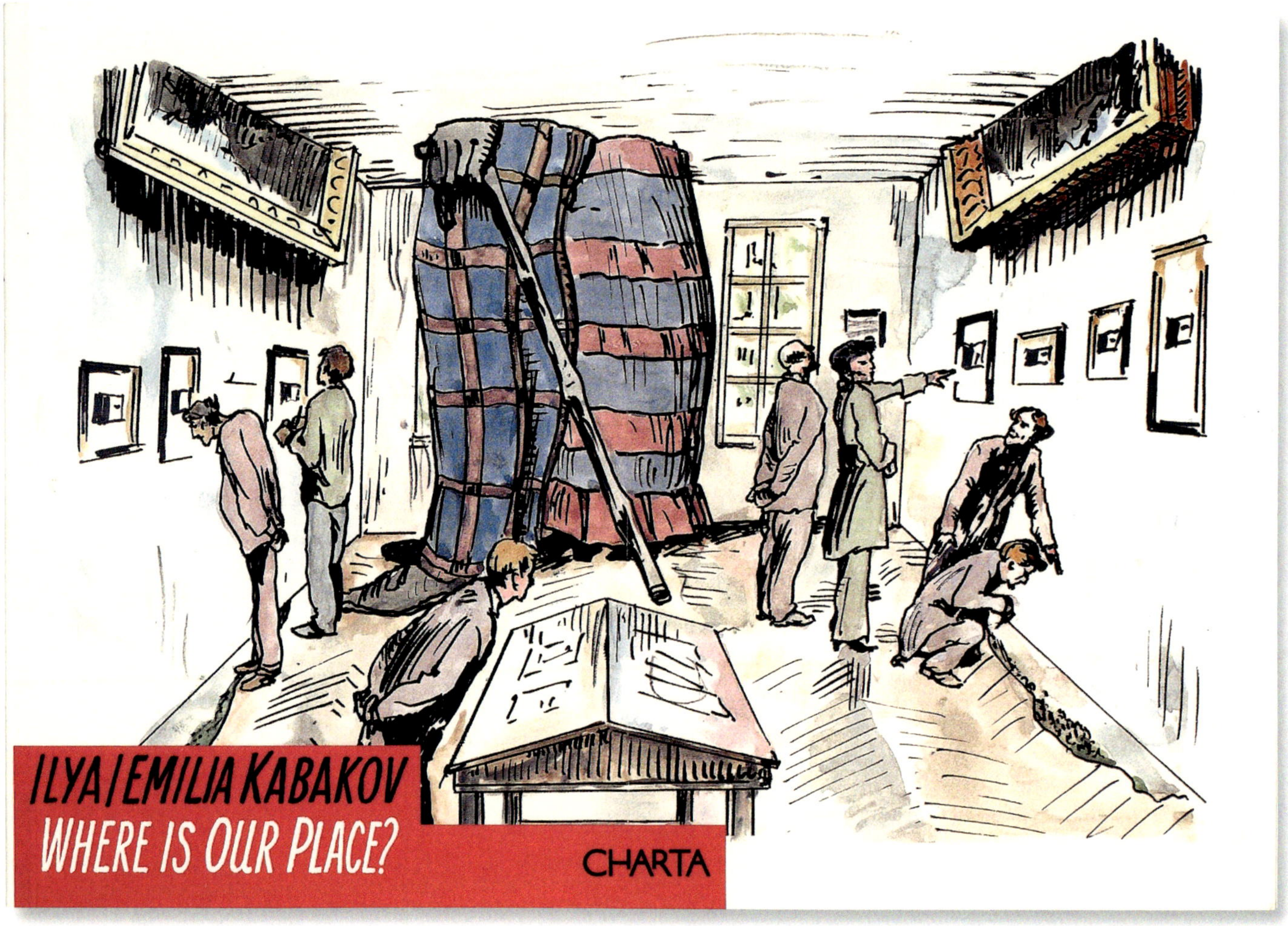

Fondazione Querini Stampalia
Milan: Charta
16.5 x 24 cm
79 pp. with 69 (31 color) ills.
stitchbound, softback
Fadenheftung, broschiert

exhibition catalogue | *Ausstellungskatalog*

layout by Ilya Kabakov | *Layout von Ilya Kabakov*

For the installation of the same name at the Fondazione Querini Stampalia, Venice, June 12 to September 7, 2003. Texts by Chiara Bertola, David Elliott, Ilya and Emilia Kabakov; Italian, English.

Zur gleichnamigen Installation, Fondazione Querini Stampalia, Venedig, 12. Juni – 7. September 2003. Texte von Chiara Bertola, David Elliott, Ilya und Emilia Kabakov; italienisch, englisch.

see also | *siehe auch* CRP, vol. 2, nos. 439–457, pp. 162–190

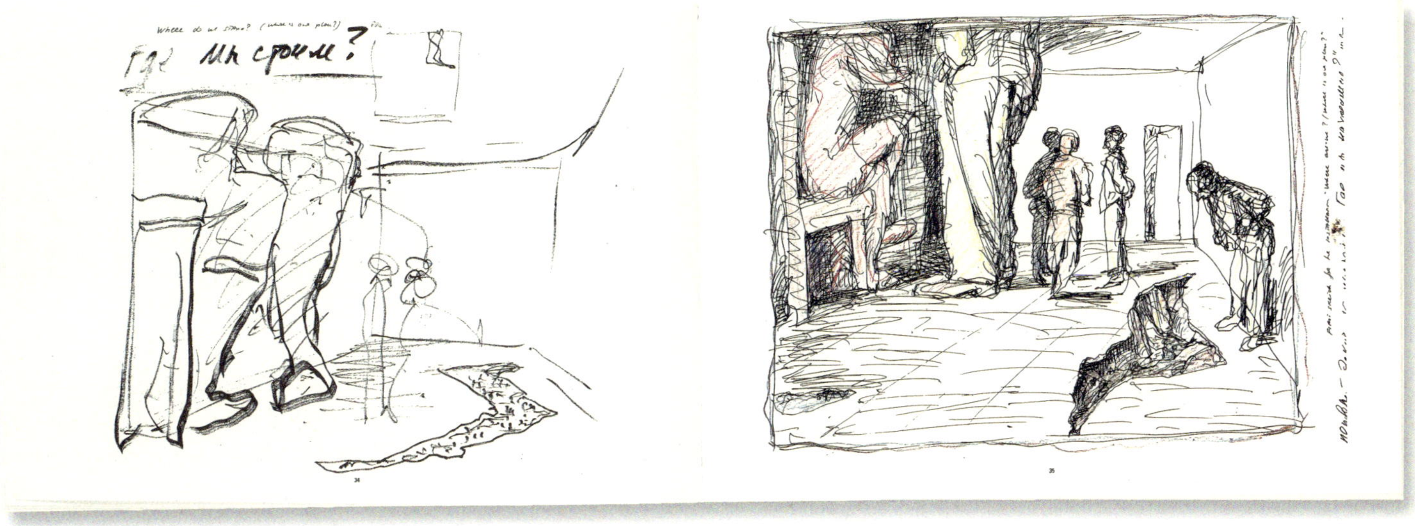

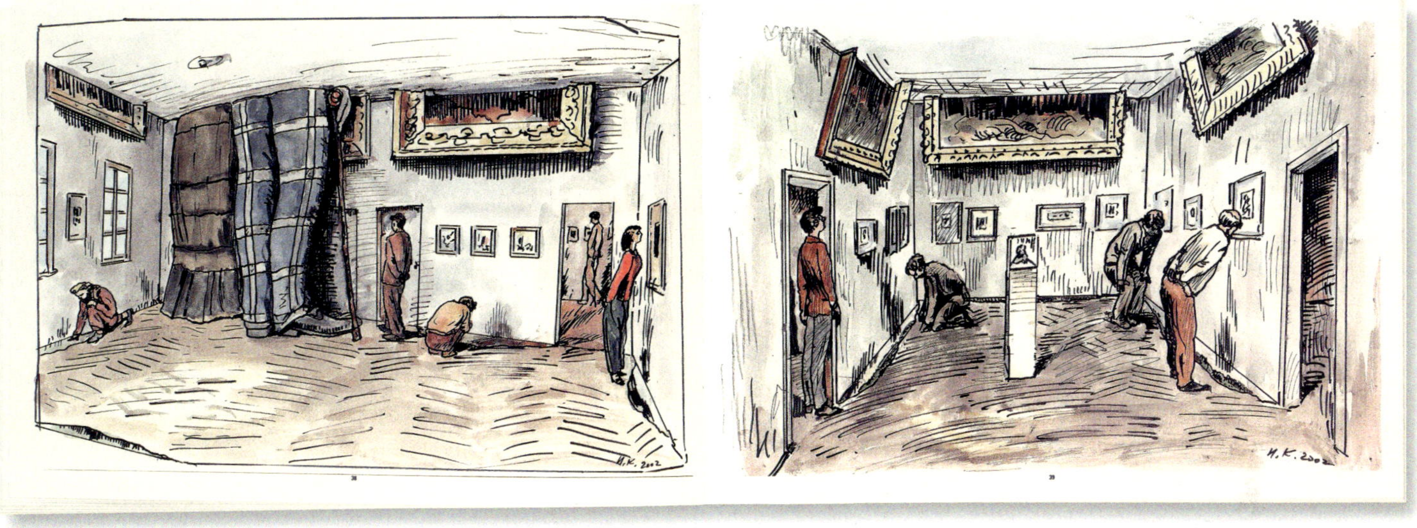

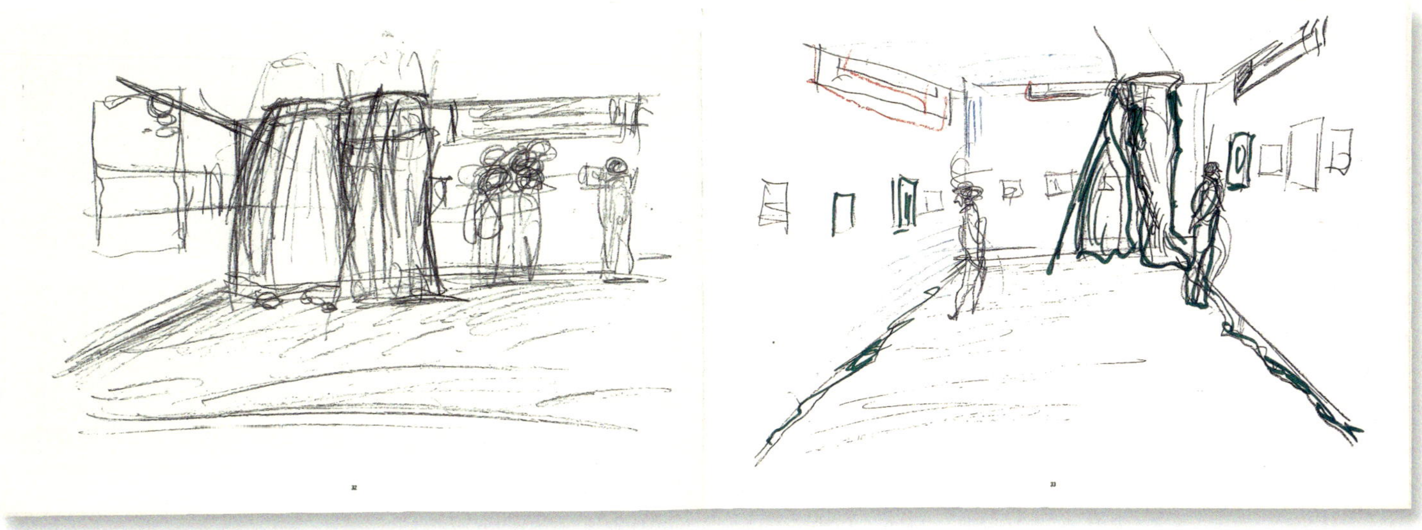

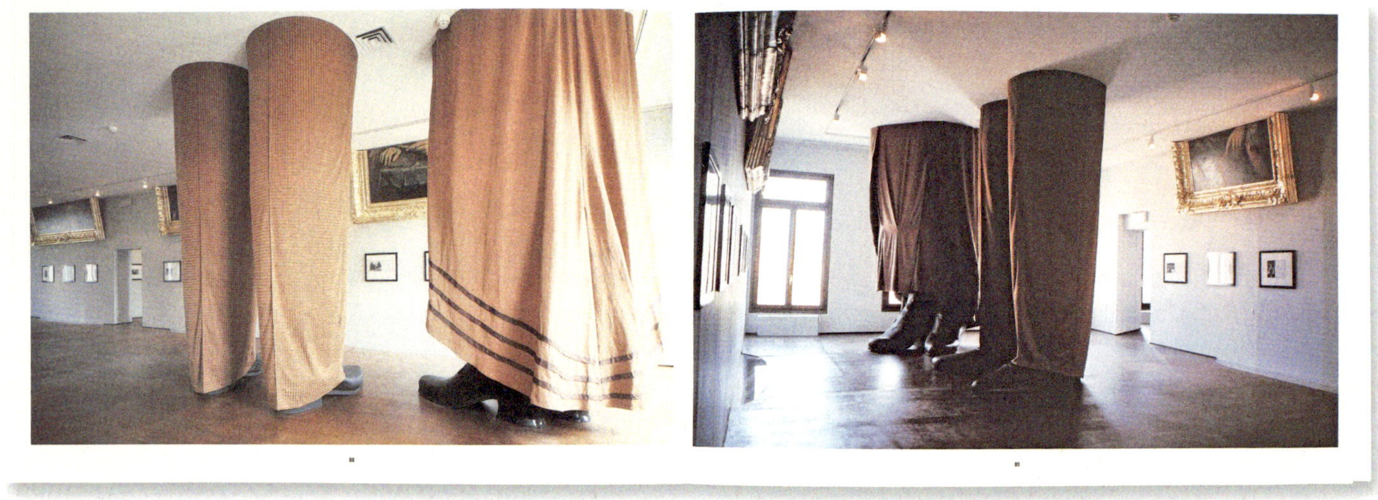

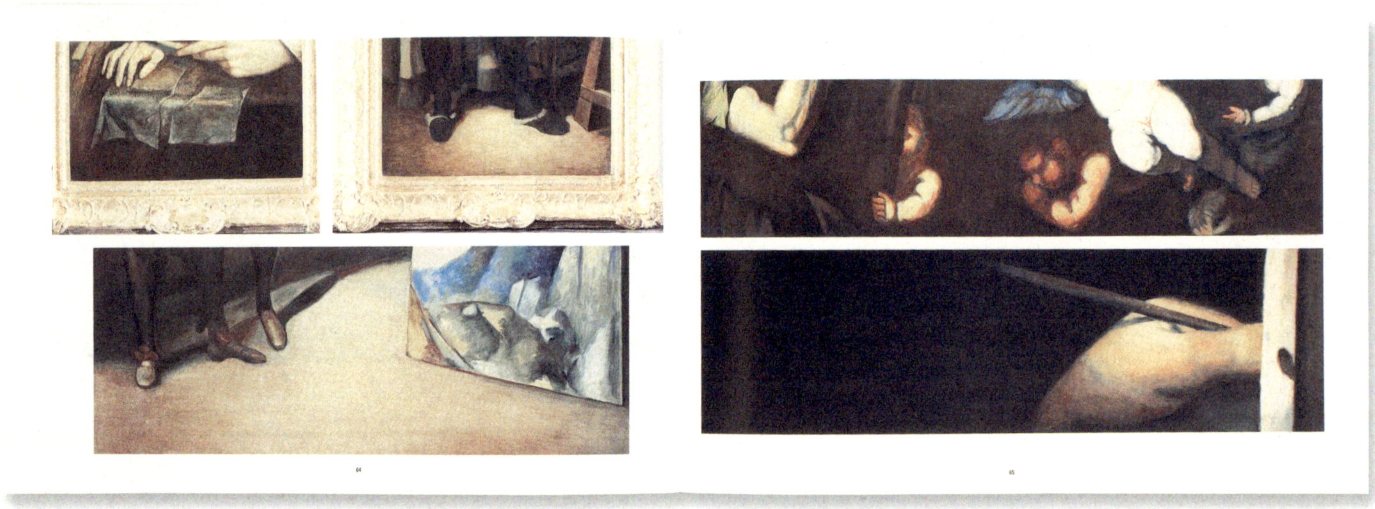

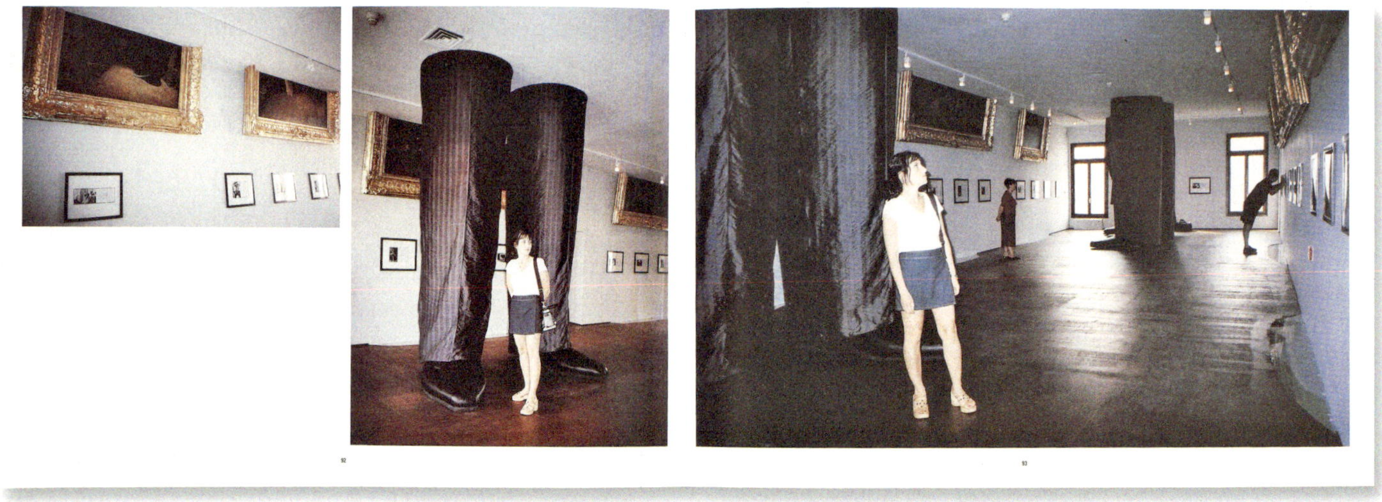

123 Installations 1983–2000: Catalogue Raisonné | *Installationen 1983–2000. Werkverzeichnis*

2003

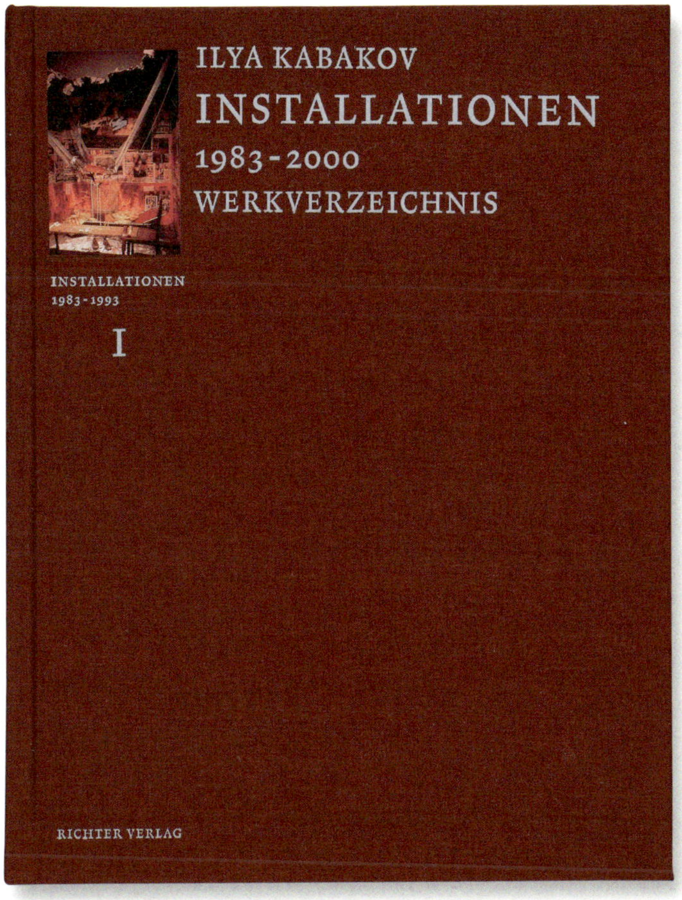

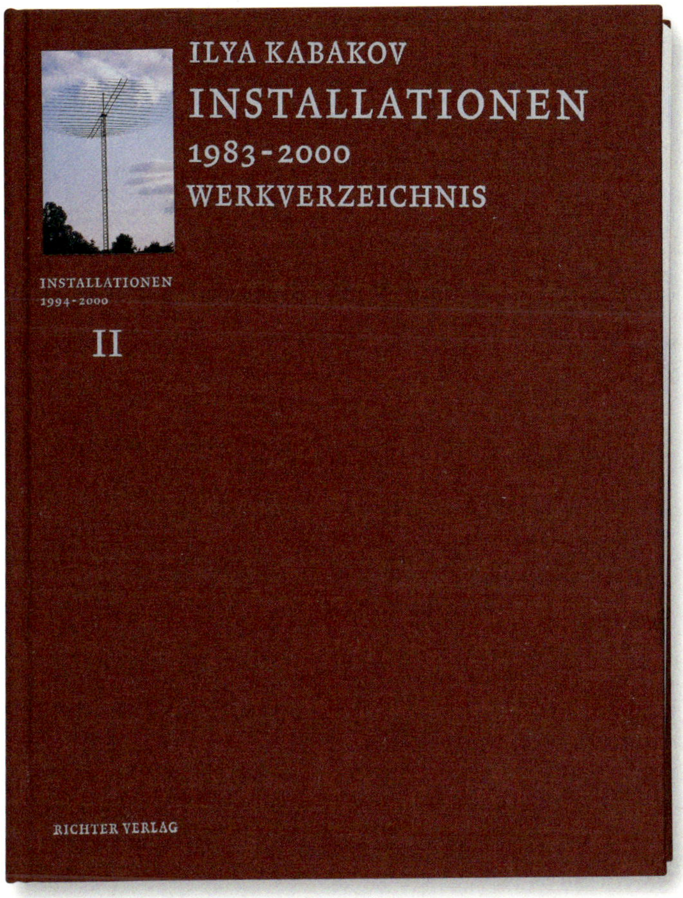

Toni Stooss, Kunstmuseum Bern
Düsseldorf: Richter Verlag
30.4 x 23.6 cm
vol. 1, 520 pp. with 543 (226 color) ills.
vol. 2, 488 pp. with 569 (247 color) ills.
stitchbound, clothbound, blind blocking with label, in cloth covered slipcase
Fadenheftung, Halbleinen, Blindprägung mit Etikette, in Leinenschuber

catalogue raisonné | *Werkverzeichnis*

layout by Ilya Kabakov | *Layout von Ilya Kabakov*

Volume 1: »Installations 1983–1993«. Volume 2: »Installations 1994–2000«. Texts by Oskar Bätschmann, Boris Groys, Ilya Kabakov, Rod Mengham, Toni Stooss, and Robert Storr; German.

Band 1 »Installationen 1983–1993«; Band 2 »Installationen 1994–2000«. Texte von Oskar Bätschmann, Boris Groys, Ilya Kabakov, Toni Stooss, Robert Storr und Rod Mengham; deutsch.

see also | *siehe auch*

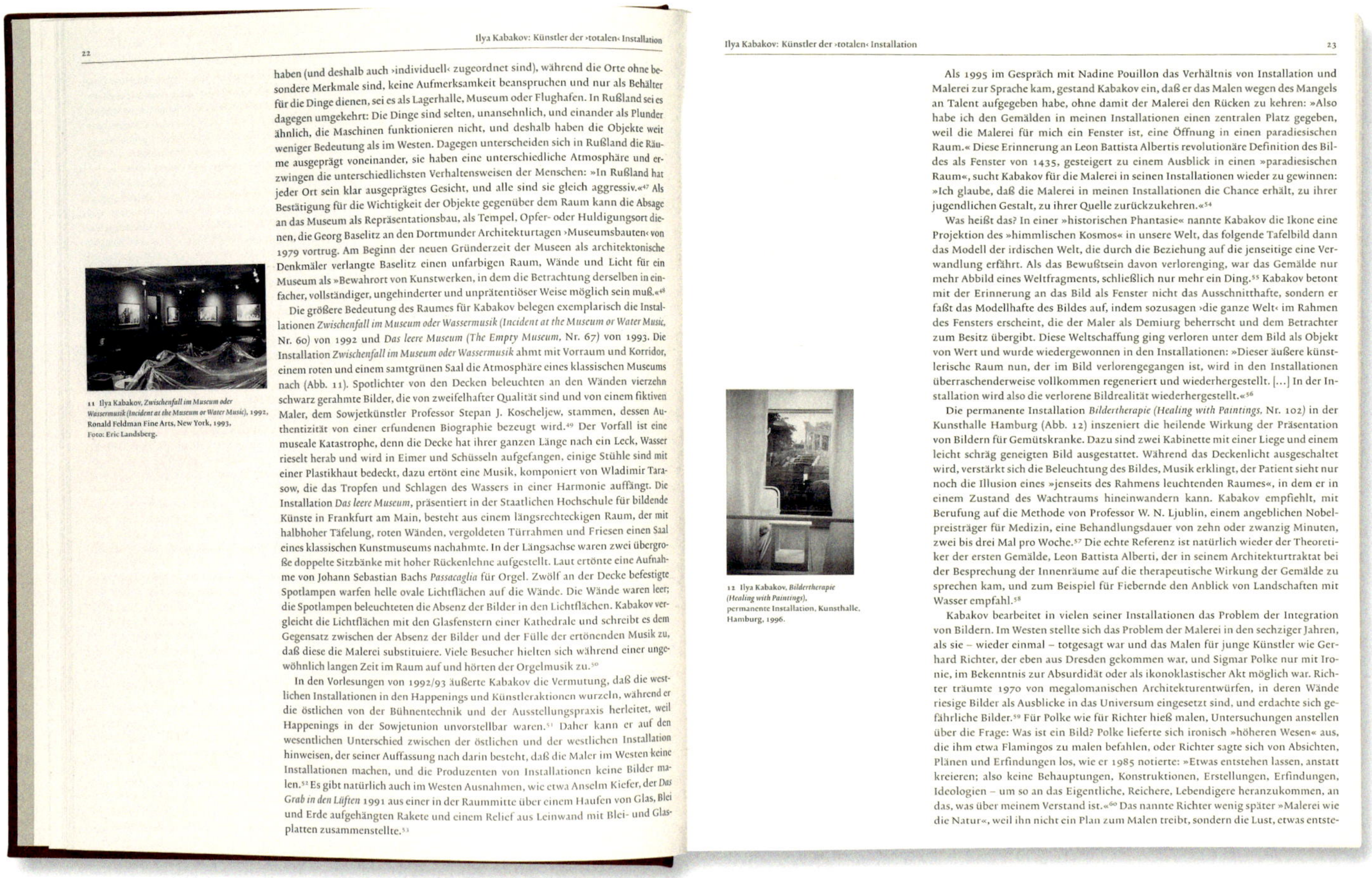

22 Ilya Kabakov: Künstler der ›totalen‹ Installation

haben (und deshalb auch ›individuell‹ zugeordnet sind), während die Orte ohne besondere Merkmale sind, keine Aufmerksamkeit beanspruchen und nur als Behälter für die Dinge dienen, sei es als Lagerhalle, Museum oder Flughafen. In Rußland sei es dagegen umgekehrt: Die Dinge sind selten, unansehnlich, und einander als Plunder ähnlich, die Maschinen funktionieren nicht, und deshalb haben die Objekte weit weniger Bedeutung als im Westen. Dagegen unterscheiden sich in Rußland die Räume ausgeprägt voneinander, sie haben eine unterschiedliche Atmosphäre und erzwingen die unterschiedlichsten Verhaltensweisen der Menschen: »In Rußland hat jeder Ort sein klar ausgeprägtes Gesicht, und alle sind sie gleich aggressiv.«[47] Als Bestätigung für die Wichtigkeit der Objekte gegenüber dem Raum kann die Absage an das Museum als Repräsentationsbau, als Tempel, Opfer- oder Huldigungsort dienen, die Georg Baselitz an den Dortmunder Architekturtagen ›Museumsbauten‹ von 1979 vortrug. Am Beginn der neuen Gründerzeit der Museen als architektonische Denkmäler verlangte Baselitz einen unfarbigen Raum, Wände und Licht für ein Museum als »Bewahrort von Kunstwerken, in dem die Betrachtung derselben in einfacher, vollständiger, ungehinderter und unprätentiöser Weise möglich sein muß.«[48]

Die größere Bedeutung des Raumes für Kabakov belegen exemplarisch die Installationen *Zwischenfall im Museum oder Wassermusik (Incident at the Museum or Water Music,* Nr. 60*)* von 1992 und *Das leere Museum (The Empty Museum,* Nr. 67*)* von 1993. Die Installation *Zwischenfall im Museum oder Wassermusik* ahmt mit Vorraum und Korridor, einem roten und einem samtgrünen Saal die Atmosphäre eines klassischen Museums nach (Abb. 11). Spotlichter von den Decken beleuchten an den Wänden vierzehn schwarz gerahmte Bilder, die von zweifelhafter Qualität sind und von einem fiktiven Maler, dem Sowjetkünstler Professor Stepan J. Koscheljew, stammen, dessen Authentizität von einer erfundenen Biographie bezeugt wird.[49] Der Vorfall ist eine museale Katastrophe, denn die Decke hat ihrer ganzen Länge nach ein Leck, Wasser rieselt herab und wird in Eimer und Schüsseln aufgefangen, einige Stühle sind mit einer Plastikhaut bedeckt, dazu ertönt eine Musik, komponiert von Wladimir Tarasow, die das Tropfen und Schlagen des Wassers in einer Harmonie auffängt. Die Installation *Das leere Museum*, präsentiert in der Staatlichen Hochschule für bildende Künste in Frankfurt am Main, besteht aus einem längsrechteckigen Raum, der mit halbhoher Täfelung, roten Wänden, vergoldeten Türrahmen und Friesen einen Saal eines klassischen Kunstmuseums nachahmte. In der Längsachse waren zwei übergroße doppelte Sitzbänke mit hoher Rückenlehne aufgestellt. Laut ertönte eine Aufnahme von Johann Sebastian Bachs *Passacaglia* für Orgel. Zwölf an der Decke befestigte Spotlampen warfen helle ovale Lichtflächen auf die Wände. Die Wände waren leer; die Spotlampen beleuchteten die Absenz der Bilder in den Lichtflächen. Kabakov vergleicht die Lichtflächen mit den Glasfenstern einer Kathedrale und schreibt es dem Gegensatz zwischen der Absenz der Bilder und der Fülle der ertönenden Musik zu, daß diese die Malerei substituiere. Viele Besucher hielten sich während einer ungewöhnlich langen Zeit im Raum auf und hörten der Orgelmusik zu.[50]

In den Vorlesungen von 1992/93 äußerte Kabakov die Vermutung, daß die westlichen Installationen in den Happenings und Künstleraktionen wurzeln, während er die östlichen von der Bühnentechnik und der Ausstellungspraxis herleitet, weil Happenings in der Sowjetunion unvorstellbar waren.[51] Daher kann er auf den wesentlichen Unterschied zwischen der östlichen und der westlichen Installation hinweisen, der seiner Auffassung nach darin besteht, daß die Maler im Westen keine Installationen machen, und die Produzenten von Installationen keine Bilder malen.[52] Es gibt natürlich auch im Westen Ausnahmen, wie etwa Anselm Kiefer, der *Das Grab in den Lüften* 1991 aus einer in der Raummitte über einem Haufen von Glas, Blei und Erde aufgehängten Rakete und einem Relief aus Leinwand mit Blei- und Glasplatten zusammenstellte.[53]

11 Ilya Kabakov, *Zwischenfall im Museum oder Wassermusik (Incident at the Museum or Water Music)*, 1992, Ronald Feldman Fine Arts, New York, 1993, Foto: Eric Landsberg.

Ilya Kabakov: Künstler der ›totalen‹ Installation 23

Als 1995 im Gespräch mit Nadine Pouillon das Verhältnis von Installation und Malerei zur Sprache kam, gestand Kabakov ein, daß er das Malen wegen des Mangels an Talent aufgegeben habe, ohne damit der Malerei den Rücken zu kehren: »Also habe ich den Gemälden in meinen Installationen einen zentralen Platz gegeben, weil die Malerei für mich ein Fenster ist, eine Öffnung in einen paradiesischen Raum.« Diese Erinnerung an Leon Battista Albertis revolutionäre Definition des Bildes als Fenster von 1435, gesteigert zu einem Ausblick in einen »paradiesischen Raum«, sucht Kabakov für die Malerei in seinen Installationen wieder zu gewinnen: »Ich glaube, daß die Malerei in meinen Installationen die Chance erhält, zu ihrer jugendlichen Gestalt, zu ihrer Quelle zurückzukehren.«[54]

Was heißt das? In einer »historischen Phantasie« nannte Kabakov die Ikone eine Projektion des »himmlischen Kosmos« in unsere Welt, das folgende Tafelbild dann das Modell der irdischen Welt, die durch die Beziehung auf die jenseitige eine Verwandlung erfährt. Als das Bewußtsein davon verlorenging, war das Gemälde nur mehr Abbild eines Weltfragments, schließlich nur mehr ein Ding.[55] Kabakov betont mit der Erinnerung an das Bild als Fenster nicht das Ausschnitthafte, sondern er faßt das Modellhafte des Bildes auf, indem sozusagen ›die ganze Welt‹ im Rahmen des Fensters erscheint, die der Maler als Demiurg beherrscht und dem Betrachter zum Besitz übergibt. Diese Weltschaffung ging verloren unter dem Bild als Objekt von Wert und wurde wiedergewonnen in den Installationen: »Dieser äußere künstlerische Raum nun, der im Bild verlorengegangen ist, wird in den Installationen überraschenderweise vollkommen regeneriert und wiederhergestellt. [...] In der Installation wird also die verlorene Bildrealität wiederhergestellt.«[56]

Die permanente Installation *Bildertherapie (Healing with Paintings,* Nr. 102*)* in der Kunsthalle Hamburg (Abb. 12) inszeniert die heilende Wirkung der Präsentation von Bildern für Gemütskranke. Dazu sind zwei Kabinette mit einer Liege und einem leicht schräg geneigten Bild ausgestattet. Während das Deckenlicht ausgeschaltet wird, verstärkt sich die Beleuchtung des Bildes, Musik erklingt, der Patient sieht nur noch die Illusion eines »jenseits des Rahmens leuchtenden Raumes«, in dem er in einem Zustand des Wachtraums hineinwandern kann. Kabakov empfiehlt, mit Berufung auf die Methode von Professor W. N. Ljublin, einem angeblichen Nobelpreisträger für Medizin, eine Behandlungsdauer von zehn oder zwanzig Minuten, zwei bis drei Mal pro Woche.[57] Die echte Referenz ist natürlich wieder der Theoretiker der ersten Gemälde, Leon Battista Alberti, der in seinem Architekturtraktat bei der Besprechung der Innenräume auf die therapeutische Wirkung der Gemälde zu sprechen kam, und zum Beispiel für Fiebernde den Anblick von Landschaften mit Wasser empfahl.[58]

Kabakov bearbeitet in vielen seiner Installationen das Problem der Integration von Bildern. Im Westen stellte sich das Problem der Malerei in den sechziger Jahren, als sie – wieder einmal – totgesagt war und das Malen für junge Künstler wie Gerhard Richter, der eben aus Dresden gekommen war, und Sigmar Polke nur mit Ironie, im Bekenntnis zur Absurdidät oder als ikonoklastischer Akt möglich war. Richter träumte 1970 von megalomanischen Architekturentwürfen, in deren Wände riesige Bilder als Ausblicke in das Universum eingesetzt sind, und erdachte sich gefährliche Bilder.[59] Für Polke wie für Richter hieß malen, Untersuchungen anstellen über die Frage: Was ist ein Bild? Polke lieferte sich ironisch »höheren Wesen« aus, die ihm etwa Flamingos zu malen befahlen, oder Richter sagte sich von Absichten, Plänen und Erfindungen los, wie er 1985 notierte: »Etwas entstehen lassen, anstatt kreieren; also keine Behauptungen, Konstruktionen, Erstellungen, Erfindungen, Ideologien – um so an das Eigentliche, Reichere, Lebendigere heranzukommen, an das, was über meinem Verstand ist.«[60] Das nannte Richter wenig später »Malerei wie die Natur«, weil ihn nicht ein Plan zum Malen treibt, sondern die Lust, etwas entste-

12 Ilya Kabakov, *Bildertherapie (Healing with Paintings)*, permanente Installation, Kunsthalle, Hamburg, 1996.

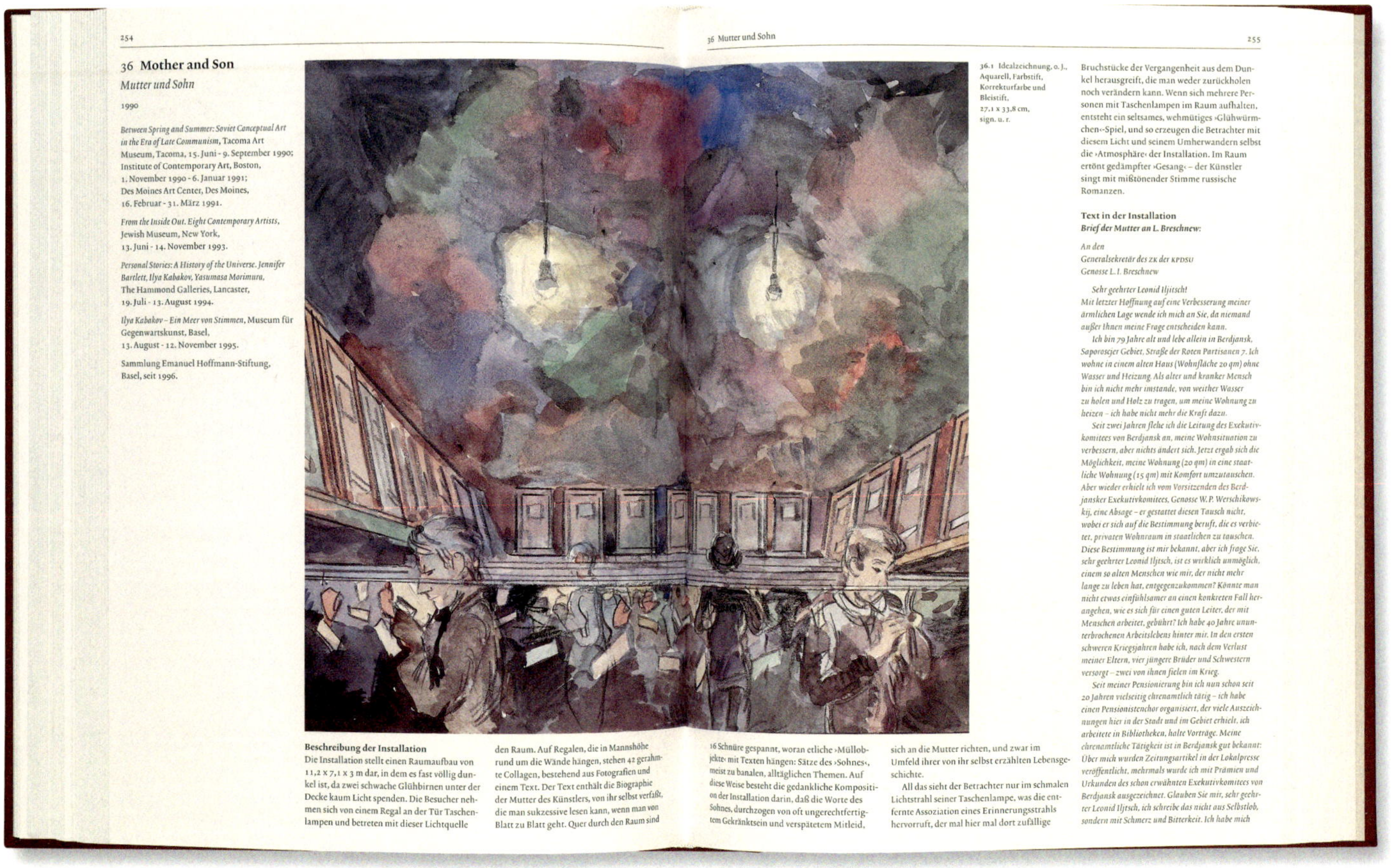

254

36 Mother and Son

Mutter und Sohn

1990

Between Spring and Summer: Soviet Conceptual Art in the Era of Late Communism, Tacoma Art Museum, Tacoma, 15. Juni - 9. September 1990; Institute of Contemporary Art, Boston, 1. November 1990 - 6. Januar 1991; Des Moines Art Center, Des Moines, 16. Februar - 31. März 1991.

From the Inside Out. Eight Contemporary Artists, Jewish Museum, New York, 13. Juni - 14. November 1993.

Personal Stories: A History of the Universe. Jennifer Bartlett, Ilya Kabakov, Yasumasa Morimura, The Hammond Galleries, Lancaster, 19. Juli - 13. August 1994.

Ilya Kabakov – Ein Meer von Stimmen, Museum für Gegenwartskunst, Basel, 13. August - 12. November 1995.

Sammlung Emanuel Hoffmann-Stiftung, Basel, seit 1996.

36 Mutter und Sohn 255

36.1 Idealzeichnung, o. J., Aquarell, Farbstift, Korrekturfarbe und Bleistift, 27,1 x 33,8 cm, sign. u. r.

Beschreibung der Installation

Die Installation stellt einen Raumaufbau von 11,2 x 7,1 x 3 m dar, in dem es fast völlig dunkel ist, da zwei schwache Glühbirnen unter der Decke kaum Licht spenden. Die Besucher nehmen sich von einem Regal an der Tür Taschenlampen und betreten mit dieser Lichtquelle den Raum. Auf Regalen, die in Mannshöhe rund um die Wände hängen, stehen 42 gerahmte Collagen, bestehend aus Fotografien und einem Text. Der Text enthält die Biographie der Mutter des Künstlers, von ihr selbst verfaßt, die man sukzessive lesen kann, wenn man von Blatt zu Blatt geht. Quer durch den Raum sind 16 Schnüre gespannt, woran etliche ›Müllobjekte‹ mit Texten hängen: Sätze des ›Sohnes‹, meist zu banalen, alltäglichen Themen. Auf diese Weise besteht die gedankliche Komposition der Installation darin, daß die Worte des Sohnes, durchzogen von oft ungerechtfertigtem Gekränktsein und verspätetem Mitleid, sich an die Mutter richten, und zwar im Umfeld ihrer von ihr selbst erzählten Lebensgeschichte.

All das sieht der Betrachter nur im schmalen Lichtstrahl seiner Taschenlampe, was die entfernte Assoziation eines Erinnerungsstrahls hervorruft, der mal hier mal dort zufällige Bruchstücke der Vergangenheit aus dem Dunkel herausgreift, die man weder zurückholen noch verändern kann. Wenn sich mehrere Personen mit Taschenlampen im Raum aufhalten, entsteht ein seltsames, wehmütiges ›Glühwürmchen‹-Spiel, und so erzeugen die Betrachter mit diesem Licht und seinem Umherwandern selbst die ›Atmosphäre‹ der Installation. Im Raum ertönt gedämpfter ›Gesang‹ – der Künstler singt mit mißtönender Stimme russische Romanzen.

Text in der Installation
Brief der Mutter an L. Breschnew:

An den
Generalsekretär des ZK der KPDSU
Genosse L. I. Breschnew

Sehr geehrter Leonid Iljitsch!
Mit letzter Hoffnung auf eine Verbesserung meiner ärmlichen Lage wende ich mich an Sie, da niemand außer Ihnen meine Frage entscheiden kann.

Ich bin 79 Jahre alt und lebe allein in Berdjansk, Saporoscjer Gebiet, Straße der Roten Partisanen 7. Ich wohne in einem alten Haus (Wohnfläche 20 qm) ohne Wasser und Heizung. Als alter und kranker Mensch bin ich nicht mehr imstande, von weither Wasser zu holen und Holz zu tragen, um meine Wohnung zu heizen – ich habe nicht mehr die Kraft dazu.

Seit zwei Jahren flehe ich die Leitung des Exekutivkomitees von Berdjansk an, meine Wohnsituation zu verbessern, aber nichts ändert sich. Jetzt ergab sich die Möglichkeit, meine Wohnung (20 qm) in eine staatliche Wohnung (15 qm) mit Komfort umzutauschen. Aber wieder erhielt ich vom Vorsitzenden des Berdjansker Exekutivkomitees, Genosse W. P. Werschikowskij, eine Absage – er gestattet diesen Tausch nicht, wobei er sich auf die Bestimmung beruft, die es verbietet, privaten Wohnraum in staatlichen zu tauschen. Diese Bestimmung ist mir bekannt, aber ich frage Sie, sehr geehrter Leonid Iljtsch, ist es wirklich unmöglich, einem so alten Menschen wie mir, der nicht mehr lange zu leben hat, entgegenzukommen? Könnte man nicht etwas einfühlsamer an einen konkreten Fall herangehen, wie es sich für einen guten Leiter, der mit Menschen arbeitet, gebührt? Ich habe 40 Jahre ununterbrochenen Arbeitslebens hinter mir. In den ersten schweren Kriegsjahren habe ich, nach dem Verlust meiner Eltern, vier jüngere Brüder und Schwestern versorgt – zwei von ihnen fielen im Krieg.

Seit meiner Pensionierung bin ich nun schon seit 20 Jahren vielseitig ehrenamtlich tätig – ich habe einen Pensionistenchor organisiert, der viele Auszeichnungen hier in der Stadt und im Gebiet erhielt, ich arbeitete in Bibliotheken, halte Vorträge. Meine ehrenamtliche Tätigkeit ist in Berdjansk gut bekannt: Über mich wurden Zeitungsartikel in der Lokalpresse veröffentlicht, mehrmals wurde ich mit Prämien und Urkunden des schon erwähnten Exekutivkomitees von Berdjansk ausgezeichnet. Glauben Sie mir, sehr geehrter Leonid Iljtsch, ich schreibe das nicht aus Selbstlob, sondern mit Schmerz und Bitterkeit. Ich habe mich

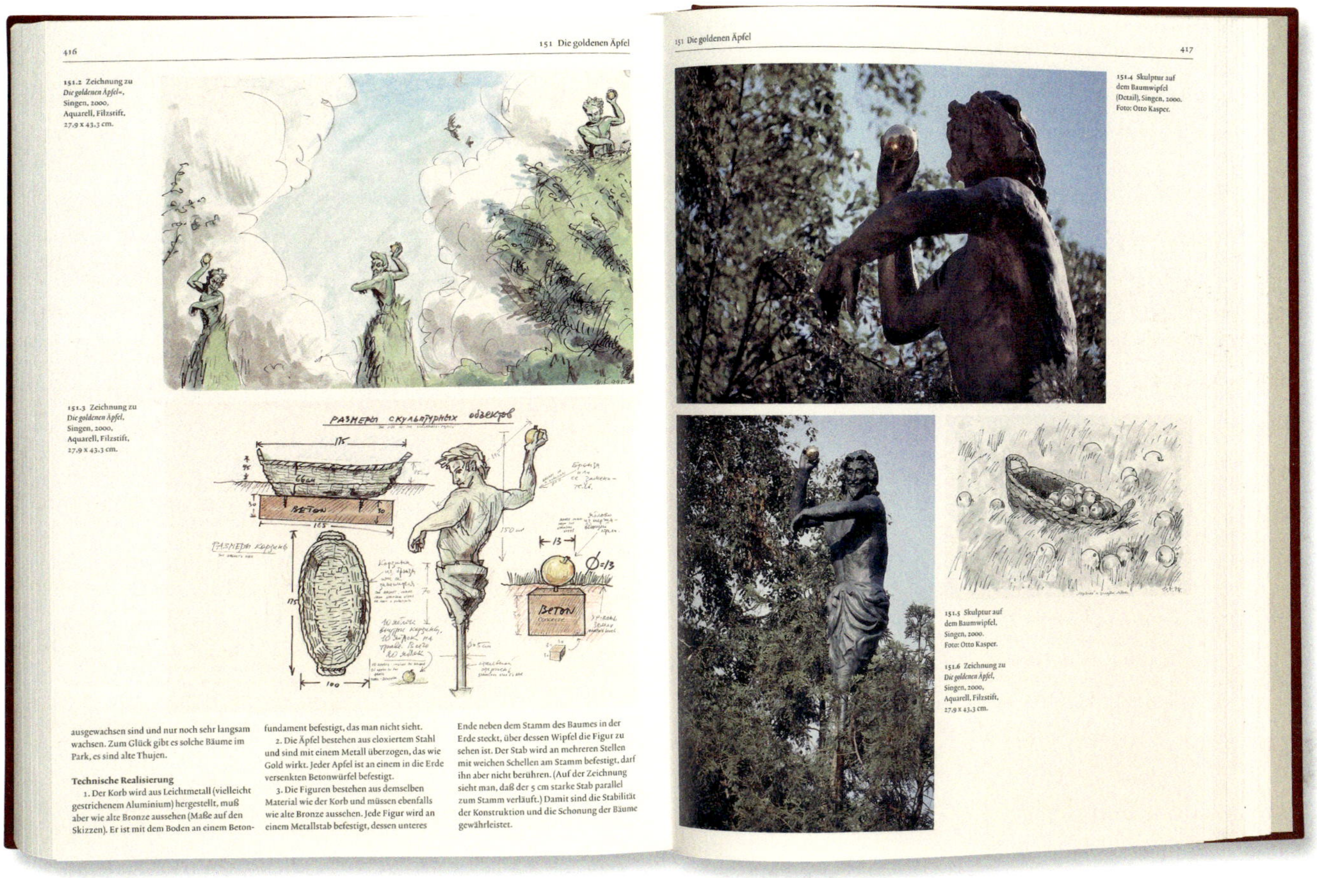

416 151 Die goldenen Äpfel

151.2 Zeichnung zu *Die goldenen Äpfel«*, Singen, 2000, Aquarell, Filzstift, 27,9 x 43,3 cm.

151.3 Zeichnung zu *Die goldenen Äpfel*, Singen, 2000, Aquarell, Filzstift, 27,9 x 43,3 cm.

ausgewachsen sind und nur noch sehr langsam wachsen. Zum Glück gibt es solche Bäume im Park, es sind alte Thujen.

Technische Realisierung

1. Der Korb wird aus Leichtmetall (vielleicht gestrichenem Aluminium) hergestellt, muß aber wie alte Bronze aussehen (Maße auf den Skizzen). Er ist mit dem Boden an einem Betonfundament befestigt, das man nicht sieht.

2. Die Äpfel bestehen aus eloxiertem Stahl und sind mit einem Metall überzogen, das wie Gold wirkt. Jeder Apfel ist an einem in die Erde versenkten Betonwürfel befestigt.

3. Die Figuren bestehen aus demselben Material wie der Korb und müssen ebenfalls wie alte Bronze aussehen. Jede Figur wird an einem Metallstab befestigt, dessen unteres Ende neben dem Stamm des Baumes in der Erde steckt, über dessen Wipfel die Figur zu sehen ist. Der Stab wird an mehreren Stellen mit weichen Schellen am Stamm befestigt, darf ihn aber nicht berühren. (Auf der Zeichnung sieht man, daß der 5 cm starke Stab parallel zum Stamm verläuft.) Damit sind die Stabilität der Konstruktion und die Schonung der Bäume gewährleistet.

151 Die goldenen Äpfel 417

151.4 Skulptur auf dem Baumwipfel (Detail), Singen, 2000. Foto: Otto Kasper.

151.5 Skulptur auf dem Baumwipfel, Singen, 2000. Foto: Otto Kasper.

151.6 Zeichnung zu *Die goldenen Äpfel*, Singen, 2000, Aquarell, Filzstift, 27,9 x 43,3 cm.

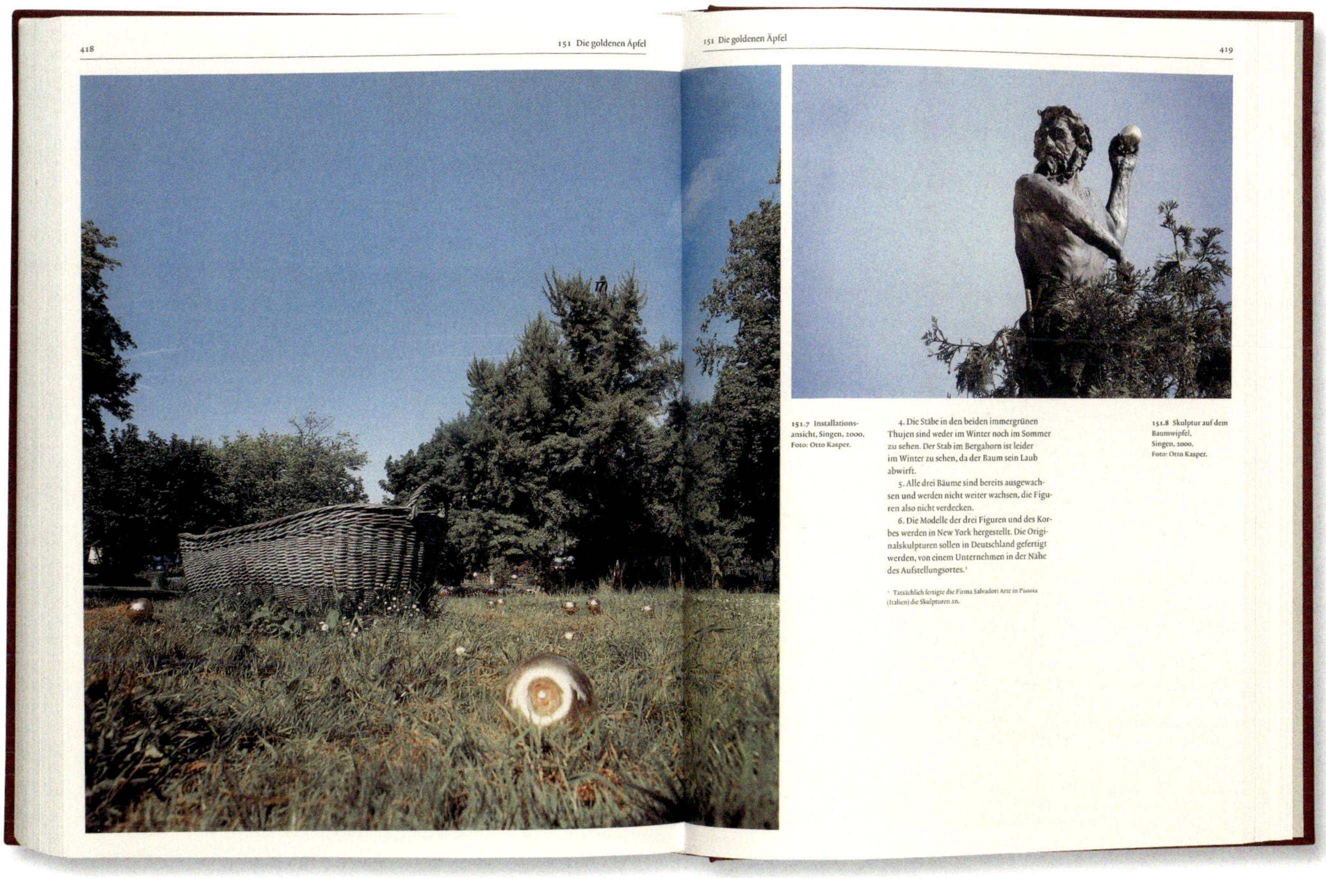

418 151 Die goldenen Äpfel

151 Die goldenen Äpfel 419

151.7 Installationsansicht, Singen, 2000, Foto: Otto Kasper.

4. Die Stäbe in den beiden immergrünen Thujen sind weder im Winter noch im Sommer zu sehen. Der Stab im Bergahorn ist leider im Winter zu sehen, da der Baum sein Laub abwirft.

5. Alle drei Bäume sind bereits ausgewachsen und werden nicht weiter wachsen, die Figuren also nicht verdecken.

6. Die Modelle der drei Figuren und des Korbes werden in New York hergestellt. Die Originalskulpturen sollen in Deutschland gefertigt werden, von einem Unternehmen in der Nähe des Aufstellungsortes.[1]

[1] Tatsächlich fertigte die Firma Salvadori Arte in Pistoia (Italien) die Skulpturen an.

151.8 Skulptur auf dem Baumwipfel, Singen, 2000, Foto: Otto Kasper.

124 Incident in the Museum and Other Installations

Zwischenfall im Museum und andere Installationen

with Emilia Kabakov | *mit Emilia Kabakov*

2004

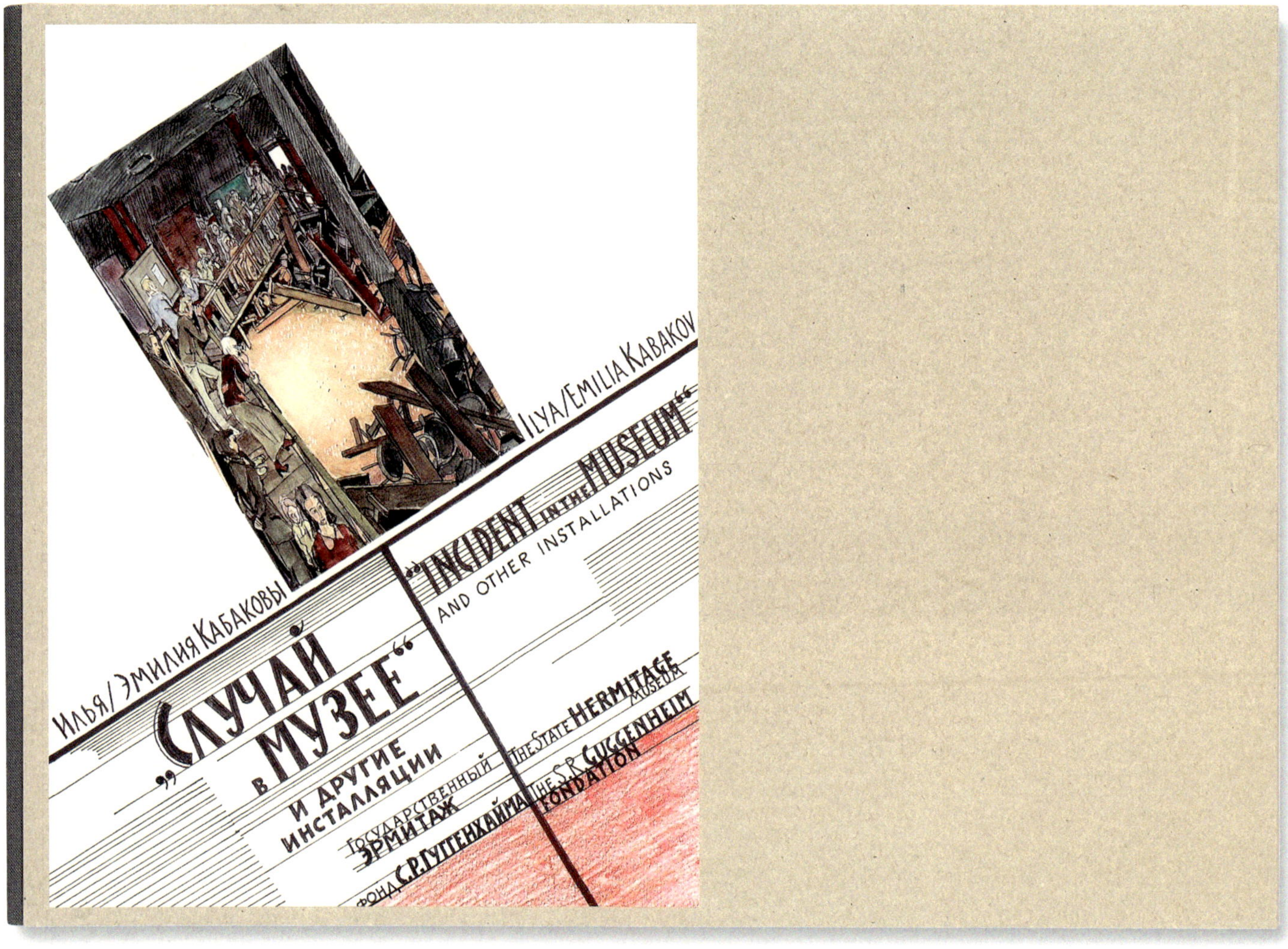

Thomas Kellein, Björn Egging, Kunsthalle Bielefeld
Bielefeld: Kunsthalle Bielefeld
23.4 x 34 cm
344 pp. with 337 (193 color) ills.
stitchbound, quarter cloth binding, blind blocking with label
Fadenheftung, Halbleinen, Blindprägung mit Etikette

exhibition catalogue | *Ausstellungskatalog*

layout by Ilya Kabakov | *Layout von Ilya Kabakov*

For the exhibition of the same name at the State Hermitage Museum, St. Petersburg, June 22 to August 29, 2004, presented by the Solomon R. Guggenheim Museum, New York, and the Art Gallery Stella, Moscow. Texts by Germano Celant, Boris Groys, Arkady Ippolitov, Ilya Kabakov, Stella Kay, Thomas Krens, Mikhail Piotrovsky, and Robert Storr; Russian, English.

Zur gleichnamigen Ausstellung, State Hermitage Museum, St. Petersburg, 22. Juni – 29. August 2004, präsentiert von dem Solomon R. Guggenheim Museum, New York und der Stella Art Gallery, Moskau. Texte von Germano Celant, Boris Groys, Arkady Ippolitov, Ilya Kabakov, Stella Kay, Thomas Krens, Mikhail Piotrovsky und Robert Storr; russisch, englisch.

see also | *siehe auch* no. 61; CRI, vol. 1, no. 60, pp. 394–401; CRP, vol. 1, nos. 225–238, pp. 295–308

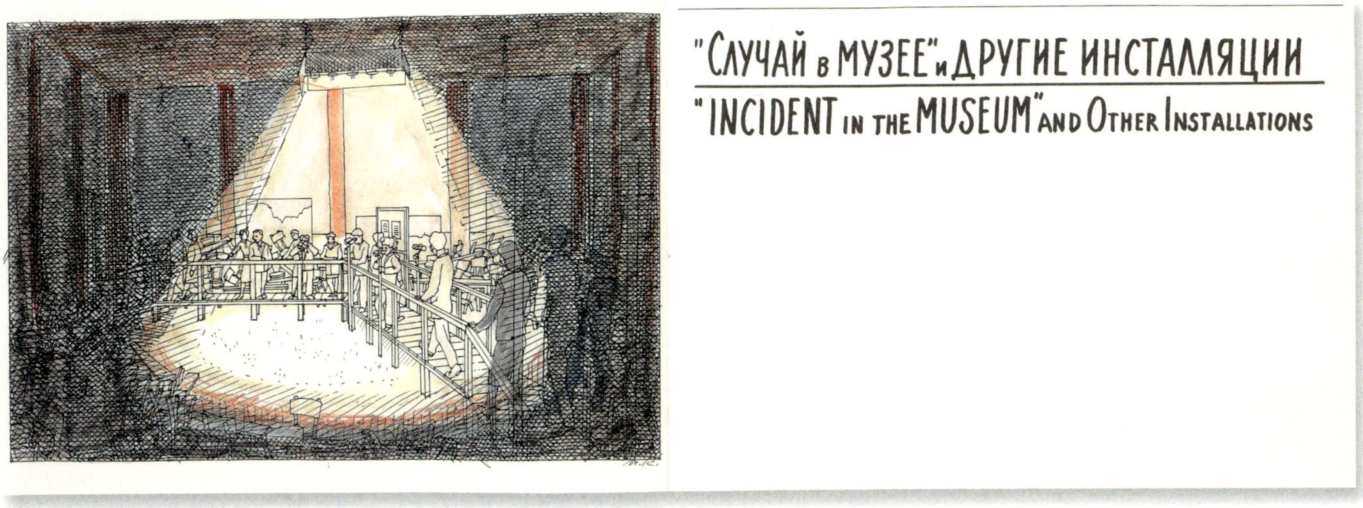
"СЛУЧАЙ в МУЗЕЕ" и ДРУГИЕ ИНСТАЛЛЯЦИИ
"INCIDENT in the MUSEUM" and Other Installations

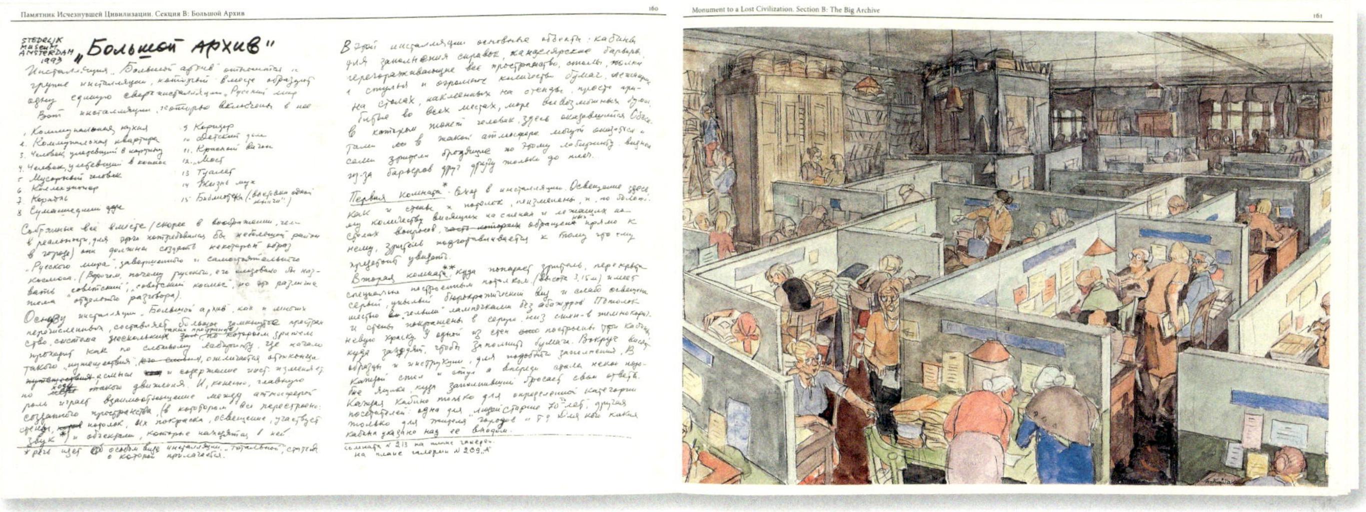
Памятник Исчезнувшей Цивилизации. Секция В: Большой Архив
160
Monument to a Lost Civilization. Section B: The Big Archive
161
„Большой архив"

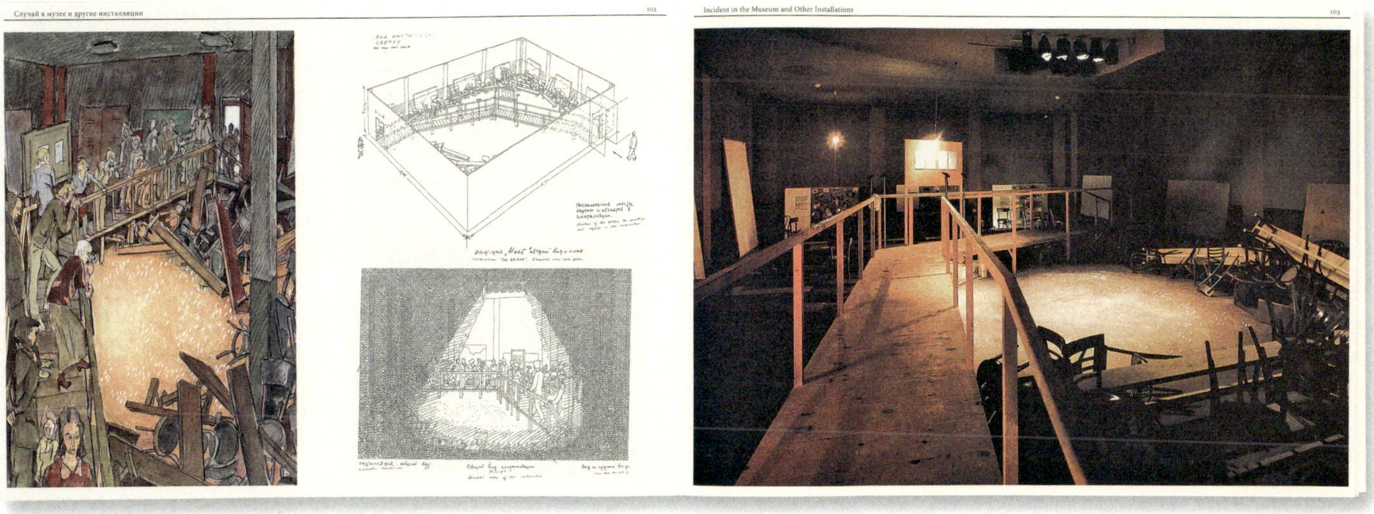
Случай в музее и другие инсталляции
102
Incident in the Museum and Other Installations
103

125 An Alternative History of Art: Rosenthal – Kabakov – Spivak

Alternative Geschichte der Kunst. Rosenthal – Kabakov – Spivak

with Emilia Kabakov | *mit Emilia Kabakov*

2004

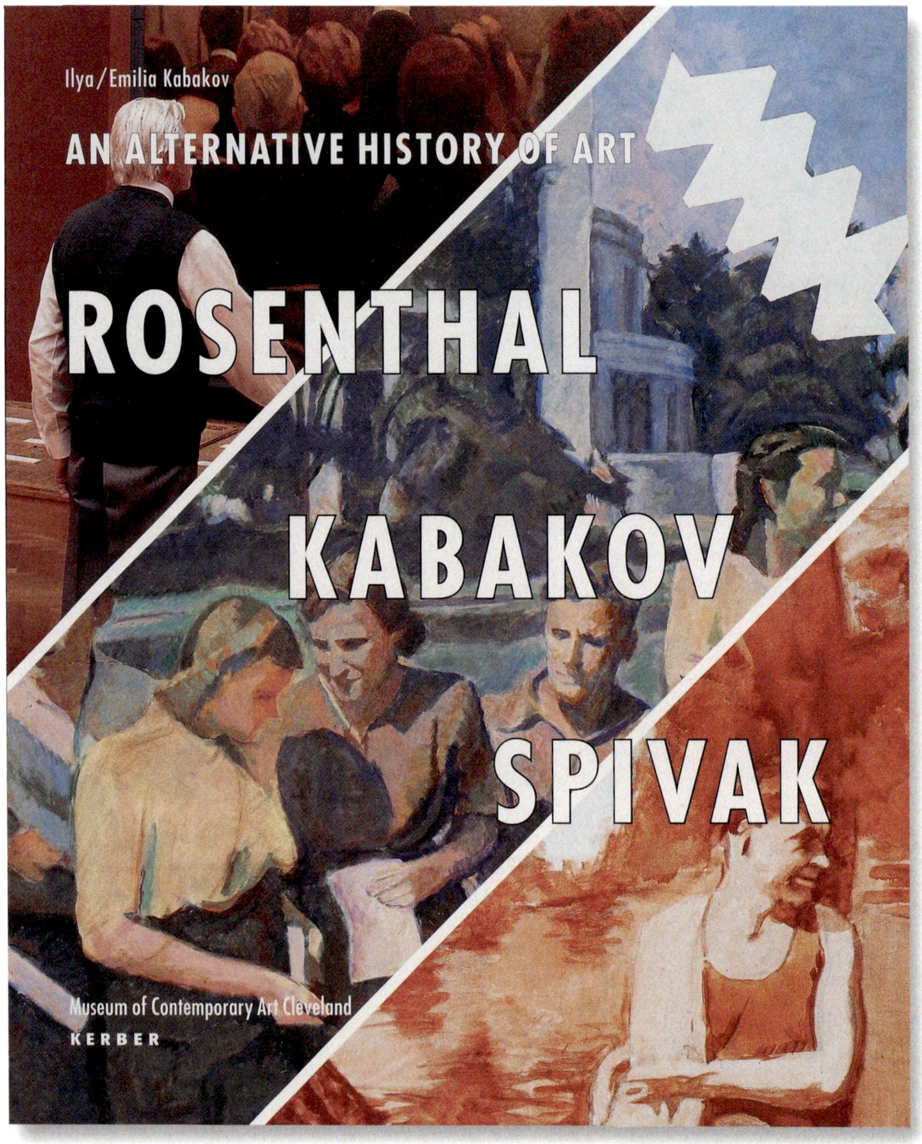

Thomas Kellein, Björn Egging, Kunsthalle Bielefeld
Bielefeld: Kerber Verlag
29 x 24 cm
272 pp. with 382 (315 color) ills.
stitchbound, softback with flaps
Fadenheftung, broschiert mit Umschlagklappen

exhibition catalogue | *Ausstellungskatalog*

layout by Ilya Kabakov | *Layout von Ilya Kabakov*

Documentation of the installation of the same name for the exhibition »The Teacher and the Student: Charles Rosenthal and Ilya Kabakov«, Museum of Contemporary Art, Cleveland, OH, September 10, 2004 to January 2, 2005. The catalogue that Kabakov designed covers the works and biographies of three fictitious artists: Charles Rosenthal, Ilya Kabakov, and Igor Spivak. Texts by Matthew Jesse Jackson, Ilya Kabakov, Ilya and Emilia Kabakov, Robert Storr, Amei Wallach. Dialogues between Ilya Kabakov and Yusuke Nakahara on »Charles Rosenthal«, between Ilya Kabakov and Margarita and Victor Tupitsyn on »Three on Two«, and between Boris Groys and Ilya Kabakov on »Igor Spivak«; English.

Dokumentation der gleichnamigen Installation für die Ausstellung »The Teacher and the Student: Charles Rosenthal und Ilya Kabakov«, Museum of Contemporary Art, Cleveland, OH, 10. September 2004 – 2. Januar 2005. Der von Kabakov konzipierte Katalog umfasst Werk und Biografie der drei fiktiven Künstler Charles Rosenthal, Ilya Kabakov und Igor Spivak. Texte von Matthew Jesse Jackson, Ilya Kabakov, Ilya und Emilia Kabakov, Robert Storr, Amei Wallach. Dialoge von Ilya Kabakov und Yusuke Nakahara

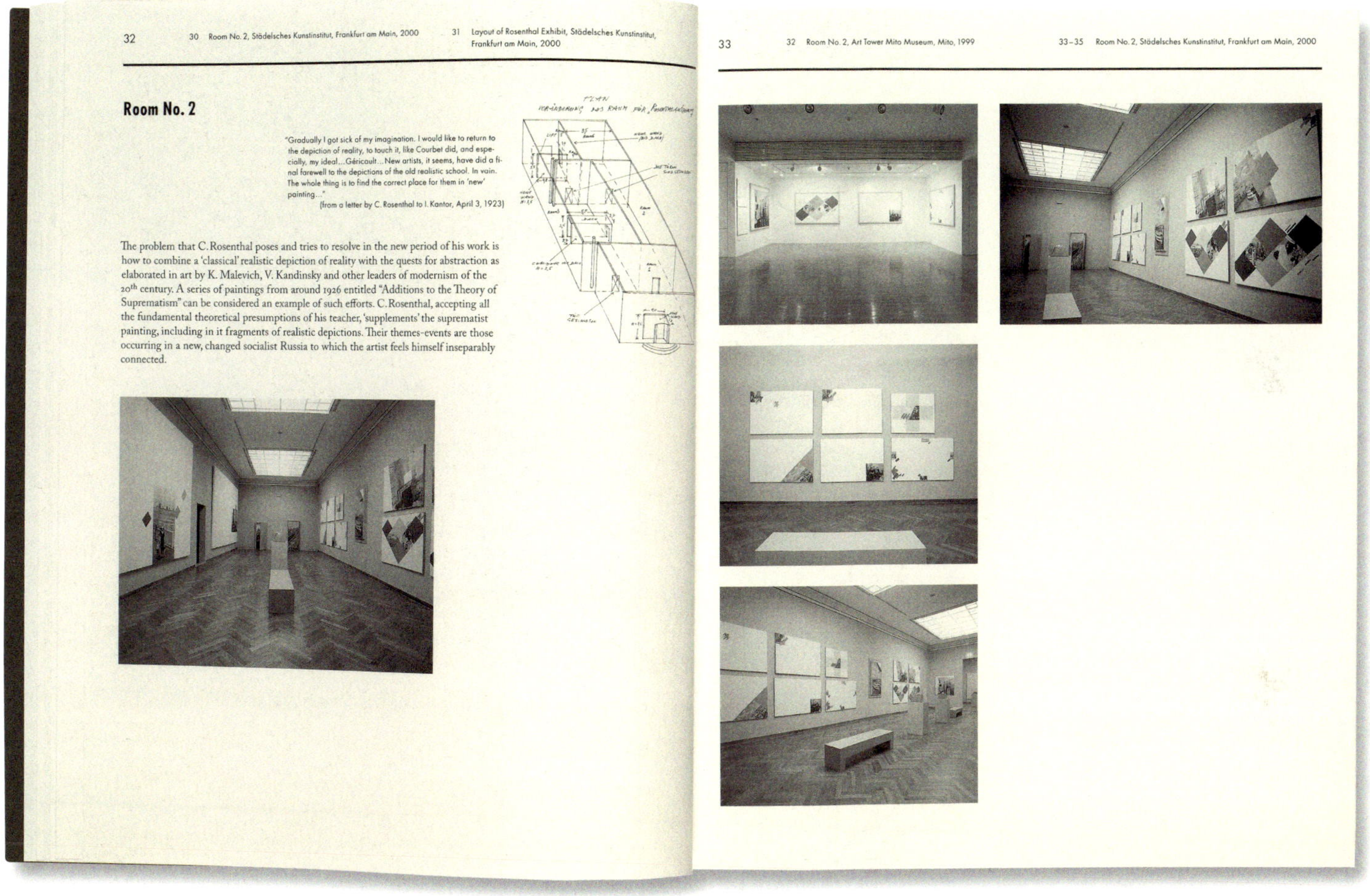
32 30 Room No. 2, Städelsches Kunstinstitut, Frankfurt am Main, 2000 31 Layout of Rosenthal Exhibit, Städelsches Kunstinstitut, Frankfurt am Main, 2000

Room No. 2

"Gradually I got sick of my imagination. I would like to return to the depiction of reality, to touch it, like Courbet did, and especially, my ideal...Géricault...New artists, it seems, have did a final farewell to the depictions of the old realistic school. In vain. The whole thing is to find the correct place for them in 'new' painting..."
(from a letter by C. Rosenthal to I. Kantor, April 3, 1923)

The problem that C.Rosenthal poses and tries to resolve in the new period of his work is how to combine a 'classical' realistic depiction of reality with the quests for abstraction as elaborated in art by K. Malevich, V. Kandinsky and other leaders of modernism of the 20th century. A series of paintings from around 1926 entitled "Additions to the Theory of Suprematism" can be considered an example of such efforts. C.Rosenthal, accepting all the fundamental theoretical presumptions of his teacher, 'supplements' the suprematist painting, including in it fragments of realistic depictions. Their themes-events are those occurring in a new, changed socialist Russia to which the artist feels himself inseparably connected.

33 32 Room No. 2, Art Tower Mito Museum, Mito, 1999 33–35 Room No. 2, Städelsches Kunstinstitut, Frankfurt am Main, 2000

über »Charles Rosenthal«, von Ilya Kabakov und Margarita und Victor Tupitsyn über »Drei über Zwei« sowie von Boris Groys und Ilya Kabakov über »Igor Spivak«; englisch.

see also | *siehe auch* no. 106; no. 132; CRP, vol. 2, nos. 304–332, pp. 21–51, nos. 335–338, pp. 54–57, nos. 340–352, pp. 60–75, nos. 354–356, pp. 77–79, nos. 403–422, pp. 123–142, nos. 424–431, pp. 144–151, nos. 433–438, pp. 154–161, no. 459, pp. 192–193

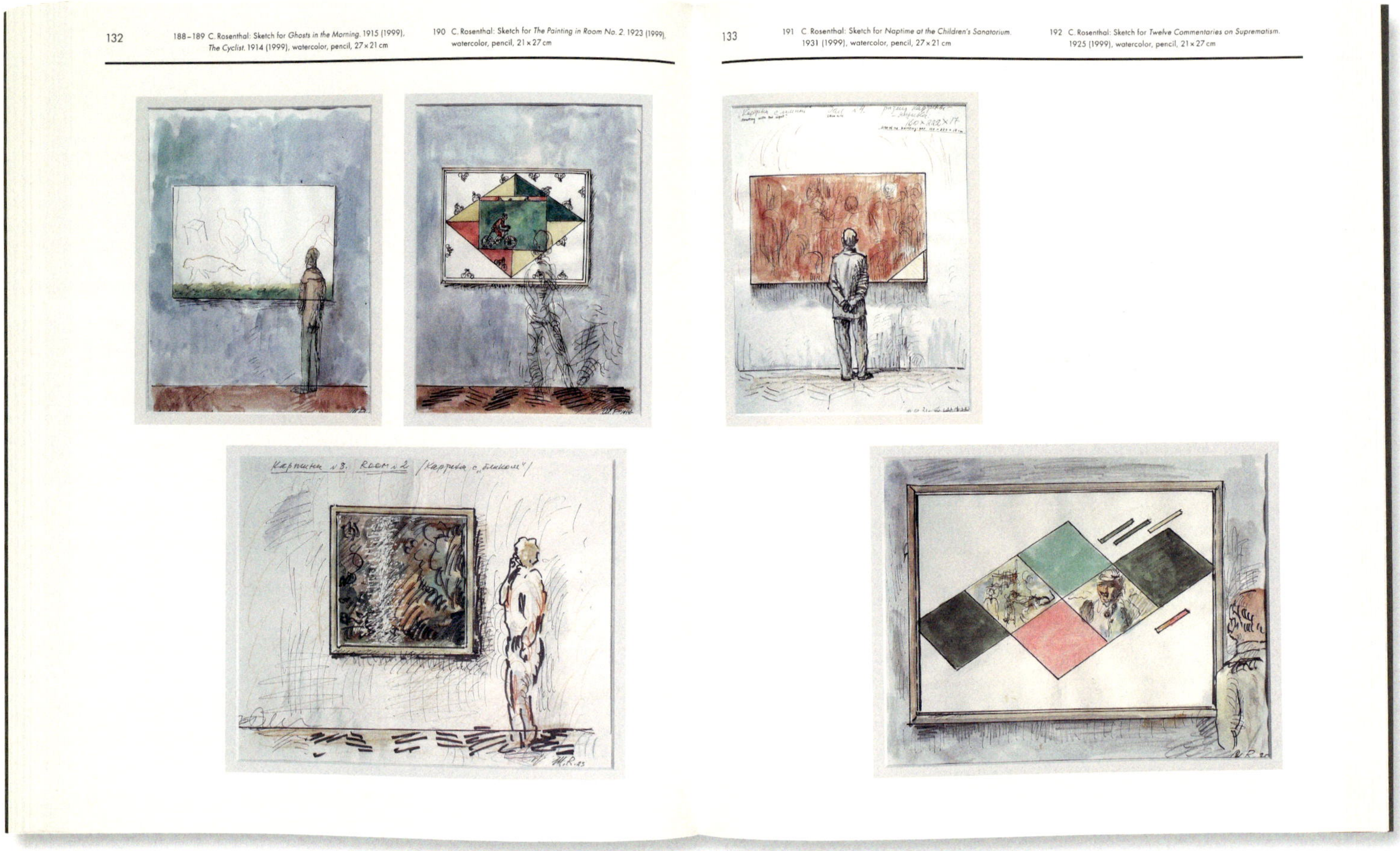
132
188–189 C. Rosenthal: Sketch for Ghosts in the Morning. 1915 (1999), The Cyclist. 1914 (1999), watercolor, pencil, 27 × 21 cm
190 C. Rosenthal: Sketch for The Painting in Room No. 2. 1923 (1999), watercolor, pencil, 21 × 27 cm
133
191 C. Rosenthal: Sketch for Naptime at the Children's Sanatorium. 1931 (1999), watercolor, pencil, 27 × 21 cm
192 C. Rosenthal: Sketch for Twelve Commentaries on Suprematism. 1925 (1999), watercolor, pencil, 21 × 27 cm

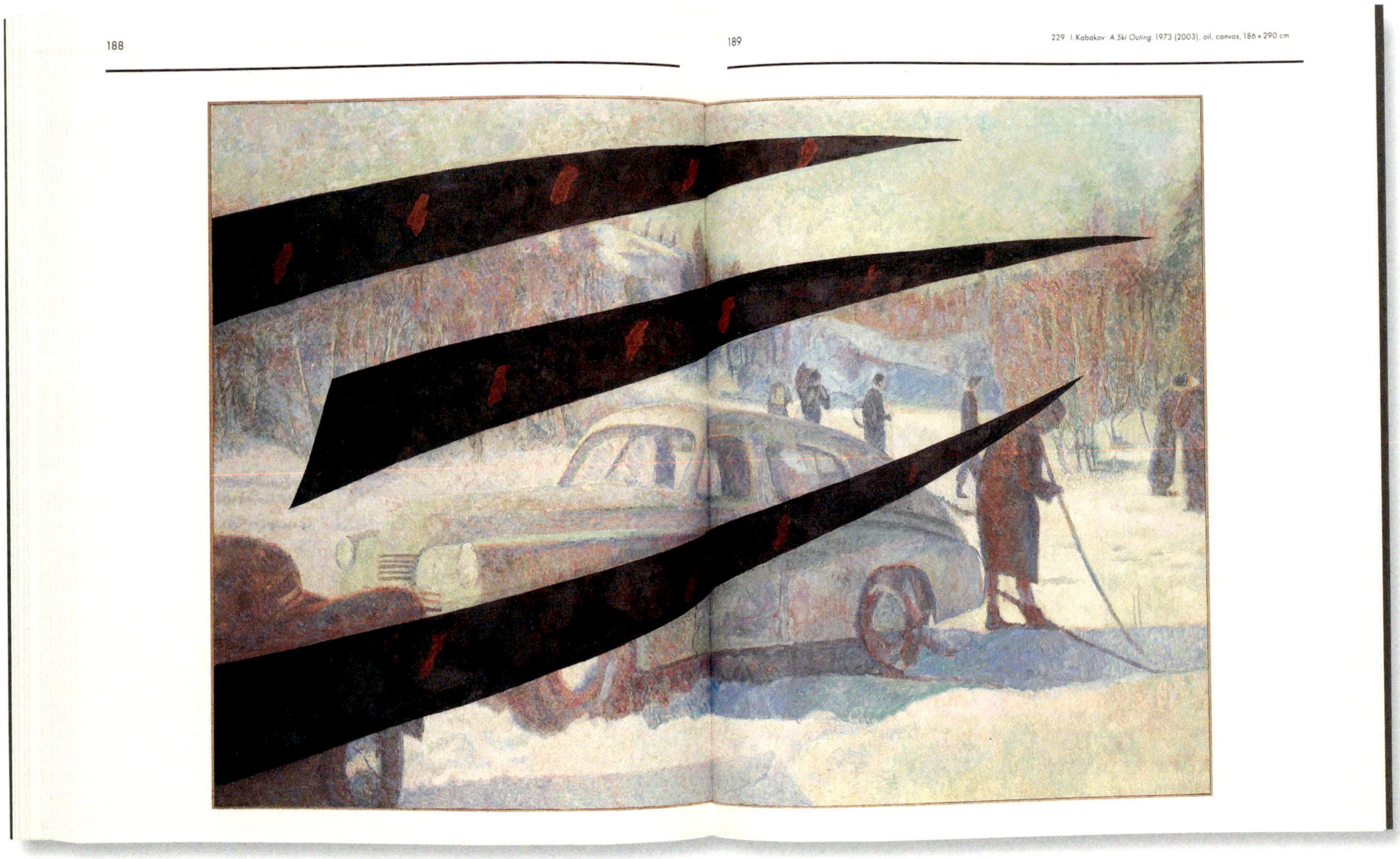
188
189
229 I. Kabakov: A Ski Outing. 1973 (2003), oil, canvas, 186 × 290 cm

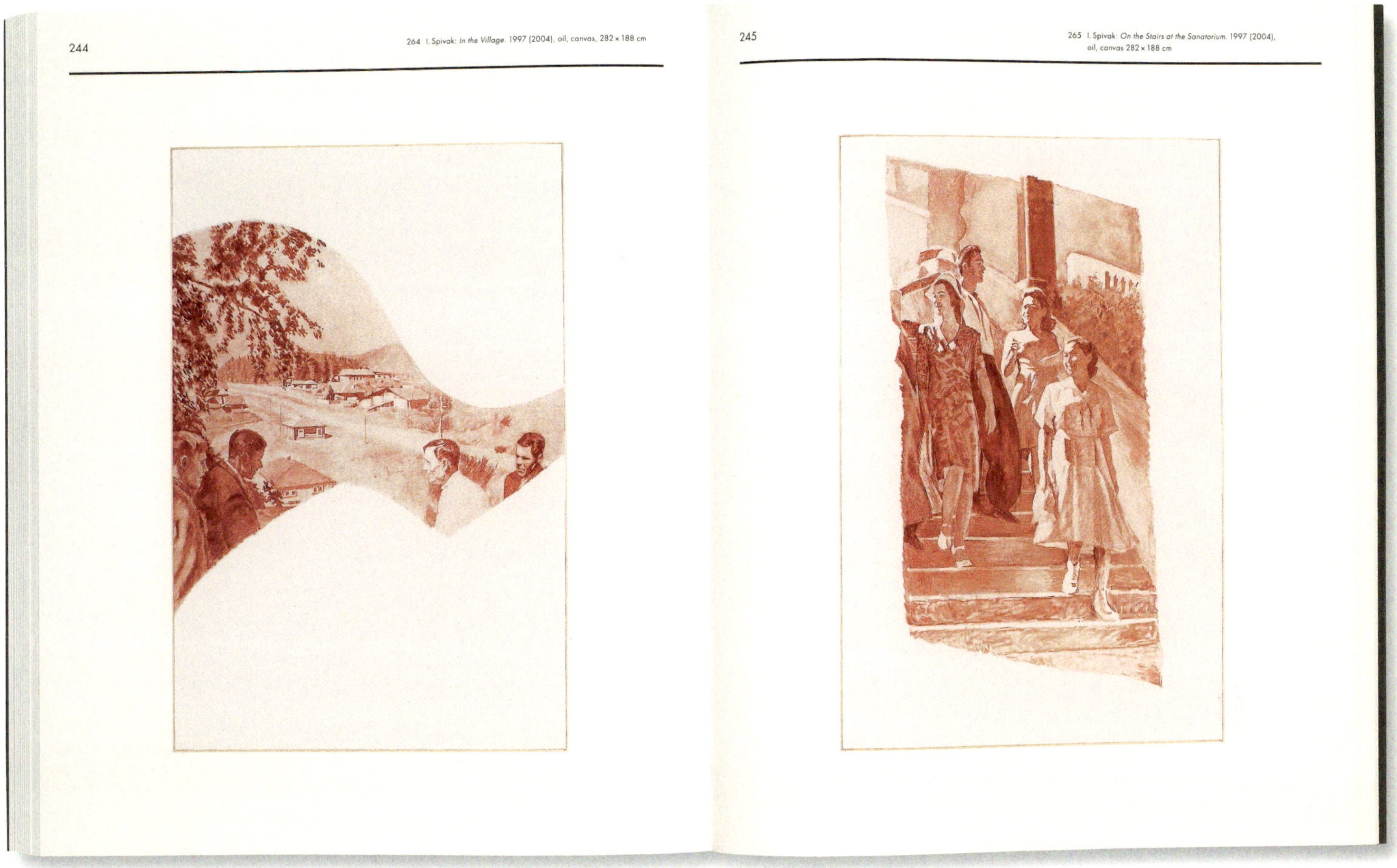
244
264 I. Spivak: *In the Village.* 1997 (2004), oil, canvas, 282 × 188 cm
245
265 I. Spivak: *On the Stairs at the Sanatorium.* 1997 (2004), oil, canvas 282 × 188 cm

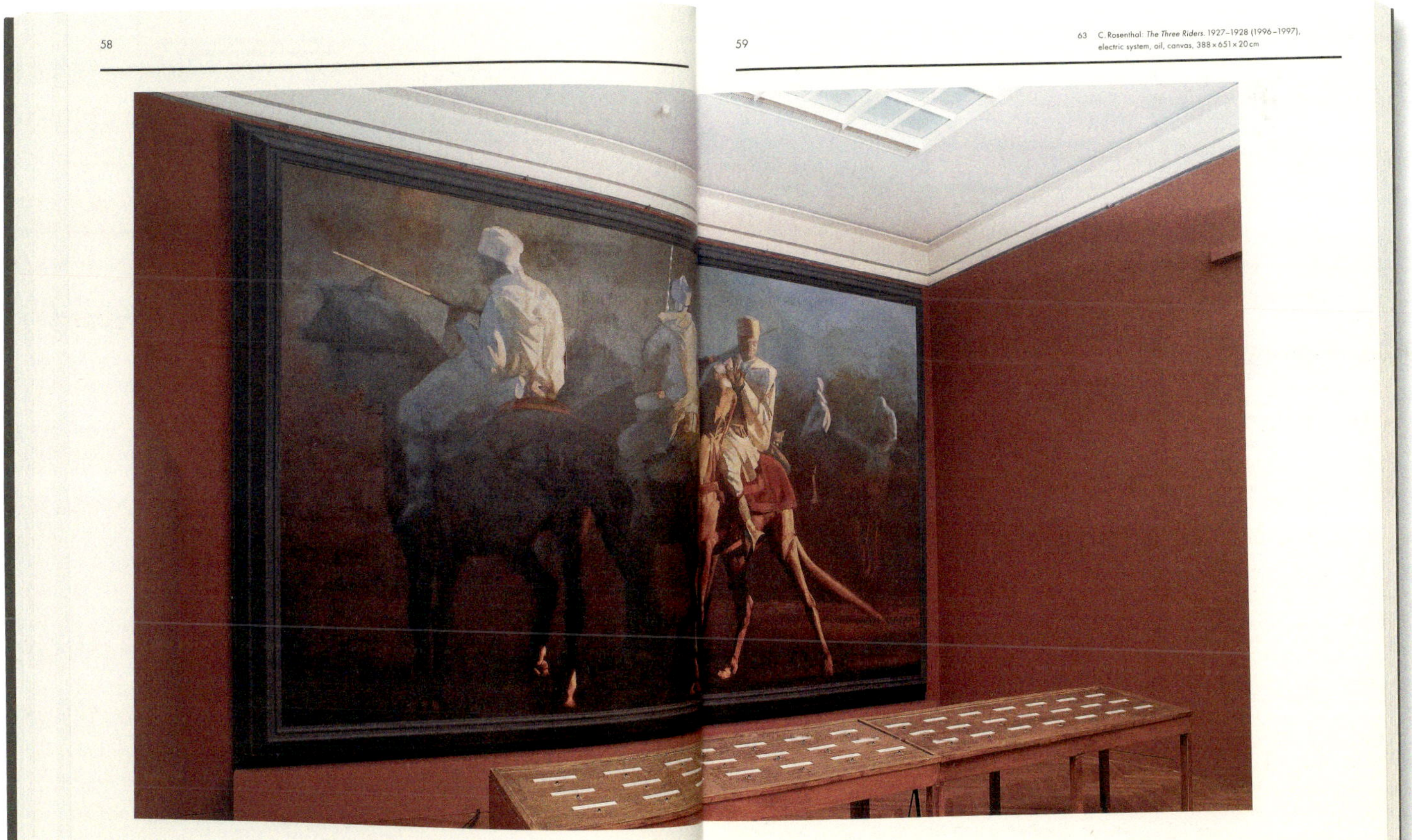
58
59
63 C. Rosenthal: *The Three Riders.* 1927–1928 (1996–1997), electric system, oil, canvas, 388 × 651 × 20 cm

126 The Utopian City and Other Projects | *Die utopische Stadt und andere Projekte*

with Emilia Kabakov | *mit Emilia Kabakov*

2004

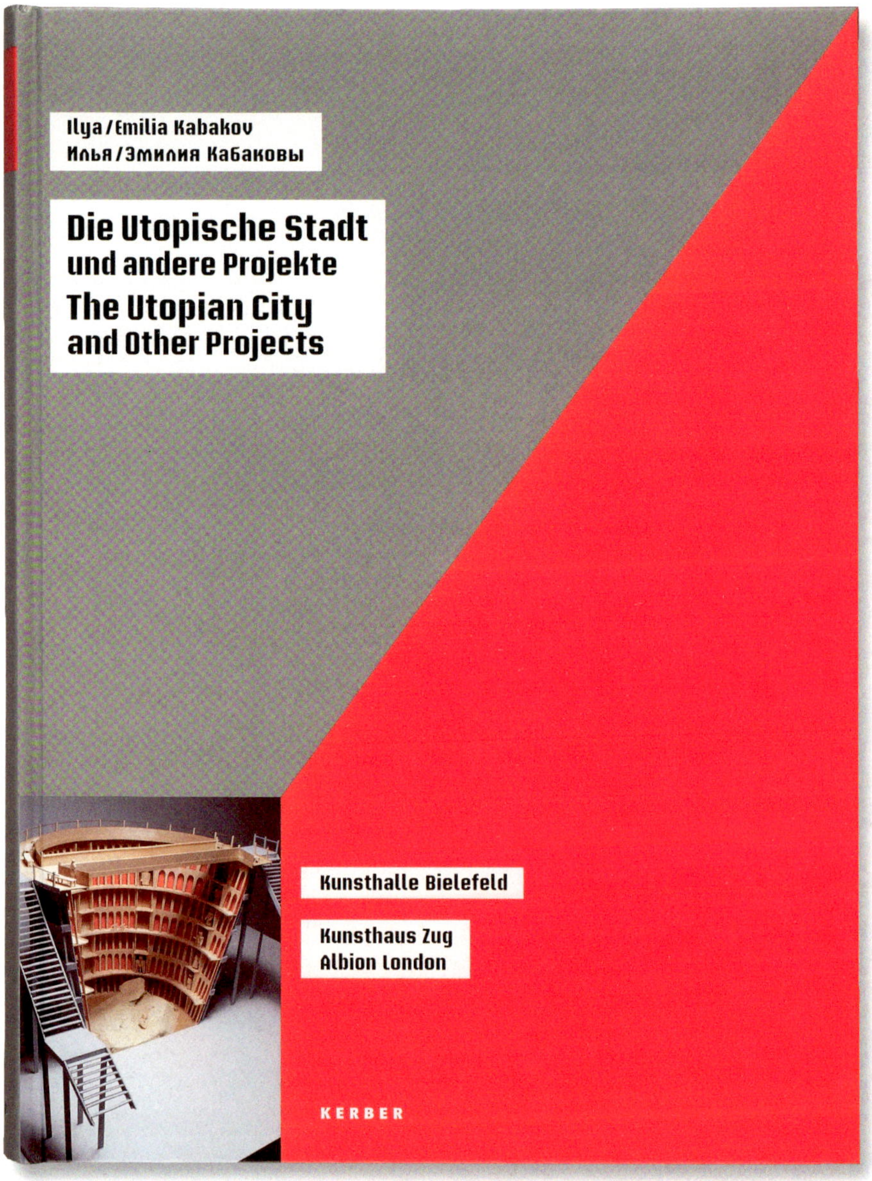

Thomas Kellein, Björn Egging
Bielefeld: Kerber Verlag
35.4 x 26.7 cm
415 pp. with 601 (454 color) ills.
stitchbound, hardcover
Fadenheftung, Hardcover

exhibition catalogue | *Ausstellungskatalog*

layout by Ilya Kabakov | *Layout von Ilya Kabakov*

For the exhibition »Ilya und Emilia Kabakov: Die Architekturprojekte«, Kunsthalle Bielefeld, Bielefeld, September 12 to November 14, 2004; Kunsthaus Zug, Zug, February 27 to June 5, 2005; and Albion London, London, October 13 to December 23, 2005. Texts by Ilya Kabakov and Thomas Kellein; German, English.

Zur Ausstellung »Ilya und Emilia Kabakov. Die Architekturprojekte«, Kunsthalle Bielefeld, Bielefeld, 12. September – 14. November 2004, Kunsthaus Zug, Zug, 27. Februar – 5. Juni 2005, und Albion London, London, 13. Oktober – 23. Dezember 2005. Texte von Ilya Kabakov und Thomas Kellein; deutsch, englisch.

see also | *siehe auch* no. 120

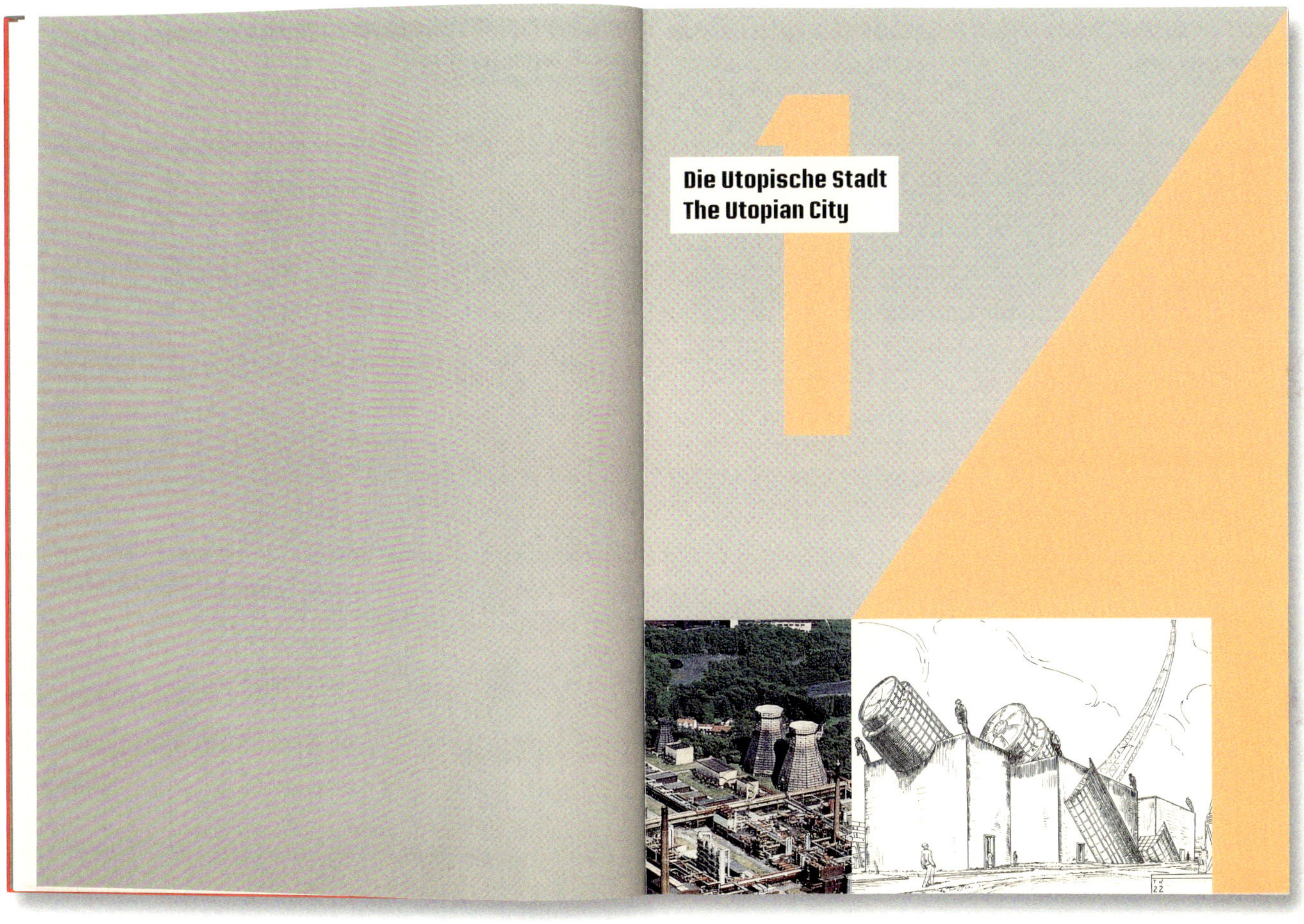
1
Die Utopische Stadt
The Utopian City

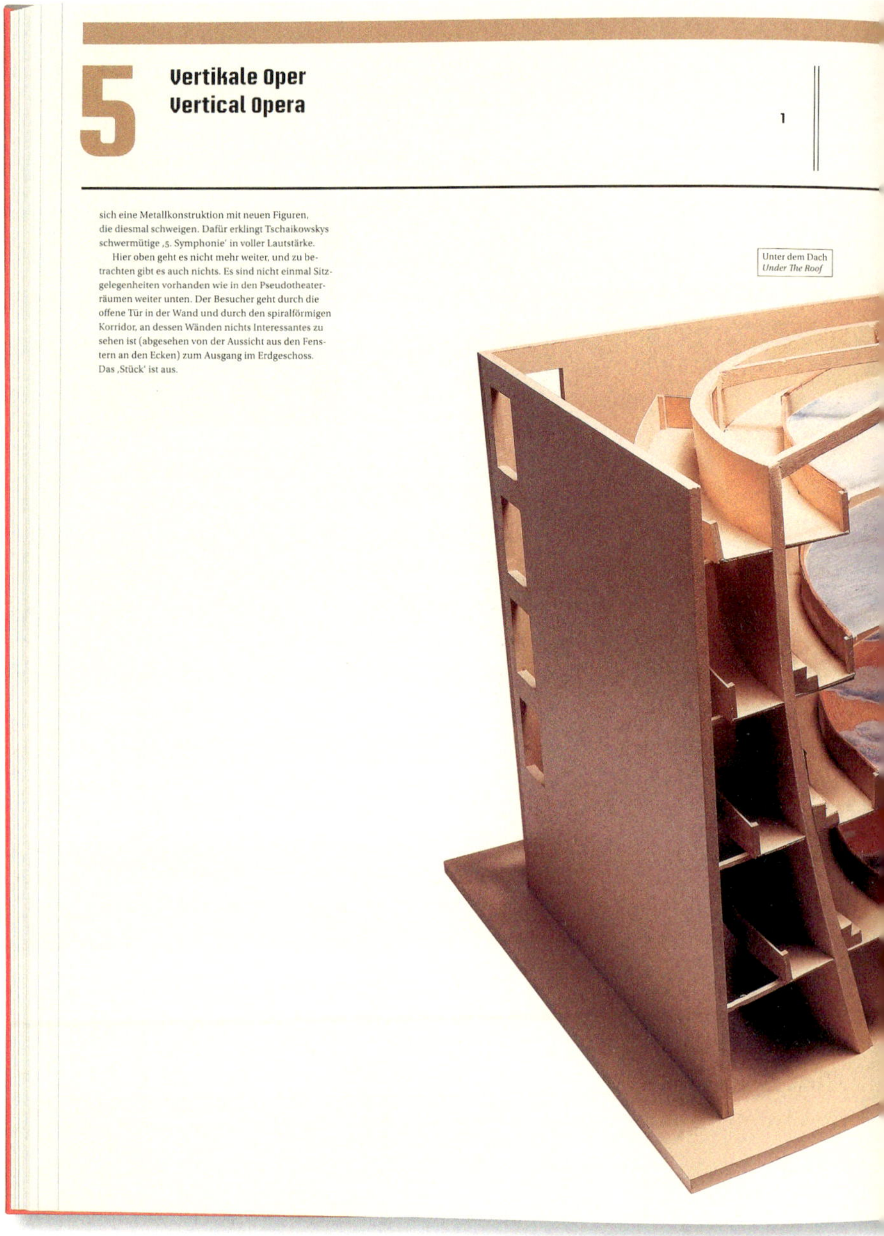

5

Vertikale Oper
Vertical Opera

1

sich eine Metallkonstruktion mit neuen Figuren, die diesmal schweigen. Dafür erklingt Tschaikowskys schwermütige ‚5. Symphonie' in voller Lautstärke.

Hier oben geht es nicht mehr weiter, und zu betrachten gibt es auch nichts. Es sind nicht einmal Sitzgelegenheiten vorhanden wie in den Pseudotheaterräumen weiter unten. Der Besucher geht durch die offene Tür in der Wand und durch den spiralförmigen Korridor, an dessen Wänden nichts Interessantes zu sehen ist (abgesehen von der Aussicht aus den Fenstern an den Ecken) zum Ausgang im Erdgeschoss. Das ‚Stück' ist aus.

Unter dem Dach
Under The Roof

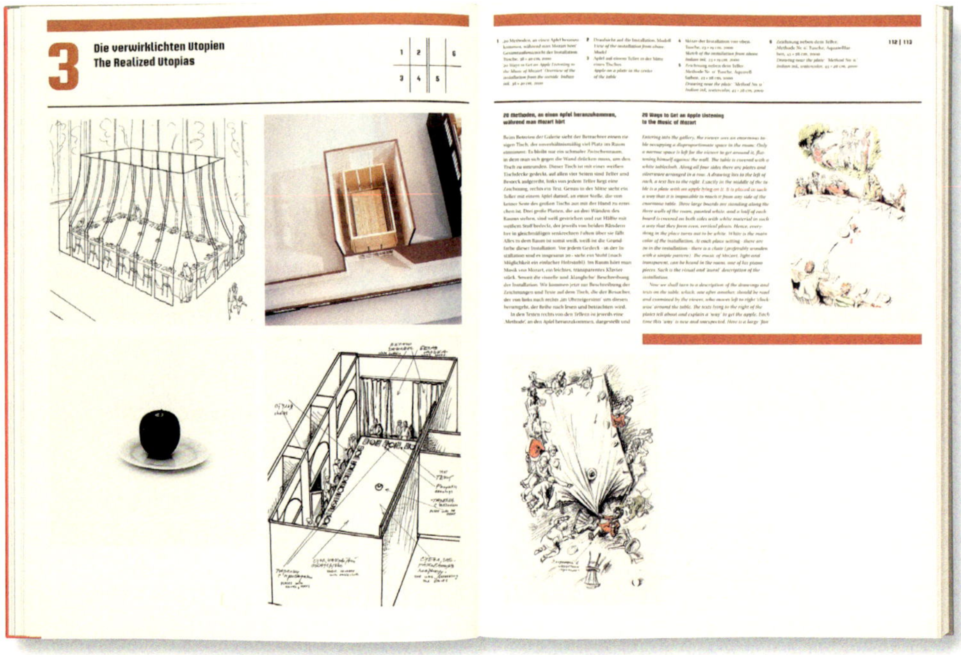

3

Die verwirklichten Utopien
The Realized Utopias

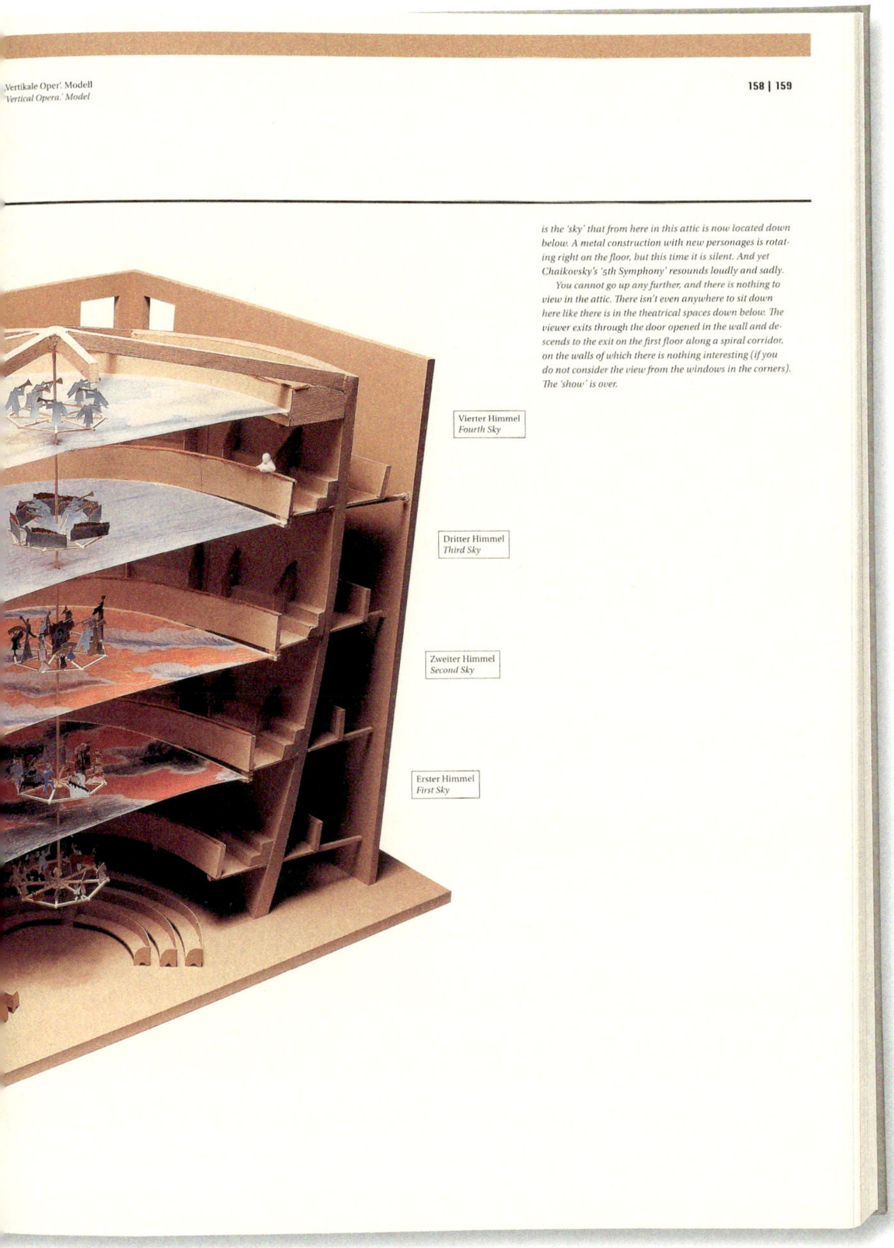

'Vertikale Oper.' Modell
'Vertical Opera.' Model

158 | 159

is the 'sky' that from here in this attic is now located down below. A metal construction with new personages is rotating right on the floor, but this time it is silent. And yet Chaikovsky's '5th Symphony' resounds loudly and sadly.

You cannot go up any further, and there is nothing to view in the attic. There isn't even anywhere to sit down here like there is in the theatrical spaces down below. The viewer exits through the door opened in the wall and descends to the exit on the first floor along a spiral corridor, on the walls of which there is nothing interesting (if you do not consider the view from the windows in the corners). The 'show' is over.

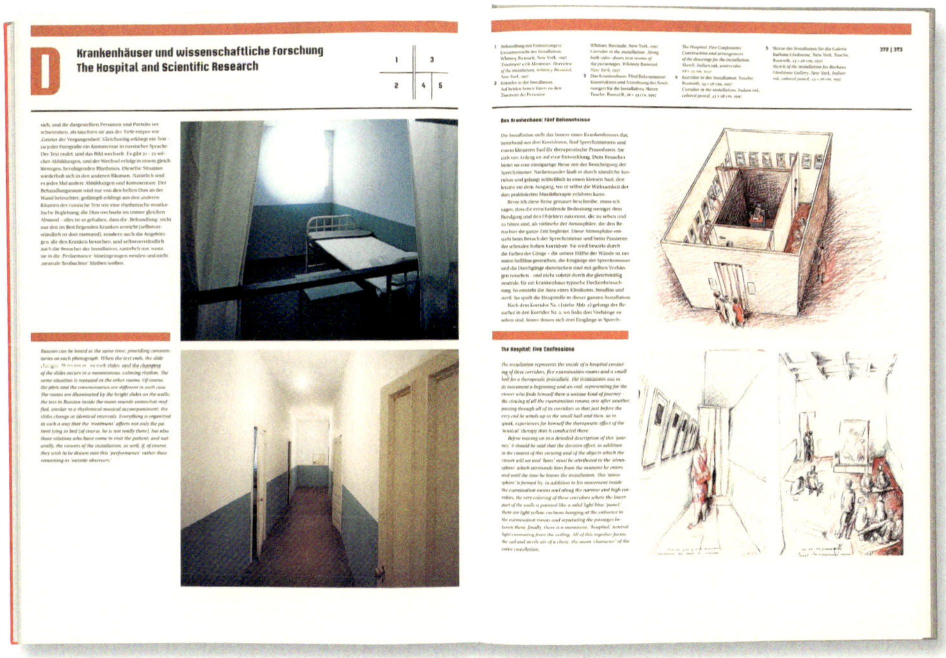

D

Krankenhäuser und wissenschaftliche Forschung
The Hospital and Scientific Research

Das Krankenhaus: Fünf Bekenntnisse

The Hospital: Five Confessions

127 "Morning, Evening, Night ..." | *„Morgen, Abend, Nacht ...“*

with Emilia Kabakov | *mit Emilia Kabakov*

2005

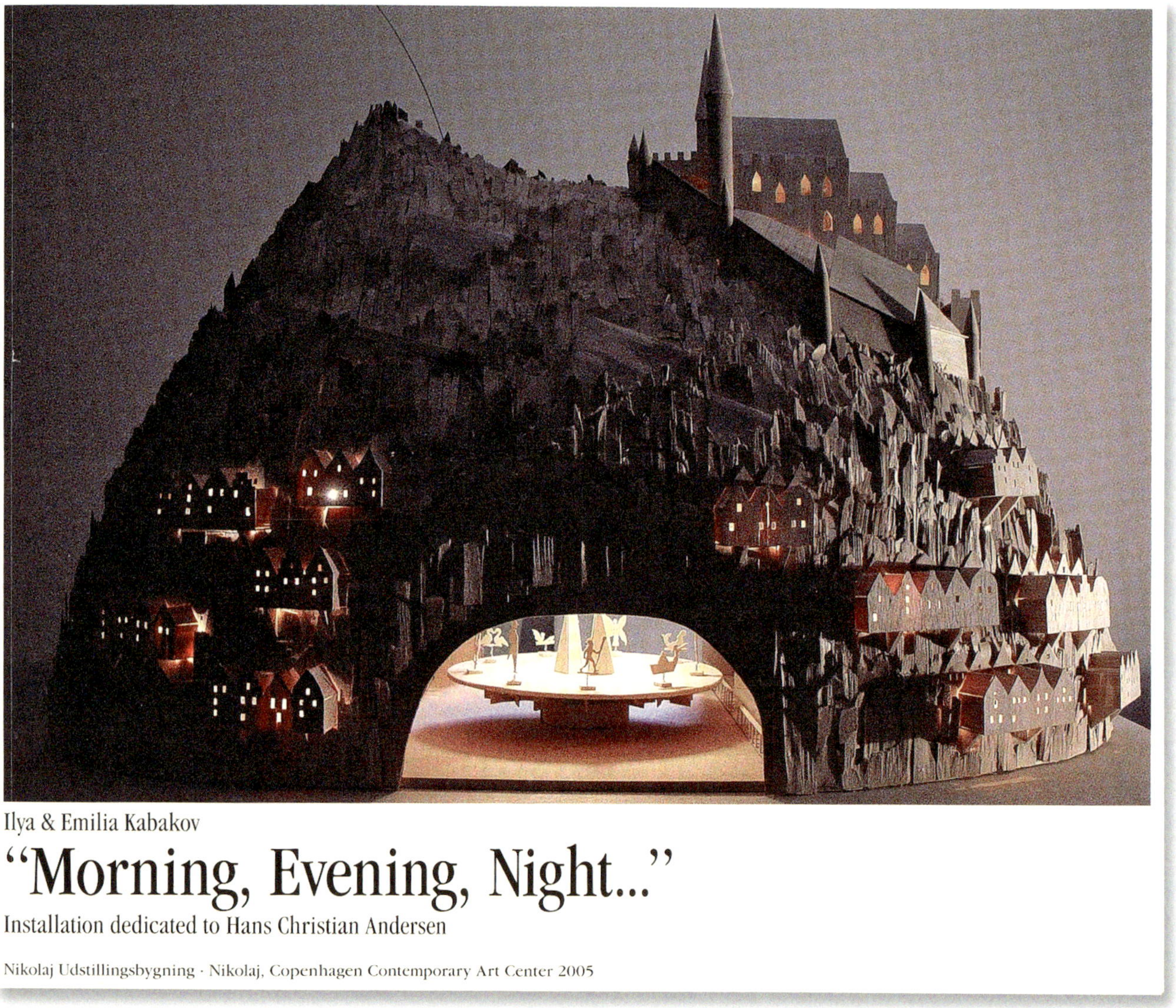

Ann Lumbye Sørensen
Copenhagen: Nikolaj, Copenhagen Contemporary Art Center
24 x 29 cm
48 pp. with 41 (33 color) ills.
stitchbound, softback
Fadenheftung, broschiert
edition: 1,500 copies

exhibition catalogue | *Ausstellungskatalog*

layout by Ilya Kabakov | *Layout von Ilya Kabakov*

Documentation of the installation of the same name for the exhibition »H.C. Andersen – En Livsverden: Installationer af Ilya & Emilia Kabakov og Joseph Kosuth«, Nikolaj, Copenhagen Contemporary Art Center, Copenhagen, June 18 to August 28, 2005. In cooperation with the Reykjavik Art Museum, Reykjavik. Texts by Ann Lumbye Sørensen, Ilya and Emilia Kabakov; Danish, English.

Dokumentation der gleichnamigen Installation für die Ausstellung »H.C. Andersen – En Livsverden. Installationer af Ilya & Emilia Kabakov og Joseph Kosuth«, Nikolaj, Copenhagen Contemporary Art Center, Kopenhagen, 18. Juni – 28. August 2005. In Zusammenarbeit mit dem Reykjavik Art Museum, Reykjavik. Texte von Ann Lumbye Sørensen, Ilya und Emilia Kabakov; dänisch, englisch.

see also | *siehe auch* CRP, vol. 2, nos. 524–535, pp. 268–273

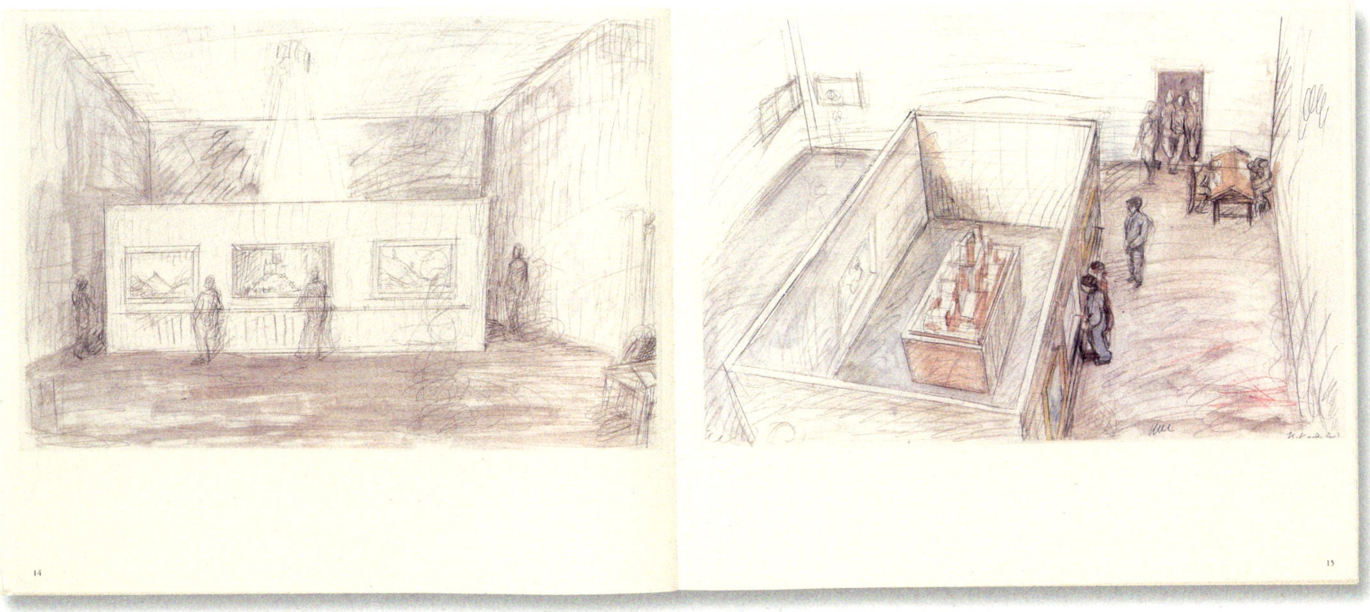
14
15

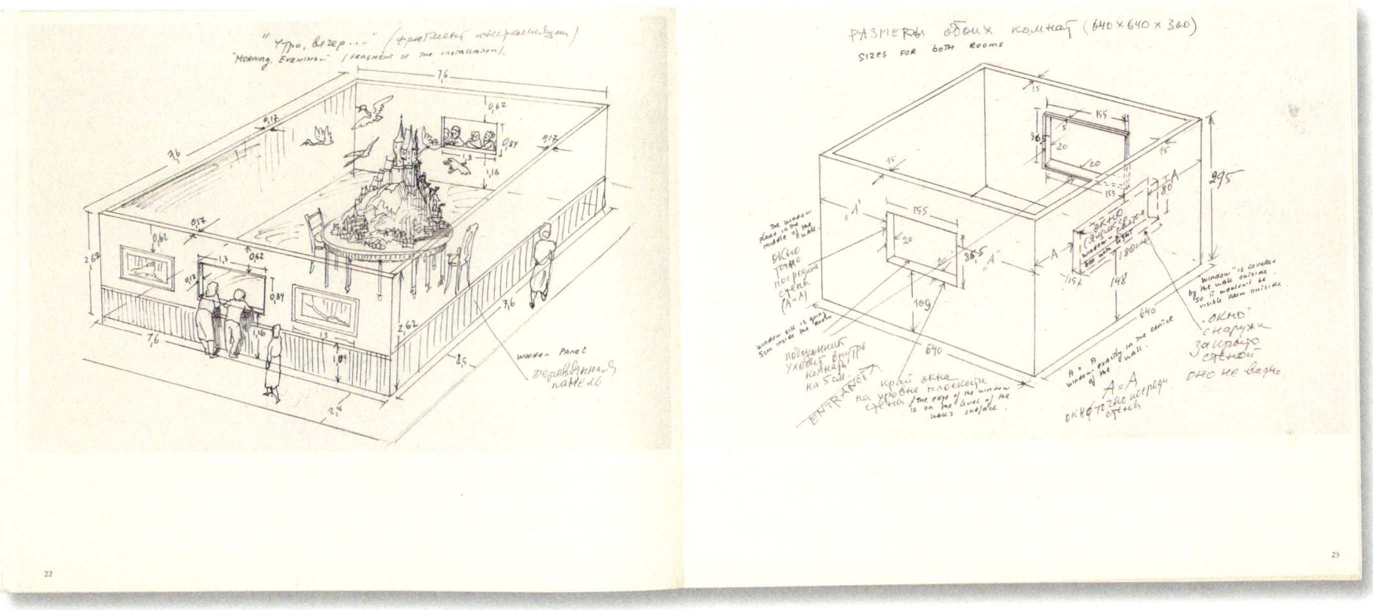
SIZES FOR BOTH ROOMS
22
23

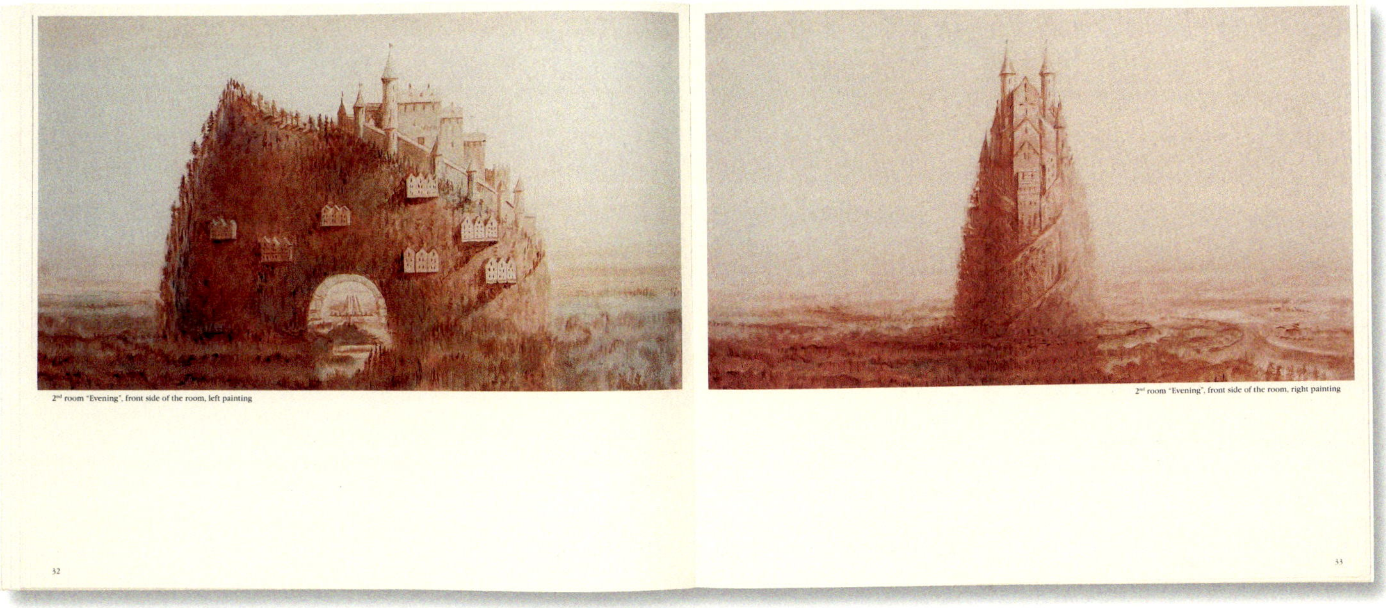
2nd room "Evening", front side of the room, left painting
2nd room "Evening", front side of the room, right painting
32
33

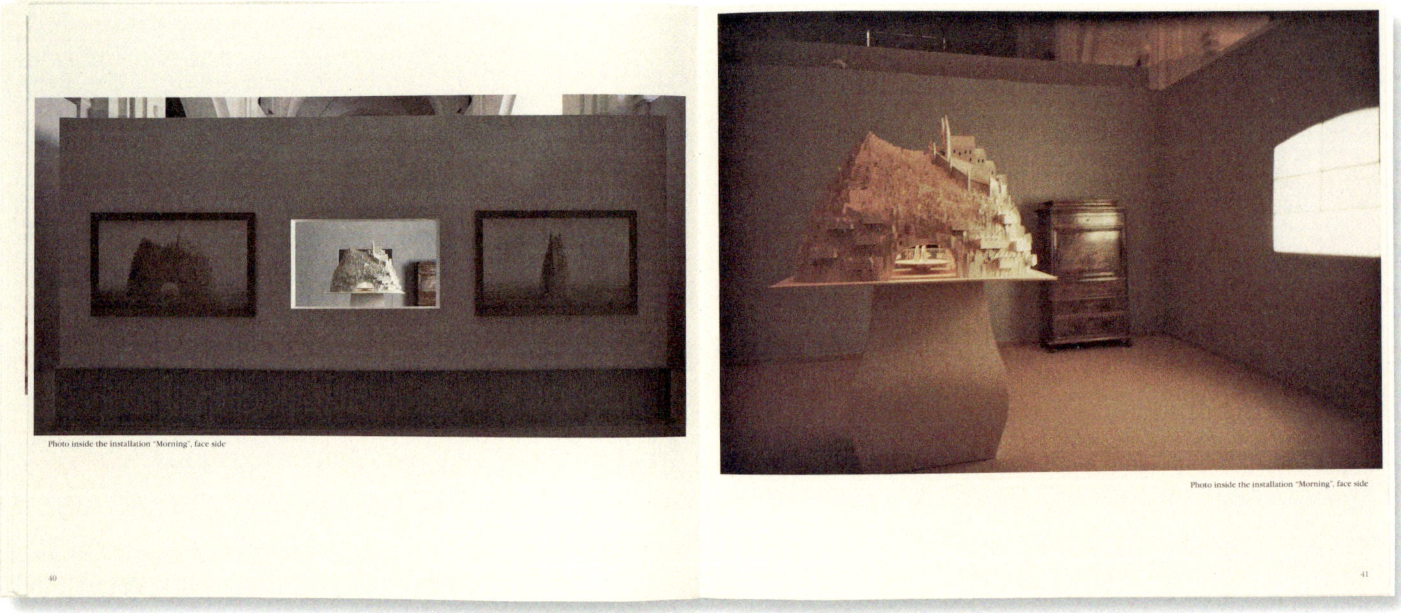
Photo inside the installation "Morning", face side
Photo inside the installation "Morning", face side
40
41

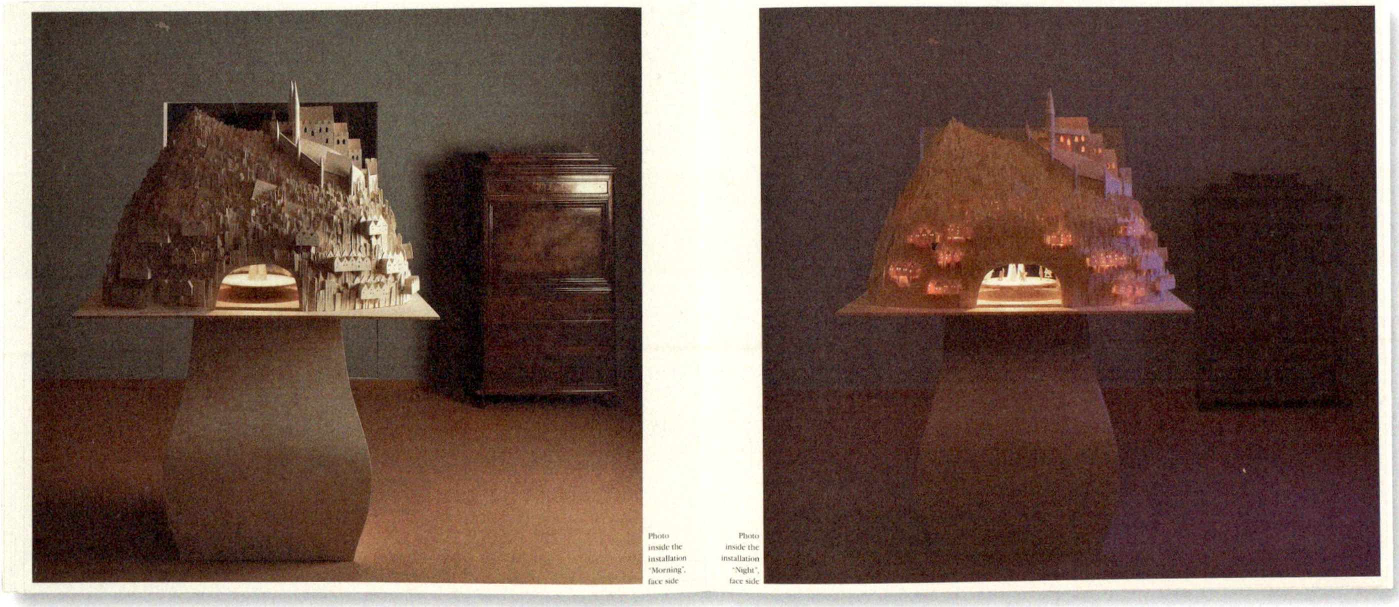
Photo inside the installation "Morning", face side
Photo inside the installation "Night", face side

128 The Thaw | *Tauwetter*

with Emilia Kabakov | *mit Emilia Kabakov*

2006

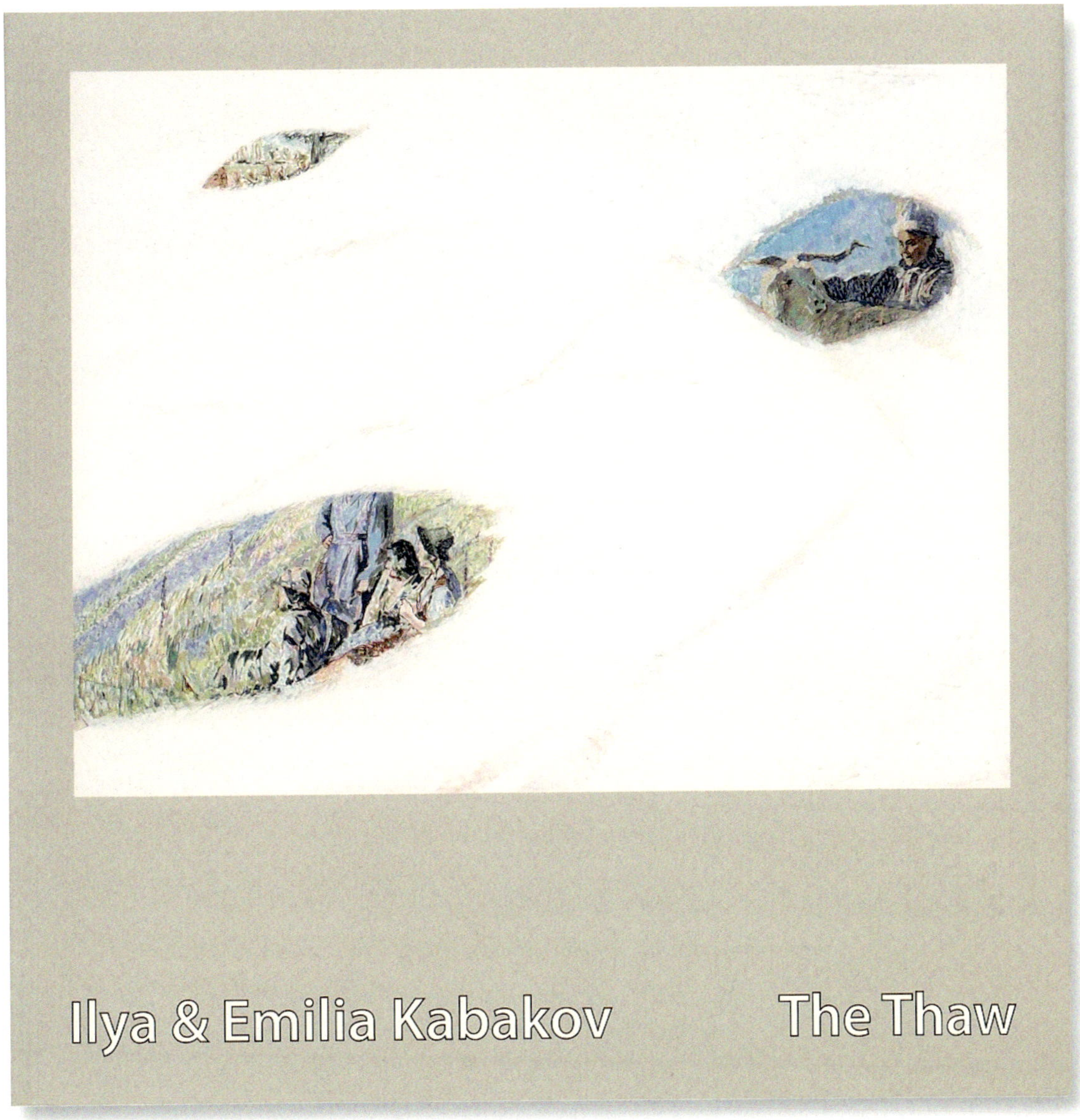

Deweer Art Gallery
Otegem: Deweer Art Gallery
21 x 21 cm
44 pp. with 16 color ills.
adhesive binding, softback
Klebebindung, broschiert

exhibition catalogue | *Ausstellungskatalog*

layout by Ilya Kabakov | *Layout von Ilya Kabakov*

For the exhibition of the same name at the Deweer Art Gallery, Otegem, Belgium, March 4 to April 23, 2006. Texts by Jo Coucke, Mark Deweer, Ilya and Emilia Kabakov; Flemish, English.

Zur gleichnamigen Ausstellung, Deweer Art Gallery, Otegem, Belgien, 4. März – 23. April 2006. Texte von Jo Coucke, Mark Deweer, Ilya und Emilia Kabakov; flämisch, englisch.

see also | *siehe auch* CRP, vol. 2, no. 501, p. 238, no. 503, p. 240, no. 505, p. 242, no. 507, p. 244, no. 508, p. 245, no. 509, p. 246, no. 514, pp. 252–253, no. 516, p. 256

Ilya & Emilia Kabakov: The Thaw

Het ensemble The Thaw (De Dooi) van Ilya & Emilia Kabakov bestaat uit 23 tekeningen en evenveel grote schilderijen, en is ontstaan in de periode 2004-2006. Voor de samenstelling van onze tentoonstelling, die de allereerste voorstelling van The Thaw is, kozen Ilya & Emilia Kabakov acht schilderijen en vier tekeningen uit. De tekeningen zijn stuk voor stuk voorstudies voor een welbepaald schilderij. Op sommige schilderijen is trouwens nog heel licht het raster van potloodlijntjes zichtbaar dat de kunstenaar hielp bij de beeldoverdracht. Maar de vier gekozen tekeningen verwijzen geen enkele keer naar een schilderij uit de tentoonstelling. Het wit van schilderijen uit The Thaw is overigens het wit van het onbeschilderde doek. Anders gesteld, Ilya heeft het wit niet geschilderd, het was er al.

Zoals aangegeven werkten de Kabakovs ongeveer drie jaar aan de volledige serie. De schilderijen dragen allemaal dezelfde titel en zijn genummerd van 1 tot 23. De eerste beelden uit de reeks vertonen duidelijk herkenbare beeldfragmenten en zijn daardoor veel realistischer dan de latere, die suggestiever en mystieker zijn. In de beeldfragmenten herkennen we o.a. drie mannen die een kaart of plan bestuderen, een mijnwerker, en een vrouw in traditionele klederdracht. Eigen aan deze motieven is hun duidelijk fragmentair karakter. Dit lijken lukraak uitgesneden delen van grotere beelden. Zonder de context van het gehele beeld verliezen de beeldfragmenten hun betekenis. Het mechanisme dat hier aan het werk is, is gelijk aan dat van de zgn. Commentaar-tekeningen, dé format waar Ilya Kabakov een patent op heeft. In die typische tekeningen worden we geconfronteerd met een flard van een fictieve uitspraak van een al even fictief personage. We herkennen de woorden en hun betekenis maar kunnen -bij gebrek aan context - over de eigenlijke betekenis van het citaat of commentaar niet veel zinnigs zeggen.

In hun statement over The Thaw (zie elders in deze catalogus) vertellen de Kabakovs ons dat er voor de serie meerdere titels bestaan. Voor Deweer Art Gallery kozen ze voor The Thaw, maar ook Under the Snow (Onder de sneeuw) of Through the Clouds (Doorheen de wolken) hadden gekund. Als titel is The Thaw poëtischer dan beide andere titels, want van een groter metaforisch gehalte. The Thaw als titel van een serie werken van een kunstenaar die heeft moeten wachten op glasnost en perestrojka alvorens zijn werk wereldkundig te kunnen maken, het kan tellen.
Zoals de Kabakovs verder in hun statement suggereren, waren er wellicht nog andere titels mogelijk. Een titel bijvoorbeeld die ons zou instrueren over het functioneren van ons geheugen: welke beelden komen onder welke omstandigheden terug in ons bewustzijn? Zijn de gaten in het wolkendek mutatis mutandis inderdaad niet te vergelijken met de gaten die de ziekte van Alzheimer in onze hersenen en hersenfunctie slaat? Of nog, een titel die ons op het spoor zou zetten van een vormelijke of esthetische analyse van de schilderijen: bijvoorbeeld wat betreft de verhouding tussen het motief op de voorgrond van het schilderij en de achtergrond van het doek, een belangrijke rode draad in de analyse van het beeldkarakter van de schilderkunst door de eeuwen heen.

Ilya Kabakov heeft gedurende zijn hele artistieke loopbaan iets met wit van doen. In het vernoemde statement verwijst hij zelf expliciet naar de oude witte schilderijen uit 1977-1978, maar een grondige studie naar het belang van het wit - al dan niet het toedekkende wit of het maagdelijk gebleven wit - in zijn gehele oeuvre, kan ongetwijfeld zeer instructief zijn voor de specifieke kunsthistorische betekenis van deze serie.
In de tentoonstelling Ilya Kabakov - 7 Ausstellungen eines Bildes (Kasseler Kunstverein, 1990) presenteerde de kunstenaar 7 grote schilderijen elk geflankeerd door een tekstpaneel en een grote hoeveelheid 'Commentaar-tekeningen'. In de catalogus van die belangrijke tentoonstelling, schrijft de eminente theoreticus en kenner van de Russische (historische én hedendaagse) avant-garde, Boris Groys, o.a. over het wit in de schilderijen van Ilya Kabakov. Mijns inziens kan de draagkracht van zijn woorden van toen zonder meer worden uitgebreid tot de schilderijen uit The Thaw: "Het wit in zijn schilderijen verwijst naar de Russische avant-garde, naar het suprematisme van Malewitch bijvoorbeeld, voor wie het wit een directe ervaring van de mystieke diepte, van de innerlijke verlichting, van de extatische sprakeloosheid, van het oorspronkelijke Niets, van de bevrijding van de wereld zoals hij is, betekende". Kabakov is zich altijd terdege bewust van zijn (kunst)historische positie.

6

Interessanter nog dan de tekst van Groys is het voorwoord dat de kunstenaar zelf in de betreffende catalogus liet opnemen. Ik citeer. "Ook het 'witte' van het schilderij wordt dan dubbelzinnig: als we het schilderij als iets ruimtelijk beschouwen, verandert het wit zich moeiteloos in licht; beschouwen we het wit echter als iets vlak, dan springt meteen de (...) verf als verf in het oog (en in het geval van The Thaw het witte schilderdoek, inclusief de daarop geschilderde arceringen, nvdr). Het is het een of het ander. De keuze voor het ene sluit het andere uit: het is 'of – of'. Het hangt niet alleen van de instelling van de ogen af, maar ook van de instelling van het bewustzijn, van diens beslissing voor wat het dit doek wil houden. Het geheel herinnert een beetje aan de zogenaamde 'Vexierbilder' (zoekprentjes; bijvoorbeeld in de voorbijdrijvende wolken een gezicht of een dier zien, nvdr): de ene keer zien we het, de andere keer niet, al naargelang de instelling van ons oog...Het belangrijkste dat we voor ons zien, in feite het enige...is het wit van het schilderij. Het is er altijd en het aanvaardt het ene zowel als het andere, alsof het zich uitspreekt zowel voor als tegen. Zijn betrokkenheid is echter slechts 'schijnbaar' passief, zoals het daar als het ware onberoerd blijft voor zowel het ene als het andere. Eenmaal we ons op het wit hebben afgestemd, kunnen we het onbewogen aanschouwen, en het zal onbewogen voor ons staan, het zal beide mogelijkheden in gelijke mate bewaren en in zich dragen, en tegelijk ook alle andere mogelijkheden, zonder daarbij zichzelf te veranderen. Het blijft in zekere zin onverschillig voor dat waarvoor men het houden wil, voor de volheid van een geheel of voor iets volkomen leeg".
Het wit, de flard tekst uit de Commentaar-tekening, het beeldfragment uit The Thaw, het is er zoals het is, en niet meer dan dat.

Ik heb hier maar een heel summiere aanzet willen geven tot een begrip van de betekenis van het hier getoonde werk, voor zover de beschouwer van deze prachtige schilderijen daar al behoefte aan heeft. Maar het is duidelijk dat Ilya Kabakov met de conceptuele schilderijen uit The Thaw andermaal het belang bewijst van zijn bijdrage aan de ontwikkeling van de beeldende kunst in het algemeen en van de schilderkunst in het bijzonder. Ilya Kabakov is één van die zeldzame kunstenaars die aan dat verhaal een echt consistente bijdrage weten te leveren. Hij is onder andere om die reden één van de grootste conceptuele kunstenaars ooit. Dat Deweer Art Gallery de primeur van deze serie nieuwe werken hebben gekregen, is een hele eer. Het belang van deze tentoonstelling ligt mijns inziens tenslotte ook in het feit dat we hier het beeld van de kunstenaar, die in onze contreien meer bekend staat om zijn installaties, vervolledigen.

Jo Coucke
Deweer Art Gallery

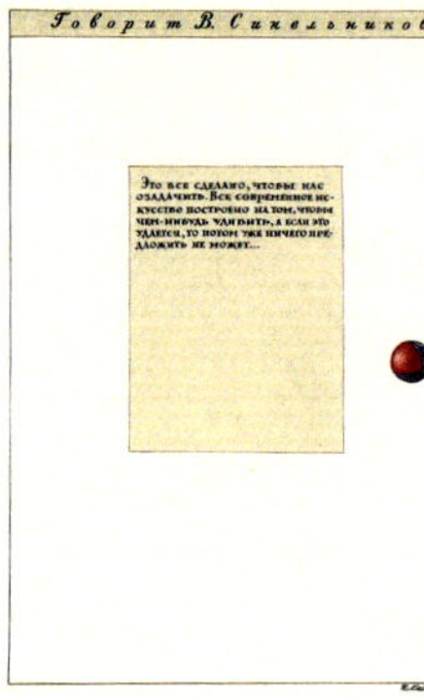

Ilya Kabakov, *Zegt V. Sinelnikov...* ,1991, kleurpotlood, gouache en inkt op papier, 33 x 23 cm

Zegt V. Sinelkov:
"Dit is allemaal gedaan om ons van slag te brengen. Alle hedendaagse kunst is erop gericht ons te verrassen, en als dat niet lukt, hebben ze ons niets anders aan te bieden..."

7

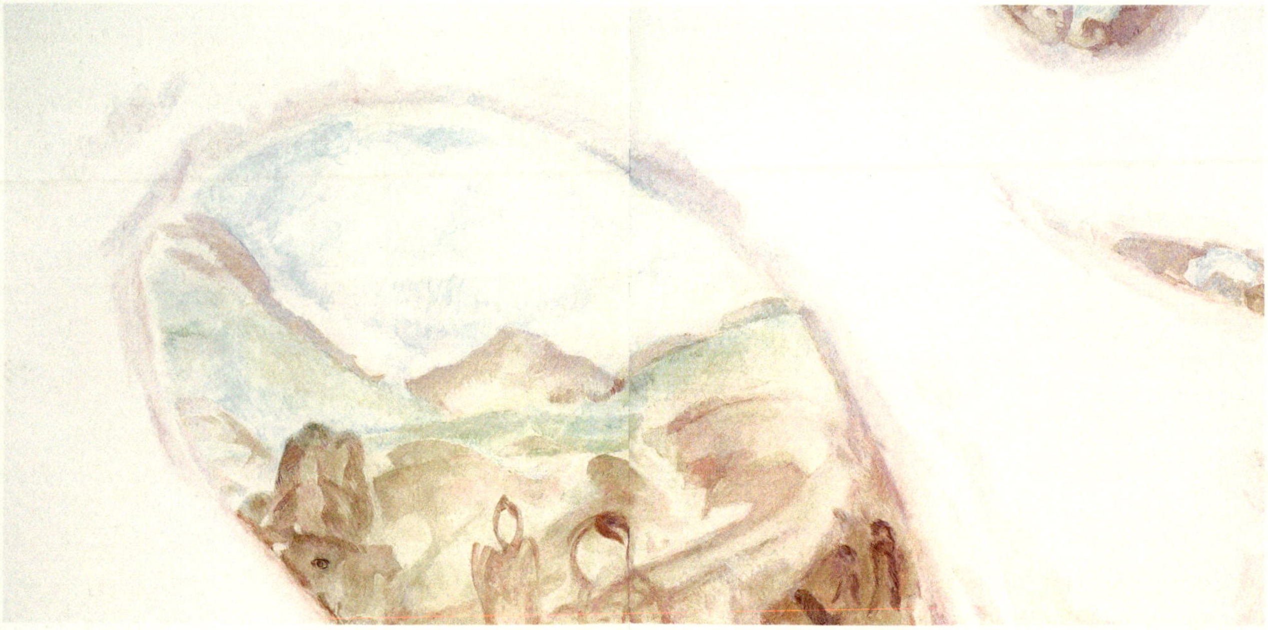

30

31

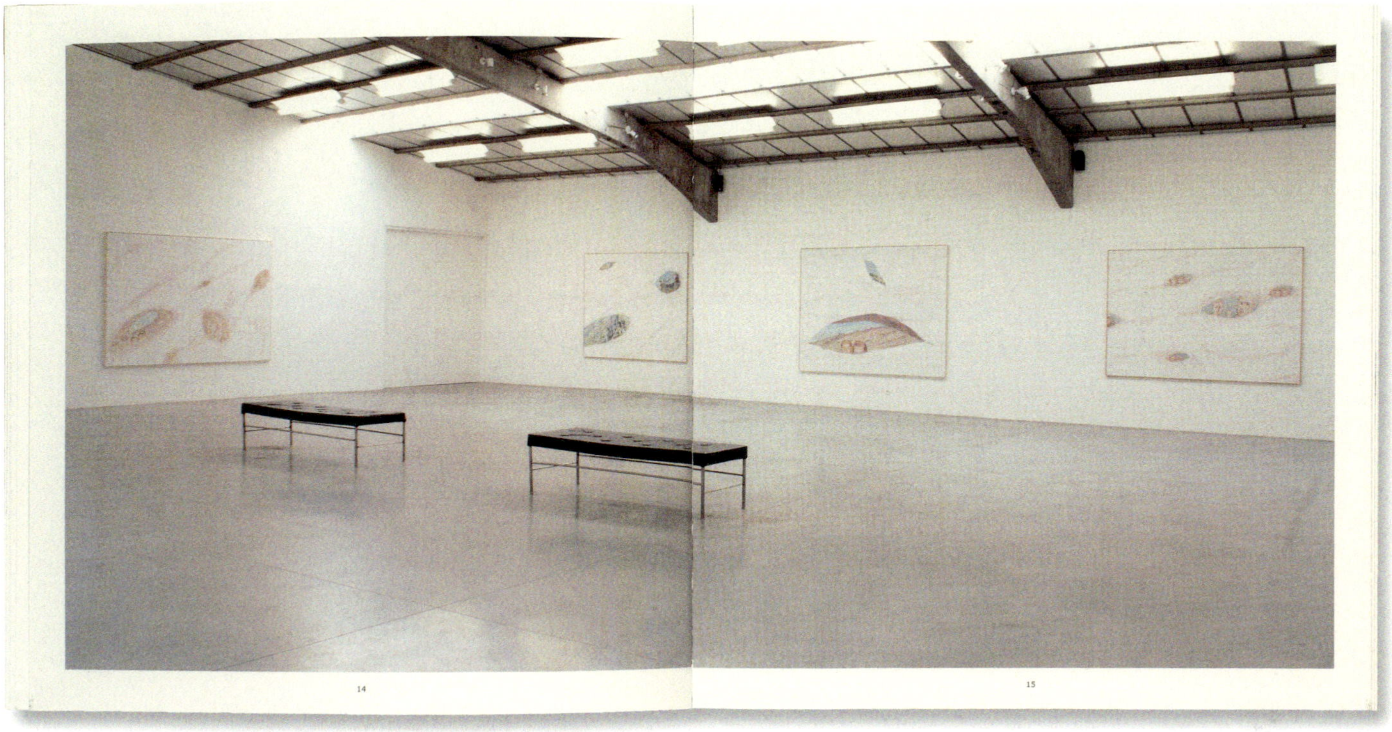

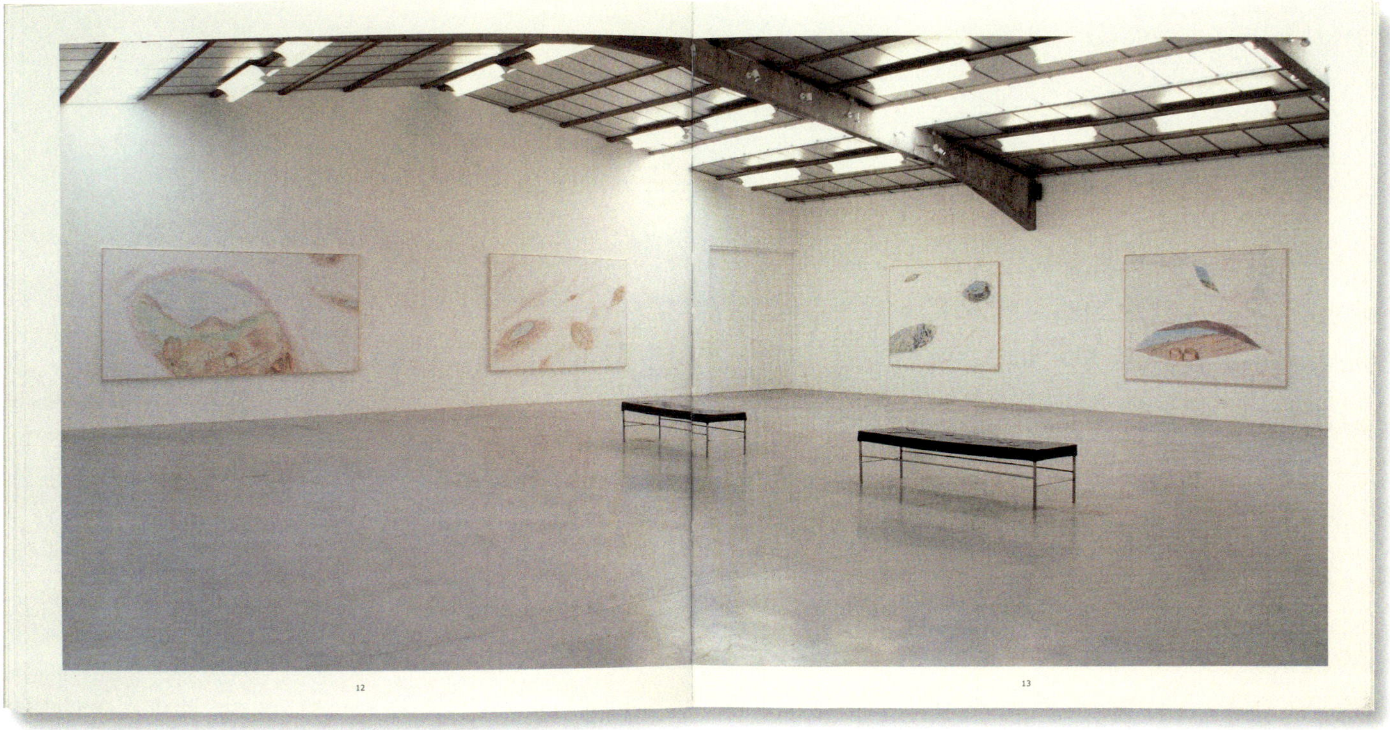

129 Orbis Pictus: Children's Book Illustrator as a Social Character

Orbis Pictus. Der Kinderbuchillustrator als sozialer Charakter

with Emilia Kabakov | *mit Emilia Kabakov*

2007

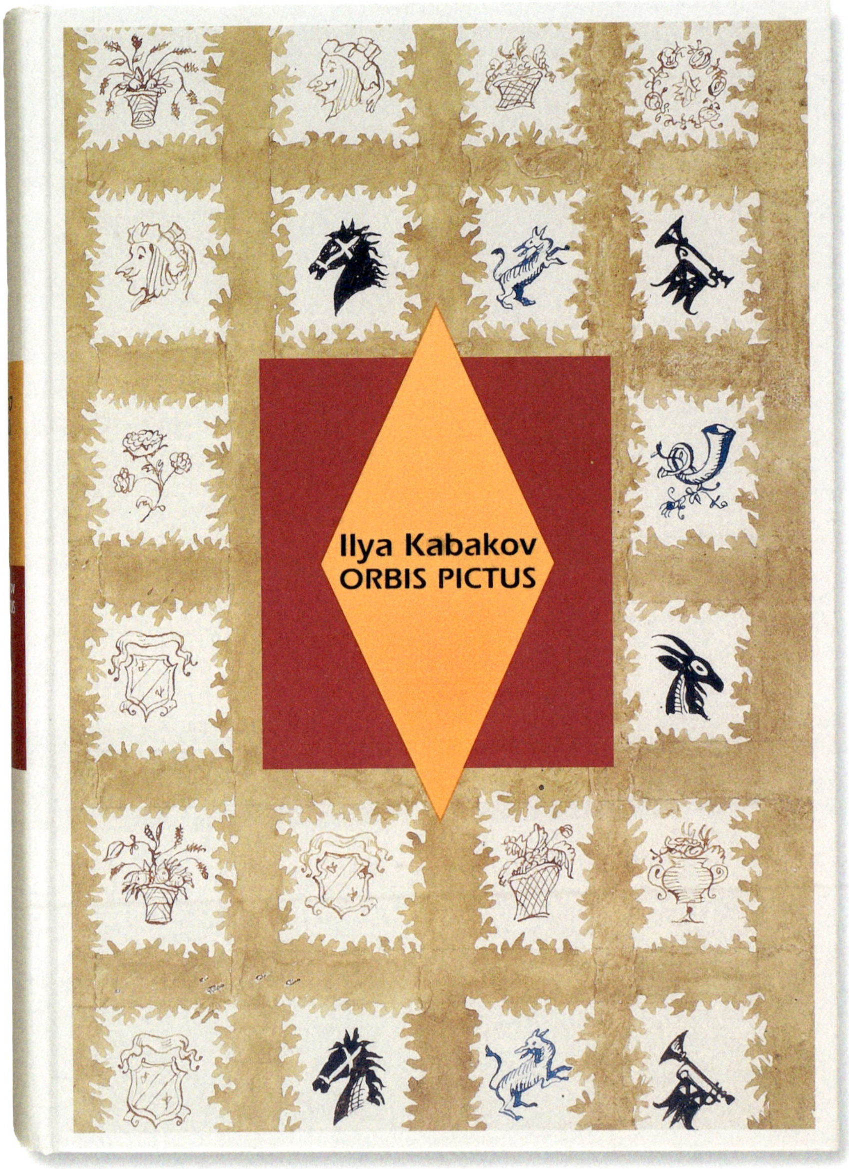

The Museum of Modern Art, Kamakura and Hayama; Hiroshima City Museum of Contemporary Art; The Setagaya Art Museum; Ashikaga Museum of Art; The Tokyo Shimbun; Wakana Kono
Tokyo: The Tokyo Shimbun
26.6 x 19.6 cm
455 pp. with 1,229 (935 color) ills.
stitchbound, hardcover, front and back fly leaf with illustrations by Ilya Kabakov
Fadenheftung, Hardcover, Vorsatz vorne und hinten mit Illustrationen von Ilya Kabakov

catalogue raisonné | *Werkverzeichnis*

layout by Ilya Kabakov | *Layout von Ilya Kabakov*

For the exhibitions of the same name in Japan, Museum of Modern Art, Hayama, September 15 to November 11, 2007; Hiroshima City Museum of Contemporary Art, Hiroshima, December 8, 2007 to January 27, 2008; Setagaya Art Museum, Tokyo, February 9 to April 6, 2008; and Ashikaga Museum of Art, Ashikaga, July 19 to September 14, 2008. Catalogue raisonné of the children's books illustrated by Kabakov between 1956 and 1989 and officially commissioned by the Soviet Union. Texts by Boris Groys, Ilya Kabakov, Wakana Kono, Tsutomu Mizusawa and Masao Momiyama; Japanese, English.

Zu den gleichnamigen Ausstellungen in Japan, Museum of Modern Art, Hayama, 15. September – 11. November 2007, Hiroshima City Museum of Contemporary Art, Hiroshima, 8. Dezember 2007 – 27. Januar 2008, Setagaya Art Museum, Tokyo, 9. Februar – 6. April 2008, und Ashikaga Museum of Art, Ashikaga, 19. Juli – 14. September 2008. Werkverzeichnis der von Kabakov im offiziellen Auftrag zwischen 1956 bis 1989 in der Sowjetunion illustrierten Kinderbücher. Texte von Boris Groys, Ilya Kabakov, Wakana Kono, Tsutomu Mizusawa und Masao Momiyama; japanisch, englisch.

see also | *siehe auch* CRP, vol. 2, nos. 524–535, pp. 268–273

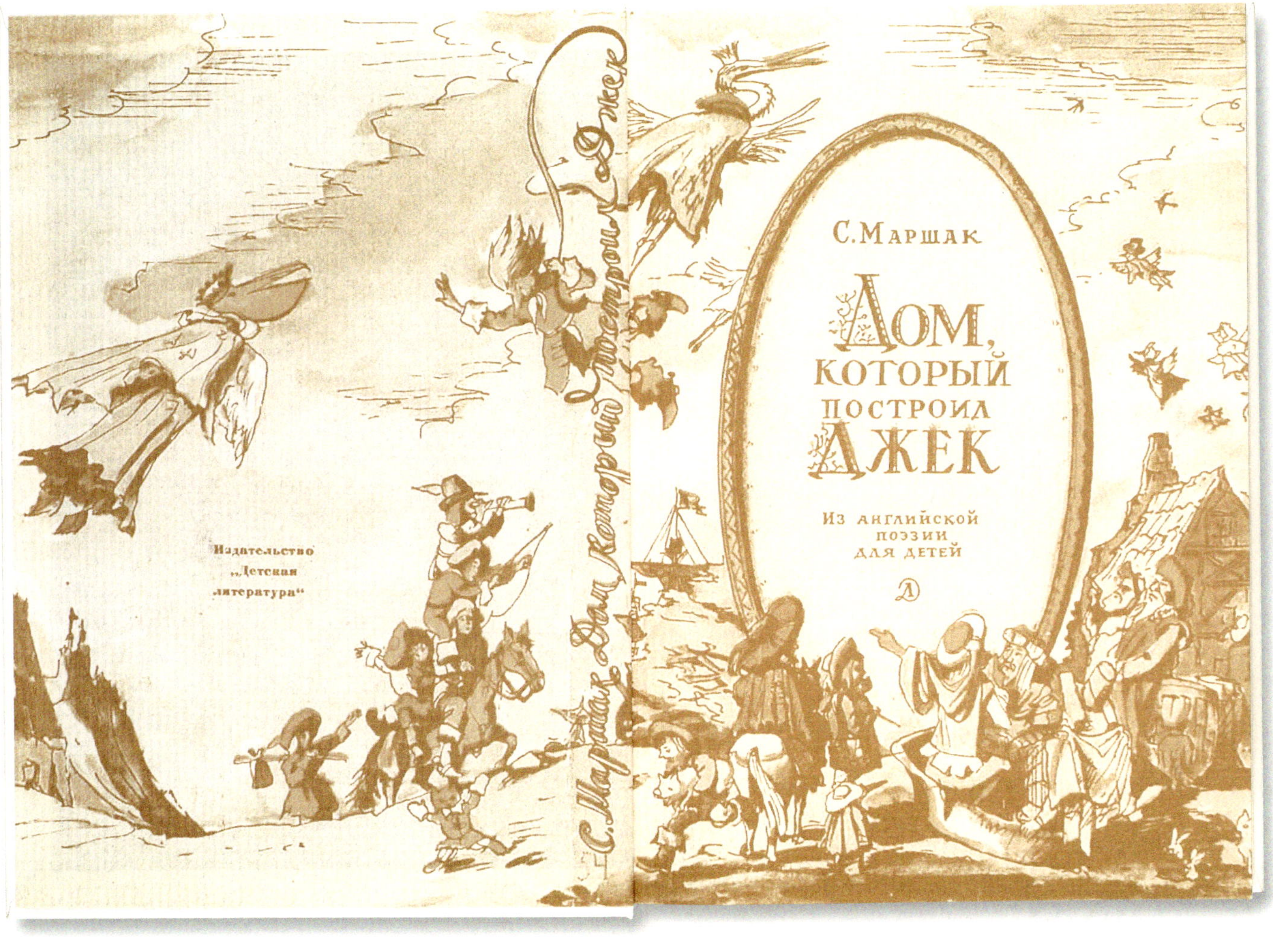
С. Маршак
Дом, который построил Джек
Из английской поэзии для детей
Издательство „Детская литература"
С. Маршак Дом, который построил Джек

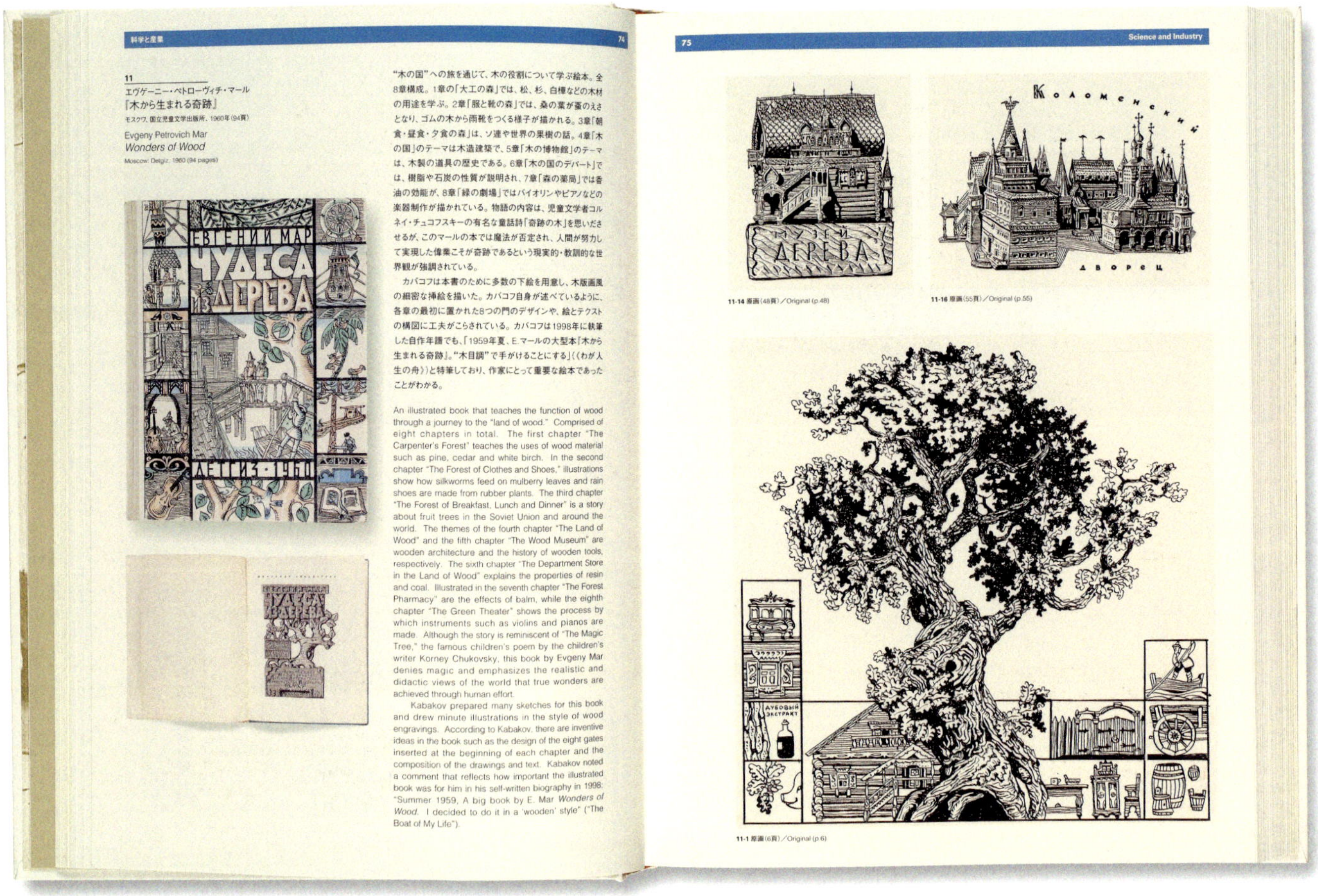

11

エヴゲーニー・ペトローヴィチ・マール
『木から生まれる奇跡』
モスクワ、国立児童文学出版所、1960年（94頁）

Evgeny Petrovich Mar
Wonders of Wood
Moscow: Detgiz, 1960 (94 pages)

"木の国"への旅を通じて、木の役割について学ぶ絵本。全8章構成。1章の「大工の森」では、松、杉、白樺などの木材の用途を学ぶ。2章「服と靴の森」では、桑の葉が蚕のえさとなり、ゴムの木から雨靴をつくる様子が描かれる。3章「朝食・昼食・夕食の森」は、ソ連や世界の果樹の話。4章「木の国」のテーマは木造建築で、5章「木の博物館」のテーマは、木製の道具の歴史である。6章「木の国のデパート」では、樹脂や石炭の性質が説明され、7章「森の薬局」では香油の効能が、8章「緑の劇場」ではバイオリンやピアノなどの楽器制作が描かれている。物語の内容は、児童文学者コルネイ・チュコフスキーの有名な童話詩「奇跡の木」を思いださせるが、このマールの本では魔法が否定され、人間が努力して実現した偉業こそが奇跡であるという現実的・教訓的な世界観が強調されている。

カバコフは本書のために多数の下絵を用意し、木版画風の細密な挿絵を描いた。カバコフ自身が述べているように、各章の最初に置かれた8つの門のデザインや、絵とテクストの構図に工夫がこらされている。カバコフは1998年に執筆した自作年譜でも、「1959年夏、E.マールの大型本『木から生まれる奇跡』。"木目調"で手がけることにする」（《わが人生の舟》）と特筆しており、作家にとって重要な絵本であったことがわかる。

An illustrated book that teaches the function of wood through a journey to the "land of wood." Comprised of eight chapters in total. The first chapter "The Carpenter's Forest" teaches the uses of wood material such as pine, cedar and white birch. In the second chapter "The Forest of Clothes and Shoes," illustrations show how silkworms feed on mulberry leaves and rain shoes are made from rubber plants. The third chapter "The Forest of Breakfast, Lunch and Dinner" is a story about fruit trees in the Soviet Union and around the world. The themes of the fourth chapter "The Land of Wood" and the fifth chapter "The Wood Museum" are wooden architecture and the history of wooden tools, respectively. The sixth chapter "The Department Store in the Land of Wood" explains the properties of resin and coal. Illustrated in the seventh chapter "The Forest Pharmacy" are the effects of balm, while the eighth chapter "The Green Theater" shows the process by which instruments such as violins and pianos are made. Although the story is reminiscent of "The Magic Tree," the famous children's poem by the children's writer Korney Chukovsky, this book by Evgeny Mar denies magic and emphasizes the realistic and didactic views of the world that true wonders are achieved through human effort.

Kabakov prepared many sketches for this book and drew minute illustrations in the style of wood engravings. According to Kabakov, there are inventive ideas in the book such as the design of the eight gates inserted at the beginning of each chapter and the composition of the drawings and text. Kabakov noted a comment that reflects how important the illustrated book was for him in his self-written biography in 1998: "Summer 1959, A big book by E. Mar *Wonders of Wood*. I decided to do it in a 'wooden' style" ("The Boat of My Life").

11-14 原画（48頁）／Original (p.48)

11-16 原画（55頁）／Original (p.55)

11-1 原画（6頁）／Original (p.6)

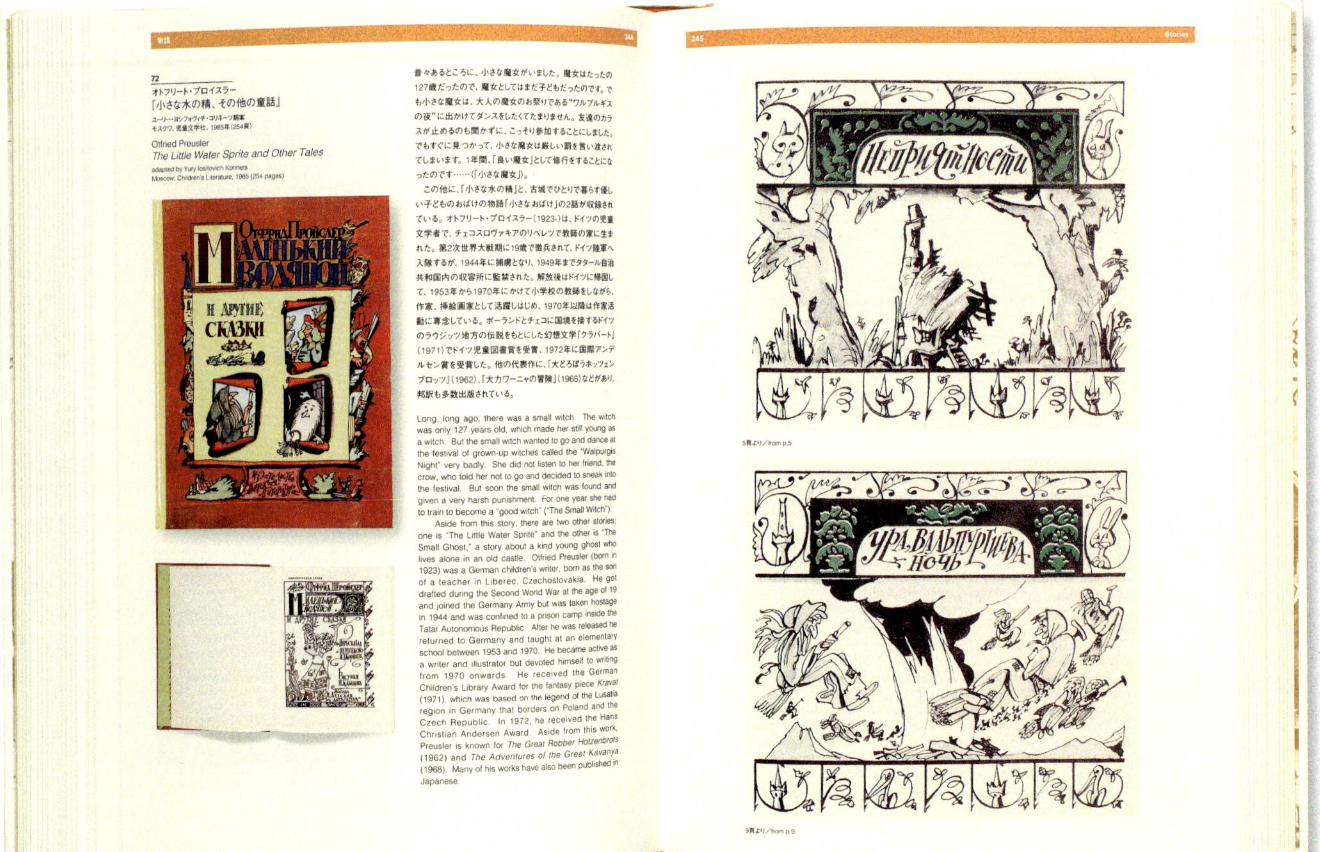

72

オトフリート・プロイスラー
『小さな水の精、その他の童話』
ユーリー・ヨシフォヴィチ・コリネーツ翻案
モスクワ、児童文学社、1985年（254頁）

Otfried Preusler
The Little Water Sprite and Other Tales
adapted by Yury Iosifovich Korinets
Moscow: Children's Literature, 1985 (254 pages)

昔々あるところに、小さな魔女がいました。魔女はたったの127歳だったので、魔女としてはまだ子どもだったのです。でも小さな魔女は、大人の魔女のお祭りである"ワルプルギスの夜"に出かけてダンスをしたくてたまりません。友達のカラスが止めるのも聞かずに、こっそり参加することにしました。でもすぐに見つかって、小さな魔女は厳しい罰を言い渡されてしまいます。1年間、「良い魔女」として修行をすることになったのです……（「小さな魔女」）。

この他に、「小さな水の精」と、古城でひとりで暮らす優しい子どものおばけの物語「小さなおばけ」の2話が収録されている。オトフリート・プロイスラー（1923-）は、ドイツの児童文学者で、チェコスロヴァキアのリベレツで教師の家に生まれた。第2次世界大戦期に19歳で徴兵されて、ドイツ陸軍へ入隊するが、1944年に捕虜となり、1949年までタタール自治共和国内の収容所に監禁された。解放後はドイツに帰国して、1953年から1970年にかけて小学校の教師をしながら、作家、挿絵画家として活躍しはじめ、1970年以降は作家活動に専念している。ポーランドとチェコに国境を接するドイツのラウジッツ地方の伝説をもとにした幻想文学「クラバート」（1971）でドイツ児童図書賞を受賞、1972年に国際アンデルセン賞を受賞した。他の代表作に、「大どろぼうホッツェンプロッツ」（1962）、「大力ワーニャの冒険」（1968）などがあり、邦訳も多数出版されている。

Long, long ago, there was a small witch. The witch was only 127 years old, which made her still young as a witch. But the small witch wanted to go and dance at the festival of grown-up witches called the "Walpurgis Night" very badly. She did not listen to her friend, the crow, who told her not to go and decided to sneak into the festival. But soon the small witch was found and given a very harsh punishment. For one year she had to train to become a "good witch" ("The Small Witch").

Aside from this story, there are two other stories; one is "The Little Water Sprite" and the other is "The Small Ghost," a story about a kind young ghost who lives alone in an old castle. Otfried Preusler (born in 1923) was a German children's writer, born as the son of a teacher in Liberec, Czechoslovakia. He got drafted during the Second World War at the age of 19 and joined the Germany Army but was taken hostage in 1944 and was confined to a prison camp inside the Tatar Autonomous Republic. After he was released he returned to Germany and taught at an elementary school between 1953 and 1970. He became active as a writer and illustrator but devoted himself to writing from 1970 onwards. He received the German Children's Library Award for the fantasy piece *Kravat* (1971), which was based on the legend of the Lusatia region in Germany that borders on Poland and the Czech Republic. In 1972, he received the Hans Christian Andersen Award. Aside from this work, Preusler is known for *The Great Robber Hotzenbrots* (1962) and *The Adventures of the Great Kavanya* (1968). Many of his works have also been published in Japanese.

5頁より／from p.5

9頁より／from p.9

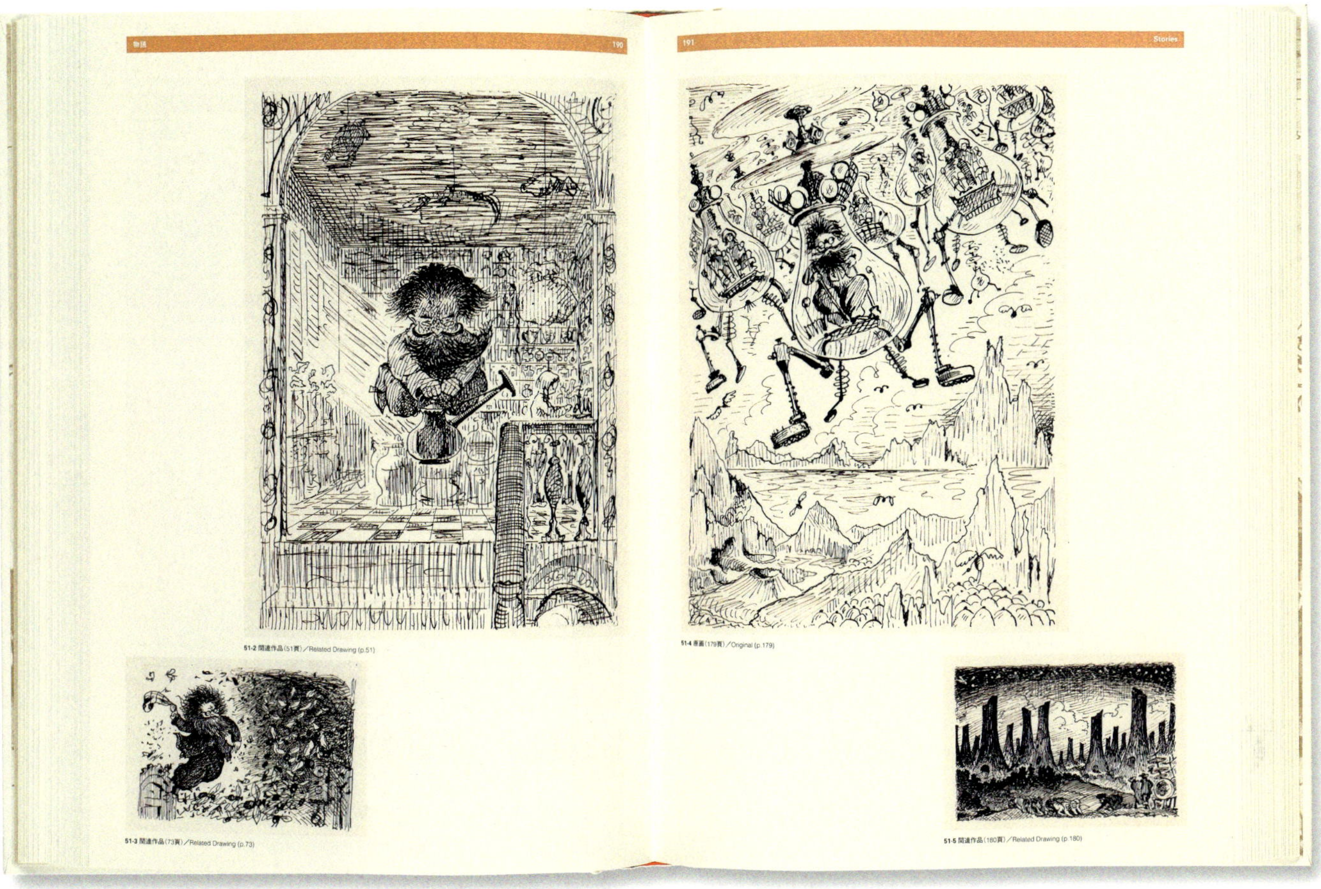
物語 190
191 Stories
51-2 関連作品(51頁)／Related Drawing (p.51)
51-3 関連作品(73頁)／Related Drawing (p.73)
51-4 原画(179頁)／Original (p.179)
51-5 関連作品(180頁)／Related Drawing (p.180)

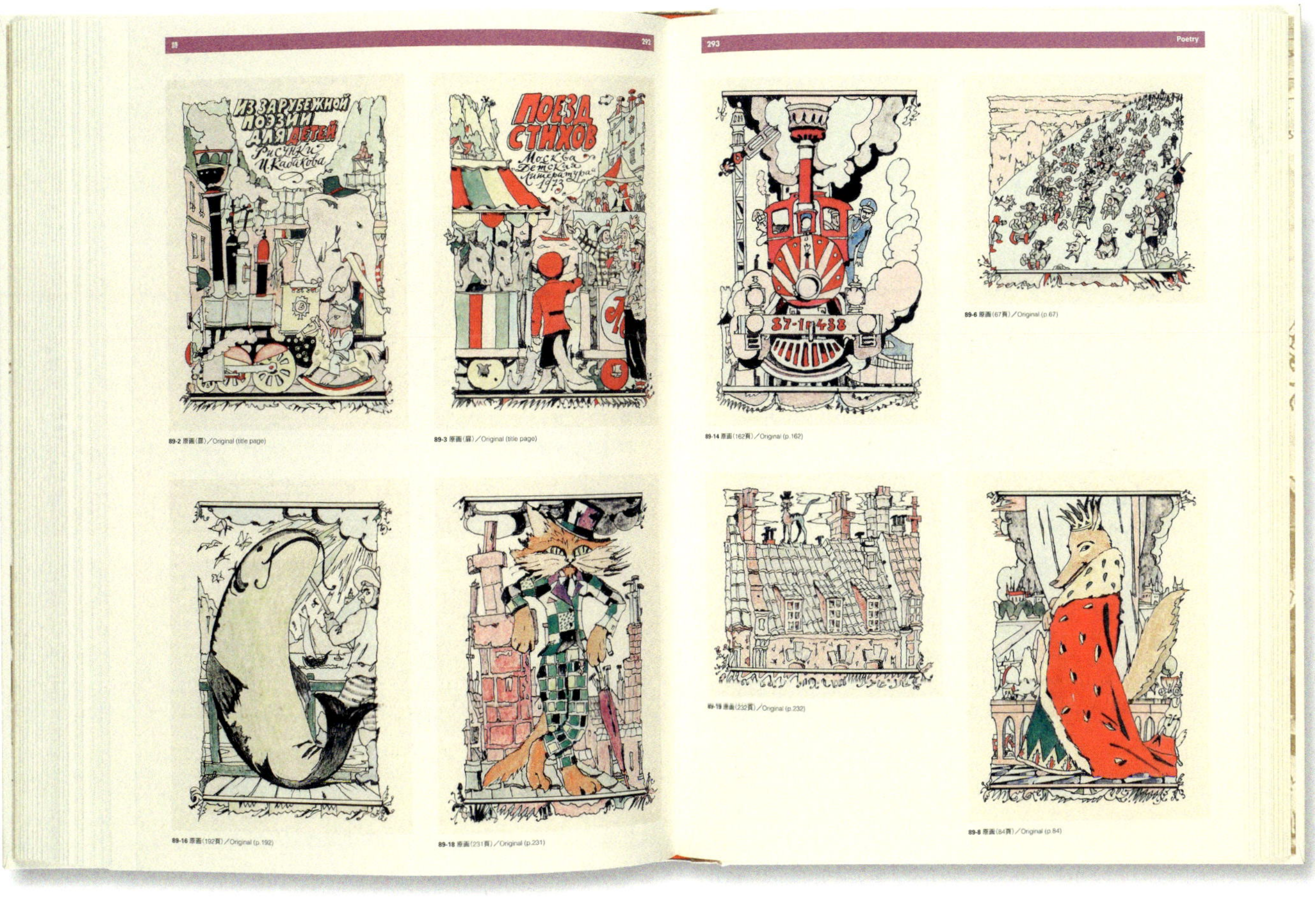
詩 292
293 Poetry
Из зарубежной поэзии для детей
Поезд стихов
89-2 原画(扉)／Original (title page)
89-3 原画(扉)／Original (title page)
89-14 原画(162頁)／Original (p.162)
89-6 原画(67頁)／Original (p.67)
89-16 原画(192頁)／Original (p.192)
89-18 原画(231頁)／Original (p.231)
89-19 原画(232頁)／Original (p.232)
89-8 原画(84頁)／Original (p.84)

130 Under the Snow | *Unter dem Schnee*

with Emilia Kabakov | *mit Emilia Kabakov*

2007

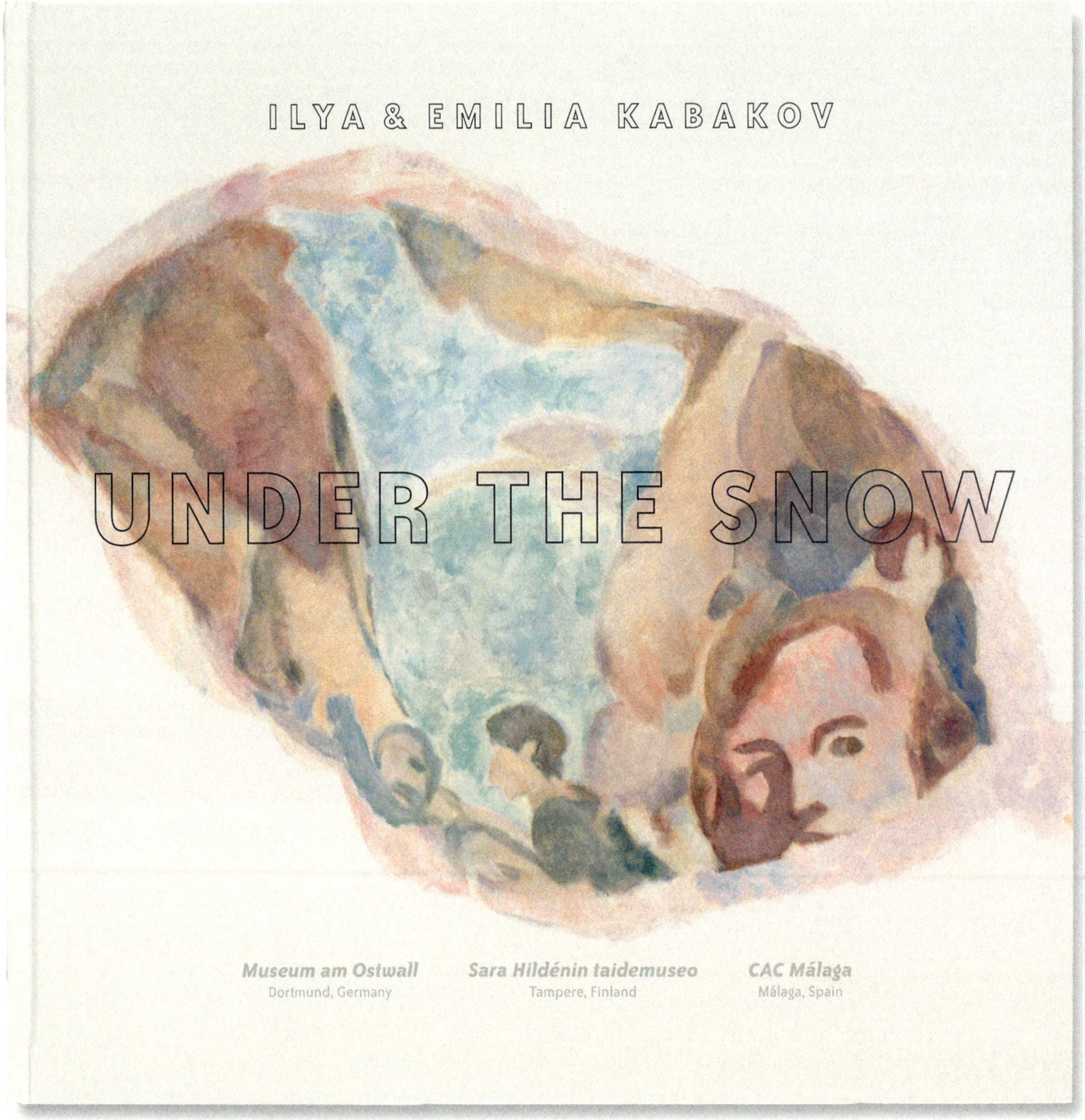

Fernando Francés, Riitta Valorinta, Kurt Wettengl
Cologne: Verlag der Buchhandlung Walther König
25.5 x 25.3 cm
100 pp. with 57 color ills.
stitchbound, hardcover
Fadenheftung, Hardcover

exhibition catalogue | *Ausstellungskatalog*

layout by Ilya Kabakov | *Layout von Ilya Kabakov*

For the exhibitions of the same name at the Museum am Ostwall, Dortmund, October 21, 2007 to January 27, 2008; Sara Hildén Art Museum, Tampere, Finland, February 15 to May 4, 2008; and Centro de Arte Contemporáneo, Málaga, November 7, 2008 to February 15, 2009. Texts by Ilya and Emilia Kabakov and Rod Mengham, and a dialogue between Boris Groys and Ilya Kabakov on »Works in the Snow«; German, English.

Zu den gleichnamigen Ausstellungen, Museum am Ostwall, Dortmund, 21. Oktober 2007 – 27. Januar 2008, Sara Hildén Art Museum, Tampere, Finnland, 15. Februar – 4. Mai 2008, und Centro de Arte Contemporáneo, Málaga, 7. November 2008 – 15. Februar 2009. Texte von Ilya und Emilia Kabakov, Rod Mengham und ein Dialog von Boris Groys und Ilya Kabakov über »Arbeiten im Schnee«; deutsch, englisch.

see also | *siehe auch* CRP, vol. 2, nos. 501–523, pp. 238–267

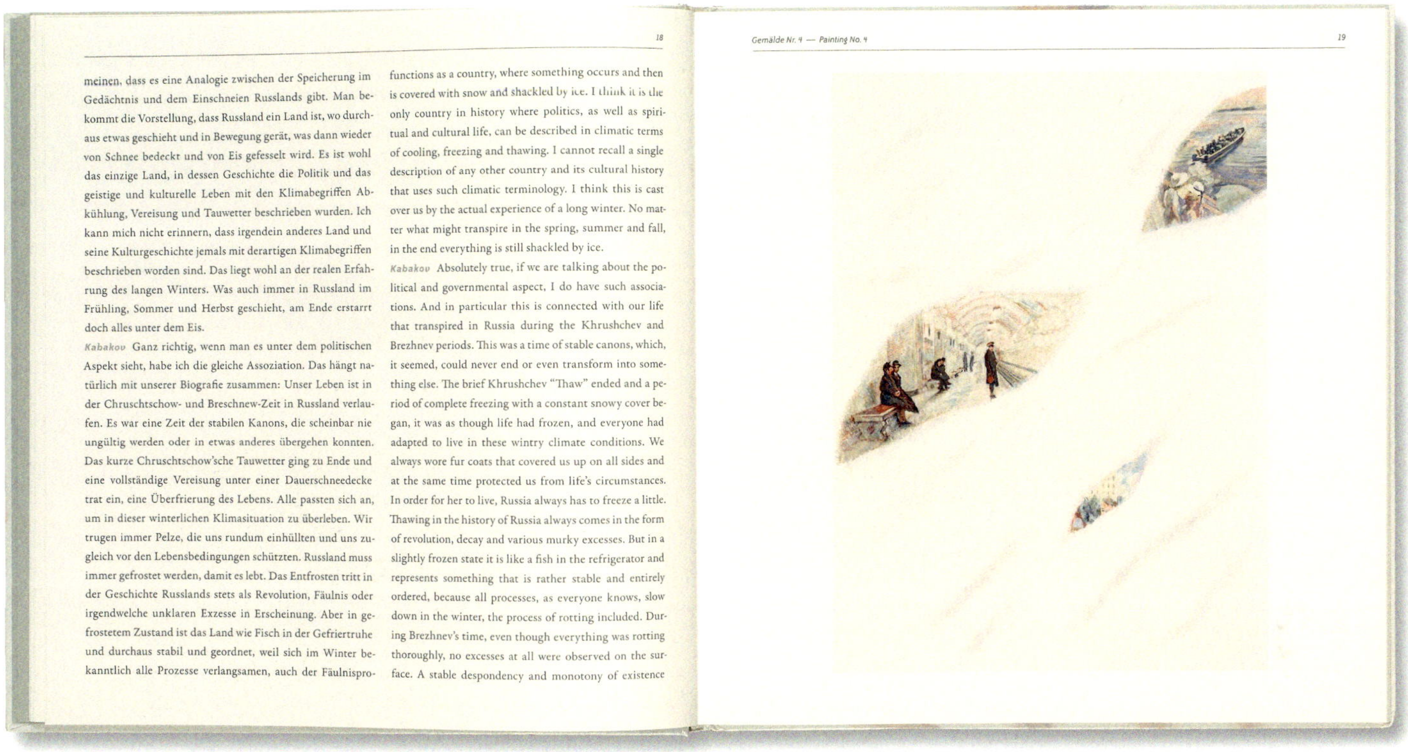

meinen, dass es eine Analogie zwischen der Speicherung im Gedächtnis und dem Einschneien Russlands gibt. Man bekommt die Vorstellung, dass Russland ein Land ist, wo durchaus etwas geschieht und in Bewegung gerät, was dann wieder von Schnee bedeckt und von Eis gefesselt wird. Es ist wohl das einzige Land, in dessen Geschichte die Politik und das geistige und kulturelle Leben mit den Klimabegriffen Abkühlung, Vereisung und Tauwetter beschrieben wurden. Ich kann mich nicht erinnern, dass irgendein anderes Land und seine Kulturgeschichte jemals mit derartigen Klimabegriffen beschrieben worden sind. Das liegt wohl an der realen Erfahrung des langen Winters. Was auch immer in Russland im Frühling, Sommer und Herbst geschieht, am Ende erstarrt doch alles unter dem Eis.

Kabakov Ganz richtig, wenn man es unter dem politischen Aspekt sieht, habe ich die gleiche Assoziation. Das hängt natürlich mit unserer Biografie zusammen: Unser Leben ist in der Chruschtschow- und Breschnew-Zeit in Russland verlaufen. Es war eine Zeit der stabilen Kanons, die scheinbar nie ungültig werden oder in etwas anderes übergehen konnten. Das kurze Chruschtschow'sche Tauwetter ging zu Ende und eine vollständige Vereisung unter einer Dauerschneedecke trat ein, eine Überfrierung des Lebens. Alle passten sich an, um in dieser winterlichen Klimasituation zu überleben. Wir trugen immer Pelze, die uns rundum einhüllten und uns zugleich vor den Lebensbedingungen schützten. Russland muss immer gefrostet werden, damit es lebt. Das Entfrosten tritt in der Geschichte Russlands stets als Revolution, Fäulnis oder irgendwelche unklaren Exzesse in Erscheinung. Aber in gefrostetem Zustand ist das Land wie Fisch in der Gefriertruhe und durchaus stabil und geordnet, weil sich im Winter bekanntlich alle Prozesse verlangsamen, auch der Fäulnispro-

functions as a country, where something occurs and then is covered with snow and shackled by ice. I think it is the only country in history where politics, as well as spiritual and cultural life, can be described in climatic terms of cooling, freezing and thawing. I cannot recall a single description of any other country and its cultural history that uses such climatic terminology. I think this is cast over us by the actual experience of a long winter. No matter what might transpire in the spring, summer and fall, in the end everything is still shackled by ice.

Kabakov Absolutely true, if we are talking about the political and governmental aspect, I do have such associations. And in particular this is connected with our life that transpired in Russia during the Khrushchev and Brezhnev periods. This was a time of stable canons, which, it seemed, could never end or even transform into something else. The brief Khrushchev "Thaw" ended and a period of complete freezing with a constant snowy cover began, it was as though life had frozen, and everyone had adapted to live in these wintry climate conditions. We always wore fur coats that covered us up on all sides and at the same time protected us from life's circumstances. In order for her to live, Russia always has to freeze a little. Thawing in the history of Russia always comes in the form of revolution, decay and various murky excesses. But in a slightly frozen state it is like a fish in the refrigerator and represents something that is rather stable and entirely ordered, because all processes, as everyone knows, slow down in the winter, the process of rotting included. During Brezhnev's time, even though everything was rotting thoroughly, no excesses at all were observed on the surface. A stable despondency and monotony of existence

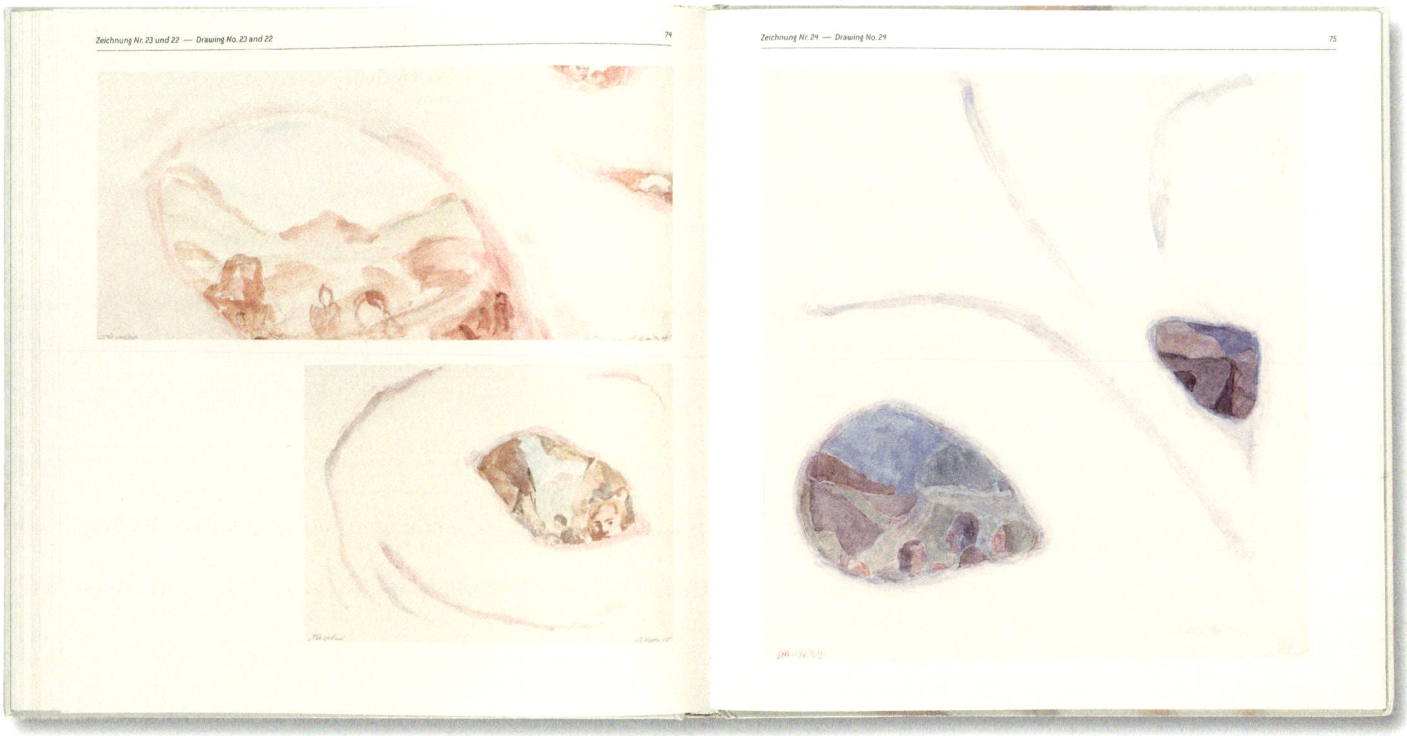

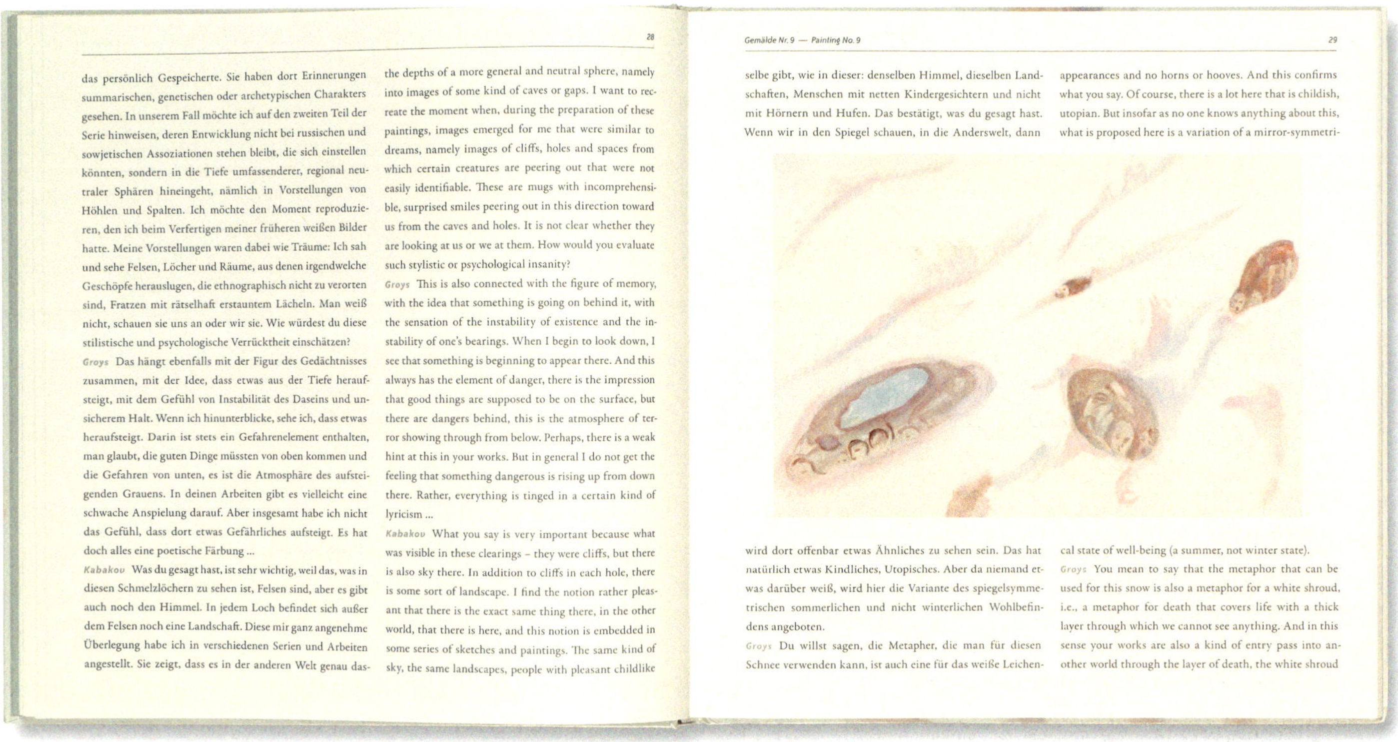

das persönlich Gespeicherte. Sie haben dort Erinnerungen summarischen, genetischen oder archetypischen Charakters gesehen. In unserem Fall möchte ich auf den zweiten Teil der Serie hinweisen, deren Entwicklung nicht bei russischen und sowjetischen Assoziationen stehen bleibt, die sich einstellen könnten, sondern in die Tiefe umfassenderer, regional neutraler Sphären hineingeht, nämlich in Vorstellungen von Höhlen und Spalten. Ich möchte den Moment reproduzieren, den ich beim Verfertigen meiner früheren weißen Bilder hatte. Meine Vorstellungen waren dabei wie Träume: Ich sah und sehe Felsen, Löcher und Räume, aus denen irgendwelche Geschöpfe herauslugen, die ethnographisch nicht zu verorten sind, Fratzen mit rätselhaft erstauntem Lächeln. Man weiß nicht, schauen sie uns an oder wir sie. Wie würdest du diese stilistische und psychologische Verrücktheit einschätzen?

Groys Das hängt ebenfalls mit der Figur des Gedächtnisses zusammen, mit der Idee, dass etwas aus der Tiefe heraufsteigt, mit dem Gefühl von Instabilität des Daseins und unsicherem Halt. Wenn ich hinunterblicke, sehe ich, dass etwas heraufsteigt. Darin ist stets ein Gefahrenelement enthalten, man glaubt, die guten Dinge müssten von oben kommen und die Gefahren von unten, es ist die Atmosphäre des aufsteigenden Grauens. In deinen Arbeiten gibt es vielleicht eine schwache Anspielung darauf. Aber insgesamt habe ich nicht das Gefühl, dass dort etwas Gefährliches aufsteigt. Es hat doch alles eine poetische Färbung ...

Kabakov Was du gesagt hast, ist sehr wichtig, weil das, was in diesen Schmelzlöchern zu sehen ist, Felsen sind, aber es gibt auch noch den Himmel. In jedem Loch befindet sich außer dem Felsen noch eine Landschaft. Diese mir ganz angenehme Überlegung habe ich in verschiedenen Serien und Arbeiten angestellt. Sie zeigt, dass es in der anderen Welt genau das-

the depths of a more general and neutral sphere, namely into images of some kind of caves or gaps. I want to recreate the moment when, during the preparation of these paintings, images emerged for me that were similar to dreams, namely images of cliffs, holes and spaces from which certain creatures are peering out that were not easily identifiable. These are mugs with incomprehensible, surprised smiles peering out in this direction toward us from the caves and holes. It is not clear whether they are looking at us or we at them. How would you evaluate such stylistic or psychological insanity?

Groys This is also connected with the figure of memory, with the idea that something is going on behind it, with the sensation of the instability of existence and the instability of one's bearings. When I begin to look down, I see that something is beginning to appear there. And this always has the element of danger, there is the impression that good things are supposed to be on the surface, but there are dangers behind, this is the atmosphere of terror showing through from below. Perhaps, there is a weak hint at this in your works. But in general I do not get the feeling that something dangerous is rising up from down there. Rather, everything is tinged in a certain kind of lyricism ...

Kabakov What you say is very important because what was visible in these clearings – they were cliffs, but there is also sky there. In addition to cliffs in each hole, there is some sort of landscape. I find the notion rather pleasant that there is the exact same thing there, in the other world, that there is here, and this notion is embedded in some series of sketches and paintings. The same kind of sky, the same landscapes, people with pleasant childlike

selbe gibt, wie in dieser: denselben Himmel, dieselben Landschaften, Menschen mit netten Kindergesichtern und nicht mit Hörnern und Hufen. Das bestätigt, was du gesagt hast. Wenn wir in den Spiegel schauen, in die Anderswelt, dann wird dort offenbar etwas Ähnliches zu sehen sein. Das hat natürlich etwas Kindliches, Utopisches. Aber da niemand etwas darüber weiß, wird hier die Variante des spiegelsymmetrischen sommerlichen und nicht winterlichen Wohlbefindens angeboten.

Groys Du willst sagen, die Metapher, die man für diesen Schnee verwenden kann, ist auch eine für das weiße Leichen-

appearances and no horns or hooves. And this confirms what you say. Of course, there is a lot here that is childish, utopian. But insofar as no one knows anything about this, what is proposed here is a variation of a mirror-symmetrical state of well-being (a summer, not winter state).

Groys You mean to say that the metaphor that can be used for this snow is also a metaphor for a white shroud, i.e., a metaphor for death that covers life with a thick layer through which we cannot see anything. And in this sense your works are also a kind of entry pass into another world through the layer of death, the white shroud

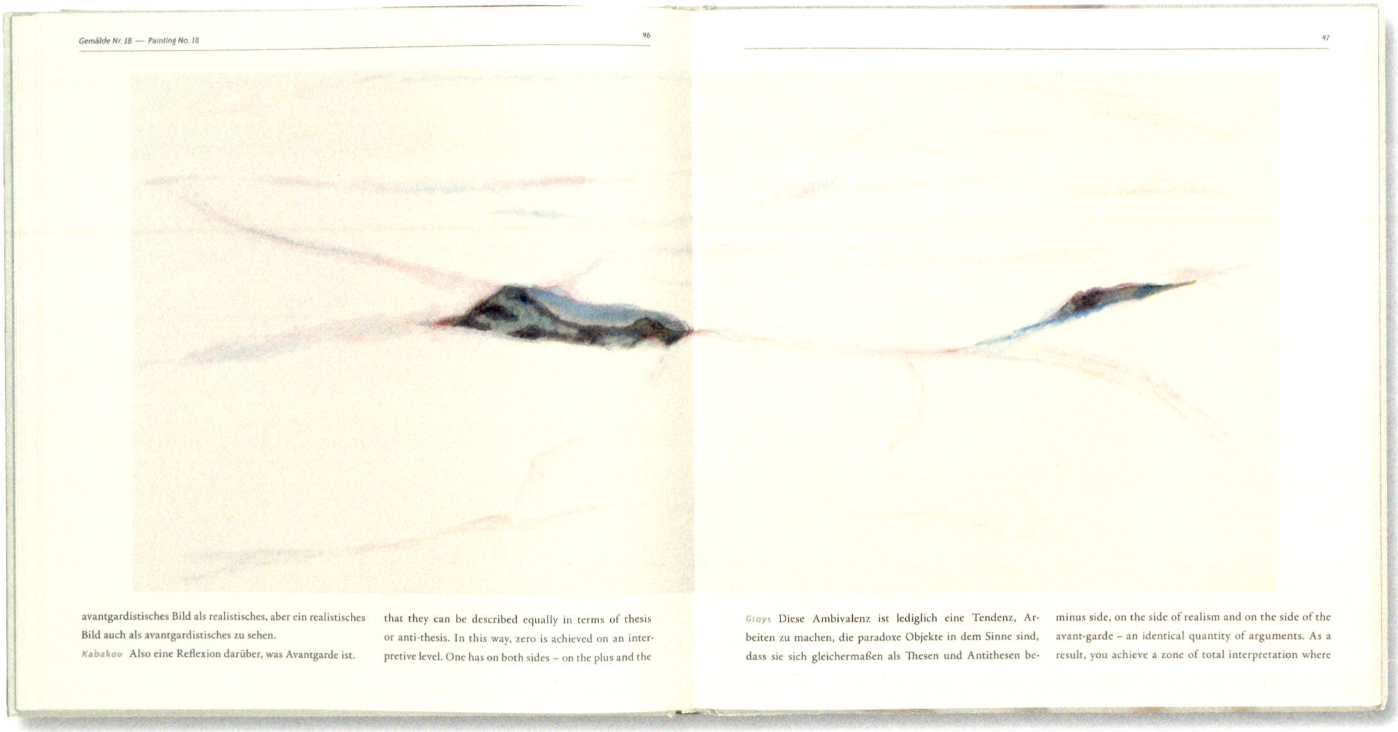

avantgardistisches Bild als realistisches, aber ein realistisches Bild auch als avantgardistisches zu sehen.

Kabakov Also eine Reflexion darüber, was Avantgarde ist.

that they can be described equally in terms of thesis or anti-thesis. In this way, zero is achieved on an interpretive level. One has on both sides – on the plus and the

Groys Diese Ambivalenz ist lediglich eine Tendenz, Arbeiten zu machen, die paradoxe Objekte in dem Sinne sind, dass sie sich gleichermaßen als Thesen und Antithesen be-

minus side, on the side of realism and on the side of the avant-garde – an identical quantity of arguments. As a result, you achieve a zone of total interpretation where

131 The Sixties and the Seventies: Notes About Unofficial Life in Moscow

Die 60er und 70er Jahre. Aufzeichnungen über das inoffizielle Leben in Moskau

2007

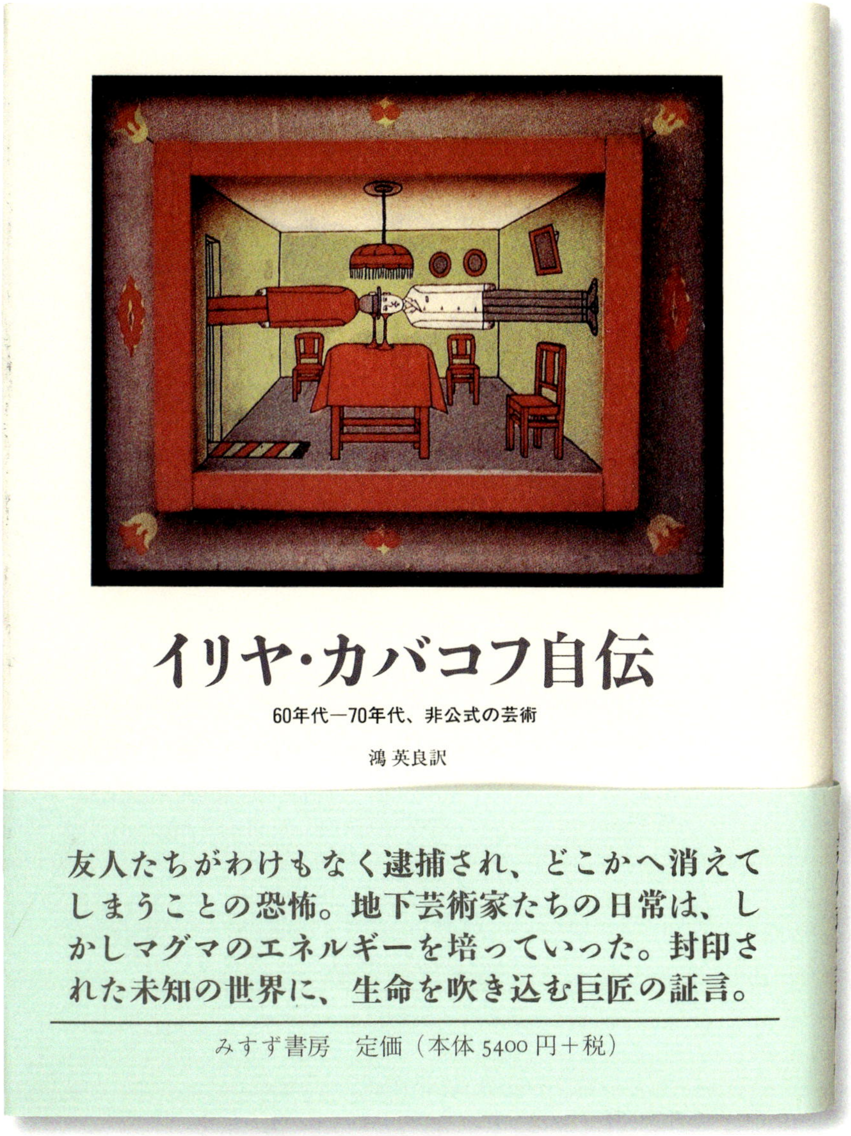

Ilya Kabakov
Tokyo: Misuzu Shobo
20.6 x 15.8 cm
395 pp. with 20 (11 color) ills.
adhesive binding, clothbound with dust jacket
Klebebindung, Leinen mit Schutzumschlag

thematic publication | *thematische Publikation*

Ilya Kabakov depicts his own artistic development within the context of the unofficial art scene in Moscow in the 1960s and 1970s. The first edition was published in Russian in 1999. Texts by Erik Bulatov, Boris Groys, Ilya Kabakov, and Oleg Vassilyev; Japanese.

Ilya Kabakov schildert den eigenen künstlerischen Werdegang im Kontext der inoffiziellen Kunst in Moskau in den 1960er- und 1970er-Jahren. Die Erstausgabe erschien russisch 1999. Texte von Erik Bulatov, Boris Groys, Ilya Kabakov und Oleg Wassiljew; japanisch.

see also | *siehe auch* no. 14; no. 107; no. 116; no. 136

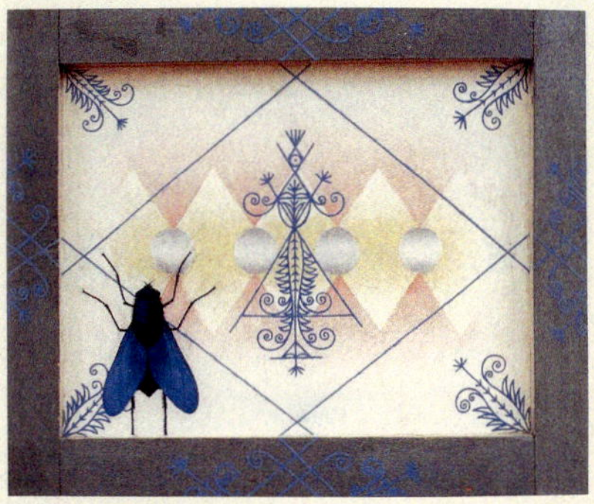

女王＝ハエ　1965年　ベニヤにエナメル　56×70cm　個人蔵（スイス）

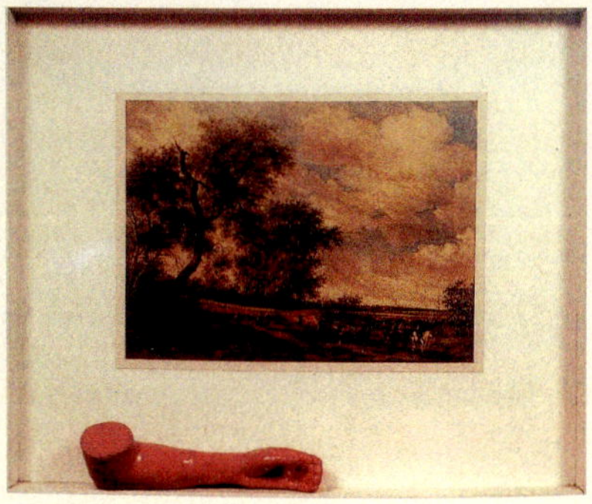

手とロイスダールの複製　1965年　オルガリート（厚手の丈夫な紙板）、紙、白いエナメル　100×120 cm

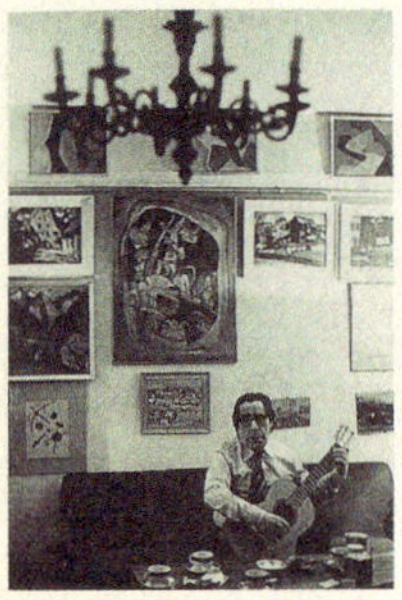

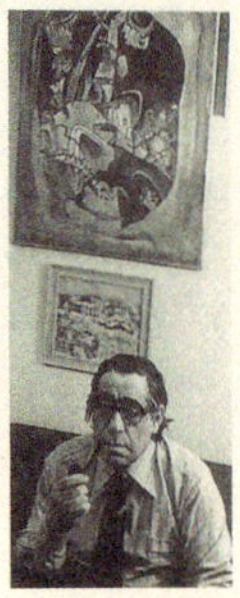

コスタキのスナップ

この写真は、1996年のカバコフのインスタレーション『屋根の上で』（デュッセルドルフ）の一角に展示され、そこには次のようなメモが添えられていた。

「われわれは著名なコレクター、ゲオルギー・コスタキの部屋に、頻繁に、たぶん週に一度ぐらい出かけていき、彼の巨大な部屋の壁に掛かっていたカンディンスキーやマレーヴィチ、ポポーワなどの、20年代のロシア・アヴァンギャルドの絵画を見た。それはソヴィエトの美術館にあったものとはまったくちがった絵だった。ゲオルギー・デオニーソヴィチ［コスタキ］のところの夕べの催しは、夕食とギターをもったコスタキの歌うロシア・ロマンスの歌唱で終わった。彼がロシアに住んでいる〈外国人〉だというのも素敵なことだった」（カバコフ）

なお、ギターを弾いているのがコスタキ本人であり、その背後の壁に飾られているのは『赤いエッジ』（中央、1919年）『抽象』（左下、1920－21年）『ムルナウ』（左上および右上、1908年）『冬の日、スモレンスク・ブリヴァール、モスクワ』（中央下、1919年）などカンディンスキーの絵画、さらに上方にはエンデルの『抽象』（1920年）『無題』（1920年）左手中央にヤヴレンスキーの『山の中の家』（1908年）などが見える。

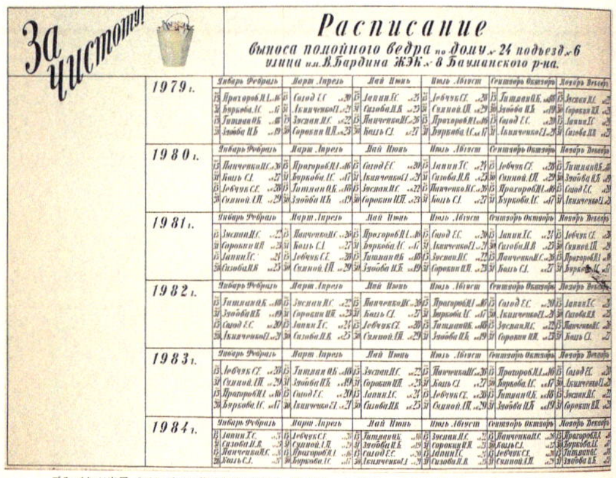

ごみバケツ当番（ごみバケツ搬出担当者氏名一覧表）　1980年　メゾナイトにエナメル　150×210 cm

左上隅に「整理整頓！」の標語がみえる。

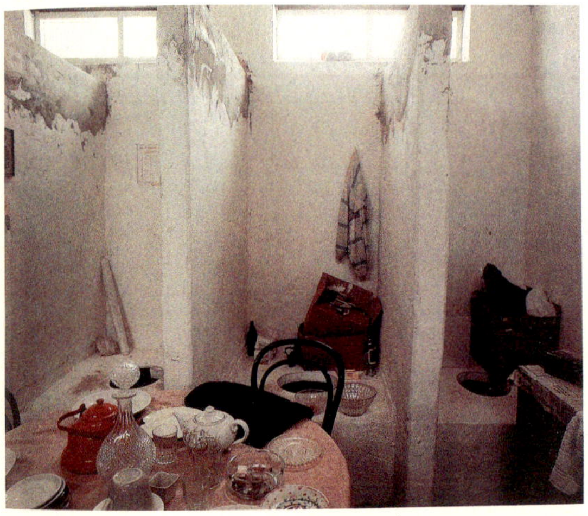

トイレ（インスタレーション、部分）　1992年

カバコフによれば、これは1960年代、70年代に、ロシアの駅やバス停の近くにつくられていた公衆便所のほとんど正確な再現である。ところが、なかに入るとそこはまったく違う世界。典型的なソヴィエトの二部屋アパートなのだ。このトイレはドクメンタ7のときに、カッセルの宮殿フリーデリヒアヌムの裏庭につくられた。正面にはボロフスキーの作品がファルスのように空にそびえていた。アメリカはつねに先端にあり、ロシアは後方にある。しかも、トイレである。それゆえ、カバコフは、ドクメンタは世界の覇権地図を象徴的に語ることになったと結論づけるのである。

132 An Alternative History of Art | *Eine Alternative Geschichte der Kunst*

with Emilia Kabakov | *mit Emilia Kabakov*

2008

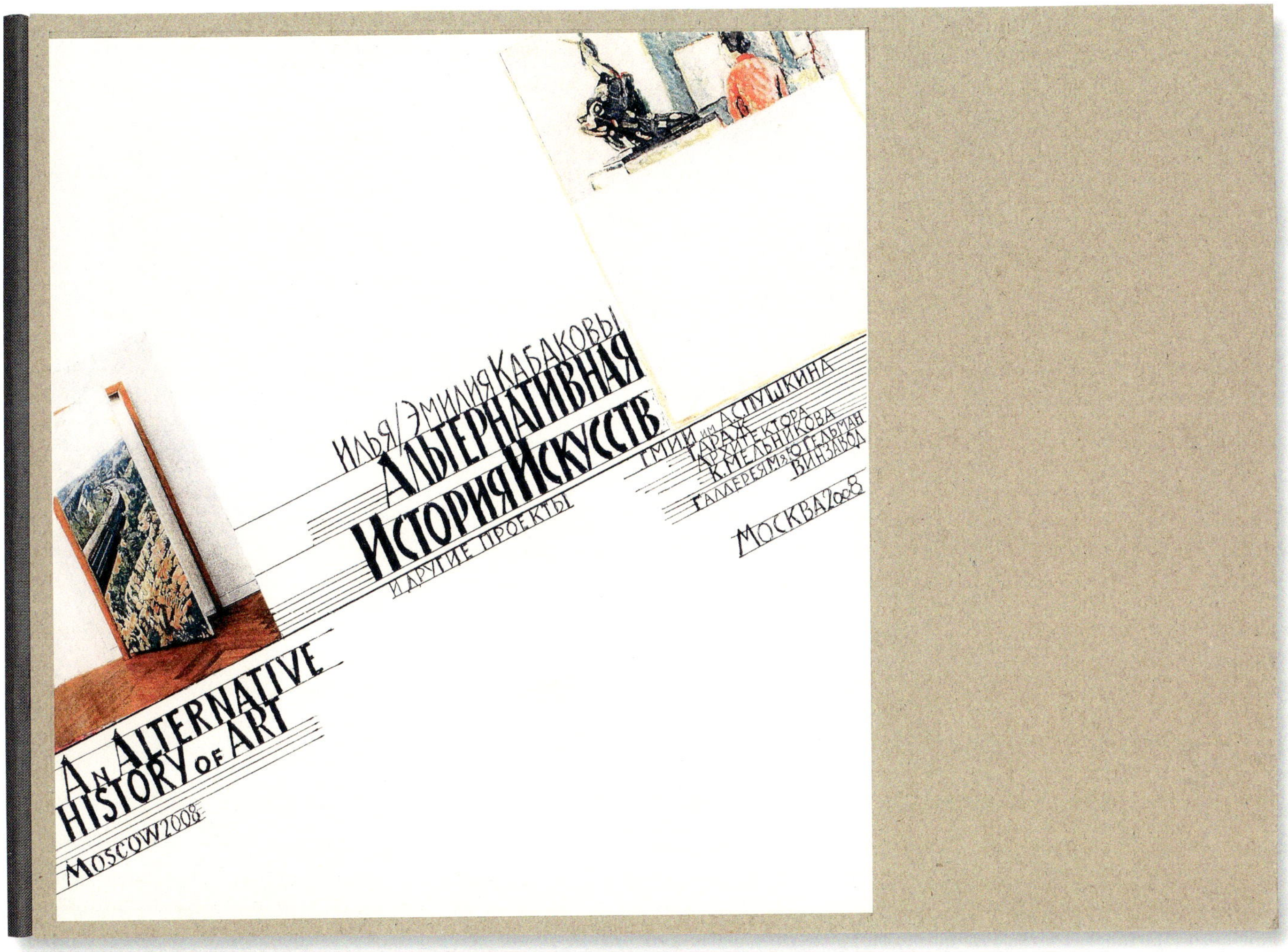

Ilya and Emilia Kabakov
Bielefeld: Kerber Verlag
24 x 34 cm
256 pp. with 288 (273 color) ills.
stitchbound, quarter cloth binding, blind blocking with label
Fadenheftung, Halbleinen, Blindprägung mit Etikette

exhibition catalogue | *Ausstellungskatalog*

layout by Ilya Kabakov | *Layout von Ilya Kabakov*

For the series of exhibitions »Ilya and Emilia Kabakov: Moscow Retrospective«, Moscow, September 15 to October 15, 2008. Documentation of the installation of the same name in The Garage, The Garage Center for Contemporary Culture Moscow. The catalogue that Kabakov designed covers the works and biographies of the three fictitious artists Charles Rosenthal, Ilya Kabakov, and Igor Spivak. Texts by Boris Groys, Ilya and Emilia Kabakov, and a dialogue between Boris Groys and Ilya Kabakov; Russian.

Zur Ausstellungsreihe »Ilya und Emilia Kabakov. Moskauer Retrospektive«, Moskau, 15. September – 15. Oktober 2008. Dokumentation der gleichnamigen Installation in The Garage, The Garage Center for Contemporary Culture Moscow. Der von Kabakov konzipierte Katalog umfasst Werk und Biografie der drei fiktiven Künstler Charles Rosenthal, Ilya Kabakov und Igor Spivak. Texte von Boris Groys, Ilya und Emilia Kabakov und ein Dialog von Boris Groys und Ilya Kabakov; russisch.

see also | *siehe auch* no. 106; no. 125; CRP, vol. 2, nos. 304–320, pp. 21–39, nos. 323–324, pp. 42–43, nos. 326–335, pp. 45–54, nos. 337–349, pp. 56–72, nos. 351–373, pp. 74–91, nos. 403–438, pp. 123–161, nos. 459–482, pp. 192–219, no. 617, p. 358

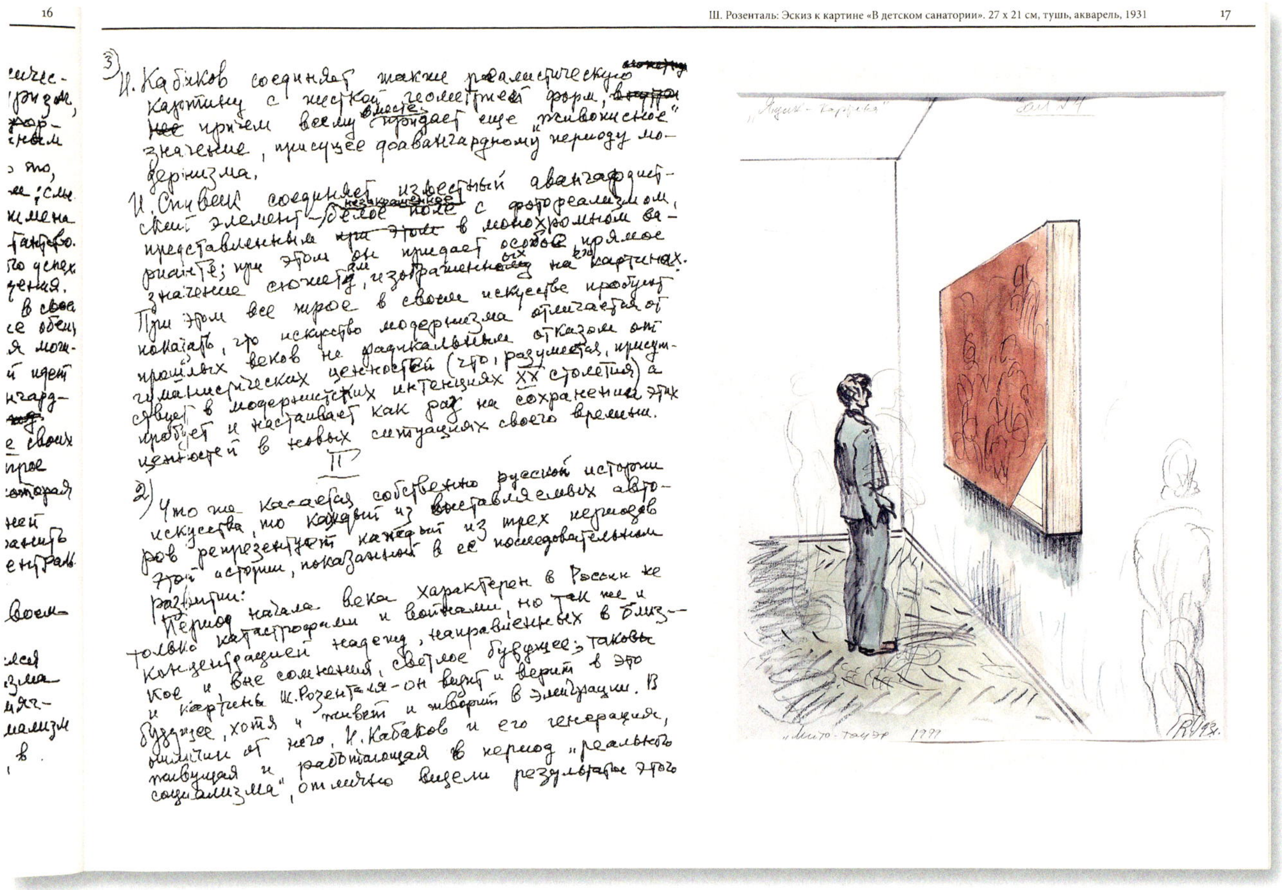

3) И. Кабаков соединяет также реалистическую
картину с жесткой геометрией форм,
причем всему вместе придает еще „живописное"
значение, присущее доавангардному периоду мо-
дернизма.
И. Спивак соединяет известный авангардист-
ский элемент – незакрашенное поле с фотореализмом,
представленным в монохромном ва-
рианте; при этом он придает особое, прямое
значение сюжетам, изображенным на его картинах.
При этом все трое в своем искусстве пробуют
показать, что искусство модернизма отличается от
прошлых веков не радикальным отказом от
гуманистических ценностей (что, разумеется, присут-
ствует в модернистских интенциях XX столетия) а
требует и настаивает как раз на сохранении этих
ценностей в новых ситуациях своего времени.

II

2) Что же касается собственно русской истории
искусства, то каждый из выставляемых авто-
ров репрезентует каждый из трех периодов
этой истории, показанной в ее последовательном
развитии:
Период начала века характерен в России не
только катастрофами и войнами, но так же и
концентрацией надежд, направленных в близ-
кое и вне сомнений светлое будущее; таковы
и картины Ш. Розенталя – он видит и верит в это
будущее, хотя и живет и творит в эмиграции. В
отличии от него, И. Кабаков и его генерация,
живущая и работающая в период „реального
социализма", отлично видели результаты этого

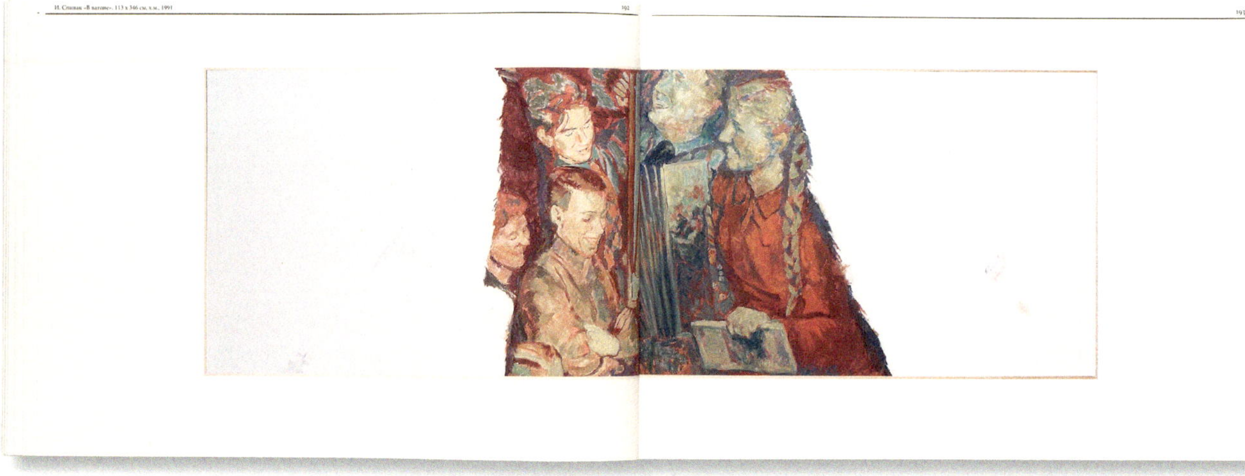

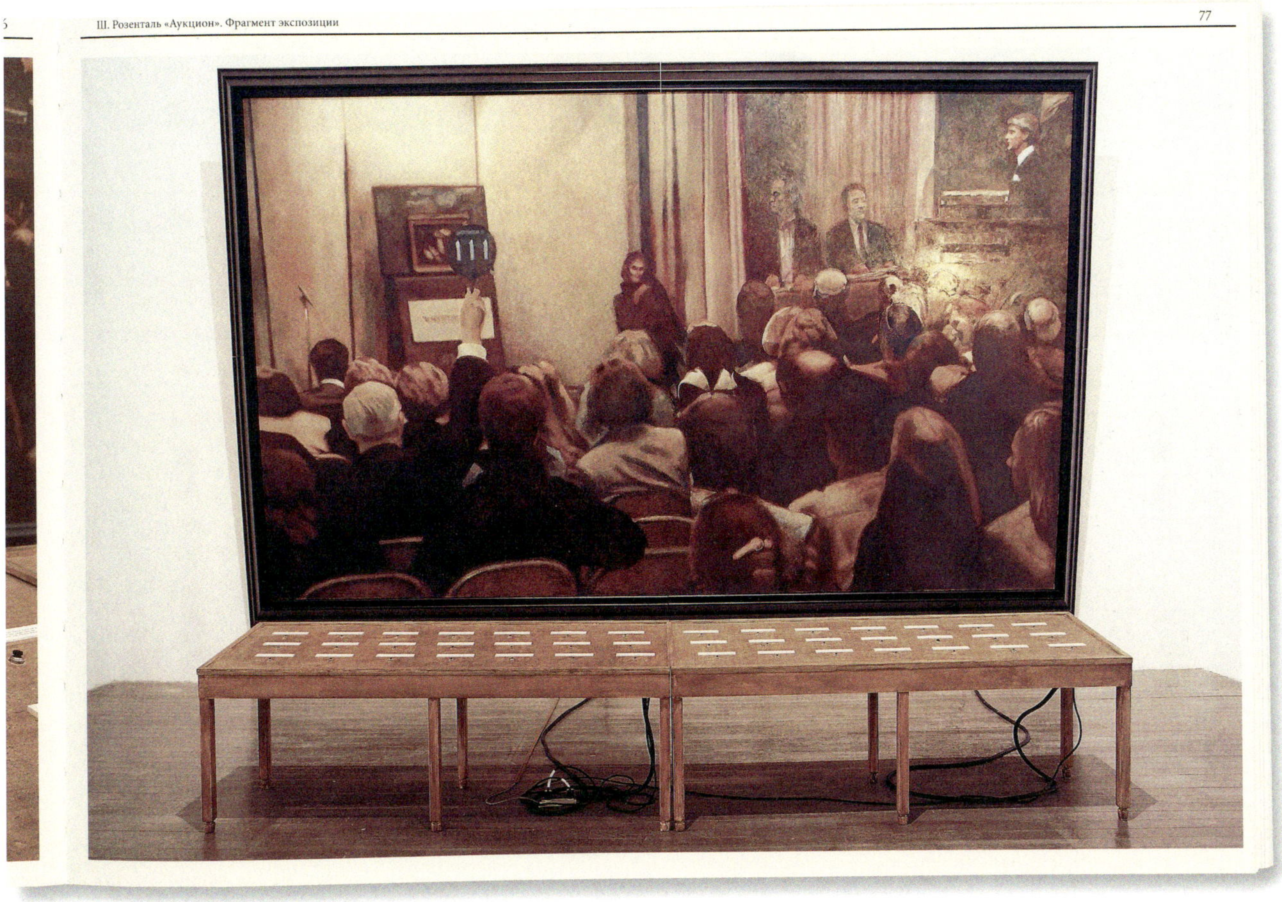
Ш. Розенталь «Аукцион». Фрагмент экспозиции
77

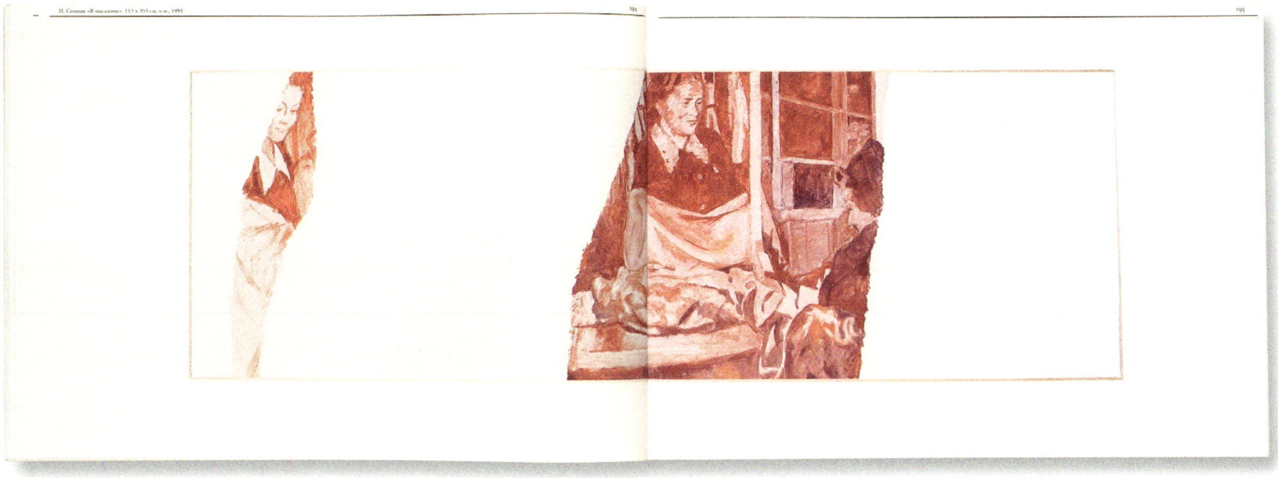

133 On the "Total" Installation | *Über die "totale" Installation*

with Emilia Kabakov | *mit Emilia Kabakov*

2008

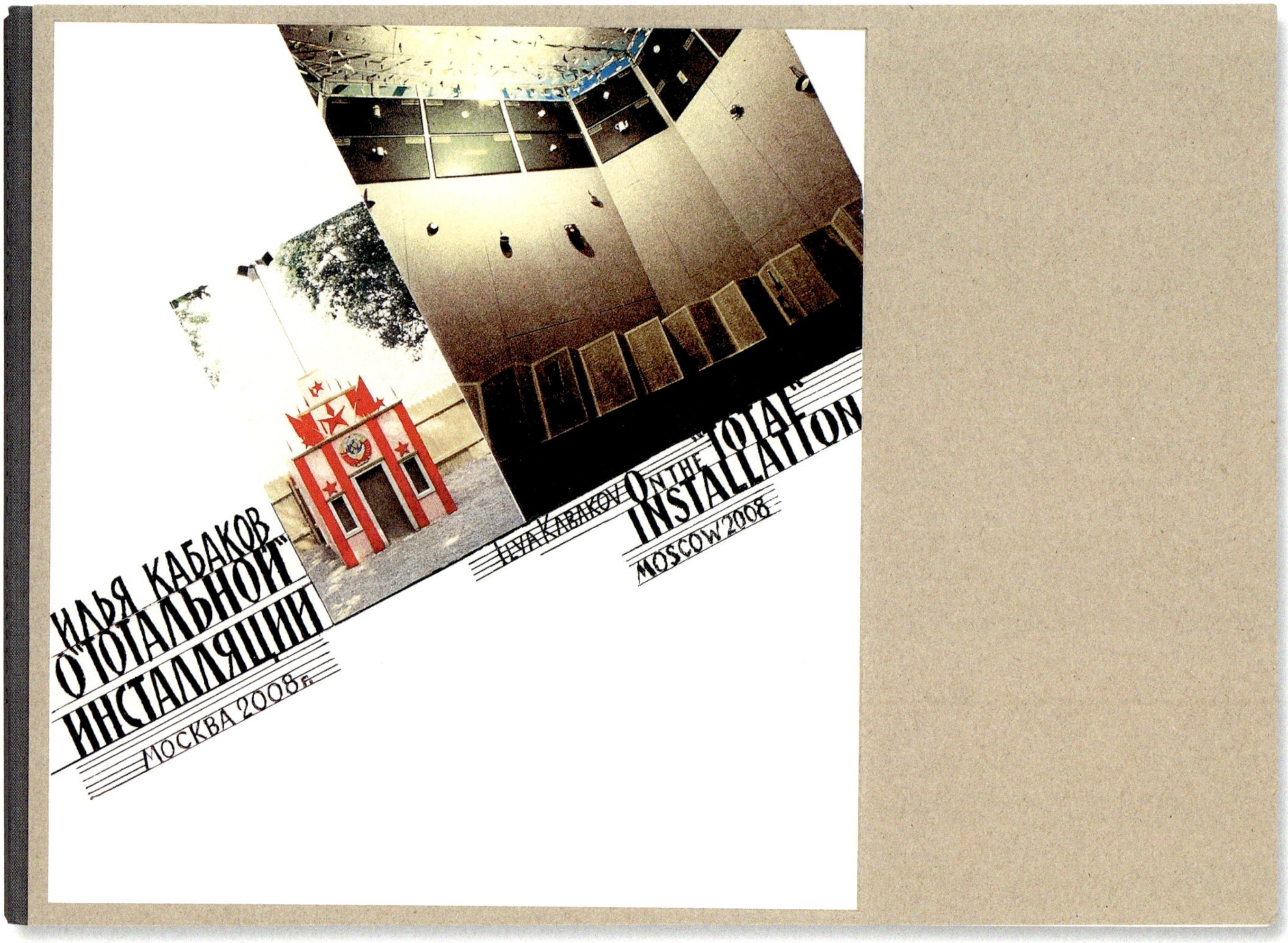

Ilya and Emilia Kabakov
Bielefeld: Kerber Verlag
24 x 34 cm
288 pp. with 238 (116 color) ills.
stitchbound, quarter cloth binding, blind blocking with label
Fadenheftung, Halbleinen, Blindprägung mit Etikette

exhibition catalogue | *Ausstellungskatalog*

layout by Ilya Kabakov | *Layout von Ilya Kabakov*

For the series of exhibitions »Ilya and Emilia Kabakov: Moscow Retrospective«, Moscow, September 15 to October 15, 2008. Texts by Jonatan Feinberg and Ilya Kabakov. The catalogue includes Kabakov's series of lectures »On the 'Total' Installation«, which he delivered at the Städelschule, Frankfurt am Main in 1992–93, and an introduction to the »General Theory of the Total Installation«; Russian.

Zur Ausstellungsreihe »Ilya und Emilia Kabakov. Moskauer Retrospektive«, Moskau, 15. September – 15. Oktober 2008. Texte von Jonatan Feinberg und Ilya Kabakov. Der Katalog enthält Kabakovs Vorlesungsreihe »Über die ‚totale' Installation«, die er 1992/93 an der Städelschule, Frankfurt/Main, hielt, sowie eine Einführung in die »Allgemeine Theorie der totalen Installation«; russisch.

see also | *siehe auch* no. 83

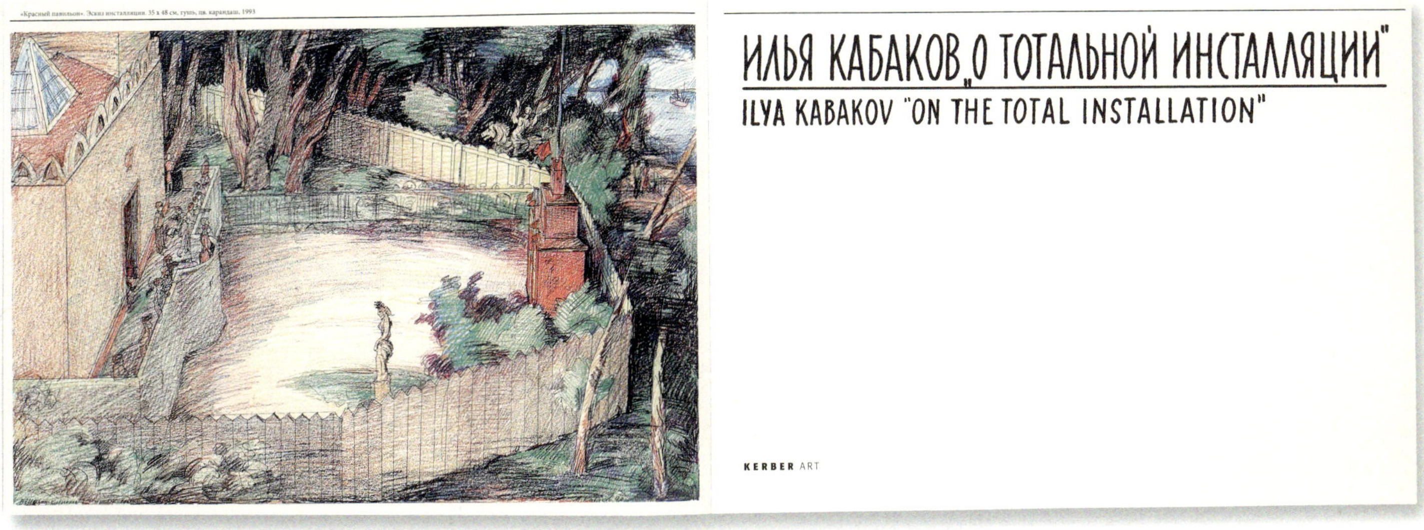
«Красный павильон». Эскиз инсталляции. 35 x 48 см, гушь, цв. карандаш. 1993
ИЛЬЯ КАБАКОВ „О ТОТАЛЬНОЙ ИНСТАЛЛЯЦИИ"
ILYA KABAKOV "ON THE TOTAL INSTALLATION"
KERBER ART

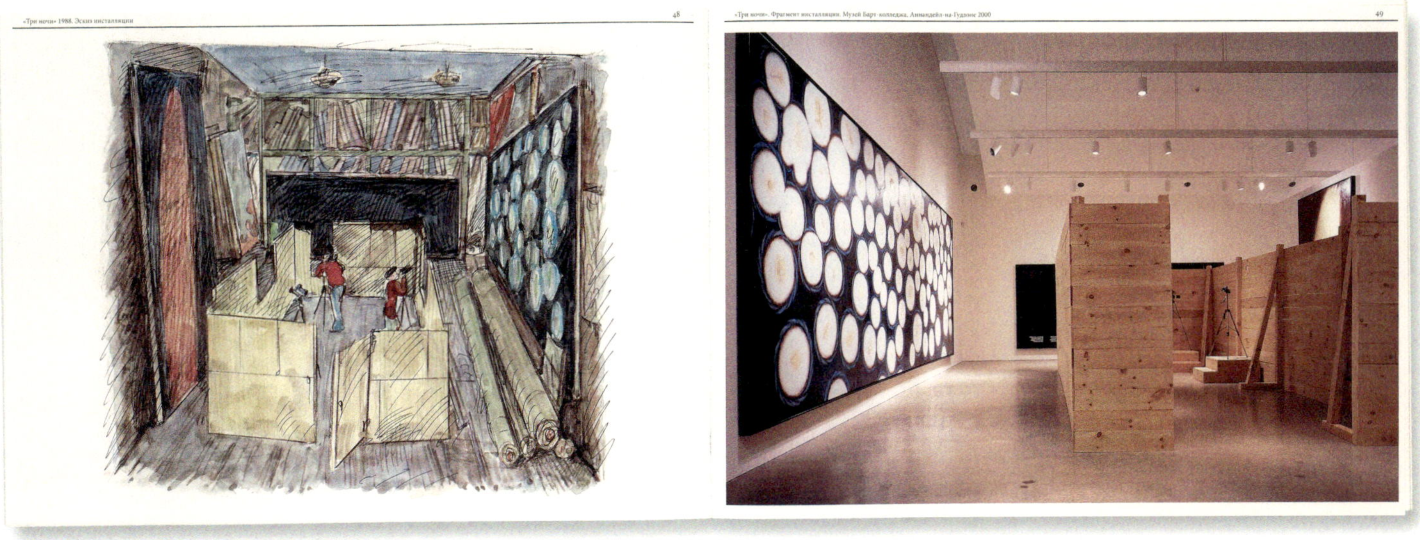
«Три ночи» 1988. Эскиз инсталляции
48
«Три ночи». Фрагмент инсталляции. Музей Барт-колледжа, Аннандейл-на-Гудзоне 2000
49

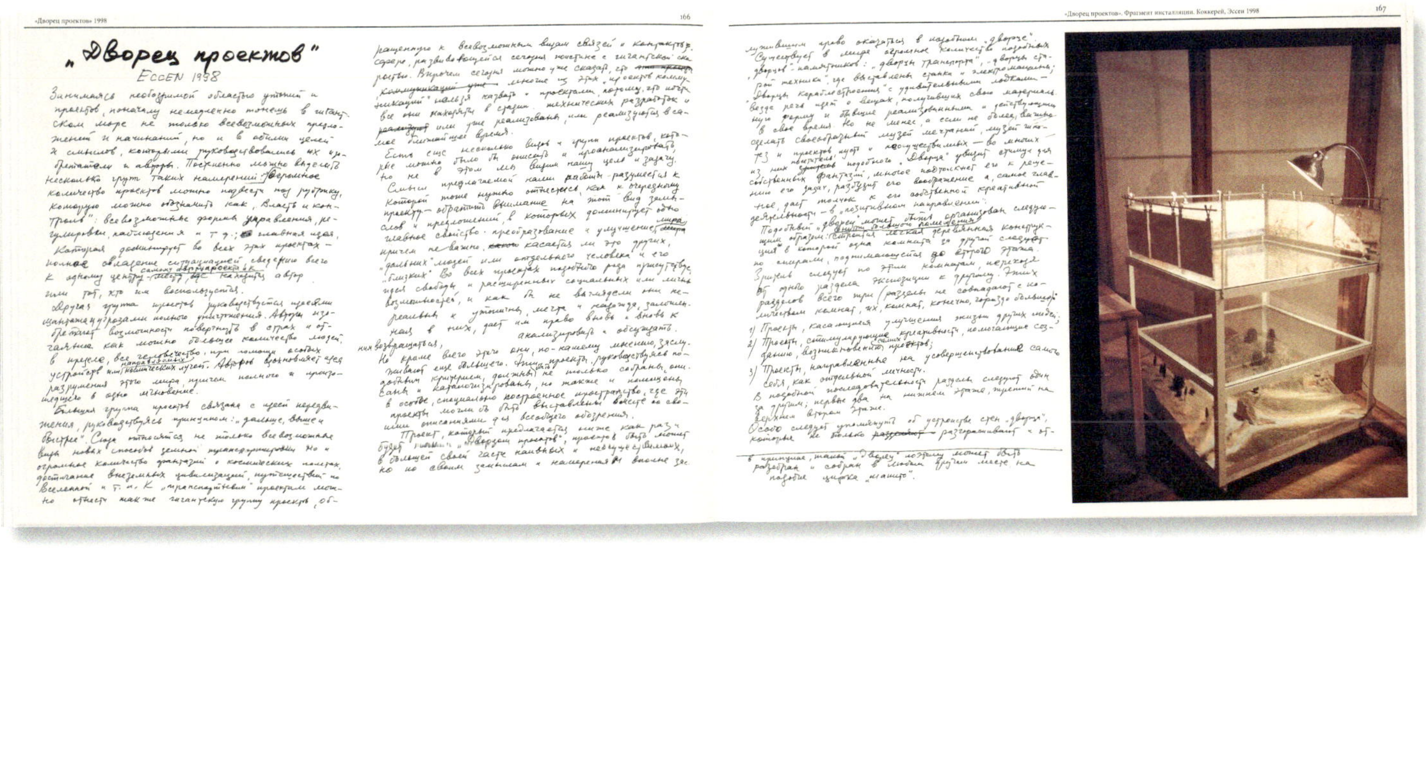
«Дворец проектов» 1998
166
„Дворец проектов"
ЕССЕН 1998
«Дворец проектов». Фрагмент инсталляции. Коккерей, Эссен 1998
167

134 The Life of Flies | *Das Leben der Fliegen*

with Emilia Kabakov | *mit Emilia Kabakov*

2008

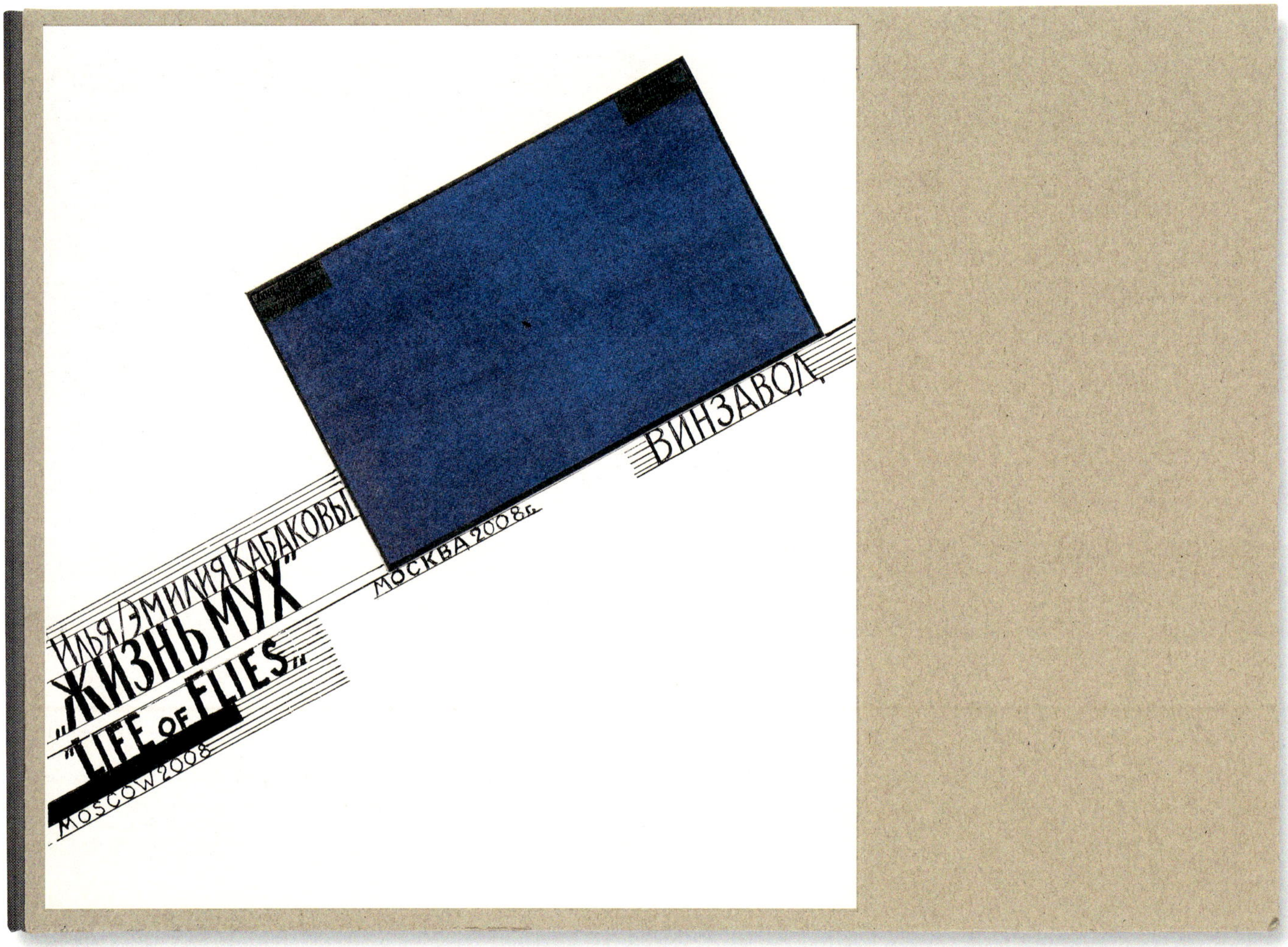

Ilya and Emilia Kabakov
Bielefeld: Kerber Verlag
24 x 34 cm
168 pp. with 123 (89 color) ills.
stitchbound, quarter cloth binding, blind blocking with label
Fadenheftung, Halbleinen, Blindprägung mit Etikette

exhibition catalogue | *Ausstellungskatalog*

layout by Ilya Kabakov | *Layout von Ilya Kabakov*

Published to coincide with the series of exhibitions »Ilya and Emilia Kabakov: Moscow Retrospective«, Moscow, September 15 to October 15, 2008. Texts by Boris Groys, Ilya Kabakov, and Robert Storr. Documentation of the installations »Concert for a Fly, Concert for a Blue Fly and a Yellow Pencil, We are Free, My Homeland; The Flies; The Life of Flies (The Fly with the Wings)«, and the play »Flies (in the Communal Kitchen): A Musical Phantasmagoria«; Russian.

Erschien zur Ausstellungsreihe »Ilya und Emilia Kabakov. Moskauer Retrospektive«, Moskau, 15. September – 15. Oktober 2008. Texte von Boris Groys, Ilya Kabakov und Robert Storr. Dokumentation der Installationen »Konzert für eine Fliege; Konzert für eine blaue Fliege und einen gelben Bleistift; Wir sind frei; Meine Heimat; Die Fliegen; Das Leben der Fliegen (Fliege mit Flügeln)« und des Theaterstücks »Fliegen (in der Kommunalküche). Eine musikalische Phantasmagorie«; russisch.

see also | *siehe auch* no. 9; no. 33; no. 35; no. 36; no. 37; no. 38; no. 50; no. 56, no. 82; CRI, vol. 1, no. 3, pp. 60–65, no. 12, pp. 114–119, no. 35, pp. 250–253, no. 40, pp. 278–283, no. 56, pp. 366–373, no. 71, pp. 460–463; CRP, vol. 1, no. 161, pp. 251, 411

«Концерт для мухи» (камерный). Рисунки «после» инсталляции. 34 х 25 см, тушь, акварель, 1996

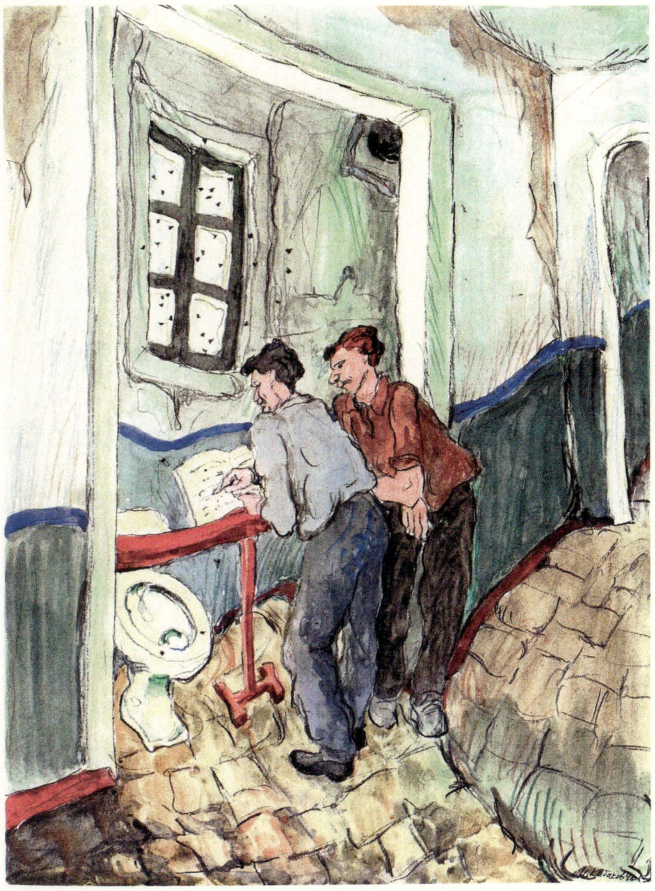

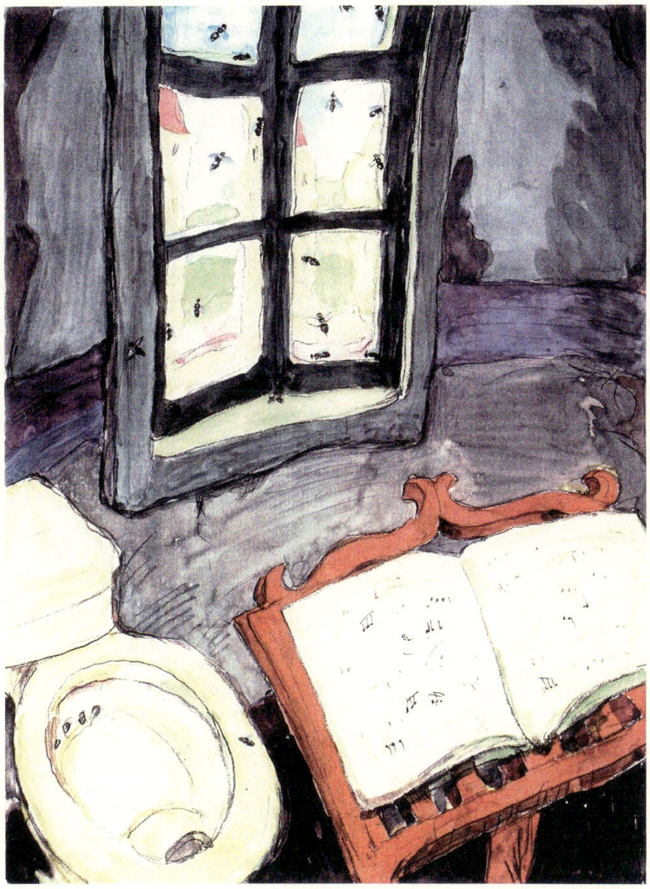

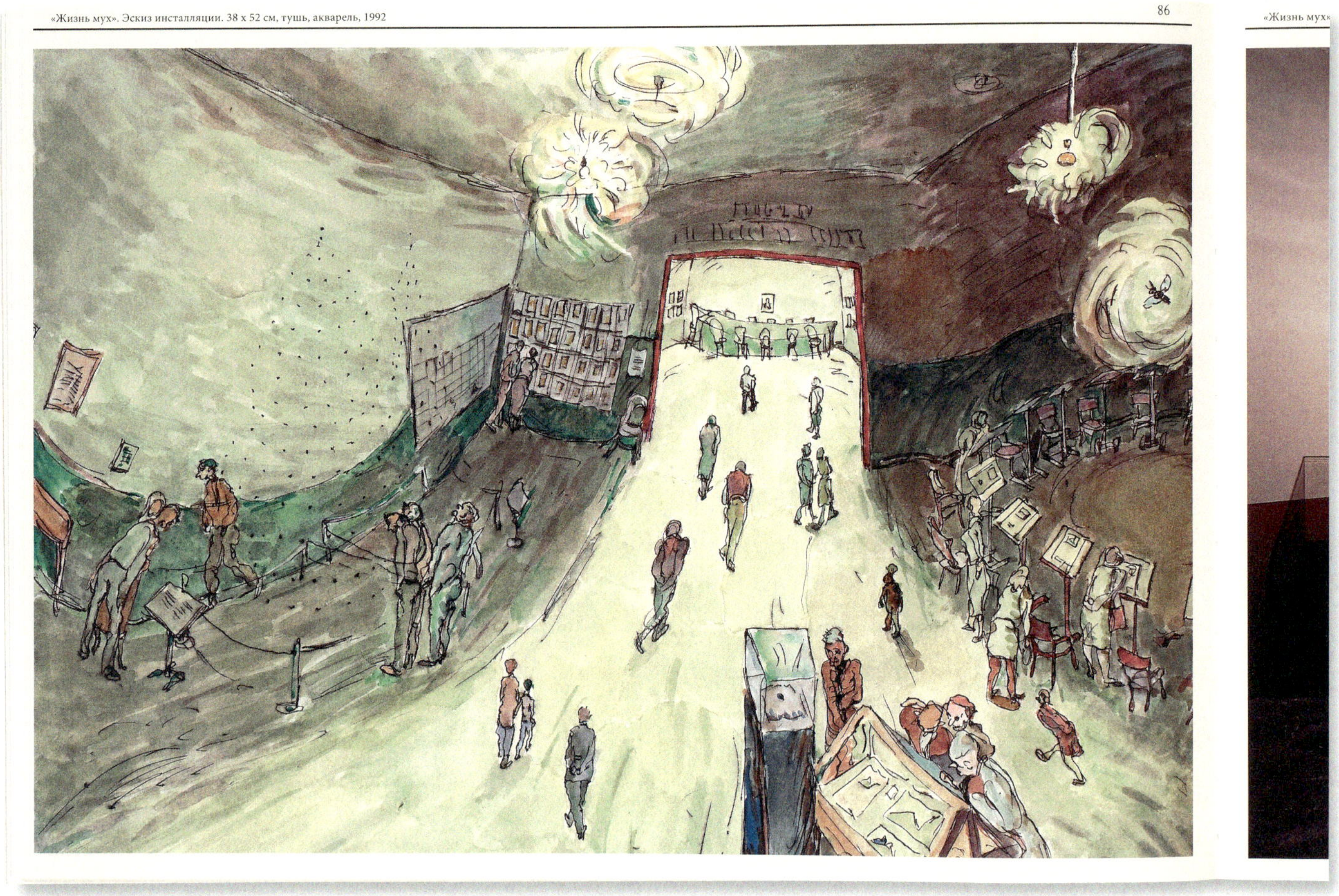
«Жизнь мух». Эскиз инсталляции. 38 x 52 см, тушь, акварель, 1992
86
«Жизнь мух»

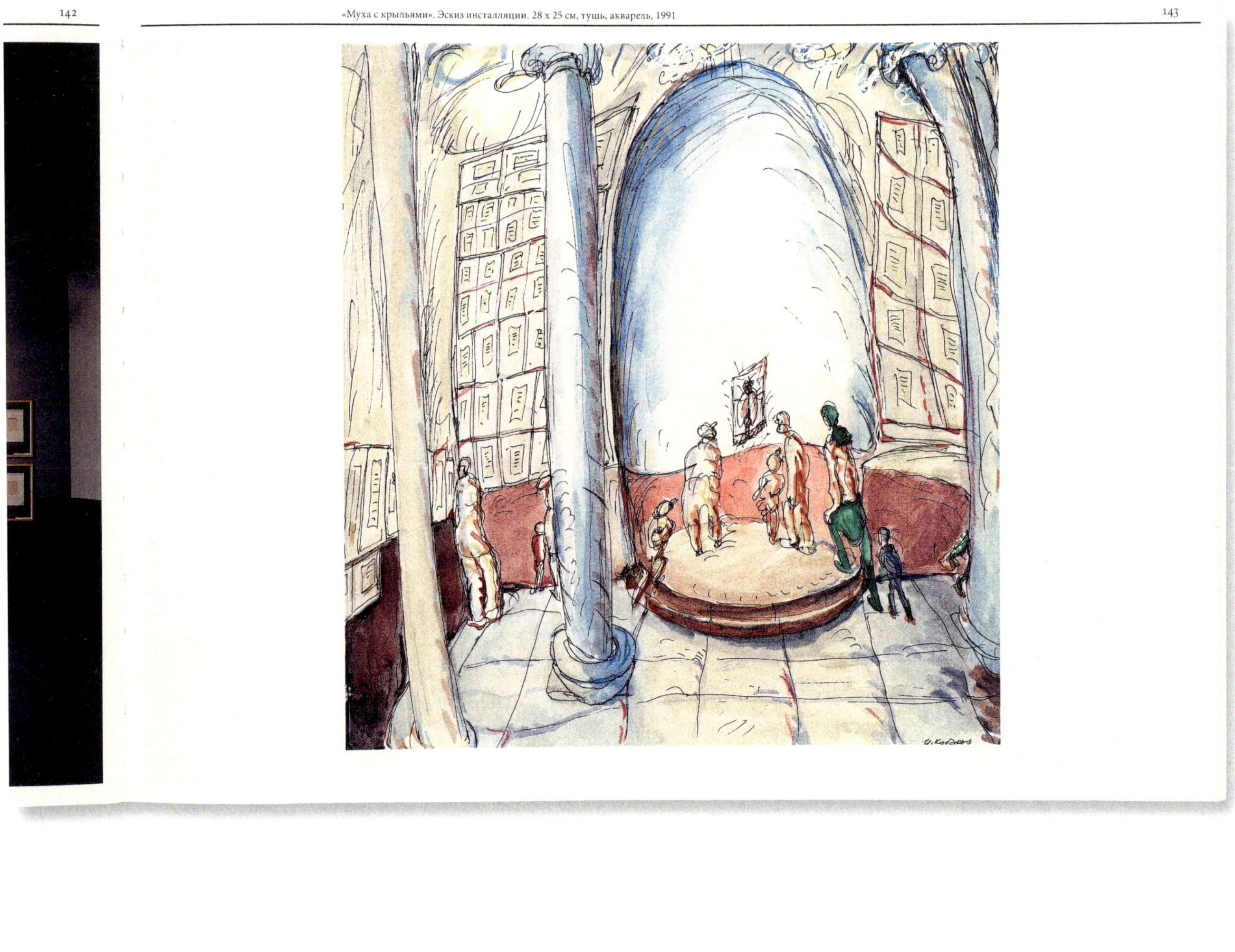
142
«Муха с крыльями». Эскиз инсталляции. 28 x 25 см, тушь, акварель, 1991
143

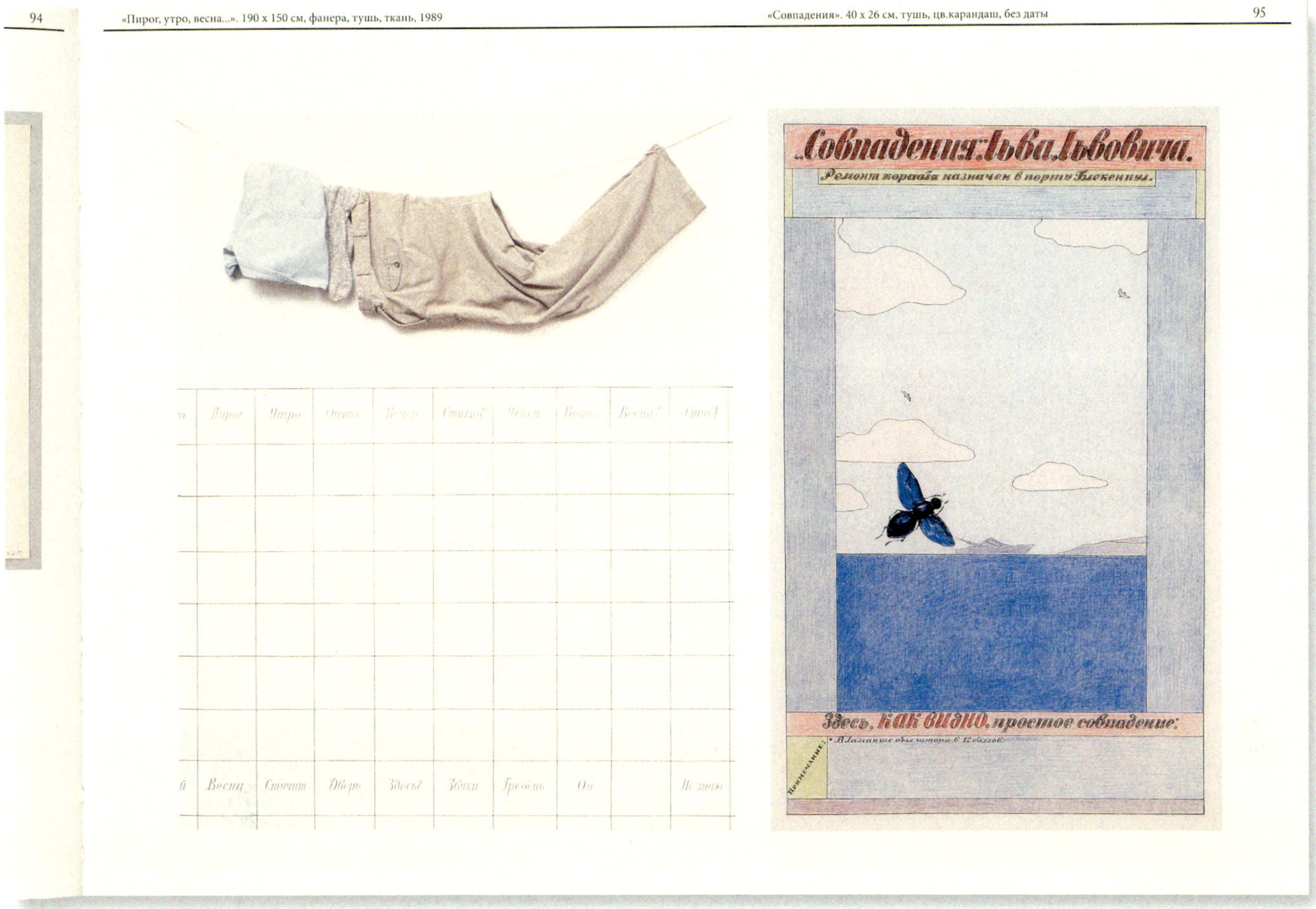
94
«Пирог, утро, весна...». 190 х 150 см, фанера, тушь, ткань, 1989
«Совпадения». 40 х 26 см, тушь, цв.карандаш, без даты
95
Совпадения Льва Львовича.
Здесь, КАК ВИДНО, простое совпадение.

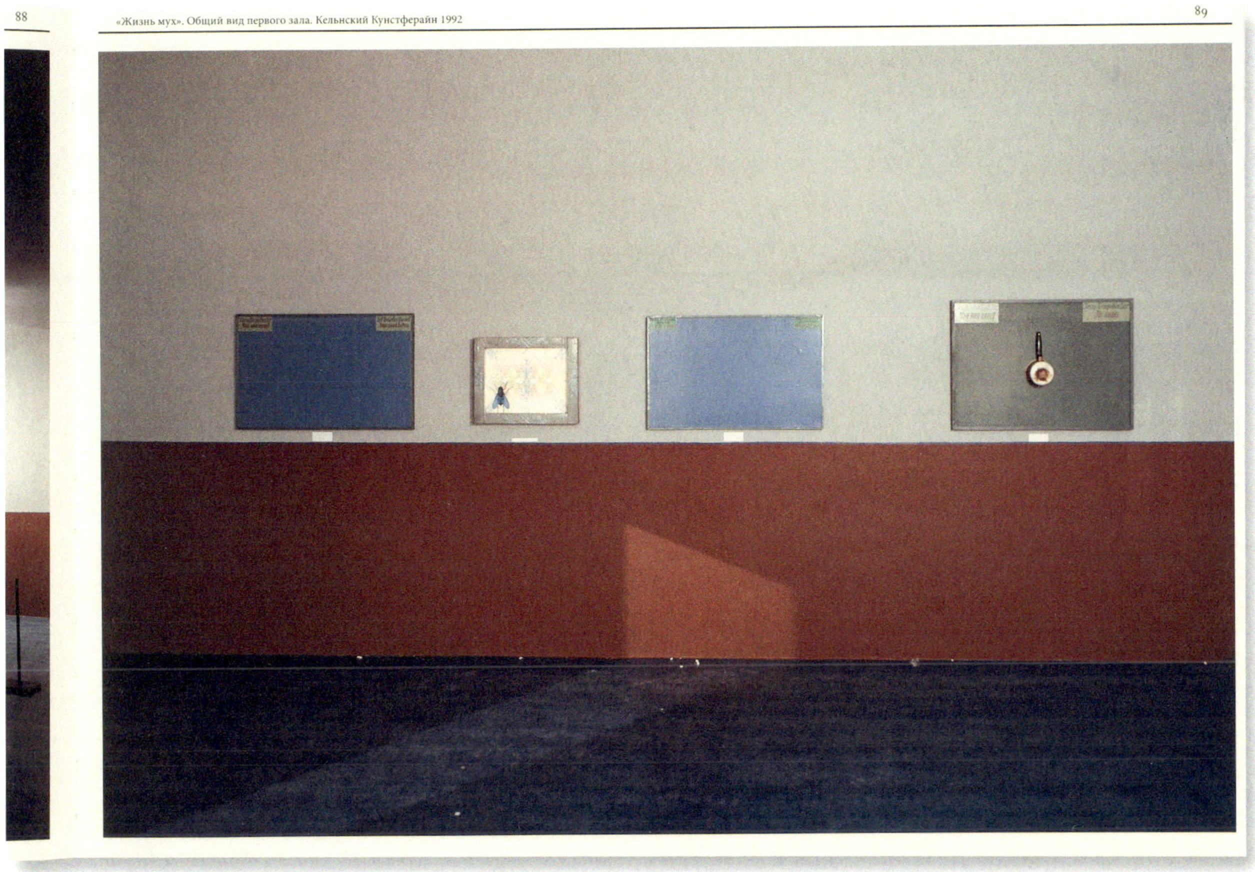
88
«Жизнь мух». Общий вид первого зала. Кельнский Кунстферайн 1992
89

135 The Red Wagon, The Toilet, The Gates, The Tennis Game

Der rote Waggon, Die Toilette, Die Tore, Das Tennisspiel

with Emilia Kabakov | *mit Emilia Kabakov*

2008

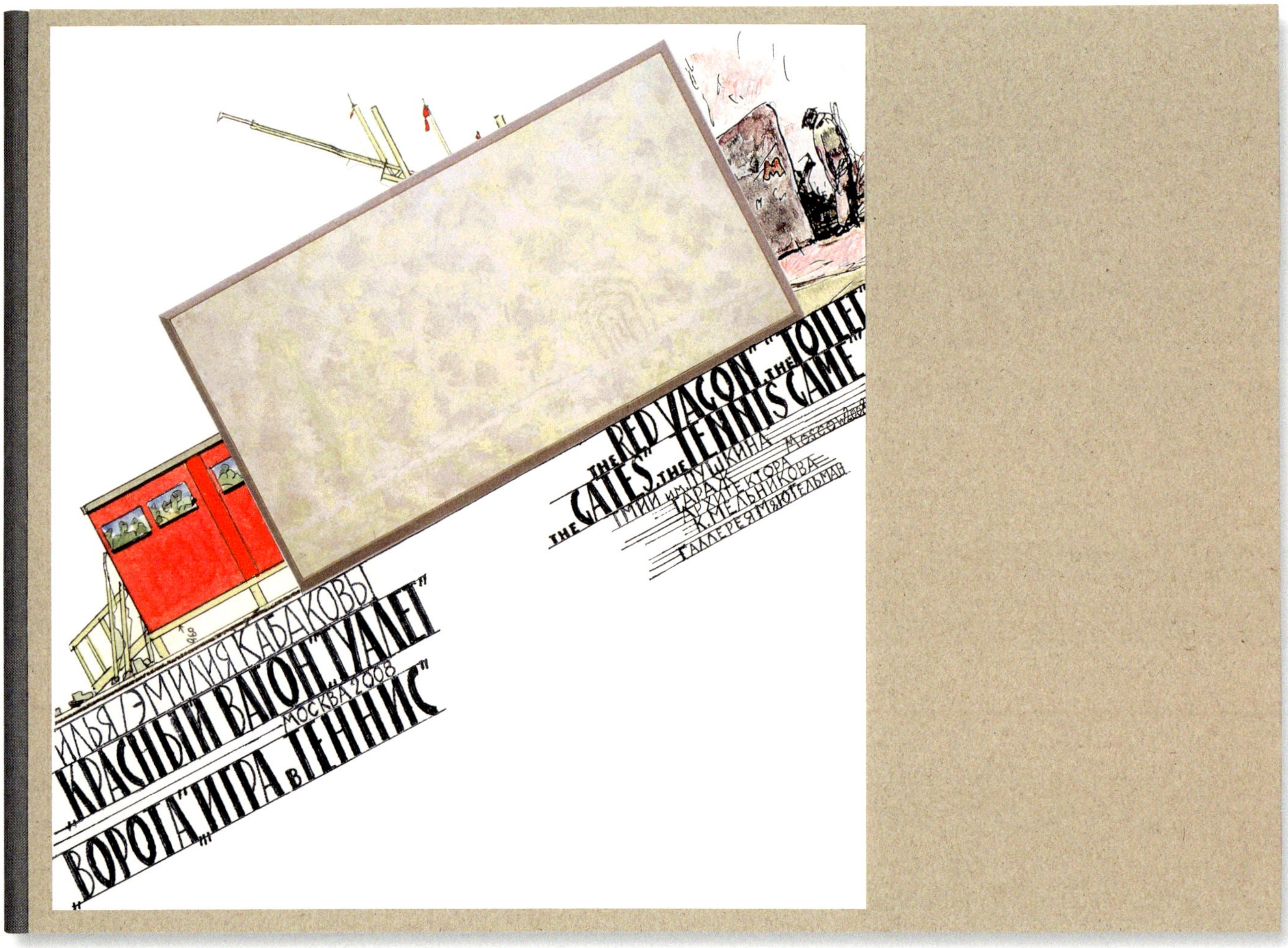

Ilya and Emilia Kabakov
Bielefeld: Kerber Verlag
24 x 34 cm
216 pp. with 204 (116 color) ills.
stitchbound, quarter cloth binding, blind blocking with label
Fadenheftung, Halbleinen, Blindprägung mit Etikette

exhibition catalogue | *Ausstellungskatalog*

layout by Ilya Kabakov | *Layout von Ilya Kabakov*

Documentation of the installations »The Red Wagon, The Toilet, The Gates, The Tennis Game«. Published to coincide with the series of exhibitions »Ilya and Emilia Kabakov: Moscow Retrospective«, Moscow, September 15 to October 15, 2008. Texts by Joseph Backstein, Ekaterina Degotj, and Ilya Kabakov, and dialogues between Boris Groys and Ilya Kabakov on »The Red Wagon« and »The Toilet« and between Ilya Kabakov and Pavel Pepperstein on »The Tennis Game«; Russian.

Dokumentation der Installationen »The Red Wagon, The Toilet,The Gates, the Tennis Game«. Erschien zur Ausstellungsreihe »Ilya und Emilia Kabakov. Moskauer Retrospektive«, Moskau, 15. September – 15. Oktober 2008. Texte von Josef Bakstein, Ekaterina Degotj und Ilya Kabakov und Dialoge von Boris Groys und Ilya Kabakov über »Der rote Waggon« und »Die Toilette« sowie von Ilya Kabakov und Pavel Pepperstein über »The Tennis Game«; russisch.

see also | *siehe auch* no. 55; no. 67; no. 94; CRI, vol. 1, no. 42, pp. 290–295, no. 59, pp. 388–393; CRI, vol. 2, no. 95, pp. 126–131; CRP, vol. 1, nos. 165–181, pp. 255–265, vol 2, nos. 549–560, pp. 287–299

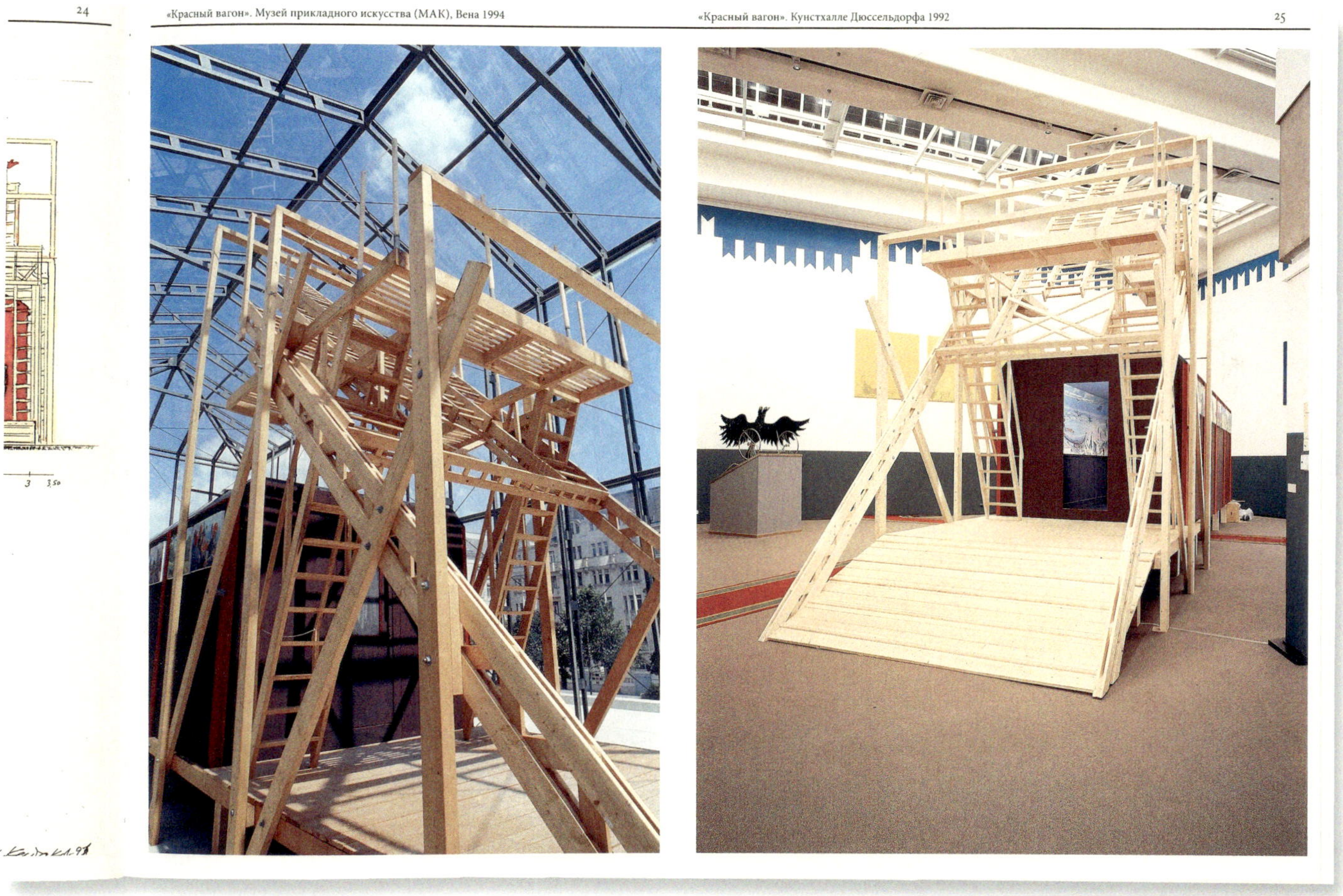
24
«Красный вагон». Музей прикладного искусства (МАК), Вена 1994
«Красный вагон». Кунстхалле Дюссельдорфа 1992
25

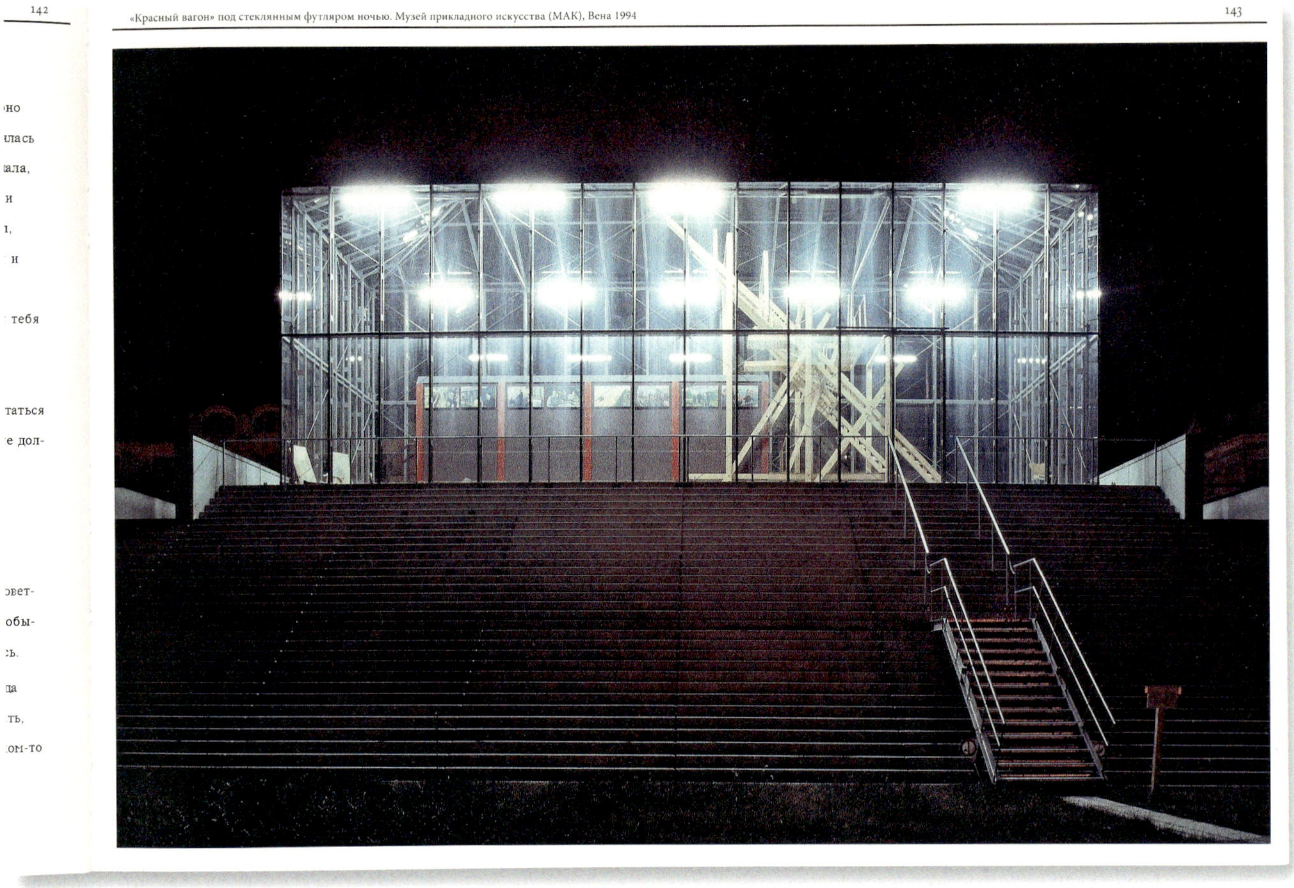
142
«Красный вагон» под стеклянным футляром ночью. Музей прикладного искусства (МАК), Вена 1994
143

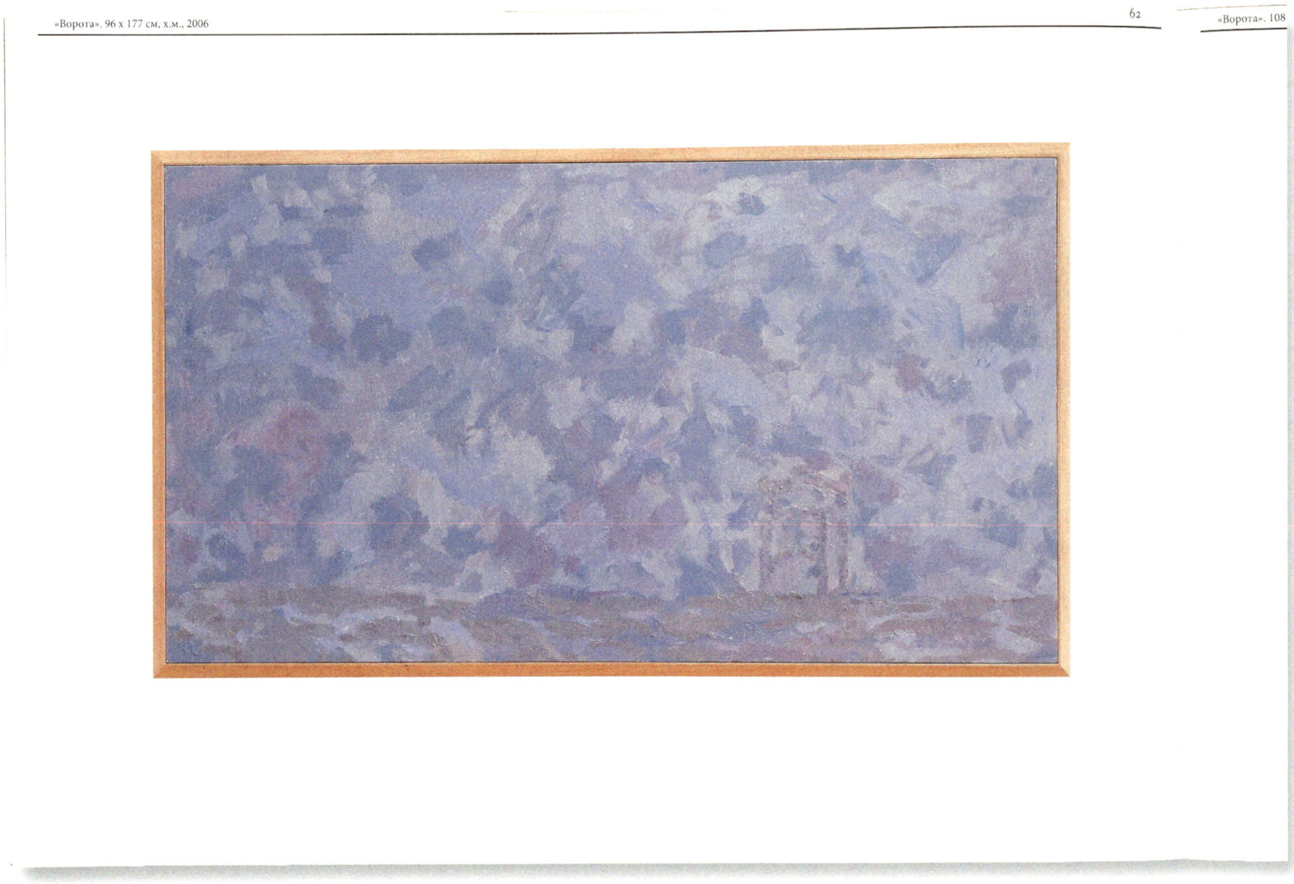
«Ворота». 96 x 177 см, х.м., 2006
62
«Ворота». 108

«Ворота» 2008. Общий вид ворот перед отправкой на выставку

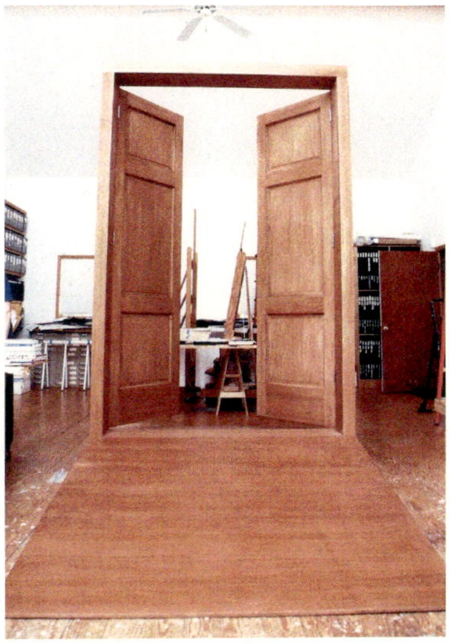

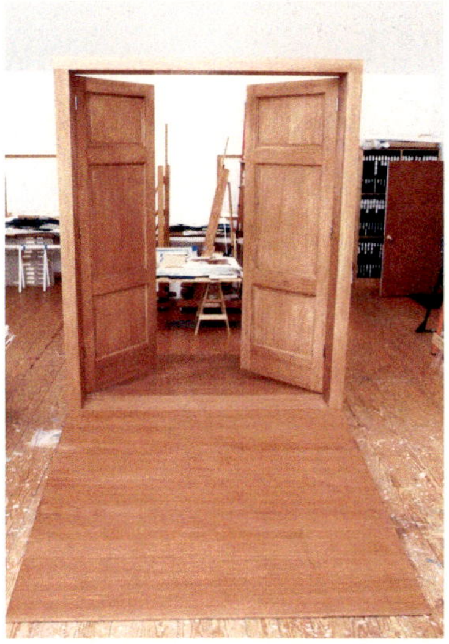

136 The Sixties and the Seventies: Notes About Unofficial Life in Moscow

Die 60er und 70er Jahre. Aufzeichnungen über das inoffizielle Leben in Moskau

2008

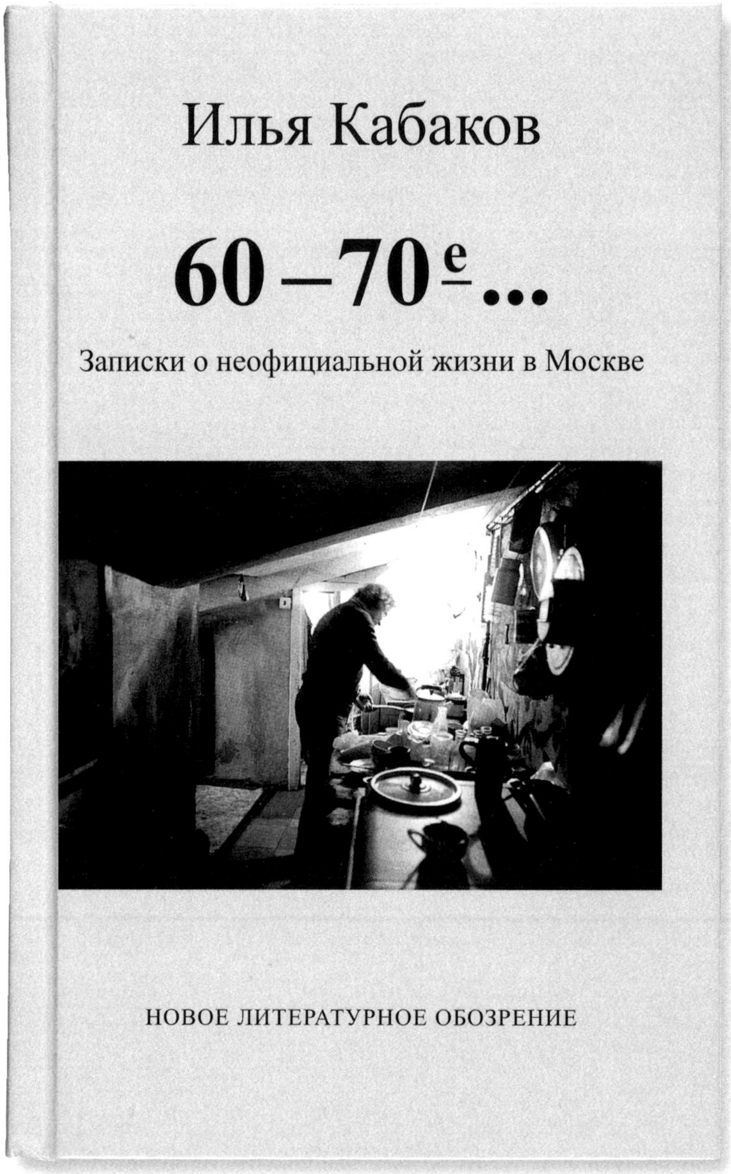

Ilya Kabakov
Moscow: Novoe Literaturnoe Obozrenie
20.8 x 13.2 cm
368 pp. with 2 b/w ills.
stitchbound, hardcover
Fadenheftung, Hardcover

thematic publication | *thematische Publikation*

Ilya Kabakov depicts his own artistic development within the context of the unofficial art scene in Moscow in the 1960s and 1970s. The first edition was published in Russian in 1999. Texts by Erik Bulatov, Boris Groys, Ilya Kabakov, and Oleg Vassilyev; Russian.

Ilya Kabakov schildert den eigenen künstlerischen Werdegang im Kontext der inoffiziellen Kunst in Moskau in den 1960er- und 1970er-Jahren. Die Erstausgabe erschien russisch 1999. Texte von Erik Bulatov, Boris Groys, Ilya Kabakov und Oleg Wassiljew; russisch.

see also | *siehe auch* no. 14; no. 107; no. 116; no. 131

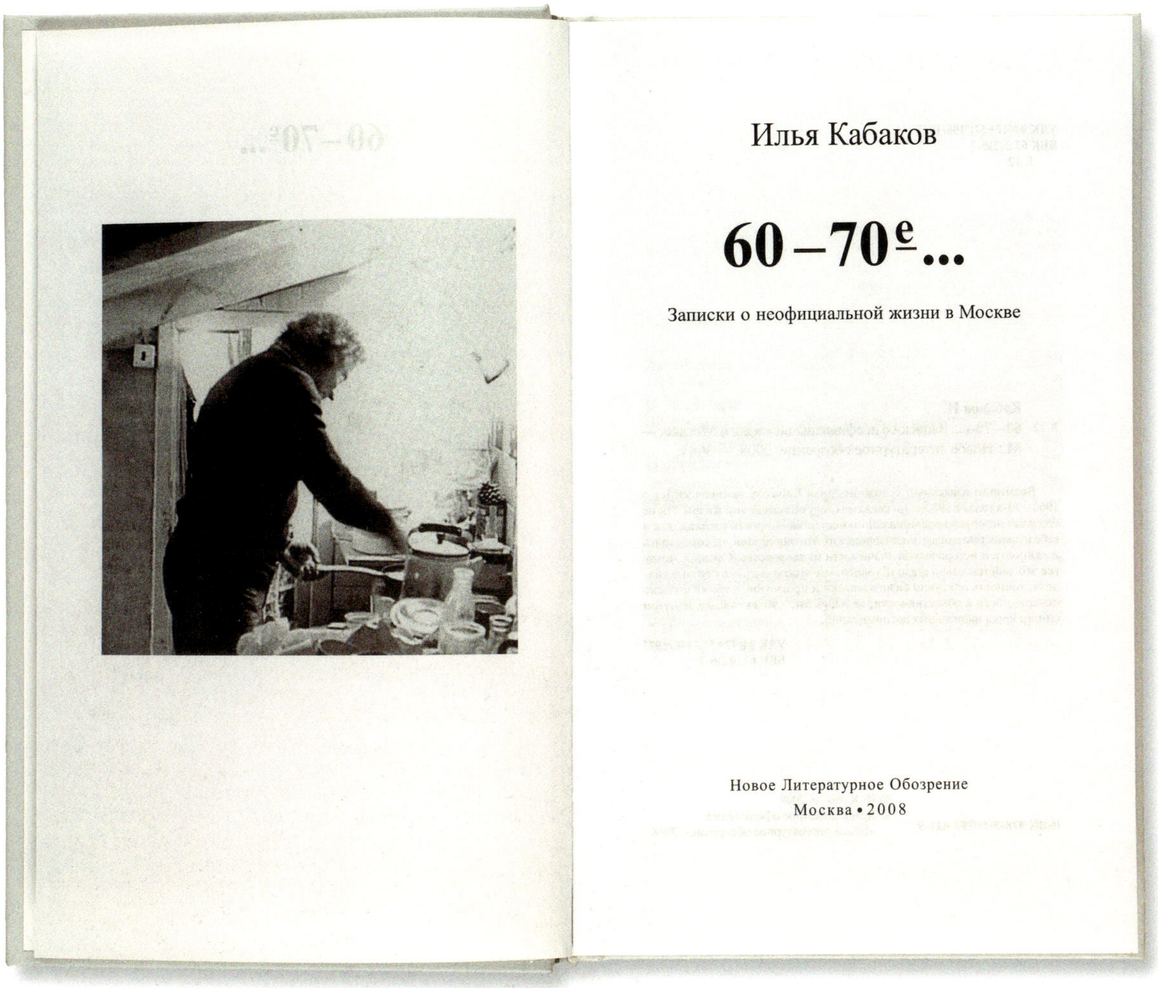

Илья Кабаков

60 – 70е...

Записки о неофициальной жизни в Москве

Новое Литературное Обозрение
Москва • 2008

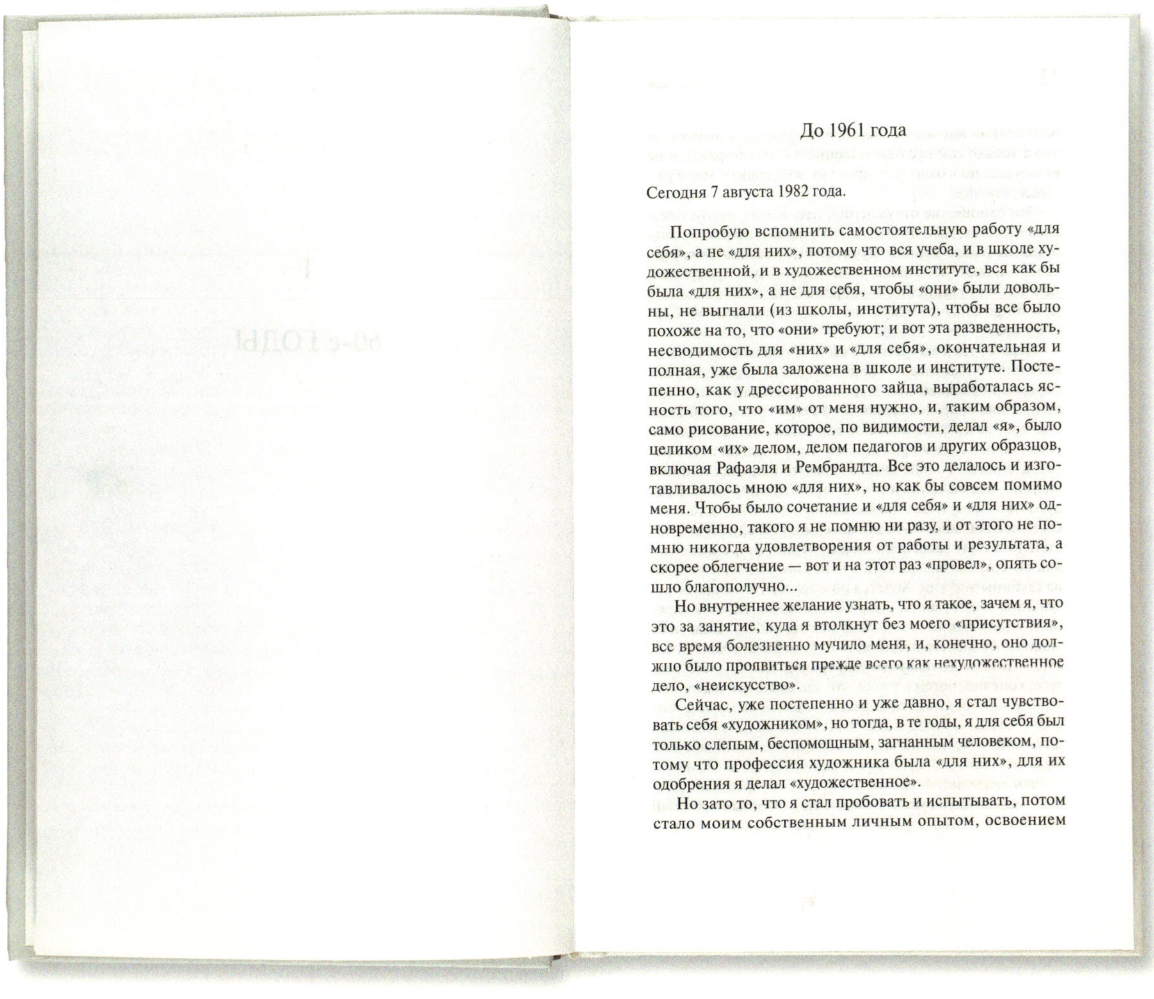

До 1961 года

Сегодня 7 августа 1982 года.

Попробую вспомнить самостоятельную работу «для себя», а не «для них», потому что вся учеба, и в школе художественной, и в художественном институте, вся как бы была «для них», а не для себя, чтобы «они» были довольны, не выгнали (из школы, института), чтобы все было похоже на то, что «они» требуют; и вот эта разведенность, несводимость для «них» и «для себя», окончательная и полная, уже была заложена в школе и институте. Постепенно, как у дрессированного зайца, выработалась ясность того, что «им» от меня нужно, и, таким образом, само рисование, которое, по видимости, делал «я», было целиком «их» делом, делом педагогов и других образцов, включая Рафаэля и Рембрандта. Все это делалось и изготавливалось мною «для них», но как бы совсем помимо меня. Чтобы было сочетание и «для себя» и «для них» одновременно, такого я не помню ни разу, и от этого не помню никогда удовлетворения от работы и результата, а скорее облегчение — вот и на этот раз «провел», опять сошло благополучно...

Но внутреннее желание узнать, что я такое, зачем я, что это за занятие, куда я втолкнут без моего «присутствия», все время болезненно мучило меня, и, конечно, оно должно было проявиться прежде всего как нехудожественное дело, «неискусство».

Сейчас, уже постепенно и уже давно, я стал чувствовать себя «художником», но тогда, в те годы, я для себя был только слепым, беспомощным, загнанным человеком, потому что профессия художника была «для них», для их одобрения я делал «художественное».

Но зато то, что я стал пробовать и испытывать, потом стало моим собственным личным опытом, освоением

137 Paintings 1957–2008: Catalogue Raisonné | *Gemälde 1957–2008. Werkverzeichnis*

2008

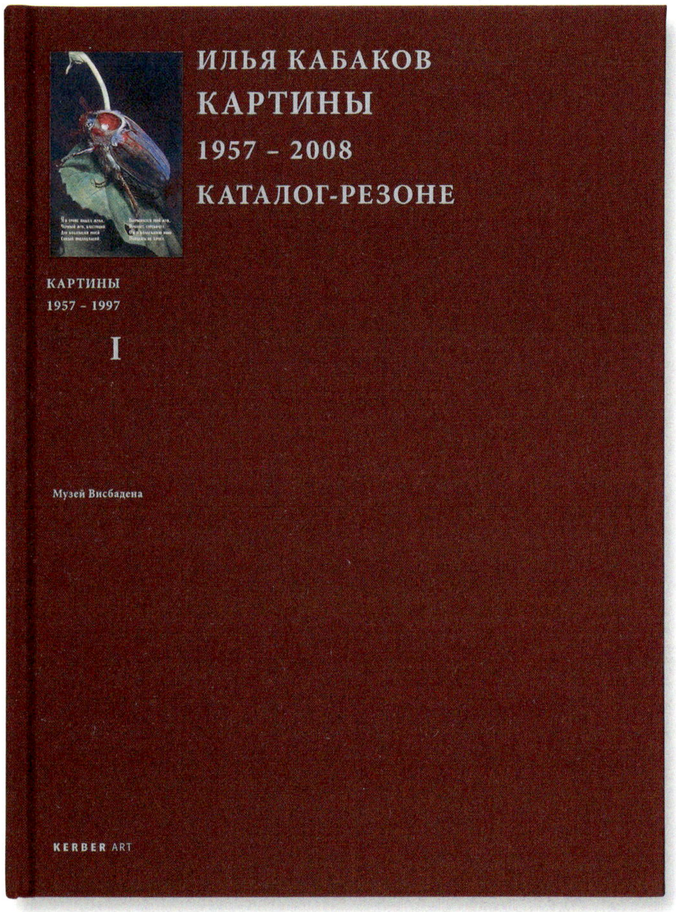

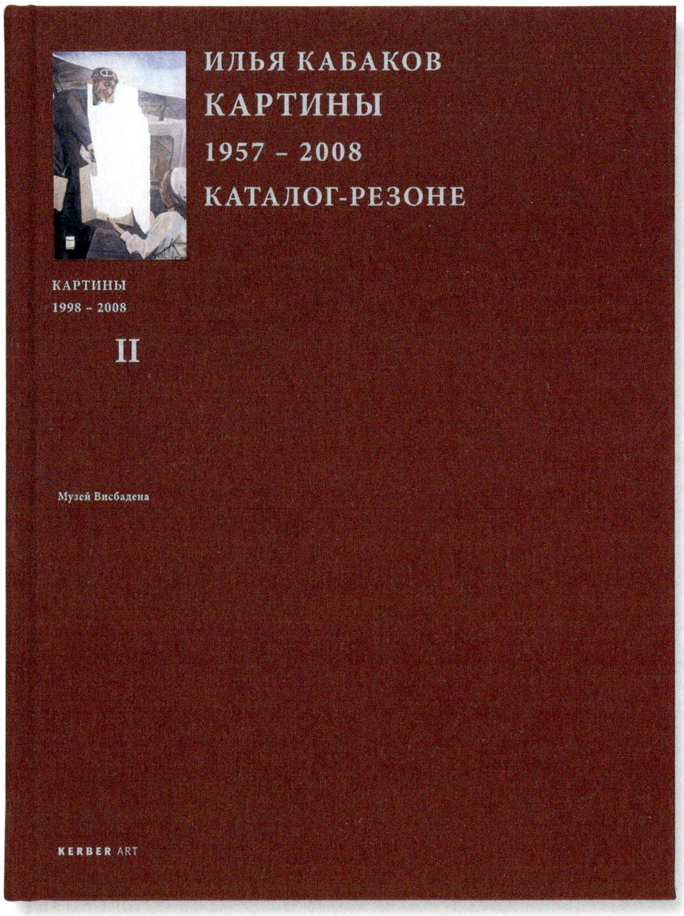

Museum Wiesbaden, Renate Petzinger, Emilia Kabakov
Bielefeld: Kerber Verlag
30.2 x 23 cm
vol. 1, 376 pp. with 383 (336 color) ills.
vol. 2, 392 pp. with 351 (337 color) ills.
stitchbound, clothbound, blind blocking with label, in cloth covered slipcase
Fadenheftung, Leinen, Blindprägung mit Etikette, in Leinenschuber

catalogue raisonné | *Werkverzeichnis*

layout by Ilya Kabakov | *Layout von Ilya Kabakov*

Volume 1: paintings from 1957 to 1997. Volume 2: paintings from 1998 to 2008. Texts by Boris Groys, Rod Mengham, Renate Petzinger, Ilya Kabakov, and Robert Storr; English, German (identical edition in Russian).

Band 1 Gemälde von 1957 bis 1997; Band 2 Gemälde von 1998 bis 2008. Texte Boris Groys, Rod Mengham, Renate Petzinger, Ilya Kabakov und Robert Storr; englisch, deutsch (identische Ausgabe in russischer Sprache).

see also | *siehe auch*

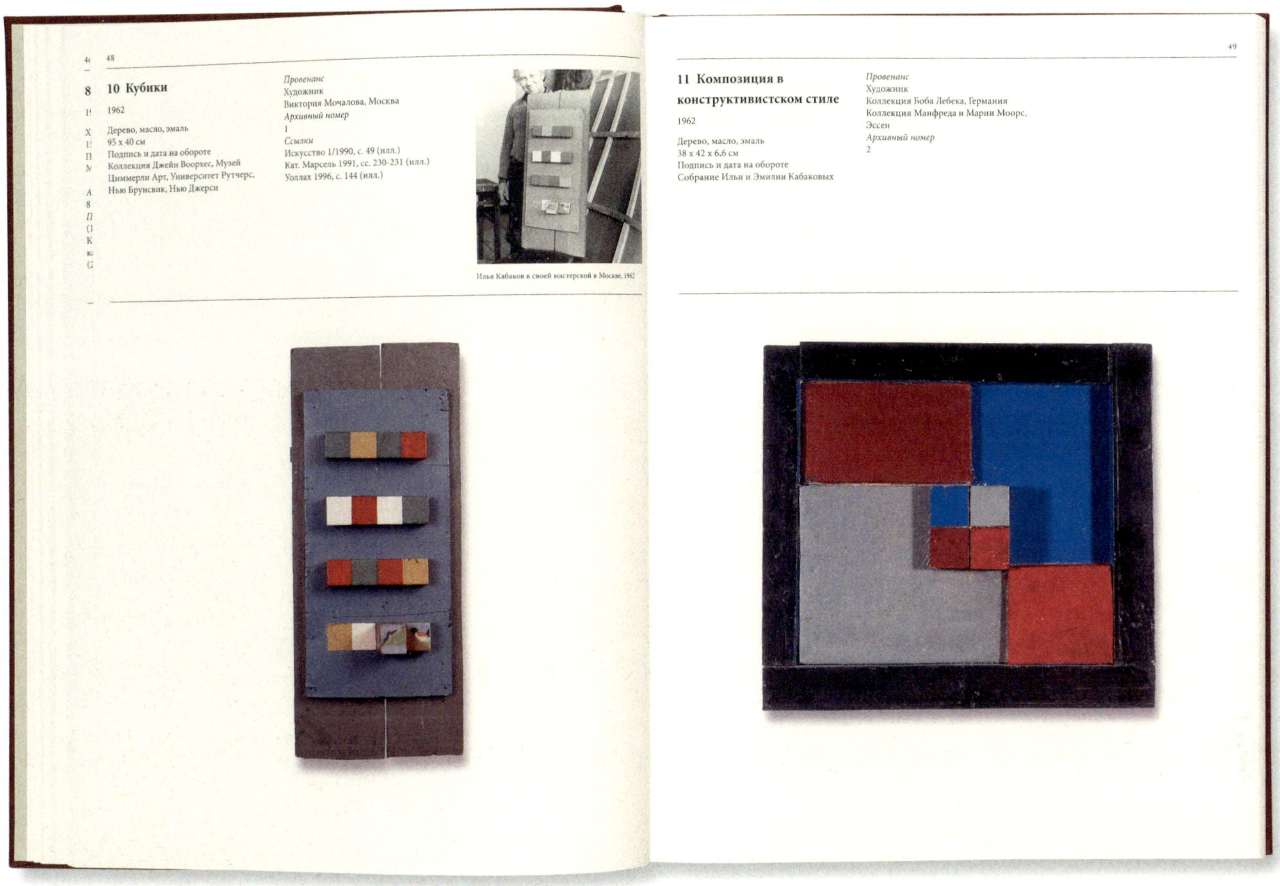
48
10 Кубики
1962
Дерево, масло, эмаль
95 x 40 см
Подпись и дата на обороте
Коллекция Джейн Воорхес, Музей Циммерли Арт, Университет Рутчерс, Нью Брунсвик, Нью Джерси
Провенанс
Художник
Виктория Мочалова, Москва
Архивный номер
1
Ссылки
Искусство 1/1990, с. 49 (илл.)
Кат. Марсель 1991, сс. 230-231 (илл.)
Уоллах 1996, с. 144 (илл.)
Илья Кабаков в своей мастерской в Москве, 1962
49
11 Композиция в конструктивистском стиле
1962
Дерево, масло, эмаль
38 x 42 x 6,6 см
Подпись и дата на обороте
Собрание Ильи и Эмилии Кабаковых
Провенанс
Художник
Коллекция Боба Лебека, Германия
Коллекция Манфреда и Марии Моорс, Эссен
Архивный номер
2

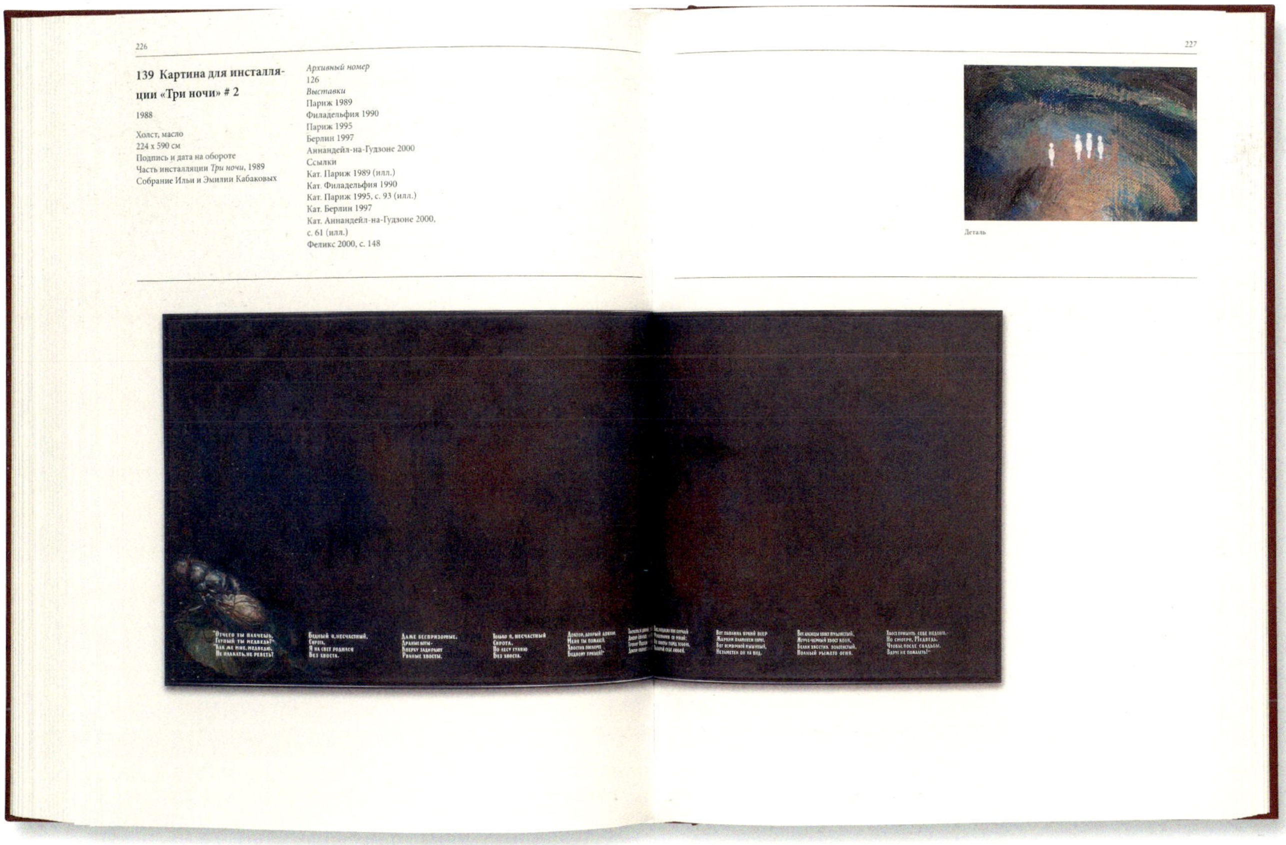
226
139 Картина для инсталляции «Три ночи» # 2
1988
Холст, масло
224 x 590 см
Подпись и дата на обороте
Часть инсталляции Три ночи, 1989
Собрание Ильи и Эмилии Кабаковых
Архивный номер
126
Выставки
Париж 1989
Филадельфия 1990
Париж 1995
Берлин 1997
Аннандейл-на-Гудзоне 2000
Ссылки
Кат. Париж 1989 (илл.)
Кат. Филадельфия 1990
Кат. Париж 1995, с. 93 (илл.)
Кат. Берлин 1997
Кат. Аннандейл-на-Гудзоне 2000, с. 61 (илл.)
Феликс 2000, с. 148
227
Деталь

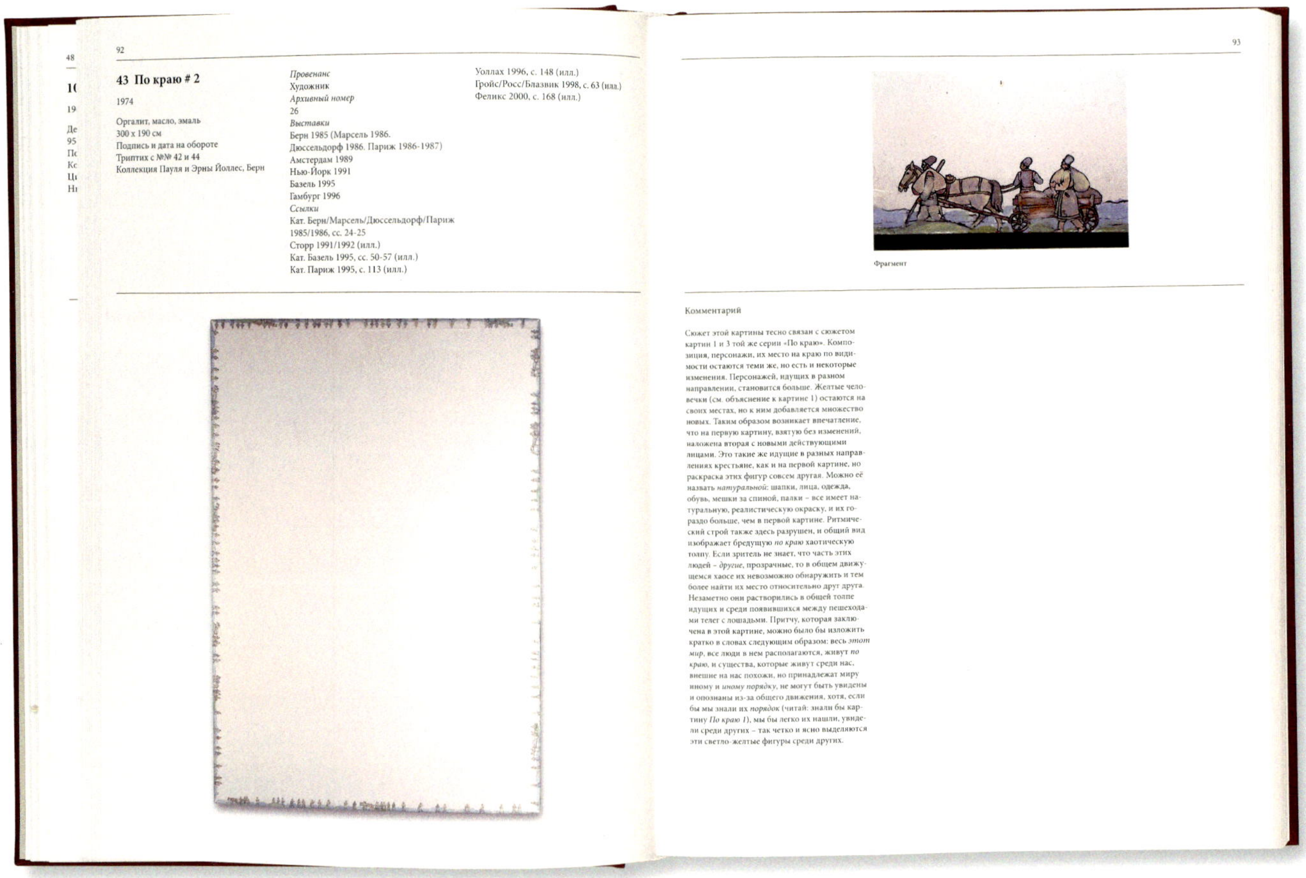

92

43 По краю # 2

1974

Оргалит, масло, эмаль
300 x 190 см
Подпись и дата на обороте
Триптих с №№ 42 и 44
Коллекция Пауля и Эрны Йоллес, Берн

Провенанс
Художник
Архивный номер
26
Выставки
Берн 1985 (Марсель 1986.
Дюссельдорф 1986. Париж 1986-1987)
Амстердам 1989
Нью-Йорк 1991
Базель 1995
Гамбург 1996
Ссылки
Кат. Берн/Марсель/Дюссельдорф/Париж 1985/1986, сс. 24-25
Сторр 1991/1992 (илл.)
Кат. Базель 1995, сс. 50-57 (илл.)
Кат. Париж 1995, с. 113 (илл.)
Уоллах 1996, с. 148 (илл.)
Гройс/Росс/Блазвик 1998, с. 63 (илл.)
Феликс 2000, с. 168 (илл.)

93

Фрагмент

Комментарий

Сюжет этой картины тесно связан с сюжетом картин 1 и 3 той же серии «По краю». Композиция, персонажи, их место на краю по видимости остаются теми же, но есть и некоторые изменения. Персонажей, идущих в разном направлении, становится больше. Желтые человечки (см. объяснение к картине 1) остаются на своих местах, но к ним добавляется множество новых. Таким образом возникает впечатление, что на первую картину, взятую без изменений, наложена вторая с новыми действующими лицами. Это такие же идущие в разных направлениях крестьяне, как и на первой картине, но раскраска этих фигур совсем другая. Можно её назвать *натуральной*: шапки, лица, одежда, обувь, мешки за спиной, палки – все имеет натуральную, реалистическую окраску, и их гораздо больше, чем в первой картине. Ритмический строй также здесь разрушен, и общий вид изображает бредущую *по краю* хаотическую толпу. Если зритель не знает, что часть этих людей – *другие*, прозрачные, то в общем движущемся хаосе их невозможно обнаружить и тем более найти их место относительно друг друга. Незаметно они растворились в общей толпе идущих и среди появившихся между пешеходами телег с лошадьми. Притчу, которая заключена в этой картине, можно было бы изложить кратко в словах следующим образом: весь *этот мир*, все люди в нем располагаются, живут *по краю*, и существа, которые живут среди нас, внешне на нас похожи, но принадлежат миру иному и *иному порядку*, не могут быть увидены и опознаны из-за общего движения, хотя, если бы мы знали их *порядок* (читай: знали бы картину *По краю 1*), мы бы легко их нашли, увидели среди других – так четко и ясно выделяются эти светло-желтые фигуры среди других.

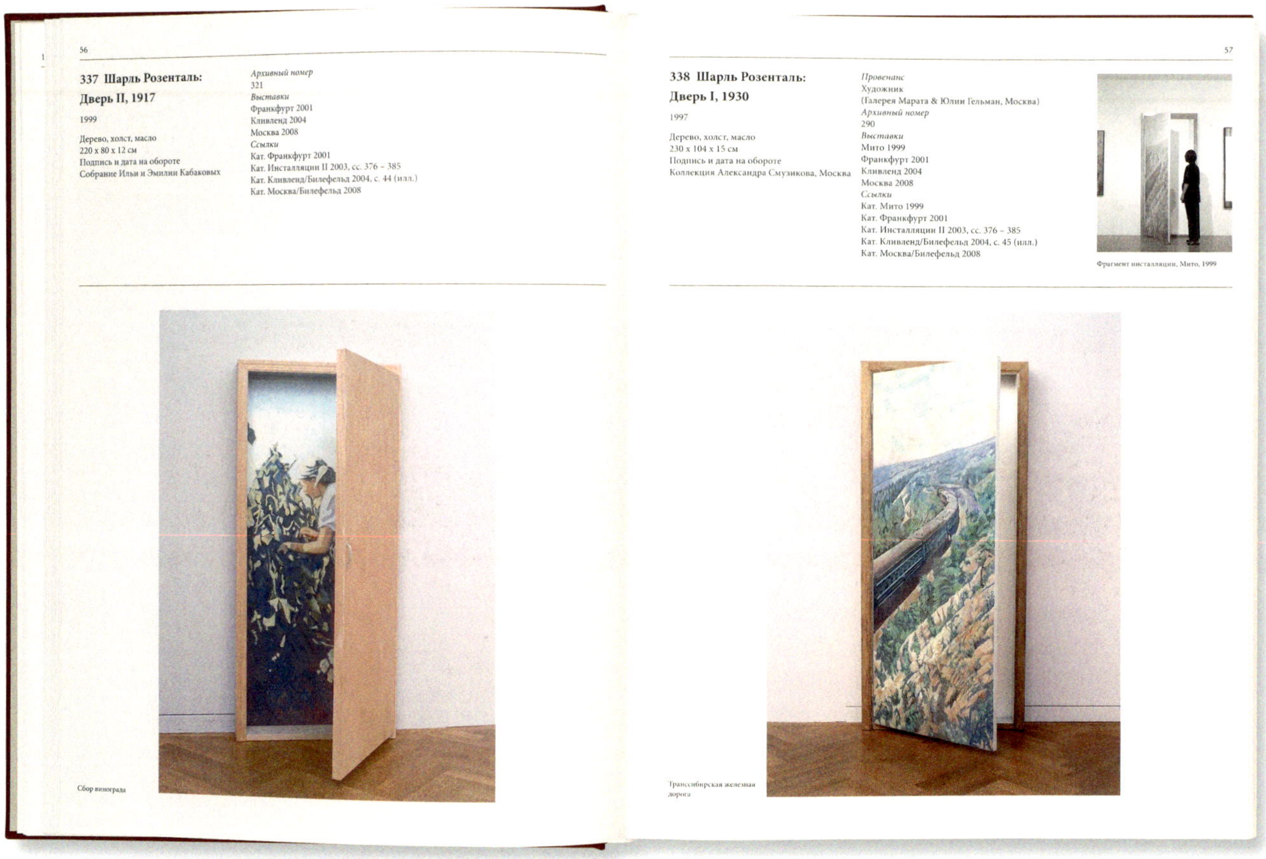

56

337 Шарль Розенталь: Дверь II, 1917

1999

Дерево, холст, масло
220 x 80 x 12 см
Подпись и дата на обороте
Собрание Ильи и Эмилии Кабаковых

Архивный номер
321
Выставки
Франкфурт 2001
Кливленд 2004
Москва 2008
Ссылки
Кат. Франкфурт 2001
Кат. Инсталляции II 2003, сс. 376 – 385
Кат. Кливленд/Билефельд 2004, с. 44 (илл.)
Кат. Москва/Билефельд 2008

Сбор винограда

57

338 Шарль Розенталь: Дверь I, 1930

1997

Дерево, холст, масло
230 x 104 x 15 см
Подпись и дата на обороте
Коллекция Александра Смузикова, Москва

Провенанс
Художник
(Галерея Марата & Юлии Гельман, Москва)
Архивный номер
290
Выставки
Мито 1999
Франкфурт 2001
Кливленд 2004
Москва 2008
Ссылки
Кат. Мито 1999
Кат. Франкфурт 2001
Кат. Инсталляции II 2003, сс. 376 – 385
Кат. Кливленд/Билефельд 2004, с. 45 (илл.)
Кат. Москва/Билефельд 2008

Фрагмент инсталляции, Мито, 1999

Транссибирская железная дорога

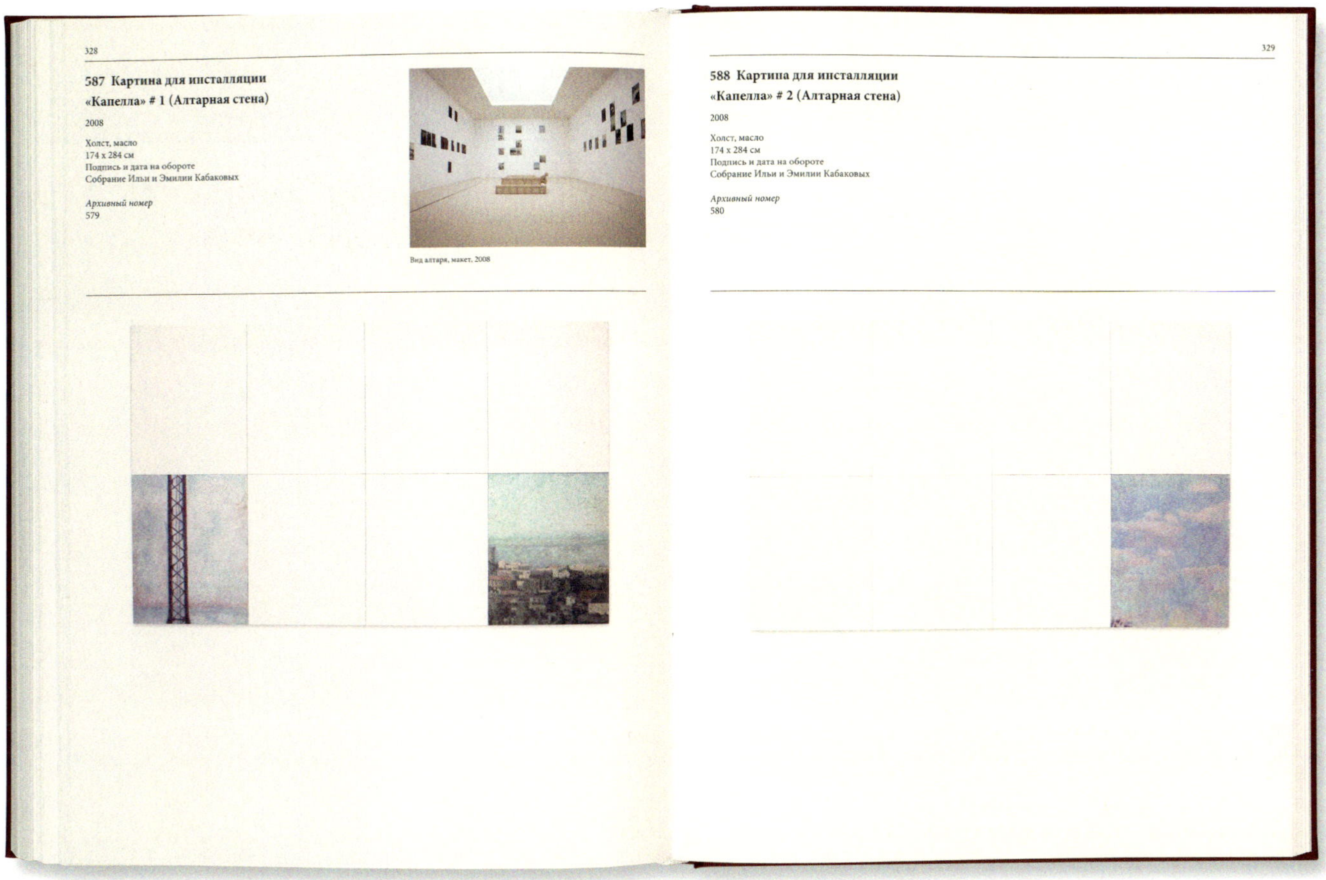
328
587 Картина для инсталляции
«Капелла» # 1 (Алтарная стена)
2008
Холст, масло
174 x 284 см
Подпись и дата на обороте
Собрание Ильи и Эмилии Кабаковых
Архивный номер
579
Вид алтаря, макет, 2008
329
588 Картина для инсталляции
«Капелла» # 2 (Алтарная стена)
2008
Холст, масло
174 x 284 см
Подпись и дата на обороте
Собрание Ильи и Эмилии Кабаковых
Архивный номер
580

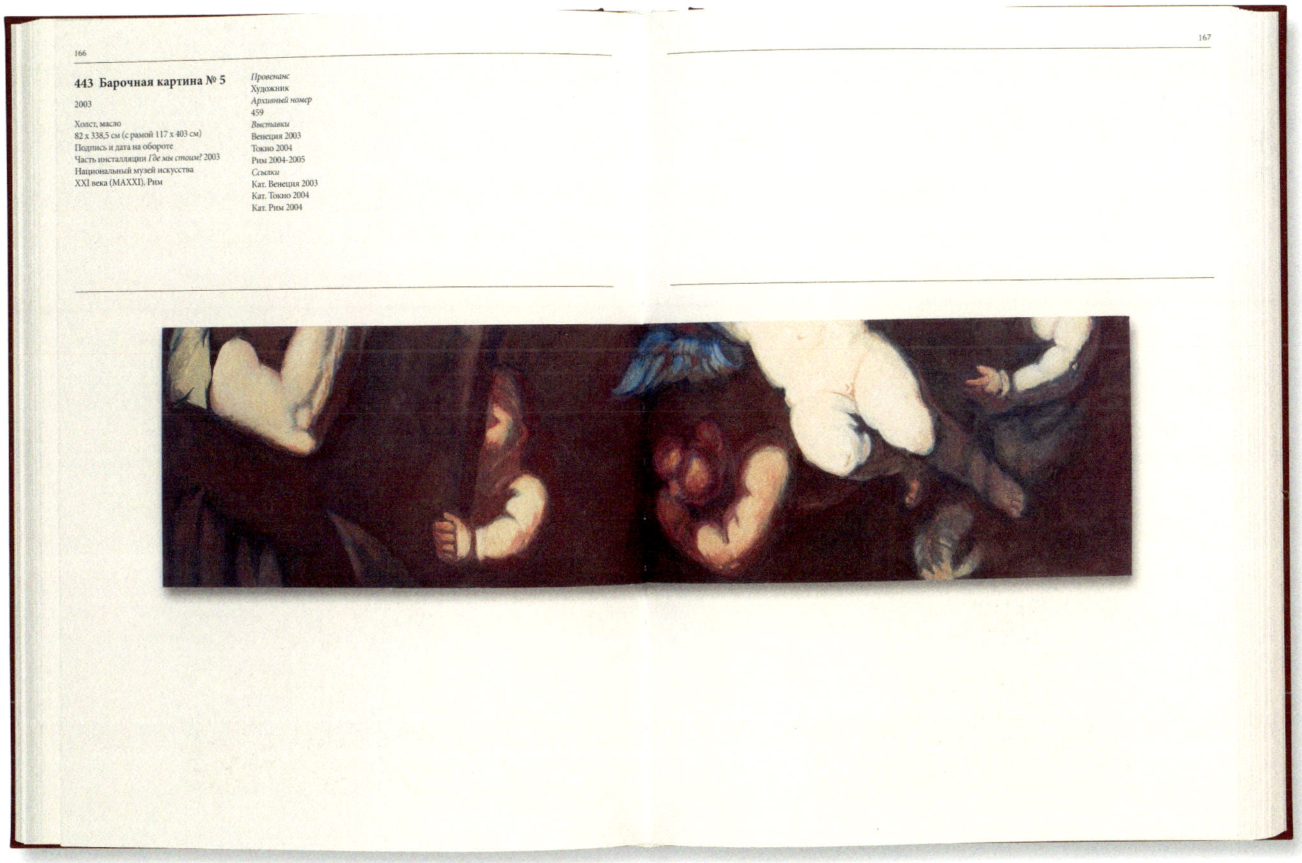
166
443 Барочная картина № 5
2003
Холст, масло
82 x 338,5 см (с рамой 117 x 403 см)
Подпись и дата на обороте
Часть инсталляции Где мы стоим? 2003
Национальный музей искусства
XXI века (MAXXI), Рим
Провенанс
Художник
Архивный номер
459
Выставки
Венеция 2003
Токио 2004
Рим 2004-2005
Ссылки
Кат. Венеция 2003
Кат. Токио 2004
Кат. Рим 2004
167

Appendix

Index of Publications not listed in this Catalogue Raisonné / Verzeichnis der nicht in diesem Catalogue Raisonné erfassten Publikationen[1]

Praemium Imperiale Grant for Young Artists, 2008 Laureates: Richard Hamilton, Ilya and Emilia Kabakov, Peter Zumthor, Zubin Mehta, Sakata Tojuro, Italian Youth Orchestra, The Japan Art Association, Japan 2008.

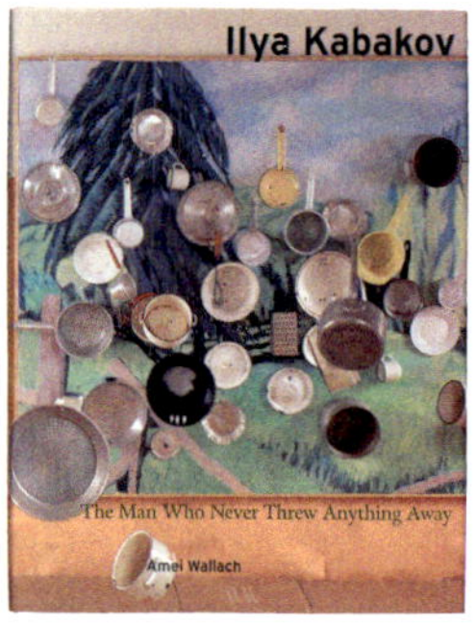

Amei Wallach, *Ilya Kabakov: The Man Who Never Threw Anything Away*, New York 1996.

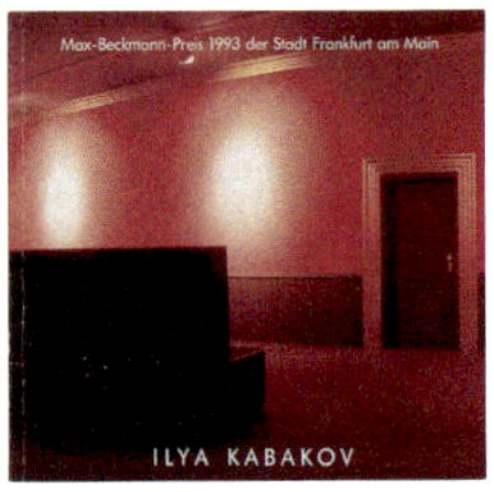

Max-Beckmann-Preis 1993 der Stadt Frankfurt am Main: Ilya Kabakov, Dezernat Kultur und Freizeit der Stadt Frankfurt am Main, Frankfurt am Main 1994.

Solo Exhibitions with Catalogues

2008

Galerie Thaddaeus Ropac, Salzburg, Austria, *Ilya and Emilia Kabakov: The Canon*, August 30 – September 27, 2008

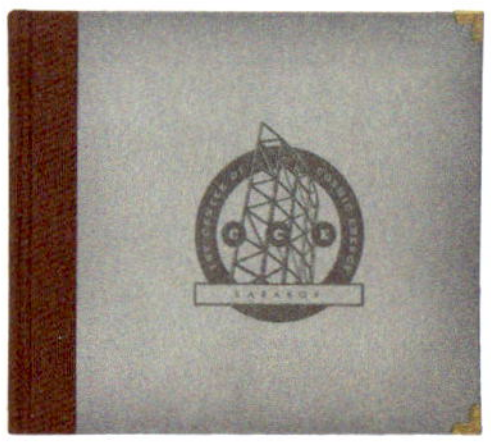

2007

Tufts University Art Gallery, Medford, MA, USA, *Ilya and Emilia Kabakov: The Center of Cosmic Energy*, September 6 – November 11, 2007.

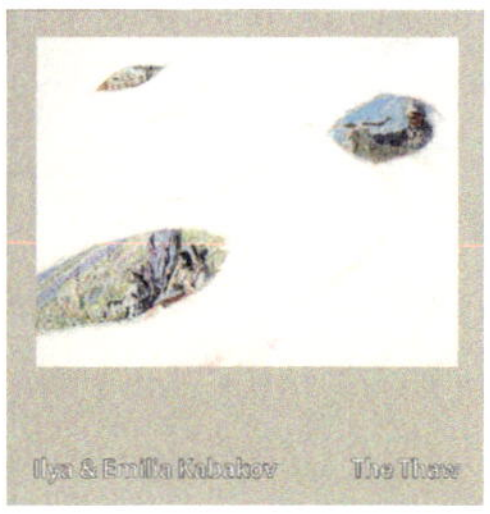

2006

Deweer Gallery, Otegem, Belgium, *Ilya & Emilia Kabakov: The Thaw*, March 4 – April 2, 2006.

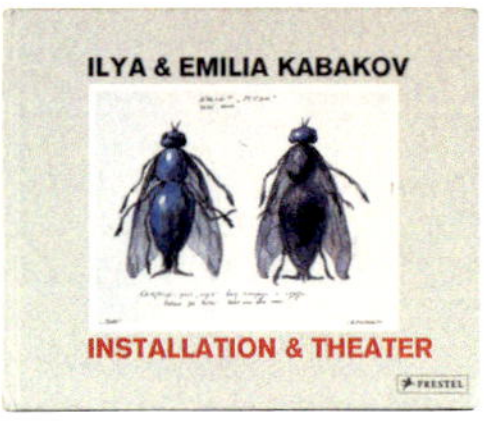

Versicherungskammer Bayern, Munich, Germany, *Ilya & Emilia Kabakov: Installation & Theater*, September 27, 2006 – March 4, 2007.

[1] This index contains all the publications that were neither written by Kabakov as an author nor conceived and/or produced by him. | *Dieses Verzeichnis umfasst alle Publikationen, die von Kabakov weder als Autor verfasst noch von ihm konzipiert und/oder gestaltet wurden.*

2005

The State Hermitage Museum, St. Petersburg, Russia, *Ilya and Emilia Kabakov: Paintings for the Label (Label for Château Mouton-Rothschild)*, February 22 – March 8, 2005 (The State Pushkin Museum, Moscow, Russia).

Musée Les Abattoirs, Toulouse, France, *Ilya and Emilia Kabakov: Où sommes-nous? (Ilya and Emilia Kabakov: Where is Our Place?)*, March 8 – June 5, 2005.

Nikolaj, Contemporary Art Center, Copenhagen, Denmark, *Morning, Evening, Night: An Installation Dedicated to Hans Christian Andersen*, June 18 – August 28, 2005 (Reykjavik Art Museum, Iceland, April 2 – June 4, 2006).

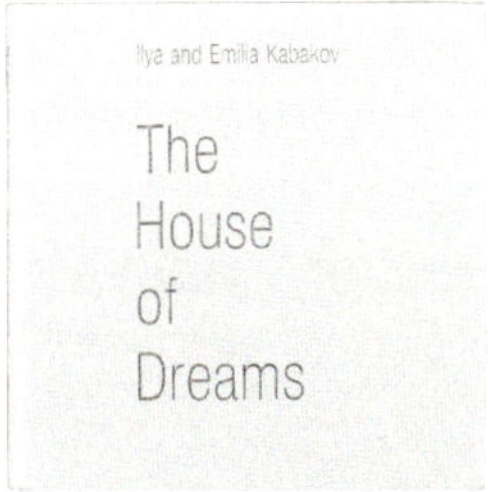

Serpentine Gallery, London, United Kingdom, *Ilya and Emilia Kabakov: The House of Dreams*, October 19, 2005 – January 8, 2006.

2004

Mori Art Museum, Roppongi Hills Mori Tower, Tokyo, Japan, *Ilya and Emilia Kabakov: Where is Our Place?*, May 29 – July 19, 2004.

Art Gallery Stella, Moscow, Russia, *We Are Free!*, December 15, 2004 – January 30, 2005.

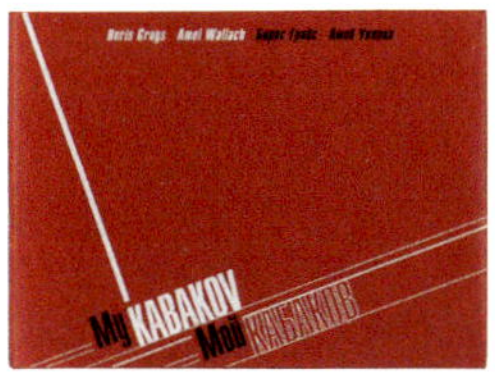

2002

Skulpturenmuseum Glaskasten, Marl, Germany, *Ausgestellt / Vorgestellt VI: Ilya Kabakov für Christian Tomaszewski*, March 9 – May 5, 2002.

2001

Fondazione Querini Stampalia, Venice, Italy, *Premio Querini Stampalia-Furla per l'Arte*, March 18 – May 13, 2001

The RISD Museum, Providence, RI, USA, *Ilya Kabakov: 10 Characters – Albums and Installation Monument to a Lost Glove*, July 13 – September 30, 2001.

2000

Center for Curatorial Studies, Bard College, Annandale-on-Hudson, NY, USA, *Ilya Kabakov: 1969–1998*, June 25 – September 3, 2000.

Städel Museum, Frankfurt am Main, Germany, *Ilya Kabakov stellt vor: Leben und Werk von Charles Rosenthal 1898–1933 (Ilya Kabakov Presents: The Life and Creativity of Charles Rosenthal 1898–1933)*, December 10, 2000 – March 4, 2001.

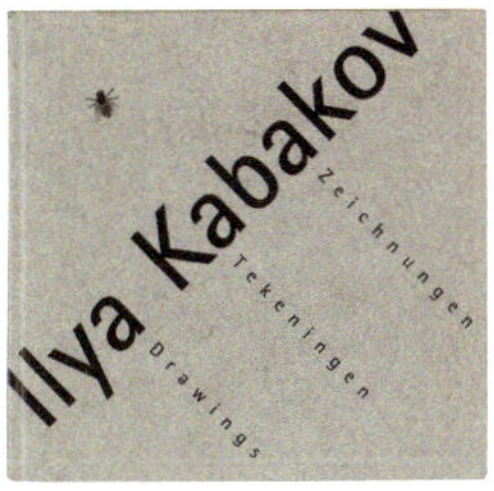

1999

Sprengel Museum Hannover, Hanover, Germany, *Ilya Kabakov: Zeichnungen (Ilya Kabakov: Drawings)*, March 14 – May 16, 1999.

San Francesco, Como, Italy, *The Old Bottle*, with Emilia Kabakov, June 25 – September 10, 1999.

Museum Wiesbaden, Wiesbaden, Germany, *Der Rote Waggon (The Red Wagon)*, October 31, 1999 – March 31, 2000.

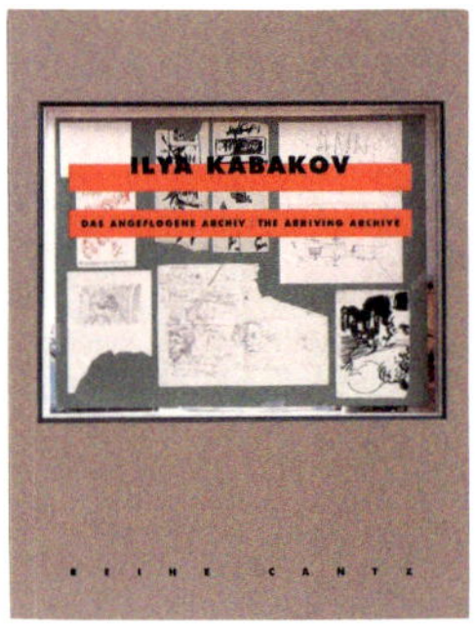

Galerie der Stadt Backnang, Turmschulhaus, Backnang, Germany, *Das angeflogene Archiv (The Arriving Archive)*, December 11, 1999 – January 30, 2000.

1998

Krannert Art Museum, University of Illinois, Champaign-Urbana, IL, USA, *The Boat of My Life*, September 17 – November 17, 1998.

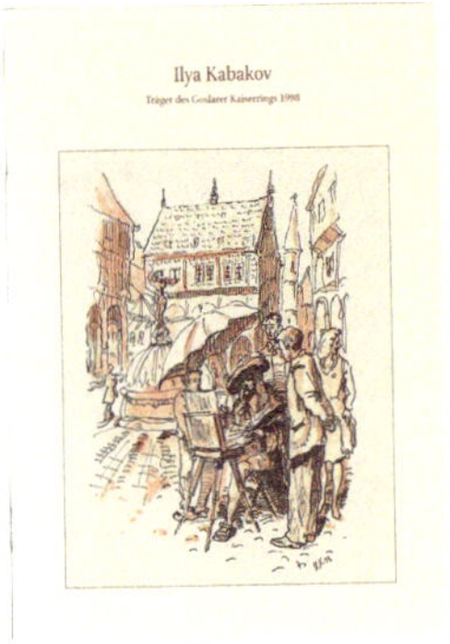

Mönchehaus Museum Goslar, Goslar, Germany, *Ilya Kabakov: My Grandfather's Shed*, permanent installation, October 16, 1998 – January 3, 1999.

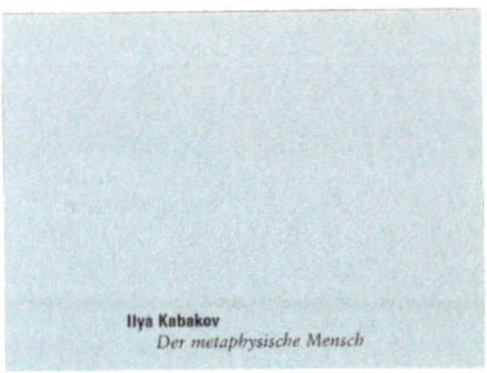

Kunsthalle Bremen, Bremen, Germany, *Der metaphysische Mensch (The Metaphysical Man)*, permanent installation, inauguration October 20, 1998.

Stadsgalerij Heerlen, Heerlen, The Netherlands, *Zeichnungen, Tekeningen, Drawings*, December 4, 1998 – February 21, 1999 (Sprengel Museum, Hanover, Germany, March 14 – May 16, 1999).

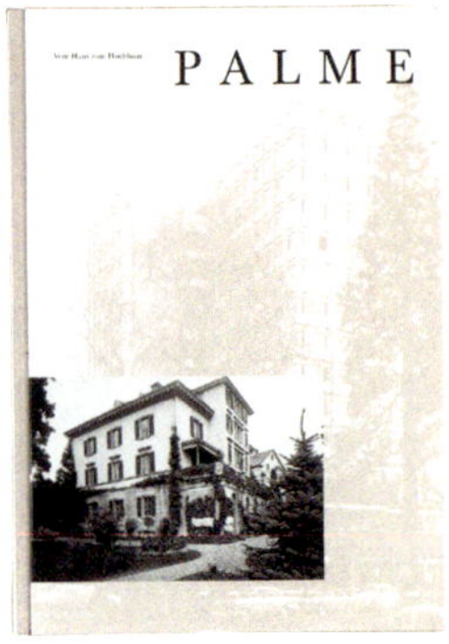

1997

Geschäftshaus zur Palme, Zurich, Switzerland, *The Fallen Chandelier*, permanent installation, inauguration April 10, 1997.

Guild Hall Museum, East Hampton, NY, USA, *The Reading Room*, June 28 – July 27, 1997.

1996

Køge Bugt, Kulturhus, Portalen i Greve, Denmark, *Ilya Kabakov: Storyteller, Installationer og ikke-realiserede projekter (Installations and Unrealized Projects)*, January 19 – March 17, 1996 (Nordjyllands Kunstmuseum, Aalborg, Denmark, April 14 – June 9, 1996).

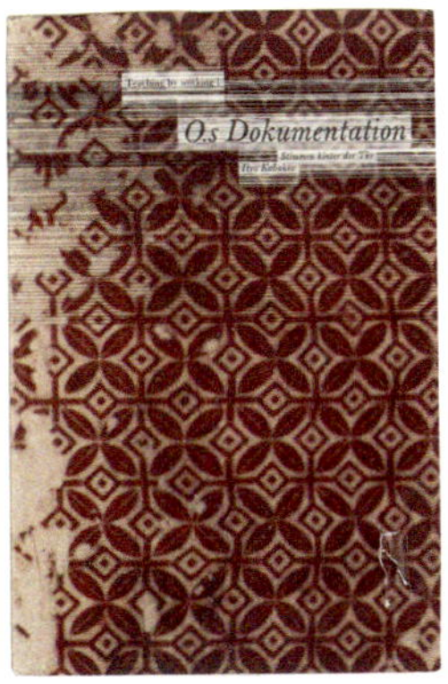

Galerie für Zeitgenössische Kunst Leipzig, Kutscherhaus der Herfurthschen Villa, Leipzig, Germany, *Stimmen hinter der Tür (Voices Behind the Door)*, November 23 – December 22, 1996.

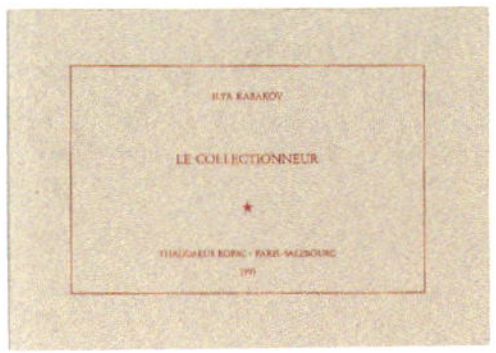

1995

Galerie Thaddaeus Ropac, Paris, France, *Le Collectionneur (The Collector)*, May 19 – July 13, 1995.

Festspielhaus Hellerau, Dresden, Germany, *Boot meines Lebens und nicht ausgeführte Projekte (The Boat of My Life and Unrealized Projects)*, July 15 – August 6, 1995.

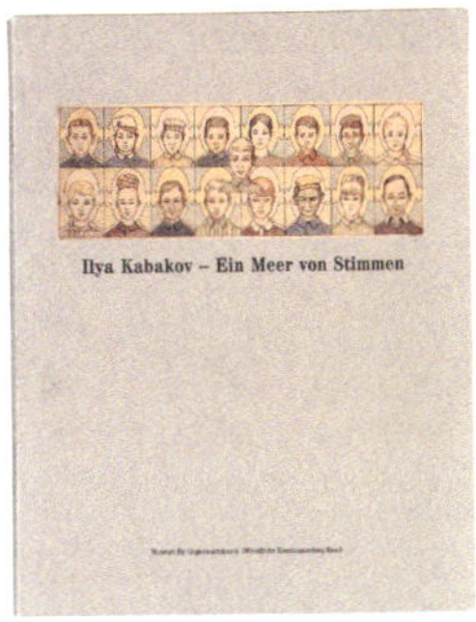

Museum für Gegenwartskunst, Basel, Switzerland, *Ilya Kabakov: Ein Meer von Stimmen, Eine Neuerwerbung der Emanuel Hoffmann-Stiftung und Werke aus der Zeit von 1965 bis 1993 in Schweizer Sammlungen (A Sea of Voices, A New Acquisition of the Emanuel Hoffmann Foundation and Works from 1965 to 1993 in Swiss Collections)*, permanent installation, August 13 – November 12, 1995.

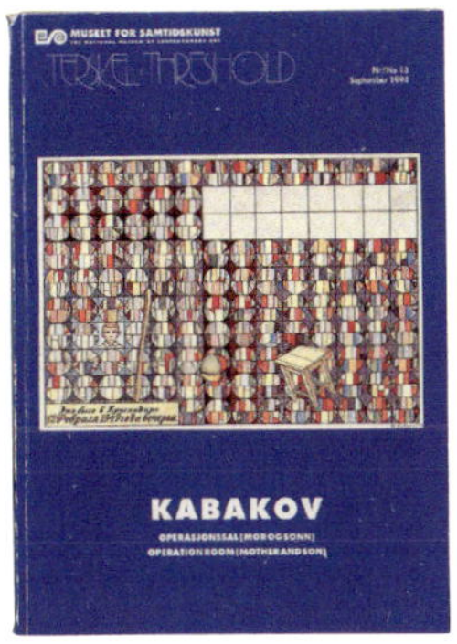

1994

Ateneum, Helsinki, Finland, *Leikkaussali – Äiti ja poika (Operation Room – Mother and Son)*, February 3 – April 10, 1994 (Museet for Samtidskunst, Oslo, Norway, *Operasjoussal – Mor og Sønn*, October 8, 1994 – January 8, 1995).

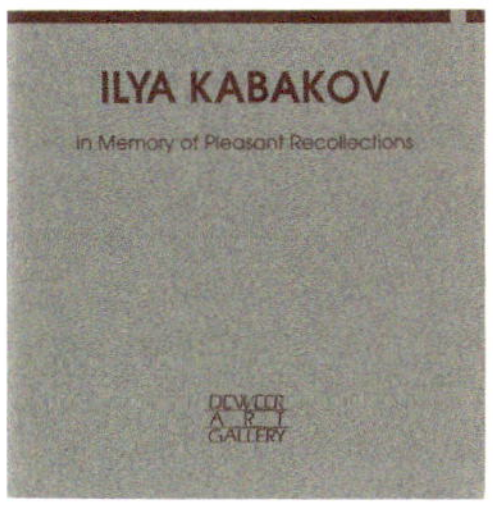

1992

Deweer Art Gallery, Otegem, Belgium, *Ter Nagedachternis aan Aangename Herinneringen (In Memory of Pleasant Recollections)*, October 10 – November 8, 1992.

1990

Hirshhorn Museum and Sculpture Garden, Washington, D.C., USA, *Directions: Ilya Kabakov – Ten Characters*, March 7 – June 3, 1990.

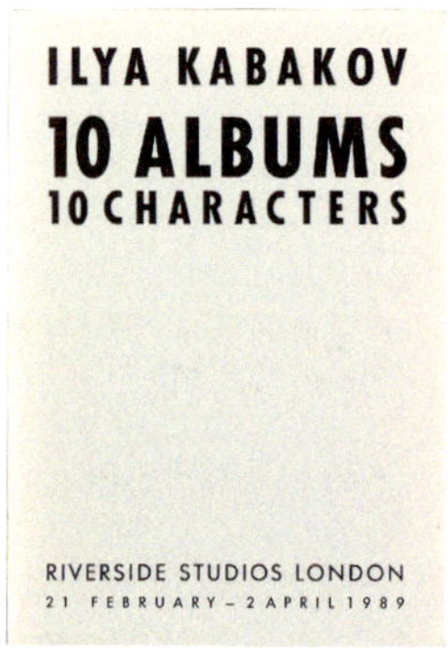

1989

Riverside Studios, London, United Kingdom, *10 Albums: 10 Characters*, February 21 – April 2, 1989.

Institute of Contemporary Art, London, United Kingdom, *Ilya Kabakov: The Untalented Artist and Other Characters*, February 23 – April 23, 1989.

De Appel Foundation, Amsterdam, The Netherlands, *Witte schilderijen en witte mensjes (White Paintings and Little White Men)*, October 6 – November 4, 1989.

Institute of Contemporary Art, Philadelphia, PA, USA, *Who Are These Little White Men?, December 14*, 1989 – January 28, 1990.

1987

Museum für Gegenwartskunst, Basel, Switzerland, *Gegenwartskunst aus der Sowjetunion: Ilya Kabakow und Iwan Tschuikow (Contemporary Art from the Sowjet Union: Ilya Kabakov and Ivan Tchuikov)*, February 14 – April 20, 1987.

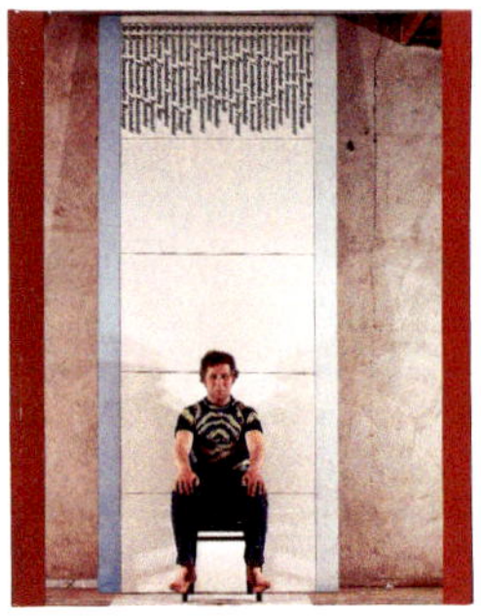

1985

Galerie Dina Vierny, Paris, France, *Ilya Kabakov*, June 11 – July 13, 1985.

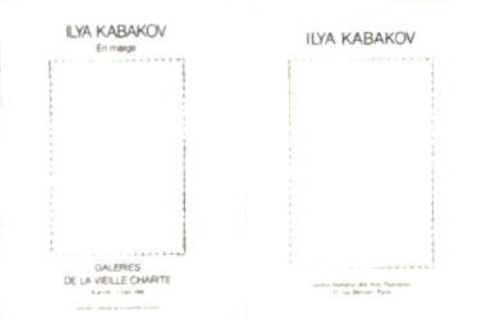

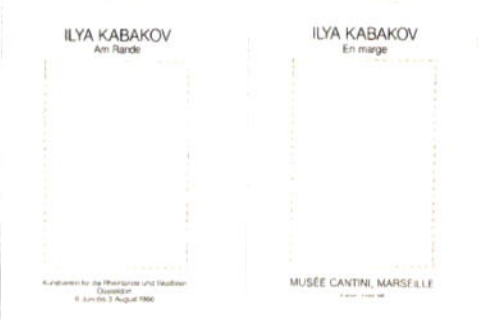

Kunsthalle Bern, Bern, Switzerland, *Ilya Kabakov: Am Rande (Along the Margins)*, August 31 – November 18, 1985 (Galerie de la Vieille Charité, Marseille, France, *Ilya Kabakov: En Marge*, January 18 – March 2, 1986; Kunstverein für die Rheinlande und Westfalen, Dusseldorf, Germany, June 6 – August 3, 1986; Centre National des Arts Plastiques, Paris, France, November 19, 1986 – January 11, 1987).

Group Exhibitions with Catalogues

2009

Musée d'Art Moderne et Contemporain de la Ville de Strasbourg, Strasbourg, France, *Silences*, installation *Labyrinth (My Mother's Album)*, with Emilia Kabakov, April 18 – August 23, 2009.

Haunch of Venison, London, United Kingdom, *Mythologies*, with Emilia Kabakov, March 12 – April 25, 2009.

2008

Royal College of Art Gallery, London, United Kingdom, *Of this Tale I Cannot Guarantee a Single Word*, installations *I Will Return on April 12* and *The Sky Is Calling*, April 10 – April 25, 2008.

2007

Yapi Kredi Sermet Çifter Hall, Beyoğlu, Istanbul, Turkey, *Freud and Contemporary Art*, January 13 – January 31, 2007.

Arcos, Museo di Arte Contemporanea del Sannio, Benevento, Italy, *We Try to Build the Future*, with Emilia Kabakov, June 1 – October 14, 2007.

52. Biennale di Venezia, Arsenale, Venice, Italy, *Think with the Senses, Feel with the Mind: Art in the Present Tense*, installation *The Manas* by Ilya and Emilia Kabakov, June 10 – November 21, 2007.

La Maison Rouge, Fondation Antoine De Galbert, Paris, France, *sots art: art politique en russie de 1972 à aujourd'hui (Soz Art: Political Art in Russia from 1972 to Today)*, October 21, 2007 – January 20, 2008.

Macro, Museo d'Arte Contemporanea Roma, Rome, Italy, *La città che sale (We Try to Build the Future)*, installation *What We Shall See After Death* by Ilya and Emilia Kabakov, October 25, 2007 – January 31, 2008.

2006

Triennale Beaufort, Oostende, Belgium, *Kust brengt Kunst (Coast Brings Art)*, with Emilia Kabakov, April 1 – October 1, 2006.

Blackwood Gallery, Ontario, Canada, *Everyday Every Other Day*, May 18 – June 18, 2006.

National Museum of Contemporary Art, Athens, Greece, *The Grand Promenade*, installation *The Fallen Angel* by Ilya and Emilia Kabakov, July 17 – September 29, 2006.

Fowler Museum at UCLA, Los Angeles, CA, USA, *The Missing Peace: Artists Consider The Dalai Lama*, with Emilia Kabakov, June 11 – September 10, 2006 (traveling exhibition).

2005

Museum of Contemporary Art, Chicago, IL, USA, *Universal Experience: Art, Life and the Tourist's Eye*, installation *The Artist's Despair* by Ilya and Emilia Kabakov, February 12 – June 5, 2005.

Museum Ludwig und Imhoff-Stollwerck-Museum, Cologne, Germany, *Kunst in Schokolade (Art in Chocolate)*, March 17 – June 19, 2005.

CCA, Wattis Institute for Contemporary Arts, San Francisco, CA, USA, *Monuments for the USA*, with Emilia Kabakov, April 7 – May 21, 2005.

MARTa Herford, Herford, Germany, *(My Private) Heroes*, May 7 – August 21, 2005.

Tate Modern, London, United Kingdom, *Open Systems: Rethinking Art c. 1970*, installation *Sitting-in-the-Closet Primakov*, June 1 – September 18, 2005.

Stiftung Archiv der Akademie der Kunste, Berlin, Germany, *Künstler.Archiv*, with Emilia Kabakov, June 19 – August 28, 2005.

Guggenheim Museum, New York, NY, USA, *Russia!*, September 16, 2005 – January 11, 2006.

2004

Centre National d'Art et du Paysage de Vassivière en Limousin, Beaumont-du-Lac, France, *Climates: cyclothime des paysages*, installation *The Toilet on the Mountain* by Ilya and Emilia Kabakov, March 10 – October 10, 2004.

State Historical Museum, Moscow, Russia, *The Man Who Flew Into Space From His Apartment*, April 6, 2004.

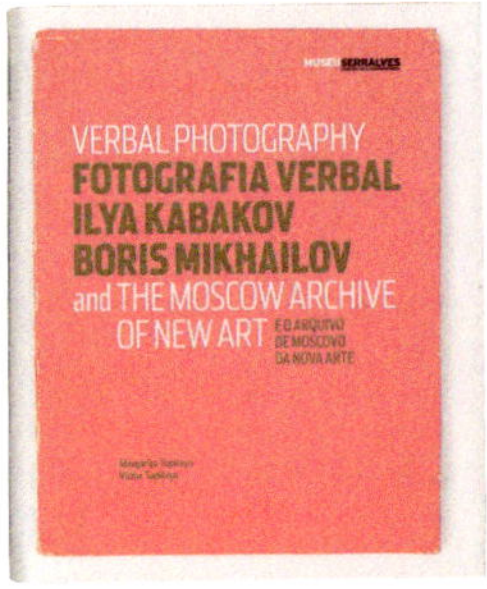

Museu de Arte Contemporânea de Serralves, Porto, Portugal, *Verbal Photography: llya Kabakov and Boris Michailov*, April 30 – July 4, 2004.

ICA, Institute of Contemporary Arts, London, United Kingdom, *Artists' Favorites* by Ilya and Emilia Kabakov, June 1 – September 5, 2004.

Parrish Art Museum, Southampton, NY, USA, *North Fork / South Fork*, installation *The Fallen Angel* by Ilya and Emilia Kabakov, July 26 – September 8, 2004.

Norton Museum of Art, West Palm Beach, FL, USA, installation *7 Characters* by Ilya and Emilia Kabakov, October 23, 2004 – January 9, 2005.

Palazzo Ducale, Genoa, Italy, *Arti & Architettura 1900–2000*, October 2, 2004 – February 13, 2005.

Fundação Calouste Gulbenkian, Centro de Arte Moderna José de Azeredo Perdigão, Lisbon, Portugal, *Vidas Imaginarias (Imaginary Biographies)*, installation *The Man Who Flew Into His Painting*, November 5, 2004 – January 2, 2005.

FRAC Limousin (Fonds Regional d'Art Contemporain), Limoges, France, *L'Artiste Editeur*, December 10, 2004 – March 12, 2005.

2003

ACCA, Australian Center for Contemporary Art, Melbourne, Australia, *The Labyrinthine Effect*, installation *10 Albums*, 1972–1975, May 23 – July 20, 2003.

Bienal de Valencia, Valencia, Spain, *La Ciudad Ideal (The Ideal City)*, installations *The Woman and Fountain* by Ilya and Emilia Kabakov, June 6 – September 30, 2003.

50. Biennale di Venezia, Arsenale, Venice, Italy, *Utopia Station*, video *The Ideal City* by Ilya and Emilia Kabakov, June 15 – November 11, 2003.

Galerie für Zeitgenössische Kunst, Leipzig, Germany, *Identität Schreiben – Autobiografie in der Kunst (Writing Identity – Autobiography in Art)*, June 21 – August 24, 2003.

Städtische Galerie im Buntentor, Bremen, Germany, *No Art – No City!*, September 20 – October 26, 2003.

Schirn Kunsthalle Frankfurt, Frankfurt am Main, Germany, *Traumfabrik Kommunismus*, installation *The Workers Club* from the installation We Are Living Here, September 24, 2003 – January 4, 2004.

Martin-Gropius-Bau, Berlin, Germany, *Berlin-Moskau / Moskau-Berlin*, 1950–2000, installation *My Motherland – The Flies*, September 25, 2003 – January 5, 2004 (State Historical Museum, Moscow, Russia, installation *The Man Who Flew Into Space From His Apartment*,
April 3 – June 15, 2004).

2002

Kunstmuseum Bern, Bern, Switzerland, *Zeitmaschine (Time Machine)*, installations *Children's Hospital* and *Medusa's Raft* by Ilya and Emilia Kabakov, March 22 – July 21, 2002.

Städtische Galerie Karlsruhe, Karlsruhe, Germany, *Europaweit – Kunst der 60er Jahre (Europe-wide – Art of the Sixties)*, April 14 – August 25, 2002 (Staatliche Galerie Moritzburg Halle, Halle, Germany, September 29, 2002 – January 6, 2003).

Kaiser Wilhelm Museum, Krefeld, Germany, *Sand in der Vaseline – Künstlerbücher II: 1980–2000 (Sand in the Vaseline – Artist's Books II: 1980–2000)*, October 27, 2002 – February 9, 2003.

CASA, Centro de Arte de Salamanca, Salamanca, Spain, *Comer o no Comer (To Eat or not to Eat)*, November 23, 2002 – January 19, 2003.

2001

Irish Museum of Modern Art, Dublin, Ireland, *The First 10 Years: Selected Works from the Collection*, installation *The Children's Hospital* by Ilya and Emilia Kabakov, April 10 – September 23, 2001.

Rooseum, Center for Contemporary Art, Malmö, Sweden, *Home / Homeless*, installation *The Final Judgement* by Ilya and Emilia Kabakov, May 17 – September 16, 2001.

49. Biennale di Venezia, Arsenale, Venice, Italy, *La Plateau of Humanity*, installation *Not Everyone Will Be Taken Into the Future* by Ilya and Emilia Kabakov, June 10 – November 4, 2001.

Art Unlimited, Art Basel 32, Basel, Switzerland, Galerie Thaddaeus Ropac, installation *Two Windows*, June 13 – June 18, 2001.

Kunsthalle Zürich, Zurich, Switzerland, *Ein Raum ist eine Welt (A World within a Space)*, with Emilia Kabakov, August 25 – October 21, 2001.

Kunsthaus Zug, Zug, Switzerland, *Projekt Sammlung (4) Pavel Pepperstein, Boris Groys, Ilya Kabakov: Die Ausstellung eines Gesprächs (Project Collection (4) Pavel Pepperstein, Boris Groys, Ilya Kabakov: The Exhibition of a Discussion)*, September 2 – November 4, 2001.

MUMOK, Museum Moderner Kunst, Stiftung Ludwig Wien, Vienna, Austria, *Die Sammlung, Museum Moderner Kunst, Stiftung Ludwig, Wien (The Collection, Museum of Modern Art, Ludwig Foundation, Vienna)*, installations *The Targets and Four Minimalist Paintings*, September 15, 2001.

2000

Kunsthalle Düsseldorf, Düsseldorf, Germany, *Das fünfte Element – Geld oder Kunst (The Fifth Element – Money or Art)*, installation *The Painting as Assignation* by Ilya and Emilia Kabakov, January 28 – May 28, 2000.

Art Museum, University of South Australia, Adelaide, Australia, *Telstra Adelaide Festival of Arts 2000*, installation *Monument to a Lost Civilization* by Ilya and Emilia Kabakov, March 3 – March 26, 2000.

Galerie nationale du Jeu de Paume, Paris, France, *L'autre moitié de l'Europe (The Second Half of Europe)*, installation *The Happiest Man* by Ilya and Emilia Kabakov, March 13 – April 9, 2000.

Rotonda della Besana, Milan, Italy, *Stanze e Segreti (Rooms and Secrets)*, installation *The Children's Hospital* by Ilya and Emilia Kabakov, April 11 – August 20, 2000.

Städtische Galerie im Zentrum für Kunst und Medientechnologie (ZMK), Karlsruhe, Germany, *Herausforderung Tier: Von Beuys bis Kabakov (The Animal as a Challenge: From Beuys to Kabakov)*, installation *The Tennis Game II*, with Boris Groys, April 15 – July 30, 2000.

Singen am Hohentwiel, Germany, *Hier, Da und Dort: Kunst in Singen (Here, Near and There: Art in Singen)*, installation *The Golden Apples*, with Emilia Kabakov, May 5 – October 8, 2000.

Art Gallery of New South Wales, Museum of Contemporary Art, Sydney, Australia, *Biennale of Sydney 2000*, installation *Monument to a Lost Civilization*, with Emilia Kabakov, May 26 – July 30, 2000.

Kunsthalle Basel, Basel, Switzerland, *Quartett:*
Baldessari, Kabakov, Kosuth, Pistoletto,
September 9 – November 12, 2000.

COCA, Center of Contemporary Art, Christchurch, New Zealand, *Art and Industry*, installation *Monument to a Lost Civilization*, with Emilia Kabakov, September 20 – December 31, 2000.

Palazzo delle Papesse, Centro Arte Contemporanea, Siena, Italy, *Artisti Collezionisti*, October 3, 2000 – January 14, 2001.

Galeries nationales du Grand Palais, Paris, France *Visions du Futur: Une histoire des peurs et des espoirs de l'humanité (Visions of the Future: A History of Fears and Hopes of Mankind)*, installation *Incident at the Museum or Water Music*, with music by Vladimir Tarasov, October 5, 2000 – January 1, 2001.

Schirn Kunsthalle Frankfurt, Frankfurt am Main, Germany, *Das Gedächtnis der Kunst: Geschichte und Erinnerung in der Kunst der Gegenwart (The Memory of Art: History and Recollection in Contemporary Art)*, installation *Monument to a Lost Civilization*, with Emilia Kabakov, December 16, 2000 – March 18, 2001.

SMAK, Stedelijk Museum voor Actuele Kunst, Ghent, Belgium, *Over the Edges*, installation *Vibrators on the Wall*, April 1 – June 30, 2000.

Echigo-Tsumari Art Triennial 2000, Niigata Prefecture, Matsudai Town, Japan, installation *The Rice Fields*, with Emilia Kabakov, July 20 – September 10, 2000.

1999

Queens Museum of Art, New York, NY, USA, *Global Conceptualism: Points of Origin 1950s–1980s*, April 29 – August 23, 1999 (Walker Art Center, Minneapolis, MN, USA, December 19, 1999 – March 5, 2000; Miami Art Museum, Miami, FL, USA, September 15 – November 26, 2000).

Whitechapel Art Gallery, London, United Kingdom, *Examining Pictures: Exhibiting Art*, May 7 – June 27, 1999 (Museum of Contemporary Art Chicago, Chicago, IL, USA, July 24 – September 19, 1999; UCLA, Armand Hammer Museum, Los Angeles, CA, USA, February 6 – April 2, 2000).

Musée des beaux-arts de Montréal, Montreal, Canada, *Cosmos: du Romantisme à l'Avant-garde, 1801–2001 (Cosmos: From Romanticism to the Avant-Garde, 1801–2001)*, installation *The Man Who Flew Into Space From His Apartment*, June 17 – October 17, 1999 (Centre de Cultura Contemporània de Barcelona, Barcelona, Spain, *Cosmos: Del romanticisme a l'avantguarda, 1801–2001*, November 23, 1999 – February 27, 2000; Palazzo Grassi, Venice, Italy, *Cosmos – Da Goya a De Chirico, da Friedrich a Kiefer: L'arte alla scoperta dell'infinito*, March 26 – July 23, 2000).

Frederick R. Weisman Art Museum, University of Minnesota, MN, USA, *World Views: Maps & Art*, installation *The Globe in a Different Topographical System*, with Emilia Kabakov, September 11, 1999 – January 2, 2000.

Kunsthalle Wien, Vienna, Austria, *Get Together: Kunst als Teamwork*, installation *The Meeting: Ilya Kabakov – Jan Fabre*, October 8, 1999 – January 9, 2000.

Art Focus 3, International Biennial of Contemporary Art, The Sultan's Pool, Merril Hassenfeld Amphitheatre, Jerusalem, Israel, installation *The Old Bottle*, with Emilia Kabakov, October 24 – November 20, 1999.

Musée d'Art Contemporain de Montréal, Montreal, Canada, *Culbutes: Œuvre d'impertinence (Heads Over Heels: Impertinent Works)*, installation *We Were in Kyoto* by Ilya and Emilia Kabakov, November 18, 1999 – April 23, 2000.

Museum Moderner Kunst Stiftung Ludwig, Palais Liechtenstein, Vienna, Austria, *Rückblick und Ausblick: Zeitwenden*, July 4 – October 1, 2000 (Kunstmuseum Bonn, Bonn, Germany, December 4, 1999 – June 4, 2000).

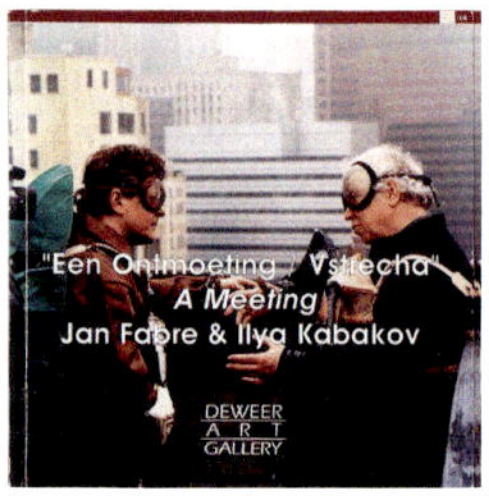

1998

Deweer Art Gallery, Otegem, Belgium, *Een Ontemoeting / Vstrecha (A Meeting): Jan Fabre & Ilya Kabakov*, January 31 – March 15, 1998 (Rozenboomkammer, Diepenheim, The Netherlands, February 28 – March 14; Ar/ge Kunst Galerie Museum, Bolzano, Italy, July 9 – September 4, 1998.

Moderna Museet, Stockholm, Sweden, *Sar: Mellan demokrati och förlösning i samtida konst (Wound: Between Democracy and Redemption in Contemporary Art)*, installation *The Man Who Flew Into Space From His Apartment*, February 14 – April 19, 1998.

Wiener Secession, Vienna, Austria, *Das Jahrhundert der künstlerischen Freiheit (A Century of Artistic Freedom)*, sketch *100 Years of the Vienna Secession* for the project *The Golden Apples*, April 3 – June 21, 1998.

Palais des Nations, organization: Art for the World, Geneva, Switzerland, *Les frontières de la conscience (The Edge of Awareness)*, installation *Did you know at least . . .?*, May 10 – July 18, 1998 (P.S.1, Contemporary Art Center and United Nations Building, Visitor Lobby, New York, NY, USA, September 13 – October 15, 1998; SESC de Pompeia, São Paolo, Brazil, December 7, 1998 – January 30, 1999; Lalit Kala Akademi, New Delhi, India, March 4 – March 30, 1999; Triennale di Milano, Milan, Italy, October 13 – November 10, 1999).

Upper Campfield Market, Manchester, United Kingdom, *Leaving Tracks: Artranspennine98, An Exhibition of International Contemporary Visual Art*, installation *The Palace of Projects*, with Emilia Kabakov, May 23 – August 16, 1998.

MMK, Museum für Moderne Kunst, Frankfurt am Main, Germany, *Szenenwechsel XIV (Change of Scene XIV)*, installations *The Rope of Life and Other Installations* and *10 Albums*, June 19, 1998 – January 1, 1999.

National Gallery of Canada, Ottawa, Canada,
Crossings / Traversées, installation *Two Windows*, August 7 – November 1, 1998.

Arte all'Arte 98, Colle di Val d'Elsa, Italy, installations *The Weakening Voice (The Column), We Are Free*, and *The Observer (The Illuminated Window)*,
September 12 – November 17, 1998.

Städelsches Kunstinstitut und Städtische Galerie, Frankfurt am Main, Germany, *Innenleben: Die Kunst des Interieurs. Vermeer bis Kabakov (Internal Life: The Art of Interior, Vermeer to Kabakov)*, installations *Toilet In The Corner* and *In The Closet*, September 24 – January 10, 1999.

Expo 2000, Hannoversch Münden, Germany,
3 Räume – 3 Flüsse: Ihr wart ins Wasser eingeschrieben (3 Spaces – 3 Rivers: You Were Inscribed into the Water), installation *The Old Bridge*, October 12, 1998 – November 30, 2000.

Centre de la Vieille Charité and Galeries Contemporaines des Musées de Marseille (MAC), Marseille, France, *50 espèces d'espaces*, installation *The Man Who Flew Into Space From His Apartment*, November 28, 1998 – May 30, 1999.

7. Triennale der Kleinplastik 1998, Südwest LB-Forum, Stuttgart, Germany, *Zeitgenössische Skulptur: Europa, Afrika*, installations *The Test of Destiny (part of Too Metaphysical)* and *Table-Painting*, October 17, 1998 – January 17, 1999.

1997

Médersa Ibn Youssef, Marrakech, Morocco, *Méditations (Meditations)*, installation *The Blue Carpet*, March 15 – April 22, 1997.

Whitney Museum of American Art, 1997 Biennial Exhibition, New York, NY, USA, installation *Treatment with Memories*, March 20 – June 15, 1997.

Henry Art Gallery, Faye G. Allen Center for the Visual Arts, University of Washington, Seattle, WA, USA, *Inside*, installation *The Collector*, April 13 – June 29, 1997.

Martin-Gropius-Bau, Berlin, Germany, *Die Epoche der Moderne – Kunst im 20. Jahrhundert (The Age of Modernism – Art in the 20th Century)*, installation *Three Nights*, May 6 – July 27, 1997.

Fondazione Querini Stampalia, Venice, Italy, *Artists for Sarajevo* (organization: Comune di Venezia, Fondazione Bevilacqua La Masa), installation *I'll Return on April 12*, June 3 – September 7, 1997.

47. Biennale di Venezia, Arsenale, Venice, Italy, *Futuro, Presente, Passato (Future, Present, Past)*, installation *We Were in Kyoto*, with Emilia Kabakov, June 12 – October 4, 1997.

Skulptur Projekte Münster 1997, Münster, Germany, installation *Blickst du hinauf und liest die Worte . . . (Looking Up, Reading the Words . . .)*, June 22 – September 28, 1997.

1996

Rundetårn, Copenhagen, Denmark, *Strangers in the Arctic: Ultima Thule and Modernity*, installation *Tennis Game*, with Pavel Pepperstein, March 8 – April 28, 1996 (Porin Taidemuseo, Pori, Finland, June 15 – September 1, 1996; Art Gallery of Ontario, Toronto, Canada, June 25 – September 1, 1997).

EV+A 1996, The Twentieth Annual Exhibition of Visual and Art, Limerick, Ireland, installation *Toilet on the River*, March 8 – May 4, 1996.

Kunsthalle Wien, Vienna, Austria, *Judenplatz Wien 1996: Wettbewerb Mahnmal und Gedenkstätte für die jüdischen Opfer des Naziregimes in Österreich 1938–1945 (Jewish Square Vienna 1996: Competition for a Monument and Memorial Commemorating the Jewish Victims of the Nazi Regime in Austria 1938–1945)*, March 19 – April 28, 1996.

Cleveland Center for Contemporary Art, Cleveland, OH, USA, *Urban Evidence: Contemporary Artists Reveal Cleveland*, installations *Three Green Paintings and Three Russian Paintings*, August 25 – October 27, 1996.

Centre Georges Pompidou, Musée national d'art moderne, Paris, France, *Les péchés capitaux: La Paresse*, September 11 – November 4, 1996.

The Israel Museum, Jerusalem, Israel, *Judenplatz Wien 1996 (Jewish Square Vienna 1996)*, July 2 – October 6, 1996 (School of Architecture, London, United Kingdom, November 5 – December 12, 1996).

23. Bienal internacional de Arte de São Paulo, Ciccillo Matarazzo Pavilion, São Paulo, Brazil, *Universalis*, installation *Two Cabinets*, October 5 – December 8, 1996.

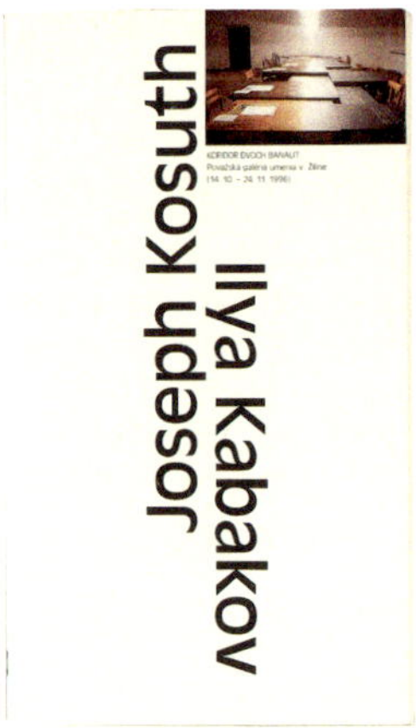

Považská galéria umenia v Žiline, Zilina, Slovenia, *Koridor dvoch banalít (Corridor of Two Banalities)*, with Joseph Kosuth, October 14 – November 24, 1996.

1995

1. Johannesburg Biennale, Johannesburg, South Africa, installation *Unfinished Installation*, February 28 – April 30, 1995.

Fundació Antoni Tàpies, Barcelona, Spain, *Els limits del museu (The End of the Museum)*, installation *Incident at the Museum or Water Music*, music by Vladimir Tarasov, March 14 – June 5, 1995.

Kunsthaus Zürich, Zurich, Switzerland, *Zeichen & Wunder: Niko Pirosmani (1862–1918) und die Kunst der Gegenwart (Signs & Wonders: Niko Pirosmani [1862–1918] and Recent Art)*, installation *This Will Happen Tomorrow!*, March 31 – June 18, 1995 (Centro Galego de Arte Contemporáneo, Santiago de Compostela, Spain, *Signos & Milagres*, July 20 – October 20, 1995).

Museum für Moderne Kunst, Frankfurt am Main, Germany, *Szenenwechsel VIII (Change of Scene VIII)*, installation *The Rope of Life and Other Installations*, June 23, 1995 – January 14, 1996.

Palais des Nations, Geneva, Switzerland, *Dialogues de paix (Dialogues of Peace)*, installation *The Fallen Sky*, permanent installation, July 3 – October 24, 1995.

95. Gwangju Biennale, Gwangju, Republic of Korea, *Art as Witness*, installations *The Test of Destiny and Too Metaphysical*, September 20 – November 20, 1995.

The Jewish Museum, New York, NY, USA, *Russian Jewish Artists in a Century of Change: 1890–1990*, September 21, 1995 – January 28, 1996.

Jane Voorhees Zimmerli Art Museum, Rutgers University, New Brunswick, NJ, USA, *From Gulag to Glasnost: Nonconformist Art from the Soviet Union*, October 22, 1995.

4. International Istanbul Biennial, İstanbul Kültür ve Sanat Vakfi, Istanbul, Turkey, *New Orientation: The Vision of Art in a Paradoxical World*, installations *The First Image of the Car and An Extraordinary Incident*, November 10 – December 10, 1995.

Galerie Hlavního Města Prahy, Prague, Czech Republic, *Létat-Odejít-Zmitet: Moskevsk Konceptuální Umení (Flight-Distance-Disappereance: Conceptual Moscow Art)*, installation *This Will Happen Tomorrow!*, November 14, 1995 – January 7, 1996 (Haus am Waldsee, Berlin, Germany, *Flug – Entfernung – Verschwinden: Konzeptuelle Moskauer Kunst*, January 27 – March 3, 1996; Stadtgalerie im Sophienhof, Kiel, Germany, June 21 – August 11, 1996).

Sala de Exposiciones de Rekalde, Bilbao, Spain, *Zubia, El Puente, MOCT*, installation *The Bridge*, November 21 – January 21, 1996.

1994

Thread Waxing Space, New York, NY, USA, *Don't Look Now*, January 22 – February 26, 1994.

Fundación "La Caixa," Madrid, Spain, *Toponimias: Ocho ideas del espacio (Toponymies: Eight Ideas of a Space)*, installation *For Sale!*, February 1 – April 10, 1994.

MAK, Österreichisches Museum für angewandte Kunst, Vienna, Austria, *Tyrannei des Schönen: Architektur der Stalin-Zeit (Tyranny of the Beauty: Architecture of the Stalin Period)*, installation *The Red Wagon*, April 6 – July 17, 1994.

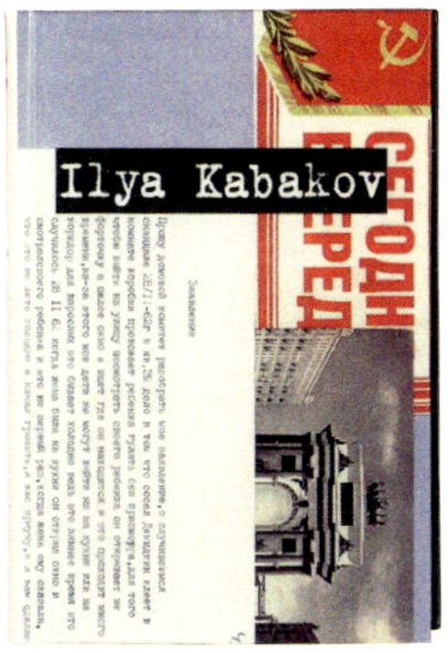

Centrum Sztuki Współczesnej Zamek Ujazdowski, Warsaw, Poland, *Korytarz dwóch banalnósci (The Corridor of Two Banalities)*, with Joseph Kosuth, April 25 – September 3, 1994.

Kunst- und Ausstellungshalle der Bundesrepublik Deutschland, Bonn, Germany, *Europa, Europa*, installation *The Man Who Never Threw Anything Away*, May 26 – October 11, 1994.

Museum der Zürcher Stadtentwässerung, Zurich, Switzerland, *Cloaca Maxima*, installation *Toilet in the Corner*, June 10 – October 30, 1994.

Galerie der Stadt Esslingen, Esslingen, Germany, *Züge, Züge: die Eisenbahn in der zeitgenössischen Kunst (Trains, Trains: The Railroad in Contemporary Art)*, June 19 – September 4, 1994.

The Hammond Galleries, Lancaster, OH, USA, *Personal Stories: A History of the Universe, Jennifer Bartlett, Ilya Kabakov, Yasumasa Morimura*, installation *Mother and Son*, July 19 – August 13, 1994.

Deweer Art Gallery, Otegem, Belgium, *Ivan Chuikov, Ilya Kabakov, Vadim Zakharov*, September 3 – October 2, 1994.

Institute of Contemporary Art, University of Pennsylvania, Philadelphia, PA, USA, *Face-Off: The Portrait in Recent Art*, installation *The Collector*, September 9 –
October 30, 1994 (Joslyn Art Museum, Omaha, NE, USA, January 28 – March 19, 1995; Weatherspoon Art Gallery, Greensboro, NC, USA, April 9 – May 28, 1995).

Kunsthalle Ritter, Klagenfurt, Austria, *Do It*, installation *The White Cube*, September 29 – November 25, 1994.

Melbourne International Biennial, Melbourne, Australia, *Virtual Reality*, installation *I Will Return on April 12 . . .*, December 3, 1994 – February 5, 1995.

1993

Louisiana Museum of Modern Art, Humlebæk, Denmark, *På kanten af kaos: nye billeder af verden (At the Edge of Chaos: New Images of the World)*, installation *Labyrinth: My Mother's Album*, February 5 – May 9, 1993.

Museum van Hedendaagse Kunst, Ghent, Belgium, *Rendez(-)Vous: Jimmie Durham, Henk Visch, Ilya Kabakov & Huang Yong Ping*, installation *Unfinished Installations*, April 28 – June 27, 1993.

Domaine de Kerguéhennec, Centre d'art contemporain, Bignan, France, *The End of Empire or the Experiments of Visual Poetry*, May 1 – September 19, 1993 (Museum van Hedendaagse Kunst, Ghent, Belgium, Mémoires de Bretagne).

Musée de la Poste, Paris, France, *L'adresse provisoire pour l'art contemporain russe (The Provisional Address for Contemporary Russian Art)*, installation *The White Cube*, May 25 – August 28, 1993.

Peggy Guggenheim Collection, Venice, Italy, *Drawing the Line Against AIDS*, June 8 – June 13, 1993.

The Jewish Museum, New York, NY, USA, *Time, Place, Memory*, installation *Mother and Son*, June 13 – November 14, 1993.

45. Biennale di Venezia, Russian Pavilion, Venice, Italy, installation *The Red Pavilion*, music by Vladimir Tarasov, June 14 – September 14, 1993.

Centre International d'Art Contemporain, Montreal, Canada, *After Perestroika: Kitchenmaids or Stateswomen* (organization: Independent Curators Incorporated of New York), August 1 – October 3, 1993 (Picker Art Gallery, Hamilton, Ontario, Canada, November 6 – December 31; DePree Art Center and Gallery, Holland, MI, USA, February 12 – March 27, 1994; Western Gallery, Western Washington University, Bellingham, WA, USA, April 18 – June 11, 1994; Iris and B. Gerald Cantor Art Gallery, Worcester, MA, USA, September 15 – October 23, 1994).

Expo '93, Taejon, Republic of Korea, *Recycling through Art*, installation *The Rope of Life*, August 7 – November 7, 1993.

Biennale d'art contemporain de Lyon, Halle Tony Garnier, Lyon, France, *Et tous ils changent le monde . . . (And They All Changed the World . . .)*, installation *Emergency Exit*, September 3 – October 13, 1993.

Kunsthalle Wien, Vienna, Austria, *Die Sprache der Kunst (The Language of Art)*, September 3 – October 17, 1993 (Kunstverein, Frankfurt am Main, Germany, December 4 – February 20, 1994).

The Rye Arts Center, Rye, NY, USA, *From Chaos to Creation: Russian Art 1971–1992*, October 3 – November 21, 1993.

Josef-Haubrich-Kunsthalle, Cologne, Germany, *Von Malewitsch bis Kabakow – Russische Avantgarde im 20. Jahrhundert: Die Sammlung Ludwig (From Malevich to Kabakov – Russian Avant-Garde in the 20th Century: The Ludwig Collection)*, installations *Before Supper* and *The Red Pavilion*, October 16, 1993 – January 2, 1994.

P.S.1 Contemporary Art Center, New York, NY, USA, *Stalin's Choice: Soviet Socialist Realism 1932–1956*, November 21, 1993 – February 27, 1994.

Haus der Kunst, Munich, Germany, *Widerstand: Denkbilder für die Zukunft (Resistance: Impulses for the Future)*, installation *Labyrinth: My Mother's Album*, December 10, 1993 – February 20, 1994.

1992

American Fine Arts, New York, NY, USA, *Just Pathetic*, installation *In The Corner*, January 18 – February 8, 1992.

Groninger Museum, Groningen, The Netherlands, *Ex USSR: Hedendaagse Kunstenaars uit het GOS (Ex-USSR: Contemporary Artists from the GOS)*, installation *The Communal Kitchen*, February 23 – April 20, 1992.

The X-Art Foundation and Blast, New York, NY, USA, *Blast Art Benefit*, April 11 – April 18, 1992.

Documenta 9, Kassel, Germany, installation *The Toilet*, June 13 – September 20, 1992.

Villa Campolieto, Ercolano, Italy, *a Mosca ... a Mosca*, installations *Commentary of O. Egorova and The Glue*, July 1 – September 13, 1992 (Galleria Comunale d'Arte Moderna, Bologna, Italy, September 26 – November 22, 1992).

LACMA, Los Angeles County Museum of Art, Los Angeles, CA, USA, *Parallel Visions: Modern Artists and Outsider Art*, October 18, 1992 – January 3, 1993.

Akademie der Bildenden Künste, Vienna, Austria, *Über Malerei – Begegnung mit der Geschichte (About Painting – Encounters with History)*, installation *The Unhappened Dialogue*, November 19 – December 31, 1992.

1991

Dominikanerkloster, Frankfurt am Main, Germany, *Bilder zur Bibel heute (Pictures for the Bible Today)*, installation *Illustrations for the Bible*, January 29 – February 20, 1991 (Evangelische Akademie Iserlohn, Germany, March 8 – April 6, 1991; Evangelische Stadtakademie, Bochum, Germany).

Karmeliterkloster, Frankfurt am Main, Germany, *MANI Museum: 40 Moskauer Künstler im Frankfurter Karmeliterkloster (MANI Museum: 40 Muscovite Artists at the Carmelite Monastery in Frankfurt)*, March 27 – April 25, 1991.

Städtische Kunsthalle Düsseldorf, Düsseldorf, Germany, *Sowjetische Kunst um 1990*, installation *The Red Wagon*, April 12 – June 2, 1991 (Israel Museum, Weisbord Pavilion, Jerusalem, Israel, *Soviet Art Around 1990*, installation *Why 'Red Wagon' Didn't Come to Israel*, August – November 1991; Tsentralny Dom Khudozhnika, *Moscow, Russia, Sovetskoe iskusstvo okolo 1990 goda*, installation *Why 'Red Wagon' Didn't Come to Moscow)*.

Centraal Museum Utrecht, Utrecht, The Netherlands, *Nachtregels / Night Lines*, installation *Whose are Those Wings?*, permanent installation, April 26 – October 16, 1991.

Auditorio de Galicia, Santiago de Compostela, Spain, *Artistos Rusos Contemporaneos (Contemporary Russian Artists)*, May 11 – June 30, 1991.

Setagaya Art Museum, Tokyo, Japan, *Soviet Contemporary Art: From Thaw to Perestroika*, May 18 – June 23, 1991.

Kunstverein Hannover, Hanover, Germany, Kunst, *Europa – Sowjetunion (Art, Europe – Soviet Union)*, installation *The Fly with Wings*, June 22 – August 25, 1991.

Sezon Museum of Modern Art, Nagano, Japan, *Art on Edge*, installations *The Communal Kitchen and Repair*, July 13 – October 6, 1991.

Rooseum, Center for Contemporary Art, Malmö, Sweden, *Trans/Mission: Konst I interkulturell limbo (Trans/Mission: Art in Intercultural Limbo)*, installation *The Mental Institution or The Institute of Creative Research*, August 27 – October 27, 1991.

FIAC, Paris, France, Galerie Dina Vierny, installation *The Communal Kitchen*, October 5 – October 13, 1991.

Carnegie Museum of Art, Pittsburgh, PA, USA, *Carnegie International 1991*, installation *We Are Leaving Here Forever*, October 19, 1991 – February 16, 1992.

MoMA, The Museum of Modern Art, New York, NY, USA, *Dislocations*, installation *The Bridge*, October 20, 1991 – January 7, 1992.

Große Orangerie im Schloss Charlottenburg, Berlin, Germany, *Schwerelos (Weightless)*, installation *Olga Petrovna Has a Dream*, November 9, 1991 – January 22, 1992.

The Power Plant, Toronto, Canada, *Ilya Kabakov / John Scott*, November 15, 1991 – January 5, 1992.

Cité Internationale des Arts, Paris, France, *50 artistes pour le 25 anniversaire (50 Artists for the 25th Anniversary)*, November 4 – December 8, 1991.

Stedelijk Museum, Amsterdam, The Netherlands, *Wanderlieder (Hiking Songs)*, installation *Before Supper*, December 8, 1991 – February 9, 1992.

1990

Museo d'Arte Contemporanea Luigi Pecci, Prato, Italy, *Artisti Russi Contemporanei (Contemporary Russian Artists)*, installations *The Underground Golden River* and *Concerto per mosca blu e matita gialla (Concert for a Blue Fly and Yellow Pencil)*, February 10 – May 14, 1990.

The Eighth Biennale of Sydney, Art Gallery of the New South Wales, Sydney, Australia, *The Readymade Boomerang: Certain Relations in 20th Century Art, installation Three Russian Paintings*, April 11 – June 3, 1990.

The Aldrich Contemporary Art Museum, Ridgefield, CT, USA, *Adaptation and Negation of Socialist Realism*, June 9 – October 7, 1990.

Tacoma Art Museum, Tacoma, WA, USA, *Between Spring and Summer: Soviet Conceptual Art in the Era of Late Communism*, installation *Mother and Son (My Mother's Album)*, June 15 – September 9, 1990 (Institute of Contemporary Art, Boston, MA, USA, November 1, 1990 – January 6, 1991; Des Moines Art Center, Des Moines, IA, USA, February 16 – March 31, 1991).

Alpha Cubic Gallery, Tokyo, Japan, *Soviet Contemporary Art 1990*, June 22 – July 27, 1990.

Orchard Gallery, Londonderry, United Kingdom, *New Works for Different Places: TSWA Four Cities Project*, installation *The Fly with Wings*, September 1 – September 29, 1990.

DAAD-Galerie, Potsdamer Platz, Berlin, Germany, *Die Endlichkeit der Freiheit: Berlin 1990, Ein Ausstellungsprojekt in Ost und West (The Finiteness of Freedom: Berlin 1990, An Exhibition Project in East and West)*, installation *Two Memories about Fear*, September 1 – October 7, 1990.

Columbus Museum of Art, Columbus, OH, USA, *The Quest for Self Expression: Painting in Moscow and Leningrad 1965–1990*, September 16 – November 25, 1990 (Weatherspoon Art Gallery, University of North Carolina, Greensboro, NC, USA, January 13 – February 1991; Arkansas Art Center, Little Rock, AK, USA, March 14 – May 26, 1991).

Stedelijk Museum, Amsterdam, The Netherlands, *In de USSR en erbuiten (In the USSR and Beyond)*, installation *The Rope of Life and Other Installations*, September 21 – November 4, 1990.

Institute of Contemporary Art, University of Pennsylvania, Philadelphia, PA, USA, *Devil on the Stairs: Looking Back on the Eighties,* installation *The Man Who Flew into His Picture*, October 4, 1990 – January 5, 1991 (Newport Harbor Art Museum, Newport Beach, CA, USA, April 16 – June 21, 1991).

Seoul Art Festival, Republic of Korea, *Works on Hanji Paper*, November 20, 1990 – February 20, 1991.

The New Museum of Contemporary Art, New York, NY, USA, *Rhetorical Image*, installations *Intellectual Screens, The Untalented Artist*, and *The Metaphysical Man*, December 9, 1990 – February 3, 1991.

1989

South East Massachusetts University, Darmouth, MA, USA, *Post-Utopia: Paintings and Installations by Soviet Conceptualists, Bulatov, Kabakov, Komar & Melamid*, January 23 – February 18, 1989.

Pervaia Galeria, Moscow, Russia, *Foto v Zhivopisi*, January 1989 (Phyllis Kind Gallery, New York, NY, USA, *Foto in Painting: Behind the Ironic Curtain*, March 11 – April 8, 1989).

Centre Georges Pompidou, Musée national d'art moderne, Paris, France, *Les Magiciens de la Terre (Les Magicians of the Earth)*, installation *The Man Who Flew Into Space From His Apartment*, May 16 – August 15, 1989.

Wiener Secession, Vienna, Austria, *Wittgenstein: das Spiel des Unsagbaren (Wittgenstein: The Play of the Unspeakable)*, September 13 – October 29, 1989 (Palais des Beaux-Arts, Brussels, Belgium, December 15, 1989 – January 28, 1990).

The Genia Shreiber University Art Gallery, Tel Aviv, Israel, *The Beautiful Sixties in Moscow*, with Michail Grobman, September 19 – December 4, 1989.

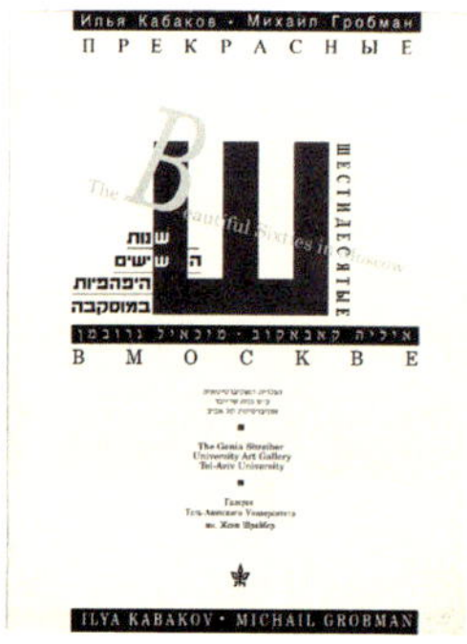

Tel Aviv Museum of Art, Israel, *Russian Art from the Michail Grobman Collection*, November 7, 1989.

Goethe-Institut Osaka, Himeji, Japan, *Pictures for the Sky. Bilder für den Himmel. Arte en el cielo. L'art prend l'air*, installation *I Will Return on April 12 . . .*, 1989 (traveling exhibition).

1988

Kunstmuseum Bern, Bern, Switzerland, *Ich lebe – ich sehe: Künstler der Achtziger Jahre in Moskau (I Live – I See: Artists of the Eighties in Moscow)*, June 11 – August 14, 1998.

43. Biennale di Venezia, Arsenale, installation *Before Supper*, June 25 – September 25, 1988.

Madrid, Spain, *ARCO 1988*, Galerie de France, February 10 – February 16, 1988.

1987

FIAC, Galerie de France, Paris, France, October 10 – October 18, 1987.

1986

Palais Attems, Graz, Austria, *Die Wahlverwandtschaften: Steirischer Herbst '86 (Chosen Affinities: Styrian Autumn '86)*.

1985

Zentrum für Interdisziplinäre Forschung der Universität Bielefeld, Bielefeld, Germany, *Ausstellung Moskauer Künstler: Jankilevskij, Kabakov, Štejnberg (Exhibition of Moscow Artists: Yankilevsky, Kabakov, Steinberg)*, June 7 – June 30, 1985 (Museum Bochum, Bochum, Germany, August 10 – September 15, 1985).

1981

Soho International Art Center, New York, NY, USA, *Russian New Wave*, December 4, 1981 – February 28, 1982.

1979

Moskovskii obedinennyi komitet khudornikov-grafikov, Moscow, Russia, *Tsvet, forma, prostranstvo (Color, Form, Space)*, February 17 – February 28, 1979.

St. Mary's College, Washington, D.C., USA, *New Art from the Soviet Union: An Exhibition of Non-conformist Art from the 1960s and 1970s*, November 3 – December 7, 1979.

1977

La Biennale di Venezia, Venice, Italy, *La nuova arte sovietica: una prospettiva non officiale (New Soviet Art: an Unofficial Perspective)*, 1977.

1976

Palais des Congres, Paris, France, *La peinture russe contemporaine (Contemporary Russian Painting)*, November 2 – November 21, 1976.

1975

Christian Brandstätter Galerie, Vienna, Austria, *Nonkonformistische russische Maler: Sammlung A. Gleiser (Nonconformist Russian Painters: The A. Gleiser Collection)*, opening November 29, 1975 (Graphotek, Kunstamt Charlottenburg, Germany, opening December 5, 1975; Konstanzer Kunstverein, Konstanz, Germany, January 25 – February 29, 1976; Städtische Galerie Die Fähre, Saulgau, Germany, March 21 – April 11, 1976; Kunstverein Brunswick, Brunswick, Germany, May 11 – June 12, 1976).

1974

Museum Bochum, Bochum, Germany, *Progressive Strömungen in Moskau, 1957–1970 (Progressive Tendencies in Moscow, 1957–1970)*, January 12 – February 10, 1974.

1973

Galerie Dina Vierny, Paris, France, *Avantgarde: Moscow-73*, May – June 1973.

Museum am Ostwall, Dortmund, Germany, *Russische Kunst der Gegenwart – Grafiken der Avantgarde (Contemporary Russian Art – Graphic Works of the Avant-Garde)*, August 12 – September 30, 1973.

1970

Galerie Gmurzynska-Bargera, Cologne, Germany, *Die Russische Avantgarde in Moskau heute (The Russian Avant-Garde in Present-day Moscow)*, January 30 – March 25, 1970.

Galerie Renée Ziegler, Zurich, Switzerland, *6 Sowjetische Künstler (Six Soviet Artists)*, May 1 – May 30, 1970.

Museo delle Belle Arti, Lugano, Switzerland, *Nuove correnti a Mosca: Rassegna di 58 artisti della giovane avanguardia (New Currents in Moscow: A Survey of 58 Artists of the Young Avant-Garde)*, September 11 – November 1, 1970.

1969

Galleria Pananti, Florence, Italy, *Nuova Scuola di Mosca: 30 Artisti non ufficiali (The New Moscow School: 30 Non-official Artists)*, January 4 – January 16, 1969 (Interior Galerie, Frankfurt am Main, Germany, *Die Neue Schule von Moskau (The New Moscow School)*, May 3 – May 28, 1969; Galerie Behr, Stuttgart, Germany, Spring – Summer 1969).

1966

Sopot, Poznan, Poland, *16 plastyków moskiewskich (Sixteen Moscow Artists)*, October 1966.

1965

Castello Spagnolo, L'Aquila, Italy, *Alternative attuali II: 2. Rassegna internazionale di pittura, scultura, grafica: omaggio a Magritte, omaggio a Mirko, omaggio a Baj: retrospettive antologiche' (Current Alternatives II: 2nd International Survey of Painting, Sculpture and Graphic Art: Hommage to Magritte, Hommage to Mirko, Hommage to Baj: Anthological Retrospectives)*, August 7 – September 30, 1965.

Imprint / Impressum

Editor / Herausgeber
Matthias Haldemann, Kunsthaus Zug

Editing / Bearbeitung
Nicole Seeberger, Marco Obrist, Matthias Haldemann

Editorial Staff / Redaktion
Marco Obrist, Emilia Kabakov, Monika Kümin

Translations / Übersetzungen
Hubert Beck, Ann Marie Bohan, Andrew Ennis,
Gabriele Leupold, Maria Porudominskaja, Judith Rosenthal

Copyediting / Lektorat
Katrin Günther, Kathleen Herfurth, Kerber Verlag, Leipzig
Dawn Michelle d'Atri

Conceptual Design / Konzept
Ilya Kabakov

Layout
Ilya Kabakov; Polina Bazir, Kerber Verlag, Bielefeld

Photographs / Fotografien
Bertram Kober

Cover Illustration / Umschlagfoto
The Window. Arkhipov Looking Through the Window
Das Fenster. Der aus dem Fenster schauende Archipow, 1985,
32.6 x 24.7 cm, Bern: Benteli Verlag

Photo p. 16 / Foto S. 16: Nicole Seeberger, Zug

Lithography / Lithografie
Klaus-Peter Plehn, Polina Bazir, Kerber Verlag, Bielefeld

Generous financial support provided by / Dank für die großzügige finanzielle Unterstützung

Nord Stream AG, Zug

Tatneft Europe AG, Zug

UBS AG, Zug

Wasserwerke Zug AG

Printed and published by / Gesamtherstellung
Kerber Verlag, Bielefeld
Windelsbleicher Str. 166–170
33659 Bielefeld
Germany
Tel. +49 (0) 5 21/9 50 08-10
Fax +49 (0) 5 21/9 50 08-88
info@kerberverlag.com
www.kerberverlag.com

Kerber, US Distribution
D.A.P. / Distributed Art Publishers, Inc.
155 Sixth Avenue, 2nd Floor
New York, NY 10013
Tel. +1 212 627-1999
Fax +1 212 627-9484

Bibliographic information / Bibliographische Informationen

The Deutsche Nationalbibliothek holds a record of this publication in the Deutsche Nationalbibliografie; detailed bibliographical data can be found under: http://dnb.ddb.de.

Die Deutsche Nationalbibliothek verzeichnet diese Publikation in der Deutschen Nationalbibliografie; detaillierte bibliografische Daten sind im Internet über http://dnb.ddb.de abrufbar.

ISBN 978-3-86678-372-0

Printed in Germany